P9-ECL-305

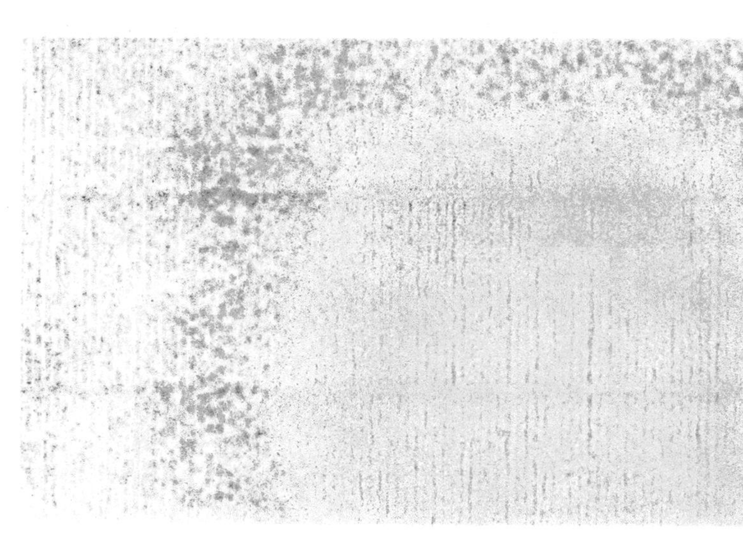

ENGLISH RECUSANT LITERATURE
1558–1640

Selected and Edited by
D. M. ROGERS

Volume 248

JACQUES DU PERRON
The Reply of the Most Illustrious Cardinall of Perron
1630

JACQUES DU PERRON

The Reply of the Most Illustrious
Cardinall of Perron
1630

The Scolar Press
1975

ISBN 0 85967 238 7

Published and printed in Great Britain by
The Scolar Press Limited, 59-61 East Parade,
Ilkley, Yorkshire and
39 Great Russell Street,
London WC1

NOTE

Reproduced from a copy in Cambridge University Library, by permission of the Syndics. In this facsimile the text has been slightly reduced: the type area in the original measures 10$\frac{5}{8}$in. by 6$\frac{1}{8}$in. Although this volume is described as 'The First Tome', no subsequent volumes were published.

References: Allison and Rogers 288; STC 6385.

THE REPLY
OF THE MOST ILLVSTRIOVS CARDINALL
OF PERRON,
TO THE ANSVVEARE
OF THE MOST EXCELLENT
KING
OF GREAT BRITAINE

THE FIRST TOME.

TRANSLATED INTO ENGLISH

Imprinted at DOVAY, by MARTIN BOGART,
vnder the signe of Paris. 1630.

An admonition to the Reader.

COurteous reader, (for so I will esteeme of thee, whosoeuer out of a true desire of vnderstãding the truth, takest this learned work into thy hands, to peruse it with iudgment, and yet without preiudice,) vouchsafe before thou begin the perusall thereof, to take these few obseruations from me.

First, whereas the most eminent authour thereof, had proiected to diuide it into twelue seuerall bookes or partiall treatises, and died before he could make a compleat end thereof (being often diuerted from it, by manifold employments, which his high estate & calling was subiect vnto, & by some more necessary dispute & writings, which the cõdition of France did then affoord: his frinds, either not marking this his proiect, or because all the work was not ended, neglecting that diuision; set is foorth reparted into six bookes only, and those so vnequally sorted, that the first book alone, is in the French edition farre bigger then all the other ensuing fiue bookes taken together. This vnproportionable partition we haue amended in this English translation; as we might easily do by the citations, or quotations with which the authour him self bordered his margent: for in them, he sometimes referres him self to such a chapter of the second, seuenth, eleuenth, twelft booke, whereby he sufficiently insinuates into how many bookes he intended to diuide this his excellent worke, & at what matter euery booke should take its beginning: which his intention we haue obserued in this that now we present to thy view, that the fit diuision of matters therein handled, may make it more intelligible and lesse tedious.

Secondly the humour of the French demanded for their satisfaction that the many places which are cited out of learned, holy, and classicall autours, hould not only be faithfully translated in the text, but also placed at large in their originall languages in the margen: that the learned reader might without recourse to the seuerall volumes (which required a copious library, whereof few are furnished) out of hand examin the faithfullnes of the trãslatiõ, & cõsequẽtly how fitly the alleged authority made for the purpose. But this humour not yet (for ought I haue seen) much raigning in our country, we haue thought it sufficient, to cite the places only in the margen, which are fully expressed in the text; the rather because the excellent translatresse copy, which we haue faithfully expressed contayned no more; and more beseemed not her translation, as not desiring to make shew of skill in greek, and other such learned languages; but only of that which was sufficient, for her assumpt that it is of a faithfull translation according to the significant expressement of the French.

Thirdly, we haue not presumed to alter or change any one word of her translation, but in some few places, where the French allusions could not be so well vnderstood, if they were expressed in English properly corresponding thereunto: for euery tongue hath some peculiar graces and elegancies, which be lost in the translation, yf they be put word for word; And yet this haue we done (as we sayde) very seldome, and that especially in the word *Church*, wich we English men vse deriued from κυριακὴ, as the house dedicated to our Lords seruice, which tropically we vse also to signify the congregation of the faithfull, most solemnly and vsually made in the Church; The French expresse it by the name of *Eglise* from ἐκκλησία *cætus vocatus ad professionem fidei*, the company of the faithfull called by Christ to professe his lawe, by which word they secundarily, or tropically vnderstand and call the Church or house of prayer. So in the name of S. Peter, in Frenche S. *Pierre*, which word also signifies a rock or stone in French, as πέτρος in greek, and Cephas in Syriak do; but in our English we haue no such allusion. No other change, but in these few, and such like haue we made; neither was it needfull, the translatresse hauing so fittly, and significantly expressed the autours meaning, that it would haue been lost labour to striue to do it better, and rather marring, then mending so perfect an expression.

Lastly, I desire thee (gentle reader) to beare with the faults of the presse: The printers being Wallons, and our English strange vnto them it was incredible to see how may faults they committed in setting: so that in ouerlooking the proofes for the print, the margins had not roome enough to hold our corrections: and do what we could, yet the number of our corrections being so many, a great many of them remayned vncorrected by the fastidious fantasy of our workman. Yet we iudge there is no fault that may hinder, or change the sence, but is amended; and for the rest we desire thee to pardon vs, considering how hard it is to make a stranger here to expresse our ortography, Farewell in our Lord, and he of his goodnes giue thee grace to take profit by reading these learned discourses.

Thy Wellwisher in Christ Iesus
F. L. D. S. M.

APPROBATIO.

Translatio hæc operis excellentissimi (quod eminentissimus Cardinalis Peronius, pro fidei catholicæ doctrina ad potentissimum Regem ac Dominum nostrum Jacobum totius Britanniæ, Franciæ, & Hiberniæ, Monarcham, summa cum eruditione pariter & modestia conscripsit) facta a nobilissima quadam Heroina prouinciæ nostræ, & serenissimæ, Reginæ Dominæ nostræ, Mariæ Henriettæ Borboniæ dicata: per omnia fideliter concordat cum ipsa autoris mente verbis, & sententiis, Quapropter dignã eam indico, quæ typis tradatur, vt ex tanti Præceptoris accuratissimis eloquentiaque incomparabili vestitis disputationibus fructum copiosum capiatur Anglia nostra, qualem vniuersa Gallia cum perpetua Magni autoris veneratione se percepisse protestatur.

2. Decemb. 1631

F. Leander de S. Martino, sacræ Theologiæ Doctor, Hebrææ linguæ in alma Academia Duacena professor Regius, Benedictinorum conuentus S. Gregorij Angliæ, Prior.

IN *LAVDEM NOBILISSIMÆ HEROINÆ,*

QVÆ HAS EMINENTISSIMI CARDINALIS DISPVTATIONES ANGLICE REDDIDIT.

SSE quid hoc dicam, quod in vno fœmina menſe
Tam varium, doctum, grande crearit opus?
Nonne hoc eſt ipſam curſu præuertere lunam
Quæ ſimili ſpatio circuit omne ſolum?
An vero Elixir, quod tactu protinus ipſo
Maxima in auratas pondera mutat opes?
Sic eſt, illa ſui fere Quinteſſentia ſexus
Quod micat in reliquis omnibus, vna tonet.

The ſame in English.

NE woman, in one Month, ſo large a booke,
In ſuch a full emphatik ſtile to turne:
Iſt not all one, as when a ſpacious brooke,
Flowes in a moment from a little Burne?
Or is't not rather to exceede the Moone
In ſwift performance of ſo long a race,
To end ſo great and hard a worke as ſoone,
As Cynthia doth her various galliard trace?
Or is ſhe not that miracle of Arts
The true Elixir, that by onely touch
To any metrals, worth of gold imparts?
For me, I think ſhe valewes thrice as much.
A wondrous Quinteſſence of woman-kind,
In whome alone, what els in all, we find.

ANOTHER.

ELEEVE me reader, they are much deluded
Who think that learning's not for ladies fitt;
For wiſdome with their ſexe as well doth ſitt,
As orient pearle in golden chace included.
T'will make their husbands, yf they haue true eyes,
Wiſe beauty, beauteous wiſdome deerly prize.

Who doth not prayſe th' Empreſſe *Eudoxias* fame,
That made old *Homer* tell our Ghoſpells ſtory?
Or noble *Proba* Romes immortall glory,
That taught sweet *Virgil* ſing our Sauiours name?
Or gracious *Elpis*, ſage *Boetius* loue,
Whoſe ſacred hymnes holy Church doth approue?

But will you ſee in one braue Ladies mind
Theſe three great gracious Ladies full compriz'd,
Their worth, their witte, their vertue equaliz'd
Look on this work, and you shall plainly find
Eudoxia, *Proba*, *Elpis* yeeld in all
To this *Tranſlatreſſe* of our Cardinall.

F. L. D. S. M.

Axoxgx

ΑΧΟΧΑΧΘ-

To the most noble Translatour.

I Would commend your labours and J finde
That they were finis'd with such ease of minde
As in some sence the praise J giue must fall
Vnder the title of Mechanicall,
When those who reade it come to vnderstand,
The paines you tooke were onely of your hand
Which though it did in swiftnesse ouergoe
All other thoughts yet to your owne was slow.
As the Sunne Beames no sooner do appeare
But they make that which stands in their light cleere
Your bright soule did but once reflect vpon
This curious peece, and it was cleard', and done.
But that a Woemans hand alone should raise
So vast a monument in thirty dayes
Breeds enuie and amazement in our sex
Of which the most ore weening witts might vex
Themselues thrice so much time and with farre lesse
Grace to their Workmanshipp or true successe.
Why should J not speak truth without offence ?
Behold this Mirrhor of French *Eloquence,*
Which shee before the English view doth place
Fill'd with the whole Originall *truth and grace*
That the most curious Author would auow
It were his owne well pleas'd, if hee liu'd now
And though you know this where to weack a frame
To rayse vp higher the greatnesse of your name
Which must from your owne rich inuentions grow,
As Riuers from the springs whence they first flow:
Yet hee who truly knowes your noblest will
To profitt others and your various skill
In choseing and in marking out the wayes
May thinck this might add something to your praise
As hee who coppying a rare Picture, shall
Equall, if not exceede, the Originall,
By many shalbee held in as high fame
As was the first inuentour of the same.
Nor can your worke bee any whit disgrac't
By those who think it done with too much hast;
For had it beene in Michaell Angells power
To perfect his great iudgment in one hower,
Hee who for that should valew it the lesse,
His owne weake iudgment would therein expresse,

And though wee in a common Prouerb say,
That Rome was not built all vp in one day:
Yet could wee see a Citty *great as* Rome
In all her splendor in one minute come
To such perfection, wee might more expresse,
Our wonders, and not make the glory lesse.
So I conclude with modest truth, and dare
All their free Censures who can but compare
And whosoere shall try may spend his Age
Ere in your whole work hee shall mend one Page.

A TABLE OF THE TITLES AND SVMMARIES OF THE CHAPTERS CONTAYNED IN THESE FOWER FIRST BOOKES OF THE REPLIE TO THE MOST EXCELLENT KING OF GREAT BRITAINE.

THE FIRST BOOKE.

THE SECOND BOOKE.

X. Of

THE THIRD BOOKE.

THE FOVRTH BOOKE.

XXXIII.

TO THE MAIESTIE OF

HENRIETTA MARIA OF BOVRBON

QVEENE OF GREAT

BRITTAINE

YOVR MAIESTIE.

MAY please to be informed, that I haue in this dedication deliuered you that right, that I durst not with-hold from you: your challenge hath so manie iust titles, as had I giuen it to anie others protection, I had done your Maiestie a palpable iniurie. You are a daughter of France, and therefore fittest to owne his worke who was in his time, an Ornament of your countrie. You are the Queene of England, and therefore fittest to patronize the making him an English man, that, was before so famous a Frenchman. You are Kinge Iames his Sonns wife, and therefore, since the misfortune of our times, hath made it a presumption, to giue the Inheritance of this worke (that was sent to the Father in Frēch) to the Sonne in English, whose proper right it is, you are fittest to receiue it for him, who are such a parte of him, as none can make you two, other then one. And for the honor of my Sexe, let me saie it, you are a woeman, though farr aboue other wemen, therefore fittest to protect a womans worke, if a plaine translation wherein there is nothing aimed at, but rightlie to expresse the Authors intention may be called a worke. And last (to crowne your other additions) you are a Catholicke, and a zealous one, and therefore fittest to receiue the dedication of a Catholicke-worke. And besides all this which doth appropriate it to you for my particular, your Maiestie is she, to whom I professe my selfe.

A most faithfull subiect, and a most humble seruant.

TO THE READER.

READER

THOV shalt heere receiue a Translation wel intended, wherein the Translator could haue noe other end, but to informe thee aright. To looke for glorie from Translation, is beneath my intention, and if I had aimed at that, I would not haue chosen so late a writer, but heere I sawe stored vp, as much of antiquitie, as would most fitlie serue for this purpose. I desire to haue noe more guest at of me, but that I am a Catholique, and a Woman: the first serues for mine honor, and the second, for my excuse, since if the worke be but meanely done, it is noe wonder, for my Sexe can raise noe great expectation of anie thing that shall come from me: yet were it a great follie in me, if I would expose to the view of the world, a worke of this kinde, except I iudged it, to want nothing fitt, for a Translation. Therefore I will confesse, I thinke it well done, and so had I confest sufficientlie in printing it: if it gaine noe applause, hee that writt it faire, hath lost more labour then I haue done, for I dare auouch, it hath bene fower times as long in transcribing, as it was in translating. I will not make vse of that worne-out forme of saying, I printed it against my will, mooued by the importunitie of Friends: I was mooued to it by my beleefe, that it might make those English that vnderstand not French, whereof there are maine, euen in our vniuersities, reade Perron; And when that is done, I haue my End, the rest I leaue to Gods pleasure.

THE LETTER OF THE LORD CARDINALL OF

PERRON.

SENT TO MONSIEVR CASAVBON INTO ENGLAND.

SIR. the letter that you deliuered to Monsieur de la Bodery, was deliuered to me by him, euen as I was vpon my departure for a voyage into Normandy; and since my returne from thence, I haue bene almost perpetuallie sicke, which hindered me from answering with more speede. Now that my disease begins to be at some truce with me, I will paie the arrerages of this delaie, and will first thanke you for the good office that you haue done me, in shewing the lettet I writt to you, to the most excellent king of great Brittaine, and in procuring me an interest in his fauour: I will striue so to husband it by my humble seruices, (and particularlye by celebrating his praises, which is the only fruite that good and vertuons kinges, such as hee doe gather from all the labours and thornie cares, that the burden of a kingdome loades them with,) as his maiestie shall haue noe cause to be sorrie, that it be declared to after ages, how he hath honord mee with his well wishes, ād how I haue had his vertues in reuerence and admiration. As for the translation of the verses of Virgill, whereof you writt to me that he desires a Copie, that which I sent you being lost; I deferr yet for some daies, to acquit myself of that dutie, because I haue put it to the presse, with the addition of a part of the fowrth, which I haue ended expressely for his maiesties sake, to inlarge my presēte to him. As soone as those few Copies which are in doing, shall be finished, I will not faile to addresse one of them to you, to offer vp to him on my behalfe The third point of your letter yet remaines; which is, that his Maiestie was astonishr at those wordes in my letter; That, excepting the title of Catholicke, I knew nothing wanting in him, to expresse the figure of a perfect and compleate Prince: and that he pretendes, that since he beleeues all thinges that the Ancientes haue with an vnanimous consent esteemed necessarie to saluation, the title of Catholique cannot bee denied him. Now as on the one side, I can not but greatlie praise his maiesties pietie and Christian humilitie, in not disdayning to submitt his iudgement, adorned with so manie lightes naturall ād acquired, to that of those cleare beames of antiquitie; (imitating therein the wisdome of that great Emperor *Thodosius*; who thought there was noe better meanes to agree the dissentions which disturbed the Church of his time, then to exact from either part an answere; whither thy beleeued that the Fathers which had flourish'd in the Church before the separation, had bene orthodoxall; and that being confessed, to summon them to submitt themselues to whatsoeuer they should be found to haue beleeued:) so on the other side, there are manie obseruations to be made vpon this Thesis, before wee passe to the hypothesis; which since I Cannot represent to his maiestie, I shall be gladd to informe you of them for your particular satisfaction.

The first is, that the name of Catholicke, is not a name of beleefe simplie, but of Communion also; else antiquitie would not haue refused that title to those which were not separated from the beleefe, but from the Communion of the Church: nor would they haue protested, that out of the Catholicke Church, the Faith and Sacramentes may be had, but not Saluation. *Out of the Catholicke Church*, saith S. Augustin, in his treatie " of Conference with Emeritus, a man may haue orders, hee maie haue Sa" craments, he may sing Alleluya, he may answere Amen, he may keepe the " Gospell, he may haue and preach the faith in the name of the Father, of " the Sonn, and of the holie Ghost, but he can no where finde Saluation, but " in the Catholicke Church. And in the Booke, De vtilit. credendi, There " is a Church as all men graunt, if you cast your eyes ouer the extent of the " whole world, more full in multitude, then all the rest; and as those, that know themselues to be of it, affirme, more sincere in the doctrine of truth. *But of the truth, that is an other question: That will suffice for this search, that there is one Catholicke Church, vpon which seuerall heresies impose seuerall names; whereas they are all call called euery one by his particular name, which they dare not disauow; from whence it may appeare to the iudgment of anie arbiter (that is not prepossessed by fauour,) to whom the name of Catholicke, whereof all are ambitions, ought to bee attributed.* And in the Booke against the fundamentall Epistle: *Then to omitt this wisdome which you denie to bee in the Catholicke Church, there are manie other things, which doe most iustlie retaine me in her bosome: the consent of people and nations retaine me therein; the authoritie begũn by miracles, nourished by hope, increased by charitie, confirmed by antiquitie, retaines me therein: the succession of Prelates euen from the verie seate of Peter, to whom our Lord deliuered his sheepe to be fedd after his Resurrection, euen to the present Bishops seate, retaines me therein: and finallie; the verie name of Catholick retaines me therein, which not without cause this Church alone, amongst so manie heresies, hath in such sorte obtained, as though all heretickes would be called Catholiques; neuerthelesse, when a stranger askes where the Catholicke Church doth assemble, there is not one hereticke that dares shew his tẽple, or his howse.* And in his treatise of Faith, and of the Creede: Wee beleeue the holie " Church and that Catholick; for heretickes and schismatickes, call their " Congregations Churches: but hereticks beleeuing of God false thinges, " violate faith; and Schismatickes separate themselues from brotherly " charitie by vniust diuisions, allthough they beleeue the same things that " we beleeue: and therefore neither can the hereticke belonge to the Ca" tholicke Church, because she loues God; nor the schismaticke, because " she loues her neightour. And in the Booke, Of the vnitie of the Church: " All those that beleeue, as hath bene said, that ouer Lord IESVS is come in " the flesh, and is risen againe in the same flesh wherein he was borne, and " hath suffered and that he is the sõne of god, god with god, ãd one with the " Father, and the onlie immoueable word of the Father, by which all things " haue bene made; but yet dissent so from his bodie, which is the Church, " that theire communion is not with the whole; or is spread in deed, but yet " is in some part found to be separate; it is manifest, they are not in the Ca" tholick Church. And Prosper, his scholler: Hee, saith hee, that Commu" nicates with this vniuersall Church, is a Christian and a Catholicke; " but he that communicates not therewith, is an hereticke and Antichrist.

And for this cause wee see, that the Fathers denied the title of Catholique to the Donatists, because of the separation of Communion, and yet graunted it to those, from whom the Donatists had taken their doctrine, because of the vnitie of Communion. *Cyprians people, saith* S. *Pacian, hath neuer bene called otherwise then Catholicke. And Sainct Vincentius Lerinensis: O admi-*

rable

rable change! the authors of one selfe same opinion, are adiudged Catholickes; and the Sectaries hereticks! And S. Augustin; *Dissention and diuision*, saith hee, *makes you heretickes, and peace and vnitie makes Catholiques.* And that in the fowrth Coūcell of *Carthage*, this article was inserted into the triall of the promotion of Bisshops; whither they beleeue, that out of the Catholicke Church none cā be saued. And that in the Epistle of the Councell of Cyrtha, it was repeated by S. Augustin, who was Secretarie thereto, in theses wordes: *Whosoeuer is separated from this Catholicke Church, how praise-worthie soeuer he conceaue his life to bee, by this onlie crime, that he is separated from the vnitie of Christ, he shall not haue life, but the wrath of God shall remaine vpon him.* And after by *Fulgentius* in these wordes: *Beleeue firmelie and doubt it not at all, that no hereticke or Schismaticke baptized in the name of the Father, of the sonne, and of the only Ghost, if he be not reconciled to the Catholicke Church, what almes soeuer he may giue, yea though he should shedde his blood for the name of Christ; can in any sort be saued.* That I say was against, or principallie against the Donatists. And neuerthelesse, the Donatists agreed in all the doctrine of the Creede, and of the Scripture with the Catholicks: *You are with vs, saith* S. *Augustine, in Baptisme, in the Creede, and in all the other Sacraments of our Lord; but in the spirit of vnitie, and in the bond of peace, and finallie in the Catholicke Church, you are not with vs* And yet they differed only in one pointe of vnwritten tradition, which, as S. Augustin himself (who principallie triumphes ouer this heresie) confessed, could not be demonstrated by Scripture. This, saith hee, in the Booke of the vnitie of the Church, *neither thou, nor I, doe euidentlie reade.* And in the first Booke against *Cresconius; though for this there be noe example in the scriptures, yet euen in this wee follow, the truth of the Scriptures, when wee doe that which hath pleased the vniuersall Church, which the authoritie of the same scriptures doth recommend.* And in the secōd Booke of Baptisme against the Donatists: *And ourselues*, saith hee, *durst affirme no such thing, but that we are vpheld by the vnanimous authoritie of the Church.* And in the fift. *The Apostles haue in this, prescribed vs nothing; but this custome which was opposite to* Cyprian, *ought to be beleeued to haue taken it's originall from their tradition; as manie other things, which the vniuersall* Church *obserues, and for this cause are with good right beleeued to haue bene commaunded by the Apostles, although they haue not bene vvritten.* From whence it appeares, that to obtaine the name of Catholicke, it sufficeth not to hold, or rather to suppose to hold the same beleefe that the Fathers held, vnlesse they communicate with the same Catholicke Church, wherewith the Fathers did communicate, and which by succession of persons, and, as wee pretend, of doctrine, is deriued downe to vs: and if she haue lost anie thing of her extent in our hemisphere, she recouers as much and more daily in the other hemisphere, that these prophecies may be fulfilled: *a In thy seede, shall all the nations of the earth be blessed. b In the last daies, the mountaine of the howse of our Lord, shall bee vpon the topp of mountaines, and shall be exalted aboue all the highe hills, and all nations shall come vp to her. c This Ghospell of the Kingdome must be preached ouer all the world, and then the end shall come;* and such like, in right whereof the Church, as saith S. Augustin, hath obtained the title and the marke of Catholicke.

[Margin: Contra literas Petil. l. 2. c. 95 — Epist. 152 — De fide ad Petr. c. 39. — Epist. 48. — Cap. 29. — Cap. 33. — Cap. 4. — Cap. 23. — a Gen. 12. 26. — b Gal 3. Isa. 2. — c Matt 14. — De vnit. Eccles. ca. 2. & 3. & alibi.]

The SECOND obseruation is vpon the restriction in Cases necessarie to saluation: For besides pointes necessarie to saluation, there are two other degrees of thinges, the one sort profitable to saluation, as it is (according to the opinion of your owne ministers) to sell all our goods and giue it to the poore: to fast in affliction to appease the wrath of God: to pray our Bretheren in the faith to praie to God for vs; and the other sort lawfull, and not repugnant to saluation, as to fly from persecution; to liue by the Altar, since we serue at the Altar, to putt awaie our wiues for adulterie, and other the like: for I alleadge these for examples, and not for instances. Now it is needefull to be cōformable to the integritie of the beleefe of the Fathers, to beleeue all thinges that they haue beleeued, according to that degree wherein they haue beleeued them: to witt, to beleeue for thinges necessarie to saluation those thinges that they haue esteemed to be necessarie for saluation: and for thinges profitable to saluation: those things that they haue esteemed to be profitable to saluation: and for things lawfull and not repugnant to saluation, those thinges that they haue holden to be lawfull and not repugnant to saluation: and not vnder colour that the two last kindes, are not things necessarie to saluation, but only profitable or lawfull, to condemne them, and to separate ourselues for their occasion from the Church, which then had thē in practise, and still practiseth thē to this day.

The third obseruation is vpon the ambiguitie of the word *necessarie to saluation*, which because of the diuers kindes of necessitie which haue place in matters of religion, is capable of diuers sences: for there is an absolute necessitie, and a conditionall necessitie; a necessitie of meanes, and a necessitie of precept; a necessitie of speciall beleefe, and a necessitie of generall beleefe; a necessitie of act, and a necessitie of approbatiō. I call an absolute necessitie (not simplie, but by vertue of Gods institution,) that which receiues no excuse of impossibilitie, nor anie exception of place, time or persons: as in regard of those that are of age, capable of knowledge, the beleefe in Christ mediator betweene God and man: for neither the circumstance of being in a place where wee cannot be instructed in that article; nor the preuention of time, in dying before wee are informed thereof; nor the condition of being an ignorant person, vnlearned, dull not apt to comprehend; a sheepe and not a shepheard, can warrant those from damnation, that beleeue it not actually, for as much as *who beleeues not in the onlie Sonn of Gods, is alreadie iudged*: And in regard of little Children, baptisme only according to our doctrine, may supplie the defect of Faith in Christ in their behalfe, agreeing with that sentence of S. Augustin: *Doe not beleeue, doe not saie, doe not teache if thou wilt be a Catholick, that little children which are preuented by death, from being baptized, can come to the remission of originall sinne.* And of this kinde of necessitie the examples are in small number. I call that conditionall necessitie, which obligeth not but in case of possibilitie, and receiues exception of place, time and persons: and that againe hath diuers branches: For first in regard of Faith there are manie points that are necessarie to be beleeued, if a man be in place where he may be instructed in them, or who hath time to be informed of them, which are not necessary for a man that liues in a wildernesse, or so pressed with the instant of death, as he hath noe leasure to receiue instruction: as that Christ was borne of a virgin that he was Crucified vnder Pontius Pilate, that hee rose againe the third daie. And manie thinges are necessary to be beleeued and holden for pointes of Faith, either by the bodie of the Church in generall, or by the order of the ministers and pastors, which are the eyes of the Church: which are not necessary for euery particular person to knowe, and hold to be points of Faith; as that the persons of the Trinitie, are the same in essence, and distinct in subsistence; that the Father hath begotten the sonn necessarily and not freely; that they are the diuine persōs which produce, and are produced, and not the essence which doth neither produce, nor is produced: that the workes of the trinitie without are vndiuided: that the only persō of the sonn hath been incarnate, and not anie of the others: that in Christ there are two substances, and one subsistence: that the diuinitie was not to him in the steede of a soule, but that besides his Bodie and his diuinitie, he had a Soule sensible and reasonable that what he once tooke in hypostaticall vnion hee hath not abandoned: that the diuell was created good, and made hinself euill by the freedome of his will: and other such like. And in regard of action, there are manie things necessarie in case of possibilitie, and according to the oportunity of places, times and persons, which are not absolutely necessarie, when the commoditie to accomplish them is wanting, as the assistance at Church Seruice, the actuall participation of the Eucharist. And manie are necessarie to some, as mission and imposition of handes to the Pastors of the Church; and marriage to those that will haue issue which are not necessary to others. And in breefe, some thinges are necessary to obtaine Saluation others some to obtaine it more easilie for ones-selfe, and others to procure and mediate it for other men: some for the constitution of the Church, and others for the edification and more ample propagation of the Church: some for the simple being of Christian Religion; others for the better being, that is to saie, for the comlynesse, dignitie, and splendour of Christian Religion. I call necessitie of meanes that, that is in behalfe of the thinges them selues as that of Sacraments to which god hath graunted power to Conferr some grace and reall operation to saluation, that of the Commandementes of the morall lawe whose necessitie is imposed vpon vs by the law of nature, that of repenting sins, which is a meanes necessarie to obtaine their remission. I call necessitie of precept, that which is only obligatorie in regard of the Commaundement, as the celebration of the first daie of the weeke in memorie of that wherein our lord did rise againe, which wee for that cause, call our Lords daie, and other such like obseruations, the omission whereof, could be noe hindrance to Saluation, but in respect of disobedience, and breach of the Commaundement. I call necessitie of speciall beleefe, that of thoses pointes, which all Faithfull, if they be not preuented by death, are obliged to beleeue with faith expresse, distinct and determinate, which the Schoolemen call explicit faith; as the twelue articles, of the Creede. I call necessitie of generall beleefe, that of those thinges which euery particular man is not obliged to beleeue with a distinct ād explicite faith: as the doctrine of originall sin the article or the two wills in Christ, the article that the holy Ghost proceedes frō the Father and from the Sonne; the beleefe that Baptisme giuē forth of the Church (prouided it be in the forme of the Church) is true Baptisme, and that heretickes which haue receiued Baptisme, must not be rebaptised when they returne to the Church: and other such like, when the simple sort of faithfull people, are not obliged to beleeue, with a distinct and explicit faith, but it sufficeth that they beleeue them generallie in the Faith of the Church; that is to saie, that they adhere to the Church that beleeues them, by whose faith they liue whiles they remaine in her Communion, as Children liue by their mothers nourishmēt whilst they are in her bowells. I call necessitie of act, that of those thinges which euerie particular person is obliged to execute actuallie, as to Confesse the name of Christ, to forgiue offences done to them, to restore the Goods of an other man. I call necessitie of approbation, that of those thinges which euerie particular man is not bound to execute actuallie but onlie not to contradict them, and not to condemne those that doe them nor the church that approoues thē, ād not to separate thēselues frō her vpō this occasiō, vpō paine of separating themselues frō their owne saluation, as the choice to liue in virginitie and single life, and other the like. Of all which kindes of necessitie, the Fathers haue holden manie thinges (euerie one according to it is degree) diuerslie necessarie to saluation as wee shall make manifest in those occasions that will offer themselues wherein to examine them: it is not to be conformable to the ancient beleefe and practise of the catholicke church, to hold the pointes of doctrine or actiō that the Fathers haue holden to be necessary to saluation, according to some of these kindes of necessitie, and to reiect the others; but to conforme our selues to the ancient beleefe and catholick practise, we must hold for necessary to saluation, all those things that the Fathers haue holden to be necessarie to saluation, in that degree, and according to those kindes of necessitie, as theyhaue holden them.

The fowrth obseruation is vpon the word FATHERS, which some, when it comes to the effect of their promise, to submit themselues to the iudgment of antiquitie, would restraine to the first or second age after the Apostles, not that they hope to finde in that space of time, anie thing in their behalfe: but because the Church being then oppressed with persecutions, there remaines to vs so fewe writinges of that date, and those against persons, and about points, for the most part so differing from the disputations of this present age, as the face of the ancient doctrine and practise of the Church, cannot euidentlie appeare to be therein represented. Now equitie would, that being to compare the state of the Societies of this age, wich pretend to the title of the Catholick Church, with the state of the ancient Church; wee should looke to take such a time, wherein not only our competitors might agree with vs, that the Church of the Fathers was still the true Church, the true Spouse of Christ, she in whom resided the lawfull authoritie to iudge questions in Religion: but also those monuments doe sufficiently remaine to vs, to manifest throughly all her doctrines and all her obseruations. Which can neuer be better chosen for both partes, then in the time wherein the fower first Councells were holden; that is to saie, from the Emperour Constantine, who was the first Emperour that was publicklie a Christian, to the Emperour Marcian. And it seemes to me, that his Maiestie hath yielded to this, and also more liberallie in some of his writinges, hauing extended this space, to the first fiue ages. For besides that the deliuerie from the yoake and subiection of the Pagans, then gaue the Church meanes to speake lowder, and to haue more communication with all her partes, situated in so manie different regions of the earth, and to flourish in a greater multitude of learned and excellent writers, which is the cause that there remaine to vs without comparison more monuments of those ages, wherein to view the entire forme of the ancient Christian Religion, then of the former ages: Besides this, I saie, our aduersaries cannot denie, but that church which nursed vp the first Christian Emperours, which rooted out the Temples and seruices of the false Gods, which exercised the Soueraigne Tribunall of Spirituall authoritie vpon earth, by the condemnation which she denounced vpon the fowre most famous heresies in the fowre first generall Councells, which were the fowre first Parliaments and
Isa.60.62. 54. Estates generall of Christs Kingdome; must bee she of whom it hath bene foretold, that Kinges should be her nursing Fathers: that the nations should walke in her light, and Kings in the brightnes of her rising: that, euery engine sett vp against her, should be destroyed: that she should iudge euery tongue that should resist her in iudgment: that God had sett watchmen vpon her walles, which neuer should be silent by daie or
a Matth. 16. 18. 1. Tim. 3. night: a that the gates of hell should not preuaile against her: that whosoeuer should not obey her should be holden for a heathen and a publican: and in breefe, that she was the Pillar and foundation of truth. *Shall we*
De vtilit. Cred. c. 17 *doubt*, Sayth S. Augustin, who liued in the betweene-times of these first

fowre Councells, *to sett our-selnes in the lapp of that Church, which by succession of Bishops from the seate of the Apostles euen to the confeßion of all mankinde, (the hereticks in vaine barkiug about her, and being condemned partlie by the iudgment of the people themselues, partlie by the grauitie of Councells, and partlie by the maiestie of Miracles) hath obtained full authoritie: to whom not to giue the preheminence, must be an act of extreame impietie or of a headie arrogancie?* And againe, [b] *The Catholick Church fighting against all heresies, may be opposed, but she cannot be ouerthrowne: all heresies are come forth from her, as vnprofitable branches cutt From their vine, but she remains in her roote, in her vine in her charitie.* Let that then bee holden for trulie anciēt, and marked with the character of the primitiue Church, which shall be found to haue bene beleeued and practised vniuersallie by the Fathers, which liued in the time of the first fowre Councells; and principallie when it shall appeare to vs, that the things testified to vs by the authors of those ages, were not holden by them for doctrines, or obseruations sprung vp in their time but for doctrines or obseruations, which had bene perpetuallie practised in the Church from the age of the Apostles: although perchance, there can not be found for euerie of them in particular, so expresse testimonies in the former ages, as in those of the first fowre Councells, because of the fewe writinges which the persecution of those times, haue suffered to come to our handes. For it sufficeth to assure vs of the perpetuall vse of such thinges that the Fathers of the first fower Councells, who had more knowledge of the ages before them, then wee can haue, doe testifie to vs, to haue beleeued and practised them, not as thinges instituted in their age, but as thinges that haue alwaies had place in the Church, and had come to them by a succession of obseruation from the Apostles downe to their time; and that there is not to be found in former authors anie testimony against them, but contrariwise in all places, where there is occasion to mention them, agreable and fauorable testimonies; that is to saie in breefe, that, is to be holden ancient by vs, which those whom we account ancient, haue themselues holden to be ancient.

[b] De Symb. & Catec. l. 1. c. 5.

The fifth obseruation is vpon the consent of the beleefe of the Fathers, which some contentious spirits would haue to be, when one selfesame thing is actuallie found in the writings of all the Fathers, which is an vniust and impertinent pretence. For to haue a doctrine or obseruation to bee trulie holden by the Fathers for vniuersall and Catholicke, it is not necessarie it should be in the writinges of all the Fathers, who haue not all written of the same matters, and of whose writinges, all haue not come to our handes: but there are two other lawfull waies, to secure our selues of them: The one is, when the most eminent Fathers of euery country agree in the affirmation of the same doctrine or practise, and that none of the others that haue bene without note of dissention from the Church, haue opposed it: As when S. Augustin hath cited against the Pelagians the testimonie of eleuen eminent Fathers, all consenting in one and the same doctrine; he supposeth hee hath sufficientlie produced against them, the Common beleefe of the Catholicke Church: and when the Councell of Ephesus had produced tenn Fathers of former ages, they conceiued they had sufficiently expressed the consent of the former Church against Nestorius his doctrine: *Because none,* saith Vincentius Lerinensis, *doubteth but that those tenn, did trulie hold the same with al their other bretheren.* The other is, when the Fathers speake not as Doctors, but as witnesses of the Customes and practise of the Curch of their times; and doe not saie, I beleeue this should be soe holden, or so vnderstood, or so obserued; but that the Church from one end of the earth to the other, beleeues it so, or obserues it soe:

Contr. Iul. l. 5. & 2.

Vincent. Lirin. c. 41

it soe: For then we noe longer hold what they saie, for a thing said by them, but as a thing said by the whole Church, and principallie when it is in pointes whereof they could not be ignorant, either because of the Condition of the thinges, as in matters of fact, or because of the sufficiencie of the persons: and in this case wee argue noe more vpon their wordes probablie, as wee doe when they speake in the qualitie of particular Doctors, but we argue therevpon demonstratiuelie. That then shall remaine trulie vniuersall and Catholicke, that the most eminent Fathers of the times of the fowre first Councells, haue taught in seuerall regions of the earth; and against which, none (except some persons noted for dissention from the Church) hath resisted; or that the Fathers of those ages doe testifie to haue bin beleeued, and practised by the whole Church in their times: And that shall remaine trulie antient and Apostolicke, that the Fathers of those ages doe testifie to haue bin obserued by the whole Church, not as a thing sprung vp in their time, but as a thing deriued downe to them either from the immemorial succession of former ages, or from the expresse tradition of the Apostles. For these thinges hauing bin holden vniuersallie by the Catholicke Church in the time of the first fowre Councells, they could haue noe other originall, but from an vniuersall authoritie; for as much as in the Catholicke Church, which did then so strictlie obserue the rule mentioned by *Saint Vincentius Lirinensis*, of opposing vniuersalitie to particularitie; a doctrine or obseruation from a particular beginning could not be slipt in, ād spread into an vniforme and vniuersall beleefe ād Custome, through all partes of the Earth; and principallie soe as the Fathers that were next after these vniuersall innouations, could not perceiue it: but it must needes be, that all that was then vniuersallie obserued in the Church, must haue come from an vniuersall beginning. Now there were in those ages, according to the beleefe of your ministers, but two beginnings of vniuersall authoritie in the Church; to wit, either the Apostles, or the generall Councells; for they Will not yeild that the Sea Apostolicke had then anie vniversall authoritie. And therefore whatsoeuer was vniuersallie and vniformly obserued in the Church, by all the Prouinces of the Earth in the time of the first fowre generall Councells, and had not begun in that time, but had bin before practised; that is to saie; before there had bin anie generall Councell in the Church; must necessarilie haue bin from the tradition of the Apostles, following these rules of S. Augustin: *Those thinges, said hee which we obserue, not by writeing, but by tradition, which are kept ouer all the extent of the earth, must be vnderstood to haue bin retained from the appointemēt and institution, either of the Apostles themselues, or from the generall Councells, whose authoritie is most wholsome in the Church. And elsewhere; what custome soeuer, men looking vpward can not discerne to haue bene instituted by those of later times, is rightlie beleeued to haue bin instituted by the Apostles: and there are manie such, which would bee too longe to repeate. And againe; If anie one herein seeke for diuine authoritie, that which the vniuersall Church obserues, and which hath not bin instituted by the Councells, but hath alwaies bin held, is iustly beleeued not to haue bin giuen by tradition, but by Apostolicall authoritie, &c.* Which Rules of S. Augustin, if they haue place in those things which the Fathers of the time of the first fowre Councells testifie to haue bin obserued iu the Church before the fowre first Coun cells, how much more ought they to haue it in those things, that the same Fathers affirme not in termes equiualent, but expresslie to haue bin instituted and ordained by the Apostles?

Epist. 118.

De Bapt. cont. Don. l.4.c.6.

Ibidem c. 24.

These fiue obseruations then made vpon the theses, I will saie, to passe vnto the hypothesis, that your ministers to whose societie his Maiestie

outwardlie

outwardlie adheres, are so farr from holding all the same thinges that the Fathers haue beleeued and practised as necessarie to Saluation, that in the only Synaxis or Church Liturgie, which is the Seale of Ecclesiasticall Communion, the fowre principall thinges for which they haue seperated themselues from vs, which are the reall-presence of the Bodie of Christ in the Sacrament, the Oblation of the Sacrifice of the Eucharist, prayer and oblation for the dead, and the prayers of the Saints, the Fathers haue all vniuersallie and vniformely beleeued, holden and practised as things necessarie (but in different kindes of necessitie) vnto saluation. By which meanes, if your ministers had bene in the time of the Fathers, as they haue for these thinges renounced our Seruice and our Communion; so must they for the same causes haue renounced the Seruice and Communion of the Fathers, and Consequently, the title and Societie of the Catholicke Church. I haue said the reall presence of the Bodie of Christ in the Sacrament, not but that I could haue gone farther, and said, the Substantiall transition of the Sacrament into the Bodie of Christ, which wee call transubstantiation but I haue been content to saie, the reall presence, because it is not precisely and particularlie vpon the transubstantiation, but vpon the reall presence of the Bodie of Christ in the Sacrament, that we ground the importance and necessitie of this Sacrament to Saluation; to witt, the Communion and Substantiall vnion to the Bodie of Christ; which S. Cyrill calls, the knott of our vnion with god. Nor is it particularly and precisely vpon transubstantiation, but vpon the reall presence that the two inconueniences depend, for which your ministers, in this article, seperate themselues from our Lyturgies; which are, one, the adoration of the Bodie of Christ in the Sacramēt, which they will haue to be only sought and adored in heauen: and the other, the pretended distraction of the vnitie of the Bodie of Christ, by existence in manie places in the Sacrament. Neither haue I spocken of the prerogatiue of the *Roman* Church, which all the Fathers haue holden for the center and roote of Episcopall vnitie, and of Ecclesiasticall Communion; because I will beleeue you are sufficientlie read in antiquitie, to knowe that the first Fathers, Councells, and Christian, Emperors, haue perpetuallie granted therevnto, the primacie and supereminent ouersight, ouer all religions and ecclesiasticall things; which is all that the church exacts as a point of Faith, from their confession that enter into her communion, to the end to discerne her societie from that of the Greekes and other complices of their Sect, wich haue deuided themselues for some ages, from the visible and ministeriall head of the Church.

In Ioan. lib. 11. cap. 27.

These fowre points then, which are the principall Springes of our dissention and which being agreed vpon, it would be easie for vs to agree vpon the rest; I saye, that the Fathers of the time of the fowre first Councels haue all holden and practised as necessary to Saluation, though with diuers kindes of necessitie. The reall Presence, of the Bodie of Christ; and the oblation of the sacrifice, they haue holden as necessary with necessitie of meanes, for the Bodie of the Church absolutely, and for euery particuler person conditionnallie. Prayer and oblation for the dead they haue holden as necessarie, by necessitie of meanes for those for whom it is done that soe their deliuerãce from temporall paines, which remaine after this life for sinne cōmitted, after baptisme, ād for which thy haue not done such penances as it hath pleased God whollie to accept, may be hastned by the prayers and sacrifices of the Church: and necessarie with necessitie of precept and to exercise christian charitie and pietie both to the Church that offers them, and to the ministers and Pastors by whom she offers them.

The prayer of the Saintes, they haue holden as necessarie to the bodie of the Church, and to the ministers by whõ they are made, with necessitie of precept, to exercise the commerce betweene the Church Militant, and the Church Triumphant: and to particular persons out of the offices of the Church, and in their priuate deuotions not necessary with necessitie of act, but only profitable, that they may the more easilie obtaine pardon for their sinnes, by the concourse of their prayers who are alreadie in the perfect and assured possession of the grace of God: but necessary to them and all others with nesitie of approbation; that is to saie, they are obliged not to contradict them, and not to condemne the custome and doctrine of the Church in that article: and not to separate themselues from her vpon this occasion, vnder paine of falling into Anathema, and to be holden for heretickes. All which things I will not now stand to proue, least I make a Booke of a letter; but I doe oblige myselfe to iustifie them, whensoeuer you shall desire it; and to make it appeare both by the vnanimous consent of the Fathers, that haue flourished in the time of the first fowre councells, and by the formes which remaine to vs in their writings of the ancient Church Seruice, that all the Catholicke Church of their times hath vninersallie and vniformely beleeued, holden and practised them, throughout all the regions and prouinces of the earth. I oblige myself I saie, to make it appeare to you, that she hath holden these fower thinges in the same sence, and in the same forme, and for the same end, as our Lyturgies are, and not as obseruations that then sprung vp, but as things that the same Fathers testified to haue bene beleeued and practised from all antiquitie, and to be deriued to them by an vninterrupted continuance from the tradition or approbation of the Apostles. Soe as they cannot renounce the Communion of our Church vnder pretence of anie of these fowre points, without renoũcing the Communion of the ancient catholick Church, and consequently the inheritance of saluation: and that by authors and testimonies, all able to abide the touch; as you know I am curious to make vse of noe other; and with cleare and ingenuous answeres to all obiections, collected out of the Fathers of the same ages, or of ages before them. A thing that will be the more easie for me, because the proofes that wee will avouch out of the Fathers, are proofes which containe in expresse termes the affirmatiue of what wee saie: whereas our aduersaries cannot finde one only passage which containes in expresse terme the negatiue, but only in termes from whence they pretend to inferr it by consequence; and which at a iust tribunall, would not merit so much as to be heard. For who knowes not, that it is too great an iniustice, to alleadge consequences from passages, and euen those euill interpreted and misvnderstood, and in whose illation, there is alwaies some paralogisme hidd, against the expresse wordes, and the liuely and actuall practise of the same fathers, from whom they are collected, and that may be good to take the Fathers for Aduersaries, and to accuse them for want of Sence or memorie; but not to take them for Iudges, and to submitt themselues to the obseruation of what they haue beleeued and practised? To this I will also adde whensoeuer you shall desire it, the present Conformitie of all the other Patriarchall Churches in these fowre cases with the Roman, and of all those which haue remained euen to this daie, vnder their iurisdiction; to witt, those that are vnder the Patriarchall iurisdiction of the Patriarck of *Constantinople*; as the *Grecians, Russians, Muscouites, and Asians of Asia-minor*, separate from vs neere eight hundred yeares: Of those that are vnde the Greeke Patriarch of *Antioch*; as the *Syrians, Mesopotamians*, and others yet more Easterne nations: (for those that obey the *Syrian* Patriarch, as the *Maronites*, perseuer in the

Com

Communion of the *Roman* Church; of those that relye vpon the *Egiptian* Patriarch of *Alexandria*, as the Egiptians whom they call *Cophtites*, and the Ethiopians which haue bene diuided both from vs, and from the greekes more then eleuen hundred yeares, euen from the time of one of the fowre first Councells, to witt, of the Councell of *Chalcedon*. For all these hold these fower pointes; yea, with more iealousie, if it be possible, then the latine Churches, and particularlie, the article of the Sacrament, where of they doe not only beleeue transubstantiation, which the greekes at this daie call in the very selfsame sence and phrase, μετουσίωσις, but also exercise the adoration with externall gesture, more full of humilitie then ours. A manifest proof that these fowre pointes were vniformely holden and obserued by the ancient Cahtholicke Church, since all the partes, whereinto the ancient Catholicke Church is dismẽbred, doe retaine them vniformly to this daie; notwithstanding soe manie distances, separations, and diuisions through all the regions of the Earth.

These are in generall, the causes that haue moued me to vse that exception in my letter, that you obiect to me in yours: whereof if the Excellent King of great Brittaine had as well leasure to heare the particularities, as he hath capacitie to comprehend them, I assure myselfe he would not thinke it strange, that I should desire in him the title of *Catholique*; but he would desire it himsefe, and put himsefe in state to obtaine it, and to cause it to be obtained by those, that are depriued of it: that is to saie, he would add yet to is other Crownes, that of making himsefe a mediator of the peace of the Church; which would be to him a more triumphant glorie then that of all the *Alexanders*, and of all the *Cæsars*, and which would gaine to his Isle, noe lesse an honor in hauing bredd him, thẽ to haue bredd great *Constantine*, the first deliuerer and pacifier of the christian Church. I praie god that he will one daie Crowne all the other graces wherewith he hath indowed him, with that; and heare to this effect the prayers of his late Queene Mother, whose teares like those of *S.* Augustins Mother, doe not onlie intercede for him in heauen, but her blood also;

And likewise keepe you Sr. in his safe and holie protection.

From Paris, 15. Iulij. 1611.

AN ADMONITION TO THE READER.

This letter to Mons. Casaubon, occasiond the whole discourse ensuing. For the letter being shewed to his most excellent maiesty our Souuerain Lord king Iames of glorio us memory: it pleased him not only to read it, but to take paines to answer it, as he thought most conuenient. To which answer of his maiesty the Cardinall replieth with that modesty and submission, which is due to the person and worth of so high and mighty a Monarch. and with that learning, and solidyty, that might be expected from so great a maister of truth as that most eminent Cardinall was, in behalf of so glorious a cause, as is the doctrine of the catholique Church.

THE L. CARDIN. PERRONS

REPLIE TO HIS MAIESTIES

ANSWER TO THE LETTER WRITTEN TO

MONS CASAVBON.

THE FIRST OBSERVATION

Reduced into an abridgement by the Kinge.

THE name of *Catholicke* doth not simplie designe Faith, but also Communion with the Catholicke Church; for this Cause the Fathers would not suffer that those shouldbee Called *Catholickes*, which had separated themselues from the communion of the Church, though they retained the Faith thereof: For there is one only Catholicke Church, out of the which, Faith and Sacramentes may be had, but not Saluation. To this end there are manie places alleaged out of S. AVGTSTIN.

OF THE VSE OF THE WORD CATHOLIQVE

THE ANSVVERE OF THE KINGE.

CHAPITRE I.

TO beleeue the Catholicke Church, and to beleeue the Communion of Saintes, are put distinctly, as diuers thinges in the Creede; and it seemes the first was ptincipallie inserted to discerne the Iewish Synagogue from the Christian Church; which ought not to be, (as that was) inclosed within the lymittes of one only nation, but to be spread in length and breadth, through all the regions of the world. And therefore the reason is not manifest, enough why in the beginning of this obseruation it is said, that the title of Catholicke designeth Communion. These two thinges are very neere one an other, but different notwithstandinge, as wee haue shewed.

THE REPLIE.

WHEN the Philosopher FAVORINVS disputed against the Emperor ADRIAN, and that his hearers were amazed, and reproached it to him that he suffered the Emperor to confute him, and yielded to him; he answered them, *should not I yield to a man, that commaundes twentie legions*? Soe if there were noe question in this worke, but of humane philosophie & secular learninge, it should be easie for me to stop my selfe at FAVORINVS boundes, and to abstaine to contest with his maiestie, or to resist him. But since heere wee treate of his interest, who hath, not legions of men, but of Angells, and which hath for his title, THE KINGE OF KINGES, AND LORD OF LORDES; and from whom this excellent Kinge himselfe makes profession to holde in Fee his life and Crownes; that is to saie, the cause of IESVS CHRIST, and of his Kingdome, which is the Church: I will promise myselfe from his Maiesties bountie, that he will not mislike, where it shall be needefull, that I resist and contradict him, with all the respectiue libertie, that the lawes of disputation yield me.

Then for the argument of the Creede, I will saie, after I haue kist my weapones, three thinges for my defence; FIRST that it is vncertaine, whither the cause of the Communion of Saintes, be an article aparte, or an explication of the precedinge cause, and a declaration that the Catholicke Church consistes not in the simple number of the faithfull, euery one considered a parte; but in the ioinct Communion of all the bodie of the faithfull, in such sorte as both clauses make but one article as it seemeth sainct IEROM, [a] RVFFINVS, [b] and [c] Sainct AVGVSTINE, who haue omitted the latter, haue esteemed it. The SECOND, that it is vncertaine, whether it signifie the Communion, that the faithfull liuinge haue one with an other, or the Commerce that the Saintes of the triumphant Church doe exercise with the Saintes of the militant Church, by the prayers, that the Saints of the triumphant, offer for the Saints of the militant; and the commemoration that the saints of the militant make of the saints of the triumphant, which is that, that wee in our Liturgie call, *to communicate with the memory of the Saintes*. And the THIRD, that whatsoeuer it signifie, it is most certaine, that the word CATHOLICKE was not added to that of the Church, to distinguish the Christian Church from the Iewish Synagogue, which had neuer borne the name of Church in qualitie of a title of a Religion when the creed was Composed, and by consequence did not oblige the Christian Church to take the Epithete of Catholicke, to bee discerned from that, from which in all cases she had bene sufficientlie distinguished by the title of *Christian*; but it was added to discerne the true Church from hereticall, and schismaticall Societies, which vsurpe equiuocally, and by false markes, the name of *Church*, for that our Lord was the first that affected and consecrated the word ECCLESIA (which we vsually translate in Englishe *Church*) to signifie a societie of Religion; whereas before, neither it, nor the Hebrewe word that answeres to it, had anie other vse, but that which prophane authors giue it, which is to signifie. *Assemblies, conuocations, Generall Estates*; as when [d] DEMOSTHENES said to ESCHINES, *thou wert dumbe to the* assemblies where the greeke word is *Ecclesijs*, the conuocations or general meetings. And as when Aristotle [e] called the conuocations of Creete ecclesias And as when the Scholiast of HOMER said, *Iupiter gathered together Ecclesias the Assemblies of the Gods*: It appeares first by the testimonie of MOSES, who forbids bastardes to enter *into* the Church of Israell; And of DAVID who singes, *I hate the Church of the malignant*; And of S. STEPHEN, who said MOSES was in the Church in the solitarie place; that is to saie, with the multitude of the people in the desert. It appeares secondlie, by the testimonie of S. IEROM, and of S. CYRILLVS, who interpretinge this verse of ESAY, *Thou shalt bee called by a new name, that the mouth of our Lord shall pronounce*, Doe affirme, that this new name, must be the name of Church *It shall noe more* (saith S. IEROM) *be called* Ierusalem *and* Sion, *but it shall receiue a new name, that the Lord shall impose vpon it, sayinge to the Apostle* PETER, *thou art* PETER, *and vpon this* PETRA *or rock I will build my Church*. And S. CYRILL; *It shall be noe more called Synagogue, but the Church of the liuinge God*. And finallie, it appeares by the verie testimonie of our aduersaries, that not only in all the textes of the old Testament, where the Greeke

[a] Hier. adu. Lucifer. [b] Ruffin. in Symbol. [c] August. de fide & symbol & de Symb. ad Catec.

[d] Demost.

[e] Arist. polit 2.

Deuteron. 23. Psal. 25. Act. 7.

Hieron. in Esai c. 62.

Cyril. ibid.

translation of the Seuentie, vse the word *Ecclesia*; but also in all those of the new, where that word hath relation to anie other multitude, beside the Christian Church, they expresse it by *Congregation* or *Assemblies*. And if since the cominge of IESVS CHRIST, and the edition of the creede the Fathers haue sometymes called the Synagogue, by the name of *Ecclesia* or *Church*, it hath bene by anticipation, to shew the successiue vnitie of the one and other societie; but not that the Iewish Church while it lasted, hath euer vndertaken to attribute to herselfe, the title of a Church, in the qualitie of a title of Religion. Neither consequently, when the creede was composed, was there neede of an Epithete, to distinguish the Christian Church from her: for as the starr that the authors call *Lucifer*, although it be the same with that, that is called *Vesper*, yet when it goes before the Sonne, it beares one name; and when it followes him, it hath an other: soe although the Iewish congregation hath bene in some sorte one same societie with the Christiā Congregatiō, neuerthelesse, whē this societie hath gone Before her SVNNE, which is CHRIST, she hath borne one name, to witt, the *Synagogue* and when she followes him, she beares an other, to witt; the *Church*. And therefore when our Lord said to S. Peter *Dic ecclesiæ, tell it to the Church, and if he heare not he Church, let him be to thee, as an heathen or a publican*; And when S. LVKE, relates, that HEROD sett himselfe to Persecute *quosdam de ecclesia some of those of the Church*; and when saint Paul writes; *I teach it so in all the Churches*; And againe, *bee without scandall to the Iewes, and to the Gentiles, and to the Church of God*: And when S. Iames proclaimes; *If anie one be sicke, lett him call the priestes of the Church*: And when S. Ireneus saith, *there haue bene sacrifices among the people, there are sacrifices in the Church*; they thought they had sufficiently distinguished, without anie other additiō, the Christian Church frō the Iewish Synagogue. And contrariwise when the Church of SMYRNA in an age neighbouringe vpon that of the Apostles intitles her Epistle, to the Church of PHILOMILION, and to all the [a] Diocesses of the Catholique Church, that are throughout the world: And when CLEMENT ALEXANDRINVS writes, *There needes not manie wordes to shewe that the mocke-Councells of heretickes, are* [b] *after the Catholicke Church*. And when TERTVLLIAN saieth; *Marcion gaue his money to the Catholique Church, which reiected both it and him, when he strayed from our truth to heresie*; And when sainct CYPRIAN aduertised the Bishops of Aфricke that passed in to Italie, *to acknowledge and hold fast the roote and matrice of the Catholicke Church*. And when Saint EPIPHANIVS reporteth that vnder the persecution of DIOCLESIAN *those that held the ancient Churches, called themselues,* [a] *the Catholicke Church, and the Militians the Church of the martyres*; And when the Emperor CONSTANTINE ordained, *that all the* [b] *Oratories of the Heretickes should be taken from them, and presently after deliuered to the Catholicke Church*: they pretended not by the word *Catholicke*, to distinguish the Christian Church from the Iewish, but to distinguish the great and the originall bodie of the Church, from the particular and later sectes.

Yet wee acknowledge, that the word, *Catholicke*, in distinguishing by her vniuersalitie the true Church from the hereticall and schismaticall sectes, distinguisheth her alsoe by accident from the Iewish Synagogue: as a speciall difference in distinguishing her species from other species of the same genders, doth also distinguish it from that of other genders, though that be not her proper office; for the word *reasonable*, discerninge men from birds, fishes, serpentes, and other beastes, leaues him not vndiscerned accessarily from plantes, metalls, and stones.

Matth. 18.
Act. 12.
1. Cor. 4
1. Cor. 10.
Iacob. 5.
Iren. cont. Valen. lib. 4. c. 34.
Euseb. histor. eod. l. 4. cap. 13.
b Tertull. cōtra Marcion. lib. 4. c. 4.
Clem. Alex: Strō. lib. 27.
Tertull. cont. Marc. lib. 4. cap. 4.
a Epiph. hær. 65.
b Euseb. de vita Constant. l. 3.

But we maintaine, the expresse and direct end for which the *Surname of Catholik* hath bene added to the Church, (I saie to the Church and not to the figures of the Church) hath bene to distinguish it from hereticall and Schismaticall sectes. *If I should this daie by chance enter into a populous towne* saith S. PACIANVS, an author celebrated by saint Ierom, *and finde there Marcionistes and Apolinarians (* it must be reade, *Apellecians) Cataphrigians, Nouatians, and other such like, which call themselues Christians; by what surname should I knowe the Congregation of my people, if it were not intitled Catholicke:* and againe, *Christian is my name, Catholicke is my Surname; that names me, this markes me out; by that I am manifested* (prodor & non probor) *by this I am distinguished.* And saint CYRILL of Ierusalem, an author the same age, expoundinge the creede; *For this cause (* saith he *) thy faith hath giuen thee this article to holde vndoubtedlie, and in the holie* Catholicke Church, *to the end thou should'st flie the polluted Conuenticles of heretickes.* And a little after: *And when thou comst into a towne, inquire, not simplie where the temple of our Lord is, for the other heresies of impious persons, doe likewise call theire dens, the temples of the Lord, neither aske simplie where the Church is, but where is the Catholique Church? for that name is the proper name of this holie Church.* And saint AVGVSTINE in his booke of the Faith and the creede *Wee beleeue* (saith he) *the holie Church, and that Catholicke; for the heretickes and Schismatickes name also theire Congregations, Churches; but heretickes beleeuing in God in a false manner, violate the faith; and Schismatickes by theire vniust Diuisions, seperate themselues from brotherlie Charitie, although they beleeue the same thinges that we beleeue; therefore the hereticke appartaineth not to the Catholicke Church, because she loues God; nor the Schismaticke, because she loues her neighbour.* So that it amazeth me, that I haue had soe little industrie to explaine my selfe, as to haue giuen his Maiestie occasion to answere, that the reason for which I had said in the beginninge of my first obseruation, that the *word Catholicke was not a title of simple beliefe but of communion,* was not enough manifest. For hauinge alleaged these fower places of saint AVGVSTINE; *Schismatickes appertaine not to the Catholicke Church, although they beleeue the same thinges with vs. Those that disagree soe from the bodie of Christ which is the Church, as theire communion is not with all; or that it spread it selfe, but is found separate in some part; it is manifest they are not in the* Catholicke *Church. There is a Church, if you cast your eyes ouer the extent of the whole world more aboundant in multitude; and also, as those that know themselues to be of it affirme, more sincere in truth, then all the others; but of the truth is an other disputation. Diuision and dissention makes you heretickes; and peace and vnitie makes vs* Catholickes. And hauinge accompanied them with these wordes of saint VINCENTIVS Lirinensis; *O admirable conuersion,* (*or change*) *the authors of one selfe opinion, are called* Catholiques*, and the followers of it heretickes!* And with those of saint PROSPER; *He that communicates with the vniuersall* church, *is a* christian *and a catholicke; and he that communicates not therewith, is an hereticke and Antichrist.* It seemed to me that I had sufficiently shewed that the title of Catholicke is not a simple title of beliefe, but of communion also. It is true, I expected not, that a question that had bene anciently moued and adiuged euen with the interuention of the authoritie of Emperors, should againe haue bene contested against, and put into dispute. For in the controuersie of Catholickes and Donatistes vpon the word C*atholicke* (before the decision whereof, as saint Austin saith, the Church was neuer perfectly treated of, no more then before the questions of the Arrians, the Trinitie had neuer bene perfectlie treated of) the *thesis* or *tenet* of the Catholickes, was that the word, C*atholicke*, was a word of C*ommunion*, and not a word of *Simple beliefe*. The Christian Africans are called saith

Pacianus ad Sympr. ep. 1. Hier. descript. Eccles.

Cyril. Hierosl. Catecheses 15. ibidem.

Aug. de fide & Symb c. 10.

De fide & Symb. c. 10

De vnit. eccles. c. 4.

De vtilit. cred. c. 7.

Cont. lit. Petil. l. 2. c. 95.

Vin. Lirin. c. 9.

Prosp. de promis. & bened. Dei par. 4. l. 5.

Aug. in psal. 54.

Saint AVGVSTIN, *and not with out good right, Catholickes*, proteſting by *theire proper Communion the word* καθόλου: And againe *wee shew by the teſtimonie of our Cōmunion, that wee haue the Catholicke Church*: & the *theſis* of the Donatiſtes contrariwiſe was, that the word *Catholicke*, was not a word of *Cōmunion* but of *beliefe* and obſeruation of precepts. *The Donatiſtes* (ſaith Saint AVSTIN) *anſwered that the word Catholike was not deriued from the vniuerſalitie of nations, but from the fulnes of the Sacramentes*; that is to ſaie, from the integritie of the doctrine. [g] And in the Epiſtle to VINCENTIVS Rogat. *Thou thinkeſt* (*ſaid he*) *then to ſaie ſome ſubtile thing when thou interpreteſt the name of Catholicke, not from the Communion of the whole world, but from the obſeruation of all the preceptes and diuine Sacramentes.* And againe: *you are thoſe that hold the Catholicke faith, not from the Communion of the whole world, but from the obſeruation of all the preceptes aud diuine Sacramentes.* And the iudgement that was made vpon this difference, was that the word, Catholicke, was a title, not of *ſimple beliefe*, but of *Communion alſo*. *After a contention of* 40. *daies*, (ſaith [a]OPTATVS Mileuit. ſpeaking of the firſt diſputation of the Donatiſtes, *the finall ſentēce of the Bishops Eunomius and Olimpius*, (whcih were the Bishops deputed to iudge the poſſeſſiō of the word, *Catholicke*, betweene the Catholickes of Africa and the Donatiſtes) *was that that was Catholicke, that was ſpread throughout the world*. And Saint AVSTINE ſpeaking of the Conference of Carthage; *The Commiſſarie*, ſaid he, *anſwered, that he could not by prouiſion, attribute the name Catholicke to anie other then to thoſe, to whom the Emperor* (*from whom he had his Commiſion*) *had attributed it*. And in an other place, citing the law of the Emperors, made vpon this Conference: *The Emperors*, ſaid he, *haue forbidden, that thoſe that vſurpe the name of Chriſtians out of the Communion of the Catholicke Church, and will not in peace adore the author of peace, should dare to poſſeſſe anie thing vnder the title of the Church.* And againe, [d] *The Emperors of our Communion haue ordained lawes againſt all heretikes: now they call heretickes, thoſe that are not of theire Communion, amongſt which you are.* And after, diſputing with the ſame Donatiſts: *Thou askeſt* (ſaid he) *of a ſtranger, whether he be a pagan or a Chriſtian; he anſweres thee, a Chriſtian; thou askest him whether he be a catechumenus or one of the faithfull, leaſt he should intrudehimſelfe vnlawfullie to the Sacraments; he anſwers thee, one of the faithfull; thou askeſt him of what Communion he is, he answers thee, a Chriſtian Catholicke.*

Ang. Collat. Carth. l 3. Auguſt. ibid. Aug. ibid. g. Aug. Epiſt 48. g. Aug ibid a Optat. Mileuit. cont. Parm l 1. b. Aug. breuin. col l. 3. c. In Ioan. tract. 6. d. Aug. Pſal. 57. e Aug. de paſtor. c. 13

CHAP. II.

Of the Conditions of the Catholicke Church. The purſuite of the kings anſwere.

NOw the King belieues ſimplie, without colour or fraude; that the Church of God is one only by name and effect, Catholicke and vniuerſall, ſpread ouer all the world, out of which he affirmes himſelfe, there can be noe hope of Saluation: he condemnes and deteſtes thoſe, which either heeretofore, or ſince, haue departed from the faith of the Catholicke Church, & are become heretickes, as the Manichees: or from her Communion, and are become ſchiſmatickes, as the Donatiſts. Againſt which two kindes of men principally ſainct AVGVSTINE hath written the things alleaged in this obſeruation.

THE REPLIE.

TELESIVS a Stripling of Greece, hauing won the prize and victorie of the Combate in the Pythian games, when there was question of leadinge him in triumph, there arose such a dispute betweene the diuers natiõs there present, euery one being earnest to haue him for theire owne, as the one drawing him one waie, the other an other waie, insteed of receiuing the honor which was prepared for him, he was torne and dismembred euen by those that stroue who should honor him most. Soe happenes it to the Church: All those that beare the name of Christians auow that to her only appertaines the victory ouer hell, and that whosoeuer will haue parte in the prize and glory of this Triumph, must serue vnder her ensigne; But when they come to debate of the true bodie of this societie, then euery sect desirous to draw her to themselues, they rent and teare her in peeces; and in steed of embracing the Church which consistes in vnitie, they embrace schisme and diuision, which is the death and ruyne of the Church. The cause, or rather the pretext of this euill, comes from two faultes, that the aduersaries of the Church commit in the distinction of the word Ecclesia, or *Church*, which makes the possession vncertaine and disputable: The one is the fraudulent *restriction* of the terme of the *Church* to the only *inuisible number* of the predestinate, by which (when they feele themselues pressed to represent the succession of theire Church) they saue themselues like Homers Æneas, or Virgils Cacus, in obscuritie and darknes. The other is the equiuocall and captious *extension* of the same word, *Church*, to all Sectes, which professe the name of Christ, by which (when they see themselues excluded from the refuge of theire *inuisible Church*) they haue recourse from darknes to confusion, and confesse that there hath bene alwaies a visible Church, but sometymes pure in faith, and sometymes impure, that is to saie now a Church, and now noe Church. And therefore I attribute it to a singular care of the prouidence of God, that his Maiesty saying he beleeues the catholicke Church, hath added as to preuent all theses shiftes, *without colour or fraude*. For to beleeue the catholicke church *without colour or fraude*, is to beleeue her in the sence that the Fathers haue beleeued and vnderstood her the Fathers I say which haue left vs these sentences pronunced sometymes, as in the hypothesis against the Manichees and Donatists; but as in the thesis against all kindes of heretickes or schismatickes in generall that out of the Catholicke Church there is noe saluation; that whosoeuer is separate from the Catholicke Church cannot haue life, and other such like, which his Maiestie protested to approue. Now first by the word Catholicke Church, these Fathers haue beleeued and intended such a Church, as these wordes of Esay designe: *In the last daies, the Mountaine of the Lord, shall be on the topp of all the Mountaines, and all the hills shall flowe to her. The people shall walke in thy light, and the kings in the brightnes of thy Orient. Theire seede shall be knowne amongst the people, and theire kinge in the middest of the nations. And these* of our Lord; *The Citie built vpon the mountaine cannot be hid. Tell it to the Church., and if he heare not the Church, let him be to thee as a heathen or publican*: that is to saie, a Church visible, manifest, and eminent, and not a Church either perpetually inuisible, or (as if she had Giges ring), now visible and now inuisible.

Esai.2. Esai.60. Esai.61. Matth.5. Matth. 18. Cypr. de vnit. Eccl.

The

The Church (saith Sainct CYPRIAN) *clothed with the light of our Lord, sheds her beames through the whole world.* And S. CRISOSTOME g *It is more easie to extinguish the Sunne, then to obscure the Church.* And againe; h *The Sunne is not soe manifest, nor the ligh thereof, as the actions of the Church.* And Sainct AVGVSTINE a *The Church is not hidden, for she is not put vnder a bushell, but in a Candlesticke, that she may giue light to all those which are in the house.* And of her our Lord hath said, *The Cittie built vpon the Mountaine cannot be hidd.* And in an other place b *It is a condition common to all heretickes, not to see the thinge that is in the world the most manifest, and built in the light of all the Nations, out of the vnitie whereof, all that they doe (though they seeme to doe it very exactly) can noe more warrant them against the wrath of God, then the Spiders webb against the rigor of the cold.* And againe; *he hath this most certaine marke, that she cannot be hidden; she is then knowne to all nations. The sect of Donatus is vnknowne to manie Nations, then that cannot be she.* And in deede how could it be that the Fathers had not had neede to be purged with Hellebore, who imployed these sentences against the heretickes and Schismatickes of theire ages, to presse them to returne to the Church. *That he shall neuer come to the rewardes of Iesus Christ, that hath abandoned the Church of Christ:* d *that he shall not haue God for his Father, that hath not the Church for his Mother:* e *That he cannot liue, that withdrawes himselfe from the Church, and buildes to himselfe other seates and other dwellinges;* f *That Christ is not with those who assemble themselues out of the Church:* g *That he who shall not be in the Arcke, shall perishe at the comminge of the floud:* h *that he which eates the lambe out of his howse, is prophane:* i *That out of the Catholicke Church none can be saued:* k *whosoeuer is separate from the Catholicke Church cannot haue life:* l *That the Catholicke Church alone is the body of Christ:* m *That out of this bodie, the holy Ghost quickens none:* n *That whosoeuer then will haue the holy Ghost, should take heede of beinge separated from her, and likewise take heede of entring into her fainedly,* if they had beleeued that the Catholicke Church had bene an inuisible flocke of predestinate persons, knowne only to God, and into whose Rolle as appointed from all eternitie none could enter or be added thereunto?

Chrif. in Esai. hom. 4. idem in Esai c. 2. Aug. de vnit. Eccles c. 14. Aug. cont. Parm l. 2. cap 3. Cont. lit. Petil lib. 1. cap. 104. Cypr. de vnit. Eccles. Ibid. Ibidem. Ibidem. Ibid. & Hier. cont. Lucifer. Hier. cont. Lucif. 1. Conc. Carth. 4 c. 1. Aug. ep. 152. Idem ep. 50 Ibidem. Ibidem.

SECONDLY by the word *Catholicke Church* the Fathers did not intend the Chaos and generall Masse of all Christian Sectes & Societies, as well pure as impure, as well heretickes as Schismatickes; as our aduersaries doe when they feele themselues excluded from theire refuge of an inuisible Church: but by the word *Cacholicke Church* the Fathers intended a Societie, such both for doctrine and Communion, as these propheticall Oracles painted her forth: o *Thou art wholie faire, and there is noe spott in thee.* p *Thou shalt be called the citie of Iustice, the faithfull citie.* q *Through thee shall noe more passe anie that is vncircumcised or vncleane. I will espouse thee in faith, and thou shalt know that I am the Lord.* And these Euangelicall decrees; s *The gates of Hell shall not preuaile against her.* t *The Church is the pillar and foundation of truth.* u *There is noe communion of Christ with Belial, nor of light with darknesse.* x *If anie one bring not this doctrine, saie not to him so much, as well be it with thee; for whosoeuer shall saie to him, well be it with thee, communicates in his wicked workes:* that is to saie they vnderstood by that terme, socitie of Christians, extracted and contracted by the iust and sufficient meanes of externall vocation to saluation; and distinct and purified, from the impurity and contagion of all the hereticall & schismatical sectes. y *If thou hearest in any parte* (saith saint IEROM) *of men denominated from anie but from Christ, as Marcionites, Valentineans, Montayners or Campites, know that it is not the Church of Christ, but the Synagogue of Antichrist.* & OPTATVS Mileuitanus z *besides*

Cant. 4. Esai. 1. Esai. 52. Ose. 2. Matth. 16. Tim 3. 2. Corinth. 6. 2. Ioan. Hier. cont. Lucifer.

Optat. l. 1. *the only Church which is truly Catholicke, the others amongst the heretickes, are esteemed to be, but are not soe indeed.* And againe, *The Church is one, which cannot* Idem l. 2. *be amongst vs, and amongst you; it remaines then that it be in one only place;* And De vtilitat. cred. c. 7. Sainct AVGVSTINE to Honoratus; *Although there be manie heresies of Christians, and that all would be called Catholickes, yet there is alwaies one Church, if you cast your eies vpon the extent of the whole worlde, more abundant in multitude, and also as those that know themselues to be of it, more sincere in truth, then all the rest: but of the truth, that is an other Dispute. That which sufficeth for the question, is, that there is one Church, to which different heresies impose different names, whereas they are all called by there particular names that they dare not disauow; from whence it appeares in the indgment of anie not preoccupate with fauour, to whom the name of Catholicke, whereof they* De vera relig. cap. 6. *are all ambitions, ought to bee attributed.* And in the booke of the true Religion: *Wee must holde the Christian Religion, and the Communion of that Church, that is called Catholicke both by her owne, and by strangers: for whether heretickes and Schismatickes will or will not, when they speake not with theires, but with stranges they call the Catholickes noe otherwise then Catholickes.* And in the Comentary vpon the 149. Psalme; *The Church of the Saints is the Catholicke Church: The Church of the Saintes is not the Church of heretickes; she hath bene marked out before she was seene, and she hath bene exhibited to the end she should be seene.* And De fide & symb, c. 10. in the booke of Faith and of the Creede; *Wee beleeue one Church, and that, the Catholicke: for the heretickes and Schismatickes, call also theire congregations Churches; but the hereticke beleeuinge of God false things violate the Faith; And Schismatickes by vniust dissentions separate themselues from brotherly Charitie, although they belieue the same thinges that we belieue and therefore neither the heretickes doe appertaine to the Catholique Church because she loues God; nor the Schismatickes because she loues her neighbour.* And certainly how could the Fathers without making themselues ridiculous te theire auditors; beate downe the heretickes and Schismatickes with these sentences, [a] *That out of the Catholicke Church there is noe Saluation; that* [b] *whosoeuer is not in the Catholique Church, canot haue life:* [c] *that he shall not haue God for his father, who wil not haue the Church for his mother:* [d] *That Christ is not with those that assemble out of the Church:* [e] *That although they should be slaine for the confession of Christ, this spot is not washt awaie euen with bloud:* [f] *That he cannot be a martyr, that is not in the Church:* [g] *That out of the Catholicke Church, one may haue Faith, Sacraments, Orders, and in summe, euery thing, except saluation:* [h] *That he that communicates not with the Catholicke Church, is an hereticke and Antichrist:* [i] *That noe hereticke nor Schismaticke, that is not restored to the Catholicke church before the end of this life, can be saued:* if they had belieued, that all the Sectes that professe the name of Christ both heretickes and Schismatickes, had bene in the Catholicke Church. THIRDLY by the word Catholicke Church, they did not intend a Church interrupted and intermitting, as that of the protestantes, which is borne and dyes by fittes, like the Tyndarides, but such a Church, as these wordes of the prophet describe; [a] *As in in the daies of Noe, I swore that I would no more bring the waters of the floud vpon the earth; soe haue I sworne I will no more be angrie against thee:* [b] *Thou shalt noe more be called the forsaken:* [c] *I will place my sanctification in the midst of them for euer.* [d] *I will noe more doe to the rest of this people as in tymes past.* And these of our Lord: [e] *The gates of hell shall not preuaile against her.* [f] *I am with you vntill the consummation of all ages.* [g] *The Spirit of truth shall dwell with you eternally.* [h] *Let the one growe with the other, vntill the haruest;*

[a] Concil. Carth. 4. cap. 1. [b] Aug. ep. 152. [c] De cym. ad Catech. lib. 4. [d] Cyp. de vnit. Eccl. [e] Ibidem. [f] Ibidem. [g] Aug. de gest. cum Emerit. [h] Prosp. promis. & prædic. Dei par. 4. cap. 5. [i] Fulhent. de fide ad Pet. c. 19. [a] Esai. 54. [b] Esai. 92. [c] Ezech. 37 [d] Ezech. 8. [e] Matt. 16. [f] Matt. 28. [g] Ion. 14. [h] Matt. 13.

that is to saie, a Church permanent eternall, and not capeable of ruine. *i Wee acknowledge* (said that great ALEXANDER Bishop of Alexandria) *one only Catholicke and Apostolicke Church which, as she can neuer bee rooted out though all the world should vndertake to oppose her, soe she outhrowes disperseth all the wicked assaulth of heretickes.* And Sainct ATHANASIVS; *l The Church is inuincible though hell it selfe should arise with all the power thereof, against her.* And THEOPHILVS; *n God in all tymes grants one selfe grace to his Church, to witt; that that Bodie should be kept intire, and that the venome of the Doctrine of heretickes shall haue noe power ouer her.* And Sainct AVGVSTINE. in the comentary vpon the 47. psalme; *God* (saith he) *hath founded her eternallie, let not heretickes deuided into factions boaste; let them not lift themselues vp, that saie heere is Christ and there is Christ.* And againe; *But perchance this Cittie, that hath possessed the whole world, shall be one daie ruined; neuer may it happen: God hath founded her eternallie: If then God hath founded her eternally, wherefore fearest thou that her foundation should fall?* And in the Comentary vpon the 101. psalme; *But his Church, which hath bene of all nations, is noe more, she is perished; soe saie they that are not in her; O impudent voice!* And a little after; *this voice soe abominable, soe detestable, soe full of presumption and falshood, which is sustained with noe truth, illuminated with noe wisedome, seasoned with noe salt, vaine, rash, headie, pernicious, the holy Ghost hath foreseene it.* And in the treatie of the Christian combate: *They saie the whole Church is perished, and the relickes remaine only on Donatus his side. O prowde and impious tongue!* And in the worke of Baptisme against the Donatists: *If the Church vere perished in Cyprians tyme, from whence did Donatus appeare? from what earth is he sprung vp? from what Sea is he come forth? from what heauen is he fallen?* And in the third booke against Parmenian; *How can they vaunt to haue anie Church, if she haue ceased from those tymes?* And in the explication of the Creede to the Cathecumenistes: *The Catholicke Church is she, that fighting with all heresies may be opposed, but cannot be ouerthrowne. All heresies are come out from her, as vnprofitable branches, cut from the vine: but she staies in her vine, in her roote, in her Charitie; And the gates of hell shall neuer ouerthrow her.* Behold *without colour or fraud*, what the Fathers vnderstood by the word Catholicke Church to witt; a Church visible and eminent, aboue all other Christian societies; A Church pure from all contagion of schisme and heresie; A Church perpetuall, and which had neuer suffered nor neuer could suffer anie interruption, neither in her faith, in her Communion, nor in her visibilitie; This Church if the most excellent King haue, let hin giue her to vs; if not, lett him receiue her from vs: *Aut det*, (as saint AVSTINE said, to the Donatists,) *aut accipiat.*

i. Alex. ep. ad Alex. Theodoret hist. l. E Eulex l. 1. cap. 4. *l.* Athan. orat. *n* Theof. ad Epiph apud Hierom. Ep. 67. Ang. Psal. 101. Ang. de agō. Christ c. 29. *r.* De bap. cont Do. l. 3. c. 2. Cont. Parm. l. 3. capt. 3. De Symbol. ad Catech. l. 1. c. 5. Angust. de vnit. Eul. c 6.

Of the proceeding of the Father, for the preseruation of the vnitie of the Church.

CHAP. III.

The pursute of the Kinges Answere,

THe Kinge commendes allso the prudence of the religious Bishops, who in the 4. Councell of Carthage, (as it is heere truly obserued,) added to the forme of the examination of Bishops, a particular interrogatory vpon this point, And his Maiestie is not ignorant, that the Fathers of the ancient Church haue oftentymes done manie thinges by forme of accommodation for the good of peace, and to the end to preuent the breach of vnitie and mutuall

Com-

Communion, whose example he protesteth he is readie to imitate, and to followe the steps of those that procure peace euen to the Altars, that is to saie: as much as in the present estate of the Church the integritie of his Conscience will permitt him. For he will giue place to none; either in extreame griefe, he suffers for the separation of the members of the Churdh, which the good Fathers haue soe much detested; or in his desire, to communicate, if it were possible for him, with all the members of the mysticall bodie of our Lord Iesus-Christ.

THE REPLIE.

IT was not by way of prudence, as prudence signifies a human vertue, that the Fathers pronounced this decree, *that out of the Catholicke Church saluation could not bee obtained;* but by way of decision, and as an article of faith. For this cause (saith sainct AVGVSTINE vpon the Creede,) *The Conclusion of this Sacrament is determined by the holie Church, for as much as if anie one be found out of it he shall be excluded from the number of the Children: And he shall not haue God for his Father, that will not haue the Church for his Mother; and it shall serue him for nothing to haue belieued or done soe manie, and soe manie good workes, without the true end or butte of the soueraigne good.* And sainct FVLGENTIVS in his booke of the Faith, *Holde this firmely, and doubt it not, that euery hereticke and Schismaticke baptized in the name of the Father, the Sonne, and the holy Ghost, if before the end of this life he be not reunited to the Church Catholicke, whatsoeuer almes he distribute, yea though he should shed his bloud for the name of Christ, cannot be saued.* And that which the Fathers haue done to hinder the breache of peace, and of mutuall communion, hath passed noe further then either to tolerate some locall and particular customes, which brought more burden then profit, as the custome some Africans had, not to touch the ground with theire naked feete in the Octaues of theire Baptisme; or to endure the manners and conuersation of some vitious men, without applyinge the iron & corrosiue of excommunication, for feare of diuidinge the Church, insteede of purginge it from wicked persons; From whence proceeded that famous sentence of sainct AVGVSTINE: *They tolerate for the good of vnitie that, which they hate for the good of equitie.* As for that which they haue done for the reestablishmēt of peace, it hath beē extēded to the yeeldinge somethinge, in the seuerity of discipline. For when Arrian or Donatist Bishops came backe to the Church, the Church in fauour of the people which followed them, receaued them by a forme of generall rehabilitatiō with facultie to exercise theire Episcopall power; Now this was against the ordinary rigor of the Canons. And therefore sainct AVGVSTINE hath from thence taken occasion to say, Thas as the trees, that are inoculated, receiue a wound in their barke, to giue waie to those branches that should be graffed in; soe the Church receiues a wound in her discipline, to the end to take in, and reincorporate hereticall people which were conuerted, and returne together with theire Bishops; but not that the loue of peace, hath euer transported the Fathers so farr, as to yield neuer so little in matters of Faith. Contrarywise sainct BASILE witnesseth; [a] *That they haue alwaies rather chosen to suffer a thousand deathes then to* [b] *betraie one sillable thereof.* And sainct EPIPHANIVS recited by sainct IEROM saith: [c] *That for one word, or two contrary to faith, manie heresies haue bene cast forth of the Church.* And S. AVGVSTINE; [d] *That the thinges contrary vnto faith and good manners, the Church doth neither approue them, conceale them, nor doe them.* Therefore his Maiestie ought not to haue feared to imitate wholy the zeale of the Fathers for the good of peace, and to doe for the restoringe the vnitie of the Church all things that the ancient Catholicke church hath approued practised, & taught. Neither ought he to haue added

Aug. de Symb. ad Cathech. l. 4. c. 10.

Fulg. de fid ad Petr. Diac. c. 39.

Aug. ep. 162

Aug. ep. 50.

a i Basil. apud Theod hist. Eccl. l. 4. c. 19.

d Aug. ep. 119.

c Hieron apol. cont. cont. Ruff. l 3.

to his, offer the exception of that prouerbe; *euen to the Altars*; since out of the true Church (such as was that of the Fathers to whose only Conditions wee exact his Maiesties communion with ours:) there are noe true Altars, but only Altars agaiust Altars; that is to saie prophane and Schismaticall Altars, as those of Ieroboam were, and the high places in the time of the law. Nor finally should he limit the desire he hath to communicate with all the true members of the misticall bodie of Christ, within this Condition, *if it were possible*; for it is so possible to communicate with all the actuall members of the misticall bodie of Christ, that contrariwise it is impossible, (except in case of error of fact) to communicate with anie one of them, but you must communicate either immediately or mediatly with all the rest; for the Church is that Societie whereof DAVID said; *Ierusalem which is built as a Cittie, whose participation is in vnitie*. And saint CYPRIAN; *The Catholicke Church, which is one, is not dismembred nor diuided, but keepes herselfe vnited, and is glewed together by the cement of the Prelates adheringe the one to the other*. And saint AVGVSTINE; *Those, whose Communion is not with all; or that doe spread themselues but yet find themselues in some parte diuided; it is manifest, they are not in the Catholicke Church*. And againe; *Whosoeuer defendeth one parte separate from the rest, let him not vsurpe the title of Catholicke*. And in an other place; *It may be, will some one saie, that there are other flockes of God, I knowe not where, whereof God hath care, but I knowe them not: But he is too absurd, euen in Common sense, that imagins such thinges*.

Psal. 122. Cyp. epist. ad Pupp. Aug. de vnit. Eccl. cap. 4. Coll. Carthag. p. 3. c. 101. De Pastor. c. 13.

Of the necessitie of communicatinge with the Catholicke Church.

CHAP. IV.

The pursute of the kinges Answere.

THese thinges beinge soe, the kinge neuerthelesse esteemes that he hath very iust cause to dissent from them who without anie distinction and exception incessantly presse this Communion.

THE REPLIE.

a THere is saith saint AVGVSTINE *noe iust necessitie to diuide vnitie*; b *and there is* (saith againe the same Doctor) *noe assurance of vnitie but in the Church, which built according to Gods promise vpon the mountaine cannot be hidden*. For besides that the examination of the Church is soe easie and soe certaine as saint AVSTIN saith: c *I haue the most manifest voice of my pastor who expresses to me, and pointes me out the Church without anie ambiguitie*: And againe, d *this is noe obscure question, wherein they may deceiue you, of whom the lord hath foretolde, that they shall come and saie heere is Christ*: And that the particular examination of Faith contrariwise is soe dangerous and difficult as yet most learned haue deceaued themselues in it; And as saint Ierom cryeth out; *There is great danger in speakinge in the Church, for feare least by a wronge interpretation, the Ghospell of Christ may be made the Ghospell of a man, or which is worse, the Ghospell of the diuell*. There is further this difference, which is, that he who hath the Church, is sure to adhere to the true Faith

a Cont. Parm. l. 2. cap. 11. b Cont. Parm. l. 3. cap. 4. c De vnit. Eccl c. 10. c De vnit. Eccl c. 10. d Ibid. c. 20 e Hieron. in ep. ad Galat. l. 1.

though he know not distinctly all the articles thereof, and that he is in the waie of Saluation; where he, that hath Faith, and is not in the Church, hath noe hope of Saluation. *If I haue all Faith* saith Sainct PAVLE *and haue not Charity, I am nothinge.* And Sainct AVGVSTIN, *He that hath Charitie is secure, and none can transporte charity out of the Catholique Church.* And elswhere *b If Schismatickes had Charitie, they would not rend the bodie of Christ, which is the Church.* By meanes whereof, as much as Charitie is more excellent then Faith, (followinge that oracle of the Apostle, *c but the greater of the three is Charitie,*) soe much the instance of the Church is more necessary, then that of Faith. *d Aboue all these thinges*, saith sainct PAVLE, *holde Charitie, which is the bond of perfection; and lett the peace of Christ, whereby you haue bene called into one bodie, holde the principall place in your hartes.* And againe, *lett vs not forsake our Congregation as some haue accustomed to doe.* And sainct Iude, *Woe be to those, that perish, in the Contradiction of Core.* And a while after, *people that separate themselues, sensuall men not hauinge the Spirit.* And it is a thinge so acknowledged by the Fathers, that they affirme, that faith it selfe turnes to increase of damnation to those, that possesse it out of the Church; yea they holde the cryme of Schisme to be worse then that of infidelitie and Idolatrie. *e Those,* saith Saint AVSTIN, *whom the Donatists doe heale from the wound of infidelity and Idolatrie, they hurt them more greevously with the wound of Schisme.* And for a proofe of his saying, he alleadgeth the example of Core, Dathan, and Abiron, and other Schismatickes of the old Testament, who were all sent quicke into hell, and punished more greevouslie, then the Idolators. *f Who doubtes,* saith he, *but that was committed most criminally that was punist most seuerelie?* And therefore, as the ancient heretickes haue alwaies against the vnitie of the Church pressed and Cryed out, *the Faith, the Faith;* soe the ancient Fathers against the diuisions of heretickes and Schismatickes, haue alwaies pressed and cried out, *the Church the Church. g He shall iudge,* saith S. IRENEVS *those that make Schismes in the Church, ambitions men, not hauinge the honor of God before theire eyes; but rather embracing theire owne interests, then the vnitie of the Church, and for little and light causes deuidinge the great and glorious bodie of Christ.* And a little after, *For in the end they cannot make anie soe important a reformation, as the euill of the Schisme is pernicious.* And sainct DENIS of Alexandria, writinge to Nouatian *h Certainly all thinges should rather be indured, then to consent to the diuision of the Church of God; those martyrs beinge noe lesse glorious, that expose themselues to hinder the dismembringe of the Church, then those that suffer rather then they will offer Sacrifice to Idolls.* And sainct CYPRIAN; *i Doe those, that assemble themselues without the Church of Christ, suppose Christ to bee with them in theire assemblie? Allthough they should be dragged to death, for the confession of the name of Christ, yet this spott is not washt awaie from them with bloude: the inexpiable and inexcusable crime of discord is not purged vith death it selfe; he cannot be a martyr that is not in the Church.* And sainct PACIAN; *k Although* (saith he) *Nouatian hath bene put to death, yet hath he not bene crowned: Wherefore not? because it was out of the peace of the Church, out of concord, out of this mother, whereof whosever will be a martyr must be a portion.* And Saint CHRYSOSTOME; *l nothinge stirrs* (saith he) *so sharpely the wrath of god, as the diuision of the Church; so as when wee haue done all other kindes of good workes, wee shall deserue no lesse cruell punishment deuidinge the vnitie and fulnes of the Church, then those that pierced and deuided his owne blessed bodie.* And S. AVGVSTINE: *m Out of the Catholike Church all thinges may bee had except Saluation etc. They may haue and preach the faith in the name of the Father, the sonne and the holy ghost; but they can noe where haue Saluation, but in the Catholicke Church.* And a little after: *I saie more, if a man out of the Church suffer the enemies of Christ, I saie not his Catholike brother that de-*

sires

1. Cor. 13. — a Aug in Psal. 21. — b De serm. Dom. in mont. c. 5. — c 1. Cor. 13. — d Hebr. 10. — e De bapt. cont Donat. l. 1. c. 8. — f Ibid. l. 2. c. 6. — g Iren. cōt. Hær. l. 4. c. 62. — h Apud Euseb. hist. eccl. l. 6. — i Cyp. de vnit. Eccl. — k Ad Sympr epist. 2. — l Chrys. in ep. ad Ephes. hom. 11. — m De gestis cum Emerit. — Ibidem.

sires his Saluation, but the enemie of Christ; if he suffer him without, and that he being out of the Church, the enemie of Christ saie to him, offer incense to Idolles, adore my Gods, and for not adoring them he be put to death by the enemie of Christ; he may well shedd his bloud, but he cannot obtaine the Crowne. And in an other place: *Being constituted out of the Church, and separated from the heape of vnitie, and the bond of Charitie, thou shouldest be punisht with eternall death, though thou shouldest haue bene burnt aliue for the name of Christ.* Aud againe: *I goe not to worship the diuells, I serue not stockes and stones, but I am of Donatus his partie. What will it serue thy turne, that the Father is not offended, since he will reuenge the Mothers iniuries?* And in his worke against the Aduersarie of the law, and the Prophets: [n] *If he heare not the Church, let him be to thee as a heathen or publican; which is more grieuous, then if he were stricken by the sword, consumed with flames, exposed to wilde beastes.* And in the booke of Pastors: [o] *The diuell doth not saie, let them be Donatistes, and not Arrians; be they heere, be they there, they appartaine to him, that gathers without any distinction. Let him, saith the diuell, adore Idolls, he his mine; let him remaine in Iewish superstition, he is myne: let him abandon vnitie, and enter into such or such an heresie, he is myne.* And in the professionto be made by the Donatistes returninge to the Church: [p] *Wee thought it had not imported in which part we had held the Faith of Christ; but thanckes be to our Lord, that hath taken vs in from the diuision, and taught vs, that it belonhgs to God who is one, to be serued in vnitie.* And FVLGENTIVS the second Sainct AVGVSTINE, and the Phenix borne a new out of his ashes: [q] *Out of this Church neither doth the title of Christian warrant anie bodie, nether doth baptisme conferr Saluation, nor can they offer a Sacrifice acceptable to God, nor receiue remission of Sinnes, nor obtaine life eternall: For there is one only Church, one only doue, one only well beloued, one only sponse.* And againe [r] *Beleeue this stedfastly without doubting, that euery hereticke or schismaticke baptized in the name of the Father, the Sonne, and the holy Ghost, if before the end of his life, he be not reconciled to the Catholikke Church, what almes soe euer he geueth, yea though he should shed his bloud for the name of Christ, he cannot obtaine saluation.* Faire, but fearefull lessons for those, who thinke, that in what communion soeuer they be, so they beleeue in Christ, they may be saued.

Aug. epist. 204.

In Psal. 88.

n. Contra aduers. leg. & proph. l. 1. c. 17.

o. Lib. de past. c. 12.

p. Epist. 48

q. Fulg. de remiss. pec. c. 22.

r. De fide ad Petr. Diac. c. 39.

Of the marks of the Church.

CHAPTER V.

The continuance of the Kinges answere.

AMongst the proper markes of the Church, the King confesseth, that that is greatly necessary; but his Majesty is not of opinion, that it is the true forme of the Church: and as the philosopher termes it, Τὸ τί ἦν εἶναι, that wherein it consisteth.

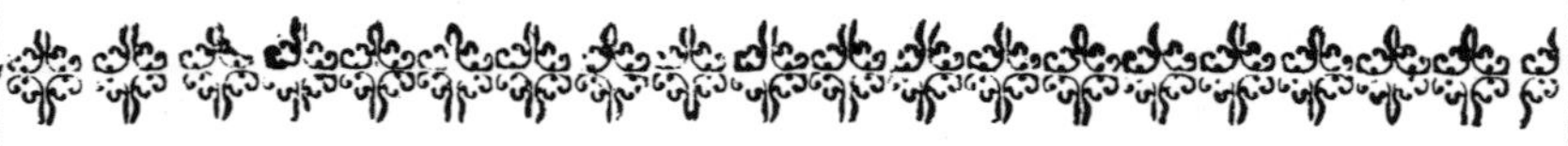

THE REPLIE.

Neither is it neceſſarie, that a condition, for to be the marke of anie thing, should be the eſſentiall forme of the thing: for then we should haue noe marke of anie ſubſtantiall thing. For we know not the eſſentiall forme of anie one of them, except only of man, and for more then three thouſand yeares, the true eſſentiall forme of man was vnknowen; witnes the ieaſt of Diogenes, vpon the definition of a man giuen by Plato. And therefore Saint BASILE reprocheth it to *Eunomius*, (who had boaſted that he knew the eſſence of the Father,) that he knew not ſoe much as the eſſence of the ground whereupon he walked euery daie; and that what comes to the knowledge of men, are but accidents. Neither on the other ſide is it neceſſary, that the eſſentiall forme of a thing should be the marke of the ſame thing. Nay contrarywiſe, to be the eſſentiall forme of anie thing, and to be the marke of the ſame thing; are commonly repugnant, and incompatible conditions. For the marke doth demonſtrate the thing to the ſenſe; and the eſſential forme doth shewe it to the vnderſtandinge; the marke deſignes the thing in the exiſtence, the eſſentiall forme deſignes it in the eſſence: The marke teacheth where the thinge is; and the eſſentiall forme teacheth what it is; the marke is ſooner knowne, then the thing; and contrarywiſe the thing is ſooner knowne, then the eſſentiall forme of the thing: for the thing defined (as Ariſtotle ſaith) preceedes in knowledge the definition; that is to ſaie; the whole is knowne before the reſolution of the thing into his eſſentiall partes. And therefore to ſaie, that the eminencie of the Communion is not the eſſentiall forme of the Church, hinders it not from being a marke of the Church: and a marke likewiſe not only greatlie neceſſary, but abſolutely neceſſary: [a] *She hath* (ſaith Saint AVGVSTINE) *this moſt certaine marke, that shee cannot be hidden; shee is then knowne to all nations, the Sect of Donatus is vnknowne to many nations, therefore that is not shee.* Againe, on the other ſide, to ſaie that the doctrine is the eſſentiall forme, or belongeth to the eſſentiall forme of the Church, makes not, that therefore it should be a marke of the Church: for a marke muſt haue three conditions: The *firſt* is, to be more knowne then the thing, ſince it is it that makes the thing knowne: the *ſecond*; that the thing neuer bee found without it; And the *third*, as we haue ſaid elſwhere, [b] that it be neuer found, either alone, if it be a totall marke, or with its fellowes, if it be a marke in part, without the thing. Now the truth of doctrine in all inſtances thereof is much harder to be knowne, then the ſocietie of the Church. I ſaid in all inſtances thereof; becauſe to know the right of the cauſe of the Church in one particular queſtion, with one or other Sect, ſufficeth not to knowe the Church by the doctrin, but it is neceſſary to know the truth of the doctrine of the Church, in all her particularities, conteſted by hereſies, as well paſt as preſent; before we can iudge by vertue of the examination of the doctrine, where the true Church is. For there needes no more, but that shee goe wrong in anie one controuerſie, to make her fall from the title of the true Church.

Cont. Eun. lib. 1.

1. Phyſ. c. 1.

a. Aug cõt. Lit. Petil. lib. 1. c. 104.

b. In the treatise of the vocation of Paſtors.

Now

Now who is he that can vaunt to know the integritie of the doctrine of the Church in all her instances, and to haue made the examination against euery one of the other societies, by infallible and insoluble proofes to all theire answeres, and by inuincible and irrefutable answeres to all theire obiections? And if anie could doe this, who knowes not, that the simple people, and ignorant and rusticall persons, (of whose Saluation neuerthelesse God hath the same care, that he hath of the learned, and to whom the markes of the Church should be equally common, since they are equallie obliged to obay her;) are not capable of this examination? [a] *For the rest of the people* (saith Saint AVGVSTINE) *it is not the quicknes of vnderstandinge, but the simplicity of beliefe, that secures them.* And by consequent, who seeth not, that they must haue other markes to know the Church by, then that of her doctrine; to wit, markes proportionable to theire capacitie, that is to saie, externall and sensible markes, as *eminencie*, *antiquitie*, *perpetuitie*, and such like; euen as children and ignorant persons must haue externall and sensible markes, and other then the essentiall forme of a man, to know and discerne a man from other liuing creatures: [b] *By what manifest marke* (cries out Saint AVGVSTINE, speaking in the person of a Catechumenist) *by what demonstration shall I (that am yet little and weake, and cannot discerne the pure truth, from the manie errors) know the Church of Christ, to which I am constrained to believe by the euent of soe manie things heeretofore presaged? for these causes* (saith he) *the Prophet goes forward, and as it were collecting methodically the motions of that spiritt, saith, that she is foretolde to be that Church, which is eminent and apparent to all.* And a little after; *and also because of the motions of these little ones, who may be seduced and diuerted by men from the brightnes of of the Church, our Lord goes before them saying; The Citie built vpon the Mountaine cannot be hidd.* And indeede how is it that Esaie should prophecy, that [c] *In the last daies the Mountaine of the Lord should be on the topp of all the Mountaines, and that all the hills should flow to her, and that the Nations should come and saie; let vs goe vp into the Mountaine of our Lord, and into the howse of the God of Iacob, and he will teache vs his waies*; if the only marke to know assuredly the howse of the Lord, that is to saie, the Church, were the especiall knowledge of his waies? And how should Saint PAVL say [d] *God hath placed in the Church Apostles, Prophetes, Euangelists, Pastors, and Doctors, &c. to the end we should be noe more little children, blowne about with euery winde of doctrine*; if he had not giuen vs other markes to know the Church, then the puritie of doctrine.

Besides, suppose the doctrine to be the marke of the Church; it must be either the doctrine contested betweene the parties that pretend the title of the Church; or the doctrine not contested: now it cannot be the doctrine not contested, because both sides haue it; And lesse yet the doctrine contested; for while the truth of the doctrine is contested, it remaines vndecided of which side it is; and the certaine and assured decision, cannot be made but by the Church: by which meanes it is necessary, that, duringe the cõtestation of the doctrine, there must be other markes to know the Church by, which being acknowledged, the question of the doctrine may be decided. And you cannot saie, that the contested doctrine can be decided by Scripture only, for besides, that there are matters of Religion which are not anie waie touched by the Scripture, (as that whereof Saint AVGVST speaketh, [e] *The Apostles in truth haue prescribed nothing of that, but this cu*

[a] August. cont. epist. Fund. c. 4.

[b] August. cont Faust. lib. 13 c. 13.

Matth. 5.

[c] Esai. 2.

[d] Ephes. 4

[e] Cõt. Do-

nat. l. 5. cap. 23. *stome, (which was opposite to Cyprian,) ought to be belieued to haue taken its originall from theire tradition.* Saint IEROME protests, *f that the Scriptures consist not in the reading, but in the vnderstanding*; and, *g that by a wrong interpretation, the Ghospell of God may be made the Ghospell of a man, nay (which is worse) the Ghospell of the diuell.* Wherefore to iudge surely of the doctrine by the Scripture, it is necessarie, to be first assured of the interpretation of the Scripture; and that by an infallible meanes. For all the conclusions of Faith, which are not found in termes expresse, and incapable of ambiguitie, in the Scripture, but are drawne by interpretations to make them conclusions of Faith and decisions infallible and equall to the authoritie of theire principles, must be drawne from it by an infallible meane. Now there are but three waies whereby we may pretend to be assured, that a conclusion drawne from the Scripture should be infallible, and necessarily agreeable to its principle; to witt, either *human discourse*, or *priuate inspiration*, or *the authoritie of an externall meane* interposed frō God, betweene the Scripture and vs; as the magistrate betweene the law of the Prince and the people: to interpret to vs the wordes, to gather the sense, and to forme and propound the conclusions. For to saie that one passage of Scripture should be interpreted by an other, (besides that there be diuers singular texts wherein this pretention can haue noe place;) this is still to returne to the same difficultie: because one will haue the controuerted place interpreted by one passage; and the other, will haue it interpreted by an other; and the very sense of the passage, which shal be brought to cleer the controuerted places, will againe be brought into dispute, and cannot be infallibile decided, but by an infallible meane, which must necessarily be one of these three, to witt either humane discourse, or priuate inspiration, or the authoritie of an externall Iudge. And from this the verse of NEHEMIAS derogateth not, which is accordinge to the impression of Geneua, *and they interpreted the law by the Scripture*: for it must be read with Saint IEROME, *They whilst it was reading, vnderstood it* the word *Mikra* neuer hauinge bene employed in the Scripture to signifie scripture; but only in the Rabines, [a] as Rabby Elias and [b] Munster, [c] and wee after them, haue other where demonstrated. Now as for humane discourse, if in the conclusions drawne from principles, which are knowne and vnderstood naturally, (as are the principles of naturall Philosophie and metaphisicke) it be subiect to commit so many errors; what shall it doe in that, whose principles are not knowne and vnderstood, but by a supernaturall light? DAVID said to God [d] *Enlighten mine eyes, and I will consider the meruailes of thy law*: And thereupon Saint IEROME cryes out, [e] *If so great a Prophet confesse the darknes of his ignorance, what shall become of vs little babes?* And the Scripture teacheth vs, that the principles of Faith ought to be vnderstood by the very same authority, either mediate or immediate, of him that reuealed them. *f Iesus*, (saith saint Luke,) *opened the sense of the scriptures to the disciples*. And saint IOHN, *g the Lambe was found worthie to open the booke sealed with seauen seales*. And the Eunuche of the Queene of Ethiopia beinge demaunded by S. PHILIP, whether he vnderstood what he read; [h] *how should I vnderstand* (said he) *heere being none to expound it to me?* And Sainct PEETER, [i] *The Scripture is not of priuate interpretation*. And againe [k] *There are in the Epistles of our brother Paule things hard to be vnderstood, that ignorant and light-minded men depraue as the rest of the Scriptures*, (marke, *as the rest of the Scriptures*) *to theire owne perdition*. And not only ignorant and light-minded men too (glorious Peter) but euen the learned and most learned. For who where euer more learned then those, whose falls S. VINCENTIVS

f. Ier. cont. Luci.
g. In epist. ad Galat. lib. 3.

a. Rabbi Elias in Tisbi in voce, Kara
b. Munster in dict. Hebre. & in dict. Rabb.
c. In the articles of the conference for Madame.
d. Psal 118.
e. Hieron. ad Paulin. de institut. mon.
f. Luc. 24.
g. Apoc. 5.
h. Act. 8.
i. 2. Pet. 1.
k. 2. Pet. 3.

Lyrinensis

Lyrinensis doth propound for examples of the temptation of the faithfull? What Tertullian, of whom he saith *l as many wordes, so many Sentences; as manie Sentence so many victories?* What Origens? of whom he writes *m What Christian did not honour him as a Prophet? philosopher did not reuerence him as a Maister? What Apollinarius?* of whom he cries out: *n* What spirit did euer surmount him in subtilitie, excercise, and doctrine? If soe manie great and admirable personages, eminent in pietie; and incomparable in all kinde of Science, Tertulians, Origens, Appollinares assoone as they haue withdrawne the raynes of theire Spirit from the guide of the Church, to put them to the guidance of theire particular discourse are fallen into so deepe and fearefull precipices, and pitts of heresies; who shall dare to assure himselfe vpon his owne particular sense concerning the true and infallible vnder standing of the Scripture, and that in all the controuersies of Faith; in anie one of whiche to erre, and make a Sect, is to fall from the title of the Church, and to loose Saluation in all?

l Vincent. Lyrin c. 24
m. Idem c. 23.
n. Idem c. 16.

But why should we haue recourse to arguments where experience speaketh? for as naturally all men agree in confessing the conclusions of the Mathematicks, because in that kinde of Science, humane discourse is infallible; so if in the consequences, which are drawne by interpretation from Scripture, humane discourse were an infallible meanes, all men would naturally agree in the conclusions of Scripture. Now how farr they are from that, the only state of the controuersies of this age doth manifest; wherein the Lutherans, the Caluinistes, the Simple Anabaptists, the Seruetians or new Arrians, (which all professe to tye themselues to the Scripture,) cannot by the Scripture agree in anie one of theire questions; and doe noe more accord one with an other, then if they had borne awaie the lawrell from the tombe of Bibrias.

And as for the inspiration of the particular Spirit, (besids the danger of those strong imaginations, that saint AVGVST calleth *o prowd and perillous temptations*, which may be mistaken for inspirations; And besides that it is necessarie, that the meanes, whereby the contentions about the interpretation of scripture are to be decided, should be common, either in deede, or in right to both parties contesting (where as the priuate inspiration, that one of the parties pretendes is noe common meanes neither in deede nor in right to the other) the Scripture aduertiseth vs, that *p the angell of Sathan transformes himselfe into the angell of light*, and commaunds vs *q to examine the Spirits and discerne whether they be of God*. Now by what shall the Spirits be examined, to trie whether they be of God? If by the Church; then we must first know the Church: if by the Scripture; we must first be assured of the true interpretatiō of the Scripture: for to examine them by the Scripture, is to examine them by the true sense, and by the true interpretation of Scripture; And therefore it is not from the particular inspiration of the Spirit of God that we must learne what the true interpretation of te Scripture is: since contrarywise it is from the Scripture truly interpreted, that we ought ro learne whether the Spirit that inspires vs be the true Spirit of God. And then these aduertisements of sainct PETER: *r The Scripture is not of priuate interpretation*; And of sainct AVGVSRINE, *s Hold not priuates truthes, least you be depriued of the truth*; exclude as well the refuge of particular inspirations, as the certaintie of humane discourse. Now if neither humane discourse, nor priuate inspiration be infallible meanes to assure a particular man of the true interpretation of Scripture in euery point of Faith, but that he must haue recourse to an externall meanes interposed from

o. Aug. de Doctore Christ. in prol.
p. 2. Cor 11.
q. 1. Ioan. 4.
r. 2. Pet. 1.
s. August. confess. l. 12. c. 25.

God betweene the Scripture and vs, as the authoritie of the magistrate betweene the law of the Prince, and the people, to draw out, to forme, and to propound the decisions for vs: What can this meanes be, but that where of God saith by the mouth of Esay: [t] *Thou shalt iudge euerie tongue that shall resist thee in iudgement?* And by his owne; [u] *The gates of Hell shall not preuaile against her.* And againe [vv] *Let him that heares not the Church be vnto thee as a heathen or a publicā.* And by that of S. PAVL: [x] *God hath placed in the Church, Apostles, Prophets, Pastors and Doctors &c. that we may noe longer be little Children, waueringe with euerie winde of doctrine*; And againe, [y] *The Church is the Pillar and foundation of truth?* doth not [z] RVFFINVS write, that Saint Basile and Saint GREGORY Nazianzene tooke the interpretation of the Scriptures, not from theire owne sense, but from the tradition of the Fathers? And doth not Saint AVGVSTINE crie out; [a] *within the wombe of the Church is the dwellinge of truth.* And againe; [b] *All the fulnesse of authoritie, and all the light of reason for reparation of human kinde, consistes in the only healthfull name of Christ, and in his only Church:* And doth not VINCENTIVS Lirinensis say, [c] *because all vnderstand not the holie Scripture, (by reason of the depth thereof) in one sense; but one interprets it in one fashion, an other in an other; so that it seemes, there may be as many seuerall opinions drawne out of it, as there are seuerall men, for Nouatiā expounds it one waie, Photinus an other waie; Sabellius an other, Donatus an other, Arrius, Eunomius, Macedonius an other, Apollinaris, Priscillianus an other, Iouinian, Pelagius, Cælestius, and finally Nestorius an other: for these causes it is verie necessarie, to auoid the perill of so manie great Labyrinths of so diuers errors, that the line of the propheticall and apostolicall interpretation, should be drawne according to the rule of the Ecclesiasticall and Catholique sense.* And haue not the ministers of *Geneua* themselues, noted this in the margent of theire last Bibles? [d] *The doctrine of Faith requires a domesticall and particular instruction, namely in those that are ordained to deliuer it into the Church, least they should take it in theire owne particular sense, vnder colour of the Scripture. And this is it, that was anciently called TRADITION in the Church.* Now if the certainty of the interpretation of the Church ought to be takē, (according to the exposition of the very *Geneua* Bibles) not from the sense of euery particular man, but from the traditiō of the Church: how can it be that the truth of the vnder standinge of the Scripture should be the only certaine and infallible marke to discerne and know the Church?

But against these proofes, the aduersaries of the Church propound obiections which we had best cōfute before we proceede to an other article. The first obiection is, that Saint AVSTINE in his writinge against the *Manichees*, after he hath made a longe list of the markes of the Church, addes this; [e] *Among you, where no such thing is found as holdes and tyes me, there soundes only a promisse of the truth; which, if it be soe manifestly demonstrated, as none can call it in question, ought to be preferred before all those things, whereby I am retained in the Catholicke Church.* And from hence they conclude, that S. AVGVSTINE held not the other markes for necessary and infallible, but onelie for probable and coniecturall: since he offered to depart from them if they could demonstrate to him vndoubtedly, that the truth was of the other side,

To this I make two answeres, one that the truth, whereof Saint AVGVSTINE speakes, makes nothing for theire purpose that alleage it. For Saint AVGVSTINE speaketh not there of the truth demonsttated by scripture, which is that whereof the Protestants vaunt: but of the truth demonstrated by the light of naturalle reason, which was that, that the Manichees promised: as it appeares by what he said three lines belowe;

t. Esa. 54.
u. Matth. 18
vv. Ibid.
x. Ephes. 4.
y. 1. Tim. 2.
z. Ruff. hist Eccl. l. 2. c. 9.
a. In Psal. 57.
b. Ep. 56.
c. Vinc. Lir. c. 2.
d. In 2. Tim. c. 2.
e. Aug. cōt. ep. fundam. cap. 4.

f I would not beleeue the Ghospell, if the authoritie of the Catholicke Church did not moue me to it. And a little after: g And therefore, if thou must yeeld me a reason set aside the Ghospell; if thou wilt tye thy-selfto the Ghospell, I will tye myselfto those, by whom I haue beleued in the Ghospell. And againe; h The authoritie of the Catholiks being destroyed, I could not beleeue the Ghospell, because it is by them that I haue beleeued it. And in an other place; i That which remaines for you, is, to saie, that you will produce a reason soe certaine and inuincible, as the truth thereof being manifested by it selfe, it shall haue noe neede of the authoritie of anie witnes, nor of the veritie, (vertue you must reade) of anie miracle. The other answer is that Saint AVGVSTINE did not propound this in the forme of a possible condition, (for contrarywise he disputes of deliberate purpose against the *Manichees*, that the naturall light of reason could not be the waie to come to the knowlege of the truth of saluation;) but in the forme of an impossible condition: and which consequentlie diminisheth nothing from the efficacie of the markes of the Church, as it appeares by what he addes immediatelie after; k *But if it be only promised, and not exhibited, none shall separate me from this Faith which by so manie and so great bondes* (so calls he the externall and sensible markes of the Church) *bindes my Spirit to the Christian Religion.*

f. Ibid. c. 5. g. Ibid. h. Ibid. i. Cont. Faust. l. 13. c. 6. k. Cont. ep fundam. c. 4.

The second obiection, that the aduersaries of the Church oppose, is, that the externall and sensible marks, that the Fathers assigne to the Church, as *antiquitie, perpetuitie, eminencie and succession*, belong not to the Church only; for as much as manie other things may claime *antiquitie*, as the Sunne, the Sea, the mountaines, and manie other; *succession*, as the Springs, the brookes, the riuers, and manie other; *vniuersalitie*, as the aire the earth and the other Elements: and euen amougst Religions, that of the pagans, hath heeretofore had *eminencie* and *vniuersalitie*; and that of the Iewes, hath still *antiquitie* and *perpetuitie*. Certainlie a childish and ridiculous obiection; for first the marks that God hath giuen to his Church, haue not bene imposed vpon her, to distinguish her frō all kindes of things, but to distinguish her only from those things that are contained, though equiuocally, vnder the same next kinde, and may be supposed and taken for Churches, that is to saie, from other Christian societies; to witt, from hereticall and Schismaticall Sects, which challenge and pretend by false markes the title of the Church: no more then the markes that Golodmithes giuen to golde that it will not euaporate in the fire, and that it will resist the coupelle and the water of separatiō, are not giue it, to discerne it from all kinde of bodies; for there are other bodies, to which these conditions are common, as glasse and diamondes; but to discerne it from false gold, that is from metalls made and sophisticated, that may be supposed and made to passe for golde. And this alsoe Saint AVGVSTINE esteemes the Church would insinuate in the Canticle, where after she hath demaunded of her spouse markes of the place, where he dwells; she saith, *Least I be as hidden amougst the flockes of thy competitors, that is to saie* (saith saint AVGVSTINE) *of those, that being in the beginninge with thee, would assemble without, not thy flocke, but theire flocks.* For what is this but to saie, that the Church demaundes marks of her spouse, not to be discerned from all kinde of things, but to be discerned only from the societie of heretickes which beare by false markes the name of Christ, and the title of Churches? And secondly, it is not necessary, that the markes in parte, (that is to saie, those, that taken separatlie, haue not the entire office of markes,) may not be found euery one a parte, without the thing marked; but that the thing may not be found without euery one of them, nor they, taken iointly and altogether, without the thing whose marke

Aug. de vnit. Eccl. c. 14.

they are. And therefor the argument of the markes in parte separated, is good to argue negatiuely, and to saie with sainct Austine against the Donatistes; *l The Church hath this most certaine marke, that she cannot be hidden, she is then knowne to all nations; the sect of Donatus is vnknowne to manie nations; then that is not she.* Or with saint IEROM against the *Luciferians*, *m Hilarius being dead a deacon, he could ordaine no Priest after him, now that is noe Church that hath noe Priestes*; or with the same saint AVGVSTINE against all heresies in generall; *n euerie heresie. that sitts in corners, is a concubine, and no matron.* But the argument of the markes in part, taken iointlie is good to argue both negatiuely and affirmatiuely; and to conclude with saint AVGVSTINE; *o Suppose then, that I omitt this wisedome, that you denie to be in the Catholicke Church, there are many other thinges, that retaine me most iustlie in her lappe: The consent of people and nations retaines me: The authoritie begun by miracles, nourished by hope, increased by charitie, confirmed by antiquitie, retaines me: The Succession of Prelates since the sea of Peter (to whom or Lord consigned the feeding of his sheepe after his resurrection) to the present Bishops Sea retaines me: and finallie the very name of Catholicke retaines me, which not without cause this Church alone amongst soe manie and soe great heresies, hath so maintained, as when a stranger askes where they assemble to comunicate in the Catholicke Church, there is no hereticke, tha dare shew him his owne temple, or his owne howse.*

l. Cont. lit. Pet. l. 2. c. 104.
m. Hier. cot. Lucif.
n. De Sym. ad Cathech l. 4.
o Cont. ep. fund. c. 4.

From what places of the voice of the sheepeheard the markes of the Church ought to be taken.

CHAPTER VI.

The continuance of the Kinges answere.

The king hath learnt from the reading of the holie Scripture (and all the Fathers heretofore none excepted held noe otherwise) that the true and essentiall forme of the Church is, that the sheepe of Christ doe heare the voice of theire pastor.

THE REPLIE.

To heare the voice of the Pastor, is the office of the sheepe, but not the essentiall forme, either of the Church, or of the sheepe. For the essentiall forme of the Church, (I meane essentiall forme analogically, as that of the supposts constituted by aggregation) is *vnitie in the meanes of vocation to saluation*, and the essentiall forme of the flocke, is the communion and participation to this vnitie. *a The name of Church* (saith saint CHRISOSTOM) *is a name of agreement and vnion.* And saint AVGVSTINE: *b God is one, the Church is vnitie, nothing agreeth with this one, but vnitie.* But if the essentiall forme of the flocke, were to heare the voice of the Pastor, doth not he heare the voice of the Pastor, that heares her voice, of whom the Pastor said by the mouth of Esay, *c Thou shalt iudge euerie tongue that resisteth thee in Iudgement*; And by his owne mouth; *d The gates of Hell shall not preuaile against her?* And, *e whosoeuer heares her not, shall be held as a heathen and a Publican?* And by the mouth of saint PAVL: *f He hath placed in the Church, Apostles, Prophets, Euangelists, Pastors, and Doctors, &c. that we may no more be little children, fleeting and wauering with euerie wind of Doctrine?* And doth not saint AVGVSTINE cry out; *g The truth of Scripture is held by vs, when we*

a. 1. Cor. hom. 1.
b. In Psal. 100.
c. Esa. 54.
d. Matth. 16.
e. Matth. 18
f. Ephes. 4.
g. Cont. Cresc. l. 1. c. 33.

doe that which pleaseth the vniuersall Church, whom the authoritie of the same scriptures recommends? And againe; [b] *There are manie thinges that the vniuersall Church obserueth, and which therefore are lawfullie belieued to haue bene deliuered by tradition of the Apostles, although we finde them not written?* And then againe, *to heare the voice of the Pastor*, is it not to heare it according to true vnderstanding? for doth not TERTVLLIAN pronounce [i] *An adulterate glosse doth as much outrage to the truth, as a false penne?* And doth not Saint Hilarie saie; [k] *The heresie is in the vnderstanding, and not in the Scripture; the sense, and not the word becomes the crime?* And doth not saint Ierome write; [l] *The Ghospell is not in the words but in the sense?* And doth not saint AVGVSTINE cry out; [m] *All the heretickes which receiue the scriptures, thincke to follow them, when they follow theire owne errors?* And in an other place; [n] *Heretickes were no heretickes, but that misvnderstanding the Scripture they defend obstinately theire owne false opinions against the truth thereof?* And againe, [o] *Manie things are spoken by Christ in the Scriptures in such a manner, as the impions Spirits of heretickes, who will needs teach before they are taught, are thereby lead into error?* And vpon saint Iohn; [p] *The heresies and peruerse doctrines, which intangle Soules and cast them headlong into hell, haue theire birth no where, but from good Scriptures euilly vnderstood?* And so is not the question still, to whom it belongs to iudge infalliblie of the true sense of the Scripture? Moreouer the first voice of the shepheard, that the Fathers summond the sheepe to heare, is it not that, whereby he designes the markes of his Sheepefolde, that is of his Church? [q] *I haue* (said saint AVGVSTINE) *the most manifest voice of my pastor, who recommends and expresses to me his Church without anie ambiguitie. I must blame my self, if for the wordes of men I straie from his floke, which is the Church, since principallie he admonishes me, saying, My sheepe heare my voyce.* Now which is this voice of the pastor, wherein Saint AVGVSTINE will haue vs seeke for the markes of the Church, but that wich expresses, not the doctrine contested betweene him and his aduersaries, which was that of the truth of the baptisme, giuen by hereticks; but the prerogatiues of *eminencie, perpetuitie, vniuersalitie*, and other externall and sensible markes, and conditions promised to the Church? [r] *If the holie Scriptures* (saith saint AVGVSTINE) *haue designed the Church only in Africa, and in a little medly of men dwelling in the rockes and Mountaines neere Rome, and in the howse and territorie of a spanish* Ladie: *though whatsoeuer other pamphlets may be produced; there are none but the Donatists that haue the Church; if the Scripture haue bounded her to a little number of Moores of the Cesarian prouince, then we must goe to the Rogatists; if to a little compaine of Tripolitans, Byzacenians, and prouincialls, the Maximianists haue gotten her. If onlie to those of the East, we must seeke her amongst the Arrians, Macedonians, Eunomians and others, if there be others to be found; for who can number the particular heresies of euerie nation? But if by the diuine and most certaine testimonie of the holie Scriptures she is designed to be in all Nations; whatsoeuer is alleadged to vs, or from whence soeuer it is alleadged, by those that saie, heere is Christ, there is Christ; if we be sheepe, lett vs rather heare the voice of our shepheard, who saith, beleeue them not: for these arenot tobe found in manie places where she is, and she who is euerie where, is also wheresoeuer they are.* And againe, [s] *My sheepe heare my voice and follow me. You haue heard his most manifest voice recommendinge his future Church, not only in the psalmes, and in the prophets, but by his owne mouth alsoe.* And a little after, [t] *This is no obscure question, and wherein they may deceiue you, of whom our Lord hath foretolde, that they should come and saie, lo heere is Christ, behold he is there; lo he is in the desert, that is to saie, out of the frequeneie of the multitud; beholde him heere in the secret places; that is, in hidden traditions and darke Doctrines. You heare that the Church must be spread ouer all, and grow to the haruest; you haue the citie, of which himselfe, that built it, said,*

the

b. De bapt. cont. Don. l.5.c.2.

i Tert. de prese.

k. Hil de Trin l 2.

l. In ep. ad galat. c 1.

m. Epist. 222.

n. De Gen. ad lit. l. 7. c. 9.

o. De fid. & Sym. c. 9.

p. In Ioan. Tr. 18.

q. De vnit. Eccl. c. 10.

r. Ibid. c. 4

s. Ibid c. 20

t. Ibidem.

the Cittie built vpon a hill cannot be hidden; it is then she that is not in anie single parte of the earth, but is well knowne euery where. Beholde the markes of the Church, that saint AVGVSTINE affirmes to be designed by the voice of the pastor; and soe cleerely designed, as they neede noe interpreter, to the end, that the Church beinge knowne by them, we may after by the Church be informed of the sense of the other voices of the pastor, which

u. Ibid.c. 16. neede interpretarion. u *Produce to vs (* said he) *something for your cause, which cannot be interpreted more truly against you; nay which at all needes no interpreter; as these wordes, In thy seede all nations shall be blest, neede no interpreter:*

Gen. 26. Luc.22. *As these wordes, It behoued that Christ should suffer and rise againe the third daie, and that in his name there should be preached penãce and remissiõ of Sinnes through*

Mat. 24. *all nations, beginning from Ierusalem; haue no neede of an interpreter, &c. As these wordes, And this Ghospell of the kingdome shall, be preached through*

Mat.13. *the whole world in testimonie to all people, and then the end shall come, haue noe neede of an interpreter. As these wordes, Let both grow together till haruest, haue noe neede of an interpretor: For when they had neede of an interpretor, our Lord himselfe ineerpreted them.* for euen as when a testator ordaines some one to interpret the difficulties of his testament, and that the name o this interpreter being common and equiuocall to manie, the testator assignes marks in his testament to make him, knowne; the clause, whereby he designes the markes to know him must be so cleere, as they shall need no interpreter, since it is by them that he should be knowne, to whom it is necessary they should addresse themselues, to make them vnderstand those thing that shall neede interpretation: So God hauing promised in his testament, to giue the interpretatiõ of his testamẽt to the Church, the wordes, whereby the markes of the Church are there designed, must be so cleere, that they shall neede noe interpreter; so that by them the Church beinge knowne, we may after by the Church learne the vnderstanding of those things that neede an interpreter. And therefore the order and course of S. AVGVSTINE was, to verifie by places of Scripture, which had not need of an interpretor, the externall and sensible markes of the Church; by the externall and sensible markes of the Church, the Church itselfe; and by the Church, the vnderstanding of those places of Scripture,

vv. Ibid.c. 16. which had need of interpretation. w *This point*, said he, *we reade it not plainely and euidẽtly neither I nor thou: but if there were heere some mã indued with wisdome, to whom our Lord himselfe had giuen testimonie; and that he were consulted with by vs about this question: I beleeve we would nothinge doubte to doe as he would direct vs, for feare of beinge iudged repugnant, not soe much to him, as to our Lord Iesus Christ, by whom he was recommended. Now he giues testimony to his Church:* And

x. Cont. Cresc.l.c.33 elswhere; x *Whosoeuer then feareth to be deceaued through the obscuritie of this questiõ, lett him cõsult with that Church, which the holy Scripture hath designed without anie ambiguitie.* But this was, when hee disputed, with the Donatists, who agreed with the Catholicks concerninge the truth of the Scripture: for when he disputed with the Manichees, or with the Infidells which denied or questioned it: then he changed his method, and did not proue to them

y. De vtil. cred. & alib. the Church by the Scripture, but the Scripture by the Church, and to that end he vsed two kindes of proceedinge y *The one* was, to put it for a ground, that if god haue care of the Saluation of man, (as without this principle all discourse of Religion is in vaine;) there can be noe doubt, but he hath appointed a meanes, howe they might attaine it; and that this meanes not cõsisting in thinges knowne by naturall reason, for as much as thẽ natutallie all men would agree in it: it is thẽ of necessity that it should consist in authority; and then, this ground benig laid, to verifie, that amonge all the Societies of Religion, that bee in the world, the onely

Catho-

Catholicke Church hath the true markes of authority. z *The other* proceedinge was, to propose to them the accomplishment of profecies, touching the extirpation of Idolles, and the ruyne of the false Gods of the paganes, and touchinge the abolishment of the Iewish Ceremonies, and the disperfinge of the people of the Iewes, and touchinge the comeinge of a newe lawe maker, and of a newe Religion; and to represent to them, that these prophecies were written before the birth of our Lord, and kept by the enemies of the Church, and were couched in termes soe cleere, that it was a wonder, that the Iewes, which kept them, were not persuaded by them; but that within the same bookes it was foretolde, that they should be stricken with blindnes, and that in seeinge they should not see; And by this meanes to proue to them, that these were sacred and inspired from God; and then this obtained, to shewe them in the same prophecies the markes, whereby, amongst soe manie Societies which should vsurpe the title of Christian Societies, shee was to be discerned, to whow appertained the right of beinge the true Common wealth of Christ. And she beinge finally acknowledged, to addresse them to learne from her what the true lawes of the Christian Religion are, and what ought to be theire true sence and vnderstandinge.

z. Cont. Faust. l. 13. & alib.

Of the Examples vvhich vve haue from the practise of the Apostles.

CHAP. VII.

The continuance of the Kings answere.

And that the Sacraments are duely and lawfullie administred, that is to saie; as the Apostles haue shewed the example, and those who haue next succeeded them.

THE REPLIE.

It is true: the due and lawfull administration of the Sacraments, is, that they be administred as the Apostles haue shewed the example, and those which haue next succeeded them; but that the examples, that the Apostles haue tracked to vs for patternes and myrrors to imitate, are not all contained in theire Writinges, Saint AVGVSTINE teacheth vs, when he saith: *There are manie thinges, which are belieued by good right to haue bene recieued by tradition from the Apostles, though we finde them not written.* And Saint CHRISOSTOME when he proclaymed, [b] *The Apostles haue not giuen vs all thinges by writinge, c but manie things also vnwritten.* And Saint Basile when he protests. [d] *Wee haue somethinges in written doctrine, and other some we haue receiued in misterie,* (that is to saie, rituall, and vnwritten obseruations) *e from the tradition of the Apostles.* And Saint Epiphanius when he saith: *f All thinges cannot be taken from the Scriptures, and therefore the holy Apostles of God haue giuen vs somethings g by writinge, and other some by tradition.* And his maiesty himselfe, when he answeres, [h] *that he is farr from the opinion of those, that would shutt vp all the historie of the primitiue Church into the sacred indeed, but yet one onely booke of the Acts of the Apostles.*

a. De bapt. cont. Donat. l. 5. c. 32.
b. Chrisost. 2. Thess. hom. 4.
c.
d. Basil. de S. Spirit. c. 27.
f. Epiph. hær. 61.
g.
h. The answere to the 4. obseru.

And as for the Authors, which haue followed next after the first perſecution of the pagan Emperors, vnder whom they lived, which gaue them much leſſe leaſure to write, then thoſe had, that flourished after the tẽpeſt, and in the tyme of the firſt peace of the Church; and then the very ſtate of the moſt part of the controuerſies of theire ages employed either againſt the pagans, or againſt the Iewes, or againſt hereſies, much differing from thoſe, which are ſince riſen vp; and thirdly the shipwracke of theire workes, which the flood of the ſame perſecution hath ſoe ſwallowed vp, as the leaſt part of them is come to our handes: And finallie the care, that the authors, which ſucceeded them, haue had, to reduce into writing the thinges, which they haue receiued from them, by vnwritten tradition: And by ſucceſſion of cuſtome tyme out of mynde; witnes enough how much wee muſt want, of being able to perceaue by the relicks of theire writinges, that followed next after the age of the Apoſtles, all the tracts and lineaments of the face of the auncient Church.

And therfore equitie wills, and the moſt excellent King, who is equitie it-ſelfe, conſents to it, that not only the monuments, which remaine to vs from the firſt or ſecond age after the Apoſtles, shall be receiued as teſtimonies of the ſtate of the primitiue Church; but alſo the writinges of the Fathers of the third and fourth age, after that of the Apoſtles; and principally, when they ſpeake of the cuſtomes of the Church of theire tymes, not as of things of a new inſtitutiõ, but as of things come to them from the vniuerſall and immemoriall practiſe of fore-goeinge ages. For behold his Maieſtiés anſwere vpon this article; *i this demaunde will ſeeme to haue little equitie, to thoſe, that would that all the hiſtorie of the primitiue Church should be contained within the diuine* indeed *but yet onely one booke, and that a litle one, of the Acts of the Apoſtles.* From theire opinion the moſt iuſt aud wiſe king is very farr: who in his monitory epiſtle hath ingenuouſly declared, how much hee eſteemeth the Fathers of the fowrth, nay euen of the fifth age.

i. The kings anſwere to the 4. obſeru.

Of the definition of the Church, and in what vnion it conſiſts.

The continuance of the Kings anſwere.

He Churches, that are inſtituted in this manner, it is neceſſary, that they should be vnited amongſt them ſelues, wth diuers kindes of communion.

THE REPLIE.

Plutarch. de amor. prol.

THoſe that obſerue the proprieties of liuing creatures affirme, that the neſt of the *Halciõ* is woué, and built in ſuch a ſymmetrie, that is to ſaie, the entrie of it is ſo fitted and equald to the meaſure of the birdes bodie, that it can ſerue for no other bird either greater or leſſe. A definition muſt be iuſtlie ſoe, it muſt cõprehend exactly the thing thereby defined, without ſtretching it ſelfe to anie thing more, or reſtrayning it ſelfe to anie thing leſſe, it muſt be fitt, it muſt agree only with the ſubiect thereof: And therefore ARISTOTLE writes, that to frame a definition, is verie difficult, and to deſtroy one, is contrariwiſe verie eaſie; for to eſtablish a good definition, all the conditions, that limitt and inclose the nature of the subiect, must meete together; and to confute it, it is sufficient that anie one be wanting. And for this cause *Plato* saith, that if he could haue found a man, that knew how to define, and deuide well, he wold haue cast himselfe at his feete to adore him. For definition is an Epitomie and abridgement of the intire knowledge of euery thing, which is reduced and epitomized from the more ample consideracon of the effects, and accidents, which accompanie it, to that which is precisely of the essence thereof: iust in such sort, as in the constitution of the numbers, (which the philosophers propound for types and patternes of essentiall formes) euerie addition or substraction, (be it neuer soe little) varies the being, and the caracter, and destroyes, the precise species or kind of the number; so in the iust turne of wordes, and in the lawfull reuolution of language, whereby the essence of euery thing should be bounded, as in an horizon; or bourning line, all additiō or omissiō of wordes, ruineth and destroyeth the definition. † *For when the definition aboundes,* (saith DAMASCENE) *in the excesse of wordes; it wants in the conception of things: and when it wants in sufficiencie of wordes, it is superfluous in the extent and cōprehension of things.* Where-in, as he addes, *nature hath inuented a merueilous arte, to witt, a plentifull pouertie, and an indigent and defectiue plentie.* Now (as *Aristotle* notes) those are the worst seruantes, that steale the corne, not out of the garner, but from thence, where it is kept for seede, because this theft is measured, not by the quantity of the thing stolne, but by the vsury and multiplicatiō of the returne or income depending theron; so the errors, which are cōmitted in principles, (which are as the seede-corne of cōclusiōs) are more pernicious and hurtfull, then those, that are cōmitted in anie other part of doctrine. For in other parts the faults may be particular: but the vices in principles, (amongst which the definitiō holdes the Scepter and Empire,) are necessarily cōmunicated to all the bodie of the disputatiō. And therefore Clemēs Alex. cries out, *that the ignorance of the definition is a spring of errors and deceites.* † Damasc. dial. c. 8. Strom. l. 8.

Now if this be graunted in other controuersies, experience teacheth vs, it must principally be graunted in that of the Church: from the false definitions of which are bred all the sophismes and paralogismes, which fall out in the rest of the disputation. For from the *too strict* definition, that the protestants giue to the Church, when they restraine her *to the only number of the predestinate*, proceede the illusions of the obscurity and inuisibilitie of this societie, by which all the markes, promises, and prerogatiues, that God hath appropriated to his Church ([a] *to haue power to iudge all tongues that shall resist her in iudgement:* [b] *not to be ouerthrowne by the powres of hell:* [c] *to be heard vnder paine of anathema:* [d] *to be the pillar and foundation of truth:*) are turned into smoke, for to haue them in this manner, that is *inuisiblie*, is to haue them without vse, or rather not to haue them at all. And from the definitiō *too vaste and indeterminate*, which they giue her, whē they say, she is *the multitude of those that liue vnder the profession of seruing God in Christ*, without adding, *by lawfull and sufficient meanes*, there ariseth in steede of the Church a medly and chaos of all kinde of heresies. Now this they doe (as hath bene said) to delude the questiōs of the perpetuitie and succession of theire Church: for when you demaunde of them, where that Church hath bene these 1000. or 1200. yeares, whereof God had said, [e] *That he would build her for perpetuitie;* [f] *that he would espouse her for euer:* [g] *that he would neuer roote her out of the earth:* [h] *that she should noe more be called the forsakē;* [i] *that euerie engine addressed against her, should be without effect:* [k] *that she should be a plentifull habitatiō: a tabernacle that can neuer be carried awaie, and whose nailes can neuer be vnfastned, nor her cordes broken in anie time to come:* [l] *that the gates of hell shall neuer pre-* a. Esa. 54. b. Matt. 16. c. Matt. 18. d. 1. Tim. 3 e. Psa. 47. f. Ose. 1. g. Ierem. 31 & Amos 9. h. Esa. 60. i. Esa. 54. k. Esa. 33. l. Matt. 16.

m. Matt. 28 *against her:* [m] *that he would be with her to the and of the world.* They fly to the *obscuritie and darknes of the first definition* and saie, that the Church is the compagnie of the predestinate, and consequently that they are not bound to proue her succession, because she hath bene inuisible. Then when they finde themselues excluded from this refuge, and that it is demonstrated to them, that the same contracts of God, which promised perpetuitie to the Christian Church, haue also promised her brightnesse and eminencie, that it is declared, that in the daies of the new alliance, [n] *the mountaine of the Lord shall be vpon the topp of all the mountaines, and all the hills shall flow to her, and shall saie; let vs goe vp into the mountaine of the Lord, and into the howse of the the God of Iacob, and he will teache vs his waies.* That it is written: [o] *That the kinges should walke in her light, and the people in the splendor of her Orient:* [p] *That her seede should be knowne among the people, and her posteritie in the middest of the generations: That all that should see her, should know she was the seede blessed by the Lord.* And [q] that *the nations should know, that God is the sanctifier of Israel, when his sanctification should be in the midst of her for perpetuitie.* Then they haue recourse to the *medly and confusion of the second,* and answere, that the Church is the multitude of those, that make profession to serue God in Iesus Chr. and by consequence, that to maintaine the perpetuitie thereof, it sufficeth, that there hath alwaies bene a multitude of men making profession to serue God in Christ, be it pure or impure

n. Esa. 2. o. Esa. 54. p. Esa. 61. q. Ezec. 37.

In psa. 80. Now this shift is one of the shifts, that Saint AVGVST. witnesseth to be common, to foxes and heretickes; *For as foxes (* saith S. AVG.) haue two holes in theire terriers, to saue themselues by one, when they are driuen from the other: soe heretickes, (whom the Scripture figures out by foxes when the spouse doth sing: *Let vs take the young foxes that destroy the vines)* haue a double issue in theire solutions, to scape by one, when they are prest and assaulted in the other; soe as who will catch them must sett theire netts before both issues, and must besiege both theire passages. To the end then we may take them, and hinder the excellent king from being taken by them, we will sett the nettes before both the breaches of this definition, and will examine first, the 4. inuisible vnions, wherein his Maiestie conceiues the essentiall forme of the Church may consist; and we will shew, that that vnitie, which constitutes the formall being of the Church, is that of externall vocation; and not that, either of *predestination,* or of *internall faith,* or of the *coniunction of spirits* by the offices of charitie and mutuall prayer, or of the participatiō of one same hope: & secōdlie, we will make it appeare that this vocatiō, in the vnitie of which, the essentiall forme of the Church consistes, is not the simple professiō of the name of Christ, but it is the vocation to saluation by iust and sufficient meanes, which are the professiō of the true faith, the sincere administratiō of the Sacraments, and the adherence to lawfull pastors. So as the definition of the Church shall be, *the Societie of those, that God hath called to saluation, by the profession of the true faith, the sincere administration of Sacraments, and the adherence to lawfull pastors.* Now of this definition, the first part, to witt that the forme of the Church cōsistes *in the vnitie of externall vocation,* and not in the vnitie of anie inuisible condition, we will treat of in the examinatiō of the three articles following, where his Maiestie propoundes the internall vnions, in the which he pretendes that the essence of the Church may be cōserued. And the 2. to witt, that the vocatiō wherein the essentiall forme of the Church consistes, is not the simple professiō of the name of Chr. but it is the *vocatiō by iust and sufficiēt meanes;* we will reserue to the article of false externall vnions † where his Maiesty esteemes; that the hereticall societies (as the Egyptiās & Ethiopiās, which denie the distinctiō of two natures in

Cant. 2.

† Deneith in the chapter of the exclusion of heretiques.

Christ.

Christand by this meanes destroy the foundation of the faith,) are neuertheless members and partes of the Catholique Church.

Of the vnion of the predestinate, and (by way of adiunction) of the visibility or inuisibilitie of the Church.

CHAP. IX.

The continuance of the Kings answere.

THEY are vnited in Christ theire head, who is the fountaine of life; in the which all those liue, that the Father hath elected, to redeeme them by the precious blood of his Sonne, and freely to giue them life eternall.

THE REPLIE.

THE vnion that the predestinate haue in God, *as they are only predestinate*, doth not constitute anie actuall Church amongst them: but only the vnion they haue one with an other *as they are called*. For *first*, the word *Ecclesia, Church*, is deriued from a verbe, which signifies, *to call*, and not *to predestinate*: frō whence S. Paul, (confirming the vse of this etymology) inscribes his first to the Corinthians, *To the Saints called*: And in the epistle to the Ephes. he saith; *One bodie and one Spirit, as you are called in one hope of your vocatiō*. And in the epist. to the Coloss. *Lett the peace of Christ rule in your harts, by which you are called in one-selfe bodie*. 1. Cor. 1. Ephes. 4. Coloss. 3.

And *secondly*, the Church is a *Societie*, and there is this difference betweene a simple multitude, and a societie; that the societie adds to the partes of the multitude a condition, and a certaine caracter as it were, in vertue whereof, they may cōmunicate together. Now predestination, as it is simple predestination, puts nothing into the persons of the predestinate, and is not made in them, but in God only, and by consequent doth not make them actually partes of the Church. *Our predestination* (saith S. AVGVST.) *is not made in vs, but in God; the three other things are made in vs, vocation, iustification, and glorification*. For that, that is alleadged out of saint Paul, that *God knowes those that are his, and hath marked them with his signet*; must be vnderstood, that he hath marked the predestinate in himselfe, that is to saie, in his eternall determination; and not in them: as an Architect, who designes in his spirit certaine stones, that he will imploy in his building, markes thē not by this mentall designation in them, but in himselfe, and makes thē not by this simple determinatiō actuall partes of his building. I meane (to be briefe) that the vniō, that cōstitutes men in the Church is in thē: now the vnion that the predestinate haue in God, as they are simplie predestinate, is not in thē, but in God alone. And so it is not the vnion of predestination, but that of vocatiō, that cōstitutes men in the Church. In psa. 150. 2. Tim. 2.

Thirdly S. Paul teacheth vs, that the Church is the bodie of Christ, and that by analogie to an organicall body. *God* (saith he) *constituted him head ouer all the Church, which is his bodie*. And againe; *I accomplish that, which wātes of the passions of Christ, in my flesh, for his bodie, which is the Church*. Now it is of the essence of an organicall bodie, as it is organicall, to be composed of diuers offices, members, and parts. *If all the members* (saith S. Paul) *were one member, where should the bodie be?* And by this reason the schoolemen proue, that the heauens are not animated or liuing bodies, because they are not organicall bodies; and they proue they are not organicall bodies, because they are not made vp of heterogeneall and different partes in cōposition and cōplexiō. And therefore it is of the essence of the Church to haue di- Ephes. 1. Coloss. 1. 1. Cor. 12.

stinction of members,organs,and offices is the Church,doth not arise from the hidden and eternall predestinatiō;for then the not predestinate,could not be ministers and pastors of the Church: but from externall and tēporall vocation,And by consequent, it is in the externall, visible and temporall vocation,and not in predestination (which is internall to God, hiddē, and eternall) that the being and essentiall forme of the Church consists.

1.Cor. 12. Fowrthly the same Saint Paul saith that *God hath tempered the honor of the members, that there might be no schisme in the body.* Now the predestinate are not capable of schisme, as they are predestinat, but as they are called: so it is not predestination, but vocation, that frames the bodie of the Church.

Gol. 4. Fiftly he affirmes the Church to be our mother;*the superior Ierusalem* saith he, (that is to saie, Ierusalē,taken not accordinge to the lowlynes of the legall letter, but according to the height of the Euangelicall sense) *is free,*
Esa.54. *which is our mother.* And he addes;that it is of her that Esa. writes *Reioyce thou barren woman that bringst not forth children.* Now the Church doth not engēder vs by predestination;(for God alone is the author of predestination, and not the Church;)but by vocation:and consequently it is vocation, and not predestination,that cōstitutes the Church in the state of a Church & mother of the faithfull. Moreouer the knowledge of being Children to

August. de vtil cred.c. 12. the mother, is before the knowledge of being Children to the father, *by the interposition of the mothers authoritie* (saith saint AVG.) *wee are perswaded of the true Father.* For that that Aristotle writes, [a] That in certaine partes of the
[a] Polit.2. vpper Sybia,where women were common,they discerned the children by the resēblance they had to theire fathers,was good for those people, where that similitude had place; but we,in whose nature the image of God is soe defaced by the spott of originall sinne as we can noe more be knowne to be his children by vertue of naturall similitude only;there is noe other meanes for vs to pretend to this quality, but that we are regenerated by him in our spirituall mother which is the Church,his only spouse. And for this cause the Ancientes are soe carefull to saie,that [b] *he shall not haue God*

[b] Cyp.de vnit.Eccl. *for his Father,that denies the Church for his mother.* [c] and that *if any be out of the*
[c] Aug.de Symb ad Catech.54 & alibi. *Church,he shall be excluded out of the mumber of the children,* and to exhort the Christians to doe like the [d] Xanthians in taking the Surname of theire mother, that is to say the title of *Catholicke.* [e] *We receiue the holy Ghost,* saith
[d] Plutarch. de mulier. virt. Saint AVGVSTINE. *if we loe the Church, if we be knitt in one bodie by charitie,*
[e] In Ioann. tract.32. *if we reioyce in the Catholicke name and faith.* Now the certaintie of being Children to the Church, cannot serue vs for a meanes and path way to come to the perswasion of being the children of God, if the definition of the Church consist in the hidden and inuisible secret of predestination. For by this definitiō contrarywise we must be assured to be Children of God,and comprehended in the Rolle of the predestinate,before we can be assured, that we are the Children of the Church. So the definition of the Church ought to consist,not in the hidden and inuisiblie condition of predestination, but in the externall and visible condicion of vocation.

Also we see that our Lord, who was the God-father of this Societie, and gaue it the name of the Church, in that sense that she ought to beare it, hath neuer vsed that name, neither he nor his Apostles,but to designe

Matth. 16. a visible Societie, constituted by externall and temporall vocation. For when he saith : *Vpon this rocke I will builde my Church and the gates of hell shall not preuaile against her. And I will giue thee the keyes of the the kingdome of heanen:* this word in the future tense, *I will build,* shewes he speakes of a Church constituted not by prestination , which was established from all eternitie , but by externall and temporall vocation. And the word keyes which signifies the authority of the ministery, confirmes it. And when he saith: *Tell it to the Church, and if he heare not the Church, let him be to thee as a heathen, or a publican*: And againe, *the Cittie set vpon a mountaine, cannot be hid*: And in an other place; *I will pray not onlie for these heere present, but for all those that by theire word shall beleeue in me; that they may be all one, because the world may know, that thou hast sent me*: Euen a blinde man may see, that he speakes of an externall and visible Church. And when he expresseth the Church by the parable of the barne, where the corne is mingled with the strawe; and by the parable of the fielde, where the corne and the tares should growe together till haruest; And by the parable of the nett cast into the Sea, where the euill fishes were inclosed with the good: And by the parable of the wedding, where the hall was full of guests aswell good as badd; and by the parable of the wise and foolish virgins, which staied for the Spouse in one howse: there needes noe Oedipus, to vnderstand, that he speakes of a visible Church, constituted by externall and temporall vocation. And when S. Paul saith to Timothee; *I write these things to thee, that thou maist know how thou oughtest to conuerse in the howse of God, which is the Church of the liuing God, the pillar and foundation of truth*: And againe: *In a great howse, there are not onely vessells of gold and siluer, but also of wood and earth*. This word (*to conuerse*) which cannot haue relation to an inuisible Societie; and this word *foundation*, which is not relatiue to truth, which hath no neede of foundation; but to men, to whom the Church serues for a foundation of truth: And these wordes, *of wood and earth*; doe visibly shew, that he speaketh of an externall and visible Church. And when he saith in the 6. Chapter of the first to she Corinthians; *What haue I to doe to iudge those that are without*? And in the 11. *We haue not this custome, neither the Church of God*. And in the 12. *God had placed in the Church, first Apostles, secondly Prophets, thirdly Doctors*: And in the Epistle to the Ephesians: *The truth of the wisedome of God, is manifested to the principalities and powers in the heauenly places by the Church*: And againe, *Christ clenseth his Church by the waching of water in the word*. And in the exhortation of the Priests of Ephesus; *Take heede to your selues and to all the flocke ouer which the holy Ghost hath made you Bishops, to rule the Church of God*: And when Saint Iames saith is his Catholicke epistle, *If anie one of you be sicke, lett him call the Priests of the Church, and let them anointe him with oyle*: It is more cleere then the sunne, that they spake of an externall and visible societie.

Math. 18. Matt. 5. Ioann. 17. Matth. 3. Matt. 13. Ibidem. Matt. 22. Matt. 25. 1. Tim. 3. 1. Cor. 11 Ephes. 3. Act. 2. Iacob. 5.

And in truth how could it be, that these prophesies alreadie soe often repeated: a (*In the last daies the mountaine of the Lord shall be aboue all the mountaines: The Nations shall come to her, and saie, lett vs goe vp to the Mountaine of the Lord, and into the howse of the God of Iacob, and he will teach vs his waies*: b *The people shall walke in her light, and kings in the brightnes of her Oriēt*: c *Thine eyes shall see Ierusalem a plentifull habitation and a tabernacle, that cannot be remoued*: d *Theire seede shall be knowne among the people, and thire posteritie amongst the generations: All those that shall see them, shall know that they are the seed blessed by the Lord*; e *the nations shall know that I am the holie one of Israel, when my santification shall be in the middle of them for euer*,) had not bene ilusions and oracles of the Spirit of lyes; if the Church should haue consisted only in the hidden and inuisible number of the predestinate, into whose knowledge, neither men nor angells can penetrate? And our Lord himselfe (who is the eternall wisedome of the Father) had not he bene the most imprudent of all lawemakers, to haue left his law exposed to soe manie suppositions, deprauations, and false expositions, whereto the malice of the heretickes of all ages hath subiected it, without leauing a depositary to keepe it, and a iudge to in-

a. Esa. 2. b. Esa. 60. c. Esa. 33. d. Esa. 61. e. Ezec. 37.

terpret it; or to haue left it an inuisible depositary, and an inuisible interpreter?

But against this inuincible truth there doe arise fiue principall obiectiōs. Matth. 16. The first is that our Lord said: *The gates of hell shall not preuaile against my Church*; frō whence it seemes to followe; that the reprobate are noe partes of the Church because the gates of hell doe preuaile against them. The Hebr. 12. Second, that sainct PAVL writheth; *you are arriued to the heauenly Ierusalem; to the Church of the primitiues (or first borne) which are inrolled in heauen*; from whence it seemes to follow, that the Church is only of the predestinate The *third*, that we protest in the Creede, *I beleeue the Church*; from whence it is inferred; that the Church is inuisible, because faith is of inuisible De vnitat. Eccl. De bapt. cont. Don. & alib. things. The fourth that Saint AVGVSTINE saith in some place, that *onely predestinat Catholicks are true partes of the Church, and the true members of the bodie of Christ*; and puts a distinction betweene those, which are *in the howse*, and those that are *of the howse*, and betweene the people knowne in the *eyes of God*, and the people knowne in the *eyes of men*: And the fift That Saint IEROME writes, *He that is a Sinner, and soiled with anie spott,* Hier. in ep. ad Ephes. c. 5. *cannot be said to be of the Church of Christ.*

To the first then of these obiections, which is that *the gates of hell shall not be victorious ouer the Church*, we saie; That the victories which the gates of hell obtaine against particular persons by the vices of theire manners, preuaile but against those particular persons that are spotted there with; and not against the bodie of the Church: for as much as the vices of manners are but in the persons that commit or approue them, and not in the Communion of the Church. *Those*, (saith saint AVGVST.) *whom the wicked* Epist. 162. *please in theire vnitie, communicate with the wicked; but those that are therewith displeased, communicate not with the wicked, in theire actions, but with the altar of Christ*. For the Church exacts from none of her membres, the condition of being vitious, to receiue him into her Communion; as she exacts from them, the profession of the Faith, and of the vniuersall ceremonies that she prescribeth to them, the participation of her Sacraments, and the adherence to her pastors. By meanes whereof, there is nothing but heresie and profession of error, or infidelitie, that can be pretended to make the gates of hell victorious ouer the body of the Church; because those only cortupt the conditions, vnder which the congregation is contracted or gathered, and infect the body and masse of the societie; for none can enter into anie hereticall societie, without obliging him-selfe to the doctrine, whereof it makes profession. And therefore saint EPIPHAN. interpretes iudicially these gates of hell, that shall not preuaile against Epiph. in anchor. the Church, to be heresies: *the gates of hell* (said he) *are heresies, and heresie-Masters.*

To the second, which is, that saint PAVL writes; *you are arriued to hea-* Heb. 12. *uenly Ierusalem, to the Church, of the first-borne, which are inrolled in heauen,* Wee answere, he speaketh of the *Church triumphant*, to which he writes that we Philip. 3. are arriued, in the same sorte, as he writes, *our conuersation is in heauen*; that is to saie, in hope; as when a shipp hath cast his ankor on land, which is (saith In psa. 54. saint AVGVSTINE,) the symbole of hope, it is said to be arriued to land, though it be yet in the sea; and let vs add, that the word *first-borne* Calu in ep. ad Heb. c. 2 signifies there, euen by Caluins owne confession, the holy Fathers and Patriarckes of the old testament: Or, if saint PAVL speake there of the *Church militant*, and that by the *first-borne* he intends the predestinate, we saie, he calls it the Church of the first-borne, not because it containes only the elect, but because the elect are no where els; I meane the elect inuested in the temporall grace of theire election, as we call the parliament of Paris, the Court of the Peeres, not becauſe it containes none but Peeres, but becauſe there is noe place els, wherein the Peeres are inueſted in theire qualitie of Peeres.

To the third, which is taken from this article of the Creede, *I beleeue in the Catholicke Church*, we ſaie, it ſufficeth, that faith be either of inuiſible things, or of things apprehended vnder inuiſible conditions; as thoſe are, vnder which wee conſider the Church, when we beleeue her to be the ſpouſe of Chriſt, the temple of God, the manſion of the holy Ghoſt, the gate of heauen, the treaſureſſe of ſpirituall graces. Otherwiſe to beleeue in Chriſt, had not bene an article of faith, while our lord was in this world: And neuertheleſſe he ſaith, *Who beleeues not in the ſonne, is alreadie iudged*. And when the Councell of Conſtantinople puts this confeſſion of Faith amongſt the articles of the Creede of the Church, *I beleeue one baptiſme in remiſſion of ſinnes*, they muſt conclude baptiſme to be inuiſible, againſt the vniuerſall condition of Sacraments, which is, to be viſible ſignes of inuiſible graces. Ioann. 3.

To the fourth obiection, to witt that ſaint AVGVSTINE writeth, *that only predeſtinate Catholiques are true partes of the Church, and true members of the bodie of Chriſt*: and diſtinguisheth betweene them which are in the howſe, and them which are of the howſe; and betweene the people knowne in the eyes of God, and knowne in the eyes of man: we haue three ſolutions. *The firſt* ſolution is, that ſaint AVGVSTINE intended not, that only Catholiques predeſtinate were true partes of the Church, according to the *formall* beinge of the Church, which is common to all that are called; but according to the *finall* being of the Church, that is, to the end, and in the fruits, for which the Church is inſtituted. I meane, ſaint AVGVSTINE did not intend in thoſe places to define the Church *formally*, and by what she is in this world, but *finally*, and by what she shall be in the other. Euen as he that ſaith, only good Citizens are true partes of a common wealth, doth not define a common wealth formally, and by what it is in it ſelfe; but finally, and by what it is in the intention of the law-maker: And he that ſaith, a true harueſt is only the corne, that is gathered from the ſtrawe, and not the ſtrawe wherewth it is mingled; defines not a harueſt formally, and by what it is in the feild, or in the barne: but finally, and by what it will be in the garner. *We confeſſe* (ſaith ſaint AVGVST.) *that wicked men are together with the good in the Catholick Church, but as Corne and ſtrawe*. And againe, *Wicked men may be with vs in the barne, but they cannot be with vs in the garner*. For, that ſainct AVGVST. doth not eſteeme, that the formall and preciſe condition that conſtitutes men in the Church, is that of predeſtination internall to God, and eternall; but that of externall and temporall vocation; he shewes it, when he ſaith vpon ſaint IOHN; *None can enter by the gates*, that is by Chriſt, *to life eternall, which is in viſion, if by the ſame gate, that is to ſaie, by the ſame Chriſt, he be not firſt entred into his Church, which is his sheepefolde to the temporall life which is in faith:* And in the place already alleadged vpon the pſalmes; *Our predeſtination is made, not in vs, but in God: the other three things are wrought in vs, vocation, iuſtification, and glorification*: And in his writings againſt Fauſtus: *Men can be inſerted into noe name of Religion, whether true or falſe, but they muſt be tied by the common participation of ſome ſignes or viſible Sacraments*. Contrarywiſe the verie ſame ſaint AVGVST. which diſtinguisheth betweene thoſe *in the howſe*, and thoſe *of the howſe*; teacheth vs, that all Catholickes, both predeſtinate and reprobate, are *in the howſe*, that is to ſaie, in the Church, *Thoſe* (ſaith he) *we cannot denie but that they are likewiſe in the howſe*; and then that the formall condition which

In Ioann. tract. 6.

In pſa. 119.

In Ioann. tract. 45.

In pſa. 150.

Cōt. Fauſt. l. 19. c. 12.

De bapt. cont. Don. l. 7. c. 51.

frames the Church is vocation and not predestination; but that there are none but the predestinate Catholickes which are of the howse, that is to saie, that are *finall peeces* inalienable and inseparable from the howse; or to speake in termes of lawe, that are goodes, that the father of the familie vouchsafes to put into the Inventory of his howse, the other being there but for a tyme and as by waie of loane and not to dwell there for euer. For when the Church shall passe from earth to heauen, and from the state of mortalitie to immortalitie, only predestinate Catholickes, shall remaine there and not the others. *The Church* (saith he)*is the howse, the seruant is the Sinner; now many sinners enter into the Church? and therefore our Lord did not saie, the Seruant enters not into the howse, but, he dwelles not for euer in the howse.* And againe; *None can blott from heauen the constitution of God; nor can anie blott from the earth the Church of God &c. She containes good and euill, but she looseth none on earth but the euill, and admitts none into heauen but the good.*

Aug. in Ioann. tract. 41.

Epist. 162.

The second solution is, that this distinction of partes of the Church true and not true, and of vessells which are in the howse, and not of the howse, and of people knowne in the eyes of God, and knowne in the eyes of men; is not a distinction of *Religion*, but a simple distinction of *manners*, which puts difference betweene the one and the other, in regarde of the formall being of the Church, and of the externall meanes of vocation which are the profession of the true faith, the sincere administration of the Sacramentes, and the adherence to lawfull Pastors; but only in regard of internall and finall correspondencie to these externall conditions; that is to saie, in regarde of the conformitie of manners, with the vocation, and of the perseuerance in his conformitie of manners: *They are* (saith Saint Au:) *so in the howse by the Communion of the Sacraments as they are out of it by the diuersitie of manners.* And Fulgent. after him: *The good ought not to be seperated from the wicked in the Catholicke Church, but by the dissimilitude of manners.* From whence it followes, that when there is question of representing the perpetuitie of the Church for matter, of Religion, that is, for matter of doctrine and Sacramente, and of the Communion of Pastors, it is an vnprofitable refuge to haue recourse to this distinction of predestinate, and of people knowne in the eyes of God, and in the eyes of men, and of vessells which are in the howse, and are not of the howse since this distinction puts noe barre betweene the one and the other people, for what concernes Religion, but only for what concernes manners. For although the list of the chosen is vnknowne to vs in respect of the secret ginftes, and the certainty of election: neuerthelesse, for what concernes protestation of faith, participation of Sacraments, and adherence to lawfull Pastors, it is alwaies visible; if not distinctly yet at least ioyntly with the rest of the called, with which in these three cases it constitutes alwaies, one and the same Church; it not being possible for the elect to be installed in the temporall effect of thiere election, and in the estate of saluation, vnlesse they make profession to communicate, and to be inseperablie vnited in all these things with the visible bodie of the Chnrch. For our Lord cryes out: *He that shall confesse me before men, I will confesse him before God my father*: And Saint Paul; *Were beleeue in our hartes to iustice, but we make confessiion with our mouthes to Saluation*: And Saint August. *We cannot be saued vnlesse* (*labouring also for the Saluation of others*,) *we protest with our mouthes the same faith we beare in oure harts.* by which meanes so farr is it of, that the Church should be lesse visible in regard of Religion in the persons of the predestinate, then in the persons of others; as contrarywise, if it could be either by error, or by infirmitie, and feare of persecutiō, that

De bapt. Cont. Donat. l. 7. c. 52.

De fid ad Pert. cap. 43.

Matth. 10. Rom. 10.

De fid. & Symbol. c. 1.

the externall and visible professiion of the true faith, the Syncere administration of the Sacramentes, and the adherence to lawfull pastors, should faile in the person of all others, it would be conserued in those of the predestinat, following Saint Pauls maxime; *There must be heresies, that the approued may be made manifest:* And this testimonie of Saint AVGTSTIN *The Church is sometimes obscured, and as it weredimmed by the multitude of scandall:* (that is to saie, of persecutions) *but yet euen then she is eminent in her stedfast Champions.* Onely there is this difference, that as the vocation, which is the condition that settes men in the Church, may be possessed in two sortes; the one worthily when it is answered by conformitie of manners, and inward deuotion: from whence it is, that *Saint Paul* praies for the Thessalonians, that *God would make them worthie of his holy vocation*; that is to saie, make them answere and perseuer to answere by theire inward disposition the externall vocation, wherewith he hath honored them: The other vnworthily; which is, when it is not answered by conformitie of manners and life; so there are two waies of being in the Church; the one worthie and meritorions, when theire manners answere theire vocation; and the other vnworthie and without merit, when they correspond not. Which hath giuen ground to the schoole distintion of being in the Church in mumber, and not in merit; and therefore in the place where Saint AVGVSTIN introduceth more expressely the distinction of those that are in the howse, but are not of the howse, nor are the howse, which is in the 7. booke of Baptisme against the Donatistes, euen there to take awaie all occasion of suspicion, that this house could be inuisible, he addes the keyes and the power of binding and loosing are giuen to her, that is the proprietie and practise of the ministrie; and that all are commaunded to heare her, and consequently to holde her visible vpon paine of beinge reputed heathens and publicans. *This howse* (said he) *hath receiued the keyes and the power to binde and loose; and from thence when she censures or correctes; if anie one despise her, it is said that he should be to thee, as a heathen or a publican.* And in the booke of the vnitie of the Church, where he repeates in euery period the same distinction: *The Church* (saith he) *is not hidden, because she is not vnder the bushell, but vpon the candlesticke, that she may giue light to all that are in the howse; and of her it was said: the Cittie sett on the Montaine cannot be hidd.* And in the booke of the waie to Cathecise; *We must* (said he) *instruct and incourage the infirmitie of man against temptations and scandall, whether without or within the Church itselfe; without against Gentiles or Iewes, or heretickes, and within against the chaffe of the barne of the Lord.* And againe, *Let not, the enemie seduce thee not onely by those that are out of the Church, be they pagans, Iewes, or heretickes; but also by those that thou shalt see in the Church, euill liuers.* And in the Comentarie vpon the Epistle of Saint Iohn, *How can I call those other then blinde, that see not so great a Mountaine, and shutt theire eyes against the lampe sett vpon the Candlestick?* And not only in those places, but in all his other workes, he declares, that the Church is perpetually visible; yea he pronounces that it is an hereticall position or rather the common foundation of all heretickes, to suppose, that she is inuisible. *The Church of the Saints* (saith he) *is the Catholicke Church: the Church of the Saintes is not the Church of heretickes: the Church of the Saintes, is that which God hath predesigned, before she was seene, and exhibited that she might be seene.* And in an other place; I*t is a common condition of all heretickes, not to see the thing in the world that is most cleere, contituted in the light of all nations, out of the vnitie whereof all that they doe, can noe more warrant them from the wrath of God, then the Spiders, webb from the extremitie of colde.* And againe; *She hath this most certaine mark, that she cannot be hid, she is then knowne to all nations: the sect of Donatus is*

1. Cor. 11.
Epist. 46.
2. Thess. 1.
De bapt. cont. Donat, l. 7. c. 51.
De vnit. Eccles. c. 14.
De Cathechis. true c. 7.
Ibid c. 26.
In 1. Ioann tract 2.
In Psalme. 147,
Cont. Parm. l. 2. c. 3.
Cont. Petil. l. 2. c. 104.

knowne

vnknowne to manie nations, then that cannot be she.

The *third* solution is, that besides, euen the vse of the *finall* definition of the Church, is a forced vse, and where with Saint AVG. was constrayned in the beginning to serue his turne, to withstād the fraude of the Donatists: but afterward he so corrected, or explained it both in the conference, that he had with them in Carthage, and in his retractations, as there remaines noe more colour to abuse it. For Saint AVGVSTINE in his first disputatiōs against the Donatistes, finding himself pressed with the arguments, that they brought, to proue that baptisme could not be giuen by heretickes, because heretickes were out of the Church; aduised himselfe, and particularlie, in the worke of the seuen bookes of baptisme (from whence this distinction of people knowne in the eyes of God, and in the eyes of men, is principally taken) to helpe himselfe against them, not with the *formall* definition of the Church, by which onely infidells, and hereticall and Schismaticall Christians are excluded; but by the *finall* definition of the Church, that is to saie, by the definition of the Church considered according to the finall and future number of those, of whom she should be constituted in the other world, from which wicked Catholickes are also excluded; to the end to inferr from thence against the Donatistes, that as euill Catholickes, though they were out of the Church defined according to her future permanent and principall being, did truly baptise: soe heretickes and Schismatickes, though they were out of the Church defined according to her present and passant being, yet might administer true baptisme. And for a foundation of his definition he made
Cant. 4. Eph. 5. vse of Epithetes of Salomon, and S. Paul, *hauing noe spott nor wrinkle*, and other such like elogies of the Church, which appertained either to the state of the other world, or to the puritie of doctrine, But after that the Donatistes abused both this definition and the testimonies from whence it was taken, to inferre from thence, that the Catholicke Communion, which was mingled with wicked men, was not the Church; he changed his proceding in the conference that he had with them at Carthage, and declared that this definition belonged not to the Church, considered according to the *present* and *formall* being, which she hath in this world, but
Breuic. coll part. 3. accordinge to the future and *finall* being, which she shall haue in the next. *The Catholicks* (saith he) *made it appeare by many testimonies and examples of holy Scriptures, that wicked mē are now so mingled in the Church, that although Ecclesiasticall discipline ought to be watchfull to correct them both in words and by excommunications, and degradations; neuerthelesse not onely being hidden, they are vnknowne, but euen being knowne, they are often tollerated for the vnitie of peace; and shewed that the testimonies of scriptures did in that manner well agree together: to witt, that the places whereby the Church is represented with the medly of the wicked, signifie the present tyme of the Church, as she is in this world; and the places whereby she is designed to haue no wicked persons mixt with her, signifie the future state of the Church, such as she shall eternally haue in the world to come.* And a little after: *so the Catholickes refuted the calumny of the two Churches, declaring expressely and instantly, what they intended to saie, to witt, that they had not pretended, that that Church which is now mingled with wicked men, should be an other Church then the kingdome of God, that shall haue no wicked pesons in it; but that the same one and holy Church, is now in one sorte, and shall be then in an other; now she is compounded*
De ciuit. Dei l. 20. c. 9. *of good and wicked men, and thē she shall not be soe* And in the worke of the Citie of God, made by him after the Conference of Carthage; *there, where the one and other kinde are found,* (that is good & euill,) *there the Church is as she is at this present; but where the one only shalbe, there is the Church such as she is to*
Cont. gaudent. l. 3. *be, when there shalbe no wicked men in her.* And in the answere to the second

Epistle of Gaudentias, written also after the said Conference: *You see that the Church according to Cyprian is called Catholicke, by the name of all, and it is not without manifestly-wicked men.* And in the second booke of his retractations, I wrote (said he) 7. *bookes of Baptisme against the Donatistes, attempting to defend themselues by the authority of the most happie Bishop and Martyr Cyprian; in all those bookes, where I haue described the Church without wrinckle or spott, it must not be takẽ, of the Church, as shee in her present being but as being prepared to be such, whẽ she shall appeare in glorie.* And againe: *In my writings to an vnknowẽ Donatist, speaking of the multitude of cockle, I said; by which are vnderstood all heretickes; there wantes a Coniunction, which is necessary; for I should haue said, by which are also vnderstood all heretickes &c. whereas I spake, as if there were onely cockle out of the Church, and none in the Church: And neuerthelesse, the Church is the Kingdome of Christ, from whence the Angells in the haruest tyme will plucke vp all Scandalls; which caused the Martyr Cyprian to saie; Althongh we see tares in the Church, yet ought neither our faith nor our charitie to be so diuerted, as because we see tares in the Church, we should therefore seperate our-selues from the Church: Which sense we haue also followed els where, and principallie against the same Donatistes present in the act of the Conference.* From whence it appeares, how much it is to abuse Saint AVGVSTINES wordes against the sense, whereto himselfe intendes they should be either corrected, or explained; to transferr, as the protestantes doe, that that he spake of the Church, considered according to her future and finall being in the other world, and applie it to the Church considered accordinge to her actuall being heere; and to inferr from thence, that she may consist in this world formally in the onely number of the predestinate, and remaine hidden and visible.

Retract. l. 2 ca. 18.

Ibid. c. 18.

To the fift obiection, which is that Saint Ierom writes vpon the Epistle to the Ephesians: *The Church is glorions without spott or wrinkle, or anie such like thing: he then, which is a sinner, and soyled with anie spott, cannot be called of the Church of Christ, neither subiect to Christ,* We answere, that he meanes not to saie, that wicked men are not of the Church which is the body, of Christ, which fightes heere below; but that they are not of the number of the Church which is the bodie of Christ, which shall raigne in heauen. For soe farr of is it from Saint IEROM to belieue, that the promise, to be without wrinkle or spott of manners, appertaines to the Church, considered as she is in this world: that he cryes out quite contrarilie against the Pelagians, *That what the Apostle writes, that our Lord will make his Church holy and without spott or wrinkle, shall be accomplished at the end of the world and in the consummation of vertues.* And againe. *True perfection, and without soyle is reserued for heauen, when the bridegrome shall say to the bride; Thou art wholie faire, my loue, and there is noe spott in thee.* And in the exposition of Ieremy; *Thou seest how manie places the Church hath, and that this sentence of the Apostle, that shee maie be without spott or wrinkle, is reserued for the time to come, and for the celestiall places.* And in the same Commentary vpon the Epistle to the Ephesians; *Our Lord Iesus accountethe for his members all that are assembled in the Church both Saintes and Sinners; but the Saints are his subiects voluntarily, and the Sinners by necessitie.* And therefore to the consequence, that the Protestates gather from this place of Saint IEROM, when they inferr from hence, that the Church consistes only in the number of the good: we oppose these expresse wordes of the same Saint IEROM; *As in the Arke of Noe there were liuing creatures of all kindes: so in the Church there are men of all nations & of all manners: as there where together the Leopard, and the Goates, the wolfe and the lambes: so heere are together the iust and Sinner, to witt the vessells of gold, and the vessells of wood and earth,* And againe, *if the Church be alreadie purified, what doe we reserue for our Lord?* And to the consequence, that they

In Ep. ap Eph. c. 5.

Cont. Pelag. l. 3.

In Ier. c. 31

Cont. Lucif.

Ibid.

gather thence, that the Church is inuisible; we oppose these followinge; *That is no Church which hath noe priests* And againe; *I could dry vp all the riuers of thy arguments, with the only Sun-shine of the Church.* And a little after, *We must remaine in that Church which, hauing bene founded by the Apostles, indureth till this present.* And in an other place, *I am ioyned in communion with thy blessednesse, that is to saie, with the Chaire of Peeter, I know the Church it built vpon that rocke. whosoeuer eates the lambe out of that howse, is prophane*

Ibid.
Ibid.
Ad Damas. Ep. 1.

Of the vnitie of internall faith.

CHAPT. X.

The continuance of the Kings Answere.

They are vnited in vnitie of Faith, at least in those pointes, which are necessarie for saluation.

THE REPLIE.

There are *seuen batailles* to be giuen vpon this article, but against a King that will glorie in suffering himselfe to be ouercome by truth, and in saying with Darius his Chamberlaines, ᵃ that kings are verie strong, but truth is yet more strong; And therefore I feare not to incurr Homers sentence: *When a great king is angrie with his seruant.*

a. Idr. 3. c. 3.

The *first bataile* is, that an vnitie in things necessarie for the Saluation of euery particular man, is not sufficient for the constitution of the Church. For there are pointes of faith, which are necessarie, euen with an ineuitable necessitie, for the bodie of the Church which are not necessary with the like necessitie in regard of euery particular man; as we haue shewed in our first Epistle: and those, which are sufficient for a man preuented by death, and in case of impossibilitie of better instruction; are not sufficient for him, that can haue commoditie to be more throughly instructed: and those that may suffice for a simple handy craftes man, or a labourer, cannot suffize for the bodie of the Pastors, and the vniuersall Societie of the Church.

The Epistle to Mr. Casaubon, obser. 3.

The *second bataile* is, that besides the thinges, which particular men are bound to belieue with a *distinct and explicite faith*, there are manie other, which they are obliged to belieue with a *faith of adherencie and non-repugnancie*, which Schoolemen call *implicit faith*. As, all the articles, that Councells ordaine to be belieued, or forbidd to be belieued, vpon paine of anathema. A vine dresser, a laborer, an artificer, is not bound to belieue them by retaile, and with a distinct and explicit faith: but it suffizeth that they beleeue thē in the faith of the Church, to witt that they adhere and consent with the Church which beleeueth, them. For making profession to beleeue all that the Church, (where-into they are incorporated) beleeues: faith embraceth in generall by the meritt of theire obedience, all that the same Church beleeues distinctlie, though theire knowlege discernes it not. And therefore euen as while children are in theire mothers wombe, or sucking at her brestes, they liue by the foode and nourishment of theire mother; but when they are parted from her, they can no longer liue with that communicated nourishment, or that infused foode:

so while simple persons remaine within the bosome and Communion of the Church, they liue, in those things, which are aboue theire capacitie, by the faith of the Church, which is imputed ahd applied to them by the adherence that they haue with her. *Such*, saith Saint AVGVSTINE, *if before they arriue to the spirituall age of the Soule (where they shall noe more be nourisht with milke, but with solid meate;) the last daie of theire life surprise them. he that dwells in them shall supplie what they want in theire vnderstandinge, because they haue not separated themselues from the vnitie of the bodie of Christ, which had bene made the waie to vs, and haue not withdrawne themselues from the societie of the Temple of God.* And therefore it is necessary, that the Church, to whom they ought to adhere to obtaine this supplie, should be first knowne, and visible to them; and more ouer that she not only liue with the doctrine, which is answerable to milke, (as is the profession of the articles, which simple persons are bound to belieue with a distinct and explicite faith, which Saint AVGVSTINE calles the rule of Faith, common to little and great;) but with that, which is answerable to solid meate. Epist 57. Ibidem.

The *third battaile* is, that it is not sufficient to saie in forme of an indeterminate proposition; *they are vnited in points necessary for saluation*; but it must be said in forme of an vniuersall proposition, *They are vnited in all points necessary for saluation*. For as it will not serue a man to liue, that he hath all his other partes sounde, if he be deadlie wounded in anie member necessarie to life; so it will nothing auaile to these societies we talk of to be vnited in other things necessary to saluation, if they be wanting in anie one. *If a man be brought*, saith saint AVGVSTINE, *to a Physician grieuously wounded in some necessary parte of his bodie, and the Physician saie, if he be not dressed, he will dye; I thinke, they which present him, will not be soe senselesse, as to answere the Physician, after they haue considered and reckoned his other sound partes; what, shall not so manie sound partes haue power to preserue him aliue? and shall one wounded parte haue powre to bringe him to his death?* Now amongst things necessarie to saluation, the principall and most necessary, is the knowledge and acknowledgement of the Catholicke Church. *What profitts it a man*, (saith saint AVGVSTINE) *either sound faith, or it may be the onely Sacrament of sound faith; when the soundnes of Charitie is wounded with the wound of schisme, the only distruction whereof, drawhes all the other partes to death?* And in an other place; *We had both one baptisme, in that they were with me; we both read the Scriptures, in that they were with me; we both celebrated the martyrs feastes, in that they were with me; we both frequented the solemnity of Easter, in that they were with me; but they were not with me in all things; in schisme they were deuided from me, in heresie they were deuided from me: in manie things with me, and in few deuided from me; but because of these few thinges, wherein they were deuided from me, the manie things, wherein they were with me, profited them nothing.* And so it is vnprofitable to those societies, whereof his Maiestie speaketh, to obtaine the name of Churches, that they be vnited in most pointes necessary for saluation; if they be not vnited in all: and particularly in the knowledge and acknowledgement of the true Catholicke Church; and consequently, not supposing her to be visible. De Bapt. cont. Donat. l. 1. c. 8. Ibid.

The *fowrth battaile* is, that the vniuersall distinction of things *necessarie or not necessarie* to saluation, cannot be assuredly made by the iudgement of euery particular person; but it dependes of the iudgement of the Church. For there is noe Sect, but belieues, that those thinges which they hold, are only necessary to saluation; and that all which others hold ouer and aboue, are either pernicious; or superfluous. *Pelagius and* De pecc. orig. cont. Pel. l. 2. c. 22.

De pecc. orig. cont. Pelag. l. 2. c. 22.

Celestius, (saith Saint AVG.) *desiring fraudulentlie to auoid the hatefull name of heresies, affirme that the question of originall sinne may be disputed without danger of faith*; And Saint AVGVSTINE contrarywise cryes out, that it belongs to the foundation of faith. *We may*, (said he) *indure a disputant which errs in other questions, not yet diligentlie examined, not yet established by the whole authoritie of the Church, theire errors may be borne with: but it must not passe soe farr, as to attempt to shake the foundation of the Church*. And *Luther*, speakinge of the controuersies of the *Reall presence* vnder both kindes, and of the *orall manducation* of the bodie of Christ in the Eucharist: *Zuinglius and Oecolampadius*, said he, *alleadge, that the question betweene them and vs, is a light matter, and a little difference, not worthie, that by occasion thereof Christian charitie should be broken*. But LVTHER contrarywise cryes out; *Eternallie cursed be this concord and this charitie, because it doth not only miserablie rend the Church, but after the diuells fashion, mockes her*. And againe; *I take to witnesse God and man, that I agree not with the Sacramentaries; that is, with the Zuinglians and Caluinists; nor euer did agree with them; nor, by the helpe of God, euer will agree with them; and that I desire my handes may be cleane from the bloud, of all those, whose soules by this poyson they haue turned from Christ, and slaine*. And a little after; *We will auoid them, we will resist, and condemne them, to the last breath, as Idolators, corrupters of Gods word, blasphemers, and seducers*. So that before we can be assured of entire vnitie in things necessarie to saluation, we must heare the iudgement of the Church, and consequently, suppose her to be visible.

Luther ep. 7. in defen. verb. Cœn.

Ibid. paulò post.

Ibid. paulò ante.

Ibid. paulò infra.

The *fifth battaile is*, that it is not euough for the constitution of a Church, that the persons, whereof it consistes, should be vnited among themselues in matters necessarie to saluation; if they be not also deuided from the externall communion of all other societies, which holde things repugnant to saluation. For it sufficeth that we be vnited with anie Congregation, which belieueth anie one point repugnant to Saluation, although we be well perswaded in all the rest, nay, and euen in that alsoe; to be excluded from the participation of the Church; for whosoeuer communicates in matter of Religion with anie Societie, is answerable for all the pointes, vnder the obligation whereof he receiueth men to his communion. From whence it ariseth, that a multitude of men of diuers externall communions, such as his Maiestie hereafter propounds, (as, a number of men of the Roman Communion, a number of men of the Greeke communion, and a number of men of the Ethiopian Communion;) cannot constitute a common Church: for as much as, though they are vnited in the beliefe of most things necessarie to saluation; neuerthelesse there are things repugnant to saluation, wherein some of them are vnited by the bond of theire externall Communions with the body of theire Sects; which externall vnion, though the internall went not with it, is sufficient to depriue them from the participation of the Church.

The *sixth battaile* is, that the vnitie of faith, which enters into the essentiall definition of the Church, is not simply the vnitie of *internall* faith; but the vnitie of *externall* faith. For the vnitie of faith, which concurrs to the *formall* constitution of the Church, is that, which serues for a foundation to the commerce of Ecclesiasticall Charitie, that is to saie, by meanes whereof the members of the mysticall bodie of Christ, may acknowledge and embrace one an other as brothers and members of one and the same bodie. Now this is the vnitie of *exteruall and professed faith*, and not that of *hidden and internall*, which serues for nothing, neither for Charitie, nor for saluation, if it be not made manifest and externall.

For

For our Lord cryes out: *Hee that will confesse me before men, I will confesse him before God my Father.* And saint PAVL; *We make confession with our mouthes to saluation.* And saint AGVST. *We cannot be saued, vnlesse labouring also for the saluation of others, we professe with our mouthes the same faith which we beare in our hartes.* And againe, *Peraduenture*, (said he) *some one may saie, there are other sheepe, I know not where which I am not acquainted with, but God hath care of them: But he is too absurd in human sense, that can imagine such thinges.* Matt.10. Rom.10 De fide &. Symb.c.1. De ouib.c 1.

And finally the *seuenth battaile is*, that the vnitie of faith, euen externall and professed, sufficeth not for the constitution of the Church, if the vnitie of the visible and Sacramentall Communion with the originall body of the Church, and the vniuersall societie of the true pastors, be not added to it. *You are with vs* (said Saint AVGVSTINE to the Donatists) *in baptisme, in the Creede in the other Sacraments of our Lord but in the spirit of vnitie, in the bond of peace, and finally in the Catholicke Church, you are not with vs.* And Saint IEROM; *There is this difference betweene schisme and heresie, that heresie holdes a false doctrine; and schisme, for Episcopall dissention, equallie separates men from the Church.* Epist.48. In epist. ad Tit.c.3.

Of other inuisible vnions.

CHAP. XI.

The continuance of the Kinges answere

THey are vnited by the coniunction of spirits, and by the offices of true Charitie, and aboue all by that of mutuall prayers. They are finally ioyned by the communion of one selfe-same hope, and by the expectation of one promised inheritance.

THE REPLIE.

NEITHER can there be a true *Communion of Spirits*, where the visible and sacramentall Communiõ of bodies is excluded; that is to saie, where the parties doe noe admitt one an other to the Communion and participation of the same Sacraments; *If we be in vnitie* (saith S. AVGVSTINE) *what haue two altars to doe in this Citty?* In ep. Ioa. tract.3.

Neither can the office of *mutuall prayers*, that is to saie, prayers made one for an other, constitute an Ecclesiasticall vnitie and Communion; For Catholickes, namely vpon good friday, pray for heretickes, and heretickes for Catholickes; although indeede the exercise of prayers, either made ioyntly, or exacted one from the other, be an *office* of communion, though an vnperfect one. And therefore the Councell of *Laodicea*, forbiddes Catholickes to pray with heretickes. And the first Councell of *Nicea* ordaines, that those penitentes, that had in perill of death receiued the Eucharist, theire health beinge recouered should remaine with those, that communicate by prayer onely. And the Councell of *Ancyra* admittes a Communion without Obligation. And the religious of Egipt, driuen away by *Theophilus*, being come to *Constantinople*, were not depriued by Saint CHRISOSTOM of the Communion of prayer. *He thurst them not*, (saith Socrates) *out of the participation of prayer; but he iudged it not conuenient to admitt them to the Communion of the Sacraments, before the knowledge of the cause.* Prosp ad calcem. ep. Cæles. Concil. Laod. can. 33. Conc. Nic. 1. can. 13. Cõmunio. Concil. Ancyr. Soc. hist. eal.1.6.c.9.

Neither is true *Charitie* to be found out of the Church; but only an humane affection, which can noe otherwise be called charitie but equiuocally. *None* (saith saint AVGVST. *) can transport charitie forth of the Catholicke Church.* And againe, *Thou hast proued to me that thou hast faith; proue to me likewise that thou hast charitie;* Keepe *vnitie.*

In Psam. 21 Sup. gest. cum Emerit.

Neither can the simple coniunction of *hope*, constitute anie Ecclesiasticall communiō; for all heretickes and Schismatickes agree in this pointe, that they hope eternall life, and the promised inheritance. *Wee* (saith *Petilian* the Donatist) *hauing nothinge, yet possessinge all thinges, beleeue that our soules are our reuenewe, and with out labour and bloud, we purchasse the eternall riches of heauen.*

Aug. cont. Petil. l. 2. c. 99.

Neither finally, can the coniunction in one iust *hope*, haue anie place, but amongst those, that are called and inserted into the bodie of the Catholicke Church: followinge this sentence of saint Paule, *One bodie and one spirit, as you are called in one hope of your vocation.*

Ephes. 4.

Of the knowledge, that the predestinate haue, of their predestination.

CHAP. XII.

The continuance of the Kings answere.

KNowing, (I speake of the elect,) that they are predestinate from before the foundation of the vvorld to be coheires, vnited in bodie, and copartners of the promises of God in the Ghospell, as the diuine Apostle saith.

THE REPLIE.

HEere the most excellent Kinge behaues himself like H*ippomanes*, who runninge with *Atalanta* for masterie, cast out golden apples in her way, to delaie her with takinge them vp: soe his Maiestie putts rubbes in this discourse, to staie the course of my pen, and to stoppe me to examine them. But I hope to remoue them so quickly, that I shall be time enough at the end of my carrere.

To this then I will succinctly saie fower thinges. T*he first* that philosophers teach vs that the morall passion, which wee call *hope* from whence theologicall hope hath by analogy borowed her name is alwaies mingled and tempred with *feare*: By meanes whereof, those thinges, that fall vnder the obiect of hope, as are the goods of future life in respect of euery particular man, cannot be apprehended with a certaintie of Theologicall faith (that is to saie, infaillible, & not to be doubted of) otherwise hope should noe more be a vertue distinct frō faith, against this oracle of sainct PAVL, *now remaines, faith, hope, and Charitie; and these things are three*: but ought to be embraced with an expectatiō mingled & tempered with feare, as *Dauid* exhortes vs in these wordes: *serue the* Lord *in feare, and reioyce in him with tremblinge.* And S. PAVL in these, *Thou subsistest by faith be not puffed vp, but feare. He that thinkes he stands, let him take heede least he falle.* And againe, *worke your saluation with feare and tremblinge.* And speaking of himselfe, *I chastize my bodie and bring it vnder, least when I haue preached to others, my selfe become a reprobate.*

The *second*, that faith cannot bee but of things reuealed by the word of God: for *faith* (saith saint PAVL *) is by hearing, and hearing by the word of God,*

Now

Now it is not reuealed to anie one in the word, which God hath consigned to his Church, either by writinge or tradition; that he is absolutelie of the number of the predestinate, and therefore if hee haue not expresse and particular reuelation from God, as Saint Paule had, (who vpon this occasion speakes somtimes of himselfe, according to his common condition as simply one of the faithfull; and sometymes accordinge to his extraordinary reuelatiō of a predestinate person;) he can not haue anie certaintie of Faith in this respect. For to saie that it is reuealed to vs in scripture that whosoeuer trustes in our Lord, shall not be cōfounded: And that our Lord himselfe saith *who beleeues in me hath life eternall*; all these promises, (not to speake of other modifications, which the scripture puts to them,) ought to be vnderstood with the condition, wherewith our Lord will haue them vnderstood, when hee saith: *who perseuers to the end, shall be saued* And Saint Paule when he writes, *See the goodnesse of God in thee, if thou perseuere in goodnes, otherwise thou shalt be also cutt of.* Now where is it that this finall perseuerance is particularly promised to anie one in the word of God? for if you answere that our Lord saith, *all that you aske for when you pray, beleeue you shall receiue it, and it shall be done to you*: And consequentlie if we demaunde perseuerance, we shall obtaine it: I answere that he meanes, all that you demaunde, as you should demaunde it. Now the principall condition required to demaunde perseuerance as you should demaunde it, is to perseuere in demaundinge it, and not to content our selues with demaundinge it once, but to demaunde it perpetually, followinge this precept of Saint Paule; *Pray without ceasinge.* And againe *watch and pray with all perseuerance.* Far *Salomon* demaunded wisedome and begged it in faith without staggeringe, which is the condition wherewith saint IAMES saith we should begge it, but because he did not perseuere to aske it, he lost it. Now this perseuerance to aske perseuerance, where is it promised to anie one in the scripture?

Psa. 124. Ioann. 6. Matt. 24. Rom. 11. Marc. 11. 1. Thess. 5. Ephes. 6. Iacob. 1.

The *third*, that this beliefe is pernicious, both to religion as an enemie to humilitie and good workes, and to States and common-wealthes, as an enemie to good manners. For imprinting in the spirit of euery particular man, yea which is worse, as well of those that are wicked and reprobate as of others, (because what is proposed in a Religion for a doctrine necessarie to saluation, all doe thinke themselues obliged to holde it;) that he is assuredly predestinate, and that whatsoeuer sinnes he commit, he shall infallibly haue leasure and grace to repent him before his death, this I say doth puffe vp men with arrogance and presumption aboue their fellowes of whose predestination they haue not the like certaintie, and makes them lesse diligent to stand vpon theire guarde and to practise this commaundement of our Lord; *watch and pray, for feare least you enter into temptation.* And therefore as the prince of the Roman harpe sings,

Matt. 26. & Luc. 21.

God by his wisdome, from mans nature frayle
The whole successe of future thinges doth vaile.

Horat. carmin l. 3. ad 29.

The *fowrth*, that S. AVGVST. (the greatest doctor in the point of predestinatiō, that hath bene since the Apostles, yea the organ and the voice of the primitiue Church in this questiom,) teacheth vs, that this beliefe is full of presumption and preiudiciall to saluation. *Although*, (saith he) *that the iust are assured of the reward of their perseuerance, yet they are incertaine of their perseuerance; for who is he amongst men that knowes he shall perseuere in the workes and progresse of iustice to the end, if he be not made certaine thereof by some reuelation from him, who by a iust and secret iudgement instructs not all, but deceiues none?* And in an other place, *Who is he among the faithfull,*

13. Deciuit. Deil. 11. c. 12

De corrept. & grat. 13

that will presume during this mortall life, to be of the number of the predestinate? for it is needefull that that be concealed in this world. And a little after, *Many like things are saidfor the profit of this secret, least peraduenture some might be puft vp: and that euen those that runn well might feare, while it is vncertaine, whither they shall arriue.* And againe, *Such presumption is not profitable in this place of temptations, where the infirmitie is soe great, as assurance might begett pride.* And thus much is said in regarde of proofes.

Rom. 8. It restes nowe to solue the obiections of the places of Scripture, that the aduersaryes of the Church alleage against this doctrine; They saie thẽ that Saint Paule, writes; *the spirit of God giues testimonie to our Spirit* (or accordinge to the greekes, *helpes our Spirit to testifie to vs*) *that we are the children of God: and if children, heires.* It is true, but they tell vs not, that he addes presently after, this conditionall clause; *if we goe forwarde in our sufferings.*

Ibid. They saie he writes, *I am certaine* (or accordinge to the greeke, *I am persuaded*) *that neither death nor life etc. can seperate vs from the charitie of Christ.* It is true; but they tell vs not, that he speakes there of all the predestinate in generall, into whose number he putts himselfe, and those to whome he writes, by a figure which the grãmarians call *syllepsis*; and accordinge to the rule, not of Faith, but of Charitie, which wills, that in all thinges concealed from vs, we should iudge in the better parte.

Rom. 11. They saie, he writes, *The vocation, and the guiftes of God are without repentance.* It is true, but there he speakes of the generall calling of the people of the Iewes, made in the olde Testament, wereof he saith; *God hath not repented, because yet one daie he will recall their nation into the bosome of the Church.* And euen those, that stretch this passage by analogy to the callinge of particular persons, either explicate it of vocation accordinge to predestination, which is as much vnknowne, as predestination it selfe; or they intend, that the guifts and vocation of god, are without tepentance *on his parte,* that is to saie, that God neuer withdrawes himselfe from vs, vnlesse

2. Pet. 1. wee withdrawe ourselues from him: And therefore, as Saint Paule saith *the vocation and the guifts of god are without repentance*; soe Saint Peter saith

2. Cor. 1. *take paines to secure your vocation and election by good workes.*

They saie he writes, *we haue the pledge of the holie Ghost in our hartes*; It is true; but it is not sufficient for our assurance to obtaine the inheritance of life eternall, that we haue this pledge, if we be not as well assured not to loose it; a thinge that Saint Paul is soe farr from assuringe vs that contrarily he cryes out, *quenche not the spirit.*

2. Thess. 1. 1. Ioann. 4. They saie, Saint Iohn writes: *perfect charitie driues awaie feare* It is true, but, (besides that Saint Iohn speakes there of perfect Charitie, which euery particular man ought to desire but not presume he hath it for feare of

In epist. Ioann. Tract. 9. loosinge it, in loosinge humilitie;) the feare that saint Iohn pretendes to be excluded by this excellent Charity, is (as Sanit AVGVSTINE saith) *seruile feare*; that is the feare of loosinge the grace of God, for feare of the paine of eternall fire; and not the *filiall feare* which is the feare of looseinge the grace of God for the loue of God himselfe, and for feare of being depriued and seperated from his presence. And therefore as S.

Apoc. 2. Iohn saith in the place cited by them; *perfect charitie castes out feare:* Soe he saith in an other place, *Thou hast lost thy first charitie, remember from whence thou art fallen, and doe thy first workes.* And againe. *Holde that thou hast least thy crowne be taken from thee.*

And from this is nothinge derogatory, that which they obiect, that the priuation of this certaintie, makes men despaire of theire saluation: For betweene the certaintie of saluation, and despaire, there is a middle

way,

way, which is *hope* that, while it lastes, (as it ought alwaies to laste in a Christian man,) is incompatible with dispaire, and suffizeth to comforte vs, and hinder vs, if we perseuer in it, from being confounded; And although it imprint not in vs an infallible certainty of our saluation, (for then it were *theologicall* faith, and noe more *hope*;) yet it causeth in vs *morall faith* which we call *confidence*, by the meanes of likelyhoodes & coniectures that the good motions, wherewith god inspires vs, giue vs of our predestination. *Learne in part*, saith Saint AVGVSTINE (*condiscite* as S. PAVL συμμαρτυρεῖ) *from the goodnesse and straightnes of your course, that you belonge to the predestination of diuine grace.* And againe, *you thẽ alsoe ought to hope from the father of lightes (from whom descendes euerie excellent guift, and euerie perfect present,) the perseuerance to obaie, and aske it of him with dailie prayers, and doeing so, confide not to be excluded from the predestination of his people, since it is himselfe that giues vs grace to doe it.* And a little after: *Of life eternall* (saith he) *which God, who is noe lyer, hath promised before all times to the Children of promise, none can be assured till this life be finished, but he will make vs perseuer in him, to whom we saie euerie daie, leade vs not into temptation*, that is to saie, as it ariseth from the protestation, of the preceding period) but we ought to hope that he will make vs perseuer in him, *to whom we saie euerie daie: leade vs not into temptation.*

De don. perseu. l. 2. c. 22.

Ibid.

Ibid.

Of the inequalitie of these two phrases, to communicate with the Catholicke Church, and to communicate with some member of the Church, departing from the rule of faith.

CHAP. XIII.

The continuance of the Kinges answere

BVT the king adds, that this very Church. if anie of her members departe from the rule of faith, will preferre the loue of truth, before the loue of vnitie. She knowes that the supreme lawe in the howse of God, is the sinceritie of heauẽlie doctrine, which if anie one forsake, he forsakes Christ, who is truth it self, he forsakes the Church which is *the pillar & foundation of truth.* VVith such separatistes, a man truly Catholique, neither will, nor maie communicate: *For what agreement is there betweene Christ and Belial.*

1. Tim. 3.

2. Cor. 6.

THE REPLIE.

HEERE his Maiestie must giue me leaue to saie, that he changeth the way of his disputation, and goes out of the lists, quite from the state of the question. For the question is not whether, to obtaine the name of Catholicke, & to attaine to saluation, it be necessary to be vnited with anie one of the members of the Church, when it comes to be separated frõ truth; but whether, to obtaine the name of Catholicke, & attaine to saluation, it be necessatie to be vnited with the whole masse & vniuersall Bodie of this Church, which the Fathers haue called Catholick. Neither is it the question, whether there may be anie externall and visible societie, wherewith it is vnlawfull to commuuicate: but whether such a tyme can be wherein there is noe externall and visible Societie, wherewith it is necessary to communicate. For to saie, that all

Communion are not to be desired, and that there are Congregations wherewith it is not lawfull to Communicate, which, of vs euer doubted it? Nay contrarily, doe we not daily pronounce *anathema* against those that Communicate with heretickes or Schismatickes? and, in that we exhorte his maiestie, to returne to the Communion, of the Catholicke Church from that of the Caluinists; doth it not proue sufficiently, that we holde not, that there should be Côm union helde with all kinde of sects? The state thẽ of the questiõ to ouerthrowe our Thesis and cõclude some thinge against vs, requires not to proue, that there may be Societies, wherewith we ought to haue noe Cõmunion: for who denies that? but to proue, that there may come a tyme, wherein there can be found noe externall and visible Societie, wherewith it is lawfull to communicate and that this tyme beinge come, (as *Luther* supposed it to be, when he began to pitch his ensignes in the fielde:) it is necessary to goe forth from all the Religions, that are then to be found visible in the world, and to make a new Communion, and a congregation a parte. See heere what is needefull to be proued; and in steede of this, the excellent kinge aleageth, that if anie member of the Church departe from the rule of Faith, the Church must preferr the loue of veritie before the loue of vnitie.

To this answere of his Maiesties we will answere two thinges: *the first* that there is noe incompatibilitie beweene this thesis; *we must be vnited with the vniuersall bodie of the Catholicke Church*; And this antithesis, *if anie member departe from the rule of faith we must not be vnited with it.* For the one speakes of the *bodie* of the Church; and the other speakes of some one of the *members* of the Church; and the speciall mention of some one of the Church departing from the true faith supposes the staie and perseuerãce of the rest of the bodie of the Church in the faith. Now it is with that bodie from whence that parte that forsakes the faith, deuides it selfe; that wee say we must haue Communion and vnitie: and not with the parte, that separates it selfe from the bodie; for it is not a meanes to maintaine vnitie to haue vnitie with those that deuide themselues from vnitie.

The *second* that there is great difference betweene the rightes and priuiledges of the *Catholicke Church*; & the preuiledges of *particular Churches.* For the infallible assistance of the holy Ghost was neuer promised to *euery particular* Church but to the bodie of the *Catholicke* Church. And therefore as the elements are corruptible in their partes but incorruptible in their *all*; soe the Church is corruptible in her parts, but incorruptible in her *all*; in such sorte that though some particular Churches may erre in faith and consequentlie cease from beinge Churches, neuerthelesse, there alwaies remaines one masse of a Churche exempt from corruptiõ soe greate and eminent, that she representes, and conserues in herselfe, the beinge, rightes and prerogatiues of all the whole. And soe the obligation that we haue to Communicate with the *Catholicke* Church, is one thinge; and an other the obligation that we haue to Communicate with particular Churches. For with her wee are bound to Communicate necessarily and absolutely vnder paine of anathema and damnation, because out of her Communion, none can be saued: and with others onely whiles they Communicate with her.

1. Tim. And the pretence of truth cannot be alleadged to make this obligation
In. Psalm. conditionall, since Saint Paule saith *the Church is the foudation of truth.*
57. And Saint AVGVSTINE *within the wombe of the Church, truth hath her dwellinge.* Nor can it be obiected, that the supreme lawe in the howse of

God,

God, is the sinceritie of heauenly Doctrine. For, besides that this lawe hath her Statutes written, and vnwritten: (following this precept of S. PAVL: *followe the traditions that you haue receiued from vs, whether by wordes, or by Epistles* And this testimonie of *Eusebius*: *The Apostles haue giuen some things by writing, and others by vnwritten lawes?* And this obseruation of sainct CHRYSOSTOME *From whence it appeares, that the Apostles haue not deliuered all things by writinges, but manie things alsoe without writing*:) it is not only necessary in matters contested, to haue a lawe, but it is needefull besides the lawe, to haue a iudge (with authoritie able to oblige, and subdue the sense of particular persons) to interpret the wordes of the lawe; which Iudge, as we haue alreadie demonstrated; cã be noe other but the Church.

2. Thess. 2 · De demõst. l. 1. c. 8. · In 1. Thess. 2. · Sup. c. 5.

How to vnderstand these wordes of sainct Gregory Nazianzene; There is a sacred warre,

CHAP. XIV.

The continuance of the Kings Answere.

HE Church then must flye the communion of those, and saie with sainct Gregory Nazianzene, that, *a dissention for pietie, is better, then an infected vnitie?* And will not doubt to pronoũce with the same blessed Father: that *there is a sacred warre.*

De pac. ar. 1. Orand. 150. Episc.

THE REPLIE.

THERE is noe doubt of prouing, that there may be some societie, whose communion must be auoided; for none denies it; but of prouing that there may come such a tyme, wherein there is noe externall and visible societie, wherewith we are bounde to cõmunicate. Now the places, that his Maiestie citeth out of S. GREGORIE NAZIANZENE, are soe farre from insinuatinge anie such thing; as they affirme the quite contrary. For S. GREGORIE saith not these wordes, against the externall and visible Communion of the Church of his tyme: but against the craftie practises of the *Arrians*, which demaũded, vnder pretence of peace, to be receiued into the communion of the Church with Confessions of the faith ambiguous and deceiptfull; that is to saie, he spake not this language, to shewe, that, when he writt it, there was then noe externall and visible Church, which must be communicated with vnder paine of *anathema*: but contrarywise, to shew, that they must continue to conserue the externall and visible communion of that Church impolluted and vndefiled, from the contagion of the *Arrians*.

De pac. or. 1.

And therefore in the second place alleadged by his Maiestie he representes two Combates, that the good Catholicke Pastors had in theire charges, some within the Church against the iealousie, & emulation of euill Catholickes: others without the Church, against heretickes & Schismatickes: And which heretickes, and not against the Church intituled Catholicke, he calleth the warre, *sacred warre*, in imitation of the *Phocensian* warre which was called sacred.

Orat. ad 150. Episc.

Of the pretended precepts, to goe forth from the visible communion of the Church.

CHAP. XV.

The continuance of the Kings answere.

NOw, that in the Church it was once necessarie to make such a separation, we lerrne it cleerely, as well out of other places of the Scripture, as frō that, which is opēlie declared to vs, by this admonition of the holy Ghost, made to the Church, certainely, not without cause; *Goe out of Babylon my people, least you communicate in her sinnes.* Now what this Babilon is, from whence the people of God are commaunded to goe forth: the kinge searcheth not into it nor decides nothinge in that respect. This certainly at least the thinge it self shewes manifestly, that (whether in that place by the word Babylon be meant a particular Church, or the greater parte of the vniuersall Church,) it must be she hath heertofore bene a lawfull Church, wherewith Religious men communicated Religiously: and then from whom, after her deprauation had yet past further, the faithfull receiued commaundement to goe forth and to breake the communion they had with her: Soe as it is easie to be vnderstood from thence, that the faithfull ought not to desire all kinde of communion with those which are called vnder the title of Christ, but only that, which is made retaining still the integritie of the doctrine reuealed from heauen.

Apoc. 18.

THE REPLIE.

IT was not without cause the first Grecians called their allegoricall sense ὑπονοίαι; be it that this word intend hidden & conealed senses, or whether it intend suspitions. For all senses, purelie allegoricall, are but suspitiōs & coniectures, & haue noe firme & solide foūdatiō. And it is not without cause, that the hebrew Doctors call the literall sense of the scripture, the *little word*, & the allegoricall sense the *great word*: For the literall sense is restrained by the square & straight measure of that, which is cōtained in the text: where as the allegoricall sence hath noe boūd, but is multiplied infinitly, & goes as farre as humane imaginatiō can be stretched. And therefore this *axiom* is past for a prouerbe in diuinitie, that *allegories proue nothinge* Now if there be a booke in the world writtē in an allegoricall stile, what one cā be equalled in that kinde to the Reuelation? which, as Sainct IEROM saith, *containes as manie Sacraments* that is to saie sacred riddles, *as wordes?* And if Sainct AVGVSTINE cryed out against the Donatists, who would haue found a prediction of theire Church in an allegoricall verse of the Canticles, and said to them, *who is it that dares, without a most vnbridled licence, produce for himselfe that, that is couched in an allegorie: if he haue not places more cleere by whose light to illustrate that which is obscure?* What would he saie in this age, not against his Maiestie but against the proceedinges of those, that haue built the vocation of theire Church, vpon these alegoricall wordes of the Reuelation, *goe forth of Babylon my people?*? who knowes not, that it is a solution sufficient for arguments drawne out of allegoricall expositions, to answere, I denie it, and principally, when there may be an other sense giuen to the allegoricall wordes, then that, according to which they are alleadged? *If I could not* (saith Sainct AVGVSTINE, answering an allegoricall obiection,) *proue this sense, by anie more certaine argument, yet it ought to satisfie euerie iudicious hearer that I haue foūd an issue for these wordes; by meanes whereof it appeares that they haue alleadged nothīge for thēselues that is certaine, but what may de doubted of*

Plutarc de aud poet.

And Paulin

Aug. ep. 48

And not only may there be found an other way of vnderstādinge this passage, then that which his Maiestie supposes: but antiquitie hath found two others, and both celebrated by excellent and authenticall Authors; and those which haue come after, haue yet added a third.

The *first* way of vnderstandinge it, is to interpret *Babylon* described by the Reuelation, to be the *Societie of all the wicked* in generall, as S. AVGVSTINE and many others often expound it in that sense; and to expound *Ierusalem*, described in the same booke, to be the *Societie of all the Good*; which are the two Citties whereof Saint AVGVSTINE hath composed a worke, of the Cittie of the diuell which began in *Cain*, and the Cittie of God, which began in *Abell*. For as there is the same reason in things contrary and opposite: soe must the interpretatiō of that *Ierusalem* painted out in the Reuelation; and that of that *Babylon*, which is opposed to it, be a like. *Marke*, said Saint AVGVSTINE, *the names of these two Citties, Babylon and Ierusalem. Babylon signifies confusion, and Ierusalem the view of peace &c. They are mingled from the beginninge of humane kind, and shall continue soe to the end of the world; Hierusalem tooke her beginning from Abell, and Babylon from Cain.* And a little after; *From whence can we now shew them, that is, discerne them? Our Lord will shew to vs, when he placeth them, the one on his right hand, the other on his left. Ierusalem shall heare, come you blessed of my father, take possession of the kingdome which is prepared for you from the beginninge of the world; and Babylon shall heare; goe you cursed into eternall fire, which is prepared for the diuell and his Angells. Yet we may also bringe some marke accordinge to the capacitie that it pleases God to giue vs, by which the faithfull and godlie Cittizens of Ierusalē may be distinguished from the Cittizens of Babylon. Two loues, make these two Citties, the loue of God makes Ierusalem, the loue of the world, makes Babylon: let euerie one then examine himselfe what he loues, and he shall finde of which he is a Cittizen.* And in an other place; *all the wicked belong to Babylon; as all the Saintes doe to Ierusalem.* And in the volume of the Cittie of God: *And what shall we gather from this, but that we must flie out of the middle of Babilon? which propheticall precept ought spiritualie to be vnderstood in this sense: that out of the Cittie of this world, wich is without doubt the societie of euill Angells, and wicked men, we should flie with the steps of faith, which workes by loue, and aduauncinge towards the liuing God.* And in the volume vpon the psalmes; *all those who perferr earthlie felicitie before God: all those which seeke themselues, and not Iesus Christ, belonge to that onlie Cittie, which is mysticallie called Babylon, and hath the diuell for her kinge.* And to this it is noe impediment, that she is described to be clad in purple; fore there, *purple*, signifies not the coulour of purple; but temperall powers dignities, and authoritie, which are for the most parte in the hands of the wicked, rather then of the good: the *white* and shining linnen, wherewith the bride is clothed, signifieth not the stuffe and colour of linnen, but the iustification of the saintes. As little is it repugnant to this, that she is described to be sett vpon 7. Mountaines; for that which followes imediately, after, *and those are 7. kinges*; shewes that the word Mountaines, ought not in that place to bee literally taken, but allegorically; whether for the seuen sinnes, that wee call mortall, or for anie other septenary mumber ruling ouer the societie of the wicked.

[Margin notes: In Psalm. 64. — In psalm. 86. — De ciuit. Dei l. 18. c. 18. — In Psalm. 61. — Apoc. 19.]

The second interpretation celebrated by the Fathers, is, to expound the destruction of *Babylon*, described in the Reuelation, to be destruction of Paganisme, and of the honor of the false Gods: and the descent of heauenly *Ierusalem*, to be the propagation of Christian Religion; for as much as in the tyme of the prophetes, from whose wordes this verse of the Reuelation, *goe out of Babylon my people* is taken, *Babilon* was as it were, the head of Pagan superstition, and also that the word Babylon signi-

fyinge Confusion, is more proper then anie other, to designe the Religion of the Pagans, which was a Confusion of Religions; because Rome, which in the age of the Apostles was become the head of Paganisme, had receiued into her Common-wealth and Religion the worship and Religion of all the Prouinces that she had ouercome. From whence it is that Saint AVGVSTINE attributes by a particular title the word *confusion* to
De vera Religione c.5. the Religion of the Pagans, when he saith; *We must seeke for Religion, neither in the confusion of the pagans, nor in the refuse of heretickes, nor in the läguishing of Schismatickes, nor in the blindenes of the Iewes*. And it is noe contradiction to
Apoc.18. this, that the Angell cryes, *goe out of Babylon my people*: And a little after, *and recompence her double for what she hath done to you*. For this cry is addressed to the elect, which were not yet the people of God in *act and vocation*, but in *power* and in predestination, whom God soe calls, to drawe them from paganisme, and to make them actually his people, and Commands them to repay or returne what she hath done to them; that is, not what she hath done in theire persons, for they could not be persecuted by her for the faith, if they were not yet seperated from her in faith; but in the persons of theire predecessors. And therefore Saint AVGVSVINE
In psal.149 saith; *Marke how the people of Babylon are put to death, the double of what she hath done, is rendred vnto her: for soe it is written of her; recompence her the double of what she hath done, &c. And how is the double recompenced vpon her? when she might persecute the christians, she slewe theire bodies, but she brake not theire God: Now she is recompenced double, for we roote out the pagans, and breake theire Idolls. And how, sayest thou, are the pagans put to death? how else but in beinge made Christians?*

For if some ancient Fathers haue interpreted the word *Babylon*, to be
Apoc.17. the Cittie of Rome, because of this epithet, *drunck with the bloud of the Saints, and the martires of Iesus*; whose sufferinges were soe frequent at Rome in the first ages of the Church, that it hath bene iustlie said, that *Rome was not so much a cittie of men, as a Church-yard of martires*; It was the *pagan Rome* that they intended, as the Capitall Seate of the heathen Religion, and of the Empire of the Gentiles; and not of any Church, neither particular, nor vniuersall; as it appeares by these wordes of Saint IE-
Cont.Iouin.l.2. ROME: *I addresse my speeche to thee, ô most puissant towne, which hast wiped out the blasphemies written in thy forehead, by the confession of Christ*: Which shewes vs, that whilst *Rome* was pagan, she was the same to the Christians, as *Babylon* was in the tyme of the old Testament, to the Iewes; but that, becomeinge Christian, she had ceased to be soe, and was transformed from *Babylon*, into *Ierusalem*. If any replie, that in his epistle to *Marcella*, the
Ad Marcell.ep.17. same Saint IEROM hath gone soe farr, as to applie the name of *Babylon* to *Rome*, after she was Christian: it was not to *Rome*, as the Seate of *Religion*, but to *Rome* as the seate of the *Empire*; not to the *Ecclesiasticall communion* of *Rome*, but to the *politicke State* of *Rome*; not to the *Church* of Rome, but to the *Imperiall Court*, to the *Senate*, to the *Pallace*, and to the troupe of Courtiers, Solicitors and Negotiators of Rome, and *not in matter of Faith* but in *matter of manners*; and not in regard of *Secular Christians*, but in regarde of the *monkes* to whom *Rome* was a kinde of *Babylon*, because of the diuersions, that the noyse, the confusion, the tumult of men and affaires in
Ibidem. soe great a Cittie brought to monasticall deuotion as it appeares by what he adds presently after: *It is true that in that Cittie there is the holie Church; it is true that there are the trophies of the Apostles and of the martyres: it is true there is the true confession of Christ, it is true there is the faith celebrated by the Apostle, and the Christian name euerie day exalted by the depression of paganisme troden vnder foote: but the ambition, the power, and greatnesse of this Cittie, to visitt and to be*

visited,

visited, to salute and to be saluted, to flatter and detract, to heare, and speake, nay to see, though vnwillingly, so great a multitude of men, are thinges farr from the purpose and quiet of those, that would followe a monasticall life. And againe, notinge the same discomodities in the dwelling in *Ierusalem*; *If* (said hee) *the places of the Crosse and Resurrection were not in a famous towne, where there is a Court, where there is is a garrison of Souldiers, where there are common woemen, players, ieasters, and all thinges which vse to be in other Citties, &c. it would certainly be a dwellinge much to be desired by Monkes.* Now if some-times he haue chanced to make vse of this word in his writinges, against certaine Priestes and Deacons of the Clergie of Rome, who, iealious of his fauour with Pope *Damasus*, persecuted him with slanders, reproching to him, *a* that he had translated the treaties of Didymus an hereticall author; *b* that he had conuersed too familiarly with the deuout ladies of Rome, and perswaded them to quit theire countrie, children, and kindred, that is, the confusion and tumulte of the world, to goe as recluses into the Monasteries of *Palestina*: These were all complaintes, which still remain'd within the limites of theire manners; and neither touched the faith of the *Roman* Church; nor the succession of *saint Peter*; nor the communion of the Apostolicall Sea; nor the very person of the Pope. And indeede, how could saint IEROME applie these wordes of the Reuelation, *Goe out of Babylon*, to the Cittie of Rome, for anie thinge concerninge faith and Religion? He that cryes out in his apologie against RVFFINVS: *Which faith is it, that he calls his? that, that the Roman Church holdes? or that, that is contained in Origens bookes? if he answere that that the Roman Church holdes, then we are Catholickes.* And in the Epistle to THEOPHILVS Patriarche of *Alexandria*. *Know that we haue nothinge in greater recommendation, then to conserue the statutes of Christ, and not to transgresse the bounds of our fathers, and alwaies to remember the Roman faith praysed by the mouth of the Apostle, whereof the Alexandrian Church doth glorie to partake.* And in the Epistle to DEMETRIAS. *When thou wert little, and that the Bishop Anastasius of holie and happie memorie, gouuerned the Roman Church, a cruell tempest of heretickes risen out of the Easterne partes, attempted to pollute and corrupt the simplicitie of that faith, which had bene commended by the mouth of the Apostle: but this personage* (Pope Anastasius) *riche in a most plentifull pouertie, and in an Apostolicall care, brake the pestilent head, and stopped the hissinge mouthes of this Hydra. And because I feare, yea I haue heard saie, that the budds of this venimous plante doe still liue, and springe vp in some, I thought it my dutie to admonish thee in a deuout zeale of charitie, that thou keepe fast the faith of Saint INNOCENT his sonne and Successor in the Apostolicall Chaire.* And in the Epistle to Pope DAMASVS, *I am chayned in communion with thy blessednesse; that is with Peters Chaire; I know the Church is built vpon that rocke, if anie eate the lambe out of that howse, he is prophane.* And a little after; *I know not Vitalis, I reiect Meletius, I am ignorant of Paulinus; whosoeuer gathers not with thee scatters; that is to saie, whosoeuer is not of Christ, is of Antichrist.* Far then was hee from holdinge the Church of *Rome* for *Babylon* and the *Pope* for *Antichrist*: since he held, whosoeuer did not communicate with the *Pope* for *Antichrist*.

Ad Paulin. de instit. Monach. ep 13.

a. Præfat. in Didim. de

b. Ad Asell. ep. 99.

Apol. aduer Ruffin. l. 1

Epist. 68.

Epist. 8.

Ad Damos. epist. 57.

The *third* exposition is of them, who interpret the allegoricall *Babylon*, to be the Monarchy of the *Turkes*, who with its false Prophet *Mahomet*, haue possessed all the citties, and particularly those of the seuen Churches of Asia, to which *S. Iohn* addressed his reuelatiō, and which hath *giuen vp her soule to the perished beast*; that is to saie, hath againe takē the office and ranke of the pagan Emperors, blasphmers and persecutors of the name of Christ; and hath vsurped the Seate, whither theire succession had bene transferd;

to witt *Constantinople*; and who is *clothed with purple*, that is, hath the Emperiall power and authority, whose simbole in Saint Iohns tyme was purple; and which is seated, *be it literally*, vpon seuen Mountaines for Constantinople hath seuen Mountaines as old Rome had, (for moderne Rome hath nyne;) Or *be it accordinge to the allegoricall* interpretation of Saint Iohn, vpon seuen kings, that is to say, vpon the seuen Empires, that followe the impietie of Mahomett. And in briefe which hath soe many other affinities with the *Babylon* in the *Reuelatiō*, as OECOLAMP. and BVLLINGER, are constrayned to giue her two seates, and constitute two *Antichrists*, one in the weste and an other in the East Now which of these expositiōs answeres the precise intētion of the Author; or whether the perfect accōplishment of these thinges be yet to come, (and should be vnderstood of a Societie, which shall not arise, till after the Ghospell haue bene actually preached to all the nations of the world, as all ancient writers are agreed, that the Monarchie of Antichrist, which the Protestāts esteene to be one thinge withthe *Babylon* of the *Reuelation*, shall not come till after that tyme,) it is not heere our purpose to examine.

Oecol. in Daniel. Bulling. in Apoc.

But in summe, that that *Babylon* whereof the reuelation speaketh, can be seriouslie taken for the cittie of *Rome*, the antithesis that saint IOHN makes of *Babylon* and *Ierusalem* (which teacheth vs, that as the *Ierusalem* described by the same *Reuelation*, is not a locall cittie; soe *Babylon* described by the same *Reuelation*, is not a locall and corporall cittie;) takes from vs all colour to belieue it. And therefore ARETHAS (who beinge a grecian, and a schismaticke, as he is held to bee, had had more interest, to interpret this passage of Rome;) resolues in the end, that it cannot be vnderstood, neither of *Rome* nor of *Constantinople*, but of the state of this corruptible world. *It appeares* (saies[a] he) *vndoubtlie by this place, that the thinges which are heere foretolde, should neither be vnderstood of Babylon, nor of olde nor newe Rome, that is Constantinople, nor of any other cittie, but of all this corruptible world.*

Areth. in Apoc. c. 18.

And that she may be taken for a Church, which in the beginninge was a true Church of Christ, and since growne false and adulterate, bearinge neuerthelesse still the title of a Church; the figure of *Babylon*, (which was from the beginninge founded by *Nimrod* a pagan, and infidell, and after alwaies perseuered in paganisme, and in the open profession of infidelitie, till the fall of her Empire;) cannot beare it. Contrarywise, that which saint IOHN saith, [b] that, *all those whose names are not written in the booke of life, haue worshipped the beast, vpon which the harlott sitts*; seemes to insinuate, that he speaks of the societie of all the reprobate, of what soeuer Secte, Religion, and profession they haue bene; as well Iewes, Gentiles, Heretickes Schismatickes: as euill Catholickes, and not of any determinate Communion.

b. Apoc. 13.

Yet we avowe neuerthelesse, that the Fathers haue some-tymes turned the wordes of *Isay* and *Ieremy*, (from whence those wordes of the *Reuelation* are takē,) to make vse of them against the particular Sect of the Arrians: As when OSIVS, and after him S. ATHANAS. say, *the Scripture cryes out, depart, depart; goe out from her, and touch not her vncleanesse: Withdrawe you from the midst of them; separate your-selues frō thē, you that carrie the vessells of our Lord.* But besides, that they haue neuer pretēded, that this precept should be extēded to all the multitude of Christiās; and, that there might come a tyme, wherein there were noe externall Cōmunion visible and eminent, out of which it should be vnlawfull to goe forth; (which is that which is in question;) There is great difference betweene the conceites, & allusions, that

Epist. ad solit. vit agēt.

the Fathers made vpon the allegoricall expositions of the passages of the Scripture: and the proper and direct vnderstandinge of the same passages, which is that onely, from whence we may argue seriouslie. And therefore when the *Donatists* in the conference of *Carthage*, would haue made vse of the same wordes, against the Catholicke Church: Saint AVGVST. and the other Bishops of Africa, answered them, that the separation intended by that passage, was the morall separation of faith and breach of Communion. *It was* (saith S. AVGVST.) *represented, what ought to be the separation of the good from the bad in this world; that they might not communicate in theire sinnes; to witt, separation of hart, by dissimilitude of life and manners: and that otherwise ought not to be vnderstood, that which is written, goe out from the middle of them, and withdrawe from them, and touch not theire vncleannesse; that is to saie, be distinguished in liuing in an other sorte, and consent not to theire vncleannesse.* In breuic. coll. coll. 3.

But the excellent kinge saith, that there are other places of scripture, whereby is proued, that which he pretendes to gather from the allegoricall wordes of the reuelation; to witt, that the visible Church should become soe corrupt, as the faithfull should be obliged to leaue her communion. Now the obiections that his Maiestie reserues for vs in this regard, are either taken from this interrogatory of our Lord, *In your opinion the sonne of man, when he comes, shall he finde faith vpon the earth?* or from these wordes; *the moone shall not giue vs her light:* Which S. AVGVST. interpretes of the Church; or from this prophecie of *Saint Paule*; *the Sonne of perdition shall be seated in the temple of God.* Or out of these words of the same booke of the reuelation; *two winges of a great Eagle were giuen to the woeman, that she might flye into the wildernesse;* Or from the examples of the pretended ecclipses and sincopes of the Iewish Church. And therefore, (settinge aside the obiection of the symptomes of the Iewish Church, which we remitt to treate of heereafter;) it is fitt, that we solue all the rest presently. Luc. 18. Matt. 24. Aug. ep. 80 2. Thess. 2. Apoc. 12. In the chap of the comparison of the Christiã Church with the Iewes.

To the *first* obiection then, which is to the interrogatory, that our Lord made to his disciples, when he asketh them; *In your opinion, when the Sonne of man comes, shall he finde faith on the earth?* Wee saie saint IEROM and S. AVG. haue answered it longe agoe; the one against the *Luciferians*, and the other against the *Donatists*: And haue shewed, that this passage is intended, not of confessed and *doctrinall faith*; but of *iustifiynge faith*, workinge by charitie; and yet not of the *extinction*, but of the *diminution* of this iustifiynge faith. *The Donatists* (saith saint AVG.) *alleadge, that this, that our Lord asketh, in your opinion the Sonne of man vhen he comes, shall he finde faith vpon the earth? is to be expoundad of the reuolte of all the earth: which we vnderstand to be said, either in regarde of the perfection of faith, which is soe difficult to men, that in the very Saintes who where to be admired, as in Moses, there was found some thinge wherein they haue staggered or might stagger; or for the aboundance of the wicked, and the smalle number of the good.* And saint IEROM, speakinge of the *Luciferians*; *If they flatter themselues,* (said hee,) *with this sentence written in the Ghospell; in your opinion when the Sonne of man comes, shall he finde faith vpon the earth? let them know, that the faith there mentioned, is that, whereof the same Lord said; Thy faith hath saued thee: And againe of the Centurion: I haue not found so great faith in Israell.* And a little after: *it is this faith, that our Lord hath foretoulde shall be rarelie found: it is this faith that euen in those that belieue well, is hardlie found perfect: Let it be done to thee* (said hee) *accordinge to thy faith. I would not haue that word pronounced to me; for if it be done to me accordinge to my faith, I shall perish: and yet I belieue in God the father; I belieue in God the Sonne; and I belieue in God the holy Ghost.* De vnit. Eccl. c. 13. Ieron. cont. Lucifer.

To the *second* obiection, which is, that sainct AVGVSTINE in-

Matt. 24. terpretes allegorically these other wordes of the Ghospell: *then the moone shall noe more giue her light*; to be meant of the Church, which in tyme of persecutions, whereof he speakes, shall not appeare; we answere sainct AVGVSTIN meanes, that she should not appeare in her carnall and weake members; but not that she shall not appeare in her strong and spirituall Champions; that she shall not appeare, or lesse appeare, in her terrestriall parte, in her strawe, in her drosse; because that parte will yeild to persecutions; but not that she shall not appeare in her more excellent parte, in her corne, in her golde; which contrarywise will then shine more then before. This appeares by what he writes in his Epistle to

Aug. epist. 48. *Vincentius*: *It is shee* (said hee) *that is sometimes obscured, and as it were shadowed with clowdes, by the multitude of scandalls, that is to saie persecutions: when the Sinners bend theire bowe, to wound it the obscuritie of the moone, the lawes of theire heart: but euen then she is eminent in her moste firme champions.* And a little after; *It is not in vaine that it was said of the seede of Abraham, that is should be as the starrs of heauen; and as the sand vpon the Sea-shore; that by the starrs of heauen might be meant the faithfull, lesse in number, more steddie, and more cleere; and by the sand which is on the Sea-shore, the multitude of weake and carnall men, who some-times in calme weather appeare free and quiet, and sometimes are couered and troubled with the waues of tribulations and temptations.* And therefore after he hath

Epist. 80. said, *she shall not appeare*, he adds; *for as much as manie, which seemed to shine in grace, shall yeilde to persecutions, and fall awaie; and some faithfull persons verie firme, shall be troubled.* And againe; *persecution shall so precede, as that defection of some shall followe*: that he might shew that he meanes not to saie, that the Church shall not appeare in her whole bodie; (otherwise how coulde he

Cont. Petil. l. 2. c. 104 crye out in an other place: *she hath this most certaine marke, that she cannot be hidden*) but that she shall not appeare in some of those that had bene her partes. Which neuerthelesse in matter of application of allegories, where it is permitted to bow the sense of the wordes, to accommodate it to the grace of the application: and where interpretors content themselues, if the thinge signified, answere in anie parte to that signifiyinge; it sufficeth to make him say. to the end to appropriate the allegory of the moone to the Church, that the Church then shall not appeare, that is; shall not appeare in some of her partes.

2. Thess. 2. The *third obiection* followes, which is, that saint Paul writes, that *the daie of the Lord shall not come, till the reuolte be first made, and till the man of sinne be reuealed, and the sonne of perdition, who shall oppose and exalte himselfe aboue all that is called God, or esteemed an obiect worthie of worship, euen to sitt in the temple of God, shewinge himselfe as if he where God.* Now I will not heere stand to dispute, what saint Paul meanes, by this *reuolte* or *apostasy*, to wit, whether hee meane the reuolte of the people from the Roman Empire, or the reuolte of the Christians from the Religion of Christ to that of Mahomet; or the reuolte of the Iewes, from vnder all the temporall principalities, within whose estates they are dispersed, to revnite themselues in a newe monarchie vnder theire pretended *Messias*, that is to saie; vnder *Antichrist*. As little will I stand to examine, whether this temple of God, wherein the sonne of perdition shall sitt, be to be vnderstood by the materiall temple of *Ierusalem*, when *Antichrist* shall haue caused it to be reedified (as Sainct IRENEVS *cont. hæres. lib. 5. cap. 30.* protestes in these wordes: *When Antichrist shall haue laied desolate all things heere in this world, and shal haue raigned three yeares and a halfe, and shall be sett in the temple at Ierusalem, then the Lord shall come from Heauen*: And as it seemes to be gathered from the relation of the speech of Sainct PAVLE to those wordes of DANIEL spoken of the Iewish temple and cited

by our Lord vpon the speeche of the locall temple of *Ierusalem*; *the abbomination of desolation shall be in the temple*; from whence it is that auntient writers note, that *Iulian* the *Apostata*, one of the figures of *Antichrist*, would haue attempted to reedifie it;) Or whether it be to bee vnderstood by the Iewish nation, whom God had first chosen for his liuinge temple, in which *Antichrist* shall place his throne, followinge this prophecy of our Lord to the Iewes; *I am come in the name of my father, and you haue not receiued me*; *if an other come in his owne name, you will receiue him*. Or whether it be to be vnderstood of nations heeretofore Christian, in who temples now turned into mosqueas, now there Mahomet the fore-runner of *Antichrist* sitts, and that one daie shall ioyne with the Iewes to receiue *Antichrist*. It is sufficiēt that all the fathers are agreed vpon two thinges; *the one* that *Antichrist* shall be the pretended *Christ* and *Messias* of the Iewes. *Antichrist* (saith Saint HILLARIE) *shall be receiued by the Iewes*. And Saint CYRILL of Ierusalem saith: *he shall deceiue the Iewes, as beinge the Christ expected by them*. And Saint IEROM, *Wee know that Antichrist shall be the Christ of the Iewes*. And S. CHRYSOSTOME: *Christ argues the imposture of the Iewes, by the expectation of Antichrist, in that they not receiued him that qualified himselfe, as sent from God: and him that shall not acknowledge God, but glorifie himselfe to be the soueraigne God, they will adore*. And Saint AVGVSTINE; *Christ by these words, if an other come in his owne name, you will receiue him*; *signifies, that the Iewes shall receiue Antichrist*. And againe: *The Iewes shall fall into his nett, of whom our Lord hath said; I am come in my fathers name, and you haue not receiued me; an other shall come in his owne name, and you shall receiue him*; *And of whom the Apostle writes; that the man of sinne and the Sonne of perdition shall be reuealed, who shall oppose and exalte himselfe aboue all that shall be called God*. And S. CYRILL of *Alexandria*, speakinge to the Iewes in the person of our Lord: *you shall receiue (for as God, I know all things,) him that shall come vnder a false title*. And THEODORET: *The Iewes which haue crucified our Lord because he called himself the Sonne of God, shall giue creditt to Antichrist, that shall call himselfe, h the great God*. From whence it appeares, that neither *Antichrist* shall take the title of a Christian; nor his faction the title of a Church; although they possesse many peoples and nations, which haue before possessed the name of a Church: since all the Fathers agree, that he shall be receined by the Iewes. The *other thinge* wherein the Fathers agree is, that this apostacie shall bringe noe interruption to the course and visible succession, of the Catholicke Church; that is to saie: it shall not hinder, but that there shall be alwaies a Christian Societie illustrious and eminent aboue all false and pretended Churches, from whose communion it shall be forbidden to departe; as Saint AVGVSTINE declares in these wordes: *If the Church should not be heere till the end of the world: why did Christ saie, I ame with you to the end of the world?* And in an other place, speakeinge of the very comeinge of *Antichrist*, whose raigne hee deemed should be but three yeares and a halfe: *Let none imagine*, (saith he) *that that little while that the Diuell shall be vnbounde, there shall be noe Church vpon the earth*. And shortly after, disputinge whether, while that short space of tyme lasted, the diuell should be so vnbound, as that he should hinder anie from entringe into the Church, either Children by baptisme, or men by Conuersion, but said he: *We should rather belieue, that euen then there will not want people, both to goe out of the Church, and to come into the Church; for certainly both fathers will be soe couragious as to giue baptisme to theire children; and those that then beginn first to beleeue, will be soe constāt, as they will cōquer this stronge one, euen although he be vnboūd*. Whereby he shewes plainely, that he speakes not of a Church hidden

Matth. 24.
Greg. Naz. in Iulian. orat. 1.
Ibid. orat. 2.
Ioann 15.
In Matth. can. 25.
Catech 15.
In Ezech. c. 16.
In Ioann. hom. 41.
In Ioann. tract 29.
In psalm. 105.
Cyrill. Alex. in Ioann. l. 3.
Theod. in in ep. diu. decret. c. de Antich.
In psalm. 70.
De ciuit. dei l. 20. c. 8.
Ibidem.

and vnknowne, but of a Church visible, and exposed to the eyes and knowledge of men.

Apoc. 12. The *fowrth* obiectiō is, *that the woeman, that had brought forth him, that ought to rule the nations, fledd into the wildernesse.* And againe, *that two winges of a great Eagle, were giuen to the woeman to flye into the wildernesse.* For these two retreates into the wildernesse, are but one retreate, repeated by two seuerall descriptions; betweene the which is inserted the fall of the diuell, to shewe the the cause of the reuenge, that he would haue exercised vpon the woeman. From this retreate then they conclude, that the Church shall then be inuisible. But besides, that the same answeres alreadie propounded against the argumentes, which are drawne from the allegoricall expositions of the reuelation, are alsoe of force against this allegation;
De Symb. ad catech. lib. 4. what shall hinder vs from interpretinge this passage with Saint AVGV. of the blessed virgin, who brought forth him, that ought to rule the nations; and who is described crowned with starrs, because she was descen-
Genes. 37. ded from the race of the twelue Patriarches, who in *Iosephs* dreame were figured by ste starrs: and who is represented enuironed by the Sunne; because according to the translation of the seuentie, (which is that the
Psal. 18. Apostles haue followed) the Psalmist singeth; *He hath pitched his tabernacle in the Sunn?* And who shall hinder vs from sayinge the wildernesse, wither she flew, was heauen, into which she was assumed after her death, which the Grecians call wildernesse; because it is exempt from all generation, wherefore Pindarus calleth the heauen a desert or wildernesse, in these verses:

If thou of combates honor mean'st to singe,
Seeke not, when daie on the horizon stayes,
A light more splendid then the Sunn, whose rayes
From the ethereall desert, first doe springe.

Matt. 13. And that the rest of the seede of the woman were those, of whom our Lord said, shewing his disciples; *See heere my mother and my bretheren?* For though Saint Iohn make mention of the paines of childbirth; neuerthelesse those wordes may be vnderstood to be spoken accordinge to the or-
Luc. 3. dinarie custome of the childbirth of wemen, as it is written, that the *daies*
Ibid. *of the purification of the childbirth of the virgin, were accomplished*, and that she *presented our Lord in the temple to obserue the lawe, that commaunded that euery male that opens the wombe shall be holy to the Lord.* Now if the mention of the paines of childbirth keepe vs from expoundinge this passage of the virgin, and obligeth vs to transferr it to the Church; what shall hinder vs from interpretinge still the wildernesse to be heauen? and from sayinge, that the wildernesse whither the woman fled, was heauen, into which the first of the faithfull persecuted and martyred fled euery day by theire death; and the Church in theire persons; from before the face of the serpent, and were deliuered from his Snares, persecutions, and temptations,
Apoc. 14. followeinge this exclamation of Saint IOHN; *Blessed are those that dye for the cause for the Lord, for they shall rest from thence forward from theire labors?* Or, if wee will not by the word *Wildernesse,* vnderstand heauen; who shall hinder vs frō sayinge, that this woman was the Church? who haueinge bene once amongst the Iewes, after she had brought forth Christ by the preachinge of the Ghospell; was persecuted by the Iewes, that is to saie, the people of
In Psal. 67 the Gentiles, which is often vnderstood by the wildernesse from whence it is, that S. AVG. interpretinge these wordes of the Psalmist, *Whē I passed through the wildernesse, the earth trēbled,* writes, *the wildernesse were the natiōs, that were ignorant of God, the wildernesse was there, where there was noe lawe giuen from God, where noe Prophetes had dwelt, which had foretolde, that the Lord should come.*

And

And who can hinder vs, from Supposeinge, that the relicks of the ſeede of the woman were the Iewes, who were conuerted to the Chriſtian Religion, and whoſe generall reunion with the Church shall be made before the end of the world? or who can forbidd vs to interpret this *wilderneſſe* to be the excluſion from ciuill and politicke charges, from which the Church was ſoe banished vnder the pagan Emperors, that the Chriſtians were not admitted to anie parte of the adminiſtration of the Common wealth? For our aduerſaries will not haue, that the number of three yeares and a halfe, to which this flight is limitted, should be taken accordinge to the ordinary and literall accompt. Or finally (if it permitted to the laſt commers, to hope to finde the diuination of the paſſages of the Reuelation in theire coniectures, as the cupp of prophecie in Beniamins Sacke;) Who shall hinder vs from applyinge this allegory to the Conuerſion of the Countries newly diſcouered, and to in terpret the *wilderneſſe* to be the Indias, and the other hemiſpheare, which had bene ſoe longe tyme left waſte and deſert from the knowledge of the true God? and from ſaying, that the two wings are the two nauigation of the Eaſt and weſt, by which the Church (that the diuell vnder the enſignes of Mahomet ſtriues to driue from our hemiſpheare) is gone to viſite thoſe regions, conformable to the ſtile of the Grecians, which call the ſailes of shipps *wings*, and ſay *winge a shippe* in ſteede of ſettinge to the ſailes? and who shall hinder vs from interpretinge the Eagle, from whence theſe two winges preceede, to be the weſterne part of the Roman Empire, whereof theſe two nauigations are partes? and from expoundinge the relickes of the woman to be the Catholickes, that remaine vnder the tiranny of Mahomet? For to expound the woman, to be the ſecret mumber of the predeſtinate: and the wilderneſſe to be inuiſibilitie and obſcurity, how can it agree with that, that our Lord Cryes: *If they tell you heere is Chriſt, beholde him in the deſart, goe not forth: beholde him in the ſecret places, belieue them not.* And S. AVGVSTINE after him: *It is not an obſcure queſtion, and wherein they can deceiue you, of whom our Lord foretolde, that they should come and ſaie; ſee heere is Chriſt, beholde he is there: ſee heere hee is in the wilderneſſe, that is out of the frequency of the multitude:* And a while after, *that is then the Church that is not in anie one parte of the earth, but which is well knowne ouer all?* And how can it be, that, the woman beinge retired into the wilderneſſe, that is to ſaie, the Societie of the predeſtinate, beinge shadowed, hidden and obſcured from before the face of the Dragon, shall quit the purſuite of the woman, to goe make warr with the relickes of the ſeede of the woman? for if the woman be inuiſible, how can the relickes of the woman be viſible? And if from that, that is ſaid, that the woman flied into the deſert, it be permitted to conclude, that the Church shall be inuiſible: wherefore shall we not by the ſame reaſon conclude, that the *Babylon* of the Reuelation shall be inuiſible? ſeeinge Saint IOHN writes, *And he carried me in the ſpirit into the deſert, and I ſaw the woman ſitt vpon the beaſt?* And this wee ſaie not that we pretend to warrant this interpretation more then the reſt, but to shew, how weake foundation ſuch allegoricall allegations are, to builde a reuolt, and an alteration of Religion vpon, and to ouerthrowe ſoe manie euident and literall promiſes of *perpetuall beinge, viſibilitie eminencie, and purity*, as God hath made to his Church.

Matth. 24.

De vnit eccles. ca. 20

Apoc. 17.

Of the consequence of the places alleadged by the fathers, for the aucthoritie of the Catholicke Church.

CHAPT XVI.

The continuance of the Kinges answere.

NOw to come neerer the point, the kinge denies that this exact collection of places out of Saint AVGVSTINE, doth in anie sorte touch him.

THE REPLIE.

IN truth, if the most excellent Kinge, can proue, that the Church, to which he adheares, hath bene perpetually visible, and eminent aboue all other Christian Societies; (as Saint AVGVSTINE puts this condition for one of the necessary markes of the Church, when he saith: *she hath this most certaine marke, that she cannot be hidden, she is then knowne to all nations: the sect of Donatus is vnknowne to manie nation, then that cannot be she:*) And if he can shew, that she hath bene not onely perpetuallie visible and eminent, but also perpetuallie pure from all contagion of Schisme and heresie, (as Saint AVGVSTINE protestes, that to be of the essence of the Catholicke Church, when he writes, *noe hereticke belonges to the Catholicke Church, because she loues God; nor noe Schismaticke, because she loues her neighbour.* And againe, *The Church of the Saintes, is the Catholicke Church; the Church of the Saintes, is not the Church of the hereticke; she was predesigned, that she might be discerned, and hath bene exhibited, that she might be seene.* And if he can proue, that she neuer went forth from the Communion of anie other, but that all other went forth from her, and shee alwaies remained in her roote, visible, eminent, perpetuall, immutable, and exempt from all interruption, which is a marke which Saint AVGVSTINE testifies to be inseperable from the Church, when he writes: *The Catholicke Church, fightinge with all heresies, may be opposed, but she cannot be ouerthrowne; All heresies are come out from her, as vnprofitable branches out from the vine, but she remaines in her vine, in her roote, in her Charity.* In truth I saie, if the excellent kinge can shewe these 3. thinges, I confesse freely that this Collection of passages (*that out of the Catholick Church none can be saued; that whosoeuer is separate from the Catholicke Church, how laudable soeuer he presumes his life to be: for this only Crime, that he is separated from the vnitie of Christ, he shall not haue life, but the wrath of God shall remaine vpõ him; that he shall not haue God for his Father, that will not haue the Church for his mother; and that it shall nothinge auaile him to haue beleiued or done such and soe many good workes, without the end of the soueraigne good; that out of the Catholicke Church all thinges may be had but saluation; that he that Communicates with the the generall Church, is a Christian and a Catholicke, and he that communicates not therewith is an hereticke and Antichriste; that it must be stedfastly and vndoubtedly held, that euery hereticke or Schismaticke baptised, in the name of the father, the Sonn and the holy Ghost, if before the end of his life he doe not reconcile himselfe to the Catholicke Church, what almesdeedes soeuer he doe, yea though he should shed his blood for the name of Christ, can in noe sorte be saued,*) makes not against his Maiestie. But if contrarily the excellent kinge cannot proue,

[Margin: Cont Petil. l.2.c.104. — De fid & Sym. — De Sym. ad Catech. l.1. c.5. — Cont. Cor. c.c.1. Aug. ep.152 — Aug. de Sym ad Catich. l.c. — Aug. gest. cũ Emerit. Prost. de promiss. & prœdict. part.4.c 39 Fulg. de fid. ad Petr. c. 39.]

that the Church, to which he adheres, hath taken the originall of her visible Communion, continued, and not interrupted, from aboue 60. or 80. yeares; and that betweene the tyme of the Fathers, from whom that collection of passages hath bene extracted, and the tyme of Caluins pretended reformation. there hath neuer bene anie Church anie communion, anie Societie, anie person, that hath held iointlie, vniuersally those thinges, for which England hath deuided herselfe from the visible Communion of that Church wherein she was before; then I had need be instructed to apprehend how these passages make not against his maiestie.

Of the distinction of heretickes, and Schismatickes.

CHAPT. XVI.

The continuance of the kinges answere.

For from all these testimonies there followes onely this consequently, that there remaines noe hope of saluation, for those, who are seperated from the faith of the Catholicke Church, or from the Communion of the same Catholicke Church. which the kinge (as we haue said before) grauntes him selfe.

THE REPLIE.

THe Collection of the passages, that I haue produced, doe not put this alternatiuely, that amongst those, that are seperated, either from the faith of the Catholicke Church, or from her Communiõ; there is noe saluation. Otherwise in a thinge that the Fathers would should be cleere and manifest, they had a perpetuall ambiguitie, to witt; what it were *to be seperated* from the faith of the Catholicke Church. For there would remaine alwaies this questiõ, whether the pointes of separatiõ were pointes of Faith; and the separation might be made vpon such a pointe, as the one side would say; it were a pointe of Faith, and the other; that it were not: As the Pellagians disputinge against the Catholickes, said *theire difference was not in a pointe of Faith*: And the Catholicks said the contrary; and as yet to this daie the Zuinglians and the Caluinistes disputinge against the Lutherans, *theire contestation is not about a point of faith*, and the Lutheranes saie the contrary. But the Fathers absolutely sett Downe this Maxime, that out of the Communion of the Catholicke Church, there is noe saluation; reducinge all the certainly and euidence of this proposition, *that out of the Church there is noe saluation*, to the seperation of Communion. It is true that the seperation of Communion, may proceede from either of these two causes, to witt; either from an error in faith, in which case those that forsake the Church are called heretickes: or from defect in Charity, in which case they are called Scismaticks. But because those, that sinne either in the one or in the other, cannot be soe easily conuinced, either of the one, or of the other, as of the seperation of the Communion of this visible Church eminent aboue all hereticall and Schismaticall sectes, whom God would be exposed to the view of all Nations and called Catholicke; and to whom he hath affected the promises and prerogatiues

Sus.c.10. Ibid.

gatiues of the perpetuall assistance of his holy Spirit; For this cause, the Fathers and the Councells of Africa, (Saint AVGVSEINE beinge theire Secretary,) haue pronounced this sentence, (soe often before particulariz'd by the penns of the precedinge authors,) that *out of the Catholicke Church there is noe saluation;* without makinge distinction betweene those that seperate themselues from the faith of the Church, and those that seperate themselues from her communion; for as much as all those, that seperate themselues visiblie from the faith of the Church, seperate themselues also frõ her Cõmunion. For there are noe declar'd heretickes, but they are withall Schismatickes also: Onely there is this difference, that heretickes seperate themselues from the Faith and Communion of the Church both together; and the Schismatickes onely seperate themselues from her communion: although there are fewe Schismatickes, who to the separation of communion, add not the separation of some pointe of faith. For as Sea-crabbs when they see oysters open, cast in litle stones within theire shells, to keepe them from shuttinge againe, that they may haue tyme to deuowre them; soe when Schismatickes see a breache made in the Church, to hinder it from closeinge againe, they caste pointes of heresie into theire Schisme, and from Schismaticks become accessorily heretickes. *Wee esteeme* (said Saint IEROM) *the difference betweene heresie and Schisme to be, that heresie holdes a peruerse doctrine, and Schisme for Episcopall dissention seperates men equallie from the Church; which difference may well haue place a while in the beginninge, but in tract of time, there is noe Schisme that doth not forge to it-selfe some heresie, to seeme to haue the iuster cause to seperate it selfe from the Church.* And therefore, when the *Emperors* speake of the *Donatists*, who are those principally, (for whom his Maiestie added this clause,) *or haue seperated themselues from her communion*, they taxe them accessorilie of heresie. *From thence*, saith the lawe, *it is happened, that from Schisme heresie is bred.* And when Saint AVGVSTINE disputes against them, he proues to thẽ, that they are not onely Schismatickes, but alsoe heretickes: *Thou art* (said he to *Gaudentius*) *both a Schismaticke by sacriligious dissention, and an hereticke by sacriligious doctrine.* But the principall difference that wee obserue is, that all call those, that haue begunne with dissention in faith, and to whom Schisme hath but the place of an accessory, *heretickes*; and those that haue begunne with schisme, and to whom heresie is come accessorily after the schisme, (as the feuer after the wound,) *Schismatickes.*

Conc. Carth. 4. Cõc. Carth apud Aug. ep. 152.

In ep. ad Tit. c. 3.

Cod. Theod. l. 16. tit. 6. l. 4.

Cont. Gauden l. 3.

Of the agreement of the ancient Catholicke Church, with the moderne.

CHAP. XVIII.

The continuance of the Kinges answere.

AND heere, most Illustrious Cardinall, his Maiestie requires from you, that you will represent to your selfe, how great Difference there is betweene Saint AVGVSTINS tyme, and this of ours: how the face, and all the exterior forme of the Church, (to saie nothinge of the interior,) is changed.

THE REPLIE.

THis is the request, that I would myselfe most humblie make to his Maiestie; to witt, to sett before his eyes the estate of the Catholicke

Church in the tyme of Saint AVGVSTINE and of the fower first Councells: A Church that belieued [a] the true and reall presence, and the orall manducation of the Bodie of Christ in the Sacrament vnder the kindes and within the Sacramentall kindes, as Zuinglius the principall Patriarch of the Sacramentaries acknowledgeth himselfe, in these wordes, [b] *From the tyme of* Saint AVGVSTINE (that is, 1200. yeares agoe) *the opinion of corporall flesh had alreadie gotten the masterie.* A church that in this qualitie [c] adored the Eucharist, not onely with thought, and inward deuotions, but with outward gestures and adorations actually reallie and substantiallie, the true and proper bodie of Christ. For I will not speake now of Transubstantiation, for which I reserue a treatise apart. A Church that belieued the bodie of Christ, to be in the Sacramét [d] euen besides the vse; and for this cause kept it after Consecration [e] for domesticall communions [f] to giue to sicke persons; [g] to carry vpon the Sea, [h] to send into farr prouinces. A Church that belieued [i] that the communion vnder both kindes, was not necessary for the integritie of participation, but that all the Body and all the blood was taken in either kinde: and for this cause [*] in domesticall communions, in communions for Children, in communions for sicke persons, in communions by Sea, in communions of penitentes at the hower of Death, in communions sent into farr prouinces, they distributed it vnder one kinde. A Church that belieued that the Eucharist was [k] a true, full, and intire Sacrifice, [l] it alone succeedinge all the Sacrifice of the lawe; [m] the newe Oblation of the newe Testament, [n] the externall worshipp of latria of the Christians, and not onely an Euchari-stiall Sacrifice, but alsoe a [o] Sacrifice propitiatory, by application of that of the Crosse; and in this qualitie offered it, as well for the absent as for the present, aswell for the *communicantes*, as for the *non-communicantes*; as well for the liuinge [a] as for the dead. A Church that for the oblation of this sacrifice vsed Altars both of wood and [b] stone, [c] erected and Dedicated to God in memory of the martyrs; and consecrated them by certaine formes of wordes and ceremonies, and amōgst others by the inshriuinge theire relickes. A church wherein the faithfull made voyages and pilgrimages, [d] to the bodies of the said Martirs, to be [e] associated to theire merites, and helped by theire intercessions: prayed the holy martyrs [f] to pray to God for them; [g] celebrated theire Feastes, [h] reuerenced theire relickes, [i] made vse of them to exorcise euill spirites, [k] kissed them, [l] caused them to be touched with flowers, [m] carried them in clothes of silke and in vessells of gold, [n] prostrated themselues before theire shrines, [o] offered sacrifices to God vpon theire tombes, [p] touched the grates of the places where theire relickes were kept, [q] tooke and esteemed the dust from vnder theire relickaryes, and went to pray to the martires, not onely for spirituall health, [r] but for the health and temporall prosperity of theire families, [s] carried theire Children, yea theire sicke cattell to be healed. And when they had receiued some helpe from God by the intercession of the said martyrs, [t] hunge vp in the temples, and vpon the Altars erected to theire memory, for tribute and memoriall of the obtayninge of theire vowe, images of golde and siluer of those partes of theire bodie, that had bene healed: And, when the godly and learned Bishops of the ancient tyme reporte these thinges, they celebrate and exalt them,

c 10. and those following. [b]. Zuing. tū. 2. l. de uer. & fals. relig cap. de Euch. [c]. Cyrill. Hier. catech. myst. 5. Chrys. in 1. Cor. hom. 24. Aug in Psalm. 96. Theod. dial. 2. and other see heere after. l. 7. c 8. [d]. Cyrill. Alex. ep. ad Cæsar. Patric. and others see belome. l. 7 c. 9. [e]. Tertul. vx. l. 2. Cyp. de laps. [f]. Eufeb. hist l 7. [g]. Amb. de obit. Satyr. [h] Eufeb hist. eccl. l 5 [i] See below l. 12. in the chapter of the cōmunion vnder one kind. [*] See the places aboue alledged. [k]. Cyp. ad Cæcil. ep. 63. [l]. Aug. de ciuit. l. 7. c. 20. [m]. Iren. c. 4. l. 32. [n]. Aug. cōt. Faust l. 20. c. 21. [o]. Eufeb. de vit Cō. l. 4. Cyrill. Hier and other vnder. l. 8. [a]. Chrys. in 1. Cor. hō. 41.

[b]. Greg. Nyss. de baptis. [c]. Aug. vbi sup. [d]. Basil. in 40. martyr. [e] Aug. supra. [f]. Ambr. de vid. Greg. Naz in Cyp. and other vnder l. 10. [g]. Aug. psalm. 63. and 88. [h]. Ier. ad Marcell. ep. 17. [i]. Idem. cont Vigil. [k]. Ibid. [l]. Aug. de ciuit. l. 22. c. 8. [m]. Ier. cont. Vigil. [n]. Ruff. de hist. Eccl. l. 2. c. 33. Chrys. 2. Cor. hom. 26. [o]. Hier. cont. Vigil. [p]. Ruff. hist Eccl. 2. c. 33. Chrys. 2. Cor. hom. 26. [q]. Hier. con. Vigil. [r]. Aug. vbi sup. [s]. Greg. Niss. in Theod. [t]. Theod. de Græc. aff. l. 8. Paul. Nol. in Fœl. nat. 6. Theod. super. [v]. Basil. de S. Spir. and others vnder lib. 6.

v Basil. de S. Spir. & others vnder lib. 6. vv Tert. de Mon. Aug. de Verb. Apost and others vnder l. 9. a Aug de cur. b Chrys. Phil. hom. 3 c Epiph. her 75. Aug. de heres. c. 53 d Hier. ad Marcel. ep. 54 e Epiph. in compend. & in Anaceph. f Conc. Leod. c. 52. g Epiph in compend. h Conc. Neoc. c 1. Eufeb. de demon. Euág. l. 1. c. 9 Cóc. Carth 2. c. 2 Epiph. hæres. 59. and others. i Epiph. cont. Apostol hæres. 61. k Chrys. ad Theod or 2. Ambr ad virg laps Hier. cont. Iou. l. 1 l Cyp. Cæcil. ep. 63. Cóc. Carth 3. c. 24. m Aug de pecc. orig. c. 40 n Aug. cót. Petill. l. 3. c. 4. o Ier. cont. Lucif. p Aug. de nupt. & cóc l. ca 17. q Amb. de pœnit. c. 7. Aug. de bapt. cō dó. l. 5. c. 20. r Leo. 1. ep. and others. see. below. l. 2. s Aug. con. Parm. l. 2. c. 13. Innoc.

as soe many beames, flashes, and triumphes of the glory of Christ. A Church which held v the apostolicall traditions not written, but cōsigned *viua voce*, and by the visible, and ocular practise of the Apostles to theire successors, to be equall to the Apostolicall writinges: and held for apostolicall tradions all the selfe same thinges that we acknowledge and embrace in the qualitie of apostolicall traditions. A Church that offered prayers both priuate and publicke vv for the Dead, to the end to gaine ease and rest for them, and to obtaine that God would vse them more mercifullie, then theire sinnes deserued; and held this custome for a thinge a necessary for the refreshinge of theire soules, b and for a doctrine of apostolicall tradition, and placed c those, that obserued it not, in the Cataloge of heretickes. A Church that held the fast of the 40. daies of Lent for a Custome d not free and voluntary, but necessary, and of Apostolicall tradition, e and reckoned amongst heretickes those that obserued it not, and duringe the tyme of Lent, as in a generall mourninge of Christians f forbadd the Celebration of weddinges, and the solemnisations of marriages. A Church that out of Pentecost held the fast of all the Fridaies in the yeares, in memory, of the Death of Christ, except Christmasse day fell vpon one, g which she excepted namely as an apostolicall tradition. For I speake not of wednesdaies supplyed in the west by satturdaies. A Church that held the h interdiction made to Bishops, Priestes, and Deacons to marry after theire promotion, for a thinge necessary, and of apostolicall tradition. A Church that held i marriage after the vowe of virginitie a sinne, and that by apostolicall tradition, k and reputed religious men and religious weemen that married after the solēne vowe of single life, not onely for adulterers, but for incestuous persons. A Church that held the l minglinge of water with wine in the Sacrifice of the Eucharist, for a thinge necessary, and of diuine and Apostolicall tradition. A Church that held the m exorcismes exsufflations and renunciations, which are made in baptisme, for sacred Ceremonies, and of Apostolicall tradition. A Church that besides baptisme and the Eucharist, which were the two initiatinge-Sacramentes of Christian Religion, held n *Confirmation* made with the Chrisme and the signe of the Crosse, o and allowed onely to Bishops the power to conferr it, p *Marriage* for a true and proper Sacrament, q *Pennance* for a true and proper Sacrament, r and *vocall Confession* tothe Pastors of the Church, for one of the Conditiōs necessary to this Sacrament, s *Order* for a true and proper Sacrament: and *Extreame Onction* for a true and proper Sacramēt; which are the seuen Sacramentes that the *Roman Church* acknowledges, and a the Greeke Communion alsoe makes profession to embrace with vs. A Church which in the Ceremonies of baptisme, vsed b oyle, c salte, d waxe, lights, e exorcismes, f the signe of the Crose, g the word *Epheta* and other thinges that accompanie it; to testifie by oyle, that in baptisme wee are made Christians, that is, partakers of the vnction of Christ; by salte, that God contracted with vs in baptisme an alliance for euer, followinge the stile of the Scripture, which calls eternall alliances, *alliances of salte*; by the light, that Christ is the light, that enlightens all men commeinge into the world; h by exorcismes, that baptisme puts vs out of the Diuells possession; i by the signe of the Crosse, that it is the Death of Christ that giues strength to all Sacramentes; k by the word *Epheta*, that God accomplisheth spiritually in vs by baptisme, what he wrought corporally in the deafe and

1. ad Decent c 8. a Censur. Orient Eccl. c. 7. b. Cyp. ep. 70. c Cóc Carth 3. c. 5. d Greg. Naz. de bapt. e Aug. ep. 101 f Aug con. Iul l. 6. c. 8. g Amb de Sacr l. 1. h Aug. ep. 205. i Aug. in Ioān tract. 1 8. k Amb. de Sacr. l. 1.

dumbe

dumbe man. A Church that esteemed baptisme for persons of full age necessary, with a *conditionall necessitie*; [l] and for children necessary with an *absolute necessitie*: and for this cause permitted [m] lay-men to baptise in danger of death. A Church that vsed *holy water*, consecrated by certaine wordes and ceremonies, and made vse of it [n] both for baptisme, [o] and against inchantments, [p] and to make exorcismes and coniurations against euill spirits. Frō whence it is that [q] S. Gregory the great, (who, though he were after the first fower Councells, yet not to be excepted against by English men, who tooke the originall of their mission from him.) ordained when Englād returned backe from paganisme to Christiā Religiō, that the temples should not be demolished, but expiated by the sprinkling of holy water. A Church, that in the œconomy of Ecclesiasticall ministrie held diuers degrees, [r] the Bishop, the Priest, the Deacō, the Acolite, the Exorcist, the Reader, and the Porter, and consecrated and blessed them with diuers formes and ceremonies; And in the order Episcopall acknowledged diuers seates of iurisdictiō, of positiue right, to witt, Archbishops, Primates, Patriarckes, [s] and one supereminent by diuine law, which was the Pope, without whom nothing could be decided appertayning to the vniuersall Church; & the want of whose presēce, either by himself or by his legates, or his confirmation, made all Councells pretended to be vniuersall, vnlawfull. A Church wich held a [u] succession of Bishops not interrupted since the first mission of the Apostles, for an essentiall condition of her; & reputed those, who had it not, or that communicated with those that had it not, for Schismatiks, and culpable of the same Curse, with *Core, Dathan, and Abiron*. A Church that held the distinction of Bishop and Priest, and namely in the acte of ordinatiō, for a thing of diuine law, [x] and Apostolicall tradition; [y] and condemned as hereticks those, that held it not, A Church, that held free will, for a doctrine of faith, & reuealed in the holy scripture; [b] that held that *faith onely* without Euāgelicall works, is not sufficient for saluation; [c] that wicked men perseuering to the end, were reprobates, but not predestinate to euill; [d] that the certainty that particular men presumed to haue of their predestination, was a rashe bouldnes. A Church wherein their seruice was said throughout the East, in *Greeke*, and through the west, aswell in *Africa* as in Europe, [e] in *Latine*; although that in none of the prouinces neither of *Europe* nor *Africa* (except in *Italie*, & in the citties where the *Roman* colonyes resided) the latine, were vnderstood by the simple people, but onely by the learned. In briefe a Church that vsed either in gender, or in species, either in forme or in analogie, the very same ceremonies, vvhich are the vvords vvell knovven the all men, vvhich the Catholique vseth vniuersally at this daie; [f] obserued the distinctiō of the Feasts and ordinary daies; the distinction [g] of Ecclesiasticall and lay habits; [h] the reuerence of sacred vessells; the custome [i] of shauing [k] and vnction for the collation of orders, the ceremonie of [l] vvashing their hands at the Altar before the consecration of the mysteries; [m] the kisse of peace before the communion, [n] pronounced a part of the seruice at the Altar vvith a lovv voice, and vnheard: [o] made processions vvith the relickes of the martyrs, accompained the dead to their sepulcher vvith [p] vvax tapers in signe of ioy and future certainty of their resurrectiō, had the pictures of Christ and his Saints both [q] out of Churches and [r] in Churches, and [s] vpon the very altars of martyrs, not to adore them, as adoration signifies diuine vvorship, but to reuerence by them the souldiers and champions of Christ. [t] vsed the signe of the crosse in all their conuersations, [u] imprinted it on the forehead of their catechumenists, [x] painted it on the portall of all the hovvses of the faithfull, [y] gaue the blessing to the people vvith their hand by the signe of the

[l]. Aug. de an. & eius orig. l. 3. c. 15. [m]. Tert. de bapt. [n]. Basil. de S. Sp c 27. [o]. Epiph. hær. 30 [p]. Theod. hist eccl. l. 5. c 23. [q]. l 9. ep 71. [r] Cōc. Lao c 24. Cōc. Carth. 4. c. 2. C. l. tit. 3. l. 6. Hier. ep. ad Tit. l. 3. [s]. Hier. ad Damas. ep. 77 Aug de duab. ep. Pel. l. 1. c 1. Cōc. Chalc ep. ad Leō. [t]. Socr. hist. eccl. l. 2. c. 10. Soz. l 3 c 10. [u]. Cyp ad Magn. ep. 76. Chryso. ad Epiph. ho. 11. [x]. Hier. ad Euag. ep 85. in fine. [y]. Epiph. hære. 75. Aug. de hær c. 53. [a]. Aug. de grat. & lib. arb. c. 2. & ep 46. [b]. Aug. de grat. & lib. arb. c. 8 & l. 83 quæst. q. 76 [c]. Prosp. ad artic. sibi impos. [d]. Aug. de cor. & grat. c. 13. [e]. Vnder in cap. of the seruice in the proper tougue. [f]. Aug ep. 118. Idem psal. 63 & 88. [g] Cōc. Lao. c. 22. & 23. Hieron ad Helio. ep 3. Theod. hist ecc. l. 2. c 27. [h]. Hier. præf in ep. Theo Optat. l 1.

[i]. Theod. hist l. 5. cap 8. Isid. de diu. off. l 2. c. 4. [k]. Greg. Naz. de pac. or. 1. [l]. Cyrill Hier. cat. myrt. 5. [m]. Conc. Laod c. 19. [n]. Conc Laod ibid. [o]. Aug. de ciuit. l. 22. c. 8. [p]. Gregor. Naz. in Iul. orat 2. [q] Euseb de vit cont. l. 3. [r]. Paulin. ep. 12. Basil. in martyr. Barlaam. Greg. Niss in S. Theod. [s]. Prudent. in S. Cassian. [t]. Tert de cor. milit. [u]. Aug. de symb. ad catec. l. 2. [x]. Cyril. cont Iul. l. 6. [y]. Hier. in vit. Hil.

z. Athan. cont Idol. a. Paul. ep. 11. b Chrys. in Matt. hom. 89. Euang. hist. eccl. l 4. c 7 c. Suff. c 3. d. Tert. de præscr. Iren l. 3. c. 3. & l. 4. c. 32. and others, see vnder l. 6. e. Cyp de vnit Eccl. Conc. Cart 4. c. 1. Augu st. de symb. ad Catec. l. 4 and others aboue c. 2. & 16. f. Hieron. cont. Lucif Aug. psal. 57. Idem de vtil. cred c. 8. Idem cōt. Cresc. l. 1. c. 38. g Cypr. ad Pup. ep. 69 & ad Magn ep. 76. Chrys. ad Epiph. hō. 11. Hieron. ad Tit. c. 3. and others vnder c. 37.

Crosse,z implyed it to driue away evill spirits, a proposed in Ierusalē the very Crosse to be adored on good friday, b vsed incense in their Synaxes, not particularly incēse of Arabia, but indifferently odoriferous gummes; for they held not incense for sacrifice as in the tyme of the lawe, but for a simple ceremony designed to represent the effect of prayers described by these wordes of Dauid; *Let my prayer arise, euen as incense, into thy presence:* And by these of the *Reuelation; The smoke of the incense of the prayers of the Saints, ascended from the hand of the Angell before God.* And finally a Church which held, that the Catholicke Church had the infallible promise, that she should be c *perpetually visible and eminent in her communion, perpetually pure and vncorrupted in her doctrine, and in her Sacramentes, and perpetually bound and cōtinued in the succession of her ministrie,* and that d to her onely belonges the keeping of the Apostolicall traditions, the authority of the interpretation of scripture, and the decision of controuersies of Faith; and that out of the succesion e of her Communion, f of her doctrine, g and of her ministrie, there was neither Church nor saluation. Beholde, what the excellent King, when it shall please him to consider it at sufficient leasure, shall finde the Catholicke Church to haue bene in the tyme of saint AVG. and of the 4. first Councelles. Let his Maiestie see, whether by these features he can knowe, the face of Caluines Church, or of ours.

Of the conformitie or inconformitie of the sense wherein the word Catholicke hath bene cōmon to the ancient Catholicke Church, and to the moderne. CHAP. XIX.

The continuance of the Kinges answere.

IN how differing sense the Church is now called Catholicke from what it was then.

THE REPLIE.

I haue drawne out this clause, from betweene the two that precede it, because I would frame an answere by itselfe: for as much as I beleiued the intention of the excellent King was, (as it is of other protestantes) to saie, that the Church beares the name, of *Catholicke* now, in an other sense, then she bare it in S. AVST. tyme; because then she possessed all nations, and now she possesses them not.

To this then I answere, that S. AVG. neuer pretended, that the Catholicke Church in his tyme did absolutely possesse all nations, but onely by *Synecdoche*, that is to say, by applicatiō of the name of all, to the *greater* part; and in comparison of other Christian sectes and societies, in regarde of which, the Catholicke Church was soe large, as it was called for eminencie; the Church of all the nations. Contrarywise where the *Donatistes* sett

In psal. 101

this errour on foote, *that the Church had ceased, and was perished;* the principall reason that S. AVGVST. opposed to them, was, that she was not yet spread ouer all the natiōs, and that she must last without interruptiō, from the first preaching in *Ierusalem,* till the Ghospell had bene preached throughout the earth, and then should be the end of the world. Soe as it were to giue the lye, to all the promises and prophesies of God, to suppose she were perished; since there were yet manie nations, to which she had not yet extended herselfe. And therefore the Church bore the title of *Catholicke* then, in noe other sense, then she doth nowe: For soe farr was she from being called *Catholicke* from the *actuall* possession of *all* Nations; that not onely heresies, whose numbers were very great were excluded; but there were likewise an infinite Company of pagan Nations, to which she was not yet arriued.

There are (saith Saint AVGVSTINE *amongst vs, that is in Africa, innumerable barbarous nations, to whom the Ghospell hath not yet been preached.* Which was soe confessed amongst the *Catholickes* and *Donatistes*, as the *Donatistes* made vse of it against the Catholicke Church, to question her Catholicke title. *If you pretend* (saith *Petilian* the Donatist) *that you holde the Catholick Church beholde you are not in possession of all, for you are past into a parte*, And Saint AVGVSTINE confuting the wordes of *Cresconius*, *Thou arguest vainely* (saith he) *against the euident truth, that all the worlde communicates not with vs, because there are yet manie barbarous nations, which haue not beleiued in Christ.* And againe: *how is the world (saist thou) full of your communion, where there are soe manie heresies, whereof there is noe one that communicates with you?* And againe, reporting these wordes of *Vincentius*: *Thou saist, that as for the partes of the earth, that wherein the Christian faith is named, is but a little portion in comparison of the world.* And the Catholickes on the other side, made vse of it against the Donatistes, to proue that the Church had neuer receiued interruption; *But that Church* (said the donatistes) *is noe more, she is perished; soe saie they* (said Saint AVG:) *that are not in her; ô impudent voice, &c. This abominable and detestable voice full of presūption and falshood, which is vnderpropt with noe truth, illuminated with noe wisedome, seasoned with noe salte, vaine, rash, headie, pernicious, the spiritt of God hath foreseene it.* And a litle after; *this Ghospell shall be preached: where? In all the world: to whom? in testimome to all nations: and what after? and then the end shall come. Seest thou not, that there are still nations to whom the Ghospell hath not been preached* &c. *and soe how is it that thou saist that the Church is alreadie perisht from all nations, since it is therefore that the Ghospell is preached, to witt; that it might be in all nations?* The Church thē in S. AVS. tyme was not called *Catholicke* for her *actuall* extent into *all* natiōs; but she was called Catholicke for two other causes; *the one*, that as *more aboundant*; and *the other*, that as *radicall* & *originall* Church, she held the place of all, in regarde of other Christian Societies. For in all the diuisiōs which were made from the first beginning of the Christian name, not onely she remayned soe full in regarde of euery sect, that came out from her, that she held the place of the *whole*, and the seperated sect the place of a *part*; but alsoe in the *act* of seperation, she still remayned immoueable; I meane to say, that the change for which the seperation happened, was made not in her, but in the hereticall sect; Soe as it was the hereticall sect that was seperated frō her, and not she from the hereticall sect: And by cōsequēce to her, as perseuering in the same profession, & in the same Estate (wherein the whole Church was before the seperatiō) apertained the right, to holde the place of the whole, and to inherite the being, and aduantages of the *whole*; And to the other, to be reduced into the cōdition of a *parte*, and to be cutt of, and depriued from the appellation and aduantages of the *whole*: noe more nor lesse, then in the deuisiō of a tree, that parte, wherein the trunke, the stocke, and the roote remaine, keepes the name of the *whole*, and the parte which is cutt of, the name of a branche, and of a part seperated from the whole. *They vnderstād not* (saith S. AVST:) speakeing generally of heretickes) *that there is one certaine, true, & holsome, and as I may saie, germinall & radicall societie, from whence they are seperated*, & in an other place; *Whosoeuer is separated from the whole, and defēds a part cut off from the masse, or bodie it selfe, lett him not vsurpe the name of Catholicke*: And againe: *The Catholicke Church fighting with all heresies, may be opposed, but she cannot be ouerthrowne: All heresies are come forth from her, as vnprofitable branches cutt off from theire vine; but she remaines in her vine, in her roote, in her charitie, and the gates of hell shall not conquer her.* And as OPTATVS Mileuit. before him; *Wee must consider who staies in the roote with the whole worlde, and who is gone forth.* For these causes thē,

Ep. 80.

Aug cont. Petil. l. 2. c.

Cōt Cresc. l. 3. c. 63

Ibid. ca. 66

Aug. ep. 48

In psalm. 101.

Cōt. Trāst. l. 13. c. 12.

De Sym. ad cat. l. 1. c. 5.

Opt. con. Parm. l. 1.

and alſo that the Catholicke Church was ſoe eminent, both for *perpetuitie* and *extent* aboue all others, as it was eaſie to iudge, that it was to her onely, and to noe other that the promiſe had bene made, that in her ſeede all nations should be bleſſed; and that in her should be denounced the remiſſion of ſinnes through all nations, beginninge from Ieruſalem: for theſe cauſes I ſay S. AVG. affirmed that *to her onely belonged the title of Catholique. Thou markeſt* (ſaith he againſt *Creſconius* the Donatiſt) *the reſt of the nations that the Church hath not yet poſſeſſed; and takeſt noe heede, how manie she hath poſſeſt, from whence she dailie ſpreades to finish the poſſeſſion of the reſt. For how doſt not thou denie the future perfection of theſe prophecies, thou that feareſt not to denie ſoe great an aduancement, to which the perfection is due?* And in an other place; *Although there are manie kindes of hereſies amongſt Chriſtians, and that all would ſeeme to be Catholickes, and call the reſt, except themſelues, heretickes; there is neuertheleſſe one Church (if you caſt your eyes ouer the whole worlde) more aboundant in multitude, and, (as thoſe that know themſelues to be of it affirme,) more ſincere in truth, then all the reſt; but of the truth, that is an other queſtion. That which ſufficeth for this diſpute is, that there is one Catholicke Church, to which different hereſies impoſe different names; they beinge neuertheleſſe all called by their particular names that, they dare not diſauowe; from whence it appeares in the iudgement of arbiters not poſſeſſed with fauour, to whom the name of Catholicke, (whereof they are all ambitious) ought to be attributed.* By which wordes S. AVG. elegantly declares, that the Church was not called Catholicke becauſe she was actually, and at one ſelfe-ſame tyme ouer all Natiōs; but for this cauſe amongſt, others, that in multitude of people, and in extent of nations, she exceeded each one of other Chriſtian ſocieties.

Cōt. Creſc. l.3.c.65.

De vtil. cred.c.7.

Of the compariſon of the Church with the Cittie builte vpon a Mountaine.

CHAP. XX.

The continuance of the Kinges anſwere.

FOr heretofore the Catholicke Church (like the Cittie built vpon a Mountaine, which could not be hidden) was noe way ſubiect to be called in queſtion, but was euident and certaine to all, in ſuch ſorte as noe bodie of an vndiſtracted ſpirit, could doubt of it.

THE REPLIE.

IT ſeemes that the excellent King holdes this word (*that cannot be hidden*) to haue reference onely to the Cittie built vpon a Mountaine, and will not haue it belong to the Church but by accident, that is; when she reſēbles the cittie builte vpon a Mountaine. That is to ſay, it ſeemes that his Maieſtie vnderſtandes not, that this condition, *to be like a cittie built vpon a Mountaine*, and by conſequent *not to be hidden*, belongs perpetually to the Church: but will haue it, that the Church ſometymes enioyes this condition, as when Saint AVGVSTINE writ; and ſometymes is depriued of it, as afterwardes. Neuerteleſſe Saint AVGVSTINE who is the beſt interpreter that can be of his owne wordes, ſaith that *the Church hath this moſt certaine marke, that she cannot be hidd.* And againe *that of her it is ſaid: The cittie built vpon the Mountaine, cannot bee hidd.* From whence it appeareth, that this Epithete of *beeing vnconcealeable*, belongs

Cont. Pet. l.2.c 104. De vnit. eccl.c.14.

not

not by accidét to the Church when she shall be found like the cittie built vpon a hill; but appartaines to her properly, directly and perpetually. For where his Maiestie adds, that the Church was then soe manifest, as noe man in his right wittes could doubt of her; that was true; and soe is she still at this day, in regarde of all those, that agree vpon the true markes of the Church; that is to saie, in regarde of those, that, accordinge to Gods promises, designe the Catholicke Church by the perpetuitie of her continuance; and by the eminencie of multitude and extent ouer nations aboue all other Christian Sectes. But to all heretickes and schismatickes, who reiected those markes, and would receiue noe signe for a note of the Church, but onely puritie of manners, or triall of doctrine, of which they attributed to themselues the iudgement, by interpretation of Scripture made accordinge to theire sense; the Church was not onely doubtfull, but altogether hidden. *It is* (saith S. AVG. (*a condition cōmon to all heretickes, not to see that thinge which is in the world the most apparent, ant built in the light of all nations: out of whose vnitie all that they doe, though they seeme to doe it with great care, can noe more warrant them from the wrath of God, then the spiders webbs against the extremity of colde.* Cōt. Parm. l. 2. c. 3.

Of the conformitie or inconformitie of the Donatists and Protestantes in the question of the Church.

CHAPT XXI.

The continuance of the kinges answere.

FOR she vvas not shutt vp in anie corner of the vvorld, liyng I knowe not vvhere, in the South, as the foolish *Donatistes* affirmed, but she vvas spread in leught and breadth, ouer all the space of the Earth.

THE REPLIE.

THE *Donatistes* held not, that theire Church was inclosed by right, and for euer into Africa; but onely in fact and for a certaine tyme; noe more then the Caluinistes, who haue pretended, that the true visible Church had bene reduced for manie ages into the Prouince of Albigeois, and other boundes, and afterward in some valleys of *Dolphiny*. And yet the Donatistes did not make this confession with theire good will, but in theire owne defence by constraint: Contrarywise they attempted with all theire power, to shewe, that theire Church was not restrained onely into Africa. For this cause they kept a Bishop at *Rome*, whom they had sent to a fewe *African Donatistes* that dwelt there; They had plented a pretended Church in *Spanie*, in the territory of a Lady called *Lucilla* that fauored them; They had made the false Actes of the *mock Councell* of the *Arrians* holden at *Philipopolis* neere *Sardica* to passe current insteede of the true Councell of *Sardica*; because in the letters of those Bishops, amongst the names of the Bishops, to whom they were addressed, theire was the name of *Donatus* the false Bishop of *Carthage*, one of the Bishops of the *Donatistes* party; thereby to make it credible, that the Councell of *Sardica* had communicated with them; yea when they entered into conference with the Catholickes, they grewe to be soe impudent, (but that it was confounded at the instant,) as to maintaine that theire communion was spread ouer all the earth. *Heere first* (saith Saint AVGVSTINE speaking

Optat. l. 2.

August. de vnit. Eccl. c. 3. Idem ep. 163.

Aug. ep. 163.

of the conference that he had with *Fortunius* the Donatist) *did he attemps to affirme, that his Communion was ouer the extent of the earth: I asked him there vpon, whether he could addresse cōmunicatorie letters, which we call formall, whither I would appoint; and I affirmed, (as it was manifest to all,) that by this meanes the question might be easilie determined, &c. but because the thinge was euidently false, they gott out of this discourse by confusion of langage.* And finally, when they were driuen from the *visible vniuersality* of the Church, they had recourse to the *inuisible vniuersality*, and said they communicated inuisibly with all the elect and hidden members of Christ, which were spread ouer all the world; for it is against them, that saint AVG. disputes, when he writes; *It may be, will some man saie, that God hath other sheepe which I know not, but God hath care of them: he is too absurde in humane sense, that imagins such things.* By meanes whereof, theire cause, who haue separated them-selues from vs in these latter ages, can be noe waie distinguished in the point of the Church, from that of the *Donatistes*.

De ouib.c. 16.

Of the extent of the ancient Catholicke Church, and the moderne.

CHAP. XXII.

The continuance of the Kinges answere.

FLourishinge vnder the Emperors, vvhose dominion vvas extended from the East to the VVest, and from the Northe to the South.

THE REPLIE.

THE Church was spread much beyond the boundes of the *Roman* Empire, for it was extended in *Africa*, besides the Roman prouinces, vnder many barbarous Kinges; to the endes of *Arabia* vnder *Mauuia* Queene of the *Sarazins*: in *Persia* vnder the Kinge of *Persia*: in *Gothland*, vnder the Kinges of the *Gothes*, where she was cruelly persecuted in saint AVGVST. tymes; and the vnitie of the Empire was not alwaies an occasion to make her more flourishinge and distinct; but oftentymes caused her to be the more oppressed. For vnder the Emperors, that were Apostatas, such as was *Julian*, all kinde of heresies tooke hart to assaile her; and vnder the hereticall Emperors, that heresie, which they professed, stroue to stifle her, as *Arrianisme* vnder *Constantius*, whose Sectaries did soe multiplie, as the Catholicke Church was reduced into narrower limittes, then she was when the separation of these last ages began: And to proue that it was soe, *Socrates* and *Sozomenus* doe note, that the Catholike profession remained almost shutt vp within the boundes of the Patriarckshipp of the Latine Church; and on this side the mountaine of *Tusc is* betweene *Thrace* and *Illyria*; the greater parte of the Bishops of the Easterne Empire beinge either *Arrians*, or banisht from theire Seates. In such sorte as the Catholicke Communion was then farr from beeinge soe spread, as she was when the last diuisions were raised. For besides that at Luthers comeinge, all the Regiōs of *Europe*, except some partes of *Greece*, were firme in the Catholicke cōmunion; and that in *Asia*, not onely since the expulsion of the Successors of *Godfry* kinge of *Palestina*, and of *Boemond*

Socr. hist. cul. l. 4. c. 36. August. de ciui. l. 18. c. 52.

Socr. hist. cul. l. 2. c. 22 Soc. l. 3. c. 13.

prince

prince of *Antioch*, the guarde of the holy Sepulcher of Ierusalem, did alwaies remaine to the Latines; and that yet to this day the Patriark of the Maronites, which is one of the branches of the diuision of the Patriarkeshipp of *Antioch*, with all the Bishops of his Iurisdiction, hath alwaies liued and perseuered to liue in the Communion of the Latine Church; and that in *Armenia* the greater, vnder the Kinge of *Persia*, before he was driuen thence by the Turkes, there were, and yet are manie Christians of that communion, which is Called the *Latine*, and manie Monasteries of *Saint Dominicke*; And that in the Isles of *Cypres*, *Candia*, *Zante*, *Chios*, *Naxos*, And other *grecian* and *Asian* Islandes, the *Roman* communion had place, and hath yet at this day for the most part: and that in *Africa* the Kingdome of *Congo*, whose Embassador came, and dyed a fewe yeares agone in *Rome*, made profession of the Catholicke Religion from before *Luthers*, tyme. Besides that, I saie, the Christiãs, that inhabited in all the borders of *Africa*, vnder the conquest of the kinge of *Portugale*; and in those of *Asia* at *Ormus*, at *Calicut*, at *Goa*, at *Cochin*, and in all the east Indias; and those which liue at this day vnder the king of *Spaine*, in whose Estate all is reunited, in the *Acores*, in the *fortunate* Islandes, in the Islandes of *Hispaniola* and *Cuba*, in the Continent of *America*, in the, *Phillippinas*, in the *Molucas*, and in other places; suffice to supplie the fall of the *Român* Communion in the East. Together with this, that all that the ancient Emperors possessed, was not peopled onely with the Catholicke communion: but there were infinite other Sectes, which although, euery one taken aparte none of them did equall her; neuerthelesse all ioyned together, would haue surmounted her,, witnes the *Donatistes* wordes aboue recited by Saint AVGVSTINE, *how can you saie that the whole world is replenished with your communion, wherein there are soe manie heresies, whereof noe one communicates with you?* Con. Cresc l. 3 c. 66. Soe as it may bee seene, that the Church in Saint AVGVSTINS tyme, for beinge vnder the *Roman* Emperors, was noe more distinct, nor easier to be discerned from hereticall Sectes, by externall notes, then she was when the last diuisions were formed; but contrarywise much lesse, principally in the west; for as much as the watch fullnes of the westerne princes in publishinge tẽporall lawes against heretickes, hath caused the Catholicke Church to remaine alonge tyme alone in *Europe* without the concurrence of anie other Sect; whereas before, there was scarce anie cittie, that was not infected with diuers kindes of heresies and of which we might not saie with Saint PACIAN; *Entringe in these daies into a populous cittie, and findinge there Marcionites, Valentinians, Appllecians, and other such like plagues, which call themselue Christians, how should I know the Societie of my people, if she were not intitled Catholick?* Cont. Sympr. ep. 1.

Of the communion that the Bishops of the East had by letters with those of the west.

CHAPT. XXIII.

The continuance of the kinges answere.

THen there might be seene the Bishops of the East and the VVest communicatinge by theire letters, and by theire Messengers euery daie, and when neede required, lendinge helpe, the one to the others.

THE REPLIE.

Ad Age-ruch.ep.11. Inter.ep. Aug.ep.93. Ep.106. Ep.157. Athan. Apol.2.

IT is true; but of those letters the principall were the consultations of the *Synodes* with the *Popes*, and the answeres of the *Popes* to the *Synodes*: whereof Saint IEROM speaketh, when he saith, that *he had serued Pope Damasus for a Secretary to answere the Synodicall consultations of the East and the West*: And whereof Pope INNOCENT writes to Saint AVGVSTIN, and to the other Bishops of the *Mileuitan* Councell; *Through all the prouinces, there run alwais the answeres from the Apostolicall springe, to those that demaund them*. And Saint AVGVSTINE himselfe in his Epistle to SIXTVS *Of this there was also sent the relation of the two Councells of Carthage and Mileuis to the Apostolicall Sea*. And in the Epistle to OPTATVS *Wee haue had care to conuay to you the letters which haue bene sent from the Apostolicall Sea vpon this subiect, either especially to the Africans, or vniuersallie to all the Bishops, for feare least peraduenture they be not yet come to your Holynesse*. And Pope IVLIVS recited by Saint ATHANASIVS; *Are you ignorant* (said hee to the Arrians) *that the custome is first to write to vs, and so from hence may proceede the iust decision of thinges?*

Of these wordes of the constitutions of Saint Clemen the *vniuersall Episcopat is Committed to Bishops*.

CHAP. XXIII.

The continuance of the Kinges answere.

FOR that, that is read in the Constitutions of *Clement*, that the vniuersall *Episcopat* is committed to Bishops: and by consequence that they are all in some sort *œcumenicall*, now amazed wee read it, and beleiue it not.

THE REPLIE.

Cốt.Audiã sect.70. Concill. Trull.can.2. Photie. in Biblioth.c. 113. Clem.cốst. l.6.c.14. Cont.duas. ep.Pel.l.1.

NEither is the booke, that beares the title of *Clemẽts Constitutions* of such creditt, as it can haue aucthority to decide in matters of Religion. For be it, that it was from the beginninge supposed vnder *Clements* name or that it were since alter'd and falsified by heretickes; it is certaine, that the authority, thereof is suspected. Saint EPIPHANIVS makes mention of a booke soe intitled, and saith, that *manie called it in question, yet as for him he reiected it not;* The Councell of *Constantinople* surnamed *Trullian*, held longe after, condemned it: And *Photius* the Patriarke of *Constantinople* yet later, saith, *It can hardly be iustified from Arrianisme; which makes it to be suspected that it is not the same writinge, which bore that name in Saint Epiphanius time; or that it hath since bene falsified by the Arrians*. Neither doth that booke saie, either expressely, or equiualently; that *all Bishops are in a sort œcumenicall*. He saith no more, but this, speakeinge collectiuely to all Bishops, and not distributiuely to euery Bishop; *Wee write these thinges, for confirmation of you; of you to whom the episcopat is committed ouer all*. But if the had said it, what could followe of that? doth not Saint AVGVSTINE say, that *the pastorall charge is common to all Bishops?* and for all that, doth hee forbeare to protest in the same place, that *the Pope is supereminent in a more high degree? As heretickes* (saith hee) *cease not to rore about the pastures of our Lords flocke, and to seeke euerie side for in-letts to snatch awaie the sheepe bought at soe high a price; and that to vs all which exercise the office of Bishops, the pastorall charge is common, although thou art supereminent in a higher degree*: And in an other place, that *in the Roman Church there hath alwaies flourisht the principalitie of the Apostolicall chaire*. Epist. 162.

Of the comparison of the Pope with other Bishops.

CHAPT. XXV.

The continuance of the Kings answere:

BVt then the ordinary practise shewed, that it was very true, and a thousand examples of history may yet easily demonstrate it.

THE REPLIE.

ANd wherefore then, (that we may begin this information in the age of Saint IRENEVS, which was the first age, after that of the Apostle:, and end it in that of Saint GREGORIE the great, whom *Caluin* will haue to be the laste true and lawfull Bishop of *Rome*;) when Saint IRENEVS disputes against the *Valentinians*, doth he cry: *with the Roman Church, because of a more powerfull principalitie*; (that is because of the principalitie of the apostolicall Sea) *it is necessary that euery Church should agree?* for that by this *more powerfull principalitie* Saint IRENEVS meant not the temporall principality of the Cittie of *Rome*, but an other more powerfull principality, to witt; the *Spirituall principality* of the Apostolicall Sea; wee haue learnt both from the same Saint IRENEVS, who in the foregoeing period called the *Roman* Church, *the greatest and ancientest Church, founded at Rome, by the two most glorious Apostles Peeter and Paule*: And from Saint AVGVSTINE, who saith; *In the Roman Church hath alwaies flourisht the principalitie of the Apostolical seate*: And from Saint PROSPER Saint AVGSTINS second soule, who writt, *The principalitie of the apostolicall Priesthood hath added more greatenesse to Rome, by the Tribunall of Religion, then by that of the Empire*. And why then (when VICTOR had excommunicated the Churches of *Asia* the lesser, vpon the question of Easter day, which they obserued not according to the vniuersall tradition of the Apostles, but according to a locall and particular tradition, which had bene instituted for a tyme in their Prouinces;) did not the same Saint IRENEVS reproche to him, that he could not doe it, and that he had noe more power to cast them out of the Church, then the other Bishops; onely admonishe him as it shall appeare hereafter, that he should not for soe small a matter cut of soe manie, and soe great Churches? *He exhorted him* (said EVSEBIVS) *not to cut of all the Churches of God which held the tradition of this ancient custome*: And RVFFINVS translatinge EVSEBIVS, *He reprehended him* (said hee) *to haue done amisse to cutt from the vnitie of the bodie, soe manie, and soe great Churches*. For as for the slaunders

Ad hanc enim Eccles. propter potentiorem principalitate necesse est omnem conuenire Ecclesiam Iren cont. Val. l. 3. c. 3.

Aug. ep. 162.

Prosp. de voc. gent. l. 2. c. 6.

Vnder chap 42.

Eu hist. eccl. l. 5. c. 26. Ruff. ibid.

slaunders, wherewith EVSEBIVS and RVFFINVS hereticall Authors, the one an Arrian, and the other an Origenist, both enemies to the *Roman* Church, doe poyson this history, they shall be answered hereafter; and it shall be shewed, that the censure of VICTOR was soe iust; that it was after followed by the *Oecumenicall* councells of *Nicea*, and *Ephesus*. And why then when TERTVLLIAN priest of *Carthage* in *Africa*, was fallen into the heresie, or rather frensie of *Montanus* doth he write, *that Praxeas had inforced the Bishop of Rome, who did before acknowledge the prophesies of Montanus; Prisca*, and *Maximilla, and by this acknowledgement brought peace to the Churches of Asia and Phrigia, to reuoke his letters of peace already published, and cease to admitt the spirituall guiftes, persuadinge him to belieue false thinges of these prophets and of their Churches, and opposing to him the authority, of his predecessors?* For the *Montanists* of *Asia* and *Phrigia* haueing been excommunicated by the Catholicke Bishops and Metropolitans of their Prouinces; what right could the Pope haue to receiue them into his communion, and to grante them peace, if he were not head and superintendent of the whole Church? and principally according to the ancient Ecclesiasticall discipline, which held, that noe Bishop, except he were superior, could receiue to his communion those, that had been excommunicated, by their owne Catholicke Bishops? And why then when the same TERTVLLIAN declaimes against the decree of Pope Zepherinus, (which ordayned that Adulterers hauing done penance, should be receiued into the communion of the Church;) doth he call him (though whith a *Sardonian* and hereticall scorne,) *the great high priest, and the Bishop of Bishops, and the good Shepheard, and the blessed Pope? I heare* (saith he) *that an Edict hath been propounded, and certainely peremptorilie, to witt; that the great high priest, and the Bishop of Bishops saith, I pardon the crimes of adulterie and fornication, to those that haue performed their penance* And againe; *thou dost sweeten thy sermons with all the allurements of mercie that thou canst. good shepheard and blessed Pope, and in the parable of the sheepe, thou seekest thy Goates.* And why then, when the blessed Martyr CORNELIVS had been created Pope did Saint CYPRIAN say, that the *Emperor Decius bare with more patience to see a competitor arise in the Empire, then to see an high priest of God constituted at Rome*; or according to the oldest and best Copies, *thē to see an high Priest constituted his riuall in Rome*; alluding to the two titles that the pagan Emperors assumed, the one of Emperor, and the other of high Priest; and comparing the concurrence that the Emperor receiued in the quality of Emperor, hy the creation of a riuall in his Empire, with the concurrence that he receiued in the qualitie of high priest, by the creation of a Bishop of *Rome*: And wherefore doth he call the *Roman* Church the *Chaire of Peter*, and the *principall Church*, and the *originall* of the *Sacerdotall vnitie? They durst* (saith he) *saile to Rome, and carrie letters from prophane and Schismaticall persons, to the chaire of Peter, and to the principall Church from whence the sacerdotall vnitie is deriued.* And in vertue of what power did he solicite Pope STEPHEN, to write letters to the *Gaules* whereby he should depose *Martian* Bishop of *Arles? Thou shouldest* (saith he) *write letters into the prouince and to the people inhibiting in Arles, by which Martian being deposed, an other might be substituted in his place.* And why then, when the same Saint CYPRIAN and the councell of *Africa* had embraced the error of rebaptising heretickes, which since the *Donatistes* haue conuerted into an heresie, did Saint VINCENTIVS *Lyrinensis* say; *then Pope Stephen of happie memorie prelate of the Apostolicke Sea, with, nay before his other colleagues resisted it, esteeming it a thing worthie of him to surpasse all others as well in deuotion of faith, as he surmounted them by authoritie of place.* For as for the angrie words that Saint CYPRIAN lett slip against

vnder chap. 42.

Tert. con. Prax.

Appolin. Hieropol. Episc. apud Euseb. his. eccl. l. 5. c. 16

Conc. Nic. c. 5. & Patres & Cōcilia in mille alijs locis.

De pudicit. c. 1.

Ibid. c. 15.

Ad Anton. ep. 52.

Cod. Afflig & edit. Pamel.

Ad Cornel ep. 55.

Ad Steph. ep. 67. vnder chap. 43.

Cōt. heres. c. 9.

Pope STEPHEN (which Saint AVSTIN iudges vnworthie to be reported) they shall be spoken of hereafter. And why then, the same Pope STEPHEN had depriued of his communion *Firmilianus* Arch-Bishop of *Cappadocia*, and the other Bishops: of the Religions of *Cappadocia*, *Cilicia* and *Galatia*, for the same error of S. CYPRIAN, but more obstinately defended, did *Firmilianus*, amongst his other wordes of fury, (which bare with them their owne confutation) that he spued vp against the Pope, reproch to him that he was soe senselesse; (he that boasted soe much of the place of his Bishops Sea, and gloried that he had the succession of Peter, vpon which the foundation of the Church had bene established) as to introduce many other Peters, and to cõstitute a plurality of Churches? *I am angrie* (said he) *not without cause, with soe manifest and euident a follie in Stephen, that he that glorifies himselfe soe much for the place of his Bishops Sea, and maintaines that he hath the succession of Peter, vpon which the foundation of the Church hath bene sett; hath introduced manie other Peters, and constituted new buildings of manie Churches, in sustaining by his authoritie that baptisme is amongst heretickes.* And why then when DIONISIVS Patriarch of *Alexandria* had seene, that Pope STEPHEN had shut the gate of his communion from *Firmilianus*, and the other Bishops of *Cappadocia*, *Cilicia*, *Galatia*, and the other neighbouring nations, did he write to him letters of intercession and of intreaty vpon this subiect? *I writt to him* (said hee) *beseeching him for them all, or praying him concerning all these things.* For as for that, that Saint BASILL Archbishop of *Cesarea* in *Cappadocia* omitted not to reckon *Firmilianus* amongst his Catholicke Predecessors, notwithstanding his staine; it was, because he repented afterwardes, as Saint AVGVSTINE witnesseth in these wordes: *Those of the East, that had held the opinion of Ciprian corrected their iudgement.* And Saint IEROM in these; *Finally the Bishops themselues, that had conceaued with Cyprian, that heretickes should be rebaptised, returning to their ancient custome published a new decree, saying; what doe wee? soe to them and to vs their Elders and ours haue giuen it by traditiõ.* And why then whẽ the same DIONISIVS Patriark of *Alexandria* was fallen into suspition of heresie, did the Catholickes of *Alexandria*, in steed of hauing recourse to the Synodes of their prouinces, come to accuse him at *Rome*, before DIONISIVS Bishop of *Rome*; *They went vp* (said saint ATHANASIVS) *to Rome, to accuse him before the Bishop of Rome, being of his owne name.* And a while after, *And the Bishop of Rome* (the translator hath falsely reported the surname to that of *Alexandria*) *sent to Dionisius that he should cleere himselfe from those things whereof they had accused him, and suddenly he answered and sent his bookes of defence and apologie.* And in an other place, *Some hauing accused the Bishop of Alexandria before the Bishop of Rome, to holde the Sonne for a creature, and not consubstantiall with the Father; The Synod of Rome*, (that is to say, the *consistory of Rome*, compounded of the Bishops neighbouring vpon the citty of Rome without whom the Pope iudged nothing of importance, and of the principall Church men of *Rome*) *was offended with him; and the Bishop of Rome writt to him the opinion of all the assistants; and he iustifying himselfe, addressed to him a booke of defence and apologie.* And why then when the councell of ANTIOCHE twice called from the prouinces of *Pontus*, *Capadocia*, *Cyria*, *Cilicia*, *Lycaonia*, *Palestina*, *Arabia*, and from all the other Prouinces of the East, had deposed *Paulus Samosatenus*, Patriarke of *Antioche*, and substituted *Domnus* in his steede; And that *Paulus*, would not quitt the possession of the Church, did the Emperor *Aurelian*, though a Pagan ordaine *And that* (saith EVSEBIVS *verie fitlie, that it should be deliuered to him whome the Bishops of Italie and of Rome, that is, the Bishops of Italie assembled with the Pope,*

vnder chap 42.

Di. Allex. apud Eus. hist. Eccl. l. 7. c. 5.

Firmil. ad Cyp. inter. ep. Cyp. ep. 75.

Di Allex. ep. Eu. hist. eccl. l. 7. c. 5.

Aug. cont. Cre. l. 3. c. 3 Hier. cont. Lucif.

Ath. de sẽt. Dion.

Ibid.

Id de syn. Ar. & Sel.

Euseb. hist eccl. l. 7. c. 29. & 30.

should

should direct it to by writing? For for what cause should EVSEBIVS, who was one of the Bishops of the Patriarkship of *Antioche*, and besides, as an Arrian, not well affected to the *Roman* Church, and this word *verie fitlie*; but to shewe, that the Emperor had in this action, followed the order of the Church; and that it was a thing fitt for the Ecclesiasticall lawes, that the synod of *Rome* should iudge the affaires of the East, euen after the synods of the East, and synodes compounded of a farr greater mumber of Bishops and Prouinces? *When Paule* (saith EVSEBIVS) *would not quit the edifice of the Church; the Emperor Aurelian, being called to this businesse, ordained most fitlie, that it should be deliuered to him, to whom the Bishops of Italie and of Rome, of the same lawe, should write backe.* And the Greeke manuscript of the *Synopsis* of the councels, kept in the priuate library of the most Christian Kinge; *The Emperor Aurelian, although, a Pagan sent backe the question of Paul to the Bishop of Rome, and to those that were by him, that when they had examined whether he were iustlie deposed, he might be dispossessed of the Church.* And *Zonaras* and after him *Balsomon*, not onely Grecians, but schismatickes: *The Emperor Aurelian enioyned the Bishop of Rome and the Bishops that were with him, to examine those things wherewith Paul was charged, and if he were iustly deposed, to cast him out of the Church of the Christians.* Which alsoe since, the oecumenicall councell of *Ephesus* did imitate when it reserued, (as shall appeare hereafter) the iudgement of *Iohn* Patriarck of *Antioche* to the Pope; and that *Iuuenall*, Bishop of *Ierusalem* saied, that *the ancient custome, and the apostolicke tradition bare, that the Church of Antioche, was alwaies to be ruled by the Roman:* And after the councell of *Ephesus*, the sixth oecumenicall councell of *Constantinople*, when they sent backe the cause of *Macarius* Patriarck of *Antioch* to the Pope. And why then, when the Arrians held their false councell at *Antioch* 1270. yeares agone, did *Socrates* an ancient Greeke author of 1200, yeares standing, write; IVLIVS *Bishop of Great Rome, was not there, nor sent he anie in his steede, although the Ecclesiasticall Canon forbidds to rule the Churches, without the sentence of the Bishop of Rome:* And likewise *Zozomenus* a greeke author alsoe, and of the same tyme with *Socrates*:: IVLIVS (saied he) *reprehended them, that they had secretly and priuily altered the faith of the Councell of Nicea, and for that against the lawes of the Church, they had not called him to the Synod; for there was a Sacerdotall lawe, which imported, that all things which were done without the aduice of the Bishop of Rome, should be inualid.* And why then, when *Eusebius* of *Nicomedia*, vsurper of the Bishopricke of *Constantinople*, and firebrand of the Arrian faction, and the other Arrians his complices sawe that *the deposition of Saint ATHANASIVS, that they had packed in the councell of Antioche, was argued of nullitie, because the Popes authoritie did not appeare therin;* Did they aduise themselues, to repaire this defect, to preuent the Pope, and to pray him to calle the cause to his tribunall? EVSEBIVS (saith *Socrates*) *haueing done in the councell of Antioche what he listed sent an Embassador to IVLIVS Bishop of Rome, requiring him to be iudge in the affaire of ATHANAS, and to call the cause before him.* And this, not after the voyage of *S. ATHANAS.* to *Rome* as *Socrates* and *Sozomene* and the Protestants with them pretend; but before; as IVLIVS recited by S. ATHANASIVS, & saint ATHANASIVS himselfe, and THEODORET doe writness. ATHANASIVS (said IVLIVS) *is not come to Rome of his owne motion, but haueing bene called, and hauing receiued letters from vs.* And saint ATHANASIVS, EVSEBIVS *and his partie writt to Rome, that is to saie, to the Pope; they writt alsoe to the Emperors CONSTANTINE and* CONSTANT &c. that is to saie to CONSTANTINE Emperor of the *Gaules*, whose residence was at *Treuers*, and to CONSTANT Emperor of *Itali* and *Africa*, whose residence was at *Millen*; *but the Emperors reiected them*; *and as for the*

Eu.hist. eccl.l.7.c.30.

Synop. Syn Bib. Luper. in Antioch. Syn.1.

Zon. pret. in Cōc. Antioch.

vnder in this same chap. and in chap 29. below in the same chapters. below there also.

Socrat. hist eccles.l.2. c.8.

Soc. hist. eccl l.2.c.8.

Zoz. hist. eccl.l.3.c.9

Soc.l.2.c.11.

Athan. apol.2. Athan. ad Solit.

Bishop

Bishop of Rome, he answered, that we should keepe a Councell where we would. And in an other place; *The Eusebians writt to IVLIVS, and thinkinge to terrifie vs, demaunded of him that he would call a Councell, and that himselfe, if he would should be the iudge thereof*: That is to say, they demaunded, either that the Pope would keepe a Councell out of Rome, in which the cause might be iudged in the presence of his Legates; or that he should iudge it himselfe at Rome, if he pleased; And a while after; *But when they heard the newes of our arriuall at Rome, they were troubled, not expecting our comeing thither*: And THEODORET; *Assoone as ATHANASIVS receiued the citation from IVLIVS, he transported himselfe in diligence to Rome.* Athan. apol. 2. Athan. apol. 2. Theod. hist. eccl. l. 2. c. 4.

And why then, when the same IVLIVS obiected to the Arrians the enterprise of the Councell of *Antioch*, did he reproch them, that against the custome of the Church, they had deposed saint ATHANASIVS in the Councell of *Antioch*, without attending first for a decision from *Rome*? *Are you ignorant* (said Pope IVLIVS in the second answere to the Arrians, recited by saint ATHANASIVS) *that the custome is, that we should be first written to, and that from hence the iust decisions of things should proceede? And therefore if there were anie suspicion conceiued against your Bishop there, you must haue written to this Church.* A manifest argument, that the request, that the Arrians a while after the Councell of *Antioch* had made to the Pope, to call the cause of ATHANASIVS before him, and to call a Councell to iudge it, or to iudge it himselfe if hee would; was noe newe attribution of iurisdiction to the Pope, (as the aduersaries of the Church imagine) but a truce of their rebellion to the Popes iurisdiction. For how could the Pope, haue reproached to the Arrians, that *the Councell of Antioch, against the ancient custome of the Church, had deposed saint Athanasius without stayinge for a decision from Rome*, if the Pope had not had right to iudge the cause of saint *Athanasius*, but since the Councell of *Antioch*? And how could the Arrians themselues haue inserted 15. yeares after, these wordes in the false letter, that *they inforced Pope Liberius to write against saint Athanasius*: *I haue followinge the traditions of the ancients, sent on my behalfe Lucius, Paule, and Æhanus, Priests of the Roman Church, into Alexandria to Athanasius, to cause him to come to Rome, that we might ordaine (himselfe beeing present) vpon his person what the discipline of the Church exactes*: if this right had bene from the newe attribution of the Arrians, and not from the ancient tradition of the Church, and euen from that that IVLIVS newly came from speaking of: *For the things which wee haue receiued from the blessed Peeter, I doe signifie them to you?* But let vs againe goe forward with our interrogatories. Athan. apol. 2. Fragm. Hil. de Cõc Arimin. p. 36.

And why then, when the articles of the *Eusebians* against S. *Athanasius* were brought to *Rome*, did the Pope vpon the accusation of one of the parties, as the common iudge, *adiourne or giue them both a day*, and that following the Ecclesiasticall Canon? *Julius* (saith *Theodoret*) *followinge the Ecclesiasticall lawe commaunded the Eusebians, to present themselues at Rome; and gaue assignation to the diuine Athanasius, to appeare in iudgement.* And why then when those greate Prelates; *Athanasius* Patriarke of *Alexandria*, *Paule* Bishop of *Constãtinople* MARCELLVS primate of *Ancyra* in *Galatia*; ASCLEPAS, Bishop of *Gaza* in Palestina; LVCIVS Bishop of *Andrinopolis* in *Thrace*; who had bene accused of diuers crymes, some *secular*; As *Athanasius* of the crymes of manslaughter and Rape; and other *Ecclesiasticall*, as the same *Athanasius*, to haue caused a Chalice to be brokẽ: And *Asclepas* to haue ouerthrowne an Altar; and had bene, deposed from their seates by diuers councells of *Thrace* and of *Asia*; and had bene heard at *Rome*; did the authors of the Ecclesiasticall histories say; that the bishop of *Rome* restored them, forasmuch as to him (because of the dignitie of his sea) the care Theod. hist. eccles. l. 2. c. 4. Soc. hist. eccl. l. 2. c. 15. a Ibid.

of all thinges appartained; IVLIVS *Bishop of Rome* (said Socrates) *because of the priuiledge of his Church, armed them with couragious letters, and sent them backe into the East, and restored to eache of them his place;* [a] *rebukeinge those that had rashlie deposed them.* And *Sozomene, the Bishop of Rome, haueing examined their complaints, and found that they agreed touchinge the decree of the Councell of Nicea, receiued them into his communion as conformable, and of the same beliefe; And because that to him (for the dignity of his Sea) the care of all things belonged, he restored to euery one of them his Church.* For as for the outragious letters, that those of the East (that is to say, as it shall appeare heereafter; the Bishops of the Patriarckship of *Antioch* and their complices who were Arrians) writt against IVLIVS in hate, because he had broken their Councell, and restored saint *Athanasius:* I meane to confute them particularly in an other place. It shall suffice nowe, that I say two thinges; *one*, that these letters, hauing bene written by hereticall authors, to witt, the Arrians; and reported by an hereticall historian, from whom *Socrates* and *Sozomene* tooke them; to witt by *Sabinus* a macedonian hereticke, who tooke part with the Councell of *Antioch* against the Pope, and against the Councell of *Nicea*, and was a sworne Enemie to the *Trinitie*, to saint *Athanasius*, and to the Councell of *Nicea*; they carryed their confutation on their foreheade, and are of as little weight, as those that the *Lutherans* or other *Protestantes* should nowe write against the Pope. For who knowes not that the Pope hath alwaies proued that concerning Religion, that *Cicero* said of himselfe, concerning the common wealth; to witt, *that none euer declared himselfe Enemie to the Church, but he tooke him (the Pope) for his aduerse partie at the same tyme?* And *the other*, that notwithstanding the boldnes, or (to speake with *Sozomene,*) *the impudencie of these hereticall and Arrian letters*, the restitution, that the Pope had made of these great persons, and amongst others *Athanasius* Patriarcke of *Alexandria*, and of *Paule* Archbishop of *Constantinople*, was neuerthelesse executed and imbraced, as iust, both in forme, and matter, by the vniuersall consent of all the Catholickes in the world. *Athanasius and Paule* (saith Sozomene) *recouered each one his seate:* And in an other place, speaking of the 300. Orthodoxall Bishops of the Councell of *Sardica*, who represented all the Catholicke Bishops vpon the Earth; *They answered* (said he) *that they could not separate themselues from the communion of Athanasius and Paule; and principally, for as much as Iulius Bishop of Rome, hauing examined their cause, had not condemned them.*

Socr. hist. Eccl. l. 2. c. 15. — a. Ibid. — Soz. hist. Eccl. l. 3. c. 8. — Vnder cha 50. — Ibid. — Socr. hist. Eccl. l. 2. c. græc. ed. t. 17. — Ibid. & c. 15 — Idem. l. 2. c. 7. — Soz. hist. Eccl. l. 3. c. 9. — Soz. hist. Eccl. l. 3. cap. 7.

And why then when the same Councell of *Sardica* (where assisted according to the calculation of saint *Athanasius, Socrates* and *Sozomene*) more then 300. Bishops: and which IVSTINIAN † calls an *Oecumenicall* Councell; And which *Vigilius* the ancient Bishop of *Trent*, saith *to haue bene assembled from all the prouinces of the Earth:* And where saint *Athanasius*, and the greater parte of the same Fathers that had bene at the Councell of *Nicea* assisted, proceeded *not to institute* the appeales, as it shall appeare hereafter; but to rule or *to reduce into writinge the customes* of the appeales;) did they ordaine, that when a Bishop should appeale to the Pope, it should be in the Popes choyse either to giue him iudges out of the neighbour prouinces, or to graunt him legates, which should be transported into those places? *If a Bishop* (said the Councell) *hauing bene deposed by the assemblie of Bishops of his prouince, hath recourse in forme of an appeale to the most blessed Bishop of Rome, and desires to be heard a new; and that the Bishop of Rome holdes it iust, that his cause should be re-examined; lett him vouchsafe to write to the Bishops, neighbours to that prouince.* And a little after; *and if hee thinke it fitt to send priests from about his person, which may together with the*

Athan apo 2. Hist. ecc l. 2. c. 20. — Soz. l. 3. c. 11. — † Iustin. in edict. de fid — Vigil. cont. Eutych. l. 5. — In chap. 50.

Bishops decide the businesse hauinge his authoritie from whom they are sent, that alsoe ought to be allowed. For as for what past afterward in *Africa* about the matter of *Appeales* in lesser causes, that shall be spoken of hereafter, in a chapter by it selfe.

And why then when the Fathers of the same councell of *Sardica*, yeilded an accompt of their Actes to the Pope, did they write to him according to the copy which is inserted in the fragment of saint HILARIE, and cited tacitly by Pope * INNOCENT the first, and expressely by Pope NICHOLAS the first; *It were very Good ad conuenient, if from all the princes, the Prelates of God would send relations to their Head; that is to saie to the Sea of the Apostle* Peter. Hil. in fragm. Cōc Arim. ex Bib. P. Pithoei. * Int. ep. Aug. ep. 91. Ep. ad Episc. Galliar.

And why then when V*alens* Bishop of *Murses* in *Mysia*; and *Vrsatius* Bishop of *Singidon* in *Hungaria*, two of the chiefe Whirle-windes in the Arrian tempest, would departe from the heresy of *Arius* and from the slaunders that they had inuented against saint ATHANASIVS, did they come to Rome to aske the Popes pardon, and to protest obedience to him? *To the absolution of* Athanasius (said *Sulpitius Seuerus*) *there was yet added, that Vrsatius and Valens chiefe of the Arrians, after the councell of Sardica seeing themselues excluded from the communion, came in person to craue pardon of* Iulius Bishop *of Rome, for haueing condemned an innocent.* And saint ATHANASIVS; *Vrsatius and Valens, seeing these things, were touched with remorse, and goeing vp to Rome confest their fault, and repenting craued pardon.* And themselues in the acte of their penāce giuē by writing to the Pope, and inserted in the Relations of saint ATHANASIVS and *Sozomene*; *Wee confesse* (said they) *to your blessednesse in presence of all your priests our bretheren, that all those things that are come hither to your eares against* ATHANASIVS *are false and fained, and farr from being his actions; and for this cause we earnestly desire to haue communion with him; and principallie because, your pietie, out of your naturall goodnes, hath vouchsaffed to pardon our Error: And we farther promise, that if for this occasion either those of the East, or Athanasius himselfe, doe maliciouslie call vs to iudgement, wee will not departe from what you shall ordaine.* Sulp. Seu. hist. Sacr. l. 2. Idem. Athan. Apol. 2. Soz. hist. eccl. l. 3. c. 22.

And why then when the Emperor constantius would set the last hand to the persecutiō of saint *Athanasius*, did *Amianus Marcellinus*, though a Pagan author reporte that he solicited Pope *Liberius* to condemne him not contenting himself, that he had bene deposed by a councell compounded of 300. Bishops of the East and West, vnlesse the Pope himselfe confirmed this deposition? *Although* (said hee) *that the Emperor knew this was done; neuerthelesse he procured with an earnest desire, that it might be comfirmed by the authoritie, whereof the Bishops of the eternall Cittie, are superiors.* For whereas afterward Pope LIBERIVS, ouercome by the persecutions of *Constantius* the Arrian Emperor, gaue himselfe vp to signe the condemnation of saint *Athanasius*, it was after he had bene cast out of his seate by the Emperor at the instance of the Arrians, and confined into *Thracia*; And after he had suffered an exile of two yeares, and a longe continuance of imprisonments, threates of death, and corporall afflictions, and vexatiōs. Nowe we make a great differēce, betwene those sentēces, that Popes pronounce *de Cathedra*, that is to saie, *sett in their Ecclesiasticall Tribunall*, & in the forme of *publicke and iudiciary* actes, and with solemne and canonicall preparation; and those things, that they doe in the forme of *particular and personall actes*, and not as constituted in the state and liberty of Iudges, but as reduced into the condition of captiues and prisoners; and constrayned by the violence of humane feare, such as may Amianus Marcellinus. l. 15.

Be in a spirit morally constant. And yet heere meete three miraculous circumstances, and worthy of Gods prouidence toward the Apostolicke Sea in this historie: *The first*, that as in the solemnitie of the Pythian games, wherein the Grecians celebrated the Feast of *Apollo*, when one of the strings of *Eunomius* lire was broken, the greeke fables saie, that a grashopper came and set herselfe vpon the lire, and supplied with her songe the defect of the string that wanted; so when LIBERIVS, banisht and cast out of his seate by the Arrians, began to be wanting to the conforte and harmonie of the Church; *Felix*, one of the Deacons of *Rome*, that the Arrians had caused to be substituted in his place, supplied against their expectation, the defect of LIBERIVS, and soe lifted vp his voice for the innocencie of ATHANASIVS, and the faith of the Councell of *Nicea*, that he was for this cause driuen out of Rome by the Arrians, and (if we will beleiue the ancient inscriptions) martyred. *The second*, that when the Emperor had drawne by force frō LIBERIVS what he would, he sent him backe to *Rome*, to exercise ioinctly with FELIX the gouerment of the Church; LIBERIVS in steede of persistinge in the conditions, that the Arrians had wrested from him, tooke vp againe such a zeale for the protection of the cause of saint ATHANASIVS, and for the defence of the faith, that he despised from thence forwarde, all the threatninges and persecutions of the Emperor, and did noe lesse imitate saint *Peter* in repairing the offence of his fall, then he did before in committinge it. And *the third*, that when LIBERIVS was arriued at *Rome*, FELIX, (if we will belieue *Sozomene*,) dyed; *which was* (saith the same *Sozomene*) *a notable care of the diuine prouidence in the behalfe of S. Peeters Sea. A while after* (saith Sozomene) *FELIX deceased and Liberius alone ruled the Church, which was disposed by the prouidence of God, least the seate of Peeter should be dishonored, being gouerned, by two Rulers.*

Clem. Alex. — Hier. chron in Liber. — Card. Bar. ad an. 357. — Soz. hist. eccl. l. 4. c. 15.

But lett vs returne to our interrogatories. And why then when the Arrians had caused LIBERIVS to be remoued from *Rome*, doth saint ATHANASIVS crye, *they haue not had a reuerent memorie that Rome was the Apostolicke Sea, and Metropolitan of Romania*: that is to saie of the Roman Empire? For first that saint ATHANASIVS by the word *Romania*, meant all the Roman Empire, we learne from saint EPIPHANIVS, who saith *Manes passed out of Persia into Romania.* And in an other place; *The fire of Arius tooke possession of almost all Romania.* And againe; *Constantine sent letters against Arius throughout all Romania.* And from *POSSIDIVS*, who calleth the *Vandalls* that sacked *Africa*, the destroyers of *Romania*. And *secondly*, that by the word *Metropolitā*, he meanes a spirituall and Ecclesiasticall *Metropolitan*, and not simplie a secular and temporall *Metropolitan*; a *Metropolitan* of Religion, and not simplie a *Metropolitan* of state and policie: we learne it from the allusion to the Epistle to the Arrians, that he cites in the same place; in which the Arrians, though scornefully, and ironically had called the Catholicke Church, the *Schoole of the Apostles, and Metropolitan of Religion*: And from the Epistle of saint IEROM against *Iohn* Bishop of *Ierusalem*, in which he said, that the Councell of *Nicea* ordayned that *Anthioch* should be the *Metropolitan* of all the East: that is to say, the spirituall and Ecclesiasticall *Metropolitan* of all the East.

Athan. ad solitar. — Epiph. hær. 46. — Idem hær. 49. — Ibid. — Possid. in vit. Aug. c. 30. — Soz. hist. Eccl. l. 3. c. 7. — Hier. ep. 61

And why then, when the *Macedonians* in the Councell of *Lampsacus* in *Asia* resolued to revnite themselues to the Catholicke Church, did they send EVSTATHIVS Bishop of *Sebaste* in *Armenia*; THEOPHIL. and *SILVANVS*, and other *Asian* Bishops to *Rome*, who after their confession of faith, subscribed with their handes, added these wordes to Pope *LIBERIVS*; *if anie one after this confession of faith expounded by vs, will attempt*

Soc. hist. Eccl. l. 4.

anie accusation against vs, or against these that sent vs, lett him come with letters from thy Holynesse before such orthodoxall Bishops, as thy Holinesse shall please to appoint and contest with vs in iudgement; and if there doe a crime appeare, lett the authors thereof be punished.

And why then, when the same *Eustathius* who had bin deposed from the Bishopricke of *Sebaste* in Armenia by the Councell of *Militine* in *Armenia* and shewed to the Councell of *Tyana* in *Cappadocia* the letters of restitution, that he obtained from Pope *Liberius*, was restablished in his Bishopricke? *Eustathius*, (writes S. *Basile* to those of the West,) *hauinge bene cast out of his Bishopricke, because he had bene deposed in the synod of Militine, aduised himselfe to finde meanes to be restored, to trauaile to you. Now of the things that where propounded to him by the most blessed Bishop LIBERIVS, and to what he submitted himselfe, we are ignorant; onely he brought a letter which restored him; which being shewed to the Councell of Tyana, he was reestablished in his Bishops seate.* Basil. ep. 74.

And why then, when the abrogation of the Councell of *Arimini* was in question, did saint BASILE write to S. ATHANASIVS; *It seemed to vs, to be to good purpose, to write to the Bishop of Rome, to be watchfull ouer these partes and giue his iudgement, to the end that since there is difficultie in sendinge from thence persons in behalfe of a common and synodicall decree, he may vse his authoritie in the businesse, and choose men capable of the labour of the waie &c. and hauinge with them the actes of Arimini, that they may disannull those things that haue bene done by force?* For whereas in an other place, the same saint BASILE, stunge with the intermission, that the Bishops of the west had made, in communicatinge by Ecclesiasticall letters with him, vpon an aduertisment that had bene giuen at *Rome*, that he communicated with heretickes, cryes against the pride of those of the west; and saith, that *they knew not the truth*, (that is to say, the truth of the Easterne affaires;) *neither had prtience to learne it:* And againe, *that they should not by affliction add paine to those that were oppressed and humbled, nor esteeme that dignity consisted in disdaine:* It was not to taxe those of the west, that they stretched their iurisdiction to farr, that hee spake this langage; but contrariwise to taxe them, that they tooke not sufficient notice of the *Asian* affaires, as it appeares by the letter he writt to them in the name of himselfe, and all the Bishops of *Cappadocia*, whose *Metropolitan* he was; which contained these wordes; *Wee are readie to be iudged by you, prouided that those, whieh slaunder vs, may appeare face to face with vs in the presence of your Reuerence.* And againe; *Comfort vs with your peaceable letters, and with your charitable communications, easinge, as by a sweete fomentation, the wound which your former negligence hath made in our heartes.* And that which he adds to the first complaint, that those of the west preuented with false suspicions, did the same thinges in his behalfe, as they had done in the cause of *Marcellus*, to wit, that they tooke them for aduersaries, that reported the truth to them, and established heresie in trustinge too much in their owne opinions; not that he pretended the Pope had euer approued the heresie of *Marcellus*: Only he meant to saie, that those of the west, not hauinge bene informed that *Marcellus* taught an other doctrine in *Asia*, then that he had professed at *Rome*, which was Catholicke. The restitution that the Pope had made of his person to the primacie of the lesser *Galatia*, was an accidentall cause; that in the East they adhered to his heresie.

Basil. ep. 52. — Ad Eusob. ep. 8. — Ep. 10. — Ep. 77. — Ep. 77. — Epist. 10. — Athan. Ad solit. vit. agent. Soc. l. 2. c. 15. Soz. l. 3. c. 7

But let vs goe on with our demaundes. And why then, when the Synod of the west, holden vnder Pope DAMASVS, did disannull and abolish the Councell of *Arimini*, doth he saie that the number of Bishops assembled at *Arimini*, how greate soeuer it were, could be of noe weight, because neither the Pope LIBERIVS, whose iudgement should first of all be attended; nor VINCENTIVS Bishop of *Capua*, who had bene Pope SYLVESTERS Legat in the Councell of *Nicea*, whose confirmation or information, was treated of in that of *Arimini*, and who came then from being the legate of Pope LIBERIVS for the same effect to the Emperor CONSTANTIVS; nor manie other had euer consented to it? *The multitude of the Bishops*, said the Councell, *assembled at Arimini, ought to make noe preiudication; since this confession was composed without the consent of the Bishop of Rome, whose sentence should be attended before all others; or that of VINCENTIVS, who had for soe manie yeares administred the Bishops seate worthilie or that of manie others.*

Lib. ep. ad Hos. in frag Hil. & ep. ad Const. in fine oper. Lucif. Theodor. hist. Eccl. l. 2. c. 22.

And why then, when the Emperor *Valens* had caused PETER the Patriarch of *Alexandria*, to be driuen from his Patriarkeship, and had placed *Lucius* in his steede; did PETER obtaine letters of confirmation from Pope DAMASVS, which restored him, and approued the faith of MOSES newe Bishop of the Arabians? *PETER* (saith *Socrates*) *being returned from Rome into Alexandria, with letters from DAMASVS Bishop of Rome which confirmed the faith of Moyses, and the creation of Peter; the people incouraged draue away Lucius, and restored PETER in his place.*

Soc. hist. Eccl. l. 4. c. 36.

And why thē, when the Emperor GRATIAN became an administrator of all the Empire, was the first thing he had care of, to ordaine that the Churches, that had bene possessed by hereticks, might be deliuered to the Bishops, that were of the Popes communion? *He ordained* (saith THEODORET) *that the sacred howses might be deliuered to those, that communicated with Damasus*; which was, as he further saith, *executed throughout the world.*

Theodor. hist. Eccl. l. 5. c. 2.

And why then when *Sapores* to whom the execution of this Edict had bene committed in the East, arriued at *Antioch* did hee finde three Competitors in the Patriarckship of *Antioch, Paulinus, Miletius, & Apollinarius*, which reported themselues all three to be in the communion of DAMASVS because eache of them would haue had the possessiō of the Patriarkship of *Antioch* to be adiudged to himselfe? *Sapores coming to Antioch*, (saith THEODORET) *and shewinge the lawe of Gratian; Paulinus affirmed that he was of DAMASVS his partie; the same Apollinarius affirmed, hyding the venome of his error.* And S. IEROM writinge afterward to Pope DAMASVS; *Miletius* and *Vitalis* (soe was the successor of *Apollinarius* called) *and Paulinus saie, that they communicate with thee; I would beleiue them, if but one said soe; now either two lye, or all three.*

Theod. ibi. c. 3.

Hier. ep. 58

And why then, when the Emperor *Theodosius* the great was associated to the Emperor *Gratian* did they make this famous lawe, which marches in the front of the Code of *Justinian: Wee will, that all the people ruled by the Empire of our clemencie, shall liue in the same religiō which the diuine Apostle Peter gaue to the Romās, as the religiō insinuated by him vntill this present witnesseth, and which it is manifest that the high-Priest Damasus followeth, and Peter of Alexādria, a man of Apostolicke sanctitie:* that is to saie; this *Peter* Patriark of *Alexādria*, that *Socrates* said, that Pope *Damasus* had newly cōfirmed & restored.

Cod. tit. 1. l. 1.

Socr. vbi supra.

And why then, when S. *IEROM* priest of *Antioch*, and resident in the Patriarkship of *Antioch*, and created by *Paulinus* the Bishop of *Antioch*, whom he calls an admirable man, and high Priest of Christ; addressed his first letters to Pope DAMASVS vpon the busines of the diuision of the Church of *Antioch* why I say did he write to DAMASVS: *I am ioyned in communion with thy blessednes, that is to saie; with Peters chaire; I know the Church is built vpon that rocke; whosoeuer eates the lambe out of this howse is prophaned &c. I know not Vitalis; I reiect Miletius; I am ignorant of Paulinus; whosoeuer*

Hier. adu. her. Ioan. Hier. ep. 61. Hieron. ad Eustach. ep 27. Ad Damas. ep. 57.

soeuer gathers not with thee, scatters; that is, whosoeuer is not of Christ, is of Antichirst? For whereas the Protestantes obiect, that saint IEROM saies in the *preludium* of this passage, that he followes no cheife but Christ; it is a Corruption of the copies of Bosle, and other the late Copies which reade *nullum primum nisi Christum sequens*, that is to saie, *folloving no chiefe but Christ*; where it should be read *nullum præmium nisi Christum sequens*, that is to say; *following noe reward but Christ*; as it appeares, both by the aime of S. IEROM, which is to protest, that he had not recourse to the greatnes of the Pope, for the desire he had to obtaine anie temporall reward, but for the only ambitiō he had to obtaine the reward of soules, which is Christ; and by the copies of saint IEROM, which passed currant fiue hundred yeares agoe, and which the author of the decree hath followed, which reade *præmium*, and not *primum*, that is; *reward* and not *chiefe*, conformably to the stile of the Church which sings in the hymne of the Martyrs; Caus. 24. q. c.

O God thy Soldiours only guard,
Their lott, their crowne and their reward.

Gregor.

And why then when the perfidiousnes of *Vitalis* was discouered, did saint GREGORIE NAZIANZENE write, that Pope DAMASVS, who in the beginning had receiued him into his communion vnder a profession of a captious faith cast him out of the Church, and frō the Priesthood, by a sentence of interdiction and anathema? *Let them not accuse vs*, (said saint GREGORIE Bishop of *Nazianza* in *Capadocia*) *for haueing first approued the faith of Vitalis, which at the instance of blessed DAMASVS bishop of Rome he gaue him set downe in writing, and now disallowing it* &c. *for that profession, if it be well vnderstood, is accompained with pietie, if euill with impietie.* And a little after: *Whereof DAMASVS himselfe hauing afterward bene otherwise informed, and hauing learnt that they persisted in their first exposition, interdicted thē, and blotted out their professiion of faith by anathema.* Greg. Naz. ad Cledon. ap. 2.

And why then when the councell of the one hundred and fiftie Fathers assembled at *Constantinople* intitled the *second œcumenicall councell*; where assisted all the Patriarchs, metropolitans, and principall Bishops of the Easterne Empire, had bene celebrated; did they demaund the confirmation of their decisions of Faith from the Pope; and namely that of the deposition of *Timothie*, one of the Bishops of the East, deposed for matters of Faith? *Whereas your Charity my deare children*, (saith Pope DAMASVS, in his answere to the councell) *yeildes due reuerence to the Apostolicke sea, it shall turne you to great honor?* And a while after; *But what neede was there to exact from me the deposition of Timothy, since hee was longe since deposed here, with his Master Apollinarius, by the iudgement of the Apostolicke sea, and in the presence of Peter Bishop of Alexandria!* For whereas the demaund of this confirmation is not to be found in the Epistle of the councell of *Constantinople*, reported by THEODORET; it is, because that Epistle is not the letter of the coūcell of the one hundred and fiftie Fathers, but of an other councell celebrated the yeare following at *Constantinople* by some of the same Fathers, either called backe againe, as THEODORET pretends; or remayning of the former councell as it appeares by the tenor of that letter. Theod. hist. eccl. l. 5. c. 9. Ibid.

And why then (when the same councell had confirmed the election that the *Syrians* had made of *Flauianus* insteede of *Miletius* competitor of *Paulinus* to the Patriarkshipp of *Antioch*, and had reunited in *Flauianus* person both their Rightes) did the Pope call the cause to Rome, before a councel that hee assembled there, and by his letters, accompained with those of the Emperor GRATIAN sent for the councell of *Constantinople* which had confirmed this election to cause them to come and put it againe to triall at *Rome,* and gaue assignation to both parties to appeare there, whereof one, to witt, *Paulinus* appeared, but *Flauianus* distrusting the equitie of his cause, had recourse to excuses and delaies? *The Ecclesiasticall necessitie* (saith saint IEROM) *drew me to Rome with the holie Bishops,* PAVLINVS *and* EPIPHANIVS, *whereof the one gouerned the Church of Antioch in Syria, and the other the Church of Salamina in Cypres.* And againe *When the Emperiall letters had drawne to Rome the Bishops of the East and west Paul sawe there the admirable men and Bishops of Christ, Paulinus Bishop of Antioch, and Epiphanius Bishop of Salamina in Cypres.* And *Sozomene: the Bishop of Rome* (said he) *and all the westerne Prælates bare the ordination of Flauianus verie impatiently.* And a little after; *And therefore, because it should be knowne, they together with the Emperor* GRATIAN *writt and called the Bishops of the East into the west:* And the same Fathers of the councell of *Constantinople* excusing themselues to the Pope, and the councell of *Rome* that they could not come to *Rome moued,* (said they) *with brotherly charitie, you haue called vs as your members, by the letters of the most religious Emperor* &c. *But besides that, our Churches but a while before beginning to be restored if we should haue done this, had bene wholie abandoned; it was a thing which many of vs could noe way put in execution, forasmuch as we trauelled to Constantinople vpon the letters of your Reuerence sent the last yeare after the councell of* Aquilea *to the most religious Emperor Theodosius, hauing prepared vs for none, but that onely journey of Constantinople, and hauing gotten the consent of the Bishops remayning in the Prouinces for none but that.* And towardes the end of the Epistle speaking of PAVLINVS, whom they belieued Pope DAMASVS fauored, as hauing bene created Patriarcke of Antioch by *Lucifer* Legate to the Pope LIBERIVS, his predecessor: *we beseeche you not to preferr the fauour or friendship to one particular man, before the edification of the Churches, that by this meanes the Doctrine of faith and Christian Charitie being confirmed amongst vs,* (that is to saie, of those of the East amongst themselues) *we may ceasse to haue in our mouthes these wordes condemned by the* Apostle *I am of Paule, and I of* Apollo, *and I of Cephas:* that is to saie, we should cease from saying, I am a Miletian, I am a Paulinist. I am an Appolinarist. For that it is which those signifie, I am of Paul, I am of Apollo, I am of Cephas, which doe not designe (as our aduersaries pretend,) the Pope and the Bishops of the Empire of the East, but the three factions whereinto the Churches of the Easterne Asia had bene deuided and rent vnder Paulinus, Miletius and Appollinarius. And indeede how could those of the East, meane by those wordes. *amongst vs* the Pope, and themselues; they that were soe tied in communion to the Pope, as they had not bene restored to their seates (as Theodoret said but euen nowe) but vnder condition to communicate with the pope? but that is so cleere as it needes noe proofe; let vs goe on.

Ad Princip.ep.16. Ad Eustoc. ep. 17. Soz hist. eccl.7.c.11. Ibid. Theod.hist eccl.l.5.c.9. Theod. hist. eccl.l. 5.c.9. Ibid. Ruff. hist.l. 1.c.27. Ibid. Theod.hist eccl.l.5.c.2.

And why then, when the euasions of Flauianus (who withdrew himselfe because he knew he had bene ordered against the oath made betweene *Miletius* his predecessor and *Paulinus,* that the longest liuer of them two should remaine the sole Patriarck) had bene discouered, and that the complaintes thereof were arriued to the Emperor THEODOSIVS, then only Emperor, who resided at Constantinople; did the Emperor make him come from *Antioch* to *Constantinople,* and pressed him to goe to *Rome,* euen after the departure of the councell of *Rome? The Emperor* (said THEODORET) *often called vpon, made Flauianus come to Constantinople, and commaunded him to trauaile to Rome, but Flauianus answering, it was winter and promisinge to performe his commaund in the returne of the Spring, returned into his countrie.* And a while after, *the Emperor hauing againe made him come to him, againe commaunded him to transport himselfe to Rome.* For that

Soc.hist. eccl.l.5.c. 15. Sod.hist.eccl.l.7.c.11. Theod. hist eccl.l. 5.c 23. Ibid.

THEO-

THEODORET, *Suffragan* of the Patriarkship of Antioch, and creature to one of *Flauianus* successors adds that the Emperor touched with the second answere of *Flauianus*, sent him backe to his prouince, and tooke vpon him protection of his cause, is a testimonie, that hath more relation to fauour then to truth; as it appeares by these wordes of saint AMBROSE, written after the councell of *Capua*. which was holden vnder Pope SIRICIVS Successor to DAMASVS; *Flauianus hath cause to feare, and therefore he flies a triall.* And againe, *one onely Flauianus not subiect to lawes as it seemes to him, appeares not, when we are all assembled* And a while after; *Flauianus only is exempted, as he pretendes, from the conditions of the Sacerdotall Colledge, who will neither exhibite his presence to the Sacerdotall assemblie, nor to the imperiall decrees.* Amb. ep. 78.

And why then when *Paulinus* was dead, and that *Euagrius* was substituted in his steed, did the same councell of *Capua* (which the third Councell of *Carthage* calls an vniuersall councell, and that S. AMBROSE describes, as assembled from an infinite mumber of Prouinces) continue the first proceeding of the Pope; and seeing that *Euagrius* had appeared, and that Flauianus perseuered in his contempt delegated THEOPHILVS Bishop of *Alexandria*, whose Patriarkship bordered vpon that of *Antioch* to examin it: *The sacred Synod* (saith saint AMBROSE in his Epistle to *Theophilus*) *hauing committed the right of examining this affaire to your vnanimitie and to our other colleagues of Egipt, it is necessarie that you cite againe our brother Flauianus.* And why then when the councell of *Capua* had giuen this commission to THEOPHILVS Patriarke of *Alexandria*, did saint AMBROSE write to him, that hee should, after he had iudged it procure his iudgement to be confirmed by the Pope? *Certainly*, (said hee) *wee conceaue, that you should relate the affaire, to our holie brother, the Bishop of the Roman Church, for we presume that you will make noe iudgement that can displease him.* And a litle after; *To the end that we hauing receaued the tenor of your acts, when we shall see that you haue iudged soe as the Roman Church will vndoutedly approue it, we may reape with ioy the fruite of your examination.* And why then (when it appeared that EVAGRIVS Successor to PAVLINVS had bene euill ordained, for as much as *Paulinus* only had imposed his handes vpon him, and that *Flauianus* by this occasion remained without a competitor) did *Theophilus* send a legation to *Rome* to put *Flauianus* againe into the Popes grace; and *Flauianus* an other, to obtaine the restitution of communion with the Pope? THEOPHILVS (saith *Socrates*) *hauing sent the priest Isidorus appeased Damasus* (you must reade *Anastasius*) *that was offended, and represented to him, that it was profitable for the concord of the people, to forgett the fault of Flauianus; and soe the communion being restored to Flauianus, the factions of the people of Antioch, a while after* (*that is to saie, vnder Pope Innocent the first*) *were reconciled* And *Sozomene* speakinge of saint IOHN CHSOSTOME Archbishop of *Constantinople*, who had a little before bene a priest of *Flauianus*, and for that cause affected him: IOHN (saith he) *praied Theophilus to labour with him, and to helpe him, to make the Bishop of of Rome to be propitious to Flauianus; and to this end there were deputed Acacius Bishop of Beroe and Isidorus.* And THEODORET, although for his partiality, he be not altogether to be credited in this cause, speaking of the Emperor THEODOSIVS his voyage to *Rome*: *The Emperor* (said he) *exhorted them to extinguish this vnprofitable contention* (for you must reade ἀνόνητον and not ἀνόητον *and represented to them that Paulinus was alreadie dead, and that Euagrius came not by lawfull meanes to the Prelacye.* And a little after: *Then vpon the exhortation of the Emperor, those of the west promised to lay aside all bitternesse and to receaue the Ambassadors that Flauianus should send: which the* divine

Côc. Carth 3. c. 38.

Amb. ep. 78.

Amb. Ibid

Soc. hist. eccl. l. 5. c. 15.

Soz. hist. eccl. 8. c. 3.

Theod. hist eccl. l 5. c. 23.

See Nicephorus l. 12 c. 24.

Theod. hist eccl. l 5. c. 23.

diuine Flauianus hauing learnt, he sent to Rome a legation of most famous Bishops, and priests, and Deacons of Antioch; for all which the chiefe was Acacius Bishop of Beroe in Syria, renowned through all parts of Sea and land. But here is too much of this historie: lett vs passe on to the rest.

And why then when Saint AMBROSE, Archbishop of *Milan* (a cittie where the Emperors of the west, made their residence, speakes of his brother *Satyrus*, doth he saie, that when he had escaped Shipwracke, and was cast vpon the Isle of *Sardinia*, he inquired of the Bishop of that place, whether he agreed *with the Catholicke Bishops, that is to saie* (as himselfe adds) *with the Roman Church?* And why then when he excuseth the custome of washing of feet which was practised in the Church of *Milan* although it was not vsed in the Chuch of *Rome*, doth he crye; *We follow in all things, the type and the forme of the Roman Church:* And againe *The same Peter is our warrant for this obseruation, who hath bene Bishop of the Roman Church?* And why then when he, or the author (that was of his tyme) of the comētary, that is attributed to him vpon the first Fpistle to *Timothie*, explaines these wordes of the Apostle, *to conuerse in the howse of God*, Doth he write that Pope DAMASVS was the Rector of the Church? *Although* (saith he) *the whole world belonges to God, neuerthelesse, the Church is called the howse of God, of which at this day Damasus is the Rector?*

Ambr. Or. de obit. frat.

De Sacr. l. 3. c. 1.

In. 1. Tim. c. 3.

And why then, when OPTATVS Mileuitanus, that is Bishop of *Mileuis* in *Africa*, whom saint AVSTIN calls a Bishop of reuerend memory, and whom *Fulgentius* honors with the title of a *Saint* disputes. *Thou* against the Donatists, doth he saie to *Parmenian* a Donatist Bishop; *canst not denie, but that thou knowest that the Episcopall chaire was first sett vp in Rome for Peter, in which seate was sett the head of all the Apostles, Peter; whereof also he hath bene called Cephas:* (soe saith he, to allude to the greeke word κεφαλή, which signifies he head; & ressembles the Hebrew, *Cephas*; that is to saie, *a stone*, from whence this Apostle was named) *to the end, that in this onely chaire, vnitie should be preserued to all; least the other Apostles might attribute to themselues, each one his particular chaire, but that he should be a Schismaticke and a Sinner, that would against the onely chaire, set vp an other?* And for what cause after he had cited the catalogue of Popes from saint PETER, euen to his tyme, doth he inferr from thence, the Donatists could haue noe chaire, and consequently noe Church, since they had noe communion with the Bishop of Rome? *Giue vs* (said he) *an accompt of the originall of your chaire, you that will attribute to your selues the holy Church? But you saie,* (quoth hee) *that you haue alsoe some parte at Rome; but this is a braunch of your Error, sprunge out of a lye, and not from the roote of truth: for in the end if Macrobius be inquired of* (soe was the name of the false Bishop that the Donatists kept at Rome) *where he sitts there, can he answere in the chaire of Peter, which perchance he knowes not soe much as by sight?* And a while after; *From whence is it then, that you attempt to vsurpe to yourselues the keyes of the Kingdome, you that fight against the chaire of Peter by your bould and sacrilegious presumptions?*

Opt. con. Parm. l. 2.

Opt ibid.

And why then when saint AVSTIN an African as well as he, pressed the same Donatistes, did he saie to them; *In the Roman Church there hath alwaies flourished the principalitie of the Apostolique Sea.* And againe, *Reckon the Prelates, euen since the seate of Peter, and in this order of the Fathers, see who hath succeeded one an other; this is the Rocke, that the prowde gates of Hell shall neuer ouercome.* And in an other place, considering the Popes as successors of saint PETER according to the other interpretation; to witt; according to that of the figure of the Church; *In this order of Fathers* (said he) *that is to saie from Saint Peter to Pope Athanasius, there is not one Donatist:* And in his disputations against the *Manichees*, *In the Catholicke Church I am detained*

Aug. ep. 162.
Idem. Ps. con. Part. Donat.
Id. ep. 65.
Id. con. ep. fund.

by

by the Succeßion of Prelates from the Seate of Peter to whom our Lord gaue his sheepe to feede after his resurrection, vnto the present Bishops seate?

And why then when the Empresse *Eudoxia*, wife to *Arcadius* Emperor of the East, seeing her husband would cause *Theophilus* to be degraded from the Patriarkship of *Alexandria*, (but delaied, because, saith the Emperor LEO the Learned, *that the legates of Rome and of the westerne Church staied longe ere they came*) had cast vpon saint *Chrisostom* Archbishop of *Constantinople* the tragedie, that was begun for *Theophilus*, and had caused him to be deposed by a councell of Bishops assembled at *Constantinople* vnder *Theophilus* Patriark of *Alexandria*; did this deuine Prelate haue recourse by letters of Appeale to the Pope? *Vouchsafe* (saith this sacred goulden pen, writing to Pope *Innocent* the first) *to commaund that these things so wickedly done, and we absent and not refusing iudgement, may be of noe value, as in truth they are not; and that they, that haue carried themselues so vniustlie, may be submitted to the punishment of the Ecclesiasticall lawes.* For to thinke to auoide these wordes, by saying, saint *Chrisostome* speakes in plurall termes, in his letter as writing to manie: Who knowes not that it was a common custome with the Easterne authors, and communicated by deriuation to those of the west, when they would honor or gratifie him, to whom they write, to speake in the plurall number, to signifie, that they consider him, as hauing in him the authority of many? And this in imitation of the Syrians, who to expresse master or Lord, called it Rabbi, which signifies many, that is to saie, contayning in him, the authoritie of manie? *God* (saith EVSEBIVS Archbishop of *Milan* in his Epistle addressed only to Pope LEO) *hath constituted yee Prelates of the Apostolicke sea, worthie protectors of his worship*: And the Bishops of *Siria* writing only to the Emperor *Iustinian*; *The Lord preserue yee deuout zealous and guardians of the faith*; And the bishops of the councell of *Mopsuestia*, a cittie of *Asia* in an Epistle to Pope *Vigilius* alone; *It was verie reasonable, ô yee most holie, since yee holde the first dignitie of priesthood, that those things which concerne the state of the holie Curches, should be represented to your deuinely honored, Blessednesse*: And the Pope saint GREGORIE in the Epistle addressed to Cyriacus Patriarke of *Constantinople* alone, to congratulate with him for his promotion; *In this most blessed Brethren, yee are stronge, that mistrusting your owne strength, yee trust in the power of God.* Iointly, that although the actes of the Popes were often dispatched in their name alone, neuerthelesse they were framed with the consent of the neighbour Bishops which were at their Synodes and consistories; As Pope *Iulius* testifies to the Arrians in these wordes: *Although it be I alone that haue written, yet I haue not onely written myne owne opinion, but that of all the Bishops of Italie and of these partes.* And therefore not onely the inscription of saint *Chrysostomes* Epistle is singular and directed to the Pope alone, but also *Palladius* and *Photius* cite it, as addressed to the Pope alone. And to hope also to auoide these wordes by saying, that in the end, not of the copie which is in saint *Chrisostomes* workes, but in that which is recited by *Palladius*, *saint Chrisostome* adds that he hath written the same things to *Venerius* Bishop of *Milan*, and to *Chromatius* Bishop of *Aquilea*, it is a vaine and friuolous hope. For he intendes the same things in regarde of the reporte of the historie, but not that in anie of his other letters, he vseth anie of those formes of Appeale: *Vouchsafe to commaund, that these things done against vs, may be inualid, and that those which haue done them, may be submitted to the punishment of the Ecclesiasticall Canons.* And againe; *Of one thing I beseeche your watchfull minde, that although those that haue filled all with troubles, be sicke of an impenitent and incurable disease, if yet they will remedie these things, that then they may not be punisht nor interdicted.* More vaine were it to hope to auoide them

Leo Imp. in vit. Chrys.

Chrys. ap Innoc. ep. 1

Rab: Ribbô Rabbi. Rabbuni. Inter ep. Leon. 1. post. ep. 50. Côc. Côst. sub. Men. act. 1.

Conc. Const. Oecum. 2. Act. 5.

Greg. l. 6. ep. 4.

Iul. apud Ath. in apol. 2.

Pal. in. vit. Chrys. Phot. bibl. c. 86.

Chrys. ad Innoc. ep. 2.

Chrys. ad Innoc. ep. 2.

by

by saying, that saint CHRISOSTOM before he was condemned had appealed to a generall councell, and that then after his condemnation, he could not appeale to the Pope. For what inconuenience were it, that saint CHRYSOSTOME before his condemnation, to staie the furie of those that were to be his Iudges, and his aduersaries together, appealed to a generall councell, which he knew could not be held without the assistance of the Pope, or his Legates? and that after his condemnation, seeing this refuge had failed him, and that all hope of a generall councell was taken awaie, because the Emperor and Empresse of the East, (against whose wills it could not be celebrated,) had declared themselues his aduersaries; he appealed to the Pope? And to add that the Pope also stroue to cause a generall councell to be held, and then the appeale had not deuolued to him; wat incompatibilitie was there, that the appeale should deuolue to the Pope, and that the Pope should iudge of the validitie of the appeale, and should ordaine, that the first iudgement should be disannulled, and things by prouision sett in the same estate they were before: and that to search it to the bottom to cleere it, with the satisfaction of all the Prouinces, and to hinder a schisme betweene the two Empires, he desired it might be iudged definitiuely in a generall councell? The rule of the councell of *Sardica* vpon the matter of Appeales, (which is that that *Palladius* and *Zozomene* teache vs, Pope INNOCENT followed in this case) did it not cast, two things vpon the Pope after the interiected appeale: the one to iudge whether the reason of the appeale seemed to him lawfull, and in case he found it lawfull, to annull the sentence, and to remitt by way of intire restitution, the parties in such estate, as they were before: *The other*, after he had disannulled the first sentence, to ordaine a new iudgement should be proceeded to, and to name iudges to that effect either taken from the neighbouring Prouinces, or sent from Rome to iudge the cause with the Bishops of the neighbour-prouinces? Now doth not *Palladius* (that *Photius* calls a worthie and a diligent writer of the history of saint CHRISOSEOME) witnesse that the Pope did, when he saith; INNOCENT *haueing receiued both parties to his communion, determined that the iudgement of Theophilus should be abrogated and annulled, saying, they should hold another Synod vnreprouable of the Prelates of the west and east?* And doth not the successe of the history teach vs, that saint CHRISOSTOM remained absolued vpon the Popes single sentence, without anie oecumenicall councell to followe it? And Pope GELASIVS an author of the same age, doth not he confirme this when he writes, a *Synod of prelates yea Catholickes hauing condemned Iohn of Constantinople euen the sea Apostolicke alone, because it consented not to it, absolued him:* And why then when saint CHRISOSTOME was dead, did *George* Patriarke of *Alexandria*, an author of one thousand yeares antiquity, and cited by saint DAMASCENE and *Photius* Patriarke of *Constantinople*, and printed in Greeke in England, with the greek wordes of saint CHRISOSTOME and followed by *Cedrenus*, *Nicephorus*, *Glycas Harmenopolus*, And other Greekes) write, that Pope INNOCENT, aduertised of his death, excommunicated the Emperor *Arcadius* and the Empresse *Eudoxia* in these wordes: *And therefore I, the meanest and a sinner as depositary (or Keeper) of the Throne of the great Apostle Peter I cutt off thee and her from the participation of the immaculate mysteries of Christ our God, and ordaine that whatsoeuer Bishop or Clarke, of the holy Church of God, which shall presume to administer them to you, after he hath read this my bond, shall be deposed?* For whereas *Socrates*, and after him *Prosper*, and *Marcellinus Comes*, reckon the Death of the Empresse *Eudoxia* to be manie yeares before the death of saint CHRISOSTOME, which is peraduen-

ture

Soz. hist eccl. l. 8. c. 17.

Soz. l. 8. c. 26. & 28.

Conc. Sard c. 5. & 6. Pall. in. vit. Chrys. Innoc. ap. Soz. hist. eccl. l. 8. c. 16.

Phoin bibl. c. 96. Pal. in vit. Chrys.

Gel. ep. ad Episc. dard. Dam de Imag. or. 1. Pho. in Geor. Alex Cedr. in Archad. Hic. l. 13. c. 13. Glys Annal in Archad. pag. 4. Harmen. de Syn. cō. Ioann. Chrys. apud Leonclau. iuris. canonici oriental. l. 9. Innoc. Pap. ap. Georg. Alex. in vit. Chrys. impresse. Lōd.

ture the cauſe that moued *Photius* to ſaie, that this *George* miſtakes himſelfe in ſome places of the hiſtory: this is an Error in *Socrates* a Nouatian author, and an Enemie to ſaint CHRYSOSTOMES memorie, who in ſteede of ſaying (as *Cedrenus*, *Zonarus*, *Nicephorus*, and all the later grecians ſaie) that *Eudoxia* dyed three monthes after the death of ſaint *Chryſoſtome*, and vnder the ſeaueuth conſulſhip of *Honorius*, and the ſecond of *Theodoſius*, hath ſaid, that she died three monthes after the exile of S. *Chryſoſtome*, and vnder the conſulſhip of *Honorius* and *Ariſtenetus*; perchance deceiued by the ambiguity of the greeke word ἔξοδος, which ſignifies ſometymes death, & ſometymes goeinge out; whereof it is credible, they frō whom he tooke his hiſtory, had made vſe. The proofe of the error is, that *Sozimus* a pagan author, who writt aboue 30. yeare before *Socrates*, and was eye witneſſe of this hiſtory, which *Socrates* was not; extendes the life of *Eudoxia* many yeares beyond the baniſhment of S. *Chryſoſtome*. For he ſaith plainely, that the reuolt of the *Jſaureans* was after the baniſhment of *John*, and that vpon the newes that came to *Conſtantinople* of their reuolt, the Emperor ſent *Arzabacius* with an armie into *Pamphilia* to ſuppreſſe them, who hauing had many victories and proſperous ſucceſſes againſt them, might haue wholly rooted thē out, had not *Arzabacius* degenerated from his firſt vigor, and giuen himſelfe vp to pleaſures and couetouſneſſe; for which cauſe he was called backe to *Conſtantinople*, to vndergoe a capitall iudgement; but being returned to the Court, he gaue parte of his ſpoyles to the Empreſſe, who ſaued him. Nowe, beſides that it was impoſſible, that all theſe things should happen in three monthes, (and moreouer that S. *Chryſoſtome* teſtifies, that during his ſtaie in *Cucuſus*, where he ſpent the firſt yeare of his exile, the *Iſaurians* had not yet bene ſuppreſſed by the *Romans*:) *Marcellinus Comes* ſetts downe preciſely the departure of *Arzabacius* againſt the *Iſaurians*, to be the yeare after the cōſulſhip of *Honorius* and *Ariſtenetus*; to witt, vnder the cōſulſhip of *Stilicon* & *Anthemius*, a thing wholy incompatible with what *Socrates* and himſelfe ſaie; that the Empreſſe dyed the yeare of the conſulſhip of *Honorius* and *Ariſtenetus*. For how could the Empreſſe ſaue *Arzabacius* after his returne from the *Jſaurians* warr, begun vnder the conſulſhip of *Stilicon* and *Anthemius*, if she were dead in the conſulſhip of *Honorius* and *Ariſtenetus*, which was before that of *Stilicō* & *Anthemius*? And why did not S. *Chryſoſtome* himſelfe, in ſoe many letters as he writt in his fower yeares baniſhment, make mentiō of the death of *Eudoxia*, that was the cauſe of it; if she were dead 3. monthes after his departure into baniſhment? And how could *Palladius*, (who although he extēdes not his hiſtory to the tyme of *Arcadius* his excōmunication, neuertheleſſe he goes on with it to S. *Chryſoſtoms* death) haue forgotten to put *Eudoxia's* death, amongſt the examples of the perſons that dyed, for hauing perſecuted S. *Chryſoſtom*, if she had bene dead, when he writ his hiſtory? & therefore alſo the Emperor *Leo*, ſurnamed the *learned*, & *Cedrenus*, & *Zonarus*, & *Nicephorus*, & *Glicas*, & all the other later Greekes, haue rather choſen to followe *Zozimus* & *George* of Alexādria, & their cōputation in *Eudoxia's* death, then that of *Socrates*; but this obſeruation deſerues a diſcourſe of more leaſure: lett vs gett ground.

Zoſim. hiſt. l. 5.

Marcel. Com. in Chronic.

Leo Imp. in vit. Chrys. Cedr. Zonar. & cæteri in Arcadio.

And why then when the tempeſt was appeaſed, would the ſame *Innocent* neuer receiue Alexander Patriark of Antioch, and Atticus Biſhop of *Conſtantinople* into his communion, till they had reſtored the name of ſaint *Chryſoſtome* into the recordes of their Churches? *I haue diligentlie inquired*, (ſaith Pope *Jnnocent* writing to Alexander Patriark of Antioch,) *whether the cauſe of the bleſſed Biſhop Iohn hath bene fully ſatisfied in all conditions; and being informed by thoſe of your legation, that all thinges haue bene fully performed according to our deſire, J haue (giuing God thankes) admitted the communion*

Innoc. ad Alex ep. 17

of your Church. And a little after, *As for the letters of the Bishop Atticus, because they were ioyned with yours, I haue receiued them, least the refusall of a man longe agoe suspended by vs, might be an iniurie to you; and yet we haue sufficiently, and more then sufficiently ordained in the actes, what ought to be obserued in his person*. And why doth THEODORET say, *Iohn being dead, those of the west would neuer admitt the communion neither of the Egiptians, nor of those of the East, nor of the Bishops of Bosphorus and Thrace, that is to saie, of the iurisdictiõ of Constantinople, till they had inscribed the name of this admirable personage into the roll of the Bishops his predecessors, and they esteemed Arsacius that succeeded him, not worthie of a bare salutation?* And as for *Atticus* successor of *Arsatius* after manie legations and treaties for peace, they finally receiued him, but not vntill he had first added the name of *Iohn* to the other Bishops. For that *Theodoret* saith this of those of the West, and that saint *Innocent* recites it of himselfe, are not thinges repugnant, forasmuch, that as the Greekes by the word *Easterne* meant the Patriark of *Antioch*, and the Bishops of his Patriarkship; and by the word *Egiptians*, the Patriark of *Alexandria*, and the Bishops of his Patriarkship: soe by the word *Westerne*, they vnderstood, the Pope and the Bishops of his patriarkship, because the Pope neuer decided matters of moment without some assembly either generall or particular of the Bishops of his patriarkship; from whence it is, that in the same letter of *Innocent* to *Alexander*, it is added at the end; *that twenty fower Bishops of Italie haue subscribed to it*.

Theod. hist. eccl. l. 5. c. 34. — Ibid. — Innoc. ad Alex. ep. 16.

And why then when the cause of *Pelagius* and *Celestius* had bene iudged both in the East, where *Pelagius* was, by the Synod of *Palestine*, and in *Africa* where *Celestius* had bene, by the Councells of *Carthage* and *Mileuis*, did the Councell of *Carthage* write this to Pope *Innocent*; *This proceeding then our holie Lord and brother, we conceiued we ought to represent to your charitie, that to the statutes of our mediocritie, there might be allso applied, the authoritie of the Apostolicke Sea*: And againe, *We doubt not but your Reuerence, when you shall haue seene the decrees of the Bishops, which are said to be made vpon this occasion in the East, will frame such a iudgement whereat we shall all reioyce in the mercie of God?* And why doth the *Mileuitan* Councell, to which S. AVSTIN was secretary, write these wordes to Pope INNOCENT: *For as much as God by the guift of his principall grace, hath placed you in the Apostolicke Sea, and hath graunted you to be such in our daies, as wee ought rather to feare that it should be imputed to vs for a crime of negligence, if we should conceale from your Reuerence those things, which for the Church ought to be represented to you; then to imagine that you can receiue them disdainefully or negligentlie; we beseeche you to applie your pastorall diligence to the great perills of the weake members of Christ*: And towardes the end; *But we belieue with the helpe of the mercie of our God IESVS CHRIST (who vouchsafe to direct you consulting with him, and to heare you praying to him) that those that holde these opinions soe peruerse and pernicious, will more easilie yeilde to the authoritie of your Holynesse drawne from the authoritie of the holie scriptures?* And why then when the same Pope INNOCENT answered both the Councells, did he testifie to them, that they had behaued themselues toward him in the same manner as all the other prouinces had done to his predecessors? *It was not by human sentence, but diuine* (said that great Pope in the answere to the *Mileuitans* Councell inserted amongst saint *Austins* Epistles, and cited by saint *Austine* himselfe in his writinges against the *Pelagians*) *that the Fathers haue ordained, that all things that are treated in prouinces distant and farr of, should not be determined, till first they were come to the knowledge of the Apostolicke Sea; to the end that the sentence that should be found to be iust, might the confirmed by the intire authority of the same Sea; and that from thence, the other Churches as Springes,*

Aug. ep. 90. — Aug. ep. 92. — Int. ep. Aug. ep. 91. Aug. cont. duas. Ep. Pelag. l. 2. c. 4.

all

all proceeding from their mother source, and running with the purity of their originall, through the diuers Regions of the whole world might take what they ought to ordaine? And in the answere to the *Mileuitan* Councell, which is alsoe inserted amongst saint AVSTINS Epistles: *You prouide* (said he) *diligently and worthilie for the Apostolick honor, for the honor I saie of him, that besides assaultes from without, sustaines the care of all the Churches, following in the consultation of difficult things, the forme of the ancient rule which you know hath alwaies bene practised by all the world with me:* And a while after, & princippally as often as there is question in pointes of faith; *I conceaue all our bretheren and Colleagues in the Bishops Sea, ought not to referr what may profitt in common to all the Churches, to anie but to Peter, that is to saie, to the author of their name and dignitie.* And why then to take away all occasion from replying, that he spake in his owne cause, doth saint AVSTIN, soe highlie praise both these answeres? *Vpon this affaire* (saith saint AVSTINE) *were sent the relations of the two Councells of Carthage and Mileuis, to the Apostolick Sea, &c. to all these things Pope INNOCENT answered vs as was conuenient, and as the Prelate of the Apostolick Sea should answere vs.* And in the epistle to Optatus; *Of this new heresie, Pelagius and Celestius hauing bene authors or most violent and famous promoters, they alsoe by the meanes of the vigilancie of two Episcopall Councells, with the helpe of God, who vndertakes the protection of his Church, haue also bene condemned in the extent of the whole Christian world, by the Reuerend Prelates of the Catholicke Sea; yea euen by the number of two of them, Pope INNOCENT, and Pope ZOZIMVS, if they correct not themselues, and besides doe not penance.* And why then when the *Africans* had held their last Councell against *Celestius*, did *Prosper* write: vnder the twelfth cōsulship of Honorius & Theodosius; *The decrees of the Councell of Carthage of 214. Bishops were carried to Pope ZOZIMVS, which hauing bene approued, the Pelagian heresie was condemned throughout the world?* And againe *Pope ZOZIMVS of happie memory added the power of his sentence to the decrees of the African Councells, and to cut of the wicked, armed the right handes of all the Bishops with Peters sword:* And in an other place, speaking of the Roman Church in generall: *The principallitie of the Apostolicall priesthood, hath made Rome greater by the tribunall of Religion, then by that of the Empire?* And why then when the Bishops of *Africa* were assembled at *Cesarea* in *Mauritania*, doth saint AVSTIN saie: *The necessities of the Church enioyned to vs by the Reuerend Pope ZOZIMVS Bishop of the Apostolicke Sea had drawne vs to Cæsarea.*

Inter. epist. Aug. ep. 93

Aug. epist. 106.

Epist. 157.

Prosp. in Chron.

Idem. cont Collat.

Id. de voc. Gent. l 2. c. 6.

Aug. epist. 157.

And why then when BRIXIVS Bishop of *Tours*, had bene cast out of his Seat, and IVSTINIAN created Bishop in his steede, and *Armenius* after him, had BRIXIVS recourse to *Rome* to the same Pope *Zozimus*, that gaue him letters of re-establishment, vpon which he was receiued and restored? BRIXIVS (saith saint GCEGORIE of *Tours*) *transporting himselfe to Rome, related to* the *Pope all his sufferinges.* And a little after, *Returning then from Rome the seauenth yeare with the authority of the Pope of the cittie, he disposed his way to Tours.*

Greg. Tur. hist. l. 2.

And why then when *Socrates*, a Greeke author of the same age with *Zozimus*, produced examples of the translations of Bishops, did he alleage in the head of all the other examples, the translation of *Perigenes* Bishop of *Patras*, one of the citties of *Peloponesus*, that the Pope cōmaunded to be made Archbishop of *Corinth*; And who alsoe in his qualitie assisted at the Councell of *Ephesus*? *Perigenes* (saith Socrates) *had bene ordained Bishop of Patras, but because the cittizens of Patras had not receiued him, the Bishop of Rome commaunded that he should be Bishop of the Metropolitā Church of Corinth the Bishop of that place being dead, in which Church also he gouerned all the daies of his life.*

Soc. hist. eccl. l. 7. c. 36.

And why then when Pope *Boniface* successor to *Zozimus* was raised to the Popedome, did S. AVSTIN write to him; *Thou disdainest not to be a friend to the humble, though thou rulest more highlie.* And againe; *The pastorall watch is common to vs all that exercise the office of Bishops, although thou art supereminent in a more high degree.*

Aug. cont. duas ep. Pel lib. c. 1:

And why then when Pope CELESTINE had succeeded in the Ponticall dignitie to Pope BONIFACE, did *Prosper* reporte, that he sent GERMAN the Bishop of *Auxerra* into Great *Brittanie* and made him his legate there, and instituted *Palladius* first Bishop of *Scotland? Pope Celestine* (said Prosper) *at the instance of Palladius, sent German Bishop of Auxerra in his steede, that casting out the heretickes, he might addresse the Brittaines to the Catholicke faith*: And againe; *Palladius was ordered and sent first Bishop by Pope Celestine to the Scotts belieuing in Christ.* And why then when *Nestorius*, Archbishop of *Constantinople*, begã to trouble the Faith of the Easterne Church, did the same Pope *Celestine* make S. *Cyrill* Patriark of *Alexandria* his Vicar in the East, to iudge the cause of *Nestorius*, and appointed him to excommunicate *Nestorius*, if within ten daies after the receipt of the letters from the Apostolicke Sea, he did not anathematize his error? *The authoritie of our Sea* (said he) *being added to thee, and vsing with power the representation of our place, thou shalt execute exactly and seuerelie this sentence; to wit, that if within ten daies tolde, after signification made to him of this admonition, Nestorius anathematize not his naughtie doctrines, &c. thy Holynesse prouiding without delaie for that Church, shall declare him wholy cutt of from our bodie.* And *Prosper* touching the same history; *Celestine to cut of the Nestorian impietie, ayded Cyrill the Bishop of Alexandria, most glorious defendor of the faith, with the Apostolicke sword.* And why then, when S. *Cyrill* had receiued the Popes admonition, did he send to signifie it to *Nestorius*, and to the *Constantinopolitans* in these wordes: *Wee are constrained to signifie to him by Synodicall letters, that if verie speedily, and within the tyme sett downe by the most holy Bishop of the Roman Church Celestine, he renounce not his noueltie and anathematize them by writing &c. he shall no more haue anie parte amongst the ministers of God.* And for what cause when Pope *Agapet* was come in the age following to *Constantinople*, did the Religious men of *Syria* pray him to doe the same to *Anthimus*, Archbishop of *Trebisond? We pray you* (said they) *to doe to Anthimus, as Celestine did to Nestorius, assigning him a daie as Celestine did to Nestorius.*

Prosp. in chron.

Cõc. Ephes part. 1. c. 15.

Prosp. cõt. Colla.

Cõc. Ephes p. 1. c. 17.

Cõc. Cõst. sub Men.

And why then, when the Councell of *Ephesus* proceeded to the condemnation of *Nestorius*, did they couch it in these termes, *Constrained necessarily by the force of the Canons, and by the letters of our most holie Father and fellowe minister Celestine, we are come not without manie teares, to pronounce this sad sentence against him?* And why then when the Legates of the Pope were arriued to the same Councell of *Ephesus* did they thanke the Bishops of the Councell, for hauing shewed themselues true and holy members of the Pope. *We giue thankes* (said they) *to this reuerent Synod, that the letters of our most holie and blessed Pope, hauing bene recited to you, you haue by your holie and religious voyces shewed your-selues holie members, to your holie head: for your blessednesse is not ignorant, that saint Peter was the head of all the faith, and of all the Apostles*: And againe, *none doubtes for it hath bene notorious in all ages, that the holy and most blessed Peter, Prince and head of the Apostles, pillar of the faith, foundation of the Catholicke Church, did receiue from our Lord IESVS CHRIST, the keyes of the heauenly Kingdome, and the power to binde and loose sinnes, and that he liues and decides causes yet vnto this daie, and for all eternitie by his Successors: of him then the holy Successor and ordinarie Vicar, and most blessed Pope and Bishop Celestine hath sent vs for him as his Lieutenant to this holie Councell.* And why then when there was a question to passe from the cause of *Nestorius*, to that of *John* Patriark of *Antioch* did IVVENALL Bishop of

Cõc. Ephes p. 2. act. 1.

Ibid. act. 2.

Ibid.

Ierusalem

Hierusalem say in presence of the whole Councell, that the ancient custome, and the Apostolicke tradition haue bene, that the Church of *Antioch* was to be iudged by the *Roman*? *It is fitt* (said hee) *that the Right Reuerend Bishop of Antioch, Iohn, honoring this great holy and œcumenicall Councell, should haue recourse hither to iustifie himselfe of what is obiected against him, and that he should obey and honor the Apostolicke Throne of great Rome (sittinge with vs and with the Apostolicke Throne of Ierusalem) before which principallie it is accustomed by Apostolicke tradition and practice, that the Seate of Antioch is to be ruled and iudged.* For that we must referr the laste clause of the period of IVVENALL to the Sea of *Rome*, as *Peltanus* hath done, (deceauing himselfe with this that the word *to obey* gouernes the datiue, and not considering that the verbe *to honor* which is there added, changeth the Rule) it shall be shewed heereafter by seauē necessarie and vndoubted proofes. And why then, when the Councell proceeded indeede to the cause of IOHN Patriark of *Antioch*, did they reserue the decision to the *Pope*? *Being moued* (writes the Councell to the *Pope*) *with the indignitie of the thing we would pronounce against him and the rest the same sentence that he had vnlawfullie pronounced against those, which were conuinced of noe crime: but to the end to conquerr his rashnesse with meekenesse; although he had most iustlie deserued to suffer such a sentence, yet we haue reserued him to the iudgement of thy pietie.* Which afterward the third œcumenicall Councell of *Constantinople* did imitate in the cause of *Macarius* Patriark of *Antioch*, as the Emperor *Constantine Pogonat* reportes in these wordes: *Macarius Bishop of Antioch and his adherents haue bene deposed by the consent of the whole Councell, and remitted to the discretion of the most holie Pope*?

Ibid. part. act. 4.

In chap. 29

Ibid. act. 5.

Cōt. Const 6. act. 18.

And why then when HILARIE Bishop of *Arles* vndertooke to ordaine Prelates in the prouince of *Vienna*, without the Popes leaue, did the Emperor *Valentinian* the third make a lawe, which afterward the Emperor *Theodosius* the second inserted into his new constitutions, vnder the title of the lawe of *Theodosius* and *Valentinian*; by which he forbadd that anie inuocatiō should be made in the Church without the Popes licēce? *Whereas* (saith the lawe) *the merit of Peter who is the Prince of the Episcopall societie, and the dignitie of the cittie of Rome, and the authoritie of the sacred Synod, haue soe establisht the primacie of the Apostolicke Sea; as presumption should attempt nothing vnlawfull against the authoritie thereof; for soe the peace of Churches shall be maintained by all, if the vniuersalitie acknowledge her Rector:* And a little after, *Wee decree by a perpetuall ordinance, that it shall not be lawfull, either for the Bishops of the Gaules, or those of other prouinces, to attempt anie thing against the ancient custome, without the authoritie of the Reuerend Pope of the eternall cittie: but to them and to all, those things shall be lawes which haue bene ordained, or shall be ordained by the authoritie of the Apostolicke Sea; in such sort, as whatsoeuer Bishop, being called to the iudgement of the Pope of Rome, shall neglect to present himselfe, he shall be constrained by the Gouernor of the prouince, to appeare.* For to obiect, that *Prosper* for all this attempt, did call HILARIE Bishop of *Arles* a *Saint*, it had bene somewhat, if betweene HILARIES attempt and his death, there had bene noe penance interposed: but soe farr was HILARIE from persisting in this crime to the end of his daies, that he went himselfe to make personall satisfaction to the Pope: *He vndertooke* (saith the author of his life reported by *Cuias*) *a iourney to Rome on foote, and entred into the Towne without a horse or anie beast of carriage, and presented himselfe to Pope Leo, reuerentlie offering him obedience, and requiring with humilitie that he might ordaine of the estate of the Churches, after the accustomed manner, &c. neuerthelesse, if it were not his will, he would not importune him:* And againe; *He applied himselfe wholie, to appease the spiritt of Leo, with a prostrate humilitie.*

Constit. Nou. Theod. & Valent. tit. 24.

Author vitæ Hilarij Arelatensis apud Cuias obseru. l. 15 c. 38.

And why then, when *Eutyches* who liued in the tyme of the same Emperors, pretended that he had appealed from *Flauianus* Archbishop of *Constantinople* to Pope *Leo*, did not *Flauianus* dispute that he could not appeale, but that he had not appealed? *Eutyches* (saith Pope Leo, writing to *Flauianus*) *affirmes, that in full iudgement he pretended you a request of appeale, and it was not receiued; by which meanes he was constrained to make acts of protestation in the cittie of Constantinople.* And *Flauianus* answering *Leo*; *Eutyches* (said he) *hath informed you, that in the time of iudgement, he pretended to vs, and to the holy Councell heere assembled, libells of appeale, and that he appealed to your Holynesse, which was neuer done by him.* And againe; *Moued then most holie Father with all these attempts of his, and with those which haue bene done, and are done against vs, and against the holy Church, doe you worke confidently according to your wonted courage, as it belongs to the priesthood, and making the common cause, and the discipline of the holy Churches, your owne; vouchsafe to confirme by your writings, the condemnation which hath bene regularlie made against him.* And for what cause did the Councell of *Chalcedon* embrace the iudgement that the Pope had giuen against *Eutyches* after the sentence of *Flauianus* his owne Bishop, as giuen by a competent iudge, and attributed the finall deposition of *Eutyches* to the Popes iudgement? *By the decrees of his tyranny* (saied the Councell of *Chalcedon*, writing to the Pope, and speaking of the attemptes that *Dioscorus* had made in the false Councell of *Ephesus*) *he hath declared Eutyches innocent, and hath restored to him the dignitie, whereof he was depriued by your Holynesse.* And why then when *Peter Chrissologus* Bishop of *Rauenna* writt to the same *Eutyches*, the Epistle which is annext to the front of all the Greeke and Latine actes of the Councell of *Chalcedon*, did he saie; *We exhort thee in these things Reuerend Brother, to lend an obedient attention, to the letters of the most holy Pope of the cittie of Rome, forasmuch as the blessed Peter, who liues and rules in his owne Seate, exhibits the true faith, to those that seeke it; for we for the desire we haue of peace and faith, cannot heare matters of faith, without the consent of the Bishop of Rome?*

Leo ep.8.

In epist. præam. Cōc. Chalc

Cōc. Chalc in relat. ad Leon.

In epist. præam. Cōc. Chalc

And why then, when *Theodoret* Bishop of *Tire* a towne neere *Persia*, and subiect to the Patriark of *Antioch*, had bene deposed in the false Councell of *Ephesus*, did he appeale to the Pope? *I attend* (said *Theodoret* in his letter to Pope *Leo*) *the sentence of your Apostolicke Throne, and beseeche your Holynesse to succor me, appealing to your right and iust iudgement, and commaund that I transport my selfe to you, and verifie that my doctrine followes the Apostolicke stepps.* And for what cause did *Flauianus* Bishop of *Constantinople*, hauing bene deposed by the same Councell, appeale to the same Pope? *We ought* (said the Emperor *Valentinian* the third writing to *Theodosius* the second Emperor of the East) *to preserue inuiolable in our daies, the dignitie of particular Reuerence to the blessed Apostle Peter, that the holy Bishop of Rome, to whom antiquitie hath attributed the priesthood aboue all, may haue place to iudge in matters of faith, and of the Bishops, &c. for therefore, according to the custome of Councells, the Bishop of Constantinople, had appealed to him, in the contention which is risen about points of Faith: and Liberatus Archdeacon of Carthage: Flauianus* (saith he, the sentence hauing bene pronounced against him) *appealed to the Apostolicke Sea, by petition presented to his Legates?* For to saie as the Popes aduersaries doe, that the actes of the false Councell of *Ephesus*, which were read againe in the Councell of *Chalcedon* onely bare that *Flauianus* said to *Dioscorus, I appeale from thee*, without saying; *I appeale from thee, to the Pope;* Who knowes not, that those actes, as it was represented to the Councell of *Chalcedon*, had bene all falsified by *Dioscorus*, who had put in and put out what he listed, making the Bishops signe by force to blanckes? *They haue done vs violence with woundes* (said the Bishops of the *East*, to the Councell

Theod. ep. ad Leon.

In ep. præā. Cōc. Chalc

Liberat. in breuiar. c. 12.

Cōc. Chalc act. 1.

of *Chalcedon*) *we haue signed blanckes?* And *Eusebius* Bishop of *Dorilaus* reporting the same history, to the councell of *Chalcedon*; *Dioscorus* (said hee) *inserted in the actes, things that were neuer spoken, and constrained the Bishops to signe to blanckes.*

And besides the exhibition that *Flauianus* made of his Petition of appeale to the Popes Legates, and the opposition that the Popes Legates made for him against *Dioscorus*, and againste all the Councell, as soone as he had appealed; and the appeale that *Theodoret* the neighboring bishop to *Persia*, and companion in *Flauianus* condemnation putin from the same councell to the Pope, resisting and makeing his appeale be iudged of before the Pope; doth it not sufficiently manifest, that it was to the Pope, that *Flauianus* appealed.

Moreoner, how had *Flauianus* in saying simplie I *appeale from thee*, made it vnderstood, that it was to an oecumenicall councell, that he apealed; since, the councell wherein *Dioscorus* condemned him, tooke alsoe in condemning him, the litle of oecumenicall, and had bene assembled by the Emperor THEODOSIVS the second in the qualitie of oecumenicall and after confirmed as oecumenicall; and that to be truly oecumenicall, there wanted nothing of the number and plenitude of Bishops, but the only authority of the Pope, which was distracted from it, by the seperation of his Legats, whereof some were fledd, and the rest remayned out of their ranke, and amongst the presse? Contrarywise, that all the Patriarkes of the earth, and all the principall metropolitans, and Bishops of their Patriarkshipps, were there, and that there wanted of the Patriarkes none but the Pope alone; is it not a sufficient proofe, that *Flauianus* saying, *I appeale* and presenting his libell of appeale to the Popes Legates, and the Popes Legates, protesting at the same tyme, an opposition against the sentence from which he appealed, that it was to the Pope that he appealed, though the Emperor VALENTINIAN had not also said these expresse wordes; *The Bishop of Constantinople, according to the custome of councells, hath appealed to the Pope:* and *Liberatus* these; *Flauianus sentence hauing bene pronounced against him, appealed to the Sea Apostolick?* For to obiect, that the Pope did not retaine the iudgement of the cause intirely, but desired, it might be iudged in a generall councell; haue wee not already said, that the Popes custome after appeales, was to doe two things; one to iudge of the validity or inualidity of the appeale: and in case of validity, to annull the first iudgement, and restore by prouision, the Appellant to his former Estate. The other, after he had annulled the first sentence, to ordaine to proceede to a second iudgement; and in case that the Pope would not take the paines to examin it himselfe, then not to vexe parties, to giue them iudges,, either sent from *Rome*, or taken by commission from *Rome* out of those partes; or in case of danger of schisme betwene the two Empires, to decree that the cause should be iudged, his legates being present in an oecumenicall councell? Now did not Pope Leo doe this in the cause of *Flauianus?* for first did he not declare the appeale to be lawfull, abrogating and annulling the iudgement of *Dioscorus*, and the false councell of *Ephesus*, against *Flauianus*, and setting things in the same estate they where before, that is to saie, restoring *Flauianus* euen after his title of Bishop of *Constantinople*, and excommunicating all those that did not communicate to his memory, and that without staying till the Councell of *Chalcedon* was holden?

And secondly, did he not ordaine that to passe to a newe iudgement (where all the proceedings of *Dioscorus*, and of the false councell of *Ephesus* against *Flauianus*, might againe be put to the triall, and when *Dioscorus*, if he persisted in his contumacy might be vsed according to his deserte)

Euseb. Doryl. in Conc. Chalc. act. 3.

Leo ep 23. & Liberat. c. 12.

Act. pseudo sinod. Ephes. relect. in Cōc Chalc. act. 1.

Thedor. ep ad Leon. & Cōc. Chalc act. 1.

Conc. Eph. 2 relect: in Cōc. Chalc act 1.

Lex Theodos. Conc. Chalc part 3 c. 19.

Idem.

pag. 18. 19.

the

the holding a generall councell should be procured that the matter might be iudged vnder the eye of the Legates, with the knowledge and satisfaction of all the world; for that the Pope and the Councell of *Rome*, prayed the Emperor of the *East*, to commaund, that all things might be sett in the same state, wherein they were before iudgement, till a greater number of Bishops might be called together from all partes of the world; was in regard of the temporall lawes; for as much as a little while before, the Emperor of the *East*, a Prince that signed as shall appeare heereafter Dispatches without reading them, and whose fauour *Chrisaphius* the *Eutychian* abused had made a lawe in his Empire, by which he confirmed the false conncell of *Ephesus*, which he belieued to be oecumenicke, and the deposition of *Flauianus*; and ordained that all those that in the *Easte* should holde the doctrine of *Flauianus*, that is to say doctrine contrary to *Eutyches* heresie, should be either excluded, or dispossessed from their Bishoprickes, and their bookes publickly burnt, and their adherents punisht with confiscation of goods, and perpetuall banishment.

Leo.ep. 23.

In chap.37.

The law of the Emp. Theod. 2. reported at the end of the acts of the councell of Chalcedon part.3.

For these causes then, the Pope and the councell of *Rome*, prayed the Emperor of the *East*, to reuoke this lawe, and to commaund, that all things in regard of temporall iurisdiction, might be set in the same state as they were before; but not that in regarde of spirituall and Ecclesiasticall authority, the false councell of *Ephesus* was alreadie disannulled by the decree of the Councell of *Rome*, and soe disannulled as *Anatolius*, that had bene made Bishop of *Constantinople* in the false Councell of *Ephesus*, was faine to renounce the Doctrine of *Eutyches*, and of the same Councell of *Ephesus*, and the communion of *Dioscorus*, and to restore the memory of *Flauianus* into the recordes of his Church, and the rest of the *East* that would returne to the communion of the Pope, were faine to doe the same, and this before the Councell of *Chalcedon*. *Anatolius* (saith the Emperesse *Pulcheria* writing to Pope Leo, longe before the Councell of *Chalcedon*) *hath embraced the Apostolicke confession of your letters, reiecting the error that was lately aduanced by some, as your Holynesse may see by his answere*. And Pope LEO himselfe in the first Epistle to *Anatholius* Bishop of *Constantinople*, written six monthes before the Councell of *Chalcedon*, *Your charitie must* (said he) *obserue in regard of silencing the names of Dioscorus, Iuuenall, and Eustathius at the holie altar, that which our Legates in those places tould you, ought to be done, and which shall not be repugnant to the honorable memorie of saint Flauianus*. And in the second Epistle to the same *Anatolius* written fower monthes before the Councell of *Chalcedon*, *Remember* (said he) *to keepe this rule, that all those that in the Synod of Ephesus, which neither could obtaine nor deserue the name of a Synod, and wherein Dioscorus shewed his corrupted will, and Iuenall his ignorance, &c: are grieued for hauing bene ouercome with feare, and for suffering themselues to be forced to consent to that most abhominable iudgement; and desire to be receiued to the Catholique communion, let brotherly peace be restored to them after competent satisffaction; prouided that they condemne and anathematize by an vndoubted acte Eutiches with his doctrine and his Sect. But as for those that haue more grieuously offended, in this case &c.* (he meanes *Dioscorus* Patriarke of *Alexandria*, and *Iuuenall* Bishop of *Ierusalem* and their complices) *if they perchance come to an acknowledgment, and abandonning their owne defence, conuert themselues to condemne theire owne error, and that their satisffaction shalbe such, as it shall not seeme fitt to be reiected, let that be reserued to the more mature deliberation of the sea Apostolicke.*

Ep.Pulch. Imper. ad Leon. in epist. præã. Cōc.Chalc

Leo ad Anat.ep. 38.

Id ad eundem.ep.44.

And indeed that it was not by vertue of any appeale of *Flauianus* to the Councell, that the Councell of *Chalcedon*, which likewise had neuer bene held but for the Pope, iudged of *Flauianus* cause but in vertue of

Flauianus appeale to the Pope, and the Popes commission to the councell, for the compleate reuiew of the cause, three things shewe it,

First, the Canon vpon which, Pope Leo grounded his procuring a Councell after an appeale, was a Canon of the Councell of *Sardica*, concerning appeales to the Pope; *The decrees* (said he, writing to the Emperor *Theodosius*) *of the canons made at* Nicea, *which haue bene decreed by the Prelates of the vniuersall world, and whose copies are heereunto annexed, witnesse that after the putting in of an appeale, the seeking a Synod is necessarie.* For the Canon annexed to that letter in the greeke actes of the Councell of *Chalcedon*, is a Canon of the Councell of *Sardica*, though incorrectly transcribed by those that copied it; which Canon Pope Leo calls a Canon of the Coũcell of *Nicea* for asmuch as the Councell of *Sardica* had bene as a Seale and an Appendix, to the Councell of *Nicea*. Leo ad Theodos. ep. 23. Cã. annex. ep. Leo. ad Theod in act grec. Cõc. Chalc & in manuscr. grec. libl regle Lupar.

The second, that when the Popes legates in the Councell of *Chalcedon*, pronounced their iudgement vpon the punishement that *Dioscorus* should incurr, they pronounced it in these wordes: *And therefore the most holy and blessed Archbishop of the great and ancient Rome, Leo, hath by vs, and by this present synod, together with the thrice blessed and worthie of all praise, the Apostle Peter, who is the rocke and pillar of the Catholicke Church, and the foundation of the right faith, deposed Dioscorus from all dignitie, as well Episcopall as Sacerdotall.* Cõc. Chalc act. 3 & Euang. l. 2. c. 4.

And the third that when the Emperors confirmed in the secular tribunall, the same Councell of *Chalcedon*, to make it temporally executory, they testified that it was by the Popes authority that it had iudged the cause of *Flauianus: The synod of Chalcedon* (said the lawe) *by the authoritie of the most blessed Bishop of the Citty eternall in glorie, Rome; examining exactly matters of Faith, aud strengthning the foundation of Religion, attributed to Flauianus the reward of his past life, and the palme of a Glorious death.* Now how is this anie other thing, but to saie that which Pope *Gelasius* writt forty yeares after in these wordes. *The sea Apostolicke delegated the Councell of Chalcedon to be made for the common faith, and the Catholicke and Apostolicke truth.* And againe, *Flauianus hauing bene condemned by the Congregation of the Greeke Bishops, the sea Apostolicke alone, because he had not consented thereunto, absolued him; and contrarywise by his authoritie condemned Dioscorus Prelate of the second see, who had there bene approued, and alone annulled the wicked synod, in not consenting to it; and alone by his authoritie ordained, that the Councell of Chalcedon should be kept?* But things incident, carry vs away, lett vs againe returne to our careere. Lez. Marc. in Cono. Chalc. part 3. c. 11. Gelas. de Anath. Vincull.

And why then when the Councell of *Chalcedon* was open, was the first cõplaint that was made against *Dioscorus* patriark of *Alexandria* that he had presumed to vndertake to keepe a generall Councell, and to be President there without commission from the Pope: Vpon which complaint also *Dioscorus* came downe from this Patriarkall seate, wherein he was first sett, and stood in the middest of the place, as an accused party, and not as iudge? *Wee haue in our handes* (said *Paschasinus* Bishop *of Lylibea* in *Sicilia*, and Legat from the Pope, speaking to the Councell) *the commaundments of the blessed and Apostolicke Prelate of the Cittie of Rome, who is the head of all Churches: whereby he vouchsaffed to ordaine prouisionallie, that Dioscorus sit not in the councell, and that if he attempt it, that he should be cast out.* And *Lucentius* Bishop of *Ascoli* also the Popes Legate; *Dioscorus* (said he) *must yeild an account of iudgement, for as much as hauing noe right to doe the office of a iudge, he attempted it, and presumed to holde a Synod without the authoritie of the sea Apostolicke, which neuer hath bene lawfull, nor neuer was done;* And *Euagrius*, in the narration of the history of the Councell; *The senat* (saith he) *hauing* Conc. Chalc. act. 1. Ibid.

inquired

Euag. l. 2. c.17. *inquired of the legates from Leo, what charge there was against Dioscorus; they answered, that he must yeild an account of his owne iudgement, because against right, he had vsurped the person of a Iudge, without the Bishop of Romes permission* After which answere, *Dioscorus* by the senats iudgment, stood in the middest of the place.

And why then when *Theodoret* Bishop of *Cyre* a cittie as, hath bene said, in the confines of *Persia* had bene restored by Pope *Leo* from the Deposition of the Councell of *Ephesus* from whence he had appealed to him, did the Emperors Officers (who assisted in the Councell of *Chalcedon* to cause order to be obserued) proclayme. *Lett the Right Reuerend Bishop Theodoret come in, that he may haue part in the Synod; because the most holy Archbishop Leo hath restored him to his Bishopricke, and that (supplied vpon this restitution) the most sacred and religious Emperor hath ordained, that he shall assist in the holy Councell*? For that the Emperor had made himselfe the Executor of the Popes authority in this Councell, it appeares by the protestations he had made of it a little before in these wordes: *Wee conceiued that we ought first to addresse ourselues to thy Holynesse, who hast the superintendance and principalitie of Faith*: And againe *Our desire is, that peace should be restored to the Churches by this Councell celebrated vnder thy authoritie.*

Cōc. Chalc act. 1.

Marci. Imp ep. ad le. in ep. præam. Conc. Chalc.

And why then when the Priests and deacons of *Alexandria*, presented their Petitions against *Dioscorus* in the Councell of *Chalcedon*, did they couch them in these termes; all the Councell seeing and approuing it, and ordayning that they should be registred in the Actes: *To the most holy, and most blessed Archbishop and Vniuersall Patriarcke Leo, and to the most holy and Vniuersall Councell*? For as for the instance that the Bishop of *Constantinople* made afterward, to participate in this title vnder the Pope, and in second place after the Pope, as *Constantinople* being a second *Rome* it shall be spoken of hereafter.

In chap. 34.

And why then when *Paschasinus* the Popes Legate, gaue his voice vpon the deposition of *Dioscorus* did he saie; *That the Pope had pardoned all those, who in the false Councell of Ephesus, had by force consented to Dioscorus, that is to saie, to almost all the Metropolitans and Patriarkes of the Easterne Empire? The sea Apostolicke* (saith he) *graunts them pardon for those things, that they committed there against their wills forasmuch as they haue remained vnto this time, adhering to the most holie Archbishop Leo, and to the holy and vniuersall Councell.*

Conc. Chalc. act. 3.

And why then when the actes of the false Councell of *Ephesus*, were in the Councell of *Chalcedon annulled, did Anatolius*, Bishop of *Constãtinople* pronounce, that of all that had bene done in the Councell of *Ephesus*, nothing ought to remaine entire, but the election of *Maximus* Bishop of *Antioch*, forasmuch as that had bene cõfirmed by the Pope? *My voice* (said he) *is, that none of the things ordained by the pretended Councell of Ephesus shall remaine firme, except that which was done for Maximus Bishop of great Antioch, forasmuch as the most holy Archbishop of Rome Leo, receiuing him into his communion, hath iudged that he ought to rule the Church of Antioch.* From whence it is also, that the same *Anatolius*, who had bene created Archbishop of *Constantinople* in the false Councell of *Ephesus*, held not his Archbishopricke from the false Councell of *Ephesus*, but from the confirmation of the sea Apostolicke, as Pope *Leo* writing to the Emperor *Marcian* puts him in mynde in these wordes: *It should haue sufficed him, that by the consent of my fauour, he hath obtained the Bishopricke of soe great a Cittie.*

Ibid. act. 10.

Leo ad Marci. Imp. ep. 52.

And why then when the Fathers of the Councell of *Chalcedon* framed that famous relation to Pope *Leo* (which is not only inserted in all the Greeke and latine Actes of the Westerne and Easterne libraries, but also is cited by the Greeke Schismatickes and amongst others by *Nilus* Archbishop of *Tessalonica* in his Booke against the Pope) did they write to him, that he had ruled in the Councell as the head to the members, and that the Emperors had presided there, to cause order to be obserued, that is to auoide such murthers and tumultes, as happened in the false Councell of *Ephesus*: And put a like difference betwene the Popes Presidencie, and the Emperors, as betweene the Presidencie of *Iesus* the high priest of the *Sinagogue*, and that of *Zorobabel* prince of the *Iewish* people in the building of the Temple: *You presided* (the Councell writt to the Pope) *in this assemblie, as the head doth to the members, contributing your good pleasure by those that helde your place; and the faithfull Emperor presided, to cause order to be obserued; striuing ioyntly with you, as Zorobabel with Iesus, to renew in the doctrine, the building of the Ecclesiasticall Jerusalem.* Nil. de primat. l. 2. Côc. Chalc relat. ad Leon.

And why then when they came to touch in their relation, the fact of *Dioscorus* Patriarke of *Alexandria*, did they call the Presidencie which he had vsurped in the false Councell of *Ephesus* without the Popes commission TYRANNY: and accused him, to haue attempted euen against him, to whom the guard of the vine had bene committed, that is, against the Pope? *By the decrees of his tyranny* (saith the relation of the Councell to the Pope) *he hath declared Eutiches innocent, and that dignity which had bene taken from him by your Holynesse, as from a man vnworthy of such grace, he hath restored it to him*: And againe; *And after all these things he hath extended his felonie euen against him to whom the guard of the vine hath bene committed by our Sauiour, to witt, against your Holynesse?* Ibid.

And why then when they prayed the Pope to approue the decree, by which they gaue the second ranke, to the Archbishop of *Constantinople* did they beseech him, that as they had corresponded with him that was their head when there was question of Faith, soe his soueraigntie would gratifie them in what concerned discipline, vsing to expresse the spirituall soueraignty of the Pope by the same word χορηγία which had bene vsed to expresse the temporall soueraignty of the Emperors? *Wee haue alsoe* (said they) *confirmed the canon of the 150. Fathers assembled at Constantinople vnder the great Theodosius of Religious memorie, which ordaines that after your most holy and Apostolicall Throne, that of Constantinople should haue the order of honor, moued with this, that the Apostolicke beame raigning amongst you, you according to your ordinarie gouernment doe often spread it toward the Church of Constantinople, because you haue accustomed to inrich without enuie your posteritie* (*that is to saie, the Church of Constantinople, which was extracted from the blood and linage of that of Rome*) *with the participation of your goods*: And againe; *Wee beseeche you, then to honor our iudgement with your decrees, and that as in what concernes the weale, we haue brought correspondencie to our head, soe your Soueraignty will performe in the behalfe of your children, that which concerneth comelinesse.* In Conc. Chalc. act. 1. ep. 14. Côc. Chalc relat. ad Leon. Ibid.

And why then when Pope Leo refused to approue this decree, were the Emperor *Marcian* and *Anatolius* Patriarke *Constantinople* in whose fauour it had bene propounded, constrained to forbeare it, and to leaue the businesse then without effect, as it appeares by these words of Pope *Leo* to *Anatolius*: *This thy fault, which to augment thy power thou hast committed, as thou saist by the exhortation of others, thy charitie had blotted out better and more sincerely, if thou hadst not imputed to the only Councell of thy Clergie, that which could not be attempted, without thy goodwill, &c. But I am gladd, deare brother, that thy charitie protesteth, thou art now displeased with that which euen then ought not to haue pleased thee: It sufficeth to re-enter into common grace, the profession of thy loue, and the testimonie of the Christian Prince, and lett not his correctiō seeme slowe, that hath gotten soe reuerent a suretie?* And why then when *Anastasius* Leo ad Anât. ep. 96.

Bishop

Bishop of *Thessalonica* and the Popes Vicar in *Macedanico, Achaia*, and other *Greeke* Prouinces neere *Constantinople*, had abused the authority of his Vicarship against *Atticus* Bishop of *Nicopolis* and Metropolitan of the aunciēt *Epirus*, did Pope *Leo* write to him; *Wee haue in such sort committed our vicarship to thy charitie, as thou art called to a parte of the care, and not to the fulnesse of the power*: And toward the end: *It hath bene prouided by a grand Order, that all should not attribute to themselues all things; but that in euery prouince there should be some, whose sentence might hold first ranke; and againe, that some others constituted in the greater Cities, might vse the more diligence, that by them the care of the vniuersall Church might flowe to the onely seate of Peter?*

Leo ad Anast. ep. 82.

And why then when *Ceretius* and the other French-Bishops, congratulated Pope *Leo* for the instruction of the Faith, that he had sent into the *East*, did they write to him; *By good right, the principalitie of the sea Apostolicke hath bene constituted in the place from whence there springe forth still the oracles of the Apostolicall Spiritt?*

Int. ep. Leō post ep. 49.

And why then when the Emperors Leo and *Maioranus*, had succeeded the Emperor *Marcian*, vnder whom the Councell of *Chalcedon* was kept, did the Emperor *Maioranus* residing amongst the *Gaules*, decree by an expresse lawe, that euery Bishop that should ordaine a clerke against his will, should be called before the Pope? *If anie Bishop* (saith the lawe) *doe dispence with himselfe in this respect, let him be called before the Prelate of the Sea Apostolicke, that in that reuerent Seate, he may incurre the note of his lawlesse presumption.*

Lex Maior. Imp. int. nouell. Maior. Tit 2.

And why then (when the Emperor *Zeno*, *Leo's* successor, had caused *Iohn* surnamed *Talaia* to be cast out from the *Alexandrian*, Sea, and set *Peter* surnamed *Mongus* in his place) did Iohn appeale to the Pope, who deposed *Peter* his aduersary, and Acacius Patriarke of *Cōstantinople* that adhered to him? Iohn (saith *Liberatus* an Affrican author, and of neere eleuen hundred yeares antiquity) *addressed himselfe to Calandion Patriarke of Antioch, and hauing taken from him Synodicall letters of intercession, appealed to the Pope of Rome Simplicius*. And *Victor* of *Tunes*, an author of the same tyme, and Country: after the consulship of the moste noble *Longinus*, *Acacius* Bishop of *Constantinople Peter* Bishop of A*lexandria*, and Peter Bishop of A*ntioch*, enemies to the Councell of *Chalcedon*, were condemned by *Felix* Prelate of the *Roman* Church; and by a Synod held in *Italie*, and the condemnation sent to *Constantinople* to *Acacius*. And *Euagrius* a greeke author somewhat later; *Iohn hauing taken his flight, and being come to Rome represented to Felix the successor of Simplicius, the things that Peter had done, and perswaded Felix to send a sentence of deposition to Acacius, for the Communion he had with Peter*. For though *Zacharie* an *Eutychian* author write, that *Acacius* who was supported by the Emperor *Zeno* a complice of his heresie, despised this deposition. From whence it is, that *Victor* of *Tunes* saith, *that Peter and Acacius died in condemnation*; neuerthelesse, the Popes Sentence had in the end such effect, as both their names, to wit, *Peter* Patriark of *Alexandria* and *Acacius* Bishop of *Constantinople*, they being alreadie dead, were raced out of the Recordes of their Churches, and out of the catalogue of the Patriarkes of *Alexandria*, and *Constantinople*, and excluded from recitall in the misteries.

Lib. in breuiar. c. 16. Vict. Tun. in Zen.

Euag. hist. eccl. l. 3. c. 18.

Vict. Tun. in Zen.

And why then when *Hunericus*, King of the *Vandalls*, would needes presse *Eugenius* Archbishop of *Carthage* to enter into conference with the *Arrians*, did *Eugenius* (reported by *Victor* of *Vtica*) answere him, that he might not enter into those listes, without the consent of other Churches, and namely of the *Roman* Church, which is the head of all Churches? *Let the King* (said *Eugenius*) *write to his friends, and I will write to*

Vict. Vtic. de persec. Vandal. l. 2.

my bretheren that our colleagues may come, who with vs may shew you our common faith, and principally the Roman Church, which is the head of all Churches.

And why then when *Fulgentius* an *African* Bishop of the same tyme, and the other Bishop, of *Africa* assembled with him made their answere to *Peter* a deacon and deputy of the *East*, did they say to him; *The Roman Church which is the topp of the world, enlightned with two great lights Peter and Paule, holdes it is soe?* And why then when the Emperor *Anastasius*, *Zeno's* successor, solicited *Macedonius* Patriark of *Constantinople* to suppresse in the seruice of his Church, the memorie of the Councell of *Chalcedon*, did *Macedonius* answere him, that he could not doe it without a generall Coũcell presided by the Pope? *The Emperor Anastasius* (saith *Theodorus Anagnostes*) *pressed Macedonius to abrogate the Councell of Chalcedon, but Macedonius answered him he could not doe it, without a generall Councell, wherein the Bishop of Rome must be President.*

Fulg. de incarn. & grat. c. 11.

Theod. Anagn. ad calc. hist. eccl. Theo. in edit. Robert. Steph

And why thẽ when the Bishops of the Easterne Church banded themselues against the preuarication of their Patriark *Acacius* did they write to Pope *Symachus*; *Thou art euerie day taught by thy sacred Doctor Peter, to feede the sheepe of Christ, which are committed to thee throughout the habitable earth, not constrained by force but willinglie, thou that with the most learned Paule cryest out to all thy subiects, we doe not rule ouer you in faith, but cooperate with you in ioy.*

Ep. Orient. ad Sym int Orthodoxogr impr. Basil. to. 2.

And why then when *Vitalianus* a *Scithiã* had rebelled against the Emperor *Anastasius* because he persecuted the Catholickes, & had borne armes at the gates of *Constantinople*, did *Victor* of *Tunes* say, *He would neuer promise peace to the Emperor, but vpon condition, that he should restore to their Seates, those that had bene banisht for defending the Councell of Chalcedon, and should vnite all the Churches of the East with the Roman Church.* And why then when *Iustin* a Catholicke Prince had succeeded the Emperor *Anastasius*, did he cause Pope *Felix* sentence to be executed against *Peter* Patriark of *Alexãdria*, and *Acacius* Patriark of *Constantinople*, and made their names be razed euen after their deathes, out of the records of their Churches, and from the recitall in the misteries? *We anathematize* (saith *John* Patriark of *Constantinople* in an epistle to Pope *Hormisdas*) *Timothie the parricide surnamed Ælurus, and we condemne likewise Peter of Alexandria his disciple, and partaker in all things; and we alsoe anathematize Acacius sometimes Bishop of this cittie of Constantinople, &c. and we promise heereafter not to recite in the sacred misteries, the names of those that are excluded from the cõmunion of the Catholicke Church; that is to saie, that consent not fullie with the Sea Apostolicke.* And the Emperor *Iustin* in his epistle to the same Pope; *We haue giuen order, that the reuerend Church of Cõstantinople, and manie others, should accomplish your desire, not only in other things, but also in razing the names that you haue required to be takẽ awaie frõ the sacred recordes.* And a while after praying the Pope, that he would be cõtent, that the names of those only, which had bene cõdemned by name by the Sea Apostolicke, should be blotted out, without exacting the racing of those that had cõmunicated with thẽ, for the difficulty that there would be in razing the names of soe many Bishops to be takẽ away out of the recordes of their churches; *We aske noe grace* (said he) *for the names of Acacius, nor for either the one Peter, or the other* (*that is to saie, Peter Patriark of Antioch, and Peter Patriark of Alexãdria*) *nor for Dioscorus, nor Timothie of whom your Holynesse letters addressed to vs, made speciall mention; but of those that the Episcopall reuerence hath celebrated in other citties.* And *Victor* of *Tunes*; *The Emperor Iustin* (saith he) *revnited those of the East vnder worthie satisfaction to the Prelates of the West, except the euill Bishops* (for it must be read prauos, and not paruos) *which died blinded with their ancient error, to witt, Acacius late Bishop of Constantinople, Peter Bishop of Antioch, and Peter Bishop of*

Vict. Tun. in Anest.

Ioan. Patr. Const. ep. ad Hormis.

Iust. ep. ad Hormisd.

Vict. Tun. Chron. in Iust.

Alexandria; and caused the decrees of the Councell of Chalcedon to be reuiued, that had bene banisht by the Emperors Zeno and Anastasius.

And why then when the Emperor *Iustinian*, nephew and successor to *Iustine* was come to the Empire neere eleuen hundred yeares agoe, did he make profession to acknowledg the Pope for he head of all the Churches? *Wee preserue,* (said hee in the lawe to *Epiphanius* Patriarke of *Constantinople,*) *the Estate of the vnitie of the most holie Churches in all things, with the most holie Pope of the ancient Rome, to whome we haue written the like; because we will not suffer anie thing to passe concerning the affaires of the Church, which shall not be alsoe referred to his Blessednesse, forasmuch as he is the head of all the holy Prelates of God*: And in the lawe, *Inter claras*, where the Epistle of the same Emperor to the Pope, and the expedition of *Hipatius* and *Demetrius* his Legates to the Pope against *Cirus*, and *Eulogius* Legates for the *Acæmites*, soe were certaine Religious men of *Constantinople* called because of their long watches; is inserted; *We will not suffer* (said he) *that anie thing shall be treated of belonging to the state of the Churches, though cleere and manifest, which shall not alsoe be referred to your Holynesse, who are the head of all the Churches.* For as for the shiftes of those that not being able to auoid the lawe, *Inter claras*, striue to make it suspected for false, I will not staie to confute them. It sufficeth that the defence of those two great Oracles of *Themis*, *Alciat* and *Cuias* haue, made of this lawe; and the authenticall copie which is to be found in the Greeke *Basiliques*, beginning with these wordes, Εν τῇ λαμπρότητι τῆς ὑμετέρας πραότητος: And the history that *Liberatus* an African author of the same tyme reportes of it when he saith; *Hypatius* Bishop of *Ephesus*, and *Demetrius* Bishop of *Philippi*, were sent by the Emperor *Iustinian* to Pope *Iohn* surnamed *Mercury*, to consult with the Sea Apostolicke against *Cyrus* and *Eulogius* deputed by the *Acæmites*, &c. but Pope *Iohn*, (we being then present at *Rome*) confirmed the Emperiall confession by an Epistle of his, and addressed it to the Emperor, And the testimonie that *Iustinian* himselfe giues it in the lawe to *Epiphanius*, and in the Epistle to Pope *Agapet* and the old greeke paratitles translated and published by *Leunclauius* a protestant lawyer, which reckon for the eight lawe of the *Code*, the Emperor *Iustinians* Epistle to the Pope, and the Popes answere to him, stopp their mouthes that think to call it in question. And yet lesse will I stand to solue this, that *Iustinian*, in the lawe *Constantinopolitana* writes, that the Church of *Constantinople* is the head of all the other Churches. For it shall be shewed heereafter, that he speakes of the other Churches of the iurisdiction of *Constantinople* which are treated of in the lawe; and not of the other Patriarkall Churches, amongst which *Iustinian* neuer attributed but the second ranke to the Church of *Constantinople*, as it appeares by the *Nouel. 131.* where he saieth; *We ordaine (following the definitions of the fower first Councells) that the holy Pope of the ancient Rome, is to be first of all Prelates; and that the most Blessed Archbishop of Constantinople, or new Rome, shall haue the second place after the holy Sea Apostolicke of old Rome, and shall be preferred before all the other Seas.*

Paris. Antwerp. & Geneu. tit. 1. l. 7.

Cod. tit. 1. l. 8.

Alciat. Parerg. l. 4. c. 23. Cuias obseru. l. 12. c. 16. Cuias ibid. Liberat. in breuiar. c. 20.

Cod. tit. 1. l. 7. Int. epist. Agap. tom. 1. ep. Rom. Pontific. Paratitl. græc. impr. latin. Francofurt. Cod. de Sacrosanct. Eccl. 1 Constantinop. In cap. 34 Iust. Nou. 131.

And why then when *Epiphanius* was dead, and that *Anthymus* Bishop of *Trebisond* had bene made Patriark of *Constantinople* in his steede, did *Anthymus* oblige himselfe by protestation written to all the other Patriarkes, to obey the Pope? *Anthymus* (saith the Councell of *Constantinople* held vnder *Menas*) *promiseth to doe all that the Archbishop of the great Sea Apostolick should ordaine; and writt to the most holy Patriarkes, that hee would in all things followe the Sea Apostolike.*

Conc. Cōst sub Men. act. 4.

And why thē whē Pope *Agapet* was a while after arriued at *Cōstantinople*, did he depose the same *Anthymus* Patriark of *Constantinople*, and then euen in *Constantinople*, and in the sight of the Emperor *Iustinian* that fauour'd him, and excommunicated the Empresse *Theodora* his wife, who did obstinately maintaine him; and ordained *Menas* priest of *Constantinople* Patriarke in his steede? *Agapet* (saith *Marcellinus Comes* an author of the same tyme) *being come from Rome to Constantinople, draue away* Anthymus *soone after his arriuall, from the Church, saying; that according, to the Ecclesiasticall rule he was an adulterer, because hee had left his Church, and had vnlawfully procured another; and ordained the priest Menas Bishop in his roome:* And *Liberatus* one likewise of the same tyme with *Marcellinus Comes*, saith; *The Empresse in secret promising great presents to the Pope, if he would leaue Anthymus in his Seate; and on the other side prouoking him with threates, the Pope persisted not to harken to her demaund: And Anthymus seing he was cast out of his Seate, gaue vp his Mantle to the Emperor, and retired himselfe where the Empresse tooke him into her protection, and then the Pope for the Emperors sake, ordained Menas Bishop in his steede; consecrating him with his owne hands:* And *Victor of Tunes* of the same tyme with *Liberatus* published by *Ioseph Scaliger*; Agapet (saith he) *Archbishop of Rome, came to Constantinople, and deposed Anthymus Bishop of Constantinople vsurper of the Church* (for it must be read *peruasorem* and not *peruersorem*) *and enemy to the Councell of Chalcedon, and excommunicated the Empresse Theodora his Patronesse, and made at the same time Menas Bishop of the Church of Constantinople*: And the Emperor *Iustinian* himselfe: *We knowe* (saith hee) *that the like thing hath bene done in the case of Anthymus, who was deposed from the Seate of this royall cittie, by the most holy Bishop of the Ancient Rome Agapet, of sacred and glorious memorie.* For those that from these insuing words of *Iustinians; but he hath bene also deposed and condemned first by the sentence of this Prelate of holy memorie, and after of the sacred Synod heere celebrated doe inferre, that the finall deposition of Anthymus was not made by the Pope, but by the Councell of Constantinople*: doe not consider that the first clause of *Iustinian* speakes (as shall appeare heereafter) of the deposition of *Anthymus* from the Patriarkall Seate of *Constantinople*, which was done and perfected by the Pope; And the second speakes of the deposition of *Anthymus* from the Archbishopricke of *Trebisond*, which was begun by the Pope, but hauing bene tyed to certaine conditions, which the continuance of the Popes life did not permitt him to cleere, it was finished after his death by the Synod of Constantinople. But tyme presseth vs, lett vs hasten.

In Chron

Liberat. in breuiar. c. 12.

Vict. Tun. in Chron. edit. per Ios. Scalig. ad calc. Chron. Eus.

Iust. Noe. 42.

In chap 39

Ibid.

And why then when *Menas* Patriark of *Constantinople*, gaue his voyce in the Councell of *Constantinople* vpon the second deposition of *Anthymus*, that is to say, vpon his deposition from the archbishopricke of *Trebisond*, did he say, *we followe as you knowe the Sea Apostolicke, and obey him, and haue his communicants for ours, and condemne those that are condemned by him?*

Conc Cōst sub Men. act. 2.

And why then when the body of the Councell formed a sentence against the same *Anthymus*, is it couched in these termes: *We ordaine* (*following things well examined by the holy and blessed Pope, &c.*) *that he shall be cutt off from the bodie of the holy Churches of God, and cast out of the Archbishops Seate of Trebisond; and depriued from all dignitie and Sacerdotall action, and according to the sentence of the same holy Father, stript from the title of Catholicke.*

And why then (when the Emperor *Iustinian* would at the instance of the Empresse *Theodora* his wife, who was an *Eutychian* persecute Pope *Siluerius*, Agapits Successor) doth *Liberatus* Archdeacō of *Carthage* an *Africā* author, and of the same tyme, and that *Hincmarus* an ancient Archbishop of *Rhemes* cites vnder the title of a *Saint*, say, that the Bishop of *Patara* in

Lycia one of the prouinces of *Asia*, disswaded him from it, by the remonstrance that he made him, that there was noe temporall monarchie which was equall in extent, to the spirituall authoritie of the Pope? *He represented to him* (said Liberatus) *the iudgement of God vppon the expulsion of the Bishop of soe great a Sea, admonishing him, that there were manie kings in the world, but there was not one of them as the Pope, who was ouer the Church of the whole world, who had bene dispossessed of his seate.*

Libera. in breuiar. caus. Nestor. & Eutych. c. 22.

And why then when the same Emperor *Iustinian* would erect the first *Justinianea* of *Bulgaria*, the cittie where he was borne into the forme of a supernumerarie Patriarkship, did he ground his ordinance vpon the Vicarship and concession of the Pope? *Wee ordaine* (said hee) *that the Bishop of the first Justinianea, shall alwaies haue vnder his iurisdiction the Bishops of the Prouinces of the Mediterranean Dacia, of Dacia Ripensis, of Triballea, of Dardanea, of the vpper Misia, and of Pannonia, &c. and that in all prouinces subiect to him, he shall holde the place of the sea Apostolicke of Rome, according as things were defined by the most holy Pope Vigilius.*

Iust. Nou. 131.

And why then when *Rusticus* deacon of *Rome*, of the same tyme with *Justinian*, writt his booke against the *Ascephales*; did he make this graue exhortation to himselfe; *Remember that thou art a Christian, and a Deacon, and that of the most soueraigne Church of all the world?* And why then when the Bishops of *France*, celebrated the second Councell of *Tours*, 1048. yeares agoe, did they say, *our Fathers haue alwaies obserued, what the authority of the Prelates of the sea Apostolicke hath commaunded.*

Rusticus Diac. cont. Asceph. impress. Basil. Concil. Turon. 2. c. 21.

And why then when saint GREGORIE the *Great* (to whom I haue brought downe this information, as well because the *English* men deriue from him the originall of their *Mission* Ecclesiasticall, as because *Caluine* propoundes him for true and lawfull modell of the iurisdiction of Popes) reprehended 1027. yeares agone *Natalis* Bishop of *Salona* in *Dalmatia* for the fault that he had committed, for which he after did penance in deposing *Honoratus* Archdeacon of *Salona* notwithstanding Pope *Pelagius* letters) did he write to him, that such a disobedience had bene intollerable, euen in one of the fower Patriarkes? *If one of the fower Patriarkes* (said hee) *had committed such an act, soe great disobedience, could not haue escaped without a greeuous scandall.*

Greg. ep. l. 2. ep. 37.

And why then (when *Clementius* Primat of *Bysacia* in *Africa* had bene accused before the Emperor, and sent backe by the Emperor to the Sea Apostolicke,) doth the same S. GREGORY saie; *If there be anie faulte in the Bishops, I knowe not what Bishop is not subiect, to the Sea Apostolicke, if a faulte require it not, according to the reason of humilitie, we are all equall.*

Id. l. 7. ep. 64.

And why then when *John* Archbishop of *Larissa* in *Thessalia*, had vniustly and vnworthily condemned *Adrian* Bishop of *Thebes*, one of the Bishops of his iurisdiction, and that the Bishop of *Thebes* had appealed to *Rome* from him, did S. *Gregorie* ecclipse the Bishop and Bishopricke of *Thebes* from the iurisdiction of the Archbishop of *Larissa* his Metropolitan, and declared the Archbishop of *Larissa*, if euer he attempted more to exercise anie act of Metropolitan ouer him, interdicted from the sacraments, soe as they could not be restored to him, except at the howre of death, but with the leaue of the Bishop of *Rome*? *Wee ordaine* (said hee) *that thy brotherhood abstaine from all the iurisdiction which you haue formerly had ouer him, and ouer his Church?* And a while after, *that if in anie time, or for anie occasion whatsoeuer, thou shalt attempt to contradict this our statute, knowe that we declare thee depriued from the sacred communion, soe as it may not be restored to thee, except in the article of death, but with the leaue of the Bishop of Rome.*

Greg. ep. l. 2. ep. 46.

And why then finally, when the Patriarke of *Constantinople* had gotten the vpper hand of the other Patriarkes, did he continue to suffer appeales of causes from his iurisdiction to the Popes tribunall, and to acknowledge himselfe subiect and inferior to the Pope? *Iohn* priest of *Chalcedon* (saith S. GREGORIE, in the cause that he had against our Brother colleague *Iohn* Bishop of *Constantinople*) *hath had recourse according to the Canons to the Sea Apostolicke, and the cause hath bene determined by our sentence*: and againe pronouncing the restitution of *Athanasius* a priest, and a Religious man of *Lycaonia*, who had bene deposed and cast out of his monastery by the same *John* Patriarke of *Constantinople*, and had appeald to him: *Wee declare thee* (said hee) *to be free from all spott of heresie, and a Catholick &c. and giue thee free leaue to returne into thy Monasterie, and to holde there the same ranke as thou didst before.* And againe, *who doubts but the Church of Constantinople is subiect to the Sea Apostolicke, which the most Religious Emperor, and our brother Bishop of the same towne doe continually protest?* For as for the word vniuersall Bishop, wherein the Bishop of *Constantinople* desired to participate with the Pope, but vnder the Pope, and in the Empire of the *East*, forasmuch as *Constantinople* had bene erected into the title of the second *Rome*, it shall be answered in a chapter by it selfe: & for the refusall that S. GREGORIE made, to vse the title of vniuersall Bishop, though it had bene giuen to his Predecessors in the Councell of *Chalcedon*, it shal be satisfied in the same place, and shewed that it was because of the euill sence the word vniuersall Bishop might receiue, which was to signifie (only Bishop,) and soe exclude the other Prelates from the title of Bishops in chiefe, and of ministers and officers of God, and to hold them but for committees, and deputies of the vniuersall Bishop, as the same S. GREGORIE protestes when he saith; *If there be one that is vniuersall Bishop, all the rest are noe more Bishops*: and not to depriue himselfe from the superintendencie and iurisdictiō ouer all other Bishops of which he cryes cleane contrary: *If there be anie crime in the Bishops, I knowe noe Bishop but is subiect to the Sea Apostolicke: if noe crime require it, according to the reason of humilitie, we are all equall.*

Id.l.4.ep 82.

Id.l.5.ep. 64.

Id.l.7.ep. 63.

See chap. 34.

In chap. 34.

Greg.ep.l. 7.ep.37. & alib.

Of formed letters.

CHAPT XXVI.

The continuance of the Kinges answere.

THEN were alsoe in frequent vse, formed letters: by the commerce and contexture whereof, the communion was admirably exercised, amongst all the members of the Church, how farr soeuer they were distant one from an other in place.

THE REPLIE.

IT is true, but the center of this communion and of this Ecclesiasticall vnitie, which was exercised and entertained by the commerce of formed letters, was the Sea Apostolicke and the *Roman* Church. This appeares by S. *Ireneus* who cryes *to the Romā Church because of a principality* (that is to say, as it hath bene aboue manifested, because of the principalitie of the Sea Apostolicke) *it is necessary that euery Church should agree.* This appeares by S. *Cyprian*, who calls the *Roman* Church, the chaire of PETER, and the

Iren. cout. Valent.l.3.c. 3.

Cypr. ad Corn.ep.55.

principall Church, and the originall of Sacerdotall vnitie. This appeares by the lawe of the Emperor *Gratian*, which ordained, that the Churches should be deliuered to those that were in the Popes communion: *Hee ordained* (saith Theodoret) *that the sacred howses should be restored to those that cōmunicated with Damasus*: And a while after; *and this lawe was indefinitely executed in all nations*. This appeares by S. *Ambrose*, who writes, speaking of his Brothers comeing into one of the citties of the Isle of *Sardinia*: *He asked the Bishop of that place whether he agreed with the Catholicke Bishops, that is to saie*, (added he) *with the Roman Church*. This appeares by S. IEROME, who writes to Pope *Damasus*; *I am ioyned in communion with thy Blessednesse, that is to saie, with Peters chaire: I knowe the Church is built vpon that Rocke; whosoeuer is not in the Arke, he shall perish at the coming of the floud; he that eates the lambe out of this howse, is profane*: And a while after, *Whosoeuer gathers not with thee, scatters, that is to saie; whosoeuer is not of Christ, is of Antichrist*: And againe; *Send me word with whom I ought to communicate in Antioch, for the heretickes of Campes with those of Tharses haue noe other ambition but that they might vnder the authoritie of your communion, preache the three hypostosies according to the ancient vnderstanding*: And in an other place, *The while I cry, if anie of you be ioyned to Peters chaire he is mine; Miletius, Vitalis, Paulinus*, (soe were the 3. Patriarkes of Antioch called,) *say that they communicate with thee; if but one of them had said soe, I had belieued it, but nowe either two, or all three doe lye and therefore I couiure thy Blessednesse by the Crosse of our Lord, by the necessarie ornament of our faith, by the passion of Christ, &c. that thou signifie to me by thy letters with whom in Syria I ought to communicate*. This appeares by *Optatus* Bishop af *Mileuis* in *Africa*, who saith; *At Rome hath bene setled for Peter first the Episcopall chaire, in which the head of all the Apostles Peter hath sate, &c. to the end that in that only chaire, vnitie might be obserued by all, least the other Apostles should attribute to themselues each one his seuerall chaire, but that he might be a sinner and a schismatick, that against that only chaire, should erect an other*. And a little after; *To Peter then succeeded Linus, to Linus Clement, to Clement Anacletus, to Anacletus Euaristus &c. to Damasus Syricius who is at this day our Colleague, by which meanes all the world communicates with vs by the commerce of formed letters*. This appeares by saint CHRYSOSTOME who writes to Pope *Innocent*; *Let vs enioy the continuance of your letters, and of your charity, and those of all the rest which we enioyed before*. This appeares by saint AVSTIN who saies, *Cecilianus might well dispise the conspiring multitude of his enemies, seeing himself vnited by communicatorie letters with the Roman Church, in which the principalitie of the Sea Apostolicke hath alwaies florisht, & with other Countries from whence the Ghospell came into Africa*. This appeares by *Eulalius* Bishop of *Syracusa* who a while after S. *Austins* death disswaded *Fulgentius* an *African* afterward Bishop of *Ruspa* in *Africa* frō goeing to inhabite with the monkes of *Egipt* in the desertes of *Thebaidis*, because they were not in the communion of saint *Peter*: *The countrie*, (said hee) *whither thou desirest to trauaile a perfidious dissention hath separated them from the cōmunion of the blessed Peter: All those Religious men whose admirable abstinence is celebrated, shall not haue the Sacraments of the altar in common with thee*. This appeares by *Iohn* Patriark of *Constantinople*, who writt to Pope *Hormisdas*, in abiuration of *Acacius* memory: *Following* (said hee) *in all things the Apostolicke chaire; wee declare all that hath bene thereby decreed and therefore hope to be in one communion with you declared by the Sea Apostolicke, in which there is the integritie of Christian Religion and perfect soliditie, promising heereafter not to recite amidst the sacred misteries their names, that haue separated themselues from the communion of the Catholicke Church; that is to say, that consent not in all things with the Sea Apostolicke*.

Theod hist. eccl. l. 5. c. 2. Ibid. c. 3. Amb. de ob. frat. Ier. ad Dam ep 57. Ierom. ad Dam. ep. 58. Opt. Mileu. cont. Parm. lib. 2. Chrysost. ad Innocēt. ep. 1. Aug. ep. 162 Auth. vitæ Fulg. Fæliciano successori ipsius dicatæ. Ioan Episc. Const. ep ad Hormisd. tom. 2. Cōc.

This appeares by the Emperor *Iustiniā*, who writes in the lawe addressed to *Epiphanius* Patriark of *Constantinople; We preserue in all things the estate of the vnitie of the holy Churches, with the holy Pope of old Rome.* And in the lawe addressed to the Pope; *We haue had care to vnite and submitt all the Bishops of the East to the Sea of your Holynesse, &c. who are the head of all the holy Churches.* This apperes by *Menas* Patriarke of *Constantinople,* who said in the Councell of *Constantinople; Wee follow the Sea Apostolicke and obey it, and communicate with those that communicate therewith, and condemne those that it condemnes.* This appeares by the forme that saint GREGORIE left vs of the abiuration, that the Bishopes returning from Schisme, to the communion of the Church, made into the handes of the Apostolicke Procurators, which haue these wordes: *I Bishop of such a Cittie, hauing discerned the trapp of diuision wherein I was caught, after a longe and mature deliberation, I am returned by Gods grace with my pure and free will, to the vnitie of the Sea Apostolick, and that I may not be esteemed to returne maliciously or fainedly, I vowe and promise vnder paine of falling from myne Order, and vnder obligation of anathema to thee, and by thee, to the holy Prince of Apostles, Peter, and to his Vicar the most Blessed GREGORIE, or to his Successors, that by anie perswasion whatsoeuer, or in anie other manner, I will neuer returne to Schisme, from whence by our Redeemers mercy I haue bene deliuered, but that I will alwaies remaine in the vnity of the Catholique Church, and in the Communion of the Bishop of Rome:*

Cod. Paris Antwerp. & Geneu. tit. 1. l. 7. Cod tit. 1. l. 8. see aboue. Con. Cōst. sub. Men. act 4.

Greg. ep. l. 10. ep. 31.

And this finally appeares by the extract of the Councell of *Nicea* which is to be read at the end of the latine edition of the Councell of *Chalcedon* vnder the name of the extract of the Councell of *Nicea* for the composition of formed letters made by *Atticus* Bishop of *Constantinople;* but some manuscripts of the sixt Councell of *Carthage* testifie they were sent into the west by the same *Atticus*, with the other decrees of the Councell of *Nicea,* when the *African* Bishops requested them of him. For this extract ordained, that they should take the number of the firste Greeke letters of the names *Father, Sonn,* and *Holy Ghost,* the number of the first Letter of the Apostle *Peters* name, and of the author that writt, and of him to whom he writt, and of the bearer of the letter, and of the place from whence it was written, and the day of Paske, and adding them to the number of the *indiction* which then was currant, they should thereof make a summe, whose cipher should be added to the Epistle, to serue it for a forme and character. By meanes whereof when there was noe more occasion to doubt, who was either in communion with the *Roman* Church or saint *Peters* sea, or out of it, as the diligence of the Catholicke Emperors, and Kings haue in the West left noe subiect of that doubt this many ages, the necessity of these kind of letters hath ceased. And therefore soe farr off is it, that the vse of the letters formed or cōmunicatory whereof antiquity made vse, was a marke to shew, that the Church was then more manifest then nowe, as contrarywise it was a testimonie, that she was much harder to be discerned then she is at this present. For that which constrained them to vse this meanes, was the multitude, and confusion of heresies which were then in soe great number and soe mingled in aboade, and habitation amidst the Catholicke Church, as there was almost noe Towne, where there was not to bee found, besides the true Church, a dozen Sects, and heresies, and the most of them agreeing in forme, and outward worship with the Catholicke Church; *Arians, Donatistes, Pelagians Nouatians Macedonians, Appolinaristes,* and other such like plagues.

Manusc. Conc. Carth. 6. D. Præsidis de Champigny. Attic. episc. qualiter formata epistola fiat. In fin. editionis latine Conc. Chalc.

( )

Of

Of the pretended excommunications attempted against the Pope.

CHAP. XXVII.

BVt against this thesis, to witt that the Sea Apostolicke was the Center and beginning of all the formed and communicatory letters, the Popes aduersaries obiect three instances; first, that *Stephen* Patriarke of *Antioch*, in the false Councell of *Sardica* excommunicated Pope *Julius* because he had admitted saint ATHANASIVS into his communion. The second, that saint HILARY proclaymed anathema against Pope *Liberius*, because he had receiued the *Arians* into his communion. And the third, *Dioscorus* Patriarke of *Alexandria* in the false Councell of *Ephesus*, excommunicated the Pope saint *Leo* the first, because he had condemned the heresie of *Eutyches*. And from hence they conclude, that the Pope was not then the center, and originall of Ecclesiasticall communion, since that, as the Pope excommunicated the other Patriarkes, Archbishops, and Bishops; soe the others reciprocally excommunicated him: And therefore it is best to blocke vp their obiections before we passe further.

Epist Syn. Ori.apud. Sardic.in append. fragm.Hilar. Soz hist.eccl l.3.c 10. & alij. Frag. Hil.de Syn.Arim. Cõc. Chalc. act.3.& in relat.ad Leon. Pap

To the first then of these obiections, which is that *Stephen* Patriarke of Antioch, excommunicated, Pope *Iulius*, because he had receiued saint ATHANASIVS into his communication, we bring three answeres: The first answere is, that it was not *Stephen* Patriarke of Antioch that made this excommunication, but it was all the Bishops assembled at the false Councell of *Sardica*, which pretended to be the true and whole oecumenicall Councell of *Sardica*, forasmuch as they said, the three hundred Catholicke Bishops which constituted the true Councell of *Sardica*, were fallen into the communion of *Marcellus* whom they held an hereticke of the heresies of *Sabellius* and of *Paulus Samosatenus*, and thefore imagined, that the true and intier authoritie of the oecumenicall Councell of *Sardica*, was deuolued to them. Nowe there is great difference betweene saying, that a Councell that pretendes to be oecumenicall, and conceaues it selfe to represent the vniuersall Body of ihe Church should vndertake to excommunicate a Pope, that they suppose to haue fallen into heresie, and that a particular Bishop Archbishop or Patriarke should vndertake it.

Epist.Syn. Sard & Soz vbi supra. Soc.hist.eccl.l.2.c.16.

The second that the false Councell of *Sardica*, which committed this presumption, was an *Arian* Councell, and whose entreprise consequently cannot be drawne into example, nor make any president against the discipline of the Church. For what meruaile is it that the *Arians* who trode vnder foote, the diuinitie of Christ, who is the inuisible head of the Church, should likewise tread vnder foote, the authority of his principall lieuetenant, that is to say, the Pope, who is the visible head of the Church?

Athã. Apol. 2. Aug ep. 163. Soz hist.eccl l 3.c.10

And the third, that in the same tyme, that the false Councell of *Sardica* spitt in the face of heauen, and excommunicated not only the Pope but IESVS-CHRIST himselfe, and all his Church in reiecting the communion of them, that held him to be consubstantiall with the Father; the true Councell of *Sardica*, compounded of more then three hundred Catholicke

Soc hist.eccl.l.2.c.16.

licke Bishops, acknowledged the Pope for head of the Church, and writt to him; *It seemes verie good and conuenient that the Prelates of all the Prouinces should referre the affaires to their head, that is to saie, to the Sea Apostolicke of Peter.* Ep. Conc. Sard. ad Iul. Pap. in tert. in- fragm. Hilar. & citat a Nicol. I. in ep. ad Episcop. Galliar.

To the second obiection, which is, that after that *Liberius* being cast out from the Sea of *Rome* by the *Arians*, and ouercome with the induring a farr banishment, and manie corporall persecutions & vexations forgott himselfe so farr, as to subscribe the condemnation of saint ATHANASIVS, and to receiue the *Arrians* into his communion; saint HILLARIE reciting the Epistles of the same *Liberius* insertes these clauses; *This is the Arrian treacherie, this I haue noted I that am noe Apostata*: And againe; *Anathema for my parte, to thee ô Liberius, & to thy Complices*; And a while after; *Anathema to thee the secōd, & third tyme, ô wicked Liberius*, we bring fower answeres. Hilar. in fragm. de Syn. Arim. p. 48.

The first answere is, that though it be certaine, and not to be doubted, that this is written by an ancient author, and of saint HILLARIES tyme, as besides the antiquitie of the manuscriptes, which are to be found in sundrie libraries, it appeares both by the manner of that stile, which fullie agrees with that of saint HILLARIES age, and by manie things which are there recited, which could not haue bene knowne but by the authors of saint HILLARIES age; neuerthelesse, it is not equally certaine, that it is S. HILLARIES. Contrariwise there are fower cōiectures, which seeme to intimate, that either it should be *Hillaries* the *Luciferian* deacon, of the same tyme with saint HILLARIE, or some other authors of the same Sect, and age, which haue supposed it, and made it passe vnder the name of saint HILLARIE; or that the *Parentheses* which are inserted into *Liberius* his Epistles that he cites, which also are inserted in forme of notes, and marked with signes of a crosse at the head, and enuirond with semye-circles, and written in an other character, are not saint HILLARIES, but some exemplaristes of that age.

The first coniecture is, that these *Parentheses* condemne the Faith of the Councell of *Sirmium* which *Demophilus* caused *Liberius* to signe; that is, the Faith of the first Councell of *Sirmium*, which did not err but in the omission of the word *Homousion* (for *Demophilus* as the Illustrious Cardinall *Baronius* hath obserued, abhorred the Faith of the Second, which denied both *Homousion* and *Homœusion*) and calls it, an *Arrians* treachery, where saint HILLARY contrariwise to spare and husband the demy-*Arrians*, which held the first confession, and to oblige them to bandie against the compleate *Arrians*, which held the second, stiled in his workes of the Synodes; *The faith of the first Councell of Sirmium*, or rather, *the first faith of the Councell of Sirmium orthodoxall and Catholicke*. And saith speaking of the Bishop *Eleusius*, Bishop of *Cyrica*, and of the other demy-*Arrians* which embraced it, *except the Bishop Eleusius, and a few others with him; the ten Asian prouinces wherein I dwell, for the more parte doe not know God truly.* Anual. tō. 3. ad an. 357. Hilar de Syn. Hilar. Ibid

And it will not serue for an antidote for this that *Monsieur de Feure*, who published that worke, saith that the *Arrians* yet made another profession of Faith composed at *Sirmium* in the presence of the Emperor, in the yeare of the Councell of *Arimini*, where they abolished the word. *Substance* For this last confession of Faith was made after *Liberius* his falle, and not before, as some haue thought, not considering that *Liberius* suffered two banishements, confounded by Socrates, but distinguished by *Sozomene*: The one when hee was confined into *Beroe* in *Thrace*, which began according to *Amianus Marcellinus* account, and that of *Sulpitius Seuerus*, the yeare wherein *Arbitio* and *Lollianus* were consulls; that is, fower yeare before Nic. Fab. in præf. fragm Hilar. Soc. hist. eccl. l. 2. c. 29. Soz. hist. ecc. l. 4 c. 10. & 14. & c. 18. Am. Marc. hist. l 15. Sul. Seu. hist. Sacr. l. 2.

Ath.ad Solitar. Theod.hist eccl.2.c. 17.

the Consulate of *Eusebius* and *Hypatius* vnder which the Councell of *Arimini* was held, and lasted according to saint ATHANASIVS and *Theodoret*, two yeares. And the other by which he was simplie cast out of *Rome*, which fell out after the Councell of *Arimini*, because *Liberius* refused to consent to it. *They report* (saith *Sozomene*, speaking of those who described more truly the history of the Councell of *Arimini*) *that the Arrians constained the Bishops to signe their confession, and cast out of the Church manie which resisted it, and in the first place Liberius Bishop of Rome*. Now *Liberius* falle was in the end of his first banishement as saint HILLARY insinuats, when he reproacheth to the Emperor *Cōstantius*, that he had plucked *Liberius* out of *Rome*, and that he was vncertaine whether he had shewed more impietie in his banishement, or in his repeale: And as saint IEROM affirmes when he saith, *Liberius overcome with the wearinesse of his banishment, and hauiug subscribed to the Arrian impietie, was entred into Rome in manner of a conqueror*. And thefore the faith of *Sirmium* which *Liberius* had signed before his fall, which happened at the end of his first exile; that is to saie, two yeare before the Councell of *Arimini*, could not be that which was forged at *Sirmium* the yeare of the Councell of *Arimini*, but it was the first of *Sirmium*; which *Sozomene* also ratifies when he saith, that, *Those of the East brought a forme of Faith, that they had drawne from Liberius, by which he condemned those that did not affirme, that the Sonne was like to the Father in substance, and in all things*. For that was the first Creede poposed to the Councell of *Sirmium*, and embraced by the *Demy-Arrians*, which concealed the word *Consubstantiall*, and insteede thereof, substituted, *like in substance*.

Soz.hist. eccl,l.4 c. 18.

Hilar.de Syn.

Hier.in Chron.

Soz.hist. eccl.l.4.c. 14.

The second coniecture is, that the Latine translation of the faith of the false Councell of *Sardica*, which is inserted into the Appendix of the Epistles, which is annexed to the end of this writing, which *Monsieur le Feure* will haue to bee gathered by the same *Author*, is so differing not in sence, but in wordes, from that which is found in the worke of the Synodes of saint HILLARY, that it seemes, they could not both come from one pen; and besides, it is noted with this Title; *The decree of the Arrians*; whereas saint HILLARY in his booke of the Synodes, to spare the *Demy-Arrians*, which held the Simbole of the false Councell of *Sardica*, and to oblige them to bandy against the *compleate Arrians*, whose impietie was proceeded much farther in their latter professions; reckons the Faith of the false Councell of *Sardica*, amongst the orthodoxall beleifes, supplyed by interpretation; that it might receiue, an orthodoxall interpretation, and was not hereticall by expression, but by omission.

Append ep ad Calcem. fragm.Hilar p. 27.

The third coniectures is, that in the tyme this writing intitled from saint HILLARY, was composed; that is to saie, after the Councell of *Arimini*, neither saint HILLARIE, not anie other Catholicke, could say *Anathema* to *Liberius* whose fault and repentance were both arriued before the Councell of *Arimini*; but only the *Luciferians*, who withdrew themselues from the communion of *Liberius* and of the Catholicke Church after the death of *Constantius* because that when *Constantius* was dead, *Liberius*, and the other Bishops, and Catholickes, receiued into the communion of the Church, and to the exercise of the Episcopall order, those Bishops which hauing bene induced by fraude or force, to signe the councell of *Arimini* protested to repent it. For when this writing was made; that is to say, after the Councell of *Arimini*, *Liberius* was acknowledged for a Catholicke, by all the Catholicke Bishops of the Earth, and was so, euer after the Councell of *Arimini*, euen to the end of his life, as it appeares both by the testimonie of the Councell of the West, celebrated vnder *Damasus*, imediate successor to *Liberius*, which disanulling the

acts

acts of the Councell of *Arimini*, alleaged amongst other nullities, that the Bishop of *Rome whose sentence should be attended before all others, neuer cõsented to it*. And by the testimony of saint BASILE, who solicites saint ATHANASIVS, *to write to the Bishop of Rome, to be watchfull ouer the affaires of the East, and send some to disannull the Councell of Arimini*: and testifies that the Catholicks of the *East*, and namely the Councells of *Militina* and *Tyana*, communicated with *Liberius*; and himselfe calls him *the blessed Bishop* Liberius: And by the testimonies of saint EPIPHANIVS, who writeth; *Eustathius Bishop of Sebaste in Armenia the lesse, seemed to doe the office of a Legate with many other Bishops, to the blessed Liberius of Rome; and subscribed to the proposition of the councell of Nicea, and to the profession of the orthodoxall Faith*. And by the testimonie of saint AMBROSE, who intitles *Liberius* after his Death, *Liberius of happie memory*. And finally, by the testimonie of *Siricius* imediate Successor to *Damasus*, who saith; *The generall decrees of my Predecessor Liberius of Reuerend memorie, sent through all the prouinces after the disannulling the Councell of Arimini, forbad to rebaptise the Arrians when they returned to the Church*. By meanes whereof either this writing which anathematizeth *Liberius* after the Councell of *Arimini*, is not saint HILLARIES, but of some *Luciferian* author of the same age, or these parenthesises inserted by forme of notes, in the Epistles of *Liberius*, inuironned with Semycircles, and written in other caracters: *this is the Arrian trechery, this I haue noted, I that am noe Apostata*: And a while after; *I for my parte, saie anathema to thee Liberius, and to thy complices*: And againe; *Anathema to thee for the second & third time, ô wicked Liberius*; haue bene interlaced by the *Luciferians*; or saint HILLARIE inserted the parenthesis into the Epistle of *Liberius*, before he made this writing; and hauing in this writing left the places, voide, to put iu the Epistles which he cited, whose Collection was a parte in his papers; those that caused them to be published after his death, sett into the voide blancke places which he had left, the copies of the Epistles which were amongst his papers, as they were there found.

And the fowrth coniecture finallie is; that this writing is not a compleate, and intire writing of saint HILLARIES, but a collection of diuers fragments of the intier worke of saint HILLARIES, put together in a heape, and without order; as may appeare by the transposition of the Epistles there inserted; and particularlie, of one of *Liberius* Epistles, which is sett in the place, where the Epistle of the Councell of *Sardica*, to *Constantius* should haue bene. By occasion whereof it remaines vncertaine, whether these parenthesis be of the author or of the collector; that is. either of saint HILLARIE, or of some *Luciferian* compiler, who to fauor the Schisme of the *Luciferians*, and to make the memorie of *Liberius* odious, and adhominable, hath thrust in these parenthesis. And this is spoken of the first answere.

The second answere against saint HILLARIES pretended *anathema* against *Liberius*, is that there is great difference, betweene an excommunicatiõ, and an *anathema*; for asmuch as every formall excommunication importes iurisdiction; and euery *anathema* doth not soe. For there are two kinds of *anathema*, the one iudiciarie the other executory, applicatorie, and adiuratory. Iudiciary *anathema's* are those which are pronounced by persons constituted in the Ecclesiasticall Tribunall, and which haue power to iudge of matters of Religion, and who decree what kindes of things, or persons ought to be anathematized; and these *anathema's* import iurisdiction, as when the Councell of *Nicea* pronounced *anathema* against the Arrians in these wordes: *they that saie there was a time wherein the sonn was not, the Catholick Church anathematizeth them*; that is to saie, decideth that their

Theod. hist. eccl. l. 2. c. 22.

Bas. ep. ad. Athan.

Id. ep. ad Occident. Epiph. cõt. Aer. her. 75.

Amb. de Verg. l. 3. Syric. ad Himer. Tarracou.

Fragm. Hil p. 35. & 36

Sac. hist ec. cl. l. 1. c. 5.

Communiō ought to be renounced and abhorred, and held for *anathema*. The *anathema's* executory, applicatory, and abiuratory, are those by which euery particular person doth protest, and declare, that hee will practise the sentence of the Church decreed against those persons, or doctrines which haue bene by her iudiciarily anathematized and to abiure, and hold them for *anathema*. And for this cause, iudiciary *anathema's*, cannot be pronounced but by persons grounded vpon iurisdictiō: but executory, and abiuratory *Anathema's*, may be made not only by persons destitute of iurisdiction, but by meere laie men: As in the Councell of *Ephesus*, when *Cordanepius* a lay man returned from the Sect of the *Quartodecumanes* to the Church, he anathematized all those that followed the Sect of the *quartodecumans*; *I anathematize* (saith hee) *all heresie, and namely that of the quartodecumans*. And to this day when anie one returnes from anie heresie into the Catholicke Church, he is caused to anathematize that heresy from whence he departs. But these *anathema's*, are but simple abiuratory *anathema's*; that is to saie, they are but bare executions, and applications, of iudiciary *anathema's*; and the word *to Anathematize* in such a case, signifies noe other thing, but to abiure, abhorr, and hold them for anathematized.

Conc. Ephes. part.2.act. 6.

Now it was in this second sorte that saint HILLARIE anathematized *Liberius*, for hauing signed and subscribed the communion of the *Arrians*; to wit, not with a iudiciary, but with an abiuratory *anathema*. For the iudiciarie *anathema* had bene already pronounced by the councells of *Nicea*, and of *Sardica*, against the *Arrians* into whose coummunion *Liberius* was entered, soe as there was noe more question to decree the sentence of *anathema* against him, but to execute it in abiuring and abhorring him, as fallen into the sentence of *anathema* pronounced against the Arrians in the Councells of *Nicea* and *Sardica*; and therefore saint HILLARY adds to his *anathema* this word, *for my parte*, and saith, *for my parte anathema to thee ô Liberius*; to shewe that he spake not with a iudiciary *anathema*, but with an *anathema* abiuratory, and abnegatory whereby hee did not seperate *Liberius* from the communion of the Church, who had alreadie seperated himselfe, in departing from her to the *Arrians*, but whereby he seperated himselfe from the communion of *Liberius*.

Soc. hist. eccl. l.2.c.5. Theod. hist. eccl. l.4.c.6.

The third answere containes two branches; the one is, that this *anathema* was not pronounced by saint HILLARIVS, in the tyme of vnitie and agreement of Popes, but in tyme of Schisme and duplicitie of Popes; to witt, when *Liberius* and *Felix* sate concurrently in the Pontificall chaire of *Rome*. Now there is great differēce between pronouncing *anathema* against a doubtfull Pope, and sitting in Schisme with another Pope; and pronouncing *anathema* against one only certaine and peaceble Pope: for in the first case; to witt, in case of Schisme betweene two Popes, it is an ordinary thing, that those that take parte with the one, doe pronounce abiuration and *anathema* against the other; as during the Schisme of *John* 23th. and of *Gregorie* the twelfth and of *Bennet* the 13th. for whose extinction the Councell of *Constance* was kept; those that tooke parte with any one of these three Popes pronounced abiuration, and *anathema* against the other two; without pretending notwithstanding to departe from the reuerence, and obedience due to the Sea Apostolicke. And therefore during the Schisme of *Liberius* and *Felix*, saint HILLARY might pronoūce *anathema* against *Liberius* and seperate himselfe from his communion and enter into the communion of the other Pope, without seperating himselfe euer the more from the communion of the Sea Apostolicke.

Soz. hist. eccl. l. 4.c. 14.

The other is, that this *anathema* was not pronounced by S. HILLARY in the tyme that the *Roman* Church acknowledged him for Pope, but in the tyme that *Liberius* was fallen from the Papacie, and that euen the *Roman* Church abiured, renounced, and disauowed him for Pope, and had withdrawne herselfe from his communion, and from his obedience, and had ranged herselfe with *Felix* his competitor. For the vnderstanding whereof, we must distinguish the tyme of Pope *Liberius* Popedome into thee partes; the first before his falle, the second during his fall, the third after his fall. Now during the first parte, to witt, before his falle; he was so firme a defender of the Faith of the Councell of *Nicea*, and of saint ATHANASIVS innocencie, and soe great an enemy to the heresie, and communion of the *Arrians*, as the Emperor *Constantius* for that cause made him be tiranously carried away, and transported by way of banishment into the cittie of *Beroe*, in the borders of *Thrace*; and at the instance of the *Arrians*, caused *Felix* the deacon of *Rome* to be ordained in his steede. During the second parte, which began at his banishmẽt, he ouercome with the length of two yeares exile, and other corporall vexations and persecutions, he suffered himselfe to be drawne to signe the condemnation of S. *Athanasius*, and to admitt the cõmunion of the *Arrians*, and entered into *Rome* with a promise, to continue in that resolutiõ; & then the *Roman* Church ceased to acknowledge him for Pope. For Popes that falle visiblie, and by their owne confession, or not contested signature into an heresie notorious, & cõdemned by a precedent sentence of the Church, or into cõmunion with an hereticall societie, as was that of the *Arrians* falle from the Papacie, from that tyme cease from their right of being Popes. And *Felix* on the other side, who was entred by the packe of the *Arrians* into his place, made himselfe so firme a protector of the Catholicke Faith and Communion, and so constant an aduersary of the *Arrians* as the *Roman* Church (if wee beleiue the ancient inscriptions, and the ancient martirologes, where *Felix* is intitled Pope and *Martyr*, and the ancient Catalogues of the Popes, where he is put into the ranke of the Popes, by the name of *Felix* the second) making valid by a new election, or an acceptation equiualent to a new election the ordination of *Felix*, receaued him for Pope in *Liberius* steede, I haue said, if we beleiue the ancient inscriptions, and martyrologes, and the ancient Catalogues of the Popes. For many moderne authors, and *Onuphrius* amongst the rest, hold that *Felix* was neuer true Pope, and that *Liberius* neuer fell from the Papacie, nor euer receiued the *Arrians* into his communion; And they beleiue, that all that saint ATHANASIVS, saint HILARY, and other ancient writers haue written, was grounded vpon a false rumor, that the *Arrians* had spread; And they alleadge for this purpose *Ruffinus*; that saith, he could neuer discouer the truth of it; *I cannot discouer* (saith Ruffinus) *certainly, whether the Emperor Constantius sent backe Liberius to Rome, because he had yeilded to his will, or because he was pressed to it by the Romans.* And *Sozomene* who reportes that the *Arrians* spread the rumor, that *Liberius* had condemned *Consubstantialitie*; *The Arrians* (said he) *spread the rumor, that Liberius had condemned the word consubstantiall.* Neuerthelesse for as much as saint IEROM, speakeing of *Liberius* his exile, writeth, *Liberius Bishop of the Roman Church hauing bene sent into exile for the Faith, all the Clerkes swore they would receiue noe other but Felix, hauing bene substituted in the priesthood by the Arrians; manie periured themselues, and at the end of the yeare were cast forth, because Liberius ouercome with the wearynesse of his banishement, and signing the hereticall impietie, entred into Rome in the forme of*

Theod. hist. eccl. l. 2. c. 16.

Hier. in Chron.

An. Bar. to. 3 ad an. 357. Martirol. Rom. ad quart. Cal. Aug. Martirol. tribut. Bedæ in eodem Die. Anast. Bib. in lib. de vit Pontific. Onuph. in notis. ad. platin. & alij.

Ruff. hist. eccl. l. 1. c. 27.

Soz hist. eccl. l. 4. c. 14.

Hier. in Chron.

Id. de scrip. Eccles. *a Conqueror*. And in an other place; *Fortunatianus Bishop of Aquilea, is in this reputed detestable, that he first solicited Liberius who was gone into banishment for the faith, and inclined him, and induced him. to signe the heresie.* We followe the opinion of those that hold, that during the tyme interposed betweene the returne of *Liberius*, and the death of *Felix*, *Liberius* remained fallen from the Popedome, and that *Felix* was then true Pope. For there is noe doubte, but that the Clerkes which were cast forth with *Felix*, *because* (saith saint IEROM) *Liberius hauing signed the hereticall impietie, was entred into Rome like a Conqueror*, were the orthodoxall and Catholicke Clerkes of the *Roman* Church, who did materially periure themselues because they abandoned *Liberius*, but not formally because *Liberius* first abandoned himselfe.

Soz. hist. eccl. l. 4. c. 14. And in the third tyme which began after the death of *Felix*, which if we beleeue *Sozomene*, followed soone after the returne of *Liberius*: *Liberius* not onely abiured that which the *Arrians* had constrained him to doe, but made himselfe so constant a protector of the Catholicke Faith, and cause, and so despised all the persecutions of the Emperor, as the *Roman* Church after the death of *Felix*, and all the other Churches of the Catholicke communion with her, did receiue and acknowledge him with an acknowledgement equiualent to rehabilitation, for Pope. In which appeared two actes of the prouidence of God, with had appeared in saint *Peters* fall: One, that as saint *Peter* in the rising from his fall, confirmed his Bretheren; so *Liberius* in rising from his, confirmed all the Bishops of the Catholicke Church, shewing them the way rather to suffer a thousand persecutions, then to signe the Councell of *Arimini*: And the other, that as the Fathers noted, that God permitted saint *Peter* to fall, that he might learne by his owne example to vse mercie to those that should fall, and not to vse that rigor to them, that the *Nouatians* would afterward haue introduced: so God permitted that *Liberius* should fall into the communion of heretickes, to the end that being restored, he might learne by his owne example, and serue himselfe for an example to others, not to shutt the gates of Episcopall cōmunion from those Bishops that should fall into the same faulte, when they should come to repentance, and not to vse that rigor toward them, that afterward the *Luciferians* would haue introduced. Now it was in this meane while, to witt, when the *Roman* Church, abiured *Liberius*, because he had receiued the *Arrians* into his communion, and ceased to acknowledge him for Pope, and had reduced themselues into the obedience of *Felix*, that saint HILARY (if as is abouesaid, these *parenthesis* be his) adhering to the *Roman* Church, abiured him also, and anathematized him, not with a iudiciary, but with an applicatory and abiuratory *anathema*: and by consequence, the obiection which is drawne from it, is not onely vnprofitable, but impertinent. For what meruaile is it, if in this meane while, to witt; when the *Roman* Church herselfe, abiured *Liberius*, and withdrew herselfe from his obedience, and ceased to acknowledge him for Pope, and tooke *Felix* his part; saint HILARY adhering to the *Roman* Church, did abiure him, and anathematize him also, not with a iudiciary *anathema*, but with an executory and abnegatory *anathema*, and tooke likewise the parte of *Felix*, to whom the orthodoxall Clerkes and inhabitantes of the cittie of *Rome*, had ranged themselues? The great and admirable DAMASVS, who was after successor to *Liberius* in the Popedome, and whom the *Greekes*, called the *diamond of Faith*, had not he bene one of those that had withdrawen themselues from the communion of *Liberius*, and had transferred themselues to that of *Felix*? and so what wonder is it, if *Liberius* owne successor, and all the true *Roman* Church with him, hauing ceased to acknowledge *Liberius* for Pope, and hauing abandoned and anathematized him, that is to saie, with an executory and abiuratory *anathema*, and hauing acknowledged *Felix* his Competitor for true, and lawfull Pope; S. HILARY also in their imitation ceased to account *Liberius* for Pope, and anathematized him, not with a iudiciary, but with an executory and abiuratory *anathema*, in withdrawing himselfe from his communion, and passing to that of *Felix*.

Marcel. in lib. de schis. Damas. & Vrcic. apud Baron. Annal. tom. 3. & 4. ad an. 357. & 367 & Biblioth Sereniss. Reip. Venet.

And finally the fowrth and last answere, is, that as in tyme of schisme and duplicity of Popes, S. HILARY following the orthodoxall and Catholicke part of the Clergie of *Rome*, adhered to *Felix*, and anathematized *Liberius*; so in the tyme of the vnitie of Popes, the same S. HILARY testifies, that all Catholickes acknowledged the Pope for head of the Church. For he reportes the epistle of the Councell of *Sardica*, wherein the Bishops of the Councell writt these wordes to Pope *Iulius*, *Liberius* predecessor; *It shall be esteemed verie good and conuenient, if from all prouinces the Bishops should referr the affaires to their head, that is to saie, to the Sea Apostolicke of Peter*; And thus much of the second obiection, there remaines third.

Epist. Côc. Sard. ad Iul. in frag. Hil. p. 15.

To the third obiection then, which is, that *Dioscorus* in the false Councell of *Ephesus*, did not content himselfe to excommunicate *Flauianus* the Archbishop of *Constantinople*, but went so farr as to excommunicate Pope *Leo* who vpeld him, Wee answere three things; first, that it was not vnder his owne name that *Dioscorus* Patriark of *Alexandria*, decreed this excommunication but vnder the name of all the false Councell of *Ephesus*, which had bene called in the qualitie of an *Oecumenicall* Councell, and which intitled it selfe an *Oecumenicall* Councell. By meanes whereof, this instance toucheth not the question, whether another Bishop, Archbishop, or Patriark may excommunicate the Pope, but whether a Councell *Oecumenicall*, pretẽding that the Pope is fallen into heresy, may excõmunicate him.

Côc. Chalc act. 1.

The second, that *Dioscorus* was deposed for this presumption in the Councell of *Chalcedon*, and depriued for all eternity, not onely of the title of Patriark, but also of the title of *Christian* and *Catholicke*, in such sort, as this example is so farr from making against the Pope, as it falls vpon their heades that alleadge it.

Id. act. 3. & in relat. ad Leon. Pap.

And the third, that there was so great difference betweene the enterprise of excõmunicating the other Bishops, Archbishops, & Patriarkes, and presumption of excommunicating the Pope, as although *Dioscorus* Patriark of *Alexandria* was an Arch-hereticke, and that he had approued in a full Councell the heresy of *Eutiches*, and condemned the orthodoxall doctrine, and had excommunicated, and not onely excommunicated, but put to death *Flauianus* Archbishop of *Cõstantinople*, who maintayned the true faith: Neuerthelesse, these things were not set amongst the principall causes of his deposition, but the presumption that he had committed in vndertaking *He* and his false Councell to excommunicate the Pope; and the contempt that he had added to it, in not comeing to yeild reason for this presumption to the Councell of *Chalcedon*. *Dioscorus* (saith *Anatolius* Arch-bishop of *Constantinople*, speaking to the Councell of *Chalcedon*) *hath not bene deposed for the faith, but because he had excommunicated my Lord the Arch-bishop Leo, and that hauing bene thrice cited, he would not appeare*: And the Councell of *Chalcedon* in the epistle to Pope *Leo*, saith; *After all these things he hath extended his felonie euen against him, to whom the guarde of the Vine is committed by your Sauiour*,

Euag. hist. eccl. l. 2. c. 18.
Côc. Chalc act. 5.
Côc. Chalc part. 3. in relat. ad Leon.

that is to saie, against thy Holynesse, and hath mediated an excommunication against him, that striues to vnite the bodie of the Church; or according to the other edition; againct thee, who makest haste to vnite the bodie of the Church, that is to saie, against thee that holdest the bodie of the Church in vnitie. For with the *Greeks* it is a common phrase to saie, *to haste themselues to doe some thing*, in steede of saying, *to doe some thinge*; As when the Emperor IVSTINIAN writt to Pope *Iohn*, surnamed *Mercury*; *We haue made haste to submitt and vnite all the Prelates of the east countries to your Sea*: insteede of saying; *We haue vnited all the Prelates of the East, to your Sea.* And as when the Councell of *Ierusalem* said; *Anthymus made haste, to cast vs into a worse tempest*, insteede of saying; *Anthymus hath cast vs into a worse tempest.*

Cod Iust. lib 1. tit. 1. Conc. Hier in Concil. Const. sub Mena.

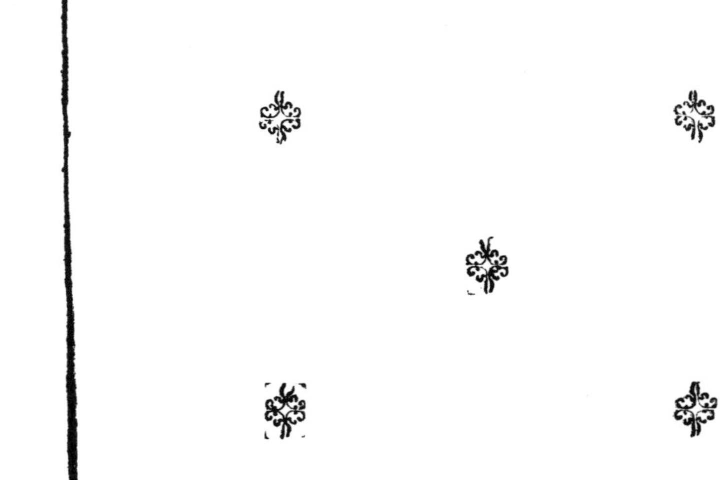

CARD PERRONS REPLIE

TO THE KING OF GREAT BRITANIE. THE SECOND BOOKE

CHAP. I.

Of Councells.

The continuance of the Kinges answere.

TO this were added alwaies, and as often as they were needefull, Councells truly Oecumenicall, and not as vve see, they haue bene often since Oecumenicall by name, but indeede assembled onely out of some prouinces of Europe.

THE REPLIE.

AND euen this also very often when there was noe neede of thē, as the Councell of *Arimini* compounded of more then 400. Bishops; the second Councell of *Ephesus*, called from all the Regions of the world, but assembled by hereticall Emperors, or gouerned by the abettors of heretickes; and from the vnlawfull celebration whereof; the one held without the Popes authority, and the other against it; the successe teacheth vs, that as much as Councells are profitable, whē the temporall authority seconds the Ecclesiasticall: as much are they pernicious, when temporall authority vndertakes to performe the office of Ecclesiasticall authority. Iointlie that as in human bodies, the multitude of medicines is not a signe of health; soe in the Ecclesiasticall bodie, the multitude of Councells, is not a signe of well being; witnesse the complaintes of S. *Gregorie Nazianz.* vpon the multitude of Councells holden after that of *Nicea*; of which he saith that he neuer sawe good come of them, that is to witt, as much because when the hereticall Emperors medled with the affaires of the Church, the ambition to please them, which was crept in among the Bishops, thwarted the iudgments of the Synod, as because the holding subsequent Councells vpon the same matter of those preceding them, was to wound and to weaken the authority of the preceding Councells. And then howe could the celebration of Councells haue bene a meanes, to make men assured of the communion of the true Church, if generall Coūcells lawfully assembled, that is, according to the externall solemne and vsuall waies, might erre in faith, as the *Protestants* pretend, and had not the infallible assistance of the holy Ghost, but that a particular man, esteeming his opinion agreeable to the sense of Scripture, and that of the Councell differing from it; might, yea ought to preferr his iudgement, before that of the Councell.

Sulp.Seu. l 2 & Soz. l 4. c. 17. Liberat in breuiar.c. 12. Theod.hist eccl.l. 2. c. 22. Libera.. c. 13. & Cōc. Chalc. act. 1.

Greg.Naz. ep. 42.

For whereas his Maiestie saith, that the Councells holden in the last ages, haue bene *Oecumenicall* in name, but in effect assembled onely from some prouinces of *Europe*, he may obserue if he please, that there are two sortes of *Oecumenicall* Councells; the one *Oecumenicall* indeede, the other *Oecumenicall* in right. I call those Councells *Oecumenicall* in deede, which haue bene assembled from all partes, wherein the succession of the Episcopall character is preserued, whether those parts haue remayned within the Body of the Church, or whether they haue bene cutt off from it. I call those Councells *Oecumenicall* in right, which are compounded onely of those partes which haue remayned within the body and Societie of the Church, and to whom onely, as such, belongs the right to iudge in matters of Faith: as the Councell of *Sardica*, at the which there assisted not the Bishops of the Patriarkeshipp of *Antioch*, because they were *Arrians*. And the second Councell of *Nicea*, at which the *Cophtes* (that is, the naturall *Egiptians* and *Ethiopians*) assisted not, because they were *Eutychians*. Now both these kindes of Councells, are of equall authority, as concerning certainty in decisions of Religion; for all the bodie of the true Church being there representatively, both in the one and the other, the assistance of the holy Ghost is there equally infallible.

Soc. hist. eccl. l. 2. c. 20.

But in regarde of euidence, the authoritie of *Oecumenicall* Councells in deede, is more powerfull and eminent, in the behalfe of those men which are deuided from the Church, then that of *Oecumenicall* Councells in right. For in Councells *Oecumenicall* in right, there are none but Catholicks, that are assured, that all the body of the Church is there assembled: whereas in Councells *Oecumenicall* in deede, each of the parties cōtesting, is of agreemēt, that all the Body of the Church is there represented. And the medley of hereticall or Schismaticall Bishops, that is prouided with the onely, succession of the Episcopall character, but cut of from the communion of the Bodie of the Church, hinders not, but that in such councells, the holy Ghost may worke by the common note of the Assemblie; because, the true Church receiuing those Bishops there (for the effect then present) into her charitie, and into her communion, while they are ioyned with her, to the end to seeke meanes to assemblish vnitie; she re-enables and restores to them for the tyme of the assemblie, the authoritie of the exercise, and of the Iurisdiction of their order whereof before, there remayned to them nothing but the character.

To say then that some of the Councells of the latter age, haue not bene *Oecumenicall*, because the Greekes or *Ethiopians* did not assist there, is not a valuable exception, vnlesse it first appeare that the *Greekes* or *Ethiopians* are true and lawfull partes of the Church, and haue not bene iustly cutt off and deuided from the Catholicke communion. For it sufficeth to make a Coūcell generall and vniuersall in right, that all the partes that remaine actuall within the Body & cōmuniō of the true Catholick church, doe concurr to it: and it is not requisite, that those that are lawfully seperated frō her either for Schisme or heresie, as are the *Greekes* who erre in the atticle of the procession of the holy Ghost, which his Maiestie himself holdes to be an article of Faith; & the naturall *Egiptians* & *Ethiopians* who erre in the Faith of the hipostaticall vnion, & in the qualitie of *Eutichians*, and *Monophysites*, are excluded frō the Bodie of the Church from before the fifth Councell, should assist to it. And notwithstanding yet euen in these last ages, there haue bene Councells *Oecumenicall* indeede, and in the sence whereto his Maiestie imployes this terme; when the partes seperated frō the Bodie of the Church whould haue conspired to some re-uniō: As that of *Lateran* vnder Pope *Innocent* the third where there where with the Pope, the Patriarckes of *Constantinople* and *Ierusalem*, and the

Matth. Paris. in Ioann. ad an. 1215. Platin. in Innoc. 3. Cēt. Magd. Ceutur. 13. c. de. Synod & alij.

legates

legates of those of *Alexandria* and *Antioch*, and more then 400. Bishops and 70. Archbishops, from all the partes of the Church, aswell *Greeke* as *Latine:* And that of *Florence* vnder *Eugenius* the fourth where assisted the *Greekes* with their Emperor and their Patriarke, and the Legates of three other Patriarkes, and the *Armenians*, and the deputies also of the *Ethiopians*; and in both these they were agreed of all the points of Faith which in these daies are againe put to question. From whence it appeareth, that the wante of Generall Councells, could not make the Church to be lesse acknowledgeable, in the last daies, then she was in the first. Act. Concil. Florent. Chalcocondyl de reb. Tur. Platin. Damiā Goes, & alij.

Of the effect of Councells for the visibilitie of the Church.

CHAPT II.

The continuance of the Kinges answere.

AND in the ancient tymes, it was a firme bond by which all the mēbers of the Catholicke Church were bound in the frame of one selfe Body, which body for this cause was meruailously noble and eminent, being so constituted in the view and knowledge of all, that none thought they would, could haue bene ignorant of her. One Faith, one policie, one Body of the Catholicke Church, a frequent visitation of the partes amongst themselues, a meruailous consent of all the members, an admirable simpathie.

THE REPLIE.

RAther some tyme these were the meanes, which heretickes, or those Emperors that fauored them made vse of, to shake and dissolue the masse and frame of the Body of the Church, frō whēce proceeded the complaintes of the Fathers, that after things had been once resolued of in the Church, they should noe more holde other newe Councells; that after the Councell of *Nicea*, euery other Councell was superfluous, and that they neuer sawe any good effect of all those Councells, as is by S. GREGORIE *Nazianzene* aboue said. And therefore these rich and magnificent amplifications of eloquence were noe impediments, but that the Church when *Luther* began might haue bene not onely as much, but more visible, illustrious, and eminent, then she was manie tymes in those ages; witnesse the obiections that the *Donatists* made to saint AVSTIN of the estate of the Church principallie in the East, in saint HILLARYS tyme, *Such was*, (said saint AVS;) *the tyme whereof Hillary hath written, from whence thou thinkest to sett ambushes for so manie deuine witnesses, as if the Church were thē perished from the Globe of the Earth.* And saint IEROM *because the East striking against herselfe by the ancient fury of her people, tore in little peeces the vnseamed coate of our Lord, wouen from aboue; and that the foxes destroyed the Vine of Christ, in such sort, as it is difficult amongst the dry pondes and which haue noe water, to discerne the sealed fountaine, and the inclosed garden; therefore I thought, I ought to consult with the Chaire of Peter and the Faith praised by the mouth of the Apostles.* For whereas his Maiestie adds that the Bodie of the Church was then set in such an eminence of view and knowledg, that she could not be vnknowne, noe not by those that would haue bene ignorant of her, this was verie true, if you tooke all Catholicke prouinces together, and com-

Aug. cont. Vinc. ep. 48.

Hier. ad Dā. ep. 57.

pared

pared them with euery particular Sect, and it had place in regarde of those that were within the bosome of the Church, which neither then nor since could haue bene ignorant of the Bodie and Societie of the true Church, for as much as they all agreed in the *hypothesis*, that the Church ought to be discerned by inimitable and indisputable markes, and that those that had them not, could not faine to haue them; as the communion with the Sea of saint PETER; the continued and not interrupted Succession of ministrie, and Doctrine; the eminencie, and vniuersalitie aboue all other *Christian* Sects taken euerie one a parte, and other such like.

Optat. Mileuit. l. 1. & 2. Hier. ad Dam. ep. 57 Aug. cont. epist. Fūd. & Psal. cōt. part Don. & alij.

But in regard of those that were seperated from it, as heretickes, and Schismatickes who would discerne the Church by markes more obscure then the thing itselfe, and such as all Sects perswade themselues to haue, to witt; by the conformitie of Doctrine with the scripture, interpreted according to the sentence of euerie particular man; there was nothing lesse euident. For to those, the Church how eminent soeuer she had been, hath alwaies been obscure, & hidden; not for the want of her light & eminencie, but because of their darknes and blindnes. *This*, saith saint AVS. *is common to all hereticks to be vnable to see the thing, that in the World is most manifest, and constituted in the light of all nations, out of Whose vnitie, Whatsoeuer they Worke, although they seeme to doe it With great care and diligence, can noe more profitt them against the Wrath of God, then the spider Webb against the extremitie of colde*. And againe *The Church is not hidden, for she is not vnder a bushell, but vpon a Candlesticke, to giue light to all that are in the HoWse*. And of her it is said; *The Cittie built vpon a Mountaine cannot be hidd, but she is as hidden to the Donatistes, Who heare so cleere and manifest testimonies Which demonstrate her to be spread ouer the Whole World, and yet had rather blindfold strike against the mountaine, then ascend it*. And other where; *hoW can I call those but blinde that see not so great a mountaine, and shutt their eyes against the lampe, sett vpon the candlesticke*.

Aug. cont. Parm. l. 2. c. 3.

Aug. de vnit. eccl. c. 14.

Id. in ep. Ioann. tract. 2.

Of the comparison of the Pope, with the other Patriarkes.

CHAP. III.

The continuance of the kinges ansWere.

IF anie one vvere fallen for heresie or Schisme from the communion of one of the Churches (I saie not one of the first, which vvere the Seates of the fovver Patriarckes, but of anie other of those, vvhich vvere much lesse) as soone as it vvas knovvne, he vvas reputed excluded, from the communion of all the Catholicke Church.

THE REPLIE.

IN the tyme of saint AVSTINE, there was yet but three true patriarchall Seates in the Church; I meane, invested with patriarchall Iurisdiction; to witt, *Rome*, *Alexandria*, *and Antioch*; *Ierusalem* hauing obtained noe patriarchall diuision, till the Councell of *Chalcedon*. For before it was but a simple Bishopricke, subiect itselfe in the first instance, to the Archbishop of *Cesarea*, and by appeale, to the

Patriarcke

Patriarck of *Antioch*: and not bearing the title of a Patiarcke, but onely as a name of honor to haue place in the Councells after the true Patriarckes, but not to exercise Iurisdiction ouer anie other diocesse.

This appeares both by the Councell of *Nicea* which perserues the title of honor to the Bishop of *Elia*, that is, to the Bishop of *Ierusalem*, alwaies sauing the dignitie of his owne Metropolitan, meaning the Archbishop of *Cesarea*. And by saint IEROM, who askes *John* Bishop of *Jerusalem* why he had recourse to the Sea of *Alexandria*, since the iudge of the Bishop of *Jerusalem* in the first instance, was the Archbishop of *Cesarea*, and in the second, hee of *Antioch*. *Thou* (saith hee) *which searchest out Ecclesiasticall rules and makest vse of the Canons of the Councell of Nicea &c. answere me, wherein doth Palestina belong to the Bishop of Alexandria? it is ordained, if I be not deceiued, that Cesarea should be metropolitan of Palestina; and Antioch of all the East: then either thou oughtest to haue referred they cause to the Bishop of Cesarea &c. or if there were cause to seeke a iudgement farther, thou shouldest rather haue writen to Antioch*: And a while after; *but thou hast rather chosen to importune eares alreadie possessed, then to yeild due honor to thy Metropolitan.* Cõc. Hic c.7. Hiero. ad Damas. con err. Ioann. Hierosol.

And finallie this appeare by the Councell of *Chalcedon* which assignes to *Iuuenall* Patriarck of *Ierusalem* for his first Patriarchall territorie, the three *Palestina's*. For that *Jerusalem* in the Councell of *Constantinople*, was called the mother of all the Churches; it was mother in antiquitie, and not mother in authoritie: And that in the Councell of *Ephesus*, *Iuuenall* Bishop of *Ierusalem* saith, according to the *Latine* translation of *Rome*, that the ancient custome, and the Apostolicall tradition was, that the Church of *Antioch* was to be directed by the Church of *Ierusalem*, it is a mistaking of the translator of *Rome*, who insteede of saying the *Roman* as *Peltanus* hath it, hath said the *Ierosolomitan*. For that the laste clause of the period, is to haue reference to the *Roman Sea*, as was done by *Peltanus*, and not to that of *Ierusalem* as the interpreter of *Rome* hath done, abusing himselfe with this that the word to obey gouernes the datiue, and not considering that the word, to honor, which is there added alters the rule, is verified by seauen vndoubted profes. Cõc. Chalc act. 7. Theod. hist eccl. l.5.c. 9. Conc. Ep. part.1.act. 4.

First it is verified by this, that the *greeke* text shoud also haue no construction, there being no verbe within the period to gouerne this *accusatiue, the throne Apostolicke of great Rome*, but the verbe *to honor*. It is secondly prooued, because alwaies the Bishops of *Rome*, and not those of *Ierusalem* haue iudged of the Councells of *Antioch*, as it hath bene aboue specified in the cause of *Paule Samosatenus*, and of of saint ATHANASIVS. It is thirdlie verified, because the nullitie propounded against the Councell of *Antioch* in saint ATHANASIVS time, was grounded not vpon the absence of the Bishop of *Jerusalem* who yet was no more there, then the Bishop of *Rome*, as *Socrates* notes, but vpon the absence of the Pope or his legates. It is verified in the fowrth place, because the Bishop of *Antioch* was so farr from being subiect to him of *Ierusalem*, that contrariwise the Bishop of *Ierusalem*, as hath lately bene shewed both by the testimonie of the Councell of *Nicea*, and by that of saint IEROM. was subiect in the first instance to the Bishop of *Cesarea* and by appeale, to him of *Antioch*. It is verified in the fifth place, because the same Councell of *Ephesus*, and in the presence of the same *Iuuenall*, sent backe the cause of *Iohn* Patriarcke of *Antioch*, to the Pope. It is verified in the sixt place, because in the Councell of *Chalcedon*, where *Iuuenall* was also present, the sentence of *Anatholius*, Bishop of *Constantinople* was, that *Maximus* Bishop of *Antioch* should remaine, for as much as Pope *Leo* hauing Soc. hist. eccl. l.2.c. 8. Cõc. Nicẽ. c.7. Hier. cont. error. Ioann. episc Hierosol. Conc. Ep. p.2. ep.5. in relat. ad celest. Cõc. Chalc act. 10.

receiued

receiued him into his Communion, had iudged that he should rule the Church of *Antioch*. And finallie it is verified, because in the generall Councell of *Constantinople* against the *Monothelites*, the cause of *Macarius* Patriarke of *Antioch* who had bene deposed by the Councell, was sent backe not to the Bishop of *Ierusalem* but to the Pope. *Macarius and his adherents* (saith the Emperor *Constantine Pogonat*,) *haue bene deposed by the consent of the whole Councell and remitted to the discretion of the most holie Pope.*

Imp. Cōst. Pog. in Cōc Const 6. act. 18.

The same may be also said of the Archbishopricke of *Constantinople*; for as much as although that the Councell of *Constantinople*, holden vnder *Nectarius*, had desired to erect it into a Patriarckship, neuerthelesse this desire had no place till after the Councell of *Chalcedon*. By meanes whereof, the Church did not acknowledge in the tyme of saint AVSTIN anie more then the three Patriarchall Chaires, which had bene acknowledged by the Councell of *Nicea*, to witt *Rome*, *Alexandria*, and *Antioch*. For whereas Socrates putts amongst the Patriarships of the Easterne Empire, the primacie of *Pontus*, and that of *Asia-minor*; from whence some inferr, that it is an impertinent thing, to goe about to restraine the number of the ancient Patriarckes, to the onely Seas mentioned by the Canons of the *Nicean* Councell, they shew their owne impertinencie, not to see, that *Socrates* there extendes by confusion of language the word *Patriarkes*, to all kinde of Primates, and imployes it not vniuocallie, and in the same sence whereto we imploy it when we speake of Patriarkes properly taken; no more then when *Cassiodorus* calls the primates, and Metropolitans of *Italie*, Patriarcks, or when *Gregorie of Tours* calls *Nicetius* Archbishop of *Lion*, Patriarcke; they intend not to speake of Patriarckes properly and strictly taken, but of Patriarckes taken largely and generally.

Soc. hist. eccl. l. 5. c. 8.

Cassiod. ep. l. 6. ep. 5. Greg. Turon. hist. Franc. l 5. c. 20. Cuiac. Parititl. in lib. 1. Codic. Titul. de Sacrosanct. Eccle.

Now these things were manifestlie distinct as *Cuias* hath plainelie noted in these termes, *the imperiall lawe separates the priuiledges Patriarchall, and metropoliticke*. For not to touch other diuersities, which were betweene the Patriarckes speciallie taken, that Antiquitie other wise calls Archbishops, and Patriarkes generally taken, that is betweene Patriarckes and those that were but simplie Primates, and Metropolitans, there was this difference betweene them; that the Seate of the Patriarckes properly and especiallie taken, was fixed, and annexed to the dignitie of their Seas, and neuer varied for anie respect of anterioritie, of posterioritie, of promotion. In such sorte as Patriarckes properly taken, neuer preceded by anie primates or Motropolitans, whatsoeuer anterioritie of promotion the simple primates, or metropolitans had before them; nor amongst the Patriarckes properly taken, the third neuer preceded the second, whatsoeuer antiquitie of promotion he had aboue him: but their Seates were annexed to the order of their Seas, and not to that of their promotion. Where Patriarckes generally and inproperlie taken, that is to saie, primates or metropolitans, had amongst them no Seates annexed to the dignitie of their Seas, but the ancientest primate, or Metropolitan preceded the others. And therefore whatsoeuer extension, and communication that the lesse curious authors haue made of the name *Patriark* to other primates, and Metropolitanes, yet when there harh been question, to speake of the *Patriarckes* properlie soe called, the Church neuer acknowledged more then fiue Patriarckes, three ancient, and originarie, *Rome, Alexandria,* and *Antioch*, and two accessorie, and supernumerarie *Ierusalem*, and *Constantinople*, as it appeares both by the testimonie of the Emperor IVSTINIAN, who writes, the most Blessed Arch-

Iust. Nouel. 123.

bishops

bishops and *Patriarckes* which are, he of ancient *Rome*, he of *Constantinople*, he of *Alexandria*, he of *Antioch*, and hee of *Jerusalem*; and by the testimonie of saint GREGORIE the *great*, who reckons fower Patriarckes besides the *Pope*, when he saith in his Epistle to *Natalis*. Bishop of *Salona*; *If one of the fower Patriarkes had committed such a disobedience, it could not haue passed without a greeuous scandal:* And by the testimonie of the sixth generall Councell of *Constantinople*, which saith to the Emperor CONSTANTINE *Pogonat*, *We praie your imperiall wisdome, that the copies of this decree, may be sent to the fiue Patriarchall Thrones.* And by the Testimonie of *Balsamon*, who compares the Patriarckes to the *Organes* of the *Senses*, and affirmes, that as there are fiue Senses in the human Bodie, so there are fiue Patriarckes in the Church; *The Patriarckes* (saith Salsamon) *are as the fiue senses in one onely and selfe-same head.* And againe, *Wee acknowledge the fiue most sacred Patriarckes for the onely head of the Bodie of all the Churches of God.* And indeede the seauenth *Canon* of the Councell of *Nicea* in saying; *Because the ancient Custome and tradition beares, that the Bishop of Ierusalem be honored, the Councell ordaineth that he haue the next place of honor, sauing the dignitie of his owne Metropolitan.* Doth it not euidently shew two things; the one that the Sea whereof the Councell spake before this *Canon* had a preeminent ranke of honor, both before the Bishop of *Ierusalem*, and before all the other Seas of the Church; And the other that the Bishop of *Jerusalem* had the next place of honor after them, that is to saie; followed them in order of ranke and precedencie, and had place of all the metropolitans, euen his owne, to witt; the Arbishop of *Cesarea*, who was Metropolitan of *Palestina*, but without anie Patriarchall Iurisdiction; but contrariwise with an obligation to remaine subiect in the first instance to the Iurisdiction of the metropolitan of *Palestina*, and by appeale to that of the Patriarke of *Antioch*?

Greg. Magn. ep. l. 2. ep. 37.

Sext. Synod. Const. act. 18.

Theod. Bals. de Patriarc. priuiledg. apud. Leunclau.

Idem. ibid.

Conc. Nic. c. 7.

Now there were but three Seas which preceded that of *Ierusalem*, and after that of *Ierusalem*, there were noe more Seas which had fixed places, but all the other Primates and metropolitans changed their Seates, according to the anterioritie, or posterioritie of their promotion. And consequentlie the intention of the Councell of *Nicea* was not to place in the rankes of Seas trulie Patriarchall, that is to saie; which had Patriarchall place, and iurisdiction, but onely the three Seas before named there and in the same ranke as they are there named; to wit, *Rome*, *Alexandria*, and *Antioch*, as saint LEO the first protests to *Anatolius* Bishop of *Constantinople* in these wordes; *I am sorrie that thy charitie is fallen into this faulte to assaie to infring the most sacred constitutions of the canons of Nicea, as if thou hadst wacht a time on purpose to make the Sea of Alexandria loose the priuiledge of the second honor, and the Church of Antioch the proprietie of the third Dignitie.* And to this it contradicts not that the same Councell of *Nicea* saith speaking of the Sea of *Antioch*; *Likewise both in Antioch, and in other prouinces the priuiledges to be preserued to the Churches.* For hee meanes by the other prouinces the Easterne prouinces which he would should be subiect to the Bishop of *Antioch*, sauing the right of those, who by reason of the too great distãce; or incommoditie of the waies, had accustomed to take the ordination of their Metropolitans from their Synods, which hath giuen subiect to Pope *Innocent* the first to write, that by the Councell of *Nicea* the Bishop of *Antioch* was established not ouer a Prouince, but ouer a Diocesse; that is to saie, according to the Stile of the ancient lawiers, ouer a Bodie and a great number of Prouinces: and to saint IEROM to saie, that the Councell of *Nicea* had decreed; that *Antioch* should be the Metropolitan of all the *East*: And to *Alexander* Patriarke of *Antioch* to complaine, that the

Leo. ad Antol. ep. a 51.

Conc. Nic. c. 6.

Innoc. ad Alex. episc. Antioc. ep. 16.

Hier. ad Pam. Cōt. error. Ioann. Ieros. ep. 77.

Innoc. ad Alex Episc Antioc. ep. 16. Conc. Eph.

Conc. Eph. part. 2. Act. 7.

the *Cyprians* against the Canons of the Councell of *Nicea* ordained their Bishop without his permission: And to the *Cyprians* contrariwise to protest, that by the Canons of the Councell of *Nicea*, the right of the ordination of their Bishops had bene preserued to them. The true Patriarkes then ancient, and originarie, in regard of Iurisdiction were the onely three Seas of saint PETER, *Rome*, *Alexandria*, and *Antioch*, which were all three, in some sorte one Sea, as saint GREGORIE the great witnesseth to *Eulogius* Patriarke of *Alexandria* in these wordes; *Although* (said hee) *there be manie Apostles, yet for principalitie, the onely Sea of the prince of the Apostles hath obtained the authoritie, which is in three places from one onlie; for hee exalted the Sea, wherein he vouchsafed to set vp his rest, and end his present life; he hath adorned the Sea to which he ordained the Euangelist his disciple; and he hath established the Sea, wherein he was resident seauen yeares, although he were to depart from it.* which our *Hincmarus* long after repeated in these termes; *the Seas of the Roman,* Alexandrian, and Antiochian *Churches, are one same Sea of the great Prince of the Apostles, Peter.*

Greg. ep. lib. 6 ep. 36.

Hincmar. in op. 55. capit. 6.

In Chapt. 57.

And of this ternary number, the reason was, that saint PETER of whose authoritie, and superintendencie wee will treate els where, willing in his life time to cast the first foundations of the Ecclesiasticall Iurisdiction, which ought to be obserued after him, and the other Apostles, iudged that the easiest meanes to establish it, was to settle the principall Seates in those places; where the principall Tribunalls of the temporall Iurisdiction were constituted, because of the correspondencie which the inferior Citties alreadie had to those Seates. Now there were then, three principall Citties Metropolitan and Capitall in the Empire, bredd from the vnion of the Easterne Empire, that is to saie; the Monarchie of *Alexāder* & of his Successors, with the Empire of the *West*. That of *Alexandria* which *Dion Chrisostome* calleth the second Cittie beneath the Sunne, which was the Seate of the Empire of *Egipt*, and of the other neighbour-Regions after conuerted into the prefecture of *Egipt*: That of *Antioch* which *Iosephus* calls the third Cittie of the *Roman world* (and which is intitled by saint *Chrisostome*, the head, and mother-Cittie of the *East*) which was the head of the particular Empire of the *East*, that is to saie, of the *Asian East*, after conuerted into the gouermnent of *Siria*, and other *Easterne* prouinces; and that of *Rome*, which was the head of the *Westerne* Empire from whence the ancient Iewes called *Rome* the Empire of *Edom*, that is, the Empire of the *West*, by allusion to *Idumea*, which was situate toward the *West* from the *Southerne Iudea*; And they called *Titus* who sackt *Ierusalem*, *Titus* the *Idumean*, a thing which gaue occasion to the latter Rabbies, to deriue the race of *Titus* from *Idumea*; and that the *Chaldean* Paraphrast turnes these wordes of *Ieremias*: *He will visit thee daughter of Edom* into these; *I will visit thee, impious Rome.* For the diuision of *Alexanders* Empire hauing been finallie reduced to two principall Empires, the one the Empire of *Egipt* holden by the posteritie of *Ptolomeus* sonne of *Lagus* whereof *Alexandria* was the head; the other the Empire of *Asia* possessed by the Successors of *Seleucus*, who after he had conquered *Demetrius* king of *Asia*; made (saie *Eusebius* and saint IEROM) of the two Kingdomes of *Syria* and *Asia*, one Empire, whose capitall cittie was *Antioch*. Then when those two Empires came to be vnited with that of the common wealth of *Rome*, which before held the Empire of the *West*, there where three principall Citties Metropolitā and capitall in the Empire, two subalterne, to witt *Alexandria*, which was head of the Empire of the *South*, that is the Empire of *Egipt*: and *Antioch* which was the head of the Empire of the *East*, that is the Empire of *Asia*. And one supereminēt,

Dio Chrys. Or. 32.

Ioseph. de bell. Iud. l. 3. c. 3.

Chrys. ad. pop. Antioch. hom. 5.

Paraphr. Chaldaic. in lam. Hierem. c.

Euseb. & Hier. in Chron.

to

to witt *Rome*, which was particularly head of the Empire of the *West*; and besides had the superintendencie ouer the heades of the other two Empires. For I doe not reckon *Carthage*, for so much as she was long before made a member of the *Westerne* Empire.

For these causes then, as the Church cast her first roote in *Asia*, saint *PETER* also first planted his Episcopall *Sea* at *Antioch*, the capitall cittie of the *East*, where he was resident comprehending his voyages into the neighbour prouinces seauen yeare, and there foũded a successor or rather a succession, which was after the death of the Apostles, head of all the Ecclesiasticall iurisdiction of the *Easterne Asia*; from whence it is, that in the Councell of *Chalcedon*, the *Patriark* of *Antioch* intitleth his *Sea*, the *Sea* of *S. PETER* of the great cittie of the *Antiochians*: & that *S.* CHRYSOST. citizen of *Antioch* cryes, *God shewed by the effect, that he had great care of the cittie of Antioch, for hee ordained that Peter the superintendent of the whole world; hee, to whom he had consigned the keyes of the Kingdome of heauen; hee, to whom he had committed the dispositiõ of all things, should be a long tyme resident there*; & that S. INNOCENT the first, of the same tyme with S. CHRYSOSTOME, writes to *Alexander* Patriark of *Antioch*; *The Sea of Antioch had not giuen place to the Sea of Rome, but what that obtained onlie by the waie, this obtained absolutelie and finallie.* From whence the same saint PETER seeing that the Church began to growe further, and to spread her rootes through all the world, he trãsported himselfe to *Rome*; which was both in particular, head of the *West*, & in generall head of the world, & held there the Episcopall Chaire, cõprehending manie voyages 25. yeares. *Simon Peter* (saith saint IEROM) *sonne of Jona of the prouince of Galilee, of the borough of Bethsaida, brother to Andrew the Apostle. and prince of the Apostles, after the Episcopate of the Church of Antioch, and the preaching of the dispersion of those of the Circumcisiõ, who had belieued in Pontus, Galatia, Cappadocia, Asia, and Bithinia, came to Rome the second yeare of the Empire of Claudius, to ouerthrow Simon the Magician, and there held 25. yeares the Episcopall Chaire*: And S. LEO the first, addressing his speech in the forme of *Apostrophe* to the same S. PETER; *Thou hadst* (said hee) *alreadie founded the Church of Antioch, in which the word Christian, first receiued birth; thou hadst alreadie replenished, Pontus, Galatia, Cappadocia, Asia, and Bithinia, with the lawes of the Euangelicall preaching*. Then finallie hauing established the superintendẽcie of the Easterne Church at *Antioch*, and of that of the *West*, at *Rome*, and considering he had still one of the three capitall citties of the Empire to prouide for; to witt, that of *Alexandria*, which was the head of the Empire of *Egipt*, he appointed & placed there his second selfe, that is to saie, his Ghostlie childe, and welbeloued disciple S. *Marke* the Euangelist: From whence it is that *Julius* the first reported by S. ATHANASIVS, writes of *Alexandria*, it was not a common Church, but of the number of those that the Apostles themselues had instituted. And S. IEROM; *The Church of Alexandria doth glorie, that she pertakes in the faith of the Roman*: And againe, *that the Chaire of the Apostle Peter confirmeth by his preaching, the preaching of the Chaire of Marke the Euangelist*: And saint LEO the first, writing to *Dioscorus* Patriarke of *Alexandria*: *Since that the most blessed Apostle Peter, hath receiued from our Lord, the principalitie of the Apostleship, and that the Roman Church remaines in his institution, it is vnlawfull to beleiue that his holie disciple Marke, who first gouerned the Church of Alexandria, hath formed his decrees vpon anie other rules of tradition.*

Greg. ep. l. 6. ep 36.

Cõc. Chalc act. 7.

Chrysost. homil. in beat Ignat.

Innocen. ad Alexan. Episc. Antioch. ep. 18.

Hier. de script. eccl.

Athan. apol 2.

Hier. ad Theoph. ep. 68.

Idem ad Pam. & Marcel. ep. 78.

Leo ad Diosc. ep. 79.

And frõ thence tooke beginning these three Patriarchall Seas, correspondent to the three Imperiall Seates, vnder which the generall vnion of the Empire was made, but not so yet equall, but that amongst these three first Churches, that is to saie, first in regard of the Churches of their diuisions, there was one first, of the first & exalted, & superintendent ouer both the others; to witt, the *Roman*. From whence it is, that the Councell of *Sardica*, & the Councell of *Chalcedon*, and the Emperor *Iustinian*, & S. GREGORIE the Great, call her the head of all the Churches; & that the Emperor *Valentinian* intitles the Pope, *The Rector of the vniuersalitie of Churches*. And that the Councell of *Chalcedon* qualifies him: him to whom the guarde of the vine is committed by our Sauiour. And that the Emperor *Constantine Pogonat*, and the sixth Councell of *Constantinople* call him the [a] *Protothrone of the vniuersall Church*; [b] *the Presidet of the Apostolicall height*; [c] *the Soueraigne Pope*; [d] *the Capitaine of the sacred warfare*; *and the vniuersall Patriark, and Arch-pastor*: and call the other Patriarkes, *Sinthrones of the Pope, after the Pope*. For I will not add that which some Catholickes vse to alleadge of *Cassiodorus*; to witt, that he attributed to the Pope, the title of Bishop of the Patriarkes; as well, because *Cassiodorus* there speakes not of Patriarkes properlie taken, but extends the word to Primates, and Metropolitans; as, because I doubt it must be read disiunctiuelie *Papam vel Patriarchalem Episcopum*, and not explicatiuely *Papam vel Patriarcharum Episcopum*. It sufficeth me to saie, that as the cittie of *Rome* besides that she was head of the Empire of the *West*, a thinge which was common to her with the two other citties of *Alexandria* and *Antioch*, each in the behalfe of their ancient territorie, had yet this condition more aboue the rest, that she was also the head of the vniuersall Bodie of the Empire, soe the finall and absolute Sea of S. PETER, which he constituted at *Rome* besides the Patriarchall iurisdiction, and as correspondent to the Empire of the *West*, in which it agreed with the other Patriarchall Chaires; had yet more, the degree of head of the Church, and Prince of the Patriarkes, in which he was superior to the other patriarchall Thrones.

Conc. Sard ep. ad Iul. in frag. Hil. Cōc. Chalc ep. ad Leo. Cod. l 7. & 8. Greg. ep. l. 11. ep. 54. Theod. Nou. Const tit. 24. ad calcem. Codic. Theod. Cōc. Chalc ep. ad Leo. a. Cōc. Cōstantin. 6. act. 18. ep. ad Agath. b. Ibid. in acclam. ad Imper. c. Ibid. d. Constan. Pog. ep. ad Syn. Apost. Idem ibid. Id. ep. ad Agath Cassiod. ep. l. 9. ep. 15.

And when there was question of things that went beyond the Patriarchall iurisdiction, that is of greater causes, and which concerned the vniuersall Churches, as were causes of Faith, or of the generall customes of the Church, or those of the finall deposition of Bishops; or those of iudging the verie persons, of the Patriarkes, exercised Ecclesiasticall iurisdiction ouer them, & iudged both of their iudgements & of their persons. For S. PETER hauing purposed to followe in the distributiō of spirituall iurisdictions, the order alreadie established in the distribution of temporall iurisdiction; it must followe that the same proportion that was betweene the seate of *Rome*, & the seates of the other two Empires, in case of politicke & secular iurisdictiō, must likewise be maintained betweene the Sea of the Bishop of *Rome*, and those of the other Patriarkes in case of Ecclesiasticall & spirituall iurisdiction: & that for two causes, the one occasionall & remote, to witt, the secular dignity of the cittie of *Rome* which had moued S. PETER to sett the spirituall soueraigntie of the Church, in that place; where alreadie the temporall soueraigntie of the commonwealth was setled: & the other neere, formall & immediate, to witt, the spirituall dignitie of S. PETER, for the eminencie whereof, it was fitt, that he that was the head of the episcopall societie, should establish his finall & absolute Throne, & plant the stock of his direct succession in that place, where the stocke & principall Seate of the human & temporall iurisdiction, was alreadie planted: As the Emperors *Theodosius* and *Valentinian* note in these wordes; *The primacie of the Sea Apostolicke hath bene established both by the merit of Peter, who is the Prince of the Episcopall societie; and by the dignitie of the cittie, and by the sacred authoritie of the Synod.*

Nauel. Theod tit. 34 ad calcem codic. Thod.

Now

Now, there was this difference betweene the seate of the cittie of *Rome*, and the seates of the other prefectures, in matter of secular & temporall iurisdiction, that not only the Emperor of the *Roman* common-wealth, commaunded the Prefects and Presidentes of the other Seates, but also that the cittie prefect of *Rome*, besides the iurisdiction of his ordinary territorie which was limitted in regarde of iudgement, in the first instance, to a certaine number of prouinces, had yet as head of the Senate, and vicar to the Emperor, the right of examining by appeale the causes of all the prouinces of the Empire. For when *Augustus*, and the Emperors following, establisht, or re-establisht the office of Prefect of the cittie of *Rome*, they gaue him power to iudge of the appeales of all the prouinces of the *Roman* circle, as the interpreter of the notice of the Empire; and euen the aduersaries of the *Roman* Church doe acknowledge, alleadging; *be it well, be it euill, these words of Mecenas reported in Dion, that the Prefect of the cittie shall iudge of the appeales and prouocations of all the Magistrates aboue mentioned*: And those of *Statius* addressed to the cittie prefect vnder *Domitian*.

Guid. Pancirol. com. in notit. Imp. Occ. c. 4. l. de Suburbic. region. impr. Francofurt ann. 1618. c. 1. Dio. Cassi. l. 52. Stat. Sylu l. 1.

Inque sinum, quæ sæpe tuum fora turbida quæstu
Confugiunt legesque, vrbesque, vbicunque togatæ,
Quæ tua longinquis implorant iura querelis.

And those of an epistle from the Senat to the iudges of *Carthage* reported by *Vopiscus* in the tyme of the Emperor *Tacitus*: *All appeales shall belong to the cittie Prefect, which shall yet proceede from the Proconsulls, and ordinarie Iudges*. And these of an other epistle of the Senat, to the Iudges of *Treues*, and to the *Antiochians*, *Aquileyans*, *Milaneses*, *Alexandrians*, *Thessalonians*, *Corinthians, and Athenians*; *The right of appeale hath bene vniuersallie decreed to the Prefecture of the cittie*: And these of an epistle of *Tiberianus*; *The appeales from all the powers, and from all the dignities, are returned to the cittie Prefect*. And these from a lawe of *Constantine* to *Iulian* the cittie Prefect: *Wee will not that the iudges from whom the appeale shall remitt the causes to our clemencie, but they shall haue recourse to the sacred auditorie of thy grauitie, to whom we haue committed our Vicarship*; which was after abolished by the translation of the appeales to the Pretoriall Prefects; from whence wee haue a lawe of *Constantius* in the *Theodosian-Code*, which ordaines the Prefect of the Pretory of *Italie*, to examine the appeales from *Sicily*, from *Sardinia*, from *Calabria*, from *Prussia*, and from the prouinces now called *Lombardy*, and adds for the cittie Prefect informed by our answere hath bene aduertised to depart from it. By meanes whereof, as the cittie of *Rome*, besides that she is head of the Empire of the *West*, leaues not to haue dominion ouer the heades of the two other Empires; or to reduce the matter into more strict termes; as the Prefect of *Rome* in the first ages of the Empire, besides the ordinary iurisdiction that he had ouer the prouinces of his territory, yet left not as Vicar to the Emperor and head of the Senat to iudge of the appeales of all other prouinces: so the Pope, beside the iurisdiction he had in qualitie of Patriark of the *West*, ouer the prouinces of the patriarkship of the *West*; yet left not as head of the Church and successor of saint PETER, and principall Vicar of Christ to haue the supereminence, and generall superintendence, ouer all the other prouinces. *To the* Roman Church (saith saint IRENEVS) *because of a more mightie principalitie*; that is to saie, as hath aboue appeared, because of a principalitie more mightie then the temporall) *it is necessarie, that all Churches should agree*. And saint CYPRIAN; *The Roman Church is the Chaire of PETER, and the principall and originall of the Socerdotall vnitie*. And Sainct

Vopisc. in vita Floria.

Vopisc. ib.

Vopisc. ib. Codex Theod. l. 11. tit. 30. l. 13.

1. Codex Theod l. 11. tit. 30. l. 27.

Iren. l. 3. c. 3.

Cypr. ad Corn. ep. 52.

Athan. ad solit. *Athanasius; They haue had noe reuerent esteeme that Rome was the Sea Apostolick, and metropolitan of Romania.* And saint GREGORIE *Nazianzene*; *The* Greg. Naz. Carm. de vita sua. *ancient Rome treads rightlie in the faith, houlding all the West bound by the healthfull word, as it is conuenient for her to doe, that ruleth all the world.* And sainct IEROM, a priest of the Church of *Antioch*, and disciple of S. *Gregorie Nazianzene*, writing to Pope *Damasus*; Hieron. ad Dam. ep. 57. *I know the Church is founded vpon that stone: whosoeuer eateth the lambe out of that howse, is profane*: And a little after; Aug. ep. 162. *I know not Vitalis; I am ignorant of Miletius; I reiect Paulinus: whosoeuer gathers not with thee scatters.* And S. AVST. *In the Roman Church hath alwaies flourisht, the principalitie of the Sea Apostolicke.* And *Prosper* whom saint *Austin* Prosp. de voc. Gent. l. 2. c. 6. reputes his second selfe, and whom *Joseph Scalager* calls the most learned man of his age; *The principalitie of the Apostolick priesthood, hath made Rome greater by the Tribunall of Religion, then by that of the Empire*; & els where changing his prose into verse:

Prosp. de ingrat.

Rome, great Apostle Peter's sacred Seate,
Head, of the Churches-Bodie, heere below;
Hath by Faithes Empire, made her selfe more great,
Then she by all her armed powres, could grow.

Leo ad Anast. Episcop. Thess. ep. 82. And S. LEO the first, in the epistle to *Anastasius* Bishop of *Thessalonica*; *It hath bene prouided by a grand order, that all should not attribute all things to themselues, but that in euery prouince, there should be some whose sentence might holde the first place amongst their bretheren*: And againe; *that there might be others constituted in the greater citties, who might vse a greater diligence, by whom the care of the vniuersall Church might flow to the onely Seate of Peter.* And therefore whẽ the *Allexandriãs* would accuse *Dionisius* Patriark of *Alexandria* their Bishop, they went vp to *Rome*, saith S. ATHANASIVS, & accused him Athan. de sent. Dyon. before *Dionisius* Bishop of *Rome*. And when the same ATHANASIVS, likewise Patriark of *Alexandria*, *Paul* Bishop of *Constantinople*; and *Marcellus* Primat of *Ancyra* in *Galatia*, had bene deposed by diuers Councells Soz hist. echl. l 3. c. 7 of the *East*; *The Bishop of Rome* (saith *Sozomene*) *restored to each one his Church, because to him, for the dignitie of his Sea, the care of all things belonged.* And when the cause of *Iohn* Patriark of *Antioch*, had bene propounded to the Councell of *Ephesus*, the Councell remitted the iudgment to the Pope: And *Juuenall* Bishop of *Jerusalem* said, that *the ancient custome and Apostolick tradition bare, that the Church of Antioch should be ruled by the Roman.*

And when the Councell of *Chalcedon* disanulled the actes of the false Gõc. Chalc act. 10. Councell of *Ephesus*, they excepted the creation of *Maximus* Patriark of *Antioch*, because saith *Anatolius* Archbishop of *Constantinople*; *The Pope hauing receiued him into his communion, hath iudged that he should rule the Church of Antioch.* And when *Theodoret* Bishop of *Cyre* in the borders of *Persia*, and subiect to the patriarkship of *Antioch*, had bene deposed in the same Councell of *Ephesus*, he appealed to the *Pope*, and the Coun- Ibid. cell of *Chalcedon* receiued him; because saith the Senat, *The Pope had restored him to his dignitie.* And when *Flauianus* Archbishop of *Constantinople*, had bene deposed by *Dioscorus* Patriark of *Alexandria*, and by the false Councell of *Ephesus*, he appealed likewise to the *Pope*; and that Valẽt. 3. ep. ad Theod. in ep. præã. Cõc. Chalc saith the Emperor *Valentinian* following the custome of the Councells. And when *Iohn* Patriark of *Alexandria*, had bene driuen from his Sea, by the plott of the Emperor *Zeno*, he also appealed to the *Pope*, & that with the intercessiõ of the *Patriark* of *Antioch*, as *Liberatus* Archdeacon of *Car-* Liber. c. 12 *thage* a writer of a thousand and one hundred yeares antiquitie, reportes

in these

in these wordes; *John* (saith *Liberatus*) *hauing taken Synodicall letters of intercession from Calendian Patriarke of Antioch, appealed to Pope Simplicius.* And thus much of the comparison of the Pope, with the other Patriarkes: For as for the canon of the Councell of *Nicea*, which seemes to rule the Bishops of *Alexandria* & *Antioch* ouer the Bishop of *Rome*, it shall be spoken of heereafter. Liberat. c. 2. In chap. 32.

Of the difficulties of the Scripture, concerning the tyme of S. Peters staie at Antioch, and at Rome.

CHAPT. IV.

BVT against this that wee haue affirmed of the sitting of Saint PETER at *Antioch*, and at *Rome*; *Caluine*, and the other aduersaries of the Church, forme twelue principall obiections; eight from the Scripture, and fower from the Fathers. The first obiection is, that S. PAVL found S. PETER in *Ierusalem* the two first voyages that he made thither; the one, three yeare after his conuersion; & the other, when he carried the almes for the famine foretould by *Agabus*; & then that the Episcopall staie of S. PETER at *Antioch*, which after S. *Ieroms* computation betweene these two voyages, could not be seauen yeares, as S. *Gregorie* affirmes it, & as wee suppose it; for asmuch as S. *Paules* conuersiõ happened at the soonest, three yeares after the death of IESVS CHRIST; & S. PETER departed from *Jerusalem* to goe to *Rome*, the secõd yeare of the Empire of *Claudius*, which was the eleauenth yeare after the death of Christ. The seconde obiection is, that S. PETER still assisted at *Jerusalem*, at the Councell holdẽ for the legall causes about twentie yeare, saie they, after the death of our Lord and was crucified as we saie, the fourteenth yeare of the Empire of *Nero*, that is the seauen & thirtith yeare after the death of our Sauiour, & then he could not haue bene 25 yeare at *Rome* as wee saie. The third, that S. PAVL addressing the principall of his epistles to the *Romans*, doth not there salute S. PETER, whom he would not haue forgottẽ, if he had bene there. The fourth is, that S. PAVL writing from *Rome* to the *Philippians*, complained that euery one sought his owne, & not that which was of Christ. And to *Timothie* that all had abandoned him: which he would not haue done if S. PETER had bene there. The fift, that when S. PAVL came to *Rome*, the bretheren went to meete him, amongst whom there is noe mention of S. PETER, and the *Iewes* prayed him to declare to them his opinion of the sect of the *Christians*, a thing they would not haue required, if S. PETER had preached at *Rome* before him. The sixt; that S. LVKE who writ the history of the Actes of the Apostles, maketh no mention of S. PETERS voyage to *Rome*. The seauenth that S. PAVL who hath described the enterview betweene S. PETER and him at *Jerusalem* and *Antioch* speakes not of their enter-view at *Rome* which was the most famous cittie of the world. And the eigth, that S. *Iohn* made mention of the kinde of death by which S. PETER should glorifie God, but makes no mention of the place of his death. Now lett vs first dispatch the obiections taken out of scripture, and after we will proceede to those taken out of the Fathers.

Galat. 1. Act. 12. Hier. de script. eccl. in Petro. Greg. ep. l. 6. ep. 36. Hier. ibid. Act. 15. Rom. 16. Philip. 2. 2. Tim. 4. Act. 28. Galat. 1. & 2. Ioan. 21.

To the first obiection then from Scripture, which is that S. PAVL still found Saint PETER in *Jerusalem* in the two first voyages that he made thither; Calu. inst. l. 4. c. 6.

Galat.2. thither; the one, three yeares after his conuersion; and the other, when
1.Act.11. he carried thither the almes for the famine, foretould by *Agabus*; and cõsequently, that the Episcopall staie of S. PETER at *Antioch*, which was betweene the two voyages, could not bee of seauen yeares: I answere, that the conuersion of S. *Paul*, happened not in the third yeare after the death of our Sauiour, as they pretend, a thing which troubles all the harmonie of the history, but the first. And this I proue in this manner. Betweene the Councell of *Ierusalem*, and S. *Paules* departure to goe to *Rome*, S. *Paul* remained besides the tyme imployed in his iourneys, six yeare in the *East*;
Act.18. to wit, a yeare and a halfe at *Corinth*; three moneths in the Synagogue
Act.19. Ibid. of the Iewes at *Ephesus*; two yeares in the schoole of *Tyrannus*, three mo-
Act.20. neths againe in *Greece*; and two other yeares finallie in the prison at
Act 24. Ibid. *Ierusalem*: for this word, *and came forth two yeare after*, hath reference to the tyme of saint *Paules* imprisonment, and not to the tyme of the insti-
Ibid. tution of *Felix*, as it appeared by saint *Paules* testimonie, who saith, that *Felix* had iudged *Iudea* many yeares. Now saint *Paul* departed from
Act 27. *Ierusalem* to come to *Rome* the fower and twentith yeare after the death of Christ, for saint *Luke* witnesseth that he came forth of prison, when *Festus* gouernor of *Iudea* was substituted in *Felix* steed; and *Iosephus* notes, that *Felix* being returned to *Rome* was absolued from his faultes committed
Ioseph antiq.l.2.c.7. in *Iudea*, by the credit that his brother *Pallas* had with the Emperor *Nero*:
Corn.Tac. annal.13. And *Cornelius Tacitus* quoteth, that *Pallas* was fallen from *Neros* fauour vnder the consulship of *Antistius*, which was the second yeare after the death of Christ; or if we comprehend the yeare of Christs death, within our reckoning, the fiue and twentith. And to this S. IEROM agrees,
Hier.de scrip. eccl. in paulo. who saith; *Paul was sent prisoner to Rome the fiue and twentith yeare after the passion of our Lord*; that is the second yeare of *Nero*, when *Festus* Procurator of *Iudea* succeded *Felix*. From the fower and twentith yeare then after the death of Christ, if you subtract the six yeares interposed betweene the Councell of *Jerusalem*, and the voyage of S. *Paul* to *Rome*, there will remaine, that the Councell of *Jerusalem* was holden at the latest, the eighteenth yeare after the death of our Lord, & not the twentith, as they suppose. Now betweene the conuersion of S. *Paul*, & the Councell of *Ierusalem*, the same S. *Paule* teacheth vs, that there were seauenteene yeares,
Galat.2. when he writt to the *Galathians*; *three yeares after I went to Ierusalem to see Peter*. And againe; and then after *fourteene yeares I went vp againe into Jerusalem*. For where *Caluin* will haue it that the voyage of *Ierusalem* whereof S.
Caluin. in ep.ad Galat.c.2. Act. c. 11. *Paul* speakes in the Epistle to the *Galathians*, when he saith, againe after *fourteene yeares I went vp to Ierusalem*, should not be the voyage of the Councell, but the voyage of the almes for the famine is a grosse ignorãce, since the voyage of the almes for the famine, was made before the death of *Herod* surnamed *Agrippa*, who deceased as it shall heereafter appeare, twelue yeare after the death of Christ. And whereas the same *Caluin* saith, that the fourteene yeare quoted by S. *Paul*, should not be added to the end of the three yeares before mẽtioned but should be coũted frõ his conuersiõ, it is coufuted by the greeke phrase, which insinuates, that these fourteene yeare were interposed betweene the voyage for the visit of S. *Peter*, & the
Bez.in ep. ad Galat. c. 2. voyage to the councell; which gaue *Beza* occasiõ to translate it thus: *And fourteene yeare hauing interuented, I went vp againe into Ierusalem*. And to saint
Ier.in ep. ad Galat. c. 2. IEROM to saie, *Paul testifies that after seauenteene yeares he conferred fullie with the Apostles*. Then let vs defalke from the foure and twentie yeares after the Death of Christ, at the end whereof saint PAVLE went to *Rome*, the six yeares which passed betweene the Councell of *Ierusalem*, and the departure of saint *Paule* to goe to *Rome*, and from the remainder

which will bee eighteene yeares, subtract the seauenteene yeare, which passed betweene the Conuersion of Saint PAVL, and the Councell of *Jerusalem*, it will appeare that the conuersion of saint PAVL happened the first yeare after the death of our Lord, as the *Chronicon* of *Eusebius* reckons it: and then that the third yeare after the conuersion of saint PAVL, which was that wherein saint PAVL transported himselfe first into *Jerusalem*, and from *Ierusalem*, as saith the Epistle, to the *Galathians* into *Syria* and *Cilicia*, that is to saie, according to the historie of the Acts, to *Tharsus* and *Antioch*, was the fowrth yeare after the death of Christ, and consequentlie that the staie of S. PETER at *Antioch* began the fourth yeare after the death of Christ. For S. LEO the first saith plainelie, that *the name of Christian had the originall at Antioch, Saint Peter preaching there, which could not haue bene so, if Saint Peter had not bene come to Antioch, within the compasse of the same yeare that saint Paul arriued there, during the which saint Luke testifies, that the disciples were first called Christians at Antioch.* Galat. 1. Act. 11. Leo ad Anatol. Const. Episc. ep. 51.

And against this it can not be said, that saint LVKE toucheth nothing of this voyage of saint PETER to *Antioch*, for saint LVKE doth no more touch the conference of Saint PETER and saint PAVL at *Antioch*, which neuerthelesse wee learne out of the Epistle to the *Galathians*; nor that saint PAVLE recites, in the Epistle to the *Galathians* the enterview betweene saint PETER and him at *Antioch*, after the Councell of *Jerusalem*. For besides that saint AVSTIN maintaines, that the enterview betweene saint PETER and saint PAVL at *Antioch*, was before the Councell of *Ierusalem*, though it be recited after it, saint PAVLE doth no where saie, that saint PETER and hee neuer mett more then once at *Antioch*. Now the voyage that saint PAVL made into *Ierusalem* when he carried the almes for the generall famine foretould by *Agabus*, & found S. PETER prisoner there, was the eleauenth yeare after the death of our Sauiour. For the Scripture saith, that this famine fell out vnder *Claudius*: and *Dion* reckons the beginning of the generall famine, which happened in *Claudius* his time vnder the 795.th yeare of the foundation of *Rome* which was the second yeare of *Claudius* his Empire; that is to saie, the eleauenth after the Death of our Lord: And *Iosephus* obserues, that *Herod* called *Agrippa*, author of saint PETERS imprisonment, deceased the seauenth yeare of his Raigne, which was the third yeare of the Empire of *Claudius*. And therefore betweene the first voyage of saint PAVL to *Ierusalem*, and the second, there was seauen yeare, that is to saie, fiue whole yeares, and two imperfect yeares, which is the time that the Fathers, and wee after them, assigne for saint PETERS staie at *Antioch*. For that the Latin *Chronicon* of *Eusebius* saith, that he was there twenty fiue yeares, it is a deprauution of the copies of *Basle* in which insteede of fiue, they haue set in 25. as it may bee seene by the accompt of the yeares noted by retaile, which, are fiue, to wit, from the three and twentith of *Tiberius*, to the second of *Claudius*; or possiblie (a frequent chance in chronologicall tables) an intire addition, as it is coniectured by the *Armenian* copie, and diuers latine manuscripts of the same *Chronicon* of *Eusebius*, which are kept in the librarie of the *Vatican*; and by the *Greeke* and *Latine* edition of *Scaliger*, in none of which, this quotation is to be found. And to this there is no repugnācy in that, that the historie of the Acts following the custome of the Scripture, which is often to recite immediatly things farr from that tyme, placeth the voyage of saint PAVL to *Jerusalem* presently after the prophecie of *Agabus*: for saint LVKE speaking of the famine foretould by *Agabus*, adds, *which also happened vnder Claudius* Act. 11. Aug ep. 19. ep. con. Faust. l. 19. c. 17. Act. 12. Dio. hist. l. 60. Iof. ant. l. 19. c. 7. Greg. ep. l. 6. ep. 36. Act. 11. verse. 30. Ibid. vers. 28.

Cesar

Cesar, to shew that the prophecie had bene longe before the Empire of *Claudius*: by meanes whereof, betweene the prophecie of *Agapus*, and the tyme of the famine which began but the second yeare of the Empire of *Claudius* there were past many yeares: nether that the same historie notes, that PAVL and BARNABAS conuersed a yeare at *Antioch*: for that should not be taken from their arriuall vntill the voyage of the Almes; which was executed manie yeares after the prophecie of *Agabus*; but it is meant, that they staide a whole yeare at *Antioch*, without departing from it, and then came againe: nor that it saith that *Agabus* came at the same tyme to *Antioch*; for this note of tyme is refer'd in generall to the tyme before the Empire of *Claudius*; and it is put to discerne the tyme of the pronunciation of the prophecie, which was vnder the Empire of *Caius*, from the tyme wherein it was accomplished, which was vnder the Empire of *Claudius*.

(Act 11. vers 19. — Ibid. verses 26. & 27.)

To the second obiection, which is, that Saint PETER assisted at the Councell of *Ierusalem* which was celebrated twenty yeare after the Death of Christ; and consequentlie could not bee arriued at *Rome* the second yeare of the Empire of *Claudius*, which was the eleauenth after the Death of Christ; neither could then haue, bene Bishop there twentie fiue yeare; Wee answere there is nothing incompatible betweene these two histories For *Suetonius* writes, that *Claudius* draue the Iewes out of *Rome* which moued tumults, said hee, at the instance of Christ. Now *Orosius* notes, and that as he saith, after *Iosephus*, that this banishment happened the ninth yeare of the Empire of *Claudius*, which was the eighteenth yeare after the Death of our, Lord; that is to saie, as wee haue demonstrated in the solution last past, the same yeare of the Councell of *Ierusalem*. And saint LVKE confirmes, who writes, that saint PAVL being come to *Corinth*, a little after the Councell of *Jerusalem*, found *Prisca* and *Aquila* there, who were, said hee new returne'd out of *Italie*, because *Claudius* had commaunded all the Iewes to goe forth of *Rome*. And therefore what wonder is it that saint PETER beiug arriued at *Rome* the second yeare of the Empire of *Claudius*, and hauing bene constrained to auoid *Rome* with the other Iewes seauen yeare after; that is to saie, the ninth yeare of the Raigne of *Claudius*, because of the Edict publisht by him against the Iewes; were in the East at the Councell of *Jerusalem*, which was celebrated that same yeare, and afterward, the heate of the Edict being cooled, returned to *Rome*?

(Caluin. inst. l. 4. c. 6. The author of the treatise vpon the Church c. 8. — Oros. hist. l. 7. c. 6. — Act. 19. — Rome. 16.)

To the third obiection, which is, that saint PAVL writing to the *Romans*, saluted not saint PETER, which he could not haue forgotten to doe, if he had bene there: wee answere, that the Epistle to the *Romans*, was written in the time of the Iewes exile from *Rome*, and during saint PETERS being in the East, to wit, betweene the Councell of *Ierusalem*, and the death of *Claudius*, for it was written at *Corinth*, when saint PAVL passed by there, to make his last iourney to *Jerusalem*. And therefore although *Prisca* and *Aquila*, and some other lesse notable Iewes, were alreadie returned to *Rome*, neuerthelesse it followes not that saint PETER, who was the principall author of the Iewes conuersion, for which their nation was banisht, should so soone returne. Iointlie that if this argumēt were of weight, we must withall conclude, that *Timothie* was not Bishop of *Ephesus*, for S. PAVL writing to the *Ephesians*, makes no mention of him: and that saint, *James* was not Bishop of *Ierusalem*, for in the Epistle to the *Hebrewes*, written in saint *Iames* his life tyme as appeares by these worde, *know that the brother Timothie hath bene licenced, with whom, if he returne shortlie, I will visit you: there is no mention made of saint James*. And therefore so

(Rom 15. Rom. 16. — Heb. 13.)

farr is *Theodoret* (an author of the same tyme, with the Councells of *Ephesus* and *Chalcedon*, and one of the most famous writers of the Ecclesiasticall historie) from takeing one argument from the Epistle to the *Romans*, as the Popes aduersaries doe, to call in question *S.* PETERS staie at *Rome*; as contrariwise, commenting the Epistle to the *Romans*, he saith, that saint PAVL *there vseth the word, to confirme, for as much as S. Peter had alreadie founded the Ghospell amongst them. Because* (saith Theodoret) *that the great Peter, had alreadie declared to them the euangelicall doctrine, therefore saint Paul necessarilie adds, to confirme you.* Theod. in p. ad Rom c. 1.

To the fourth obiection, which is that S. PAVL writing from *Rome*, not onely toucheth no word of S. PETER, but also in the epistle written to the *Philippians* from *Rome* saith; *that all sought that which was of themselues, and none sought which was of Christ*: And in the second to *Timothie*, written from the same place, *that all had forsaken him.* Wee answere, that in the one he speakes of those that he might haue sent to the *Philippians*, and that in the other he speakes, either of his familiars, as S. CHRYSOST. saith, and of those which were accustomed to follow him, or of those that had power to defend him, at the Emperiall Tribunall, of which number S. PETER was like to be none. And besides wee maintaine, that S. PAVL speakes by *Synecdoche* saying, *all*, insteede of saying, *many*, as S. IEROM acknowledgeth in these words; *For as much as saint Paul had bene forsaken by manie, hee therefore writes, that all had forsaken him*: And *Bullinger* minister of *Zurich*, In these; *I doubt not, but the Apostle vsed a Synecdoche, in this passage, saying he had bene forsaken of all, when as, onely some had forsaken him.* And finally wee will adde, that if from the silence of S. PAVL, it be permitted to inferre, that saint PETER was not at *Rome*, when saint PAVL writt these epistles; wee must then also conclude by the same argument that saint PAVL was not there. For in anie one of the epistles, that S. PAVL hath written from *Rome*, he neither makes mention of the cittie, nor Church of *Rome*; and wee onely know that he writt them from *Rome*, because in the epistle to the *Philippians*, hee speakes of *Cesars* howse; and because in the epistle to the *Ephesians*; and to the *Colossians*; and in the second to *Timothie*, he speakes of his prison. Philip. 2. 2. Tim. 4. Chrys. in 2 Tim. c. 4 Hier. in ep ad Eph. c. 1. Bulling. in 2. Tim. c. 4 Philipp. 4.

To the fift obiection, which is, that when saint PAVL arriued at *Rome*, the bretheren went to meete him, amongst whom there is no mention of S. PETER; Wee answere, that all the *Roman* Church, went not to meete S. PAVL, but some particular Christians, the Church then not being so free and quiet at *Rome*, as they could make those publicke demonstratiõs; but contrarily so oppressed & inclosed, as the most part of the faithfull, were constrained to hide themselues in caues, and places vnder ground, to auoid the persecutions & tyrannies of the infidells. Iointlie that wee say not, that S. PETER remained alwaies fixed and tied to *Rome*, while he was Bishop thereof, but that he went from tyme to tyme, planting the Ghospell in the lesser citties, and placing Bishops ouer them, and that during these voyages he administred the *Roman* Church, by the ministrie of *Linus* and *Cletus*, whom he had there establisheth for his Coadiutors; which is the cause for which (if wee belieue *Ruffinus*) they are sometimes reckoned in the order of the Bishops of *Rome*, before S. CLEMENT, and sometymes after him. And whereas the Iewes prayed S. PAVL when he came to *Rome*, to informe them of the sect of the Christians, which they obiect to vs they would not haue done, if saint PETER had already bene Bishop there; Wee answere, that they prayed S. PAVL to informe them, not of the sect of the Christiãs, but of the opiniõ that he (whom they reputed to be greatly versed in the Iewish doctrine) had of them. Otherwise, Act. 18. Ruff. præf. in Clem. Act. 28. Calu. inst. l. 4 c. 6. The author of the trea. vpon the Church. c. 8.

how could S. PAVL say in his epistle to the *Romans*, aboue fower yeare before his arriuall at *Rome*; *your faith is declared through the whole world?*

Rom. 1.

To the sixt obiection; which is, that S. LVKE, who hath written the historie of the Apostles, speaketh not of the voyage of S. PETER to *Rome*; we answere, S. LVKE purposed to write particularlie the actes of saint PAVL his master, and not these of the other Apostles. For except that which past betweene the death of our Lord, and the conuersion of saint PAVL, where he treates the historie of the Apostles in cōmon, to make it serue for a foundation to the particular relation of the actes of S. PAVL, and except the discourse of the conuersion of *Cornelius*, which hee adds there, for as much as this conuersion, was the ouerture of the Ghospell to the *Gentiles*, for whose vocatiō S. PAVL had bene called; S. LVKE doth not, after that to the end of his booke, make mention of anie other Apostle, vnlesse in as much as hee was in the place where S. PAVL was; and yet he omitts the voyage of S, PAVL to *Jerusalem*, to visit S. PETER, & S. PETER & S. PAVLES meeting at *Antioch*, and the right hand of association giuen by S. PETER, S. IAMES, & S. IOHN to S. PAVL; & the voyage of the same S, PAVL into *Galatia*, which caused *Beza* to saie, *Luke hath omitted manie thinges, and principallie S.* PAVLES *voyage to the Galathians*. And therefore so farr is S. IEROM from making vse of S. LVKES silence, to weaken the credit of S. PETERS staie at *Rome*, as contrariwise he argues the staie of S. PETER at *Antioch* and at *Rome*, to shew how *S. LVKE* hath passed manie thinges vnder silence, and takes this foundation for a certaine and vndoubted principle of historie. *Finallie* (saith S. IEROM) *we haue learnt, that Peter was the first Bishop of the Church of Antioch, and that from thence, he was transferred to Rome, which Luke hath vtterly omitted.*

Bez. annot. in act. ep. ad Galat.

Hier. in ep. ad Gal. c. 2

To the seauenth obiection, which is that S. PAVL speakes of the enterview betweene S. PETER and himselfe, both at *Ierusalem* and *Antioch*, but speaks of no meeting, betweene S. PETER and him at *Rome*, which was the famousest cittie of the world; wee answere, that the epistle to the *Galatiās*, which is the onely place where S. PAVL speaks of the enterviews betweene S. PETER and him, to dissipate the reproaches that they that would seduce the *Galatians*, laid vpon him, that he had not bene instituted Apostle by Christ, but by S. PETER, & by the other Apostles who gaue him their right hands for associatiō; was written (if wee belieue S. CHRYSOSTOME before the epistle to the *Romans*; and then we must not thinke it strange that S. PAVL touched nothing there, of the enterview of S. PETER & him at *Rome*; since it was written, before the voyage of S. PAVL to *Rome*.

The auth. of the trea. vpon the Chr. c. 8.

Chrys. præfat. in ep. ad Rom.

To the eighth obiection, which is that S. IOHN makes mention of the kinde of death of S. PETER, but makes noe mention of the place of his death: we answere two things; the one, that S. IOHN makes mentiō of the kinde of S. PETERS death, & not of of the place where, because the kinde, and not the place of the death of S. PETER, belonges to the explication of this prophecie of our Lord; *When thou shall be olde, thou shalt stretch forth thy hands*: And the other, that so farre is this clause of S. IOHN from weakning the beliefe of S. PETERS death at *Rome*, that it fullie confirmes and authoriseth it. For S. IOHN hauing writt his Ghospell manie yeares after the martyrdome of S. PEEER, and hauing explained, and proued this prophecie of our Lord, *thou shalt stretch forth thy hāds*, by the kinde of S. PETERS death, without specifying it particularly; it must be, that when S. IOHN writt his Ghospell, the kinde of S. PETERS death was knowne and euidēt to all partes of the Church. Now, the kinde of S. PETERS death could not be knowne to all partes of the Church, but the place of his death must likewise be knowne to them, nor could the place of S. PETERS death be

The authe. of the trea. vpon the Chr. c. 8.

Ioann. 21.

knowne

knowne to all the Church, & bee anie other then *Rome*. For how could it happen, that not onely all the ancient authors, yea those that writt in the next age after S. IOHN as [a] S. DIONISIVS of *Corinth*, [b] S. IRENEVS, [c] *Caius*, [d] *Tertullian*, & infinite others, but the very stones also, & the inscriptions of the sepulchres of S. PETER & S. PAVL, which were yet preserued, and publickly shewed at *Rome* in the tyme of *Caius*, should witnesse with a cōmon voice, that S, PETER had bene martired at *Rome*, & that noe other Church but the *Roman*, did euer glorie in his Relicks, and his martirdome, if frō the time wherein S. Iohn writt his Ghospell, the place of S. PETERS death had bene knowne to all the partes of the Church, & had bene anie other then *Rome*? And therefore, what remaines in all the texts obiected to vs from scripture, which agrees not perfectly with the Chronology of the Church, concerning the history of S. PETER? Saint PAVL affirmes that three yeare after his conuersion, he trauelled to *Ierusalem* to visit S. PETER; consents not that exactly with our computatiō, which reckons the conuersion of S. PAVL, the first yeare after the death of our Lord; & the voyage of S. PETER to *Antioch*, the fifth? S. LVKE reportes, that S. PAVL being come to *Ierusalem* for the distributiō of the almes during the famine, which began the eleauenth yeare after the death of Christ, found S. PETER there prisoner; doth not that wholie agree with our Chronologie, which supposes, that the Episcopall Seate of saint PETER at *Antioch*, was seauen yeare, fiue compleate, & two imperfect? The same S. LVKE writes, that S. PETER withdrawing himselfe from *Ierusalem* at his deliuery, which was the second yeare of the Raigne of *Claudius*, *went into an other place*; that is to saie, into an other place proper to goe out of *Iudea*; & from the iurisdiction of *Herod*, such as was *Ioppa*, where those vsed to imbarke, that would saile to *Rome*, & into the west: doth not that excellently agree with S. IEROMS computatiō, who reports that S. PETER came to *Rome*, the second yeare of the Empire of *Claudius*? For that S. LVKE saith onely, that he went into an other place, & expresses not whither, but leaues him seauen yeare after without mention, it is not to abandon the historie of S. PAVL his master. The same S. LVKE testifies, that S. PETER was againe at the Councell at *Ierusalem* holden for legall causes. Fitts not that iust with that, that *Suetonius* saith, that *Claudius* draue the Iewes from *Rome*, which raisd tumults for Christs cause, & to that, that *Orosius* notes, that this banishment was in the ninth yeare of *Claudius*; that is, the eighteenth yeare after the death of Christ, which was the verie yeare of the Councell? S. IOHN expounds this prophecie of our Lord to S. PETER; *Thou shalt stretch forth thy hands, and an other shall girde thee*, by the kinde of S. PETERS death; and adds, that our Lord foretelling enigmaticallie the martirdome of S. PETER, said to him, *follow mee*; doth not this agree, with that *Tertullian* saith, speaking of the *Roman* Church: *Happie Church, in which the Apostles haue shedd all their doctrine, with their bloud, in which Peter is equalled to the passion of our Lord*: And with what S. AMBROSE writes that *S. Peter being come forth of Rome to flie persecution, our Lord appeared to him; and said; I goe to Rome to be crucified againe?*

S. PETER insinuates in his first epistle, that he writt it from *Babylon*; & many greeke copies contrarily date it from Rome: Is not this solued by that, that *Eusebius* and S, IEROM saie, that *S. PETER calls Rome allegorically Babylon, for as much as Rome was then in regard of the Iewes, the same as the Asian Babylon had bene in the tyme of the Prophets?* He adds the salutation of MARKE: *The Church* (said hee) *which is in Babylon, and Marke my sonne, salute you*: doth not that agree, both with the vse of the word *Marcus*, which was a *Roman* name, and not a *Babylonian*; and with these wordes of *Papias*

[Margin notes: a Dion Cor. apud Eus. hist. eccl. l. 2. c. 25. — b Iren. aduers. hæres. l. 3. c. 3. — c Caius apud Eus. hist. eccl. l. 2. c. 25. — d Tert. de præscrip. — Galat. 1. — Act. 12. — Ibid. — Hier. de script. eccl. in Petro. — Act. 15. Sueton. in Claud. Oros hist. l. 7. c. 6 — Ioann. 21. — Tert. de præscript. Amb. orat. in Auxent. de non trad Basil. ep. l. 5 — 1. Pet. c. 5. Exep græc. Oecum. & alia. — Euseb. hist. eccl. l. 2. c. 14. Hieron. de script. eccl. in Marc. 1. Pet. ibid.]

Auditor

Papias Hierap. & Clemen. Alex. l. 7. Hypotyp. apud Euseb hist. eccl. l. 2. c 14

auditor of S. IOHN, reported by *Clemens Alexandrinus*; *Marke being requested at Rome by the bretheren, writ a short Ghospell which Peter hauing read approued?* For whereas *Erasmus* saith, that S. IEROM attributes the name of *Babylon* to *Rome* in choller, for as much as hee had bene euill intreated there; and will haue that *Babylon*, whereof *S.* PETER speakes, to be the *Asirian-Babylou*; These are two childish ignorances, the one not to know that S. IEROM had alreadie interpreted that *Babylon*, whereof S. PETER speakes to be *Rome*, both in his commentarie vpon *Esay*, and in his catalogue of the Ecclesiasticall Authors, written long before the euill intreaty that he receiued at *Rome*, which happened vnder *Syricius*: And the other, not to know, that when S. PETER writ this epistle; *Iosephus* witnesseth, there were then no Iewes in *Babylon*. But this is enough of the instances of scripture; lett vs proceede to those of the Fathers, which consist in fower principall obiections.

Erasm. annot. in ep. 1. Pet. Hieron. in Esai. c. 47. Hier. de script. eccl. in Marc. Ios. Ant. l. 17. c. vlt. The author of the trea. vpon the Ch. c. 8.

The first, that *Clemens Comanus* writes to IAMES brother of our Lord, Bishop of Ierusalem, the death of S. PETER at *Rome*, a thing repugnant (saie the obiectors) to scripture, which witnesseth that IAMES was martired longe before the death of PETER. The second, that S. IEROM writes, that S. PETER was crucified in *Iudea*. The third, that S. AVST. affirmes, that the history of the battle of S. PETER and *Simon Magus* at *Rome*, proceeded from an opinion, or as they saie, from a fabulous narration: And the fowrth, that in the order of PETERS successors, some place *Linus* & *Cletus* before *Clement*, & some after: to which they farther add for the banquet and confectes after the Feast, that *Eusebius* and the *Legend*; vpon which they charge vs, that we found the Papacy contradict one an other; for as much as *Eusebius* saith, that S. PETER was crucified; and the *Legend* saith, he was beheaded.

Idem.

Ibid.

To the first of these obiectiōs; which is, that *Clement* writing to IAMES brother to our Lord, declares to him, the martirdome of *S. PETER*; Wee answere three things; first, that that epistle is *apocripha* and supposed; for though it was translated frō *Greeke* into *latine* by *Ruffinus*, & that it is cited by the first Councell of *Vaison* which was holden vnder the Emperor *Valentinian* the third, contayning manie good doctrines, neuerthelesse it is certaine, thar the *Greeke* originall of the recognitions of *Clement*, to which it was annexed & relatiue, was apocripha, & had bene either supposed or corrupted by the *Hebionites*. The second, that the Bishop of *Ierusalem*, to whom this epistle is addressed, was not IAMES the Apostle, brother to our Lord, but *Simon* brother & successor in the Bishoprick to IAMES the Apostle intitled the brother of our Lord; whom this epistle calls IAMES brother of our Lord, according to the custome the *Hebrewes* had to beare manie names, & sometimes to inherit names one from an other; as it appeares both by the repugnancie of the tyme of the death of the Apostle IAMES brother of our Lord, which *Ruffinus* interpretor & aduocate for his epistle, who had translated the Ecclesiasticall history of *Eusebius*, could not be ignorāt of; & by the inscription, in the which the author of the epistle intitles him, to whom he addresses it, IAMES *brother of our Lord, and Bishop of Ierusalem*, & intitles him not Apostle, which he could not haue forgottē to doe in that place, if it had bene the Apostle IAMES brother to our Lord. And the third, that those that obiect this, strayning forth a gnat, swallow a Camell; that is, in thinking to taxe the ignorance of others in the matter of the Chronologie of the Fathers, discouer their owne in the historie of the Scripture; for the Apostle S. IAMES, whose martirdome they saie, the Scripture reportes, was the Apostle IAMES, brother of IOHN, martir'd by *Herod*, in the twelfth of the Actes, & not the Apostle IAMES brother of our Lord, who was ten yeares after

Ruffi. præf. in ep. Clem Conc. Vasion. 1. c. 6. Lib. recognit. citat. à Clem. ad Iacob. ep. 1. Gelas. decr. de lib. apocriph. Epiph. cōt. Hebion. hæres. 30.

Euseb, hist. eccl. l. 2. c. 22.

Ios. ant. c. 8

still

ſtill in *Ieruſalem*, and of whoſe death, the Scripture neuer ſpeakes in anie part of it, the Church hauing learnt what she knowes of it, not from the Scripture, but from *Ioſephus*, and from *Hegeſippus*, and from *Clement Alexādrinus*, & from *Euſebius*, & from S. IEROM, who teſtifie that IAMES the Apoſtle, brother of our Lord, dyed vnder the *Pontificate* of *Ananus* the young, and in the ſeauenth yeare of the Empire of *Nero*.

To the ſecond obiection, which is, that S. IEROM writes, that *S. PETER was crucified in Iudea*; we anſwere that S. IEROM doth no where write, that S. PETER was crucified in *Iudea*, but contrarily he plainely affirmes, that he was crucified at *Rome*: *PETER* (ſaid he) *held the Sacerdotall Chaire at Rome, till the fourteenth yeare of Nero, by whom he was crucified.* And againe; *He was buried at Rome, in the Vatican, neere the triumphall Streete, where he is celebrated by the veneration of all the Cittie.* Onely after he hath reported the wordes of our Lord; *Behould, I ſend you prophets, and wiſe men, and Scribes, and you will kill them, and crucifie them, and whip them, in your Synagogues*: hee adds, *note likewiſe that there are diuers Guifts in the diſciples of Chriſt, according to the Apoſtle to the Corinthians; Some are Prophets, who foretell things to come; ſome are wiſe men, who know when they should pronounce the word; others Scribes well learned in the law; whereof Steuen hath bene ſtoned, Paule beheaded, Peter crucified.* But that *S. PETER* was crucified in *Iudea*, he hath, no where ſaid; and if he had bene crucified by the Iewes, hee had intēded it (in the ſame ſence wherein S. PAVL cryes, that *the Iewes crucified the Lord of Glorie*, that is to ſaie,) the Iewes cauſed him to be crucified, but not that hee had bene crucified in *Iudea*; otherwiſe, they muſt alſo haue concluded, that S. PAVL was not beheaded at *Rome*; but in *Iudea*, for S. IEROM ſaith it equallie of the one, and of the other, *whereof PAVLE hath bene beheaded, and PETER Crucified.*

To the third obiection, which is, that *S.* AVGVSTINE writ, that the hiſtorie of the combatt of S. PETER, and *Simon* the *Magitian* at *Rome* had taken ground from an opinion. Wee anſwere that *S.* AVGVSTINE ſaith no ſuch thing. And indeede how should he ſaie it, that had for ſuertie and forerunners in this hiſtorie, not onely S. IVSTIN *Martir*, an author of the next age after *Simon Magus*, who writt thus to the *Pagan* Emperors, from, and in the name of all the *Chriſtians*: *One Simon a Samaritan, hauing by the Diuells art, done workes by enchantment, vnder the Emperor Claudius, in your imperiall Cittie of Rome, was accoūted, a God, and, honored by you with a Statue as a God*; And [a] S. *Ireneus*, and [b] *Tertullian*, which writ the like, but alſo [c] *Arnobius*, [d] *Euſebius*, [e] S. CYRILL of *Ieruſalem*, [f] *S. EPIPHANIVS*, [g] *Philaſtrius*, [h] *S. IEROM*, [i] *Sulpitius ſeuerus* who all affirme, that *Simon*, hauing vndertakē, by art magicke to flie at *Rome*, was hindred from it, and cauſed to fall by S. PETER? he ſaith only that whereas ſome held, that the particular cuſtome obſerued by the *Roman* Church to forbeare dinner on Saturdaies, proceeded from a faſt celebrated by S. PETER the *S*atturdaie before this act, was an opinion. Behold his words; *It is* (ſaid hee) *the opinion of manie, although manie Romans hould it to be falſe that the apoſtle Peter being on the Sundaie to combat againſt Simon the magitian for the perill of ſo great a temptation, faſted the daie before, both he and the Church of the ſame Cittie, and that hauing obtained ſo proſperous and glorious a ſucceſſe, he continued the ſame cuſtome, and that ſome Churches of the weſt imitated him.* But that the hiſtorie of the conflict of S. PETER and *Simon Magus* at *Rome*, was grounded vpon an opinion, he ſaith nothing neere it, cōtrariwiſe he ſetts it downe for the firſt principle in his booke of hereſies in theſe words: *Simon would haue made it belieued that he was Iupiter, ad that a common woman, whoſe names was Helen, with whom he had ioyned himſelf for a complice of his crimes, was Minerua, and gaue the images of himſelf and his Copeſmate to be adored to his deſciples, and had obtained that they*

Hegeſip. hiſt. l. 5. apud Euſ. hiſt. eccl. l. 2. c. 22. Clem. Alex l. 7. Hypotyp. apud. Hier. de ſcrip. eccl. Euſ. hiſt. eccl. l. 2. c. 22. Hier. de ſcript. eccl. in Iacob. The auct. of the trea. vpon the Ch. c. 8. in the old editions. Hier. de ſcrip. eccl. in Petr. Idem ibid. Hier. in Matth l. 4. c. 23. Cor. c. 2.

The auct. of the treat of. the voc. of. Miniſters.

Iuſt. Martyr apol. 2. [a] Iren. aduers. hæres. l. 1. c. 20. [b] Tert. in apol. aduers gent. [c] Arnob. cōt. gent. l. 2 [d] Euſ. hiſt. eccl. l. 2. c. 14. [e] Cyrill. Hier. catich 6. [f] Epiph. hæres. 21. [g] Philaſtr. Brix. in Symon. [h] Hier. de ſcript. eccl. [i] Sulp. Seu. hiſt ſacr. l. 2 Aug. ep. 86 Aug. in Cat hæres. hæres. 1.

might be constituted by publicke authoritie, amongst the images of the Gods at Rome, in which Cittie the blessed Apostle Peter extinguished him, by the power of God Almightie. Which it seemes, the prophane authors themselues, though curious to bury the memorie of all the miracles of Christianitie, haue obliquely pointed at, when Suetonius saith, that there was a spectacle exhibited in a full theater in Nero's time, whereby they should haue made the Icarian-flight appeare, but the Icarus fell against Nero's chamber, and watred it with blood: and when Dion Chrisostome saith, that Nero had a long time neere him in his pallace, a certaine man who promised to flie.

Sueton. in vit Cæsar. l. 6
Dio. Chrys de pulchri. orat. 1.
The auct. of the trea. vpon the Ch c 8.
Epiph. cõt. Carp. hæres. 27.

To the fowrth obiection, which is, that amongst the Successors of S. PETER, some place *Linus* and *Cletus* before *Clement*, and some after: wee answer, that S. EPIPHANIVS hath preuented and solued it, 1250. yeares agone, in these worde: *At Rome were first Apostles and Bishops Peter and Paul, and then Linus, then Cletus, and then Clement &c. and lett none wonder that others receiued the Bishopricke before Clement.* And a little after; *whether that the Apostles being still aliue, Clement had receiued the ordination of the Bishopricke from Peter, and hauing refused it, abstained from it*; for hee saith in one of his Epistles; *I goe my waies and withdraw myselfe, till the people of God be erected, &c.* or whether after the decease of the Apostles, he haue bene instituted by *Cletus*, wee doe not euidently know, but it may be, that hauing bene promoted to the Bishopricke, & hauing refused it &c. he was againe cõstrained, after the death of *Linus* and of *Cletus* to accept of it. For that which the obiectors add for the banquet, and to make vp their mouthes, that *Eusebius* saith that S. PETER was crucified, and that the *Legend*, where vpon wee ground the Papacie saith, he was beheaded, there are two ridiculous ingredients in this last Seruice; the one to impute to vs, that we ground the historie of S. PETERS seate at *Rome*, which is testified by all the first ages of the Church vpon the *Legend*, which is a booke written in the last ages by a *Jacobin* called *Jacobus de voragine*: And the other, not to discerne, that, that S. PETER, that the *Legẽd* said was beheaded, is S. PETER the *Iacobin Martir*; who was beheaded for the Catholick faith, in the time of the *Albigeses*, about 400. yeare agone, and not S. PETER the Apostle, whom it affirmes to haue bene crucified.

Legend. Aur. in Petr Mart.
Legen. Aur in Petr. Apost.
Eus. hist. eccl. l. 2. c. 25.
Ibid.
Iren. l. 3. c. 3.

But now let vs leaue the obiections of the Popes aduersaries, and let vs heare the testimonies of the Fathers. S. DIONISIVS Bishop of *Corinth*, writing to be Church of *Rome* in the next age after the Apostles; *you haue* (said hee) *mingled the plant of the Roman & Corinthian Church made by PETER and PAVL*: And a little after; *for hauing taught together in Italie, they were both martired at one and the same time.* And S. IRENEVS; *We represent the tradition apostolick, of the greatest and most ancient Church, founded at Rome, by the two glorious Apostles PETER and PAVL*: And againe; *The blessed Apostles then founding and instructing the Church, consigned the Episcopat of the administration of the Church to Linus.* And TERTVLLIAN; *Happie Church wherein the Apostles haue shed all their doctrin with their bloud, in which PETER is equalled to the passion of our Lord.* And CAIVS of one tyme with *Tertulian*; *If thou wilt goe to the Vaticane, or to the waie of Hostia, thou shalt finde the trophies, (that is the Sepulchers) of those, which haue founded this Church.* And CLEMENT *Alexandrius*, & before him *Papias* the hearer of S. IOHN; *Marke being intreated at Roman by the bretheren, writt a briefe Ghospell, which PETER haueing read, approued.* And ORIGEN; *PETER was crucified at Rome, with his head downewards.* And saint CYPRIAN; *The Romeã Church, is the Chaire of PETER, and the principall Church, from whence proceeded, the Sacerdotall vnitie.* And EVSEBIVS; *Vnder the Empire of Claudius, the prouidence of God, brought the great Apostle Saint PETER to Rome*: And againe; *the histories beare, that*

Tert. de præsc.
Caius apud Eus. hist. eccl. l. 2. c. 15.
Apud. Eus. hist. eccl. l. 3. c. 1.
Cyp. ad Cornel. ep. 55.
Eus. hist. eccl. l. 2. c. 14.

PAVL

PAVL was beheaded, and PETER crucified at Rome, vnder Nero; and the titles of PETER and PAVL preserued to this daie in their sepulchers, confirme it. And LACTANTIVS; *PETER and PAVL preached at Rome, and their preaching remained written for memorie.* And S. ATHANASIVS; *though it were declared to PETER and PAVL, that they should suffer martirdome at Rome; yet they forbare not to trauell thither.* And S. CYRILL of *Ierusalem*; PETER *and* PAVL *presidents of the Church, came to Rome.* And saint EPIPHANIVS; *At Rome were first Apostles and Bishops,* PETER *and PAVL, and then Linus, and then Cletus, and then Clement.* And saint AMBROSE; PETER *is our warrant for this custome, who hath bene Bishop of the Roman Church*: And againe; *Christ haueing answered PETER, I goe to Rome to be crucified againe; PETER vnderstood, that this answere belonged to his Crosse*: And the Emperors GRATIAN, and VALENTINIAN, and THEODOSIVS; *Wee will that all the people ruled by the Empire of our clemencie, liue in such Religion, as the Religion insinuated hither-to by the diuine Apostle PETER declareth, that he gaue to the Romans.* And OPTATVS *Mileuitanus*; *Thou canst not denie, but that thou knowest, that in the Cittie of Rome, the Episcopall Chaire was first conferred to Peter, wherein Peter head of the Apostles sate.* And saint IEROM; *Simon* PETER, *Sonne of Iona, of the Prouince of Galilee, of the Borough of Bethsaida, brother to the Apostle Andrew, and Prince of the Apostles, after the Episcopat of the Church of Antioch, and the preaching of the dispersion of those of the Circumcision, which had belieued in Pontus, Galatia, Cappadocia, Asia, and Bithinia, came to Rome the second yeare of the Empire of Claudius, to ouerthrow Simon Magus, and held the Sacerdotall Chaire* twentie fiue yeares there. And againe, *Hegesippus* affirmes; *That he came to Rome vnder Anicetus, who was tenth Bishop of Rome after* PETER. And else where, *Cyprian addressed the Councell of affrica, to Steuen Bishop of the Roman Church, who was the twentie sixth after the Blessed* Peter. And RVFFINVS; *Peter ruled the Roman Church, for the space of twentie fower yeares.* And SVLPITIVS *Seuerus*; *The Christiā Religion had then taken roote in the Cittie of Rome Peter being Bishop there.* And S. CHRISOSTOME: *What spectacle shall* Rome, *see in the daie of Iudgemeut, Paul comeing forth of his graue, risen againe with* PETER. And OROSIVS; *Nero putt* PETER *to death by the Crosse, and* PAVL *by the sword.* And saint AVGVSTIN; *Wee see the most eminent height of the thrice noble Empire, submitting his diadem, bend his knee to the supulcher of the fisherman* PETER: And in an other place; *I thinke this part of the world ought to suffice thee, wherein our Lord would crowne, with a most glorious martirdome, the first of his Apostles.* And else where; *What hath the chaire of the Roman Church done to thee, wherein* PETER *hath bene set, and wherein now Anastasius sitts?* And againe *To* PETER *hath succeeded Linus, to Linus Clemēt; to Clemēt, Anacletus, to Anacletus Euaristus.*

Lactan inst l.4.c.21. Athan. apo 2. Cyril. Hier catech.6. Amb. de Sacram. l 3 c.1. Cod. l.1. Opt. cont. Parm. l.2. Hier. de scrip. eccl. in Petr. Idem. ibid. in Hegesippo. Id. in dial. aduers. Lucif. Ruffin. inuect. Sulp. Seu. hist. sacr. l.2. Chrys. in ep. ad Rom hom.32. Oros l.7. c.7. Aug. ep.42. Id. cont. Iul Pelag. l.1. Id. cont. Petil. l.2. c.51. Id. ep.165.

Of the Canon of the Councell of Nicea, touching the gouernment of the Patriarches.

CHAPT. V.

HAuing dispatched the difficulties of the Scripture, and of the Fathers, cōcerning S. PETERS staie at *Antioch*, & *Rome*; there remaines to solue the obiections, that the aduersaries of the Church, make against what wee haue said of the Popes superioritie, ouer the other patriarkes: whereof the principall is taken frō one of the Canōs of the coūcell of *Nicea*, which ordaines, that the anciēt customes obserued in *Egipt*, *Lybia*, and *Pentapolis*, should goe on; to witt, that the Bishop of *Alexandria* should haue the power of all those things, because it was also so accustomed to the Bishop of *Rome*. Now the aduersaries of the Church, doe more willinglie make vse of the Councell of *Nicea* in such like cases, then of anie other; because the actes of the Councell of

Cōc. Nic. c.6.

Nicea, (which, if wee had them, might cleere the sence of the Canons of the same Councell) are loste; & that there remaine to vs of the acts of the first fowre generall Councells no more but those of *Ephesus*, and of *Chalcedon*. And therefore wee must supplie what wants in the breuitie and omission of this Canon, by conferring it with the acts of the other councells, or by the examination of the histories of their ages.

To this obiection then wee bring two Answeres, the first is, that it hath alreadie bene aboue shewed in the Chapter of the patriarkes, that the pope had two distinct qualities, the one of patriarke of the *West*, & the other of head of the Church, vniuersall, as the Prefect of the Cittie Prefecture; by which the aduersaries of the Church, would measure the spirituall Iurisdictiõ of the *Pope*, who had 2. distinct qualities, the one of prefect of the Cittie Prefecture, in which he was equall to the prefect of the other prouinces; & the other, of head of the senate, & Vicar of the Emperor, in which he was superiour to the prefects of prouinces, and iudged by appeale, of the cause of all their Iurisdictiõs. By meanes whereof, although in things that concerned but the patriarchall Iurisdictiõ, as were the celebratiõ of prouinciall, or nationall coũcells; the correctiõs of mãners, of the simple priests or deacõs; the confirmatiõs either mediate, or immediate, of the Bishops of the Patriarkship, and the subalterne iudgements of the causes euen of Bishops. All the other Patriarkes were squared out by the modell and paterne, of that of *Rome*; neuerthelesse, when there question of things that went beyond the limitts of *Patriarchall* iurisdiction, that is to saie, of *Maior* causes, and which conuerned the vniuersall Church; as were causes of Faith, or generall customes of the Church, or those of the finall depositions of Bishops, or that of the iudgements euẽ of the persons of the *Patriarkes*, the Bishop of *Rome* as head of the Church, and superintendent of the other Patriarkes, exercised Ecclesiasticall Iurisdiction ouer thẽ and iudged of their iudgements and persons. And therefore when the coũcell of *Nicea* ordained that in *Egipt*, *Lybia*, and *Pentapolis*, the Bishop of *Alexandria* should remaine in possessiõ of the authority he had for all the causes, whereof the councell thẽ spake; that is to saie, for the celebration of Prouinçiall and nationall *Synods*; for the correctiõ of *minor*, and particular causes; & for the confirmation either mediate or immediate of the Bishops of the same prouinces; & addeth, for as much as this alsois accustomed to the Bishop of *Rome*; it is certaine that the intention of the coũcell was not, by that to square the Bishop of *Alexandria* by him of *Rome*, in things that wẽt beyond the limitts, and authoritie of Patriarchall iurisdictiõ, and concerned the iurisdictiõ of the head of the Church, and the gouernment of the vniuersall societie but in those things onely, that were withim the boũdes, and within the facultie of Patriarchall iurisdiction. No more then when they measured the power that the other Prefects of the Empire had within the cõpasse of their prouinces by the power that the prefects of the cittie of *Rome* had within the prouinces of his *Prefecture*, they pretẽded not by that, that in matters that wen forth by appeale from the other prouinces, the cittie Prefecte, as head of the Senate and Vicar to the Prince, was not Superior to all the others: nor that whẽ in a nationall Councell, they square out the power that the Archbishops haue ouer the Bishops of their prouinces to the modell of that which the *Primate* of the natiõs, hath, as particular Archbishop ouer the Bishops of his quarter, they pretẽd not by that, that in things which goe beyõd the iurisdictiõ of the prouinces, & regard the generall interest of the natiõ, the Primat should not be superior to the other Archbishops; nor finallie, whẽ in a regiment of men of warre, they measure the power that euery particular Captaine hath to

Lib. de Suburb. im presſ. Francofurt 1618. differtat 2. c. 2. Ibid differtat. 1. c. 1.

Conc. Nic. c. 6.

commaund his company, by the paterne and modell that the Campe-Master of the Regimēt hath ouer his; they intend not by that, in things which are not in the particular comaund of euerie companie, but haue regard to the order, the disposition, and gouernemēt of the Regiment in generall, the Campe-Master should not be superiour to all the other captaines. For both before the Councell of *Nicea*, when the Church-men of *Alexandria*, would accuse *Dionisius* the Patriarke of *Alexandria* their Bishop, who was the first Patriarke of the Church after the Pope, *they transported themselues* (saith *Athanasius*) *to Rome*, *& accused him before Dionisius Bishop of Rome*; & presently after the Councell of *Nicea* when the councell of *Antioch*, Sea of the third Patriarkeship had bene celebrated, it was argued of nullitie, *because* saith SOCRATES, *the Ecclesiasticall law forbad, to rule the Churches without the sentence of the Bishop of Rome*. And when the same Councell of *Antioch*, & the other councells of the *East*, had deposed S. ATHANAS. Patriarke of *Alexandria*, and *Marcellus* Primate of *Ancyra* in *Galatia*, and *Asclepas* Bishop of *Gaza*, in *Palestina*, a cittie of the Patriarkeship of *Antioch*; *The Bishop of Rome* (saith *Sozomene*) *restored them euerie one to his Church, because to him, for the dignitie of his Sea appertained the care of all things*. And when the Councell of *Sardica* within twentie yeare of that of *Nicea*, and holden for the Confirmation of that of *Nicea* and composed of the like or a greater number of Bishops thē that of *Nicea*, and at which assisted the same *Osius* Bishop of *Corduba*; the same saint ATHANASIVS then Patriarke of *Alexandria*, & the same *Protogenes* Bishop of *Sardica*, which had assisted at that of *Nicea*, proceeded to the direction of ecclesiasticall causes; it did not onely authorize the appeales, from the Bishops of all the Earth to the Pope, but also declared that it was a very good and conuenient thing, that from all the Prouinces, the Bishops should referre the affaires, to their head; that is to saie, to the Sea of the Apostle PETER. And whē the Councell of *Capua* which the third Councell of *Carthage* calls a generall councell, deputed *Theophilus* Patriarke of *Alexandria*, because of the neighbourhood of his Patriarkship, to examine the cause of *Flauianus* Patriarke of *Antioch*; saint AMBROSE writ to him, that after he had iudged it, he must get the Pope to confirme his iudgement. And when the generall councell of *Ephesus* passed to the cause of *Iohn* Patriarke of *Antioch*; *Iuuenall* Bishop of *Ierusalē* said that the ancient custome bare, that the Church of *Antioch* was alwaies gouerned by the *Roman*: and the councell in the Bodie of it, remitted the iudgement of the Patriarke of *Antioch*, to the Pope. And when *Dioscorus*, Patriarke of *Alexandria*, had in the false Councell of *Ephesus* condemned and deposed *Flauianus* Bishop of *Constantinople*; *Flauianus* appealed frō him to the Pope; and that, saith the Emperor *Valentinian* following the custome of the Councells. And when the Councell of *Chalcedon* disanulled the false Councell of *Ephesus* it was voted by *Anatolius* Bishop of *Constantinople*, that of all the acts of that councell, none should remaine in force, except the creation of *Maximus* Patriarke of *Antioch*, because the Pope hauing receiued him into his cōmunion, had iudged that he should gouerne the Church of *Antioch*, & whē *Theodoret* Bishop of *Cyre* neighbour to *Persia*, and one of the Subiects of the Patriarkship of *Antioch*, who had bene deposed by the same coūcell of *Ephesus*, & had, frō it appealed to the Pope, presented himselfe at the coūcell of *Chalcedon*; the senators, to cause order to be obserued there, commaunded he should come in, for as much as the Pope had restored him to his Bishopricke. And when the Popes Legates bare the first word in the Councell, not onely they intitled the Pope the head of all the Churches; but also when the Fathers of the councell in their Bodie, sent their Relation to the Pope, they

Ath. de sent. Dionis. see aboue in Chap. 25.

Soc. hist. eccl. l. 2. c. 8.

Soc. hist. eccl. l. 3. c. 7.

Cōc. Sard can 5. See Balsamon vpon this Canon.

Cōc. Sard. ep. ad Iul. in fragm. Hilar.

Amb. ep. 78

Conc. Eph. part. 2. act. 5. in relat. in Cælest.

Valēt. apud Theod. in ep. pradm.

Cōc. Chalc

Cōc Chalc act. 10.

Cōc. Chalc act 1.

Ib. & Euag. l. 2. c. 4.

Cóc. Chalc apud. Leó. part. 3. intreated him as the head of the vniuersall Church; *Thou hast guided vs* (said they) *by the legats, as the head doth the members.* And againe; Ibid. *As in this, which is for the weale, we haue brought correspondencie to our head, so thy Soueraigntie may fulfill, in the behalfe of thie Children, that which concernes decencie:* and they treated *Dioscorus* Patriarke of *Alexandria*, as ghostly vassall to the Pope; Ibid. *Dioscorus* (said they) *hath extended his felonie euen against him, to whom the guarde of the Vine hath by our Sauiour bene committed: that is to saie, against thy Holynesse.* Euident and manifest arguments, that the Pope had two qualities distinct; the one of Patriarke of the *West* and the other of Soueraigne Vicar of Christ, and head of the vniuersall Church; and that when the other Patriarkes were compared to him, it was in qualitie of Patriarke of the West; and not in the quality of Soueraigne Vicar of Christ, and head of the vniuersall Church.

The second Solution is, that the Councell of *Nicea* speakes of the Conc. Nic. c. 6. Bishop of *Alexandria* with restriction; and of the Pope without restriction; from whence it is, that the Senators assisting at the Councell of *Chalcedon*, to cause order to be obserued there, after they had heard the Cóc. Chalc act. 16. lecture of the sixth Canon of the Councell of *Nicea*, and of the third Canon of the Councell of *Constantinople*, inferred thereupon; *thus it apppeares from hence, that all primacie, and principall honor, hath alwaies bene yelded to the Bishop of Rome:* a thing that amazes, me that the *Greeke* Hil. Arch. Thessa. de Prim Pap. l. 2. Schismatickes, and *Nilus* amongst the rest, did not perceiue it. For *Nilus* Archbishop of *Thessalonica*, disputing against the Pope, saith: *If the Canon of the Councell of Nicea, had distributed the Climates of the earth to euerie one of the Bishops-Generall,* (so he calls the Patriarkes) *and had determinately setled nothing vpon the Sea of the Pope, but had contented it self with saying, that he had receiued the primacie, there had bene some reason to esteeme that all the earth had bene vnder him.* And neuerthelesse, not onely the Councell of *Constantinople* ordaines that the Bishops should not exceede their limitts, but that Cóc Const c. 2. according to the Canons of the Councell of *Nicea*, the Bishop of *Alexandria gouerned onely, the affaires of Egipt*; And the Bishops of the *East*, that is, of the Patriarkship of *Antioch*, onely the affaires of the *East*, And the Councell of *Chalcedon* ordaines, to the Bishop of *Ierusalem*, the three *Palestina's*; And to him of *Constantinople*; *Asia minor*, *Pontus*, and *Thrasia*, and the Cóc. Chalc act. 7. Barbarous prouinces, that is to say, *Russia* and *Muscouia*; without euer Cóc. Chalc c. 28. goeing about, either that or anie other Councell, to sett out a part to the Bishop of *Rome*, nor prescribe limitts, out of which he might not exercise his authoritie: But euen the Councell of *Nicea* speakes of the Bishop of *Alexandria* with restriction, assigning him the prouinces of *Egipt Libia* and Conc. Nic. an. 6. *Pentapolis*, and of the Pope without restriction, leauing him the waie free, and assigning him noe limitts; nor anie determinate number of prouinces. The customes said the Canon obserued from antiquitie in *Egipt*, *Libia*, and *Pentapolis*, are to be maintained, to wit, that the Bishop of *Alexandria*, haue the power, of all those things, for as much as this is also accustomed to the Bishop of *Rome*. By meanes whereof, it remaines in the libertie of the Reader to supplie the word, *ouer all the Church*, and to expresse the Canon in this sence; that the customes obserued from antiquitie in *Egipt, Libia*, and *Pentapolis*, should be maintained; to wit, that the Bishop of *Alexandria*, haue the power of all those things, for as much as this is also accu- Iren. cont. Valent. l. 3. c. 3. stomed to the Bishop of *Rome*, ouer all the Church. For what was this custome practized by the Bishop of *Rome*, but that whereof saint IRENEVS speakes, when he saith to the *Roman* Church; Aug. ep. 262. *because of a more mightie Principalitie, it is necessarie that all the Church should agree.* And saint AVSTIN when he writes; *In the Roman Church hath alwaies flourisht, the*

principalitie

principalitie of the Sea Apostolicke: And *Socrates* when he affirmes; *that the Ecclesiasticall lawe bare, that no decrees might be made in the Church, without the sentence of the Bishop of Rome*. And *Sozomene* when he notes, that *to the Bishop of Rome, because of the dignitie of his Seate, the care of all things appertained?* Soz. hist. eccl. l. 3. c. 8.

And so who sees not, that the intention of the Councell, was not to compare the Bishop of *Alexandria* with the Pope formallie, but anologically; that is to saie, that the intention of the Councell, was not to compare the authoritie of the Bishop of *Alexandria*, ouer the prouinces of *Egipt, Libia* and *Pentapolis*, with the authority of the Pope, ouer anie determinate territorie; but to compare the authoritie of the Bishop of *Alexandria* ouer the prouinces of *Egipt, Libia*, and *Pentapolis*, with the authority of the Pope ouer the whole Church? It is certaine that in this clause; *for as much as this is also accustomed to the Bishop of Rome*, there is an omission which should be supplied, either by the extent of an vniuersall word, of particular restriction. Now that the designe of the Councell was not to compare the Sea of *Alexandria* as head of the particular Prefecture of *Egipt*, with the sea of *Rome* as head of an other particular prefecture, but to compare the Sea of *Alexandria*, as head of the particular prefecture of *Egipt*, with the Sea of *Rome*, as head of all the Empire; the decree of the Councell of *Chalcedon*, which shall be spoken of hereafter, shewes it, when it saies, designing the temporall cause of the priuiledges of the Church of *Rome*, *The fathers yeilded the priuiledges to the Sea of the ancient Rome, for as much as that Cittie helde the Empire*: And the Confronting of these wordes of *Socrates*, *The Ecclesiasticall rule bare, that no lawes should be introduced into the Church, without the sentence of the Bishop of Rome*: with these of the Bishops of *Egipt*, to the Councell of *Chalcedon*: *Permitt vs to attend the ordination of our Archbishop, to the end, that according to the ancient customes, we may follow his sentence*: And againe: *It is the custome in the prouinces of the prefecture of Egipt, to doe noe such ting, without the sentence and ordinance, of the Archbishop of Alexandria, confirmeth it*. For to saie, that there could be nothing established in the vniuersall Church without the sentence of the Bishop of *Rome*, and to saie there could be nothing established in the prouinces of the Prefecture of *Egipt*, without the sentence of the Bishop of *Alexandria*, was it not to make the Bishop of *Alexandria* that in the prefecture of *Egipt*, that the Bishop of *Rome* was ouer the whole Church? And therefore the Councell saying simplie, *for as much as this is also accustomed to the Bishop of Rome*, and not specifying where, nor bringing in anie restriction, what should hinder vs from supplying, ouer all the Church, and from answering, that the intention of the Councell was, to ordaine, that the Bishop of *Alexandria*, who in *Egipt, Libia*, and *Pentapolis*, was as Vicar bred from the Sea of saint PETER, who had there established his second selfe; that is to saie, his sonne, and welbeloued disciple, the Euangelist saint MARKE, should haue the superintendencie of the Ecclesiasticall affaires in all these prouinces; for as much as the Bishop of *Rome* to whom (as *Sozomene* saith) because of the dignitie of his Seate, the care of all things appertained; had it generally ouer all the Church? or if they will presse vs to reduce the enthymeme of the Councell into the forme of a complete sillogisme, what can hinder vs from reducing it into this: The same priuiledges that the Bishop of *Rome* hath in regard of the whole Church; the other Patriarkes haue proportionablie euery one, in regard of his Patriarkship: Now the Bishop of *Rome* hath this priuiledge that to him, because of the dignitie of his Sea, the care of all things pertaines, and that without him, nothing can be decided, of things which

Conc. hist. c. 6. In chap. 34. Côc Chalc act. 16. can. 18. Côc. Chalc act. 4. Ib. Conc. Nic. c. 6. Soz. l. 3 c. 8. Soz. Ibid.

concerne the gouernment of the vniuersall Church: the Bishop of *Alexadria* then ought to enioy by proportion, the same priuiledges in the prouinces of his Patriarkship; that is to say, in the prouinces of *Egipt*, *Libia*, and *Pentapolis*; to witt, that to him, because of the dignitie of his Sea appertaines the superintendencie of the Churches of the same Prouinces; and that without him nothing should be decided in causes which concerne them. For that the Patriarkes in their diuisions were as images and modells of the Popes authoritie, and as Vicars borne from the Apostolicke Sea; that is to saie, were, euery one in the extent of his Patriarkship, that, that the Pope was vniuersallie ouer the whole Church. And then, that as the Riuer *Melas* in *Greece* produced the same kindes of animals and plantes, as *Nilus* in *Egipt*, but lesser and proportionable to the quantitie of his course, so the same authoritie, that the Pope had ouer all the Church; to wit, that without him nothing might be decided, in things which had regard to the vniuersall Church; the Bishop of *Alexandria* had it, proportionablie in his diuision; to witt, that without him, nothing could be decided of the Ecclesiasticall causes of *Egipt*, and of all the deuision of *Alexandria*; it appeares by ten meanes besides many others.

Soc. hist. eccl. l. 2. c. 8

It appeares first by the diuersitie of the conditions vnder which the Pope, and the other Patriarkes participated to the succession of the Sea of Saint PETER, who was the head and superintendent of Episcopall iurisdiction; for the Pope onely bare the title of absolute successor, and ordinary Vicar to saint PETER, as being constituted in the Tribunall, where saint PETER had established his finall and absolute Sea, & where he had planted the stocke of his direct Succession: from whence it is, that saint CYPRIAN calls the *Roman* Church, *the Chaire of Peter, and the principall Church, and the originall of the Sacerdotall vnitie*; and that the councell of *Sardica* exhortes the Bishops of all the prouinces, to referr the causes to their head; that is to saie, to the Sea of the Apostle PETER: and that *Sozomene* saith, that the Death, of *Pope Felix*, was the prouidence of God, least the Sea of PETER might be dishonored, being gouerned by two *Rectors*: and that saint IEROM writes to Pope DAMASUS; *I am ioyned in communion with thy blessednesse*; that is to saie, with the Chaire of PETER: and that Pope *Innocent* the first reported, and approued by saint AVSTIN, writt to the Bishops of *Africa*; *I conceaue that all our bretheren and colleagues, can referre causes, and principallie concerning faith, to none but to PETER; that is to saie; to the author of their name and dignitie; and that the Legates of Pope Celestine, in the oration that they made to the Councell of Ephesus, and which was coufessed and registred by the ordinance of the Councell called the Pope, the Successor, and ordinarie Vicar of saint PETER*; And that the councell of *Chalcedon* intitled the Epistle of the Pope saint LEO the first; *The Sermon of saint PETERS Sea*: whereas the part that the other patriarkes had to the Successioin of saint PETER, was an oblique and collaterall part, and founded vpon subalterne and particular causes; to witt, that of the patriarke of *Antioch* vpon the passing and transitorie Sea of saint PETER at *Antioch*; from whence it is that saint CHRYSOSTOME saith; *Peter the superintendet of the whole world, he to whō Christ had cōsigned the keyes of the kingdome of heauen, to whom he had committed the disposition of all things, was a long time resident at Antioch*: And that the Pope *Innocent* the first, tyme sellow to the same saint CHRYSOSTOME, writt to *Alexander* the Patriarke of *Antioch*: *The Sea of Antioch had not giuen, place to Rome, had it not bene, that what that obtained but by the waie, this hath obtained absolutely and finallie*: And that of the patriarke of *Alexandria*, vpon the commission that saint PETER gaue to his

Cyp ad Cornel. ep. 55.
Conc. Sard. ep. ad Iul. in fragm. Hilar. p. 15.
Soz. hist. eccl. l. 4 c. 14.
Hier ad Dam. ep. 58
Aug. ep. 106.
Innoc int. ep. Aug. ep. 93.
Conc. Eph. part. 2. act. 3.
Cōc. Chalc part. 3.
Chrys. hō. in beat. Ign
Innoc ad Alex. Episc Antioch ep 18.

his second-selfe; that is to saie, to his deare, and welbeloued disciple saint MARKE, to goe found the Church of *Alexandria*, the Metropolitan cittie of *Egipt*, and of the prouinces adiacent; from whence saint GREGORIE the *great* cries out; *The sea of Peter in three places, is of one alone; for he had exalted the Sea, wherein hee vouchsafed to staie, and finish his present life: he hath adorned the Sea, to which he hath ordained the Euangelist his disciple; hee hath established the Sea, wherein he was resident seauen yeare, though he were to depart from it.* By which meanes, as the Pope represented the Stocke of the direct succession of saint PETER; and the other Patriarkes represented the branches of the oblique and collaterall succession of saint PETER; so what the Pope was in regard of the vniuersall Church, the other Patriarkes were in the behalfe of their particular Patriarckships; and reciprocally what the other Patriarkes were, in the behalfe of their particular Patriarkships, the Pope was, in regard of the vniuersall Church. Greg. Magn. l. 6. ep. 37.

It appeares secondly by the analogie of the ancient order of the Church, which bare that the same priuiledges that the Patriarkes, Primats, and Metropolitans had, to wit, that without them nothing could be decided, of the affaires of their deuisions; and that the Prouinciall, nationall, or Patriarchall Councells, which were held in their territories, could not be esteemed perfect, if they assisted not there, the Popes had thē for the affaires which regarded the gouernment of the vniuersall Church, and for the celebration of generall Councells; and reciprocallie that the same priuiledges that the Popes had, as that the care of all the Church pertained to them, and that without them nothing could be decided of points concerning the vniuersall Church, nor generall Councells bee celebrated; the Patriarkes, Primats, and Metropolitans, had them proportionablie in their limitts, to witt, that the care of all the affaires of their deuisions, belonged to them, and without them nothing could be decided, in the affaires of their iurisdictions, nor the Councells of their territories bee celebrated. For as the Councell of *Antioch*, which I alledge because it borrowes this decree, not from the discipline of the *Arrians*, but from the ancient forme of the Church, saith, that *the care of all the Prouince belongs to the Metropolitan.* Soe *Sozomen* saith that *the Bishop of Rome restored Athanasius, Patriarke of Alexandria; Paule Bishop of Constantinople; Marcellus primate of Ancyra in Galatia, for that to him because of the dignitie of his Sea; the care of all things appertained.* And as the same Councell of *Antioch* saith, speaking of particular Councells; *That Sinod is perfect, at which the Metropolitan assists;* Soe *Socrates* witnesseth; *That Generall Councells, and which were to prouide for the Generall lawes of the Church, could not be celebrated without the Pope. JVLIVS,* (saith he) *had not assisted at the Councell of Antioch; nor had sent anie in his place, although the Canon of the Church forbids to make Ecclesiasticall lawes without the sentence of the Bishop of Rome* or according to the translation of EPIPHANIVS, followed by *Cassiodorus, to celebrate Councells without the sentence of the Bishop of Rome:* And *Sozomene; There was an eccclesiasticall lawe, which annulled all things that were instituted in the Churches, without the sentence of the Bishop of Rome.* And the Emperors *Theodosius* and *Valentinian; Wee decree, that accoding to the ancient custome, nothing shall be innouated in the Churches, without that sentence of the reuerend Pope of the Cittie of Rome.* Now, how was this anie other thing, but to make the Pope what the same lawe of *Theodosius* and *Valectinian* calls him: to witt, *the Rector of the vniuersalitie of Churches:* and what the Councell of *Chalcedō* intitles him, to witt, *the Guardian of the Lords Vine:* and what the Councell of *Sardica*, the Councell of *Chalcedon*, and the Emperor *Justinian* qualifie him; to wit, *the head of Bishops?* For if as the Prouinciall, Nationall; or Patriarchall

Conc. Antioch. c. 9.

Soz. hist. eccl. l. 3. c. 7

Conc. Antioch c. 16.

Soc. hist. eccl. l. 2. c. 8.

Soz. hist. eccl. l. 3. c. 8.

Const. nou. Theod. tit. 24.

Ibid.

Cōc. Chalc apud Leō.

Cōc Sard. in fragm. Hil.

Cōc. Chalc in. ep ad Leon.

Cod. l. 7.

Councells,

Councells, could not be reputed perfect; nor decide the affaires of the Region, or of the nation, or of the Prouince, without the Metropolitan assisted there; so the generall Councells could not be generall, nor decide the things which concerned the vniuersall Church, without the assistance and sentence of the Bishop of *Rome*: And if as S. IEROM saith that the Councell of *Nicea* had ordained, that *Antioch* should be the metropolitan, supplied spirituall of all the *East*; so not only saint ATHANASIVS calls *Rome, the Sea Apostolicke and metropolitan of* Romania; that is, of all the *Roman* Empire, & beates the *Arrians* with the epistle which they had writen to the Pope, in the which, though fainedly, ironically, they had called the Roman Church, *the Schoole of the Apostles, and the Metropolitan of religion*; but also S. GREGORIE *Nazianzene* cries out; *the ancient Rome marcheth right in the faith, houlding all the West tied by the healthfull word, as it is conuenient that Cittie should doe, which rules all the world*: And if, as the Bishops of *Egipt* protested at the Councell of *Chalcedon*, that it was the custome in the prouinces of the Prefecture of *Egipt*, to doe nothing without the sentence & ordinance of the Archbishop of *Alexandria*; So *Socrates* saith, that the Coūcell of *Antioch*, was argued of nullitie, for as much as the ancient Ecclesiasticall law bare, that the Churches could not bee ruled, without the sentence of the Bishop of *Rome*: how is it that the Bishop of *Rome* was not metropolitā of the vniuersall Church, & such in regard of the whole Church, as euerie Patriark & Metropolitan was, in regard of his diuision? And if the Pope reciprocallie, as heire to the principall Sea of S. PETER, & Metropolitan of the vniuersall Church, was Rector of the vniuersality of Churches; how could it be that the originall Patriarks, which were heires of the subalterne Chaires of S. PETER, & the Metropolitans of the secōd Seas of the Empire, were not by proportion in the behalfe of their diuisions, that which the Pope was ouer the whole extent of the Church?

Hier. ad Apamach. Athan. ad solit. vit. agent. Id. ibid. Soz hist. eccl. l. 3. c. 7. Greg. Naz. carm de vita sua. Cōc. Chalc act. 4. Soc. hist. eccl l. 2. c. 8 Coc. Theo. nouel. constit. 24.

It appeares thirdlie by the proceeding of the same Councell of *Nicea*, and in the same Canon. For what cause had the Councell of *Nicea* to represse the rebellion of *Meletius* Bishop of *Sycopolis* in *Egipt*, who refused to obey the Bishop of *Alexandria* his Patriarke, alledged the custome of the Pope, & not that of the Patriark of *Antioch*? The Patriark of *Antioch*, was in person at the Councell, which the Pope was not, hee was neerer both to the cittie of *Nicea* wherein the Councell wae holden, & to the Sea of *Alexandria*, in whose fauour this Canō was made, then the Pope: he had the superintēdēcie ouer fifteene great prouinces, whereof the least conteined more countries, then the *Protestants* attribute to the Patriarkship of the Pope. For what cause doth the Councell to suppresse *Meletius*, alledge the custome of the Bishop of *Rome*, and not that of the Bishop of *Antioch*, but because the Bishop of *Antioch* his authoritie, was of positiue right, as well as that of the Bishop of *Alexandria*; by which meanes, the same rashnesse that carried *Meletius* to denie the one, might likewise haue carried him to denie the other; where the Popes authoritie was of diuine right; that is to saie, as S. AVSTIN & the *Mileu.* Councell speake; *drawne frō the authoritie of the holie scriptures*? Moreouer for what cause did the Coūcell of *Nicea* confirme the custome of the Patriark of *Alexandria*, & that of the Patriark of *Antioch*, & not confirme that of the Pope, but because the Popes authoritie depends not of the authoritie of Councells, but proceeded from the verie mouth of our Lord, as Pope *Gelasius* whō S. *Fulgentius* the secōd S. AVS. or rather the second Oracle of the *African* Church calleth the Reuerēd Prelat of the Sea Apostolicke, hath since expressed it in these words: *The holie Romā Catholicke Apostolick Church, hath not bene preferred before other Churches, by anie synodicall constitutions, but hath obtained the primacie*

Aug. ep. 92 Fulgent. ad Ferrand Diac. Resp. 2. Gelas. in Decret. de apocryph. Script.

by the

Euāgelicall voice of our Lord and Sauiour, when he said; Thou art Peter, and vpō this rocke I will builde my Church? Now, this being so, how is it not manifest, that the intention of the Councell was not to restraine the authoritie of the Pope, to the limits of a simple particular Patriarkship, as that of the other Patriarkes; but to propound the authoritie that the Pope had in regard of the vniuersall Church, for a type and patterne of the authoritie of the other Patriarkes, in regard of their patriarkships; for either the law diuine gaue nothing to the Pope ouer the other Bishops; or if it gaue him anie thinge, it was giuen him ouer all the Earth, although for the cōmoditie of the vniuersall gouernement of the Church, the Pope abstained from the immediate administratiō of the other Patriarkships, & cōtented himselfe, with the onely immediate gouernement of the patriarkship of the West; and with the mediate & generall superintendencie ouer the rest.

It appeares fowthly, by the possession wherein the Pope remained, after the Canon of the Councell of *Nicea*, of iudging the persons and iudgements of the other Patriarkes, and that in the view, & with the applause, euen of those that had made the canon, & of their successors, & without that anie euer murmured, that this practise contradicted it: for how had Pope *Iulius* the first, who was created Pope fiue yeares after the Coūcell of *Nicea*, restored those great Champions of the Councell of *Nicea* saint ATHANASIVS Patriark of *Alexandria*; *Marcellus* Primat of *Ancyra* in *Galatia*, & *Asclepas* Bishop of *Gaza* in *Palestina, because to him* (saith *Sozomen*) *for the dignitie of his Sea, the care of all things apperteyned*; if the intentiō of the Councell of *Nicea*, had bene to restraine the authoritie of the Pope into the onely limitts of a particular Patriarkship, as well as that of the other Patriarkes? And how had those great Chāpions, & defendors of the Coūcell of *Nicea*, made vse of the Popes restitution, to re-enter their Seas, if it had bene contrary to the canon of the Councell of *Nicea*, the which themselues had helped to compose, & S. ATHANASIVS amongst the rest, who had bene the soule and pen thereof, & was then heire & successor to *Alexander* Patriark of *Alexandria*, in whose fauour and vpon whose particular the article had bene sett downe? And how could Pope *Iulius* haue reproched the *Arrians*, that they had altered the decrees of the Coūcell of *Nicea*, if himself, in restoring S. ATHANASIVS Patriark of *Alexandria*, *Paul* Bishop of *Constantinople*, *Marcellus* Primat of *Ancyra* in *Galatia*, *Asclepas* Bishop of *Gaza* in *Palestina*, *Lucius* Bishop of *Andrinopolis* in *Thrace*; & in disannulling the Councells of *Tyre*, *Antioch*, & *Constantinople*, which had bene holden against them; had violated the canō of the councell of *Nicea*? And why did not the *Arrians* replie to him, that it was himself that infringed the decrees of the Councell of *Nicea*, if the intention of the Councell of *Nicea* had bene to restraine the Popes authoritie, to the only limits of a particular Patriarkship, as well as that of the other Patriarks? And how had the Councell of *Sardica*, wherein the Councell of *Nicea* was againe put to the triall; & which was holden twenty two yeares after the Councell of *Nicea*, & to defend the authoritie of the Councell of *Nicea*, & by many of the same Fathers that had assisted at the Coūcell of *Nicea* reduced into a written lawe; that Bishops deposed by the Councells of their prouinces, might appeale from thē to the Pope: & declared that it was a very good & fitt thing, that frō all the prouinces, the Bishops should referr the affaires to their head; that is to saie, to the Sea Apostlick of S. PETER; if the intentiō of the Coūcell of *Nicea* had bene, to restraine the Popes authoritie, into the onely limits of a particular Patriarkship, as well as that of the other Patriarkes? And how had the generall Councell of *Ephesus* reserued the cause of *John* Patriark of *Antioch*, to the iudgmēt of the

[Margin notes: Soz. hist. eccl. l. 3. c. 7. — Ibid. — Cōc. Sard. c. 5. — Cōc. Sard. ep. ad Iul. in frag. Hil. p. 15.]

the Pope? And how had *Flauianus* Bishop of *Constantinople*, after he had beé deposed by *Dioscorus* Patriark of *Alexandria*, & by the second Councell of *Ephesus*; appealed from them to the Pope, *and that* (saith the Emperor *Valentinian* the third) *according to the custome of the Councells?* And how finally had *Theodoret*, one of the Bishops of the Patriarkship of *Antioch*, hauing bene deposed in the same second Councell of *Ephesus*; and hauing thence appealed to the Pope, bene receiued into the Councell of *Chalcedon*, because the Pope had restored him to his Bishopricke, if the intention of the Councell of *Nicea* had bene, not to propose the authoritie of the Pope, in regard of the vniuersall Church for type and patterne of the authoritie of the other Patriarkes in regard of their Patriarkships, but to restraine the Popes authority, into the onely limits of a particular Patriarkship, as well as that of the other Patriarkes.

Valent.ep. ad Theod. in ep. præá. Cóc.Chalc Theod ep. ad Leon. Cóc.Chalc act. 1.

It appeares in the fifth place, by the title of vniuersall Patriarke, and vniuersall Pope, that the Churchmen of the other Patriarkships, and particularly those of *Alexandria*, who had more interest in the obseruation of the sixt Canon of the Councell of *Nicea*, then anie other, as hauing bene made in fauour of their Church, yeilded to the Pope. For when the Priests and deacons of the Patriarchall Church of *Alexandria*, presented their requests to the Councell of *Chalkedon*, from which the person of the Pope was as farre distant, as it is betweene *Rome* and *Asia*, they couched them in these termes; *To the most holie, and most blessed vniuersall Patriark of great Rome, Leo; and to the holie and vniuersall Councell.*: And this they did, all the Councell seeing and approuing it, and ordayning that they should be inserted into the Acts, and consequently not holding them for strange new, and vnwonted things. And when the Religious men of *Antioch*, presented in *Constantinople* their requests to Pope *Agapet*, they couched them, and made them to be inserted into the Actes of the Councell of *Constantinople*, holden against *Anthymus*, and celebrated vnder the Emperor *Iustinian*, in these wordes; *To our most holie and blessed Lord Agapet, Archbishop of the ancient Rome, and vniuersall Pairiark.* And when the great scourge of the *Nouatians*, *Eulogius* Patriark of *Alexandria*, and heire of the Rights conferred vpon the patriarkship of *Alexandria* by the Councell of *Nicea*, sett hand to penn, he did not onely saie (disputing against the *Nouatians*) that PETER onely had receiued the keys, that is to saie, originally; but also writing to the Pope S. GREGORIE; he called him *vniuersall Pope*. Now how is this anie other thing, then to protest, that what the other Patriarkes were euerie one, in the behalfe of his owne Patriarkship, the Pope was the same in the behalfe of the world? For as for the part that the Bishop of *Constantinople* challenged in this title afterward, it shall be heereafter shewed, that it was by vertue of the right of the Bishop of *Rome*, that he pretended it to be communicated to him, by the erection of *Constantinople* into the title of the second *Rome*: And as for the refusall, that the Pope S. GREGORIE made of the vse thereof; it shall be answered in the same chapter.

Cóc. Chalc act. 3.

Conc. Cóstant. sub Men.act. 1. Eulog. Alex. apud Phot.in Bibl. c.280.

Greg. l. 7. indict.1.ep. 30.

Chap. 7.

It appeares in the sixth place, by the proceeding of *Theodosius*, the second Emperor of the *East*, who resoluing at the instance of *Atticus* Bishop of *Constantinople*, to make the cittie of *Constantinople* enioy the title of Patriarkship, which he pretended had bene attributed to him in the Councell of *Constantinople*, published a law, which hath alwaies (as shall heereafter appeare) remained without effect; by which he alleadged, that *Constautinople* had the priuiledges of the ancient *Rome*; and ordained that she should exercise them, not only in all the prouinces of *Pontus*, *Asia minor*, and *Thracia*, but also in all the prouinces of *Illiria*. The one of the

Chap. 6.

heades

heades of this lawe, we learne from *Socrates*, who said, the Bishop of *Cyzica* being dead, *Sisinnius* Archbishop of *Constantinople*, ordained *Proclus* Bishop of *Cyzica*; but the *Cyzicenians*, that is to saie, the Bishop of the diuision of *Cyzica*, seeing he went about it preuented him, and ordained a religious man called *Dalmatius*, and this they executed, despising the law, which forbad to ordaine Bishops without the sentence of the Bishop of *Constantinople*; alleadging, it had bene made onely for the person of *Atticus*: And the other we learne from the lawe *omni innouatione cessante*, which is a fragment of that whereof Socrates makes mention, which forbids, that euen in all the prouinces of the *Easterne Illyria*, any thing should passe, but with the knowledg of the Bishop of *Constantinople*; *Wee ordaine* (saith the lawe) *that all innouation ceasing* (so speakes the Emperor, because *Atticus* abusing the simplicitie of his youth, had ginen him to vnderstand falsely, that the refusall that the Bishops of *Illeria* made, to acknowledg him for Patriarke, had begun but since the schisme of *Arsacius* his predecessor) *the antiquitie, and the precedent Ecclesiasticall Canons, which haue bene obserued hitherto* (he meanes the Canons of the Councell of *Constantinople*, holden vnder *Nectarius*, which had attributed to the Sea of *Constantinople*, euen in spirituall causes, the title of the second *Rome*; and it had bene admitted in some prouinces of *Pontus*, *Asia Minor*, and Thracia) *shall also haue place through all the prouinces of Illiria; that is to saie, of the Easterne Illiria; to witt, thae if there doe anie controuersie arise, it may not be referred to the holy iudgment and sacerdotall councell, without the knowledg of the most holy, and right Reuerend the Bishop of the cittie of Constantinople, which hath the priuiledges of the ancient Rome.* And *Photius* Patriarke of *Constantinople* reporting the same lawe; *The sixth constitution* (said hee) *of the second title of the first booke of the Code ordaineth, that all the Canonicall questions, that shall arise in all Illiria, may not be decided without the sentence of the Bishop of Constantinople, and of his Synod, which hath the priuiledges of the ancient Rome.* Now, what was this priuiledge of the ancient *Rome*, to whose imitation nothing could be decided, not onely in all the prouinces of *Thracia*, *Pontus*, and *Asia Minor*, but also in all the prouinces of the *Easterne Illiria*, without the knowledge, or according to the text of *Socrates* and of *Photius*, without the sentence of the Bishop of *Constantidople*, and of his Synod, but that which we now come from speaking of with the same *Socrates*, that the Ecclesiasticall lawe gaue the Pope through the whole earth; to witt, that without the sentence of the Bishop of *Rome*, there might be made no new definition in what part of the world soeuer: and which the law of *Valentinian* inserted into the new constitutions of the same *Theodosius* renewes in these wordes: *We decree, that according to the ancient custome, nothing shall be innouated in the Churches, withont the sentence of the Bishop of Rome*? And therefore, what other thing was it to graunt to the Bishop of *Constantinople* in Ecclesiasticall matters, the priuiledges of the cittie of *Rome*, but to make the Bishop of *Constantinople*, particularly in his diuision, what the Bishop of *Rome* was, ouer all the Earth?

Soc. hist. Eccl. l. 7. c. 28.

Cod. Iust. de sacrosanct. eccl. l. 1. tit. 2. l. 6

Phot. in Nomocan. tit. 8.

Soc. hist. eccl. l. 2. c. 8.

Cõst. nou. Theod. tit. 24.

It appeares in the seauenth place, by the possession wherein the Pope continued notwithstanding the erection of the Patriarkship of *Constantinople*, to iudge of the iudgements, and of the persons of the Patriarkes of *Constantinople*, and to receiue the appeales in *maior* causes from their diuisions. For not onely the Popes, as well after the Councell of *Constantinople*, wherein the erectiõ of the Patriarkship of *Constãtinople* was attempted; as after that of Chalcedon, where it was againe sett vpon, remained in perpetuall possession to iudge of the iudgements, & of the persons of the

Patriarkes of *Constantinople*; and to receiue the appeales of the maior causes from their diuisions; but also the Patriarkes of *Constantinople* remained in perpetuall profession of obedience and of subiection to the Pope. The one of these pointes shall be seene heereafter, both by the appeale that S. CHRYSOSTOME Archbishop of *Constantinople* cast in, from the Councell of *Constantinople* to Pope *Innocent* the first; and by the appeale that *Eutiches* Abbot of *Constantinople* cast in from *Flauianus* Patriark of *Constantinople* to Pope *Leo* the first; & by the appeale that the same *Flauianus* Patriark of *Constantinople* cast in, from the second Councell of *Ephesus* to the same Pope *Leo* the first; & that saith the Emperor *Valentiniã* the 3rd. according to the custome of Councells, & by the condemnatiõ that Pope *Felix* the third made of *Acacius* Patriark of *Constantinople*; in vertue whereof he was raced, yea after his death, out of the records of the Church of *Constantinople*; and by the deposition that Pope *Agapet* made of *Anthymus* Patriarke of *Constãtinople*; & by the iudgemẽt that the Pope S. GREGORIE the *Great*, gaue in the causes of *Iohn* priest of *Chalcedon*, and *Athanasius* a Regular of *Lycaonia* appealing to him from the tribunall of the Patriarke of *Constantinople*. And the other shall appeare in the same chapter, by the protestations that [a] *John* the second [b] *Anthimus*, [c] *Menas*, & [d] *John* the fowrth Patriarkes of *Constantinople*, euery one in his tyme made, to acknowledge thẽselues submitted & subiect to the Pope, & to the *Roman* Church. Now how was this anie other thing, but a perpetuall testimonie, that the Patriarkall dignitie exempted not those that were thereof prouided, from the iurisdiction & superioritie of the Pope; & then, that the intention of the Councell of *Nicea*, had neuer bene, to restraine the Popes authoritie, within the simple limitts, of a particular patriarkship, as well as that of other Patriarkes, but to propose the Popes authority, in regard of the vniuersall Church, for a type and patterne of the authoritie of the other Patriarkes, in regard of their patriarkships?

In chap. 7. Chrys. ad Innoc. ep. 1. Valent. ep. ad Theod. Marcell. com. in Chron. Greg. l. 5. ind. 14 ep. 24. & 64. In chap. 7. a. Ioann. Const. ep. ad Horm. b. Concil. Const. sub Men. act. 4 c. Ibid. d. Gregor. Magn. l. 7. ind. 2. ep. 63.

It appeares in the eight place, by the proceeding of the Emperor *Iustinian* the first, who desiring to erect the first *Justinianea* of *Bulgaria* the cittie of his Birth, into the forme of a supernumerary patriarkship, ouer the six Archbishoprickes of the six prouinces, neere to that towne, ordained, that in those six prouinces, she should hold the place of the Sea Apostolicke of *Rome*, following the definitions of Pope *Vigilius*: *Wee decree* (saith the Emperor) *that the blessed Bishop of the first Justinianea, shall haue vnder his proper iurisdiction, the Bishops of the Mediterranean Dacia, of Dacia Rypensis, of Triballea, of Dardania, of vpper Misia, and of Pannonia; and that they shall be ordained by him, and by his proper Synod; and that in the prouinces subiect to him, he shall hold the place of the Sea Apostolicke of Rome, following the things defined by the holie Pope Vigilius.* For that the intention of the Emperor *Iustinian*, was to erect by this lawe, the Bishoprick of the first *Iustinianea* of *Bulgaria*, into the forme of a Patriarkship of honor, although this honor remained to him but in shadowe and smoake wee learne from two cases. The one, that in the Councell of *Constantinople* surnamed *Trullian* holden vnder *Iustinian* the second, before *Bulgaria* was possest by the Infidells, *John* Bishop of *Iustinianopolis*, signed in the ranke of the Patriarkes in this order; *Paul* of *Constantinople*, *Peter* of *Alexandria*, *Anastasius* of *Jerusalem*, *George* of *Antioch*, and *John* of *Iustinianopolis*. And the other, that euer after the returne of *Bulgaria* to be *Christian*, the latter *Greekes* did in some sorte, continue this title to him, as *Curopalates* a *Greeke* Author acknowledgeth, when he coupleth the Archbishop of *Bulgaria*, with the Patriarkes in these termes; *The designatiõ of the other Patriarkes, is made without anie diuersitie, as well of him of Alexandria, of*

Iust. nou. 131. Subscript. Cõc. Trull.

him of Antioch, of him of Ieruſalem, as alſo of the Archbishop of the firſt Iuſtinianea called Achrida, and of all Bulgaria: And as *Barlaam a Greeke Author,* natiue of *Peloponoſus* confirmes it in his diſputations againſt the *Greeke* ſchiſmaticks, when hee writes, that in the part ſeparate from the Pope, there were fiue Patriarkes; on the other part, ſaith he, the are fiue Patriarkes, reckoning him of *Bulgaria.* And that this priuiledge to hold the place of the Sea Apoſtolick in the ſix prouinces neere the firſt *Iuſtinianea,* was not by co-ordination with the Pope, but by ſubordination to the Pope; that is to ſaie, it was not by forme of exemption from the authoritie of the Pope, but by forme of ſubmiſſion and ſubſtitution to the authoritie of the Pope. Wee learne from the epiſtles of S. GREGORIE the *Great,* which teſtifie, as it ſhall appeare in the chapter following, that the ſame S. GREGORIE cōfirmed, yet fiftie yeare after this law, the electiō of the Biſhop of the firſt *Iuſtinianea,* ſent him the Archiepiſcopall mantle, renewed to him the Vicarship of the Sea Apoſtolicke, iudged by appeale of the Biſhops of his diuiſion; & chaſticed himſelfe, when he had iudged amiſſe.

[Mich. Codin. dictus vulgo Curopalates c. de Patr. deſignat. Barlaam ep. Gyrac. ep. 1. — Greg. l. 4. ep. 6. & 15. Item l. 2. ep. 6.]

It appeares in the ninth place, by the proceeding of the Biſhop of *Conſtantinople,* who hauing obtained in the Councell of *Conſtantinople,* holden vnder *Theodoſius* the *Great,* a decree which ordained, that his Sea should bee the ſecond after *Rome,* becauſe *Conſtantinople* was the ſecond *Rome;* and hauing made this decree to be explained by a ſurreptitious Canon, in the Councell of *Chalcedon,* in ſuch ſort as he was permitted to enioy the ſame priuiledges with the Pope, after the Pope; attempted to participate with the Pope, the title of vniuerſall Patriarke, and to inſcribe himſelfe vniuerſall Patriarke, not in regard of the Pope, but vnder the pope, and in regard of the other patriarkes, and to this the other patriarkes, & the Emperors themſelues, and the Councells of the *Eaſt,* conſented, & communicated to him this nomination. For in the Councell of *Conſtantinople* holden againſt *Anthimus,* not onely the title of *vniuerſall Patriarke* was attributed to the Pope, but alſo to the Biſhop of *Conſtantinople.* And in the ſeauenth law of the *Code,* the Emperor *Iuſtinian* called *Epiphanius* Patriarke of *Conſtantinople, Oecumenicall Patriark,* but vnder the Pope, whom he calls in the ſame lawe, the head of all the holie miniſters of God. And in the ſixth generall Councell, not onely the Emperor *Conſtantine Pogonat,* intitles the Pope, *Generall Arch-paſtor, and the Protothrone of all Patriarkes;* but alſo the epiſtle of *Cyrus* Patriarke of *Alexandria,* read in the ſame Councell, qualifies *Sergius* Patriarke of *Conſtantinople,* with the title of *Oecumenicall Patriarke.* Now how was this anie other then to preſuppoſe, that the Pope had alwaies bene vniuerſall & *Oecumenicall Patriarke?* For if the Patriarke of *Conſtantinople,* by vertue of the erection of *Conſtantinople* into the title of *ſecond Rome,* made as he pretended for ſpirituall Rights in the firſt Councell of *Conſtantinople,* attributed to himſelf ioyntly with the Pope, though vnder the Pope, the title of *vniuerſall Patriarke;* & that all the other Patriarkes, & the Emperors themſelues, & the Councell of the *Eaſt,* conſented to it, & cōmunicated to him, this nomination: how doth it not appeare manifeſtly, that they then acknowledged, that before the holding of the firſt Councell of *Conſtantinople,* the Biſhop of *Rome* was *vniuerſall* and *Oecumenicall Patriarke;* and by conſequent, that the intention of the Councell of *Nicea* had not bene to reſtraine the Popes authoritie to the onely limits of a particular patriarkship, as that of the other patriarkships, but to propound the Popes authoritie, in regard of the vniuerſall Church, for a type and patterne of the authoritie of the other Patriarkes, in regard of their patriarkships?

[Cōc. Chalc act. 15 can. 28. — Conc. Cōſt ſub Men. act. 1. Ibid. act. 5. Cod. l. 1. tit 1. l. 7. Cod. Paris Antuerp. & Gen. tit 1. l. 7. Conſt. Pog ep. ad Synod. Apoſt. Cōc. Conſt 6. act. 18. epiſt. ad Agath. Cōc Conſt 6. act. 13.]

It appeares in the tenth place, by the epiſtle of *Innocent* the firſt, whom

[Aug. ep. 106.]

S. AVSTIN calleth *Pope of happie memorie,* to *Alexander* Patriarke of *Antioch*, wherein he writes to him, that the Councell of *Nicea* had established the Patriarkship of *Antioch*, not ouer a Prouince, but ouer a Bodie, and a masse of Prouinces; and adds, that *Antioch* had not yeilded to *Rome*, but that what *Antioch* had trāsitorilie (to wit, S. PETERS Sea,) *Rome* had it finallie and absolutely: and by the testimonie of S. IEROM priest of the Patriarkship of *Antioch*, who saith that the Councell of *Nicea* had ordained that *Antioch* should be the metropolitan of all the *East*; and neuerthelesse cries, that the Church is built vpon the Popes cōmunion, and vpon the chaire of S. PETER, and that he will not acknowledge the Patriarks of *Antioch*, but whiles they communicate with the Pope: from whence it ariseth, that the intentiō of the Councell of *Nicea* had not bene to make the Popes authoritie, and that of the Patriarke of *Antioch*, equall.

Innoc ad Alex Epist Ant. ep. 18. Ibid.

Hier ad Pammac. Idem ad Damas. ep. 57. & 58.

And finally it appeares by the difference that the Councell of *Chalcedon*, (where this very decree of the Councell of *Nicea* was read,) put betweene *Dioscorus* Patriarke of *Alexandria*, who possest the Sea, in whose fauour the Canon had bene made, and the *Pope*; accounting the Pope for Guardian of our Lords Vine, & the Patriarke of *Alexandria* for one of his subguardians. For not onely the Coūcell of *Chalcedon* writing to the Pope, calls him the head of Bishops: *We beseech thee* (saith the Councell) *to honor our iudgement with thy decrees, that as wee haue brought consent in matters of weale to our head, so thy Soueraigntie,* ἡ κορυφὴ, or according to the other copies ἡ κορυφὴ, *the Soueraigntie maie fulfill in the behalfe of thy children, that which is for decencie:* But also speaking of the presūptions of *Dioscorus* Patriarke of *Alexādria*, adds for the last, to make his insolence cōpleat, that he durst sett vpon the proper person of him to whom our Lord had committed the guard of the Vine; *hee hath* (said they) *extended his felonie, euen against him, to whom the guard of the vine, was committed by our Sauiour, that is to saie,* (added they) *against thy Holynesse*. Now was not this to protest, that what *Dioscorus* Patriarke of *Alexandria*, was ouer the Churches of *Egipt*, *Libia*, and *Pentapolis*, the Pope was the same ouer all the Churches of the world; and to authorize what the Emperor *Valentinian* the third had said but a while before, *that the Pope was Rector of the vniuersalitie of Churches*. And what the Bishop of *Patara* in *Lycia*, one of the Prouinces of *Asia*, said afterward to the Emperor *Iustinian*, that there was noe kinge in the world, which was ouer all the world, as the Pope was ouer the Church of all the earth? For this occasion then; to witt, that the Patriarkships, and namely those of *Alexandria*, and *Antioch*, which had bene founded from the tyme of S. PETER, and by S. PETER himselfe, were as Vicarships (I meane Vicarships borne and perpetuall, and not Vicarships delegate and arbitrary) of the Sea of S. PETER; or rather to repeate S. GREGORIES words, *one same Sea of S.* PETER *with that of Rome*; whē the Fathers of the Councell of *Nicea* confirmed the priuiledges of the Bishop of *Alexādria*, troubled by *Meletius* head of the Schismaticks of *Egipt*, they decreed that the Bishop of *Alexandria* in the Prouinces of his Patriarkship, should enioy the Rights of the Bishop of *Rome*, as the Sea of *Alexandria* in *Egipt*, *Libia*, and *Pentapolis*, being an originarie and perpetuall Vicarship of S. PETERS sea, but not that they thereby pretended in things that exceeded Patriarchall authoritie, either to equall him with the Pope, or to exempt him frō the Popes iurisdiction. Otherwise how could *Pope Iulius* the first in the view of the Fathers of the same coūcell of *Nicea*, who were still for the most part liuing & breatihng haue re-established S. ATHANAS. Patriarke of *Alexandria*; *Paul* Bishop of *Constantinople*; *Marcellus* Primat of *Galatia*; and *Asclepas* Bishop of *Gaza* in *Palestina*, Prelats who had all assisted at the Councell of *Nicea*, could not bee ignorant of the

Conc. ep. ad Leon. part. 3. c. 2.

Côc. Chalc ibid.

Ad calc. Cod. Theod. nouel. const. tit. 24. Liberat in Breuiar c 22 the Canons thereof, since they helped to compose them: for *that* (saith *Sozomene*) *to him, because of the dignitie of his Sea, the care of all thinges appertained*? And how could S. ATHANASIVS haue alleadged for his defence these words of the same *Iulius*; *Are you ignorant that the custome is, that you first write to vs, and so from hence must proceede the iust decision of all things*; and therefore, if there were anie suspition raised against the Bishop there; that is to saie of *Alexandria*, you must haue written of it to the Church heere; that is to saie, the Church of *Rome*? And how could *Peter* Patriark of *Alexandria*, and S. ATHANASIVS successor, hauing bene driuen from his Sea, haue bene restored vpon the letters that he brought from Pope DAMASVS, *which confirmed* (saith *Socrates*) *the faith of Moyses, and the ordination of PETER*? And how, when *Flauianus* Bishop of *Constantinople*, hauing bene deposed in the false Councell of *Ephesus* by *Dioscorus* Patriarke of *Alexandria*, could the Emperor *Valentinian* haue said; *Antiquitie hath yeilded to the most holie Bishop of Rome, the Priesthood ouer all, &c.* For this cause the Bishop of *Constantinople*, according to the custome of the Councells, hath appealed to him? And how could Pope *Leo* the first, haue written to *Anatolius* Bishop of *Constantinople*, that if *Dioscorus* Patriarke of *Alexandria*, and *Iuuenall* Bishop of *Ierusalem*, *should come to repentance, and accompanie their conuersion with such satisfaction, as it should seeme ought not to bee despised, the thing should be reserued to the more mature deliberation of the Sea Apostolicke*? And how could the Fathers of the Councell of *Chalcedon*, addressing their relation to the Pope, and speaking of *Dioscorus* Patriarke of *Alexandria*, and of the false Councell of *Ephesus*, haue said; *He hath extended his frensie euen against him, to whom the guard of the vine was committed by our Sauiour; that is to saie, against thy Holynesse*? And when a little after the celebration of the same Councell, *Peter* surnamed *Mongus*, and *John* surnamed *Talaia*, hauing bene created by diuers factions, Patriarkes of Alexandria, how could the Pope haue committed the care of the prouinces of *Egipt* to *Acasius* Patriarke of *Constantinople*? And how could *John* hauing bene deposed from the Patriarkship of Alexandria by the Synod of *Egipt*, and by the complot of the Emperor *Zeno*, and appealed to the Pope, and taken with him *Synodicall* letters of intercession from *Calendion* Patriarke of Antioch to fauour his appeale? And the same *John* Patriarke of *Alexandria*, hauing appealed to the Pope, how could the Pope haue deposed *Peter* his aduersary, and with him *Acacius* Bishop of *Constantinople* who adhered to him, & that with such effect, that euen after their death, they were raced in *Constantinople* & in *Alexandria*, out of the Catalogue of the Patriarkes of *Alexandria* and *Constantinople*, and their names blotted out of the records of their Churches, and excluded from the recitall of the misteries.

Soz. l. 3. c. 8

Athanas. apol. 2.

Soc. l. 4. c. 37.

In epist. praeamb. Côc. Chalc.

Leo 1. ep. 44.

Gelas. ep. ad Episc. Dardan.

Liberat. in breuiar. c. 18.

Euag. l. 3. c. 15.

Iust. Imp. epist. ad Hormisd.

Of the addition of the word Churches suburbicary made by Ruffinus, in the latine translation of the Canons of the Councell of Nicea.

CHAP. VI.

Against these thinges, neuerthelesse the Popes aduersaries obiect the translation of *Ruffinus* priest of *Aquilea*, who adds to the Epilogue that he hath made of the latine translation of the Canon of the Councell of *Nicea*, the word *Churches suburbica-*

ry, which is neither in the Greeke text, nor in the ancient compleate and formall latine editions, & turnes the article in these termes, *that the Bishop of Alexandria, should haue the care of the Churches of Egipt; and he of Rome, of the Churches suburbicary:* from whence they drawe this impertinent conclusion; that the Pope had there no iurisdiction, but ouer the Churches neighbouring to this cittie; and they triumph so vpon it, as after a thousand writings which they haue published vpō this subiect, they haue euen this last yeare caused to be imprinted a topographicall mapp of the ancient Patriarkship of the Pope, & haue accompanied it with a discourse, intitled; *Of the regions suburbicarie*; where they haue assigned him for all iurisdictiō, a hundred thousand paces about the cittie of *Rome*; that is to saie, about as much Ground, as is betweene *Paris*, and *Orleans*: But I hope soone to sett a *Catastrophe* to their Tragedie, and to turne their triumph into obsequies;

Ruffin. hist. l. 2.

De suburb. Regio &c. Francofur. apud Ioan. Carol. vnck ann. 1618.

Superbos
Vertere funeribus triumphos.

Horat. 1. carm. 35.

For who sees not, that it is a wilfull blindnesse, hauing the greeke text, and the ancient latine editions compleate, and in forme, of the Canon of the Councell of *Nicea* in their handes, to tye themselues to the Epilogized translation of a man, that S. IEROM auoucheth to haue bene, a verie euill translator; and whoe bsides for his errors, had bene excommunicated, and noted (saith the same S. IEROM) with the brand of heresie by Pope *Anastasius*, and by the *Roman* Church?

Hier con. Ruffi. apol. 2.

There are three things which principall e make a Translator vnfitt to be credited, *passion, ignorance*, and *rashnes*. Now, as for *passion*, who hath euer better deserued to be reproched in this regard, in matters that concerne the *Roman* Church, then *Ruffinus*, who had bene excommunicated for his errors in faith by Pope *Anastasius*, and by the *Roman* Church, and that before he writt his historie, which was written after *Alaricus* comming into *Italie*; that is to saie, vnder the Popedome of *Innocent* successor of *Anastasius*? *Ruffinus* (saith Pope *Anastasius*) *is soe excluded from our communion, as wee are not curious to knowe, neither what he doth, nor where he is; let him looke to himselfe, where he can be absolued.* And S. IEROM; *Pope Anastasius in the epistle he writt against thee to Iohn Bishop of Ierusalem, hath taxed this default, iustifying me, me that did it, and condemning thee, thee I saie that wouldest not doe it.* And againe, speaking of the confession of *Ruffinus* faith, which he fallie affirmed to haue bene approued by the Bishops of *Italie*; *How should Italie* (said hee) *haue approued that which Rome hath reiected, how should the Bishops receiue that, which the Sea Apostolicke hath condemned?* And a little after; *Thou doest soe auoid the iudgment of the cittie of* Rome, *that thou chosest rather to support a siege of Barbarians*, (this he spake because of the coming of *Alaricus* to *Aquilea*, whither Ruffinus had retired himselfe) *then the sentence of a peaceable cittie.* For whereas *Gennadius*, placeth Ruffinus amongst the Orthodoxall Authors, it was because *Gennadius* was of the Sect of one of the branches of *Pelagius heresie*, whereof *Ruffinus* had cast the rootes; but not, that *Ruffinus* did not dye an hereticke, and anathematized by the *Roman* Church, as saint IEROME insinuates when he saith, describing enigmaticallie the reuolte, anathema, and the sepulcher of Ruffinus, who was dead in *Sicilia*; *The Scorpion is pressed vnder the Sicilian earth, betweene Enceladus and Porphirus*, it must be read, betweene *Enceladus* and *Porphirion*, who were two of the Giants that the Poeticall fables had said to be reuolted against *Jupiter*,

Ruffin. ep ad Chrom in hist. Eus. Anast. ep. ad Ioann. Hier. Hier. aduers. Ruffin. l. 2. Id. ibid. Id. ibid.

Hier. præf. in 1. comment. Ezec

and had bene ſtrucken dead with thunder bolts, and couered with the Mountaines of *Sicilia*. With what faith then can they alleadge the words of *Ruffinus*, when the authoritie of the *Roman* Church is in queſtion, by whoſe Tribunall he had bene condemned and excommunicated? you can ſcarce light vpon a place in *Ruffinus* tranſlations, where there is an occaſion preſented to ſpeake of the Pope and of the *Roman* Church, but he sharpens and enuenoms it, as particularly when *Euſebius* reporting the hiſtory of Pope *Victor*, who had excommunicated the Church of *Aſia*, becauſe of the queſtion about keeping the paſch; ſaith, *There are yet to be found letters of the Biſhops, which handled Victor ſomewhat roughlie*, (*Ruffinus* adds of his owne,) *as prouiding vnprofitablie for the affaires of the Church*; and in the verſe following, where *Euſebius* writes; *Ireneus exhorted Victor not to cut off all the Churches of God which helde the tradition of this ancient cuſtome*: *Ruffinus* turnes it; *Ireneus reprehended him that he had not done well to cutt off from the bodie of vnitie ſo manie and ſo great Churches of God*: and ſees not, that in thinking to calumniate Pope *Victor*, he callumniates the councell of *Nicea*, who renewed the ſame excommunication, a thing poſſibly pardonable in *Euſebius*; who beſides that he was an *Arrian*, writt his hiſtories before the Councell of *Nicea*: but inexcuſable in *Ruffinus*, who made his tranſlation afterwardes. With what colour then, would they ſquare the intention of the originall *Greeke* of the canons of the Councell of *Nicea*, by the addition that *Ruffinus* a paſſionate tranſlator, incenſed againſt the Church of *Rome*, hath made thereto? Eus.hiſt.eccl.l.5.c 24 Id ibid.

And as for *ignorance* what tranſlator was euer more worthie to be refuſed in that regard, then *Ruffinus*, whoſe clauſes are almoſt as manie prooffs of ignorãce and impertinencie? for what could be imagined more vnapt, then to make of, *Iames, Biſhop of Ieruſalem*; *Iames*, *Biſhop of the Apoſtles*: of the *Greeke* word, μακαρος which ſignfies *Bleſſed* or *happie* a *Saint* called *Macarius*: of *Euſebius Pamphilus*, an heretick and an *Arrian*, *Pamphilus*, a Catholicke and a Martyr: of *Xiſtus* a *pithagorian* and *Pagan* Philoſopher, XISTVS Pope and *Martir*. An error that S. IEROM bitterly reproues, and which gaue occaſion to ſaint AVSTIN to ſtumble and retract vpon the ſame matter: of *queſtion* which comes of *quæro*, a verbe *actiue*, *querimony*, which comes of *queror*, a verbe *deponent*, of *Corepiſcopus*, whereof the *Nicea* Councell ſpeakes, *the vacant place of a Biſhop*; and ſo of infinite others, which moued ſaint IEROM to ſaie, that *Ruffinus* was ſo vnapt, in both tongues, as the *Romans* tooke him for a *Grecian*, and the *Greekes* for a *Roman*? Ruff in hiſt.eccl. Euſeb.l.1. c 1. Ibid.l.5.c. 24. Hier.ep.ad Cteſiph. Ibidem. Ibidem. Aug. Retr. l 1 c.42. Hier.aduers. Ruff. apol 2.

And as for *bouldneſſe* and *rashnes*, what interpreter euer shewed leſſe Religion or Faith in obſeruing the text of his Authors then *Ruffinus*, who hath alwaies taken libertie to add, or diminish, as it ſeemed good to him? *Thy conſcience* (ſaith ſaint IEROM, ſpeaking to *Ruffinus* of the tranſlation hee had made of *Origen*) *knowes what thou haſt added, and what thou haſt taken away, and what thou haſt changed from one place to an other, as it hath pleaſed thee.* And *Eraſmus* in his preface vpon ſaint HILARY; *Ruffinus hath attributed to himſelfe, the ſame authoritie, in the tranſlation of all the bookes which he hath tranſlated, and principallie in that of Origens writings, and in that of Euſebius hiſtorie, but this is not the libertie of an interpreter, but the licence of a defiler of an others workes*. And *Scaliger* in his annotations vpon the Chronicle of *Euſebius*: *It is the cuſtome of Ruffinus* (ſaith hee) *to omitt, to peruert, and to change the texts as he liſt*. With what face then, can they now leaue the *Greeke* text of the Councell of *Nicea*, to haue recourſe to *Ruffinus* tranſlations, a perpetuall corrupter of the tranſlations of antiquitie, and particularlie of that of the Canons of *Nicea*, whereof he *Suppreſſes* ſome; *diuides* others; *mangles* ſome; *adds* to others; *depraues* ſome, *miſtakes* the ſence of others? I haue ſaid Conc Nic. Hier Apol. con.Ruff.l. 2. Idem.Ibid. Eraſm.Rot præfat.in Hilar. Ios.Scal. annot.in Chro.Eus. num. MMLXV. Ruff hiſt. eccl.l.10. c 6.

Suppresses some; for he suppresses the twentith Canon of the Councell of *Nicea*, which containes the Ordenance to adore standing in the Sundaies seruice, and during the fiftie daies of Pentecoste: And that in hate of the resurrection of the very flesh, which as an *Origenist* he opposed, no more remembring what he had written of it, when he was yet a Catholicke. I haue said *diuided*, and *multiplied others*; for he diuided the eigth and the ninteenth Canons, into two others, and of either of them made two different Canons: I haue said *mangles* some, for he mangles the sixt, and ecclipseth from it, the Rights of the Bishop of *Antioch*, in fauour of *Iohn* Bishop of *Jerusalem* whom he pretended to be an *Origenist* as himself was; And maymes the end of the thirteenth. And that which the fathers saie of Dying penitents, to whom the Councell regrauntes the communion of the Sacrament, after the examination of the Bishop, with condition notwithstanding, that if they chance to suruiue, they shall be admitted but to the communion of prayers: he interprets it, of the examination of the Bishop for penitents recouered. I haue said, *adds to others*; for he adds to the eighteenth this whole clause, *That Deacons in the absence of Bishops and priests, might distribut the Eucharist*. And to the ninth this; *or haue bene conuinced thereof by others*: which are no more within the Greeke text of the Councell, then this of the Churches suburbicary. I haue said *depraues some*; for he depraues the ninteenth and saith of Deaconesses in generall, that which the Canon onely saith of the Paulianist deaconesses. I haue said *mistakes the sence of others*, for in the eigth he is ignorant of the sence of the word *Corepiscopus*, and turnes it, the *vacant place of a Bishop*. And in the ninth that of the word, ἀνεξετάστως, and interprets, of confession of priests after promotion, That, which the councell saith, of the Confession of Priests before promotion; that is to say, of the Confession made in the triall of those that were to be promoted to priesthood.

For whereas some to warrant the clause of the *Churches Suburbicary* alleadge, that Pope *Gelasius*, writing about the end of the same age, approued the workes of *Ruffinus*, excepting those things that saint IEROM had reprehended. It is a vaine and friuolous warrantie; for as much as Pope *Gelasius* intended to speake of the workes, or dogmaticall translations of *Ruffinus*, as was the *Commentary* vpon the *Creede*, and the translations of the treatises of some *Greeke* diuines, and not of his historicall workes or translations: Otherwise how could Pope *Gelasius* in the same decree haue condemned the ten bookes of the recognitions of *Clement*, which had bene translated by *Ruffinus*? and how could he haue written in the same place, the holy *Roman* Catholicke and Apostolicke Church hath not bene preferred before other Churches by anie Synodicall Constitutions, but hath obtained the primacie by the Euangelicall voice of our Lord and Sauiour, saying; *Thou art Peter, and vpon this rock J will build my Church*? And how could he haue writté elsewhere speaking of the ancient canons of the Church: *These are the Canons which ordaine, that from all partes of the world, the appeales shall be brought to the Sea Apostolicke*? And how could he haue said, that the care of the Regions of *Egipt*, and of *Antioch*, had bene by Pope *Felix* committed to *Acacius* Patriark of *Constantinople*? And whereas they add that saint CYRILL sending the Canons of the Councell of *Nicea*, to the Bishops of *Africa*, writt to them, that they might finde them in the Ecclesiasticall historie; which they pretend must be vnderstood of the history of *Ruffinus*; for as much as those of *Socrates*, *Theodoret*, and *Sozomene*, were written since, and besides containe nothing of the canons of the Councell of *Nicea* this is yet a more feeble and deceiptful caution.

Lib. de Suburb. Reg. Impr. Franc an 1618. dissert. 2. c. 6. Gelas. Pap. 1. in decret de apocryph. script. Id. ibid.

Id in commonit. ad Faust. magistr. Id. ep. ad. Episc. Dard. Lib. de Subic. Reg. vbi supra.

caution. For besides that many others had made collections of the Ecclesiasticall historie (as amongst the Catholickes, saint ATHANASIVS Bishop of *Alexandria*, who had composed a volume intituled, *Synodica*. *Theodorus* Bishop of *Mopsvestia*, not yet then noted for heresie, who had framed a particular historie of the Councell of *Nicea*, *Philip* of *Sida*, who had compiled an vniuersall Ecclesiasticall history: And amongst the heretickes *Philostorgius* the *Arrian*; and *Sabinus* the *Macedonian*) where is the article of the Bishop of *Antioch*, and the precept to adore standing on the sundaies, and during the fiftie daies of Pentecoste, which were contained in saint Cyrills Copie, to bee found in *Ruffinus* edition? and contrariwise where are the permission to deacons to distribute the Eucharist in the absence of priests and Bishops: and the restitution of the communion to penitents, before the accomplishement of their pennance: and the extension of the canon of the *Paulianist deaconesses* to all deaconesses in generall: and the equiuocation and mistaking of the confession of priests after promotion, which are all in the edition of *Ruffinus* to be read in the copie of saint CYRILL? contrarywise, if saint CYRILLS intention had bene to approue the edition of *Ruffinus* by this remittment; why did not the *Africans* which turned, or caused to be turned, from *Greeke* into *Latine*, saint CYRILLS *Greeke* Copie, followe *Ruffinus* in their translation, and put in the Clause of *Churches Suburbicarie*? And saint CYRILL himselfe, if he had beleiued that the clause of, *Churches suburbicary*, should haue bene added to the Canō of the Councell of *Nicea*, how could he haue taken, a Vicarship and commission from Pope *Celestine*, to execute the sentence of the Sea Apostolique against *Nestorius* Archbishop of *Constantinople*? And how could hee and the other Bishops of the Councell of *Ephesus*, haue approued of the oration of the Popes Legates, by which they called the Pope, the head of the Church, and the Vicar and ordinary Successor of saint PETER? and why had they reserued the iudgement of the cause of *Iohn* Patriarke of *Antioch* to the Pope?

Soc. hist. eccl. l. 1. c. 13. Theod. Mopsuest. apud. Nicet. Thesaur. l. 5. c. 7. & 9. Phillip. sid. apud. Soc. hist. eccl. l. 7. c. 27. Philostorg apud. Niceph. l. 9. c. 19. & l. 12. c. 29. & Nicet. l. 5. c. 7. & 9. Sabin Maced apud. Soc. hist. eccl. l. 1. c. 7. & alibi. Conc. Eph. p. 1. in ep. Celest. Pap Conc. Eph. act. 3. Ibid. Conc. Eph. p. 2. act. 5. in relat. ad Celest.

And then, what proofe is there, that *Ruffinus* by the word suburbicary, did intend the Churches within a hundred thousand paces of the Cittie of *Rome*, and not the Churches of all the Citties subiect to the Empire of the Cittie of *Rome*, Is there anie likelyhood, that the Bishop of *Alexandria*, should haue had *Egipt Libia*, and *Pentapolis*, vnder which were yet intended many other great prouinces, either annexed or subalterne as *Ammoniaca*, *Marœotides*, *Thebaidis*; and besides the immense Region of *Ethiopia* from whence the *Greeke* Emperor *Leo*, surnamed the Philosopher, saith in the life of saint CHRYSOSTOME, that *the Emperor* Arcadius *caused* Theophilus *Patriarke of* Alexandria *to come to Cōstantinople, accompanied with Indian and Egiptian Bishops*; And that the Bishop of *Rome* by whom they squared him, had no more but those onelie Churches, that where neere the Cittie of *Rome*? *Theocritus* writeth, that *Ptolomeus*, *Philadelphus*, king of *Egipt*, of whose Empire the Prouinces since attributed to the Patriarkship of *Alexandria* made the principall parte, commaunded 33339. citties.

Epiph. Hier. Milet Leo imp. in. vit. Chrys.

Of townes, thirtie three thousand, three hundred thirty nine;
Vnder the yoake of his decrees; their seruile heads incline.

Theocr. Idyl 17. Strab. geogr. l. 17. Diodor. sicul. bibl. l. 2.

And *Strabo*, and *Diodorus Siculus*, and the interpreter of the notice of the Empire after them saie, that the ancient diuision of *Egipt*, was diuided into thirtie six prouinces whereof *Delta* in *Egipt* contained ten; and the Emperor *Theodosius* the second writing to *Dioscorus* Patriarke of *Alexandria*, to cause him to come to the false Coũcell of *Ephesus*, sent to him to bring his ten metropolitan Bishops, or ten of his metropolitã Bishops; that is to saie, heades of Prouinces with him. And the Bishop of *Antioch* who was but the third Patriarke, had vnder him the two *Syria's*, the three *Palestina's*, the two *Cilicia's*, the three *Arabia's*, the Region of *Euphrates*, *Mesopotamia*, *Isauria*, and *Osrhoene*. and more as he pretended the Isle of *Cyprus*,, without reckoning manie other prouinces, which though he ordained not their metropolitans, yet neuerthelesse acknowledge him. For there were manie prouinces which acknowledged their Patriarks, and were obliged to appeare at their patriarchall Synods, although they tooke not from them the ordination of their metropolitans; from whẽce it is that *Balsamon* writes, that the Councell of *Antioch* holden vnder the patriark *Peter*, *Iberia Asiatica* otherwise called the prouince of the *Georgians* was made *Autocephalus*, that is to saie, exempt from takeing the ordination of their Metropolitan, anie other where, then from the Synod of the prouince, and neuerthelesse still remained subiect to the patriarke of *Antioch*. And when the Councell of *Chalcedon* would erect *Constantinople* into a patriarkship, they assigned him for his patriarchall Diuision the prouinces of *Trace*, *pontus*, *Asia minor*, with the Barbarous prouinces; that is to saie, *Russia* and *Muscouia*, which together contained more ground then all *Europe*; principally if we giue Credit to *Herodotus*, who saith, that the *Thracians* were the greatest nation of the world next the *Indians*. And the Pope who was the first patriarke, and the patterne and modell of all the patriarkes, to haue bene restrained to the onely Churches neere the Cittie of Rome, what a Birth-right had that bene? For to saie that the Pope had in his portion the Cittie of *Rome*, which recompenced in splendor and dignitie, the extent of the other patriarkships; and besides that the prouinces neere the Cittie of *Rome* were much more peopled, then the prouinces neere the other patriarchall Citties: who knowes not first, that the Cittie of *Rome* being vnder the Popes gouernement, is not because of his dignitie of patriarke, but because of his qualitie of Bishop? And secondlie, who knowes not, that *Diodorus Siculus* writes, that manie placed *Alexandria* the first or second of all the Citties of the world; and affirmes, that in his tyme, there were aboue three hundred thousand. Freemen inhabitans in *Alexandria*: and that *Herodian* saith, that *Geta* esteemed, that *Alexandria* and *Antioch*, were not farr short of *Rome*: and that *Claudian* calls *Constantinople* equall to *Rome*? And as for the prouinces neere *Constantinople* and *Alexandria*, who knowes not that they were no lesse peopled then the prouinces neere and contiguous to *Rome*; and principallie, if we belieue *Iosephus*, wherein *Agrippa* saith, that *Egipt* contained Seauenty fiue hundred thousand of men, without accompting the inhabitantes of *Alexandria*: And *Diodorus Siculus* who saith; that the ancient *Egipt* contained aboue eighteen thousand Citties or famous Boroughes?

Cõc. Chalc act. 1. Zon. in Conc. Nic. c 6. Nil. de Prim. Pap. & aliie Conc. Eph part. 2. act. 7. Balsamon. in Conc. Const. 1 c 2. Cõc. Chalc act. 15 c. 28. Herodot. in Terpsichor. Diod. Sic. bibl hist. l. 1 Idem ibid. l. 17. Herodian. hist. l. 4. Claud. de Bell. Gildon. Ios. de Bell Iud. l. 2. Diod. Sic. bibl hist. l. 1.

The word *Suburbicary* being deriued as *Grammar* teacheth vs, from the word *vrbs*, the lawes of *Etimology* will, that the varietie of the significations, should be ruled according to the difference of the acceptions of the word *vrbs* the primitiue: Now the word *vrbs* precíselie taken for the Cittie of *Rome*, had two Offices; the one, to distinguish her from all Citties contained vnder the Empire of the same Cittie of *Rome*, which was Called by excellencie and absolutely *vrbs*; from whence it is that S. CYPRIAN calls the Clearks of *Rome*, *Clearkes of the Cittie*, and the first Councell of *Arles*, intitles the Deacons of *Rome*, *the deacons of the Cittie*.

Cyp. ep. 40. Conc Arelat. can. 18.

And *Optatus Mileuitanus* calls *Zepherinus* Bishop of *Rome*; *Zepherinus of the Cittie*. And GREGORIE of *Tours*, saith, *Papam Vrbis*; intending the Pope of *Rome*; and that conformablie both to the eminencie of the Cittie, and to the Councell that *Mecenas*, reported by *Dion*, gaue to *Augustus*, to make all other people take their Citties, but for Countrie howses and Villages and to beleiue that there was but one Cittie, trulie a Cittie, to witt, *Rome*: And the other, to distinguish it from the onelie Citties, subiect to the Prouostship of *Rome*, which they called the Prefecture of the Cittie, which contained the next hundred thousand paces to the Cittie of *Rome*. And therefore as the word *vrbs*, taken precisely for the Cittie of *Rome*, had two vses; one relatiue to the Imperiall territorie of the Cittie of Rome, and the other, relatiue to the prouostall territorie of the Cittie of *Rome*: so the word *suburbicary* taken according to the reason of the etymology, ought to haue two offices; the one generall, to witt, to designe all the Citties situate within the emperiall territory of *Rome*, that ancient writers called *Romania*: from whence it is that saint ATHANASIVS said, that *Rome* was the Sea Apostolick and Metropolitan of *Romania*: the other particular, and more proper to lawyers; to witt, to designe the onely Citties, situate within the prouostall territorie of Rome; that is to saie, within a hundred thousand paces about *Rome*, which they called *suburbicary*, to distinguish thē from the Citties of *Italie*, subiect to the Pretoriall prefect of *Italie*, who held his Seate at *Milan*; the which, and principallie since the tyme of *Constantine*, was partycularly called *Italie*; for before *Constantines* tyme, the pretoriall Prefecture was not yet diuided into fowre Pretoriall Prefectures, of *Italie*, of *Gallia*, of *Illiria*, and of the *East*, but consisted in one onely Prefecture though it were sometymes solidarily administred by two persons. Now to pretend that it were in this second sence; to wit, not by relation to the Imperiall territory of *Rome*; but by relation to the Prouostall territory of *Rome*, that *Ruffinus* hath translated, that the Bishop of *Rome* should haue the care of the Churches suburbicary; what were this but to finde the Readers some what to laugh at? For besides that this terme was not in vse, but in the authors that haue written since *Constantin*, and the Councell of *Nicea*, who euer heard of shutting vp the Popes authoritie within the next hundred thousand paces of the Cittie of *Rome*? is there so simple a scholler that knowes not, that the Pope setting aside his qualitie, of head of the Church, was Patriarcke of the *West*; whence it is, that saint BASILE considering him as Patriarke, calls him the *Corypheos* of the *westerne* people, And that S. IEROME speaking of him in the same qualitie, cries out, *let them condemne me of heresie with the West; let them condemne me of heresie with Egipt*; that is to saie with *Damasus* and with PETER, vnderstanding by *Damasus*, Pope *Damasus*, and by *PETER*, *Peter* Patriarke of *Alexandria*; whom *Socrates* saith, Pope *Damasus* had newly then restored. And euen the *Greeke Scismaticks*, did not they anciētly acknowledge, that the Patriarkship of the Pope, did anciently cōtaine all the prouinces of the Empire of the *West*, that is to saie, all the Prouinces of *Italie*, *Africa*, *Spaine*, *France*, and the *Germanies*, *England*, & the *Western Illiria*, vnder which was vnderstood *Dalmatia*, *Hūgaria*, & the neighbouring prouinces? *Thou Seest*, saith *Nilus* Archbishop of *Thessalonica*, disputing against the Latins, *that the Canon of the Councell of Nicea esteemes, that the rules of the Fathers ought to be confirmed, which haue distributed to euery Church their priuiledges, to witt, that some of the Nations should be submitted to the Bishop of Alexandria, others to the Bishop of Antioch, as those of Syria, & the two Cilicia's, Cœlosiria, & Mesopotamia: And to the Bishop of Rome is giuen the same, to wit, that he haue the superintendencie of those of*

Opt. Mil. con. Parm. l. 1. Greg. Tour. hist. Franc. l. 2. Dio. hist. Rom. l. 52.

Epiph. hæres. 46. & 49. Possid. in vita. August. c. 30. & alij. Athan. ad Solit. vit. agent.

Bas. ep. 10. Ier. ad. Marc. presb. Celed. ep. 77. Soc. hist. eccl. l. 4. c. 37.

Nil. de Prim. Pap.

the West. And *Zonarus* a Greeke commenter and a Schismatick, expounding the sixth Canō of the Coūcell of *Nicea* long before *Nilus*; *The Councell* (saith hee) *ordaines, that the Bishop of Alexandria, should haue the superintendencie of Egipt, of Libia, and Pentapolis &c. as the ancient custome had giuen to the Bishop of Rome, to commaunde in the prouinces of the West*. yea, doth not the same *Zonarus* write, that the patriarkship of *Rome*, comprehended not onely all the prouinces of the Empire of the *West*, but also almost all the *Westerne* prouinces of the Empire of the *East*? *To the Roman Church* (saith *Zonarus* comenting the fifth Canon of the Councell of *Sardica*) *were then subiect almost all the Westerne Churches; to wit, those of Macedonia, those of Illiria, those of Hellada, those of Peloponesus; those of Epirus, which haue since bene attributed to the Sea of* Constantinople. For those prouinces that *Zonarus* calls *Westerne*, were all of the Empire of the *East*; but they were called *Western*, and appertained to the Patriarkship of the *West*, for as much as they had bene of the ancient Empire of the *West*, such as it had bene possessed by the common-Weale of *Rome*, before the Empire of *Asia*, holden by the *Seleucides* & other neighbour-Princes, & that of *Egipt* were vnited to it, & such as it had bene limited by the Emperors *Antonius* and *Geta*, when they proiected to diuide the *Roman* world, and set the *Bosphorus* for a barr betweene the two Empires: and such as it remained in the portion of the Emperors of the *West*, when the heires of *Constantine* shared the bodie of the State, and assigned the mountaine of *Thuscis* in *Trace*, for a bound betweene both Empires. From whence it is, that saint ATHANASIVS reckons *Eremius* Bishop of *Thessalonica* amongst the Bishops of the *West*. And that *Socrates* saith that *Paul* Bishop of *Constantinople* was banished from the Empire of the *East*, and confined to *Thessalonica*. And therefore when in the last diuision of the Empire they added the eleauen prouinces of the *Esterne Illyria*, to the fortie nine prouinces of the Pretoriall Prefecture of the *East*, to make thereof the Empire of the *East*; they remained within the *Popes* patriarkship, though they were become parts of the Empire of the *East*, and were called the *Westerne* prouinces of the Empire of the *East*, to distinguist them from those of the same Empire, which were vnder the pretoriall prefecture of the *East*.

Zō.in Cōc. Nic.can.6.

Idem.in Cō.Sard. c.5.

Herodian. hist. l. 4. in Antonin. & Get.

Soc. hist. eccl. l. 2. c. 21.

Athan. apol. ad Const.

Soc. hist. eccl. l. 2. c. 16.

And it is not to be obiected, that the law *Omni innouatione cessante*, made by *Theodosius* the second at the instance as it hath bene aboue said of *Atticus* Bishop of *Constantinople*, attributes to the patriarkship of *Constantinople*, not onely the prouinces of *Thracia*, *Asia minor*, and *Pontus*, but also those of the *Easterne Illyria*. For it appeares by a thousand testimonies, that this law remained without effect, and had no place after the death of *Atticus*. It appeares first by the testimonie of *Socrates*, who saith, first that the inhabitants of *Cyzica* a Cittie of *Hellespont*, would not receiue *Proclus*, that the Bishop of *Constantinople* had ordained Bishop of *Cyzica*, alleadging that the lawe of the Emperor *Theodosius* the second whereof the law *Omni innouatine cessante* is but a paragraph inserted into the *Code* by the heedlesnes of *Triboniam*, had bene made but for *Atticus*, his life tyme. *They ordained* (saith *Socrates*) *Dalmatius*, *despising the law which commaunded that the ordinatiō of Bishops should not be made without the sentence of the Bishop of Constantinople, and slighted this lawe, as hauing bene graunted to Atticus onely for his life*. It appeares secondly by the testimony of the Pope sainr LEO, who was created *Pope*, eighteene yeares after this lawe, who teacheth vs, that the causes of the *Easterne Illyria* went euen then to the Archbishop of *Thessalonica* Vicar of the Sea Apostolicke, in the *Easterne Illyria*, and that with the good likeing, and the strong hand of the ministers of the Empire of the *East*; and reprehends *Anastasius* Archbishop of *Thessalonica*

Soc. hist. eccl. l. 7. c. 28.

his

his Vicar in *Illyria*, because hauing sent for *Atticus* the Metropolitan of the old *Epirus*, *Atticus* hauing excused himselfe vpon his sicknes, and vpon the extreamitie of the winter, he had imployed the armes of the Empire of the *East*, to bring him by force. *Thou hast* (said hee) *had recourse to the Tribunall of the Prefecture of Illyria, and hast moued the Soueraigne power, amongst all worldlie powers, to make an innocent Bishop appeare, and to pull him from the sacred grates of his Church: and neither for the indisposition of his person, nor for the sharpnesse of the winter, could be obtaine anie respit, but hath bene constrained to put himself into waies full of perills, and through impenitrable snowes*: And againe; *Wee haue in such sort committed our Vicarship to thy Charitie, as thou art called to a part of the care, but not to the fulnesse of power.* Leo ad Anast. ep. 82. Ibid.

It appeares thirdly, by the testimonie of the Councell of *Chalcedon*, holden thirtie yeares after this lawe, which decrees that the Bishop of *Constantinople*, shall ordaine but onely the Metropolitans of *Pontus*, *Asia minor* and *Thracia*; that is to saie, declares that the law of *Theodosius* the second and particularlie the Paragraph *Omni innouatione cessante*, should haue no place; and that the prouinces of the *Easterne Illyria*, should remaine to the Patriarkship of *Rome*, and not to that of *Constantinople*. It appeares fowrthlie, by the testimonie of the Emperor *Iustinian* the first who erecting the Bishoprike of the first *Iustinianea* into the forme of a Primacie, or supernumerary Patriarkship; and attributing to him manie of the Prouinces of the *Easterne Illyria*; yeilds for a reason of this attribution, the difinition of Pope *Vigilius*, and not that of the Patriarke of *Constantinople*; and ordaines, that the Bishop of the first *Iustinianea*, shall there hold the place, of the Sea Apostolicke of *Rome*, and not of the Sea of *Constantinople*. *Wee ordaine* (said hee) *that he shall haue vnder his iurisdiction, the Bishops of the Mediterranian Dacia, Dacia Dypensis, Triballea, Dardania, vpper Mysia, Pannonia, &c. and that in the prouinces subiect to him, he shall holde the place of the Sea Apostolicke of Rome, following the definition of the holy Pope, Vigilius*. It appeares fifthy by the testimony of saint GREGORIE the *great*, who writes to the Bishops of *Illyria*: *Following the desires of your demaund, we confirme by the consent of our authoritie, our brother Iohn in the Bishopricke of the first Iustinianea.* And in the Epistle to himselfe; *The relation of our bretheren and fellow-Bishops, hath declared to vs that thou art called to the Episcopall dignitie, by the vnanimous consent of all the Councell, and by the will of the most Excellent Prince; that is to saie, of the Emperor Mauricius, third Successor to Iustinian; whereto wee also giue our consent in the person of thy fraternitie, &c: and send thee the Pall according to custome, and decree by a reiterated innouation, that thou exercise the Vicarship of the Sea Apostolicke*: And elsewhere, iudging the appeale from the sentence of the same Iohn Bishop of the first Iustinianea against Adrian Bishop of Thebes, one of the Bishops of his primacie; *because* (said he) *that wee see, that vnder the shadow of our Vicarship, thou presumest to doe vniust things; wee reserue with the helpe of Christ, to determine againe of this qualitie; &c: and the while, abrogating and disannulling the decrees of thy sentence, we ordaine by the authoritie of the blessed Prince of the Apostles, that thou remaine depriued of the sacred Communion for the space of thirtie daies?* Cōc. Chalc act. 15. c. 28. Iust. nouel 131. Greg. Magn. ad Episc. per. Illyr. l. 4. ep. 9. Idem. ad Ioān. episc. prim. Iustin. l. 4. ep 15. Idem. l. 2. ep. 6.

It appeares in the sixt place, by the testimonie of *Iohn* Bishop of *Thessalonica*, who in the third generall Coūcell of *Constantinople*, which we call the sixt generall Coūcell signed with the title of Vicar of the sea Apostolick of

Cõc. Cõſt. ſext. act. in ſubſcript.

Rome, in theſe words: *Iohn by the mercie of God, Biſhop of Theſſalonica, and vicar, and natiue Legat of the Sea Apoſtolicke of Rome, haue ſubſcribed.* It appeares in the ſeauenth place, by the teſtimony of *Leo* the *Learned* the *Greeke* Emperor, who reckons amongſt the Churches ecclipſed, a little while before him, from the Sea of *Rome*, and ſubmitted to the Sea of *Conſtantinople*; that of *Theſſalonica*, Metropolitan of *Macedonia*; that of *Nicopolis* metropolitan of the ancient *Epirus*, that of *Patros*, that of *Corinth*, and that of *Athens*: *The Metropolitans* (ſaid hee) *which haue bene ſubtracted from the Patriarkship of Rome, and which are now ſubiect, they and their Biſhop to the Sea of* Conſtantinople *are theſe: the Archbiſhop of Theſſalonica; the Archbiſhop of Syracuſa the Archbiſhop of Corinth; the Archbiſhop of Rhegium; the Archbiſhop of Nicopolis; the Archbiſhop of Athens; the Archbiſyop of Patros.* And finally it appeares by the teſtimonie of *Zonarus*, the moſt famous Canoniſt of the *Greekes*, who interpreting the words of the Councell of *Chalcedon*, that the Biſhop of *Conſtantinople* should ordaine but onely the metropolitans of Pontus, *Aſia*, and *Thracia*, adds, for the Dioceſſes, to witt; thoſe of *Macedonia*, *Theſſalia*, *Hellada*, *Peloponeſus*, *Epirus*, and *Illyria*, were at that tyme ſtill ſubiect to the Biſhop of *Rome*. And then if the lawe *Omni innouatione ceſſante*, had bene executed, and that the Prouinces of the *Eaſterne* Illyria should haue remayned after that diſpoſed to the Biſhop of *Conſtantinople* would not the conſequence haue bene yet worſe for the Popes aduerſaries? for that Pope *Leo* the firſt, who was made Pope eighteen yeare after this lawe, reproues the Archbiſhop of *Theſſalonica* his vicar in *Illyria* (becauſe hauing called *Atticus* Metropolitan of the ancient *Epirus*, and he excuſing himſelf vpon his ſicknes, and vpon the winters colde, he had employed the arme of the *Eaſterne* Empire, to make him come by force) and writt to him; *Wee haue in such ſort committed our Vicarship to thy charitie as thou art called to a part of the care, and not to the fulneſſe of power:* And that the Emperor *Iuſtinian* being willing to exalt the Biſhop of the firſt *Iuſtinianea* of *Bulgaria* ouer diuers Prouinces of the *Eaſterne* Illyria, alleadgeth for a reaſon of his ordinance, the definition of Pope *Vigilius*, and not that of the Patriark of *Conſtantinople*, and conſtitutes him vicar of the Apoſtolicke Sea of *Rome* in theſe very Prouinces; doth it not neceſſarilie shew, that either the lawe of the Emperor *Theodoſius* the ſecond had remained without effect, or that the Pope had iuriſdiction out of his Patriarship? and that before the Councell of *Nicea*, ſaint CYPRIAN ſolicited Pope *Steuen* to write to the *Gaules*, that *Marcian* Biſhop of *Arles* might be diſcharged; and reproued the ſame *Steuen*, for that he had vpon a falſe reporte reſtored *Baſilides* and *Martial* Biſhop of *Spaine*, depoſed for hauing abiured in the perſecution time: And that a while after the Councell of *Nicea*, *Valens* Biſhop of *Murſes* in *Pannonia*, and *Vrſatius* Biſhop of *Singidon* in *Myſia*, asked the Popes pardon for the ſlaunders they had published againſt ſaint ATHANASIVS: and that *Socrates* ſaith, that *Perigenes* Biſhop of *Patros* in *Achaya* was by the Popes commaundement made Biſhop of *Corinth*: And that ſaint PROSPER writes, that Pope *Celeſtine*, ſent *Germanus* Biſhop of *Auxera*, his vicar into *Scotland*: and that the Biſhop of *Theſſalonica* had bene from time to time, till Pope *Leo* the firſt; and from Pope *Leo* the firſt, to the time of Pope GREGORIE the *great*, vicars of the Sea Apoſtolicke in *Macedonian*, *Achaya*, *Epirus*, and other *Greeke* Prouinces, and not vicars of ſimple negotiation as *Balſamon* pretends; [a] but Vicars of iuriſdiction as *Zonarus*,

Leo philos Imper. in diſpoſit. eccl, thron. Conſtant. ſubiectar. apud. Leũclau. in iure Oriental.

Cõc. Chalc c. 28. Zon. in Cõc. Chalc c. 28.

Leo ad Anaſt. ep. 28.

Iuſt. nou. 131.

Cyp. ad Steph. ep. 67.

Id. ad Cler. & pleb. Hiſp. ep 68.

Sulp. Seu. hiſt. ſacr. l. 2

Soz. hiſt. ecl. l. 3. c. 23.

Ep. Conc. Sard. apud. Theod. hiſt. eccl. l. 2. c. 8.

Soc. hiſt. ec. cl. l. 6. c. 36.

Proſp. in Chron.

Leo ad Anaſt. ep. 82.

a Bals. in Comment. Cõc. Chalc c. 28. & poſt. orat. allocut. Synod.

and the *Greeke* Emperor *Leo*, [c] more learned and more ancient then hee, and the very Epistle of Pope *Leo* [d] beare witnes: shew they not plainely; either that the Pope had iurisdiction out of his Patriarkship; or that his Patriarkship extended further, then the Prouostship of *Rome*? For as for the new Critickes that obiect, that the Emperor *Valentinian* the third commaunded by one of his lawes the prefect of the Cittie, that he should banish those which were not in the Popes Communion from the space of an hundred thousand paces about the Cittie of *Rome*, and inferr from thence, that the Popes authoritie, did then extend but an hundred thousand paces about *Rome*; they shew themselues blinde with two more then *Tiresian* blindnesses: the one not to see that there was difference betweene this, that the Emperor *Valentinian* the third did; which was to beare so great a respect to the Popes, as not to permit to those, that were out of their Communion, the very temporall dwelling within the Prouostships of the Cittie of *Rome*; and the consequence that they inferr from it; which is to saie; that the Popes had not power to exclude those which were not in their communion, from the spirituall communion of all the Church: And the other not to perceiue, that the bound of an hundred thousand paces, is fitted to the lawe, not because the Popes iurisdiction extended no further; but because the ordinarie iurisdiction of the Prouost of the Cittie of *Rome*, to whom the lawe was directed, extended no further then ouer the next hundred thousand paces to the Cittie of *Rome*. Otherwise, how could saint PROSPER haue said, speaking of Pope *Celestins* proceedinges against *Cœlestius*: *he commaunded Cœlestius should be driuen from the vtmost endes of Italie*? and how could saint, AVSTIN haue written, that Pope *Innocent* and Pope *Zosimus*, condemned *Pelagius* and *Cœlestius*, *through all the Christian world*? and how should the same Emperor *Valentinian* the third haue said in an other lawe; *Wee ordaine by a perpetuall sanction, that neither to the Bishops of the Gaules, nor to those of other prouinces, it shall be lawfull against the ancient custome. to attempt anie thing, without the authoritie of the Reuerend Pope, of the eternall Cittie; but that to them, and to all, that be for a lawe, that the authoritie of the Sea Apostolick shall haue ordained*? But why should wee haue recourse to reason, to confute that which ruins and destroies it selfe by the proper hippothesis thereof? for had not the Cittie of *Constantinople* bene formed and made, by the patterne of the ancient *Rome*? had she not the same offices, priuiledges, and politicke orders with the ancient *Rome*? from whence the ancient *Rome* saith by the mouth of *Claudian*;

Cum subito par Roma mihi, diuisaque sumpsit
Æquales aurora togas.

Had she not a Senat as *Rome* had? had she not one of the Consulls as *Rome* had? had she not a Prouost of the Cittie, whose ordinarie iurisdiction was inclosed within the next hundred thousand paces to the Cittie of *Constantinople*, as *Rome* had? and when they would honor her with spirituall priuiledges, and erect her into the title of a Patriarkship; did they not rule her, by the square and by the modell of the Patriarkship of *Rome*, alleadging, that as she was honored with like temporall priuiledges as *Rome* was; so it was reasonable to honor her (that is to saie, in a Patriarchall degree) with like Ecclesiasticall priuiledges? If then the Patriarkship

[b] sext. in Trull. Zon. in Cōc. Sard. c. 5. & in Cōc. Chalc c. 28.
[c] Leo Imp. de ordin. eccl. thron. Const. subiectar.
[d] Leo ep. 82.
Lid. de Suburbic. region. impress. Frāc. an: 1618. differt. 2 c. 3.
Cod. Theod. l. 16. tit. de heretic. l. 62.
Prosp. Aquit. l. cōt. Collat.
Aug. ad. Opt. ep. 1. 57.
Theod. nou. Cōst. tit. 24. ad calcem Cod. Theod.
Claud. de Bell. Gild.
Cōc. Chalc act. 15. can. 28.

of *Constantinople*, were squared by that of *Rome*; and *Constantinople* had her Prouost of the Cittie, whose ordinary iurisdiction was contained within the next hundred thousand paces to the Cittie of *Constantinople*, as well as that of *Rome*; who sees not, that either the Patriarchall iurisdiction of the Pope, must not be restrained, within the ordinary territory of the Prouostship of the Cittie of *Rome*; that is to saie, within an hundred thousand paces next the Cittie of *Rome*; or that the Patriarchall iurisdiction of the Bishop of *Constantinople* must likewise bee restrained within the ordinarie territorie of the prouost of the Cittie of *Constantinople*, that is to saie; within an hundred thousand paces next the Cittie of *Constantinople*? for that *Constantius* Sonne of *Constantine* attributed to the Prouost of the Cittie of *Constantinople*, the appeales from the diuisions of *Thrace*, of *Pontus* and *Asia*, it was not of the ordinary iurisdiction of the Prouostship of the Cittie of *Constantinople*, noe more then the appeales of all the Prouinces of the Empire, that the ancient Emperors had attributed to the Prouost of *Rome*, were of the simple and precise ordinary iurisdiction of the Prouostship of the Cittie of *Rome*. By meanes whereof, to forme and mould the spirituall authoritie of the Bishop of *Constantinople*, by the patterne and modell of that of the Bishop of *Rome*; it was necessarie, either that the spirituall authoritie of the Pope; should be extended ouer all that which was of the extraordinarie iurisdiction of the Prouost of the Cittie of *Rome*; or that the spirituall authoritie of the Bishop of *Constantinople* should be inclosed within the onely boundes of the ordinarie iurisdiction of the Prouost of the Cittie of *Constantinople*, that is to saie; within the next hundred thousand paces of the Cittie of *Constantinople*. Now, so farr was this from being so, that the patriarchall territory of the Bishop of *Constantinople* was confined within an hundred thousand paces next the Cittie; as contrarywise the Patriarckship of *Constantinople* had for diuision, the prouinces of *Pontus*, *Thracia*, *Asia minor*; and the barbarous Prouinces; that is to say; *Russia* and *Muscouia*; which contained more ground, then all *Europe*?

Cod. de appel. l. 23.

Cōc. Chalc act. 15. can. 28.

And against this it is not to be said, that *Constans* sonne of *Constantine*, and brother to *Constantius* had depriued the Prouost of the Cittie of *Rome* from the right of examining by appeale, the causes of all the prouinces, and had attributed it to the pretoriall Prouosts. For if the Pope had bene squared by the patterne of the prouost of the Cittie of *Rome*, it had bene by the patterne of the prouost of the Cittie of *Rome*, not such as he was since the Empire of *Constantine*, but such as he had bene vnder the Empire of the Predecessors of *Constantine*: Otherwise how had the Councell of *Nicea* confirmed the ancient prerogatiues of the Bishop of *Alexandria* in *Egipt*, *Lybia*, and *Pentapolis*; for asmuch as they were grounded vpon the custome of the Bishop of *Rome*?

Cod. Theod. l. 11 tit. de appel. l. 27.

Conc. Nic. c. 6.

Moreouer, the same lawe of *Constans* sonne of *Constantine*, which tooke awaie the appeales of the prouinces of *Italie* from the prouost of the cittie, and attributed them to the pretoriall prouost of *Italie* cōprehended by names *Sicilia*, *Sardinia*, *Campania*, *Calabria*, and *Brusse*. And neuerthelesse it is certaine, that these prouinces, and particularly *Sicilia*, remained alwaies in the Popes patriarkship, as longe as the Latine and Greeke Churches were vnited. For those that saie that *Sicilia* was added to the patriarkship of *Constantinople*, when *Iustinian* attributed the Secular appeales of *Sicilia* to the pretor of *Constantinople*,

Cod. Theod. l. 11. tit. de appel l. 27. Lib de Suburb. reg. impr. Frāc. an. 1618. diss. 2. c3. Iust non. 75 & 104.

commit

committ two grosse ignorances; the one, not to knowe that the spirituall iurisdiction of *Sycilia*, was not transferred to the Patriarkship of *Constantinople*, till after the Greeke Emperors infected with the heresie of the *Iconoclasts*, had bene driuen from *Rome*, and in reuenge had depriued the Pope, not onely of the exercise of spirituall authoritie, but also from the temporall reuenew that he had in *Sicilia*, which remained to them: and the other, not to perceiue, that seeing *Sicilia* (which was out of the ordinary territorie of the Prouost of the Cittie, and belonged before the vsurpation of the *Vandalls*, to the Pretoriall Prouost of *Italie*; and since the expulsion of the *Vandalls* to the Pretor of *Constantinople*, to whom *Iustinian* had attributed it; for asmuch as when hee re-conquered *Sicilia*, the *Gothes* still held *Italie*) was of the Popes Patriarkship, the Popes authoritie was not then restrained to the onely territory of the Prouostship of the Cittie of *Rome*; for that *Sicilia* both before and after *Iustinian*, had bene and remayned vnder the Patriarkship of *Rome*, till the tyme of the *Iconoclast* Emperors, wee learne both from the Epistles of saint LEO, the first, written neere a hundred yeares before *Iustinian* which ordained the Bishops of *Sicilia*, to send euery yeare three Bishops of their prouinciall Synod to Rome the third of the *Calends* of *October*: and from the Epistles of saint GREGORIE the *Great*, written fiftie yeares after *Iustinian*, whereby he made *Maximian* Bishop of *Syracusa*, his Vicar ouer all the Churches of *Sycilia*: and from the sixth generall Councell, where the Bishops of *Sicilia* signed amongst the Bishops of the Popes Patriarkship: and from the Councell *Trullian*, celebrated vnder *Iustinian* the second where the description of the Patriarkship of *Constantinople* was repeated without anie mention of *Sicilia*: and finallie from the very confession of the Greeke Emperor *Leo*, surnamed the *Learned*, who placeth amongst the Churches subtracted from the Sea of *Rome*, and attributed to the Sea of *Constantinople*, the metropolitan Church of *Syracusa* and all her subalterne Churches?

Leo ad Episc. Sicil ep. 4. Greg. Magn l. 2. indict. 10. ep. 4. & alibi. Cōc. Cōst. sext. act. 4. Cōc. Trull c. 36. Leo. Imp. in ordin. eccl. thron. Const. subiect. apud Leunclau. in iur. Orientall.

And so what remaines but that *Ruffinus* an author that saint IEROM saith is full of impietie of language; and that *Ioseph Scalager* calls a slanderous and ignorant interpretor; and who was so little curious in the stile of the lawyers, as hee employed (with *Lampridius* and the other authors of the declination of the latine tongue; yea, as saint IEROM reproacheth it to him, with the vulgar) the word *parentes*, to signifie *Kinsmen*, setts therein the adiectiue *Suburbicary*, not according to the speciall vse of the lawyers, but according to the etymologie of the word? and then that as the generall office of the word *vrbs* absolutely taken, and by excellencie for the Cittie of *Rome*, was to distinguish her from all the Citties subiect to the *Roman* Empire, from whence it is, that they called the Bishop of *Rome* for distinction from all other Bishops; the Bishop of the Cittie; so *Ruffinus*, by the Churches *Suburbicary*, intends not the Churches within an hundred thousand paces of the Cittie of *Rome*; but the Churches of all the Citties, subiect to the Empire of the Cittie of *Rome*; which saint ATHANASIVS calls the Sea Apostolick, and Metropolitan of *Romania*? And indeede, that *Ruffinus* in translating, or rather in epilogizing the Canon of the *Nicean* Councell omitts the clause of the Patriarkship of *Antioch*; and translates onely, that the Bishop of *Alexandria* shall haue the

Acyrologijs. Hier. aduers. Ruff. apoll. 2. Ios. Scal. ano. in chro. Eus. num. LXXXIIII Hier. aduers. Ruff. apol. 2. Opt. Miliuit. cont. Parm. l. 1. & Greg. Turon. hist Franc. l. 2. Ath. ad Solit vit. agent.

care of the Churches of *Egipt*; and hee of *Rome*, that of the Churches *Suburbicary*: is it not a manifest proofe that he vseth these words, not in forme of diuision, but in forme of Subordination; and that this which he saith, that the Bishop of *Rome*, should haue the care of the *Suburbicary* Churches, and that which *Socrates* and *Sozomene* saie, that to the Bishop of *Rome*, because of the dignitie of his Seate; the care of all thinges belonge, is one and the same language: or rather that this that *Ruffinus* saith here, that the Bishop of *Rome* is to haue the care of the *Suburbicary* Churches; and this that he saith elsewhere; *Rome by the grace of God, is the head of all the Christrians*; is one and the same thing? But graunt that *Ruffinus* by the word *Churches Suburbicarie* doth intend in generalll all the Churches of the prouinces, subiect to the Empire of *Rome*; nor in particular, the onely Churches of the Cittie, subiect to the Prouoitship of *Rome*; but intends the Churches of the Prouinces or Nations, where the Metropolitans or Primats acknowledge the Pope immediatly without the intermedling of anie the Patriarks; to wit, the Churches of the Patriarkship of the west, would that hinder that besides the immediate superintendencie that the Pope hath ouer the prouinces of his Patriarkship, hee might not haue a mediate superintendencie ouer all the prouinces of the others?

Soc. hist. eccl. l. 2. c. 8. Soz. hist. eccl. l. 3. c. 7. Ruff. in Hier. inuect. 2.

Homer, if it be lawfull to compare thinges sacred to prophane, doth not he teach vs, that besides the Commaund *Agamemnon* had, as a particular King ouer the compaines of his owne subiects; and the other kings like him, euerie one ouer their owne; hee had yet beyond that, as head and Captaine generall, ouer the Armie of the *Greekes*, the vniuersall authority and superintendencie ouer the other kinges, and ouer their Companies? And will not the aduersaries of the Pope haue it, that the Prouost of the Cittie of *Rome*, to whose temporall proportion they pretend to square the Popes spirituall authority, besides the ordinarie iurisdiction of his Prouostship, wherein they equall him to other Prouosts had besides in the first ages an other extraordinary iurisdiction, by which as head of the Senate, and Vicar of the Emperor, he was superior to other Prouosts, and iudged of the appeales of all the Prouinces? And saint BASILL that great Archbishop of *Cappadocia* did not hee consider the Pope some tymes as Patriarch of the *West*, where hee calls him the *Corypheos* of those of the *West*; and sometymes as head of the vniuersall Church, when he writes to those of the *West*; *Be it that you repute yourselfe head of the vniuersall Church; the head cannot say to the feete, you are not necessarie to me: be it that you place yourselues, in the ranke of the other members of the Church; you cannot say to vs, that are constituted in one same bodie With you, you are not necessarie to me?* for that he vseth this disiunctiue particle (be it) it is not there to cast anie doubt, but to distinguish the addresse of his speache into two branches; whereof the one, to witt, *be it that you repute yourself head of the vniuersail Church*; had regard to the Pope: and the other, to witt; *be it that you place yourselues in the ranke of the other members*; had regard to the other Bishops of the *West*. And doth not hee himself reporte, that *Eustathius* Bishop of *Sebaste* in *Armenia* hauing bene deposed by the Councell of *Melitina* in *Armenia*, a Catholicke and orthodoxall Councell and hauing brought letters of restitution from Pope *Liberius*, was receiued without forme of processe into the Councell of *Tyana* in *Cappadocia*? And doth not saint IEROM, who was priest of

Lib. de Suburb. reg. impr. Frãc. ano. 1618. diss. 1. c. 1. Bas. ep. 10. Bas. ad transm. ep. 77. Basil. ep. 74.

Antioch

Antioch and creature to *Paulinus* the Bishop of *Antioch*, and resident within the diuision of the Patriarkship of *Antioch*, say; *What should the Churches of the East doe, and those of Egipt, and that of the Sea Apostolicke?* designing by the Churches of the Sea Apostolicke, those which were subiect immediatly, without acknowledging anie other Patriarke betweene, to the Patriarkship of the Pope: And by the Churches of *Egipt*, those which answered to the Patriarkship of *Alexandria*: & by the Churches of the *East*, those which were submitted to the Patriarkship of *Antioch*? And yet for all that, doth he not write to Pope *Damasus* about the contention of *Vitalis, Meletius*, and *Paulinus*, Competitors in the Patriarkship of *Antioch*; *I am ioyned in communion with thy blessednesse*; that is to say: with the Chaire of PETER; *I know the Church is built vpon that rocke*. And a little after; *I know not Vitalis, I reiect Meletius, I am ignorant of Paulinus; whosoeuer gathers not with thee, scatters?* That is to saie, doth he not teach vs that the distinction of the Popes patriarkship, from the other patriarkships, hindred not the Popes superioritie ouer the others? And did not *Flauianus* Archbishop of *Constantinople* write to Pope *Leo*; *Wee haue giuen aduertisment to your Holynesse, of the excommunication of Eutyches, that you may make his impietie knowne to all the Bishops, resident vnder your pietie?* And yet for all this, did he not, when *Eutyches* pretended to haue appealed to the Pope, submitt his iudgemēt to that of the Pope? And did not himselfe in the second Councell of *Ephesus*, appeale to the Pope? And *Iohn* the second, and *Anthimus*, and *Menas*, and *Iohn* the fourth his successors, did they not aknowledge and protest, that they were subiect to the Pope? And the Popes that came after *Leo*, did not they depose *Acacius*, and *Anthimus*, Patriarkes of *Constantinople*, and iudge by appeale the causes of *John* & *Athanasius* subiects to the Patriarkes of *Constantinople*? And did not the Pope S. GREGORIE the *great*, call the Bishops of the *West* his Bishops? *If the causes* (said hee) *of the Bishops, which are committed to me, are treated by the religious Emperors, by the intercessions of strangers; miserable man that I am, what doe I in this Church? but that my Bishops dispise me, and haue recourse to secular iudges against me, I thāke God almightie for it, and I impute it to my sinnes.* Yet did not he saie of all the Bishops in generall; *If there be anie fault in the Bishops, I know noe Bishop, but is subiect to the Sea Apostolicke?* And *Iulian* the former, who liued 1050. yeares past, did he not turne the hundred thirtith one new cōstitution into these words; yet more rawe, thē those of *Ruffinus*; *That the Bishop of the first Iustinianea should haue the same right ouer the Bishops subiect to him; as the Bishop of Rome had ouer the Bishops submitted to him?* And yet by this doth he pretend to equall the Bishop of the first *Iustinianea* to the Pope, or to exempt him and his Bishops from the Popes iurisdiction? Nothing lesse; but by the Bishops submitted to the Pope, he intended, the Bishops submitted immediately to the Pope without the interposition of other Patriarks, as it appeares both by the originall greeke of the law, which beares this: *We ordaine, that in all prouinces subiect to him, he holde the place of the Sea Apostolicke of Rome, following the things defined by the most holie Pope Vigilius*: And by the lawe of the same *Iustinian* to *Epiphanius*, which saith; *We will suffer nothing to passe, concerning the state of the holy Churches, which shall not be also referred, to the blessednesse of the most holy Pope; for as much as he is the head of all the most holy Ministers of God*: And by the places aboue cited of saint GREGORIE the *great*, which witnesse that the Pope confirmed euen then; that is to saie, fiftie yeare after *Iulian* the former, the election of rhe Bishop of the first *Iustinianea*; and sent him the Archiepiscopall mantle, and the reuocation of the Vicarship of the Sea Apostolicke, and iudged by appeale of the causes of his Bishops, & chasticed him himselfe, when he had misiudged.

Hier. cont. Ioan. Hier.

Id. contra Vigil.

Id. ad Dam ep. 57. Ibid.

In ep. præā. Cōc. Chalc Ibid. Ibid. & Lib. in breuiar. c. 12. See chap. 7 Vict. Tun. in Zen. & Euag. hist. eccl. l. 3. c. 18.

Greg. Mag. l 4. ep. 82. & l. 5. ep. 64. Id. e. l. 4. ep. 64.

Iul. antecess. nou. 119. in ver. nou. Iust. 131.

Iust. nou. 131. Cod. tit. 1. l. 8.

Greg. Mag. l. 4. indict. 13. ep. 9. & 15. Item. l. 2. indict. 11. ep. 6.

But

But in summe whatsoeuer the sence of this addition of *Ruffinus* bee, it imports little to knowe it. For hauing bene excommunicated for his errors in faith, by the Pope and the *Roman* Church; who doubtes but if he could insert into his translation, anie thing to the Popes preiudice, he hath done it?

It sufficeth before the Councell of *Nicea*, which wills that to euery Church the prerogatiues thereof, be preserued; the *Roman* Church was she, whereof S. IRENEVS cryes out, *to this Church because of a more mightie principalitie*; that is to saie, because of a principalitie more mightie then the temporall, *it is necessary that all the Churches should agree*. It was she, that S. CYPRIAN called *the Chaire of Peter, and the principall Church, from whence the Sacerdotall vnitie proceeded*. It was she of whom S. IEROM writt; *I know the Church is built vpon this stone; whosoeuer eates the lambe out of this howse, is prophane*. It was she of whom S. AVSTIN said, *In the Roman Church hath alwaies flourisht the principalitie of the Sea Apostolicke*. It sufficeth that before the Councell of *Nicea* which ordaineth that the ancient customes should remaine entire; the law Ecclesiasticall forbad, to canonize Churches; that is to saie, to make canons touching the generalitie of Churches, without the sentence of the Bishop of *Rome*: that the Ecclesiasticall custome bare, that the finall depositions of Bishops, could not be proceeded to without attending the decision from *Rome*, and that from the tyme of the Emperor *Gallienus*, that is to saie, more then sixtie yeares before the Councell of *Nicea*, the Churchmen of *Egipt*, desiring to accuse *Dionisius* Bishop of *Alexandria* their Patriarke, went vp saith saint ATHANASIVS Patriarke of the same Sea of *Alexandria* to *Rome*, and accused him before *Dionisius* Bishop of *Rome*. It sufficeth that presently after the same Councell of *Nicea*, when S. ATHANASIVS Patriarke of *Alexandria*, *Paul* Bishop of *Constantinople*, *Marcellus* Primate of *Galatia*, *Asclepas* Bishop of *Gaza* in *Palestina*, had bene deposed by diuers Councells of the *East*; *Julius* Bishop of *Rome*, restored to euery one his Church, *because to him* (saith *Sozomene*) *for the dignitie of his Sea, the care of all things appertayned*. It sufficeth, that after the death of ATHANASIVS, Pope *Damasus* confirmed the ordination of *Peter* Patriarke of *Alexandria*, successor to the same saint ATHANASIVS, and restored him to his Sea of *Alexandria*, It sufficeth, that in the Councell of *Sardica* holden for the defence of the Councell of *Nicea*, & whereat assisted besides more then three hundred other Bishops, the same *Osius*, that was President at the Councell of *Nicea*; the same saint ATHANASIVS which had helped to frame the acts of the Councell of *Nicea*; the same *Protogenes* Bishop of *Sardica*, which was at the Councell of *Nicea*, the Episcopall appeales to the Pope,, were authorized by a written lawe, and the Bishops of all the prouinces exhorted to referr the affaires to their head, that is to saie, to the Sea of the Apostle PETER. It sufficeth that in the Councell of *Lampsacus* in *Asia* the *Macedonians* purposing to returne to the Catholicke Church, sent their Legats from *Asia* to *Rome*, to protest obedience to the Pope, & to oblige themselues to come vp to his Tribunall, or to the iudges delegated by him in all causes that should be attempted against them. It sufficeth, that in the Councell of *Tyana* in *Cappadocia*, *Eustachius* Bishop of *Sebastia* in *Armenia*, who had bene deposed by the Councell of *Melitina*, the Metropolitan cittie of *Armenia*, bringing letters of restitution from Pope *Liberius*, was receiued without forme of processe, and had place as a Bishop in the Councell. It sufficeth, that when the Emperor *Constantius* had caused S. ATHANAS. Patriarke of *Alexandria*, to be deposed in a Councell of more then three hundred Bishops of the *East* and *West*, he thought he had not satisfied his

Conc. Nic. c. 6.
Iren. l. 3. c. 3.
Cypr. ad Corn. ep. 55.
Hier. ad Dam. ep. 57.
Aug. ep. 162.
Athanas. apol. 2.
Athan. de sent. Dion. & de Synod. Arim.
Socr. hist. eccl. l. 2. c. 15.
Soz. hist. eccl l. 3. c. 8.
Soc. hist. eccl l 4. c. 37.
Id. l. 2. c. 20
Conc. Sard c. 3. 4. & 5
Ep. Conc. Sard. ad Iul in relat Hilar. de hist. Conc. Arim. & apud Nicol. 1. ep. ad Episc. Gall.
Socr. hist. eccl. l. 4. c. 12.
Bas. ep. 70.
Socr hist. eccl. l. 2. c 36 & Soz. l. 4. c. 8.

desire; *if the thing* (saith *Amianus Marcellinus*) *were not confirmed by the authority whereof the Bishops of the eternall cittie are superiors.* It sufficeth that when the same Canon of the Councell of *Nicea*, which is now in question, was renewed in the Councell of *Constantinople*, the other Patriarkes and Primats were forbidden to meddle, beyond their diuisions: *Let the Bishop of Alexandria* (said the Synod) *gouerne onely what belongs to Egipt; and let the Bishops of the East*, that is to saie, of the patriarkship of *Antioch*, *administer onely to the East*; where neuer Coũcell interdicted the Pope from medling in matters which were out of his patriarkship: Cõtrariwise the Pope in importãt occasiõs, hath alwaies takẽ notice of the ecclesiasticall affaires of the Empire of the *East*, & iudged by appeale the causes of other patriarkships, the Catholicke Councells of the *East* thẽselues, yeilding to be solicitors & executors of his sentences: & oppositely neuer anie of the other Patriarks once attempted, to examine the Ecclesiasticall causes of the Empire of the *West*, and of the patriarchall diuision of the Pope. It sufficeth, that in the *Mileuitan* Councell holden by the Bishops of *Africa*; and by S. AVSTIN amongst others, it was affirmed, *that the Popes authoritie was of diuine right, and drawne from the authoritie of the holy Scriptures*: and then not to be restrained to the simple patriarkship of *Rome*, but vniuersall; and such as the law of the Emperor *Valentinian* the third describes it, when it calls the Pope, *the Rector of the vniuersalitie of Churches.* And the Emperor *Iustinian* when he writes, that the Pope is the head of all the most holy ministers of God. And the Bishop of *Patara* in *Lycia*, one of the prouinces in *Asia*, when he saith to the same Emperor *Iustinian*, *that there were many kings and princes in the world, but there was noe one of them, that was ouer all the earth, as the Pope was ouer the Church of all the world.* It sufficeth, that in the generall Councell of *Ephesus*, when the Fathers had executed the sentence of deposition, that the Pope had pronounced at *Rome* against *Nestorius*; when they should haue passed to the cause of *Iohn* Patriark of *Antioch*, the Councell reserued the iudgement thereof to the Pope, and that according to the ancient custome and tradition Apostolicall. It sufficeth, that in the false Councell of *Ephesus*, after *Dioscorus* Patriarke of *Alexandria*, and his pretended generall Councell, had deposed *Flauianus* Archbishop of *Constantinople*, and *Theodoret* Bishop of *Syre*; *Flauianus* (saith the Emperor *Valentinian*) according to the custome of Councells, appealed from him to the Pope; and *Theodoret* did the like: & that the Pope vpon these appeales, replaced *Flauianus* alreadie dead, into the Catalogue of the Bishops of *Constantinople*, and restored to *Theodoret* his Bishopricke, and annulled all the acts of the false Councell of *Ephesus*, except the creation of *Maximus* Patriark of *Antioch*, which remained in force, because said *Anatolius* Bishop of *Constantinople*, *the Pope hauing receiued him into his communion, iudged that he should rule the Church of Antioch.* And finally it sufficeth, that when the greeke text of the same canon of the Councell of *Nicea*, translated by *Ruffinus*, had bene read in the Councell of *Chalcedon*, a Councell composed of aboue six hundred Greeke Fathers, who vnderstood both Greeke, and the Greeke Canons better then *Ruffinus*, who was so vnapt and barbarous in both the tougues, as S. IEROM saith; the *Latins* tooke him for a *Grecian*, and the *Greekes* for a *Latine*: so farr were the Fathers of that Conncell from inferring from thence, anie equallitie betweene the Pope and the Patrirake of *Alexandria*, that contrariwise in their Synodicall relation, they protested they held the Pope for the head of their societie; *Thou rulest ouer vs* (said they) *as the head doth ouer the members.* And againe; *We praie thee to honor our iudgement, with thy decrees, and that as in what concernes the weale, we haue brought correspondencie to our head, so thy Soueraigntie*

would

Amian. Marc. hist. l. 15.

Cõc. Const. c. 2.

Aug. ep. 92.

Cod. Theo nou. Theo. & Valent. tit. 24.

Cod. Paris. Antuerp. & Gen. tit. 1. l. 7.

Lib. in breuiar. c. 22.

Conc. Eph. p. 2. act. 5. in relat. ad Cæl.

Ibid. act. 4.

Valent. 3. Imp. in ep. præamb.

Cõc. Chalc Theodor. ep. ad Leõ.

Ibid.

Cõc. Chalc act. 16.

Hier. aduers. Ruffi. apol. 2.

Cõc. Chalc part. 3. in relat. ad Leon.

Ibid.

would fulfill to thy children, what concernes decency: And on the other side, they vsed *Dioscorus* Patriarke of *Alexandria* as subiect, and ghostly vassall to the Pope, in these words; Ibid. *Dioscorus hath extended his frensy, euen against him to whom the guarde of the Vine hath bene committed by our Sauiour; that is to saie, against thy Holynesse.*

Of the claime of the Bishops of Constantinople.

CHAPT. VII.

BVT the aduersaries of the Church not finding anie foundation in the history of the other Patriarkes, to establish the equallitie, that they would introduce, betweene the Pope, and the simple Patriarkes, had recourse to the claimes of the Bishops of *Constantinople*, which are to be reduced principallie into two. The first claime was that of *Anatolius*, who packed in the Councell of *Chalcedon* by the fauor of the Emperor *Marcian*, and of the Senat of the cittie of *Constantinople*, to be declared the second Parriarke, and to enioy after the Pope, the like priuiledges of honor as the Pope; because *Constantinople* was a second *Rome*, that is to saie, packed to be declared equall to the Pope, not in regard of the Pope, to whom contrariwise he and all his Catholicke successors, alwaies protested themselues inferiors, but in regard of the other Patriarkes ouer whom he affected to be, what the Pope was ouer him and them. For that is it that Cōc, Chalc act. 15. c. 28 these words of the Councell of *Chalcedon* signifie that the cittie of *Constantinople* should be honored in Ecclesiasticall causes, as the *Roman*, being the second after her; to witt, that as the Bishop of *Rome*, had the primacie absolutely ouer all the Patriarkes, so the Bishop of *Constantinople* should haue it after him, ouer all other Patriarkes. Euag. hist. eccl. l. 2. c. 4. *It was ordained* (saith *Euagrius*, repeating the same Canon) *that the Sea of new Rome, because of the second place she held after the ancient Rome, should haue the primacie before the other Seas.* The second Clayme was, that of *John* and of *Cyriacus* Patriarkes of *Constantinople*, who in the tyme of *Pelagius* the second and of Sainct GREGORIE, would participate in the title of vniuersall Bishop, which in the presence, & with the consent of the Councell of *Chalcedon* had bene attributed to the Pope; pretending, that by the same Councell of *Chalcedon*, it had bene said, that the Bishop of *Constantinople* should enioy the like priuiledges of honor as the Pope, after the Pope: and then, that as the Pope had the right to beare the title of vniuersall Bishop through all the world; so the Bishop of *Constantinople* should haue the right to beare it in the Empire of the *East*. For that such was their Clayme, it appeares besides a thousand other proofes, by the capitulation of the great Comentor of Homer *Eustathius* Patriarke of *Constantinople*, and the other Greekes would haue renewed with the Latins, vnder the Greeke Emperor *Basilius* six hundred yeares agone; to witt, that the Bishop of *Constantinople*, might be called vniuersall in the Empire of the *East*, as the Pope ouer all the world. Glaber Rodulph. hist. l. 1. c. 1. *The Bishop of Constantinople* (saith *Glabar*, an author of the same age) *with his Princc Basilius and some other Greekes, held a Councell that it might be lawfull for them with the Popes consent, to haue the Church of Constantinople to be held and called in that compasse vniuersall, as the Roman is, in the compasse of the whole world.*

Now may I in two words, not onely confute these two obiections, but also retort them against the Popes aduersaries. For if the Bishop of *Constantinople* pretended to obtaine the second place after the Pope, be cause *Constantinople* was a second *Rome;* that is to saie, a part and a branche of the cittie and Church of *Rome*, for what cause is it not manifest, that the Church of *Rome* before his challenge, had then the primacie before all other Churches; as also the officers of the Emperor *Marcian* acknowledged in these termes; euen when they protected *Anatolius*: *By the proofes which haue bene produced on both sides, it appeares that the primacie before all, and the principall honor hath bene preserued by the canons, to the most beloued of God, the Archbishop of the ancient Rome?* And if the Bishop of *Constantinople* would participate in the title and nomination of vniuersall Bishop, because *Constantinople* was a second *Rome*, how could it be, but that the title of vniuersall Bishop, did appartaine primitiuely and originally to the Bishop of *Rome*? But for as much as the beginning of these contentions, came from the Councell of *Constantinople*, it is best to take the busines at the source of the history, which is thus: At the Councell of *Constantinople* held vnder the great *Theodosius*, the Greeke Bishops ordained in fauor of the Cittie of *Constantinople*, and in fauor of the Emperor of the *East*, who resided there to make a new Sea of the Empire that the Bishop of *Constantinople*, should haue the prerogatiues of honor after him of *Rome*, because *Constantinople* was a second *Rome*. Now this Canon was noe Canon of a Generall Councell; for be it that it was framed by the Councell of *Constantinople* that we call *Generall*; or be it was made by that which was reassembled at *Constantinople* the yeare following; the Councell of *Constantinople* that wee call *Oecumenicall*, hauing bene composed onely of the prouinces of the Empire of the *East*, and being become *generall* but by the adiunction and confirmation of that which was celebrated at the same tyme at *Rome*, and this Canon not hauing bene sent thither it could not hold the place of a Canon of a generall Councell And therefore when *Anatolius* Bishop of *Constantinople*, would haue caused it to be renewed in the Councell of *Chalcedon*, the Popes Legates answered, that is was not to bee found in the *Code* of the Synodicall Canons of the vniuersall Church and added, that is was neuer put in practise. *If the Bishops of Constantinople* (said they,) *haue enioyed, it what would they haue more? and if they haue not enioyed it, why doe they demaund it?* and for this very cause, Pope *Leo* writt backe to *Anatolius*: *The signatures of certaine Bishops made as thou pretendest more then threescore yeares agone, cannot vphold thy intention, to which being tardie and longe agoe fallen, thou hast sought weake and feeble proppes: for neuer hauing bene transmitted to the knowledge of the Sea Apostolicke, it could obtaine noe force.* And saint GREGORIE to the Patriarkes of *Alexandria* and *Antioch*; *The Roman Church hath neuer hitherto, neither now doth receiue the Canons or acts of the Councell of Constantinople; but she hath admitted that Synod in what it hath defined against Macedonius.* *Anatolius* then seeing this Canon had remained without effect, for want of hauing bene confirmed by the Pope, and by the *westerne* Church, resolued to take the occasion of the Councell of *Chalcedon*, celebrated at the gates of *Constantinople*, and of the deposition of *Dioscorus* Bishop of *Alexandria* and second Patriarke of the Church, which ranke he desired to possesse, to attempt to cause it to be renewed. And therefore spying out at the Euening of the twelfth daie, the time that the assemblie of the Councell was seperated, and that the legates of the Pope, and the Senate were retired, and that there were none remayning, but the Bishops that he thought he could easily bring to his Bowe; makeing vse of the absence of the Prelates of *Egipt* and of *Libia*, who assisted not

[Margin notes: Côc. Chalc act. 16. — Côc. Const c. 3. — Côc Chalc act. 16. — Ibid. — Leo ad Anatol. Episc. Côst. ep. 51. — Greg. Magn. l. 6. indict. 15. ep. 31.]

at the last Sessions of the Councell; for as muche as there was yet noe Patriarke of *Alexandria* established in *Dioscorus* his steede; and preuailing with the fearefulnes of *Maximus* Bishop of *Antioch*, created in the false Councell of *Ephesus*, who for the sence he had of the vice of his election, durst not open his mouth against *Anatolius* who had ordained him, he made a decree be particulariz'd which renewed the pretended Canon of the Councell of *Constantinople*, and made it be signed by certaine Bishops of the prouinces neere *Constantinople*. *There was that daie* (saith *Liberius*) *an other Session, when after the departure of the Iudges and the Senate, and the Legates of the Sea Apostolicke, certaine priuiledges were adiudged to the Church of Constantinople by Anatolius his vsurpation, takeing aduantage* of *Dioscorus condemnation*. The next day the Popes Legates stood vpon the forme of this surprise to the Councell, and represented that the Bishops themselues that had signed this decree, had signed it by constraint. But the plott was so well laid for *Anatolius*, borne out by the Emperor, and by the Senat of *Constantinople*, and by the Prelats of his diuision, that their resistance was in vaine. For part of the Bishops being absent, as those of the Patriarkship of *Alexandria*, who had the principall interest in it, and part dissembling their opposition, as *Maximus* Patriarke of *Antioch*, who afterward complained to the Pope of the preiudices that the priuiledgs of his Church had receiued in the Councell of *Chalcedon*, and part confessing against their will, that they had signed it with their will, as the Bishops of *Asia minor*, who had already protested in the fowrth action, that they had as lieue dye, as permitt that the Bishop of *Constantinople* should ordaine their metropolitans. And besides that *Eusebius* Bishop of *Dorylaus*, one of the Bishops of the diuision of *Constantinople*, assuring falsely, that the Pope was of agreement with the Article; the Councell passed forward to the approbation of the Canon; and when the legates of the Pope opposed it, they writt to the Pope to pray him to confirme it, in these termes: *We praie thee to honor our decree with thy iudgement, and as wee haue brought correspondence to our head for matters of weale, so thy soueraigntie may fulfill to thy children in matters of decencie; for in so doeing, the religious Emperors shall be gratified*. Now the Pope had bene allreadie desired not to giue consent to such enterprizes, for vpon this, that in the Councell of *Ephesus, Iuuenall* Bishop of *Jerusalem* abusing the absence and contumacie of *Iohn* Patriarke of *Antioch*, and assaying to vsurpe the iurisdiction of *Palestina*, against the Canon of the Councell of *Nicea*, which attributed the superintendencie of *Palestina*, and of the Bishop of *Ierusalem* himselfe, to the Archbishop of *Cesarea*, one of the metropolitans of the Patriarkship of *Antioch*: saint CYRILL Patriarke of *Alexandria*, praied the Pope, to consent that such attempts should take place. *In the Councell of Ephesus* (saith Pope LEO the first, in his Epistle to *Maximus* Patriarke of *Antioch*) *Iuuenall Bishop thought to haue found out a sufficient occasion, to obtaine the principalitie of Palestina, and to cause his audacious, insolence to be confirmed by surreptitious writings which saint Cyrill of holy memorie iustly haueing in honor, represented to me, and declared to me by his letters, what Iuuenalls ambition had attempted, and requested me with great earnestnesse and care, that no consent might be giuen to such vnlawfull attempts.*

Liberat. in breuiar c. 13.

Leo. ep. 50

Côc. Chalc part. 3.

Leo. ad. Maxim. Episc. Antioch. ep. 60.

For those causes then, and allso that *Maximus* Patriarke of *Antioch* had renewed the same request vnto him, the Pope insteede of confirming the decree of the Councell of *Chalcedon*, seeing it inviolated the order of the Councell of *Nicea*, which had giuen the second place to the Bishop of *Alexandria*; and the third place to the Patriarke of *Antioch*, annulled and abrogated it, by these words addressed to the Empresse *Pulcheria*; *The pietie of your Faith ioyned with vs wee annull the plotts of the Bishops repugnant to the rules of the holy canons established at Nicea, and by vertue of the authority of the blessed Apostle PETER, wee wholy abrogate them by a generall sentence.* And that with such effect, as the Emperor and the Bishop of *Constantinople*, were constrained for the tyme to depart from their pursuite, as it appeares by these words of the same Pope to *Anatolius*: *This thy fault which thou hast committed to augment thy power, as thou saist by the exhortations of others, thy charitie had better and more sincerely blotted out, if that which could not be attempted against thy will, thou hadst not imputed it onely to the Councell of thy Clergie &c. but it is an agreable thing, to me most deare brother, that thou dost now protest to be displeased with what should not euen then haue pleased thee; but the profession of thy loue, and the testimonie of the Christian Prince shall suffice to cause thee to re-enter into common grace, and let not his correction seeme tardie, that hath gotten so reuerent a suertie.* And from hence it comes, that in manie greeke and latine copies, this canon is onely in the historie of the acts, but not in the Catalogue of the Canons noe more then the twenty ninth and thirtith, and that it is manifest to haue bene transferred from the history of the acts into the rolle of the Canons, which possible is the subiect that hath giuen saint GREGORIE occasion to complaine, that the Councell of *Chalcedon* had bene altered by the Greekes.

Ibid.ep.53. Ibid.ep.69. Greg.Mag. l.5.ind.14 ep.14.

Afterward when *Rome* was fallen into the seruitude of the northerne nations, a people barbarous and hereticall, the Patriarkes of *Constantinople* makeing vse of the oportunitie or rather importunitie of the tyme, againe sett forward the instance of this Canon, and obtained from the Emperor *Zeno*, who raigned in the *East*, a lawe, whereby he confirmed the precedency to the Bishop of *Constantinople*, before the other Patriarkes; that is to saie, before the other Patriarkes of the *East*. And one from the Emperor *Iustinian* after the recouery of *Rome*, by which he ordained, that the Bishop of *Constantinople* should hold the second place in the Church: *Wee ordaine* (said the Emperor *Iustinian*) *that the blessed Archbishop of Constantinople new Rome, shall haue the second place after the holie Sea Apostolicke of the ancient Rome, and shall be preferred before all other Seas*: From whence it is, that *Liberatus* time-fellowe with *Iustinian* speaking of the Councell of *Chalcedon* adds, *And although the Sea Apostolicke to this daie contradicts this decree, neuerthelesse the decree of the Synod, doth in some sort remaine by the Emperors protection.*

Iust.nouel. 131. Liberat. in breu.c.13.

Now *Anatolius* had procured that the Clerkes of the Councell of *Chalcedon*, in renewing the Canon of the Councell of *Constantinople*, should insert a word therein. For whereas the Councell of *Constantinople* had simplie ordained, that the Bishop of *Constantinople* should haue the prerogatiues of honor after the Pope; those that renewed it, added thereto (*Equall*) and couched the reuocation of the Canon in these words: *that the Chaire of Constantinople should haue the prerogatiues equall to that of the ancient Rome, and shall haue the same aduantages in Ecclesiasticall causes as she hath, being the second after her*: that is to saie, ordained that the same prerogatiues, as the Pope had absolutely ouer all Patriarkes, the Bishop of *Constantinople* should haue them after the Pope, ouer the other Patriarkes.

Cōc.Chalc act.15.c.28

The Bishops of *Constantinople* then seeing, that this Canon not onely granted them, to hold the second place after the Bishop of *Rome*, but also to enioy the same priuiledges with him as *Constantinople*, being a diuision of *Rome*, and a second *Rome*; went so farr as to desire to participate in the same titles of honor, which had bene yeilded to the Bishop of *Rome*, to possesse them in a second place; and in forme of adiunctes and colleagues with him; and finding that in the Councell of *Chalcedon*, the title *Oecumenicall* or *vniuersall* had bene offerd to the Bishop of *Rome*, they insisted as second Popes and Bishops of the second *Rome*, to participate therein, not in intention to exercise it, in regard of the Pope, but vnder the Pope, and in regard of the other Patriarkes, and were openly fauor'd therein by the Emperors. For not onely the Councell of *Constantinople* holden vnder the Emperor *Justin* predecessor to *Iustinian*, yeilded the title of vniuersall Patriarke to *Iohn* the third Patriarke of *Constantinople*; but also the Emperor *Justinian* in the lawe, to *Epiphanius* Patriarke of *Constantinople*, exhibited to him the title of vniuersall Patriarke; and after vnder the same *Justinian* the Councell of *Constantinople* holden against *Anthimus*, attributed the name of vniuerfall to *Menas*; & still after vnder *Mauritius*, *Iohn* Bishop of *Constantinople* surnamed the *Faster*, held a kinde of Councell at *Constantinople*, where he began to intitle, and inscribe himself, *Vniuersall Bishop*; and then the Popes displaied their censures against this title; for although the Synods of the *East*, had before this time yeilded the title of vniuersall Bishop, to the Bishop of *Constantinople*, neuerthelesse the Bishop of *Constantinople*, had neuer yet presumed, to inscribe and subscribe himself *Vniuersall Patriarke*, vntill the Councell of *Constantinople*, holden vnder *Mauricius* the Emperor. And therefore the Pope *Pelagius* the second, predecessor to saint GREGORIE, abrogated and annulled all the decrees of that Councell, except what had bene decided concerning the cause of *Gregorie* Patriarke of *Antioch*. *It hath bene reported to the holy Sea Apostolicke* (saith Pope *Pelagius* the second) *that John Bishop of Constantinople, intitles himself Vniuersall, and that vpon this presumption of his, he hath called you to a generall Councell, notwithstanding that the authoritie of calling generall Synods, hath bene consigned by a singular priuiledge to the Sea Apostolicke, of the blessed Peter.* And a little after; *And therefore all that you haue decreed, in that noe Synod of yours, for Synod so attempted, it could not be, but a conuenticle; J ordaine by the authoritie of the blessed PETER, that it be annulled and abrogated.* And saint GREGORIE successor of the same *Pelagius*: *Our predecessor Pelagius of blessed memorie, hath disannulled by a sentence intirely valid all the acts of that Synod, except what concerned the cause of Gregorie Bishop of Antioch of reuerend memorie.* When Pope *Pelagius* was dead, and saint GREGORIE his successor establisht in the Popedome, the same *John* Bishop of *Constantinople* assisted by the fauour of the Emperor *Mauricius* still continued his challenge, and perseuered to attribute to himselfe, the qualitie of vniuersall Bishop; not to exercise it in the Popes behalfe, but to exercise it in the Popes absence, and as colleague and adiunct to the Pope in the vniuersalitie, ouer the Empire of the *East*, and toward the other Patriarkes. For it shall be shewed heereafter, that he alwaies acknowledged the Pope for head and stock of the vniuersalitie, and for absolutely vniuersall ouer all the Church, and did protest himself to be his subiect and inferior; and did not pretend to enioy the title of vniuersall, but vnder the Pope, and by association subalterne and subordinate to the Popes authoritie; which was soone after interdicted him by the Emperor *Phocas* immediate Successor to *Mauricius*, who declared that the

Cōc.Chalc act. in libel Clericor. Alexand.

Cōc.Const relatū sub Men. Cod.Iust. Paris. & Geneu. impress. tit. 1. l. 7. Cōc.Const sub Men. act. & seq. Greg. l. 7. indict. 2. ep. 69.

Pelag.Pap. 2. ep. 1.

Greg.Mag. l. 4. indict. 13. ep. 38. & l. 7. ep. 69.

title of vniuersall Bishop, appertained but to the Bishop of *Rome* onely, and could not be communicated to him of *Constantinople*. And so much of the truth of the history; Now let vs come to the obiections which are drawne from it.

To the first then of these obiections, which is that in the Councell of *Chalcedon*, *Anatolius* packed to be declared equall to the Pope after the Pope; wee bring three Answeres. The first answere is, that he pretended not, to be declared equall to the Pope in regard of the Pope; but vnder the Pope, and in regard of the other Patriarkes; that is to saie, that he did not pretend to haue like aduantage ouer the Pope, as the Pope had ouer him; but to haue the same priuiledges ouer the other patriarkes, as the Pope had ouer him and them; and by this meanes to be equall to the Pope, not in regard of the Pope, but in regard of the other patriarks. And this is testified by the vniuersall historie of the Bishops of *Constantinople*; which haue bene from the first contention to the second; that is to saie since *Anatolius* vntill *Cyriacus*; ouer all which the Pope hath exercised a perpetuall iurisdiction, and iudged continually both of their iudgements, and of their persons. For not to speake of *Paul* Bishop of *Constantinople*, that Pope *Iulius* restored to his Seat; *for as much as to him* (saith *Sozomene*) *for the dignitie of his Sea, the care of all things appertained*: Not to speake of saint CHRISOSTOME, who hauing bene deposed from the Sea of *Constantinople*, appealed by writing to the Pope, that he might cause the iudgement of his deposition to be made void: Not to speake of *Eutiches*, who hauing bene iudged by *Flauianus* Bishop of *Constantinople*, and hauing alledged that he had appealed to the Pope, was againe iudged by the Pope, *Flauianus* and the Councell of *Chalcedon* consenting to it; where *Anatolius* himself was in person, approuing the iudgement: Not to speake of *Flauianus*, who hauing bene deposed in the false Councell of *Ephesus* appealed from it to the *Pope*, and that saith the Emperor *Valentinian, following the custome of* Councells: Not to speake of *Anatolius*, who hauing bene chosen Bishop of *Constantinople* in the false Councell of *Ephesus*, and consequently his election being void, was made valid by the Pope; as Pope *Leo* testifies to the Emperor in these words: *It ought to haue sufficed him, that by the helpe of your pietie, and the consent of my fauour he hath obtained the Bishopricke of so great a Cittie.* And in briefe, not to speake of all the former examples, but to restraine myselfe to the onely tyme betweene *Anatolius* and *Cyriacus* when *Acacius* who was created Patriarke of *Constantinople*, thirteen yeare after the death of *Anatolius*, fell into the faction of heretickes, had not the Churches of the Patriarkship of *Constantinople* recourse to Pope *Symmachus*, as to the superior both of them and their Patriarke? *Seeinge thy Children to perish* (said they) *in the preuarication of our father Acacius, delay not or rather to speake with the prophet, slumber not, but make hast to deliuer vs*: And againe; *Thou art taught daily, by thy sacred doctor, Peter, to feede the flock of Christ, which is committed to thee through the whole world, not constrayned by force, but willinglie, thou that cryest with the blessed Paul to vs thy subiects; wee will not haue dominion ouer you in the faith, but will cooperate with you in ioy*? And did not Pope *Felix* depose the same *Acacius* from the Patriarkship of *Constantinople* yea with such effect, that although *Acacius* borne out as longe as he liued by the hereticks, despised the Popes Sentence, neuerthelesse after his death, his name euen in *Constantiuople* it-self; was raced out from the records of his Church and excluded from the recitall of the mysteries?

Soz. hist. eccl. l. 3 c. 8.

In ep. proœamb. Cõc. Chalc

Leo ep. 52.

Ep. eccl. Orient. ad Sym. in volum. Orthodoxograph. impress. Basil.

Teod. Anagnost. ad calcem hist. eccl. Theod. in edit. Rob. Steph.

And when *Macedonius* Patriarke of *Constantinople*, was solicited by the Emperor *Anastasius*, to take out of the seruice of his Church, the memory of the Councell of *Chalcedon*; did not he answere him; *that he could not doe it without a generall Councell, wherein the Bishop of great Rome must be President*? And when *Iohn* Patriarke of *Coustantinople* executed the sentence of the Sea Apostolicke against the memorie of *Acacius* his Predecessor; did he not write to Pope *Hormisdas*: *I promise, in time to come, no more to recite amongst the sacred Mysteries, those who are seperated from the Communion of the Catholique Church; that is to saie, that doe not wholie consent with the Sea Apostolicke: that if in anie thing I attempt to depart from this my profession, I protest my-self to be comprehended, by mine owne condemnation, in the number of those whom I haue condemned*? And when *Anthymus* was installed in the Patriarkship of *Constantinople*, did hee nor oblige himselfe *to doe all that the Soueraigne Pope of Great Rome should decree*? And did he not write to all the Patriarkes *that he wholy followed the Sea Apostolike*: And when Pope *Agapet* was arriued at *Constantinople*, did he not depose the same *Anthymus* from the Patriarkship of *Constantinople*; and did he not excommunicate the Empresse *Theodora*, who sustained him? And when *Menas* Patriarke of *Constantinople*, gaue his voice in the Councell of *Constantinople*, did he not saie; *We follow in all things the Sea Apostolicke, and obaie it*? And when the Emperor *Iustinian* pressed by the Empresse, who was an *Eutychian* would persecute Pope *Siluerius*, did not the Bishop of *Patara* in *Lycia*, one of the subiects to the Pattriarkship of *Constantinople*, represent to him, *that there was no king in the world, that was ouer all the world, as the Pope was ouer all the earth*? And euen in the tyme of saint GREGORIE, vntill whose Popedome, the temporall dignitie of the Citty of *Rome* grew into such a diminution, and that of *Constantinople* contrarywise to such a height, that *Constantinople* then exceeded *Rome*, and all the other Citties of the world,

Ioan. Cōst. ep. ad Hormisd. Cōc. sub Men. act. 4.

Ibid.

Iust. nou. 24. Vict. Tun. in Iust. Conc. Cōst sub Men. act. 4.

Liberat. in breuiar. c. 22.

As the high Cypres sharpe-head doth outgrow
The crooked wreathes of Shrubbs that spread below.

The Churchmen of the deuision of *Constantinople*, after they had bene iudged at the Tribunall of the Patriarke of *Constantinople*, did they not goe by appeale, to that of the Pope? And did not the Emperor and the Patriarke of *Constantinople* themselues, Confesse *that the Church of Constantinople, was subiect to the Sea Apostolicke*?

Greg. l. 5. indict 2. ep 24. & l. 7. ep. 64. Idem. l. 7. ep. 63.

The second answere is, so farr of is it that from this Canon there may bee drawne anie arguments to oppose the primacie of the Pope, as contrarywise there may from hence be drawne, strong reasons to defend it. For from this, that the first Councell of *Constantinople*, and the Councell of *Chalcedon* ordained, that the Bishops of *Constantinople*, should hold the second place after the Bishop of *Rome*, and should enioy after him the same priuiledges, because *Constantinople* was a second *Rome*, doth it not appeare that before the Councell of *Constantinople* and *Chalcedon*, the Pope was the first of all the Patriarkes, and the first not in simple primacie of order, but in primacie of iurisdiction; since the equalitie that these Canons gaue to the Bishop of *Constantinople* with the Pope, was excepting the primacie of order, which they reserued to the Pope: And since, by vertue of this equalitie in the second degree, the Bishops

Cōc. Const c. 3. Cōc. Chalc act. 15. c. 28.

of *Con-*

of *Constantinople* attributed to themselues, the right of receiuing appeales from the Patriarkships of the *East*, and to ordaine in extraordinary occurrences the persons of their Patriarkes, and to participate in the title of vniuersall Bishop, and to call the generall Councells of the Empire of the *East*, and to iudge the Patriarkes of the *East*? For was it not vnder this pretence that *Anatolius*, before the Councell of *Chalcedon* ordained *Maximus* Patriarke of *Antioch*? *Anatolius* (saith Pope *Leo* the first) *without anie example, and against the Constitutions of the Canons, hath presumed to ordaine the Bishop of Antioch, which we would not reuoke, for the desire of repairing faith, and for the zeale of peace.* And was it not vnder this pretence, that he would haue brought vnder the Patriarkships of *Alexandria* and of *Antioch*; from whence it is, that the same Pope *Leo* reproached it to him, that he had packed this decree, not simplie to exalte his ranke, but to increase his power? *This thy fault* (said hee) *which to augment thy power, thou hadst committed as thou saist by the exhortation of others, thy charitie had better and more sincerely blotted out, if thou hadst not imputed that which could not be attempted without thy will, to the onely Councells of thy Clergie.* And elsewhere; *After the vicious beginnings of thy promotion, after the ordination of the Bishop of Antioch, which against the rules of the Canons thou hast attributed to thy self, I am greeued that thy dilection hath fallen so farre, as to infringe the holy Constitutions of the canons of Nicea; as if thou hadst watched a time for thy purpose, wherein the Sea of Alexandria was fallen from the priuiledge of the second honor, and wherein the Church of Antioch had lost the proprietie of the third dignitie; to the end that those places being subiected to thy iurisdiction, all the Metropolitans might be depriued of their proper honor.* And was it not vnder this pretence, that the Patriarkes of *Constantinople* attributed to themselues the appeales from other Patriarkes? *That which was defined* (saith Balsamon) *in the Councell of Sardica for the Pope concerning appeales, ought also to be extended to the Patriarke of Constantinople, forasmuch as hee hath bene by diuers canons,* (meaning the canon of the Councell of *Chalcedon*, and that of the Councell *Trullian*) *honored in the same sort as the Pope.* And againe; *This priuiledge belonges not to the Pope alone, that euerie Bishop being condemned should haue recourse to the Sea of Rome, but it ought also to be vnderstood, of the Patriarke of Constantinople.* And *Nilus* Archbishop of *Thessalonica*; *the twentie eight canon of the Councell of Chalcedon, and the thirtie sixth of the sixth Councell, honoring the Sea of Constantinople, with the same priuiledges with that of Rome, grant also manifestly the appeales to that of Constantinople.* And in briefe was it not vnder this very pretence, that when *Gregorie* Patriarke of *Antioch* had appealed to the Emperor and to the Councell from the persecutions of the Gouernors of *Syria*; *John* Patriarke of *Constantinople* presumed to call a generali Councell of the Church of the *East*, and to assigne the other Patriarkes and Metropolitans of the Empire of the *East*, to be there, and there to iudge with them, the cause of *Gregorie*, and there to intitle himself vniuersall Bishop? Now is not this to protest, that before that *Constantinople* was erected into the title of second *Rome*, and that the Councells of *Constantinople* and *Chalcedon* had made this pretended extension of the priuiledges of the Bishop of *Rome* to him of *Constantinople*; the vniuersall primacie and superintendencie of the Church, belonged to the Pope? For to say, that at least it appeares from these words of the Councell of *Chalcedon*; *The Fathers did iustlie exhibit the priuiledges to the Sea of the ancient Rome, forasmuch as that cittie had the Empire; and the hundred and fiftie Religious Fathers, moued with the same conside-*

Leo ad Martian. ep. 52.

Idem ad Anatol.

Idem ad eund.

Balsam. in Conc. Sard c. 3.

Ibid.

Hilar. de prim. Pap. l. 2.

Euag. hist. Eccl. l. 6. c. 7.

Pelag. 2. ep. 1.

Greg. ep. l. 7. ind. 2. ep. 69.

Cōc. Chalc act. 15. c. 28

ration, haue attributed equall priuiledges, to the holy Sea of the Cittie of Constantinople. That the cause wherefore the Fathers which had preceded the first Councell of *Constantinople*, had giuen the primacie to the Pope was not the Succession of saint PETER, but the dignitie of the cittie of *Rome*; besides that heere, the question is not of right, but of possession, nor of deuining the cause, wherefore the Fathers which liued before the first Councell of *Constantinople*, had granted the primacie to the Pope; but to knowe whether indeede, they had graunted it him, when the Bishop of the Councell of *Chalcedon* said: that the primacie had bene exhibited to the Church of *Rome*, because the cittie of *Rome* was the Seat of the Empire; they intended not that the dignitie of the cittie of *Rome* had bene the next conioyned and immediate cause of the primacie of the Bishop of *Rome* but the cause *antecedent*, *obiectiue*, and *remote*, contrarywise, the next and conioyned cause of the primacie of the Church of *Rome*, they acknowledged to be the Succession of saint PETER, as it appeares both by the title that they gaue to the Popes Epistle, calling it the *sermon of the Sea of saint PETER*: and by the protestation that they made, that the Popes primacie was of diuine right, and instituted by the proper mouth of our Lord, when they said, speaking of *Dioscorus*; *He hath extended his felonie euen against him, to whom the guarde of the vine was committed by our Sauiour*, But the cause of the cause; that is to saie, the cause that moued saint PETER, head of the Apostles, to place and settle his Sea at *Rome* rather then in an other place, they pretended to haue bene the dignitie of the Cittie. By meanes whereof these two causes were not exclusiue but inclusiue one to the other: As also the lawe of the Emperors *Theodosius* & *Valentinian*, made six yeare before the Coūcell of *Chalcedon*, conioynes them in these wordes: *Three things haue established the primacie of the Sea Apostolicke; the Merit of saint Peter, who is the Prince of the Episcopall Societie; the dignitie of the Cittie; and the Synodicall authoritie.*

Cōc.Chalc in allocut. ad Imperat. Cōc.Chalc in relat. ad Leon. Nou. Theod. tit.24.

And to this there is no repugnancie in that which the Fathers of the same Councell argued also of the dignitie of the cittie of *Constantinople*, and they alleadged that it was second *Rome*, to inferr from thence, the second place to the Bishop of *Constantinople*: for they grounded not their instance simplie vpon the temporall dignitie of the cittie of *Constantinople*, which was, saith saint AVSTINE, *daughter to the cittie of Rome*: but also vpon the spirituall dignitie of the Church of *Constantinople*, which was daughter to the Church of *Rome*, forasmuch as a part of the Clergie of *Rome*, were transferr'd to *Constantinople*, with the other *Roman* inhabitants, when one of the halues of the Empire was transported thither; that is to saie, they did not leane onely vpon this, that the Cittie of *Constantinople* was an other Seate of the Empire; but vpon this, that the Church of *Constantinople* was a Swarme and a collonie of the Church of *Rome*, and the Episcopall Sea of *Constantinople* a member and part of the Sea Episcopall of *Rome*; or rather, one and the same Sea Episcopall. and one and the same Throne of saint PETER with that of *Rome*, as *Iohn* Patriarke of *Constantinople* protesteth to Pope *Hormisdas*, in these words: *I esteeme the Church of your ancient and this new Rome, to be one self-same Church; and I make account that that Sea of saint Peter, and this of this Imperiall cittie, is one selfe-same Sea:* And as it seemes the title of the lawe of the Emperor *Heraclius* confirmes it, when he calls the Sea of *Constantinople*, *the Sea Apostolick*: and *Zonarus* when he saith, that in the tyme of the Councell intitled the 8th. Oecumenicall, *the Bishop of Rome and him of Constantinople were yet homodoxall and homothronall*; that is to saie, vnited in one selfe-same faith, and set in one selfe-same Sea. And therefore, the Fathers of the

Aug.de ciu.dei. l.5. Ioann. Episc.Cōst ep.ad Hormisd. Conc tom.2. Titulus legis 4. Heracl.apud Leunclau. iur.Orient l.2 in nouel Imp. Zonar.in Syn habitam.in æde Sanct.Sophiæ. can.1

Councell

Coũcell of *Chalcedon*, did noly alleage in their Canõ, that it was reasonable that *Constãtinople* being adorned by the Empire and the Senate, should enioy alsoin the secõd place after the Cittie of *Rome*, the same priuiledges in Ecclesiasticall causes; but addeth thereto in their relation two other reasons, taken frõ the spirituall affinitie of the Church of *Constantinople*, with that of *Rome*. The one, the facilitie of the influence of the gouernment of the Church of *Rome* into that of *Constãtinople*; forasmuch as the beames of the Sea Apostolicke, might spread more commodiouslie from *Rome* to *Constantinople*, then to the other Patriarchall Seas, because of the communication that those two cities, which made one selfe-same head of the Empire, had together. By meanes whereof, it was more conuenient, that the rules which the other Patriarkships should take from the *Roman* Church the Church of *Cõstantinople*, where resided in ordinary the *Nuncios* of the Sea Apostolicke, and which was neerer the Patriarkship of *Rome*, should receiue them first and immediatly from the *Roman* Church, and then communicate them to the other Seas, which were farther off. The other, that the Church of *Constantinople*, was daughter and extract frõ the *Roman* Church; *Wee haue* (said they,) *bene incouraged to doe this, for that the Beame Apostolicke raigning amidst you; and you by your ordinary gouernment spreading it to the Church of Constantinople, you may cause it to shine the oftner into these partes, because you are wonted without enuie to inriche those of your linage, with the participation of your Goods.* And therefore Pope *Leo*, with a purpose to cutt off in a word, all their hope of this pretence, writt to the Emperor that *Constantinople*, what soeuer *Anatolius* might attempt, could neuer be made a Sea Apostolick: *Let Anatolius* (said he) *not disdaine the imperiall cittie, which he cannot make a Sea Apostolicke*: which moued the latter *Greekes*, to add another deuise. For considering that the pretence of the vnitie of their Sea with that of saint PETER, could not serue for a good Colour of a Spirituall title, to perserue thereto the second place in the Church, they haue had recourse, to deriue by a fabulous list, and which hath noe testimonie in antiquity, the Succession of the Bishops of *Bizantium* from saint ANDREW, brother to saint PETER, to maintaine to the Church of *Constantinople*, built vpon the foundation of *Byzantium* the second Sea after that of saint PETER.

Cõc. Chalc act. 15 c. 28.

Cõc. Chalc apud Leon

Leo ad Martian. Aug. ep. 52.

Catalog. Episcop. Byzant. apud Leũclau. in iur. Greco-Roman. l 4 Niceph. Patriarch. Constant. in. Chron.

The third Answere is what soeuer the ayme and sence of this Canon may be; there can noething be inferred from it, either lawfull or Canonicall; forasmuch as it was a surreptitious Canon, and obtained by fraude and by surprize; and against which there were thirteen nullities, whereof the least is sufficient to impose a perpetuall silence, to all those that alleadge it. The first nullitie is, that they were neither the presidents of the Councell, nor the Bishops of the Councell which propounded and particularized this Canon, but the Clerkes of the Church of *Constantinople*, and particularly *Aetius* Archdeacon of *Constantinople*, as it appeares both from the eleuenth action, in which one of the clauses which was after entered into this Canon to witt, *that the Metropolitans of Asia minor, should receiue their ordination from the Bishop of Constantinople*, hauing bene contested by the Bishops of *Asia*, the onely Clerkes of the Church of *Constantinople*, with lowde voices cried out; *Lett the ordinance of the hundred and fiftie fathers* (so called they the Canon of the Councell of *Constantinople*, falsely alleadged to that purpose) *stand*; *let not the priuiledges of Constantinople perish, lett the ordinations be made, according to the custome, by our Bishop*: And from the words of *Aetius* Archdeacon of Constantinople, when he would haue excused the obreption of this Canon, which were; *It is a thing accustomed in Synods, after principall matters haue bene defined, to questiõ and*

Cõc. Chalc can. 28.

Ibid. act. 11.

Cõc. Chalc act. 16.

decide

decide some other necessary things. Now we haue; to witt the holy Church of Constantinople, some articles to propound: And from the excuse that *Anatolius* Bishop of *Constantinople* made, when he departed from this canon, which was that he had bene set on to solicit it, by the importunitie of his clergie. *This thy fault* (saith Pope *Leo* answering *Anatolius*) *which to augment thy power, thou hadst committed, as thou saist, by the exhortation of others, thou hadst better and more sincerelie blotted out, if thou hadst not imputed to the onely councell of thy clergie, that which could not be attempted without thy consent.*

Leo ad Anatol. ep. 69.

The second nullitie is, that this decree was made at an vndue hower, and after the assemblie of the Councell had bene separated; and when the Popes Legates and the Senators which assisted there on the Emperors part, were retired; as it appeares both by the complaint that the Popes Legates made thereof the morrowe after, to the Emperors officers, deputed to keepe order in the Councell, which contained these words: *Yesterdaie after the departure of your excellencie and of our humilitie, they saie there were made certaine articles, that we pretend to be contrarie to the canons, and to Ecclesiasticall discipline*: And by the answere of the Emperors officers, which was; *If there were anie articles framed after our departure, let them be read.* And by these words of *Liberatus*; *There was that daie, another session, wherein after the departure of the Judges, and the Senat, and the Legats of the Sea Apostolicke, certaine priuiledges were adiudged to the Church of Constantinople, takeing aduantage of the condemnation of Dioscorus.* And to that, is not repugnant the excuse that *Aetius* Archdeacon of *Constantinople* alleadged to the Emperors officers in these words: *Wee requested my Lords the Bishops of Rome to assist to it, they refused saying, they had noe commaundement to that effect: Wee reported it also to your magnificence, you commaunded the Synod should examine it, when your excellencie was gone forth, the holie Bishops which are heere, risinge as for a common businesse, required that the action should be made; now it is in our hands, nothing hath bene done in a corner or by stealth, but the action hath bene competent and canonicall.* For either the clerks of *Constantinople*, had made no such request to the Popes Legates & the Emperors officers; or it was not that daie, nor vpon the point of the action, otherwise the Emperors officers would not haue answered the Popes Legats, as being ignorant of the historie; *If there be anie article framed since our departure, let it be read.*

Cóc. Chalc act. 16. Ibid. Liberat. in breuiar. c. 13. Cóc. Chalc act. 1. Ibid.

The third nullitie is, that this canon was made, the Bishops of all the other Patriarkships being absent, & in the onely presence of the Bishops of the Patriarkship of *Antioch*, and of the prouinces neere *Constantinople*. That it was so, besides that the Bishops of the westerne prouinces of the Empire of the *East*; that is to saie, of the Easterne *Illyria*, and of the naturall Greeke prouinces; as of *Macedonia*, of *Hellada*, of *Peloponesus*, of *Thessalia*, and of the Isle of *Creete*, who had assisted at the other actions, were there omitted; neither were the Popes Legates, (who represented all the Bishops of the Empire of the west) there, *Anatolius* hauing watched the time of their absence; nor anie of the Bishops of the Patriarkship of *Alexandria*, which were those that had the principall interest in the busines. For as for this that *Caluin* saith, that *Proterius* Patriarke of *Alexandria* was there, it is an ignorance disproued by the signatures of the canon, and by all the histories of antiquitie, which teach vs, that *Proterius* was not created Patriarke of *Alexandria*, till after the councell of *Chalcedon* had bene finisht, and till the Egiptian Bishops were returned from *Chalcedon*, into *Alexandria*.

Calu. inst. l. 4. c. 7. Liberat. in breuiar. c. 14.

The fourth nullitie is, that euen those that signed this canon, signed it against their wills, as the Popes Legates protested when they complayned *that they had made the Bishops subscribe by force*, or *to vnwritten canons.*

Cóc. Chalc act. 16.

And it is no opposition to this, that the next day when the Senators asked the Bishops of *Pontus*, and of *Asia*, whether they had signed this canon with their will or against it, they answered *that they had signed it without constraint*. For this interrogatory and this answere had bene procured by *Anatolius*, and by the Clerkes of *Constantinople*, abusing the fauor of the Emperor, and the support of the Senat, as it appeares by the protestation that the Bishops of *Asia* had made in the eleauenth Session of the Councell, against the right that the Bishop of *Constantinople* would haue attributed to himself, to ordaine the Archbishop of *Ephesus*, Metropolitan of *Asia Minor*; which was afterward one of the principall articles of this decree. *The Reuerend Bishops of Asia* (saith the eleauenth Action of the Councell of *Chalcedon*) *prostrated themselues before the* Councell *and cried out; haue compassion vpon vs; haue compassion vpon our children*. (that is to saie, either of their Ghostly children, which were their Diocesans; or of their children borne by wiues, married before their Priesthood) *least by our occasion, and by our Sinnes, they should dye &c. for if a Bishop of Ephesus be ordained here, both our children will die, and the cittie will be rooted out*. And againe; *The most glorious Senators said; The most reuerend Bishops of Asia present in this Councell, protest that if there be here an other Bishop ordained, there will be a sedition in the cittie of Ephesus. Let the Synod then declare, where the canons will that the Bishop of* Ephesus *be ordained*. And a little after; The most Reuerend Bishops answered; *In the Prouince. And Diogenes the most reuerend Bishop of Cyzica said; such is the custome, if the Bishop of Ephesus tooke his ordination from the Bishop of Constantinople, these things would not happen*, &c. *And Leontius right Reuerend Bishop of Magnesia added; Since S. Timothie vntill this present, there haue bene twentie seauen Bishops created, all haue bene ordained at Ephesus; one onely Bassianus, hath bene violently ordained heere, from whence there haue ensued manie murthers*. And in the end, *The Right Reuerend Bishops cryed out; Let the canons stand*, &c. *And the Clerkes of Constantinople contrariwise; Let the ordinance of the hundred and fiftie Fathers stand; Let not the priuiledges of Constantinople perish; Let the ordination acording to custome be made by our Archbishop*. From whence it appeares euidentlie, that the Bishops of *Asia*, and the Clerkes of *Constantinople*, were directly contrary in this article: And that what *Diogenes* Bishop of *Cyzica*, and the other *Asian* Bishops said then when the canon was read ouer againe, to witt, that they had signed voluntarily, was so farr from being true, that contrariwise the same *Diogenes* Bishop of *Cyzica*, and the other *Asian* Bishops had protested, that if they should consent, that the Bishop of *Constantinople*, should ordaine the Metropolitans of *Asia*, which was one of the principall clauses of the Canon, their Diocesans would perish, and their citties would be put to fire and sword.

Id. ibid.

Ibid. act. 11

Ibid.

Ibid.

Ibidem.

The fifth nullitie is, that the Clerkes of *Constantinople* faigning to renew by this decree, the canon of the Councell of *Constantinople*, which is called the canon of the hundred and fiftie Fathers, did insert therein two manifest falshoods; the one was, that they added thereto the word *equall*, which was not in the canon of the Councell of *Constantinople*. For whereas the Councell of *Constantinople* had said simplie; *That the Bishop of* Con*stantinople should haue the prerogatiues of honor after the Bishop of* Rome; those that renewed the canon, supposed that it had said; *that the Bishop of* Con*stantinople, should haue the prerogatiues of honor equall after the Bishop of Rome*: And the other, that they imputed to the Councell of C*onstantinople*, that it had adiudged the ordination of the Metropolitans of *Pontus*, and *Asia minor*, to the Bishop of C*onstantinople*; a thing, whereof the Councell of *Constantinople*, had not onely spoken nothing to that purpose, but had pronounced cleane contrary, *that the Bishops of Asia, should gouerne the affaires*

Côc. Const c. 3.

Côc. Chalc act. 15 c. 28.

Côc. Const c. 2.

Socr. hist. eccl. l. 5. c. 9. *of Asia. And the Bishop of Thracia, that is to saie, of Constantinople, should onely gouerne the affaires of Thracia*; which *Socrates* repeates in these words: *Nectarius obtained the great cittie and Thracia: And Helladius successor to Basilius in the Bishopricke of* Cesarea *in* Cappadocia, *obtained the diuision of Pontus, &c. And Amphilochius Bishop of Iconia, and Optimus Bishop of Antioch in Pisidia, that of Asia.* And is it not to be said, that those that renewed the decree annexed therevnto, the ordinatiō of the Bishops of *Pontus*, & *Asia*; not as a thing decreed by the Councell, but as a thing added by them. For besides this, that their text beares; *The hundred and fiftie religious Fathers moued with the same designe, haue granted equall prerogatiues, to the most holy Sea of new Rome; reasonably iudging, that the Imperiall cittie, which is adorned by the Senate, and hath the same priuiledges with the ancient Rome, should also be equally exalted in Ecclesiasticall affaires, being the second after her, and that she shall ordaine the Metropolitans in the Dioceses of Pontus, Asia, and Thracia*: words which haue manifest relation to the canon of the Councell of *Constantinople*, when the Bishops of *Asia* protested, they could not suffer, that their Metropolitans should be ordained by the Bishop of *Constantinople*, the Clerkes of *Constantinople* cryed out; *Let the canon of the hundred and fiftie Fathers stand; let not the priuiledges of* Constantinople *perish; let the ordination be made, according to custome, by our Bishop.*

Côc. Chalc act. 15. c. 28.

Ibid.

Act. 11.

The sixth nullitie is, that when this canon was againe put to the touch, and propounded to bee reuiewed in the Councell, the libertie of the assistants had already bene prepossessed by the tēporall officers of the cittie of *Constantinople*. For the Senators of the cittie of *Constantinople*, that the Emperor had deputed, to maintaine order in the Councell, considered so much their owne interest in the challenge of *Anatolius*, esteemeing they might by this meanes, still augment the dignitie of their cittie, and in such sort imprinted into the spirits of the assistants, that it was the desire and passion of the Emperor; that the Bishops of the Councell belieued, they could not resiste this decree, without offending the Emperor, and the Senat of *Constantinople*, and all the Imperiall Court of the *East*; as it appeares by the relation of the Bishops of the Councell to the Pope, in these words: *Wee gratifieing the most religious and* Christian *Emperors, who take pleasure in this decree, and all the illustrious Senat, and in a word, all the royall citty; haue esteemed it to purpose, that this honor should be confirmed by the generall Councell.* And a little after; *Wee pray you then to honor our iudgement, with your decrees; and that as in what concerned the weale we haue brought correspondencie to our head; so your soueraigntie may accomplish toward your children, what concernes decency; for in so doeing, the religious* Emperors *shall be gratified.*

Côc. Chalc relat. ad Leon.

Ibidem.

The seauenth nullitie is, that *Eusebius* Bishop of *Dorylaus*, and abettor to *Anatolius* his Claime, vsed a manifest surprise, to cause this decree to be approued by the Councell, which was, to testifie to the Councell, that it was agreable to the Pope: *I haue* (said *Eusebius* of *Dorylaus*) *voluntarily signed this canon, because I haue read it at Rome to the most holie Pope, in the presence of the clerkes of Constantinople, and he approued it.* From whence it is, that the Bishops of the Councell writt to the Pope, in the relation that they addressed to him, that it was vpon this foundation that they had proceeded to the confirmation of the decree: *Wee haue* (said they) *taken the boldnesse to confirme it, as a thing begun by your Holynesse, in fauour of those that you haue alwaies desired to cherish, knowing that in whasoeuer children doe well, it is referred to their Fathers.* And neuerthelesse this testimony, was a testimonie full of falsehood and imposture, as it appeares both by the instruction that the Pope had consigned to the Legates which bare; *Suffer not the canon of the holie Fathers to be violated by anie rashnes*: And a little after;

Côc. Chalc act. 16.

Relat. Côc. ad Leon.

Ibid. act 16

And if anie perchance trusting in the power of their owne citties, shall attempt to vsurpe anie thinge; represse them as agreeth with iustice: And by the words of the same *Leo*, who writt in the epistle to *Maximus*; *If they saie, that the bretheren which I haue sent in my steede, to the Synod, haue done anie thing beyond what concernes Faith, it shall be no force, for as much as they haue bene sent by the Sea Apostolicke to this end onely, to roote out heresies, and to defend Faith*: And in his epistle to *Anatolius*; *Neuer maie my conscience consent, that so depraued a couetousnesse, shall be helped by my fauor; but rather that it be suppressed by me, and by those that allow not the prowde, but consent with the humble.* Leo ad Max. Episc Ant. ep. 60 Idem ad Anat. Episc Cost. ep. 51.

The eight nullitie is, that when they would proceede to the approbation of the canon, the Popes Legates protested a nullitie against it, and made their protestation to be registred within the acts of the Councell. This appeares first by the verball processe of the Councell; where their opposition is couched in these words: *Wee require your excellence to commaund, that the things which were yesterdaie done against the canons in our absence, may be cutt of; or if not, that our contradiction may be inserted into the acts, that we may know what wee haue to reporte to the Apostolicke Bishop, and to the President of the whole Churches, that hee may pronounce the iniurie done to his Sea, and to the subuersion of the canons*: This they added, not that this decree gaue anie authority to the Patriarke of *Constantinople* but after the Pope, and in regard of the other Patriarkes, but forasmuch as to propound it without the Popes consente, who was the protector of the rightes of the other Patriarkes, and preseruer of the canons; and to make it passe against the opposition of his Legates, it was to wound the dignitie of the Sea Apostolicke, and to infringe the ancient discipline, *which annulled the rules of the Church, made without the sentence of the Bishop of Rome.* And secondly it appeares by these words of the Pope to *Anatolius*: *Our bretheren sent in behalfe of the Sea Apostolicke, which presided in my steede at the Councell, resisted pertinently and constantlie to those vnlawfull attempts, crying out with a lowd voice, that the presumption of a pernicious noueltie, might not be exalted against the canons of the Councell of Nicea*: *And their contradiction cannot be doubted, since thou thy-self complainest in thy letters, that they haue desired to crosse thy enterprise, wherein thou dost greatelie recommend them to me; but thou accusest thy-selfe, for not obeying them.* And thirdly it appeares by the relation of the Councell itselfe, to the Pope, which containes these words; *Daigne most holy and blessed Father, to embrace these things, for the most holy Bishops Paschasinus and Lucentius, and the most religious Priest Boniface, holding the place of your Holynesse, haue greatlie striued to contradict this rule, desiring that such a good might take the intire originall from your prouidence; to the end that as the rule of Faith, so that of good order, might be attributed to you.* Cōc. Chalc act. 16. Socr. hist. eccl. l. 2. c. 8 Leo ad Anatol. ep. 51. Cōc. Chalc ep. ad Leō.

The ninth nullitie is, that the Pope insteede of consenting to the request that the Councell solicited hy *Anatolius*, and by the Emperor, and the Senate, had made to him to confirme this canon, disannulled & abolished it: *Ioyninge with vs* (said the Pope in his epistle to the Empresse *Pulcheria*) *the pietie of your faith, wee annull the plotts of the Bishops repugnant to the rules of the holy canons establisht at Nicea, and by vertue of the authoritie of the blessed Apostle Peter, doe wholie abrogate them by a generall sentence*: And Pope *Gelasius* fortie yeares after repeating the same historie, *That which the authoritie of the Sea Apostolicke hath confirmed in the Councell of Chalcedon, hath remained in force; and what she hath refused, could obtaine noe stedfastnesse*: *And onely she hath disannulled that, which the Synodicall congregation had adiudged against order should be vsurped.* And it is not to be said, that the Pope abrogated this canon for passion, or out of desire to contradict, and not in zeale to preserue the right of the other Seas, and to maintaine the canons Leo ad Pulcher. ep. 53. Gelas. Pap. 1. tom. de anathem. vincul.

of the Councell of *Nicea*; for the Pope did not abrogate it of his owne motion, but hauing bene already prayed before by saint CYRILL Patriarke of *Alexandria*, and since by *Maximus* Patriarke of *Antioch*, not to permitt that such attempts should take place, and that the rights of the Churches setled by the Councell of *Nicea*, should be violated. *Thy charitie* (saith Pope *Leo* in his epistle to *Maximus* Patriarke of *Antioch*) *hauing esteemed that some what ought to be done for the priuiledges of your Church, let it take care to explaine it by letters, that wee may answere absolutelie and fitlie to thy consultation; for the present it shall suffice to pronounce in generall, that if anie thing seeme to haue bene attempted, or euen for a time exhorted by anie one, in what Synod soeuer it be, against the canons of the Councell of Nicea, it cannot doe preiudice to the inuiolable decrees.* And a little after; *In the Councell of Ephesus, Iuuenall the Bishop thought to haue found a sufficient aduantage;* (to witt, that of the schisme of *Iohn* Patriarke of *Antioch*) *to obtaine the principalitie of Palestina, and to cause his insolent boldenes to be confirmed with surreptitious writinges; which Cyrillus of holy memorie iustly abhorring, represented to me, and intreated me with great instance and care, that noe consent should be giuen to such lawlesse attempts.*

Leo ad Max. Episc Antioc. ep. 60.

Ibid.

The tenth nullitie is, that *Anatolius* Bishop of *Constantinople* seeing this canon could not subsist if it were discouered that it had bene annulled by the Pope, concealed from the Bishops of the Councell of *Chalkedon* the abrogation that the Pope had made of this decree, and kept backe the Popes letters, whereby he had annulled and abolished it, a fraude so perillous, as it had like to haue turned vpsidowne all the Church of the Empire of the *East*. For the Pope hauing ioyned in one letter the abrogation of this decree, with the confirmation that hee made of the other acts of the Councell, *Anatolius* because he would not shewe the censure of his ambition, concealed the Popes letters, where the one and the other clause was contained; which was the clause that the Easterne Churches remained in such doubt, whether or not the Pope had confirmed the Councell of *Chalcedon*, as infinite people for this cause making difficultie to receiue it; the Emperor was faine to request the Pope, to dispatch new letters confirmatiue of the Faith of the Councell of *Chalcedon* to all the Bishops who had assisted there, and to send them to each one of them in their Churches. *This* (said Pope *Leo* in his answere to the Emperor *Martian*) *your clemencie thinks will be more easilie fufilled, if throughout all the Churches we signifie, that the definitions of the Councell of Chalcedon haue pleased the Sea Apostolicke, a thing whereof there was noe occasion of doubt, &c. seeing I haue written to your Glorie, and to the Bishop of Constantinople, letters which euidentlie shewed, that I approued those thinges which had bene there defined concerning Catholicke Faith: but because by the same letters I had reproued those things, which vnder the occasion of the Synod had bene euilly attempted, he rather chose to conceale my applause, then to publish his ambition.* And in his epistle to the Empresse *Pulcheria*: *Whereas the most Religious Emperor, hath willed that I should write letters to all the Bishops, which assisted at the Councell of Chalcedon, whereby I should confirme what was then defined concerning Faith, I haue willinglie accomplished it, least the deceiptfull dissimulation of some, should pretend to put people in doubt of my sentence, although by the meanes of the Bishop of Constantinople, to whom I had largelie testified my ioy, that which I had written, might haue come to the knowledge of all, if he had not rather chosen to conceale my contentment, then to publish the rebuke of his ambition.*

Leo ad Mart. Aug. ep. 57.

Id. ad Pulcher. Aug. ep. 58.

The eleauenth nullitie is, that *Anatolius* Bishop of *Constantinople*, euen he that had packed this Canon, he himself in whose fauour it had bene particularized, departed from it, as is seene by the text of the epistle that Pope *Leo* the first writt him, which is such: *This thy fault which to increase*

Leo ad Anat. ep. 59

thy power thou hast committed, as thou saist, by the exhortation of others, thy charitie had better and more sincerelie blotted out, if that which could not be attempted without thy consent, thou hadst not imputed it, to the onely Councells of thy Clergie, &c. But it contents me much deare brother, that thy dilection protests to bee agreeued with that which euen then ought not to haue pleased thee; it sufficeth to re-enter into common grace: the profession of thy charitie together with the attestation of the most Christian Prince; and let not his correction seeme tardie that hath gotten so reuerent a suretie: And by these words of Pope *Gelasius* written fortie yeares after against *Acacius: That which the Sea Apostolicke consented not to, nor did the Emperor impose it, nor Anatolius vsurpe it: and all was put into the power of the Sea Apostolicke; and therefore what the Sea Apostolicke confirmed in the Councell of Chalcedon, hath bene in force, what it refused could not be stedfast.* Gel. Pap. tom- de Anath. vinc

The twelfth nullitie is, that this Canon hath bene falselie inserted into the catalogue of the Canons of the Councell of *Chalcedon*, by the latter Greekes, which perchance made Sainct GREGORIE to saie; *The Councell of Chalcedon hath in one place bene falsified by the Church of Constantinople*; for during all the age of the Councell of *Chalcedon*, this Canon which had bene but proiected and not confirmed, remained in the onely historie of the Acts, and was not inserted into the catalogue of the Canons, till a long time after; as it appeares both by the testimonie of the most ancient Greeke and latine copies; in all which, the Rolle of the Canons containes but twentie seauen Canons. And by the collection of *Theodoret*, an author of the same age, in which the list of the Canons of the Councell of *Chalcedon*, is but of twentie seauen Canons. And by the Edition of *Dionisius Exiguus* time-fellow with the Emperor *Iustinian*, whose catalogue of the Canons of the Councell, comprehend but twentie seauen Canons: And by the acknowledgement that *Theodoret Anagnostes*, a Greeke author makes thereof in these words: *The Councell of Chalcedon published twentie seauen* Canons. Greg. l. 5. indict. 14. ep. 14. Theodor. in Synagoge cannon. in bibliotheca regia Medicea. Dionis. Exig. in Cod. can. Theodor. Anagn. ad calc. hist. Eccl.

And the thirteenth nullitie is finally, that the number of thirtie Canons, which the Greekes of following ages haue attributed to the councell of *Chalcedon*, to comprehend this, and to make it come in vnder the title of the twentie eight is a supposed number. For it is euident that the two last canons, to witt, the twentie ninth and the thirtith are noe canons, but are, the one of them, an interlocution betweene *Paschasinus* the Popes Legate, and *Anatolius* Bishop of *Constantinople*: and the other a prohibition prouisorie, to anie of the Bishops of *Egipt*, which had excused themselues, from signing the epistle of Pope *Leo*, because they remained without a Patriarke, not to depart from *Constantinople*, before the arriuall of the newes of the creation of a new Patriarke of *Alexandria*: which haue bene taken out of the historie of the Acts of the Councell, and transferred into the catalogue of the Canons. Whereunto it serues not to alledge for counterbattery, that the councell *Trullian* which was holden two hundred and fortie yeares after the councell of *Chalcedon*, citeth this canon as a canon of the Councell of *Chalcedon*: for besides that in saying, *wee renewe the decree made by the hundred and fiftie Fathers assembled in this religious and royall cittie; and by the six hundred and thirtie Fathers assembled at* Chalcedon, it shewes sufficientlie how this canon had bene till then disputed and called in question; the Councell *Trullian* was a schismaticall, ignorant, and vnlawfull Councell, as it shall heereafter appeare, both by the testimony of BEDA an author of the same time; who calls it an impious Councell; and by the approbation which was Theod. in edit. Rob. Steph. col. lect. l. 1. Cōc. Const. 6. in Trull. can. 36. In chap. 15 Bed. de sex ætatibus.

made there of the Councell of *Africa* concerning the Anabaptisme of heretickes, which had bene an erroneous and reprouable Councell, as Saint AVGVSTINE, and all antiquitie doe testifie, and as the Popes aduersaries themselues doe acknowledge: And this sufficeth for the first obiection. Now let vs goe forward to the second.

To the second obiection then, which is that the Bishop of *Constantinople,* went about to participate in the title of *Oecumenicall* or *vniuersall,* whereof the Pope had receiued the nomination in the Councell of *Chalcedon*; wee bring fower Answeres: The first answere is, that it was not to possesse this title by the exclusion of the Pope; but to possesse it by the association of the Pope, and in regard of the other Patriarkes; for not onely in the Councell of *Chalcedon,* the title of vniuersall had bene offered the Pope, before the Bishop of *Constantinople* had euer presumed to aspire to it; but in the Councell of *Constantinople* holden vnder *Menas,* which is the first Councell where the name of *Vniuersall* had bene giuen to the Patriarke of *Constantinople*, bee it directly, or be it from the relation of a Councell holden a little before it; there were read the requests of the Churchmen of *Constantinople*, of *Antioch*, and of *Jerusalem*, presented in *Constantinople* it self to Pope *Agapet,* and couched in these termes: *To our most holie and most blessed Lord Agapet, Archbishop of the ancient Rome and vniuersall Patriarke*; And during the contention of saint GREGORIE, and the Patriarks of *Constantinople*; *Eulogius* patriarke of *Alexandria*, writing to Pope GREGORIE calls him *Vniuersall Pope.* And in the next age after saint GREGORIE, the Emperor *Constantine the bearded*, residing at *Constantinople,* and assisting at the third generall Councell of *Constantinople,* intituleth the pope, *Vniuersall Patriarke, and Arch-Pastor: You haue* (said hee in the epistle to the councell of the West) *seconded your captaine the vniuersall Hierarch and Patriarke.* And againe; *You haue bene present by your Procurators, you and the vniuersall Arch-Pastor at our councell.* And after, when the Emperor *Basilius* the *younger*, and *Eustachius* Patriarke of *Constantinople* would haue reconciled themselues to the *Roman* Church, they capituled, *that it might be lawfull for them to obtaine with the consent of the Pope, that the Church of* Constantinople should be called *Vniuersall in the compasse thereof, as the Roman was in the compasse of the whole world.* And still after them *Balsamon*, although puft vp with his imaginarie title of Patriarke of *Antioch*, and a great enemy to the Latins which possessed his pretended patriarksip, he fauoured the Pope as little as he could; and attempted to proue all the patriarkes equall, for that which concernes the ordinary administration of their patriarkships; neuerthelesse he confessed that the custome of the Greekes, was to attribute to the Pope, the title of *Vniuersall Pope*; and to the Bishop of *Constantinople*, that of *Vniuersall Patriarke, I haue* (said hee) *a purpose to tell, wherefore the Pope of Rome is called, Vniuersall Pope; and likewise the patriarke of* Constantinople, *Vniuersall patriarke.* And a little after: *But because the Deuill of self-loue hath separated the Pope from the societie of the other most holy Patriarkes, and hath restrained him onely into the West, I omitt this discourse as vnprofitable.*

Cõc. Const sub Men. act. 1.

Greg. l. 7. ind. 1. ep. 30

Conc. 6. Const. act. 18.

Ibidem.

Glaber. Rod. hist. l. 4. c. 1.

Theod. Bals. medit 7.

Ibid.

The second Answere is, that by the word *Vniuersall,* the Bishop of *Constantinople* neuer pretended to exempt himself from the Popes iurisdiction, but acknowledged himself subiect and inferior to the Pope, as it appeares by those very peeces where the name of *Vniuersall* is attributed to the Bishop of *Constantinople*; which doe all testifie, that he was subiect and inferior to the Pope, and that the instance that he made

made to be adioyned and associated to the Pope in the participation of the vniuersalitie, was not to the end to possesse it in regard of the Pope, but vnder the Pope, and in regard of the other Patriarkes; alwaies acknowledging the Pope for stocke and head of the vniuersalitie, and protesting himselfe his subiect and his inferior. For in the law of the Emperor *Iustinian* to *Epiphanius* Patriarke of *Constantinople*, which is the first where the word vniuersall is offerred to the Patriarke of *Constantinople*, doth not *Iustinian* write to him: *Wee haue in all thinges preserued the Estate of the vnitie of the holy Churches, with the most holy Pope of ancient Rome, to whom wee haue written the like. For wee suffer not that anie thinge should passe touching the Ecclesiasticall Estate, which shall not be also referred to his Blessednesse, for as much as he is the head of all the most holie Prelats of God?* And in the Councell of *Constantinople* holden vnder *Menas* which is the first Councell in forme, where we see the title of *Vniuersall*, giuen to the Patriarke of *Constantinople*: *Is it not* (saith *Anthimus Patriarke of Constantinople*) *protested to doe all that the Soueraigne Pope of great Rome should decree: And writt to all the most holy Patriarkes, that hee would altogether followe the Sea Apostolicke?* And *Menas* Patriarke of *Constantinople*, doth noe hee himself pronounce these words; *Wee will in all things follow and obay the Sea Apostolicke?* And in the heate of the question of the word *Vniuersall*, doth not saint GREGORIE reporte, that *Iohn* Priest of *Chalcedon* a Cittie situate in *Asia*, and at the gates of *Constantinople*, hauing bene iudged at the Tribunall of *Iohn* Patriarke of *Constantinople*, appealed from him to the Sea Apostolicke, and was againe iudged at *Rome*, and the Bishop of *Constantinople* giuing his helping hand to it, euen then when he tooke vpon him, the qualitie of vniuersall, and sending the Acts of the first iudgement to *Rome*, to be reuiewed by the Pope? *Knowest thou not* (Saith sainct GREGORIE) *that in the cause of John the Priest, against our brother and fellow-Bishop, Iohn of Constantinople, he had recourse according to the Canons to the Sea Apostolicke, and that it hath bene defined by our sentence?* And elsewhere; *John Bishop of Constantinople, hath gone soe farr as vnder pretence of the cause of John the Priest, he hath sent hither Acts, wherein almost at the end of euerie line, he calls himselfe vniuersall Patriarke.*

Cod. Iust. impress. Paris. Antvverp. & Geneu. tit. 1. l. 7.

Cōc. Const sub Men. act. 4.

Ibid.

Greg. l. 5. indict. 14. epist. 24.

Id. l. 4. ind. 13. ep. 39.

And finally the Emperor, and the Patriarke of *Constantinople*, did they not themselues acknowledge in the strenght of this dispute, that the Church of *Constantinople* was subiect to the *Roman* Church, as saint GREGORIE reportes it in these words: *Who is it* (saith hee) *that doubts, but that the Church of* Constantinople, *is subiect to the Sea Apostolicke; which the most Religious Lord the Emperor, and our brother Bishop of the same cittie, continuallie protest?* For as for the illusion of those, who to weaken the credit of this passage, cauill vpon the word *Eusebius*, which is in the printed copies before these words, *Bishop of the same cittie*; and obiect, that the Bishop of *Constantinople* then being, was not called *Eusebius*, but *Cyriacus*: I will not stand vpon it, to say that there was noe inconuenience in it that *Cyriacus*, might haue had two names, and be called *Eusebius Cyriacus*, as Sainct IEROME was called EVSEBIVS IEROME: And besides that the word, *Eusebius* might there be taken adiectiuely, and signifie pious and religious, as when *Arrius* writt to *Eusebius* Bishop of *Nicomedia*: *Farewell Eusebius trulie Eusebius*; that is to saie, farewell *Eusebius* truly *Religious*. It will be a shorte cutt to answere at the first, that it is an error of the *Exemplarists*, who of an (*eiusdem*) euill written, and for that occasion blotted out, and written

Id. l. 7. ind. 2. ep. 63.

Theod. histor. Eccl. l. 1. c. 6.

againe, haue made *Eusebius*: for the copies of this epistle which had bene currant two hundred yeare after saint GREGORIE read simplie, (*and our brother Bishop of the same cittie*) without makeing anie mention of *Eusebius*, as is seene by the relation of *Amalarius* Bishop of *Treuers*, who liued eight hundred yeares agone; who inserting into his Booke of the Ecclesiasticall offices, this epistle of saint GREGORIE whole and intire, from the beginning to the endinge, reports the period now in question in these onely words, without anie mention of *Eusebius*; *for as for that which is spoken of the Church of Constantinople; who doubts but it is subiect to the Sea Apostolicke, which the most Religious Lord the Emperor, and our brother the Bishop of the same Towne continually protest?* And therefore alsoe when the Patriarkes of *Constantinople*, were in anie Synodicall action with the Popes Legates; yea, within *Constantinople* it selfe, they abstayned from the title of *Vniuersall*, and left it to the Popes Legates alone for their master, to the end to shew, that they held the Pope for head and stocke of the *Vniuersalitie*; and did repute themselues *Vniuersall* but in the absence of him, or of those that represented him; as appeares by the signatures of the third generall Councell of *Constantinople*, which was celebrated vnder *Constantine Pogonat* in the next age after Sainct GREGORIE; wherein the Popes Legates signed in the qualitie of Legats to the vniuersall Pope; and the Patriarke of *Constantinople*, in the qualitie of onely Bishop of *Constantinople*: for though the epistle of the Emperor to the Patriark of *Constantinople*, written before the holding of the Councell, attributes to him, the title of *Vniuersall*, neuerthelesse in the signatures of the Councell, the onely Legats of the Pope, take the title of *Vniuersall* for their master, and signe in this forme; *Theodorus, humble Priest of the holy Church of Rome, and holding the place of the blessed and vniuersall Pope of the cittie of Rome Agatho, I haue subscribed. George humble Priest of the holy Church of Rome, and holdinge the place of the blessed and Vniuersall Pope of the Cittie of Rome Agatho, I haue subscribed. Iohn humble Deacon of the holy Church of Rome, and holding the place of the blessed and vniuersall Pope of the Cittie of Rome, Agatho, I haue subscribed.* And the Patriarke of *Constantinople* forbare it, and signed thus; *George by the mercie of God Bishop of Constantinople new Rome, I haue voted and subscribed.*

Amalar. de diu. offic. l. 4. c. 36

Cóc. Const act. 18.

The third Answere is, that whatsoeuer was the intention of the Patriarke of *Constantinople*, so farr was hee from doeing anie thinge against the Popes authoritie, as contrarywise he confirmed and fortified it altogether. And that it is so, how from this, that the Bishop of *Constantinople*, pretended to be vniuersall Bishop, because *Constantinople* had bene associated to the Rights of *Rome*, can it chose but followe, that the Bishop of *Rome*, was so primitiuely and originallie? For as for those that saie, that the Patriarke of *Constantinople* was called *Oecumenicall* Bishop in the same sence, wherein the other Patriarkes were so called, (not knowing that there is great difference betweene the word, *Catholicke Bishop*, which *Nilus* attributes to the Patriarkes, which signifies generall Bishop of a Region, and the word, *Oecumenicall Bishop*, which signifies vniuersall Bishop, either of all the Imperiall Orbe, or of the particular Orbe of the Empire of *Constantinople*;) I will not stand to confute them; it shall suffice me to aske them, why then the Patriarke of *Constantinople* neuer gaue the name of vniuersall Patriarke, to the other Patriarkes of the *East*? And why the other Patriarkes of the *East*, neuer gaue it one to another,

Nilus de prim. Pap. l. 2.

but haue yeilded it onely to the Bishops of *Rome*, and of *Constantinople*? And why the Bishops of *Constantinople*, haue stirred vp so many tragedies to participate therein, and haue alleadged that *Constantinople* was the second *Rome*, and ought after her to enioy the same Rights and priuiledges? And in briefe, it shall suffice me to aske them; why then both anciently and euen to this day, the Patriarke of *Constantinople* doth attribute to himself, by vertue of his *vniuersalitie*, this aduantage aboue the other Patriarkes of the *East*; to call the generall Councells of the *East*, and to preside in them, and to iudge by appeale of the sentences of the other Patriarkes? *It hath bene reported* (saith Pope *Pelagius* in the epistle before alleadged to those of the *East*) *to the Sea Apostolicke, that Iohn Bishop of Constantinople inscribes himselfe Vniuersall; and by vertue of that his presumption, hath called you to a generall Councell.* And the Emperors *Constantine* and *Leo*; *The care and the iudgement of all the Metropolitanships, and Bishopricks, and of all the Monasteries and Churches, appertaine to their proper Patriarke; but the Patriarke ol Constantinople, may in the territorie of the other Seas, when there hath bene noe precedent consecration plant the Crosse; and not onelie soe, but also may decide and determine the controuersies bredd in the other Seas.* And *Nilus*; *The twentie eight canon of the Councell of Chalcedon; and the thirtith six of the sixth Councell honoring the Sea of Constantinople with like priuiledges to that of* Rome, *graunt also manifestly, the appeales to that of* Constantinople: And *Balsamon*; *This priuiledge is not giuen to the Pope alone; to witt, that euerie condemned Bishop should haue recourse to the Sea of Rome, but it ought also to be vnderstood of the Patriarke of Constantinople.* And elsewhere; that which neuerthelesse is but a claime bredd amongst the Greekes, since the schisme; *The fifteenth canon of the councell of Antioch, was abolished by the fourth* Canon *of the councell of Sardica; or at least is to be vnderstood of the Synods, which are subiect to noe appeale, as those of the Pope, and of the Patriarke of Constantinople.* For as for the place of *Photius* from whence they inferr that the Patriarkes were as the Prefects of the Pretorie, from whence there was noe appeale, that shall be satisfied heereafter, and shewed that it is a vice in the transcription of the copies.

Pelag. Pap. 2. ep. 1.

Leo & Cõstantinus apud Leunclau. tit. 3. de Pat.

Nilus de prim. Pap. l. 2.

Balsam. in Cõc. Sard. c. 5.

Id. in Cõc. Ant. c. 15.

See belovve. in the chapt. of the Councell of Sardica.

And the fourth and last Answere is, that this claime was not longe suffered in the Bishop of *Constantinople*, for the Emperor *Mauricius* who fauored it, hauing bene extinguished by the conspiracie of *Phocas*, the same *Phocas* interposed his temporall authoritie, and forbadd him anie more to call himselfe *Vniuersall Bishop*, reseruing that title onely to the Pope alone. It is true, that afterward the Empire being againe fallen into the hands of two hereticall Emperors *Heraclius* and *Constans*, successors to *Phocas*; the Greekes againe sett abroache this custome, and not onelie sett it abroache, but haue since continued it euen to the last ages, as it appeares by the inscriptions of *Sisinnius*, *Germanus*, *Constantius*, *Alexius*, and other Patriarkes of *Constantinople*, reported in the Canon lawe of the Greekes, where they inscribe and signe, *Vniuersall Patriarks*. Onely they vse this distinction, that they call the Pope, *Vniuersall Pope*; and the Patriarke of *Constantinople*, *Vniuersall Patriarke*: And that if it be lawfull to giue way to coniectures for two reasons; the one, because the antiquitie of the title of *Vniuersall Patriarke*, was euidently restrained by this distinction, to the superiority onely ouer the simple Patriarkes; wherein the Pope was not comprehended, as it appeares when saint GREGORIE saith; *that if one of the fowr Patriarkes had done that against the Popes letters, that was done by the Bishop of Salona, such a disobedience could not haue past without a most*

Ius Canon. Orient. l. 3. Ibid.

Greg. l. 2. indict. 10. ep. 17.

grieuous scandall. And the other, forasmuch as the *Constantinopolitans* esteemed the word POPE, except amongst the monkes, to be a title more exalted, then that of PATRIARK; because the name of Pope was more reuerend amongst the *Bythinians*, a people neere *Constantinople*, who had accustomed in the time of Paganisme, to call *Jupiter* πάππας then that of Patriarke; from whence it is, that the latter *Greekes* haue belieued, although ignorantlie, that the reason why the Patriarkes of *Alexandria* bare the title of Pope, came from this, that sainct CYRILLVS Patriarke of *Alexandria*, had bene legat to the Pope in the Councell of *Ephesus*, as *Balsamon* noteth in these termes: *The Bishop of Alexandria hath bene called Pope, forasmuch as saint CYRILLVS in the third* Councell *receiued the priuiledges of the Pope of Rome* Celestinus. And *Nicephorus* in these; *Celestinus Bishop of Rome, refused to assist at the Councell of Ephesus, for the danger of nauigation; but he writt to Cyrillus, that he should hold his place there, and since that time the same goes, that Cyrillus receiued the Tyara, and the name of Pope, and of iudge of the world.*

Arrian. in Bythiniac.

Theod. Bals. medit 7. apud Leunclau, in iur. Orient. Niceph. Calixt. hist Eccl. l. 4. c. 34.

For whereas *Beda*, *Paul* the Deacon, *Theophanes*, and *Anastasius* the *Bibliothecarie*, and after *Anastasius* the *Bibliothecary*, all the latine *Chronologists* say, that *Phocas* iudged; *that the Sea of the Roman and Apostolicke Church, was the head of all the Churches; forasmuch as the Church of Constantinople intituled herself, the first of all the Churches*; It is a mistake that *Beda* an English author, and later by an hundred yeare then *Phocas*, hath made of the question, which was about the word, *Vniuersall*, and not about the word, *First*; And of this wee haue two certaine and vndoubted proofes; the one that saint GREGORIE, who is he onely of all the authors of the age that hath spoken of this contestation, and who was himself one of the parties contesting, testifies that the dispute was about the word *Vniuersall*, and not about the word *First*. And the other, that the Patriarkes of *Constantinople* haue alwaies remained within the termes of the second Sea; and haue perpetually yeilded the first, to the Bishop of *Rome*. For neuer can it be found in anie monumẽt of antiquitie, that the Church of *Constantinople*, hath at anie tyme taken the title of the first of all the Churches: contrarywise, all the pens of antiquitie haue witnessed that the Church of *Constantinople* neuer affected more then the second in the Church, and hath alwaies giuen the first to the Church of *Rome*; for in the Councell of *Constãtinople*, which was the source of all those pretẽces, it was ordained, that the Bishop of *Constantinople* should haue the prerogatiues of honor after the Pope; because *Constantinople* was a second *Rome*. *They decreed* (saith *Socrates*) *that the Bishop of* Constantinople *should haue the prerogatiues of honor after the Bishop of Rome, because* Constantinople *was a second Rome.* And in the Councell of *Chalcedon* it was ordained, she should be honored as the Church of *Rome*, being the second after her: *It was esteemed fitt* (saith *Euagrius*) *that the Sea of new Rome, because of the second ranke it held after that of ancient Rome, should be preferred before the others.* And in the third generall councell of *Constantinople*, which was the sixth generall councell; the councell called the Pope, *the Protothrone of the vniuersall Church*: & the Emperor *Constantine Pogonat*, called the Patriarks *Synthrones of the Pope, after the Pope*; that is to saie, *sett in one same throne with the Pope, after the Pope.* And in the councell intituled *Trullian*, the canon of the councell of *Chalcedon* was renewed in these words: *Wee decree that the Sea of Constantinople, shall haue equall priuiledges to the Sea of ancient Rome, and shall be honored in Ecclesiasticall causes like it, being the second after it.* And when *Nicephorus* Patriarke of *Constantinople* writes against the *Iconoclasts* he calls the Sea of *Rome*, the first and Apostolicke Sea. The *diuine Patriarke Nicephorus* (saith *Zona-*

Bed. de sex ætat. mund.

Soc. hist. Eccl. l. 5. c. 8. Euag. hist. Eccl. l. 2. c. 4.

Cõc. Const 6. act. 18. ep. ad Agathon, Ep. Imp. ad. Occ. ibid.

Conc. in Trull. c. 36.

rus

rus) speaking of the Icconomaks writes thus; their being cutt of from the Catholik Church, appeares clearely (amonst other things) by the letters of the blessed Archbishop of Rome; that is to saie, of the first and apostolicke Sea. Zon.in Cóc.Chalc c.28.

And against this it is not to be obiected, that the Emperor *Zeno* calls *Constantinople, the mother of all the Orthodoxall;* For he speakes of the orthodoxall of his Empire; that is to say, of the Empire of the *East*; within the which there remained the yeare before, noe Patriarchall Sea except that of *Constantinople*, but was possessed by hereticall Patriarkes. As little is it to be obiected that *Justinian* saith, *that the Church of Constantinople is the head of all the other Churches*; For he speakes, not of the Church of *Constantinople* in regard of the Churches of the whole world, but of the Cathedrall Churche of the Cittie of *Constantinople*; that is to saie, *of the Church of saint Sophia* that he calls the great Church of *Constantinople*, in regard of the other Churches of the Patriarkship of *Constantinople*, as it appeares both by the next following discourse of the *Chartularies*, and by the Seauenth lawe of the foregoeing title, where he writes to the Bishop of *Constantinople*; *That the Pope is head of all the holie Prelats of God;* And by the 131. Nouel. where the same *Justinian* ordaineth, that the Sea of *Constantinople*, should be the second after Rome: *Wee ordaine (* saith hee *) according to the definition of Councells, that the holy Pope of olde Rome, shall be the first of all Prelates; and that the blessed Archbishop of* Constantinople *new Rome, should haue the second place, after the Sea Apostolick of olde Rome.* Lesse yet is it to be obiected, that some latter *Greekes* saie, that the Councells of *Constantinople & Chalcedon*; adiudged the primacie to the Church of *Constantinople*; for they will not saie, that the intention of those Councells was then, to iudge the primacie to the Church of *Constantinople*, but by propheticall spirit, to iudge the primacy to the Church of *Constantinople*, after the *Roman* Church should haue lost it. And to this end they pretend, that the word, *after*, which the Councell of *Constantinople* made vse of when it saith, *the Bishop of* Constantinople *should haue the priuiledges of honor after him of Rome*, was not a note of order, but a note of tyme; that is to say, that the Fathers of the Councell foreseeing by diuine inspiration, that the Sea of *Rome* should one daie fall into the heresie of the double procession of the holy Ghost (so call they the doctrine of the procession of the holy Ghost, by deriuation from the Father, and from the Sonne) and by that occasion fall from her ranke; they ordained, that after the Bishop of *Rome* should haue lost his primacie, the Bishop of *Constantinople* should possesse it. Which *Zonarus*, although a Greeke and a Schismaticke reportes and confutes in these words: *Some (* said he *) believe that the preposition (after) is a marke of time, and not a submission of honor to the Church of Rome; and they make vse for the proofe of their opinion, of the twentie eigth Canon of the* Councell of Chalcedon, &c. *But the* 130. *Nou. of Iustinian, inserted in the third title of the fift booke of the Basilickes, giue the* Canons *otherwise to be vnderstood.* And a little belowe; *From hence it appeares manifestly, that the preposition (after) signifies submission and inferioritie.* And elsewhere: *the Councell of Chalcedon ordaines, that newe Rome should be honored with the same Ecclesiasticall prerogatiues as old Rome, and should be preferred in honor before all the other Churches, being the second after her; for it is impossible, that she should be equallie honored in all thinges; vnlesse they will saie, that those diuine Fathers foreseeing by the light of the holy spirit, that the* Church *of* Rome *should be cutt off, from the bodie of the orthodox, and bee banisht from the* Societie *of the faithfull, because of the diuersitie of the doctrine, they destined that of* Constantinople *to be one day the first, and so esteemed it then worthie to enioy in all things equall priuiledges; to witt when she should haue receiued the primacie, as the Roman Chuch had in former*

Cod.l.1. tit 2.l.16.

Ibid.l. 24.

Cod.l.1.tit 1.l.7. Iustinou. 131.

Zon.in Cóc.Const 1.c.3.

Ibid.

Ibid.

Zon.in Cóc.Chalc c.28.

time

Ibid. *time had it*. And againe; *But to this sence the thirtie sixth canon of the councell Trullian doth oppose it self; which hauing placed the Sea of Constantinople second after that of old Rome, adds; And after it, that of Alexandria; and after that of Alexandria, that of Antioch; and after that of Antioch, that of Ierusalem*. And therefore not onely *Nilus* Archbishop of *Thessalonica* writing against the latines, confesseth ingeniously, that the *Greekes* neuer disputed for primacie with the *Roman* Church: *Wee are not* (said hee) *separated from peace, for attributing to ourselues the primacie, nor for refusing to holde the second place after the principalitie of Rome; for wee neuer contested for primacie with the Roman Church*, But euen amongst the Authors of the last age, *Duaren* although a greate enemie to the Pope, acknowledgeth, that the sentence of *Phocas* interuened vpon the word, *Vniuersall*, and not vpon the word, *First*. Behold his words: *Boniface the third* (said hee) *obtained with great contention from Phocas to be made œcumenicall and vniuersall Bishop*. Onely he shewes his galle in saying that *Boniface obtained from* Phocas *to be made vniuersall Bishop*; where hee should haue said, that he obtained of *Phocas*, that the title of *vniuersall Bishop*, should be preserued to him alone; and that the Bishop of *Constantinople* who desired to participate in it, might be excluded frō it, For neither did the Bishop of *Constantinople*, dispute the title of *Vniuersall Bishop* with the Pope, but pretended he ought to be therein associated with him: neither did the title of *Vniuersall Bishop*, begin to be attributed to the Pope by *Phocas*, but from the tyme of the Emperor *Marcian* aboue an hūdred fiftie yeare before *Phocas*, it had bene exhibited to him in the councell of *Chalcedon*: and after that, vnder the Emperor *Iustinian*, aboue fiftie yeares before *Phocas*, it had bene giuen him in *Constantinople* it selfe; as it appeares both by the Acts of the Councell of *Chalcedon*, wherein the petitions of the Clerkes of *Alexandria* presented to the Councell, bore; *To the most holie and vniuersall patriarke Leo, and to the holie generall* Councell: And by the testimonie of saint GREGORIE, who wrote to *Eulogius* Patriarke of *Alexandria*: *Your Holynesse knowes, that the title of vniuersall Bishop, hath bene offerred in the councell of* Chalcedon, *and by the following Fathers to my predecessors*. And by the Acts of the Councell of *Constantinople* holden vnder *Menas*, & confirmed by *Iustinian* where the petitions of the Regulars of *Constantinople*, and of *Syria*, and of the Bishops of the Patriarkships of *Antioch*, and of *Ierusalem* to Pope *Agapet*, were inserted with this inscription: *To our holy aud blessed Lord, the Archbishop of old Rome, and vniuersall Patriark, Agapetus*. In such sort, as be it that *Phocas* sentence, were vpon the word, *vniuersall*, it cannot be said, that *Phocas* was the author of the attribution of this title to the Pope, since from the time of the Councell of *Chalcedon*, and since vnder the Empire of *Iustinian*, it hath bene attributed to him: or be it that it interuened vpon the word, *First*, the originall thereof, could not be imputed to *Phocas*, since the Emperor *Iustinian* more then fiftie yeare before *Phocas*, had written: *Wee ordaine, following the definitions of the Councells, that the holy Pope of olde Rome, be the first of all the Prelates; and that the blessed Archbishop of Constantinople new Rome, haue the second place after the Sea Apostolicke of old Rome, and be preferd before all the other Seas*.

Nil. de prim Pap. l. 1.

Duaren. de Sacr. Eccl. Min. l. 1. c. 10.

Cōc. Chalc act. 3.

Greg. l. 7. indict. 1. ep 30. & l. 4. indict. 13. ep. 32. & 34

Cōc. Const sub Men. act. 2.

Iust. nou. 131.

But it may be replied, that S. GREGORIE did not onely condemne the vse of the word *vniuersall* in the person of the Btshop of *Constantinople*, but refused it himself, in his owne. For hauing admonisht the Bishop of *Alexandria*, that he should giue this title neither to him, nor to the Bishop of *Constantinople*; and the Bishop of *Alexandria* hauing written to him, that hee had abstained according to this admonition,

from

from attributing it to the Bishop of *Constantinople*; he replies: *I said you should giue such a title neither to me, nor to anie other; and behold in the front of your Epistle, which you haue addressed to myselfe, which haue made you this prohibition, you haue imprinted this title of prowd nomination; Calling me Vniuersall Pope, which I praie your most deare holynesse noe more to doe.* And a little after; *And certainely your holynesse knowes, that this title was offered in the Councell of Chalcedon, and since againe by the Fathers followinge to my Predecessors, but none of them would euer vse this word, because in preseruing in this world the honor of all Bishops, they might maintaine their owne toward God Almightie.* To this then, to make an end, wee answere; that the word *Oecumenicall* or *vniuersall* hath two meaninges; the one proper, litterall, and grammaticall, whereby it signifies *onelie Bishop* And the other transferred and metaphoricall, wherby it signifies *superintendment ouer all Bishops*: And saint GREGORIE censered this title in the first sence, forasmuch as it would haue ensued, from the vse of this word grammaticallie taken, and measured by the letter, that there had bene but one Bishop onely, be it in all the Empire, or be it in the particular Empire of *Constantinople*; and that all the rest had bene but his commissioners and deputies, and not true Bishops in title, and true offices of Christ. *If there be one that is vniuersall Bishop* (saith saint GREGORIE) *all the rest are noe more Bishops.* Now saint GREGORIE maintained that all Bishops were true titularie Bishops, and true ministers, and officers of Christ, although concerning iurisdiction, they were subordinate one to an other; as the inferior iudges of a Kingdom, although concerning iurisdiction, they be subalterne to the superior Iudges, and that there be appeales from the one to the other, yet are they not their commissioners or their deputies; but are also themselues Iudges in title, and ministers and officers to the Prince: And therefore he opposed this title, as a title full of sacriledge and arrogancie; by which he that vsurpes it putts himself into the place of God, makeing of Gods officers; and euen in that by which they are Gods officers; and exalting himselfe for that which is of the Episcopoll order, aboue his Bretheren; that is to saie, denying to his Bretheren, the Essence and the proprietie of Bishops; and holding them, but for commissioners and substitutes in the Bishops Sea, and not for true Bishops in title, and true ministers and officers of Christ: And in briefe reputing himselfe, not as *Seruant constituted ouer his fellowe seruants*, whereof the Ghospell speakes, but as the Master and Lord of his fellowe seruants. And it is not to be said, that the Bishop of *Constantinople*, pretẽded not to the title of vniuersal Bishop in this first sence: for when a title hath two sences, whereof the one is euill and pernicious; it is easie for him that is in possession of such a title, to transferr it abusiuelie from one sence to the other. And therefore saint GREGORIE reiected absolutelie, the vse of the word Vniuersall, for feare least vnder pretence of an acception in processe of time, it might be captiouslie drawne to the other: And for this cause he withstood it, not according to the metaphoricall sence which was giuen it, but according to the naturall and originall sence which it had. For that it was in this sence, that saint GREGORIE cried out; *That he that intituled himselfe, Vniuersall Bishop, exalted himselfe licke Lucifer aboue his Bretheren, and was a fore-runner of Antichrist*; to witt in as much, as the word *Vniuersall Bishop*, tooke from others the qualitie of Bishops, and the title of officers of Christ; And not to deny in case of iurisdiction, the prelature and superioritie of one Bishop ouer others, he shewes it sufficiently when hee writes; *For as much as it is notorious, that the Sea Apostolicke, by Gods institution is preferred, before all other Churches, so much, amongst manie cares, we are most diligent in that*

Greg. l. 7. ind. 1. ep. 30

Id. ibid. & l. 4. ind. 13. ep. 32. & 34

Greg. ind. 13. ep. 36. & l. 7. ind. 2. ep. 69.

Matt. 24.

Greg. l. 6. ind. 15. ep. 30. & alibi.

Id. l. 2. ind. 21. ep. 30.

which we must haue, when for the consecration of a Bishop, they attend our will: And when he alleadges, to distinguish betweene these words, *Principalitie* and *Vniuersalitie*, the example of S. PETER, who was indeede Prince of the Apostles, and head of the vniuersall Church, and notwithstanding, was not vniuersall Apostle. *The care of the Church* (said hee) *hath bene committed to the holie Apostle, and Prince of all the Apostles Peter; the care and principalitie of the vniuersall Church, hath bene committed to him, and yet he is not called vniuersall Apostle:* And when he adds, that none of the Saints vnder the lawe was euer called vniuersall; *The Saints before the lawe* (said hee) *the Saints vnder the lawe, and the Saints vnder grace, compounding one Bodie of Christ, haue all bene constituted amongst the members of the Church, and none would euer be called Vniuersall.* Certaine proofes, that by the vniuersalitie that S. GREGORIE opposed, he intended not to exclude the principality and superintendence of one Bishop ouer others, not to depriue himselfe of the qualitie of head of the Church; noe more then in denying that saint PETER was vniuersall Apostle, he denied him to be head of the Apostles, & that the principalitie & superintendẽcie of the vniuersall Church was committed to him; he that contrarywise came from saying; *The principalitie of the vniuersall Church is committed to Peter*; nor in denying that any vnder the lawe was called vniuersall; hee meanes not to denie, that the highest Priest of the lawe, was head of the Iewish Church, & had the superintendencie ouer all the other Priests & Leuites. And therefore what pretence is left, to the Ministers of the excellent King to abuse this passage, to calumniate the Sea Apostolicke? They saie S. GREGORIE cries out, *That a Bishop that intitles himselfe, Vniuersall Bishop, exalts himself like Lucifer, aboue his bretheren, and is a forerunner of Antichrist*; it is true, but besides, this is so too, that S. ATHANASIVS cries yet with a stronger voice; *That an Emperor that makes himself Prince of Bishops, and presides in iudgments Ecclesiasticall, is the abbomination foretolde by Daniel:* Who knowes not that there is great difference betweene *Forerunner* and *Predecessor*: And that Antichrist should not sit in the Seate of his *Forerunners* (for so are all hereticks and schismaticks) noe more then our Lord sate in the Seate of S. IOHN, who was yet his *Forerunner*, but not his *Predecessor*? otherwise *Antichrist* must sit in the Episcopall Seate of *Constantinople*; for it was the Bishop of *Constantinople*, that S. GREGORIE pretended by this clause to qualifie the *Forerunner* of Antichrist. And then what blindnes is it, to strike vpon the refusall that S. GREGORIE made of the title of *Vniuersall*; and not to see that the same S. GREGORIE protests, that by the refusall of this word, hee intends not to refuse the qualitie of head of the Church, nor superintendencie & iurisdiction, ouer all the other Bishops, Archbishops, and Patriarks? for what age of S. GREGORYS epistles is not full of testimonies, that the *Roman* Church, is the head of all the Churches?

Id. l. 4. ind. 13. ep. 32.

Id. l. 4. ind. 13. ep 38.

Greg. l. 6. ind. 15. ep. 30.

Athan. ad solit. vit. agent.

Heauen, in her bosome, not so manie Starrs embow'rs;
The Sea so manie sailes, th'Earth so manie Flow'rs.

Greg. l. 7. ind 2. ep. 63.

He writt in the epistle to *Iohn* Bishop of *Syracusa; Who doubts but the Church of Constantinople, is subiect to the Sea Apostolicke? which the most Religious Lord the Emperor, and our brother the Bishop of the same cittie protest continuallie.* Hee writes in the Epistle following, to the same Bishop; *If there be anie cryme found in Bishops; I know noe Bishop but is subiect to the Sea Apostolicke; but when crimes exact it not, all according to the condition of humilitie, are equall.* He writes in the Epistle to *Iohn* the defendant, correcting the iudgement which had bene giuen against the Bishop *Steuen*;

Greg. l. 7. ind. 2. ep. 64.

If they

If they answere he had neither Metropolitan nor Patriarke, it must be replied, that the cause should haue bene heard and determined by the Sea Apostolicke, which is the head of all the Churches. He writes in the Epistle to *Iohn* Bishop of *Panormus: Wee admonish thee, that the Reuerence of the Sea Apostolicke be not troubled by the presumption of anie. For then the state of the members remaines intire, when noe iniurie is done to the head of the faith.* He writes in the Epistle to *Natalis* Bishop of *Salona; If one of the fower Patriarks had committed such an act, so great a disobedience, could not haue passed without a grieuous scandall.* He annulled in his Epistles to *Iohn* Bishop of *Constantinople* the Iudgement of the Church of *Constantinople*, against *Iohn* Priest of *Chalcedon*; *Reprouing* (said he) *the sentence of the foresaid Iudges, we declare him by our definition, to be Catholicke and free from all hereticall crime.* And elsewhere; *Knowst thou not that in the cause of Iohn the Priest, against our brother and Colleague, Iohn of Constantinople: He had recourse according to the Canons, to the Sea Apostolicke, and it hath bene defined by our sentence?* He abrogated in his Epistle to *Athanasius* a Regular of *Lycaonia* the decree of *Iohn* Bishop of *Constantinople* against him, and restored him to his place: *Wee decree thee* (said he) *to be exempted from all blott of hereticall frowardnes, and doe grant thee free leaue to returne into thy Monasterie, and to holde the same place and ranke as thou didst before.* He abrogated in the Epistle to *Iohn* Archbishop of *Larissa* in *Thessalia*, the sentence of the same Archbishop of *Larissa* against *Adrian* Bishop of *Thebes*, and one of the suffragans of the Archbishopricke of *Larissa*, and ecclipsed the Bishopricke of *Thebes* from the iurisdiction of the Archbishopricke of *Larissa*; and ordained that if the Archbishop of *Larissa* should euer more vndertake to exercise iurisdiction ouer the Bishop of *Thebes*, he should be depriued of the communion of the Body of Christ, and that it might not be restored to him, except at the point of death, but by the leaue of the Bishop of *Rome*. *Wee ordaine* (said hee) *that thy brotherhood obtaine from the power thou hadst before ouer the Bishop of Thebes, and ouer his Church, and according to the letters of our Predecessor: for if anie cause either of faith, or of crime, or of money, be pretended against our said Colleague Adrian, it may be iudged, if it be a matter of meane importance, by our Nuncios, which are, or shall be in the Royall Cittie*; that is to saie, in *Constantinople*; *and if it be a matter of Weight, that it should be reported hither to the Sea Apostolicke to be decided by the sentence of our audience. And if at anie time, or for what occasion soeuer, thou doe attempt to contradict this our decree, know that we declare thee depriued from the sacred Communion, soe as it maie not be restored to thee vnlesse in the article of death, but with the leaue of the Bishop of Rome.* And finally he abrogated in his Epistle to *John* Patriarke of the first *Iustinianea*, who had confirmed the sentence of the Archbishop of *Larissa*, the iudgement of the said *Iohn* Primate of the first *Iustinianea*, and condemnes him to remaine depriued of the communion of the Bodie of Christ for the space of thirtie daies: *Abrogating* (said hee) *and annulling the decrees of thy sentence; Wee decree by the authoritie of the blessed Prince of the Apostles, that thou shalt be depriued of the sacred communion, for the space of thirtie daies.* Nowe, what was this, but to crye with a lowde voice, that in refusinge the title of *Vniuersall*; he refused not therefore the title of Head *of the Church*, and the Iurisdiction and superintendency ouer all other Bishops, Archbishops, and Patriarks?

Ibid. ep. 42.

Id. l. 2. ind. 10. ep. 37.

Id. l. 5 ind. 14. ep. 15.

Ib. ep. 24.

Ib. ep. 64.

Id. l. 2. ind. 11. ep. 7.

Greg. l. 2. ind. 11. ep. 6.

Of the Order of sitting in the Councell of Nicea.

CHAPT. VIII.

BVT *Caluin*, to fight against this doctrine, and to proue that the Pope is not head of the Church, nor Superior to the other Patriarkes, vseth fower principall meanes; first, that the Popes legates haue not presided, in the ancient Generall Councells. The secōd that the Pope called them not. The third that the appeales of Bishops were not to the Pope. And the fourth that the Canons of *Africa* forbadd the Bishop of the first Sea; by which *Caluin* impertinently vnderstands the Pope, to call himselfe Prince of Bishops: and the first meanes he striues to proue by Seauen examples, which wee had best confute all at a clapp, for els they will obiect them to vs in a second Answere.

The first obiection of Caluin against the precedencie of the Pope in the Councells. Soc. hist. eccl. l. 4. c. 11. Id. edit. græc. l. 2. c. 37. Theod. hist. eccl. l. 2. c. 21. Soz. hist. eccl. l. 4. c. 18. Am. Marc. l 31. Theod. hist eccl l. 2. c. 16. Soc edit. grec. l. 2. c. 27.

He produceth then before all things, the order of the Councell of *Nicea*, which he ignorantly calls the Councell of *Nice*, not knowing that the Councell of *Nice* was an hereticall Councell, that the Arrians held at *Nice* in *Thrace*, to deceiue the Catholicks by the affinitie of the words *Nice* and *Nicea*, νίκη and νίκαια compounded almost of the same letters. *The Arrians* (saith the Epistle of the *Asians* to *Liberius*) *caused to be signed by fraude and periuries at Constantinople a faith contrarie to that of the holy Councell of Nicea, which had bene brought from* Nice in Thrace. And *Socrates*: *They transported themselues into a cittie of Trace called Nice, and after a longe staie, held there an other Councell &c. to surprise the simple, by the affinitie of the words. For the simple people belieued that it was the faith of Nicea in Bithinia.* And *Theodoret*: *They brought manie Bishops against their wills, into a Towne of Thrace, whose name was Nice.* And *Sozomene*; *Passing through Thrace, they came into a cittie of the Countrie called Nice, and there kept a Conuenticle &c. And this they did expressely at Nice, to the end to perswade the simple people to cōsent to it, deceined by the neerenes of the words, and belieuing it to be the decree which was made at* Nicea. For although *Stephanus* doe indeede, put in a Cittie of *Nicea* in *Thrace*, neuerthelesse, besides that *Ammianus Marcellinus* saith, that the Garrison of *Thrace*, situate vpon the passage from *Italie* to *Constantinople*, which was the same wherein the *Arrians* had held their false Councell, was called *Nice*; The *Greciā* Ecclesiasticall historians very notablie marke this difference, betweene the Councell of the Catholiques and that of the *Arrians*, vpon the name whereof the fraude was founded; that that of the Catholicks was holden at *Nicea* ἐν νικαίᾳ and that of the hereticks at *Nice* ἐν νίκῃ; and reporting the two impostures of the *Arrians*, vse in the first (which was to hold a mocke Councell at *Nice* in *Thrace*) the word, *affinitie of name*, and saie, that the *Arrians* aduised themselues of this fraude, to surprise the simple, by the affinitie of the names. And in the second, which was to hold a mocke-Councell at *Nicea* in *Bithinia*, they vse the word, *identity of names*, and say, that they committed this fraude, to surprise the simple *by the identity of names*. By which meanes, that in the writings of saint HILLARY, the Towne of *Nice* in *Thrace* where the Conuenticle of the *Arrians* was held, is called *Nicea*, It is a vice of the Copists, which haue imposed it vpon some learned men. But in Summe what soeuer the cittie of *Nice* in *Thrace* be, it is Certaine, that that of

Nicea in *Bithinia*, where the Catholicke Councell was holden, was called, νίκαια, and not νίκη, *Nicea*, and not *Nice*. Which I would not reproche to *Caluin*, were it not, that all the Authors of the Ecclesiasticall historie, agreeing in this note, he is as inexcusable for hauing bene ignorant of it, as many Catholickes which are deceiued after him, are excusable for hauing followed him *bona fide*. But heere is to much of this digression; let vs come to the point.

The french translator Nicephorus aud others.

He alleadges then, that in the Councell of *Nicea*, S. ATHANASIVS presided, and that the Popes Legates had onely the fourth place. *I praie you* (saith *Caluin*) *if they had acknowledged Iulius for head of the Church, would those that represented his person, haue bene cast backe to the fourth place? Had Athanasius presided in the generall Councell, where the order of the Hierarchie ought to be singularly obserued?* Now, what should I answere to this, but what the oracle said of *Chalcedon*; to witt, that *heresie is the land of the blinde?* For all the Authors of Ecclesiasticall antiquitie, [a] S. EPIPHANIVS, [b] *Ruffinus*, [c] *Socrates*, [d] Theodoret, [e] *Sozomene*, and [f] S. ATHANASIVS himselfe, and the Councell of *Alexandria*, reported by him, to whom wee may ouer and aboue add S. HILLARY; testifie, that S. ATHANASIVS was yet Deacon, in the time of the Councell of *Nicea*, and was not made Bishop of *Alexandria*, till fiue moneths after the Councell of *Nicea*; and that *Alexander* Bishop of *Alexandria* his Predecessor, assisted at the Councell of *Nicea*, and did not preside there, (so farr was S. ATHANASIVS that was then but his Deacon from presiding) but onely held the second place there, and was preceded by the Popes Legates. It is true, *Caluin* may easily be pardoned this error, since he is soe ignorant in the Ecclesiasticall historie, as to haue belieued that *Sabellius* who was aboue threescore yeares before *Arrius* and the Councell of *Nicea*, was since both the one and the other. But let vs leaue the error there, and passe forward to the consequence.

Calu. inst. l. 4. c. 7. a Epiph. hær. Melet. b. Ruffin. hist. Eccl. l. 1. c. 5. & 14. c. Soc. hist. Eccl. l. 1. c. 15. d. Theod. hist. Eccl. l. 1. c. 27. e. Soz hist. Eccl. l. 1. c. 17. f. Athan. apol. 2. Hillar. in frag. Syn. Arim. Theodor. hist. Eccl. l. 1. c. 26. Socr. hist. Eccl. l. 1. c. 23.

Caluins argument then against the Legates of the Pope is, that *Sozomen* writes; *At this Councell assisted from the Sea Apostolicke, Macarius Bishop of Ierusalem, Eustachius Bishop of Antioch, Alexander Bishop of Alexandria; and as for Julius Bishop of Rome, hee assisted not at it, because of his age: but in his steede, there assisted Vito and Vincentius Priests of the same Church.* And from thence *Caluin* infers, that the Legats of *Julius* were onely then in the fourth place; and consequently that *Iulius* did not preside there, Now could I note in passing by, that the Councell of *Nicea* was not holden vnder *Julius*, as *Caluin* thought, but vnder *Syluester* the predecessor of *Julius*, and that it is a deprauation of *Sozomens* copies, that hath deceiued *Caluin*; and before him *Cassiodorus*, *Beda*, and many others. For first [a] *Eusebius*, [b] saint IEROM, [c] *Socrates*, [d] *Theodoret*, [e] *Gelasius* of *Cyzica*, and the ancient latine subscriptions: and after all those *Hincmarus* Archbishop of *Rheims* testifie, the Councell of *Nicea* was holdē in the time of *Syluester*, and not of *Iulius*. And secondly *Sozomene* notes, that vnder the third consulship of *Crispus* and *Constantine Cæsars*, which is he by whom he hath begun his historie, *Syluester was Bishop of Rome*. Now the third consulship of *Crispus* and *Constantine* ended but fower moneths before the ouerture of the Councell of *Nicea*, which begun in the moneth of May vnder the cōsulship of *Paulinus* & *Julianus*; by which meanes *Julius* could not haue sent his Legats, seeing betweene *Syluester* and *Julius*, *Sozomene* reports, that there was a Papacy interposed; which was that of *Marcus*, which according to S. IEROM

Calu. inst. l. 1. c. 23. sect. 4. Soz. hist. Eccl. l. 1. c. 16. a. Eusеb. in Chron. b. Hier. in Chron. c. Soc. hist. Eccl. l. 2. c. 27. d. Theod. hist. Eccl. l. 1. c. 3. e. Gel. in act. Conc. Nic. Hincmar. opusc. 55 c. 20. Soz. in præf. oper. Soz. hist. Eccl. l. 1. c. 2. Socr. hist. Eccl. l. 1. c. 9. Id. ibid.

Soz. l. 1. c. 25. Conc. Chalc. act. 2. Soz. hist. Eccl. l. 2. c. 20. Hier. in Chron.

Theodor. hist. Eccl. l.1. c. 7. Soz. hist. Eccl. l. 4. c. 7. Socr. hist. Eccl. l. 2. c. 27. Soz. ibid. Soc. ibid. Id. ibid. Ibid.

lasted eight moneths. And thirdly the cause wherefore *Sozomene* obserues that the Bishop of *Rome* assisted not at the Councell, which was his extreame age, or as *Theodoret* saith, *his profound age*, could not agree with the person of *Iulius*, who liued till thirtie yeares after the Councell. And fourthly *Sozomene* assignes but twentie fiue yeares to *Julius* Papacie, in which place we must reade but fifteen with *Socrates*; and consequently he could not presuppose, that *Julius* had bene Pope, in the tyme of the Councell of *Nicea*; seeing aswell hee, as *Socrates* affirme, that *Iulius* dyed, after the death of *Magnentius Gallus* and *Siluanus*; that is to saie, thirtie yeares after the Councell; for *Magnentius* was slaine, according to *Socrates*, vnder the sixth consulship of *Constantine*; and the second of *Gallus*, which was the twentie eigth yeare after the Councell, and *Gallus* vnder the seauenth of *Constantine*, Am. Marc. l. 15. and the third of his owne, which was the twentie ninth yeare after the Councell, and *Siluanus*, according to *Amianus Marcellinus*, after *Gallus*. Soz. l. 3. c. 9. I add, that *Julius* would neuer haue reproched to those of the *East*, that they did not request him to assist at the Councell of *Antioch*, which was holden sixteen yeares after the Councell of *Nicea*, if he had bene so old Soc. edit. græc. l. 2. c. 7. at the tyme of the Councell of *Nicea*, as he could not be there. I add, that *Sozomene* had had much more cause to impute it to *Julius* his age, Id. c. 20. that he was not at the Councell of *Sardica*, which was holden twentie two yeare after that of *Nicea*, then that he was not at that of *Nicea*. And finally I add, that *Sozomene* himselfe decides the point of the question, and teacheth vs, that it is a vice in the writing, which is slipt into the text of the historie. For after he had finisht in the closing vp of the first booke, the whole narration of the Councell of *Nicea* with Soz. hist. Eccl. l. 2. c. 1. these words: *Heere in this place ends all that concernes the Councell of Nicea*: And after he had employed all the ninteen first chapters of his second booke, to sett downe what past betweene the Councell of *Nicea*, and that of *Antioch* against *Eustathius*: when he had finished the recitall of the Councell of *Antioch* against *Eustathius*, he begins the twentith chapter Id. c. 20. of his second booke with these words: *In this time, Marcus hauing for a short space holden the Bishops Sea of Rome, after Syluester; Julius tooke the gouernment of the Sea of Rome: and Maximus after Macarius, of that of Ierusalem.* From whence it appeares manifestly, either that the word, *Iulius*, which is in the precedent booke, where *Sozomene* saith, speaking of the Councell of *Nicea*, *Julius Bishop of Rome because of his age, was not there*, is a note which slipt out of the margent, into the text; and that Euseb. de vit. Const. l. 3. c. 7. *Sozomene* had simplie said, as *Eusebius*; *The Bishop of Rome, because of his age was not there*: or that, insteede of ἰούλιος, wee must reade πόλιος, that is to saie; *ancient*, or *venerable*: But because we haue handled this matter more at large elsewhere; to witt, in the preface, composed by vs Cōc. græc. Imp. Com tom. 1. at *Rome*, but published without our name, before *Gelasius* of *Cyzica*, wee will heere content ourselues to remitt the Readers to that; and the while wee will examine the place of *Sozomene*.

Soz. hist. Eccl. l. 1. c. 16. *Sozomene* then (saith *Caluine*) writes; *At this Councell assisted of the Seas Apostolicke, Macarius Bishop of Ierusalem, Eustathius Bishop of Antioch, Alexander Bishop of Alexandria; and as for the Bishop of Rome, he was not there because of his age; but in his steede, there assisted Vito, and Vincentius, Priests of the same Church.* This is true, but so farr of is it, that from hence it followes, that *Sozomene* puts the Popes Legats in the fourth place; As contrarywise it is euident, euen there, that he attribures to them the first. For being constrained to followe the tract of his discourse, which obliged him, since he had

purposed

purposed to speake of the Apostolicke Prelats which assisted at the Councell, to beginne with those that were there in person; before he would make mention of those which were there but by their Legats; he inuerted of sett purpose the order of the enumeration; and began with the fourth and last of all the Patriarkes, which was the Bishop of *Jerusalem*, who was then but a Patriarke of honor; and then went vp increasing to him of *Antioch*, who was the third and then came to him of *Alexandria*, who was the second, to the end to keepe the last place of the progresse, for the Popes Legates. Now, what could be done more expressely, and with more note to testifie the primacie of the Pope? A man that being to describe an Emperiall diet, where the Emperor assisted but representatiuelie, would begin with the Princes of the Empire, who had assisted there in person; but to keepe the greater dignitie to the Emperor, would inuert the order of the other Princes; and would saie, rising from the last to the first of the Princes of the Empire, there assisted at the Emperiall diet, the Marquesse of *Brandenbourg*, the Count *Palatine*, the Duke of *Saxony*, the Archbishop of *Collen*, the Archbishop of *Treuers*, the Archbishop of *Ments*, and the Kinge of *Bohemia*; and as for the Emperor, he was not there, but deputed two Vicars there to hold his place: should hee in doeing so, giue the last ranke to the Emperor, or the first? For that the order reported in *Sozomene*, was the inuerted order, and not the direct order of the Seat of the Patriarkes, it appeares both by the confession of *Caluin*, who cryes out; *Amongst the Patriarks, Jerusalem hath bene the last*: and by all the Ecclesiasticall histories, which teach vs, that *Ierusalem* was the fourth of the patriarkships, and *Antioch* the third, and *Alexandria* the second. And by the Canons of the Councell of *Nicea* it selfe, which setts *Alexandria* before *Antioch*, and *Antioch* before *Jerusalem*. And by the expresse report that *Socrates* made of the direct order of the Councell, taken by the very Synodicall booke of S. ATHANASIVS, which is thus: *Osius* Bishop of *Cordua*, *Vito* and *Vincentius* Priests, *Alexander* of *Egipt*, *Eustachius* of great *Antioch*, *Macarius* of *Jerusalem*. In which Catalogue Sainct ATHANASIVS, and *Socrates*, put *Osius* the Bishop, and *Vito*, and *Vincentius* Priests; as holding but one and the same place in the first ranke: And *Alexander* Patriarke of *Alexandria*, who was the second Patriarke, in the second place; and *Eustachius* Patriarke of *Antioch*, who was the third Patriarke, in the third: And *Macarius* Patriarke of *Jerusalem*, who was the fourth Patriarke, in the fourth place.

Calu. inst. l. 4. c. 6.

Socr. hist. Eccl l. 1. c. 12.

But they will replie, that *Eusebius*, and after him *Theodoret*, and *Sozomene* make mention but of two Legats of the Pope *Vito* and *Vincentius*; and consequently that S. ATHANASIVS and *Socrates* could not place *Osius*, *Vito*, and *Vincentius*, as being all three Legats to the Pope, in one same place: to this replie then, the answere shall be, that the Popes had accustomed to send two sortes of Legates to the generall Councells celebrated in the *East*; the one Bishops, taken out of the bodie of the *Roman* Patriarchall Church: As *Arcadius* and *Proiectas* Bishops, to the first Councell of *Ephesus*. *Iulian* Bishop of *Pozzoly*, to the second. *Paschasinus* Bishop of *Lilybea*, to the Councell of *Chalcedon*; and the other Priests taken out of the body of the particular *Roman* Church, as *Vito* and *Vincentius* to the Councell of *Nicea*: *Archidamus* and *Philoxenus*, to the Councell of *Sardica*: *Phillip* to the first Councell of *Ephesus*: *Boniface* to the Councell of *Chalcedon*. And the reason of this was, that the body of the *Westerne* Church, was neuer at the generall councells celebrated out of the Patriarkships of the *West*; but the Pope held at *Rome* a Councell of the Bishops of the *West*, whose resolution he sent by a legation to the Councell, of the other Patriarchall diuisions assembled in the *East*; or at least, confirmed by a Councell holden afterward, that which had bene decided at the Councells of the other patriarchall diuisions assembled in the *East*: And from this concourse, arose the absolute title of generall Councell. The Legats then, that the Pope sent, to carry the voice of the *Westerne* Church, to the generall Councells assembled in the *East*, were of two sortes; the one taken from the body of the Bishops, to represent in generall the whole bodie of the *Westerne* Church, that is to saie; aswell the person of the Pope, as of the other Bishops of the *West*, and the other Priests and Deacons, taken from the particular Clergie of the *Roman* Church, to represent particularly the intention and person of the Pope: And this was some times the practise of those of the *East* in the *Westerne* expedition: For when *Flauianus* Patriarke of *Antioch*, sent his embassage to *Rome*, to recouer the grace of the Pope; hee added to it, besides the Priests and Deacons of the Church of *Antioch*, *Acacius* Bishop of *Beroe* in *Syria*, one of the Bishops of his patriarkship, *who was* (saith *Theodoret*) *head of the legation*; and some other Bishops of the same diuision; to the end to shew the consent of his patriarchall Church with his particular Church. But let vs leaue those of the *East*, and returne to the Pope.

Theodor. hist. Eccl. l. 5. c. 23.

The Pope then to cause the voices of the *Westerne* Church to be carried to the generall Councells, celebrated in the *East*, sent a legation compounded of two kinde of Legats; the one internall, and taken from the bodie of the particular *Roman* Church, whom wee with the Councell of *Sardica* call, *Legats taken out of the Popes owne side:* and the other externall, and taken out of the order of the Bishops: And this legation was sometymes made by two distinct commissions; as in the sixth generall Councell; the Legats from the popes particular person, and those from the Councell of *Rome*, were deputed seuerally: And sometymes by a ioynt deputation, as in the Councell of *Ephesus* and *Chalcedon*. Now were those Legats that we call internall (that is to saie taken out of the particular Clergie of the *Roman* Church) the principall Legats, not in honor; except when the Popes legations, and those of the Councell of *Rome*, were distinct; but as for the instructions, and in the report of the Popes intentions. And therefore also when there was question of the particular voice of the Pope, they were often named alone; as in the historie of *Sozomene*, and in the list of the signatures of the Councell of *Sardica*, because, they were onely Legats deputed both from the person of the Pope, and from the bodie of his Church. And of those examples we haue one remarkable in the commission that the Councell of *Ephesus* gaue to the Bishops that it sent to *Constantinople:* for by this commission, the Councell of *Ephesus* intituled *Phillip* Priest of the *Roman* Church, Legate from the Pope in these words: *To Phillip Priest, holding the place of the Bishop of Rome, Celestine; to Arcadius, to Iuuenall, &c.* And intituled not *Arcadius* Legat to the Pope, though he were both Bishop and Legat to the Pope altogether; because *Phillip* was *Legat à latere*, from the Pope; that is to saie, a Legate taken out of the very bodie of the particular *Roman* Church; and *Arcadius* was Legat from the Patriarchall *Roman* Church; that is to saie, Legat

Cõc. Sard. can. 5.

Soz. hist. Eccl. l. 1. c. 17. Athana. apol. 2.

Cõc. Eph. edit. græc. inter epist. Catholic.

from the Pope and Councell of *Rome*; by meanes whereof, when *Sozomene* and *Theodoret* say, there were two Legats from the Pope at the Councell of *Nicea*; to witt, *Vito* and *Vincentius*; and that S. ATHANASIVS and *Socrates*, put *Osius*, *Vito*, and *Vincentius* into one place; they contradict not one an other; for as much as the one speakes onely of the internall Legats, that we call *Legats à latere*, of which *Osius* was none; and the other speakes of the Legats, aswell internall as externall, whereof *Osius* was one. And in this the ancient Greeke and Latine Canonists, agree with vs: For not onely *Hincmarus* Archbishop of *Rhemes*, who flourished in the time of *Charles* the *Balde*, and was not suspected to fauour the Pope much, writes; *At the Councell of Nicea in the place of Syluester, Osius Bishop of Cordua, and Vito, and Vincentius Priests of the cittie of Rome presided*: But alsoe *Dalmatius* Bishop of *Cyzica* in *Asia*, one of the Fathers of the Councell of *Ephesus*, who liued neere a thousand two hundred yeares agoe; and after him *Gelasius* Priest of *Cyzica*, who liued vnder the Emperor *Zeno* a thousand one hundred and fortie yeares agoe; that is to saie, in the next age to the Councell of *Nicea*; and from whose pen is come to vs the famous Canon of the *Eucharist*, so much cited by *Caluin* and by all the *Sacramentaries*, written in the extract of the same Councell of *Nicea*, that *Osius* was the Popes Legat in the Councell of *Nicea*; and that *Vito* and *Vincentius* were his Colleagues. *At this Councell* (saith *Gelasius* of *Cyzica*, speaking after *Dalmatius* of *Cyzica* of the Councell of *Nicea*) *assisted Osius Bishop of Cordua, who held the place of the Bishop of great Rome Syluester, with the Priests Vito and Vincentius.* And not onely *Gelasius* of *Cyzica* vseth these words; but *Photius* Patriarke of *Constantinople*, the greatest enemie to the *Roman* Church that euer was amongst the *Greekes*, alleadgeth them neere eight hundred yeares agoe, in these words: *I haue* (said he) *read a booke in forme of a historie intituled, The Acts of the Councell of Nicea, containing three tomes, and bearing* (added he a little after) *the title of Gelasius of Cyzica; in this booke* (saith he) *the Author writes, that Osius Bishop of Cordua, and Vito and Vincentius Roman Priests assisted at the Councell from the part of Syluester Bishop of Rome.* And not onely *Photius* alleadgeth them; but himselfe in his treatie of the Synods, dedicated to *Michell* King of the *Bulgarians*, and reported by *Euthymius*, writes; *With Vito and Vincentius was ioyned Osius Bishop of Cordua.*

Hincmar. opusc. 55. capitul. c. 20.

Gel. Cyz. in prolog. Syntag. Conc. Nic.

Gel. in Syn Conc. Nic. l. 2. c. 5.

Phot. Biblioth. Ibid.

And indeede, for what other cause, should *Osius* simplie a Bishop of the patriarkship of the *Roman* Church; and subiect in the first instance to the Metropolitan of *Seuilla* in *Spaine*, and by appeale to the Patriarke of the *West*, haue preceded all the Patriarks of the *East*; yea, in the *East* it selfe he that in the Councell of *Eluira* that we call *Elibertin*, composed of ninteene Bishops of *Spaine* had held but the secōd or according to others, the eleauenth place. And in the Councell of *Arles* compounded of two hundred Bishops, had had noe ranke amongst the principall Bishops of the Councell, but for the same cause, for which *Vito* & *Vincentius* simple Priests of the *Roman* Church, preceded them; to witt, for the order of his legation? for to precede them by vertue of the particular conditions of his person, neither age, nor antiquitie of promotion, nor learning, nor desert, hath euer giuen ranke in generall Councells to anie simple Bishops before Archbishops, much lesse before the Patriarks; otherwise the distinction of the Seas had bene introduced in vaine, and the personall condition of *Osius* were good to make his person reuerent, but not to make him preside in a generall Councell,

Phot. ep. de 7. Syn. in Panopl. Euthym. p. 2. tit. 24. Catalog. Conc. Elib. Conc to. 1. Collect. Cōc. Hisp. a Garf. Loais. Aug. cont. Parm. l. 2. c. 5.

Calu.inst. l. 4. c. 7.

where the order of the Hierarchy (saith Caluin) *ought to be singularly obserued.* Iointly, that euen in all these qualities, there were manie in the Councell, that surpassed him. For if wee speake of persecutions for the Faith, *Paphnucius* Bishop of one of the citties of *Thebaida*, who had lost a knee vnder the persecution of *Maximinus* and an eye, whose skarre the Emperor *Constantine* was wont to kisse; was not he there? *Potamon* Bishop of *Heraclea* in *Egipt*, whom S. EPIPHANIVS calls, *great Bishop and great Confessor*, and who in the same persecution, had had an eye put out; was not he there? *Paul* Bishop of *Neocesarea* vpon *Euphrates*, whose handes had bene maimed with a hott iron, in the persecution of *Licinius*; was not he there?

Ruffi. hist. Eccl. l. 1. c. 4. Soc. l. 1. c. 11. Epiph. 68. Melet. hær. 68. Theod. hist Eccl. l. 1. c. 7.

And if we speake of the guiftes of prophetie and working of miracles, *Spiridion* Bishop of *Trimithunta* in *Cyprus*, that *Ruffinus* calls *a man of the order of the Prophets*; was not he there? *James* that great Bishop of *Antioch* in *Mygdonia*, otherwise called *Nisibis*, that *Theodoret* saith [a] *had raised againe the dead*, and whom hee intitles *the prince of the troupe of the Councell*; was not he there? S. NICHOLAS Bishop of *Myra* in *Lycia*, a man for manners and for miracles Apostolicall; was not he there? And if wee speake of credit and estimation, with the Emperor; euen he whose credit wee learne from *Osius*; to witt *Eusebius* Bishop of *Cesarea* in *Palestina*, whō the Emperor from his childhood had knowne in the *East*, [c] and whom he testified in his conceit to be worthie of the Bishopricke of the whole earth, [e] and to whom besides so manie other letters and markes of familiaritie, he directed the first commission, for the re-establishment of the Churches in the *East*, [f] and the charge of the transcription of the sacred bookes [g] for the Churches of *Constantinople*; was not he there? *Eusebius* Bishop of *Nicomedia*, who afterward baptized the Emperor, and who was Metropolitan of the prouinces where the Councell was held, and Bishop of the Seate of the Empire in the *East*, and of the cittie where the Emperor resided, *a man* (say *Socrates* and *Sozomene*) *indued with great authoritie, and very prudent, and honored in the pallace of the Emperor* (for the ecclipse of his fauour with the Emperor, happened not till after the Councell, and lasted but a moment) was not he there? *Alexander* Bishop of the future Imperiall cittie of *Byzantium*, conuerted by exchange of name into *Constantinople*; was not he there? *Paphnutius* of whom *Socrates* saith, *the Emperor honored him extraordinarily, and kept him ordinarily in his Court*; was not he there? *Protogenes* Bishop of *Sardica*, to whom the Emperor had addressed his first lawe for the manumission in Churches, and to *Osius* the second lawe; was not he there?

Ruffi. hist. Eccl. l. 1. c. 5. a. Theod. hist. Eccl. l. 1. c. 7. b. Theod. hist. Sanct. Pat. c. 1. c. Euseb. de vit. Const. l. 1. c 13. e. Ep. Cōst. apud Eus. de vit. Cōst. l. 3. c. 59. f. Eus. de vit. Const. l. 2. c. 44. g. Id. l. 4. c. 36. Socr. hist. Eccl. l. 1. c. 6. Soz. l. 1. c. 15. Soc. l. 1. c. 1. Cod Iust. l. 1. tit. de his qui in Eccl. manumittuntur. Cod. Theo l. 4. tit 70.

And if wee speake of learninge; the same *Eusebius* Bishop of *Cesarea*, of whom the Emperor said, *that he more then admired his knowledge and his studies*; was not he there? *Alexander* Patriarke of *Alexandria*, whom *Theodoret* calls, *the admirable Bishop*; was not he there? *Eustachius* Patriarke of *Antioch*, who made the oration of the Councell, and whom *Sozomene* intitles *the miracle of eloquence*; was not he there?

Euseb. de vit. Const. l. 4. c. 35. Theod. histor. Eccl. l. 1. c. 26. Id. l 1. c. 7. Soz. l. 2. c. 19.

And if wee speake of reuerence for age; the same *Alexander* of *Alexandria*, whom the histories of the Councell call, *the old man*; and whom the epistle of the Councell exalts, *for hauing at that age sustained so manie labours*; was not he there? *Alexander* Bishop of *Constantinople* of threescore and three yeares of age, whether he were then Bishop in cheife, or as the Patriarkes of the Church of *Constantinople* will haue it Coadiutor, and Legate of *Metrophanes*, yet elder then himself; was not he there?

Ruffi. hist. Eccl. l. 1. c. 5 Theodor. hist. Eccl. l. 1. c. 9. Soz. hist. Eccl. l. 3 c. 3.

And if we must speake of the antiquitie of promotion; Zeno

whom

whom saint EPIPHANIVS calls, *antique Bishop of Phenicia*, euill qualified by the lists of the signatures of the Councell, *Bishop of Tyre;* was not he there? *Eusebius* Bishop of *Nicomedia*, before Bishop of *Berith*, whom saint EPIPHANIVS calls, *the ancient old-man of* Nicomedia; was not he there? And in briefe, an infinite number of other Bishops, that *Eusebius*, for the antiquitie aswell of their age as of their promotion, comprehends in the first clause of this passage; *some where honored: because of their length of tyme; others flourished in the rigor of their age and spirits; others were newly entred into the course of their charges,* were not they there? For that in the Councell of *Sardica*, the age of *Osius* was accompted amongst those things that purchased him Reuerence; that was more then twentie yeare after the Councell of *Nicea*. And that saint ATHANASIVS calls him, *the Father of Bishops*, and saith he died a centenarie it was neere fortie yeare after the Councell of *Nicea*, But if none of these, what personall qualitie soeuer he had, noe not *Alexander* Patriarke of *Alexandria*, whom the Epistle of the Councell calls, *the master of the Councell*; that is to saie, Master for sufficiencie, did aduance himselfe a finger breadth, beyond the degree of his dignity: for what cause should *Osius* for his particular cõditiõs, haue bene President of all the Assemblie? For to saie *Osius* presided there as the Emperors deputie, the Emperor was in person at the Councell, and so could haue noe deputy; and besides that, he presided not there, but was sett there beneath the Bishops and in a lower Seate; and after he had attended, and desired the leaue of the Bishops, to shew that in matter of *Religion*, he was of the number not of the Iudges, but of those that were to be iudged. And in the first Councell of *Arles*, where the Emperor *Constantine* assisted also in person, and *Osius* with him, as it appeares by the reproches of the Donatists against the Iudges of that Councell wherein *Osius* was inwrapped; not onely *Osius* who was alreadie then in as great Credit with that Emperor witnesse the Epistle of the iudowing the Churches of *Africa*, did not preside there, but euen in the letter of the Councell was not placed amongst the first Bishops, but comprehended vnder the curtaine of silence with the troupe and multitude of the Bishops. And in the Councell of *Sardica*, where *Osius* presided, aswell as at the Councell of *Nicea*, he was so euill willed by *Constantius* the Lord of the Empire, who was an *Arrian* that he could not be said there to preside, in qualitie neither of a fauorite or of a Deputie to the Emperor; contrarywise the care he had to make himself Procurator and Promoter of the Popes Rights, and the instance he made for the appeales to the Pope, and for the honor of saint PETERS memory, and the iustificatiue relation of the Councells, which *Protogenes* Bishop of *Sardica* and he, dedicated to the Pope; and the protestation that he and the other Bishops inserted into the Epistle of the Councell to the Pope, to hold him for head of the Church, and to acknowledge, *That it was a conuenient thing, that from all Prouinces of the earth, the Prelats of God should referr all affaires to their head; that is to saie, to the Sea of the Apostle Peter;* shew sufficiently that it was from the part of the Pope, and not of the Emperors that he presided there.

And from this it derogates not, that saint ATHANASIVS makeing the recitall of the signatures of the Councell of *Sardica*, puts the signatures of *Osius*, without a title of Legation, and before that of the Pope in those words: *Osius of Spaine, Iulius of Rome, by Archidamas and Philoxemus*: For besides that, this recitall followes not the rankes of the dignities, as it appeares by *Nessus* an African Bishop, who is placed there before *Gratus* Archbishop of *Carthage*. And moreouer, that hee vseth this

Epiph. her 69. Epiph. ibid. Eus. de vit. Cont. l. 3. c. 9. Theod. hist. Eccl. l. 2. c. 8. Athan. ad solit. vit. agent. Theod. hist. eccl. l. 1. c. 9. Eus. de vit Const. l. 3. c. 10. Soc. l. 1. c. 1 Aug. cont. Parm. l. 1. c. 4. 5. 6. 7. Eus. hist. eccl. l. 10. c. 6 Pars. act. Concil. Arelat. sub Constantin in ep. ad Syluestr. Cõc. Sardic. Can. 3. 4. 5. Soz. hist. eccl. l. 3. c. 12. Epist. Cõc. Sard. ad Iul. in fragm. Hilar. de gest. Concil. Arim. & apud. Nicol. 1. ep. ad Episcop Gal. Athan. apol. 2.

order for as much as *Osius* signed the Epistle of the Councell immediately, and by himselfe and the Pope mediatelie, and by another the legates of the Pope, who were Bishops, had a vote of their owne in the Councell, and the Priests not. From whence it is, that when the legations of the Pope and of the Councell of *Rome* were distinct, as in the sixth generall Councell, the legates of the Councell of *Rome* because they where Bishops, tooke the qualitie of difinitors, and signed in this forme: *John vnworthie Bishop of the holy Church of Port, and legate of all the Synod of the holy and apostolicke Sea of the cittie of Rome, I haue defined and subscribed.* And the Legats from the particular person of the Pope abstained from it, and signed thus: *Theodorus humble Priest of the holie Church of Rome and holding the place of the most blessed and vniuersall Pope of the cittie of Rome, Agatho, I haue subscribed.* Now, saint ATHANASIVS had an interest, not to diminish the number of those that voted for his iustification in the Coũcell of *Sardica*, and not to loose that of *Osius*. For this cause then he procured him to signe, not as a simple reporter of the Popes voice, but as hauing right himselfe to vote, and say his opinion in the Councell, and reserued to *Archidamus* and *Philoxemus*, who were but simple Priests, and had noe voice of their owne in the Councell, the office to represent the voice and the signature of the Pope; and in truth with what a face could *Osius* haue accepted to preside in the Councells, whether of *Nicea* or *Sardica* in the behalfe of the Emperors, he that writt to the Emperor *Constantius*; Goe *not about to meddle in Ecclesiasticall affaires, and commaund not vs in such matters, but rather learne of vs:* God *hath committed the Empire to thee, and the gouernment of the Churches to vs.* And S. ATHANASIVS, How could he haue past without censure, hee that cries out; *that an Emperor presiding in Ecclesiasticall iudgements, is the abhomination foretold by Daniell.*

Conc. 6. Const. act. 18. Cõc. Cõst. act. 18.

Epist. Osij. ad Cõst. in Script. Athan. ad solit. Athan. ad solit.

For that afterward in the Councell of *Chalcedon*, the Emperor *Marcian* presided; the Fathers of the Councell declared, that it was not for things Ecclesiasticall, but for order and temporall policie; to the end, to hinder such seditions, as had happened in the false Councell of *Ephesus*, and testified, that the presidencie of the Emperor, whas not of the essence of the Councell, as that of the Pope, but onely for comelynesse and ornament. *Thou gouernest vs there* (said they to the Pope) *so the head doth the members, contributing thy good will by those that hold thy place; and the faithfull Emperors presided there for ornament, or to cause good order to be obserued there.* And in the sixth generall Councell holden vnder the Emperor *Constantine Pogonat*, it is said in the Rolle of the causes of the *Laycks*: *the most religious and Christian Emperor presiding*; that hath reference not to the assemblie of the Synod, but to the assemblie of the Senate, and of the imperiall offices. For there were two distinct assemblies in the hall of the Councell: the one, that of the Senators, and officers of the Empire, wherein the Emperor presided; and the other; that of the Synod of the Bishops, wherein the Popes Legats presided, as it appeares, both by the verball processe of the Councells, which after it had decreed, the assemblie of the officers of the Empire, added; *the holy and generall Councell being also assembled, called by the imperiall ordinance in this Royall and God-protected Cittie: to witt the most reuerend Priests Theodore and George, and the most Reuerend Iohn the deacon holding the place of the most holy and sacred Archbishop of old Rome, Agatho; and George the most holy and sacred Archbishop of this famous cittie of Constantinople new Rome*; And by the protestation that the same Emperor sent to *Rome* for the holding of the Councell in these wordes: I *will not sitt as Emperor with them, and I will not speake Emperiouslie, but as one of them, and what the Prelates shall ordaine, I will execute*: And finally

Ep. Conc. Chalc. ad Leon. act. 1. & seqq.

Cõc. Cõst. 6. act. 1. & seqq.

In ep. Greg 2. ad Leon Imp. ep. 1.

by the modestie which he vsed in the signatures, in signing last, and after all the Bishops. For whereas in the false Councell intituled *Trullian*, the Emperor *Iustinian Rhinotmete* his sonne signed contrary to his Fathers modestie, before all the Prelates: it was an irregular action, and done in an erroneous and illegitimat Councell, as it shall appeare hereafter; And then, if creditt with Emperors, should haue giuen anie Bishop the prerogatiue to preside in Councell, what Bishop had euer more credit with the Emperor *Constantius* then *Valens* Bisohp of *Murses*; to whose meritts, and not to his Souldiers valour, he said he ought the victorie ouer *Magnesius*, and the preseruation of his Empire; And vpon whose industrie and counsells, he depended in all affaires of Religion: Who notwitdstanding, neuer presided in anie one of the manie Councells, holden vnder *Constantius*? Or what Bishop had euer more creditt with the Emperor *Iustinian*, then *Theodorus* Archbishop of *Cesarea* in *Cappadocia*, who was his deare and trustie Counsellor and Assessor; or rather, the soule and Oracle of all his Counsells; who notwithstanding presided not, in the fifth Generall Councell, but sate there in his simple ranke of Metropolitan, belowe all the Patriarks and legates of the Patriarkes?

In.cap. 15.

Sulp.Seu. hist.sacr. l. 2.

Euag. hist. eccl.l. 4. c. 37.

Cōc. Cōst. œcum.5. act.1.2.3.4 5.6.7.8.

Now if *Osius* had presided in the Councell of *Nicea*, for the meritts and conditions of his person, must not the election haue bene made before by a solemne and authenticall act in the Councell? or if he had presided there by delegation from the Emperor, must not the same Emperor haue signified it, and inrolled his commission in the Councell? for if they saie, there is noe mention found of it, because the acts of the Councell are lost, wherefore should they rather exact testimonies of the delegation of *Osius* by the Pope, then by the Emperor, and not content themselues that the analogie of the ancient Ecclesiasticall order, and that which is saued from the Shypwracke of the acts of the Councell in the memorie of the following ages, and hath bene collected by *Dalmasius* or others yet more ancient; and by *Gelasius* of *Cyzica*, *Greeke* and *Thrace* authors, the one writing a hundred yeare, & the other an hundred & fiftie after the Coūcell of *Nicea*; and the Confession of the latter, and Schismaticall *Greekes* themselues, as *Photius* and others doe plainely informe vs of it, in affirming that *Osius*, was *Syluesters* legate, with *Vito*, and *Vincentius*; And that saint ATHANASIVS and *Socrates*, doe tacitly informe vs so, in setting *Osius Vito*, and *Vincentius*, in one and the same place, and before the second Patriarke? For where *Eusebius*, and after him *Socrates*, and *Sozamene* saie, that from before the Councell of *Nicea*, the Emperor *Constantine* had sent *Osius* from *Nicomedia* into *Egipt*, to assaie to pacifie the difference of the Church of *Alexandria*, which commission happened not seauen yeare before the Councell of *Nicea*, as they conceiue that would salue the actes intituled from *Siluester*; but the next yeare before the Councell of *Nicea*, as it appeares by *Sozomens* historie, who putts the calling of the Councell of *Nicea*, presently after the returne of *Osius*, what can assure vs, that it had not bene with the aduise and authoritie of Pope *Siluester*? or rather, what can assure vs, that it was not Pope *Siluester*, that sent him to the Emperor into the *East*, to prouide for the trouble of *Arrius*; whereof the Bishop of *Alexandria* had written to the same *Siluester*, and to solicite the Emperor, to interpose his authoritie, and that what remaines to vs from the authors of the Ecclesiasticall history, more attentiue then in the first conuersion of the Emperors to note their actions, then those of the Popes; to the end, to strengthen the Church, with the temporall authoritie of the Empire, hath not past it ouer in silence? or to saie better who can assure vs, that the same *Eusebius* with an hereticall

Euf.de vit. Const.l.2. c.62.

Soz.hist. eccl.l.1.c. 17.

Epist. Lib. ad Const. in opusc. Lucif.

malice

malice, as being an *Arrian*, and for that cause an Enemie to the *Roman* Church, hath not dissembled it, as well as he dissembled, that *Alexander* Patriarke of *Alexandria*, sent the relation of the trouble of the Church of *Alexandria*, to Pope *Siluester*, and an other relatiō then the circular letters addressed to the principall Bishops of the *East*, as it appeares from the number and the degrees of those that were excommunicated, where of there is mention made; which neuerthelesse, wee learne euidently from Pope Liberius, who writes to the Emperor *Constantius*: *Wee haue still in our hands the letters of the Bishop Alexander, heeretofore sent to Siluester of holy memory*; and tacitely, from saint CYRILL, Patriarke of the same place of *Alexandria*, who writes to Pope CELESTINE: *The longe custome of the Churches, exhorts me to communicate those things to your Holynesse*?

Epiph.cōt. Ar.hær.69 Soc.hist.eccl.l.1.c.6. Theod.hist eccl l.1.c.5. Epist. Lib. ad.Const. vbi sup. Cyril.ep. ad Celest. in Concil. Ephes. part.1.

The Fathers of the third generall Councell of *Constantinople*, which was the sixth generall Councell, *Greekes* Fathers, and which liued neere a thousand yeare agoe, and had read manie *Greeke* Ecclesiasticall histories, that the iniurie of the tymes haue robbed from vs, and in whose eares there sounded yet the memory of the acts of the Councell of *Nicea*, doe not they throughly testifie, that not onely the Emperor *Constantine*, but also Pope *Siluester*, wrought for the preparation of this Councell; when they saie, *The most sacred Coustantine, and the famous Siluester, called the great and notable Councell at Nicea*? And doth not the analogie of the historie informe vs, that the Pope before the celebration of the Coūcell of *Nicea*, must first haue holden a Patriarchall Councell of the westerne Church; that is to saie; a Councell compounded of the deputies, from the particular Councells of the *westerne* Prouinces, to send by delegates, carrying the voice of that Councell the sence of all the westerne Church to the Councell of *Nicea*, as it was done when there was question of holding the Councells of *Ephesus*, and *Calcedon*? otherwise, how had the Councell of *Nicea*, which was compounded but onely of the Easterne Prouinces, and where there were but fiue or six Bishops of all the *West*, bene originallie vniuersall and Oecumenicall; (I say originally, and not by accession, as that of *Constantinople*,) if some one of them had not bene deputed, to carrie the voice of all the westerne Church? And which of those Bishops could it bee, except *Osius*, who onely had his Seate with the Popes legates, before the heads of all the other Patriarkships? For if the authors of the Ecclesiasticall historie, for the most part *Grecians*, which remaine to vs, haue spoken of noe Councell of the *West* preambulary to that of *Nicea*; what meruaile is it, since that of the Councell of *Capua*; that the Councell of *Carthage* calls a generall Coūcell, and that saint AMBROSE describes as assembled from all the partes of the world, and for the affaires of the *East*, there is found noe author of the ancient Ecclesiasticall historie that speakes a word? And if *Eusebius* and those that haue followed him, haue made noe memorie of the Councell of the *West*, holden for the preparation of the Councell of *Nicea*; what meruaile is it, if they haue made noe mention, of the deputation of the Bishop, sent from the Pope; and the Councell of the *West*, to represent their person at the Councell of *Nicea*? Wee finde indeede, that *Eusebius* Bishop of *Vercelles* in *Italie*, and *Lucifer* Bishop of *Cailira* in *Sardinia*, two Bishops of the Popes Patriarkship, where banisht into the, *East* and that at the issue of their banishment, one of them, to wit, *Lucifer*, created in *Syria*, *Paulinus* Patriarke of *Antioch*, and assisted by one of his deacons, at the Councell of *Alexandria*, holden for the restitution of the Churches: And the other; to witt *Eusebius*, assisted there in person, but that they bare the

Cōc. Cōst. œcum. 6. act. 18.

Cōc. Carth 3.c.38. Amb.ep. 78.

Ruff.hist. eccl.l.3. c.27. Soc.hist.eccl l.3.c.27. Ibid. Ibid.

qualitie of the Popes Legates, when they were banisht into the *East*, or since wee finde nothing in all the *Grecian* antiquitie: And neuerthelesse, saint IEROM describing the life of *Lucifer*, saith; *Lucifer Bishop of Calaris, sent Legat for the faith with Pancratius and Hyllarius, Clerkes of the Roman Church, by the Bishop* Liberius *to Constantius, because he would not vnder the name of Athanasius condemne the Faith of* Nicea, *was banisht into Palestina.* And describing that of *Eusebius*: *Eusebius* (saith hee) *made, from a* L*ecturer in the Roman Church, Bishop of Vercelles, was for the confession of his faith, confined by the Emperor Constantius to Scythopolis, and from thence to Cappadocia.* And saint HILLARIE describing the Councell of *Millan*, from whence they where both sent into the *East* by *Constantius*: *Eusebius Bishop of Vercelles* (saith hee) *is there with the clerks of Rome, and* Lucifer *Bishop of Sardinia.* And *Liberius* himself, in an Epistle to the Emperor *Constantius*, which remaines to vs in the workes of *Lucifer*; I *haue* (said hee) *sent to you my holie Brother and fellow-bishop* Lucifer, *with Pancratius my fellow-Priest, and* Hillary *Deacon.* And *Nicetas* a graue *Greeke* Author, and who had seene manie Ecclesiasticall histories, that tyme hath enuied to vs, expounding these words of saint GREGORIE *Nazianzene*: *There were at Cesarea in Coppadocia, Bishops of the west, which drew all that were orthodoxall to them*; adds, *These Bishops were* L*ucifer and Eusebius, who had bene sent from Rome.*

Hier. de script. Eccl in Lucif.

Idem Ibid. in Euseb.

Hilar. ad Constant. l. 1.

Liber. epist ad Cōstant. in oper. Lucifer. & in fragm. Hilar.

Greg. Nazian. Or. in Basil.

Nicet. Serr ibid.

And why then, as all the ancient *Greekes* cōcealed the deputation of *Lucifer* and *Eusebius* Bishops of *Vercelles*, from the Pope, to the Emperor *Constantius*; so could not *Eusebius* and those that haue followed him conceale the deputation of *Osius* from the Pope, be it to the Emperor *Constantine*, or be it to the Church of *Alexandria*? And if from this, that *Eusebius* notes not, that *Osius* (whom in hate to Catholicke doctrine, he vouchsafes not so much as to name in all the historie of the life of *Constantine*) was sent by the Emperor into *Egipt* as the Popes legate, or from this that hee doth not relate that *Osius* assisted at the Councell of *Nicea* as the Popes Legat, it doe ensue, that it was not in the qualitie of the Popes legate, that *Osius* presided at the Councell of *Nicea*; must wee not conclude by the same meanes, that he presided not there at all? for *Eusebius* saith not, that *Osius* presided at the Councell of *Nicea*; he onely saith, that he sate there, with manie others: *From Spaine itselfe* (said hee) *there was one verie famous Bishop sett with manie others.* Two onely historians doe informe vs of it; the one is *Socrates*, who saith after saint ATHANASIVS, *At this* C*ouncell assisted* O*sius Bishop of* Cordula, *Vito and Vincentius Priests:* The other *Dalmatius* of the same tyme with *Socrates*, who writes; and *Galatius* of *Cyzica* fiftie yeares after him; *At this Councell assisted* O*sius* L*egat of the Bishop of Great Rome Siluester; with the Priests Vito, and Vincentius*; but as for *Eusebius* hee saith thereof nothing at all; contrariwise, hee affirmes cleerelie that the Priests of the Bishop of *Rome*, whom he reserues to name last, as the seale and the Crowne of the Councell, held there the ranke of their Bishop. *The Bishop of the cittie regnant* (saith hee) *assisted not there because of his age, but his priests kept his ranke there.* Now by what arithmeticke could the priests of the *Roman* Church, keepe there the ranke of the Bishop of *Rome*, if *Osius* possessed the first place, otherwise then in the qualitie of their Colleague, and filling vp one selfesame place with them?

Euseb. de vit. Const l. 3. c. 7.

Gel. in Synt. Conc Nicen. l. 2. c. 5.

Euseb. de vit. Const. l. 3. c. 7.

Moreouer, howe had not the Patriarkes of *Alexandria, Antioch* and *Ierusalem* lost at the Councell of *Nicea* their rightes of the second, third, and fowrth Seates in the Councells, against the expresse protestation, that the Councell of *Nicea* made to preserue their priuiledges; if *Osius Vito*,

Conc. Nicen. c. 6. 7.

and

and *Vincentius*, had held diuers places there and not one and the same place? And how had the Councell of *Constantinople*, celebrated in the same age, that the *Grecians* call the second generall Councell, when they would erect *Constantinople* into a Patriarkship, ordained that the Patriarke of *Constantinople* should hold the second place after the Bishop of *Rome*; if in the first generall Councell the Bishop of *Rome* had not held the first place? And how could the legates of the Pope in the Councell of *Chalcedon* haue complained, that *Dioscorus* had presumed to vndertake to preside in a pretended generall Councell, without the Popes authoritie, which had neuer bene lawfull nor euer had bene done, if *Osius* had presided in the Councell of *Nicea* without the Popes authoritie? And how could the Emperor *Iustinian* haue said; *Wee decree following all the fower holie Concells, that the most holy Pope of olde Rome, be the first of all the Prelates*; if in the first of all the generall Councells, a simple Bishop of *Spaine*, had bene the first, otherwise then in the qualitie of delegate by the Pope?

Cõc.Chalc act.1.

Iust.nou. 131.

And finallie, how came it that an Action so irregular, as that by which a man who was neither Metropolitan nor Patriarke, had preceded all the Patriarkes of the *East*; and euen in the *East* was not noted amongst the extraordinary examples of antiquitie? And how came it, not to speake of the interest of the Patriarkes, that *Theognis* Bishop of *Nicea*, the Cittie wherein the Councell was celebrated, and *Eusebius* Bishop of *Nicomedia* head of the *Arrian* faction, and Metropolitan of the Prouince of *Bithinia* wherein the Councell was holden, and Bishop of the Seate of the Emperors in the *East*, did not oppose it: as well as when *Fortunius* Archbishop of *Carthage* was at *Constantinople* the Metropolitans subiect to the Patriarkship of *Constantinople*, opposed this that the Archbishop of *Carthage*, should haue caused the acts of the second generall Councell of *Constantinople* to be searched, to see what place the legate of *Primosus* Archbishop of *Carthage* had there; And how chanced it, that they, and the other *Arrians*, who after the death of *Constantine* and *Constans*, the Catholicke brothers to *Constantius* the hereticall Emperor stirred heauen and earth to reuerse the auctoritie of the Conncells of *Nicea* and *Sardica*, could not alleage for a meanes of nullitie, that *Osius* had presided irregularly in the one and the other, if he had presided otherwise, then as representing the person of him, to whom the right to preside did appertaine?

But the question in the matter that *Caluin* propounds, is not betweene the Pope and *Osius*, who at least was one of the Suffragans or reare Suffragans of the Pope; that is to saie, one of the Bishops of the Popes Patriarchall diuision; And by consequence, what ranke soeuer he held, it could not tend to the Popes preiudice? For were it that the Pope sent him from the *West* into the *East*, with the title of legat; or were it, that being alreadie there, the Pope had chosen and designed him by letters to represent his person; or were it, that neither the one nor the other had chanced, but that being at the Councell, he had bene intreated as the most ancient Bishop there present of the Popes Patriarkship, to ioyne himselfe with his deputies, to helpe them to present him; it could be noe waie to the disaduantage of his Patriarke: It is betweene the Pope and the other patriarks, and consists in this, whether at the Councell of *Nicea* the Popes deputies were sett after the other three patriarks, or before them. Now of this ATHANASIVS and *Socrates* put vs out of doubt, when they saie, that the order of the Councell was: *Osius Bishop of Corduba Vito and Vincentius priests, Alexander of Egipt, Eustachius Patriarke of great Antioch, and Macarius Bishop of Ierusalem.* For to

Soc.hist. Eccl.l.1.c. 12. Soz hist. Eccl. l.1.c. 18.

this that *Eustachius* Patriarke of *Anthioch*, or as others saie, *Eusebius* Archbishop of *Cesarea*, made the oration of the Councell to the Emperor, and was sett at the head of the Bishops on the rigth hand in respect of the Emperor to whom his speeche was directed; it sufficeth to answere two things; the one, that the highest qualified were not chosen to preach the oration, but the most eloquent, amongst whom *Eustachius*, that *Sozomene* calls admirable in eloquence, held the first ranke; And the other, that the right hand at the coming in, and reckoning from the place where *Constantine* was, who had his backe turned towards the doore, and his face to the Fathers; at the first incounter of whom in coming from the doore, he staied, was not the most honorable place in the Councell, but the right hand at goeing forth; and to reckon from the place where the Ghospell was sett, as appeares by the order of the Councell of *Chalcedon* and of the Councell of *Constantinople*, holden vnder *Menas*, where the Presidents were sett at the left hand from the side where they came in, which was the right hand from the side of the Ghospell; and the others at the right hand. Idem l.2. c.18. Eufeb. de vit. Const. l.3.c.10. Cõc.Chalc Cõc. Cõst. sub Men. Act 1.& seqq.

Of the order of the sittings in the first Councell of Ephesus.

CHAPT. IX.

THE second obiection of *Caluin*, is taken from the first Councell of *Ephesus*, and couched by him in these wordes; *Att the first Councell of Ephesus*, saith Caluin, *Pope Celestin vsed an oblique practise, praying saint* CYLILL B*ishop of Alexandria, who otherwise was to preside there, to hold his place; And the Popes Ambassadors were there in an inferior place.* But with what oblique faith was this done? For first Pope *Celestine* had made saint CYRILL Patriarke of ALEXANDRIA his Vicar in the *East*, before anie Councell was spoken of to be kept at *Ephesus*, and had giuen him commission to execute at *Constantinople*, the iudgement pronounced at *Rome* against *Nestorius* Archbishop of *Constantinople*; *Adding to thee* (said Pope *Celestine* in his Epistle to saint CYRILL;) *the authoritie of our Sea, and vsing with power the representation of our place, thou shalt execute exactlie and constantly this Sentence; to witt, that if within ten daies, reckoned since the day of this monitory, Nestorius doe not anathematise by writing his wicked doctrines &c. thy holynes should prouide for that Church without delaie, and declare him to be wholie cutt off from our Bodie.* And in the Epistle to *Nestorius*, read and inserted into the Acts of the Councell: *Wee haue sent the forme of this iudgement with all the verball processe to our holy fellow-Bishop of* A*lexandria, to the end that he being made our Vicar, may execute these things.* And in the Epistle to the Clergie of *Constantinople*; *Wee haue conferred our Vicarship, because of the farr distance of places, to our holie brother* C*yrillus.* And the Councell of *Ephesus* in the relation to the Emperor; *The sentence of him and his before there was anie Synod assembled at Ephesus, the most holy* C*elestine* B*ishop of great Rome had testified by his letters, and had committed to the most holy and most beloued of* G*od,* C*yrill Bishop of* A*lexandria, to be his Vicar.* And saint CYRILL himselfe in the Epistle against *Nestorius*, addressed to the Inst.l.4.c.7 Côc.Ephes impress. Heidelb. c. 16. Ibid.c.17. Ibid.c.17 Ibib.c.65.

[Ibid c.15.] *Constantinopolitans; Wee are constrained* (said hee) *to signifie to him by Synodicall letters, that if verie speedilie, that is to saie, within the time defined by the most holy Bishop of the Roman Church, hee renounce not the nouelties of his doctrine, he shall haue noe more communion with vs, nor place amongst the Ministers of God?*

[Ibid. c. 65 Marcell. Com. in chron. Liberat. in Breuiar. l. 5 Theoph. hist. Eccl. ante Conc. Eph. imp. Heid. Basil. in Nomoc. Phot. tit. 8. c. 1. Niceph. hist. Eccl. l. 14. c. 34.] And secondly *Celestine* making saint CYRILL his vicar, it was by forme of commission, and not by forme of intreaty. *Hee committed to him* (saith the Councell of *Ephesus*) *to be his Vicar.* And *Marcellinus Comes* of the same tyme with *Iustinian; Nestorius was condemned at Ephesus in a Synod of two hundred holie Fathers, Celestine declaring to the Councell, Cyrill Bishop of Alexandria, his Vicar for the time.* And *Liberatus*, the African author of the same age: *Celestine signified to Nestorius that he had giuen his Vicarship to* CYRILLVS. And *Theophanes* the *Greeke*-historian; *Celestine of Rome writt to Cyrill of Alexandria to holde his place in the Synod.* And *Balsamon*, not onely a *Grecian* but a Scismaticke: *Celestine, when he could not assist at Ephesus, and iudge Nestorius in person, thought good to permitt saint* CYRILL, *to preside in his place at this Councell.* And *Nicephorus; Celestine Bishop of Rome refused to assist at the Councell of Ephesus, for the perill of the nauigation, but he writt to* CYRILL *to holde his place there; and after that time the fame goes, that Cyrill receaued the Tyara and the name of Pope, & of iudge of the whole world.*

And thirdly, who reuealed to *Caluin* that it was not, in the qualitie of the Popes Legats but in his owne name, that saint CYRILL presided in the Councell? For did not *Prosper* an author of the same tyme say, [Prosp. in Chron. Id. cont. Collat. Cōc. Ephes impress. Heid. c. 45.] *To the heresie of Nestorius,* CYRILLS *industrie, and Celestines authoritie principallie resisted.* And againe, *Celestine cutt of the Nestorian impietie, aided* CYRILL *with the Apostolicke sword.* And the letters of the Bishops, writing from *Constantinople* to the Councell; *Doe they not beare this superscription; To the most holie and beloued of God, Bishops and Fathers, who by Gods grace are assembled in the Metropolitan Cittie of Ephesus; Celestine Cyrillus Iuuenall, and others;* to shew that the Pope though absent, preceded saint CYRILL, euen in the person of saint CYRILL? And [Cōc. Ephes part. 1. Act. 2. Ep. Cyril. ad Celest. in Conc. Ephes. part 1. Conc. Eph. p. 1. Act. 1. in depos. Nestor. Socrat. hist Eccl. l. 1. c. 12.] did not the Popes legates thanke the Fathers of the Synod, because they had shewed themselues, *holie members to their holie head,* that is to saie, to the Pope. And saint CYCILL writing to Pope *Celestine*; Doth he not call him his Father, though himselfe were an ancienter Patriark by tenn yeare then Celestine? And did not the Councell in the Bodie of it make themselues executioners of the Popes Indgements against the same *Nestorius*, when they said; *Wee are come not without teares to pronounce this sadd sentence, constrained by the force of the Canons, and by the letters of our holy Father and fellow-Minister, Celestine?* And then if *Alexander* Bishop of *Alexandria*, had not presided at the Councell of *Nicea*, but was there preceeded by two simple priests of the Roman Church *Vito* and *Vincentius*, why should *saint* CYRILL one of his successors, and Patriarke of *Alexandria* as he was, and noe lesse enemie to *Nestorius* then *Alexander* was to *Arrius*, haue presided at that of *Ephesus*, a cittie that was in *Asia*, and out of the Patriarkship of *Alexandria*, as well as *Nicea* was? And if that appertained by right to saint CYRILL, for what cause did *Dioscorus* his Successor obtaine surreptitious letters from the Emperor vnder pretence of the refusall that *Eutyches* made of the Popes [Concil. Ephes. 2. lect. in Cōc Chalc Act. 1.] legates, forasmuch as they had bene intertained, feasted and gratified with presents by his aduersarie; that is to saie, by *Flauianus* Archbishop of *Constantinople* to preside at the false Councell of *Ephesus?* And for what cause, notwithstanding the said letter, was hee accused

for

for this attempt at the Councell of *Chalcedon*, as for a newe and vnheard of enterprize: *He must* (said Lucentius Bishop of *Ascoli*) *giue vp an accompt of his iudgement, forasmuch as hauing noe right to doe the Office of a Iudge, he hath vsurped it, and hath presumed to hold a Synod without the authoritie of the Sea Apostolicke, which hath neuer bene lawfull, neither was euer done?* And for what cause did the Councell of *Chalcedon*, call his presidencie *Tyrannie*; and *Victor* of *Tunes* author of the following age; *vsurped principalitie?* for whereas *Caluin* adds, that at the Councell of *Ephesus*, the other legates of the Pope, sate after saint CYRILL; that was, because saint CYRILL had bene first deputed, and before the Councell, and that the others came thither but at the end thereof; and besides, that amongst colleagues of one same legation, he that of himselfe was alreadie in greatest dignitie, was to precede.

Côc.Chalc Act.1.

Epist. Côcil. Chalc.ad Leon. pag. 25. Victor. Tun.in Consulat. Postumian. & Zenon.

Of the order of the sittings of the second Councell of Ephesus.

CHAPT. X.

THE third obiection of *Caluin* is; *That in the second Councell of Ephesus, Dioscorus Bishop of Alexandria presided; and that although the issue of this Councell was vnlawfull; neuerthelesse at the beginning when order was yet obserued, the Popes deputies did not question him for the first place*: An obiection that containes as manie falshoods as wordes: For first the second Councell of *Ephesus*, that the *Greekes* call the *Councell of robbery*, was all disordered from the beginning to the ending; *Those things shall cease* (said the lawe) *which haue taken their originall from iniustice*. And indeede, how could it be otherwise hauing begunn by practises, by Steele and weapons? for *Chrysaphius*, Master of the imperiall pallace, who was an *Eutychian*, and *Eutyches* his God-sonne, [a] sent thither from the beginning, [b] regiments of Souldiers, to authorise by force *Dioscorus* the abbettor of the *Eutychian* heresy, and to exclude from iudgement, all those that were suspected by *Eutyches*. Now *Eutyches* refused the Popes legats amongst others, aswell because the Pope had confirmed the sentence of *Flauianus* Bishop of *Constantinople* against him, as in their owne interest, because that being arriued at *Constantinople*, *Flauianus* that *Eutyches* held for his aduersarie, had entertained and feasted them; *The legates* (saith *Eutyches*) *sent by the most holie and most beloued of God the Archbishop of Rome, Leo, are suspected by me, for they haue bene entertained, and feasted, and gratified with presents by the most beloued of God the Bishop Flauianus*. For these causes then *Chrysaphius* desirous to exclude them from the iudgment of the Councell, obteyned by surprise letters from the Emperor *Theodosius* the second (a man that signed dispatches without reading them, wherefore his sister to reproach him for his simplicitie, once made him signe the bondage of his wife) by which, vnder colour of refusing those that had alreadie iudged *Eutyches*, he ordained *Dioscorus* to preside there, and accompained them with men of warr to haue the sway there. Now, how vnlawfull this beginning was, there needes noe other iudge but the same Emperor, who afterward informed of the deceipt that *Chrysaphius* had made vse of to him-ward, punisht him by exile and confiscation of goods and offices. And

Calu.inst. l.4.c.7.

Lex Valêt. & Marc. contra. 2. Concil. Ephes.in fin.Concil. Chalc.c.11 [a] Liber.in Breu. c.11. [b] Id.Ib.c. 12. Zonar.in Theod.2. Niceph.l. 14.c.47. Act.1. Côcil.Ephes.2 lecta in Concil. Chalc.Act. 1. Cedren. in Theod.2: [a] Epist. Theodos. ad Elpid & ad Diosc. lect in Côc Chalc.Act. 1.

[Cedrenus in Theod.l.] ſecondly where *Caluin* ſaith, that the Popes Legates did not diſpute for
the firſt place there, is manifeſtly falſe. For *Liberatus* an author of the
[Niceph.l. 14.c 49.] next inſuing age writes exppreſſely, *The Popes deputies would not indure*
[Liber.in] *to ſitt there becauſe the precedence had not bene giuen to their ſacred Sea.*
[Breu c. 12.] And when the Acts of the ſame Councell (all which *Dioſcorus* had
falſified) were read ouer in the Councell of *Chalcedon*, when they
came to name *Julian*, legate to Pope *Leo*; it was ſaid that the Act
[Concil. Chalc. Act 1.] was falſe, *and that the name of Leo, had not bene there receiued.* And
thirdly, the firſt complaint that the Popes Legates propounded to the
[Ibidem.] Councell of *Chalcedon* againſt *Dioſcorus*, was; *That he had preſumed to hold*
an Oecumenicall Councell without commiſsion from the Sea Apoſtolicke, which
had neuer bene either done, or lawfull to be done. And finally the primacie
that *Dioſcorus* had vſurped in the falſe Councell of *Epheſus*, though
by ſurreptitious letters from the Emperor, and vpon the refuſall of
the Popes Legates, was declared, *Tyrannie*, and himſelfe depoſed,
[Concil. Chalc. Act 5.] amongſt other cauſes, for hauing ſett vpon the Pope. *By the decrees of*
his tyrannie; (ſaid the Fathers of the Councell of *Chalcedon* writing to
[Ibidem ad Ibid.] Pope *Leo*) *he hath abſolued Eutyches, who for his impietie had bene condemned,*
and hath reſtored to him the dignitie whereof he was depriued by your Holyneſſe,
And a little after; *And to make vp all this, he hath extended his felonie, euen*
againſt him to whom the guarde of the Vine hath bene commited by our Lord, that
is to ſaie, againſt your Holyneſſe. Is not this a goodly example for *Caluin*
againſt the Pope?

Of the order of the ſittings of the Councell of Chalcedon.

CHAPT. XI.

[Iuſt.l. 4. c. 7.] CAluins fowrth obiection is taken from the Councell of
Chalcedon. In the Councell of Chalcedon (ſaith he) *Pope Leo asked*
it of Grace of the Emperor, that his Ambaſſadors might preſide there,
becauſe the Biſhops of the Eaſt who had preſided in the ſecond Councell
of Epheſus, had misbehaued themſelues there, and had abuſed their power:
And I for my part muſt needes aske him, how longe hee will abuſe
our patience? For Leo did nothing leſſe, then to pray the Emperor that
his deputies might preſide at the Councell of *Chalcedon*, but hauing
[a Leo. ep. 42.] ſent in the firſt month of the ſame yeare a legation to *Conſtantinople* of
Lucentius a Biſhop and *Baſilius* a prieſt;[a] and after haueing added to them
[Leo ep.47] vpon the occurrence of the celebration of the Councell *Paſchaſinus*
[Leo ep.39. & 54.] Biſhop of *Lylibea* in *Sicilia*; and hauing aſſociated with him *Iulian* a latine
Biſhop of the Iſle of *Cos* in the Grecian Sea, who was alreadie in
thoſe partes, and reſided as *Nuntio* at *Conſtantinople* with the Emperor; he declared to the Emperor not in forme of a requeſt, but in forme of
a reſolution, that it muſt be this *Paſchaſinus* Biſhop of *Lylibea*, of whoſe
ſufficiencie and conſtancie to maintaine the truth, he had more aſſurance
then of the reſt that ſhould preſide in his name at the Councell; as alſo he
was there the head of the legation, and carried the vote in the concluſion of the Coũcell, though he had bene laſt ſent. Now who ſeeth not that
this was not to demaund, that his legates might preſide there, but to

appoint which of his legates should preside there? I *haue* (said he) *sent my Brother and fellow-Bishop Paschasinus of the Prouince, which seemes to me most secure, that he may fulfill my place, and haue associated with him our brother and fellowe-Priest Boniface, comprehending with them, those that we had alreadie formerly sent; to whom I haue added for a Colleague the Bishop Iulian.* And a litle after; *Because some of our bretheren, a thing which we can not speake of without griefe, could not keepe their Catholicke Constancie, against the whirlewindes of falsehood, it is Conuenient that my said brother and fellowe-Bishop Paschasinus should preside in my place in the Synod.* For whereas *Caluin* saith, *That by those bretheren that could not maintaine their Cōstancie against the whirlwindes of falsehood*, he intended not the legates of the Pope which had withdrawne themselues, but the Bishops of the *East*, who had presided at the false Councell of *Ephesus*; to witt, *Dioscorus*; it is an ignorance that deserues the *Ferula*, since *Dioscorus* and his complices, were themselues the whirlewindes of falshood. And indeede why should Pope *Leo* in the Epistle that *Caluin* citeth of him which was written vnder the Consulship of *Adelphius*, haue prayed the Emperor that he might preside by himself, or by his legates at the Councell of *Chalcedon*, since from the precedent yeare, that is to saie, vnder the consulship of *Valentinian* and *Abienus*, and before it was knowne there should be anie Councell holden at *Chalcedon*, the Emperor had written to him; *Our desire is, that all impietie being banisht by a Councell assembled vnder your authoritie, an intire peace may be restored to all the Bishops of the Catholicke faith.* And againe, *It remaines, if it pleasse your Holynesse, that you trauell into these partes, and celebrate a Synod heere &c. or if it be troublesome to come hither, your Holynesse may please to signifie it by your letters*: Which *Theodorus Anagnostes* citing the same letters, repeates in these termes; *Marcian and Pulcheria writt to Leo Pope of Rome, yeilding to him all authoritie:* And how could he haue prayed the Emperor, since without attending the Emperors answere, and the next day after he had sent him the letter, he writt to the Councell: *The Emperor hath inuited vs by his letters, to cōtribute our presence at the reuerēd Synod, which the necessitie of time and Custome will not permitt; neuertheless, your brotherhoods may make account, that in these brothers of mine, Paschasinus and* Lucentius *Bishops, and Boniface and Basilius priests, sent from the Sea Apostolick, I doe preside in your Councell?* For the letter the Pope writt to the Emperor, was dated the sixth of the calends, of Iulie; and that he writt to the Councell, was dated the fifth. And why should he haue praied him, since in the secular confirmation of the Actes of the Councell, the same Emperor saith: *The Councell of Chalcedon hath examined matters of faith, by the authoritie of the* B*lessed* Leo *Bishop of the Cittie eternall in glorie Rome?* And why, since the Fathers of the Councell writt to the Pope; *Thou didst preside in the Councell, as the head to the members, exhibiting there thy good will by those that held thy place; And the faithfull Emperors presided there, for policie and ornament?* And why since the Emperor *Anastasius* a while after, pressing *Macedonius* Patriark of *Constantinople* to race out of the Rolle of his Church the name of the same Councell of *Chalcedon, Macedonius* answered him; *That he could not doe it without a generall* Councell *wherein the* Bishop *of great Rome did preside.*

Leo. Ep. 47.

Marcian. Imp ad Leon. ep. 33. in proœm. Concil. Chalc. Id. ep. 34. ib

Theodor. Anag. Collect. l. 1. ad calc. hist. Eccl. Theodor. in edit. Græc. Robert. Steph.

Leo ep. 45

Lex. Imp. Marcian in fiu Conc. Chalc.

Cōc. Chalc ep ad Leon. p. 3.

Theodor. Anagn. vbi supra. l. 2.

Of the order of the sittings of the fifth Councell of Constantinople.

CHAPT. XII.

Inst.l.4. c.7.

Caluins fifth obiection is, *That Menas presided at the, fifth Councell of Constantinople; And that the Pope being called thither, debated not the first place, but without anie difficultie, suffered Menas Patriarke of the place to preside.* Which is an obiection, wherein ignorances march by troupes. For first *Menas* was dead fiue yeares before, the fifth Councell of *Constantinople* was holden as appeares by the Acts of the sixth Councell of *Constantinople*, which say *Menas dyed the one and twentith yeare of the Empire of Iustinian: but the fifth Councell of Constantinople was holden the twentie seuenth.* And by *Victor* of *Tunes* an author of the same age, who, saith, *That the fifth Councell of Constantinople, was holden vnder Eutychius Successor to Menas*: And by the very Acts of the fifth generall Councell in all the Sessions whereof *Eutychius* is named, and not *Menas*. For what we haue from the Councell of *Constantinople* vnder *Menas*, are but particular acts and preambulatory to the Generall Councell, which was after holden vnder *Eutychius*, which hath giuen occasion to *Euagrius* and to *Nicephorus*, to mistake and to thinke that the fifth Councell of *Constantinople* had bene begun vnder *Menas* and finisht vnder *Eutychius*, as impertinently as the same *Euagrius* placeth *Epiphanius* betweene *Anthymus* and *Menas*, and maketh *Epiphanius* succeede *Anthymus*, whereas contrariwise he was his predecessor. And secondly Pope *Agapet*, who went to *Constantinople*, not to assist at anie Councell, but to treate a peace betweene the Emperor *Iustinian* and *Theodat* king of the *Gothes*, was dead, when the Councell of *Constantinople* holden vnder *Menas*, was celebrated; And by conseuqent had noe occasion to debate for the first place; and *Siluerius* his Successor in whose tyme this Councell was holden neuer was at *Constantinople*. And suppose *Agapet* had bene liuing and present at the Councell, how could *Menas* haue presumed to preside in his presence; hee that said in the same Councell; *Wee followe the Sea Apostolicke & obey it?* And who had bene made Patriarke of *Constantinople*, and his Predecessor *Anthymus*, deposed from the Patriarkship of *Constantinople* by Pope *Agapet*; And who calls Pope *Agapet*, *his Father of most holy memory?* And how would the Emperor *Iustinian* haue permitted it, he that said; *Wee will not suffer that anie thing shall passe concerning the estate of Churches, but what should be referred to the blessednesse of the holy Pope of old Rome; forasmuch as he is the head of the holie Prelates of God*: And againe; *Wee decree according to the definitions of the fower Councells, that the holie Pope of old Rome, be the first of all the Prelates; and wee ordaine, that the blessed Archbishop of Constantinople new Rome shall haue the second place after the holie Sea Apostolicke of old Rome, and shall preceede all the other Seas.* Also how would hee haue permitted it, hee that forsooke his great friend *Anthymus*, whom he had exalted from the Bishops Sea of *Trebysond*, to the Patriarkship of *Constantinople*, and suffered him to be deposed in his presence from the Patriarkship of *Constantinople* by Pope *Agapet*? *Wee know* (saith he lawe of the

Conc.œcu. 6.Act.3. Vict. Tun. in Chron. anno 13. post. Cons. Basil. Conc.5. œcum.Act. 1.2.3.4.& seqq. Euagr. hist Eccl.l.4.c. 36. Cõc. Cõst. sub.Men. Act.1. Menas.in Cõc. Cõst. Act.4. Marcel. Com in Chron. Men. in Cõc. Cõst. Act.4. Cod l.7. Iust.nouell 131.

Emperor

Emperor *Iustinian*) *that the same hath bene done to Anthymus, who hath bene deposed from the Sea of this Royall cittie, by the most holy Bishop of old-Rome Agapet of holy and glorious memorie, because that against all the sacred canons he had intruded himself into a Sea that appartained not to him.* For what hee adds presently after (*but he hath also bene deposed and condemned by the common sentence, first of that person of holy memorie, and then of the holie Synod heere celebrated, because he had straied from the right doctrine,*) hath reference not to the deposition of *Anthimus* of the Patriarkship of *Constantinople* as the Patriarke *Nicephorus* and *Cedrenus* supposed, authors farr from the age of *Iustinian*, but to the deposition of *Anthimus* from the Bishops Sea of *Trebisond*. Iust. nou. 42.

For the vnderstanding whereof, you must knowe, that there were two depositions of *Anthymus*, one from the Patriarkship of *Constantinople*, which was made and perfected by the Popes onely action, and wherein the Councell of *Constantinople*, whereof *Iustinian* speaketh, had noe hand; and the other from the Bishops Sea of *Trebyzond*, which was indeede begun by the Pope, who ordained, that if *Anthymus* did not purge himself of the heresie which was imputed to him, he should be deposed also from the Bishops Sea of *Trebisond*, which had bene reserued to him by the first deposition, and should be withall excommunicated and depriued of all Sacerdotall title, and of all Catholicke nomination. But because the Pope could not finish this second deposition, by reason death preuented him before he had the leasure to be fully cleered from the condition that was thereunto apposed, it was finished and executed in the Councell. This appeares by the Acts of the same Councell, whereof *Iustinian* speaketh, to witt, of the Councell of *Constantinople* holden by *Menas*; for the confirmation whereof, was published two moneths after, this lawe which is annexed to the end of the Councell. For the action that precedeth it, is the last, although it be first recited. *God* (saie the Regulars of *Syria*, in their petition to the Emperor, reported by the same Actes) *sent into this cittie Agapet, truly Agapet, that is to saie, beloued of God and man, Pope of old Rome, for the deposition of Anthymus, and of the foresaid hereticks, as heeretofore he sent great Peter to the Romans for the destruction of the witchcraft of Simon. This reuerend person then knowinge by the requests of many of ours, the thinges iniustly attempted vpon the Churches, and knowinge them by sight, would not so much as admitt into his presence Anthymus transgressor of the canons, but iustly deposed him from the Episcopall Sea of this cittie.* And a little after; *After the Bishops of Palestina assembled in this cittie, and the other Easterne Bishops, that is to saie, of the Patriarkships of Antioch and Ierusalem, and the deputies of the others Bishops, and we, did againe present petitions touching Anthymus and the other hereticks, and demaunded that Anthymus should certifie his belieue by libell to the Sea Apostolicke, and should purge himself from all hereticall errors, and in this case should returne to the Church of Trebisonde; or if he would not doe it, that he should be finallie condemned and deposed from all sacerdotall dignitie and action.* And a little beneath; *These our iust requests, the same most holy personage, to witt Agapet, preuenting them, and seeing Anthymus had failed to appeare, he condemned him with the foresaid hereticks, and despoyled him of all office and dignitie sacerdotall, and of all title orthodoxall, euen till the pennance of his errors.* And the Fathers of the Councell it self in the sentence of the Synod; *The blessed Pope Agapet of most holie and happie memorie, settinge with God his hand to the sacred canons, deposed Anthymus from the Sea which appartained not to him, pardonning those which had participated or communicated in this act*; that is to saie, *Peter* Patriarke of *Ierusalem*, and other of the *East*. And a little after; *But because that euen in doctrine, Anthymus was burdened with infinite accusations, and that manie petitions and supplications were presented against him, and by diuers*

Cōc Const sub Men. act. 1.

Conc sub Men. act. 1.

Ibid.

Ibid. act. 4.

Ibid.

by diuers reuerend personages to a most religious Emperor, and to the most blessed Pope; the same most blessed Pope, after much paine taken with a fatherly care, to call backe his soule &c. pronounced a sentence by writinge against him full of clemencie and seemely holynesse, grauntinge him time of repentance, and ordaining, that till he had changed his opinion, and satisfied the doctrines canonically defined by the Fathers, hee should neither haue the title of a Catholicke nor a Prelate. From whence it appeares, that the Pope had made two diuers depositions of *Anthymus*, and in two differinge tymes, one from the Patriarkship of *Constantinople*, and that grounded vpon discipline, because against the canons *Anthymus* was exalted from the Bishops Sea of *Trebisond*, to the Patriarkship of *Constantinople*. And the other from the Bishops Sea of *Trebisond*, which had bene reserued to him by the deposition from the Patriarkship of *Constantinople*, and that grounded vpon doctrine, because *Anthymus* was accused and defamed for heresie. But the difference that was betweene these two depositions, was that the first, I meane, that from the Patriarkship of *Constantinople*, was absolute and definitiue, and made and perfected by the Pope, without the helping hand of anie Councell. For whereas within the petition of the Bishops of the Patriarkships of *Antioch* and *Jerusalem* to the Pope, the latine interpreter hath vnaptly translated *Exossauimus Anthymum*, you must saie, *you haue cast forth Anthymus* ἐξοςρακίσαντας, and not ἐξοςρακίσαντες, as it appeares by this that follows; *And our Emperor hath participated in your good worke.* And the second; to wit, that from the Bishopricke of *Trebisond* was by prouision, and conditionall, and tempered with this clause *vntill pennance*, which left the sentence depending, and subiect to reuocation, in case that *Anthymus* should appeare and purge himselfe of heresie. Now the Pope died before he had leasure to attend whether *Anthimus* would come to repentance, and purge himself both of the contempt and of the heresie, which was imputed to him. For this cause then, the Councell of *Constantinople* holden vnder *Menas*, takinge it vp where the Pope left it, and making an end to fulfill all the formalities required to cleere the doubt of the condition, cited *Anthymus* againe, and seeing he appeared not, executed the second sentence of the Pope against him, and deposed him from the Bishopricke of *Trebizond*, and from all Sacerdotall and Catholicke title, but without touching in anie sorte the deposition alreadie made and perfected from the Patriarkship of *Constantinople*: *Wee* (saie the Fathers of the Councell) *followinge those thinges well examined by the blessed Pope, ordaine that he shall be cast out of the bodie of the holy Church of God, and despoyled of the Bishopricke of* Trebizond, *and depriued of all Sacerdotall dignitie and action, and according to the sentence of the most holy Pope of the appellation of Catholicke.* For whereas the narration of the sentence of the Councell, & the lawe of *Justinian* reporting the historie of the same sentence, places amongst the causes of *Anthymus* deposition, the transgression that he had made of the Canons in vsurping the Sea of *Constantinople*, that makes nothinge toward inferringe, that the deposition that the Councell decreed against him, should be the deposition of the Patriarkship of *Constantinople*; forasmuch as the Councell reported the memory of this vsurpation, not to depose him then from the Patriarkship of *Constantinople*, from which the same Councell testifies, that he had already bene entirely excluded; but to aggrauate the crime for which it would depose him from the Archbishoprike of *Trebizond*, to witt heresie, by a commemoration of his fore goeing crimes, as it appeares both from the disposition of the sentence of the same Councell, and from that of the sentence of *Menas* who presided there, and from the repetition which was made of it in the

Conc. sub Men. act. 1.

Ibid.

Côc. Const sub Men. act. 4.

Councell

Councell of *Ierusalem* holden vnder *Peter* Patriarke of *Ierusalem*: In all which places there is nothing spoken of, but the deposition of *Anthymus* from the Archbishopricke of *Trebizond*, and not from that of the Patriarkship of *Constantinople*. And indeede, how could the Councell of *Constantinople* where *Menas* presided, touch the deposition of *Anthymus* from the Patriarkship of *Constantinople*, and *Menas* vote there in qualitie of Patriarke of *Constantinople*, since *Menas* had bene promoted to the Patriarkship of *Constantinople* by the deposition of *Anthymus*? For of this all the ancient monuments are of agreement: *Agapet* (saie the *Syrians* to the Emperor) *hath iustly deposed Anthymus from the Episcopall Sea of the cittie of Constantinople; and with the helpe of your Imperiall authoritie cooperatinge and lendinge a hand to the diuine canons, haue proposed the holy Menas to the same Church.* And *Marcellinus Comes* of the same time with *Menas*: *Agapet beinge come from Rome to Constantinople, draue awaie soone after his arriuall Anthymus from the Church, sayinge, that accordinge to the Ecclesiasticall rule, he was an adulterer, because he had left his Church, and had packt for another, and ordained the Priest Menas Bishop in his place.* And *Liberatus* of the same time with *Marcellinus*: *The Empresse promisinge in secrett great presents to the Pope, if he would suffer Anthymus in his Sea; and on the other side tempting him with threates; the Pope persisted in not harkninge to her request; and Anthymus seeinge hee was cast out of his Sea, gaue vp the mantle that he had to the Emperors, and retired himself to a place, where the Empresse tooke him into her protection. And then the Pope in fauour of the Emperor, ordained Menas Bishop in his steede, consecrating him with his owne hand.* And *Victor* of *Tunes* of the same time with *Liberatus*: *Agapet Archbishop of Rome, came to Constantinople, and deposed Anthymus Bishop of Constantinople, vsurper of the Church, and enemie to the Councell of Chalcedon, and excommunicated the Empresse, and made Menas Bishop of the Church of Constantinople.* An admirable effect of the power of S. PETERS Successor in the time that the Church of *Constantinople* was most flourishing and triumphant, & the Church of *Rome* contrariwise, most abated & afflicted; when *Constantinople* was the Seate of the Empire, & the mansion of *Iustinian* the Emperor conquering and victorious; and that *Rome* on the other side was noe more a cittie, but a tombe and carkasse of a cittie, a seruant and slaue of the *Gothes* a barbarous and *Arrian* people, a poore Pope, that the tyrannie of *Theodat* king of the *Gothes*, who otherwise threatned him to roote out the *Roman* Church, had forced to transport himself into the *East*, to solicite the Emperor *Iustinian* to withdrawe his armes out of *Italie*; and so poore, as he was faine to sell the sacred Vessells of his Church, to performe his voyage, beeing in *Constantinople* a stranger and without support, yea euill receiued and entertained by the Emperor; neuerthelesse deposeth and casts out of his Sea, *Anthymus* Patriarke of *Constantinople*, powerfull in meanes and fauour about the Emperor, and whom the Emperor and the Empresse had exalted from the Bishopricke of *Trebizond* to the Patriarkship of *Constantinople*, and pardons the Bishops of the *East*, who had communicated with him; and excommunicates the Empresse, who obstinately defended him, and established *Menas* in his place: And *Caluin* will haue it, that *Menas* who was *Agapets* creature, preceded *Agapet* in the Councell of *Constantinople*, in whose time *Agapet* was already dead; and wherein there is neuer mention made of him, but with this title of *Agapet of holy memory*: What an *Argus* is he in antiquitie?

Cōc. Const sub Men. act. 1.

Marcell. Comes in Chron.

Liberat. in breuiar.c. 21.

Vict Tun. in Chron.

But, at the least will *Caluin* replie; the Bishops of *Italie* that assisted with *Menas* at the Councell of *Constantinople* after the death of *Agapet*, did not preside there. It is true: But what will this replie serue him for,

but

but to increase his shame? for these Bishops were noe more the Popes deputies when the Councell was holden, and had noe commission to be there, but were Bishops, Priests, and Deacons which were long before come out of *Italie* for other businesses, [b] and whose legation was finisht both by the arriuall and by the death of *Agapet*, and who assisted not at the Synod, which was noe generall Councell, but a simple councell of the Patriarkship of *Constantinople*, and of some strange Bishops resident at *Constantinople*; but for honor sake; and by vertue of the Emperors commaundement as exlegates, and not as Legates. Neither must he hope to escape by this excuse, that he pretended to speake of *Vigilius* and not of *Agapet*, for *Vigilius* was neither Pope nor present at *Constantinople*, when the councell of *Constantinople* holden vnder *Menas* was celebrated.

b. Conc. sub Men. act. 1. & seq.

Lesse yet can *Caluin* saue himselfe, by sayinge that his intention was to speake of the councell holden vnder *Eutychius*: for *Vigilius* who was then Pope, was neither present by himselfe, nor by his Legates, and consequently had not occasion to hold the second place; but confirmed it by writing: [c] *Vigilius* (saith *Euagrius*) [d] *consented by letters with the Councell*: And *Photius*; [e] *Vigilius approued by writing, the faith of the Fathers*. And that he refused to assist there, it was not (as *Nicephorus* a Schismaticall author [f] and later by manie ages pretends) *because hee disdayned to receiue the Bishop of Constantinople into one Seate with him, that is to saie, that he would haue sate in a seate more exalted*. For how should that haue bene put in dispute, since the same *Nicephorus* saith, [g] *it had bene practised twentie eight yeares before by Pope John, who had sate within Constantinople in a throne exalted aboue Epiphanius Patriarke of the place, and that* (adds he) [h] *not to abandon the prerogatiue of the Sea Apostolicke*, But forasmuch as he sawe the Emperor resolute to cause the three chapters to be condemned, so were called certaine writinges of *Theodorus* of *Mopsuestia*, of *Ibas*, and of *Theodoret*, which had bene read in the councell of *Chalcedon*, and feared that if this condemnation should be made, the Bishops of the Prouinces of the *West* not being present, it might begett a schisme betweene those of the *West*, and those of the *East*. For those of the *West* held, that to condemne those three chapters, it was to giue aduantage to the *Eutychians*, and to make a breach in the Councell of *Chalcedon*, who had receiued into their communion, *Ibas* and *Theodoret* authors of those writinges and defendor of *Theodorus* of *Mopsuestia*; and those of the *East* contrarywise held, that to maintaine them, was to giue aduantage to the *Nestorians*, and to oppose the Councell of *Ephesus*, which had condemned the doctrine therein contained, and denied that to censure them, was to doe wronge to the Councell of *Chalcedon*, who had indeede receiued *Theodoret* and *Ibas* into their communion, but after they had made them detest the doctrine of *Nestorius*. For this occasion, though Pope *Vigilius* in his particuler condemned these three chapters, yet he would not assist at a Councell, wherein they should goe about to condemne them publicklie, vnlesse it had bene a generall Councell, and wherein the Bishops of the *West* had bene present, aswell as those of the *East*: And he admitted not the reason alleadged by the Legates of the Councell, that in the other generall Councells there had bene fewe Bishops of the *West*, forasmuch as those fewe Bishops of the *West* which had bene in other generall Councells, went thither after Councells holden vpon the same matter in the *West*, whose resolution they bearing with them, they carried the voice of all the westerne Church into the *East*.

c. Concil. Const. 6. act. 18.
d. Euagr. hist. Eccl. l. 4. c. 37.
e. Phot. de sept Synod
f. Niceph. hist. Eccl. l. 17. c. 27.
g. Id. c. 9.
h. Ibid.

Conc. 5. act. 7. & 8.

Conc. 5. act. 2. in relat. Legator. Conc.

To this feare there concurred also that that *Vigilius* had to renew the opinion that was held of him during his Antipapacie, I saie during his

Antipapacie, because in the beginning *Vigilius* was intruded into the Papacie by the priuate sute of the Empresse, who was an *Eutychian*, his predecessor *Siluerius* a true and lawfull Pope, *a* still liuing, & with this simoniacall and hereticall couenant not onely to condemne the three chapters, but to approue the faith of *Anthymus*; which he did; and therefore sometymes as false Pope, and sometymes as an abettor of heretickes, he was excommunicated by the true Pope *Siluerius*, *b* and by the Bishops that adhered to him, and amongst others by the Prelates of *Africa*. *c* For those that suspect that *Liberatus*, *d* the most exact monument that we haue of antiquity hath bene depraued in the fall of *Vigilius*, are mistaken; seeing *Victor* of *Tunes*, *e* time-fellowe of them both, recites the same historie; but after, *Siluerius* being dead, and *Vigilius* hauing bene for the good of peace accepted by the election of the clergie of *Rome*, he became true Pope, and then so farr was he from communicating with *Anthymus*, that contrarywise he rather chose to suffer all kinde of disgraces, then to consent to it; yea, he went so farr, as to condemne the same Empresse, who had exalted him to the Papacy, as S. GREGORIE testifies in these words: *f* *The Pope Vigilius constituted in the royall cittie*, (that is to saie, at *Constantinople*) *published a sentence of condemnation against Theodora then Empresse, and against the Acephales.*

a. Liber. in breuiar. c. 22.
b. Syluer. ep. ad Vigil
c. Victor Tun. qui Chronic.
d. Laurent. Sur. in not. ad Liber.
e. Victor in Chron. an. 2. post Consul. Basil.
f. Greg. l. 2. indict. 10. epist. 36. Paul. Diac. siue Theophan. hist. l. 17. & alij.

This then was the cause why *Vigilius* assisted not at the fift Councell, but if he had assisted there, who doubtes but he had presided, since the letters that *Eutychius* Patriarke of *Constantinople* writt to him to obtaine the celebration of the Councell, imported thus much: *Wee require that your Blessednesse presiding ouer vs vnder the Sacerdotall tranquilitie and meekenes, the holie Ghospell being sett in the middle* (which was a forme of obligation by oath, to vote according to conscience) *the three chapters which are in question, may bee examined?* Well doe I knowe that the minister *Iunius* would correct these words; *presidente nobis vestrâ beatitudine*; and change them into these, *residente nobiscum vestrâ beatitudine*. But who seeth not, this is a corruption, and noe correction? For besides that this clause, *vnder the Sacerdotall quiet and peace*, presuppose *presidency*, and not simple *residency*, doth not the Pope repeate the request of *Eutychius* in these words: *Your brotherhood hath required that we presiding (vobis præsidentibus) the three chapters might be examined?* And after when the Councell deputed all the Patriarkes who were there in person, *Eutychius* Patriarke of *Constantinople*, *g* *Apollinarius* Patriarke of *Alexandria*, *Domnus* Patriarke of *Antioch*, and seauenteene of the principall Metropolitans with them to the Pope, to beseeche him to assist at the Councell: is it not enough to testifie, that they acknowledged the Pope for the Chiefe of the Patriarkes, and that if he had assisted at the Councell, he had presided there? And when the Emperor *Iustinian* writes to the Bishops of the Councell of *Mopsuestia*, that they should informe what had past about the rasure of the name of *Theodorus* of *Mopsuestia*, from the recordes of his Church, and adds; *And sendes two relations thereof, one to vs, and the other to the most holy Pope*: Is not this enough to testifie, that if the Pope had bene at the Councell, he had presided there? And when the fift Councell it selfe inserts within the acts thereof, the relation of the Councell of *Mopsuestia* to the Pope, and inrolles it in these words; *They made also a relation to the most holie Pope Vigilius which contained these words*; *It is verie conuenient, ô most holies*, (so called they the Pope in the plurall number, to giue him the more respect) *since you holde the first dignitie of the priesthood, that those things which concerne the state of the holy Churches, should be represented to your diuinely honored Blessednesse.* Is it not enough to testifie, that the Pope had primacie ouer all the other Bishops,

Concil. 5. act. 1.
Ibid. act. 5. in histor. Concilij Mopsuest.
g. Conc. 5. act. 1.
Ibid. act. 5.
Ibid.

and that if he had bene at the Councel, he had presided there? And when *Marcellinus Comes* an author of the same age, saith; that within the cathedrall Church of *Constantinople*, where the Patriarke of *Constantinople* should principallie keepe his ranke, Pope *John* predecessor to *Agapet*, was sett at the right hand, that is to saie, at the right hand in regard of the altar, and within the right Tribunall of the Church; *dexter dextro insedit Ecclesiæ solio*: And if wee believe *Nicephorus*, in a seate more eminent and exalted. Is not this enough to shewe, that if the Pope had assisted at the councell of *Constantinople*, he had presided there? And when the Greeke historians reporte, that *Macedonius* Patriark of *Constantinople*, who lived forty yeares before the fift generall Councell, findinge himself pressed by the Emperor *Anastasius* to blott out of the recordes of his Church, the name of the coũcell of *Chalcedon*, answered, *That he could not doe it, without a generall Councell, wherein the Bishop of great Rome should preside*: Is not this enough to testifie, that if the Pope *Vigilius* had assisted at the Councell, he had presided there? And when the Emperor *Justinian* himself, who caused the Councell to be celebrated, saith; *Wee ordaine according to the definitions of the fower holie Councells, that the most holie Pope of old Rome, should be first of all the Prelates; and that the blessed Archbishop of Constantinople, should be the second after the holy Sea Apostolicke of old Rome, and should precede all the other Seas*. And elsewhere; *The Pope is the head of all the holie Prelates of God*: Is it not enough to shew, that if the Pope had bene at the Councell, he had presided there?

Theodor. Anagnost. Collect. l. 2. ad calcẽ hist. Eccl. Theod. in edit. græc. Robert. Steph. Iust. nou. 151. Cod. tit. 1. l. 7. impr. Parif. Antuerp. & Geneu.

But the Councell (saie the Popes adversaries) was celebrated notwithstanding the Pope was neither at it by himselfe, nor by his deputies. It is true, forasmuch as the Fathers of the Councell had alreadie drawne a writing from the Pope, whereby he had promised them to consent to the holding of a regular Councell, that is to saie, compleate, and to assist at it: *Wee agree* (said hee) *that assembling a regular Councell, equitie being observed, and the sacred holy Ghospells being sett in the middle, we united with our bretheren will conferr of the three chapters*. But those that make this observation, add yet fiue more to it; the first, that it was not held for generall, but since the Pope confirmed it; & that while it was celebrated, although all the other Patriarkes assisted at it either personally or representatiuely; in anie of the acts, it neuer tooke the title of Generall. *Vigilius* (saie the Fathers of the sixth generall Councell) *consented to Iustinian; and the fift Councell was established*. The second, that howsoeuer Pope *Vigilius* refused to be there, although he was in *Constantinople* itselfe and vnder *Justinians* halberds, the Councell neuer past to proceede against him. The third, that the great African light *Primasius* Bishop of *Adrumeta*, whose writinges doe to this day illustrate the Catholicke Church, being within *Constantinople*, and being cited by the Councell to assist at it, preferred the Popes authoritie before the citations of the Councell, & answered those that summond him from the Councell; *The Pope not being there present, I will not goe*. The fourth, that the strongest and last persuasion that the Emperor vsed to the councell, to dispose them to the condemnation of the three chapters, was to send them particular writinges of Pope *Vigilius*, whereby he had condemned them. And the fifth, that till three or fower Popes after *Vigilius*, whose intention was a long while called in question; *Pelagius*, S. GREGORIE, and *Sergius* had confirmed this councell, there were both in the *West* and *East* so many schismes and oppositions against it, and so manie Bishops and councells, that supposed that it was to gaine the crowne of martirdome, to dye for resisting it; some believing Pope *Vigilius* neuer confirmed it, and others believing that Pope *Vigilius* who was said to confirme it, was not true Pope, forasmuch as he had in-

Concil. 5. act. 1.

Cõc. Const œcumen. 6. act. 18.

Concil. 5. act. 2.

Ibid. act. 7.

truded into the Papacy, his predeceſſor being yet liuing, that whatſoeuer threatnings, banishments and puniſhment the Emperor *Juſtinian* employed vpon it hee could neuer compaſſe it, neither hee nor his next ſucceſſors; but this is enough for this obiection of *Caluin*, let vs goe on to the reſt.

Of the order of the ſittings in the ſixth Councell of Carthage.

CHAPT. XIII.

Aluins ſixt obiection is taken from the ſixth Councell of Carthage: *In the ſixth Councell of Carthage* (ſaith *Caluin*) [a] *Aurelius Archbishop of the cittie preſided, and not the Ambaſſadors of the Sea of Rome.* Now wee might ſend him to diſpute this matter with *Hincmarus* Archbishop of *Rheims* of almoſt eight hundred yeares antiquitie who ſaid contrarywiſe, ſpeaking of the ſixth Councell of Carthage: [b] *The Councell of Carthage where the Sea Apoſtolicke preſided by his Vicars.* Neuertheleſſe leaſt it should ſeeme to be a delaie, the beſt will be to trie it out in the field. To this obiection then wee will bring three anſweres; the firſt that there is nothing more vncertaine then the Rolles of the ſittings, and ſignatures of Councells, where the copies varie and miſtake at euery turne, ſometymes following the order of the perſons ſending, ſomtymes the order of the perſons ſent, ſomtymes the order of the tyme of their arriuall, ſomtymes the errors in the writing which ſlipp in, in the tranſcription of liſtes and Catalogues as it appeares, beſides an hundred other proofes by the repetition of one of the Seſſions of the firſt Councell of *Epheſus*, inſerted into the latine copie of the Councell of *Chalcedon*, in which *Arcadius*, *Proiectus* and *Phillippus*, the Popes legates, [a] are named, not onely after all the Bishops, but euen after *Beſſula* Deacon and legate of *Carthage*, which was the order of the tyme of their arriuall; and neuertheleſſe, the greeke originall of the ſame Councell of *Epheſus*, placeth them in all the Seſſions whereat they aſſiſted immediately after ſaint CYRILL firſt legate of the Pope; and as it appeares by the thing itſelfe which is preſented by the teſtimony of *Hincmarus*; for *Hincmarus* affirmes particularly, that the Sea Apoſtolicke preſided by legates, at the Councell of *Carthage*, in theſe words; [b] *The Councell of Carthage where the Sea Apoſtolicke preſided by Vicars.* The ſecond that there where diuers kindes of legates, ſome which repreſented the negotiating perſon of the Pope, as Procurators, Agents, Nuntios, Apocriſaries, and Ambaſſadors; and others, which repreſented the iudiciary perſon of the Pope, as Cathedraticall Vicars and legates, a kinde onely neceſſary for generall Councells, where the Bodie of the Church ſpeakes with her head, and not for particular Councells, as this of *Carthage* was. Now amongſt theſe deputies, ſome held the ranke of thoſe that ſent them, and others not, for in the Councell of *Chalcedon*, [c] *Iuſtinian* Biſhop of *Cos*, legat or rather *Nuntio* and Ambaſſador from the Pope to *Conſtantinople*, although he bore the title of the Pope legate at the Councell, neuertheleſſe ſate not with the other legates of the Pope, but after the Patriarkes and among the Bishops; and at the Councell of *Conſtantinople* holden vnder *Menas*, the Ambaſſadors of the Patriarkes of *Antioch* and *Ieruſalem* were not ſett in

[a] Inſt. l. c. 7.

[b] Hincmar. ep. ad Nicol. apud Flodoard. hiſt. Eccl. Rem. l. 3.

[a] Concil. Chalc. Act. 1.

[b] Hincmar vbi ſupra.

[c] Concil Chalc. Act. 1. & ſeqq.

a Conc. Const. sub. Men. Act. 1 2. 3. & 4.

b Conc. Carth. 6. c. 6. & 5.

c Conc. Afric. c. 100.

the ranke of their *Patriarkes*, but in the ranke of their simple personall dignitie, and after the Archbishops and Bishops. a And the third Answere finally is, that in the sixth Councell of *Carthage*, the legation of the Popes deputies was finished by the death of *Sozimus*, who had sent them the yeare before, and had not bene renewed by *Boniface* his Successor, whose creation they knewe well, for they procured b and charged themselues c to carry him the Councells letters, but they had not yet receiued anie commission from him, and treated onely vpon the memories that they had brought from his predecessor. By meanes whereof, they were noe more the Popes legates, but *Exlegates*, continuing neuertheles in office to solicite for the rights of the Roman Church that they had begun in the former Councell; and for this cause bearing for honor sake in the signatures, the title of the Legates of the Roman Church, but not the title of legates or Vicars of Pope *Boniface* then sitting. And indeede if they had bene then, in the actuall qualitie of the Popes Vicars, and Cathedraticall Vicars; that is to saie, representing the iudiciary person of the Pope, they had bene sett one with an other, and had all signed in the ranke of Bishops. Now this was not soe, for *Faustinus* Archbishop of *Potentia* assisted but in his simple ranke of Archbishop, belowe *Aurelius* Archbishop of *Carthage* and *Valentine* Archbishop of *Numidia*, and *Phillippus* and *Asellus* were not there in the ranke of Bishops; but sate and signed as simple priests after all the Bishops; where as in the Councell of *Ephesus* which was generall, the same *Phillip* priest d as Vicar, deputed to represent the iudiciarie person of the Pope, was set with saint CYRILL and *Arcadius* likewise the Popes legates before all the other Primates, Archbishops, and Bishops. It it true that *Faustinus*, *Phillippus*, and *Asellus*, had bene either nuntios or legates to Pope *Sozimus* in a Councell holden the yeare before at *Carthage* vnder the twelfth consulship of *Honorius* and the eigth of *Theodosius* as it appeares from the discourse and from the Epistle of the sixth Councell of *Carthage*, but of this Councell (for that which is inserted vnder the date of the same consulls in the Rapsodie of the Councells of *Africa* speakes not of the Popes legates) there remaines to vs noe piece whereby wee may iudge whether the Popes agents presided, or presided not; onely it appeares, that the authority of the Pope was very eminent there, for it was sent to *Rome* and confirmed by the Pope, as *Prosper* an author of the same age testifies in these words: e *Vnder the* 12th. *Consulship of* Honorius, *and the eigth of Theodosius*, *a* Councell *of two hundred and fourteen Bishops, hauing bene holden at Carthage, the Synodicall decrees were carried to Pope* Sozimus. *which hauing bene approued by him the heresie of Pelagius was condemned throughout the world.* And againe; f *Pope Zosimus annexed to the decrees of the African Councells, the force of his sentence, and for the extirpation of the wicked, armed the right hand of all the Prelates, with the sworde of Peter.*

d Conc. Ephes. impress. Hejd. Act. 1. & Rom. Act. 4.

e Prosp. in Chron.

f Id cont. Collat.

Of the order of the sittings in the Councell of Aquilea.

CHAPT. XIV.

THE seauenth obiection of *Caluin* is, *That there was a generall Councell kept euen in Italie, to witt,* (adds hee) *the Councell of Aquilea, wherein saint AMBROSE presided for the credit that he had with the Emperor.* Now this obiection, is the crowne & master-piece of all *Caluins* obiections for matter of impertinency: For first S. AMBROSE did not preside there, but *Valerianus* Bishop of *Aquilea*; the Bishop of *Milan* and the Bishop of *Aquilea* hauing bene in such sorte equalls & paralells vntill the tyme of *Iustinian*, as when the Bishopricke of *Milan* was vacant, as Pope *Pelagius* the first tyme-fellowe to *Iustinian* notes it, the Bishop of *Aquilea* ordained him of *Milan*: And when the Bishopricke of *Aquilea* was vacant, the Bishop of *Milan* ordained him of *Aquilea*; by meanes whereof, each of them in his Diocesse had his ranke before the other, and in anie third place, the ancienter of the two preceded, as at the Councell of *Rome*, S. AMBROSE preceded *Valerian*, and at the Councell of *Aquilea*, *Valerian* preceded S. AMBROSE. It is true S. AMBROSE disputed there more then the rest because of his learning: And *Aurelius* Bishop of *Bologna* after him which deceiued the author of *Synodica*, publisht by the Minister *Pappus* a greeke author & meanely instructed in latine affaires, & many others with him. But he presided not there, if we giue credit to the actes of the Councell, which are couched in these termes; *Vnder the consulship of Eucherius and Euagrius in the nones of September, there were sett in the Church of Aquilea, Valerian, Ambrose, Eusebius, Limenius and others.* And then if he had presided there to what purpose was it to interpret that it was for the fauour the Emperor bore him. Was not S. AMBROSE an Archbishop, & Archbishop of *Milan*, a cittie saith S. ATHANASIUS, *metropolitan of Italie*, that is to saie, not of all *Italie*, but of that part of *Italie* which was subiect to the pretoriall Prefect of *Italie*, and which was particularly called *Italie*, to distinguish it frõ the prouinces subiect to the Prouost or Vicar of *Rome*? and therefore what meruaile had it bene, that the Councell of *Aquilea* being celebrated in the metropolitan cittie of *Istria*, which was one of the prouinces of *Italie*, and subiect to the Vicar of *Italie*, that is to saie, to the Vicar of the Prouost of the Pretory of *Italie* in *Italie*, and the Pope not being there, neither by himselfe, nor his Legates, if S. AMBROSE, who was both the most ancient Archbishop, & the Archbishop of *Milan*, metropolitã of *Italie* had presided there? And secondly the councell of *Aquilea* which lasted but halfe a day, was not a generall councell, but a particular Councell, compounded onely of the Bishops of *Lombardie* & of *Prouence*, & of one Bishop of *Illiria*, and of some deputies of *Africa*, & of the *Gaules*: for there were in all but thirtie Bishops, amongst which there was but one onely Legat, neither of the Pope, nor of the other Patriarks. Now how could it be generall if there were noe Bishop of the *East*, nor any Patriark nor Patriarkes Legat? Nay how could it be generall, since the onely reason that *Palladius* the hereticke made, that he would not answere there was, that it was not a generall Councell? *Wee haue promised* (said hee) *that wee will proue that we are Christians, but in a generall Councell; wee answere you not, least wee should preiudice a future Councell.* Nay, how could it haue bene vniuersall, since the Fathers of the Councell themselues confessed in their Epistle to the Emperor; *That is was not reasonable that for two wretched hereticks, the Churches of the whole world should be abandoned*

Calu. inst. l. 4. c. 7.

Pelag. Pap. 1. apud Grat. c. 24 q. 1.

Act. Conc. Aquil.

Athan. ad solit. vit. agent.

Act. Conc. Aquil.

Ibidem.

by their Bishops? Nay how could it haue bene generall; since the same yeare the generall Councell of *Constantinople* was celebrated? for the Councel of *Aquilea* was held in September vnder the consulship of *Euagrius* and *Eucherius*; and the Councell of *Constantinople* was assembled the same yeare, not in the month of May as *Socrates* and those that haue followed him haue conceiued, but vpon the end of Autumne as it appeares by the words lately cited from *Palladius*, and by the verie epistle of the Councell of *Constantinople* to the Pope, n where the Fathers testified, that the Councell of *Constantinople* had bene called after the holding of that of *Aquilea*. It is true it had bene proiected at the beginning to haue holden a larger Councell at *Aquilea*, but because the aduersaries were not iudged worthie that for them there should be called a quantitie of Bishops necessarie neither for a generall Councell, nor for a Patriarchall Councell, the Pope not onely abstained from sending, but also presently after the celebration of the Councell of *Aquilea*, as being nothing lesse then vniuersall, set himselfe to cause a generall Councell to be celebrated; and to this effect called by his letters addressed to the Emperor *Theodosius*, the Bishops of the *East* to the Councell of *Constantinople*; Witnesse these wordes of the same Bishops to Pope *Damasus*; o *Wee were come to Constantinople at the arriuall of the letters from your Reuerence sent after the Councell of Aquilea to the most religious Emperor;* And held himselfe a Councell of the Bishops of the *West* at *Rome*, where assisted the chiefe of those that had bene at *Aquilea*; And amongst others saint AMBROSE Archbishop of *Milan* and *Valerianus* Archbishop of *Aquilea*; and in the which presiding, he approued what had bene done at *Constantinople*; and by this approbation, made the Councell of *Constantinople* œcumenicall. For whereas it is obiected that in this concourse of Councells it was not the Councell of *Rome* whereat the Pope was present, that obteyned the title of a Generall Councell, but the Councell of *Constantinople*; It sufficeth to saie, that it was because the Simbole of faith which was published there against *Macedonius*, was composed in the Councell of *Constantinople*, whereat there assisted the Bishops of the Prouinces, where the question was disputed and was but confirmed, and not composed at the Councell of *Rome*; and that the Councells œcumenicall by concourse tooke their name from the place where the Simbole of the Faith was composed, and not from the place where it was onely confirmed.

n *Theod. hist. Eccl. l. 5. c. 9.*

o *Theod. hist. Eccl. l. 5. c. 9.*

Of the calling of Councells.

CHAPT. XV.

THere followeth the calling of Councells, that *Caluin* affirmes to haue bene onely done by the Emperors: *The Generall Councell* (saith Caluin) a *was neuer declared but by the Emperor, and the Bishops were called by his authoritie.* Now from whence doth he inferre this? Vpon this, that the Councells bare on their brow the conuocations of the Emperors. Fine and subtile logique!

a *Caluin. Inst. l. 4. c. 9.*

as if it had bene an incompatible thinge that the Emperors should call the councells, in regard of temporall authoritie, to make them obligatorie to the secular Tribunall, and executory by the ministrie of the officers of the Emperor, and to take away the crime of treason and the hinderance of politicke lawes, which forbad them to make anie assemblies, b but with permission of the Emperors; And that the Popes (*without whom* (said *Socrates*) c *the Churches cannot be ruled*; or according to the translation of *Epiphanius* followed by *Cassiodorus*, d *the councells cannot be celebrated*) should call them in regard of spirituall and Ecclesiasticall authority. But rather, as if it had not bene a thing perpetually vsed and practised, that the spirituall authoritie of the Popes, should be required with the temporall authoritie of the Emperors; that is to saie, that there were two conuocations of Councells; the one Ecclesiasticall to make them obligatorie in conscience, and spirituallie; and the other Politicke, to make them executory by the secular arme, and temporally.

b. D. de collegijs illicitis.l.1. c.Soc. hist. Eccl.l. 2.c. 8. d.Hist. tripart.l.4.c. 9.

For first, as for the ensigne bearer and forerunner of all the generall Councells, which is that of *Nicea*, the Fathers of the third generall Councell of *Constantinople*, otherwise called the sixth generall Councell, Greeke Fathers, as hath bene alreadie often noted, of neere a thousand yeares antiquitie, and inlightned by manie histories that tyme hath subtracted from vs, did they not saie; *The most sacred Constantine, and the praise worthie Siluester, called the famous councell of Nicea?* And as for the Councell of *Sardica*, which was the appendix and supplie of that of *Nicea*, the demaund that *Eusebius* of *Nicomedia* head of the Arrian faction made after the Councell of *Antioch* to Pope *Julius* of a Councell which since it could not be generall at *Rome*, was afterward appointed at *Sardica*; and the complaint of those that blamed the same *Julius* for the little tyme that was giuen them to assemble at *Sardica*, doth it not teach vs, that the Pope had cooperated with the Emperors in the calling the Councell of *Sardica*: *Eusebius* (saith S. ATHANASIVS) *and his writt to Iulius, and to amaze vs, required that he would calle a Councell*: For you must reade there with the greeke text, *that he would call a Councell*; and not with the latine translation, *that a Councell might be called*. And againe, e *Iulius writt backe, that there should be a councell held where we would*. And the same *Julius* reported by S. ATHANASIVS; *Your deputies* (said he, answering the *Eusebians*) f *haue solicited me to call a Councell, and to write to Athanasius into Alexandria, and to those of the Eusebian partie, to the end that in the presence of all, the cause might be defined in iust iudgement*. And *Socrates*; g *There was a generall Councell published at Sardica a cittie of Illyria by the ordinance of the two Emperors*. And a little after; *Others complained of the breuitie of the tyme*, h *and laide the blame vpon Julius Bishop of Rome*. Which *Harmenopolus* himselfe, though a late greeke and a schismaticke, acknowledgeth in these words; *By the aduise of the Emperors, and of the Bishops of Rome, there assembled a Councell of three hundred forty one holy Fathers at Sardica, which confirmed the Councell of Nicea*. For that he accounts not the Councell of *Sardica* for vniuersall, because the *Arrians* separated themselues from it, makes nothing to the purpose of the conuocation, which at least was vniuersall. *There was* (said *Socrates*) *a generall Councell published*.

Concil. oecumen. 6. act. 18.

Athan. de fuga sua Apol.

e. Idem ad solit. f. Id. apol. 2.

g. Soc. l. 2. c. 20. h. Ibid.

Harm. in epitom. can

And as for the Councell of *Constantinople*, these words of the epistle of the Bishops of *Constantinople* to Pope *Damasus*, and to the Synod of *Rome*, celebrating by the will of God the Synod of *Rome*; *You haue called vs with a brotherlie Charitie, as your owne members, by the letters*

Theodor. hist. Eccl. l. 5. c. 9.

Theodor. hist. Eccl. l. 5. c. 9.

of the most Religious Emperor: And a little after; *But the execution of this desire was impossible to manie, for we were gone to Constantinople vpon your Dignities letters sent the yeare last past, after the councell of Aquilea, to the most religious Emperor Theodosius;* Doe they not sufficiently demonstrate, that Pope *Damasus* by his letters written the yeare before; that is to saie, before the Synod of *Rome*, and when he was yet alone, had concurred with the Emperor, or rather the Emperor with him, for the calling the Councell of *Constantinople*, and for the first councell of *Ephesus*, which onely of the name, deserues the title of councell (for the second was excluded from the ranke of councells.) Doe not those wordes of *Liberatus* Archdeacon of *Carthage*, an African Author, and of neere a thosand one hundred yeares antiquitie; *Cyrill with his, prouided with the Vicarship of the Sea Apostolicke, hauing called a Councell of two hundred Bishops cited Nestorius:* Doe they not testifie that it had bene called at the instance, and with the cooperation of S. CYRILL Patriarke of *Alexandria*, alreadie before made Vicar and executor of the Popes authoritie in the *East*?

Liberat. in breuiar. c. 5

And as for the councell of *Chalcedon* these declarations of the Emperor *Martian* to Pope LEO, when there was a question of holding the councell afterward transferred to *Chalcedon*; a *Our desire is; that all impietie being banisht by this councell celebrated vnder your authoritie, an entire peace may be restoredto the Bishops of the Catholicke faith:* And againe; b *There rests, if it please your Holynesse that you come into these partes, and heere celebrate the Synod, that you will daigne to doe it for the zeale of Religion.* And a little after; *Or if it, be burdensome to you, to come hither, that you will signifie it to vs by your letters that we maie dispatch our sacred Patents into the East, and into Thracia and Illiria, that all the most holie Bishops may assemble in some such place as shall seeme good to vs, and decree by their sentences, things profitable to Christian Religion and Catholicke faith, as your Holinesse according to Ecclesiasticall rules hath defined it.* And these of the same LEO; *It hath pleased, both to the ordinance of the most Religious Emperors and to the consent of the Sea Apostolicke, that the generall councell of Chalcedon should be called.* And these of the Bishops of the second *Mœsia*, to the Emperor *Leo*, translated from greeke into latine by *Epiphanius*, at the instance of *Cassiodorus*; *The faith of the incarnation of our Sauiour, hath bene confirmed by manie Bishops assembled by the commaundement of the Roman Pope Leo, who is trulie head of Bishops and of Anatolius Patriarke of Constantinople, in a councell celebrated vnder the two Emperors:* Doe they not euidentlie proue, that Pope LEO cooperated with the Emperors for the calling of the councell of *Chalcedon*?

a. Concil. Chalc. p. 1.
b. Ibid.
Ibid.
Epist. 59.
Cassiod. de diuin. lect. c. 11.
Ep. Episc. Mœs. pro Cōc. Chalc

And for the second generall councell of *Constantinople*, which we call the fifth generall councell; this answere of the Pope *Vigilius* to the letters of the Patriarke of *Constantinople*; *Hauing knowne your desire by your demaunds; wee agree, that for the three chapters in question, there shall be made a regular councell, where preseruing equitie, the holie Ghospell being set in the middest, wee vnited with our bretheren, may conferr.* Doth it not make plaine that the holding this Councell had bene preceded by the Popes consent and permission? For the Councell was assembled in the month of May, the twelfth yeare after the Consulship of *Basilius*; and the Popes answere had bene made in the moneth of Ianuary before. And these words of the sixth Councell; *Vigilius consented to Iustinian, and the fifth Councell was established:* Doe they not conuince, either that the conuocation or the confirmation of the Councell, was taken from the Pope? And that a while after, *Iohn* Patriarke of *Constantinople* hauing gone about as Bishop of the second *Rome*, to participate with the Pope, in the title of *Vniuersall Bishop*, would attribute to himselfe the authority of calling

Cōc. Const 5. act. 1.
Ibid.
Cōc. œcum 6. act. 18.

Generall Councells in the *East*; is it not a manifest proofe that the authoritie of the spirituall calling of Councells, appertained to the Popes? *It hath bene* (saith Pope *Pelagius* the second in his Epistle to those of the *East*, z cited by saint GREGORIE) *reported to the Sea Apostolicke, that Iohn Bishop of Constantinople, hath intitled himselfe Uniuersall Bishop, and by vertue of this his presumption, hath called you to a generall Councell although the authoritie of calling Generall Councells be attributed by a singular priuiledge to the Sea Apostolik of saint PETER.*

z Pelag. 2. ep. 1. a Gregor. l. 7. Indict. 2. ep. 69.

And for the sixth generall Councell, which was holden vnder the Emperor *Constantine Pogonat*, and in the same cittie of *Constantinople* that the Emperor would not call the Bishops of the Easterne part of the Empire which was seperated for the Monothelite heresie, from the obedience of the Sea Apostolicke, till first the Pope had called the Bishops of the westerne part to *Rome*; b and till the legates from the Pope, and from the Councell of *Rome*, were come to him; doth it not presuppose that the spirituall authoritie of the Pope, did flowe together with the temporall authoritie of the Emperor, or rather preceded it for the celebration of Councells? And that the same Councell speaking to the Emperor alleadgeth to him for the image and paralell of his Actes, as well as of his name the example of the great *Constantine* in these wordes; *Constantine Augustus, and Pope Siluester of Reuerend memorie, called the famous Councell of Nicea*, Doth it not confirme it? And for the second Councell of *Nicea* which is the seauenth generall Councell, what Pope *Gregory* the second had answered a while before to the Emperor Leo the *Iconoclast*, who desired to cause a Councell to be holden for the busines; d *Thou hast written that a generall Councell might be holden, but it seemeth not fitt to vs.* And againe; e *Put case we had harkened to thee, and the Prelates had bene gathered from all the earth, and that the Senat and the Councell had bene sett, where had the religious Emperor the louer of Christ bene, to sitt there according to custome?* And that which the Fathers of the Councell alleadge amongst the nullities of the Synod of the *Iconoclasts*; f *It had not for cooperator, as that had which now is celebrated, the Pope of Rome nor his Prelates, neither by his Legates, nor by circular letters* (that is to saie, addressed to all the prouinces) *as is the lawe of Councells*; doth it not insinuate, that the Popes authoritie was required with that of the Emperors for the lawfull celebration of Councells. Now these are all the generall Councells which haue bene celebrated from the age of the Apostles till the seperation that *Photius* made of the *Greeke* church from the latine. For as for the Councell of *Constantinople* surnamed *Trullian*, that the Greekes call, *the supplie of the sixth Councell*; For asmuch as the sixth Councell which was holden vnder *Constantine Pogonat*, hauing made noe canons; some of those Bishops that had bene present, reassembled themselues ten yeares after vnder *Iustinian* the second his Sonne; and made some certaine canons which they published with the title of canons of the sixth Councell; I meddle not with it because none of the Bishops of the *West* assisted there and consequently it was not generall. It is true, that *Balsamon*, g and after him *Nilus* h Archbishop of *Thessalonica* saith, that he had seene in one of the copies of the same Councell *Trullian*, a catalogue of signatures, which also is at *Rome* and which hath bene printed with the Greeke Texts of the Councell; from whence it is collected, that *Basilius* Bishop of *Gortina*, Metropolitan of the Isle of *Creete*, and legate of the Councell of *Rome*, and a certaine Bishop of *Rauenna* assisted there. But he forgetts like a Greeke Schismaticke as he is, to tell two other things; the one, that the title of legate of the Councell of *Rome* that this *Basilius* bore, had noe reference to

b Epist. Cõst. Imp. ad Patriar. Constant. Concil. 6. Act. 1.

c Concil. 6. Act. 18.

d Greg. 2. ad Leon. ep. 1.

e Ibid.

f Concil. œcum. 7. Act. 6.

g Balsam. in prœf. Concil. in Trull.

h Nil. de prim. Pap. l. 2.

what

what he was then; for there was noe Councell holden in the weſt for the preparation of the Councell ſurnamed *Trullan*; but to what hee had bene in the ſixth Councell whereto he had ſigned with this title; *i* *Baſilius*

i Concil.6. Act.18.

vnworthie Biſhop of Gortina, Metropolitan of the Iſle of Creete, and Legate of all the holie Synod of the Sea Apoſtolicke of olde Rome: And the other, that euen in the ſixth Councell, he bore this title, but as a title of honor, and not as actuall Legate either of the Pope, or of the Councell of *Rome*; I ſaid, neither of the Pope, nor of the Councell of *Rome*, becauſe the Pope, and the Councell of *Rome* at the expreſſe requeſt of the Emperor ſent two diſtinct legations, *k* a thinge neuer before heard of to the ſixt Councell;

k Epiſt. Imp ad. Domin. Pap. in proœmb. Conc.6.

whereof the one, to witt that of the Pope, was of two Prieſts, a Deacon, and a ſubdeacon, who ſate before all the Patriarkes of the ſixth Councell. And the other, to witt; that of the Councell of *Rome*, was of three Biſhops, who ſate after the Patriarkes, to ſhew that they were two diſtinct legations. Nowe neither in the one nor other of theſe two legations, had *Baſilius* Biſhop of *Gortyna*, (who was neither of the Bodie of the Clergie of *Rome*, nor of the bodie of the Councell holden at *Rome*,) bene named, as it appeares aſwell by the Popes letters, as by thoſe of the Councell of *Rome*. *l* Onelie it happened that this *Baſilius* being the Popes ordinary le-

l Concil. œcum.6. Act.4.

gate in the Isle of *Creete*, for thoſe things which concerned the iuriſdiction of the Sea Apoſtolicke in his Prouince; as he of *Theſſalonica* in the prouince of *Macedonia*; and he of *Corinth* in the Prouince of *Achaia*: The legates of the Councell of *Rome* finding him in thoſe partes, for honors ſake aſſociated him, and him of *Corinth* not with the legates of the Pope, but with them; For he ſubſcribes with the legates of the Councell of *Rome*, who ſigned after all the Patriarkes, and not with the Popes Legates, who ſig-

m Concil. œcumenic. Act.18.

ned before all the Patriarkes. *m* But this aſſociation was onely for the ſixth generall Councell. And that afterward in the Councell ſurnamed *Trullian* he continued to attribute to himſelfe the name of legate of the Councell of *Rome*; it was as a memoriall of the honor he had receiued in the ſixth Councell following the cuſtome of the *Greekes*, who when they haue borne a title in anie ſolemne action, preſerue it many yeares after in memory of the honor they haue once receiued. And it will nothing auaile to ſaie, that at leaſt he was the Popes legate in the Isle of *Creete*, when he aſſiſted at the Councell ſurnamed *Trullian*; for there was greate difference betweene the Metropolitans, honored with the Title of the Popes legates in their Prouinces, and whoſe legation was attributed to their Seas; As the Archbiſhop of *Arles* amongſt the *Gaules*; *n* The Arch-

n Greg. Magn.l. 4. Indict. 14. ep.52. & 53

o Leo ad Anaſt. Theſſ. ep. 82.

biſhop of *Theſſalonica* in *Macedonia*; *o* The Archbiſhop of *Corinth* in *Peloponeſus*; And the Synodicall Legates deputed from the Pope or the *Weſterne* Church to the generall Councells, foraſmuch as the one contributed to the vniuerſalitie of the Councells, the authoritie of thoſe that ſent them; and the others conferred noe more, but that of their owne perſons, or their particular Prouinces. And therefore the aſſiſtance of *Baſilius* Biſhop of *Gortyna* at the Councell ſurnamed *Trullian*, wherein he held not the place of the Pope, but ſigned after all the other Patriarkes, yea after ſome Metropolitans, *p* did nothing auaile to make it generall.

p Concil. in Trull. in ſubſcript.

And as for the Archbiſhop of *Rauenna*, he ſigned not: from whence it is, that *Balſamon* could not tell his name, but becauſe his predeceſſor had aſſiſted by Atturney at the ſixth Councell, whereof the Councell *Trullian* pretended ro be a ſupplie; a place to ſigne in, was reſerued for him, as one abſent, in theſe words: *q* *The place of the Biſhop of* Heraclea, *of him of* Rauenna, *and of him of Corinth*. Therefore euen from that, from whence

q Concil. Trull. in ſubſcript.

Balſamon inferrs, that the Biſhop of *Rauenna* aſſiſted at the Councell

ſurnamed

surnamed *Trullian;* to witt, from the Rolle of the subscriptions; wee collect the contrarie, that hee assisted not there at all. And indeede, if the Bishop of *Rauenna*, or anie other Westerne Bishop had assisted there, how could that Councell haue commtited the error it did committ, besides, manie others, in approueing the Councell of *Carthage* holden vnder saint CYPRIAN, for the rebaptisation of Heretickes? *r* For there was not a Bishop in the *West* soe ignorant, as not to knowe, that the Councell holden vnder saint CYPRIAN was an erroneous Councell, whose doctrine was condemned by the *Roman* Church, and had bene the seede and originall of the *Donatists* heresies. For if they obiect with *Balsamon* and *Nilus*, that the Councell surnamed *Trullian*, that would be taken for a supplie of the sixth generall Councell, and passe the Canons thereof, for canons of the sixth Generall Councell, attributes to it selfe in the forefrõt of their decrees, the title of Generall; Cõucell we answere that it was not because it was soe, but because it expected to be soe, by the addition of the *Westerne* Church, and of the Pope, for whom there was a blanke left to signe in, aboue all the Patriarkes, in these wordes, *s* *A place for the most holie Pope of Rome;* A thing that plainlie shewes, that the Pope had noe deputies there. Now soe farr was the Pope and the *Westerne* Church from signing to it, as contrarywise they prepared themselues rather to indure Martyrdome. For the Emperor hauing sent the copie of the Councell *Trullian* to *Rome*, to praie the Pope to sett to his subscription, the Pope rather chose to incurre all the Emperors hatred and persecution, then to cõsent to it, as BEDA an author of the same age testifies in these wordes: *The Emperor Iustinian the second* (saith he) *t hauing sent Zacharie his Constable, commaunded him to confine Pope Sergius to Constantinople, because he would not fauour the erraticall Councell that he had made at Constantinople, and had refused to signe it. But the Garrison of* Rauenna, *and of the neighboring place preuented the impious commaunds of the Emperor, and repulsed Zachary with outrages and iniuries, from the Cittie of Rome.* And it is not to be said, either that Pope *Adrian* praised the allegation that *Tarhasius* Patriarke of *Constantinople* had made in his synodicall Epistle of the eightith two canon of that Cõucell against the *Iconoclasts*: Or that the legates of the same Pope *Adrian* did not oppose themselues against the apologie that *Tarhasius* Patriarke of *Constantinople* made for the canons of that Councell, at the second Councell of *Nicea*. For that Pope *Adrian* praised the allegation of *Tarhasius*, it was not because of the authoritie of this Councell that *Tarhasius* had cited vnder the title of the sixth Councell, but because of the doctrine of the canon which was sound and orthodoxall; and that not onely the Popes legates, did not oppose themselues against it, but alsoe some Popes haue alleadged it, against the *Iconoclasts*, it was because the arguments taken from those canons were good, in regard of the Greekes that had receiued them; And besides that if the authoritie of the Sea Apostolicke had bene wounded in the Councell *Trullian* by the proceedings of the Emperor *Iustinian Rhinotmete* this wound had bene in some measure repaired by the same Emperor with his other crymes; when at Pope *Constantines* arriuall in the East, He *prostrated himselfe* (saith BEDA) *v on the Earth before him, and praying him to intercede for his Sinnes, renewed to him all the priuiledges of his Church.*

But against this prescription, the aduersaries to the Sea Apostolicke, frame three principall obiections; The first, that *Ruffinus* speakeing of the Councell of *Nicea* saith, *vv that the Emperor by aduise of the Churchmen called a Coucell at Nicea,* and maketh noe particular mention of the Pope. The second, that *Iulius* reproached the Bishops of the Councell of

r Concil. Trull. c. 1.

s Concil. Trull. in subscript.

t Bed. de sex ætatib.

v Beda de sex ætatib.

vv Ruff. hist. Eccl. l. 1. c. 1.

x Socrat. hist. Eccl. l. 2. c. 17. & Soz. l. 3. c. 10.
y Hier. contr. Ruff. Apol. 2.

Antioch, x *That they had not called him to their Councell.* And the third that saint IEROM treating of a Councell holden amongst the *Gaules* cries; y *What Emperor commaunded this Synod to be called?* To the first then of these obiections; which is, that *Ruffinus* saith; *That the Emperor by the aduise of the Clergie, called a Councell at Nicea;* Wee answere, that although *Ruffinus*, because of the hate he bore to the *Roman* Church, from whence he had bene excommunicated for his errors, whould not expresse the historie but in generall termes, and by these words; *by the aduise of the Church-men*; Neuerthelesse, he alwaies giues it to be inferred from thence, that the ecclesiasticall authoritie preceded the Emperiall conuocation; and that the Emperiall conuocation, was but an execution of the Ecclesiasticall aduise; For whereas saint EPIPHANIVS saith; z *That the care of Alexander, Bishop of Alexandria, moued Constantine to assemble the Councell*; this word, *moued*, excludeth not the meanes and interuention of the Pope, to whom *Alexander* had written of it by especiall letters; as *Liberius* testifies to the Emperor *Constantius* in these termes; a *Wee haue the letters of the Bishop Alexander to Siluester of holie memorie*, & by consequent is not incompatible with these words of the third generall Councell of *Constantinople*; b *Constantine Augustus and Pope Siluester of Reuerend memorie, called the famous Councell of Nicea.*

z Epiphan in hæres. Melet.
a Liber. epist. ad Constant. in fragm. Hilar. & apud. Lucif Caral.
b Conc 6. œcum. Act. 18.

To the second opposition, which is, that *Julius* reproached it to the Bishops of the Synod of *Antioch*, that they had not called him to their Councell; from whence the Aduersaries of the Sea Apostolicke inferre, that it did not belong to the Pope to call Councells; Wee answere, that the obiection is not valide; and the reason of the nullitie is; that this was not a generall Councell, to which the conuocation of the Pope, either mediate or immediate was necessary; but a particular Councell of the Bishops of the Patriarkship of *Antioch* which the Patriarke of *Antioch* might call alone, and at which the other Bishops who were but in small number, assisted but by aggregation. And therefore the Pope doth not reproach it to them, that their Councell was not called by him, or at his instance, but forasmuch as that Councell which was a particular Councell, had vndertaken, as compounded of Arrian Bishops, who violated all order and discipline, to decide things that concerned the vniuersall Church ordayning in hate to saint ATHANASIVS; That euery Bishop, that after he had bene deposed by a Synod, should continue still to performe episcopall functions, without hauing bene first reestablisht by an other greater Synod, should be incapable of restitution; and that the lawes of the Church bore, that there could noe decrees be made in the Churches; that is to saie, as *Caluin* himself interprets it, d for things regarding the vniuersall Church, without the Sentence of the Bishop of *Rome*, he reproacheth it to them, that they had exceeded the power of a particular Councell; That is to saie, had decided the affaires which concerned the generall gouernement of the Church, without hauing inuited him to assiste at it, either by himself, or by his Legats. A thing, that if we were stript of all other argumentes, would sufficiently shewe the Popes authoritie; for if the absence of the Pope alone and not of anie other Patriarke or Metropolitan, were an impediment to the makeing of decrees, to oblige the vniuersall Church; how can it bee, but the Pope must be head of the Church, and Superior of the other Patriarkes?

c Socr. histor. l. 2. c 17.
d Inst. l. 4. c. 7.

To the third obiection, which is, that saint IEROM speaking of a certaine Councell holden amongst the *Gaules*, cryes; *What Emperor hath commaunded this Synod to be assembled?* From whence they inferre, that the Emperors onely called the generall Councells. Wee answere, it is a

e Hier. Apol. aduers. Ruff. l. 2.

very

very Sophisme; for the Councell whereof saint IEROM spake, was not a generall Councell, but a particular, that *Ruffinus* pretends to haue bene holden in *Gaule* against saint HILLARY. Nowe wee agree of all sides, and *Caluin* himselfe confesses it, *f* that the Metropolitans, Primates, and Patriarkes called particular Councells. And the Councells of the *Westerne* Church holden at *Rome* by Pope DAMASVS in the tyme of the heresie of the *Macedonians*; by Pope *Celestine* against the heresie of the *Nestorians*; by Pope LEO against the heresie of the *Eutychians*; by Pope *Agatho* against the heresie of the *Monothelites*, inforced the most obstinate to confesse, that the Pope, if not as head of the vniuersall Church, yet at least as Patriarke of the *West*, called the Patriarchall Councells of the *Westerne* Church; and not onely called the Patriarchall Councells of the *Westerne* Church, but alsoe when there was neede, caused to be called extraordinarily, the nationall or prouinciall Coũcells of such a Natiõ or Prouince of the *West*, as he thought to be necessarie; as it appeares; for *Africa* frõ these wordos S. AVGVSTINE; *g The Ecclesiasticall necessitie enioyned vs by the Reuered Pope Zosime Bishop of the Sea Apostolicke, had drawne vs to Cæsaria*; And for *Macedonia*, *Achaia*, and *Thessalia*; from these of Pope LEO to *Anastasius* Bishop of *Thessalonica*, his Legat in those prouinces; *h If There be anie maior cause moued, for which it shalbe necessarie, to cause an Episcopall assemblie to be called, let it suffice thee to call two Bishops of euery Prouince such as the Metropolitans shall choose*. And for *Spaine*, from these of the same LEO; *i Wee haue sent letters to our bretheren and fellow Bishops of Arragon, of Carthagena, of Portugall, and of Galitia, and haue declared to them the assemblie of a generall Councell*; that is to saie, generall for *Spaine*. In which place, they must not cauill vpon the word, *Councell*, and conuert it into *Counsell*; For the first Councell of *Bracara*, reporting the same historie, saith, *k By the commaundement of Leo the Bishops of* Arragon; Carthagena, *Portugall and* Andaluzia *held a Councell amongst them*. But besides the spirituall authoritie, were it of Metropolitans, Primates, and Patriarkes for the calling of particular Councells, be it of the Popes as wee pretend for the calling of generall Councells, the temporall authoritie of the Emperors was alsoe requisite aswell to auoid state iealousies, and hinder suspitions of conspiracies against the Empire, as to take order for the Charge of transportations, Staples, and prouisions, and to furnish the costes of the voyages, which the Churches then newlie out of the persecution of the Pagans could yet hardlie beare. And therefore when there was question of calling not onely generall Councells of all the Earth, but alsoe the generall Councell of the *Westerne* Church, the temporall authoritie of the Emperors, concurred with the Spirituall authoritie of Popes for the execution of the conuocation. *The Emperor Valentinian*, saith Pope *Sixtus* the third tymefellowe to saint CYRILL, *l hath commaunded by our authority, that the Synod should be called*. And when there was question of calling *Nationall* Synods, if it were within the countries of the Empire, the authoritie of Emperors or of their lieuetenans, was allso required; and if it were within the ecclipsed countries or not depending from the Empire, that of the Kings of the nations where it was to be celebrated, must be ioyned thereto; as when the first Councell of *Bracara* in *Spaine* was called, it is said it was called, *m by the commaundement of the glorious King* Ariamira, or according to others, *Theodomira*. And when the second Councell of *Tours* speakes of the first Councell of *Orleans* holden vnder *Clouis* it is said, it was done, *n at the request of the most inuincible king* Clouis. And when the second Councell of *Mascon* was holden vnder King *Gontran*, it was ordained, *o* that the ordinarie *Nationall* Councells should be celebrated from three yeare to three

f Caluin. Inst.l. 4. c. 7.

g Aug. Epist. 157.

h Leo ad Anast. Epist. 82.

i Id epist. 91.

k Cõc Brac 1. in præfac

l Ep. ad Orient.

m Conc. Brac. 1. in præf.

n Cõc. Turon. 2. c. 22

o Concil. Matisc. 2. c. 20.

yeare; *and that the care to cause them to be assembled, appertained to the Bishop of Lion, and the disposition to the most magnificent Prince.* Now if the temporall conuocation of Nationall Councells made by the Emperors, or by the Princes of the Nations, were noe impediment, but that the spirituall conuocation of the same Councells might be due to the Primats of the Nations; Why should the temporall conuocation of generall Councells made by the Emperor be an impediment why the authoritie to call them spiritually; that is to saie, in behalfe of spirituall and ecclesiasticall power, might not belong to the Pope?

For that then as we haue newlie said, the authoritie of Emperors was necessary; and alsoe to make the decisions of Councells executorie by the Secular arme, and by the ministers and officers of temporall iustice, who otherwise would not haue labored to punish corporallie those that should contradict. And that is the cause wherefore the Fathers of the Councells were soe carefull to sett this title in the forefront of their acts; *The most holie and generall Councell called by the authoritie of the most religious Emperor;* to the end to make their decrees executorie temporallie, and by the ministrie of the Secular Tribunall, but not to make them obligatorie in conscience and spirituallie. *For when was it* (saith saint ATHANASIVS) [p] *that the iudgement of the Church hath euer taken authoritie from the Emperor?* And indeede who can doubt, but that if there had bene any generall Councell holden vnder the Pagan Emperors, the Christians had bene obliged in conscience and to the spirituall Tribunall of the Church, though it had not bene called by them. And that if the Turke should euer make himselfe vniuersall monarch of the world, and that there should be a generall Councell holden vnder his Empire, the Christians should be obliged in conscience, and to the spirituall Tribunall of the Church, though it were not called by him. And then if the authoritie necessarie to make generall Councells obligatorie in conscience, ought to be perpetuall and alwaies to haue place; how can that be by imperiall authoritie, which hath bene deuided into soe manie parcells, as at this daie in a manner the least part of it belonges to the Empire. For the conuocation of the pluralitie dispersed, must depend from an vnitie, and from an vnitie that hath authoritie ouer euerie indiuiduall of the pluralitie: as the ancient Emperors themselues acknowledged that of the Pope to be, when they ordayned, [q] *That euery Bishop that being called to the Popes iudgment, should neglect to come, should be constrained by the Gouernor of the Prouince to appeare.* And therefore as often as our aduersaries crie out; such an Emperor called such or such a Councell, so often they loose their tyme and their labour. For wee are agreed, that whilst the Emperors were Monarchs of the world, or of the greater part of the world, they called them all in regard of temporall authoritie; but we saie besides, the secular authoritie of the Emperor, which was necessarie to make the conuocations of Councells authenticall temporally must an other authoritie interuene; to witt, a spirituall and ecclesiasticall authoritie, to make it lawfull and authenticall spirituallie, and to make that the Councells may be said to be called from God, and obligatorie in conscience, and to the Spirituall Tribunall of the Church. Now that we maintaine to haue bene the authoritie of him who was the principle & center of ecclesiasticall vnitie, [r] and the head of all the Bishops, and without whose sentence it was vnlawfull to make definitiue lawes in the Church; to witt, the Pope, whose authoritie for this regard ought to concurr with the authoritie of the Emperors, either actuallie or virtuallie. I said either actuallie or virtuallie, for as much as it sufficed for the spirituall validitie of the conuoca-

tion

[p] Ath. ad solit. vit. à gent,

[q] Nou. Theod. Tit. 24.

[r] Cypr. ad Cornel. ep. 55.

[s] Inst. Cod. Tit. 1. l. 7.

[t] Socr. hist. Eccl. l 2. c. 8.

tion of Councells, that the Popes did either call them or cause them to be called, or approued their conuocation. For when the Emperors called them, either at the Popes instance, or with the consent and approbation of the Pope: the spirituall conuocation of the Pope was alwaies reputed to interuene as also the Catholicke Emperors, and which abstained from tyranizing ouer the Church neuer called them but whē the Pope required it of them, or they required it of the Pope; And when they were required by the Pope, they were alwaies readie to call them, although that for the places where they should be celebrated, the Emperors because of the commodities or incommodities of the State, reserued the election to themselues. For whereas the Emperor *Constantius* refused Pope *Liberius*, who demaunded of him that a generall Councell might be holden for saint ATHANASIVS cause; it was the refusall of an *Arrian* Emperor, noe lesse an enemie to the Sonn of God, then to saint ATHANASIVS. And whereas the Emperor *Arcadius* refused Pope *Innocent*, *who sent*, (saith *Sozomene*) *fiue Bishops and two priests of the Roman Church to the Emperors, to demaund of them a Councell for the cause of saint Chrisostome,* and sent saint CHRISOSTOME into a more remote banishment, it was a tyrannicall act of an Emperor possest by the Enemies of this holy man.

Theod. hist. Eccl. l. 2. c. 16.

Sozom. hist. Eccles. l. 8 c vlt.

For this then the temporall conuocation of the Emperors was necessary, to wit, that the ministers of the Empire who were obliged by the politicke and imperiall lawes not to suffer anie assemblies without the Emperors permission, should not hinder them; & that the Estate should haue noe colour of iealousies; and that the officers of the cittie should furnish the charges Staples, and transportations of the Bishops, and that the Councells should be kept at the expences of the imperiall Exchequer; and that finallie the decrees of Councells might be obligatorie to the secular Tribunall, and executory temporallie, and by the Ministrie of the politicke Magistrate; but not that the conuocation of the Emperors was of the essence of the Councell, as that of the Popes was; nor serued to make them obligatorie in conscience, and to the spirituall Tribunall of the Church, noe more then the Presidency of the same Emperors at the Councells, either by themselues or their Officers was of the essence of the Councells, as that of the Pope was, but onely for comelynes and ornament, and for keepeing order and temporall policie; witnes this language of the Councell of *Chalcedon* to Pope LEO the first; *Thou didst preside by thy legates in the Councell, as the head to the members, and the Emperors presided there for seemelynesse and ornament, striuing with thee as Zorobabel with Jesus, to renew in doctrine the building the Jerusalem of the Church.* For what meanes this comparison of Pope LEO with *Jesus* high Priest of the Iewish lawe, and of the Emperor *Marcian* with *Zorobabel* Prince of the Iewish people, but that there was like analogie in Christian Religions, betweene the Pope and the Emperor for the holding of Councells, as there was in the Iewish Church betweene the high Priest which was *Jesus*, and the Prince of the people, which was *Zorobabel* for the building of the Temple; that is to saie, that the one, to witt the Pope should concurr there as head of the Priesthood and spirituall iurisdiction: and the other, to witt the Emperor; should concurr there, as head of the politicke and temporall iurisdiction; and therefore when there is question of the calling of Councells, there must be a distinction betweene the spirituall calling of Councells, and the temporall calling of Councells; that is to saie, betweene the conuocation necessarie to make their

Cōc. Chalc ep. ad. Leon.

assemblie authenticall temporallie, and the conuocation necessarie to make their assemblie authenticall in conscience and spirituallie. In the first case there was nothing to be determined betweene the Popes and the Emperors; for none doubtes, but the authoritie necessarie to call generall Councells temporallie, and to make them executory by the secular arme, was the authoritie of the Emperors, noe more then at this daye anie doubtes, but the authority necessary to make the conuocation of *Nationall* Councells authenticall temporally must be that of the Kings or Princes within whose estates they are to be holden. In the second case, there was yet lesse, for as much as it is euident, that the authoritie necessarie to legitimate in conscience the conuocation of Councells; and to make them obligatorie spirituallie, must be a spirituall and ecclesiasticall authoritie, a temporall Magistrate not being able to conferr anie spirituall authoritie to Councells. And indeede when the Emperors haue pretended to call generall Councells without being moued thereto, or seconded by the iust ecclesiasticall authoritie, those Councells haue bene declared illegitimate, not onely by the finall issue of their iudgements, but by the originall vice of their forme, if the Popes confirmation did not come in to correct the defect. For the Councell of *Arimini* which was compounded of fower hundred Bishops, and which had bene called by the Emperor *Constantius*, was declared inualid, not onely for the issue of the iudgement, but for this cause amongst others, saith the Councell of those of the *West*, reported by *Theodoret,* That it had bene holden without the consent of the Bishop of *Rome*, *whose sentence should first of all haue bene attended.* And in the Councell of Chalcedon, the first complaint that was made against the false Councell of *Ephesus*, that the Emperor *Theodosius* the second, surprized by the fraude of the *Eutychians*, had called without the Popes authoritie, although with a request to the Pope, to assist at it, or to send to it was, *That Dioscorus presumed to hold a Councell without the Bishop of Romes permission, which had neuer bene lawfull or before done,* By meanes whereof, all the question of the spirituall and ecclesiasticall authoritie necessary from the part of the conuocation to make Councells lawfull in conscience and obligatory to the internall Tribunall of the Church, is betweene the Pope and the other Patriarkes; and consistes in this to witt, to whom, either to the Pope, or to the other Patriarkes it belonged to call Councells spiritually. Now who doubtes but it must be to him of the Patriarkes that ought to preside there, and the defect of whose presence either mediate or immediate, rendred the Councells inualid? And who sees not, that euen if the Pope had not bene the direct Successor of saint PETER; if he had not bene his Vicar, in whose name all Councells ought to be called; if he had not bene the center of the ecclesiasticall vnity and Communion, if he had not bene the Bishop as saint CYPRIAN saith, *of the chaire of Peter, and of the principall Church, from whence the Sacerdotall vnitie proceeded*; and in breefe, had he not bene superior in authoritie to the other Patriarkes, but onely the first of them in order, it belonged to him to call them, as it did anciently to the Presidēt of the senate, to call the Senate? And therefore whē Pope *Gelasius* saith; *The Sea Apostolicke onely decreed that the Councell of Chalcedon should be holden*; It is not to the exclusion of the Emperor, that he makes this restriction but to the exclusion of the other Patriarkes. And when Pope *Pelagius* S. GREGORIES predecessor writes; *The authority to call generall Councells, hath bene attributed by a singular priuiledge, to the Sea*

Theod. hist. Eccl. l. 2. c. 22.

Concil. Chalc. Act. 1.

Cyp. ad Cornel. ep 55.

Gelas. Epist. ad Episc. Dardan.

Aposto-

Apostolicke of holie Peter. It is not to the exclusion of the Emperors, that he makes this limitation, but to the exclusion of the other Patriarkes, and particularly of the Bishop of *Constantinople*; for the Bishop of *Constantinople* pretending by the creation of his cittie, into the title of the second *Rome*, to haue bene made equall to the Pope, not in regard of the Pope, as hath bene aboue said, but in regard of the other Patriarkes had dared to presume to participate in the *East*, in the title of vniuersall Patriark; which title the Pope had receiued at the Councell of *Chalcedon*; and in continuance of this presumption, had endeuored to call a generall Councell; that is to saie, a generall Councell of the Empire of the *East* in the *East*. To the end then to represse his arrogance, the Pope put him in mynde that the power to call generall councells; that is to saie, the generall councells, aswell of all the Empire, as of the particular Empire of *Constantinople*, as a case exceeding the simple patriarchall authoritie, belonged to the onely direct and absolute successor of S. PETER; *It hath bene reported to the Sea Apostolicke* (saith the same *Pelagius*, writing to the Bishops of the *East*) *that Iohn Bishop of Constantinople hath intituled himselfe vniuersall, and by vertue of this his presumption, hath called you to a generall Councell*: he meanes, the generall Councell of the *East* whereof *Euagrius* speakes, called for the cause of *Gregorie* Patriarke of *Antioch*) *notwithstanding that the authoritie of calling generall Councells, hath bene attributed by a singular priuiledge to the Sea Apostolicke of the holy Peter.* And alittle after; *And therefore all that you haue decreed in this your not Councell, but conuenticle; I ordaine by the authoritie of holy PETER Prince of the Apostles, &c. that it be disanulled & abrogated.* Which S. GREGORIE the *great* also reportes in these words: *Our predecessor Pelagius of happie memorie, hath abrogated by a sentence intirely valid, all the actes of this Synod, except what concerned the affaire of Gregorie Bishop of Antioch of happie memorie.* Now doth not this alone suffice to decide the whole question? For if the Bishop of *Constantinople* vnder pretence of the equalitie that he challenged to haue obtained with the Pope in superioritie ouer the other Patriarkes, presumed to call the generall Councells of the *East*: why is it not manifest, that the authoritie to call generall Councells, forasmuch as concernes spirituall and Ecclesiasticall power, belonged to the Pope? And if it were soe, when the Emperors possest almost all the Regions of the Empire, and when the Catholicke Church was spread almost ouer all the other patriarkships, how much more nowe when that the Emperors hold but the least part of the Estates of the ancient Empire, and that the Catholicke Church is almost reduced into the prouinces of the patriarkship of the Pope, or to those, that by the conuersion of countries newlie discouered, haue drawne their mission and Ecclesiasticall iurisdiction from them? But heere is enough of the calling of Councells; lett vs goe forward to the other Articles.

Pelag. 2. epist. ad Orient.

before c.7.

Pelag. 2. epist. ad Orient.

Euagr. hist. Eccl. l. 6. c. 7.

Gregor. Magn. l. 7. indict. 2. ep. 69.

CARD. PERRONS REPLIE

TO THE KING OF GREAT BRITAINE, THE THIRD BOOKE.

Of Appeales.

CHAPT. I.

The continuance of the Kings Answere.

F*Or vvhereas there are some examples of a contrarie obseruation*; (that is to saie, of a contrary obseruation to vvhat his Maiestie had said, that those vvhich vvere excommunicate by anie of the Churches, vvere presently acknovvledged to be cutt of through all the Catholicke Church,) *it vvas not common right, but vsurpation.*

THE REPLIE.

AND what doth this then signifie, that *Theodoret* speaking of the accusation that the *Eusebians* made of saint ATHANASIVS Patriarke of *Alexandria*, at the tribunall of Pope *Julius*, writeth: *Julius follovving the lavve of the Church commaunded them to come to Rome, and cited the deuine Athanasius in iudgement?* And what doth this then signifie that *Sozomene* saith, that after the same ATHANASIVS; Patriarke of *Alexandria*; *Paul* Bishop of *Constantinople Marcellus* Primat of *Ancyra* in *Galatia*; *Asclepas* Bishop of *Gaza* in *Palestina*; And *Lucius* Bishop of *Andrinopolis* in *Thrace*, had bene deposed by diuers Councells of the Bishops of the *East*, *The Pope restored them euerie one to his Church; because to him for the dignitie of his Sea, appertained the care of all things?* And what then doth this signifie, that the Emperor *Valentinian*, writ to the Emperor *Theodosius*, *that Flauianus Bishop of Constantinople deposed in the second Councell of Ephesus had according to the custome of Councells, appealed to the Pope?* And what then doth this signifie, that the senators of the Councell of *Chalcedon* saie in the restitution of *Theodoret* Bishop of *Cyre*; a towne bordering vpon *Persia*, who had bene deposed in the same Synod of *Ephesus*, and had appealed from it, to Pope LEO: *Let the most religions Bishop Theodoret come in, that he maie partake of the Councell, for as much as the most holie Archbishop Leo hath restored him to his Bishopricke?*

Theod. hist Eccl. li. 2. c. 4.

Soz. hist. Eccl. l. 3. c. 7.

In ep. pæamb. Conc. Chalced.

Côc. Chalc Act. 1.

For

For as for the impertinent shift of those that answere, that the restitution that the Pope makes of Bishops which had bene deposed by the Councells of their Prouinces, was but a simple declaration, that he was of opinion they ought to be restored, and not a formall and iuridicall restitution; And likewise, that the deposition that he made of the Bishops or Priests of other Prouinces, was but a declaration, that his opinion was, that they ought to be deposed, and not a formall and iuridicall deposition; what can there be imagined more vnapt and more ridiculous? Is there soe young a Nouice in the lawes, that knowes not how differing these things are, to be of opinion that a man ought to be absolued, and to absolue; or to be of opinion, that a man ought to be condemned, and to condemne him: And that if all the Parliaments of the world had pronounced that it was their opinion, that a criminall person ought to be condemned, he were not condemned thereby, vnlesse they pronounced planelie, *wee haue condemned and doe condemne him*? for as much as the one is an act of science and the other is an acte of authoritie; and that the least doctors can doe the one, and onely Iudges the other. But why said I soe younge a Nouice in the lawes? Is there a man soe destitute of common sence as can not discerne, that when the Pope restores anie one, who had bene deposed by the Councell of his prouince, if the Popes restitution were but a simple aduice, that he ought to be restored; he that had bene deposed, had not more right to returne into his Bishopricke after the restitution then before; And that his diocesans were noe more obliged in conscience to receiue him, then they were before. Moreouer, if the Popes restitution, were but simplie an aduise, that he that was deposed, ought to be restored, what end would there be of Ecclesiasticall contentions? for the Bishops that had deposed him, being of opinion that he ought to bee deposed, and the Pope being of opinion that he ought to bee restored, if the Popes restitution were but a simple aduise, that he ought to be restored, to whose aduise should the restored person be obliged to yeild? If to that which seemed most iust to him, then it was he himselfe that was the iudge of his deposition or restitution; if to that of the Pope, then it were noe more an act of aduise and Councell, but an act of iurisdiction and authoritie, and not a simple act of iurisdiction and authoritie by which the Pope restored him for his part, and as much as was in him; but an act of iurisdiction and operatiue authoritie vpon the precedent sentence, and abrogating the first iudgement. O strange glosse to saie; that when Pope *Iulius* restored saint ATHANASIVS Patriarke of *Alexandria*; *Paule* Bishop of *Constantinople*; *Marcellus* Primate of *Ancyra* in *Galatia*; *Asclepas* Bishop of *Palestina*; or that when Pope LEO restored *Theodoret* Bishop of *Cyre*, then liuing; and *Flauianus* Patriarke of *Constantinople* after his death; he did noe other thing then to declare, that his opinion was, that they ought to be restored. Or to saie, that when Pope *Felix* opposed *Acacius* Patriarke of *Constantinople*: or that when Pope *Agapet* deposed *Anthimus* Patriarke of *Constantinople*, he did noe other thing then to declare, that his opinion was, that he ought to be deposed? And wherefore then, to recapitulate what hath soe often bene alleadged, when saint CYPRIAN solicites Pope *Steuen* to depose *Marcian* Bishop of *Arles*, did he write to him; [e] *Let there be letters from thee directed into the prouince, and to the people inhabiting at Arles by which Marcian being interdicted, an other may be substituted in his steede*? And wherefore then when *Theodoret* speakes

[e] Cyp. ep. 67.

of the cause of saint ATHANASIVS Patriarke of *Alexandria*, doth hee saie; *f Iulius according to the Ecclesiasticall lawe, commaunded the Eusebians to appeare at Rome, and gaue a daie to the diuine Athanasius, to appeare in iudgement?* And wherefore then when *Sozomene* speaketh of the restitution of the same saint ATHANASIVS Patriarke of *Alexandria*; of *Paule* Bishop of *Constantinople*; of *Marcellus* Primate of *Ancyra* in *Galatia*; of *Asclepas* Bishop of *Gaza* in *Palestina*; and of *Lucius*, Bishop of *Andrinople* in *Thrace*, doth he write; *g Iulius Bishop of Rome restored each of them to his Church, because to him for the dignitie of his Sea, the care of all things appertained?* And for what doth he add, *h that he commaunded those that had deposed them, to appeare at a sett daie at Rome, to yeild an accompt of their iudgement, and threatned them not to let them scape vnpunished, if they would not leaue to innouate?* And againe; that in the pursuite of this restitution, *i Athanasius*, Patriarke of *Alexandria*, and *Paul* Bishop of *Constantinople*, *recouered their Seas*: And besides, that the Councell of *Sardica* answered, that they could not abstaine from the Communion of ATHANASIVS Patriarke of *Alexandria*, and *Paul* Bishop of *Constantinople*; *because Iulius Bishop of Rome hauing examined their cause, had not condemned them?* For as for the rebellious and outragious letters that the Bishops of the *East*; that is to saie, the Bishops of the Patriarkship of *Antioch* and their complices who were Arrians writ against this restitution, it hath bene alreadie aboue spoken of, and shall againe be treated of heereafter. It sufficeth that the complaint which they made, *l that the Pope had iniured their Councell, and abrogated their sentence*, sheweth that the Popes action had not bene a simple aduise, but a formall iudgement. And wherefore then when the great Councell of *Sardica*, for soe saint ATHANASIVS calleth it, *m* holden for the defence of the same saint ATHANASIVS, and of the other Bishops that the Pope had restored, would conuert the discipline of appeales into a written lawe did they ordaine, that when a Bishop should be deposed by the Councell of his Nation, and should appeale from it to the Pope, they should not establishe a Successor in the place of the Bishop deposed, till the Pope had iudged of the appeale? *If a Bishop* (saith the Canon) *n hath bene deposed by the iudgement of the Bishops of the neighbour prouinces, and pretends that he ought to be heard againe, let noe other be substituted in his Sea, till the Bishop of Rome examining the affaire, haue pronounced the definition.* And wherefore then when *Valens* and *Vrsacius* the two principall aduersaries to saint ATHANASIVS would depart from their pursuite, did they come to *Rome* to aske pardon of the Pope for the slaunders they had laied vpon saint ATHANASIVS? *They came in person* (said *Sulpitius Seuerus*) *o to aske pardon of Julius Bishop of Rome?* And themselues in the acte of their pennance; *p your Pietie in your naturall goodnesse, hath daigned to pardon our error.* And wherefore then when the same *Vrsacius* and *Valens* had obtained the Popes pardon, did they add this protestation at the end of their acte; *And besides this we promise, that if vpon this occasion either those of the East, or Athanasius himselfe will malciouslie appeale vs in iudgement, q we will not depart from what you shall ordaine?* And the legates of the *Asian* Bishops to Pope *Liberius* in like manner; *If anie one after this profession of faith expounded by vs, will attempt anie accusation against vs, or against those that haue sent vs; r let him come with letters from your* Holinesse *before such orthodoxall Bishops as your* Holynesse *shall thinke fitt, and contest with vs in iudgement; And if a crime appeare, let the author be punisht?* And wherefore when the Arrians constrained Pope *Liberius* to condemne saint ATHANASIVS, did they insert these words into the false letter that they made him signe; *f I haue following the tradition of the Elders, sent in my behalfe, Lucius, Paul, and Ælianus priests of*

f Theod. hist. Eccl. l. 2. c. 4.
g Sozom. hist. l. 3. c. 7
h Ibid.
i Ibid.
k Id. ib. c. 10
l Soz. hist. Eccl. l. 3. c. 7.
m Athan. in Apol. 2.
n Concil. Sardic. c. 4.
o Sulpic. Seuer. hist. sacr. l. 2.
p Athan. Apol. 2.
q Ibidem.
r Soc. hist. Eccl l. 4 c. 12.
f Fragm. Hilar. de Concil. Arim. p. 36

the Roman Church into Alexandria to Athanasius, to cause him to come to Rome to the end I might appoint he being present vpon his person, what the discipline of the Church exacts? And for what cause doth S. BASILE testifie, that when Pope *Liberius* had restored *Eustathius* Bishop of *Sebaste* in *Armenia*, who had bene deposed by the Councell of *Militina* in *Armenia*, an orthodox and Catholicke councell, the councell of *Tyana* in *Cappadocia* receiued him without inquiring of the condition; by meanes whereof he had bene restored: *The things* (saith hee) *which were propounded to him by the blessed Liberius, and those whereto he submitted himselfe, we know not, sauing that he brought a letter which restored him, which hauing bene shewed to the Councell of Tyana, he was reestablished in his Bishopricke?* [Basil. ep. 74.] And wherefore then when S. IOHN CHRYSOSTOME had recourse by letters to Pope *Innocent* to procure the sentence to be abrogated that the mocke councell of *Constantinople* had pronounced against him, did he write to him; *One thing, I require of your vigilant soule, which is, that although those that haue troubled the world, be sicke of an impenitent and incurable disease yet if they will remedie it they maie neither be punisht, nor interdicted?* [Chrysost. ad Innoc. ep. 2.] And wherefore then when the councell of *Ephesus* had excommunicated and deposed *Iohn* Patriarke of *Antioch*, and his adherents, did it reserue the definitiue iudgement to the Pope, to correct or confirme the action, and besought the Pope to conceiue a iust indignation against him, that soe he might punish him for his rashnesse? *Wee haue* (saie the Fathers of the councell) *reserued him to the iudgement of thy pietie; and the while we haue declared them excommunicate and depriued of all Sacerdotall power.* [Côc. Eph. p. 2. act. 5. relat. ad Cœlest.] And a while after, *May it then please thy Holynesse to conceiue a iust indignation against these things; for if it be lawfull for euerie one to doe outrage to the greatest Seas;* (so spake they because of the Sea of *Alexandria*, which preceded that of *Antioch*) *and to pronounce sentences vnlawfull and not canonicall, or rather contumelies, against those ouer whom they haue noe power &c. Ecclesiasticall affaires will fall into an excessiue confusion; but if those that committ such enterprises may be punished according to their desert, all tumult will cease.* [Ibidem.] And wherefore then when the Emperor *Valentinian* the third would suppresse by one of his lawes *Hilarie* Bishop of *Arles*, who had presumed to consecrate Bishops of the *Gaules* without the Popes licence, doth he saie; *That the Popes clemencie alone permitted Hilarie still to beare the title of a Bishop?* [Nouell. Theod. tit. 24.] And againe; *Wee ordaine, that whatsoeuer the Sea Apostolicke shall decree, shall be a lawe,* (that is to saie, shall be executed by the ministers of the Imperiall iustice) *and that euerie Bishop who being called to Rome by the Pope, shall refuse to appeare, shall be constrained by the Gouernor of the prouince?* [Ibid.] And wherefore then when *Flauianus* Archbishop of *Constantinople* had bene condemned by the false Councell of *Ephesus*, did the same *Valentinian* the third write to the Emperor *Theodosius* his Father in lawe; *We ought in our daies to preserue to the blessed Apostle Peter, the dignitie of the Reuerence proper to him, inuiolate, that the blessed Bishop of the cittie of Rome, to whom antiquitie hath yeilded the Priesthood ouer all, may haue waie to iudge of Bishops, and of faith: For for this reason Flauianus Bishop of Constantinople, following the custome of Councells, hath appealed to him by petition in the contention moued concerning faith?* [Ep. Valent. Imper. in ep. præam. Côc. Chalc.] And wherefore then when *Theodoret* had bene condemned in the same Councell of *Ephesus*, did he write to the Pope; *I attend the sentence of your Apostolicke Throne, and doe beseeche your Holynesse to succour me appealing to your right and iust iudgement, and to commaund that I maie be transported to you, and verifie that my doctrine followes the Apostolicall pathes?* [Theod. ep. ad Leon.] And for what cause when the Pope had restored him, did the Senators that assisted at the Councell of *Chalcedon* saie; *Let the most Reuerend Bishop Theodoret come in, because the most holy Archbishop Leo hath restored him to his Bishops* [Côc. Chalc act. 1.]

Sea?

Ibid.act.8. *Sea?* And the Councell euen the same; *Theodoret is worthie of his Sea; Long liue Archbishop Leo; Leo hath iudged the iudgment of God?* And wherefore then when Pope *Leo* would sett his hand to the restitution of the Bishops, that had inclined to the false Councell of *Ephesus*, did he write to *Anatolius* Archbishop of *Constantinople*; (Leo ad Anatol.ep. 44.) *But as for those that haue more grieuouslie sinned in this cause, if perchance they come to repentance, and abandoning the defence of themselues, being conuerted to condemne their owne error, and that their satisfaction maie be such, as it seemeth they ought not to be reiected, let the matter be reserued to the more mature determination of the Sea Apostolicke?* And for what cause when *Paschasianus* the Popes Legate, voted vpon the same subiect, did he pronounce in the presence of the Councell of *Chalcedon*, that the Pope had pardoned all the Bishops and Archbishops of the *East*, which had suffered themselues to be ouerborne by the violence of *Dioscorus*? (Conc.Chalc act. 3.) *The Sea Apostolicke* (saith hee) *hath graunted them pardon for what they haue against their wills committed, forasmuch as they haue hitherto remained adhering to the most holy Archbishop Leo, and to the most holie and vniuersall Councell?* And wherefore then when *Dioscorus* and the false Councell of *Ephesus* had restored *Eutyches*, who had bene iudged in the first instance, by the Archbishop of *Constantinople*, and in the second instance by the Pope, did the Councell of *Chalcedon* cry out, that *Dioscorus* and the false Councell of *Ephesus* had restored to *Eutyches* the dignitie that the Pope had depriued him of; *He hath* (said they) *declared Eutyches innocent, and hath restored to him the dignitie taken from him by your Holynesse?* (Ibid.p. 3.) And wherefore then when *John* Patriarke of *Alexandria*, had bene deposed from his patriarkship, and *Peter* surnamed *Mongus* established in his place, did *John* appeale to Pope *Simplicius*, and tooke Synodicall letters from *Calendion* Patriarke of *Antioch*, to accompanie his appeale? *John* (saith *Liberatus*) *addressed himselfe to Calendion Patriarke of Antioch, and hauing gotten from him Synodicall letters of intercession, appealed to Pope Simplicius?* (Liberat. in breuiar. c. 16.) And wherefore then when Pope *Felix* successor to *Simplicius*, had deposed the same *Peter Mongus* Patriarke of *Alexandria*, and *Acacius* Patriarke of *Constantinople*, and *Peter* surnamed the *Tanner*, Patriarke of *Antioch*: and that these three Patriarkes trusting vpon the support of the Emperor *Zeno*, who was an hereticke like themselues, dispised the Popes sentence; doth *Victor* of Tunes saie, *that they dyed all three, vnder damnation?* (Vict.Tun. chron in Zenon.) And wherefore then when the Emperor *Justin* a Catholicke Prince was come to the Empire, was the sentence that the Pope had pronounced against them executed soe exactlie, that their names euen after their deathes were blotted out of the records of the Churches of *Alexandria*, of *Antioch*, and of *Constantinople*: And that for the rest that had communicated with them, but were not comprehended by name within the Popes letters, the Emperor was faine to demaund pardon of the Pope for them? (Iust. ep.ad Hormisd.) *Wee aske grace* (saith the Emperor, writing to Pope *Hormisdas*) *for the names, not of Acacius, not of either Peter*; that is to saie, not of *Peter* Patriarke of *Antioch*, and of *Peter* Patriarke of *Alexandria*, *not of Dioscorus, or Timotheus, of whom your Holynesse letters to vs directed, made especiall mention, but of those whom the Episcopall Reuereuce hath celebrated in the other cities?* And wherefore then when Pope *Agapet* deposed within *Constantinople* itselfe *Anthimus* Patriarke of *Constantinople*, doth *Liberatus* saie; (Liberat. in breuiar.c. 12.) *The Empresse Theodora wife to the Emperor Iustinian on the one side secretlie offered great presents to Pope Agapet, and one the other side tried him with threates, to hinder him from deposing Anthimus; but the Pope persisted in not hearing her request: And Anthimus seeing himselfe cast out of his Sea, rendred vp the Archiepiscopall mantle to the Emperors, and retired himselfe into a place, where the Empresse tooke him into her protection?* And for what cause when the Councell of *Constan-*

tinople

tinople, holden vnder *Menas*, speakes of the deposition of the same *Anthimus* Patriarke of *Constantinople*, doth it saie, that the Pope had pardoned *Peter* Patriarke of *Ierusalem*, and the other Bishops of the *East* that had communicated with him? *It must not be wondred at* (saith the Councell) *if the great Sea Apostolicke still continue to followe the first tract, preseruing the Rights of the Church inuiolate, and maintayning the faith, and granting pardon to those that haue sinned.* And againe; *The blessed Pope Agapet of holie aud Reuerend memorie, comeing into this Royall Cittie, hath next God giuen his helping hand to the sacred Canons, and hath cast Anthimus out of the Sea which appertained not to him, and hath pardoned those who had participated or communicated with him?* And wherefore then when *John* Archbishop of *Larissa*, and *Iohn* Primate of the first *Iustinianea* had iniustly condemned the one in the first, and the other in the second instance *Adrian* Bishop of *Thebes* in *Thessalia*, did Sainct GREGORIE depriue the Bishop of the first *Iustinianea* of the communion, for the space of thirtie daies, and Ecclipsed the Bishopricke of *Thebes* from the iurisdiction of the Archbishopricke of *Larissa*; and ordained, that if the Archbishop of *Larissa* should anie more attempt to enterprise anie thing vpon the Bishop of *Thebes*, he should remaine depriued of the sacred communion, soe as it might not be restored to him, except at the point of death without the leaue of the Bishop of *Rome*? And wherefore then when the same S. GREGORIE restored *Athanasius* Abbot of *Tamnaca* in *Lycaonia*, who had bene deposed by *John* Patriarke of *Constantinople*, and had appealed from him to the Sea Apostolicke, did he saie to him; *Wee declare thee free from all crime of heresie, and giue thee free leaue to repaire to thy Monasterie, and there to holde the same place as thou didst before?* But for as much as these shiftes are more then sufficiently confuted by the onely Canons of the Councell of *Sardica*, which were framed to iustifie the restitution of S. ATHANASIVS, and in the presence of S. ATHANASIVS himselfe, wee remitt the Reader to the Chapter wee shall heereafter make thereof: And the while we will examine the obiections that *Caluin* alleadges against the appeales to the Sea Apostolicke, which consist in fiue principall instances; which though they are treated of vnder two titles; the one of corrections, & the other of appeales: Neuerthelesse for as much as the right of appeales dependes from that of corrections; and besides that *Caluin* mingles the instances of the one with the instances of the other, we will treate of them vnder one Title; to witt, vnder that of Appeales.

Cōc. Const sub Men. act. 1.

Ibid. act. 4.

Gregor. Mag. l. 2. indict. 11. ep. 6.

Ibid. ep. 7

Id. l. 5. ind. 14. ep. 64.

In the chapter of the Councell of Sardica.

Calu. inst. l. 4. c. 7.

Of the opposition of S. Ireneus to Pope Victor.

CHAPT. II.

THE first instance then that *Caluin* alleageth against the Popes censures, is taken from *Eusebius* an Arrian author, and from *Ruffinus* enemie to the *Roman* Church his translator; who writt, that S. IRENEVS reprehended Pope *Victor* for hauing excommunicated the Churches of *Asia* for the question of the daie of Pasche, which they obserued according to a particular tradition that S. IOHN had introduced for a tyme in their prouinces, because of the neighbourhood of

Id. ibid.

the Iewes, and to bury the Synagogue with honor, and not according to the vniuerſall tradition of the Apoſtles. *Ireneus* (ſaith *Caluin*) *reprehended Pope Victor bitterlie, becauſe for a light cauſe he had moued a great and perillous contention in the Church.* There is this in the text that *Caluin* produceth; *He reprehended him, that he had not done well, to cutt of from the bodie of vnitie, ſoe manie and ſoe great Churches.* But againſt whom maketh this, but againſt thoſe that obiect it? for who ſees not, that S. IRENEVS, doth not there reprehend the Pope for the wante of power, but for the ill vſe of his power; and doth not reproache to the Pope, that he could not excommunicate the *Aſians,* but admonisheth him, that for ſoe ſmale a cauſe he should not haue cutt of ſoe manie prouinces from the bodie of the Church? *Ireneus* (ſaith *Euſebius*) *did fitlie exhort Pope Victor, that he should not cutt of all the Churches of God which held this ancient tradition.* And *Ruffinus* tranſlating and enuenoming *Euſebius,* ſaith; *He queſtioned Victor, that he had not done well in cutting of from the bodie of vnitie ſoe manie and ſoe great Churches of God.* And in truth, how could S. IRENEVS haue reprehended the Pope for wante of power; he that cries: *To the Roman Church, becauſe of a more powerfull principalitie;* (that is to ſaie, as aboue appeareth, becauſe of a principalitie more powerfull then the temporall: or as we haue expounded otherwhere; becauſe of a more powerfull Originall) *it is neceſſarie that euerie Church should agree?* And therefore alſoe S. IRENEVS alleadgeth not to Pope *Victor* the example of him, and of the other Biſhops of the *Gaules* aſſembled in a councell holden expreſſelie for this effect, who had not excommunicated the *Aſians,* nor the example of *Narciſſus* Biſhop of *Ieruſalem,* and of the Biſhops of *Paleſtina* aſſembled in an other Councell, holden expreſſely for the ſame effect, who had not excommunicated them, nor the example of *Palmas*, and of the other Biſhops of *Pontus* aſſembled in the ſame manner, and for the ſame cauſe in the Region of *Pontus,* who had not excommunicoted them, but onely alleadges to him the example of the Popes his predeceſſors: *The Prelates* (ſaith hee) *who haue preſided before Soter in the Church where thou preſideſt, Aniſius, Pius, Hyginus, Teleſphorus, and Sixtus, haue not obſerued this cuſtome, &c. and neuertheleſſe none of thoſe that obſerued it, haue bene excommunicated.* And yet, ô admirable prouidence of God, the ſucceſſe of the after ages shewed, that euen in the vſe of his power, the Popes proceeding was iuſt For after the death of *Victor*, the Councells of *Nicea*, of *Conſtantinople*, and of *Epheſus,* excommunicated againe thoſe that held the ſame cuſtome with the prouinces, that the Pope had excommunicated, and placed them in the Catalogue of heretickes, vnder the titles of heretickes *Quarto decumans!*

Calu. vbi ſupra. — Ruffin in verſ. hiſt. Ecel. Euſ. l. 5. c. 24. — Euſeb. hiſt. Eccl. l. 5. c. 24. — Ruffin. ib. c. 24. — Iren. l. 3. c. 3. 1. booke. Chapt. 25. — Euſeb hiſt. Eccl. l. 5. c. 23. — Iren. apud Euſeb. hiſt. Eccl. l. 5. c. 26. — Conc. Antioch. c. 1. Cōc. Conſt c. 7. Cōc. Eph. p. 2. act. 6.

But to this inſtance *Caluins* Sect doe annexe two new obſeruations; the firſt, that the Pope hauing threatned the Biſhops of *Aſia* to excōmunicate them, *Polycrates* the Biſhop of *Epheſus* and Metropolitan of *Aſia,* deſpiſed the Popes threates, as it appeares by the anſwere of the ſame *Polycrates* to Pope *Victor*, which is inſerted in the writings of *Euſebius*, and of S. IEROM, & which S. IEROM ſeemeth to approue, when he ſaith, hee reportes it *to shewe the ſpirit and authoritie of the man.* And the ſecond, that when the Pope pronounced anciently his excommunications, he did noe other thing but ſeparate himſelfe from the communion of thoſe that he excommunicated, and did not thereby ſeparate them from the vniuerſall communion of the Church. To the firſt then we ſaie, that ſoe farr is this epiſtle of *Polycrates* from abating and diminishing the Popes authority, that contrarywiſe it greatly magnifies and exaltes it. For although *Polycrates* blinded with the loue of the cuſtome of his nation, which he beleeued to be grounded vpon the word of God, who had aſſigned the

Euſeb. hiſt. Eccl. l. 5. c. 24. Hieron. in ſcript. Eccl. in Polycr.

fourteenth

of the Month of March for the obseruation of the *Pasche*, and vpon the example of saint IOHNS tradition maintaines it obstinately; Neuertheles, this that he answeres, speaking in his owne name, and in the name of the Councell of the Bishops of *Asia*, to whom he presided; *I feare not those that threaten vs, for my elders haue said, it is better to obaie God then man*. Doth it not shew, that had it not bene, that he belieued the Popes threate, was against the expresse word of God, there had bene cause to feare it, and he had bene obliged to obaie him; for who knowes not, that this answere; *it is better to obaie God then men*, is not to be made but to those, whom we were obliged to obaie, if their commaundements were not contrarie to the commaundments of God; And that he adds, that hee had called the Bishops of *Asia*, to a Nationall Councell, being summoned to it by the Pope; doth it not insinuate, that the other Councells whereof *Eusebius* speakes, that were holden about this matter, through all the prouinces of the Earth, and particularly that of *Palestina*, which if you beleiue the act that *Beda* said came to his handes, *Theophilus* Archbishop of *Cesarea* had called by the auctoritie of *Victor*, were holden at the instance of the Pope, and consequently that the Pope was the first mouer of the vniuersall Church? And that the Councells of *Nicea*, of *Constantinople* of *Ephesus* embraced the censure of *Victor*, and excommunicated those that obserued the custome of *Polycrates*: doth it not proue, that it was not the Pope; but *Polycrates* that was deceiued, in beleiuing that the Popes commaundement, was against Gods commaundement? And that saint IEROM himselfe, celebrates the Paschall homelyes of *Theophilus* Patriarke of *Alexandria*, which followed the order of *Nicea* concerning the *Pasche*; Doth it not iustifie, that when saint IEROM saith; that he reportes the Epistle of *Policrates, to shew the spirit, and authoritie of the man*; he intends by authoritie, not authoritie of right, but of fact; that is to saie, the credit that *Polycrates* had amongst the *Asians* and other *Quartodecumans*?

Exod. 12.

Hieronym. vbi supra.

Euseb. hist. Eccl. l. 5. c. 23.

Beda in frag. de Æquinoctio. vernali.

To the second obseruation; which is, that when the Pope excommucated other Bishops, Archbishops, or Patriarkes, he seperated himselfe from their communion, but did not thereby seperate them from the communion of the Church; Wee will doe noe other thing, then examine examples that they alleadged for proofe of their hypothesis; And yet we will not examine them all, for we haue alreadie confuted the most part of them in the Chapters preceding; as that of saint HILARY against *Liberius*, and others the like? We will onely treat of those that they propound to vs a newe, which consist in three principall heades. The first is, that the fifth Coũcell of *Carthage* ordained, that euery Bishop that should fall into the cases mentioned by the tenth and thirteenth canons of the same Councell, should content himselfe with the communion of his one Church alone, from whence they conclude, that euerie excommunication, did not import priuation of Sacraments. The second, that *Nicephorus* writes, that Pope *Vigilius* hauing excommunicated *Menas* Patriarke of *Constantinople* for fower moneths, *Menas* yeilded him the same measure. And the third, that *Sigesbert* speaking of the proceeding of Pope *Innocent* in the cause of saint CHRISOSTOME saith, that Pope *Innocent* and the Bishops of the *West* suspended themselues from the communion of those of the *East*.

Aboue 1. booke chap. 27.

Niceph. hist. Eccl. l. 17. c. 26.

Sigebert in Chron. ad ann. 409.

To the first then of these examples, which is; *That the fifth Councell of Carthage odaines, that euerie Bishop that should fall into the case of Canons aboue mentioned, should content himself with the communion of his owne Church onelie*; Wee answere two things, The one, that the censure whereof the Canons

of this

of this Councell ſpeake, was not an excommunication, but a reſtitution of communion, by which thoſe that did fall into the caſes whereof there is queſtion, might adminiſter the Euchariſt in their owne Dioceſſes, and to their owne People, but not out of their dioceſſes. And the other, that the Pope himſelfe, often vſed this reſtriction, as it appeares by the Epiſtle of ſaint AVGVSRINE to Pope *Celeſtine* where ſpeaking of the Biſhops of *Africa*, that the Popes his Predeceſſors had reſtored, whether by iudgement, or by confirmation into their Seas, he reckons amongſt the reſt, *Victor* one of the Biſhops of *Mauritania Ceſarea*, who had bene reſtored, conditionallie not to communicate but in his owne Dioceſſe. And by the Epiſtle of Pope LEO the firſt, to *Anatolius* Patriarke of *Conſtantinople*; who ordained that the Biſhops of the *Eaſt*, who had ſinned in the falſe Councell of *Epheſus*, and deſired to returne to the communiō of the Sea Apoſtolicke, they ſhould remaine till they had made ſufficient ſatisfaction, incloſed within the communion of their owne Dioceſſes onely, and barred from communicating with other Catholicke Biſhops From whence it appeares, that the Pope had the Soueraigne iudgement, aſwell of the Biſhops that ought to be admitted to the Catholicke commuuion, as of thoſe that ought to be admitted to the communion of their owne Dioceſſes. For whereas *Balſamon* interpreting one of theſe Canons, ſaith, that it was a cuſtome particular onely to *Africa*, and that it was practiſed noe where els; it was an ignorance of one that had learnt but halfe his leſſon.

August. Epist. 162. edit. Plantin. tom. 2

Leo ad Anatol. Cōst. epist. 38.

Balsam. in Cōc. Carth c. 79.

To the ſecond example, which is, that *Nicephorus* ſaith, that Pope *Vigilius* hauing excommunicated *Menas* Patriarke of *Conſtantinople* for fower Moneths, and that within *Conſtantinople* itſelfe, *Menas* did the like in his behalfe; And that the Emperor *Juſtinian* angrie with *Vigilius* act, ſett men to apprehend him, by meanes whereof he fledd into the Temple of ſaint SERGIVS, where he ſtucke amongſt the organ Pipes becauſe of his groſſenes: Wee anſwere two things; the one, that *Nicephorus* is an author not onely remoued from *Iuſtinians* age more then ſeauen hundred yeares but a Schiſmaticke, and often fabulous, and ſoe dimſighted in the eccleſiaſticall Chronologie of that age, as he placeth a Pope called *Agatho* in the ſame Chapter, and in the Chapters before, betweene *Agapet* and *Siluerius*, and will haue it that this *Agatho* held a Councell at *Conſtantinople* after *Agapets* death; and that he and *Menas* preſided there, againſt all hiſtorie, which teacheth vs, that there was neuer anie Pope called *Agatho*, either that ſucceeded *Agapet*, or was tyme-fellowe with *Menas*, nor that euer was at *Conſtantinople*; And that the firſt Pope that bore the name of *Agatho*, was aboue an hundred and fiftie yeare after *Agapetus*, and neuer ſett foote in *Conſtantinople*; And that if by *Agatho Nicephorus* meane *Boniface* the ſecond who was created in *Iuſtinians* tyme, and whoſe name ſeemes to haue ſome affinitie with the Greeke ſignification of the word *Agatho*, neither was *Boniface* the ſecond Succeſſor, but Predeceſſor to *Agapetus*, nor euer ſawe *Conſtantinople*. And the other that this particular hiſtorie of *Nicephorus* is a fable; as it appeares as well, becauſe neither *Procopius*, nor *Liberatus*, nor *Victor Tunonenſis*, nor *Marcellinus Comes*, nor *Euagrius*, ſome Grecians and ſome latines that haue written the hiſtorie of *Juſtinian*; and all either of the ſame tyme, or of the ſame age, with *Juſtinian*, ſaie nothing of it, as becauſe it is diſproued by the dates of Chronologie. For *Nicephorus* ſaith, that *Inſtinian* repented this action becauſe the Empreſſe *Theodora* interpoſed her interceſſion, and obtayned that *Juſtinian* ſhould receiue *Vigilius*, and *Vigilius* ſhould admitt *Menas* to the communion; and adds, that this fell out the ſame yeare of the

Niceph. vbi supra Ibidem.

fifth

fifth generall Councell, which was the twentie ſeauenth yeare of the Empire of *Iuſtinian*. a Now beſides that the Empreſſe was not likely to ſolicit either for *Vigilius*, who had excommunicated her, b becauſe ſhe would haue inforced him to haue receiued *Anthymus* Patriarke of *Conſtantinople*, whoſe hereſie ſhe followed; or for *Menas*, who had bene eſtabliſhed in ſteede of *Anthymus*; c *Procopius* d and *Victor* of *Tunes* e Authors of the ſame tyme, and *Theophanes* f after them affirme, that the Empreſſe *Theodora* was dead in the beginning of the two and twentith yeare of *Iuſtinian*, that is to ſaie, more then fiue yeare before the fifth Councell of the ſame ſtampe, it is that *Anaſtaſius Bibliothecary*, g an Author noe leſſe fabulous in things remote from this tyme, and fower hundred yeare diſtant from the age of *Iuſtinian*, ſaith, that the Emperor in the beginning receiued *Vigilius* with great honor & went to meete him, the Clergie of *Conſtantinople* ſinging: *Beholde the Lord, the Ruler cometh*: But that afterward the Empreſſe who was an *Eutychian* hauing wonn her husband to cauſe *Anthymus* to be reſtored, the head of the *Eutychian* faction, and *Vigilius* hauing called them, *Diocleſian Eleutherius* one of the aſſiſtants ſtrucke *Vigilius* vpon the face, and ſaid to him, *Manſlayer knoweſt thou to whom thou ſpeakeſt? art thou ignorant that thou sleweſt Pope Siluerius?* By occaſion whereof *Vigilius* being fledd into *Chalcedon*, the Empreſſe made him be plucked out of the Temple of S. EVPHEMIA, and made him be dragged with a cord about his necke through the ſtreetes of *Conſtantinople*; for firſt, neither *Procopius*, nor *Victor* of *Tunes*, nor *Liberatus*, nor *Marcellinus Comes*, nor *Euagrius* reporte anie ſuch thing. And ſecondlie, the ſame repugnancie as is in the fable of *Nicephorus*, is in this alſoe; to witt, that the Empreſſe was then alreadie dead. And it is not to be ſaid, that the acts that runn vnder *Vigilius* his name againſt *Menas*, h make mention of the euill entertainement that *Vigilius* receiued frō the Emperor. For beſides this, that the date of the acts which is of the fiue & twentith yeare of the Empire of *Iuſtinian*, ſeemeth to be diſproued by the acts of the ſixth generall Councell, where the legats of the Pope did proue, that the writing which the *Monothelites* had ſuppoſed vnder this title, i *A diſcourſe of Menas to Vigilius, in the fifth Councell*, was falſe, *for as much as the fifth Councell had bene holden the twentie ſeauenth yeare of the Empire of Iuſtinian, and that Menas was dead the one and twentith.* If it be not ſo, that in ſteede of εἰκοςῷ πρώτῳ, which ſignifies one and twentith, it should be read εἰκοςῷ πέμπτῳ, which ſignifies fiue and twentith, which were yet ſufficient for the concluſion, that the Popes legats would drawe from it; to witt, that *Menas* was dead before the fifth Councell. Beſides this I ſaie, theſe acts ſpeake not but of the flight of *Vigilius* to the Temples of S. PETER and of S. EVPHEMIA, and affirme that it happened, not for the quarrell of *Anthimus* and the Empreſſe, but becauſe *Vigilius* had condemned the Emperors Edict, concerning the three chapters; and they noted, that the retreate of *Vigilius* into the Temple of S. EVPHEMIA, was but the fiue and twentith yeare of the Empire of *Iuſtinian*, more then three yeare before which tyme *Theodora* the Empreſſe was dead: And thē ſuppoſe that *Vigilius*, the memorie of whoſe intruſion made him the more apt to be diſpiſed, for as much as he got into the Papacie by the plott of the Empreſſe, & with hereticall & ſimonicall couenants, his predeceſſor *Siluerius* being ſtill aliue, and was become true Pope but after the death of *Siluerius*; after which the Clergie of *Rome* for the benefit of peace had accepted him, had bene perſecuted and vnworthily vſed at *Conſtantinople* by the Emperor, with whom he was conſtrained to ſpend his life in exile, becauſe the *Gothes* vnder the conduct of their new King *Totilas*, had againe taken *Rome*; whereto would this turne, but to the glorie of *Vigilius*, and to the

a Concil. Conſt. 6. œcumenic. act. 3. & Vict. Tun. in Iuſtin.
b Gregor. magn. l. 2. indict. 10. epiſt. 36. Paul. Diac. ſiue Theophan. hiſt. l. 17. & alij
c Concil. Conſt. ſub Men. act. 1. Marcellin. Com. in Chron. Liberat. in breuiar. c. 21. Victor Tun. in Chron.
d. Procop. de boll. Goth. l. 3. de bello Perſ. l. 1. & de bell Ital aduerſus Goth. l. 4.
e. Victor Tunenſis Chron. in Iuſtin.
f. Theoph. vel ſecundū alios, Paul. Diacon. in Iuſtinian.
g. Anaſtaſ. Bibliothec. de vit. Pontific. in Vigil.
h. Vigil. ep. ad vniuers.
i. Concil. Cōnſt. 6. œcum. act. 3.

Vigil. ep. ad vniuers

Niceph. vbi supra. shame of the Emperor? For saith not *Nicephorus*, that the Emperor repented it, and doe not the same actes shew, that he sent the principall ministers of his Empire to *Vigilius* to praie him to returne? And that Vigil. ep. ad Vniuers. *Vigilius* during this persecution, remained so constant, that he would neuer giue anie waie to the Emperors violences, but deposed in *Constantinople* it self *Theodorus* Archbishop of *Cesarea*, the principall Gouernor of the Emperor; and excommunicated *Menas* Patriarke of *Constantinople*, and all that adhered to him. Did it not throughlie shew, the confidence Vigil. Pap. in fragm. damnat. Theod. to. 2. Concil. he had in the dignitie of his Sea? *Wee decree thee* (saith hee) *ô Theodorus, late Bishop of Cesarea, by the publication of this sentence, depriued as well of Sacerdotall honor, and of the Catholicke communion, as of all Episcopall power and function; and wee ordaine, that thou shalt heereafter applie thy-self to nothing, but to the teares of pennance, by which hauing obtained remission of thy crimes, thou maist recouer; if thou deseruest it, the place of indulgence, and of communion with me, or after my death, with my successor. And thou Menas Bishop of the cittie of Constantinople, which art inwrapt with the same crime, with all the Bishops, Metropolitans, and Micropolitans, &c, wee suspend you from the sacred communion, till eache of you, acknowledging the error of his preuarication, haue blotted out before vs his proper fault with a competent satisfaction.* And this that he cries out, numbring *Theodo-* Ibidem. *rus* his crimes; *Thou art come in despising the authoritie of the Sea Apostolicke, which had pronounced interdiction by vs into the Church where there hung the Emperors Edicte, and there hast celebrated the solemnity of Masse.* Idem ep. ad vniuers. And this that he adds; *Wee haue charged the Ministers of the most clement Emperor, to signifie to him from vs, that he ought not to communicate with those which haue by vs bene excommunicated, least he thereby runne, which God forbid, into a grieuous sinne.* Doth it not shew that the Pope in excommunicating the other Bishops, Archbishops, and Patriarks, did not onelie pretend to separate himselfe from their communion, but to separate them, and cutt them of from the communion of the Church? And as for the persecution of the Empresse which happened long before, and for an other cause, to witt, forasmuch as *Vigilius* after his predecessor *Siluerius* was dead, and that he was become true Pope, would not keepe the promise that he had made, and secretlie accomplisht to her during his Antipapacy, to admitt *Anthymus* and the other *Eutychians* into his communion. What greater glorie could *Vigilius* receiue, then that whereof S. GREGORIE speakes when Gregor. Magn. l. 2. indict. 10. ep. 36. he writes; *Pope Vigilius constituted in the Royall cittie, that is to saie, at Constantinople, publisht a sentence of condemnation against Theodora then Empresse, and against the Acephales?* And what more visible punishment could the Empresse receiue, then that whereof *Victor Tunonensis* writes; Vict. Tun. in Chron. *The ninth yeare after the Consulship of Basilius, the Empresse Theodora, enemie to the Councell of Chalcedon strucken her whole bodie ouer with the wound of an vniuersall canker; (that is to saie, with leprosie) prodigiouslie ended her life?* For whereas the same *Victor*, who was a Schismaticke, and tooke part with *Rusticus* the Deacon, and other *Roman* Clerkes reuolted against Pope *Vigilius*, and against the fifth generall Councell, writeth that the Bishops of *Africa*, that is to saie, the schismaticall Bishops of *Africa* (for the Catholicke Bishops of *Africa* tooke the Ibidem. other part) excommunicated *Vigilius*, there hath alreadie bene two things spoken of concerning this; the one that they held not *Vigilius* for true Pope, but for an intrusiue Pope, because he had vsurped the Papacie, his predecessor *Siluerius* being yet aliue, as it appeares by this, that the same *Victor* placeth a little after amongst the nullities of the fifth

generall

generall Councell, the vice of the creation of *Vigilius*, *who had*, said he, *bene ordained Bishop of Rome*, *Siluerius being still aliue*. And the other, that Pope *Siluerius* had alreadie long before excommunicated *Vigilius* for hauing intruded himselfe into the Papacie in these termes; *Doe thou then receiue, and those that consent with thee the sentence of paine of condemnation, and know that being condemned by vs, by the iudgement of the holy Ghost, and by the Apostolicke authoritie, that the name and office of Sacerdotall ministery, is taken from thee.* And againe; *Cælius Siluerius Pope of the cittie of Rome giuing consent to all the statutes, I haue signed this decree of Anathema against the vsurper Vigilius.* By meanes whereof, the act of the Schismaticall Bishops of *Africa* against *Vigilius*, was rather a renouation and an application of the excommunication of Pope *Siluerius*, then a primitiue and originall excommunication. Vict. Tun ad ann. 13 post cõsul. Basil. Syluer. Pap ep ad Vigil Ibidem.

To the third example, which is, that *Sigebert* writes, that Pope *Innocent* the first, and the Bishops of the *West*, suspended themselues from the communion of those of the *East* for the quarrell of Saint CHRYSOSTOME; from whence the Protestants inferr, that when the Pope excommunicated the other Bishops, Archbishops, or Patriarks, he separated himselfe from their communion; and did not separate them, from the communion of the Church: Wee haue three answeres; the first, that it is a ridiculous thing, to alleadge for the testimonie of the historie of Pope *Innocent*, and of S. CHRYSOSTOME, *Sigebert*; who writt seauen hundred yeares after them, and who was an open enemie to the Sea Apostolicke, and partaker with the Emperor *Henry* the fourth against Pope *Gregorie* the seauenth and his successors. The second, that Pope *Innocent* the first, did not suspend himselfe from the communion of those of the *East*, but suspended those of the *East* from the Ecclesiasticall communion: the which although they still continued in fact with some of their Diocesans according to the custome of Schismatickes, this hindred them not from being suspended by right, and that they should send to demaund restitution of the Pope, as it appeares by these words of the same *Innocent* in the epistle to *Boniface*; *Know* (saith he, speaking of those of *Antioch*) *that we haue receiued them into our bowells, least the members which had a long while required health, should be excluded from the vnitie of the bodie.* And in the epistle to *Maximianus*; *What we haue done in the behalf of those of Antioch, we will doe it in the behalfe of others, if they will accomplish the same treaties and conditions, and send as those did, to beseeche by a solemne legation, that the communion might be restored to them.* And in the Epistle to *Alexander* Patriarke of *Antioch*; *I haue diligentlie inquired, whether the cause of the blessed Bishop Iohn had bene satisfied in all conditions, and hauing learned from those of your legation, that all things had bene accomplished according to our desire I haue by the grace of God, admitted the communion of your Church.* And a little after; *As for the letters of the Bishop Atticus, because they were ioyned with yours, we haue receiued them, least the refusall of a man, alreadie a long while suspended by vs, should turne to your preiudice; and yet we haue sufficiently, and more then sufficiently ordained in the acts, what ought to be obserued in his person.* And *Theodoret* treating of the same matter; *Iohn being dead, those of the West, would neuer admitt the communion, either of the Egiptians, those of the East, nor of the Bishops of Bosphorus and Thrace; that is to saie, of the diuision of Constantinople, till they had inscribed the name of that admirable personage into the rolle of the Bishops his predecessors; and esteemed Arsacius, that succeeded him, scarce worthie of a salutation; and as for Atticus successor of* Sigebert. in Chron. ad ann. 409. Innoc. ad Bonif. ep. 14. Idem ad Maximian. epist. 16. Theodor. hist. Eccl. l. 5. c. 34.

Arſacius, after manie legations and requeſts for peace, they receiued him finallie but when he had added the name of Iohn to the other Bishops. And the third, that if what *Sigebert* writes were true, there were great difference betweene ſuſpending themſelues from the communion of anie one, which was ſometymes done by intermitting the commerce of communicatory letters, and excommunicating him, or making him incommunicable, ἀκοινώνητον ποιεῖν and that in the matter of verie excommunications there was great difference betweene *minor* excommunications, which depriued thoſe that were ſmitten with them from the vſe of the Sacraments, but depriued them not as is aboue ſaid, from the other fruits of the

Aboue 1. booke Chap. 27. Churches communion; and the *maior* excommunications, which tooke awaie not onely the vſe of the Sacraments, but caſt out thoſe that were therewith attainted, from the bodie and ſocietie of the Church. Now it was with this kind of excommunication, wherewith Pope *Victor* excommunicated the Bishops of *Aſia*, who obſerued the Paſche

Euſ. hiſt. Eccl. l. 5. c. 25. according to the Iewish computation. *Victor* (ſaith *Euſebius*) *moued with the anſwere of Polycrates, attempted to cutt of at one blowe from the common vnion, all the Dioceſſes of Aſia, and the neighbouring Churches as Heterodoxall, and proſcribed them by letters, declaring all the bretheren which inhabited thoſe Regions,*

Ibid. c. 26. *incommunicable.* And againe; *Ireneus exhorted Victor, that he should not cutt of* μὴ ἀποκόπτειν *all the Churches of God, that obſerued the tradition of this ancient cuſtome.* By which wordes it maie appeare, that the meaning of *Victors* cenſure was, not ſimplie to ſeperate himſelfe from the communion of the *Aſians*, but to diuide and cutt of the *Aſians* from the bodie and ſocietie of the whole Church; and that the remonſtrance and exhortation that S. IRENEVS and others made him, was not to keepe him from ſeperating himſelfe from the cōmunion of the *Aſians*, but that he should not cutt of the *Aſians* from the bodie and common maſſe of the Church for the verbes, to *proſcribe*, and to *declare* incommunicable, expreſſe an other thing, then to ſeperate himſelfe from them; & the Greeke word ἀποκόπτειν whereof *Euſebius* makes vſe, ſignifieth to diuide and cutt of from the bodie and from the maſſe; for which cauſe *Ruffinus* hath

Ruffi. hiſt. Eccl. l. 5. c. 24. tranſlated it; to cutt of from the vnitie of the bodie; *He reproued him* (ſaith *Ruffinus*) *for not doeing well in cutting of from the vnitie of the bodie, ſo manie and ſo great Churches of God.* And certainlie, what ſubiect of terror had Pope *Victor* giuē to the Bishops of *Aſia* in threatning to excōmunicate them, if he had intended onely to ſeperate himſelfe from them? And why

Polycrat. apud Euſeb hiſt. Eccl. l. 5 c. 24. & apud Hieron. in catal. ſcrip. Eccleſ. should *Polycrates* haue ſaid, that hauing the word of God for him, he feared not thoſe that threatned him; if this threat had bene noe more but to ſeperate himſelf from their communion, and not to ſeperate and cutt them of, from the communion of the bodie, and from the ſocietie of the Church? For what greater wound had the *Aſian* Bishops receiued in the Popes ſeperation from them, then the Pope in the *Aſian* Bishops ſeperation from him, if the Popes excommunication had bene noe other thing, then a declaration, that ſeperated himſelfe from their communion? Contrariwiſe, the Bishops of *Aſia minor*, and of the neighbouring prouinces, that the Pope comprehended in his cenſure, being ſo great number as *Polycrates* ſaith, that if hee should repreſent their names, the multitude would ſeeme too great; why had it not bene more opprobry for the Pope, to be ſeperated from them, then for them to be ſeparated frō the Pope, if the Popes excōmunication, had bene but a ſimple declaration that he departed from their cōmunion? And it can not be ſaid, that *Euſebius* writes, that *Victor* attempted to cutt them of; for the queſtion is not of the diminutiue termes, which *Euſebius*, whom S. IEROM calls *the ensignebearer of the Arrian faction*, vseth with an Arrian enuie and malignitie against the *Romane* Church; but of the intention of *Victor*, & of the Bishops that made their remonstrances to him. And yet lesse can it be replied that the other Bishops opposed themselues against it, for they opposed it not, but in the forme of remonstrances and exhortations, representing to him not that he could not doe it, and that he enterprized beyond his iurisdiction; but that for soe small a cause he ought not to cutt of soe manie Churches from the vniuersall bodie and societie of the Church. Wherein was discouered the euill will of *Eusebius* against the *Roman* Church, who saith that the other Bishops did bitterly reproue *Victor*; & when there is question to produce an example of the bitternes of their reprehensions, he alleadges for his onely patterne; the words of S. IRENEVS, where there is not one bitter word to be found, & which containeth onely simple & gentle remonstrances, and full of submission to the person of *Victor*, and to the authoritie of his Sea. For to represent to the Pope that he ought not to cutt of so manie Churches from the bodie, and from the societie of the vniuersall Church; was it anie other thing then to confesse, that if the cause had bene sufficient, as afterward the Councells of *Nicea* and of *Ephesus* shewed it to be, it belonged to him to cut them of, and chiefely in the time of the pagan Emperors, vnder whom noe generall councells could be celebrated? And to vse the word ἀποκόπτειν, which signifies to diuide and cutt of from the bodie and from the masse; what was it, but to saie, that it was the Roman Church; that as the stocke and roote did not cutt her selfe of from the Churches, that she excommunicated, but cutt them of from her selfe, and in cutting them of from her selfe, cutt them of from the communion of the whole bodie, noe more nor lesse, then the head in cutting of anie member from the communion thereof, cutts not it selfe of from that, but cutts of that from it selfe; and in cutting it of, doth not onely cutt it of from the communion of the head onely, but from the communion of the whole bodie; or that the stocke and roote, in cutting of some branche, cuts not of it selfe from that, but cutts that of from it selfe, and in cutting it of, cutts it not of onely from the communion of the roote, but from that of the whole tree? And therefore we alsoe see, that in all the breaches of communion which haue bene betweene the *Roman* Church and the other Churches, there hath happened fower things? The first, that when other Churches haue separated themselues from the *Roman*, all the Catholicke Churches haue alwaies remained vnited with the *Roman*, and haue separated themselues from those which haue forsaken her. The second, that when it hath bene the *Roman* Church, which hath excõmunicated others, all the Catholicke Churches haue forsaken them; or if they not thought the cause of the excommunication grieuous, haue had recourse to the *Roman* Church with remonstrances, and intercessions to beseeche her to suspend and reuoke her censure; as it appeares both by the words of S. IRENEVS to Pope *Victor* vpon the excommunication of the *Asians*: he exhorted him not to cutt of all the Churches of God which held the tradition of this ancient custome. And by those of *Dionisius* Bishop of *Alexandria*, to Pope *Steuen*, vpon the condemnation of the Bishops of *Cappadocia*; *I haue* (said hee) *written beseeching him for all these things*; or occording to the other translation; *beseeching him for them all*. And by these of *Socrates* vpon the Popes censure against *Flauianus* Patriarke of *Antioch*; *Theophilus Patriarke of Alexandria hauing sent the Priest Isidorus appeased Damasus* (you must reade *Anastasius*) *his indignation, and represented to him, that it was profitable for the concord of the people, to forgett the fault of Fla-*

Eufeb. cõt. Ruffin. Apol. 1.

Cõci Antioch c. 1. Conc. Eph. p. 2. act. 6.

Iren. apud. Eufeb. vbi supra.

Dionif. Alexãd. apud Eufeb. hist. Eccl. l. 7. c. 5.

Socr. hist. Eccl. l. 5. c. 15.

uianus; and soe the communion hauing bene restored to Flauianus, the factions of the people of Antioch, were soone after revnited. And by these of the Councell of *Carthage* vpon Pope *Innocents* sentence against *Theophilus* Patriark of *Alexandria* for S. CHRYSOSTOMES cause; *It had bene agreed vpon, that concerning the dissention of the Roman and Alexandrian Churches, Pope Innocent should be written to, that both Churches may obserue the peace that our Lord hath commaunded.* For why should it be ordained, that Pope *Innocent* should be written to, and not *Theophilus* Patriarke of *Alexandria*, but because it was the Pope that kept the key of the Ecclesiasticall communion; and that it was the *Roman* Church to whom it belonged to receaue the *Alexandrian* Church into her communion, and not to the *Alexandrian* Church to receiue the *Roman* into her communion? And in briefe, that it belonged to the *Roman* Church to prescribe to the *Alexandrian*, the lawes of the revnion, and not to the *Alexandrian* to prescribe them to the *Roman*; as *Theodoret* witnesseth, that it happened a while after in these words; *John being dead, those of the West would neuer admitt the communion nether of the Egiptians, nor of those of the East, nor of the Bishops of Bosphorus and Thrace till they had inscribed the name of this admirable personage into the rolle of the Bishops his predecessors?* And the third, that when the separation hath continued, those that were excluded from the communion of the *Roman*, haue alwaies bene cast out from the communion of the other Catholicke Churches, and reputed for heretickes or schismatickes; as it appeares euen in the busines of the *Asians* excommunicated by *Victor*, whose Sectaries were afterward constrained to abiure their heresie in these termes; *I anathematize all heresie, and particularlie that of the Quartodecumans?* And the fowrth, that when the deuided partes were to be revnited, the other Churches haue alwaies sent to take and demaund their restitution into the commnnion of the *Roman* Church, and that the *Roman* Church neuer sent, to take or demaund that of other Churches? *Those of the West* (saith *Theodoret*, speaking of *Flauianus* Patriarke of *Antioch*) *promised to laie by all bitternesse, and to receaue the Embassadors that Flauianus should send. Which the diuine Flauianus hauing heard, he sent a legation of famous Bishops, and Priests, and Deacons of Antioch to Rome.* And *Socrates*; *The communion hauing bene restored to Flauianus, the parts of the Church of Antioch, were soone after reunited,* And Pope *Innocent* the first, writing to *Alexander* Patriarke of *Antioch* vpon S. IOHN CHRYSOSTOMES cause; *I haue diligentlie inquired whether the case of the blessed Bishop Iohn, had bene satisfied in all pointes, and hauing found by those of your legation, that all things had bene accomplished according to our desire, I haue by the grace of God admitted the communion of your Church.* And *Theodoret* treating of the same matter. *Iohn being dead, those of the West would neuer admitt the communion, neither of the Egiptians, nor of those of the East, nor of the Bishops of Bosphorus and Thrace; that is to saie, of the diuision of Constantinople, till they had inscribed the name of that admirable personage, into the rolle of the Bishops his predecessors, and scarcely esteemed Arsacius who had succeeded him worthie to be saluted; and as for Atticus successor to Arsacius, after manie legations and requests for peace, they finallie receaued him, but when he had first added the name of Iohn to the other Bishops.* And Pope *Leo* in his Epistle to *Anatolius* Patriark of *Constantinople* concerning the Bishops of the false councell of *Ephesus*; *Wee will* (said hee) *that by our Legats, the care of the affaire being communicated to thee, it be ordained, that those that with full satisfaction shall condemne their euill actions, and rather chose to accuse, then to defend themselues, shall enioy the vnitie of our peace and cōmunion.* And else where; *But as for those that haue more grieuously sinned, if they after such satisfactiō, as it shall seeme it ought not*

Cōc. Cart. sub consul. Honor. 7. & Theodos. 2.

Theodor. hist. Eccl. l. 5. c. 34.

Conc Eph. p. 2. act. 6.

Theodor. hist. Eccl. l. 5. c. 23.

Soc. hist. Eccl. l. 5. c. 15.

Innocent. ad Alexan. ep. 17.

Theodor. hist. Eccl. vbi supra.

Ibid.

Leo ad Anatol. ep. 38.

Id. ad eund. ep. 44.

to be

to be refused &c. let the things be reserued to the more mature determination of the Sea Apostolicke. And Pope *Hormisdas* tyme-felowe with the Emperor *Iustin* in his Epistle to *Epiphanius* Patriarke of *Constantinople*; *You must* (said hee) *put on my person, and of those that shall ioyne with you in communion, and by you to the Sea Apostolick, informe vs by your letters therein, inserting therein the tenor of the libells which they shall haue preseted.* And againe; *Which we thought we ought to impose vpon you, laying our charge vpon your diligence, because you haue giuen noe small proofe of your resistance to hereticks.* And *Victor* of *Tunes* reporting the same historie: *The Emperor Iustin reunited those of the East &c. with meete satisfaction for those of the West.* And the Emperor *Iustinian* nephew and Successor to *Iustin*, in the Epistle to Pope *Iohn* surnamed *Mercurius*; *Wee haue hastned to submitt and vnite to your Holynesse Sea, all the Prelates of the East Countries.* And certainelie if the Pope had holden noe other ranke in the ecclesiasticall communion then the other Patriarkes, Archbishops, or Bishops, for what cause was it, that when the Pope excommunicated anie other Patriarkes, as when he excommunicated *Flauianus, Porphirius*, and *Peter* Patriarkes of *Antioch* or as when he excommunicated *Nestorius Accacius* & *Anthimus* Archbishops of *Constantinople*, or as whē he excōmunicated *Theophilus, Peter*, and other Patriarkes of *Alexandria*, hee did for all this incurr noe censure, from the Bishops, or Catholicke Councells, but was reputed to doe, what he might doe? Whereas, when anie other Patriarke, yea vnder the pretence of a generall Councell, did excommunicate the Pope, he was punished and deposed for this presumption, as for an enormious and extraordinary Sacrilege. For what had not *Dioscorus* Patriarke of *Alexandria* done in his false Councell of *Ephesus*? he had embraced the heresie of *Eutyches*; he had condemned the Catholicke doctrine; he had excommunicated *Flauianus* Archbishop of *Constantinople* who maintained it; and had not only excommunicated him, but alsoe slaine him: And neuertelesse, ô eminent dignitie of the Sea Apostolicke! these Sacrileges were not the principall causes of his deposition, but that he and his pretended Councell had dared to excommunicate the Pope; *Dioscorus* (saith *Anatolius* Archbishop of *Constantinople*) *hath not bene deposed for the faith, but because he excommunicated my Lord, the Archbishop Leo, and that hauing bene cited thrice before the Councell, he appeared not.* And the Fathers of the Councell of *Chalcedon* in their relation to the Pope; *After all these things* (said they) *he hath extended his frensie euen against him; to whom the guard of the Vine hath bene committed by our Sauiour; that is to saie, against thy Holynesses, and hath meditated an excommunication against him, who laboreth to vnite the bodie of the Church.* But why should wee haue recourse to particular examples, since the common voice of antiquitie teacheth vs, that in all the tumults, and in all the confusions of the Schismes and heresies, which haue perturbed the Christian Religion, the *Roman* Church hath alwaies bene as the center, the principle, and originall of the ecclesiasticall communion, and as the Ensigne colonell of the armie of Iesus Christ, vpon whom all the other Catholick Churches haue cast their eyes, and to whom they haue gathered themselues separating themselues from the communion of those that, communicated not with her and embracing the communion of those, who communicated with her? For what meane these wordes of saint IRENEVS *With the Roman Church because of a more powerfull principalitie, it is necessarie that euerie Church should complie*: And these of saint CYPRIAN; *The Roman Church is the Chaire of Peter, and the principall Church, from whence the Sacerdotall vnitie hath proceeded*: And these of saint AMBROSE; *Hee asked whether the Bishop of that place, consented with the Catholick Bishops, that is to saie, with the Roman*

Conc. sub. Men. Act. 5. Ibid.

Vict. Tun. in Chronic

Codic l. 1. Tit. 1. l. 8.

Concil. Chalced. Act. 5.

Côc. Chalc relat. ad Leon.

Iren. l. 3. c. 3

Cypr ad Corn. ep. 55

Ambros. de obit. Frat.

Church

Church: And these of *Theodoret*; *The Emperor Gratian commaunded that the Churches should be deliuered to those, that held communion with Damasus, which was* (added hee,) *executed throughout the world*: but that the *Roman* Church, was the center, the beginning and the roote of ecclesiasticall communion, and that whosoeuer was admitted to her communion, was likewise admitted to the communion of the whole Bodie of the Catholicke Church; and that those, who were excluded out of her communion, were excluded out of the communion of the whole Bodie of the Catholicke Church? And what meane these wordes of saint HIEROM: *I am ioyned in communion with thy Blessednes; that is to saie, with the Sea of Peter, I know the Church is founded vpon that Rock, &c. whosoeuer eateth the lambe out of this howse, he is prophane*. And a little after; *I know not Vitalis, I am ignorant of Paulinus, I reiect Meletius whosoeuer gathers not with the, scatters*. And againe: *In the meane time I crie; If anie one be ioyned to Peters Chaire, he is mine*. And these of Optatus *Mileuitanus*: *At Rome there hath bene setled to Peter the Episcopall Chaire, in which there was sett the first of all the Apostles, Peter, &c. to the end that in this onlie Chaire, the vnitie of all, might be preserued*. And a litle after: *In the person of Cyricius, all the world cõmunicates with vs, by the commerce of formed letters*. And againe; *From whence is it, that you pretend to vsurpe to your selues, the keyes of the Kingdome, you that combate against Peters Chaire by your presumptions and bold Sacriledges?* But that the *Roman* Church was the center, the principle, and the roote of Ecclesiasticall communion, and that those that were admitted into her communion, were admitted into the communion of the whole Catholicke Church; and that those, that were excluded from her communion, were excluded from the communion of the whole Bodie of the Catholicke Church? And what meane these words of saint AVSTIN, *In the Roman Church hath alwaies flourisht the principalitie of the Apostolick Sea*. And those of *Eulalius* Bishop of *Syracusa* to saint FVLGENTIVS to turne him from goeing to the Monasteries of *Egipt*: *The Countries whither thou desirest to trauell, a perfidious dissention, hath separated them from the communion of the blessed Peter; all those Religious persons, whose admirable abstinence is celebrated, should not haue the Sacraments of the Altar common with thee?* And these of *Victor* of *Tunes*, speaking of the rebellion of *Vitalian* against the Emperor *Anastasius*, the hereticke: *Hee would neuer promise peace to the Emperor, till first he had restored the defendors of the Councell of Chalcedon, who had bene banisht into their owne Seas, and till he had vnited all the Churches of the East, to the Roman*: But that the *Roman* Church was the center, principle and the roote of the Ecclesiasticall communion; and that those who were admitted to her commuuion, were admitted to the communion of the whole Catholicke Church; & that those who were excluded from the communion of the whole Bodie of the Catholicke Church? And what doe these wordes of *John* Patriarke of *Constantinople* intend; *We promise, not to recite amidst the sacred misteries, the names of those, who are seperated from the communion of the Catholick Church: that is to saie, who doe not fullie consent with the Sea Apostolicke?* And those of the Emperor IVSTINIAN; *Wee preserue in all things, the vnitie of the most holie Churches with the most holie Pope of old Rome?* And these of *Menas* Patriarke of *Constantinople*: *Wee follow the Sea Apostolick and obeie it, and communicate with those that communicate therewith; and condemne those, that it condemneth?* And these of the Bishops returning from the Schisme to the Church in the time of saint GREGORIE the *Great*: *I promise I will neuer returne to the Schisme, from whence, by the mercie of our Redeemer, I haue bene deliuered; but that* I *will remaine alwaies in the vnitie of the Catholick Church, and in the communion of the Bishop of Rome*; but that the *Roman* Church was the center, the principle, and the Roote, of the

Theod. histor. Eccl. l. 5. c. 2.

Hieron. ad Damas. ep. 57.

Ibid. ep. 8.

Optat. Mileuit. cont. Parm. l. 2.

Idem ibidem.

Idem ibidem.

Aug. ep. 162.

Autor. vit. Fulgent. Fœliciano Successori ipsius, dicatæ.

Vict. Tun. Chronic. in Anast.

Ioan. Patr. Constant. ep. ad Hormisd. tom. 2. Concil.

Cod. l. 1. tit. 1 l. 7.

Concil. Const. sub. Men. act. 4

Greg. Magn. l. 10 indict. 5. ep. 31.

the ecclesiasticall communion; and that those that were admitted into her communion, were admitted into the Communion of the whole Catholicke Church: and that those that were seperated from her communion, were seperated from the communion of the whole Bodie of the Catholick Church?

Of the oppositions of saint Cyprian.

CHAPT. III.

THE second instance of *Caluin*, is taken from saint CYPRIAN, and consistes in seauen heades produced by him, or by his disciples; The first; that saint CYPRIAN calls Pope *Steuen*, Brother. The second that he complaines, because *Basilides* a Bishop of *Spaine*, hauing bene deposed by a Synod of his Prouince, for hauing bowed vnder persecution, and an other hauing bene ordained in his place, Pope *Steuen* restored him. The third, that he saith, there were but a small number of lost and desperate persons, who beleeued that the authoritie of the Bishops of *Africa*, was lesser. The fowrth, that he saith, that the ecclesiasticall causes ought to be determined, where they were bredd. The fift, that hee affirmes, that the Episcopall power is one thing, whereof euerie one holdes his portion, vndiuidedly. The sixth, that hee cries, none of vs constitutes himselfe Bishopp of Bishopps. And the seauenth, finallie that he vseth rude wordes against Pope *Steuen*, and accuses him of ignorance and of presumption. To the first then of these heades, which is that saint CYPRIAN calls Pope *Cornelius* brother: Wee answere, he calls him Brother, not to denie to him the superintendencie of the Ecclesiasticall gouernement; but for two other causes: The one to insinuate that the Popes superintendencie ouer other Bishops, was not a Lordly Monarchie, as that of temporall princes ouer their subiects; but a gentle and brotherly Monarchie, as that of an elder brother ouer his younger Bretheren, which is the title that our Lord himselfe would beare when he made himselfe be called the first borne amongst manie bretheren, and which is the memoriall of humilitie, that God had giuen to the Kings of his people, when he had pronounced; *Thou shalt take a king from amongst thy bretheren*. And againe *that the kings heart, may not be exalted aboue his bretheren*. From whence it is, that the Scripture, to represent this brotherly Monarchie, as well in the Sacerdotall, as in the politicke order, saith in the first booke of *Esdras: And Josua sonne of Josedeck rose vp, and the priests his bretheren, and built vp the Altar of* God. And the other to signifie the vnitie of the communion, that *Tertullian* calls the nomination of brotherhood and to shew that he spake not of the Antipope *Nouatianus*, to whom the Schismatickes adhered; but of the true Pope *Cornelius* and of *Steuen* his successor, with whom the Catholicke Bishops communicated as *Erasmus* hath acknowledged vpon the same place of saint CYPRIAN in these termes: *The word*, BROTHER *doth not there signifie equalitie, but societie of Religion*: For that it was a familiar thing for ancient authors to vse the word Brother not to exclude the superioritie of iurisdiction, but to expresse the vnitie of communion, it appeares by a thousand testimonies. It appeares first by the testimonie of saint AMBROSE, who calls the Bishop of *Rome*, his holy Brother, and neuerthe-

[Margin notes: Inst. Calu. 4 c. 7. — Cyp. in ep. ad Cornel. — Rom. 8. — Deuter. 17 — Ibidem. — Esdr. 1. c. 3. — Erasm. annot. in ep. Cyprian. ad Cornel. — Ambros. ep 78.]

lesse in the same place aduertiseth *Theophilus* Patriarke of *Alexandria*, who was a committee from the Councell of *Capua*, to iudge the cause of *Flauianus* Patriarke of *Antioch*, to procure his iudgement to be confirmed by the Pope. *Wee conceaue* (said hee,) *that you ought to referr the affaire to our holy brother Bishop of the Roman Church, for wee presume you will iudge soe as can not displease him*. And a little after that; *Wee hauing receaued the tenor of your acts, when wee shall see that you haue iudged things soe, as the Roman Church shall vndoubtedlie approue, we will receiue with ioy the fruite of your examination*. It appeares secondly by the testimonie of the Catholicke Bishops of *Africa* who answered the *Donatists* in the conference of *Carthage*, that *Cecilianus* Archbishop of *Carthage* had bene their brother: *Hee was* (saith saint AVSTIN) *our brother because of the communion of the Sacraments*. And neuertheles, the Archbishop of *Carthage* was head and Superintendent of all the Bishops of *Africa*. It appeares thirdly by the testimonie of saint AVGVSTINE, who calls *Aurelius* Archbishop of *Carthage* his brother; and neuerthesse, saint AVGVSTINE was the spirituall subiect to *Aurelius*, and had bene made Bishop of *Hippo* by meanes of the dispensation that *Aurelius* had giuen to *Valerius*, to take him for coadiutor, and himselfe acknowledged that he was obliged to executehis commaundemēts. *I haue* (said hee) *obeied thy commaundements my holie brother Aurelius*. It appeares fowrthlie, by the testimonie of *Epigonius* one of the Bishops of the third Councell of *Carthage*, who calls the same *Aurelius*, his brother; and neuertheleſſe acknowledgeth in the same place, that *Aurelius* had superintendencie ouer all *Africa*. It appeares in the fifth place by the testimonie of *John* Patriarke of *Constantinople*, who writing to Pope *Hormisdas*, intituleth him his Brother, and neuertheles protests; *Wee doe in all things followe the Sea Apostolicke, and preach all that hath bene thereby decided; And promise in the tyme to come, not to recite amidst the sacred misteries, the names of those that are seperated from the communion of the Catholicke Church; that is to saie* (addeth hee) *that doe not altogether agree with the Sea Apostolicke*. And finallie, it appeares by the testimonie of the Emperor *Justinian*, who writes to Pope *John* surnamed *Mercurius*; *Wee demaund that your Fatherlie affection may declare to vs your intention by your letters, directed to vs, and to the most holie Bishop and Patriarke of this famous cittie your brother*. And neuertheles in the same Epistle, and in the Epistle to the Patriarke of *Constantinople*, he affirmeth that *the Pope is the head of all the holie Prelates of God*. And the same may be said of the words *Colleague*, or *Fellow-Minister*; that the ancient Catholique Bishops sometimes attribute to the Pope, not to weaken the Superioritie of the Gouernment, but to designe the societie of the Ministrie, and to shew that the faithfull and wise seruant, that the Master hath substituted ouer the companie of his seruants to giue them their nourishment in due season, is not Lord, but fellowe Seruant to his fellowe Seruants. For that the Fathers doe so vnderstand it, it appeares by manie Examples: It appeares first, by the Epistle of the Synod of *Alexandria*, where the Bishops of Egipt call saint ATHANASIVS Patriarke of *Alexandria* their *Colleague*; who neuertheleſſe, was their head, and had iurisdiction ouer all the Bishops of Egipt and *Libia*; as it appeares both from the sixth *Canon* of the Councell, which giues perfect authoritie to the Bishop of *Alexandria* ouer all the Bishops of *Egipt*, *Libia*, and *Pentapolis*; And from the Remonstrance that the Metropolitans of *Egipt* made to the Councell of *Chalcedon*, that they could enterprise nothing without the authoritie of the Bishop of *Alexandria*. It appeareth secondlie by the Epistle of *Proclus* Archbishop of *Constantinople*, who intreateth *Domnus* Patriarke of *Antioch* that he would beare with the infir-

Id. ibid. — Id. ibid. — Collat. Carthag. Act. 3. — Possid. in vit. Aug. — August de oper. Monarch. — Conc. Carthag. 3. c. 45 — Ioan Constant. Patr. ep ad Hormisd. — Codic. l. 1. tit. 1. l. 8. — Cod l 1. t. 1. l 7. — Matth. 24. — Athan. de fuga. sua Apolog. Cōcil Nicen. can. 6. & Concil. Chalced. Act. 4. Concil. Chalced. Act. 4.

mities of *Athanasius* Bishop of *Perhes*, his fellowe-Minister, and to graunt him for his iudges, other Bishops then his Metropolitan, who was suspected by him. It appeares thirdly by the sentence of the Bishops of the Councell of *Ephesus*, who called Pope *Celestin*, their most holy Father and fellowe-Minister; and nenerthelesse made themselues the executioners of his Decrees: *Constrained Necessarilie* (said they) *by the force of the Canons, and by the letters of our most holie father and fellow-minister Celestin, wee are come not without teares to pronounce this heauie sentence against Nestorius*. And finallie, it appeares by the writings of *Optatus* Bishop of *Mileuis* in *Africa*, who calls the Pope *Siricius* companion of Societie with the Catholicke Bishops: and neuertheles acknowledgeth him in the same place, for the heire of saint PETERS Chaire, and for center and principle of Ecclesiasticall vnitie. Ibid. Act. 14. Concil. Eph. p. 1. Act. 1. Optat. Mileu. cont. Parm. l. 2.

To the second head, which is, that saint CYPRIAN complaines, that *Basilides* a Bishops of *Spaine* hauing bene deposed by the Councell of the Prouince, for hauing yeilded vnder the persecution, and an other hauing bene ordained in his place, Pope *Steuen* had restored him: Wee answere, that this complaint, insteede of wounding the Popes authoritie, wholie confirmes it. For saint CYPRIAN complaines not of the enterprize made by the Pope, but of the surprize made vpon the Pope by *Basilides*, who had misinformed him concerning that affaire. Behold his wordes; *That Basilides*, said hee, *after the discouerie of his crimes and the ignominie of his conscience, made naked by his owne confession trauailing to Rome hath deceiued our brother Steuen remote by a farr distance, of place, and ignorant of the historie in fact and the truth of the matter, which hath bene concealed from him to procure that he might be vniustly restored to his Bishopricke from which he had bene iustlie deposed, cannot annull an ordination lawfully made &c. Neither is he so worthie of blame who hath by negligence suffred himselfe to be misinformed, as he is worthie of execration that hath fraudulently imposed it vpon him*. Now who sees not, that this manner of speeche is not to reproue, the interprize made by the Pope, but the suprize made vpon the Pope: And indeede how could saint CYPRIAN reproue the enterprize made by the Pope, he that writes to him; *Lett there be letters directed from thee into the prouince, and to the people that inhabite Arles, whereby Marcian being deposed, an other may be substituted in his place?*. Cyp. ad Cler. & pleb. Hispa ep. 68. Ib. ibid. Id. ad Steph. epist 67.

To the third head, that is, that saint CYPRIAN writes; *Since it hath bene ordained to vs all, or by vs all, and that it is iust and equitable that euerie cause should be heard where the crime hath bene committed, and that to euerie pastor there should be assigned a part of the flocke which he may rule and gouerne before he come to yeild an accompt of his actions to God, those that we rule, must not runne heere and there, and cause the well vnited concord of the Bishops to knocke one against an other by a fraudulent and deceiptfull rashnes, but pleade their cause where there may be accusers and wittnesses of their crimes*. Wee answere, that he speakes heere of minor and particular causes, whereof it was afterward ordained in the Councell of *Carthage*, *That particular causes should be determined within their prouinces*; that is to saie, causes of manners, and which concerned nothing but the liues of Clerkes, and of inferior Clerkes onely; that is to saie, of Priests, deacons, subdeacons, and other ecclesiasticall persons constituted to the lesser orders, as it appeares both by these wordes; *Those whom we rule*, and by the qualitie of *Fortunatus* person of whom the question was, who was a priest of the Church of *Carthage*, who had bene excommunicated for his crimes by saint CYPRIAN and had made a Schisme against him at *Carthage*. And not of Maior causes as those of faith, or of the Sacraments, or of the generall customes of the Church, or of the Id. ad Cornel. ep. 55. Concil. dict. African. c. 62.

depositions of the persons of Bishops; the definition of which causes might be reserued for the iudgements beyond the Seas. For that there was euer this difference in *Africa* betweene the inferior Clerkes; that is to saie, Priests, deacons, subdeacons and other ecclesiasticall persons constituted to the lesser orders; and the superior Clerkes, that is saie Bishops; that the causes of the inferior Clerkes of *Africa*, ought to be determined in *Africa*, and not passe beyond the Seas; but that the causes of the superior Clerkes, that is to saie of Bishops, might be transferred to the iudgement beyond the Seas, wee learne it from saint AVGVSTINE, who cries out, that *Cecilianus* one of saint CYPRIANS Successors in the Archbishoprike of *Carthage*, and within fortie yeares of S. CYPRIANS tyme, who had bene condemned in *Africa* by a Councell of seuentie Bishops, might reserue his cause beyond the Seas, for as much as he was of the order of Bishops, and not of that of Priests, deacons and other inferior Clerkes. *There was noe question then* (saith saint AVGVSTINE) *of Priests or Deacons, or other Clerkes of the inferior order, but of the Colleagues that is to saie, of Bishops who might reserue their cause intire to the iudgement of the other Colleagues, and principallie of the Churches Apostolicke.* For whereas saint AVGVSTINE vseth the word *Churches Apostolicke* in the plurall number, wee answere that, in the Chapter following, and shew, that it is not to exclude the eminencie of the Roman Church ouer the rest, whereof contrarywise he said but three lynes before. *In the Roman Church hath alwaies flourisht the principalitie Apostolicke.* But to preuent the malice of the *Donatists* who refused the iudgement that Pope *Melchiades* had giuen of the cause of *Cecilianus*; for as much as they said, that *Melchiades* had sacrificed to Idolls, and consequenrlie, could not iudge of the cause of *Cecilianus*, who was accused of a crime of the like nature, or equiualent to it. It sufficeth at this tyme to inferr from the wordes of saint AVGVSTINE that there was this difference betweene the superior and inferior Clerkes of *Africa*, that the causes of the superior Clerkes might be iudged beyond the Seas, and not those of the inferior Clerkes; And therefore, where saint CYPRIAN saith, that euery cause should be iudged where the crime had bene committed; he spake of the causes of inferior Clerkes; that is to saie, of Priests, Deacons, subdeacons, and other Ecclesiasticall persons constituted to the lesser order; and not of the causes of superior Clerkes; that is to saie, of Bishops.

Ang.ep. 162.

Id.ibid.

To the fowrth head, which is, that saint CYPRIAN complaines, *That the authoritie of the Bishops of Africa seemed lesse to some lost and desperate persons, who had alreadie the yeare before bene iudged by them*; Wee answere two things, the one, that the word lesser, hath noe reference heere to the *Roman* Church, and is not a Comparatiue of relatiue signification, but it is a comparitiue of positiue signification; which hath noe other meaning, but lesse then it should be; that is to saie, little, or not great enough; as when the same S. CYPRIAN writeh in the Epistle to *Antonius: If the number of Bishops resident in Africa seemed lesse sufficiet*; that is to saie, *not enough sufficient:* And the other that if it were a comparison of the comparatiue signification, it should noe more haue reference to the Roman Church, but to these wordes; *paucis desperatis & perditis*, interpreting them in the ablatiue and not in the datiue; and translating the period in this sence; *If it be not peraduenture that the authoritie of the Bishops constituted in Africa, who had alreadie iudged of them be esteemed lesse then a small number of desperate and lost, men*: it seemes, that the continuance of the period doth afterward declare which compares the number of the Bishops of *Africa*, who had iudged of *Fortunatus* with those that tooke part with *Fortunatus* and not with

Cypr. ad Cornel. ep. 55.

the

the Roman Church in these wordes; *If the number of those that iudged of them the yeare past, comprehending the Priests and deacons, be reckoned, it will be found there were more assistants present at the iudgement and at the examination of the cause, then of those that tooke Fortunatus part.* And indeede if saint CYPRIAN had intended this word in a comparatiue signification, and in regard of the *Roman* Church; how could he haue said three lines aboue, *they presumed to saile to the Roman Church which is the Chaire of Peter, and the principall Church, from whence the Sacerdotall vnitie hath proceeded?* And how coul *Optatus Mileuitanus* an *African*, as well as hee saie; *At Rome hath bene constituted to Peter the chiefe, the Episcopall Chaire, that in this onely Chaire, the vnitie of all might be preserued?* And howe could saint AVGVSTINE, an *African* as well as either of them, say; *That Cecilianus might despise the conspiring multitude of his Enemies*: that is to saie, of seauentie Bishops of *Africa* assembled in the Councell of *Numidia* with him, *For as much as he sawe himself vnited by letters communicatorie with the Roman Church, in which had alwaies flourisht the principalitie of the Sea Apostolicke; and with the other Countries, from whence the Ghospell came into Africa.* And againe; *That he doubted not, but that Pelagius and Celestius*, who had bene iudged by two Councells of *Africa*, *whould more easilie yeild to the Popes authoritie drawne out of the authoritie of the holie Scriptures.* Ibid. Opt. Mileu. cont. Parmen l. 2. Aug. ep. 162. Id. ep. 92.

To the fifth head, which is, that the same S. CYPRIAN saith; *That there is but one Bishopricke whence euerie one holds his portion vndiuidedlie*, Wee answere, hee vseth this language, to insinuate that the Bishopricke cannot be possessed separatelie, out of the vnitie and societie of the Episcopall Bodie; but not to denie, but that in the vnitie of this Episcopall Bodie, the functions of Episcopall power are exercised in a more principall and eminent manner in the Roman Church, then in the other Churches; noe more then when wee saie, that the soule is possessed by all the partes of the bodie inseparablie and vndiuidedly; wee intend not to, saie, that for the exercise of her functions, she resides not in a more principall and eminent fashion in the head, then in the other partes; otherwise, why should hee call the *Roman* Church, *the Chaire of PETER, and the principall Church, and the originall of Sacerdotall vnitie?* Cypr. de vnit. Eccl. Id. ad Cornel. ep. 55.

To the sixth head, which is, that S. CYPRIAN saith in the Councell holden for the rebaptization of heretickes, *None of vs constitutes himself Bishop of Bishops*; Wee answere he speakes there onelie of the Bishops of *Africa*, to whom hee directs his speach, and whom hee exhorts to tell their opinion freelie in the Councell without being held backe by the respect of the authoritie that as Primate of *Africa* hee had ouer them. And wee will add, that if hee had holden this language euen to taxe and preuẽt the Pope obliquely, who afterward condemned him, the matter would be of noe weight, for as much as this Coũcell was an erroneous Coũcell, where S. CYPRIAN cast the foundations of the Donatists heresie; and that as such, it was not onelie condemned by the Pope, and by all the rest of the Church, but euen by those that had adhered to saint CYPRIAN; witnes these wordes of saint HIEROM; *The Blessed Cyprian stroue to auoide the myrie lakes, and not to drinke of the strainge waters; and vpon this subiect, addressed the Synod of Africa to Steuen Bishop of Rome. who was the twentiesixth after saint PETER, but his strife was in vaine. And finallie, those that had bene of the same opinion with Cyprian, sett forth a newe decree saying; What shall wee doe? Soe hath it bene deliuered to them by their Ancestors and ours?* Cypr. in præfat. Concil. Carth. Hier. cont. Lucif.

To the seauenth head, which is of the inuectiues that S. CYP. suffered to slipp out of his mouth after the contention that hee had with Pope *Steuen* for the rebaptizatiō of hereticks, taxing him of ignorance and presumption. Wee answere, it is impietie in *Caluin* to alleadge them, since S. AVSTINE holds them vnworthy to be reported, and couereth them with this excuse: *The things which Cyprian in anger hath spread against Steuen, I will not suffer them to passe vnder my penn*. And we adde, the resistance that Pope *Steuen* made to the error of S. CYPRIAN, was the safetie of the church, as saint *Vincent, Lerin:* witnesseth in these wordes; *Then the Blessed Steuen resisted, with, but before his Colleagues; iudginge it as I conceaue, a thing worthie of him that he should surmount them as much in Faith as he did in the authoritie of his place.*

Augustin. de Bapt. cont. Donat. l. 5. c. 25.

Vincent. Lyrin in. Com. part. 1.

Of the Commission of the Emperor Constantine the Great, for the iudgement of Cecilianus Archbishop of Carthage.

CHAPT. IV.

THe third instance of *Caluin*, is taken from *Optatus Mileuitanus* and from saint *AVGVSTINE*; who saie, that the *Donatists hauing accused Cecilianus Archbishop of Carthage, and Felix Bishop of Aptunge, his Ordinator, and besought the Emperor Constantine, who thē was resident amongst the Gaules, to giue them Iudges of the Gaules: the Emperor gaue them three Bishops of the Gaules whom he sent to Rome to iudge the affaire with Pope Melchiades.* But whom doth this Instance combate against, but those that alleadge it. For the Emperor being constrained by the importunitie of the Donatists, and that as himselfe protested against all Ecclesiasticall order, to giue them Iudges; and hauing giuen them according to their demaund, Iudges of the *Gaules*, what could he more expressely doe, to testifie the Popes authoritie, then to remitt them to *Rome*, and to ordaine that the same Iudges of the *Gaules* that hee had giuen them should transporte themselues from the *Gaules* to *Rome*, to the end the cause might be iudged at the Popes *Tribunall*, and vnder the presidencie and direction of the Pope. Was there a Stronger meanes to proue what wee reade in S. ATHANASIVS; *That antient custome of the Church was that the causes of Bishops cou'd not be determined, till first the decision had bene made at Rome* And in *Sozomene*: *That the Sacerdotall lawe required, that those things which were constituted without the Bishop of Romes sentence should be annulled.* Neuerthelesse for as much as *Caluin* obiectes, that if this cause had belonged to the Popes Ordinary iurisdictiō he ought not to haue iudged it by the Emperors commission; it is necessarie to cleere it. To this obiection then, before wee sound the matter to the bottom, wee will answere in forme of a prologue fiue thinges: first, that it was not a commission except in regard of the three Assessors of the *Gaules*, that the Emperor named to content the importunitie of the *Donatists* & to the end that they might serue for witnesses & warrants of the sinceritie of the proceedings of the Councell of *Rome* but a remittmēt: as it appeares both by the Emperors confessiō, who avowed, that it belōged not to him to examin this cause, & by the electiō that the Pope made of fifteene other Bishops that he tooke for his assistāts, besides those that the Emperor had nominated. And therefore although S. AVG. in regard of the *Donatists* intētiō sometimes calls this remittmēt a

Calu. Inst. l. 4 c. 7. Opt. Mileu. cont. Parm. l. 1. Aug ep. 162.

Inl ep. ad Eusebian. apud. Athan. apol. 2. Sozom. l. 3. c. 9.

delegation neuerthelesse hee sheweth sufficientlie, that it was rather a relegation, then a delegation, when he notes that the reason wherefore the Emperor did it, was for as much as he durst not iudge the cause of a Bishop: *Your Superiors*, (said he to the Donatists) first brought the *cause of Cecilianus to the Emperor Constantine*. And a little after; *But because Constantine durst not iudge the cause of a Bishop, hee delegated the examination and decision thereof to Bishops*. I add, that hee vsed this language by *Synecdoche*, and referringe the word delegation to the Iudges of the *Gaules* onelie, that were deputed to assist at the Councell of *Rome*, and not to all the Councell of *Rome*, as hee witnesseth elsewhere by these wordes: *The Emperor gaue to the Donatists the Iudges that themselues had demaunded:* that is to saie, *the Iudges of the Gaules*. And againe, *Donatus was heard at Rome by the Iudges that himself had demaunded*. For of the ninteene Bishops of the Councell of *Rome*, there were but three of the qualitie of those that *Donatus* had demaunded. *Donatus* had demaunded but three: but saint AVSTIN extendes this clause by *Synecdoche* to all the Coūcell, for as much as the three Iudges demaunded by *Donatus*, had iudged in Common with all the Councell, and were found soe conformable to the rest, as the iudgement of the Councell, which passed all with one voice, and without anie diuersitie of opinions, and theirs was one selfe same thing.

Aug. ep. 166.

Aug ep. 171.

Aug. de Agon. Christ. c. 29.

Optat. Mileuit. cont. Parm l. 1.

The second answere is that *Constantine* did not interpose his authoritie in this affaire as Maister by himself of the cause, but as an Arbiter sought by the *Donatists*, and assuringe himself as a Catholicke that he should be avowed by the Catholicks. *This Matter*, (saith saint AVGVSTIN) *belonged greatly to the Emperors care whereof he ought to giue an accompt to God; for the Donatists had made him arbiter and iudge of the cause of the tradition, and of the Schisme*. From whence it appeares, that the Emperors interposition in this cause, was a matter of fact, and not of right, and whose example cannot be alleadged for a paterne of the ancient discipline of the Church. The third, that it was not a controuersie questioned amongst the Catholicks, and according to the ordinarie lawes of the Church, but a Sute commenced by the heretickes against the Catholicks, and by waies extraordinarie to all the lawes and formes of the Church. For the *Donatists* had alreadie broken the bond of vnitie, and shaken off the yoake of the Churches authoritie. *They were* (saith saint AVGVSTIN) *alreadie culpable of the Schisme, and alreadie stained with the horrible crime of the erection of Altar against Altar*. By meanes whereof, there being noe iudge common betweene them, and the Catholicks in the Church, there remained nothing for them to doe, but to haue recourse to the Arbitrements of the secular powers, whose examples could noe more be drawne into consequence against the ordininarie authoritie of the Christian Church, then the iudgment that *Ptolomeus Philometor* king of *Egipt*, gaue betweene the Iewes and the *Samaritans*, could forme a president against the ordinarie authoritie of the high priest, and of the Sacerdotall colledge of the Iewish Church. The fowrth, that the cause questioned in this processe, was not a cause of right, and that should be proued by ecclesiasticall meanes, such as the testimonies of Scripture, or the traditions of the Apostles, or the Custome of the Church, or the sentences of the Fathers, but a question of fact, and whereof the hypothesis was mingled with accessories that belonged not to the causes of the Church, and could not be examined by ecclesiasticall meanes onelie, but must be iustified by human and secular meanes, as the confronting of witnesses, the acts

Aug. ep. 162.

Aug. ibid.

Ioseph. antiquit. l. 13. c. 6.

Opt. Mileu. cont. Parm. l. 1. August. ep. 162. Gest. purgat. Fælic. & Cecilian. Aug. ep. 152. Aug ep. 162.

of Notaries (yea Pagan and heathen ones) the Recordes of Clerkes, and euen the applications of questions, and corporall tortures. For the accusation of the *Donatists* was principallie grounded vpon the framing of a false letter, that they had forged against *Felix* Bishop of *Aptunge*, for the examination whereof there must be a secular and proconsulary iudgement interposed betweene the ecclesiasticall iudgements; that is to saie betweene the Councell of *Rome* and that of *Arles* to conuince the forgers of the falshood by the application of rackes and tortures. *Wee haue vndertaken* (saith saint AVSTIN) *the defence of the cause of Cecilianus, although it belong not to the cause of the Churche, that we may make their calumnies appeare euen in that.* And againe speaking of the torture which was offered to the scriuener *Ingentius* or *Vigentius*, to make him confesse whether he had falsified the letter of the *Ædile Alfius Cecilianus* to *Felix* Bishop of *Aptunge*: *The Proconsull* (said hee) *amongst the fearefull cries of the vshers, and the bloudy hands of the hangmen would not haue condemned a Colleague of his being absent.* And the fifth, that all the actes that the *Donatists* extorted from the Emperor in this cause hee protested them to be soe manie irregularities and nullities and so manie vnlawfull enterprises vniust and extraordinarie, wherein he suffered himselfe to be constrained against his will, to giue waie to the passion and malice of the *Donatists*, and in yeilding to them, to assaie to reduce them to the peace and vnitie of the Church; and he was soe farr from desiring to haue the example thereof serue for a lawe to the Bishops, as contrarywise he promised to aske the Bishops pardon; the historie is this:

The *Donatists* hauing accused *Cecilianus* Archbishop of *Carthage*, of treason, or communication with traytors; that is to saie, with those that had deliuered the holie Bookes, and the sacred Vessells to be put into the fier in the persecution tyme; yea, euen to haue bene ordained by a traytor; soe did they intitle *Felix* Bisop of *Aptunge*, they first obtained a iudgement of seauentie Bishops in *Africa* against him. Then discerning that *Cecilianus* dispised this iudgement, as well because it was giuen against an absent person, as because (as saint

Aug. ep. 162.

AVSTINE saith) that he sawe himselfe vnited by communicatory letters with the *Roman* Church, in the which (adds the same saint AVGVSTINE) hath alwaies flourisht, the principalitie of the Sea Apostolicke, and with the other Countries from whence the Ghospell came in to *Africa*, they resolued to pursue beyond the seas a new iudgement. Now they feared the Popes Tribunall both in generall, because all *Italie* had bene trobled with persecutions vnder the Empire of *Dioclesian* by meanes whereof they figured to themselues that there would be manie Bishops that had bowed or bent, and consequentlie would supporte the cause of *Cecilianus*; and in particular if wee beleiue the *Donatists* in the conference of *Carthage*, because the Pope *Melchiades* was suspected by them as a complice, as they pretended of the same crime, or one equiualent to that of him that ordained *Cecilianus*.

Aug. in Breuic. Collar. Carth. part 3.

They began (said saint AVGVSTINE, speaking of the *Donatists* of the conference of *Carthage*) *to charge Melchiades of the crime of Treason, and to saie that their superiors had shunned his iudgement, because he was a Traytor.* For these causes then, that is to saie; be it for the suspition that they had in common against all *Italie*, be it for that they had in particular against the Pope, they addressed themselues to the Emperor *Constantine*; who then was resident amongst the *Gaules*, and besought him to giue them iudges from amongst the *Gaules*, because in that

prouince

prouince whereof his Father *Constantius* had had gouernment, there had bene noe persecution, which was to refuse in generall all the prouinces, where *Dioclesians* persecution had taken place, amongst which *Italie* was one of the principall. *Your Superior* (saith *Optatus Mil.*) *presented to the Emperor, yet ignorant of the affaire, the request which followes: Wee beseeche thee ô excellent Emperor Constantine, because thou art of a iust race, whose father amongst all the Emperors, neuer practised anie persecution, and that the Gaules are freed from this crime, for in Africa there are contententions amongst vs, let there be giuen to vs Iudges from amongst the Gaules.* And what meruaile is it, if they addressed themselues to *Constantine*, since after they had recourse to the Emperor *Iulian* the *Apostata*, a pagan and an infidell prince, the Emperor *Constantine* amazed and angrie with this proceeding, reproached it to the *Donatists*, and obiected to them that they would receiue iudgement from him, who himselfe did attend the iudgement of Christ. *He durst not,* (saith saint AVSTINE) *iudge the cause of a Bishop.* And *Optatus Mileuitanus* from whom S. AVGVSTINE borrowed this historie; *Hee answered them* (saith hee) *with a spirit full of indignation; you aske of me iudgement in this world; of me I saie, that doe my self attend the iudgement of Christ; that is to saie, you would haue me constitute my selfe for a Iudge of the Ministers, of Christ, I that doe my self attend the iudgement of Christ.* Which was the same protestation that he made afterward at the Coūcell of *Nicea* in these wordes, repeated by our glorious CHARLEMAINE; *To me, who am constituted in a lay condition, it is not lawfull to iudge of Bishops.* And this the Emperor *Valentinian* renewed in these wordes, repeated by saint AMBROSE; and by the same CHALEMAINE; *Your businesse ô Bishops, is farr, aboue vs; and therefore treate amongst you of your causes.* And that S. ATHANASIVS remēbred to the Emperor *Constātius* in these termes; *What hath the Emperor in common with the iudgement of Bishops?* And againe; *when did the iudgements of the Church take their force from the Emperor?* And saint MARTIN to Maximus; *This is a new and neuer heard of impietie, that a secular iudge should iudge a cause of the Church*, And this was the first protestation of irregularitie, made by the Emperor *Constantine* against the *Donatists*; to witt, that leauing the waie, and the ordinarie progresse of the iudgments of the Church, they had recourse to him to obtaine Iudges, and which hath, bene alwaies followed since by the pious and religious Catholicke Emperors.

Optat.cōtr Parm.l.1. c.72.

Aug.contr. lit.Petil.l. 2.c 92.

Aug.ep. 166. Optat.l. 1.

Capitul. Carol. Magn.1.6. Ambros. Epist 32. & capit. Car.Magn. ibid. Athan. ep. ad Solit. Ibidem. Sulpit. hist sacr.l.2.

This request neuerthelesse of the *Donatists*, that the Emperor reiected as a iudge, he beleiued, that hee ought not altogether to reiect as an arbiter and compounder of the busines, but thought it to bee to purpose in some sorte to make vse of the arbiterment that the *Donatists* referred to him, to assaie to reconcile them to the Catholickes whose communion he held, and for that occasion assured himselfe that he ought to be auowed and agreed vnto by them. And therefore desiring on the one side to preserue the forme of the ordinarie iudgements of the Church; & on the other side being constrained to giue some waie to the hardnes of those that he desired to bring backe by faire meanes, he remitted them from the Gaules, to Rome, to be iudged by the Pope *Melchiades*, with the assistance of three Bishops of the *Gaules* that he caused to trauaile thither, *Maternus* of *Cologne*, *Rheticius* of *Autun*, and *Marinus* of *Arles*, that they might be wittnesses and warrants of the sinceritie of his proceedings: *I haue ordained* (saith the Emperor in his Epistle to *Melchiades*, euill inscribed to *Mechiades* and to *Marcus*) *that Cecilianus with ten of his accusers, and ten of his abetters; that is to saie, ten Africā Bishops which opposed him, and ten of Africk Bishops which maintained him, trauelled so farr as to Rome,*

Eufeb hist. Eccles.l.10 c.5.

that

that in your presence, ioyning with you Rheticius, Maternus and Marinus your Colleagues, whom for this effect I haue enioyned to trasport themselues to Rome, he may be heard so as you shall know that it belonges to the most religious lawe. I haue said in the Epistle, euill inscribed to *Melchiades* and to *Marcus*, for there it must be read καὶρὸν μακρὸν, and not καὶ μαρκῳ, as well because *Marcus* was not Bishop of *Rome* till after *Siluester*, Successor to *Melchiades*, as because, if this *Marcus* had bene anie other then a Bishop, the Emperor would not haue said, ioyntlie with you, your colleagues *Rheticius*, *Maternus* and *Marinus*. And if he had bene Bishop, hee had not directed his letter to *Melchiades* Bishop of *Rome* and to *Marcus*, without adding to it the qualitie of Bishop. These three Bishops of the *Gaules* then hauing bene vpon the nomination of the Emperor, admitted by the Pope, and called by him to the Councell of Rome became iudges of the right of the affaires. Now to whom doth it not heereby appeare quite contrarie to that which the *Caluenists* pretended to inferr? For first, if the Emperor, as he protests himselfe, had noe right to iudge the causes of Bishops, howe could hee in right giue them Iudges? I saie in right, and not in fact, for as much as the Emperor could well giue them Iudges in fact, and whose iudgement should be obligatorie to the secular Tribunall, and executory by the officers of the Empire, and vnder the imposition of paines and temporall punishments; but hee could not giue them Iudges in right, whose Iudgements should bee obligatorie in conscience, and to the Tribunall of the Church, and should make those that contradicted, culpable of spirituall censures and punishments. And secondly the *Donatists* hauing specified in their request, that they demaunded Iudges of the *Gaules*, and that of purpose to exclude particularlie the iudges of *Italie*; the Emperor harkening to their request, and giuing them Iudges of the *Gaules*, how had he sent them to *Rome* to iudge the cause with the Pope, and vnder his Presidencie and direction, who was hee against whom, if wee giue creditt to the *Donatists* in the conference of *Carthage*, their petition was principallie presented, if hee had not acknowledged that the Pope was naturall and ineuitable Iudge of the cause? Is there any likelyhood, that the Emperor beeing resident amongst the *Gaules*, and the Iudges whom he nominated for the *Donatists*, being risident there, that hee would haue sent them from about his person where they were, to the Popes person, from whom they were seperated by so large a distance of Sea and land to serue him for assistants, if hee had belieued that it was himselfe and not the Pope, that was the Naturall Iudge of the affaire. To what purpose should he haue made the *Donatists* take so much paines, who came to him out of *Africa* into *Gallia*; and the three Iudges that hee graunted them, who were also in *Gallia*, to trauaile from thence to *Rome*, if hee had not acknowledged that which wee read latelie in saint ATHANASIUS; *That the causes of the Bishops could not be determined, till de decision had bene made at Rome.* And in *Sozomene*; *That those things that were constituted without the sentence of the Bishop of Rome, were nullities.* And in saint AUGUSTINE vpon the same place, *that in the Roman Church had alwaies flourisht the principallitie of the Sea Apostolicke*? But let vs kintt vp our historie. To these three Bishops nominated by the Emperor, the Pope yet added fifteene more; whose names *Optatus* reportes; *Merocles* Bishop of *Milan*; *Florian* Bishop of *Cesena*; *Zoticus* Bishop of *Quintian*; *Stemnius* Bishop of *Arimini*; *Felix* Bishop of *Florence*; *Gaudensius* Bishop of *Pisa*; *Constantius* Bishop of *Faensa*; *Proterius* Bishop of *Capua*; *Theophilus* Bishop of *Beneuentum*; *Sauinus* Bishop of *Terracina*; *Secundus* Bishop of *Preneste*; *Felix* Bishop of the three lodges; *Maximus* Bishop of *Hostia*; *Euander*

Optat. contr. Parm. l. 1.

Iul. ep. ad Eusebian. apud. Athan. see aboue. Sozom. l. 3. c. 10. See aboue.

Opt. cont. Parm. l. 1.

Bishop of *Vrsin*, and *Donatian* Bishop of *Foro-Clodi*. Now if the Pope had not bene iudge of this case but by deputation, and that the Emperors addresse to him had bene but a simple commission, and not a remittment, how could he haue taken fifteene others Bishops for his assistants, besides those that had bene nominated by the Emperor, and Bishops of *Italie* also, which was the prouince that the *Donatists* had principallie pretended to refuse by their petition? And why did not the *Donatists* reproach to him, that hee had exceeded the boundes of his commission? For as for *Caluins* saying, that the Emperor nominated Iudges out of *Gallia*, *Spaine*, and *Italie*, it is an ignorance disproued by *Optatus* who affirmes that the Councell of *Rome* was compounded but of ninteen Bishops in all; to witt, of the Pope, three Bishops of *Gaules*, and fifteen Bishops of *Italie*; and that there were noe Bishops of *Spaine*; and teacheth vs, that the Emperor nominated but onely three Bishops of the *Gaules*. *Iudges* (saith *Optatus*) *were giuen; Maternus of Cologna, Rheticius of Autun, and Marinus of Arles*. And indeede, how could the *Donatists* haue desired Iudges out of *Spaine*, where the persecution had bene soe cruell? Wherefore although S. AVGVSTINE extendes as farr as he can the Emperors commission to the iudges of the Councell of *Rome*, of purpose to make that Councell not capable of refusall by the *Donatists*, who hauing taken the Emperor for their arbiter, it seemed they could not decline a iudgement wherein his authority had interuened; yet he extends it noe farther then to saie; that the Emperor sent Bishops to *Rome*, to iudge the cause with *Melchiades*, and neuer goes so farr as to say, that he gaue commission to *Melchiades*, or gaue him for a iudge. Contrarywise, speaking of the iudges giuen by the Emperor, he restraines them, as hath bene alreadie aboue noted to the Bishops of the *Gaules* onelie. *Iudges* (saith hee) *were giuen to the Donatists, those that they had demaunded, that is to saie, the Bishops of the Gaules*: Insinuating thereby, that the Pope was none of the iudges that were giuen; and that the Emperors delegation extended it selfe noe farther, then onely to the iudges of the *Gaules*, which he had deputed, to the end they might bee witnesses and colleagues of the Popes iudgement, and did not comprehended the Pope. From whence it appeares, that when he said, that the Emperor delegated the examination of *Cecilianus* his cause to the Bishops; or that the Councell of *Rome* absolued *Cecilianus*, by the Emperors commaundement; he speakes by *Synecdoche*, that is to saie, by extending the part to the whole, for as much as the Bishops delegated by the Emperor, and enabled by the Emperors commission, which was valid in respect of the *Donatists*, that had sought it, made a part of the Councell of *Rome*, where *Cecilianus* his cause was examined, & a part so conformable to the opinion of the whole, as the iudgement of the Emperors Commissioners, and that of the whole Councell, was one selfe same thing. Otherwise we must conclude by the same reason, that *Donatus* had demaunded for iudges, all those that assisted at the Councell of *Rome*; that is to saie, both the Pope, and the fifteene iudges of *Italie*; for S. AVGVSTIN saith in the like wordes; that *Donatus* was heard at *Rome* by the iudges that he had demaunded: And yet it is certaine that *Donatus* had demaunded none but the three iudges of the *Gaules*; yea, with the exclusion of the others. But S. AVSTIN saith, that he had bene heard by the iudges, that he had demaunded; for as much as amongst the iudges that heard him, were those that he had demaunded; who being conformable in their opinions with the rest, it was as much as if he had demaunded them all. Let vs finishe our historie; The Pope assisted by these eighteen Bishops, three nominated by the Emperor, and

Instit. l. 4. c. 7.

Opt. cont. Parm. l. 1.

Aug. ep. 162.

Id. ep. 171.

Id. ep. 166

De vnic. bapt. cont Petil. c. 16

August. de agon. Chr. c. 29.

fifteen chosen by him, iudged the cause of *Cecilianus*, and iudged it soe soundlie, as saint AVSTIN takes occasion from thence to call him the FATHER of the Christian People. *How innocent* (saith saint AVSTIN) *was the last sentence pronounced by the blessed Melchiades; how intire, how prudent, how peaceable?* And a while after; *O blessed man, ô Sonn of Christian peace, and Father of Christian people!* From this iudgement of the Popes, notwithstanding the *Donatists* appealed to the Emperor; and that was the second irregularitie, and so great and enormious an irregularitie, that it made the Emperors haire stand on end. *To this appeale* (saith *Optatus Mileu.*) *the Emperor answered thus: O, madd impudence of furie, they haue put in an appeale* (that is to saie, a secular appeale, & to the imperiall Tribunall) *as in the causes of the Gentiles.* And the Emperor *Constantine* himselfe, in the Epistle to the Catholicke Bishops:: *What so great frensie* (saith hee) *perseuers in them, as to perswade themselues with an incredible arrogance of things which are not permitted, either to be spoken or heard.* And a litle after; *They seeke for secular iudgements, and leaue those that are celestiall; ô madd impudence of furie!* And againe; *What will these detractors* (you must reade *detrectators*) *saie of the law, who refusing the heauenlie iudgement, haue demaunded mine? is this the account they make of Christ our Sauiour?* He was farr enough then, from approuing the appeale from the Popes iudgement to his; since he calls this Appeale, *a thing not fitt to be spoken or heard, madd impudence of furie, a recourse from heauenlie to earthly iudgement, and a contempt of Christs authoritie.* Neuertheles, pressed by the *Donatists* importunitie, he graunted them an other Councell at *Arles*, not in the forme of a iudgement of appeale, as the *Donatists* pretended; but in the forme of a ciuill request, and of a more ample review of the cause, which the *Donatists*, who complaining for the omission of *Felix* his crime, said had not bene fullie heard. And this againe irregularly; that is to saie, against the ordinarie course of the iudgements of the Church, and to giue way to the *Donatists* fury. *He gaue them* (saith saint AVSTIN) *an other iudgement at Arles; that is to saie, of other Bishops not that it was necessarie, but giuing waie to their peruersnesse.* At this Councell, compounded of two hundred Bishops, assisted the Popes legates, as appeares by the Catalogue of the Bishops of the first Councell of Arles, although confusedly and ill applied to the Canons of the the second. And *Marinus*, *Rheticius* and *Maternus* assistants at the first iudgment; for that the Popes legates are not named in the Epistle from the Councell to the Pope; it is because themselues were the Messengers that carryed them. And the relation of the Councell was directed to Pope *Siluester* Successor to *Melchiades* in these wordes; *Being come to Arles, by the will of the pious Emperor, from thence, most Religious Pope* (or according to other copies) *most glorious Pope, we salute thee with all due reuerence.* And the Fathers of the Councell, testified to the Pope in their Epistle, a great griefe, that he could not assist there in person; and protested, that if he had bene there present, they would haue pronounced, yet a more rigorous sentence against the slanderors. But that, said they, could not be, for as much as thou mightest not remoue from the place where the Apostles sitt continuallie, and where their bloud without intermission, giues testimonie to the glory of God. And they sent their decrees to the Pope, that he might spread them through all the partes of the world. *It hath pleased* (said they) *according to the ancient custome these things should be intimated to thee, who holdest the maior administrations and by thee principallie to all.* For insteede of these maimed and corrupted words; *Placuit etiam, antequam ante qui maiores Dioceses tenes, per te potissimum omnibus insinuare*; You must restore, *Placuit etiam hæc iuxta consuetudinem antiquam, ad te qui maiores dioceses* (or *maiores Dioceseos*)

Marginal notes: Aug. ep. 161. — Optat. cótr Parm. l. 1. — Const. Ep. ad Episc. Cathol. ad calc. Gestor. Purgat. Cæcil. & Fœlic. — Epist. Cóstant. ad Ablau. — Aug. ep. 68 & lib. de vnic. bapt. c. 16. — Aug. ep. 162. — Aug contr. Parm. l. 1. c. 5. — Epist. Cóncil. Arelat. 1. — Ibid. — Ibid. — Ibidem.

Dioceseos) tenes, & per te potissimum omnibus, insinuari; That is to saie; *It hath pleased, according to ancient custome, that these things should be insinuated to thee, that holdest the maior administrations, or the maioritie of the administration, and by thee to all.* For the proper and originall signification of the word *Diocese*, is to signifie, administration. From whence it is, that *Zonara* speaking of the Empire of *Constantine*, and *Irene*, say; *All the Diocese of the Empire, meaning all the administration of the Empire*. From whence appeares *Caluins* extreame ignorance, who saith that *Marinus* Bishop of Arles iudged by appeale of the sentence of Pope *Melchiades*, and that Pope *Melchiades* indured it, and neuer opposed himselfe against it. For besides *Melchiades* was dead before the Councell of *Arles* (which was holden vnder *Siluester* his successor) was celebrated, and had neede of a strainger miracle, then that of *Caluins* to raise him vp againe, if it had bene an appeale from the Pope, the Popes Legates would not haue assisted there, and would not haue iudged by appeale of their Maisters iudgement; and the Councell would not haue addressed their relation to the Pope; and would not haue bewailed the Popes absence; and would not haue said, that if the Pope had bene present, they had pronunced a more heauie sentence against the delinquents. And then how could *Marinus* Bishop of *Arles*, who had bene one of Pope *Melchiades* assistants, at the iudgement giuen at *Rome*, haue iudged by appeale of the Councell of *Rome*? And how could the other assistants of the Pope haue iudged by appeale of the Popes iudgement, or rather of their owne? For not onely the same *Marinus* Bishop of *Arles*, who had bene one of the Popes assistants at the Councell of *Rome*, assisted at the Councell of *Arles*; but also the other Bishops who had acompanied the Pope at the iudgement of *Rome*, as well those that the Emperors had nominated, as *Maternus* Bishop of *Cologna*, *Rheticius* Bishop of *Autun*, *Marinus* Bishop of *Arles*, as those that the Pope had associated there; as *Merocles* of *Milan*, *Proterius* of *Capua*, and others were present, voted, and signed at the Councell of *Arles*. And besides how could *Marinus*, and all the Councell haue written to the Pope, *That he held the maior dioceses*, or, *the maior administrations*; a thing that whatsoeuer it signifie, attributes to the Pope a prerogatiue, that the Bishop of *Arles* and the other Bishops of the Councell had not, if *Marinus* had bene iudge by appeale of the Popes iudgement? for whereas some of *Caluins* disciples saie that is was not the same *Marinus* Bishop of *Arles* that was at the Councell of *Rome*, who iudged of the Popes sentence; but *Martian* Bishop of *Arles* his Successor; this is an ignorance, yet greater then the former; for there is not so meane a Scholler, but knowes, that *Martian* Bishop of *Arles* was dead more then fiftie yeares before *Marinus*, and before the Councell of *Arles*. Ioyntlie, that the Bishop of *Arles*, and particularly *Martian*, could not iudge of the Pope by appeale, since the same *Martian* being fallen into the Sect of the *Nouatians*, saint CYPRIAN had addressed himselfe in these words to Pope *Cornelius*, to praie him to depose him. *Let there be letters written from thee, into the prouince, and to the people inhabiting Arles, whereby Marcian being deposed, an other may be placed in his steede.* And indeede that which saint AVSTIN saith to the *Donatists*; *put case that the Bishops which iudged at Rome, had not bene good Iudges, yet there remained the vniuersall Councell of the whole Catholicke Church*; Doth it not verifie, that after the Popes iudgement (supposing and not graunting that it had bene subiect to appeale) there remaines noe other iudgement but that of the generall Councell of the whole Church? But let vs returne to the Councell of *Arles*: From this Councell then, the *Donatists* had againe recourse to the Emperor,

Zonar. Annal. tom. 3. in Constāt. & Iren.

Inst. l. 4. c. 7.

Epist. Concil. Arelat. 1

The author of the tract of the Church chap. 8. Edit. 2.

Cypr. ad Steph. ep. 67.

Ep. 162.

and forced him to examine the cause himselfe. And this was the fowrth irregularitie, as it appeares by the protestation that the Emperor made for which he would aske pardon of the Bishops. *He gaue waie* (saith saint AVGVSTINE) *to their importunitie, to stopp their mouthes, and yeilded soe farr, as to iudge this cause after the Bishops, but with an intent afterward to craue pardon of the holie Bishops.* Now how can an example for which the emperor protests that himselfe will craue the Bishops pardon, serue for a lawe to the Bishops: yet this was not all, for the *Donatists* did noe more obey the iudgement of the Emperor then they had done to that of the Councell of *Rome* holden in the Popes presence; or to that of the Councell of *Arles*, holden in the presence of the Popes legates, but disavowed the Petitions that they had presented to the Emperor *Constantine* and said that that busines was not for the emperors examination, and that it was not their solicitation that brought it before him, and cast this imputation vpon the Catholickes; soe as the last dispute was whether the Catholickes, or the Donatistes had caused the Emperor to intervene in this cause, both disavowing it *If he be culpable*, (saith saint AVSTIN, speaking of the Bishop *Felix*, who ordained *Cecilianus* whō the Emperor had caused to be heard before the Procōsull of *Africa*) *that hath bene absolued by an earthlie iudge not hauing demaunded it, how much more are those culpable, that would haue an earthlie king to be iudge of their cause For if it be noe crime to haue appealed to the Empero,rit is noe crime to haue bene heard by the Emperor, neither thē by him to whom the Emperor had delegated the cause*, that is to saie, by the Proconsull. And againe; *know that your superiors haue first brought Cecilianus his cause before Constantine, oblige vs to proue it to you; and if wee proue it not, doe with vs what you can.*

Ep. 162.

Aug. ibid.

Ep. 162.

Ep. 166.

Now let vs recapitnlate all the heades of this historie: The first head, saie the *Caluinists*, was that the *Donatists* addressed themselues to the Emperor *Constantine* to aske Iudges of him; it is true, but what consequence can you drawe frō this exāple? For were not the *Donatistes* alreadie Schismatickes, and separated from the obedience and from the communion of the Church? And besides, had not they recourse afterward to the Emperor *Julian* the Apostata, a pagan and infidell Prince to recouer their Churches,, that the Christian and Catholicke Princes had taken from them, and with this Elogie, *that in him onely all iustice remained*? And did not saint AVGVSTINE crie out to them; *If it were in your power, you would not now call against vs the Emperor Constantine, because he fauors the truth, but you would rather call Iulian the Apostata out of hell?* The second head was, that the Emperor partlie yeilding to their importunitie, graunted them Iudges from the prouince that they had demaunded; that is to saie, from the *Gaules*; it is true, but did not the Emperor protest before he graunted this to them; *that it belonged not to him, who attended the iudgement of Christ, to meddle with the iudgements of Christ's Ministers?* And after he had graunted them this, did he not remitt them to *Rome* to iudge the cause with the Pope, and vnder the Presidencie and direction of the Pope? The third head was, that the *Donatists* appealed from the Popes iudgement, to the Emperors iudgement; it is true: But doth not the Emperor crie out, *that this appeale was a thing not fitt to be spoken or heard? that it was a madd impudence of furie; that it was a recourse from heauenlie to earthlie iudgement, and a manifest contempt of Christ's authoritie?* The fowrth head was, that notwithstanding this protestation, the Emperor graunted them a Councell at *Arles*; it is true: but doth not saint AVGVSTINE testifie, that it was an irregular action, when he saith that the Emperor did it, *giuing waie to the peruersnes of the Donatists?* And that the Popes legates and the assistants

Aug. ep. 162.

Aug. contr liter. Petil. l. 2. cap. 92. Ep 166

Optat. cōt. Parm. l. 1.

Ibidem.

that were with him at the Councell of *Rome*, were present at that of *Arles*. And that the Fathers of the Councell, bewailed that the Pope could not assist there, and said, that if he had bene there present, they had pronounced a more severe sentence against the *Donatists*; doth it not proue, that it was not a iudgement of appeale, but a more ample reuiew of the cause which the *Donatists* said was not fullie heard: The fift head was that the *Donatists* had recourse againe from the councell of *Arles* to the Emperor, and prayed him to take the examination of the cause himselfe, which he did, it is true; but doth not saint AVGVSTIN saie that he protested the he would afterward craue pardō of the holy Bishops? And doth he not further testifie that the *Donatists* did noe more agree to the Emperors iudgement then to the former? *The Emperor* (saith hee) *is chosen iudge; the Emperor iudging is dispised*. With what ingenuitie then, can *Caluin* and his disciples saie, that this historie is enough to end the question, and fully to cleere the busines; for who sees not, that these proceedings, not hauing bene at the instance of the Catholicke partie, and according to the ordinary formes of the Church, but at the instāce of the hereticall partie, and by extraordinarie waies and against which the Emperor himself protests for iniustice, for furie, for impietie, and obligeth himselfe to aske the Prelates pardon: And hauing finally bene reiected and disauowed, euen by those that had solicited for them, and as it were snatched it out of the Emperors handes, there is noe more iustice in makinge vse of them, to the preiudice of the ordinarie lawes of the Church, and to propound them for copies and paternes of the anciēt forme and ecclesiasticall discipline, then to alleadge against the present authoritie of the Pope and the Councell the audience and conference that King *Charles* the ninth graunted at *Poissy* to the Protestants of his Kingdome, after the councell of *Sens* and *Trent*, to the end to proue to bring them backe to the church, by way of mildenes and accommodation, and to inferr from thence, that the Conference of *Poissy*, was giuen aboue the Councells of *Sens* and *Trent*.

Ibidem.

Ibidem.

Ibidem. Aug. ep. 162.

Caluin. Inst. l. 4. c. 7.

The author of the tracte of the Church c. 8.

Of the decree of the Mileuitan Councell concerning the beyond-Sea Appeales.

CHAPT. V.

THE fowrth instance of *Caluin* is; that in the *Mileuitan* Councell holden vnder Pope *Innocent* the first thousand two hundred yeares agoe, the Bishops of *Africa* forbad the clerkes of their Prouinces the appeales beyond Seas. *In the Mileuitan Councell, saith Caluin, where saint* AVGVSTINE *assisted; those that should appeale beyond Sea; were excommunicated*. It is true, but to this instance we bring two sharpe and decisiue answeres: the first. that the canon is meant but of appeales in minor and personall causes, as were causes as well pecuniarie as morall, that is to saie, as well ciuill as criminall of clerkes, and not in maior causes, that is to saie, in common and Eclesiasticall causes, as were causes of Faith and Sacraments, or of the vniuersall customes of the church. And the second, that he speakes but of the Appeales of Priests deacons, and other clerkes of the inferior order; and not of the Appeales of the Clerkes of Superior orders; that is to saie,

Calu. Inst. l. 4 c. 7. Concil. Mileuit. can. 22.

of

of Bishops. For the cleering then of the first of these doubtes; which is, that the Canon is meant but of Appeales in minor causes, it must be knowne, that the ecclesiasticall Tribunalls, did then examine not onely the spirituall and religious causes of the Church, but also all the temporall and secular causes of ecclesiasticall persons, as well ciuill as criminall. This appeares both by the first Councell of *Constantinople*; which ordaines, *That if anie one doe begin a particular processe against a Bishop, as hauing receiued losse or iniurie from him, the person and* Religion *of the accuser shall not be examined, but if it be an ecclesiasticall crime, the accusers person shall be examined, and first it shall not be lawfull for herетickes to accuse orthodox Bishops for ecclesiasticall causes*: And by the third Councell of *Carthage*, celebrated ninteen yeares before the *Mileuitan* Councell; which decrees, *That euery Clerke that leauing the Ecclesiasticall gouernment, would purge himselfe in the publicke iudgements, although the sentence be to his aduantage, if it be in a criminall iudgement, he shall loose his degree; and if it be in ciuill iudgement, he shall loose that which hath bene adiudged to him.* And by the Epistle to the Emperor *Theodosius* the second who to aduance the iudgement of the controuersie of *Nestorius*, imposed truce to the Councell of *Ephesus* of all pecuniarie and criminall causes, and ordained that they should handle noe cause, neyther ecclesiasticall nor other, till that of Faith were determined. Now these different sortes of causes, were not reputed to be all of a weight; but the one, to witt those that regard Faith, or the generall customes of the Church, were called maior causes, maior businesses, maior affaires. And the others, to witt, those that regard the particular persons of clergy men, and consisted in accusation of manners, or pursuite of pecuniarie interests, were called minor causes, minor businesses, and minor affaires; And that by a distinction taken from the analogie of the Scripture, which reportes that *Jethro* aduised *Moyses* to suffer the minor causes of the Israelites to be iudged by the inferior iudges, and to reserue to himselfe onely the maior causes: *Those that shall be maior causes, said hee, lett them bring to thee, but let themselues iudge the minor causes*, The vse of this distinction may be seene in a thousand places of antiquities. It appeares in these wordes of the Epistle of the same Pope *Innocent*, vnder whom the *Mileuitan* Councell was holden, to *Victricius*; *If they be maior causes that are in question, after the Episcopall iudgement, lett them be referred to the Sea Apostolicke, as the Synod and ancient customes (* vetus and not *beata) ordaine*. Which Epistle I the rather alleage, because it was cited by the Bishops of *France* in the second Councell of Tours a thousand and seauen hundred yeares agone. It appeares in these wordes of the Epistle of the Pope saint LEO the first to *Anastasius* Bishop of *Thesalonica* his Vicar in *Macedonia* and other prouinces neere *Constantinople*; *If anie maior cause be moued for which it maie be reasonable and necessarie to call an Episcopall assemblie, lett it suffice thee to cause two Bishops to come to thee out of euerie prouince, such as the Metropolitans would choose*. And a litle after; *And if their iudgement be found differing from thy opinion let the acts be sent to vs with authenticall testimonie, that all dissentions taken awaie, a sentence pleasing to God may be decreed.* It appeares in these wordes of the Epistle of saint GREGORIE the *Great*, to *John* Bishop of the first *Justinianea*: *If anie cause of faith, or of crime, or of pecuniary matter be obiected against our Colleague Adrian Bishop of Thebes, lett it be iudged if it be a matter of light importance by our Nuncios, which are or shall be in the royall Cittie; that is to saie, at Constantinople; and if it be a matter of weight, let it be referred hither to the Sea Apostolicke*. And finally it appeares in the capitularie of our great Emperor *Charlemaine*, where the wordes of Pope *Innocent* the first, are repeated by forme of lawe, in these wordes: *If they be maior*

[Margin notes: Côc. Côst. 1.c.6. — Conc. Charth.3. c.7. — Conc.Eph. Act.1. — Exod.18. — Innoc.ep. ad Victric. — Conc. Turon 2.c.21 — Leo ep.82 — Greg.l.2. Ep.46. — Cap. Carol Magn.l. 6. c 287.]

the Sea Apostolicke, as the Synod and the blessed (or to reade better, *the ancient*) *custome ordaines*. And from thence it is that *Hincmarus* Archbishop of Rheims, writing a little after, that is to saie vnder *Charles* the *Balde* to Pope *Nicholas* the first, maketh him this protestation; *Let it not please God, that wee should soe despise the priuiledge of the first and soueraigne sea of the Pope of the holie Roman Church, as to wearie your soueraigne auctthoritie with all the Controuersies and with all the quarrells of the Clergie, as well of the Superior as inferior order, which the canons of the Councell of Nicea and the decrees of Innocent, and of the other Popes of the holy sea of Rome, commaund to be determined in their prouinces* And againe; *Wee Metropolitans trauailinge in our prouinciall Councells, decide carnall controuersies, and haue care after iudgement to referr the maior causes, and of maior persons, to the examination of the Pope of the Souueraigne Sea*. And from hence it is alsoe that *Gerson* declaming longe tyme after against the disorders in the court of *Rome* during the schisme of *Iohn* the twentie three, cryes out; *If the iudgement of minor causes be reproued in Moyses by Iethro, how would it be in the Pope and in his Court of soe manie continuall and importune imployments of most prophane and vnworthie processes*.

Hincm. ep. ad Nicol. I. apud Flodoard. hist. Eccl. Rem. l. 3.

Gers. de Protest. Eccl. Consid. 8.

The first solution then that wee bring to the prohibition that the Bishops of the *Mileuitan* Councell made to their clerkes from appealing beyond Sea, is that the wordes of the Councell were intended not of appeales in maior causes; that is to saie, in causes that concerne faith or the vniuersall customes of the church; but of appeales in minor causes; that is to saie in causes morall or pecuniarie of Ecclesiasticall persons. And this solution, besides the places alreadie alleadged, wee drawe first from the text of the canon which saith precisely; In the cause that they shall haue to shewe, that he speakes of their particular causes, and not of the causes of the church. And secondly from the argument that hath bene sett before one of the places of the Greeke translation of this canon neere thousand yeares agoe, which saith in their proper causes, to distinguish them from Ecclesiasticall causes: for the first councell of *Constantinople*, that the Greekes held for the *Palladium* of their discipline; And the third Councell of *Carthage*, oppose proper causes to ecclesiasticall causes, not that proper and temporall causes of ecclesiasticall persons were not sometimes called ecclesiasticall causes but because when the word ecclesiasticall cause was speciallie taken, it was restrained onely to ecclesiasticall matter. And thirdlie wee collect it from the practise and proceedinges of the same *Mileuitan* Councell. For after that *Pelagius*, whose cause was a maior cause, and belonging to the Faith, had bene iudged in the East by the Bishops of *Palestina*, and that *Celestius* his disciple had bene heard and excommunicated for the same cause in *Africa*, by the *African* Bishops, the *Mileuitan* Councell remitted the finall iudgement thereof to the Pope, in these words: *Because God by the guift of his principall grace, hath placed thee in the Sea Apostolicke, and in our daies, giuen thee for such as wee ought rather to feare that it should be imputed to vs for a crime of negligence if wee chould conceale from they Reuerence, those things that ought to be represented for the good of the Church, then to apprehend that they would seeme troublesome or contemptible to thee: Wee beseech the to applie thy pastorall diligence to the great perills of the sick members of Christ* And a little after; *Insinuating these things into they Apostolicall breast, wee neede not extend our-selues in language, and to amplifie so great an impietie with words, being assured that they will so moue thee, as thou canst not delaie their correction, least they should spread farther*. And againe; *But we hope, with the helpe of the mercie of our Lord Jesus Christ, who vouchsafe to gouerne thee consulting with him, and to heare thee praying to him, that those*

Edit. Græc Conc. Carth. c. 26. Côc. Côst. I. c. 6. Côc. Carth 3. c. 7.

Epist. Côcil. Mil. ad Innoc. inter. Ep. Aug. ep. 92

that holde these doctrins so peruerse and pernicious, will more easilie yeeld to the authoritie of thy Holynesse, drawne out of the authoritie of the holie scriptures, in such sort as we may haue more cause to reioyce in their correction, then to afflict ourselues in their ruine. A meruailous encounter of the effects of Gods prouidence, which willed that the same *Mileuitan* Councell, which the *Lutherans* and *Caluinists* abuse to ouerthrowe the Popes authoritie, not onely puts it in practise, but also witnesseth that it is of diuine right, and grounded vpon the authoritie of the holie scriptures. For to thinke, to shift off this Epithete, *drawne from the authoritie of the holie scriptures*, by saying that the Councell speakes not of the cathedrall and Iudiciary authoritie of the Pope, but of the authoritie of the passages of the scripture, alleadged by the Pope against *Pelagius*, it is a childish and ridiculous shifte, aswell because, the Pope had not then alleadged anie thing against the *Pelagians*, as because it had bene a singular impertinencie that the *Pelagians* would rather yeild to the Popes authoritie, then to that of the other Bishops, doctors, and Catholicke Councells, and amongst the rest, of saint IEROM, saint AVGVSTINE, and of the two Councells of *Africa*, whereof bookes are full saith saint PROSPER, Prosp. de Ingr.

Of Channells that wee bring,
From the eternall Spring.

Because the Popes authoritie was drawne from the authoritie of the holy scriptures; If by the Popes authoritie, they had intended the passages alleadged by the Pope, and not the authoritie of the Popes chaire. Iointly that the fiue Bishops of *Africa* who accompained the relation of the *Mileuitan* Councell with their letters, did sufficientlie explicate of what authoritie the *Mileuitan* Councell intended to speake, when they writt to the Pope; *If the abettors of Pelagius knew, that the booke, which they belieue or knowe to be his, hath bene anathematized and condemned by the authoritie of the Catholicke Bishops, and principallie by that of thy Holynesse, which wee doubt not, but it is of greater weight in his behalfe; wee will imagine, that they will noe more dare to disturbe the soules of the faithfull which are simplie Christian.* And fowerthlie, wee collect it from the words of the same saint INNOCENT the first, to whom the *Mileuitan* Councell addresse their relation, who not onely in the Epistle alreadie cited, to *Victricius*; saith, *That the ancient custome bare, that the maior causes after the Episcopall iudgement, were referred to the Sea Apostolicke;* but also in the verie answere of the *Mileuitan* Councell witnesseth, that causes of Faith, were wont to haue recourse to the Sea Apostolicke; *As manie tymes* (said hee) *as there is question of anie matter of faith, I make accounte that all my bretheren and fellowe Bishops cannot chuse but referr it to Peter; that is to saie, to the origiaall of their name and dignitie.* Which wordes are not to be argued of ambition, since saint AVSTIN commendes them as iust and lawfull, in these wordes; *Vpon this the relations of the two Councells of Carthage and Mileuis were sent to the Sea Apostolicke.* And a little after; *Wee writt also to Pope Innocent of blessed memorie, familiar letters, wherein wee treated the affaire somewhat more amplie.* To all these things he answered vs in the same manner as was conuenient and fitt, that the Prelate of the Sea Apostolicke should answere vs. And finallie we drawe it from the issue of *Celestius* his cause, which was that Pope *Innocent* hauing bene preuented by

Aug. ep. 95

Innoc ep. ad Victric.

Inter. ep. Aug. ep. 93.

Aug. ep. 106.

death before he could bring it to effect, Pope *Zosimus* his Successor and that euen at the instance of the Councells of *Africa*, who sent to *Rome* the verball processe of that, that past betweene them, and *Celestius* finisht it. And after he had heard *Celestius* in person, and deliberated whether hee would absolue him or not absolue him from the excommnnication that the Bishops of *Africa* had pronounced against him, he finallie confirmed the sentence of the Councells of *Africa*, and declared him condemned and excommunicated through the whole earth. *Celestius* (saith saint AVGVSTINE, speaking of the answeres that *Celestius* made to the Interrogatories of Pope *Zosimus*) *would not condemne the things that had bene obiected to him by the Deacon Paulinus in the Councell of Carthage; but he durst not resist the letters of the blessed Pope Innocent, but promist to comdemne all, what that Sea would comdemne. And therefore hauing bene gentlie fomented like a franticke person, to the end to giue him a little rest, it was not yet thought fitt that he ought to be absolued from the bondes of excommunication, but for the space of two moneths attending an answere from Africa, leasure for repentance was giuen him, vnder a certaine medecinall sweetenes of iudgement.* And againe: *Of this newe heresie Pelagius and Celestius hauing bene the authors, or the most famous and violent promoters, they themselues by the meanes of the watchfulnes of two Episcopall Councells, with the helpe of God, who takes the protection of his Church, haue also bene condemned in all the Christian world, by the Reuerend Prelates of the Sea Apostolicke; yea euen to the number of two, Pope Innocent, and Pope Zosimus, if they doe not correct themselues, and besides doe pennance.* And Prosper his disciple; *Vnder the twelfth consulship of Honorius and of Theodosius; the decrees of the Councell of Carthage two hundred and fourteen Bishops, were carried to Pope Zosimus, which hauing bene approued, the Pelagian heresie, was condemned throughout the world.* And againe; *The Pope, Zosimus of blessed memorie, added the force of his sentence to the decrees of the Councells of Africa; and to cutt of impious persons, armed the right hands of all the Bishops, with the sword of Peter.*

Aug de pecc.orig. cont Pelag & Celest. c.7.

Aug. ep. 157.

Prosper. in Chronic.

Id contr. Collator.

The second solution that whe bring to the place of the *Mileuitan* Councell is, that the Canon speakes but of inferior clerks, which were Priests, deacons, subdeacons, and other lesser Orders, and not superior Clerks; that is to saie, Bishops, whose causes, because of the importance and dignitie of their persons, were reputed maior causes; as Pope *Nicholas* the first, though longe after, writes to the Bishops of France, in these wordes. *The more the Bishops are in a principall degree. and more exalted in the Church of God, the more when their preseruation is treated of, or their deposition, ought their causes to bee reckoned amongst maior and difficult causes: for they are the first in the Church; they are those which holde the reede in their hand, to measure the holie Jerusalem; they are those that rule in Gods buildings.* And this solution we drawe first from the very wordes of the *Mileuitan* Councell, which are; *It hath bene thought fitt, that the Priests, Deacons, and other Clerks of the inferior order, in the causes that they shall haue, if they complaine of the iudgements of their Bishops, appeale not but to the Councells of Africa, or to the Primates of their prouinces.* By which words restrained to onely priests, deacons, and other Clerkes of inferior order; it is manifest that the Councells except the Clerkes of the superior order; that is to saie, Bishops And secondly, wee drawe it out of the Epistle of Pope *Julius* the first, reported by saint ATHANASIVS, which saith; that saint ATHANASIVS, could not be definitiuely iudged without the Roman Church, because he was of the order of Bishops: *They were* (said he) *Bishops, and not of vulgar Churches*

Nicol.1.ep ad Episc. Gallic.

Conc. Mileuit.c.22.

Ibid.

And a little after; *If then there were such a suspition conceaued against the Bishops there, it must haue bene written of, to this Church here.* Hereby testifying to vs; that there was this difference betweene the Bishops and the inferior Clerkes, as the causes of inferior clerkes were determined in particular Councells; but the causes of Bishops could not be iudged definitiuely without the Pope. And thirdly wee collect it from saint AVGVSTINE, who teacheth vs, as wee note in the appendix of the conference of *Fontaine-bleau*, that the prerogatiue of Bishops, and that of priests, deacons, and other inferior Clerkes were distinct in *Africa*, for matter of appeale; and that the one, to witt Bishops, might appeale beyond Sea, and not the others; yea groundes the iustice of the Catholickes of *Africa*, who tooke part with *Cecilianus* Archbishop of *Carthage* against the *Donatists*, who opposed him vpon this, that *Cecilianus* hauing bene iudged by a Councell of seauentie *African* Bishops assembled at *Carthage* could haue appealed beyond Sea; for as much as he was not of the number of Priests, deacons or other inferior Clerkes, but was of the order of Bishops: *He might* (saith saint AVSTIN) *despise the conspiring multitude of his enemies because he sawe himselfe ioyned by communicatorie letterrs with the Roman Church, in which hath alwaies flourisht the principalitie of the Sea Apostolicke, and with the other transmarine Churches. For* (adds he a little after) *there was noe question of Priests, deacons, or other Clerkes of the inferior order, but of the colleagues;* (*that is to saie,*) *of Bishops, who might reserue their cause intire to the iudgement of other Bishops, and principallie of the Churches Apostolicke.* In which place saint AVSTIN vseth the word *Churches Apostolicke*, in the plurall number, not to denie the eminencie of the *Roman* Church ouer the other Apostolicke Churches, of which contrarywise he had newlie said, that *Cecilianus* might dispise the conspiring multitude of his Enemies, for as much as he sawe himselfe vnited by communicatorie letters, with the Sea of *Rome*, in which had alwaies flourisht the principalitie of the Sea Apostolicke, but to the end to shutt vp the gate against the shift of the *Donatists*, which calumniated and reiected the iudgement that Pope *Melchiades* had made of *Cecilianus*, because they said that *Melchiades*, not onely was culpable of the crime of treason as well as *Cecilianus*, and by consequent capable of refusall in this case; but also whilst he was yet a deacon had Sacrificed to Idolls, with Pope *Marcellinus*. For although this reproach were false, as appeares by the computation that saint AVGVSTINE giues it elswhere, and by the testimonie that *Theodoret* giues to *Marcellinus*, to haue bene most excellent in persecution: Neuertheles it gaue colour to the *Donatists* to reuolte against the Popes iudgement; therefore saint AVSTIN without tying himself to the specialitie of the *Roman* Church, contents himself to saie in generall, that *Cecilianus* might reserue his cause to the iudgement of the transmarine Churches, and principally those that are Apostolicke; to inferr thẽce, that the *Donatists*, (who vpon the onelie sentence of the Councell of *Africke*, & without attending a iudgement frõ beyond Sea had instituted an other Archbishop at *Carthage*,) were Schismatickes. For the priuiledge that the Bishops of *Africke* had, that they might appeale beyõd Sea, was such, that their causes could not be determined, either till the *Roman* Church should examine them, or in default of the *Roman* Church, (putting it in the forme of a case giuẽ, not graũted that they had iust cause to refuse the Pope in anie affaire;) till the iudgemẽt of all the other trãsmarine Churches, & principallie Apostolicke, had interuened as S. AVS. declares a while after, in these wordes: *Put the case that the Bishops that iudged the cause at Rome, had not bene good iudges*

Refut. de l'obiect. 1. du Decret.

Aug. ep. 162.

Aug. de vnic. Baptism. Theod. hist. Eccl. 1. c. 3.

Aug. ep. 16..

there remayned yet the vniuersall Councell of the whole Church. For this cause then the *Mileuitan* Councell, willing according to the ancient *African* discipline, (witnessed by saint AVSTIN himselfe) to except at the Canon where the defence of the appeales beyond Sea is questioned; the clerkes of the superior order, that is to saie, the Bishops, put in by waie of barr, the specification of priests, Deacons and other Clerkes of the inferior order, to hinder Bishops from being comprehended therein. *It hath bene thought fitt* (saith the Councell,) *that the Priests, Deacons, and other clerkes of the inferior order, should not appeale but to the Councell of Africa, or to the primates of their owne prouinces.* For whereas the Greekes in their rapsody of the *African* Councells, which they call the Councells of *Carthage*; doe add at the end of a place, where the canon is reported out of his place, these words; *as it hath bene often ordained of Bishops*; a clause that if it were true, shewes plainely, that the bodie of the Canō speakes not of Bishops, it is a false addition made by the Greekes, and followed in the forme of diuers reading by some latine copists. Conc. Mileuit. c. 22 Edit. Græc. Conc. Carthag. c. 28. vel. secundum alios 31.

Our waies to disproue this are seauen. The first is, that neither in the originall texts of the *Mileuitan* Councell, nor in *Gratians* citations, nor in the copies that are transcribed in forme by the centuriators of *Germanie*, nor in the Councell of *Carthage*, holden vnder the twelfth Consulship of *Honorius* where the canons of the *Mileuitan* Councell were reported; nor in all the hundred and fiue chapters of the latine rapsodie of the Councells of *Africa*, this cause is not to be found. The second, that in the very rapsodie of the Greekes, in the place where the Councell of *Carthage*, relatiue to that of *Mileuis* is inserted, there is noe mention made of this clause. The third, that neuer before the *Mileuitan* Councell, there had bene anie speech of interdicting the appeales beyond the Sea to the Bishops; contrarywise, saint AVSTIN testifies, that the ancient discipline of *Africa*, bare, that Bishops had right to appeale beyond Sea; by meanes whereof the *Mileuitan* Councell could not add to their decree; *as it hath often bene ordained of Bishops.* The fowrth, that they had neuer begun to make this *Defence* for Bishops, before it had bene done for Priests, deacons, and the inferior clerkes, who were much lesse priuiledged then the Bishops. The fift, that these wordes; *As it hath bene often ordained of Bishops*, can not be compatible with the text of the Canon; which wills, that the appeales whereof it speakes, should haue recourse to the Primates of prouinces. For the causes of Bishops went not by appeale, but in in the first instance, to the Primates of the Prouinces. *If anie Bishop be accused* (saith the Councell of *Hippo* and after that the third Coūcell of *Carthage*;) *lett the accuser bringe the cause to the Primate of the prouince.* And it is not to be replied, that the Canon *importes; to the African Councells, or to the Primates of their Prouinces*; for besides that by the *African* Councells, he intēds the prouinciall Councells of *Africa*, as it appeares by this alternatiue, *or to the Primates of their prouinces*; which was put there, because the Primates iudged with the Councells of their Prouinces: The Greekes, to finde a place for their addition, without multiplying the wordes of the article, haue taken awaie in this place, the clause of the *African Councells*, and left that onelie, *of the Primates of Prouinces*, as being one same thing. Yet will it lesse auaile to obiect, that in two most incorrect manuscripts; there is, *or to the Generall Councell*; that is to saie, to the Generall Councell of *Africa*, For besides that, all the greeke and latine impression, disproue this different reading, euen the addition of the other clause can not sufferr it. For as much as these words; *as it hath often bene ordained of Bishops*, shew, that the precedent period spake not of Bishops, but of inferior

Impress. Paris. apud Galliot. du Prè. 1524. & Francisc Regnaut. 1553 & Guillel. Thibout 1555. Impress. Basil. per Ioan Opoporin. 1535. Impress. Venet 1585. Decret. Grat. c. 2. q. 6 & c. 21. q. 3. Centur. Magdeburg Centur. 5. col. 839. Cōc. Afric. c 93. Edit. Græc. Cōc. Carth c. 126. vel secundum alios 127. Aug. ep. 162. Conc. Hipon c. 7. Conc. Carthag. 3. c. 7. Edit. Græc. Concil. Carth. c. 26

Clerkes whose causes went not to the generall Councells of *Africa*. And because euen those that alleadge the canon with the first addition, and amongst others *Hincmarus*, and the Conuenticle of *Rheims*, the one vnder *Charles* the *Bald*; the other vnder *Hugh Capet*, are ignorant of the second, as not contayned in the copies of their tyme: And the rapsodists of the Greekes, euen the same. And it serues for nothing to saie, that in the Epistle to Pope *Celestine*, there is found a like clause. For neither doth that epistle speake seperately of the inferior clerkes, as doth the first period of this Canon; but speakes iointlie of the inferior Clerkes and of the Bishops; and it is to bee vnderstood respectiuely of the one and of the other; neither was it done as it shall appeare heereafter, before the controuersies of the Bishops appeales, as was the *Mileuitan* Councell, but after. The sixth way of disproofe, is, that Pope *Innocent* the first, commended the *Mileuitan* Councell, for hauing carryed themselues worthilie for the honor of the Sea Apostolicke; *You prouided* (said hee) *diligentlie and worthily for the Apostolicall honor*. And againe; *You shall enioy the glorie of hauing obserued the Canons*. Which he had neuer done, if in the prohibition of appeales beyond Sea, the *Mileuitan* Councell had comprehended the causes of Bishops. And the seauenth finallie, that *Cresconius* an *African* author and ancient, of a thousand yeares, in the Epitomie that he compiled of the Canons, registers the title of this Canon in the same termes of the originall latin of the *Mileuitan* Councell, and of the Councell of *Carthage*, holden vnder the twefth consulship of *Honorius*, where the Mileuitan was inserted; that is to say, restraines it to onely priests and deacons in these words; *For priests* (said he) *And deacons, lett not them appeale, but to the Councells of Africa*. I add, that if this addition should be true, it would not belonge to the *Mileuitan* Councell, which toucheth, not one word of Bishops appeales, but to the sixth Councell of *Carthage*, where the busines of the Bishops appeales was questioned. For the place of the Greeke rapsody that containes it, is noe relatiue, either to the *Mileuitan* Coũcell nor to the Councell of *Carthage*, holdẽ vnder the twelfth Consulship of *Honorius*, where the *Mileuitan* was reported; but to the sixth Councell of *Carthage*, and the copie of some latine collections, whither it hath bene transferred, beare the title of the sixth Councell of *Carthage*. And finallie, I saie it is soe farr from being true, as the very place where it is found, is forged. For neither the sixth Councell of *Carthage* made anie Canon concerning Bishops appeales, but ordained, that the resolution of the affaire, should be put off, till the Greeke copies of the Councell of *Nicea*, which arriued long after, had bene brought out of the East, and that when they should come, there should be a new Councell called to deliberate of it, and the while that the Bishops appeales should continue, neither was the collection of thirtie three Canons annexed by the Greekes, before the rapsodie of the Councells of *Africa*, and published in some latine copies, vnder the name of the sixth Coũcell of *Carthage* made in the sixth Councell of *Carthage*, but is a mingle mãgle of diuers *African* Canons, peeced together by some impertinent compiler, and publisht, as shall hereafter appeare, vnder the name of the sixth Coũcell of *Carthage*. But for as much as the clereing of these two last pointes, depends vpon the order and distinction of the Councells of *Africa*, that the ignorance of the Copyer and compilers, hath strangelie confounded, it is necessarie to informe the Readers therein before I passe further.

Hincm. in ep. 55. cap. 17. Centur. Magdeb. cent. 10. coll. 494. Edit. Græc. Conc. Carth. c. 26. Cõc. Afric. c. 105. Beneath. chap. 10.

Cresc. in Breuiar. can. capit. 285.

See beneath. chap. 7.

Conc Carthag. 6. c. 9. Conc. Carthag. 6 c. 7.

Beneath. chap. 49.

Of the order and distinction of the Councells of Carthage;

CHAPT. VI.

TO bring some light to this confusion, you must note, that there are three waies by which the Canons of the Councells of *Africa* are come to our handes; the first, the originall text of the Councells of *Africa*, which are come in forme to vs, amongst which are seauen Councells of *Carthage* which are escaped from the iniurie of tyme, and some Councells of *Numidia*. The secōdis this latine rapsodie of the Canōs of the Coūcells of *Africa*, cōtained in an hūdred & fiue chapters which we call the coūcell of *Africa*. And the third is this greeke rapsodie of the same Canons of the Councells of *Africa*, contained in a hundred thirtie eight whereof the first thirtie three are translated from a latin collection, falsely attributed to the sixth Councell of *Carthage*. And the hundred and fiue others, are translated from the latine rapsodie; And therefore according to those three waies, wee will distribute the discourse of the distinction of the Councells of *Africa* into three partes.

Of the Councells of *Africa* then, which are come in forme to vs, the first is the Councell of *Carthage* holden vnder *Gratus* Archbishop of *Carthage* in the tyme of the Emperor *Constantine*, sonne to the Great *Constantine*, when *Paulus* and *Macarius* were sent into *Africa*, and whose Canons are cited by *Fulgentius Ferrandus* an ancient *African* Canonist, with this title: *The Councell of Carthage, holden vnder saint* GRATVS; which Councell wee call the first, because it is the first of the orthodox Councells of *Africa* that hath come to our handes; for that, that was held by saint CYPRIAN, was an erroneous Councell, and reproued by the Church. The second is the Councell of *Carthage*, celebrated vnder *Genetlius*, during the Empire of *Valentinian* the first. The second is the Councell of *Carthage*, assembled in the tyme of *Cornelius* vnder the Consulships of *Cesarius* and *Atticus*. The fowrth is the Councell of *Carthage* called vnder the Consulship of *Honorius* and *Eutychianus*, where the conditions of those that ought to be receiued into ecclesiasticall orders were decided. The fifth is the Councell dated after the consulship whether of *Stilicon* and *Aurelianus*; or whether as the Illustrious cardinall *Baronius* will haue it, of *Cesarius* and *Atticus*; where was decreed the legation to the Emperors, for the destruction of the relickes of *Idolatrie*. The sixth is, the Councell that was gathered after the twelfth consulship of *Honorius* the eigth of the calends of *Iune* for the cause of *Apiarius*. And the seauenth is that that was kept the third of the calends of *Iune* of the same yeare, after the Bishops assembled at the sixth Councell of *Carthage* were retired, and had left with *Aurelius* one & twētie deputies of all their assemblie, to the end to frame rules necessary for *Africa*. Now in the busines of these seauen councells, we shall meete with seauen principall difficulties, which we will assaie to remoue all in this chapter; the first difficultie is, concerning the second and third councell of *Carthage*, whereof some authors of this age, reuerse the order, and will haue the second to be the eigth, or the ninth; and the third to be the second, and

Fulg. Ferr. in Breu. Can. art. 4. 24. 123. & alibi.

from

from the third they cutt of manie canons, which they attribute to the sixth. A thing that not onely disturbes the order, and the credit of the ecclesiasticall historie, but also diminisheth the antiquitie of manie canons, aduantageous to the Catholicke cause, which are contained in the second and third, by meanes whereof, the interest of the same cause, obligeth me to replace them in their ranke, and the rather because the last impression of the councells which hath bene made vpon this new chronologie, begins to take such footing in mens spirits, as the more parte of the moderne writers, sufferr themselues to be carried awaie with it. Now, I cannot sett to my hand to correct it, without shouldering and remouing the computation of the most learned and Illustrious cardinall *Baronius*: for it is hee, vnder whose authoritie, they couer themselues, and out of whose writings they take all their arguments; and therefore before I enter into the matter, I will beseeche that great *Ornament* of the Church now that he discernes from heauen his obliuions and ours, to pardon me, if I bee in anie thing different from the course of his nanalls. For who can be such a *Homer*, as in soe long and prodigious a labour not sometymes to slumber? but wee must alwaies remember, that his defects are beneath his glory, and that if within the great and immense masse of his workes, there be found (as within the bodie of the moone) some markes and spotts, they hinder him not from shyning aboue all other Ecclesiasticall historians,

Edit. Conc. Colon. 1606.

As Luna, when the nights dimme Curtaine shrines
The skies; the fainter light of Starrs out-shines.

The reasons then, for which the Illustrious Cardinall *Baronius* hath departed, in the second Councell of *Carthage* from the ordinarie chronologie, are fower: the first, that the inscription of this councell is *Valentinian*, being the fowrth tyme consull with *Theodosius*, which can not be vnderstood of *Valentinian* the first, and of the great *Theodosius*, who were neuer together consulls, and therefore ought to haue reference to *Theodosius* the second & *Valentinian* the third who were consulls together the yeare of Christ three hundred twentie fiue. And for as much, as whē *Valentinian* is named before *Theodosius* it is *Valentinian* the first, and *Theodosius* the great which are intended; he will haue it, that the order hath bene inuerted, and that insteede of *Valentinian* and *Theodosius*, it should be restored *Theodosius* and *Valentinian*. And because the fowrth consulship of *Valentinian* the third fell out after the possession of *Africa* by the *Vandalls*, and after the death of *Aurelius* Bishop of *Carthage* he conceaues that in steede of IIII. we should read IV. and that these two letters, are not markes of cyphering, but an abridgement of the word *Iunior*: and that the inscription speakes of the young *Valentinian*. The second reason is that this Councell was holden vnder *Genedius*, Archbishop of *Carthage*, which cannot be before *Aurelius*, for before *Aurelius* there was noe Bishop of *Carthage*, that bare the name of *Genedius*. The third reason is, that there is mention made in this Councell of *Aurelius* and of *Genedius*, as being both present there; by meanes whereof, it must bee that this *Genedius* was condintor to *Aurelius*, which could not haue bene but in the extreame old age of *Aurelius*; and by consequent, longe after the date of the second Councell of *Carthage*. And the fowrth which is the strongest of all, that *Alipius* Bishop of *Tagast*, and *Valentin* Primate of *Numidia*, are there nominated as present and speaking in the Councell, which cannot agree to the Chronologie of the second Coun-

Annal. tom. 5. ann. 397. Et in appendic ad Tom. 5. ann. 397. Et in Epito D. Spond. ad eund. ann. & in Edit Conc. Col ex recogn. Seuerin Binn. Tom I.

cell of *Carthage*, in the time whereof, neither *Alipius* as appeares by saint AVGVSTINE was Bishop of *Tagast* nor *Valentin* as appeares by the *African* Councell, Primate of *Numidia*. Aug.ep 8. Conc. Afric.c.53.

Now to the first of these obiections, which is of the date, it hath bene alreadie answered by manie and amongst the rest, by *Monsieur le Feure*, afterward Tutor to the most Christian King, that in steede of these wordes *Valentinian for the fowrth tyme, and Theodosius Consulls*, it must be read *Valentinian for the fowrth time, and Neoterius consulls*, the copiers hauing ignorantlie from the abridgement of these letters *Neot*: made *Theod*: Præfat in Frag.Hilar

To the second obiection, which is of the name *Genedius*, which is not found attributed to anie Bishop of *Carthage* before *Aurelius*; it hath likewise bene answered, that it must not be read *Genedius*, but *Genetlius*, which is the name of *Aurelius* predecessor, and so the ancient Manuscriptes haue it; And so *Fulgentius Ferrandus* an *African* Author, reades it, whose antiquitie is of aboue a thousand two hundred yeares. To which there may be added that the appendix of the capitularie of *Charlemaine* citeth the ninth canon of the same Councell with these termes, *The Bishop Genilius hath said*; which is a word corrupted from the name *Genetlius*. Fulg.Ferr. in Breuiar. Can c.4.& alibi. Capit. Carol.Magn. add.4.

To the third obiection, which is of the presence of *Aurelius* mentioned in some canons of this councell; *Monsieur le Feure* answereth, that he hath seene some Manuscripts, which insteede of *Aurelius* haue in the second canon *Epigonius*, and in the fifth and sixth *Genetlius*. Though it should be read *Aurelius*, it doth not therefore followe, that the councell intended to speake of *Aurelius* Bishop of *Carthage*; for the name of *Aurelius* was a name very common to the Bishops of *Africa*, as in the councell holden vnder the consulship of *Cesarius* and Atticus, *Aurelius* Bishop of *Carthage* maketh mention of an other Bishop, called *Aurelius*: *Reginus* (saith hee) *hath brought me letters frõ Crescentianus Bishop of the first Sea of Numidia, as he pretends and from* Aurelius *our fellow Bishops*: And in the conference of *Carthage* with the *Donatists*; *There was amõgst the Catholicke Bishops* Aurelius *Bishop of Carthage, and* Aurelius *Bishop of Macomades*. And if this same *Aurelius*, had bene Bishop of *Carthage*, it neede not followe therefore, that *Genetlius* had bene his coadiutor. Contrarywise it would follow from thence, that it should be *Genetlius* that had bene Bishop of *Carthage* in Chiefe, and *Aurelius* his coadiutor; For the Councell intituled the second of *Carthage*; had bene called by *Genetlius*, as he testifies in these words: *You haue trauailed to* Carthage *according to the request of my letters*. Now the letters to call the councell had not bene dispatched in *Genetlius* his name, and principally *Aurelius* being present and resident at *Carthage*, if *Aurelius* had bene chiefe Archbishop, and that *Genetlius* had bene but his coadiutor. For the priuiledge to call Generall Councells of *Africa*, belonged of right to the Archbishops of *Carthage*; and to them it apperteyned to signe the letters which they called in greeke *Synodicall*, and in latin *tractatorie*; and not *tractorie*, as *Erasmus* supposed, and some new censors after him, not considering the difference that was betweene the *tractory* letters that the Emperors dispatched to send for their officers, and to cause them to be defraied by the waie; and the tractatory letters, that the Primates write either to their Suffragans, to call them to the Councells of their Prouinces; or to strainge Bishops, to aduertise them of what they had done in the Councells of their Prouinces; for the one was called *tractory*, of the word, *traho*; and the other was called *tractatory*, of the word, *tractatus*, which signifies *Synod*, or *Councell*: From whence it is that saint AMBROSE, and the Councells of *Carthage*, call the Councell of *Nicea*, *Tractatus Nicenus*; and that the Councell of *Zelles* in *Africa* In Concil. Africant. c.1. Collat. Carth.Act. 1. Conc.Carthag.2.c.1. Ambr.ep. 32 & 82. Conc.Carthag.3.c. 48.& Conc. Afric.c.14

calls

Conc.zel-len. Vulg. vocat. Te-lens.in proœm. Conc. Afric.c.43. & c.57. Edit. Græc Côc.Carth c.90.

cal's the Epistle that Pope *Siricius* writt to the *Africans*, not to the end to call them, but to the end to aduertise them of what had bene ordained in the Councell of *Rome*, *tractatory*. And that saint AVGVSTIN intitleth the *Synodicall* Epistles of the Councell of the *Maximianists* holden at *Carthage*, TRACTATORIE. And therefore in all the places of the *African* Councells, where this word is vsed, not onely the latine editions, say *tractatory*, but euen the greeke translation made before the tyme of *Iustinian Rhinotmete*, that is neere a thousand yeares, agone, hath it *Sinodicall*.

To the fowrth obiection, which is that in the Councell intitled the second of *Carthage*, there is mention made of *Alipius* Bishop of *Sagast*, and of *Valentine* Primate of *Numidia*, to which there hath as yet bene nothing answered, and which is in truth such, as if the edition of this place were correct, the Illustrious Cardinall *Baronius* his reason had bene inuincible; I answere these two wordes; *Alypius* Bishop of *Sagast* and *Valentine* Primate of *Numidia* are not of the originall text of the second Councell of *Carthage*, but they are two quotations which haue bene added to the repetition of one of the canons of this Councell, which was made in the collection intitled the sixth Councell of *Carthage*. I will take the busines at the spring, to make the readers vnderstand it the better: Amongst the monuments of antiquitie which are come to vs, there it found as is alreadie aboue said, a Collection of thirtie three Canons, taken out of diuers precedent Councells; And amongst the rest, from the first Councell of *Carthage* holden vnder *Gratus* Archbishop of *Carthage*, from the second Councell of *Carthage*, holden vnder *Genetlius* Archbishop of *Carthage*; and from the third and fifth Councells of *Carthage*, holden vnder *Aurelius* Archbishop of *Carthage* Successor to each of them, but which haue bene since compiled and assembled into a collection, be it as we pretend by a particular rapsody; be it as some others pretend by the sixth Councell of *Carthage*. Now it is happened, that the copyers of this collection, intituled the sixth Councell of *Carthage*, belieuing that the canons that are inserted there, had bene made in the sixth Councell of *Carthage*, and not borrowed and repeated out of the preceding Councells, haue accommodated in their copies, the most parte of the quotations of the articles, to the time and to the persons of the sixth Councell of *Carthage*. For example; in the fifte Canon of the collection, intituled the sixth Councell of *Carthage*, which is a canon taken from two places, out of the first Councell of *Carthage*, celebrated vnder the Archbishop *Gratus*, as it appeares, both by the text of the first Councell of *Carthage* of whose truth both sides are agreed; and by *Fulgentius Ferrandus*, who alleadges the second part of this canon, with the title of the Canons of the Councell holden vnder saint GRATVS; and by the Councell of *Ayx* in *Germany*, called in the tyme of *Lewis* the *Debonnaire*, who citeth the last part with this inscription; *Gratus hath said*, the copiers to fitt it to the time of the sixth Councell of *Carthage*, haue changed the ticket of the article; and in steede of these wordes, *The Bishop Gratus hath said*, haue put it. *Aurelius hath said*. In the third canon of the same collection, intituled the sixth Councell of *Carthage*, which is taken, out of the second canon of the Councell holden vnder *Genetlius* Archbishop of *Carthage*, after these wordes: *As in the councell last past, the rule of continence and chastitie was treated of*, which could not haue bene pronounced in the sixth councell of *Carthage*, for as much as in the councell holden vnder the twelfth consulship of *Honorius*, which did immediately precede the sixth Conncell of *Carthage*, there was nothing or-

Concil. Carthag. 1. c. 10. & 13. Ful.Ferr.in Breu. Can. art.24 & 123. Concil. Aquisgran. c.61. Côcil.dict. Carthag. 6 c.5. Concil. sub Honor 12. & Theodos.8. Coss in Concil. Afric c.76 & deinceps vsque ad cap.94.

dained

dained concerning the continence of the Clergie: the copyers of the collection notwithstanding to fitt them to the time of the sixth Coũcell of *Carthage*, where *Faustinus* the Popes Legat assisted, haue changed the following clause, and in steede of these wordes, *all the Bishops saie*; haue put; *Faustinus, Bishop of Potentia saith*. In the ninth canon of the same collection, which is a canon taken out of the second Councell of *Carthage*, where after the proposition of *Felix* and *Epigonius*, *Genetlius* spake againe; the exemplifiers of the collection to applie this Canon to the time of the sixth Councell of *Carthage*, haue suppressed the word *Genetlius*, and insteed of these wordes *Genetlius Bishop*, haue put, *Augustine Legate of the prouince of Numidia hath said*. And finallie in the thirteenth Canon of the same collection, which is a centon taken from the three last canons of the Councell holden vnder *Genetlius*, which we call the second of *Carthage*; the exemplifiers to make the wordes of the canon agree with the tyme of the sixth of *Carthage*, haue chainged the word *Genetlius*, which was in all the three places of that Councell which we call the second of *Carthage*, and haue put *Aurelius* in steede of it. And they cannot say, that the canons of the Councell holden vnder *Genetlius* are not repeated in the collectiõ intituled, the sixth Councell of *Carthage*; but that the canons of the collection intituled the sixth Councell of *Carthage*, are repeated in the Councell holden vnder *Genetlius*. For besides that the Canõs of the Councells of *Carthage* holden vnder *Genetlius*, & repeated in the collection intituled, the sixth Councell of *Carthage*, are cited by *Fulgentius Ferandus*, as canons of the councells holden vnder *Genetlius*, and placed before the canons of the Councell of *Carthage* holden vnder *Aurelius*; the words of the same canons are couched in the councell holden vnder *Genetlius* in their order, and at their length; and with their reasons and relations to the antecedent and subsequent clauses; whereas in the collection intituled, the sixt Councell of *Carthage*, they are compiled in forme of centons of diuers canons of the councell holden vnder *Genetlius*, and couched as shall heereafter appeare impertinentlie, and without order of relation or dependencie one vpon an other. Now the abuse of Scriueners hath not yet staied there, for this first error hath by reflection produced a second; to witt, that the Exemplifiers of the Councell holden vnder *Genetlius*, which we call the second of *Carthage*, finding in the collection, intituled the sixth Councell of *Carthage*, the canons of the second repeated, and noted with these new quotations, haue transferred them, & made some of them retrograde into the copies of the second; sometimes in forme of diuers readings, as those of the canõ of the celibat, where the writers in steede of these wordes, *all the Bishops said*, haue put in the marget, *Other copies saie; Faustinus Bishop of Potentia did saie*: sometimes in the forme of a continued text, and without the note of diuers reading; as in the second, third, fowrth, and sixth canon of the second councell of *Carthage*; in the first whereof the ancient manuscripts of the second Councell of *Carthage*; cited by *Monsieur le feure*, haue *Epigonius*; and in the three others, *Genetlius*; the exemplifiers haue taken awaie *Epigonius* and *Genetlius*, and put in *Aurelius*. Now of this kinde doe wee maintaine the two quotations to be, that are heere in question; that is to saie, that the two names *Alypius Bishop of Tagast*, and *Valentine Primat of Numidia*, are not of the originall text of the Councell holden vnder *Genetlius*, which we call the second of *Carthage*, but haue bene transferred thither, from the repetition of the Canons of the same Councell, which had bene made in the collection intituled, the sixth councell of *Carthage*. And thus much for answere to the last of the Illustrious

Cõc. Carth 2. c. 7.

Cõc dict. Carth. 6. c. 9.

Cõc. Carth 2. c. 11. 12. & 13.

Fulg. Ferr. in Breuiar. Can artic. 4. 96. 194 & alibi.

Cõc. Carth 4. ad marg. c. 2.

Præfat. in frag. Hilar.

Cardinall

Cardinall *Baronius*. We are now to passe forward to ours.

The reasons then, by vertue whereof wee seperate ourselues from the chronology of the Illustrious Cardinall *Baronius*, who placeth the Councell of *Genetlius* vnder the emperor *Valentinian* the third, and adhere to the ordinarie computation, which placeth it vnder the emperor *Valentinian* the second, consists in tenne principall proofes: The first proofe is that, we haue nowe some what touched; to witt, that manie of the canons of the Councell holden vnder *Genetlius*, are repeated in the Collection intituled *the sixth Councell of Carthage*; from whence it appeares, that the Councell holden vnder *Genetlius* preceded the sixth Councell of *Carthage*. Now the Councell holden vnder *Genetlius*, could not precede the sixth Councell of *Carthage*, vnlesse *Genetlius* had bene chiefe Bishop of *Carthage*, before *Aurelius*: for in the tyme of the sixth Councell of *Carthage*, *Aurelius* had noe coadiutor, and *Genetlius* could not haue bene Predecessor to *Aurelius*, but he must haue liued, not vnder the Empire of *Valentinian* the third who began not his Raigne, till six yeare after the sixth Councell of *Carthage*, but vnder the Empire of *Valentinian* the second.

The second proofe is, that the Councell intituled, the second of *Carthage*, was called by *Genetlius*, as it hath bene aboue said, and as he declared it himselfe in these wordes: *You haue trauailed to* Carthage *vpon the instance of my letters*: by meanes whereof he must necessarily be Archbishop of *Carthage* in chiefe, and not coadiutor to *Aurelius*; and consequentlie, that the Councell intituled the second of *Carthage*, was holden vnder *Valentinian* the second, and not vnder *Valentinian* the third. The third proofe is, that saint AVGVS. hauing repented that he was made coadiutor with identitie of title to *Valerius* Bishop of *Hippo*, because he belieued that it was forbidden by the Councell of *Nicea*, and hauing vpon this occasion procured in the sixth councell of *Carthage*, that those that ordained Bishops, should be obliged to read the decrees of the Coũcells to them, before they ordanied them; there is noe appearance, that after the third Councell of *Carthage*, *Aurelius* should haue made *Genetlius* his coadiutor, with identitie of title. The fowerth proofe is, that after *Aurelius* there was noe Bishop of *Carthage* which bore the name of *Genetlius*, nor anie roome vacant where to place him: For to *Aurelius* succeeded *Capreolus*, to *Capreolus*, *Quod-vultDeus*; to *Quod vult-Deus*, *Deo gratias*: Whereas betweene the promotion of *Gratus*, who assisted at the Councell of *Sardica*, which was holden the three hundred and fortie seauenth yeare, and the death of *Aurelius*, who still liued according to the computation of the Illustrious Cardinall *Baronius*, the yeare fower hundred twentie fiue, there was so long a space, as there must necessarily be one or more Bishops betweene both. The fifth proofe is, that *Fulgentius Ferrandus* an *African* author of more then a thousand one hundred yeares antiquitie, not onely placeth *Genetlius* betweene *Gratus* and *Aurelius*, but also placeth the Councell of *Carthage* holden vnder *Genetlius*, before the third Councell of *Carthage*, and other Councells of *Carthage*, assembled vnder *Aurelius*. For in the fourth article of his *Epitomy*, speaking of the ordination of Bishops, which ought to be done by three Bishops, with the *Metropolitans* consent, he alleadgeth for the credit of this decree, *the Councell of Carthage holden vnder the Prelate Genetlius, the tenth title, and the generall* Councell *of Carthage, title fortie seauenth; and the* Councell *of Zelles*: which generall Councell of *Carthage* was the third Councell of *Carthage*, as it appeares both by the words of the decree alleadged, which are there; and because it is placed

Cõc. Carth 2. c. 2.

Act. design. Erad apud August. ep. 110. Possid. in vit. August. Cõc. Carth 3. c. 3.

Ep. Capreol. Episc. Carth. ad Concil Ephes. Victor. Vtic. persec. Vandal l. 1. Id. Ibidem.

Fulg. Ferrand. in Breuiar. Can. art. 4.

before the Councell of *Zelles*, which was holden vnder the twelfth consulship of *Honorius*; that is to saie, the yeare before the sixth Councell of *Carthage*. And in the twentie fowrth article speaking of the decree which forbids Bishops to vsurpe one an others people, he alleadgeth for warrãt to that lawe, the Councell of *Carthage* vnder S. GRATVS, title the ninth and the Councell of *Carthage* vnder the Prelate *Genetlius*, title the ninth. And the Councell of *Carthage* title the fifth, putting the Cõucell of *Carthage*, celebrated vnder S. GRATVS; which was the first Councell of *Carthage*, in the first place; & the Councell of *Carthage* celebrated vnder *Genetlius* in the second place; and the other Councell of *Carthage* in the third place. The sixth proofe is, that in the third Councell of *Carthage*, holden vnder the consulship of *Cesarius* and *Atticus*; whereof the preface is reported in the Rapsody of the Councell of *Africa*; *Victor* Bishop of *Pupputa*, is nominated amongst the Bishops of the Councell, with the Epithete of *old man*, whereas in the Councell of *Carthage* holden vnder *Genetlius* he is named without anie mention of age; a thing which shewes that the Councell holden vnder *Genetlius*, had preceded the third Councell of *Carthage*. For there is noe appearance that in the third Councell of *Carthage*, *Victor* of *Pupputa* should haue bene called old man, and that in the Councell holden vnder *Genetlius*; if this Councell had bene celebrated, as the Illustrious Cardinall *Baronius* would haue it, twentie seauen yeares after the third Councell of *Carthage*, the mention of his age should haue bene omitted. The seauenth proofe is, that in the third Councell of *Carthage Epigonius* calls the same *Victor* of *Pupputa*, the father of the *African* Bishops, and the most ancient in promotion; And neuerthelesse in the Councell of *Carthage*, holden vnder *Genetlius*, he is mentioned after *Victor* Bishop of *Abdera*, a cittie of *Africa* soe called, otherwise called *Gemanicia*, that S. CYPRIAN calls, *Abbir* of *Gemanicia*; and *Victor* of *Vtica*, *Abdir*, and *Ptolomy*, *Abdeira*. A thing that euidently shewes, that the Councell of *Carthage* holden vnder *Genetlius* preceded the third Councell of *Carthage*. For the *Africans* were so curious to obserue the orders of promotion in the Catalogues of their Cõucells, that they neuer inuerted it, as appeares by the cõplaint that S. AVGVS. made to *Victorinus*, that in his *tractatorie*, or according to *Erasmus* Editiõ, *tractorie*, he had named him before some Bishops, in promotion more ancient then himselfe. The eigth proofe is, that *Victor* Bishop of *Abdera*, who assisted at the Councell holdẽ vnder *Genetlius*, that we call the secõd Councell of *Carthage* was dead before the tyme of the Emperor *Valentinian* the third, & consequentlie that the Emperor mentioned in the Date of the same coũcell, could be noe other then *Valentinian* the second; for from the tyme of the seauenth Coũcell of *Carthage* which was holden six yeares before the Empire of *Valentiniã* the third, it was noe more *Victor*, but *Candidus* that was Bishop of *Abdera*. The ninth proofe is, that *Victor* Bishop of *Pupputa*, & *Epigonius* Bishop of *Bulla regalis*, who were present in the second and third councell of *Carthage*, were deceased long before the Empire of *Valentinian* the third, which began the yeare foure hundred twentie fiue. For in the cõference of *Carthage*, which was holdẽ the yeare foure hũdred and eleauen is was noe more *Victor*, but *Pãnonius* that was Bishop of *Pupputa*; nor *Epigonius* but *Dominick*, that was Bishop of *Bulla regalis*. The tenth proofe is, that in the second Councell of *Carthage*, there is mention made of the Coũcell celebrated the yeares before in the pretory, which could not agree with the tyme of *Aurelius*, vnder whose *Pontificate* all the Councells of *Africa* were celebrated, within the diuisions of the *Basilickes*. The 11th. proofe is, that in the same 2d. councell of *Carthage*

Fulg. Ferrand. in Breuiar. Can. artic. 24.

Cõc. Afric. in Conc. hab. 6. Cal. September sub. Coss. Cæsar. & Attic.

Cõc. Carth 3. c. 44. Cõc. Carth sub. Cypr. art. 16 Vict. Vtic. de persecut. Vand. l. 2. Ptolem. Greg. l. 4. Aug. de Vict. ep. 217. Cõc. Carth 7. in catalog. & in subscrip. Et Cõc. Afric. ante c. 95 & post. c. 100. Cõc. Carth 2. in process' verbal. & Conc. Afric. in process. verbal. Concil. sub Cesar. & Attic. Concil. Carth. 2. c. 7. & Conc. Carth. 3. c. 42. 44. & 50. Coll. Carth Act. 1. Cõc. Carth 2. c. 1.

Cõc Carth 2.c.2.

Cõc.Carth 5.c.3.

Cõc.Zellenſ male inſcript. Telenſ.in procem. Fulg. Ferrand.iu Breu. Can. art.4.6. & alibi.

Conc. Tolet.12.c. 4.

Ibidem.

it is ſaid,that the decree of clergy continence had bene made; that is to ſaie,reduced into a written lawe in the former councell:which could not agree with the tyme of the Emperor *Valentinian* the third,ſince more thẽ twelue yeare before he came to the Empire, the fifth Councell of *Carthage*,had cited the decrees of the clergies continence, as made in former councells, but in the tyme of the Emperor *Valentinian* the ſecond vnder whom the letter of *Siricius* to the *African* Bishops concerning the clergies continence, was carried into *Africa*. For whereas the councell of *Zelles* holden onelie ſeauen yeares before the Empire of *Valentinian* the third cauſed to be read and inſerted into the acts thereof,two letters of Pope *Siricius*,that was not particularly for the Statute of clergie continence, which had bene publiſhed long before in *Africa*; but for the other articles which were therein contained. And the twelfth proofe finallie is,that the twelfth councell of *Toledo* a generall councell for all *Spaine*,a prouince neere to *Africa*, holden vnder the King *Flauius Eruigius*, and in the age of the Emperor *Conſtantine Pogonat*, and of the third generall councell of *Conſtantinople*;that is to ſaie, neere a thouſand yeares agone,citeth the councell of *Carthage* holden vnder *Genetlius*, which we call the ſecond councell of *Carthage*,with the title of the ſecond coũcell of *Africa*,in theſe wordes, *In the ſecond councell of Africa the fifth canon, Felix the Bishop of Selempſela ſaid; I inſinuate alſo,if you pleaſe to your holynes, that the dioceſes that neuer had Bishops,may haue none.* And a little after; *Genetlius* Bishop ſaith; *If the motion made by our brother and fellow Bishop* Felix, *pleaſe you, let it be confirmed by vs all*; and cites the councell celebrated vnder the cnſulship of *Ceſarius* and *Atticus*, that we call the third councell of *Carthage*, with the title of the third Councell of *Africa* in theſe wordes; *In the third councell of Africa, the two and fortith Canon, Epigonius Bishop pronounced this amongſt other things; I conceaue that a people that hath alwaies bene vnder the ſubiection of a Bishop, and neuer had a proper Bishop, ought not to be admitted to haue a Bishop.* All which is ſaid neuertheles with ſo much reſpect,as the world ſhall knowe, that we admire the great cardinall *Baronius*, euen when we reproue him; and we doe acknowledge that his dreames are more learned, then the cleereſt ſight of others.

The ſecond queſtion concerning the councells of *Africa* in chiefe, is about the number of the Canons of the third Councell of *Carthage* and conſiſts in this; whether the third Councell of *Carthage* hath publiſht all the fiftie Canons that are in the ordinary editions;and amongſt the reſt, the canon of the Canonicall booke,which is the fortie ſeauenth; or whether it hath publiſht but twentie one. The new promulgators of the canõs of the *African* church will haue it,that it publiſht but 21. amongſt which that of the canonicall bookes, which they pretend to haue bene framed by the ſixth coũcell of *Carthage*, is not comprehended. And we contrarywiſe maintain that the third councell of *Carthage* hath publiſht all the fiftie canons contayned in the ordinarie edition; & amongſt the reſt, that of the canonicall Bookes. Their pretẽces are grounded vpõ two reaſons; the one, that there are but twentie one Canons, or few more of the third coũcell of *Carthage* inſerted into the *African* Rapſody, amõgſt the which, the canon of the canonicall bookes is none; and the other that in the continuance of this canõ, it is ſaid that they muſt cõmunicate with Pope *Boniface* and with other Bishops beyond Sea; which *Boniface* was of the tyme not of the third Councell of *Carthage*, but of the ſixth. To the firſt then of their reaſõs we anſwere that whereas they ſaie there are but twẽtie three canons of the third councell of *Carthage* in the rapſody of the coũcells of *Africa*, it is becauſe the rapſodiſt, as it hath aboue appeared, hath inſerted there but the Canons of the third Councell of *Carthage*, which had added some amplification or modification to the canons of the councell of *Hippo*, and hath not sett in those that had first bene instituted in the Councell of *Hippo*, and had bene but repeated in the third of *Carthage*, amongst which was that of the canonicall bookes, as it appeares by the thirtith canō of the councell of *Hippo*, whose quotation remaines to vs in these wordes; *What are the canonicall Scriptures which ought to be read in Churches, and besides which, noe others ought to be read*. To the second reason which is taken out of the Illustrious Cardinall *Baronius*, who saith, that the fiftie canons contained in the copies of the coūcell of *Carthage*, cannot be all of this councell, and particulaaly the canon of the number of the canonicall Bookes; for as much as in the end of the same canon, there is mentiō made of Pope *Boniface*, who was long tyme after; wee answere two things; the one that it is not in the originall canon of the copies of the third councell of *Carthage*, wherein this mention is found of Pope *Boniface*; but in the repetition that is made of the same canon, in the collection of the thirtie three Canōs, attributed to the sixth Coūcell of *Carthage*, holden vnder Pope *Boniface*; frō whence certaine ignorant exemplifiers haue takē it awaie, & made it retrograde in forme of a diuers reading in the margent of some of the copies of the third Coūcell of *Carthage*; & the other, that if this continuāce were of the originall text of the canon, it must haue bene read *Syricius* & not *Bonifacius*; as it appeares both by the canon following, where the Fathers speaking of an other matter, saie, *It hath bene concluded that we should consult with our bretheren and colleagues Cyricius and Simplicianus*: And because that Pope *Innocent* the first, a little after *Cyricius*, who dyed six moneths after the third coūcell of *Carthage*, had alreadie made a catalogue of the canonicall bookes, cōformable to that of the third Councell of *Carthage*, more then fifteen yeare before *Boniface*, and the sixth Councell of *Carthage*; which the fathers of the sixth Councell of *Carthage*, whereat the Popes legates assisted, could not be ignorant of. By meanes whereof, there was noe more neede to demaund the Popes confirmation in this regard; in the tyme of the sixth Councell of *Carthage*: But it is not sufficient to solue the reasons of the contrarie opinion, but we must propound our owne. The conterbattery then, that wee make to conuince that the third Councell of *Carthage* hath publisht the fiftie Canons that are in the ordinarie editions; and amongst others, that of the catalogue of the canonicall bookes is grounded vpon fower reasons; the first reason is, that the twelfth Coūcell of *Toledo*, which was holdē neere a thousand yeare agoe, citeth the 42th. canō of the third Coūcell of *Carthage* in these words; *In the 42th. canon of the third councell of Africa, it is said; that a people that hath bene alwaies subiect to a diocese, shall receaue noe other Bishop for Bishop*. Which are the proper words of the two & fortith Canon of the third Councell of *Carthage*, which we haue in our haudes. The second that in the repetition of twentie three of the canons of the Councell of *Carthage*, holden vnder *Cesarius* & *Atticus* the sixth of the calends of *September*; that is to saie, of the third Councell of *Carthage*, which is made in the *African* Rapsody, there is a canon repeated which saith, *That it shalbe also lawfull to reade the passions of the Martyrs*; which canon being bound by the aduerbe (*alsoe*) to some Canon from whence it hath bene seperated, can haue noe relation, but to the Canon, that forbidds anie other scriptures, but the Canonicall Scripture to be read in Churches; and consequently supposeth, that the Canon of the canonicall Scriptures, had bene publisht in the Councell holden vnder the consulship of *Atticus* and *Cesarius*, which is the third Councell of *Carthage*; but that it hath bene

Cōc. Hippon. c. 30.

Cōc. Carth 3. c. 48.

Innoc. 1. ep ad Exup.

Cōc. Tolet 12. c. 4.

Cōc. Afric. c. 13.

omitted in the Rapsody, because it reportes none but those Canons that haue added some amplification or diminution to the Canons of the Councell of *Hippo*, which the Illustrious Cardinall *Baronius* could not see, for the impediment that was giuen him by the vitious collocation that the Exemplifiers of the latin Rapsody haue made of the preface of the Councell holden after the Consulship of *Stelicon*, which they haue interposed betweene the exordium of the Councell, holden vnder *Atticus* and *Cesarius*, and the first Canon of the same Councell: a thing which gaue him occasion to thinke, that all the thirtie two canons following were of the Councell celebrated after *Stilicons* consulship; whereas the twentie three first, were of the Councell celebrated vnder *Cesarius* and *Atticus*, as we will proue heereafter, by the order of the dates, and by conferring of the *Greeke* edition, and as it is confirmed also, by the fowrteenth of the same Canons, which makes mention of *Syricius* and of *Simplicianus*, which were not Bishops together but vnder the consulship of *Cesarius* and *Atticus*. The third reason is; that *Fulgentius Ferandus* citeth these two Canons; to witt, that of the reading of the canonicall bookes; and that of the reading of the passion of Martyrs, as two consequent canons; and the one vnder the title of the fortie fifth, and the other of the fortie sixth Canon of the Councell of *Carthage* in these wordes; *That there should be nothing read in the Church but the canonicall scriptures; the Councell of Laodicea Canon fiftie sixth and the Councell of Carthage Canon fortie fifth. That it shall be also lawfull to reade the Martirs Passions on the daies of their Martyrdome; the Councell of Carthage Canon fortie sixth.* Which cannot be meant, but of the third Councell of *Carthage*, as well because the collection intituled the sixth Councell of *Carthage*, contayneth but thirtie three Canons; as because the last of these two Canons is not found in the collection intituled the sixth Councell of *Carthage*; and that there is but onely in the third councell of *Carthage* where they are couched one next after the other. And the fowrth finallie, because saint AVSTIN teacheth vs, that the first amongst the councells of *Carthage*, wherein the rolle of the canonicall bookes was published, was the third Councell of *Carthage*, and not the sixth, for he writes in the Epistle to *Quintianus*; That in the same Councell, where the rolle of the canonicall bookes was entered, it was also ordained that a Bishop should not vsurpe the clerke of an other Bishop; *I am amazed* (said he) *that thou dost admonish me to commaund that those that come from your quarters into our Monasteries, should not bee receiued; that, that which hath bene decreed in the councell by vs, may be obserued; and that thou remembrest not, that in the same councell it was determined, what the canonicall Scriptures are, which ought to be read to the people. Then reuiew this councell, and bring to thy memorie all things that thou shalt reade there, and thou shalt perceaue it was so decided onely of the clergie, and not of the laitie, that coming from other dioceses, they should not be receiued into our Monasteries, not that there is a word of a Monastery, but because it hath bene decreed, that none should receiue the clerke of an other.* Now the canon that prohibits Bishops to receiue the clerkes of other Bishops, is in the third Councell of *Carthage*, but not in the sixth. Moreouer he adds, that in a later Councell it had bene ordained, that those that departed from a monastery should not be admitted to be clerkes or superintendents of an other monasterie. *In the Coũcell,* (said he) *where it was determined, what were the canonicall scriptures, there was noe mention made of a Monastery; onely it was ordained, that none should receiue the Clerke of an other; but in a later Councell it hath bene decreed, that those that haue retired themselues, or haue bene expelled out of any monastery, should not be made clerkes in anie other place or superintend*

[Margin notes: Annal. tom 5. ad ann. 401. — Beneath in the Chapt. of the African Councell. — Fulg. Ferrand in Breu. Can. art. 228. & 229. — Aug. ep. 235. — Conci. Carthag. c. 21. — Aug. ibidem.]

anie monasteries: which shewes againe that the Councell of *Carthage* where the catalogue of the canonicall Bookes was published whereof saint AVSTINE speakes, was the third Councell, and not the sixth: for the canon that forbidds to receiue a Religious man that retires from a monastery, and to make him clerke or superintendent of an other monastery, was instituted in the fifth Councell of *Carthage*, which preceded the sixth neere eighteen yeares.

The third controuersie is concerning the fowrth Councell of *Carthage*, holden vnder the consulship of *Honorius*, and of *Eutychianus*; that is to saie, the next yeare after the consulship of *Cesarius* and *Atticus*; the which not the Illustrious cardinall *Baronius*, but the new publishers of the greeke edition of the Councells of *Africa* race from the number of the ancient Councells; moued thereto, because it is not inserted into that Rapsodie of the Councells of *Africa*, that we call the *African* Councell. Now this coniecture is soe weake, that it is not worth the confutation. For besides that the collection that we call the *African* Councell, is farr from comprehending, either in generall, all the Councells of *Africa* witnes the Councell of *Suffetula*, the Councell of *Septimunica*, the Coūcell of *Marazan*, the Councell of *Tusdra*, the Councell of *Macri*, the Councell of *Zelles*. the councell of *Tunis*, the coūcell of *Iuca* or rather *Tuca* cited by *Fulgentius Ferandus*, which are not spoken of in the bodie of the *African* rapsody; or in particular all the councells of *Carthage*, and principallie, if we belieue the edition of the same *Ferandus* who alleadgeth the fifth canon of the fiftie fift Councell of *Carthage*. There are two euident reasons wherefore the fowrth councell of *Carthage* ought not to be inserted into the collection of the councells of *Africa*, that we call the *African* coūcells; the one, that he, that collected them, had restrained himselfe of deliberate purpose as it appeares by the diuision of the nintie ninth canon of his rapsodie which is the last of the seauenth Councell of *Carthage*; which to finde the rekoning iust he diuides in two, to make but one century of *African* canons, within which the fowrth Councell of *Carthage* which onely contayned a hundred and foure canons, could not enter; and the other, that the fowrth councell of *Carthage*, hauing prescribed the lawes, vnder which all the ecclesiasticall persōs of *Africa* ought to be promoted to the order of Priestood; there was noe neede to inserte it into the bodie of this Rapsodie, to keepe them frō wandring frō the matter; for as much as all ecclesiasticall persons, and particularly Bishops were obliged to keepe it in their hands. To those two reasons I will yet annex two others, which conuince that it is truly ancient, and due to the age whereto wee attribute it; the one is that the things there decided, agree wholie to the Estate of *Africa* in S. AVG. tymes, as the profession which this councell obligeth Bishops to make, coming to the Bishops Sea, *That one selfe same God, is the author of the old and new testamēt, and that the diuell is become ill by the libertie of his will*: to exclude the *Maniches*: as the beleefe that is exacted from them, *that out of the Catholicke Church one is saued* to exclude the *Donatists*; as the prohibition that he made, *to driue the Gentills, or the Jewes, or the hereticks out of the Church before the masse* (that is to saie, the dimission) of the catechumens; which shewes that this councell was holden while paganisme lasted. Yet amongst the prouinces of the Christians, or as the canons that he instituted, *that the Clerkes should not nourishe, either their haire of their head, or their beard and might gett their meate drinke and cloath, by a trade, or by hushandrie, without derogating from their office*, which were composed, to impugne certaine Religious persons slothfull and long heared, that saint AVSTIN

Cōc. Carth 5. c. 13.

Fulg. Ferr. in Breu. Can. art. 2. Id. art. 11. Id art. 44. Id. art. 23. Id art. 76. Id. art. 65. Id. art. 61. Id. art. 26. Fulg. Feraud. in Breu. Can. artic. 13.

Cōc. Carth 4. c. 1.

Ibidem. c. 84.

Ibid. cap. 44. Ibid. cap. 52.

Aug de oper. Monach.

combats in the worke of the trauaile of Religious persons, who held it for an oprobry, that Religious men should labour with their handes or shaue their heades. The other reason is, that the decrees of this councell are acknowledged, and cited not onely by all the canonists that haue written since six hundred yeares, as *Burchard, Iuon*, and *Gratian*, but also by *Isidorus* Bishop of *Hispalis*, now called *Seuill*, a cittie neighbouring vpon *Africa*, who liued a thousaud yeares agone; who reported the canon of the ordination of Exorcists, in these wordes. *When the Exorcists are ordained, they take* (as saith the canon) *from the Bishops hand, the little Booke where the exorcismes are written, receiuing the power to impose hands vpon the Energumenes, whether they be baptized or Catechumens.* Which are the very words of the seauenth Canon of the fowrth Councell of *Carthage*: And by *Hincmarus*, ancient Archbishop of *Rheims*, who cites the Canon where it is forbidden to the Bishop to iudge the cause of anie without his clergie, in these termes: *Let the Bishop heare noe mans cause, without the presence of his Clergie*; which are the very wordes of the twentie third canon of the fowrth Councell of *Carthage*.

Isidor. de offic. Eccl. l. 2. cap de Exorcist.

Hincmar. opusc. 55.

The fowrth difference is, vpon the order of the fifth Councell of *Carthage*, that the Illustrious cardinall *Baronius*, pretends to haue bene transferred from the degree; and that it ought to be placed againe in the third place; that is to saie betweene the Councell of *Carthage*, holden vnder the consulship of *Cesarius* and *Atticus*, that he places in the second ranke, and the fowrth. The reasons of the Illustrious Cardinall *Baronius* are, the one that the date of this Councell which is not filled vp in the printed editions, but onelie beares, *The sixth of the calends of Iune after the Consulship*, without specifying the consulls names, is found in some manuscripts filled vp with these wordes *Cesarius and Atticus*: by which meanes this councell must haue bene holden the next yeare after the celebration of the Councell, that we call the third of *Carthage*, and he, the second which was holden vnder the consulship of *Cesarius* and *Atticus*; and the other, that there is a canon in the fifth Councell of *Carthage*, which ordaines that the Emperor may be besought to roote out the relickes of Idolatry. From whence it followes, that this Councell hath preceded the commaundement that the Emperors gaue to abolish the remainder of Idolatrie. Now this Commaundement was giuen vnder the consulship of *Theodosius*, the yeare of our Lord, according to our computation three hundred nintie nine by two edicts, the one addressed to *Apollodorus* vicar of *Africa*, where the Emperors commaund that the pagans Idolls, should be taken out of their temples and their sacrifices abolisht. And the other addressed to *Eutychianus*, prouost of the Easterne Pretory; where they commaunded, that the temples of the pagans that were in the fieldes, should be demolished without trouble or tumult; And consequently saith he, the Councell had bene holden the yeare before, which was the yeare after the Consulship of *Cesarius* & *Atticus*. To the first then of these reasons, we answere that the manuscript which saith, after the Consulship of *Cesarius* and *Atticus*, is not confirmed by the vniuersall consent of the other manuscriptes; for there are collections in manuscripts of *Mercator*, as the new publishers of the Councells of *Africa* haue noted; which saie, after the Consulship of *Flauius Stelicon*. And to the secōd we saie, that the Canō that ordaines the request for the abolishmēt of the remainders of Idolatrie hath nothing in it common with the Edicts of the Emperors of the yeare three hūdred nintie nine. Forasmuch as the Emperors had onely ordained by one of the Edicts; that the Sacrifices should be taken

Côc. Carth 5. c. 15.

Cod. Theod. l. 16. Titul. De pag. l. 16. Ibid. l. 18.

out of the Temples; and the Idolls deposited into the handes of the Ministers of the Empire, but that the buildings should still be kept intire; and by the other, that the Temples of the pagans which were in the fieldes, should be demolished. And the fifth Councell of *Carthage* demaundes, that the remainder of Idolatrie, should be abolished, not onely in the Idolls, but also in the woods and in the trees. For the pagans adored not onely the similitudes of the false Gods, but also adored certaine shady thicketts, and certaine ancient Trees, that they belieued to be the dwellinges and mansions of the presence of their Gods. From whence it is, that *Quintilian* speaking of *Ennius*, said, *Wee adore Ennius, as we doe thicketts that are become sacred through age.* These trees then, and these groues polluted by the worship that the *Pagans* yielded to thē, the canon demaunded to be rooted out, as well as the Idolls and similitudes. From whence may be drawne, that it is soe farr from following thence, that this canon was before the Emperors Edictes; as contrarywise it appeares hereby, that it was after them. For as for the decree, where was required the distruction of the temples built in fieldes, which gaue noe ornament to citties; which seemes to haue preceded the Edict of the Emperors, addressed to the prouost of the *East*, it is not in the fifth Councell of *Carthage* in cheefe, but in the onely Rapsody of the councell of *Africa*, which hath transferred this canon and manie others, from the Councell holden after the consulship of *Honorius* and *Eutychianus*, where the first legation to the Emperors was decreed, to the Councell holden after the consulship of *Stelicon*, where the second was decreed. By meanes whereof the obseruation of the Illustrious Cardinall *Baronius* is good to ouerthrow the order of the *African* Rapsody, and to shew that it was made by some grosse and ignorant Rapsodist; and not to remoue the chronologie of the fifth Councell of *Carthage*. But we haue said enough of these reasons; it is tyme to propound ours. The motiue then that incites vs to belieue, that the Councell that we call the fifth of *Carthage*, hath bene holden in the tyme wherein we place it; that is to saie, betweene the fowrth Councell of *Carthage* and the sixth consists besides the common consent of copies, and the vniuersall voice of *Canonists* in two reasons; the one is, that S. AVGVSTIN in his Epistle to *Quintianus*, after he hath spoken of the Councell, where there were ioyntly publisht the Canon of the canonicall Bookes; and that of the prohibition to Bishops, to vsurpe one an others Clerkes, which was the third Councell of *Carthage*, saith, *And after in a fresh Councell it hath bene ordained, that those who retire from a monastery, or are driuen from it, shall not be receiued elsewhere to be clerkes, or to be superintendents in an other Monastery*; which are the wordes of the thirteenth Canō, of the fifth Councell of *Carthage*: from whence it is gathered, that the fifth Councell of *Carthage* that saint AVGVSTIN calls freshe, in regard of the third Councell of *Carthage*, was not holden the next yeare after the third councell of *Carthage*, but a longe while after: and by consequent, ought to keepe the ranke of the fifth and not of the fowrth Councell of *Carthage*. The other reason is, that in the Epistle two hundred thirtie sixth written to *Xantippus* Primat of *Numidia*, the same saint AVGVSTIN cites the canon, by which those that had neglected to followe their cause a whole yeare together, were excluded from goeing forward with it, which is the twelfth canon of the fifth Councell of *Carthage*, as a canon newlie instituted. From whence it appeares, that the fifth Councell of *Carthage* was holden after that, that we call the fowrth. For saint AVGVSTINE testifies, that the yeare in which he writt this Epistle, the

Cōc. Carth 5. c. 15.

Instit. Orat l. 10.

Concil. Afric. c. 25.

Concil. Afric. in Præfat. Cōcil. Celebr. post. Consul. Honor. & Eutych. Concil. Afric. c. 35

August. ad Quintian. Ep. 235

Pasch should be the eigth of the Ides of Aprill. *I haue* (said he,) *heard the cause of Abundantius, there being yet a hundred daies to Pasch Sundaie, which shall be this yeare the eigth of the Ides of Aprill. This I haue had care to insinuate to your Reuerence, because of the Councell, and I haue not concealed it from himselfe, but haue faithfullie aduertised him, of what was there instituted, that if within a yeare, in case hee thinkes he should be prouided of a iudgement, he neglect to pursue his cause, none may after giue him audience.* Now *Pasch* neuer fell out vpon the eigth of the Ides of Aprill while *Xanthippus* was Primat of *Numidia*, but the yeare of our saluation four hundred and two, which was the yeare of the fifth consulship of *Archadius* and *Honorius*, and consequently the fifth Councell of *Carthage*, that had bene holden the yeare before, fell out in the yeare foure hundred and one, that is to saie in the yeare after the consulship of *Stelicon*; which was two yeare after the yeares of the consulship of *Honorius* and *Eutychianus*, in which the fowrth councell of *Carthage* had bene celebrated.

August. ad Xanthip. ep. 236.

Pro. & legendum vt.

The fifth question is concerning the second *Mileuitan* Councell, holden vnder the Consulship of *Honorius* and *Constantius*, that the new publishers of the Councell of *Africa* pretend to haue made noe canons, moued by three coniectures; the first, because in the Rapsody of the *African* canons, there is noe mentiõ made of this Councell. The second because the canons that are thereto attributed, are in part taken from the first *Mileuitan* Councell; and in part from the Councell holden vnder the twelfth consulship of *Honorius*. And the third, that amongst the Canons that are thereto assigned, there are some, that cannot agree, either with the place or tyme wherein it was celebrated. To these three coniectures, we haue also three answeres. The first answere is, that the Councell celebrated vnder the twelfth Cõsulship of *Theodosius* against *Pelagius* & *Celestius*, was rather a repetition and confirmation of the *Mileuitan* councell, which had bene holden the yeare before against the same heretickes, then a new Councell. By meanes whereof, it must not be held strange, if the *African* Rapsody whereinto the Coũcell celebrated vnder the twelfth consulship of *Hou orius* is inserted, hath not reported the Canons of the second *Mileuitan* Councell; and principally the second *Mileuitan* Councell, hauing bene but a prouinciall Councell of the Bishops of *Numidia*, which had not the force of a nationall Councell of *Africa*, but by the concurrencie of the Councell of the Proconsulary Prouince, celebrated the same yeare at *Carthage*; and by the emologation that was made thereof the yeare following in the generall Councell of all *Africa* assembled at *Carthage* For the Bishop *Aurelius*, who is mentioned in the inscription of the *Mileuitan* Councell, reported by saint AVGVSTIN, is not *Aurelius* Bishop of *Carthage*, but *Aurelius* one of the Bishops of *Numidia*, whereof mention is made in the Councell holden vnder *Cesarius* and *Atticus*, otherwise he could not haue bene put in the third place, and named after *Siluanus* and *Valentinus*. For *Aurelius* Bishop of *Carthage* presided in all the Episcopall assemblies of *Africa* as well at *Carthage*, as out of *Carthage*, as it appeares both by the commaundement read in the conference of *Carthage*, which saith, *Aurelius* Bishop of *Carthage* presiding, and *Siluanus* Primat of *Numidia*; and by the first *Mileuitan* Councell, where *Aurelius* Bishop of *Carthage* presided, and preceded *Xanthippus* Primate of *Numidia*, Predecessor to *Siluanus*, and *Nicetius* Primat of *Mauritania Sitifensis*, and *Valentine*, and all the other Bishops. The second answere is, that the writers finding in the *African* Rapsody the Canons and the preface of the fist *Mileuitan* Councell, and belieuing there was noe other *Mileuitan* Councell, but that, that was holden against *Pelagius* and not being

Concil. Afric. in Præf. Cõcil hab. 5. Calend. sept. sub. Coss. Cesar. & Attic.

Collat. Carthag. Act. 1.

Cõc. Afric. in Præf. c. 53.

enough conuersant in historie to discerne them by the distance of dates, haue mingled a part of the preface, and of the decrees of the one, with the text of the other. And the third, that the same Bookebinders, finding the greater part of the canons of the *Mileuitan* Councell in the Councell holden vnder the twelfth consulship of *Honorius*; and vpon this occasion conceiuing that the Coũcell holden vnder the twelfth Cõnsulship of *Honorius* was but a repetition of the *Mileuitan*, haue added to the *Mileuitan* what they haue found more in the Coũcell holden vnder the twelfth consulship of *Honorius*, and haue yet added thereto, some other canons taken out of other Councells. But that for this cause it followes, that the second *Mileuitan* Councell hath made noe canons, wee denie, and denie it with the authority of the second Councell of *Tours*, celebrated a thousand and fifteene yeares agone, which cites the canons of the second *Mileuitan* Councells, in these words; *It hath bene ordained in the ancient Mileuitan Canons, that euerie Bishop that in case of necessitie etc. vailes a virgin before the age of twentie fiue yeare, shall not be holden culpable of breaking the Councell, were this number is prescribed.* Which are the very words of the twentie sixth canon of the *Mileuitan* Councell, that we haue in our handes at this daie. Conc.Turon.2.cap. 21.

The sixth controuersie is, concerning the durãce of the sixth Councell, of *Carthage*, which not onely the Protestants, but the Illustrious Cardinall *Baronius* himselfe, and the doctors of *Collen* which haue followed him in the last impression of the Councell, will haue, to haue continued fiue yeares; to witt, to the tyme of the Epistle of the Bishops of *Africa* to Pope *Celestine*, which was written vnder the consulship of *Victor* and of *Castinus*. And we contrarywise maintanie, that it ended the same yeare wherein it began; to witt, the yeare after the twelfth Consulship of *Honorius*; that is to saie, the yeare of the Consulship of *Monaxius* and *Plinta*; and that all the assemblies which were made aftervpon the subiect of appeales, were as many distinct & seperated Councells; and for proofe of our intention, wee will imploy two reasons: the one, that the Bishops of the sixth councell of *Carthage* protested that they would answere nothing concerning the appeales till the copies of the exemplifications of the councell of *Nicea*, kept at *Constantinople*, and in *Alexandria*, had bene brought out of the East; and that when they should come, they whould assemble a councell to aduise vpon it. From whence, it appeares that the sixth councell of *Carthage* was finished the same yeare wherein it began, and lasted but till the copies came out of the East, which arriued in the month of *Nouember* of the consulship of *Monaxius* and *Plinta*; and the other, that when there was question of the last processe of *Apiarius*, and of the second voyage of *Faustinus* into *Africa*; the Bishops of *Africa* writt to Pope *Celestine*, that they had assembled a councell, expressly vpon the occurrence of this Businesse; from it may be gathered, that the sixth councell of *Carthage* had not continued till then: *Our holy brother & fellowe Bishop Faustinus*, saidthey, *coming to vs, wee haue assẽbled a councell.* Whereto there may yet be added, that betweene the first appeale of *Apiarius*, when he was pursued by the inhabitants of *Sicca*, which was determined in the sixth councell of *Carthage* in the presence of *Flauianus*; and the second appeale of the same *Apiarius*, when he was pusued by the inhabitants of *Thabraca*, which was determined in the Councell holden after the returne of *Faustinus* into *Africa*; there did againe interuene an other Councell, by which he had bene depriued a second time, of the Communion of all the Bishops of *Africa*. And it is not to bee replied, that the sixth Councell of *Carthage* chose twentie two deputiesto finish

Edit. Concil. Colon. 1606. pag. 619. & 621.

Conc Carthag 6.c. 10.

Epist. Cõcil. Afric. ad Cælest.

Præf. Concil Carth. 7

what

what had not bene determined in the generall assemblie of the Councell, for it was an ordinarie thing for the generall Councells of *Africa*, when they had bene some daies together, to auoide the wearysomnes, and the expences of so great a multitude of Bishops, to choose three or fower deputies from euerie prouince, who should prepare and put into forme the actes of the Councell: as in the Councell holden the yeare before vnder the twelfth Consulship of *Honorius* after the constitution of the decrees, there was chosen three deputies of euery prouince, to determine the other businesse of the Councell, and to reduce into forme, the actes of what had bene there resolued. And neuerthelesse, soe farr is it from appearing from thence, that this Councell lasted to the yeare following, as contrarywise the yeare followinge, which was the yeare after the twelfth consulship of *Honorius*, there was assembled a newe Councell, the eigth of the calends of *June*, which was that that we call the sixth of *Carthage*.

Coccil. Afric. c. 94.

Cõc. Carth 6. in Præfat & cap. 1.

The seauenth skirmish is about the collection intituled, the sixth Councell of *Carthage* which is a gathering of thirtie three of the principall canons of the former Councells of *Carthage*, which manie thinke to haue bene made in the sixth Coũcell of *Carthage* and we cõntrarywise pretend it to be compiled by some impertinent Rapsodist, whether an *African* during the last and most barbarous tyme of the dominion of the *Vandalls* in *Africa*; or an *Europian*, while the heresie and tyrannie of the *Vandalls*, hindred the catholickes on this side the Sea, from beinge able to haue exact communication and knowledge of the ecclesiasticall things of *Africa*. And we are grounded in this beliefe by infinite reasons: The first reason is that *Fulgentius Ferandus* an *African* deacon, and very conuersant in the *African* antiquitie, who writ a little before the expulsion of the *Vandalls* out of *Africa*, not onely makes noe mention of this collecton that they intitle the sixth councell of *Carthage* but also citinge some of the canons that are there, alleadgeth them vnder the title of canons of the former Councells of *Carthage*. As when he citeth the canon of the canonicall Bookes, he cites it from the Councell of *Carthage* where there was added the permission to reade the Passions of the martyrs, which is the third Councell of *Carthage*; and doth not note that this canon hath bene published in anie other Councell of *Carthage*: when he registers the prohibition of ordayninge Bishops without the consent of their Primate; he alleadgeth it with these quotations, *The Councell of* Carthage, *vnder the Prelate Genetlius, title tenth, the Generall* Councell *of* Carthage, *title fortie fowerth: And the* Councell *of Zelles in the recitall of the Popes Epistle*: and maketh noe mention amongst the places where this canon of the Councell is, that we call the sixth Councell of *Carthage*, which was holden the yeare after that of *Zelles*. When he inrolls the canon of the celibate of Bishops, Priests and deacons, he inserts it with this quotation, *The* Councell *of* Carthage *title the first, and* Councell *of Zelles*; And of the Coũcell of *Carthage*, holden after that of *Zelles*; which is that which we call the sixth, he speakes not one word. And it is not to be obiected, that these fragments are found in the collection of *Dionisius Exiguus*. For besides that the collection of *Dionisius Exiguus*, was compiled not by a naturall *African*, as was *Fulgentius Ferandus*, but by a *Scythian*, it was made after the Register of *Ferandus*, as it appeares both by the canons of the Apostles which are there inserted, which in Pope *Gelasius* his tyme, and in *Fulgentius Ferandus* his tyme who were both *Africans*, were neither receiued in the church of *Rome* nor in the *African* church; and for this cause are not mentioned in the Register of *Ferandus*: and by the diuision

Fulg. Ferand in Breu. Can art. 4.

Ibid. art. 16

of the laſt canon of the ſeauenth councell of *carthage*, which the collection of *Dioniſius*, and the Greeke edition that followes it, doe diuide inpertinently into two canons: whereas *Fulgentius Ferandus*, and the originall text of the ſeauenth Councell of *Carthage*, doe place them vnder one onely title. And to this there is noe oppoſition, in this, that *Victor* Bishop of *Tununes*, or according to others *Tunnes*, extendes the life of *Fulgentius Ferandus*, if the quotations be not tranſpoſed, to the one & twẽtith yeare of the Empire of *Juſtinian*. For it is certaine that *Fulgentius Ferandus* writt from the tyme of the Emperor *Anaſtaſius*, and of *Fulgentius* Bishop of *Ruſpa*, to whom he dedicated the Epiſtle of the fiue queſtions.

The ſecond reaſon is, that theſe fragments intituled the ſixth Councell of *Carthage*, are not in the collection of *Iſidorus Mercator*, and in the ordinary volumes of the Cõucells, where the Cõucells of *Africa* in chiefe, are reported, and all the other ancient Councells of the latine church, whereof wee make vſe. Contrarywiſe, that the ſixth Councell of *Carthage* which is there inſerted containes noe canons, and comprehends but the verball proceſſe of what paſſed betweene the Popes legates, and the Bishops of *Africa*, about the matter of appeales; which verball proceſſe is reduced onely to tenn Chapters; after which immediatly followes in the ordinarie copies, the ſeauenth Councell of *Carthage*. The third reaſon is, that the ſixth Councell of *Carthage* and the ſeauenth, were not two different Councells, but two actions of one and the ſame Councell, the one celebrated the eigth of the calends of *June* vnder the twelfth conſulship of *Honorius*; and the other celebrated three daies after; to witt, the fifth of the calends of *June*, vnder the ſame twelfth conſulship of *Honorius*; but that they are reckoned as two different Councells, for as much as the firſt was holden by all the two hundred & ſeauenteen Bishops that were come to the Councell: and the ſecond was holden by the twentie two deputies, that ſtaied to finish the affaires of the Councell, after the two hundred & ſeauenteen bishops had bene licenced to depart. For that the Illuſtrious Cardinall *Baronius*, and the Doctors of *Coloigne* write, that the two hundred and ſeauenteen Bishops aſſiſted not at the firſt action of the Councell, but by their deputations and ſignatures; and that there was none preſent at the firſt act but the twentie two deputies that were at the ſecond, moued with this, that the verball proceſſe of the firſt ſaith, *Aurelius and the ſeuerall legates of the African prouince then ſitting*, is contradicted both by the ancient cuſtome of the Councells of *Africa*, which teacheth vs, that there was great difference betweene the deputies that the prouinces elected to aſſiſt at the Councells, and the deputies that the councells elected to finish the reſt of their affaires: And by the ouerture of the firſt act, where *Aurelius* gaue thankes to God for the arriuall of ſo great a companie; and by the ouerture of the ſecond where it was ſaid, that the twentie two deputies had bene choſen, becauſe the other Bishops had complained that they could not ſtaie the end of the affaires of the Councell; by meanes whereof, if theſe thirtie three canons had bene made in the ſixth Councell of *Carthage* as the quotations of the tymes and perſons ſeeme to shew; that they haue not onely bene compiled there, but made there, and as the new publishers of the *African* councells maintaine, they muſt haue bene made either at the firſt acte, or betweene theſe two acts, and before the ſeperation of the entire companie of the Councell. For *Fauſtinus* the Popes legat who is repreſented pronouncing one of the thirtie three Canons, departed the morrow after the ſecond act, which containes but the fiue Canons, that bare the title

of

Collect. Dionys. in Conc. dict. Afric. c. 99 c. 100. Edit. Græc. Cõc. Carth. c. 133. Fulg. Ferand. in Breu. Can art. 73. Concil. Carth. 7. c. 5. Iſidor. de Scriptor. Eccl. c. 14. Annal. tom 5. ann. 419. num. 59. Impreſſ. nou. Concil. Colon. tom. 1. pag. 626. Concil. Carth. celebrat. v. Calend. Sept. Ceſar & Attic. Coſs. relat. in Conc. Afric. Cõc. Carth. Theodos. & Rumorid. Coſs. relat. in Conc. Africk poſt. cap. 57. Concil. Carth. Honor. 7. & Theodos. Coſs. relat. in Afric. poſt. c. 63. Cõc. Carth Honor. 12. & Theod. 8. Coſs. relat. in Afric c. 94. & Conc. 7. Carth. relat. in Afric poſt. c. 94. Cõc. Carth 6 c. 1. Edit. Græc Cõc. Afric. Paris. apud Abraham. Pacard. ann 1615. in Præf. p. 35. & 38. Concil. dict. Carth gg. 6. c. 4. Con. Afric c. 100.

of the seauenth Councell of *Carthage*; & consequently, it is necessarie that the edition of the thirtie three canons should haue bene made in the whole assemblie of the generall Councell of *Africa*, that is to saie, in the presence of all the two hundred seauenteen Bishops; and before the Rapsody of the hundred canons that we call the *African* Councell, into which the fiue canons of the second acte are inserted; and which also the collection of *Dionisius* and the Greeke translation place after the collection of the thirtie three canons intituled the sixth Councell of *Carthage*. Now this is against the expresse distinction that *Cresconius*, one of the principall maintainers of the collection of *Dionisius*, setts betweene the collection of the thirtie three canons attributed to the sixth Coūcell of *Carthage*, and the Rapsody of the hundred canons, that they call the *African* Councell. For cyting the order of the voyages of the Bishops beyond Seas, which in the collection of the thirtie three canons attributed to the sixth Councell of *Carthage* is the twentie third, and in the collection of the hundred canons that we call the *African* Councell, is the seauentie third, he cites the twentie third, & all the rest of the same collection vnder the simple title of the Councell of *Carthage*; and the seauentie third with the title of the generall Councell of *Carthage*. The fourth reason is, that yf euen the thirtie three canons attributed to the sixth Councell of *Carthage*, should not be pretended to haue bene made, but onely collected in the sixth Councell of *Carthage*, there is noe appearance that those two collections to witt, that of the thirtie three canons, that is intituled the sixth Councell of *Carthage*; and that of the hundred canons, that they call the *African* Councell, hauing bene both compiled in one Councell as the new publishers of the Coūcell of *Africa* maintaine, & as *Dionisius Exiguus* and those that haue follwed him suppose, that they would haue registred the same canōs in thē both. Contrarywise the diuision of the inscriptions would, that into the first should be inserted, the onely canons of the Councells celebrated before the promotion of *Aurelius*; and into the second the canons of, the Councells holden after the promotion of *Aurelius*. For the collection of *Dionisius*, and the greeke translation that followes it, putts this inscription in the front of the first collection, *After this, the thinges publisht in diuers African Councells, are acknowledged to haue bene inserted into the present actes:* a clause that shewes plainely, that it is a Rapsodyst, and not the clerke of a councell that speakes: And in the front of the second this; *There were recited also in this Synod, diuers Councells of the whole Prouince of Africa, celebrated in the tymes preceding Aurelius.* And neuerthelesses, not onely the first collection doth indifferently imbrace the Canons of the Councell holden both before and after the promotion of *Aurelius*; but also the most part of the Canons that are inserted into the first collection, are soe also into the second; as the Canon of the celibat of Bishops, Priests and deacons, which had bene made in the fifth Councell of *Carthage*, is reported in the collections of the thirtie three Canons, vnder the title of the twentie fift Canon, and in the collection of the hundred Canons, vnder the title of the thirtie seauenth Canon; of the prohibition of Priestes, deacons, and other inferior clerkes to appeale beyond Sea, which had bene made in the second *Mileuitan* Councell, and confirmed in the Councell holvnder the twelfth consulship of *Honorius*, is reported in the collection of the thirtie three canons, vnder the twentie eigth Canon; and in the collection of the hundred Canons vnder the title of the ninetith two canon; and so of manie others.

Crescon. in Breu. Canon art. 154 & alibi. Id. ibid.

Noua Editio Græca Codicis Canon Afric. impress. Paris apud Abraham Pacard. Anno 1615. in Præf. Pag. 35. & 38. Collect. Dionys. in Concil. Carthag. in inscrip. cap. 1. Edit Cræc Concil. Carth. ibid Collect. Dionys. in inscript. Concil. Afric. Edit. Græc Concil. Carth. post can. 33. Conc dict. Carthag. 6 c. 25. Conc. dict. Afric. c. 73 Conc. dict. Carthag. 6 c 28. Conc. dict. Afric. c. 92

The fifth reason is, that the preface of the collection of the thirtie three Canons is all taken from the discourse, that *Genetlius* made in the beginning of the second Councell of *Carthage*, which after some wordes, containes these, *because you are heere present vnder the auspices of Gods fauour, the ecclesiasticall faith that wee consigne ought to be before all things vniformely confessed in this glorious assemblie.* And then afterward, *the order of euerie point of ecclesiasticall discipline, ought to be establisht and fortified by the consent of all, to the end that the Spirits of our bretheren and fellow Bishop newly promoted, should be confirmed in the resolution of the things propounded, and that as we haue receiued from our Fathers by an assured trust, the Trinitie which we retaine consecrated in our breasts; that is to saie, the vnitie of the Father, the Sonne, and the holie Ghost, which is acknowledged to haue noe noueltie; in the same sort as wee haue learnt it, soe wee teache it to the people of God.* After which words, these immediatly followe, *It was said by all the Bishops; so certainely haue we receiued it, soe we hold it, following the faith Apostolicke.* From this former discourse then, the compilers of the collection intituled the sixth Councell of *Carthage*, haue stolen their prologue, except that in steede of these wordes; *Genetlius the Bishop said;* they haue sett downe to fitt their theft to the sixth Councell of *Carthage; All the Councell saith.* And in steede of this answere, *It was said by all the Bishops;* they haue sett; *it was said by all the Bishops newly promoted.* Behold their language; *All the Councell saith; vnder the auspices of Gods fauour, the ecclesiasticall Faith that we consigne ought to be before all things vniformely confessed in this glorious assembly, and then the order of euery point of Ecclesiasticall Discipline ought to be establisht by the consent of all, and to confirme the spirits of our bretheren and fellowe Bishops, newlie promoted; those things must be propounded which we haue receiued from our Fathers by an assured deposition, to the end that the vnitie of the trinitie that wee retaine consecrated in our sences* (so haue they corrected the word *finibus* which was in the second Councell of *Carthage*, not discerning that in the steede of *finibus*, must be read, *sinibus*, that is, breasts) *to witt of the Father, sonne, and holie Ghost; which is acknowledged to haue noe difference* (so haue they corrected the word *notitiam*, not seeing that in steede of *notitiam*, must be read, *nouitatem*, which is an allusion of cadence that *Genetlius* would make to the word, *vnitatem*) *In the same sort as we haue learnt it, soe we teache it to Gods people.* And immediatly after, *Item it was said, by all the Bishops newly promoted; Soe certainely haue we receiued it, soe we hold it, so we teache it, following the Euangelicall faith, with your doctrine.* Now this fragment cannot subsist neither in the place nor forme where it is coucht, For besides that the Fathers of the sixth Councell of *Carthage* had alreadie, yea from the ouerture of the Councell, and before all other things, caused the creede of the Councell of *Nicea* to be read, by meanes whereof this instance of propounding the faith of the Trinitie was to noe purpose; how could it be all the Councell that said, *to confirme the spirite of our Bretheren and fellow Bishops newly promoted; those things must be propounded which we haue learnt from our Fathers?* And how could the Bishops newly promoted answere; *so haue we receiued it, soe wee holde it, soe wee teache it following the Euangelicall faith with your doctrine?* For the Bishops newly promoted which made this Answere; where they not parts of the Bodie of the Councell? and then what likelyhood is there, that all the Bishops in a Councell should pronounce word for word, one selfe-same speach? There is often tymes noted in the front of the Canons; a *all the Councell saith*; for as much as such Canons hauing bene propounded and read by some of the Fathers of the Councell,

Cōc.Carth. 2.c.1.

Legendum depositione & nō dispositione.

Legendum sinibus, & non finibus

Legendum nouitatem, & non, notitiam.

Conc. dict. Carth. c. 2.

Concil. Carthag. 6. c. 1. 9. & 10.

all the reſt haue giuen their conſent vnto it. And there are alſo ſometimes Clauſes of two or three wordes, pronounced together by all the Bishops of a Councell; And principallie in the acclamations to Princes; where one of the Bishops hauing begun a period, all the reſt repeate with him in the forme of an *Eccho* the ſame wordes. There are alſo ſometymes orations compoſed and pronounced by the deputies of Councells, which are attributed to the whole bodie of the Councells, but that a whole Councell hath made and pronounced, immediately one ſame oration, and principallie an oration that had bene ſpoken word by word by one Bishop in an other Councell neere thirtie yeare before, there is noe ſparke of likelyhood in it.

Concil. Conſt. ſub. Men. & alibi. Concil. Conſt. 6. Act. 18.

The ſixth reaſon is that the moſt part of the Canons of this pretended Councell, are taken from diuers Clauſes of former Councells; ſticthed together, and threded as it were in the forme of Centons, one at the end of an other, and ioyned with ſoe little relation, and ſo vnaptlie and impertinently as the Collection can but be attributed to the ignorance of a particular Rapſodiſt, and not to the ſufficiencie and napacitie of the Fathers of the Councell. I will content myſelfe with producinge two examples, to the end that from thence, the readers may coniecture the reſt. The firſt example shall be drawne from the fifth Canon, whereof this is the tenor: *Aurelius Bishop ſaith, there is none doubtes, but that the greedines of Couetouſnes, is the mother of all euills; and therefore it muſt be interdicted, that anie should vſurpe the bounds of an other, or for hope of profitt to trench beyond the limitts eſtablisht by the Fathers, neither shall it be lawfull for anie to take vſurie of anie thing whatſoeuer: although the new propoſitions which are either obſcure or hidden vnder the generalitie of words being conſidered by vs, shall receiue a rule. But for the reſt thoſe whereof the Scripture hath cleerely determined muſt noe longer be delayed, but rather to execute iudgement. And therefore that which is reproued in laymen, ought by as much ſtronger reaſon to be condemned before all others in eccleſiaſticall perſons, all the Councell ſaith; None can labour without danger either againſt the prophets or the Ghoſpell.* Now this Canon is a centon compiled of two clauſes, taken the one from the tenth Canon of the firſt Councell of *Carthage*, which forbidds Bishops to trench vpon the lymitts of their fellowe-Bretheren; and the other from the thirteenth which forbidds Clerkes to lend vpon vſury; betweene which the Rapſodiſt hath vnaptlie interpoſed this interlocution; *although the new propoſitions which either are obſcure or hidden vnder the generalitie of wordes, being conſidered by vs, shall receiue a rule, yet thoſe where the ordonance of the ſcripture is cleere, muſt not be delayed, but rather the iudgement muſt be executed*; which is not of the bodie of the originall Canon, but is an anſwere to the demaund that *Abundantius* Bishop of *Adrumeta* had made, that they should confirme in the firſt Councell of *Carthage*, which was a generall Councell of all *Africa*, the decree that had bene propounded in the Councell of *Adrumeta*, which was a particular Councell of one of the prouinces of *Africa*; *that it was not lawfull for Clerkes to lend vpon vſurie.* To this demaund then *Gratus* anſwered that new propoſitions and the deciſions whereof were either obſcure or ambigious in the Scripture, it was reaſonable to deliberate of before they should be reſolued. But that thoſe where the ordonance of the Scripture was cleere, as in the caſe of vſurie, which was euidently forbidden both by the old and new Teſtament, there needed noe deliberation but execution. And the Rapſodiſt hath

Cốc. Carth dict. 6. c. 4.

Cốc. Carth 1. c. 10. Concil. Carth. 1. c. 13.

Cốc. Carth 1. c. 13.

inſerted

inserted the answere into his centon without makeing mention of the question. And to tye it to the rest of his fagot, he hath put in there the word, *although*, which hath noe relation either to the wordes before or after; But this will best appeare by confronting the Texts. The first clause then of this centon, is taken from the tenth Canon of the first Councell of *Carthage*, where the text saith. *Gratus Bishop said, that none doubts, but that the greedines of auarice, is the roote of all euills; and therefore it must be forbidden, that anie man should vsurpe the ends of nother, or trench vpon an other Bishop his colleague.* And the second is taken from the thirteenth Canō of the same Coūcell, whereof the wordes are these: *Abundantius Bishop of adrumeta said, It hath bene ordained in our Councell, that it is not lawfull for clerkes to lend vpon vsurie: and if it seeme to your Holynesse and to this Councell to be to purpose, let it be appointed by this present decree. Gratus the Bishop said, new propositions, which are either obscure or hidden vnder the ambiguitie of anie generall wordes; wee deliberate of, before we sett downe a Rule concerning them; but those wherein the ordinance of the diuine Scriptures is cleere, it is not needefull to delay the iudgement, but rather to execute it. And soe that which is reproued euen in the laitie, ought by a much stronger reason to be condemned in ecclesiasticall persons, before all others. All the Bishops said, None can doe anie thing contrary to the prophets, nor contrary to the Ghospell without perill.* And out of these two Canons of the first Councell of *Carthage*, seperated by the interposition of two other Canons, and distant by more then twelue periods one from an other, the gatherer of the collection *intituled the sixth Councell of Carthage*, hath made this continued text vnder the title of the fifth Canon of the sixth Councell of *Carthage*. *Aurelius the Bishop said, none can doubt, but that the greedines of Auarice is the mother of all euill, and therefore it must be forbidden, that anie man should vsurpe the ends of an other, or for hope of profitt trench beyond the lymittes prescribed by the Fathers; and that that also it shall not be lawfull for anie clergie man to lend vpon vsurie; although new propositions, which are either obscure or hidden vnder the generalitie of wordes, should be considered by vs, before wee sett downe a rule concerning them: yet those where, the ordinance of the diuine Scripture is cleere, must not be delayed, but rather proceeded in to Judgement: and so that which is reproued euen in laymen, ought to be by stronger reason much more condemned in Clergy-men. All the Councell said, none can act anie thing without perill contrary to the lawe or the prophets.* In which place yet to accommodate this confusion to the tyme of the sixth, Councell of *Carthage* he hath changed, either he or the exemplifiers which came after him, the word *Gratus* into *Aurelius*, against the credit of all antiquitie, which teacheth vs, that the first Councell of *Carthage* was holden vnder *Gratus*, and not vnder *Aurelius*; and contrary to the copies of the first Councell of *Carthage*, in the truth whereof wee all agree on both sides, which saith *Gratus* and not *Aurelius*; and against the testimonie of *Fulgentius Ferandus*, who cites the two Canons whereof this centon is compounded with the title of canons of the Councell holden vnder saint *Gratus*. The second example, shall be drawne from the thirteenth Canon of the same collection, which consists in these wordes: *Aurelius the Bishop said; that we ought, to obserue the decrees of the ancient Fathers; as also, that without consulting with the Primat of euery Prouince, many Bishops assembled presume not so easily to ordaine a Bishop, vnlesse in case of necessitie three Bishops, in what place soeuer they should bee, ought by his commaundement, to ordaine a Bishop; and if anie one doe in anie thing contradict his profession or signature, he depriues himselfe of this Societie.* Now this gallymaufery is a medley stitched and

Cōc. Carth 1. c. 10.

Cōc. Carth 1. c. 13.

Conc. dict. Carth. 6. c. 5.

Fulg. Ferrand in Breu. Can. art. 24. & 123.

Conc. dict Carth. 6. c. 13.

patched together from the three different clauſes of the ſecond Councell of *Carthage,* where they are couched with their reaſons, relations, and dependancies; whereas in this centon, they are inſerted without anie relation or connexion one to an other. The firſt clauſe is taken from the tenth Canon of the ſecond councell of *Carthage*, where after *Felix* Biſhop of a cittie of *Africa* called *Selemſela,* or according to the collation of *Carthage*, *Silemſila* ſhewed that the ancient Councells decreed, that a Biſhop ſhould be iudged by twelue Biſhops; a Prieſt by ſix; and a deacon by three; there follow theſe wordes: *Genetlius* Biſhop ſaid; *what ſaith your Holyneſſe to this?* All the Biſhops ſaid, that the decrees of the ancient Fathers ought to be obſerued. The ſecond clauſe is taken from the twelfth Canon of the ſame ſecond Councell of *Carthage*, wherein after the complaint that *Numidius* Biſhop of *Maſſilia,* (or according to the collation of *Carthage, Maxulia*: for *Maſculia*, whereof the Biſhop *Victorianus* was at one of the actes of the third Councell of *Carthage* was an other Biſhoprike) had made to *Genetlius that ſome Biſhops diſpiſing the Primats of their prouinces ordained Biſhops without receiuing letters frõ thẽ;* & the anſwere that *Genetlius* gaue him, *that this was a thing that concerned their common honor, and they muſt all giue their votes;* there followe theſe wordes: *It was ſaid by all the Biſhops, It pleaſeth vs all, that the Primate of the Prouince not hauing bene conſulted with, none ſhould preſume ſoe eaſilie (though with manie Biſhops) to ordaine a Biſhop, &c. but in a caſe of neceſſitie, three Biſhops in what place ſoeuer they ſhall bee, with the commaundement of the Primat, may ordaine a Biſhop.* The third is taken out of the laſt Canon of the ſame Councell, where after *Genetlius* had demaunded, *will it pleaſe you then, that all things that haue bene decreed in your moſt glorious aſſemblie, ſhall be obſerued by all?* and that all the Biſhops, had anſwered; *It pleaſeth vs, it pleaſeth vs, that they ſhould be obſerued by all,* theſe wordes follow, *Genetlius Biſhop ſaid, and if (againſt our expectation) it happen that they ſhould be violated in anie point, what doe you ordaine ought to be done? It was ſaid by all the Biſhops: Whoſoeuer ſhall contradict his proteſtation or his ſignature, ſhall make himſelfe incapable of this Societie.* And of theſe three diuers clauſes repeated in three ſeuerall canons, and which haue noe relation one to an other, he that gathered the collection intituled the ſixth Councell of *Carthage*, had made this centon as a continned Canon; *Aurelius the Biſhop ſaid, what ſay your Holyneſſe to this? All the Biſhops anſwered; that we ought to obſerue the Canons of antiquitie, as alſoe; that without conſulting with the Primate of euery Prouince, manie Biſhops aſſembled, ought not to preſume, ſo eaſily to ordaine a Biſhop, vnleſſe in caſe of neceſſitie, three Biſhops in what place ſoeuer they be, with his commaundement ought to ordaine a Biſhop; and if anie man happen in anie thing to contradict his profeſſion or his ſignature, he ſhall thereby make himſelf incapable of this Societie.* And to the end to fitt it to the tyme of the ſixth Councell of *Carthage*, either he, or the Exemplifiers which haue come after him, haue changed the name of *Genetlius* into that of *Aurelius*, againſt the credit of the copies of the ſecond Councell of *Carthage*, which ſay, *Genetlius*; and of *Fulgentius Ferrandus*, who citeth theſe Canons with the title of the Councell holden vnder *Genetlius*.

The ſeauẽth reaſon, but one that cõprehendes vnder it a legiõ of others, is that almoſt all the canõs that are inſerted into this collection, are there inſerted with preciſe notes of Canons cõpoſed & pronoũced in the ſixth Councell of *Carthage*; & neuertheleſſe, there is ſcarce one of them; where there are not ſome clauſes, that cannot agree neither with the tyme, nor with the perſons, nor yet with the diſcipline of the Fathers of the ſixth coũcell of *Carthage*: As for example; in the third canõ, it is ſaid, *when in the*

Creſc. Epiſc. Silemſilenſis Collat. Carthag. in recent. Epis. Donatiſt. Act. 1 art. 176.

Concil. Carthag. 2 c. 10.

Numid. Maxulit. Collat. Carthag Act. 1. art. 112.

Donatus Maſculitan Optat. Mileuit. l. 1. Fœlix. Epiſc. Mozulitanẽſis & Vitalis epiſcop. Maſcul. Donatiſtæ in Collat. Carth. Act. 1 art. 188. & 202.

Concil. Carth. 2. c. 12.

Cõc. Carth 2. c. 13.

Cõc. Carth dict. 6. c. 13.

Fulg. Ferãd in Breu. Can. art. 55. & 96. & artic. 4.

Cõc. dict. Carth. 6. c. 3.

Councell past, the continence of the clergie was treated of, these three degrees were restrained by the consecrations, as to one kind of conscription of Chastitie; to witt, Bishops, Priests, and deacons. Now it hath alreadie bene shewed, that these wordes cannot be of the sixth Councell of *Carthage*, as well because they are word by word in the second Councell of *Carthage* which had bene celebrated thirtie yeare before, & with this same remitment to the past Councell; as because in the Councell of *Carthage* holden vnder the twelfth consulship of *Honorius*, which had immediately preceded the sixth councell of *Carthage*, there had bene nothing ordained concerning the continence of the clergie. And it cannot be said, that by this phrase in the councell past, they intended to speake of the Councell assẽbled vnder the consulship of *Vincentius* & *Flauitas*, which had bene celebrated eighteen yeares before the sixth councell of *Carthage*. For besides that this note of tyme, *in Concilio præterito*, determinately taken, & to saie, *in the past councell*, hath reference to the councell last past; and indeterminately taken, & to saie, *in a councell past*, it cãnot haue bene vsed by the sixth councell of *Carthage*, in the tyme whereof, the decree of clergie continẽce had bene published not in one, but in manie and seuerall Councells; as the twentie fifth canon of the same collection declares; when it saith, *That hath pleased vs, which hath also bene confirmed in seuerall Councells; that the subdeacons which handle the Sacraments, and the Deacons, Priests, and Bishops, according to the former decrees, shall abstaine euen from their wiues.* The word, *in Concilio præterito*, cannot be expounded of the Councell holden vnder the Consulship of *Vincentius* and *Flauitas*; for as much as the canon of the celibat, published vnder the consulship of *Vincentius* and *Flauitas*, is wholie reported in the same collection, more then twentie chapters after. In the fifth Canon the text sayth, *Faustinus Bishop of Potentia of the Prouince of Vrbin, Legat of the Roman Church, saith; It pleases that Bishops, Priests, and Deacons, or those that handle the Sacraments, keeping chastitie, shall abstaine euen from their owne wiues.* Now this Canon is not a Canon by itselfe, but the trayne of a former Canon; that is to saie, of the second canon of the second Councell of *Carthage*, in the which the compiler of the collection, or his exemplifiers, in steede of these wordes; *It was said by all the Bishops, it pleaseth all, that the Bishops, Priests, and Deacons, or those that handle the Sacraments, keeping chastitie, shall abstaine euen from their owne wiues*; hath put to fitt the decree to the tyme of the sixth Councell of *Carthage*; *Faustinus Bishop of Potentia, of the Prouince of Vrbin, Legat of the Roman Church, saith; It pleases that Bishops, Priests, deacons, or those that shall handle the Sacraments keeping chastitie, shall abstaine euen from their owne wiues.* A thing that can noe waie subsist. For besides, that if it had bene the Popes legat that had spoken this language, he would neuer haue forgotten to mention the decrees of the celibate, sent to the Bishops of *Africa* by Pope *Syricius*; It is euident, that this clause is not a Canon a parte, but it is the approbation and conclusion of the proposition of the Canon; and therefore alsoe in the second Coũcell of *Carthage*, it is ioyned in one and the same canõ with the preceding article. And neuerthelesse the author of the collection intitled the sixth Councell of *Carthage*, not onely hath thereof made two canons in chiefe, but the better to distinguish and make manifest his impertinẽcie, hath intituled thẽ with two differing titles, and hath placed before the one of them this inscription: *Of continence, chapter the third.* And before the other, *Of the diuers orders that ought to abstaine from their wiues, chapter fourth.* And the Greeke Interpreter the very same. In the ninth canon, the text of the collection is, *Augustin Bishop Legat of the prouince of Numidia said, Vouchsafe to ordaine that if anie*

Cõc. Carth. c. 2.

Cõc. Carth celebr. Honor. 12. Theod. 8. Coss. relat in Afric. Concil. Carth. 5. c. 3. & Cõcil dict Afric. c. 37.

Cõcil dict. Carth. 6. c. 25.

Con. dict. Carth. 6. c. 5.

Cõc. Carth 2. c. 2.

Syric. Ep. ad Afric. citat. in Cõc. Zell. & apud Fulg Ferr. in Breu. Can. art. 130. Conc. dict. Carthag. 6. in titul. c. 3. Ibid in titul. d. 4. Edit. Græc Cõc. Carth in titul. c. 3. & 4. Cõcil. dict. Carthag. 6. c. 6.

in respect of their crimes be cast out of the Church, and that anie Bishop or Priest receiue them into communion, he may be held to be inuolued in the like crime, as those that shunne the regular iudgement of their Bishop. Now these are the wordes of the second Councell of *Carthage*, where after *Felix* Bishop of Selemsela, and *Epigonius* Bishop of *Bulla Regia* (for it must be read *Bullensium regiorum* and not *Bullensium regionum* as it appeares both by the acts of the conference of *Carthage* which saie, *Bullensium regiorum*; and by the *Geograficall* tables of *Ptolomy*, where there is a cittie of *Africa* called *Bullaria*, which is a corrupt abridgement of the word *Bulla regia*) had made the proposition of the article; *Genetlius* Bishop of *Carthage* replied; *With good cause then doe our Bretheren and fellowe Bishops propound, that those that in respect of their crimes are cast out of the Church, if auoyding the regular iudgment of their Bishop, they be receiued to the communion by anie Bishop or Priest, he shall be held to be inuolued in the like crime.* Onely there is this difference, that whereas the second Conncell of *Carthage* saith: *Genetlius Bishop saith*; the compiler, or his exemplifers, to accommodate the Canon to the time of the sixth Councell of *Carthage*, haue sett, *Augustin Bishop Legat of the prouince of Numidia saith*; which is a metamophosis, that cannot take place as well because *Epigonius* was dead, as it hath bene aboue shewed, a long tyme before the sixth Councell of *Carthage*; as because saint AVGVSTIN would not haue said in the sixth Councell of *Carthage*, *Vouchsafe to ordaine*, of a thing alreadie ordained, and in the same termes thirtie yeare before. In the fourteenth canon the collection saith; *Item, it hath pleased, that from the prouince of Tripolis, in regard of the small number of Bishops, there one onelie Bishop may come in legation, and that in the same prouince, a Priest may bee heard by fiue Bishops, and a Deacon by three, the proper Bishop of the Diocesse, as hath bene aboue-said, sitting with them.* Now the first clause of this decree, is a traine of the second Canon of the third Councell of *Carthage*, where after the Fathers had ordained that there should be sent to the nationall aniuersarie Councells, three deputies from euery prouince, they added this exceptation; *But from Tripolis, because of the small number of Bishops, there shall come but one onely Bishop.* From this canon then, the Rapsodists of the sixth Councell of *Carthage* haue seperated and torne the traine from the head, and haue set, by an order reuersed, the head, which ordaines that there should come to the nationall Councells but three deputies from euery prouince, in the eighteenth canon of their collection, and the traine which excepts the prouince of *Tripolis*, and the dispensation of sending but one deputie, in the fourteenth, that is to saie, after the thirteenth with which it hath noe relation. For that this exception hath bene made in the third Councell of *Carthage* and not in the sixth; and that it is a traine of the second canon of the third Councell of *Carthage*, it appeares both by the text of the third Councell of *Carthage*, where it is in the same wordes; & by the Coūcell of *Carthage*, holdē vnder the twelfth consulship of *Honorius*, which preceded the sixth Councell of *Carthage*, where it is said, *that Plautius was come onely Legat from the prouince of Tripolis according to custome*; a thing that euidentlie shewes, that the exception of the prouince of *Tripolis*, had preceded the sixth coūcell of *Carthage*. The other clause is, an ignorant addition, that the Rapsodist hath thrust in, by which hee will haue it, that in the prouince of *Tripolis*, fiue Bishops with the diocesan, that is to saie, six Bishops might iudge a Priest; not considering that in the prouince of *Tripolis* there was in all but fiue Bishops. For that the Rapsodist meaneth fiue Bishops besides the Diocesan, it is apparent by these wordes: *the proper Bishop, as hath bene aboue said, being present:* Which remitts the Readers to the

Collat. Carth. Act 1. Ptolom. Geogr. l. 4. legendum. Βȣλλα ῥια id est Βȣλλα ῥηγία. Concil. Carth. 2. c. 7.

Concil. dict. Carth c. 14.

Concil. Carth. 3. c. 2.

Concil. Carth. Honor. 12. & Theod. 8. Coss. relat. in Concil. Afric. c. 94

the former canons, where the diocesan Bishop is added, besides the six Bishops that ought to iudge the Priests of the other Prouinces; and by *Zonara* and *Balsamon*, who saie interpreting this canon: *Hee meanes fiue Bishops, besides the Diocesan Bishop*, which ought to preside at this act; and that there was in all but fiue Bishops in the prouince of *Tripolis*, it is manifest by the ninteenth canon of the third Councell of *Carthage* which is the sixteenth of the *African* Rapsody, where *Aurelius* saith: *In Tripolis as it is affirmed*, (or according to the Greeke, *as you know*,) *there are but fiue Bishops*. In the sixteenth Canon which is a confusion of fower articles; all the articles are as soe manie canons of the third Coūcell of *Carthage*, bound vp and patched together without order one with an other, and that cannot be presumed to haue bene transferred from the sixth Coūcell of *Carthage* into the third as the new publishers of the councells of *Africa* pretend; for as much as the most part of the same canons had bene instituted in the Coūcell of *Hippo*, which the first *Mileuitan* Councell testifies to haue bene repeated in the third Councell of *Carthage*. In the seauēteenth canon the collection saith, *It hath pleased, that Mauritania Sitifensis*, (*as it hath requested of the Primat of Numidia from whose Congregation it is now to bee subtracted*) *should haue a Primat a parte, which all Primates of African prouinces, yea all the Bishops consenting thereto, because of the length of the waie, doe permitt to be so.* Now this canon could not be made in the sixth Councell of *Carthage*, for more then twentie yeare before the sixth Councell of *Carthage*, *Mauritania Sitifensis* had a primat apart, as appeares both by the third Councell of *Carthage* which saith, that there were none but the Prouinces indued with the first Seas, that should send Legates to the Councells, and neuertelesse names the Legates of *Mauritania Sitifensis*; and by the first *Mileuitan* Councell where *Nicetius* is called, *Primat of Mauritania Sitifensis*. And therefore also *Fulgentius Ferandus* attributes this decree to an other Councell of *Carthage*. In the eighteenth canon, it is said; *Item, it hath bene decreed, that those that ordaine, shall imprint the canons of the Councells in the eares of the Bishops or Clearks, that are to be ordained*; wordes which are sillable for sillable, in the third Councell of *Carthage*, & which cannot be said to haue bene trāsferred thither frō the sixth, as the new publishers of the Coūcells of *Africa* pretend. For *Possidius* reportes, that it was saint AVGVSTIN, who hauing perceiued that he had bene created Bishop of *Hippo* ioyntly with *Valerius* his Predecessor, contrary to the prohibition of the councell of Nicea, after his promotion caused the decree of reading the canons of the coūcells, to those that were to be promoted to be made. To the same canon the Rapsodist adds, *Item, it hath pleased that the Eucharist shall not be giuen to the bodies of the dead &c. and that the ignorance of Priests doe not cause men alreadie dead to be baptized. For which cause it shall be confirmed in this holy Synod, that according to the decrees of the councell of Nicea in ecclesiasticill causes which often decaie with age, to the domage of the people, there shall be called euerie yeare a councell, whereto all the prouinces that haue Primats, shall send from their councells, two legates, or as manie as they please, that the authoritie may be intire in the companie assembled*: Which are two decrees, the one taken from the sixth canon of the third councell of *carthage*, which saith, *Item it hath pleased that the Eucharist shall not be giuen to the bodies of the dead &c.* And the other drawne from the second canon of the same third councell of *carthage*, which pronounceth; *It hath pleased that for ecclesiasticall causes, which often decaie with age to the domage of the people, there shall be called euerie yeare a councell, to which all the prouinces that haue prime Seas, shall send three Legates from their councells, to the end that the authoritie should be intire, and the assemblie lesse subiect to enuie, and lesse costlie to their hosts.* Now besides this that, the last

Concil. dict. Carrh. 6. c. 11. Zon. in Cōc. Carth c 14. Balsam. ibid. Cōc. Carth 3. c. 19. Edit. Græc. Concil. Carth. c. 49. Impress. Concil. Afric. Paris 1615. apud Abraham Pacard. in Præf. pag. 35. & 38 Concil. Mileuit. 1. relat in Afric post. c. 52. Cōcil. dict. Carth. 6. c. 17. Cōc. Carth 3. c. 2. Cōc. Carth 3. c. 48. Conc. Mileuit. 1. relat. in Afric p. c 51. Fulg. Ferand. in Breu. Can. art. 81. Cōc. Carth dict. 6. c. 18 Cōc. Carth 3. c. 3. Possid. in v. Aug. Conc. dict. Carthag. 6 c. 18. Cōc. Carth 3 c 6. Cōc. Carth 3. c. 2.

of these canons hath nothing common with the prohibition of giuing the *Eucharist*, or baptisme to the dead, with which the Rapsodist tyes it, but speakes of causes attempted against ecclesiasticall persons . And besides that the mention of the Coücell of *Nicea* which is ioyned thereto, is wholie impertinent, seeing the lawe of the Councell of *Nicea* is but of prouinciall Councells, and not of Nationall; it could haue bene neither made, nor cõfirmed in the sixth Coücell of *Carthage*, for the dereee of the *Anniuersarie* holding of the Nationall Councells of *Africa*, first intituled in the Councell of *Hippo*, and since renewed by this canon in the third Councell of *Carthage*, had bene suppressed and abrogated more then twelf yeare before the sixth Councell of *Carthage*, by the Councell holdẽ vnder the seauenth consulship of *Honorius*, in these wordes; *Because it had bene ordained in that Councell of Hippo, the there should be holden euerie yeare a Generall Councell of Africa, not onely heere at Carthage, but in all the other prouinces euerie one in his turne, it hath bene reserued to be kept, sometimes in the prouince of Numidia, and sometimes in that of Byzacia: But for as much as this hath seemed laborious to all the bretheren, it hath pleased that there should be noe more anniuersarie necessitie to trauaile-trouble the bretheren, but that when the common cause, that is to saie of all Africa, shall require it, from whatsoeuer part the letters shall be addressed to this Sea; the Synod shall be assẽbled in the prouince that shall be thought fittest.* In the ninteenth and tweentith it is said, that Bishops and Priests accused, cannot be excommunicated vnlesse after citation and refusall to appeare; which are two decrees transferred from the third Councell of *Carthage* into this collection; and not transferred from this collection into the copies of the third Councell of *Carthage*, as the new publishers of the Councell of *Africa* pretend. For S. AVGVSTIN himself notes, that the decree forbidding to excommunicate accused Priests, but after citation and refusall of appearance, was instituted in the tyme that *Proculian* was Bishop for the *Donatists* at *Hippo*. Now *Proculian* had liued and was dead a long while before the sixth Councell of *Carthage*, as it appeares both by the letters of the clergie of *Hippo* to *Ianuarius*, which testifie, that *Proculian* was Bishop of *Hippo*, before the lawes of the Emperors against the *Donatists* came into *Africa*; and by the cõferéce of *Carthage*, which was holden eight yeares before the sixth Councell of *Carthage* in which tyme it was noe more *Proculian*, but *Macrobius*, that was Bishop of the *Donatists* at *Hippo*. In the twentie fourth canon which is of the canonicall Bookes, the collection saith, *Bee it also made knowne to our brother and fellow-Bishop Boniface, and to the other Bishops of the same prouinces, for the confirmation of this canon, that these are the bookes that wee haue receiued from our fathers, to be read in the church.* Now we haue alreadie shewed by three reasons, and can yet confirme it by a fowrth that the canon of canonicall bookes had bene publisht in the third councell of *Carthage*. For the first *Mileuitan* councell testifies that the Statutes of the councell of *Hippo* which cõtained fourtie one canons, amongst which was a decree of the canonicall bookes, had bene inserted and confirmed in a more full councell assembled at *Carthage*. Which can not be vnderstood, but of the third councell of *Carthage*; that is to saie, of the councell holden the fifth of the calends of *September*, vnder the consulship of *Cesarius* and *Atticus*, in which was propounded the extract of the canons of the Councell of *Hippo*. Moreouer wee haue proued that Pope *Innocent* the first, had alreadie framed a roll of the canonicall Bookes agreable to that of the third Councell of *Carthage* more then fourteen yeare before *Boniface*, and the sixth Councell of *Carthage*. By meanes whereof, it had bene an impertinent thing, for the Bishops of the sixth Councell of *Carthage*, to

Cõc. Carth 3. c 7. Conc Nic. c. 5. Cõc. Hipp. c. 7. Cõc. Carth 3. c. 2. & 41 & Cõc. dict Afric c. 18. vbi vitio. scriptorum non aduertentium vtrumque Canonem esse eiusdẽ Concilij, pro *iam superius*, positum est *iam dudũ*. Conc. Hon 7 & Theod. 2. 11. Coss. rerelat in Afric. c. 62 Cõc. Carth 3. c. 7 & 8. Aug. ep. 137. Aug. ep. 68 Collat. Carthag. Act 1. art. 201. Cõc dict. Carth. 6. c. 24. Cõc. Mileuit. 1 relat. in Conc. Afric. post. c 52 Cõc Hipp. c 30. Cõc. Carth 5 Calend Sept. Cesar & Attic. Coss. relat in Concil. Afric c 1. Innoc. ad Exup. ep. 3.

write

write to Pope *Boniface* for the confirmation of this canon; and it cannot be ſaid, that perchance the *Africans* knewe it not; for *Fauſtinus* the Popes legat who was preſent at this Councell, and *Phillippus* and *Aſellus* prieſts of the *Roman* Church, who aſſiſted him, would not haue permitted them to be ignorant of it. In the twentie fifth, the collection containes, *Aurelius ſaith: Wee add my moſt deere brothers moreouer, as relation had bene made of the incontinence of ſome clerkes, although but readers, towardes their owne wiues; It was decreed, which alſo hath bene confirmed in diuers Councells; that the ſubdeacons which should handle the ſacraments, & the deacons and Prieſts and alſo Bishops, according to the former Statutes, should abſtaine from their owne wiues &c: which if they obſerue not, that they should be depoſed from their eccleſiaſticall office; but that the other clerkes should not be conſtrayned by this lawe, but in a riper age.* Now beſides that theſe are the wordes of the third canon of the fifth Councell of *Carthage*, which ſaith; *moreouer, as relation had bene made of the incontinence of ſome clerkes, though toward their owne wiues; It was decreed, that Bishops prieſts, and deacons, according to the former Statutes, should abſtaine euen from their owne wiues; which if they obſerue not, that they should be depoſed from their eccleſiaſticall office; but that other clerkes should not be bound by this lawe*: there are ſoe manie impertiencies in the extract of the canon, as it could not be collected by the Fathers of a Councell. For firſt, theſe wordes, *Aurelius ſaith; Wee add my moſt deare bretheren;* hath noe relation with the former canon of the ſame collection, which is of the catalogue of the canonicall bookes. And ſecondlie, this contexture; *Aurelius ſaith Wee add my moſt deare bretheren: moreouer, as relation had bene made to the incontinencie of ſome clerkes,* hath noe conſtruction, neither naturall nor gramaticall, but is a ſtrained and impertinent coniunction to bring into *Aurelius* diſcourſe the words of the third Canon of the fifth Councell of *Carthage*, which beginus with theſe wordes: *Moreouer, as relation had bene made of the incontinence of ſome Clerkes.* And thirdly this parentheſis (*although but readers*) is directly againſt the diſcipline of the Fathers of *Africa*; who neuer meant to depriue the Readers from the vſe of their owne wiues; contrarywiſe, they haue bound them, coming to the age of Manhood, either to profeſſe chaſtitie, or to marrie. *It hath bene ordained* (ſaith the third councell of *Carthage*, *that Readers hauing once attained to the age of manhood, shall be conſtrained either to take wiues, or to make profeſſion of chaſtitie.* And fowrthly this exception, *vnleſſe a riper age*, vtterlie deſtroyeth the intent of the councell; which wills that none but Bishops, Prieſts, deacons and ſubdeacōs should be obliged receiuing orders, to quit their wiues; & that the other clerkes which handle not the Sacraments, should not be obliged to this Condition. In the twentie eight Canon, which is a repetition of the canon inſtituted in the ſecond *Mileuitan* Councell, and confirmed in the Councell of *Carthage* holden vnder the twelfth Conſulship of *Honorius*, where it had bene decided, *that the prieſts Deacons and other inferior Clerkes, cannot in their proper cauſes, appeale beyond Sea*: the greeke edition and ſome latin copies add, as it hath bene often ſaid of Bishops, a thing which can haue noe ground, firſt becauſe the originall Canons of the ſecond *Mileuitan* Councell, and of the Councell holden vnder the twelfth conſulship of *Honorius*, from whence this repitition is taken, reduce the article to onely prieſts, Deacons, and other inferior clerkes, & make noe mention of Bishops: Secondly, becauſe the title of the ſame twētie eight canon which is in the collection of *Dioniſius Exiguus*, and in the greeke edition, is reſtrained preciſely to theſe wordes, *that the prieſts, deacons and clerks, that in their owne cauſe appeale beyond Sea, should not be receiued to the communion*: and thirdly becauſe the Fathers of the ſixth Councell of

Conc. dict. Carth. 6. c. 25.

Conc. Carth. 5. c. 3.

Concil. Carth. dict. 6. c. 24.

Cōc. Carth 3. c. 19.

Conc. dict. Carth. 6. c. 23.

Cōcil. Mileuit. 2. c. 22.

Cōc. Carth Honor. 12. & Theodos. 8. Coll relat. in Cōc. Afric. c. 92.

Collect. Dionys. in tit. Can 28 Conc dict. Carthag. 6. Edit. Grec. Cōc. Carth 6. in tit. c. 28.

Cõc. Carth 6.c.9.&.10 *Carthage* protested in the acts of the same Councell, that they would not meddle with this article, till the Copies of the Councell of *Nicea* should be brought out of the East, and after they should come, they would assemble a new Synod to aduise vpon it. Now these copies came but in the month of *Nouember* in the Consulship of *Monaxius* and *Plinta*, that is to saie six monethes after the calling of the sixth Councell of *Carthage*; in which tyme neither the sixth Councell of *Carthage* was on foote, neither was *Faustinus* Legat to Pope *Boniface* then in *Africa*, in whose presence this collection is pretended to haue bene made. For that which the Illustrious Cardinall *Baronius*, and the doctors of *Collen* doe suppose, (that *Innocentius* and *Marcellus* bearers of the copies of the Councell of *Nicea*, arriued not in *Africke* till after the death of Pope *Boniface*, and in the tyme of Pope *Celestine*; and vpon this occasion put backe the edition of the collection of the thirtie three Canons vntill the tyme of, *Celestine*, vnder which *Faustinus* made a second voyage into *Africa*,) is contradicted both by the inscription of the same copies, which shewes, that they were brought out of *Alexandria* into *Africa* by the priest *Innocentius*, and sent from *Africa* by the same *Innocentius* and by *Marcellus* Subdeacon of the Church of *Carthage* to *Boniface* Bishop of the Roman Church, the sixth of the calends of *december*: and by saint CYRILL that saith to the *Africans* in the end of his Epistle; *As for the Pasch, we signifie to you according to the request that you haue often made to vs in your letters, that we will celebrate it the seauenteenth* (or according to the correction of some the fourteenth) *of the calends of may, of the future indiction*; for, for what cause should the answere be made to the question that they had made to him of the daie of the next *Pasch*, if his answere were not to be returned before the same *Pasch*. And by the Epistle of the *Africans* to Pope *Celestine*, which testifies that they had sent the copies of the Exemplifications from the East to his predecessor *Boniface* by *Innocent* priest, and *Marcellus* subdeacon. And from this, that which saint IEROME writes to saint AVGVSTIN derogates not; *The holie priest Innocent bearer of this epistle, tooke not the yeare last past anie letters from me to your Dignitie. as if hee should not haue returned into Africa*. For so farr is it from appearing by this that *Innocent* staied in the East till the yeare following, as contrariwise it doth the more plainely appeare, that he returned the same yeare into *Africa*, but that he made a new voyage into the East the yeare after. And then if this collection haue bene framed in a Councell of *Carthage* where *Faustinus* was present, as the fourth canon of the same collection supposeth; it must haue bene while the first staie that *Faustinus* made in *Africa*, vnder the Popedome of *Boniface*, and not during the second staie that he made there vnder the popedome of *Celestine*: for the twentie fourth canon of the same collection ordaines, that the article of the canonicall Bookes, should be communicated to Pope *Boniface*; whose Popedome mett with the first staie of *Faustinus* in *Africa*, and not with the second.

Inscript. ep. Cyrill. ad Episc. Afric. Ann. tom. 5. ad. ann. 419. Impress. Conc. Col. ann. 1606. in not. ad Concil. Carthag. 6 Inscript. ep. Cyril. & Attic. — Conc. dict. Afric. c. 102. — Conc. dict. Afric. cap. 105. Hier. ep. 79. — Conc. dict. Carth. 6. c. 4. — Conc. dict. Carth. 6. c. 28.

The eigth reason is, that except *Aurelius* Bishop of *Carthage*, and *Valentine Alypius*, and saint AVGVSTINE Bishop of *Numidia*, there is not so much as one neither of all the two hundred seauenteen Bishops who were present at the sixth Councell of *Carthage*, nor of the twentie two deputies that staied at *Carthage* after the separation of the rest of the Councell, that is brought in to speake in this collection contrarywise all the other Bishops that are named there, as *Fortunatus*, *Felix* of *Selemsela*; *Numidius* of *Massilia*, are the Bishops that assisted thirtie yeare before in the second Councell of *Carthage*; and more then this also the names of the Bishops of the sixth Councell of *Carthage*,

which

which are mentioned in this collection, haue bene almost all supposed there in the steede of others that haue bene taken awaie to sett them in their places, as we haue shewed amongst other examples by that of the fifth canon, which is taken from the first Councell of *Carthage*, where in steede of *Gratus* Bishop of *Carthage*, there is sett into the collection, *Aurelius*; and by that of the ninth which is taken from the second Councell of *Carthage*, where in steede of *Genetlius* Bishop of *Carthage*, there is sett into the collection *Augustine* Bishop Legat of the prouince of *Numidia*: and by that of the thirteenth which is taken out of the same second Councell of *Carthage*, where in steede of *Genetlius*, there is sett into the collection, *Aurelius*. A thing which could not haue bene done by the Fathers of a Councell, who would neuer haue changed the names of those, that had first propounded the canons to sett them vnder the names of others; and that could not be attributed to the ignorance of the copies of the last ages, but ought to be imputed either to the originall Rapsodist, or to the exemplifiers of the next ages after him. For the same mistakes and changes of names which are in the latine edition of this collection, are in the collection of *Dionisius*, which was made more then a thousand yeares agoe; and in the greeke translation which was made shortlie after.

Cõc. Carth 1. Can. 10. & 13. Cõc. Carth 2. c. 7. Cõc Carth 2. c. 10. 12. & 13.

And finallie the ninth and last reason is, that the conclusion which is read in some copies at the end of the collection, intituled the sixth Councell of *Carthage*; and in others at the end of the Rapsody of the Councell of *Africa*, which wee call the *African* Councell, is taken word by word out of the conclusion of the first Councell of *Carthage*, except that in steede of *Gratus*, there is *Aurelius*. For behold the latin termes wherein it is reported in the copies of *Monsieur* the president of *Champigny*, at the end of the collection, intituted the sixth Councell of *Carthage*; and in others, at the end of the collection, intituled the *African* Councell, *Aurelius Episcopus dixit, Iuxta statuta totius Concilij congregati & meæ mediocritatis sententiam, placet facere rerum omnium conclusionem, vniuersi tituli & designati huius diei tractatum, & ecclesiæ gesta suscipiant.* And beholde how it is couched at the end of the first Councell of *Carthage*, *Gratus Episcopus dixit, Iuxta statuta concilij, & meæ mediocritatis sententiam, placet facere rerum omnium conclusionem; vniuersi tituli disignati & digesti teneant sententias suas*. In which place the Rapsodists of the collection intituled the sixth Councell of *Carthage*, haue impertinentlie taken the word, *tituli*, in the genitiue singular; and the greeke interpretors euen the same; and haue expressed the period in this sence; *Be it registred in the actes of the Church, the treatie of all the title designed & digested this daie.* Not considering that in *Gratus* his proposition, it is a nominatiue plurall; and not remembring that, *tituli*, in the Statutes of the first Councell of *Carthage*, signified *Canons*; and besides not perceiuing that the word *Vniuersi*, in the same first Councell of *Carthage*, hath reference to the Bishops, and not to the decrees. For the order of the Sence sheweth, that *Gratus* his proposition must be read by waie of interrogation and expounding it in these wordes: *Doth it please you according to the Statutes of all the Councell, & the sentence of my mediocritie, to make the cõclusion of all things*: And in the second clause after the word, *Vniuersi*, to sett in as in all the other canons of the same Councell *dixerunt*, and to interpret it in this sence; *all the Bishops did saie, that the canons designed and digested, maintaine their sentences*: and this done, to repeate, *Gratus Bishop saith*. I know well neuerthelesse, that in the verball processe of the sixth Councell of *Carthage* inserted into the ordinarie volumes of the Cõucells, there were some articles ordained to be registred, as it appeares by the wordes of the

Cod. Manusc. D. de Champig. Conc. dict. Carth 6. c. 40. qui secundum. alios. 33. Conc. dict. Afric c. 100 Concil. Carthag. 1. c. 14.

Edit. Græc

Cõc. Carth c. 133.

Cōc.Carth c.9. Councell to *Aurelius*, which are these; *The copies of the faith and of the Statutes of the Councell of Nicea, which were brought to our Councell by the Bishop Cecilian, late predecessor to your Hollinesse which had assisted there, and also the thinges that our Fathers constituted heere, following the same copies, and those that we by a common Synod constitute now remaine registred in the present Ecclesiasticall acts:* But that these wordes; *the things that we constitute now by a common Councell*, are meant of the determination to send to seeke the Councell of *Nicea* into the East, and to obserue it; (treated in the eight chapters preceding the verball processe; which the *Africans* would should be reduced into writing; and not of anie other decrees;) the rest of the speeche shewes it; which is, *To witt, that as it hath bene aboue said, your Blessednesse* (the Latin beares ita vt & le Græc. δηλονότι.) *should vouchsafe to write to the Reuerend Bishops of the Churches of Antioch, Alexandria, and Constantinople, to send vnder the testimonie of their letters, the most certaine copies of the Councell of* Nicea, *whereby the truth being cleered, the chapters that our brother and fellowe Bishop Faustinus heere present, and our fellowe Priests Phillipus and Asellus haue brought with them in their instruction, either if they bee found, they shall be confirmed by vs; or if they be not found we will assemble a Synod to aduise vpon it.* And as for these wordes; *and also the thinges that our Fathers constituted heere following the same copies,* they are meant by the confirmatiue decrees of the Councell of *Nicea* made by the Councell of *Carthage*, holden vnder *Cecelianus* and other predecessors of the Bishops of the sixth Councell of *Carthage*, where the Statutes of the Councell of *Nicea* had bene imposed both in grosse and in retaile to all the ecclesiasticall Orders of *Africa*, and not of the canons of the collection intitled the sixth Councell of *Carthage*, whereof the more parte, had bene made in the Councell holden vnder *Aurelius*, and are not contayned neither in Sense nor in wordes in the canons of the Councells of *Nicea*. Well doe I know againe, that the decrees of this collection, are alleadged both by the Epitomy of the Councells, sent in Pope *Adrians* name to *Charlemaine*, and by *Hinckmarus* Archbishop of *Rheims* in the worke of the fiftie fiue Chapters, and by manie others. But the misreckoning being come from a higher roote, and hauing had place from the tyme of *Dionisius* and *Cresconius*, and of the Greeke translation, it must not to be thought strange, if from one absurditie manie others haue ensued. It sufficeth that *Fulgentius Ferandus*, who was both before them and more versed in the knowledged of the Councells of *Africa* then they, represents no track of the collection of the thirtie three Canons, intitled the sixth Councell of *Carthage*, for that *Fulgentius Ferandus* hath preceded all the other collectors of this kinde in antiquitie; whether it were that *Ferandus* deacō of *Carthage*, that writt the workes of the fiue Questions to saint FVLGENTIVS Bishop of *Ruspia*, in the time of the Emperor *Anastasius*, Or (Isidor.Hispal.De Scriptor. Eccl.c.14.) whether it were an other deacō of *Carthage*, yet more ancient, which hath borne the name of *Fulgentius Ferrandus*, it appeares as well because hee speakes not, neither of the Canons of the Apostles, nor of the Epistles of the Popes later then *Syricius*: as because he makes mention of infinite Councells of *Africa*: as of the Councell of *Suffetula*: of the Councell of *Septimunica*, of the Councell of *Marazan*: of the Councell of *Tusdra*: of the Councell of *Macria*: of the Councell of *Tenis*: of the Councell of *Iuca*; & of many Councells of *Carthage* whereof there is found no track, neither in *Dionisius* nor in *Cresconius*. And that he hath surpassed them in the knowledg of the Councell of *Africa*, it is manifested aswell by the same citations, as by the testimonie that *Cresconius* giues of him in the Epistle to *Liberinus*, which containes these wordes; *I did remonstrate to you, that the Epitomy of the Canons had bene alreadie made by Ferandus most Reuerend* (Cresc.ep. ad Liber. in Præf. Collect. Can.)

Deacon

con of Carthage, and that it ought to suffice for our instruction, least vndertaking to make an other, it may seeme that we would steale from his wisdome. And therefore also those that haue collected the bodie of the Councell in forme, haue passed ouer the medley of the thirtie three canons, intitled by some; the sixth Councell of *Carthage*, in silence.

Of the African Councell.

CHAPT. VII.

NOW as for this medley and rapsody of the Councells of *Africa* that we call the *African* Councell, which is a century of *African* canons, gathered from diuers coũcells, there are therin two difficulties. The first difficultie concernes the author of the Rapsodie, & cõsists in this, to witt; whether this composition hath bene made by anie particular canonist; or whether it hath bene gathered in a Councell. The Greekes, & the Protestants who follow them, and some Catholickes as well ancient as moderne, belieue it to be made in a councell, which some suppose to haue bene the sixth Councell of *Carthage*, and others the seauenth, & I contrarywise incline to beleeue, that it hath bene made by some *African* canonist, and whilst the *Vandalls* possest *Africa*, in which tyme there could no nationall councell be assembled in *Africa*: And this I incline to beleeue for ten reasons amongst others: The first reason is, that the Epistle of the Councell of *Africa* to Pope *Celestine* is there inserted, which was made in a coũcell holden expressely, for the second processe of *Apiarius*, and after the last voyage of *Faustinus* into *Africa*, as appeares by these wordes; *Our holie Brother and fellow Bishop Faustinus, coming to vs, we haue assembled a Councell, and haue beleeued that the aime of his coming hath bene, that as by his procurement Apiarius had bene once before restored to the priesthood, so now by his labour, he might be purged from the accusations of the Tabracenians.* Now this Councell that we call the ninth was holden long after the sixth & seauenth which had bene celebrated vnder *Boniface*. And to saie that it was in this ninth that the Rapsodie of the Councells of *Africa* were made, it is a thing that cannot subsist, for the Fathers would not haue bene contented, to insert heereinto their Epistle only, but would haue added to it somewhat of the historie, and of the date of their Councell. The second reason is, that after the quotation of the Councell of *Hippo*, which is the first whose date is registred in this Rapsody follow these wordes: *The acts of this Councell are not heere described because the things that haue bene therein ordained, are aboue inserted which words cannot haue relation either to the rapsody of the councells of Africa, or to the sixth Councell of Carthage*; for the actes of the Councell of *Hippo*, which containe more then fortie canons, are inserted neither into the Rapsodie, which begins with the Councell of *Hippo*, and comprehends nothing that precedes it, nor in the thirtie three canons attributed to the sixth Councell of *Carthage*, but are the wordes of the Exemplifier or Rapsodist, which remitts the readers to finde the Canons of the Councell of *Hippo*, to the former collections of the Councells. The third reason is, that in the quotation of the Councell, holden the sixth of the calends of *Julie*, vnder the Consulship of *Cesarius*, and *Atticus*, there are these wordes, *Whosoeuer will search the acts of this councell, shall finde them in the authenticall copies*: A thing which shewes it is a particular collection, and not a Councell that speakes. The fourth reason is, that at the head of the sixtith one chapter, after these wordes, *Vnder the consulships of the noble cõsulls Stel: cõ for the secõd time, & Arthemius, the tenth of the calẽds of Septẽber at Carthage, in the Basilicke of the second region:* these followe, *I haue*

Cõc. Afric. cap. 105. in ep. ad Cælest.

Cõc. Afric. in not. ante. c 1.

Cõc. Afric. in notis. ante. cap. 1.

Concil. Afric. in not. ante. c 61.

not transcribed from the one end to the other, the acts of this coũcell, forasmuch as they more regarde matter of time, then anie generall ordinances, but for the instruction of the studious, I haue digested from them a briefe Summary. Frõ whẽce it appeares, that this collection was made by a particular compiler. For that the Greekes haue translated it in the third person, & in steed of these words. *for the instruction of the studious;* haue turned it, *of things studiouslie ordained;* that is to saie, in steede of σπουδάζων, haue supposed σπουδασμάτων, is a corruption too apparant. The fifth reason is, that in the thirteenth chapter of the latine Rapsody, which is the fourtie seauenth of the Greeke Rapsody, the Canon saith in either edition, *Likewise also, that it may be lawfull to reade the the passions of the Martyrs;* which hath noe relation to the words of the former Canon, which are; *that reconciliation shall not be refused to comedians:* but it is a traine that hath bene torne from his head, that the latine Rapsody hath omitted, and that the Greeke hath trãsferred from his place, to witt, from the Canon, that forbids other Scriptures then those that are canonicall to be read in Churches, as appeares both by the Councell of *Carthage* intire, where these two Canons are couched the one after the other, and by *Ferandus* his Breuiarie, where they are quoted as two canons, following one an other in these words; *That there shall be nothing read in the Churches, but the Canonicall Scriptures: the Councell of Laodicea. title fiftie sixt and the Councell of Carthage, title fourtie fifth. That it shall be lawfull also to read the Martyrs passions in the anniuersary daie of their Martyrdomes. Coũcell of Carthage, title fourtie sixt.* A thing that shewes that this collectiõ hath bene made by a particular Rapsodist, who inserting the third Councell of *Carthage* into his Rapsody, hath omitted the canõ of the canonicall Bookes; forasmuch as this canon was made in the Councell of *Hippo*, & was but repeated in the third Councell of *Carthage*, & had contented himselfe with inserting that, that the Councell of *Carthage* had added to it; to witt, the permission of reading also in the Church, the passiõs of the Martyrs. The sixth reason is, that of the fifth canon of the seauenth councell of *Carthage* (which ordaines, *That if a Bishop saith, that if anie one haue cõfessed* (that is to saie, with ciuill confession) *a crime to him alone, and that he after denie it, the Bishop shall not holde it for an iniurie, if creditt be not giuen to his only testimonie, and that if the Bishop, moued with the scruple of his owne conscience, saith that he will not communicate with him that so denies; as long as the Bishop shall not communicate with him, other Bishops shall not cõmunicate with the Bishop.*) The Rapsodist hath made two different canõs, to witt, the nintie ninth & hũdredth of his Rapsody; And to perfect the construction of the nintie ninth, which otherwise was without sence, hath added these words, that he shall notwithstãding, secretly interdict him the cõmunion, till he conforme himselfe: which are directly against the intẽtion of the Councell. See heere the words of the nintie ninth, *If a Bishop saith, that anie one hath cõfessed a crime to him alone and that he denie it, and will not do pẽnãce for it, the Bishop shall not hold it for a particular iniury, that credit is not giuen to him alone: and if moued with the scruple of his owne consciẽce, he saith that he will not cõmunicate with him that so denies, let him neuertelesse interdict him the cõmunion secretlie, till he conforme himself.* And behold heere the words of the hundredth: *Whiles a Bishop communicates not with his excommunicated Diocesan, lett not the other Bishops communicate with such a Bishop.* An error that the Fathers of the sixth or seauenth Councell of *Carthage* would neuer haue committed, if themselues had compiled this Rapsody, seeing it was themselues that had composed the whole Canon. And it is not to be said, that the later Exemplifiers perceiuing this fault, haue reunited the two Canons in one, and haue reported the canon compleate, as it is couched in the seauenth councell of *Carthage*. For the ancient latine Rapsodies, made two canons of it as it appea-

[Margin notes: Edit. Græc. Concil. Carth. ant. cap 94. vel secundum. alios 69. — Cõc. Afric. c. 13. & Edit. Græc. c. 47. — Concil. Afric. c. 12. & Edit. Græc. c. 46 — Cõc. Carth 3. cap. 46. & 47. — Fulg. Ferr. in Breuiar. art. 218. & 219. — Cõc. Carth 7. c. 5. — Cõc. Afric. in Edit. Ioan. Schoffer. c. 99. — Ibid. c. 100.]

res both by the copies of *Dionisius Exiguus* that the edition of *Schoffer* the *Almaigne* Printer hath followed, & by the Epitomy of *Cresconius* who cites them vnder two titles; the one of the nintie ninth canõ, & the other of the hũdredth; And by the words of the Greeke trãslatiõ, which distinguisheth and diuideth thẽ into two Canons. The seauenth reason is, that at the end of the same canon, follow these words; *Be it registred in the acts of the Church the treatie of all the title designed and digested this daie; and as for the things which haue not yet bene expressed, we will write thẽ the daie following by our bretheren Faustinus Bishop, and Phillip and Asellus priests, to our Reuerend brother and fellow Bishop Boniface.* Which wordes besides that they are couched after the canon of the rash excõmunications, which is the hũdredth of the Rapsodie, that is to saie, the fiftith & last of the seauenth Councell of *Carthage*, could not, if they be authenticall, be pronoũced anie other where then in the seauẽth Coũcell of *Carthage*, for they testifie that the Popes Legates, which were yet present in the seauẽth Councell of *Carthage*, departed the next daie after they had bene pronoũced. And neuerthelesse, not only they are not in the seauenth councell of *Carthage*, but also in some copies they are sett after the fortie, or according to others the thirtie three canõs, attributed seuerallie to the sixth Councell of *Carthage*, & after the prohibition to alienate ecclesiasticall Goods. The eigth reason is, that at the end of the signatures of the last coũcell of the Rapsody, which is the seauenth coũcell of *Carthage*, it is said, *And the other two hundred seauenteen Bishops Subscribed*: Which is a manifest ignorãce in the cõpiler, who remẽbred not, that in the seauenth Coũcell of *Carthage*, there were but twentie two Bishops; For to ease the two hũdred seauenteen Bishops which were at the sixth Coũcell of *Carthage*, they were sẽt backe a while after into their Prouinces; & only twẽtie two chosen in their places, to finish the rest of the affaires of the Coũcell. This appeares both by the signatures of the seauẽth Councell of *Carthage* where there did but twentie two Bishops signe, & by the inscription of the same seauẽth Councell of *Carthage* inserted into the Greeke & latine Rapsody in these words: *Manie of the Bishops cõplayning that they could not attend at the lẽgth of the other expeditiõs, & were prest to returne into their prouinces, it pleased all the Councell, that by the whole assemblie, there might be deputies chosen from euerie of the prouinces which should remaine to finish the rest.* Frõ whence it happened, that those assisted there whose signatures testifie thẽ to haue bene there present. A thing which manifestly shewes, that this clause; *And the two hundred seauenteen other Bishops signed likewise*; is of the compilers stile, & not of the acts of anie Councell. The ninth reason is, that if this Rapsody had bene cõpiled by the Fathers of the seauẽth Coũcell of *Carthage*, or anie other later; as the vse that is there made of the Canons at the seauẽth of *Carthage*, & other subsequent pieces do suppose, they would neuer haue forgottẽ to sett downe the extract of the sixt coũcell of *Carthage*, & the thirtie three Canõs which are attributed to it, if at least they be iustlie attributed to it. For with what colour should the extract of the Canõs of the seauenth Coũcell of *Carthage*, which were made by the deputies that remained of the sixth Councell of *Carthage* after the rest were dismissed, haue bene inserted into the Rapsody, & the Canõs of the sixth councell of *Carthage*, which had bene made by the whole councell, not haue bene inserted? And it will not serue to saie that the sixth Councell of *Carthage* is in an act a part: for so is the seauenth also which neuerthelesse is registred in the Rapsodie. Lesse will it auaile to saie that the Canons of the sixth Councell of *Carthage*, are inrolled in the Greeke Rapsody. For besides that the ancient & originall Rapsody is the latine and not the Greeke, as it appeares amongst other meanes by the quotations of *Cresconius*, which answere to the numbers of the latine, and

Crescon. in Breu. can. art. 288. Edit. Græc. Concil. Carth. cap. 132. 133. Concil. Afric. ad calcem. cap 100.

Concil. Afric. in subscript. c. 100.

Concil. Carth. 7. in Præf cap. 1 Et Conc. Afric. in Præfat. c. 95.

Crescon.in Breuiar. Can.

not of the Greeke; they are not inserted into the Bodie of the Greeke Rapsodie; that is to saie, into the order and chronologicall clew of the Rapsody, which begins at the Councell of *Hippo*, and ends at the Epistles of the Bishops of *Africa* to Pope *Celestine*: but in the extract and particular collection of the Canons of the sixth Councelll of *Carthage*, that the Greekes haue tacked & annexed tothe head of their Rapsody, which had not happened, if it had bene cōpiled in an actuall Councell, for as much as the Fathers of the Councell whould haue sett the extract & the Canons of the sixth Coūcell of *Carthage* in their true place, which is betweene the Councell holden vnder the twelfth consulship of *Theodosius*, & the seauenth Councell of *Carthage*, and not in a place anticipated. The tenth reason is, that if this Rapsody were a reading of diuers former Councells of *Africa*, which had bene made in a later Coūcell, there would haue bene in the same Councell some ordinance to reade them: as in the third Coūcell of *Carthage* reported by the rapsody, it was ordayned that the Canons of the Coūcell of *Hippo* should be read there; & in the first *Mileuitan* Coūcell incorporated into the same Rapsody, it was ordained that the Canōs composed in the Councell of *Hippo*, & after confirmed in the Councell of *Carthage* should be read there; A thing neuerthelesse, whereof there is no tracke to be foūd. And this may be said of the reasons which inuite me to beleeue that the *Africā* Rapsody hath bene compiled by some particular canonist; it remaines to examine the proofes of the contrary opinion.

Cōc. Afric. in Præfat. c. 1. Cōc. Afric. in Præfat. cap. 53.

The foundatiō thē of those that thinke that the *African* Rapsodie hath bene collected in an actuall Councell, is, that at the head of the century, it is said, *In this Councell were also recited diuers Councells of the prouinces of Africa, holden in the times past of Aurelius*. Which clause some pretend to be relatiue to the sixth and others to the seauenth Councell of *Carthage*: but this foundation it selfe, hath neede of a foundation; for first it is not certaine, whether this clause bee of the originall text of the Rapsodie, or whether it be a note of some exemplifier, who thought that the *African* century, that is to saie, the Rapsody of the hūdred *African* Canōs, that wee call the *African* Councell, had bene made in the sixth Councell of *Carthage*. contrarywise that at the head of the collection intituled by some, the sixth Councell of *Carthage* precedes such a like clause, in these wordes, *Then were read the Canons of the Coūcell of Nicea, as they haue aboue bene inserted; After also were registred in the presēt Acts, the things that had bene published in the African Councells*; intimates that these two clauses are of the Exēplifiers stile; for besides that this remitment, *as they haue bene aboue registred* which is in the latine addition of the first clause, sheweth that it is neitheir the sixth Councell of *Carthage*, nor the clerke of the sixth Coūcell of *Carthage*; that speakes; but the exemplifiers of the volumes of the Councells, who to saue the paines of writing out the Canōs of the Coūcells of *Nicea*, which were produced in the sixth coūcell of *Carthage*, sendes the Reader to the place, where they had bene first transcribed in their forme & in their order; to what purpose was it, after it was said at the head of the collection, intituled the sixth councell of *Carthage*; there were also recited sundrie canons of *Africa*, that is to saie, at the head of the Rapsody of the hundred canons. *In this councell were likewise recited, diuers councells of Africa, holden in the tymes past of Aurelius?* Secondly yf this second clause, were of the originall text of the Rapsodie, that is nothing to oblige the reader to referr it to the sixth councell of *Carthage*; contrarywise that the clause saith; *In this Councell were likewise recited diuers Councells of Africa, holden in the times past*, or according to the Greeke, *in the times before Aurelius*: Giues to vnderstand, that the two correlatiue termes of the clause, are not the one, the sixth Coūcell of *Carthage*, and the other the Bodie of

In Clausul. ant. Concil Afric.

In Concil. dicto. sexto Carth. ex Edit. Ioan Schoffer. inter finem Conc. Nicen. & 1 caput Conc. Carthag. 6.

In Edit. Græc. Cōcil. Carth.

the Coūcells inserted into the Rapsodie;but the one, the third coūcell of *Carthage*,& the other,the coūcells holden vnder *Aurelius* before the third councell of *Carthage*.For in the whole body of the rapsody,there are manie things which haue bene made,not in the tymes of *Aurelius* which had preceded the sixth councell of *Carthage*,but in the last tymes of *Aurelius*, and after the sixth councell of *Carthage*. And therefore also *Zonara* the Greeke canonist,not onely omitts this secōd clause,but also depriues the reader of meanes to referr it,either to the sixth or seauēth coūcell of *Carthage*.For he will haue it(although ignorantly & against the custome lōg obserued amongst the *Africans*,to celebrate euery yeare a nationall coūcell in *Africa*;)that the six councells of *Africa*,whereof according to him, the *African* Rapsody is compounded, & which containes the interim of more then twelf yeare, haue bene as manie Sessions of one and the same councell of *Africa*, seperated & reassembled in seauerall tymes,and that in these six Sessions,the Rapsody of the *African* Canons hath bene compiled. A thing which cannot agree,neither with the sixth or seauēth coūcell of *Carthage*;which were both celebrated as shall heereafter appeare, in one same yeare,& in one same moneth But it may be said, wherefore should the clause of the century haue reference to the third Councell of *Carthage*?For two causes;the one,because the third coūcell of *Carthage* is the first whose canons are inserted into the century of the *African* Canōs: for although there be diuers Councells quoted in the *African* Rapsody, neuerthelesse there are but fiue Councells that are inserted there with their canons,whereof the first is the third Conncell of *Carthage*.And the other,because the Rapsodist hath not incorporated in his Rapsodie all the Canons that were published in the third Councell of *Carthage*, but of fiftie chapters that were couched there hath only registred twentie three in his century,and that in part to make vp the nūber of the century;& in parte, because all the canons that were imployed in the third Coūcell of *Carthage* were not all first instituted there,but that manie of thē had bene framed in the Councell of *Hippo*,& had bene but renewed or accōpanied with some moderations in the third Coūcell of *Carthage*. For this cause then the compiler taking from the third Councell of *Carthage* and from what was thereto annexed,which was the answere to the instāces of *Musonius*,but the Canōs that had added either some decision,or some kindes of moderation to the Canons of the Councell of *Hippo*; and willing neuerthelesse to hinder the readers from beleeuing, that these were all the canons that had bene publisht in the third councell of *Carthage*, hath set before his Rapsodie, whereof the third councell of *Carthage* makes the first part, *In this Councell were also read diuers Councells of Africa holden in the tyme befores Aurelius*: and of those hath quoted particulaly three to wit that of *Hippo*, holden vnder the consulship of *Theodosius* and *Abundantius*,the yeare 391.that of *Carthage* holden vnder the consulship of *Arcadius* and *Honorius*,the yeare 394 And that of *Carthage* holden vnder the consulship of *Cesarius* and *Atticus*,the yeare three hundred nintie seauen the sixth of the callends of *Julie*; for that the councell of *Carthage* holden vnder the consulship of *Atticus* and *Cesarius* the sixth of the calends of *Iulie*, is quoted in the latine Rapsodie after the third Councell of *Carthage*, which was celebrated the same yeare, the fifth of the calends of *September*; it is a manifest error in those that copied it, as it appeares first by the order of the dates;the one of the fifth of the calends of *September*; and the other of the sixth of the calends of *July*. And secondlie: by the note that in that of the sixth of the calends of *July*, the Canon was decreed, *That Bishops should not saile beyond Sea*; *without letters*

Zonar.in Comm. Can.Conc. Carth.in Præfat Act 2.pag.422

Concil. Afric.in not.ante Can.I.

C6c.Carthag.3 c. 28

formed from their Primates; which Canon is repeated in the third Coũcell of *Carthage* compleate. And thirdly becauſe betweene the preface of the Councell holden vnder *Atticus* and *Ceſarius* the fifth of the calendes of *September*, in which *Aurelius* propounds, to cauſe the abridgement of the Councell of *Hippo* to be read, and the firſt Canon of the centurie; where *Epigonius* ſaith in that abridgment that is drawne from the Councell of *Hippo*; *it Seemes there ought nothing to be changed but that the ſignification of the daie of Paſch should bee made in the tyme of the Councell,* there could be nothing interpoſed. A like error haue they committed, when at the traine of the ſame Councell, holden vnder *Atticus* and *Ceſarius* the ſixth of the calends of *Iulie*, they haue alſo interpoſed betweene the preface of the third Councell of *Carthage* and the firſt canon of the third Councell of *Carthage*, the quotation of the Councell celebrated after the Conſulship of *Honorius* and *Eutychianus*, and that of the Councell celebrated after the conſulship of *Stelicon* with the preface; A thing that not only reuerſeth the order of the dates; for theſe two laſt Councells were holdẽ, the one, two yeare, and the other four yeare after the third Councell of *Carthage*, but alſo maimes the ſence of the thirtie fourth Canõ of the centuarie, which can haue no perfect conſtruction, if the date and the preface of the Councell after the conſulship of *Stelicon*, to which this canon is a relatiue, be not placed after the report of the ſignatures of the third Coũcell of *Carthage*; that is to ſay, betweene the three & thirtith canon of the latine Rapſody, & the thirtie fourth. And therefore the Greekes haue taken awaie theſe three quotations from the place where they are ſett in the latine Rapſody, and haue ſett them in the Greeke Rapſody after the canons and ſignatures of the third Councell of *Carthage*, as pertinentlie for the two laſt quotations, as impertinently for the firſt, which should precede the Regiſter of the third Coũcell of *Carthage*. But this is enough for the queſtion of the compiling, which neuertheleſſe I remitt to the Iudgement of the readers. For I know well that *Creſconius* an *African* canoniſt of neere a thouſand yeares antiquitie, hath cited the canons of a Councell, that he intitles the generall Councell of *Carthage*, with numbers anſwering to the numbers of this collection, which we call the *African* Councell. It is true that he might either be abuſed about the clauſe whereof wee haue ſpoken aboue; or elſe that he might call this collection the generall Councell of *Carthage*, for as much as it is a collection of many ſeuerall Councells of *Carthage*; as *Gratian* and the other canoniſts alleadge the collection of the Greeke Synods, made by *Martin* the ancient Bishop of *Brague* or *Bracara* in *Spaine*, vnder the ſingular title of a Councell, and intitles it the Councell of Pope *Martin*. Well know I alſo, that the *Africans* in their Epiſtle to Pope *Boniface*, ſent him the copie of ſome Canons either made or confirmed by their Councell, but there is no impediment, why this ſending may not be intended of the canons of the ſeauenth Councell of *Carthage*, which had bene holden in the preſence of the legates of the ſaid Pope *Boniface*, the day before the date of this Epiſtle. And therefore without peruerting the iudgment of the Readers, I haue contented my ſelfe with touching the cauſes of the firſt difference. Let vs goe on to the ſecond.

Edit.Græc. Concil Carth. poſt c.

Creſcon. in Breuiar. Canõ. artic

Diſt.24 c. ſi quis Preſb.& alibi.

The ſecõd difficultie hath regarde to the number of the canons of this Rapſodie, & conſiſts in this, that the latine editiõ cõtaines but an hũdred canons, which with the Epiſtles and the act ſent from the *Eaſt*, make an hũdred fiue chapters; & that of the Greekes containes an hundred thirtie three beſides the Epiſtles. And the reaſon of this difference proceedes frõ this, that the originall Rapſody not comprehending all the canons of the

Councell

Councell of *Carthage*, but being restrained to the number of an hundred, and the Greekes not hauing the copies of those other Councells of *Carthage* in cheefe, that wee haue, it seemed necessarie to them to add to this century an other collection of thirtie three Canons which goes vnder the title of the Canons of the sixth Councell of *Carthage*, but which is taken from diuers former Councells, and to sett it at the head of their Rapsodie. For that the originall rapsody containes but an hundred Canons, and was conformable to the number and to the cyphers of the latine, and not of the Greeke, it appeares by the citations that *Cresconius* an ancient *African* Canonist makes of this medley, that we call the *African* Councell, wherein the numbers and titles of the Canons, answere the order of the latine Rapsody. Crescon. in Breu. Can.

Whether the latin edition of the African Canons, be more faithfull, then the Greeke Rapsody.

( )

CHAP. VIII.

The Aduersaries of the Church will haue it, that the relation of the *Greeke* rapsody is more faithfull, then that of the latine Rapsody. And wee cötrarywise maintaine, that the Relatiö of the *latine* rapsody is much more sure, sauing some faultes in the Exëplifiers, thë that of the *Greeke.* & that for three causes; the first because the Councells of *Africa*, haue bene made in latine and not in *Greeke*, by meanes whereof reason wills, that the *latine* Rapsody which hath bene taken out of the originall it selfe, except the Epistles whereof it seemes as it shall appeare heereafter, that the *latine* hath bene translated from the *Greeke* translation, and that the old *latine* originall hath bene lost, must be more certaine then the *Greeke* Rapsody, which had bene made but vpon the extracts of the translation. The second because the *Greekes* haue bene much more ignorant in the matter of Councells of *Africa*, then the *latins*; as it appeares by the erroneous Councell holden vnder saint CYPRIAN, that the *Greekes* haue sett into the ranke of the orthodox Councells of *Africa*. And the third because that in the places, where the readings of the *Greeke* and *Latine* Rapsody differ, the readings of the *latine* Rapsody agree with the Councells of *Africa* in cheefe, which wee haue in our hands, and with the custome of the ancient *African* Church, reported by saint AVGVSTINE, by *Fulgentius Ferrandus*, and other *African* Doctors; And the readings of the *Greeke* Rapsody are repugnant thereunto. I will content myselfe to alleadge two examples besides that, which wee haue already tendred of the adition of the Bishops to the canon of the appeales. Edit. Græc Cöc. Carth c. 71 vel secundum alios 73. Phot. Nomocan. Tit 9. c. 29. Cedr. in hist. Cöcill Nicen.

The first example shall be taken from the seauentith one Canon of the *Greeke* Rapsody where the *African* Fathers hauing said: *It hath pleased that the Bishops, priests, and Deacons, according to the former determinations, shall abstaine from their owne wiues.* The *Greekes* that doe indeede forbid Priests to marry after their promotion, yea call such marriages impious and detestable; but if before their promotion they haue bene married, prouided it were but once, and besides that they be simple Priests and not Bishops; doe permitt them the continuance of the wiues that they

haue

Balsam.in Cóc Carth c.73.

haue married before their priesthood; haue aduised themselues to abuse the ambiguitie of their tongue, which maketh vse of one same word, to expresse (*determination*) and to expresse (*terme*) and haue conuerted these words, *according to the former determinations*, or, *according to their owne determinations*, into these wordes, *according to their proper termes*. And to the end to delude the sense of the canon, haue made weekely priests, who serue by turnes and alternatiue weekes, and obserue the *Celibat*, during the weekes of their Seruices, and intermit it during the rest. Now how false this interpretation is, and how contrarie to the intention of the *African* fathers who neuer knew these weekely priests, nor these alternatiue *Celibats*, it appeares first by all the Councell of the ancient *Latine* Church, holden in the Regions neere *Africa*, which oblige Bishops, Priests and deacons, without distinction of turnes and vicissitudes, to a perpetuall *Celibat*. *It hath pleased* (saith the *Elibertine* Councell celebrated in the prouince of *Grenado* in *Spaine* neere an hundred yeares before the sixth Councell of *Carthage*) *to ordaine Bishops, Priests, Deacons, and Subdeacons, establisht in the Ministrie, to abstaine wholie from their wiues, and to begett no children.* And the first Councell of *Toledo*, celebrated in *Spaine*, in the tyme of the fifth Councell of *Carthage*, from whence this canon is taken, *If anie Deacons haue liued incontinentlie with their wiues, lett them not be honored with the degree of Priesthood.* And the second Councell of *Arles*, celebrated a little after the sixth of *Carthage*: *None constituted in the bond of Marriage, can be admitted to Priesthood, without promise of Conuersion.* Secondly it appeares by all the Councells of the *African* Church which concerne the same matter: *It hath pleased* (saith the second Councell of *Carthage*) *that Bishops, Priests, Deacons, &c. practice intire continence &c. to the end that what the Apostles haue taught* (or according to the *Greeke* edition, *giuen by tradition*) *and antiquitie it selfe obserued, we also should obserue.* And againe: *It hath pleased that Bishops, Priests, and Deacons, or others that handle the Sacraments, should liue chastlie and abstaine euen from their owne wiues.* And the fifth Councell of *Carthage*: *It hath pleased that Priests, and Deacons, according to their owne Statutes* (or as the best copies haue it, *according to the former Statutes*) *should abstaine from their owne wiues.* It appeares thirdly by the testimonie of all the doctors of the *Latine* church, and especiallie the *African*, who haue liued in the tyme of those Councells; *That the Ministrie* (saith Saint AMBROSE) *must be preserued inuiolate and immaculate, without defiling it with anie coniugall embraces, you know it you that with integritie of bodie, and incorruption of modestie, abstayning your selues euen from the vse of Marriage, haue receiued the grace of the sacred Deaconship*, And saint *Hierom*; *Bishops, Priests, and Deacons, are chosen either virgins, or in widowhood, or at least are after their Priesthood, eternallie chast.* And saint AUGUSTINE; The soule and penn of the Councells of *Africa*: *Wee haue*, (said he) *accustomed to propound to lay men, that haue put awaie their wiues, the continence of Clergie men, who are often taken by force, and against their wills, to vndergoe that charge; and hauing accepted it, beare it with gods helpe lawfullie, euen to the end. Wee saie to them, what would become of you, if you were constrained and forced by the violence of the people, to vndergoe this charge? would you not chastlie preserue the office wherewith you were charged, instantlie conuerting your selues to beseeche of God such strength, as before your neuer thought of?* Wherto I might yet add the ancient *Greeke* doctors, as *Eusebius*, who writes; *Now the heraldes of the diuine word, doe necessarilie imbrace abstinence from Marriages, to attend to a better imployment practizing a generation of spirituall and incorporall children.* Or as saint EPIPHANIUS, that cryes out; *The holie Church of God receiues not him, that hath bene but once married, and conuerseth still with his wife, and begetts children, for Deacon,*

Cócil. Elibert.c.33.

Conc. Tolet 1. can. 1

Concil. Arelat.2.c.

Cóc Carth 2 c.2. Edit. Græc. Concil Carth.c 3. Ibid. Cóc.Carth 5.c.3.

Ambros. de offic.l.1. cap.vlt.

Hier.ad Pam.pro libr.adu Iouin l.1. Aug.de adulter. Coniug.l.2 c.vlt.

Eusеb.de demost. Euang.l. 1. cap 9. Epiphan. contr. noua hæres. 59.

Priest,

Priest, and Bishop. But because heere the question is of the custome of the *latine* Church; and particularlie of the *African*, & not of the *greeke* Church; I sett the *greeke* testimonies aside. It appeares fourthly by *Fulgentius Ferandus* an *African* Canonist, of aboue *1100.* yeares antiquitie, who in his epitomy of the Canons, registers the Canon of the Councell of *Carthage*, in these words; *That Bishops Priests, and Deacons should abstaine from their Wiues.* And by *Cresconius* an *African* Canonist likewise, & of neere a thousand yeares antiquitie, who registers it in these wordes, *That the priestlie and leuiticall order ought to haue no cohabitation with woemen.* It appeares fiftly by the proper text of the Canon, which plainely comprehends Bishops, which neuerthelesse the *Greekes* exclude from all coniugall acts, and to whom this condition of seruing by turnes and alternatiue weekes cannot agree. It appeares besides this, by the sixth Canō of the same Coūcell of *Carthage*, which saith; *That readers when they are come to the yeares of manhood, shall be constrained either to marrie, or professe chastitie.* A thing which necessarily shewes, that the vse of Marriage, was wholie prohibited to Bishops Priests, and deacons. And finallie, it appeares by *Andrew Gesnerus* minister of *Zurich*, and the *German Centuriators* being ashamed of this falshood; for *Gesnerus* interpreting the *Greeke* translation of the Councell of *Carthage*, hath turned it into these words; *It hath pleased, that Bishops, Priests, and Deacons, according to their statutes, should abstaine euen from their wiues:* And the *Centuriators* of *Germanie* epitomizing the same Councell of *Carthage*, reporte it in these wordes; *That the Sacerdotall and and Diaconall order, should abstaine from their wiues.* But forasmuch as this matter was treated of more largely in the appendix of the conference of *Fontainebleau* where wee confuted the fable of *Paphnucius* reported by *Socrates* and *Sozomene Nouatian* Authors, from whom the later *Greekes* haue borrowed the occasion of their fall, and expounded the Canon of the Councells of *Gangres* which seemes to fauour them: It shall suffice me for an end of this aduertisment, to remitt the readers thereunto.

> Fulg. Ferr. in Breu. Can. art. 16 Crescon in Breu. Canon art. 109. Edit. Grec. Concil. Carth. cap. 7. Concil. in Trull. c. 12 Cedre. in hist. Cōcil. Nicen. Cōcil. dict. Carth. 6. c. 16.

> Cōc. Carth ex edit. Græcolatin Andr. Gesn. c. 71. Cētur. Mag. cent. 5. col. 829

The second Example of infidelitie, shalbe taken out of the twentie fourth Canon of the *Greeke* Rapsody, which is the twentie fourth of those thirtie three *latine* Canons, whereof the collection is intituled the sixth Councell of *Carthage*, where the *Greeke* interpretor hath ecclipsed from the Catalogue of the Canonicall Bookes receiued in *Africa*, the two Bookes of the *Machabes*. Now that this subtraction is a notable falshood, appeares by six vnreprochable meanes. It appeares first by all the *latine* copies, as well printed as manuscripts of the collection intituled the sixth Councell of *Carthage*, in which the two Bookes of the *Machabes* are expressed by name. It appeares secondly by the fortie seauenth Canon of the third Councell of *Carthage*, from whence the canon of the collection intituled the sixth Councell of *Carthage* hath bene extracted, which mentions particularly the two Bookes of the *Machabes*. It appeares thirdly by the Canon of the Canonicall Bookes, inserted into saint AVGVSTINS second Booke of *Christian Doctrine*, where the two Bookes of the *Machabes* are expresly contained; and to which saint AVGVSTINE, for an impediment that the number should not be varied by anie addition, or Subtraction, setts to this seale, *In these fortie foure Bookes the authority of the old Testament is determined:* And againe repeates the same seale in the Register of his retractions in these words: *In the place haue* (said hee) *of the second booke of Christian Doctrine, where I haue written, in these fortie foure bookes, the authoritie of the olde Testament is determined; I made vse of the word olde Testament, according to the forme of speech, which the Church practiseth at this daie; but the Apostle seemes to call none the old Testament but*

> Manuscr. D. Præsid. de Champign. & alij innumeri.

> Aug. de Doctri. Christ. l. 2. c. 8.

> Aug. tract. l. 2. c. 4.

that

that which was giuen in the Mount Sinai. It appeares fourthly by the other writings, where saint AVGVSTINE speakes of the *Machabees,* as when he saith in the eighteenth Booke *of the cittie of God; Amongst the volumes seuered from this ranke, are the bookes of the Machabees, which not the Iewes but the Church, hold for Canonicall.* And in the second booke against the Epistle of *Gaudentius* the Donatist, *The scripture intituled from the Machabes, the Iewes doe not hold, as the lawe, the Prophetts, and the Psalmes, which our Lord alleadgeth for his testimonie, &c. But it hath bene receiued by the Church, not vnprofitable, if it be read or heard soberlie.* In which passage that saint AVGVSTINE saith, that the *Iewes* hold not the Scripture of the *Machabees* in the same ranke, as the *Lawe*, the *Psalmes*, and the *Prophets*, is not to weaken the authoritie of the Scripture of the *Machabees*; for the *Iewes* doe no more hold the booke of *Wisdome* in the same degree of the *Lawe*, the *Psalmes*, and the *Prophets*; and our Lord hath noe more alleadged it amongst the Testimonies, then that of the *Machabees*. And neuerthelesse S. AVGVSTINE saith; *The booke of WISDOME hath merited after so long a continuance of yeares, to be read in the Church of Christ, by the Readers of the Church of Christ, and to be heard by all Christians, euen from the Bishops to the lowest laymen, faithfull penitents, and catechumens, with the reuerence of diuine authoritie.* And againe; *All the Doctors neere the tyme of the Apostles, making vse of the testimonie of the Bookes of WISDOME, haue beleeued that they made vse of none, but a diuine Testimonie*; but the reason why saint AVGVSTINE said, that the *Iewes* held not the Scripure of the *Machabees,* in the ranke of the *lawe* the *Prophetts* and the *Psalmes*, was to shew the *Donatists* who were seperated from the Church, and yet made vse of her owne weapons to oppose her, that this Scripture hauing bene receiued into the Canon, not by the *Iewes* but by the Church, they could not imploy it against the sence and Doctrine of the Church. And that he adds, *that it was receiued by the Church, not vnprofitablie. prouided it be read soberly*; it is not to the end to diminishe the credit which ought to be giuen to it, but to represse the furious consequences that the *Donatists* inferred vpon it, and signifies no other thing, but, *prouided it be read with setled sences, aud not with madnesse and frensie*, as the *Donatists* read it, who tooke occasion from the example of *Sampson* in the history of the *Iudges*, and from the example of *Razias* in the historie of the *Machabees,* whose zeale and not his act is commended, to kill and precipitate themselues, which he confirmes a while after in these words; *Wee ought not then to approue by our consent, all things which wee reade in the Scriptures to haue bene done by men euen adorned with prayses by Gods owne testimonie, but to mingle our consideration with discretion, bringing with vs iudgment not of our authoritie, but of the authoritie, of the holie and diuine Scriptures, which permitt not vs to praise or imitate all the actions euen of those, of whom the Scripture giues good and glorious testimonie, if they haue done anie thing that hath not bene well done, or that agreeth not with the custome of the present time.* It appeares fifthly by the Catalogue of the Canonicall bookes, that Pope *Innocēt* the first, tyme-fellowe with S. AVSTINE, sēt to *Exuperius* Bishop of *Tholosa*, where the two Bookes of the *Machabees* are expressely contained. For whereas Pope *Gelasius* in renewing the decree of the Canonicall bookes, makes vse of the history of the *Machabees*, but for one only booke, it is because he speakes according to the Stile of S, AMBROSE, who reckons the first and second of the *Machabees*, for one and the same Booke. And whereas saint GREGORIE the great, in his commentary vpon *Iob*, compounded neere two hundred yeares after the Canon of the *African* Fathers, cyting the Bookes of the *Machabees*, adds *although not canonicall, yet written for the edification of the Church*; that is because

De Ciuit. l.18.c.36.

Cont. Secundum Gaudent. Epist.l.2. c.23.

Aug. de præd. Sāct. l.1.c.14.

Ibid.

Cont. 2. Gaudent. Epist.l.2.c. 23.

Ibid.

Innoc.1. ad Exup. ep.3, Gelas.in Decret.lib. veter.testam. Ambros.de offic.l.3.c. 14. Greg.in Iob.c.17.

the first draught of this comentary was made in the East. For saint *Gregorie* was not yet Pope, when he first composed the comentarie vpon *Iob*, but a simple deacon, exercising the office of *Nuntio* at *Constantinople* amongst the Greekes. For this occasion then speaking in the East, of the Bookes of the *Machabees*; he added in the forme of a case put, and not granted; *If not canonicall, yet written for the edification of the Church*; that is to saie, the which if they were not canonicall, neuertheles had bene writtē for the edification of the Church. It appeares finally, by the very continuance of the *African* canon, inserted into the *Greeke* Rapsody, which is, *Wee haue learnt from our Fathers, that those are the bookes that ought to bee read in the Church*. For not only all the ancient *African* Church, but also all the ancient *Westerne* Church, had holden from age to age, the Bookes of the *Machabees* to be canonicall, as it appeares, in regard of the ancient *African* church, by the testimonie of saint *Cyprian*, who calls the *Machabees*, duinie scriptures: and in regard of the other partes of the westerne church, by the testimonie of saint *AMBROSE*, who cryes out; *Moyses saith as it is written in the bookes of the Machabees*; And by that of the great defender of the Catholick Faith *Lucifer* Bishop of *Sardinia*, who writt to the emperor *Constantius*; *The holie scripture speakes in the first booke of the Machabees*: And by an infinite number of others, whose names I will not stand particularly to report. Only I will saie in generall that there was neuer anie latine Author which tooke liberty to remoue the authoritie of the Booke of the *Machabees* before saint HIEROME, and *Ruffinus* after him, while he was his disciple. Whereupon, there are three obseruations to be made. The first obseruation is, that as saint HIEROME, before the perfect maturitie of is studies, for afterward he changed his opinion, ecclipsed from the canon of the old testament, the historie of the *Machabees*, so did he also shake in the canon of the new testament, the epistle to the *Hebrewes*. *The latine custome*, saith hee *receiues not the Epistle to the Hebrewes, amongst the canonicall scriptures*. And againe; *If anie one will receiue the Epistle, which vnder Paules name hath bene written to the Hebrewes*. And elselwhere; *Paule in his Epistle which is written, to the Hebrewes, though manie of the latines doubt of it*. By which meanes if the authoritie of saint HIEROME not yet fullie instructed in the sence of the Church, be auaileable for the exclusion of one of these pieces; it is also auaileable for the disabling of the other. The second obseruation is, that saint HIEROME was induced to remoue this stone, by the commerce that he had with the *Iewes* of *Palestina*, amongst whom hee inhabited, and from whom he learnt the *Hebrew* letters. For *Isidore* Bishop of *Seuilla*, who writt a thousand yeares agoe, reportes; that the *Iewes* in hate of our Lord, reiected and abhorred the Booke of *Wisedome*: *The Hebrewes* (said *Isidore*, as some of the sages haue noted it) *receiued the Booke of Wisdome amongst the canonicall Scriptures; but after they had taken Christ, and putt him to death remembring that there were in the same Booke so manie euident testimonies of Christ, &c. they made a conspiracie together, and least ours should conuince them of so manifest a Sacriledge, they cutt it off frō the propheticall volumes, and prohibited theirs from reading it*. Now the *Iewes* could haue no faire colour to cutt of the Booke of *Wisdome*, from the rolle of the Canonicall Bookes, but because it was not in the Canon of *Esdras*, a thing which likewise obliged them, to cutt of all the other Posthume bookes from the old testament; so call I all the bookes of the olde Testament, which had bene writtē or published since the canon of *Esdras*; and after the death of *Esdras*, as *Ecclesiasticus*, the Booke of *Tobias*, the Booke of *Iudith*, and the two Bookes of *Machabees*. For these causes then, saint HIEROME tying himselfe to the catalogue

Edit. Græc Cōc. Carth c. 24.

Cypr. ep. 55

Ambros. de offic. l. 13. c. 14.

Lucif. lib. de non parcend. in Deum. delinq.

Hier. in Esai c. 8. In Ezech. c. 28 in ep. ad Eph. c. 3. & alibi. Hierom. in Math. in c. 26.

Isidor. de Eccles. offic. l. 1. c. 13.

of the Iewes, vpon whose text, and with whose helpe, and particularly of a certaine Rabbin called *Barabanus* or *Barhanina* whom *Ruffinus* by way of reproch calls *Barrabas*; he had made the translation of his Bible, not only excludes in his prologue vpon the booke of Kings, that he intitles the *armed prologue*, and in his prologue vpon the *Prouerbs*; all the whole bookes which were not in the canon of *Esdras*; as were *Wisedome, Ecclesiasticus*, *Tobias, Iudith*, and the *Machabees*: but also in his prologue vpon *Daniell* reiects all the partes of the canonicall Bookes, not comprehended in the text of the *Hebrewes*, as were the *Canticle* of the three Children, and the historie of *Susanna*, and that of *Bel*. *The Booke of Daniell*, saith he, *amongst the Hebrewes, containes neiter the history of Susanna, nor the Himne of the three Children nor the fables of the Dragon of Bel; which neuerthelesse, because they are spread ouer all the world, we haue annexed thereto*; but after hauing marked them with an obeliske, which precedes them, and cutts their throate. From whence it is that *Ruffinus* being growne his enemie reprocheth him thus; *All those then that supposed Susanna had furnished all married and vnmarried women with an example of Chastitie, haue erred, it is not true; all those that conceaued that Daniel yet a child had bene fulfilled with the Spirit of God, and had confuted the adulterous Elders, haue erred, it is not true. And the whole Church throughout the extent of the world, as well as those that are still vpon the Earth, as of those that are before our Lord, be they holy confessors, be they holy Martyrs, who haue sung in the Church of our Lord the Hymne of the thre Children, haue all erred and sunge false things. Now then after foure hundred yeares, doth the truth of the Lawe bought with Siluer* (Soe he saith, because saint HIEROM had giuen money to the Iewes, to be helped by them in the edition of this Bible) *come to vs from the Synagogue*? And the third obseruation finally is, that saint HIEROME being afterward more exactly instructed in the truth of the sence of the Church, changed his opinion, and retracted both in generall and particular, all that he had written in these three prologues. For in his Apologie against *Ruffinus*, answering to his reproach about the historie of *Susanna*, and of the *Dragon* of *Bel*, and of the canticle of the three Children, he saith; *Whereas I haue reported what the Hebrewes vsed to obiect against the historie of Susanna, and the Hymne of the three Children, and the fables of the Dragon of Bell, which are not in the Hebrew volume, &c. I haue not explicated what I thought, but what the Iewes were accustomed to saie against vs*. And in his preface vpon the booke of *Tobias*; *The Hebrewes* (saith hee) *cutt of the booke of Toby from the Catalogue of the diuine Scriptures*. And againe; *The iealousie of the Hebrewes doth accuse vs, and imputes it to vs, that against their Canon we transferr the booke of Toby into the latine eares: but I iudge that it is better to displease the iudgement of the Pharises, and to obay the commaundements of the Bishops*. And in the exposition vpon the fortie fourth Psalme: *Ruth, Hester, and Iudith, haue bene so glorious, as they haue giuen their names into the sacred volumes*. And in his preface vpon the historie of *Iudith*: *The booke of Iudith* (said hee) *is read by the Hebrewes amongst the* Hagiographs, *whose authoritie is esteemed lesse sufficient to decide contentious things, &c. but for as much, as the Councell of Nicea is read to haue reckoned it amongst the holy Scriptures, I haue obeyed your demaund*. Words which plainly retract what he had said in his Prologue vpon the *Prouerbs*: *As then the Church reads Iudith and Toby and the Machabees, but receaues them not amongst the canonicall Bookes: so may she reade Wisedome, and Ecclesiasticus for the edification of the people, but not for the confirmation of Ecclesiasticall Doctrines*: And which cannot be auoided, by answering that the word (*holy Scriptures*) doth not there signifie Canonicall: for the opposition that he makes of the Councell of *Nicea* to the Iewes,

Hier. ad Pam. & Ocean. ep. 65. Hier. in Prol. Galeat ep. 105 Hier. Præf. in Prouerb ep. 115.

Hier. Præf. in Daniel. ep. 120.

Ruff. in Hier. Inuect. 2.

Hier. ad Pam. & Ocean. ep. 65. & Præf. in Iob. ep. 113.

Hier. aduers. Ruff. apol. 2.

Hier. Præf. in Tob. ep. 100. Ibidem.

Hier. in exposit. Psal. ad Princip. ep. 140. Hier. præfat. in Iudith. ep. 111

Hier. Præfat. in Prou. ep. 115.

which esteemed the Booke of *Iudith* amongst the *Hagiograph* bookes; *whose authoritie is reputed lesse sufficient to diuide contentious things*, stopps the mouth of that delusion. And finallie in his commentarie vpon the Prophet *Esay* compounded long after the prologue armed, he setts the historie of the *Machabees* amōgst the canonicall Bookes, *The Scripture* (saith he) *reportes, that Alexāder king of the Macedonians came out from the land of Cethim.* Which some *Latins* that followed being ignorant of, it befell that they were seperated from the common voyce of the *westerne* Church. For although the greater part of the later *Latine* Doctors, as *Alcimus*, *Bellator*, *Cassiodorus*, *Isidorus*, haue followed the catalogue of S. AVS. & of the third Councell of *Carthage*, and sett the historie of the *Machabees* amongst the canonicall Bookes; yea that some of them, as *Bellator*, who liued in the tyme of the Emperor *Iustinian* the first, haue illustrated it with cōmentaries; neuerthelesse, some others not knowing that S. HIEROME had chāged his opinion, haue tyed themselues to that of S. HIEROME: But in summe, whatsoeuer the later *Latine* doctors haue done, it is certaine, that in the *Latine* Church, neuer anie before S. HIEROME, had remoued the authoritie of the six posthume bookes of the old Testamēt. For whereas S. HILARIE in his commentary vpon the Psalmes cōposed, or rather as S. HIEROME saith, translated by him out of *Origene*, whilst he was in the East, writes that the nūber of the canonicall bookes of the old Testamēt, is reduced according to the tradition of the Elders, either to the number of the twētie two letters of the *Hebrew* alphabet, or by the additiō of the Bookes of *Iudith* & of *Tobias*, to the nūber of twentie foure letters of the *Greeke* Alphabet; besides that these markes are not the notes of S. HILARY, but the notes of *Origene* in his cōmentary vpō the first psalme, that S. HILARY hath transcribed in part into his prologue vpon the psalmes. Hee meanes by the traditiō of the Elders, not the traditiō of the Church, but the traditions of the Iewes; whereof some, to wit, these that made vse of the *Hebrew* tongue in their Synagogues, set twentie two Bookes into their canō, according to the nūber of the letters of the *Hebrew* Alphabet: And the others, to witt, the *Hellenist Iewes*; that is to saie, those that vsed the *Greeke* tōgue in their Synagogues, sett in twentie fower according to the nūber of the *Greeke* Alphabet, which cōtaines twentie fower letters.

Hier. de Scrip Eccl c. vlt. Hier. in Esai. c. 23. Alcim. Auit. l. 6. c. 17. Bellator. apud. Cassiod. Diuin lect c. 6. Cassiodor. ibid. Isidor. Orig. l. 6. c. 1. & de Diuin. offic. l. 1. Cassiodor. de Diuin. lect. c. 6. Hier. Apol adu. Ruffin l. 1. Ad. Aug ep 89. & in exposit. Ps. 126. ad Marcell. ep 141. Hilar. Proleg. in Psalm.

But at the least will some man saie, there are amongst the monuments of the *Greeke* Church, catalogues wherein the six postume Bookes of the old Testament are omitted, Now this is a case apart: for the dispute which now is treated of is not of the custome of the *Greeke* Church, but of the the custome of the *Latine* Church, and particularly of the *African* in the times of the Councells of *Carthage*. Neuerthelesse, for as much as this chance may be mett in our waie, wee will furnish it with fower aduertisments. The first aduertisement shalbe that of the *Greeke* canons, where these bookes are omitted, there are manie which haue bene supposed by the later *Greekes*, as amongst others the Synopsis which beares the title of S. ATHANASIVS; the which also *Beda* and the copies of *Basile* cast into the *Tome* of the Bookes falsely imputed, to S. ATHANASIVS. For the Synopsis intitled from saint ATHANASIVS, defalketh *Wisedome* from the number of the Canonicall Bookes, and setts it into the rankes of the Bookes that were read by the Catechumens only; directly against saint AVGVSTINE, who saith, *That the bookes of Wisedome had merited by so long a continuance of yeares, to be read in the Church of Christ by the Readers of the Church of Christ, and to be heard by all the Christians, from the Bishops to the lowest laymen, faithfull penitents, and Catechumens with reuerence of diuine authoritie*; And against saint ATHANASIVS himselfe, who cryes out; *They feare not what is written in the holy*

Beda Præfat. in Apocalyps. & edit. Basil oper. Athanas. Aug. de prædest. Sanct. l. 1. c. 14. Athan. Apol. 2.

letters, the false witnes shall not be vnpunished, and the lying mouth slayes the soule.

The *second aduertissement* shall be, that although the neighbourhood and the confusion of dwelling with the Iewes, hath sometimes hindred the Greeks, & principally the *Asians* from setting the posthume bookes of the old Testament into their Canons, neuerthelesse there are none of those bookes, but haue bene imployed by diuers Greeke Authors, in the qualitie of a sacred and canonicall booke: as the booke of wisedome by *Melito* Bishop of *Sardes*; & by S. ATHANASIVS, and all the Synod of *Alexandria*, which saith, speaking of the *Arrians*; *They feare not that which is written in the holy scriptures, the false witnes shall not remaine vnpunished, and the lying mouth slayes the soule.* The booke of *Tobias* by the same Sainct ATHANASIVS, and the same Synod, which saith; *It is written, that the misterie of the King must be concealed.* The booke of *Iudith* by the Councell of *Nicea*, which is read (saith S. HIEROME) to haue reckoned the volume of *Iudith* amongst the holy Scriptures. The bookes of *Wisedome*, and of *Ecclesiasticus*, by S. EPIPHANIVS, who writes against *Ætius*; *Thou must turne ouer the two Wisdomes, that of Salomon, and that of the sonne of Syrach, and in summe all the diuine Scriptures.* And finallie, the booke of the *Machabees*, by the three first and greatest Antiquaries of the *Greeke* Christendome; *Clemens Alexandr. Origen*, and *Eusebius*. For *Clemens Alexandr.* reporting the historie of the Scriptures, saith; *In the captiuitie were Hester and Mardocheus, whose historie is currant, as that of the Machabees.* And *Origen* in the second booke of the worke of *Principles*, disputing against the heretickes of the sect of *Marcion*, who placed *matter* as coeternall to God; & willing to proue to them, that God had created the world of nothing, cryes out; *And that we may proue it to be so by authority of Scriptures; bearken in the booke of Machabees to the mother of the seauen martyrs.* And in his commentarie vpon the Epistle to the *Romans*, expounding this verse of S. PAVL; *None dyes for the iust*: and disputing against the same *Marcionites*, who interpreted it of the God of the old lawe, he askes; *But what will they doe? For we finde in the lawe manie martyrs, lett them reade the bookes of the Machabees.* And *Eusebius* in the worke of Euangelicall preparation, comparing the points of the doctrine of *Plato*, with the diuine Oracles of the *Hebrewes*, setts downe among the examples of cōformitie, the place where *Plato* writes; *that the soules of the iust after their death helpe the liuing*: with the place where the booke of the *Machabees* quots, *that Jeremy was seene after his death praying for the people. The twelfth booke of the Euangelicall preparation* (saith *Eusebius*) *shall containe the rest of the conformitie of the doctrine of Plato, with the oracles of the Hebrewes.* And a little after, reporting the articles of this conformitie; *Plato* (saith hee) *writes, that the soules of the deceased, are endued with a certaine vertue, and haue a care of the affaires of men,* &c. *And in the booke of the Machabees it is written, that the Prophet Ieremy after his departure out of this life, was seene praying for the people.* And from this it doth not derogate, that *Origen* alleadged also in the second booke of his worke of *principles*, the volume of *Pastor*, which manie of the auncient held for canonicall: for he adds in the fourth booke of the same worke, that some despised it, which he noe were notes of the booke of *Machabees*. Contrariwise in his apologie against *Celsus*, he cryes out; *that the historie of the Machabees is testified by the witnesse of two whole nations;* that is to say, of the *Iewes* and the *Christians*. Frō whence it is also, that the *Greeke* doctors hold it for so authēticall & vndoubted, as they affirme that the things therein described, the holy Ghost had long before foretolde, by the mouth of *Dauid*, & the other Prophets. *The Prophet* (saith S. CHRISOS) *hath indited the 43th. psal not in his person, but in the person of the Machabees, describing and prophecying the things that should happē in their times.* And S. ISIDORE of *Egipt* time fel-

Eusebius hist. Ecc. l. 5. c. 26. Athan. apol 2. Ibid. Hier. præf. in Iudith. Epiphan. Æt. hær. 76. Clem. Alex strom. l. 1. Origen. de Princip. l. 2. c. 2. Id. in ep. ad Rom. l. 4. Euseb de præp. Euāg. l. 12. c. 1?. Euseb. ibid. Origen. de Princip. l. 4 c. 2. Orig. cont. Cels. l. 8. Chrysost. in psalm. 43.

low with the same S. CHRYSOS. saith, *The Angell that discoursed with Daniell, spake of Antiochus Epiphanes that he should be manifestlie conquered and dispossessed by the Machabes.* And *Theodoret* contiguous in tyme to both of thē: *The holie Ghost* (saith hee) *hath written by the diuine Dauid the fortie third psalme of the Machabees.*

Isid. Pelus. ep. l 3. ep. 4

Thodor. in in ep. ad Rom. c. 8.

The third aduetisment shalbe, that not only diuers *Greeke* authors, but often the same *Greeke* authors in speaking of the Bookes of the old testament, follow according to the occasion of their speeche, sometimes the primitiue computation of the Iewes, & the *Rabbinicall* tradition of the canon of *Esdras*, & of the bookes inclosed in the Arke, & answerable to the number of the letters of the *Hebrew* alphabet, in which the posthumall bookes of the old testament were not cōprehended; & somtymes the accessory cōputation of the Christians, wherein they were contained, from whence it appeares, that from the lesser of these computations nothing can be inferred against the larger. To proue it so, when *Origen* in his cōmentary vpon the psalmes speakes of the Scriptures of the old Testament he followes the canon of *Esdras*, and the nūber of the twentie two *Hebrew* letters, wherin neither *Tobias* nor *Iudith* nor that of *Wisedome* had anie place. *You must not be ignorāt* (said hee) *that the bookes of the Testament according to the tradition of the Hebrewes, are 22, according to the number of their letters.* And whē he speakes in his cōmentary vpō the book of Nūbers of the volumes of the Scripture, he followes the accessory cōputatiō of the christians, & the appēdix of the posthumall bookes, & sets downe the bookes of *Iudith, Tobie* & that of *Wisedome* amongst the canonicall Bookes: *When there is presented* (saith hee to those that are newly Schollers in diuine Studies) *anie reading of the diuine volumes in which there is nothing that seemes obscure, as the booke of Hester or of Iudith, or of Tobie, or the precepts of wisedome, they receiue it willinglie; but if the booke of Leuiticus be read to them, their spirit is presentlie dulled.* And in the same place of the cōmentary vpon the psalmes, where he reckons the Canonicall Bookes of the old Testament, according to the cōputation of the *Hebrewes*, and the number of the *Hebrew* letters, hee adds; *out of this ranke are the bookes of the Machabees, which the Hebrewes call* Sarbit Sarbaneell; *that is to saie, the Scepter of the Prince of the childrē of God*, By which wordes he intēdes not to saie, that they are not of the ranke of the canonicall bookes of the old Testament, for then wherefore (hauing purposed to speake of the Canonicall Bookes) should he mentiō the *Machabees* but that they were not in the ranke of the canonicall bookes, inserted in the canon of *Esdras*. Likewise when S. EPIPHANIVS in the Booke of the Hebrew weights & measure & in the confutatiō of the Sect of *Epicurus*, speaks of the canonicalll Bookes of the old Testamēt, he followes the catalogue of *Esdras*, & the cabbale or tradition of the twentie two *Hebrew* letters, and saith, that the Bookes of *Wisedome & Ecclesiasticus*, were not of this nūber: *The Wisdome of Salomon and that of Iesus the sonne of Syrach, are vsefull and profitable, but are not sett downe amongst the bookes enrolled;* (that is to saie enrolled by *Esdras*) *And for that cause they are not placed in the Aron, that is to saie, in the Arke of the testimonie;* for so it must be read, & not; *neither in the Aron, nor in the Arke*; as it is read at this daie by the ignorance of the booke writers & interpreters, who of the word *Aron*, which in hebrew signifies *Arke*, haue made *Aaron* brother of *Moyses* And when he disputeth against *Ætius* head of the heresie of the *Anomeans*, he followeth the accessory cōputation of the Church, & setts both those amongst the diuine and Canonicall Scriptures. *You must* (saith hee) *turne ouer the twentie seauen bookes of the olde Testament, that the hebrewes reckon twentie two and the four Ghospells, and the fourteen epistles of the Apostles S. PAUL and the Acts of the Apostles made before, and during the same time, and the Catholick Epistles*

Orig. apud Euseb hist. Eccl. l. 6. c. 19.

Orig. in Numb. hom. 27.

Orig. apud Euseb. hist. Eccl. l. 6. c. 19.

Epiph. de ponder. & mens. Hebraic.

Epiphan. contr. Aet. hæres. 76.

of Iames, Peter, Iohn, and Iude, and the Apocalips of Iohn, and the two Wisdomes, that is to saie, that of Salomon, and that of the Sonne of Syrach, and in summe, all the diuine Scriptures.

And finallie, the fourth and last aduertisment shall bee, that there is not one of all the *Greeke* canons, wherein the *Machabees* are past ouer in silēce, (except those that follow the double computation, whereof wee now speake) which is not according to the verie iudgment of *Geneua* imperfect, & omitts those Bookes, the *Caluinists* thēselues confesse to be canonicall. And to proue it so, in the canon of *Melito*, the booke of *Hester* is omitted; in the canon of S. CYRILL of *Hierusalem*, & in the canō of the coūcell of *Laodicea*, the *Apocalips* is forgoten: in the *Synopsis* falsely imputed to S. ATHANAS. the booke of *Hester* is cutt of: in the canon laid to S. GREGORIE of *Nazianzenes* charge, (I say, laid to his charge, because this canon leaues out *Wisedome*, which S. GREG. of *Nazianzene* in his true writings cites as canonicall,) the Booke of *Hester*; and that of the *Apocalips* are excluded. In the catalogue, attributed to *Amphilochius*, the booke of *Hester* and the *Apocalips*, are called in question. In the catalogue of *Iosephus* (an author that was an *Hebrew* by nation, but whose Bookes are written in *Greeke*) the booke of *Job* is omitted & principallie according to their computation that will haue *Job* to haue been before *Moyses*; as *Origen* amōgst the old Christians, & *Mercerus* the Caluinist amōgst the moderne, & *Raby Moyses Kimhi* amongst the Iewes, And in all the Iudaicall antiquities of the same *Josephus*, there is no mētion made of *Iobs* history. By meanes whereof, nothing can be concluded from the silence of those imperfect rolls against the volumes by thē omitted And indeede, notwithstanding this catalogue, *Josephus* leaues not of, (if wee giue creditt to the Greeke text of the worke against *Appion*) to alleadge the booke of *Ecclesiasticus* for one of the pieces of the *Jewish* lawe, when he writes; *The lawe saith, that the woeman is in all things worse then man, and that a mans iniquitie is better thē the good worke of a woeman*; Nor to insert a great parte of the history of the *Machabes* into his treatie of the dominion of reason ouer the senses, yea with the title of a sacred Booke, if wee beleeue the finall clause of the worke, which is defectiue in the *Greeke* text, but is in the anciēt latine translation, acknowledged, & publisht by *Erasmus*. For whereas the same *Iosephus* distinguisheth betweene the bookes written before *Artaxerxes*, when the Prophets flourished in the *Jewish* Church; & the Bookes writtē since; so farr of is he frō excluding heereby the bookes of the *Machabes* frō the nūber of the bookes writtē by the Prophets: that cōtrarywise, in noting that the bookes written since *Artaxerxes*, are not reputed so worthie of credit as the former, because, the successiō of the Prophets hath not bene exact, he shewes that they were beleeued to haue bene writtē by the Prophets, but with a beleefe lesse assured, & mingled with some vncertaintie. *Since Artaxerxes*, (saith he) *euē to our tyme, other things haue bene writtē, but they are not esteemed worthie of the same credit as the former, because the Succession of the Prophets hath not bene exact.* Now this vncertaintie S. IOHN & S. PAVL seeme to take awaie; S. IOHN, whē he reportes, that our Lord assisted at the feast of the dedication of winter, whose institutiō is described in the only collection of the *Machabees*, for the historie of the dedication of winter was a thing necessary to Saluatiō, since without this dedicatiō, the ordinarie Sacrifices of the Lawe, could not be lawful, & by cōsequēce according to our aduersaries, had neede of the testimony of a canonicall Scripture; and S. PAVL when he cites in the Epistle to the *Hebrewes*, the historie of the *tympanized Martyrs*; and that not in matters of things knowne by naturall light, as when he alleadgeth *Aratus*; or in manners

Eusebi. hist. Eccl. l. 5. c. 26. Cyrill. Hierosolym. Cateches. 4. Conc. Laodicen. c. 60 Greg. Naz. de Theolog. ora. 2. & orat. de fid. Ioseph. contr. Appion. l. 1. Orig. cont. Cels. l. 6. Merc. Comm. in Iob. Rab. Mos. Kimhi in libr. vsar. ling. Sanct. Ioseph. contr. Appion. l. 2.

Vetus. vers latin. Ioseph. recognit. per Erasm. & impress. Basil. 1535. Contr. Appion. l. 1

Ioseph. contr. Appion. l. 1.

Hebr. 11. v. 35.

as when he alleadgeth *Menander* or *Epimenides*, but in matter of faith; and to verifie these two theologicall propositions, *that faith is the proofe of things not apparant*, and; *by faith the Saints haue Conquerd Kingdomes, and wrought Iustice.* For the historie and the word it self of *tympanized Martirs*, S. PAVL takes it from the second Booke of the *Machabees*, as *Theodoret* hath noted, and after him the Ministers of *Geneua*, who in their annotations vpon the Epistle to the *Hebrewes*, haue quoted in the Margent of this verse, the sixth Chapter of the second of the *Machabees*.

Hebr. 11. v. 1. Hebr. 11. v. 33. Edit. Græc 2. Mach. c. 6 v. 19. 28. Theod in ep ad Hebr c. 11. Bib. de Geneu. ann. 1588.

I know well that the *Caluinists* doe shake the Authoritie of the two Bookes, & principallie of the second they obiect fiue things; first that the author excuseth the lownesse of his stile: the secõd, that it is not an originall historie, but the extract & epitomy of a more large history: the third, that the primitiue author was called *Iason* which is a pagan and prophane name: the forth that he was a *Cyrenian* and not a *Iewe*: the fifth that this historie containes manie contrarieties, both to it selfe, and to prophane histories. But there is none of these obiections, but brings his solution with him; for to the first oppositiõ, which is in behalfe of the excuse of the stile, wee answere; that S. PAVL doth yet excuse himselfe in more expresse termes, for the stile of his Epistles, whẽ he saith, *Though I be ignorant as concerning words yet I am not so in knowledge.* To the second opposition, which is in behalfe of the qualitie of the historie, which is the abridgment of a larger history; wee answere, that the historie of *Kings*, and that of *Chronicles* are also of other larger histories of the *Kings* of *Israel* and *Iuda*; and that to make a history Canonicall, it is not necessary that the holy Ghost should immediatly indite all the matter of the Narration, but it sufficeth that he so assist it, that in the composition of the ingredients of the history, there be noe falshood mingled with it. To the third opposition, which is cõcerning the name of *Iason*, one of the authors of the originall history, which they will haue to bee a prophane name; wee answere that the name *Jesus* in hebrewe, and the name *Jason* in greeke, the one deriued from the hebrewe word *Iesa*, which signifies saluation; and the other from the the Greeke word *Iasis*, which signifies, *healing*; is one selfe-same: From whence it came, that the priest *Iesus* brother of *Onias*, was called *Jesus* amongst the *Hebrewes*; and *Iason* amongst the *Greekes* as *Onias* his brother was called *Onias*, or *Oniã* amõgst the hebrewes, which signifies the strẽgth of the people, and *Menelaus* amongst the *Greekes*; & that since, *Iason* sonne of *Eleazar*, and manie other Iewes, bore the same name. To the fourth oppositiõ, which concernes the cõutrie of this *Iason*, who is surnamed, *Iason*, the *Cyrenean*; we answere, that *Cyrene* was a prouince and peopled with *Jewes*, frõ whence it is that the Ghospell calls him that did helpe to carry the crosse of our Lord, *Symon* the *Cyrenean*; and that S. LVKE calls one of the Synagogues of *Ierusalem*, the Synagogue of the *Cyreneans*. And finally to the fifth and last opposition, which is concerning the pretended repugancie of this history either against it selfe, or against prophane histories; we answere that if this gate should be once opened, there were noe Canonicall booke whose authoritie might not be called in question. For who knowes not, that it is a thousand times more difficult to reconcile, either the historie of the *Chronicles*, which saith, that *Elias* writ to *Joram*, king of *Iuda*: with the historie of the *Kings*, which saith, that *Elias* had bene taken vp out of the world, eight yeare before the raigne of the same *Toram* King of *Juda*: (or saint MATTHEW who writes that *Ioram* King of *Juda* begat *Ozias*; and reckons from *Dauid* to *Ozias*, fourteen Generations; with the history of the *Kings*, & the *Chronicles* which testifie, that *Joram* was the Grandfather of the Grandfather to *Ozias*; and

1. Corinth. c. 11. Reg. 15. ver 36. & alibi. 2. Cronic. 27. vers 7. & alibi. Machab. 2. Ioseph. antiq. l. 2. c. 6. Theodor. in Daniel. c. 11. & alij. Machab. 8. Machab. 2. Marc. 10. Act. 6. 2. Chronic c. 21. 2. Reg. c. 2. & 3. Matth 1. 2. Reg. c. 8. 9. 11. 14. 15 2. Chronic c. 22. 23. 24. 26 Act 5. Ioseph antiquit. l. 20 c. 2.

setts downe from *Dauid* to *Ozias*, seauenteen Generations; or the historie of the *Acts*, which computes the death of *Theodas*, to be vnder the Empire of *Tiberius*; with *Iosephus*, an author, of that countrie, and tyme, who reckons it vnder the Empire of *Claudius*) then to reconcile all the seeming repugnancies, which are in the historie of the *Machabees*, either against it selfe, or against prophane histories. And if it shoud be lesse, who sees not, that it belongs not, as hath bene already said to the matter now in agitation? For the question that is in dispute in the matter of the collection intituled the sixth Councell of *Carthage*, is not, whether the bookes of the *Machabees* are in their ground Canonicall or not; nor whether the other partes of the Church haue reputed them canonicall; or not Canonicall; but whether the *African* Church hath holden them for such; and whether the *Greeke* interpreters, in ecclipsing them from the canon of the *African* Church, haue done falsely or not? Now wee proue that they haue done so, both by the Catalogue of the third Councell of *Carthage*, and by that of saint AVGVSTINE, and by a thousand other authenticall testimonies, and consequently that the *latine* edition of the *African* canons, is of better creditt then the *Greeke* Rapsody, which is that wee haue obliged our selues to proue.

Of the difficultie touching the epistles that are at the end of the African Councell.

CHAPT. IX.

Cõc. Carth 3. c. 47. Aug. de doctr. Christ. l. 1. c. 8.

THERE remaines one last difficultie, which is represented vpon the matter of the Councells of *Africa*, touching the Epistles annexed to the end of the century of the *African* Canons; to witt, whether the latine text of these Epistles which wee haue at this daie in our Libraries, haue bene translated ftom the Greeke translation, and added to the collection of *Dionisius*, the ancient latine originall being lost: or whether the ancient latine text, being come to our hands, it haue bene corrupted by the Schismatickes of *West* the whether it were in the tyme that the Church of *Aquilea*, and that of *Grada* were in Schisme, and that the Popes held for the Church of *Grada*, and the *Lumbards* for the Church of *Aquilea* or whether it were afterwards. For that it hath bene familiar with the Schismatickes of the *West*, to abuse these Epistles to the fomenting their rebellions, it appeares by the mocke-Councell of *Rheims*, holden for the cause of *Arnulphus* Bishop of *Orleans*, where the principall piece that the Schismatickes made vse of, was the Epistle of the *Africans* to Pope *Celestine*, I haue said, the mocke-Councell of *Rhemes*, for as much as the very Centuriators that caused it to be printed, confesse it to haue bene a tyrannicall Councell, holden at the instance of *Hugh Capet*, to oppresse *Arnulphus*, bastard Brother to the king *Lotharius*, Legitimate and innocẽt Bishop of *Orleans*; And besides that it was disannulled three yeares after by the authoritie of the Sea Apostolicke, and of *Seguin* Archbishop of *Sens*, and with the consent of *Hugh Capet* himself. Then whether the *Latine* text of these Epistles be a translatiõ of the *Greeke* edition; or whether the ancient latine originall being come to our hands, hath bene corrupted, be it by the ignorance of the Bookbinders, or by the malice of the Schismatickes, is the thing in question.

Centur. 10 cap. de. Syn.

Aim. seu Continuat Aim. de Gest. Frãce l. 5. c. 46.

And

And the causes of this doubt are, that whereas in the copie of the *African* Canons, the latine edition is much more correct then the Greeke, in the copie of the Epistles; contrarywise, the Greeke edition is very correct, and the latine most depraued and corrupt; and the corruptions are such as seeme to proceede from the ambiguitie, and misunderstanding of the Greeke wordes: I will alleadge fiue patterns.

The first patterne shall be taken from the Epistle to Pope *Boniface*, where the Greeke text, speaking of the canons that Pope *Zozimus* had sent into *Africa*, vnder the title of the Canons of the Councell of *Nicea*, saith; *These things haue bene rigistred in the Acts, till the more certaine Copies of the Councell of Nicea shall come, in which if they be couched in the same forme, as they are contained in the instruction, that our Bretheren haue shewed vs sent by the Sea Apostolicke, and that they be obserued in the same fashion by you in Italie, we will make no more mention thereof, nor further contest of the not suffering them*: which is the true sence of the *African* Bishops, who had newly before besought the Pope, that he would cause them to obserue in the like case, what should be found in the copies of the Coũcell of *Nicea*, which should be brought out of the *East*; And which is the sence also, that hath bene followed by the Protestants of *Germanie* in the last impression, that they haue made of the Councells of *Africa*. And the latine text contrarywise saith; *These things haue bene inserted into the Acts, vntill the coming of the more certaine copies of the Councell of Nicea, which if they be there contained, so as they are couched in the instruction, as our Bretheren sent by the Sea Apostolicke haue alleaged, and were kept in the same forme amongst you in Italie, we shall be no waie constrained to tollerate things, such as we will not now call to memory or to suffer them intollerable*. Wordes that besides the impertinencie of the construction; in the alternatiue whereof, there is no antithesis, are directly repugnant to the sence and intention of the Epistle; which is, contrarywise to saie, that if the clauses intended by the Popes instruction, were to be found in the copies of the Councell of *Nicea*, which should come out of the East, they would not so much as open their mouthes to speake of it, and would not contest of the not suffring them: and whereof the corruption seemes to proceede from the ambiguitie of the two Greeke verbes whereof the one signifies, *to make mention* or *to commemorate*; and the other, *to bee constrained* and *to contest*.

Edit. Græc. Cõc. Carth cap. 138.

Conc. dict. Afric. c. 101

The second patterne shall be taken from the exordium of the Epistle to Pope *Celestine*, where the Greeke text speaking of *Apiarius* saith; *For first he hath mainely resisted all the Councell, charging it with diuers contumelies, vnder pretence of pursuing the priuiledges of the Roman Church, and willing to cause himselfe to be receiued into our communion, because your Holynesse beleeuing that he had appealed to you, which he could not proue, had restored him to the communion. Yet this did not succeede with him, as you shall more at large vnderstand, by reading the Acts*; Which is the true sence of the wordes of the Epistle; and which also the Protestants of *Germanie* haue followed in the last impression that they haue made of the Councell of *Africa*. And the latine text contrarywise importes, referring these wordes to *Faustinus* the Popes *Legate*. *For first how much he hath resisted all the Assemblie, Charging it with manie contumelies, vnder colour of pursuing the priuiledges of the Roman Church, and willing to cause him to be receiued into our communion, because your Holynesse beleeuing he had appealed to you, which could not be proued, had restored him to the commnnion. Which notwithstanding was not lawfull, as you shall better discerne by reading the Acts*; which are three deprauations, one in the neck of an other: the first in this that the latine text referrs to *Faustinus* that which the Councell saith of *Apiarius*, as it appeares by these words: *For first*, which shew that it

speakes

speakes of him, of whom it had begun and continued to speake of in the following periods; and by this subsequent clause, *when we examine the crimes that haue bene obiected to him*, which could not be vnderstood but of *Apiarius*. And this seemes to proceede from the ambiguitie of the Greeke pronowne, which being taken in a reciprocall signification signifies, *himselfe*, and obligeth the Readers to translate, *willing to make himselfe be receiued*, which is the sence that the new editions of the Protestants of *Germanie* haue embraced; and being taken in a direct signification, signifies, *him*, and obligeth the Readers to translate; *willing to cause him to be receiued*. The second in this, that insteede of these words of the Greeke text; *Notwithstanding this hath not succeeded to him*, which are spoken of the Action of *Apiarius*, the latine text setts downe, *which yet was not lawfull*, and referrs it to the action of the Pope against the credit of this remitment, *as you shall better discerne by the reading of the Acts*: which shewes, that the Councell speakes of the issue of *Apiarius* his cause, and not of the Popes action; and this seemes to haue proceeded from the Ambiguitie of the Greeke verbe, which signifies *to succeede*, and *to be lawfull*, And the third in this, that insteede of the aduerbe, *greatlie*, which is in the greeke text, the latine edition reades, *how much*, a thing which depriues the construction both of sence and verbe, and makes the speeche suspence and defectiue.

Edit Can Concil. Viteberg. 1614.

The third paterne shall be taken from the beginning of the request of the same Epistle, where after these words, *Premising then the office of a due salutation, we beseech you affectionatly that henceforward you will no more, so easily admitt to your eares, those that come from these partes, nor restore to the communion, those that haue bene excommunicated by vs; for as much as your Reuerence will easily discerne, that this hath bene defined by the Councell of Nicea*; the latine text adds, *for although it seeme, that there should only mention bee made of Clerkes and laymen, by how much stronger reason, should this be obserued of Bishops, that those which haue bene depriued of the communion in their prouince, might not appeare to be restored rashlie and duely to the communion by your Holynesse?* And the Greeke text contrarywise makes two diuers clauses of this traine, whereof he referrs the first to the Pope, and not to the Councell of *Nicea*, and distinguisheth them by the word, *then*, which is an aduerbe of illation, in these termes; *For if it appeare that he hath had care to extend his caution, euen to clerkes and laymen by how much stronger reason would he haue it to be obserued in regard of Bishops? Let not those then that haue bene suspended from the communion in their owne prouince, appeare to be hastilie, and otherwise then is fitt, restored to the cõmunion by your Holynesse.* Now that the reading of the Greeke edition be the true one, it appeares by the branch following, which is; *Likewise also the impudent flightes of priests and inferior clerkes, let your Holynesse as a thing worthie of you, reiect them*; Which supposeth, a precedent prayer to the Pope particularly made for the Bishops.

Conc. dict. Afric. c. 105.

Edit. Græc Cõc. Carth cap. 138.

Edit. Ioan. Schoffer. 1525. & nou. impress. Paris apud Abrah. Pacard. 1615. Edit. ordin. Cõcilior. ex Isidor. Mercat.

The fourth patterne shall be taken from the middle of the same petition, where the Greeke text contayning, *the grace of the holy Ghost shall not want to euery prouision*; the latine exemplifiers of the Greeke word, which signifies there *prouision*; some of them haue made, *prouidence*; and other some, *prouince*. For that there it must be read *prouision*, and not *prouince*, it appeares by the clause that followes, which saith; *And principally since it is permitted to euery one if he finde himselfe agreeued at the sẽtẽce of the iudges to appeale to the Synod of his prouince*. The fifth patterne shalbe taken frõ the end of the same Epistle, where the Greeke text saith; *For as for the wretched Apiarius, hauing already bene for his infamous crimes cast out of the Church of Christ, by our brother Faustinus, we are no more in care; for as much as by the meanes*

Edit. Græc Cõc. Carth cap. 138.

of the approbation and direction of your Holynesse, for the preseruation of brotherly Charitie, Africa will suffer him no longer: which is the true sence of the Epistle, where the Fathers intend to expresse, that the Pope will noe longer permitt, that *Apiarius* (to whom by the first iudgement of *Faustinus* his Legat, & of the *African* Bishops reuiewing the cause with him, it had bene granted to remaine in *Africa*, and so exercise there in anie place he could or would, the office of priesthood, prouided it were not at *Sicca*; hauing bene by the second iudgement, condemned and excommunicated, yea by the very month of *Faustinus* his Holinesse legate;) should remaine in *Africa*, and exercise anie priesthood there; which sence also the protestants haue followed, as well in the Greeke, as in the latine, of the last impression of the Councells of *Africa*, which they haue made in *Germany*. And the latine edition contrarywise saith, transferring the speech to *Faustinus*; *For as for our Brother Faustinus, Apiarius hauing bene already cast out of the Church for his enormious crimes; we are assured, sauing the probity and moderation of your Holynesse, that brotherly Charitie will not permitt, that he be anie longer borne with, in Africa*. Now this translation is both against the Greeke text, which referrs the speeche to *Apiarius*, and not to *Faustinus*; and against the expresse intention of the Councell, which might well & coueniently desire the Pope, not to permitt anie longer, that *Apiarius* should remaine in *Africa*, but not desire him no more to keepe a Legat in *Africa*, & principally according to the opinion of those that will haue it, that the Councell of *Carthage* where *Genetlins* presided, was celebrated vnder the Empire of *Valentinian* the third who begun to be Emperor, but the yeare after the Consulship of *Victor* and *Castinus*, vnder the which, according to them, this letter was written, and that *Faustinus* the Popes Legate assisted at it: And against the testimonie of *Leo* the first, who was created Pope eight yeares after the death of *Celestine*, who makes mention of a Bishop called *Potentius*, who was his Legat in *Africa*. For as for the clause, *wee are no more in care of it* which wants in the Greeke printed copies, it is in the ancient greeke copies commented by *Zonara* and by *Balsamon*; And as for the word *probity* which is read in the latine text it may be it is a deprauation of the Greeke word, which signifies, *probation*, which also the *Germans* haue retained in the new edition as well Greeke as latine of their Conncells. But it is alreadie a longe while since this digression began, to exceede the proportion of the other partes of my worke; And therefore the feare to abuse the Readers patience, obligeth me to conclude and to pray them to excuse me, if I haue suffered myselfe to be carried beyond what was my purpose at the beginning of the chapter. The importance of the matter shall recompence the defect of the proportion, which perchance in these kindes of searches, will not be displeasing to spiritts curious of antiquities.

Cōc. dict Afric. cap. 101. & 105. Edit. Cōc. vviteberg. Ann. 1614.

Leo ad Episc. Afric. ep. 85.

Of the Question of Appeales, treated of in the sixth Councell of Carthage.

CHAPT. X.

THE fifth instance of *Caluin* against the Popes authoritie, is taken from the dispute that happened about the matter of Appeales in sixth Councell of *Carthage*; and consists in this; that *Apiarius* priest of the cittie of *Sicca* in *Africa*, hauing appealed to the Pope from a sentence that the Bishops of *Africa* had giuen against him; And the Bishops of *Africa* hauing complained of this Appeale, the Pope sent them the canons of the appeales made in the Councell of *Sardica*, and directed them to them vnder the title of the canons of the Councell of *Nicea*, for as much as the Councell of *Sardica*, was an appendix of the Councell of *Nicea*. By meanes whereof the *Africans* not finding these Canons in the Copies of the councell of *Nicea* that they had with them, deputed some into the *East*, to see if they could finde them in the copies of the *Easterne* Churches, and not hauing found them there, and besides finding themselues much aggreeued at the frequent appeales, which those that had badd causes cast in from their Iudgments, besought the Pope, that he would not more so easily receiue Appeales from the church-men of their prouinces. Now this instance hath bene after manie ages, the principall engine of the aduersaries against the Popes authoritie, as it appeares both by the vse that the Schismatickes of the mock-Councell of *Reimes* made of it, to the end to oppresse the innocence of *Arnulphus* Bishop of *Orleans*, which the Pope maintained; And by the calumnies where with *Zonaras* and *Balsamon* Greeke Schismatickes, vniustly charge the memorie of Pope *Zosimus*, for hauing alleadged the canons of the Councell of *Sardica*, vnder the title of the canons of the Coũcell of *Nicea*: And finally by the proceedings of the protestants, who in this slander haue followed and surpassed them. For not only the first Protestants haue caused to bee published, and republished manie tymes, this sixth Councell of *Carthage*, as a Storehowse reputed by them very powerfull to resist the authoritie of the Sea Apostolicke, but also haue vomited & disgorged with so much impudence, the venome of their inuectiues against the Popes, vnder the which, this matter hath bene treated of, as the heauens abhorre it; calling Pope *Boniface*) whom S. AVGVS. calls, *Reuerend Pope Boniface*, & to whõ he dedicated one of his principall Bookes, and whom *Prosper* qualifies, *Pope of holy memory*) insteed of *Boniface Maleface*; And Pope *Celestine*, whom the Generall Councell of *Ephesus*, calls *new S. Peter*; in the steede of *Celestine, Infernall*. And yet since these two last yeares, their Successors dissembling the learned answers of the Illustrious Cardinalls *Bellarmine* and *Barronius*, haue caused the same Councell to be twice new printed, once in *France*, & an other time in *Germanie*, as an insoluble piece against the Popes authotity. And therefore since the affaire deserues to be treated with much diligence, and read with much attention, it belongs to me to contribute the one, and to the readers to the lend the other.

Cõc. Carth Dist. 9. c. 3.

Centur. 10. c. 9 col. 494. Zonar. Cõment. in Cõc. Carth c. 5. Balsam. ibid.

Aug. contr. duas. Epist. Pelag. l. 1. Prosp. cõtr. Collat. Cõc. Eph. part. 2. Act 3.

To this instance then, before I vndertake to search this history to the bottomb, I will bring eight obseruations in forme of preseruatiues and antidotes: *The first obseruation* shall be, that whatsoeuer the aime and successe of this Councell were, nothing could be inferred from it, to trouble & shake the Popes authoritie in regard of Appeales. For in the Coũcell of *Chalcedon* which was holden by six hundred thirtie six Bishops, thirtie yeares after the sixth Councell of *Carthage*, & which was more famous & authenticall, then the sixth Coũcell of *Carthage*, as being a generall Coũcell, & one of the first four Generall Coũcells; whereas the sixth Coũcell of *Carthage*, wat but a Nationall Coũcell, the Appeales of causes which cõcerned either faith or the persons of Bishops, cõtinued to goe to the Pope according to the forme that had bene ordayned by the rule of the Coũcell of *Sardica* The Epistle of the Emperor *Valentinian* the third annexed to the head of all the copies of the Coũcell of *Chalcedon*, as well Greeke as latine, is a testimonie of this, which saith; *Wee ought to preserue in-*

uiolablie in our daies, the dignitie of particular reuerēce to the blessed Apostle Peter, to the end that the holie Bishop of Rome, to whō antiquitie hath grāted the priesthood aboue all, may haue place to iudge of faith, and of Bishops, &c. For, for this cause according to the custome of the Councells, Flauianus Bishop of Constantinople hath appealed to him, in the cōtrouersie which is mooued concerning faith. The law of the Emperor *Marcian* annexed to the end of the Acts of the same Councell is a testimonie of this, which cryes out: *The Synod of Chalcedon, by the authority of the blessed Bishop of the cittie eternall in glorie Rome, examining matters of faith exactly, and establishing the foundations of Religion, giues to Flauianus the reward of his past life, and the palme of a glorious death.* A testimonie of this, is the petition of appeale, sent to the Pope by *Theodoret* Bishop of *Cyre*, a cittie confining vpon *Persia*, and subiect to the Patriark of *Antioch*, which saith; *I attend sentence of your Apostolicke Throne, and beseeche your Holynesse to succour me, appealing to your right and iust iudgement.* A testimonie of this is the ordinance of the directors of the policie of the Councell, which was; *Let the most reuerend Bishop Theodoret come in, that he may partake of the Councell, because the most holy Archbishop Leo hath restored his Bishopricke to him and that the most sacred and religious Emperor hath ordained, that he be present at the Councell.* And finallie the relation of the same Councell is a testimonie of this, which writes to the Pope, approuing the iudgement of appeale, that he had giuen in the cause of *Eutyches* Abbot of *Constantinople*, and condemning *Dioscorus* and the false Councell of *Ephesus*, for presuming to meddle with it, *He hath restored to Eutyches, the dignitie whereof he was depriued by your Holinesse, &c.* And after all this; *He hath extended his felony euen against him, to whom the keeping of the vine had bene committed by our Sauiour, that is to saie, against your Apostolicke* Holynesse.

In Epist. præambul. Cōc. Chalc.

Lex Marcian. in Cōc. Chalc. part. 3. c. 11

Theod. ep. ap Leon.

Cōc. Chalc Act. 1.

Cōc. Chalc relat. ad Leon.

Cōc. Chalc ep ad Leon part. 3. c. 2.

The *second obseruation* shall be, that the controuersie of appeales, which was handled in the sixth Councell of *Carthage*, was not of appeales in maior and Ecclesiasticall causes, that is to saie, in causes of Faith, or of the Sacraments, or of discipline, or of the customes and ceremonies of the Church: but of appeales in *minor* and personall causes, that is to saie, in the secular and temporall causes of persons constituted in orders; as causes of adultery, drunkenes, battery, theft, debt, and others causes, as well morall as pecuniary, and as well ciuill as criminall of Ecclesiasticall persons, which the decrees of Councells, and the lawes of Emperors, submitted to the Tribunall of the Church. This appeareth both by the qualitie of *Apiarius* his cause, for which this question was moued, which was a morall cause, and wherein there were enormious and infamous crimes handled, and not an Ecclesiasticall cause; And by the remonstrance which the *Africans* made to Pope *Celestine*, *That the beyond-sea iudgments could not be assured for the difficultie of causing witnesses to passe out of Africa into Europe, which often because of the weakenes either of age or sexe could not indure sea voyages.* And by the Epistle of Pope *Innocent* the first, which S. AVGVSTINE calls, *worthie of the Sea Apostolicke*, wherein these words were contained; *And principally whensoeuer matters of faith are handled, I conceiue that all our brethren and colleagues ought not to referre them but to Peter, that is to saie, to the authour of their name and dignitie.* And finally by the very proceedings of the *Mileuitan* Councell, and of the Councell of *Carthge*, holden vnder the twelfth consulship of Honorius. For not only the Fathers of the *Mileuitan* Councell, where the prohibition was made to inferior Clerkes not to appeale beyond sea, remitted the finall iudgment of *Celestius* alreadie heard and iudged for a cause of Faith in *Africa* to Pope *Innocent* the first, with this acknowledgment, *that the Popes authority was of diuine right*; or to vse their owne owne

Conc. dict. Afric. can. 138.

Ep. Conc. African. ad Celest. Pap. in Concil. Afric. c. 105

Aug. ep. 106 Inter epist Aug. ep. 93

Conc. Mileuit. c. 22.

Aug. epist. 106.

Aug. ep. 92

termes

termes, *drawne from the authority of the holy Scriptures*: but euen Pope *Innocent* the first being dead before he could heare *Celestius* in person, and hauing only condemned him in generall, vpon the reporte of the Councells of *Africa*, the *African* Bishops reassembled in the Councell of *Carthage* holden vnder the twelfth consulship of *Honorius*, wherein the question of *Apiarius*, and the controuersie of Episcopall appeales began, caused their acts concerning *Celestius*, to be carried to *Rome*, and procured them to be confirmed by Pope *Zosimus*, successor to *Innocent*. *The reuerend Bope Zosimus* (saith S. AVGVSTINE) *pressed Celestius to condemne those things that the Deacon Paulinus* (so was he called that had accused *Celestius* in *Africa*) *had obiected against him, and to giue cousent to the letters of the Sea Apostolicke, expedited by his predecessor of holy memorie. But he would not condemne the articles that Paulinus had obiected against him, true it is that he durst not resist Pope Innocents letters: Contrarywise, he promised to condemne all that, which that Sea should condemne. And therefore after hauing bene gentlie fomented, as a franticke person to make him rest; it was neuerthelesse, not thought fitt, to vnbinde him from the Bondes of excommunication, but for the space of two moneths, attending till they writt out of Africa, time for repentance was giuen him, vnder a certaine medicinall sweetenes of iudgement.* And againe; *By the watchfulnesse of the Episcopall Councells, the Reuerent Prelates of the Sea Apostolicke, euen to the number of two, Pope Innocent, and Pope Zosimus, haue condemned Pelagius and Celestius through the whole Christian world, if they doe not correct themselues, and besides that doe penãce.* And *Prosper*, timefellow & scholler to S. AVGVST. vnder the twelfth consulship of *Honorius*, and the eigth of *Theodosius*, *The decrees of the Councell of Carthage of two hundred and fourteen Bishops, were carried to Pope Zosimus, which hauing bene approued, the Pelagian heresie was condemned ouer all the world.* And againe; *Pope Zosimus of blessed memorie, added the forces of his sentence to the decrees of the Councells of Africke, and to cutt off impious persons, armed the right hand of all the Bishops with the sword of Sainct Peter.* And the Deacon *Paulinus* him selfe, in his epistle to Pope *Zosimus*, publisht by the illustrious Cardinall *Baronius*; *I had promist* (saith he) *not to faile to appeare at Rome, if the iudgement had bene giuen against me, and not for me, but then I could pursue nothing, since he that had appealed to the Sea Apostolicke* (he meanes *Celestius*, who, as saith S. AVGVSTINE, vpon the end of the triall at *Rome*, tooke his flight) *absented him self, he that ought to haue maintained the validitie of his appeale.*

August. de peccat. origin c. 7. — Id. ep. 157. — Prosper. in Chronic. — Id. contr. Collat. — Baron. Annal. tom. 5. ad Ann. Christ. 418 — Aug. de peccat. origin c. 7. & 8.

The third cautiõ shalbe, that the *Africans* did not in this question contest the euocations, that came from the meere motion of the Pope, but the appeales that came from the simple motion of the particular men. For that the custom of euocations proceeding from the Pope hath bene knowne in antiquitie, and hath had place both before and after the sixth Councell of *Carthage*, it appeares both by the request that *Eusebius* Bishop of *Nicomedia*, and his partakers made to the Pope, to call the cause of *Athanasius*, which had bene iudged in the Councell of *Antioch*, and in many others Councells of the East, and to drawe it to *Rome*; *He writt* (saith *Socrates*) *to Iulius Bishop of Rome, and besought him to call the cause to himselfe.* And *Theodoret*: *Julius following the Ecclesiasticall lawe, commaunded them to present themselues at Rome, and summoned the diuine Athanasius in iudgement;* and by the *constitution of the Emperors Theodosius and Valentinian published a while after the sixth Councell of Carthage, which ordaines, That euerie Bishop that, hauing bene called by the Pope, shall refuse to appeare, shall be constrayned thereunto, by the Gouernor of the Prouince.* And by the euocation that the Pope S. GREGORIE the *Great* made of all the causes that *Adrian* Bishop of *Thebes* in *Macedonia* had, or might afterward haue, before *John* Bishop

Socrat. hist. Eccl. l. 2. c. 11. — Theodor. hist. Eccl. l. 2. c. 4. — Nouel. Theodos. tit. 24. — Greg. Mag. l2. indict. 11. ep. 7.

of *Larissa* his *Metropolitan*, which he ordayned to be iudged either at *Constantinople*; by the Popes *Nuncio*, if the causes were Minor or at *Rome* by the Pope himselfe if they were maior causes. And that the *Africans* contested none but the Appeales that proceeded from the simple motion of particular persons, and not the euocations that came of the Popes meere motion; it appeares by this, that the Pope hauing put four Articles into the instruction that hee had giuen to his Legates, to treate with the Bishops of *Africa*, amongst which there was one that imported thus much, To call *Vrbanus* Bishop of *Sicca* to *Rome*, or euen to excommunicate him, if he corrected not such things, as ought to bee corrected. The *Africans* stucke only vpon the Articles of Appeale, and as for the Article of euocation, they brought neither scruple nor resistance against it. Contrarywise, they answered, that *Vrbanus* had corrected those things, that ought to be corrected, without anie difficultie. And indeede, how could the *Africans* haue contested the euocation, proceeding from the Popes proper motion, they that but euen before, had solicited Pope *Innocent* the first, to call *Pelagius* out of *Palestina*, where he had bene absolued by *Eulogius* Archbishop of *Cesarea*, and by *John* Bishop of *Hierusalem*, and by all the Councell of the prouince, to be heard and adiudged by him at *Rome*: *It is necessarie then* (said they) *either that Pelagius should be called to Rome by they Reuerence; &c. or that he may haue Interrogatories by letter.* And elsewhere: *Wee are assured, that when your Reuerence shall haue seene the Episcopall Acts, which are said to haue bene made vpon this occasion in the East, thou wilt iudge of it in such sort, as we shall all reioyce in the mercie of God.* For that Pope *Innocent* answers, that *Pelagius* might be more commodiously heard by the Bishops neere *Palestina*, he intends with commission from the Sea Apostolicke, as hee shewes by these words: *Hee ought not to attend to be called by vs, but ought to come to vs, that he may be absolued.* And againe; *But care shall not be wanting, if he will giue waie to remedies, for he may condemne those things that he hath holden, and aske pardon for his errors by letter, as is conuenient for one that returnes to vs.* Now this exception was more then sufficient, to preserue the marke of Superioritie, though the minor Appeales should haue no place. For euen in secular Iurisdictions, there is great difference betweene making difficultie, that a particular man of his owne Motion, should appeale from anie Tribunall to the Prince, or that the Prince of his owne motion should call the cause of a particular man to him. And our ancient *French* haue often debated Appeales from *France* to *Rome* in minor and personall causes, without pretending for all that to debate, either euocations or Superioritie. And to proue this, when *Rothaldus* Bishop of *Soissons* appealed to *Rome* vnder the second race of our Kings, *Hincmarus* Archbishop of *Rheims* and tyme-fellow with *Charles* the *Bald* writt to the Pope: *God forbid that wee should so despise that priuiledge of the Prime and Soueraigne Sea of the Pope of the holy Roman Church, as to wearie your Soueraigne authoritie with all the Processes, and all the differences of the Clergie, aswell of the inferior as superior order; which the Canons of the Councell of Nicea and of the other Sacred Councells, and the decrees of Innocent, and of the other Bishops of the holie Sea of Rome, commaund to be determined in their prouinces.* And neuerthelesse to manifest that he pretended not to touch, vpon neither the superioritie, nor the euocations, hee added; *Wee know all, aswell young as old, that our Churches are subiect to the Roman Church.* And a little after, *It is fit and iust, that euerie Bishop, that the Roman Bishop shall send for, to come to him to Rome, if sicknesse*

Edit Græc. can. 134. Cōc. Carth 6. epist. vniuers. Afric. Synod ad Bonifac. c. 101

Ibid.

Aug. ep. 95.

Aug. ep. 90

Inter. epist. Aug. ep. 96

Ibidem.

Hincm. Epist. ad Nicol. Pap. 1 apud. Flodoard. hist Eccl. Rom. 1. 3.

Id. ibid.

Id ibid.

or anie other more grieuous necessitie, or impossibilitie hinder him not as the sacred Canons prescribe, shall doe his deuoyre to trauell thither, And elsewhere; *Wee yeelde obedience to the Sea Apostolicke, from whence is deriued the streame of Religion, Ecclesiasticall ordination, and Canonicall iudicature.* And euen to this day, in the Appeales of minor and personall causes; neither the causes nor persons of the *French* Clergie, goe to *Rome* to be iudged there; neither doth the Pope send legats from *Rome* in to *France,* but names commissaries taken out of the Prouince of *France*, and dwelling in *France,* to iudge them vpon the place, to auoide the costs and other inconueniences, that the length and difficultie of the waie, would bring vpon the witnesses and parties, which was that, that principallie did hurt the *Africans.*

Idem.in opuscul 55. Capit.l.35.

The fourth aduertisement shallbe, that it was not of sett purpose, and of the first designe, that the *African* Fathers moued the controuersie of the beyond-Sea Appeales of Bishops, but by accident, and in continuance of *Apiarius* his appeale. For the *Africans* had alwaies till then obserued this difference betweene Bishops and Simple Priests; that Bishops might Appeale beyond the Sea, and Priests not; as it appeares, both by the declaration that saint AVGVSTINE made, That *Cecilianus* might reserue the definition of his cause, to the iudgments beyond Seas, because he was not of the number of simple Priests, or other inferior Clerkes, but of the number of Bishops; And by the testimonie he giues, that manie *African* Bishops, the Sea Apostolicke iudging them, or confirming the iudgments of others, had bene preserued to the title of their Bishoprick without retayning the exercise thereof. And by the tacite exception of the order of Bishops, that the Fathers of the *Mileuitan* Councell had sett into the decree of the Appeales, when they had ordained that the Priests Deacons and other inferior Clerkes, could not appeales to the Prouinces beyond the Sea. And therefore, when *Apiarius* Priest of the Church of *Sicca* in *Africa,* came to appeale beyond Sea, the *African* Bishops opposed themselues against it. And from thence by occasion, the question of Episcopall appeales, tooke, the originall, as an incident sett on the backe of an other affaire. For vpon this opposition, the Pope sent the *Rule* of the Councell of *Sardica* concerning appeales into *Africa*, which consisted in two articles; whereof one treated of the Appeales of Bishops, and the other of the appeales of Priests. Now the Pope sent these two Canons in the qualitie of Canons of the Councell of *Nicea*, for as much, as the Councell of *Sardica* was an Appendix, and a supplie of the Councell of *Nicea.* The *African* Prelates then not finding the Canon of Bishops Appeales in the copies of the Councell of *Nicea*, that they had with them no more then that of the Priests Appeales; And besides being much vexed with the frequent Appeales of Bishops from their prouinces, besought the Pope to be pleased, that they might send into the *East*, to see if this *Rule* were to be found in the copies of the Councell of *Nicea*, which were kept in the *Easterne* Churches: and putting in compromise the Title, which was produced to them of that, which they had till then obserued by custome, in regard of Episcopall Appeales, tooke occasion also to put the continuance of the custome to compromise; that is to saie, to contest, not only the Priests Appeales, but also to beeseeche the Pope to reiect, or more rarelie to receiue the Appeales of Bishops.

Aug.ep. 162.

Concil. Mileuit. can.22.

Concil. Carth. 6. c.3.

The fifth aduertisement shalbe, that the allegation that Pope Zozimus made of the Canons of the Councell of *Sardica*, vnder the title of Canons of the Councell of *Nicea*, was not as shall heereafter appeare, by fraude; or to make an aduantage of, seeing contrarywise it had bene more aduantageable to him for the matter then in question, to haue alleadged them vnder the title of Canons of the Councell of *Sardica*, then vnder the title of the Canons of the Councell of *Nicea*; for as much as in the Councell of *Nicea*, there was but one only Bishop of *Africa*, to witt, *Cecilianus*; whereas in the Councell of *Sardica*, there were thirtie six Bishops of *Africa* present, that subscribed it: but that it was, because it was the custome of the *Roman* Church to cite the Canons of the Councell of *Sardica*, vnder the title of the Canons of the Councell of *Nicea*, because the Councell of *Sardica*, had bene an Appendix of the Councell of *Nicea*: as it is the custome of the *Greekes* to alleadge the Canons of the Councell *Trullian*, vnder the title of Canons of the sixth Generall Councell, because they pretend the Councell *Trullian* to be an Appendix to the sixth Generall Councell. And as *Gregorie* of *Tours* alleadges, and that with much lesse reason, the Canons of the Councell of *Gangres*, for Canons of the Councell of *Nicea*, when he saith; *Then arriuing at the Monasterie, I read ouer againe the decrees of the Canons of the Councell of Nicea, wherein it is contayned, because that if anie woeman leaue her husband, and she dispise the bedd wherein he hath liued honestlie, saying there is no part in the glorie of the Kingdome of heauen, for him that hath bene ioyned in marriage; lett her be Anathema*: For these words are the words of the Councell of *Gangres*, and not those of the Councell of *Nicea*, for as much as the Councell of *Gangres*, was as a branche and a slipp of the Councell of *Nicea*; and that the same *Osius*, who had presided at the Councell of *Nicea*, assisted there, if we beleeue the ancient *Latine* inscriptions of the Councell of *Gangres*, and the reporte of *Eunodius* ancient Bishop of *Pauia*.

Côc. Carth 6. c. 3.

Greg. Turon. hist. l. 9 c. 33.

The sixth aduertisement shalbe, that whereas the *African* Fathers, did not perceiue that these Canons which they found not in the copies of the Councell of *Nicea*, were in those of the Councell of *Sardica*, happened from this that the *Donatists* had suppressed in *Africa*, all the copies of the true Councell of *Sardica*, which had bene holden by the Catholicke Bishops at *Sardica*, and had substituted in their steede the copies of the false Councell of *Sardica*; which had bene holden by the *Arrians* neere *Sardica*. For in the same tyme, when the three hundred Catholicke Bishops, which represented all the Catholicke Church held their Councell at *Sardica*, where they confirmed the faith of the Coûcell of *Nicea*, & the absolution of S. ATHANASIVS; the seauentie *Arrian* Bishops which had seperated themselues from thẽ, held their hereticall mock-Councell, which they falsely and impudently intituled, the Councell of *Sardica*, at *Philippopolis*, a cittie neere *Sardica*, where they condemned the Faith of the Coûcell of *Nicea*, and the person of S. ATAANASIVS. Now it happened, that in the addresse of the Epistle of this false Councell of *Sardica*, the *Arrians* amongst the Bishops of their communion, inserted the name of *Donatus*, Bishop of the *Donatists* of *Carthage*; for as much as this *Donatus*, besides the heresie of the *Donatists*, was also infected with that of the *Arrians*. The *Donatists* then thinking, they might inferr from thence, that their communion had in former tymes bene spread out of *Africa*, & by this meanes auoid the reproaches that the Catholickes of *Africa* made to them, that their Church was imprisoned within the lymitts of *Africa*, and consequently was not *Catholicke*; aduised themselues to call in, and supprese secretly in *Africa*, all

Socrat. hist. Eccl l. 2. c. 20. &. Sozom. l 3. c 10. In frag. Hilar. p. 6.

the copies of the true Councell of *Sardica*, which had bene brought thither by *Gratus*, Catholick Archbishop of *Carthage*, and to sowe in their steedes, the copies of the false Councell of *Sardica*, which had bene addressed to *Donatus* his competitor, and wrought so in it, that in the time, of saint AVGVSTINE, and of the sixth councell of *Carthage*, as it shalbe heereafter proued by many places of S. AVGVSTINE, there were to be found in *Africa*, none of the copies of the true councell of *Sardica*, but only those of the false councell of *Sardica*.

The seauenth Aduertisement shalbe, that the *African* Fathers, neuer went so farr as to make anie decision or anie decree vpon the Article of the Episcopall Appeales: contrarywise before the cōming of the copies frō the *East*, all their proceeding was to beseeche the Pope, to cause their contentes to be obserued, with protestation the while to practise what was sett downe in his Legates Instructiōs. And after the copies had bene brought out of the East, so farr were they from making anie decree vpon the Article of the Bishops Appeales, as they hindred not those of Simple priests. For after the death of Pope *Boniface*, vnder whom the copies of the *East* were brought into *Africa*, *Apiarius* being fallen into new crimes, for which he was againe condemned, by a Councell of *Africa*, and Pope *Celestine*, vpon a pretence of Appeale, hauing againe sent *Faustinus* his Legate into *Africa*, to cause a newe Councell to be holden there, where *Apiarius* did not only forbeare to hinder it, but also to obay the Popes Bill of Appeale, assembled a new Councell, where, in his Legates presence, *Apiarius* his cause was againe put to triall; and they did not awake the contention of Appeales, but vpon the occasion that was giuen them by the subsequent and vnexpected confession of *Apiarius*, who vanquished by the remorse of his owne conscience, voluntarily discouered all the infamous crimes, whereof he was accused. This confession then, hauing renewed in the spirit of the *Africans*, the memory of the greeuances that they receiued by Appeales, which in steede of seruing, as they ought, for a shield for innocence, when the raynes were let too loose, serued for a Shield for incorrigibilitie and impunitie; they tooke occasion from thence to write an Epistle of complaint to the Pope. But yet euen then they passed not so farr, as to make anie decree of the Episcopall appeales, but contained themselues within the simple lymitts of complaints, petitions, and Remonstrances. Which the Bishops of the Councell of *Constantinople* surnamed *Trullian*, that the Greekes call the sixth generall Councell, acknowledged when they said, *wee receiue the Canons made by the holy Fathers assembled at Sardica and at Carthage*; words which shewed plainely, that they beleeued not the Councell of *Sardica* to haue bene disabled by the decrees of the Councell of *Carthage*.

Concil. dict. Afric. epist ad Bonifac. c. 101.

Epist. Cōcil. Afric. ad Pap. Cælest. c. 101. Ibidem.

Ibid.

Conc. in Trull. c. 2.

The eight and last aduertisement shall be, that the end & issue of the affaire was, that after all these contentions, searches, and proceedings, the Pope remained in full and intire possession of the Right of the Episcopall Appeales of *Africa*, and that the *Africans* were satisfied, that what they had not found in the Councell of *Nicea*, was contained in the Councell of *Sardica*, whose Canons vpon this occasion, they inserted into the Canon law of their prouinces; and in summe that all the *African* Church continued and perseuered, in the practise of yielding Episcopall Appeales to the Sea Apostolicke, and in the communion and obedience of the Pope, as long as Christianitie lasted in *Africa*: This is the history: *Apiarius* priest of *Sicca*, a cittie of the prouince of *Numidia* in *Africa*, after he had bene condemned, deposed, and excommunicated by the *African*

Bishops

Bishops in a cause,that he had against *Vrbanus* Bishop of *Sicca* cōplained to Pope *Zozimus*,that he had appealed to him,& that the *Africans* would not suffer the cause to passe beyond Sea. Pope *Zozimus* vpon this occasion sent into *Africa* the rule of the Councell of *Sardica*,vpon the matter of Appeales;which consisted in two Articles;wherof the one contained, that the Bishops after they had bene deposed by the Councells of their Prouinces might appeale to the Pope: & the other contained that the Priests which had bene deposed by the Councell of their Prouince might haue their cause reuiewed, by the Bishops of the next Prouinces, which was the point that concerned *Apiarius* his controuersie.For whereas the rule of the Councells of *Africa* imported,that the Priests should be iudged by the Bishop of their Diocesse,and by six Bishops of the same Prouince, and that in case they would appeale from it, they might not appeale but to the Primat, and to the Councell of their Prouince; to the end, that the cause might be determined within the Lymitts of that particular Prouince, where it had bene begun: The Councell of *Sardica* ordained, that after they had bene iudged by the Primat and the Councell of their Prouince, they might appeale to the Primat, and to the Councell of one of the next Prouince. Which thing being applyed to *Africa*, to witt,that it might be lawfull to euery Priest of *Africa* to appeale from the Primat and from the Councell of his Prouince, to the Primat and Councell of one of the next Prouinces; *Apiarius* pretended, that it belonged to the dignitie and the Priuiledge of the Sea Apostolicke, that it might be in the power of him that was a *Numidian* Priest, to choose amongst the Churches next the Prouince of *Numidia* the *Roman* Church,although it were out of the continent of *Africa*, before anie of the rest,because besides the neighbourhood that *Tertullian* expresses by these words; *If thou beest a neighbour to Italie, thou hast the Roman Church, whose authoritie is neere and at hand to vs*, she hath the prerogatiue and preheminence of dignitie aboue all the rest.

Côc.Carth 6.c.3.

Côc.Carth 1 c 1 & Côc Carth 2.c 10.

Concil. Sardic.c. 14.

Tertul.de præscript. c.36.

Now it happened that the Pope sent into *Africa* these canons of the Councell of *Sardica* vnder the title of the Canons of the Councell of *Nicea*. For the mention of the Councell of *Sardica* inserted into some *Latine* copies of the sixth Councell of *Carthage*, is a quotation of the copists, which slipt out of the Margent into the Text,as it appeares both by the current of the discourse,& by the latine collections of *Dionisius*, and by the copies of the Greeke edition, where it is not to be foũd. And this he did not to deceaue as is aboue said,but because it was the custome of the *Roman* Church,to cite the Canons of the Councell of *Sardica*, which was an Appendix of the Councell of *Nicea*, vnder the Title of canons of the Coũcell of *Nicea*,as it is the custome of the *Greeke*,to cite the canõs of the Councell intituled *Trullian*,vnder the title of the Canons of the sixth Generall Councell for that the Councell of *Sardica* was an *Appendix*, and a supplie of the councell of *Nicea* holden in the same age, and for the same cause with the councell of *Nicea*,the *Greekes*,yea euen those that are Schismatickes,are of agreement with vs. *It pleased* (said *Zonara*) *the two Emperors to cause a Councell to be holden to decide those things that had bene decreed in the Councell of Nicea*. At *Sardica* then assembled three hundred fortie one Bishops,who made a decree confirming the Synod of the Fathers of the councell of *Nicea*, & excommunicating those that held the contrary. And *Balsamõ*; *It pleased the Emperors, that the Bishops should assẽble at Sardica;to dispute about those thinges that had bene decided at Nicea; the assẽbly thẽ was made of three hũdred fortie one Bishops, & the holie Creede of the Fathers called at Nicea, was confirmed*. And *Glycas*; *By the aduise of the Emperors,the Coũcell was assẽbled at*

Zonar.præfat.in Concil.Sardic.

Balsam. Ibid. Glyc.Annal.l.4.

Sardica where there were three hundred fourtie one Fathers who confirmed the sacred and holie Creede made at Nicea. From whence it is, that the Emperor *Iustinian*, who intitles the Councell of *Sardica*, a generall Councell; yet neuerthelesse reckons but foure Generall Councells, as cōprehending and confounding the Councell of *Sardica*, vnder one selfe same title with that of *Nicea*, because the Coūcell of *Sardica* had made noe creede in chiefe, like the other Generall Councells, but had contented itselfe, with confirming and expounding that of the Councell of *Nicea*. Likewise also, that the custome of the *Roman* Church, was often to cite the canons of the Coūcell of *Sardica*, vnder the title of the canons of the Councell of *Nicea* (as well because the Councell of *Sardica* was annexed as an appendix to the Councell of *Nicea*, as because the Councell of *Nicea* and that of *Sardica* had bene sett downe in the *Latine* edition by one selfe same penn, and brought to *Rome* by one selfe-same Messenger; to witt, by *Osius*, who had presided at both, and they were written one following an other, yea in some copies, whereof they saie, one is to be found at *Arras*, without being distinguished the one from the other.) It appeares from the letters of the Popes *Innocent* and *Leo* the first, who alleadge the one in his Epistle to *Victricius* reported by *Charlemaine*, and by *Hincmarus*; and the other in his Epistle to the Emperor *Theodosius* the second annexed to the front of the copies of the Councell of *Chalcedon*; the decrees of the Councell of *Sardica*, vnder the title of the decrees of the Councell of *Nicea*. And indeede, if this extension of title had bene a fallacy, how came it that the *Pelagians*, which barked with so much fury against Pope *Zozimus* his ashes (who had condemned them) and slandred and defamed him of preuarication, neuer reproached him of this falshood? And how could S. AVGVSTINE, and *Prosper*, who vndertooke the defence of his memory, haue qualified him after his death, *Holy*, *Reuerent*, and *most blessed*? And how could Pope *Leo*, thirtie yeares after, haue fallen into the same crime? And then what profitt could it haue bene to the Pope, to alleadge by fallacy the Councell of *Sardica*, vnder the title of the Coūcell of *Nicea*; contrarywise if he had regarded his owne particular interest, why had it not bene of lesse aduantage to him to conceale the title of the Councell of *Sardica*, which in regard of generall authoritie, was as authenticall, and in regard of the particular discipline of *Africa*, was more authenticall, and more obligatory then that of *Nicea*? For first, as for generall authoritie, there were these equalities betweene the Councell of *Nicea* & the Councell of *Sardica*, that they had bene holden in tymes neere and contiguous one to the other, and celebrated, the one for the explication and strengthning of the other, & that the same *Osius*, which had presided at the one, had presided at the other: And that there were like number of Bishops in the one, as in the other; and that the one was called from all partes of the world, as well as the other. That it was so, not only saint ATHANASIVS, and after him *Socrates* and *Sozomene* testifie, that in the Councell of *Sardica*, there were more then three hundred Bishops, amongst which were the Patriarke of *Alexandria*, who was saint ATHANASIVS himselfe; the Bishop of *Hierusalem*, who was *Maximus*: the Bishop of *Constantinople*, according to *Sozomene* who was *Paule*: the Archbishop of *Carthage*, who was *Gratus*; and many of the same Bishops which had assisted at the Conncell of *Nicea*, as *Osius* Bishop of *Cordua* in *Spaine*; *Nicasius* Bishop of *Dina* in *Gaule*: *Protogenes* Bishop of *Sardica* in *Illyria*; *Marcellus* Primate of *Ancyra*, in *Galatia*: *Asclepas* Bishop of *Gaza* in high *Palestina*, *Ætias*, Bishop of *Lydda* in Lowe *Palestina*; *Paphnutius* of *Egipt*; *Spyridon* of *Cyprus* and others: But also saint

Iustin. in edict. de fide Orthodox. apud. Leūclaue. l. 8.

Theod. hist Eccl. l. 2. c. 15.

Capitul. Carol. Magn. addit. 4. Hincmar. in opusc. 55 capitul. c. 6 In ep. præam. Concil. Chalced. c. 9. Aug. ep. 157. & contra duas Epist. Pelagiani ad Bonifac. l. 2 c. 3. Prosp. Contra collat.

Athanas. Apol 2. Socrat. hist Eccl. l. 2. c. 20. Sozom. ibidem. c. 12. Athan. Apol. 2.

ATHANASIVS affirmeth that the Councell of *Sardica* was called by the commaundement of the two Emperors of *East* and *West*, a thing which appertained only to generall Councells; and that it was compounded of more then thirtie fiue Prouinces, and in this reckoning counting *Africa* but for one; *Spaine*, but for one; the *Gaule* and *Almany* but for one; *Great Britaine* but for one; *Macedō* but for one; *Thrace* bur for one; *Galatia* but for one; *Egipt* but for one; and the three *Arabias*, and three *Palestinas* but for one; as it shall appeare in the Chapter following, where wee will treate of deliberate purpose, of the authoritie of the Councell of *Sardica* and confute all the obiections that the *Popes* aduersaries make against it. And this is to be said of the equality of the Councells of *Nicea* and *Sardica* as concerning generall authoritie. For to the particular obligation of *Africa*, so farr of is the Councell of *Sardica* from being lesse authenticall then that of *Nicea*, as contrarywise the Councell of *Sardica* had this aduantage aboue that of *Nicea*; that in the Councell of *Nicea* there was but one only Bishop of *Africa*, to witt, *Cecilianus* Archbishop of *Carthage*, as the second generall Councell of *Constantinople* notes in these words: *Only Cecilianus Bishop of Carthage came from all Africa, to the Councell of Nicea; whereas in the Councell of Sardica, there were thirtie six African Bishops, amongst which was Gratus Archbishop of Carthage: Of Africa* (saith S. ATHANASIVS) *there signed at the Councell of Sardica, Nessus, Gratus, Magesius Coldeus, Rogatianus, Consortius, Raphinus Manninus, Cecilianus, Erennianus, Marianus, Valerius, Dinamius, Nyronius, Iustus, Celestine, Cypryan, Victor, Honorat, Marinus Pantagathus, Felix, Baudeus, Liber Capiton, Minersall, Cosmus, Victor, Hesperion, Felix, Seuerian, Optantius, Hesper, Fidetius, Salustus, Paschasius.* And *Osius* speaking to the Councell of *Sardica*; *Manie Bishops make a custome of trauailing to the court, and principallie the Africans, that as we haue vnderstood by our welbeloued brother and Colleague Gratus, receiue not wholsome Councells.* And *Gratus* himself citing in the first Councell of *Carthage* (cōcerning the credit whereof we are all agreed, and which is alleadged by *Ferandus* Archdeacon of *Carthage*) one of the Canons of the Councell of *Sardica*: *I remēber* (said hee) *that in the most holie, Councell of Sardica, it was decreed, that none should vsurpe a man of an other diocesse for his Clerke.* By meanes whereof not only the Councell of *Sardica* was of more authority then the Councell of *Africke*, as *Zonarus* himselfe acknowledgeth, when he saith speaking of the intituling of the Archbishopps: *The Councel of Chalcedon agreed rather to the Canon of the Councell of Sardica, then to that of the Councell of Africa*; but also in regard of discipline was more strong and obligatorie, in respect of the *Africans*, then the Councell of Nicea.

Conc. Const. 5. Act. 5. Athan. Apo. 2.

Concil. Sardic. can. 7.

Fulg. Ferand. in Breu. Can. artic. 24. 122. & alibi.

Cōc. Carthag. 1. c. 5. Zonar. in Concil. Carthag. c. 42.

Now it happened as we haue alreadie touched aboue, that when the Pope sent this Rule to the *Africans*, the Canons of the Councell of *Sardica* were no more to bee found in the *African* Prouinces; for the *Donatists* had soe wrought by craft, as they had suppressed and banished out of *Africa* all the true Actes of the Councell of *Sardica*, that had bene brought thither in the time of *Gratus* and of the first Councell of *Carthage*, and had supposed and slipt into their steede, the actes of the Anticouncelle of *Sardica*: that is to saie, the acts of the false Councell holden by the *Arrians* at *Philopolis* neere *Sardica*, vnder the title of the Councell of *Sardica*, because that in the Epistle of this false Councell, the *Arrians* made mention of *Donatus*, Bishop of the *Donatists* of *Carthage*. This appeares by conferring the places of S. AVGVSTINE with the rest of antiquitie. For S. AVGVST. testifies, that the Actes of the Councell of *Sardica* which were in his time currant in *Africa*, were the acts of the *Arriā* Councell & which had condēned S. ATHANASIVS & the Councell of

Aug. ep. 163. cell of *Nicea*. He offerd me (said S. AVGVSTINE, speaking of *Fortunius* the donatist) *a certaine Booke, where he would shew me, that, the Councell of Sardica had written to the African Bishops of the communion of Donatus.* And Id. ibidem. a little after: *Then hauing taken the Booke, and considering the statutes of the same Councell, I found that Athanasius Bishop of Alexandria, &c. and Iulius Bishop of the Roman Church, no lesse Catholicke, had bene condemned by this Councell of Sardica; whereby I was assured, that it had bene a Councell of Arrians.* And in the third Booke against *Cresconius* the *Donatist*, who had alleadged the same Councell of *Sardica*: Aug. cōtr. Crescon. l. 1. 3. c. 34. *The Councell of Sardica* (saith hee) *was a Councell of Arrians, as the copies that we haue in our hands doe manifest, principallie holden against Athanasius Bishop of Alexandria a Catholike.* And all antiquitie contrariwise teacheth vs, that the true Councell of *Sardica* had confirmed the Councell of *Nicea* and iustified S. ATHANASIVS, and was a most holy and most Catholicke Councell. *The holy Synod of Sardica* Athan. ad Solit. vit. agent. (saith S. ATHANASIVS, who assisted there in person) *compounded of aboue thirtie fiue Prouinces, receiued vs in our iustifieable proceedings.* And a little Id. ibid. after, *They declared Athanasius, and those that were with him pure and free from all crime, and their aduersaries slaunderers and wicked persons.* And elsewhere; Athanas. de fuga sua apol *In the great Councell of Sardica, our aduersaries were deposed as slanderers, and more then three hundred Bishops subscribed to our iustification.* And againe, *The holie councell assembled at Sardica decreed, that therein nothing of faith should be concluded, but that they should content them selues with the confession of the councell of Nicea.* And *Gratus* Archbishop of *Carthage*, who was also Conc. Carthag. 1. c. 5. there in person; *I remember* (said hee) *that in the most holy councell of Sardica it was decreed, that none should vsurpe a Clerke of an other diocesse.* And the Epist. Cōc. Sardic. apud. Athan. Apol. 2. Epistle of the same Councell of *Sardica*: *We haue declared our deare brethren and fellow-ministers, Athanasius, Marcellus, Asclepas, and others their adiuncts in the seruice of God, innocent and blamelesse.* And *Socrates*; Socrat. hist. Eccl. l. 2. 20 *The Bishops assembled at Sardica condemned before all things the desertion of those of Philopolis, and then deposed the accusers of Athanasius, and confirmed the decrees of the Coūcell of Nicea*: Sozomene: Sozom. hist. Eccl. c. 8. 1 *They answered that they would not separate themselues from the Communion of Athanasius and Paul, and principallie Iulius Bishop of Rome hauing examined their cause, and not hauing condemned them*, and the Councell of *Chalcedon*: *The fathers assembled at Sardica combated against the Relicks of Arrius*. A manifest proofe that the *Africans* in the tyme of S. AVGVSTINE, and of the sixth Councell of *Carthage* had no other but the Actes of the false Councell of *Sardica* holden by the *Arrians* at *Philopolis* neere *Sardica* which had condemned S. ATHANASIVS, and ouerthrowne the coūcell of *Nicea*, and not those of the true councell of *Sardica* wich had iustified S. ATHANASIVS and cōfirmed the councell of *Nicea*. But let vs returne to our history.

The Bishops of *Africa* then finding neither of these Canons in the copies of the councell of *Nicea*, and not being able to finde them in those of the councell of *Sardica* because they had them not, they stretched out vpon the occasion of the question of the priests, for which at the beginning the conclusion was moued, euen to Bishops; and seeing that the title vpon which that was groūded, which had vntill then bene obserued by custome concerning Bishops Appeales, did no more appeare then that of Priestes, tooke their tyme and opportunitie to complaine of the progresse of this custome, and of the greeuances that the Appeales, aswell of the one as of ther other; that is to say, as well of the Bishops as of the priests, brought vpon them, not by the fault of the appeales, but by the malice of men which is such as the gate cannot be opened for Appeales, but there wil happen great euills in the frequent, executions of this remedie,as the cōtempt of the first Iudges, the delaie and prolonging of iustice, the cost and vexation of the parties,the incommoditie of the transportation of witnesses of all sexes,and all ages: nor wholly shut it vp from them least worse may come of it. And therefore they writt to Pope *Sozimus*, whom their letters found already dead; and after to *Boniface* his successor, an Epistle by which after they had remonstrated to him the troubles that the past examples of appeales had brought vpon them; and had represented to him that they had not found the rule which was in question in the Canons of the Councell of *Nycea*, they required tyme to send into the *East* to take Copies out of the originall: but with what humilitie, and with what respect? Alwaies praying, alwaies beseeching, alwaies protesting to obserue in attending the comming of the copies of the Councell of *Nicea*, that which was contained in the instruction of the Popes legats: and in case that this Rule were not found in the Canons of the Councell of *Nicea*, requesting his *Holynesse* to cause them to obserue that which had bene decreed by the Canons of the Councell of *Nicea*: *Because* (said they) *it hath pleased God, that of the things that our holy Bretheren Faustinus our Colleague, and Phillip and Asellus our fellowe Priests haue treated with vs, our Humilitie gaue answere, not to the Bishop of Blessed memorie Zosimus from whom they brought vs commaundement and letters, but to thy Reuerence that haue bene diuinely instituted in his steed; we ought heere breefly to insinuate those thinges which haue bene determined by the reciprocall agreement of both parties.* Conc. Afric.ep. ad.Bonifac.c,101. And againe; *We request your Holynesse, that as these things haue bene done or decreed by the Fathers of the Councell of Nicea, so you will cause them to be obserued by vs, and that you will cause to be practised amongst you, that is, on thother side the sea, the points contained in the instruction.* Ibidem. And againe, *These things haue bene registred in the acts vntill the coming of the more certaine copies of the Councell of Nicea; within the which, if they be sett downe in the same sort as they are contained in the instruction that hath bene shewed vs by our bretheren, sent by the sea Apostolike and obserued amongst you in Italie wee wil no more make mention thereof* (For soe is the reading in the greeke text, and so wee haue proued heeretofore that it must be read) *nor further contest of the not induring it.* Ibidem. And presently after speaking of the Article of the Priestes appeales, which was the last article that they came from reporting, and that which most troubled them by reason of the insolence of the *African* Priests, who vnder pretence of these Appeales dispised and shooke of all their Bishops iurisdiction; *But we beleiue with the helpe of Gods mercie, that your Holynesse presiding in the Roman Sea, wee shall no longer suffer this typhe* (that is to saie, this meteor, or this vexation, or this insolence of Priests despising and shaking of the yoake of Episcopall discipline) *but that those things that brotherly charitie (yea though ourselues were silent) requires to be obserued towards vs, and which your selues according to the wisedome and Iustice that the most high hath bestowed vpon you, doe know ought to be obserued, shall be obserued to vs ward, if at least the copies of the Councell of Nicea speake otherwise then your Legats instruction.* Ibidem. For that is intended by the word, *typhe*, which being taken in his proper and naturall sence, signifies, *globe of smoke*, or *meteor*; from whence it is, that the greeke Marriners call the meteors and whirlewindes, shott from the clowdes in the forme of Globes and rolls of smoke, *Typhons*, and being taken in the figuratiue sence, signifies sometymes vexation, by allusion to the smoke with which bees are driuen; sometymes pride, sometymes insolence, and sometymes fury and madnes: termes all agreable to the persecution that the Bishops of *Africa* receiued from the insolent appeales of their priests, whereof they had newly said in *Apiarius* his case; *For as much as manie such examples haue* Ibidem.

preceeded,

caution must be vsed, that heereafter there may happen none such or yet worse. And the while to obey the present commandement of the Pope, they restored *Apyarius* to the Communion and to his Priesthood, as they testifie by these words of their Epistle to *Boniface; Apiarius crauing pardon for his faults, hath bene restored to the communion.* And againe; *It hath pleased vs that Apiarius should retire from the Church of Sicca, retayning the honor of his degree.* And by these in their Epistle to *Celestine; Apiarius had bene formerlie restored to Priestood by the intercession of Faustinus.* And not only that, but also protested in expecting the coming of the copies out of the *East*, to obserue from point to point what was contained in the instructions of the Popes legates. *We protest* (said *Alipius*) *vpon the reading of the first article, to obserue these thinges vntill the coming of the perfect copies.* And S. AVGVSTINE vpon the reading of the second; *We protest also to obserue this article, sauing a more diligent inquirie of the Councell of Nicea.* And the Fathers of the councell in the Epistle to *Boniface; Wee protest to obserue these things, vntill the proofe of the Canons of the Councell of Nicea, and wee trust in the will of God, that your Holynesse also will helpe vs in it.* By meanes whereof, the appeales remayned in the estate contayned in the instruction of the Popes legates vntill the coming of the copies from the *East*.

Ibidem. Ibidem. Ibid epist. ad Celest. cap. 105. Concil. Carthag. 6. c. 4. Ibid. c 7. Concil. Afric. c. 101.

When the copies of the councell of *Nicea* had bene brought out of the *East* wherein these Canons which also were of the Councell of *Sardica* and not of the Councell of *Nicea* were not to be found: the *African* Bishops sẽt a *Duplicat*, thereof to Pope *Boniface*, neuerthelesse without innouating anie thinge in matter of appeales. Whẽ Pope *Boniface* was dead, who deceased a few yeares after, and *Celestine* created Pope in his place; *Apiarius* who had retired himself frõ *Sicca* to *Tabraca* a Cittie of the same Prouince, to witt, of *Numidia* to exercise his priesthood there, fell in to other crimes, for which, at the instance of the *Tabracians* he was condemned, and deposed by the Councell of the Prouince, & from this Councell Appealed, or fayned to haue Appealed to *Rome* to Pope *Celestin* vpõ this pretẽce of appeale, sẽt *Faustin'* againe, who had assisted at *Apiari'* his iudgmẽt of appeale against those of *Sicca*, to cause a new Coũcell to be holden in *Africa*, where the cause of *Apiarius* against those of *Tabraca*, was in the presence of the same *Faustinus* againe put to triall, & the while restored and reintegrated *Apiarius* by forme of prouision to the Cõmunion. The *Africans* to obey the Popes commandement, assembled a last Councell, where they remitted A*piarius* his cause to examination in the presence of the Popes *Legates*, and found themselues so troubled to cleere the crimes, for which they had deposed him, which he affrontedly and impudently denied; as, if he had not conuinced himselfe, they despaired of euer compassing it: God so pressed the impostume of *Apiarius* his hart, as he broke it, and constrayned him to vomitt vp by an vnexpected confession, all the filth, rottennes, and infamyes, whereof hee was accused, and which he had denied with so much fraude and impudence. The *Africans* then pricked and stung with these infamous and insolent proceedings of *Apiarius*, and moued with this, that the Canons of Appeales that had bene sent them vnder the title of the Canons of the Councell of *Nicea*, were not in the copies of the Councell of *Nicea* that had bene brought out of the *East*; and not knowing that they were in those of the Councell of *Sardica* which was the *Appendix* and the seale of the Councell of *Nicea*, they tooke licence to write an Epistle to Pope *Celestine*, to beseeche him no more so easily to receaue the Appeales of the Clergie-men of *Africa*. Now some might call in question the credit of this Epistle, as well because it is a peece out of the worke, and annexed

Epist. ad Celest. Conc. Afric. c. 15. Ibid.

to the continuance of the sixth Councell of *Carthage* , which had bene held three yeare before, as a foundling, without anie mention of the date or of the actes, or of the history of the Councell where it was written, as, because it was full of clauses , and cannot be compatible with the discipline of the *Africans* , for it takes for a first foundation, that if the Councell of *Nicea* excluded Priests from being to be adiudged by Appeale out of their Prouinces, the Bishops may by stronger reason be excluded. And the foundation of the *Africans* contrarywise in the question that they had against the *Donatists* was, that *Cecilanus* after he had bene deposed by the Bishops of *Africa* might haue reserued the iudgment of his cause to the beyond sea Churches, for as much as he was not of the number of Priests or other inferior Clerkes; which the Coũcell of *Nicea* whereat *Cecilianus* assisted , could not be ignorant of. It takes for a second foundation that ecclesiasticalls condemned might appeale to the Councell of their Prouince , yea euen to the generall Councell of all *Africa* which is manifestly against the history and discipline of the Councells of *Africa*, and principally for the inferior Clerkes, as Priests, deacons and Subdeacõs. For, the holding of the anniuersary Councells of all *Africa*, had bene suppressed twelue yeares before *Celestine* in the Coũcell holden vnder the seauenth Consuslhip of *Honorius*; where it had bene ordained that the vniuersall Councells of *Africa* should no more be ordinary and anniuersary , and should no more be holden but for extraordinary and vniuersall causes. And that the causes that were not common, should be iudged in their Prouinces; And that if there were an appeale, the appealant and the partie should choose Iudges , from whom it should not be lawfull to appeale. And finally, it takes for a third foundation, that there was no difference of priuiledge betweene Clerkes of the Superior order, in the matter of passiue iurisdiction ; and that the same which had bene ordained concerning the one , ought by a stronger reason, to haue place concerning the others, which is directly contrary to the *African* discipline, which makes so great difference betweene the one and the other , as to iudge Priests in the second instance, there needed but six Bishops with the Diocesan, and to iudge a Bishop in the first instance , there must be twelue with the Archbishop of the Prouince. But for as much as this Epistle is in the collection of *Dionisius*, whether it haue bene added since , or whether it were inserted from the beginning ; and that after *Dionisius*, Pope *Adrian* and the Emperor *Charlemaine* made mention thereof, although there be ancient copies, where neither of these Epistles are to be found, I will not resist it. Only *I* will saie, that S. AVGVSTIN assisted not at the Councell where it was written; as appeares, as well because there is no mention made of him, neither at the beginning nor end of the Epistle, a thing which would neuer haue bene forgotten , to authorise and fortifie the action, as well as it had bene in the Epistle to *Boniface*, as because those that were after him in order of promotion, and which were wont to be enrolled after him in publicke actions, and amongst others *Theasius Vincentius*, and *Fortunatianus*, are named in the inscription of the Epistle, and not he. For that S. AVGVSTINE did vse to precede *Theasius* , appeares by the fortie fifth and two and sixtith Canon of the councell intitled *African*, and that hee vsed to precede *Vincentius* and *Fortunatianus* appeares by the collation of *Carthage* where the deputies for the Catholickes, vere *Aurelius*, *Alipius*, *Augustinus*, *Vincentius*, *Fortunatus* , *Fortunatianus* and *Possidius*. Now this Epistle containes two partes, to witt, a narration, and a supplication, which wee report from the Greeke text , for as much as the Greeke edition, as wee haue aboue shewed, is more intire

Aug. epi. 162.

Concil. dict. Afri- can. c. 62.

Con. Car. 1. c. 1. & citat a. Fulg. Ferrand. in Breu. Can. art. 244. Et Conc. Carth. 2. c. 10. & citat. eodem art. 55.

Diony. Ex. collect. Canon. diuers Concil. Afric. Prouin. tit. 138.

Adrian. Pap. collect ex Synod. & Canon diuers Capit. Carol. Mag. l. 6. c. 287.

Collat. Carthag. pag. 1.

and correct in matter of Epistles then the latine. The narration then is; *Our holy brother and colleague Faustinus coming to vs; wee beleeued that hee had bene sent with Apiarius, to the end, that as by his meanes Apiarius had bene formerly restored to his Priesthood; so now by his labour hee might be purged of so manie crimes, as had bene obiected against him by the Tabracenians, But the multitude of our Synod running ouer the crimes of Apiarius: found them to bee so great and in so great number, as they haue surmounted the protectiō, rather then iudgment: and affection of a defender, rather then the iustice of a Judge of the same Faustinus; for first he hath throughly resisted all the assemblie charging it with diuers contumelies vnder colour of pursuing the priuiledges of the Roman Church; and willing to cause himselfe to be receiued vnto our Communion, because your Holynesse beleeuing he had appealed to you, which yet he could not proue, had restored him to the Cōmunion. Yet this succeeded not with him, as you may know better by the verball processe of the actes; cōtrary wise after a laborious inquiry of three daies, during which wee examined with much anguish the diuers charges which were obiected to him, God a iust iudge powerfull & patiēt hath cut off by a great abridgemēt, the delaies of our colleague Faust. ād the tergiuersatiōs of the same Apiarius, by which he attēpted to hide his infamous villanies, &c. For our God pressing the conscience of this fraudulent denyer, and his will beinge to publish to men the Crimes that his prouidence condemned, being yet hidden in his hart, as in a bogge of vices, he hath blased out and sufferd himselfe to fall into a confessiō of all the vices, which were obiected against him &c. and hath couerted our hope by which wee beleeued and desired that he might purge himselfe from these so shamefull blotts and staines, into greef, but that our greefe hath bene eased by this only confort, that wee haue bene deliuered from the affliction of a longer labour.* After the narration marcheth the supplication which consists in three requests; The first request is, that the Pope should noe more so easily receiue those that should appeale to him from *Africa*. *Premised then* (said they) *the office of a due salutation, wee beseech you with all our affection, that you doe no more so easily admitt these to your eares, that shall come from hence, and no more receiue those to the Communion, that haue bene excommunicated by vs*, And a while after. *That so those that in their owne Prouince haue bene depriued of the Communion, may not seeme to be rashlie and vnfitly restored to the Communion by your Holynesse*, And this request they propt vp with fiue reasons. The first, that the Councell of *Nicea* had forbidden, that those which had bene excommunicated in one Prouince, should be receaued to Communion in an other: *Your Reuerence* (said they) *will easilie acknowledge that this hath bene so defined by the Councell of Nicea; for although it seemes to restraine the caution to inferior Clerks and to lay men by how much strōger reason did they intend it allso to Bishops*; A thing that the heate of contention drew from their mouthes, and which is directlie against S. AVGVSTINE, who saith speaking of *Cecilianus* Archishop of *Carthage*, who had bene deposed by a Councell of seauentie *African* Bishops assembled at *Carthage*: *Hee might contemme the conspiring multitude of his Enemies, because he knew himselfe to be vnited by communicatorie letters to the Roman Church, in which hath alwaies flourisht the principalitie of the sea Apostolick, and from the other Countries from whence the Ghospell first came into Africa*. And against the Councell of *Nicea* it selfe which precisely limitts the words to Priests and Laymē, which hauing bene excommunicated by their Bishop, could not be receiued to Communion, by anie of the other Bishops of the same Prouince. For whereas the *African* Fathers inferr, that if the Councell of *Nicea* spake these words of Priests and Laymen, they must be much more intended of Bishops; this is formally opposite to saint AVGVSTINES foundatiō, who saith that *Cecilianus* tyme-fellowe with the Councell of *Nicea*, might haue appealed beyond Sea, because hee was not of the number of Priests and other in-

Paulo post. princ.

Circa med.

Conc. Nicen. c. 5.

Aug. epi. 162.

ferior Clerkes, but of the number of Bishops, *They did not handle the cause* (saith hee) *of Priests, Deacons, or other inferior Clerkes, but of Bishops, which might reserue their causes to the iudgement of the churches beyond Sea.* Id. ibid.
The second that the Councell of *Nicea* committs the causes as well of Bishops as of Priests, to the Metropolitan; which is Concil.
true for the iudgement of Priests in the second instance, and of Bishops Nicen. c. 6
in the first. But not for the iudgment of Bishops in the last instance, as appeares by the testimonie of saint ATHANASIVS, who had assisted in person at the Councell of *Nicea*, which alleadges for his defence an Epistle, where Pope *Julius* writes, that the Councell of *Antioch*, and other Councells of the *East* could not depose ATHANASIVS from the Bishopricke of *Alexandria*, without expecting the decision of the church of *Rome*; *Are you ignorant* (saith hee) *that the custome is, that they should first write to vs and so from hence should procede the iust decision of causes, and therefore if there were anie suspition conceiued against the Bishop there*, that is to saie, of Alexandria, *they must write to the Church heere*; that is to saie, to the Church of *Rome*. Iul. ep. ad Eusebian apud Athan. Apol. 2. The third, that the *grace of the holy Ghost shall not be wanting to euery prouision*, or to euery Prouince, *to discerne the equitie of causes, and that it is not credible that God should inspire the Justice of the triall, to one only man what soeuer he be, and denie it to an infinite number in a Councell.* A certaine proofe that they spake of the causes of equitie and iustice, as well ciuill as criminall, and not of causes of faith, of which contrarywise they had written a yeare or two before to Pope *Innocent* vpon the subiect of *Pelagius* and *Celestius* his cause, which was a cause of Faith. *Wee doubt not with the helpe of Gods mercie,* Aug. ep. 92
who will vouchsafe to heare thee praying, and to guide thee consulting; but those that hold these peruerse thinges, will more easily yield to the authoritie of thy Holynesse, deriued from the authoritie of holy Scriptures. And Pope *Innocent*, to themselues: Aug. ep. 93
Alwaies, and as often as matters of faith are handled, J conceiue that all our Bretheren and colleagues can haue no reference but to Peter; that is to saie, to the author of their name and dignitie. The fourth, That it was very hard to assure beyond Sea iudgements, because of the difficultie of causing witnesses to passe the seas: *How can* (said they) *the Judgements beyond Sea be certaine, wherein the necessarie persons of witnesses for the debilitie of sexe of age, or manie other hindrances interuening cannot appeare?* An euident Argument, that they spake of particular and personall causes. And the fifth that it had neuer bene taken from the *African* Church, by any decree of a Councell, that Appeales should goe out of *Africa*, and that to send Legats from *Rome* into *Africa* to iudge them vpon the place, it was not constituted by any Councell: A thing the ignorance whereof they might well excuse, forasmuch as they had no more then in *Africa*, the true copies of the Councell of *Sardica*, but only as had bene aboue shewed those of the false Councell of *Sardica*, composed by the *Arrians*, and publisht by the *Donatists*, which gaue ground to all this question. The second request was, that the Pope should no more grante them clerkes executioners, so were certaine clerkes of the *Roman* Church called committees, to cause to be executed (with the helpe of secular power, and of the imperiall forces; that is to saie, by the strength of Vshers, Sergeants, and Souldiers) the iudgements of the Pope or of his Legats; a thing which prouoked much murmure in *Africa*. For although the malice of the *African* Poeple, who after they were fastned in the hate of anie Ecclesiasticall person would hardlie lett goe their hold, did some tymes make this remedie necessarie; Neuerthelesse, the abuse of

those, which did too violently applie it, did often conuert it into a pretence and occasion of complaint, as S. AVGVSINE testifies in an Epistle to the same pope *Celestine*, when he saith speaking of *Anthony* Bishop of *Fussala* in Numidia, who had appealed to the Pope from the iudgemet which the inhabitantes of *Fussala* had caused to be giuen against him. *He threatens them* (saith hee) *with secular power, and with the furie of souldiers, as if they should come to execute the iudgements of the Sea apostolike, in such sort as the miserable inhabitants being Christians and Catholiks feared more grieuous vsage from a Catholike Bishop, then they did when they were hereticks, from the lawes of the Emperors.* For these causes then, the *African* Bishops besought the Pope, to grant no more Clerkes executors to those which demanded them; *That you will not also* (said they) *send your clerks for executors to all those wich demaund them, nor permitt that wee should seeme to introduce the typhe or smoky meteor of the age into the Church of Christ, which propounds the light of simplicitie and the daie of humility to those that desire to see God.* Calling the force and military violence with which those executors did execute the iudgements of the Sea Apostolike, *Secular typhe*; for this is that which the marriage of these two words, *Typhe of the age* signifies; to witt, the furious and violent manner with which the worldly and secular powers were accustomed to cause themselues to be obeyed; as when the author of the life of *Fulgentius*, saith; That *Fulgentius*, commaunded nothing with the *Typhe* of secular dominion. And as when the Councell of *Ephesus* calls the vse that *John* Patriarke of Antioche, had made of the letters of *Dionisius* Gouernor of Syria, to the Captaine of the Garrison and of the souldiers of *Cyprus* to hinder the Bishops of *Cyprus*, from electing to themselues an Archbishop without the permission of the Patriarke of *Antioch*, *Secular Typhse*, and drawing from this particular case a generall lawe, ordaines, *That noe Bishop vsurpe the Prouinces which haue not bene from all antiquitie vnder his predecessors, &c: And vnder pretence of the execution of sacred thinges, introduce not the Typhe of secular power.* And a little after; *And that all letters obtained to the contrarie, may remaine disannulled, and of no effect.* And finallie, the third and last request, but expressed in termes of Confidence and assurance, is that the Pope will not suffer that *Apiarius*, to whom by the first Iudgement it had bene permitted to remaine in *Africa*, and exercise his Priesthood where he would; prouided it were not at *Sicca*, should remaine anie longer in *Africa*, and that he would not cause him to be assisted with Secular authoritie to this effect; Behold the words of the clause, which containe also the end and conclusion of the Epistle, which I haue translated from the Greeke text, because the Greek edition of the Epistles, as hath bene aboue shewed, is more correct then the latine. *For as for the wretched Apiarius, hauing alreadie bene condemned for his infamous crimes, by our Brother* Faustinus, *wee are no more in care for it, as much as by the meanes of the approbation and moderation of your Holynesse, for the preseruation of brotherly charitie, Africa will no longer indure him.* Now vpon this, what answere the Pope made them, wee haue it not, but that it is easie to be iudged by the successe, that he satisfied them of the mistaking of the Councell of *Nicea*, for that of *Sardica*, and made it appeare to them, that what they found not in the Councell of *Nicea*, had bene ordained, yea euen by their predecessors, in the Councell of *Sardica*. For, the Appeales of the *African*, Bishops, to the Pope, continued as before; as it appeares both by the Rule that Pope, LEO; onely eight yeare later then CELESTINE, made

Aug. epi. 261.

Author. vit. Fulg. c. 25.

Con. Eph. tom. 2. c. 4. in appēdic.

Ibidem.

Edit. Græ. Conc. Car. c. 138.

Leo epist. ad Episc. African ep. 8.

made vpon the appeale that *Lucifrinus* a Bishop of *Africa* had cast into the Sea Apostolike; and by the care that the *Africans* had afterward to insert into their Canon law, the Canons of the Councell of *Sardica*, vpon the matter of Appeales to the Pope. For *Fulgentius Ferandus* deacō of *Carthage*, a little later then S. AVGVSTINE, and tyme-fellow with S. FVLGENTIVS, registers into the collection that he made of the Canons, these decrees, vnder the title of the sixth and fifth Canon of the Councell of *Sardica*: *That a condemned Bishop may appeale, if he will to the sea Apostolike, and that during the appeale, an other cannot be ordained in his Chaire.* By meanes whereof, this question brought no interruption to the possession wherein the Pope was of appeales, euen in minor causes, and by consequent much lesse in maior causes, as those of Faith were, for which *Theodoret* Bishop of *Cyre*, a Cittie neere vpon *Persia* appealed in the same tyme to pope *Leo*, and was iudged and restored by him, all the Generall Coūcell of *Chalcedon* holden a while after the Councell of *Carthage*, approuing and confirming it. For I will not alleadge the Epistle of S. AVGVSTINE to *Celestine*, which is in the supplie of S. AVGVSTINS Epistles imprinted by *Plantine* where the same S. AVGVSTINE pursues in the behalfe of *Celestine*, the iudgment of the appeale, made by *Anthony* Bishop of *Fulsala*, to Pope *Boniface*; and represents to him to iustifie the sentence of the bishops of *Africa* who had left him his title, and depriued him of this Bishops Sea: *That there had bene manie like sentences in Africa, eue͂ the Sea Apostolike iudgeing it, or confirming the iudgement of others; as particularly of Priscus, Victor, and Laurence Bishop of the Cesarian Prouince*; because it seemes, that this Epistle was written before that of the Councell of *Africa* to *Celestine*. It sufficeth that neither the possession of the appeales from *Africa* to *Rome*, were interrupted by this question; neither did the Bishops of *Africa* cease to remaine in the same Communion and reuerence of the Sea Apostolike, as they were before, as the words of S. AVGVSTINE to Pope *Boniface* written in the current of the difference testifies *Thou disdainest not, thou which presumest not haughtilie, though thou presidest highlie, to be a friend to the hūble.* And these of Pope *Celestine* after the death of S. AVGVSTINE, *Wee haue alwaies had Augustine of holie memorie in our cōmunion*, which Prosper citeth to iustifie to the Bishops of the Gaules S. *Augustins* doctrine against the Pelagiās And these of *Capreolus* Archbishop of *Carthage*, & immediate successor to *Aurelius*, vnder whom the sixth Councell of *Carthage*, was holden, writing to the fathers of the Councell of *Ephesus*; *VVee praie you to resist all nouelties, with such constancie, as the authoritie of the sea Apostolicke and the seueritie of the Prelates assembled in one, seeme not to permitt that the doctrine of those that the Church hath long since ouerthrowne; come to be borne againe.* And these of *Eugenius* one of the other successors to the same *Aurelius* to the Lieutenant of *Hunnericus* Lord of *Africa*; *The Roman Church is the head of all the Churches.* And these of *Fulgentius*, and of the Bishops of *Africa*; *the Roman Church which is the head of the world.*

Fulg. Ferr in Breu. Cano 1. art 59. & 60.

Theod. ep. ad Leon. inter epist Leon post. 60. & in epist. Græ manuscr. Theodor. Concil. Chalced. I. Aug. ep. 261.

Aug. con. duas epist. Pelag. ad Bonifac. l. 1. Epist. Cœlest ad Gal. quæ extat tom 7. bea. August. & citatur a Petro Diaco. lib. de incarn. & grat. Prosp. con. Collator. Actor. Conc. Ep. tom. 2. Fulgent de incarn. & gratia c. 11.

Of the Councell of Sardica.

CHAPT. XI.

I Remember that I promised in the former chapter, to handle in this, the truth and authoritie of the Canons of the Councell of *Sardica*; the time summons me now to performe my promise, and with so much the more neede, because the Popes aduersaries haue a while agoe, caused a Greeke Code of Canōs to be imprinted, which they haue intituled, *A Code of the Canons of the Vniuersall Church*: from whence they haue ecclipsed and cutt off, the Canons of the Councell of *Sardica*, against the credit of all the Greeke Canonists *Photius*, *Zonara*, *Balsamon*, *Harmonopolus*; and against the Greeke impressions, euen of *Basle Wittenbourg*, and other Protestant Citties; and in summe, against the truth of all the Greeke codes, as well printed as manuscript, of all the westerne and Easterne libraries. Then to compasse this designe with some method, I will aduertise the readers, that there past two things in the Councell of *Nicea* which gaue an occasion soone after, for the holding of the Councell of *Sardica*: the one was the decree of the consubstantialitie of the Father and the Some; and the other the decree of Appeales. The first was inserted into the Creede of the faith publisht by the Fathers of the Councell of *Nicea*, the second into the originall acts of the Councell of *Nicea*, with which it hath bene lost; only there remaines to vs, some light track of it in an Epistle of Pope *Julius* reported by S. ATHANASIVS, and by the Councell of *Alexandria*, where Pope *Julius* writes to the *Arrians*; *It hath not bene without the prouidence of God that the Bishops assembled in the great Councell of Nicea haue permitted that the acts of a former Synod, should be examined in an other Synod*. For that this decree was not the same which is contayned in the Canons of the Councell of *Nicea* where it is ordained, that when a Bishop hath excommunicated anie Churchman or Layman of his diocesse, the cause of the excommunicated person may be reuiewed in the Synod of his Prouince: it appeares both by this, that he speakes of the reuiew of the iudgments giuen in the first instance by the Synods, & inferrs from thence; that S. ATHANASIVS hauing bene iudged in the first instance in the Councells of *Tyre* and *Antioch*, might againe haue bene iudged at *Rome* in a new Councell. And because that he adds; *That if this custome being of itselfe antient, and hauing bene renewed and sett downe in writing in the great Synod, you will not permitt that it haue place amōgst you, such a refusall is vndecent*, a thing that shewes, that this decre whereof he speakes, was resisted by the *Arrians*, which cannot be said of the reuiewe of the sentences of the diocesan Bishops by the Councell of the Prouince. And therefore it must be supposed, that this decree had bene inserted, not into the catalogue of the Canons of the Councell of *Nicea*, which contained but the twentie articles which wee haue; but into the very acts of the Coūcell of *Nicea* which haue bene lost. And of this kinde of decrees inserted not into the list of the Canons of the Councells, but into the acts of the Councells, there are manie examples, and in the matter of the Coūcell of *Nicea* it selfe. For the Epistle of the same Coūcell of *Nicea* and the Councell of *Antioch* teach vs, that the Councell of *Nicea* made a decree of the *Pasch*, and S. AMBRO. teacheth vs that the Coūcell

[Margin notes: Iust. apud Hadria Beys. 1610 — Iul. apud Athanas. ap. 2. Con. Nic. c. 7. — Iul. vbi supra. — Concil. Anthioch. c. 1. Am. ep. 82.]

of *Nicea* made a decree of the exclusion of these that were in *Digami* from Priesthood: and the Caluinists themselues are agreed, that the Councell of *Nicea* made a decree of the *Eucharist*; All which decrees are not inrolled into the Canons of the Councells of *Nicea*, but haue bene necessaryly inserted into the Acts. Now what the conditions of these following Synods ought to be, which iudged by Appeale of the iudgments of former Synods, there is nothing to be found in Pope *Iulius* his Epistles, only it is left to vs to coniecture, that the subsequent Synods should be greater then the former Synods. But wherein this Maioritie consisted; that is to saie, whether it should be a simple maioritie of number, as the *Arrians* had monopolized it in the Councell of *Antioch*; or whether it should be a maioritie as it seemes the third Councell of *Carthage* requires, when it saies, *That when there hath bene an Appeale from what Ecclesiasticall Judge soeuer, to other Ecclesiasticall Iudges, where there is greater authoritie, the disannulling of the former Sentence, hurts not the first iudges*, there is nothing found in Pope *Julius* his Epistle: only we learne from the practise of antiquitie, that the maioritie of Councells did not alwaies depend of the number of Bishops, but was often measured by the qualitie of him, that was the head thereof, although the number of Bishops were fewer as the Councell of the Primat of the Nation, was reputed greater, then that of the Metropolitan of the Prouince; and that of the Patriarke greater, then that of the Primat; and that of the Pope yet greater, then that of the Patriarke, although there were fower Bishops. For in the Councell of *Rome*, which iudged saint ATHANASIVS his cause, after the Councell of *Antioch*, there were but fiftie Bishops, whereas in that of *Antioch*, there were aboue ninetie. And in this sence *Balsamon* a Schismaticall Greeke Author, which rankes the Patriarke of *Constantinople* aboue the Pope pretends that the title of *Vniuersall Bishop*, which in the Councell of *Calcedon*, had bene giuen to the Pope, should be also communicated to the Bishop of *Constantinople*; for as much as *Constantinople*, bore the title of second *Rome*; and will haue it, that the Synod of the Bishop of *Constantinople*, should be esteemed greater, then that of all the other Patriarkes of the Empire of the *East*. *Although* (saith hee) *that the Synod of Constantinople, were not vniuersall, for as much as other Patriarkes assisted not there; neuerthelesse, it seemes to me greater then all the other Synods; and the Patriarke thereof is called vniuersall Patriarke*. Now it fell out a while after the holding of the Councell of *Nicea*, that the *Arrians* made two breaches in these two decrees: The one by abollishing the word, *Consustantiall*, which they ecclipsed from all their creedes; And the other, by the resistance that they gaue to the restitution that the Pope made of *Athanasius* Patriark of *Alexandria*; of *Paul* Bishop of *Constantinople*: of *Marcellus* Primat of *Ancyra* in *Galatia*; *Asclepas* Bishop of *Gaza* in *Palestina*; and of *Lucius* Bishop of *Adrianopolis* in *Thrace*, deposed a little before by the Councells of *Tyre*, *Antioch*, and *Constantinople*, for diuers pretended crimes: Some Secular, as *Athanasius* for the crimes of Treason, Adultery, and homicide; and other Ecclesiasticall. The history of the first contrauention appeares by all the testimonies of *Antiquitie*: And the history of the second by the report of *Sozomene*; who after he had said; *Iulius Bishop of Rome hauing heard the accusations attempted against Athanasius of Alexandria; Paul of Constantinople; Marcellus of Ancyra in Galatia; Asclepas Bishop of Gaza in Palestina; Lucius Bishop of Adrianopolis in Thrace; and hauing found them all consenting to the doctrine of the*

Cōc. Carth. c. 10.

Ath. de fug. sua Apol idem ad Solit. Sozom. hist. Eccl. l. 3. c. 5. Concil. Chalced. Act. 3. in libell. Cleric. Alex. Cōc. Const c. 3 & Cōc. Chalced. Act. 15. & 28. Balsam in Cōc. Const 1. c. 6. Theod. hist. Eccl. l. 2. c. 21. & Sozom. l. 3. c. 12. Sozom. hist Eccl. l. 3. c. 9. Id. ib. c. 7.

Sozom. hist Eccl. l. 3. c. 7.

Councell of Nicea, receiued them to his Communion, and because to him for the dignitie of his Sea, the care of all things apperteyned; he restored them each one to his Church, and writt to the Bishops of the East, chiding them for not hauing obserued the right formes in the iudgement of these men, and that they had troubled the Churches with not hauing kept within the compasse of the decrees of the Councell of Nicea, and commaunded them to send a small number from amongst them all, to appeare at a daie prefixed, and to iustifie their Sentence; Adds, *These things Julius writt, and Athanasius and Paule, receiued each one his Church, and sent the letters of Julius, to those of the East; who finding themselues sharpely toucht therewith, assembled themselues at Antioch, and writt backe to Pope Iulius an Epistle, adorned with flowers of eloquence, and composed in an orators stile full of manie figures, and not free from greeuous threatnings, for although they auouched by theyr letters, that the Roman Church obtained the prize of honor from them all, as hauing bene from the beginning the Schoole of the Apostles, and the Metropolitan of Religion; although the Doctors of the Christian world, were come thither from the East; Neuerthelesse, they did not thinke, they ought to be put behind, vnder colour that they were inferior in Greatnesse and multitude of Churches; since contrarywise they were much Superior in vertue and election of opinion;* that is to saie in *Arianisme*; *And as for Iulius they reproached it to him for a crime, that he had admitted into his communion, Athanasius and his consortes, and were offended at it, pretending that by that Acte, their Councell had bene iniuryed, and their Sentence abrogated; a thing that they calumniated as vniust, and repugnant to the ecclesiasticall Rule.* For that the authors of that Epistle that *Sozomene* argues of *ironia*, because they fained by their *exordium*, to confesse the primacie of the *Roman* Church, which they denied by their conclusion of slander because they pretended, that the abrogation that the Pope had made of their Councell, was a thing outragious, and contrary to the lawe of the Church, and of impudence, for as much as they set vpon him, to whom for the dignitie of his Sea, the care of all things belonged, were *Arrians*, it appeares both by the testimonie of S. ATHANASIVS who called them *Eusebians*, that is to say, of *Eusebius* his Sect, the chiefe firebrand of the *Arrians* heresie: And by the reproache that *Iulius* made to thẽ, that they had altered the decision of the Councell of *Nicea*; and by the answere that themselues made to that reproach; to witt, that as for the things they had done against the decisiõ of those that had bene assembled at *Nicea*, they Answered nothing; although they signified that they had manie causes to excuse their Actions, but that it was superfluous then to enter into defence of it, since they were suspected to haue violated iustice in all things, by the glorie that they attributed to them selues, to be more excellent in beleefe then the *Roman* Church: And finallly, by the offer that they made to *Julius*, to enter againe into peace and communion with him, if he would admitt the deposition of S. ATHANASIVS, and of his cõsortes. And that *Sozomene* calls them, those of the *East*, it is in parte, because the principall Seate of the *Arrians* heresie was the *East*; and in part, because they were the Bishops of the Patriarkship of *Antioch*, and other *Arrians* their adherents, who after the Councell of *Antioch*, holden in the dedication, reassembled themselues at *Antioch*, to answere Pope *Iulius*; which Patriarkship of *Antioch*, was called the Patriarkship of the *East*, because amongst the *Asian* prouinces, which acknowledged the *Roman* Empire, the diuision of *Antioch* held the place of the *East*; from whẽce it is, that *Cornelius Tacitus*, & *Amianus Marcellinus*, say that *Antioch* was the head of the *East*; and that the Councell of *Constantinople* ordaines, *That the Bishops of the East; that is to saie, of the Pa-*

Idem. Ibid

Athan. apol. 2. Statim. post. epist. Iul. & alibi. Iul. apud Athan. apol. 2.

Sozo 4. hist Eccel. l. 3. c.

Ibidem.

Cornel. Tacit. Ammian Marcel. l. 22. Concil. Const. c. 2.

triarkshipp of Antioch, should only rule the East. And that *Iohn* Patriarke of *Antioch* saith, in the Schismaticall Councell of *Ephesus* speaking of the Bishops of his Patriarkship: *wee that are called of the East.* And it is not to be said, that *Iulius* in the Answere that he sent to *Danius* (it must be read *Dianus*) and to *Phlacillus* (it must be read *Placitus*) and to *Narcissus*, and to *Eusebius*, and to *Maus*, and to others which had written to him from the second mock-councell of *Antioch*, stiles them his Bretheren; For he calls them his Brothers because of the communion of the Episcopall charac-ter; As S. AVGVSTINE calls the *Donatists* his Bretheren, because of the Commnunion of the charactar of Baptisme, but not, but that all those Bishops were *Arrians*, and the most impious of all the *Arrians*, for this *Dianius* was a Bishop of *Cesaria* in *Capadocia* an *Arrian*; and this *Placitus* was a Bishop of the *Arrians* of *Antioch*, and this *Narcissus* was an *Arrian* Bishop of *Veroniade* in *Cilisia*; and this *Eusebius* was Bishop of *Nicomedia*, Ensigne-bearer of the *Arrian* faction, who procured as S. ATHANA-SIVS notes the second Councell of *Antioch*, and the Councell of *Sardica* and likewise the others. But lett vs againe pursue the course of our histo-ry of *Arrianisme*; vpon the complaint propounded by the Catholikes a-gainst the *Arrians*, of the woundes made in these two decrees of the Councell of *Nicea*, the two Emperors, the one Catholike, and the other *Arrian*, agreed vpon the holding of a Generall Councell and called from the two Empires to *Sardica*, a Cittie situate in the confines of both the Empires, to decide it; *Paul and Athanasius* (saith *Socrates*) *demanded to haue an other Councell called, to the end, that as well their cause as that of faith, might be reuewed in a generall Councell shewing that their depositions had bene made with a purpose to destroy the Faith.* Then vpon their request, a generall Councell was publisht at *Sardica*; Now of this Councell the issue in regard of Faith was; that the fathers assembled at *Sardica*, confirmed the Creede of the Councell of *Nicea*, as *Harmenopolus* a Greeke author and a schismatike reportes after thousand others in these words; *By the aduise of the Emperors and of the Bishop of Rome, the Synod of Sardica was assembled, composed of three hundred fortie one Fathers, which confirmed the Councell of Nicea, and pu-blished the Canons.* For that which S. ATHANASIVS saith, that, the Coun-cell of *Sardica*, would not permitt that anie thing of faith should be re-duced into writing, ought to be vnderstood, that it would not permitt, that there should be anie new Creede made, but ordained that they should hold themselues to that of *Nicea* which they amplified, not by waye of innouation, but by way of exposition. And as for the matter of Appeales, they approued the restitution that the Pope had made of *Paul*, of *Athanasius*, and of the other Bishops with had bene deposed in the Councells of *Tyre* and *Antioch*, and receiued them into their Commu-nion vnder this title, that the Pope having examined their cause had not condemned them. *They answered* (saith *Sozomene*) *that they would not re-iect the Commnnion of Athanasius and of Paul for as much principally, as Iulius Bishop of Rome hauing examined, their cause, had not condemned them: and to pre-uent the Churches trouble thereafter in like accidents, reduced into writing three Ca-nons vpon the matter of appeales;* whereof the first was propounded by *Osius*, Presidét of the Councell, and concluded by all the Councell in these ter-mes. *If anie Bishop in anie cause in likelyhood ought to be condemned and that hee presume to haue, not an euill but a good cause to the end the iudgement may be re-newed, if it please your charitie that we should honor the memorie of the Apostle Pe-ter, lett it be written to Iulius Bishop of Rome by the same Bishops that haue giuen the iudgemét, to the end that if it be needefull, it may be renewed by the next Bishops; and lett the Bishop of Rome giue the Iudges: but if the affaire be such, as there is no*

Collat. Carth. Act. 3. & breu. coll. p. 3.

Athan app. 2.

Socrat. hi. Eccl. l. 2. c. 20.

Harmeno. in epi. tom. can.

Sozo. hist. Eccl. l. 3. c. 9.

Concil. Sar. c. 3.

neede of a new iudgement, lett not the things once iudged be disabled, but remaine firme. The second was propounded by *Gaudentius* and authorized by all the Councell, in these wordes: *If it seeme to you necessarie to add to this sentence full of sincere charitie that you haue propounded; That if anie Bishop be deposed by the next Bishops, and saie that his affaire ought to be iudged a new, lett no other be installed in his sea, till the Bishop of Rome haue pronounced vpon it, with examinatiō of the cause.* Which Canō was made as *Balsamon* notes, to disanull the Canō that the *Arriās* had published in the Councell of *Antioch* against S. ATHAN. which ordained that it should not be lawfull for a Bishop after he had bene deposed by all the votes of a Synod to exercise anie Episcopall functiō, nor to hope for restitutiō; and to condēne the intrusiō the Arians had made of *Gregorie* in steede of S. ATHAN. without attending the reuiew of the processe. And the third was againe propounded by *Osius*, and confirmed by all the councell, in these words: *It hath pleased, that if a Bishop haue bene accused, and that he haue recourse by waie of Appeale, to the Blessed Bishop of the Roman Church, and that he will heare him, and doe esteeme it iust, that the examinatiō of the affaire should be renewed, let him vouchsafe to write to the Bishops neighbouring that prouince, that they should carefullie and with diligence examine all things, and iudge the affaire according to the creditt of the truth: and if anie one demaund that his cause shou'd be heard againe, and seeme to moue the Bishop of Rome by his prayer, that he should send Priests from his owne side it shall be in the power of the Bishops, of Rome, to doe what he shall think fit and if he conceiue that he should send to iudge with the Bishops, persons hauing the authoritie of him that sends them, lett it be so done; and if he thinke it will suffice, that those that are alreadie vpon the place should examine the affaire and the iudgment of the Bishop; lett him doe what shall seeme best in his most wise iudgment.* Now these words do so dazle the eyes of the Popes aduersaries as they cannot supporte their light, and therefore they attempt to resist and weaken them with seauen obiections.

Concil. Sar. c. 4.

Balsom. in Concil. Sardic. c. 4.

Concil. Sardic. c. 5. or. 7.

The first, that the Councell of *Sardica* propounds the ouerture of Appeales to the Pope, not as a thing before practised; but as put to deliberation, and instituted at that present tyme, and in words of the future tense; from whence they inferr, that the Right of Episcopall appeales, was not from all Antiquitie yielded to the Pope, but only since the Councell of *Sardica*; and add that the Councell specifying the name of Pope *Julius* and saying, *let it be written to Iulius Bishop of Rome*: shewes that this institution began only in the Papacie of *Julius*, and had no place in his predecessors tymes. To this obiection then wee saie, that it is ordinary to antient Councells when they renew vnwritten customes, yea euen the verie written lawes of the Church, to propound them as if they did new institute them, and to take the notes of the assistants to conclude them, and to declare them, by words of the future tense: As in the same Councell of *Sardica* the prohibition to passe from one Cittie to an other renewed because of *Eusebius* of *Nicomedia*, head of the *Arrian* faction, who was past from the Bishoprik of *Nicomedia* to that of *Constantinople*: and the prohibition to a Bishop to receaiue a Clerke from an other Bishop excommunicated by him, and others the like, were propounded in future words, and with receauing the votes of the assistants, although the custome were tyme out of mynde in the Church, and that they had bene euen sett downe in writinge in the Councell of *Nicea*. And Pope *Julius* after he had cited the Canon of the Councell of *Nicea* for the reuiew of the iudgements of Synods, adds: *that this Canon had bene formerly practised by custome in the Church, and after reduced into writing at the Councell of Nicea.* And the Councell of *Constantinople* writing to Pope *Damasus*: Doth it not saie

The first obiection against the Canon of appeales to the Pope.

Concil. Sardic. c. 1.

Ibid. c. 16.

Conc. Nic. c. 6.

of the ordination of Bishops by the metropolitans, *It is as you know, both a lawe grounded vpon ancient custome, and decision of the Councell of* Nicea; For as for the name of Pope *Iulius*, which is specified in the first of the three canons of the Councell of *Sardica*, besides that it is not found in the ancient latine Editions, which were produced in the Councell of *Africa* in saint AVGVSTINES tyme, where the text saith simplie as in the other following canons: *The Bishop of Rome*, and not *Iulius Bishop of Rome*: By meanes whereof there is a Ground for suspition, that it is a quotation of the exemplifiers, which is slipt out of the margent into the Text; there can be nothing inferred from it but this, that the Fathers of the Councell of *Sardica* inserted the name of *Iulius* there, to shew that the Councell by this canon, ratified not only in generall Appeales to the Pope, but iustified and ratified in particular, the restitution that Pope *Iulius* had made of saint ATHANASIVS; *Paule* of *Constantinople*; *Marcellus* of *Ancyra Asclepas* of *Gaza*, and other Bishops, that the *Arrians* had deposed in their false Councells, agreeably to the Answere that they had made to the *Arrians*, that they could not reiect the comunion of *Athanasius* and the other Bishops, deposed by the Councells of *Tyre*, *Antioch*, and *Constantinople*; because *Iulius* Bishop of *Rome* hauing examined their cause, had not condemned them. And indeede if the Councell of *Sardica* had giuen beginning to the Right of Appeales, how could Pope *Iulius* manie yeares before haue written to the *Arrians*; *Are you ignorant that it is the custome that wee be first written to, that from hence may proceede the iust decision of things; and therefore if there were anie suspition conceiued against the Bishop there*, that is to saie, against the Bishop of Alexādria, *you should haue written to the church heere*; that is to saie, to the church of Rome? & how could *Socrates* & *Sozomene* haue said, *that Pope Iulius, many yeares before the Cōucell of Sardica, restored Athanasius Patriarke of Alexandria; Paule Bishop of Constantinople; Marcellus Primat of Galatia, and other Bishops, deposed by the Councells of the East, because to him for the dignity of his Sea the care of all things belonged.*

[Conc. Const. 1. ep ad Damas. & alios Episc.]

[Soz. lib. 3.]

[Iul. apud Athan. Apol. 2.]

[Soc. hist. Eccl. l. 2. C. 11. Sozom. hist. Eccl. l. 3 C. 7.]

The second obiectiō is, that the Councell of *Sardica*, grounds the canon of appeales to the Pope not vpō diuine right, but vpon the desire of honoring of saint Peters memory; from whence they inferr that the attributiō of the Episcopall appeales to the Pope, is not by diuine Right: but who sees not, that euē this is to ground it vpon diuine Right; for to saie, that to honor the memory of S. PETER, it was to purpose to yield Episcopall Appeales to the Pope, what is it but to saie, that the Pope was S. PETERS successor, and that in this qualitie, Appeales ought to be yielded to him, as to him that had the succession of head of the church, and by this succession was himselfe made head thereof? And in truth what the Fathers of the councell of *Sardica* expresse in their Canon by these words; *That we may honor the memorie of Peter, lett it be written to Iulius the Bishop of Rome*; do they not expresse in their Epistle to the same *Iulius*, by these? *It is verie good and fitt that from all the prouinces, the Bishops haue reference to their head, that is to saie to the sea of the Apostle Peter*? And doth it not from thence appeare, that to honor in the persons of the Bishops of *Rome*, the memory of *Peter*, and to ackdowledge the sea of *Peter* in the persons of the Bishops of *Rome*, for head of the Church, is according to the Councell of *Sardica*, one and the same thinge, and by consequent that the right of Appeales which was implicitly contained in the title of, *Head of the Church*, had belonged to the Pope by diuine right from all antiquitie, although the custome had bene first reduced into an expresse lawe but in the Councell of *Sardica*? For who knowes not that all the prerogatiues that are implicitly contained in anie Title, belong to him to whom the

[The second obiection against the Canon of Appeales.]

[Epist. Concil. Sardic ad Iul. Pap. insert. in fragm. Hilar. & citat. a Nicol. 1. in Epist. ad Episcop. Galliar.]

The third obiection against the Canon. Title is giuen, from the verie tyme it is giuen him, though the lawes that are made for the explicit declaration of anie of those prerogatiues be later? The third obiection is, that saint HILARIE and saint EPIPHANIVS, and the second Councell of *Constantinople*, call the Councell of *Sardica* the Councell of those of the west; From whence *Zonara*, *Hormenopolus*, and some other later Greekes and Schismaticks, and the Protestants who ioyne with them conclude, that the Councell of *Sardica* was not Generall. To this obiection then we answere two thinges; the one, that the word of the west, did then extend much farther, then it doth now, for by the word of the *West*, the fathers intended not onely, all the Prouinces of *Africa*, of *Italie*, of *Spaine*, of the *Gaules*, of *England*, of *Germanie*, of *Hungaria*, of *Dalmatia*; but also all the Prouinces of *Greece*; as *Achaia*, *Peloponesus*, *Macedonia*, the *Isle* of *Creete*; and left nothing for the East; but *Thrace*, *Egipt*, and *Asia*. And the other; that their calling the Councell of *Sardica*, the Councell of the west, is not to distinguish it from the Generall Councells, as some late Greekes haue supposed, but to distinguish it from the false Councell of *Sardica*, which was called the Councell of those of the East. For after the whole Councell, composed of three hundred Cotholicke Bishops, and of seauentie six *Arrian* Bishops, was arriued at *Sardica*, these seauētie six *Arrians* seperated themselues from the Bodie of the Councell, and retired them selues to *Philopopolis*, a cittie neere *Sardica*, where they kept an *Anti-councell*, which was called the Councell of those of the East; Not that all the Bishops of the East assisted there, but for two other causes: the one, for as much as the principall Bishops of this mock-councell, were *Steuen* Patriarke of *Antioch*, and the other Bishops of his Patriarkship, which was called the Patriarkship of the East. And the other; because of the two citties; whereinto this Councell was diuided, situate on the two sides of the mountaine of *Thuscis* which was the bound of the two Empires of the East, & of the west; the cittie of *Sardica* wherein the catholicks remayned was situat in the westerne side of the mountaine; and the cittie of *Philopopolis* into which the *Arrians* retired themselues, was situate on the Easterne side. For so farr of were all the Bishops of the East from assisting at this *Anti-synod*, as the *Arrians* themselues confest that held it, that there were but eightie of them there, and auowed, that the Bishops of the Empire of the East, which were present at the true Councell of *Sardica*, were an immense number. *There came* (saie they) *to Sardica, an immense number of wicked and lost Bishops, flowing from Constantinople, and from Alexandria, whom Osius and Protogenes held assembled with them in their Conuenticle.* And yet euen to take the East particularly for the Patriarkship of *Antioch*, many of the Bishops of the East, though taken in this sence, assisted not at the false Councell of *Sardica*. Contrarywise all the Catholick Bishops, as well of the Patriarkship of *Antioch*, as of the neighbouring Prouinces, as *Diodorus* Bishop of *Asia minor*; *Asterius* Bishop of *Petra* in *Arabia*; *Maximus* Bishop of *Hierusalem*; *Ætius*, Bishop of *Lydda*; *Arius* Bishop of *Petra* in *Judea*; *Theodosius*, *Germanus Siluanus*, *Paul*, *Claudius*, *Patrick*, *Elpidus*, *Germanus*, *Eusebius*, *Zenobius*, *Paule*, and *Peter* Bishop of *Palestina*, assisted and subscribed with the body of the catholicke Bishops at the true Councell of *Sardica*; By meanes whereof this distraction, consisting in so small a number of Bishops, and being made by the *Arrians* only, could not hinder the true Councell of *Sardica*, which represented all that were catholicke Bishops in the world, from preseruing the title of Generall which had bene imposed vpon it at the calling it; no more then the di-

S. Hilar. l. cont. Const. Aug. Epiphan. hæres. 71. cont. Photinian. Concil. Constant. 1 c5. zonar. in Conc. Const. 1. c. 5.

Socrat. his. Eccl. l. 2. c. 20 Et Soz. l. 3 c. 10.

Decret. Synod. Oriental. apud Sardic. in fra. Hilar. p. 10.

straction of those of the East; that is to saie, the *Bishops* of the Patriarkship of *Antioch*, which maintained *Nestorius*, and held an *Antisynod* in his fauour at *Ephesus*, hindred the true Councell of *Ephesus* from being perfectlie and absolutely generall; and from taking this qualitie euen then, when those of the East; that is to saie, the Bishops of the patriarkship of *Antioch*, held their mockcouncell a part. And therfore saint ATHANASIVS, not only calls it, the Great Councell of *Sardica*; and *Socrates* and *Iustinian*, a Generall Councell; but also saint ATHANASIVS, and after him *Sulpitius Seuerus*, *Theodoret* and *Vigilius* ancient Bishop of *Trent*, affirme that it was composed from all the christian Prouinces of the Earth. *The holie Councell of Sardica* (saith saint ATHANASIVS) *assembled from more then thirtie fiue Prouinces, knowing the malice of the Arrians, receaued vs in our iustifiable acts*, And elsewhere, explicating the list of the same Prouinces: *In the Great Councell of sardica, called by the commaundement of the Religious Emperors, Constantius and Constans, There subscribed for vs more then three hundred Bishops of the Prouinces of Egipt, of Libia of Pentapolis, of Palestina of Isauria, of Ciprus, of Phamphilia, of Licia, of Galatia, of Dacia, of Misia, of Thracia, of Dardania, of Macedonia, of the Epiruses, of Thessalia, of Achaya, of Creete, of Dalmatia of Siccia, of Pannonia, of Horica, of Italie, so they called the Prouostship of Milan, of Picena, of Tuscany, of Campania, of Calabria, Apulia, of Brussa of Sicilia, of all Africa entirelie, of Sardinia, of Spaine, of France, and of the Brittans.* And *Theodoret* registring the inscription of the same Councell: *The holie Synod assembled by the Grace of God at Sardica, from Rome, from Spaine, from France, from Italie, from Campania, from Calabria, from Africa, from Sardinia, from Pannonia, from Misia, from the first Dacia, from Dardania, from the second Dacia, from Macedonia, from Thessalia, from Achaya, from the Epiruses, from Thracia, from Rhodope, from Asia, from Caria, from Bithinia, from Helespont, from the first Phrigia, from Pisidia, from Capadocia, from Pontus, from the second Phrigia, from Cilicia, from Phamphilia, from Lydia, from the Cyclades Ilands, from Egipt, from Thebaidis, from Lybia, from Galatia, from Palestina, and from Arabia.* And elsewhere exagerating the obstinacie of *Acacius*, Archbishop of *Cesarea* in *Palestina*, one of the heads of the *Arrian*, faction. *The Councell assembled at Sardica, deposed this Acacius* (said hee) *but hee obeyed not the deposition, despising so great a number of Bishops.* And *Sulpitius Seuerus* describing the conuocation of the Councell of *Sardica*, first proiected, as he pretends by *Constantine*, and after executed by his children; *Hee commaunded* (said hee) *that from all the world, the Bishops should assemble themselues at Sardica.* And *Socrates* reporting the historie of the Councell of *Sardica*; *Paule and Athanasius demaunded, that their Cause & that of faith might be examined in a generall Councell. By the ordinance then of the two Emperors, there was a Generall Councell called at Sardica.* And the Emperor *Iustinian* in the Edict of faith indited as Hincmarus notes, by the second Councell of *Constantinople*, that wee call the fifth Generall Councell; *They were* (said hee, speaking of the Aduersaries to the Councell of *Nicea*) *anathematized; some whiles they liued, and some after their death, by Damasus of holy memorie, Pope of olde Rome, and by the Generall Councell of Sardica.* And *Vigilius* the old Bishop of *Trent*: *The holie Bishops* (said hee) *assembled at Sardica; from all the prouinces, that is; from Rome, from Spaine, from France, from Italie, from Campania, from Calabria, from Africa from Sardinia, from Panonia, from Missia, from Dacia, from Dardania from the other Dacia, from Macedonia from Thessalia, from Achaya, from Epirus, from Thrace, from Rhodope, from Asia, from Caria, from Bithinia, from Helespont, frō Phrigia, from Pisidia, from Capadocia, from Pontus, from Cilicia, from the other Phrigia, from Pamphilia, from Lidia,*

Athan. ad Solit vit. agent.

Id. de ap.

Theodor. hist. Eccl. l. 2. fug. c. 8.

Id. l. 2. c. 27.

Sulp. Seue. hist. Sacr. l. 2.

Socrat. hist. Eccl. l. 2. c. 20.

Hincm. opusc. 55. c. 26.

Apud Lenclau l. 8.

Vigil. cōtr. Eutych. l. 5.

from

from the Islands of the Cyclades, from Egipt, from Thebaides, from Lybia, from Galatia, from Palestina, and from Arabia, expounded this faith. To which I will add aboue my bargaine for an ouer measure, that the title that saint HILLARIE and saint EPIPHANIVS giue to the Councell of *Sardica*, of the Councell of those of the West, is so farr from abating anie thing of the qualitie and authoritie of a generall Councell, as contrariwise *Monsieur le Feure* a great Reader and Examiner of saint HILLARIES writings, causing a new fragment of the workes of the same saint HILLARY to be printed, doth iugeniouslie acknowledge the Councell of *Sardica* for a generall Councell in the preface of his Edition by these words; *Athanasius approued his innocencie in the Synods of Alexandria, and of Rome, and in the Generall councell of Sardica.*

Hilar. l. cont.Côn. Aug. Epiphan. hæres. 71. contra Photinian. Faber præfat. fragm. Hilar.

The fourth obiection, against the Canon of Appeales.

The fourth Obiection is, that in the Code of the Canõs of the Greeke church, which was produced in the Councell of *Chalcedon* in the cause of *Bassianus* and *Steuen*, the Canons of the Councell of *Sardica* were not contained: to this obiection wee bring three answeres; the first, that there were two volumes of Canons produced in the Councell of *Chalkedon*; the one where the Councells were sett downe in heades, and with the inscriptions of their titles and the particular number of their Canons, as appeares by the fourth and fifteenth act of the same Councell of *Chalkedon*, where the fourth and sixth Canons of the Councell of *Nicea* were read with the titles of the fourth and sixth Canons of the most holy three hundred and eighteen Fathers assembled at *Nicea*. And the third Canon of the Councell of *Constantinople*, with the title of Synodicall of the second synod held by the hundred and fiftie Fathers at *Constantinople* vnder *Nectarius*. And the other where the canons were annexed one after an other vnder a continued Cypher in the forme of a chaine and of a rapsody and without inscription of the titles of the Councells whence they were taken, and without distinction of the particular number of the Canons of euery Councell, as appeares in the fourth and eleuenth act, where the third, forth, sixteenth, and seauenteenth Canons of the Councell of *Antioch* were read vnder a simple quotation of Canon 84. 85. and 94. and 95. without anie mention neither of the title, or of the particular cyphers of the Councell from whence they were taken. Now it is not of the volumes in heads where the Canons of the Councells were inserted with inscription and distinction of the titles of their Coũcells, but of this rapsodie where the Canons were annexed one at the end of an other without inscription and distinction of the titles of their Councells, that the aduersaries to the Sea Apostolike speake: and therefore it is but the onely copie of this rapsodie that raiseth all this question. The second answere is, that there is noe proofe that euen in the copie of this rapsodie, the Canons of the Councell of *Sardica* are not cõprehended with the Canons of the other Councells. For that the fower Canons which are cited of this copie, which are the fourth, the fifth sixteenth, and seauẽteenth Canõs of the Coũcell of Antioch, are cited vnder the title of rule, eightie fourth, eightie fifth, nintie fourth, nintie sixth is good to shew, that before those Canons, there were but the twentie Canons in the same volume of the Councell of *Nicea*, the twentie of the councell of *Ansyra*: the fifteene of the councell of *Neocesarea*, the twentie one of the councell of *Gangres*, and the fiftie nine of the councell of *Laodicea*. And therefore *Hincmarus* antient Archbishop of *Rheims* argues pertinentlie out of this copie, that the councell of *Nicea* had made but twentie Canons, but not to conclude that the Canons of the councell of *Sardica*, which had bene made after those of the councell of *Antioch*

Hincmar. in opusc. 55. c. 21.

were

were not in the same volume. And the supplie of proofe which they pretend to drawe from *Dionisius Exiguus*, is nothing as shall appeare heereafter; contrariwise, there are manie proofes that the Councell of *Chalcedon* had both acknowledged and obserued the canons of the Councell of *Sardica*. For not onlie the first Councell of *Constantinople*, which was alleadged in the Councell of *Chalcedon*, confirmes the tome of those of the West, that is to saie, (if wee beleeue *Zonara* and *Balsamon*,) the Councell of *Sardica*, and not only the Epistle of *Valentinian* the third addressed to the Emperor *Theodosius* the second for the holding of the Councell of *Chalcedon*, and inserted with the Greeke Acts of the same Councell of *Chalcedon* saith; That *Flauianus* Bishop of *Constantinople*, had appealed to the Pope, following the custome of Councells,, which had principallie reference to the Councell of *Sardica*, and not only the Senate of *Constantinople*, deputed to cause policie to be obserued in the Councell of *Chalcedon*, receiued *Theodoret* Bishop of *Cyre*, who had appealed to Pope *Leo*, and made him enter and haue a seate in the assemblie of the Councell; because Pope *Leo* had restored his Bishopricke to him; a thing which was grounded vpon the canons of the Councell of *Sardica*: but also *Zonara* explaining the canon of the Councell of *Sardica*, which calls Metropolitans, Archbishops, And conferring it with the sixth Councell of *Carthage* which reiects the vse of this word; saith that the Councell of *Chalcedon* hath retained it; yielding rather to the authoritie of the Councell of *Sardica*, then to that of the Councell of *Carthage*. And *Balsamon*, *Nilus*, and other Greeke Schismatiks, will haue it, that the Councell of *Chalcedon* yielded the appeales of the Easterne prouinces, to the Patriark of *Constantinople*, pretending that it was grounded vpon the canons of the Councell of *Sardica*, which gaue the appeales to rhe Pope; and they haue extended this right to the Patriark of *Constantinople*; for as much as *Constantinople*, was a second *Rome*. For as for the supplie of proofes, that the Popes aduersaries pretend to collect from *Dionisius Exiguus*, it shall be satisfied heereafter. The third Answere is, that the verie copie of this Rapsodie which was produced in the Councell of *Chalcedon*, was a falsified code, as appeares by the canons thereof, that were produced in the same Councell; for the fowre canons which were read in the Councell of *Chalcedon* vnder the title of, Rule eightie fourth, eightie fifht nintie fourht and nintie sixth, were fowre canons of the Councell of *Antioch*, celebrated vnder *Constantius*. Now this Councell was an hereticall Councell holden by the *Arrians*, and at the instance of *Constantius* an *Arrian*, against saint ATHANASIVS. And of these fowre canons, that which was quoted vnder the cypher of the canon eightie fifth that is to saie; vnder the cypher of the canon correspondent to the fowrth canon of the Councell of *Antioch*, had bene partycularly framed against saint ATHANASIVS. This appeares both by the historie of *Socrates*, which reportes, that the fifteenth canon of this councell of *Antioch* hauing bene produced against S. CHRISOSTOME when the Emperor *Arcadius* would haue caused him to be deposed; S. CHRISOSTOME answered, that this canon was come out of the shopps of the *Arrians*, and had bene forged by them against S. ATHANASIVS. *Iohn (saith Socrates) answered, that this Canon was not of the Church, but of the Arrians: For those that assembled themselues at Antioch, for the distruction of the faith of consubstantialitie, publisht this canon out of hate to saint* ATHANASIVS; And by that of *Sozomene*, who writes; *And for that of the Ecclesiasticall*

Cō. Const. 1. c. 5. Con Chal. Act. 1. Zonar. in Conc. Cō. 1. c. 5. Balsam. ibidem.

Valent. 3. ep ad Theo. in ep præá. Con. Chal. Con. Chal. ep 1. Con. Sard. c 6.

Zona. in in Concil. Cart c. 42.

Balsam in Con. Sar. c. 5. Nil. de primat. Papæ l. 2.

Sozom. hi. Eccle. l. 3. c. 5. Athan. de Synod. Ar. &c.

Socrat. hi. Ecc. l. 6. c. 18. Sozo. hist. Eccle. l. 8. c 20.

Canon, Iohn refusing it, they receiued not his apologie, but deposed him although hee insisted (for it must be read ἐνεςάμενον and not ἐνιςάμενοι) *that it was a Canon of hereticks*. And by the Epistle of Bope *Innocent* the first, to the *Constantinopolitans*, reported in the same *Sozomene*, were Pope *Innocent* saith, speaking of the canons of the Councell of *Antioch*, that were produced against saint CHRISOSTOME; *These canons ought not to be receiued by catholicke Bishops for wee must not patch vp the inuention of hereticks, with the canons of catholicks*.

Soz. hist. Eccl. l. 8. c. 26.

And by the testimonie of *Paladius* a Greeke author, and tyme-mate with saint CHRISOSTOME, who saith in the life of saint CHRISOSTOME, and vpon the subiect of the same canons; *Theophilus had sent Canons composed by fortie of the Complices of Arrius*.

Pallad. in vit. Chryst.

Soe spake he, because that of nintie Bishops which assisted at the Councell of *Antioch*, there were but fortie or according to the Epistle of *Iulius* thirtie six, which actually comdemned saint ATHANASIVS: *but these fortie did so oppresse the rest, by the force and tyranny of Constantius an Arrian Emperor, who was there present, that they alone caused, to be ordained and publisht what they listed*. And a little after; *Elpidius Bishop of Laodicea and Tranquillus, shewed the Emperor Arcadius, that these Canons were hereticall*.

Id ibid.

And finally this appeared, by all the authors of saint CHRISOSTOMES life; who saie that his defendors, offered the Emperor *Arcadius*, to quitt his protectiõ, if his aduersaries would signe, that they held the same Faith with those that framed these canons. And this is alsoe acknowledged by the ministers of *Germanie*, who in the laste Greeke impression of the canons of the Councell, that they haue made at *Witenberge*, saie vpon the fourth canon of the Councell of *Antioch*, which is that that was read in the Councell of *Chalcedon*, vnder the name of canon eigthtie three; *This canon seemes to bee made in hate and ruine of the pious Athanasius*; And vpon the eleuenth; *This canon was likewise framed against saint Athanasius*. And vpon the fifteent; *This canon was also vndoubtedly made against the Good Athanasius, to take from him the power of Appealing to an other Synod*. And vpon the twentie fifth; *This Councell of Antioch, not only neglected the faith of the Councell of Nicea, touching Christs diuinitie, but also stroue cautelouslie to disanull it*.

Hic Canõ in odium & detrimẽtum pij Athanasij factus esse videtur. Et hic Canon contra S. Athan. compositus est. Et hic Canõ haud dubiè contra virum optimum Athan. factus est, vt illi appellatio ad aliũ Synodum adimeretur Fuit autem Concilium Antiochenum &c. Nicenum verò fidem Orthodoxam, de filij Dei diuinitate non modo neglexit verũ etiam callidè abolere studuit.

By meanes whereof it is cleere, that the Rapsodie which was produced at the Councell of *Chalcedon*. in the cause of *Bassian*, and *Steuen*, where these canons were inserted, was not the true vniuersall Code of the canons of the Greeke Church which had bene preserued in the Episcopall Bibliotheque of *Constantinople*, since the time of the Councell of *Constantinople*, to that of saint CHRISOSTOME, but was the same falsified code that *Cyrinus* Bishop of *Chalcedon* who was an *Egiptian* by extraction, and for that cause a partaker which *Theophilus* and a cruell aduersarie to sainr CHRISOSTOME; And other *Asians* Enemies to saint CHRISOSTOME, conspiring, and assembled with *Theophilus*, had produced against the same saint CHRISOSTOME, and which remained after the death of *Cyrinus* in the Episcopall Bibliotheque of *Chalcedon*; a thing whereto the fathers of the Coũcell of *Chalcedõ* tooke noe heede, because the canõs which were inserted into this Rapsodie, were there inserted without inscription of titles, and without distinction of Councells, and with suppression of the name of the Councell of *Antioch*.

Con. Cal. Act. 11.

And against this it auailes not to saie, that S. HILARIE speaking of the *Synod* of *Antioch* holden in the dedication, calls it, the *Synod* of the Saints; for he saith it to accomodate himselfe to the infirmitie of *Eleusius* Bishop of *Cyzica* and other secret catholicks of the *Asian* prouinces amongst whom he inha-

Hylar. de Synod.

bited

bited; for foundation whereof you must knowe that *Eleusius* and the other couert catholicks of the *Asian*, prouinces, that were called *Demy Arrians*, for as much as to shunne the Emperors, persecution, they communicated with the *Arrians*, in the Sacraments, and were different from them in beleefe, seeing themselues constrained by the tyranny of *Constantius*, an *Arrian* Emperor, to adhere to some one of the formes of faith of the Councell, that he had caused to be published, rather chose to adhere to that of the Councell of *Antioch*, then to any of the rest, as being the least pestilent, and the least, estranged from Catholicke, doctrine. For of all the Councells, holden by the *Arrians*, the most moderate in impietie, was the Councell of *Antioch*, holden in the dedication, whereinto the *Arrians* had infused noe other thing of their venome, but that they had taken away the word, *Consubstantiall*, which had bene inserted into the creede of the Councell of *Nicea*, and had sett in steede thereof, *inuiolable image of the substance, and one in concord*; without instilling into it anie proposition which besides the omission of the word, *Consubstantiall*, might not be auowed by the catholicks. For those causes then, when the *Arrians*, and amongst others *Acacius* Bishop of *Cesarea* in *Palestina*, would in the Councell following, and namely in that of *Seleucia*, propound other creedes, wherein they did more plainely expresse their impietie; *Eleusius* and the other couert catholicks of the *Asian* prouinces opposed themselues to it, crying out that they must hold to the creede of the Councell of *Antioch*. With such words, saith *Sabinus*, and after him *Socrates*, *Eleusius* opposed himselfe to *Acacius*, calling the faith of the Fathers, the faith publisht in the *Synod* of *Antioch*. (Socrat. l. 2. c. 40.) And therefore saint HILARIE desiring to suffer the infirmitie of *Eleusius*, and of the other couert catholickes of the *Asian* prouinces, amongst whom he was confined, and which he maintayned against the other *Asians*, who were compleate *Arrians*, as himselfe testifies in these words; *Except the Bishop Eleusius, and a few others with him, the tenn Asian prouinces amongst whom I inhabit, know not God, trulie*. (Hylar. de Synod.) And choosing rather to retaine them within the bounds of the Councell of *Antioch*, and to prouoke the rest of the *Asians*, by their Example, to returne to it and to come one stepp neerer by this meanes to the catholicke doctrine, then to lett them fall into the precipices of the other more impious creedes of the *Arrians*, speaks lesse hardly of the *Synod* of *Antioch* and calls it (in comparison of the other *Arrians*, *Synods*) *the Synod of the Saints*; because there were in this *Synod*, some, Catholiks for whose respect, (although they were oppressed by the force and, violence of the *Arrians* who comaunded there, and held there both the scepter and the pen, and by the tyranny of *Constantius* the *Arrian* Emperor, who was there present, the *Arrians* durst not at the first blowe, vomitt vp all their impietie; (Athanas. de Synod. Ar. & Seleu.) But not that the *Arrians*, had not bene the sole masters, authors, and directors of this councell, and had framed the draught and indited all that was there ordained: for not only saint ATHANASIVS, who was he against whom the Councell had proceeded, and who should better knowe the historie, then anie other, witnesseth that the Councell of *Antioch*, in the dedication, was an *Arrian* Councell, and celebrated by the *Arrians* in the presence of *Constantius* the *Arrian* Emperor. (Athan. ep. de Synod. Arimin. & Seleu. Socrat. hi. Ecc. l. 2. c. 8) But he also affirmes, and *Socrates* after him, that those that indited the faith of the Councell of *Antioch* publisht in the dedication; that is to saie, that whereof saint HILLARY speakes; were *Eusebius* Bishop of *Nicomedia* and *Acasius* Bishop of *Cesarea* in *Pale-*

stina, the two principall maintainers of *Arrian* heresie, and their complices. *The Eusebians* (saith saint ATHANASIVS) *after they had in the Synod of Tyre extolled all the peruerse doctrine of Arius; and after they had ordained to receiue the Arrians to the communion, and had themselues first executed it, esteeming neuerthelesse, that there yet wanted some thinge to their intention, held a new Synod at Antioch, vnder pretence of the dedication of the Church of* Antioch. And a while after; *The Bishops agreeing to the dedication were nintie vnder the consulship of Marcellus and Probinus, the impious Constantius being present.* And againe; *With what face could Eusebius and Acasius and their Complices, after they had vsed words not formerlie written, and had said that the first of all creatures, was the inuariable image of the substance, power, Councell and glorie, murmure against the Fathers, for making vse of words not formerlie written; and that they vsed the word substance*. And Socrates answering by waie of Apostrophe to the same *Eleusius* of whom S. HILARY speakes; *How* (said hee) *ô Eleusius dost thou call those that assembled at Antioch, Fathers, and abiure those that had bene their Fathers? for the Bishops that mett at Nicea, and decreed consubstantialitie, ought more properly to be Fathers; aswell for hauing bene before them, as because they had promoted them to Priest-hood then if those that held the Councell of Antioch, rooted out their Fathers, doe not they forgett themselues, that following them, they follow Paracides for Fathers?* As little doth it auaile to saie; that *John* Bishop of *Antioch*, and the other Easterne Bishops; that is to saie, *Syrians* that were with him at the mock Councell of *Ephesus* erected in the face of the generall Councell of *Ephesus*, and amongst others *Theodoret* Bishop of *Cyr*, alleadged against saint CYRILL, the same canon of the Councell of *Antioch* which had bene framed against saint ATHANASIVS; and after produced against saint CHRISOSTOME; And that *Theodoret* also in the collection of Councells that he hath made, insertes the canons of the Councell of *Antioch*, with the canons of the other Councells of the Easterne Church. For *Malesius* Patriarke of *Antioch*, in whose branch *John* Patriarke of *Antioch* had succeeded, and to whose Successors *Theodoret* and the other Easterne Bishops that were at *Ephesus*, adhered, had bene of the number of the couert Catholicks, which communicated with the *Arrians*; and euen when he was made patriarke of *Antioch* was ioyned in externall communion with the *Arrians*, although he held the catholicke doctrine. By reason whereof to haue meanes to resist the *Arrians*, vnder pretence of some confession of faith authorised by the lawes of the *Arrian* Emperors, vnder whose tyranny *Asia* groaned, they protected and defended the Councell of *Antioch* against the other Councell of the, *Arrians*, and gaue it the greatest authoritie they could in their Patriarkshpp; to the end that weake catholicks might haue meanes to shadowe themselues vnder the authoritie of his Councell against the *Arrian* Emperors that persecuted them; And from thence it came, that the libertie of catholicke Religion hauing bene restored in the East, this Councell yet remayned in authoritie amongst the couert catholiques of *Syria*, who during their oppression, had made vse of it, as a bulwarke against the *Arrians*, and other *Asian* prouinces, neere the Patriarkship of *Antioch*. Lesse auaileth it, to saie, that in the generall Councell, of *Constantinople*, holden vnder the Emperor, *Theodosius* the great, the Councell, of *Antioch*, was approued in these words; *As, for the tome of those of the West, wee receiue it, and also those that at* Antioch, *haue confessed one Deitie, of the* Father, *of the sonne, and of the holie Ghost*.

Athan. vbi supra. Athan. ibid. Ibidem. Socrat. hist. Eccl. l. 2. c. 40. Concil. Const. 1. c. 5.

For

For it is not of the councell of *Antioch* holden in the dedication and vnder the Emperor *Constantius*, that they speake: as it appeares as well because they sett it after the tome of those of the West, which was holden longe after the Councell of *Antioch* in the dedication; as because they saie, that this Councell confessed one and the same deitie of the Father, of the Sonn, and of the holy Ghost; whereas the councell of *Antioch* in the dedication, calls the vnitie of the Father, of the Sonne, and of the holy Ghost, an vnitie of Concord: but of an other Councell of *Antioch*, holden in the beginning of the Empire of *Iouian*; which conformed the faith of the Councell of *Nicea*, as it appeares both by the Epistle of the Bishops of *Constantinople*, assembled the yeare after the generall Councell of *Constantinople*, and by *Socrates* who reportes the whole historie, and by S. GREGORIE of *Nisea*; and by *Cassianus*, and manie others. To thinke also to escape by saying, that it is from this Councell of *Antioch* holden vnder the Emperor *Iouian*, that the Canons of the Councell of *Antioch* haue bene taken, that we haue at this daie in our handes, is a thing wholie vaine: for these very Canons of the Councell of *Antioch*, that wee haue, were in vse amongst the *Arrians*, and *Demy-Arrians* from before the Councell of *Seleucia* which was holden vnder *Constantius*, as appeares by the reproch that *Sabinus*, the *Macedonian*, made to *Cyrill* of *Jerusalem*, that against the Ecclesiasticall lawe; that is to saie, against the fifteenth Canon of the Councell of *Antioch*, he had recourse to the Emperor, *Constantius*, to appeale to the Councell of *Seleucia*. It is yet more vaine to saie, that *Fulgentius Ferandus*, *Yuon*, *Gratian*; and other latin canonists, haue inserted the canons of the Councell of *Antioch*, in the dedication amongst the canons of the Councell receiued in the latine Church. For it is certaine, that in the time of Pope *Innocent* the first, and of saint CHRISOSTOME, the latine Church receiued them not, as appeares by the Epistle of Pope *Innocent* to the *Constantinopolitans*, about the matter of the Canons of the Councell of *Antioch*, which were produced against saint CHRISOSTOME, of which *Sozomene* reportes these wordes aboue cited, *such Canons are reiected by the catholicke Bishops, for wee must not patch the inuentions of Heretickes with the canons of Catholickes*. And whereas afterward some latine collectors haue inserted them into their copies, it was in part, because they were deceaued about the Canon of the Councell of *Constantinople* not considering that the Councell of *Antioch* which was there approued, was the Councell of *Antioch* holden vnder the Emperor *Iouian*, and in part because in those Canons, there was nothing either against faith nor against the greater part of Ecclesiasticall discipline. Contrariwise in regarde of Ecclesiasticall discipline, there were manie good things, and which had bene taken from the customes and constitutions of the former Church. And that if there were anie canon that hurt the policie of the church, it had bene corrected and medicined by the Councell of *Sardica*. But aboue all it is an impertinent thing to saie that the Bishops of the Councell of *Antioch* ordained by the first of their canons, to obserue the canon of the great Councell of *Nicea*, concerning the daie of the celebration of *Pasch*; and so that they were not *Arrians*. For this Coūcell of *Nicea* hauing bene holden as *Eusebius* testifies for two causes, the one to decide the controuersies of faith, and the other to reconcile the difference of the *Pasch*, the *Arrians* did imbrace ioyntlie with the catholickes the decree of the Councell of *Nicea*, concerning the obseruation of the *Pasch*, & reiected only that of the Faith: And therefore

Socrat. hist. l. 3. c. 25.

the ministers of *Germanie* in the last greeke impression of the canons of the councells, that they haue made at *Wittenberg*, doe iustlie note, that although the councell of *Antioch* approues the decree of the councell of *Nicea*, touching the celebration of the Pasch; neuerthelesse, that hinders it not from being *Arrian*. For behold what they saie vpon the first canon of the same Councell of *Antioch*, *These Antiochian Fathers, excommunicated and deposed those that sinned in indifferent things*; soe spake the ministers ignorantlie following *Socrates* his error, and the other *Nouatians*, who put the decree of the Councell of *Nicea* concerning the obseruation of Pasch amongst indifferent things, *and excommunicated not, nor deposed those that haue presumed to reuerse the pious decree, and grounded on the Word of God of the Councell of Nicea concerning the eternall and Consubstantiall diuinitie of the Sonne of God: but the Arrians Would not condemne the Arrians.*

Hi patres Antiocheni eos excommunicant & deponunt qui in rebus adiaphoris peccant: eos verò neque excommunicant, neque deponunt, qui pium & in verbo Dei fundatum Decretum Synodi Nicenæ de Filij Dei æterna & & consubstantiali diuinitate conuellere ausi sunt. Sed Ariani noluerunt damnare Arianos.

The third obiection that the aduersaries of the church make against the canons of the Councell of *Sardica*, is, that they were not contained in the Greeke Code of the Canons of the vniuersall Church, compiled and authorised by the Emperor *Iustinian:* which obiection as it containes two heads; the one that *Iustinian* compiled and authorised a Code of Canons; and the other, that in this Code, the canons of the Councell of *Sardica* were not compreheded; so they accompanie it with two proofes, for that the first head; to witt, that the Emperor *Iustinian* compiled and authorised a Code of canons contayning the Bodie of the canons of the vniuersall Church, they produce the hundred thirtith one new constitution of *Iustinian*, where he vseth these words, *Wee decree, that the holie Ecclesiasticall Canons, Which haue bene constituted and confirmed by the fower holie Councells, shall holde the place of a Lawe.* And for the proofe of the second, to witt, that the canons of the Councell of *Sardica*, were not in the code compiled and authorised by *Iustinian*, they alleadge the Epistle of *Dionysius exiguus*, time-fellowe with *Iustinian*, who saith, that to the translation that he had made of the Greeke code, he had added the canons of the Councells of *Sardica* and *Africke*, which had bene framed in latine: To the first proofe then wee auswere, that it is a proofe, wouen with the threde of a Cobwebb; for *Iustinian* speakes not there of anie volume of canons confirmed by the first fowre councells, and intends not to saie, that he authorises aswell the canons that are actually contained in the first councells, as those which are there contained but relatiuelie; that is to saie, by the confirmation which is there made in grosse of the councells where they are contained; but that he authorises, and erects into the title of a temporall lawe all the canons actuallie contained in the fowre first councells, aswell those that were there first composed, as those that hauing bene before obserued by an vnwritten tradition, haue bene there confirmed, and reduced into writing: for so signifies there, this alternatiue, *constituted*, or, *confirmed*, which is sett there for as much as the more part of the canons of the fowre first councells had bene before obserued, by an vnwritten lawe, as the Fathers of the councell of *Constantinople* testifie, when they saie, speaking of the Oeconomy of the Ecclesiasticall ordinations: *It is as you knowe both a lawe descended from antiquitie, and a Canon of the Councell of Nicea.* Now, that this is the intention of *Iustinian*, to witt, to speake onlie of the fowre first generall councells, it appeares both because he saith that he receiues their *Dogma's* as the holy scriptures. A phrase since practised by S. GREGORIE vpō the matter

Epist. Cōcil. Const. 1. ad Damas. Ambros. & alios.

Gregor. Mag l. indict. ep.

of

of the first fower generall coūcells, and which cānot be stretched to anie of the other councells holden before the Emperor *Iustinian* and by this that he adds, that he receiues their Canōs as lawes; *VVee receiue* (saith hee) *the dogma's of the four Synods aboue named, as the holie scriptures, and receiue their Canons as lawes*. And by this that he concludes: *For these causes wee ordaine, that according to their distinctions, the holie Pope of olde Rome, be the first of all the Prelates, and that the Bles. Bishop of Constantinople the second Rome haue the second place after the Sea Apostolik of old Rome, and be perferr'd before all the Seas*. A thing which euidentlie shewes, that he speakes precisely of the fowre Generall councells onlie, where the order of the Patriarkes had bene obserued, and not of the particular coūcells, where there had bene noe concurrence of Patriarkes. And indeede, how could *Iustinian* haue pretended to haue giuen by this constitution, the force of an imperiall lawe to all the Canons of particular Councells; hee that disanulls and infringes the fifteenth Canon of the Councell of *Neocesarea?* for the Councell of *Neocesarea*, had made a Canon by which it ordained, that according to the Booke of the actes, there should be but seauen deacons in one cittie, how great soeuer it were. Where *Iustinian* ordaines, that there shall be an hundred Deacōs in the cathedrall church of *Constantinople*. And that is not to be reckoned of, which *Balsamon* saith that *Iustinian* and the councell of *Trullio* after him, interpret the Canon of the councell of *Neocesarea*, for they doe indeede interpret the place of the acts wich they pretend to be euill vnderstood by the Coūcell of *Neocesarea*, and that it ought to be expounded, of the dispensers of almes and not, of the ministers of the Altar; but they correct and abrogate the Canon of the councell of *Neocesarea*, as *Zonora* acknowledges in these termes: *From before the Councell Trullian, the Canon of the Councell of Neocesarea was noe more obserued; for Iustinian instituted sixtie priests, and an hundred deacons, and fortie Deaconesses in the great Church of Constantinople*. And therefore *Balsamō* is constrained to confesse, that the Councell *Trullian* correctes the Canon of the councell of *Neocesarea*; *The present Canon* (saith hee) *interpreteth, or rather correcteth the fifteenth Canon of the Councell of Neocesarea*. And then if *Iustinian* in saying; *Wee ordaine that the Canons constituted or confirmed by the fower first Councells, shall holde the place of a lawe*; had pretended to meane not onlie the Canons contained in the catalogues of the fower first councells, but also those of the other Councells which they pretend to haue bene confirmed in grosse by these fower first. What caution can they giue that he did not intend to comprehend the Canons of the councell of *Sardica*, that hee, and the fifth councell of *Constantinople* call a generall councell, comprehending it consequently vnder the title of the councell of *Nicea*; and whereof the first councell of *Constantinople* canoniseth the authoritie in these termes: *Wee receaue the Councell of those of the West*: that is to saie, (if wee beleeue *Zonara* and *Balsamon*) *the Councell of Sardica*. But this is enough for the first head; let vs examine the second.

Concil. Neocæsar. c. 15. Act. c. 6. Lib. 3. Im. Constitut. tit. 2.

Balsam. in Concil. in Trull. c. 16 Zonar. in Conc. in Trul. c. 16. Balsam in Conc. Iust. in edi. fid. Ortho. apud Leū. clau. l. 8. Conc. Cō. 1. c. 5. Zonar. in Conc. Cō. 1. c. 5. Bal Ibid.

To the proofe then of the second head, which is that *Dionisius Exiguus* a *Scithian* monke, but habituated at *Rome*, and versed in the Greeke and Roman letters, who liued in the time of *Iustinian* the Emperor, in translating the Canon of the councells saith; that he hath taken the councell of *Sardica* from the latine edition, and hath not taken it from the Greeke text, because it was not in the Greeke edition, a proofe that hath seemed so strong to the Popes aduersaries; that two yeare since they haue caused to be printed a greeke Code of the Canōs of the vniuersall church, from which they haue ecclipsed and cutt of the councell of *Sardica* against the

Chr. Iust. apud Adr. Beys Paris 1610.

credit

credit of all the greke editions of the councells, both antient and moderne, which are at this daie to bee found in the world. Wee answere that the greeke copie that *Dionisius Exiguus* had in his handes, was a maimed and defectiue copie, as appeares, besides manie other lamenesses, by the omission of the Canōs of the coūcell of *Ephesus*, which are wanting there; for *Dionisius Exiguus* passes immediatly from the Canons of the councell of *Constantinople*, to those of the councell of *Chalcedon*, and omitts the Canons of the councell of *Ephesus*; a thing which manifestlie shewes, that the greeke copie that he had in his handes, and which he had brought out of *Scithia*, was lame and imperfect, for as much as not onlie the councell of *Ephesus* was the third of the first generall councells: and that in this qualitie the canons thereof are inserted into all the collections and mentions of the greeke collections: as in the greeke collection of *Theodoret*; and into the concordances of *Iohn Scholasticus* Patriarke of *Constantinople*; and into the catalogue of the Councell *Trullian*, and into the *Nomocanon* of *Photius*; and into the greeke copies of *Zonara*, *Balsamon*, *Alexius*, *Blestares*, *Simon Logotheta*, *Harmenopolus*, and others; But also that the Emperor *Iustinian* quotes and expresses them by name in the lawe produced for the proofe of the first head which hath these wordes: *Wee ordaine that the holie Ecclesiasticall Canons that haue bene constituted or confirmed by the foure holie Councells, shall holde the place of a lawe; to wit, those of the Councell of Nicea, celebrated by the three hundred and eighteen Fathers; and those of the Councell of Constantinople celebrated by the hundred and fiftie Fathers; and those of the first Councell of Ephesus; and those of the Councell of Chalcedon.* And to the end to conuert our defence into an act, wee will arme it with seauen counter-Batteries, which doe not onlie destroie the proofe drawne from *Dionisius Exiguus*, but also shewes expressely, that in the Emperor *Iustinians* age and long before him, the Canons of the councell of *Sardica* were acknowledged by the greeke church and inserted into the greeke collections of councells. The first is, that *Paladius* Bishop of *Helenopolis* in *Bithinia*, an Author greeke in stile, and *Asian* in nation, (who liued a thousand two hundred yeares yeares agoe; that is to saie, a hundred and fiftie yeare before *Iustinian*, and whom *Photius* Patriarke of *Constantinople*, calls a most diligent Writer of the life of S. CHRISOSTOME;) And *George* Patriarke of *Alexandria*, (who liued a thousand yeare agoe) witnesse not only, (as hath aboue appeared) that the Canon of the Councell of *Antioch* that the Schismatickes of the East produced against S. CHRISOSTOME, had proceeded from the Shopp of the *Arrians*; but also that it had bene abrogated with the common voice of the Greeke and Latine Bishops, by the Canons of the Councell of *Sardica*. *This Canon* (saith *Palladius*, and after *Palladius*, *George* Patriark of *Alexandria*, and after *George*, Patriarke of *Alexandria*, *Photius* Patriarke of *Constantinople*) *was as impious, and the worke of impious men, abrogated in the Councell of Sardica, by the Romans, Italians, Illyrians, Macedonians, and Greekes.* The second that *Sozomene*, an antient Greeke historian, and who liued neere an hundred yeares before Iustinian, reportes for the defence of the same S. CHRISOSTOME, an Epistle of Pope *Innocent* the first, to the *Constantinopolitans*, where hee writes speaking of the canons of the Councell of *Antioch*; *We saie not onlie that they are not to be followed, but also that they must bee condemned with hereticall and Schismaticall doctrins, as was done in the councell of Sardica, by the Bishops that haue bene before vs.* The third that *Balsamon* Patriarke of *Antioch* and guardian of the charters of the Church of *Constantinople*, notes after all them, that the fifteenth canon of the Coūcell of *Antioch*, was abolished by the fowrth canon of the Councell of *Sardica*;

Nouel. Iust. 131.

Phot. in Georg. Alex.

Pallad. dial de vit. Chris.

Sozom. hist. Eccl. l. 8. c. 20.

Note (saith *Balsamon* commenting the fourth Canon of the councell of *Sardica that by this Canon, the fifteenth Canon of the coũcell of Antioch, was abrogated.* And comenting the fifteẽth Canon of the councell of *Antioch; This Canon* (saith hee) *was disannulled by the fourth canon of the councell of Sardica.* Balsam. in Conc. Sar. c. 4. Id. In. Cõ. Antioch. c. 15.

The fowrth counterbattery is, that the greeke edition of the Canons of the coũcell of *Sardica*, is not a translation of the antient latine edition, which was currẽt, whether in the time of Pope *Zosimus*, or whether since, in the time of *Dionisius Exiguus*; but that it is a greeke edition, primitiue and originall, which was made in the councell itself, whereof (as holden vpon the confines betweene both empires) the Canons were publisht from the beginning in both tongues: This appeares by manie differences which are betweene the old latine edition: and the greeke edition; not in substance, but in the order, in the phrases, formes, and circumstances: and amongst others in the seauenth Canon of the latine edition, which is the fourteenth in the greeke; for the latine edition produced by Pope *Zosimus* his legates in the sixth councell of *Carthage*, and inserted into the collection of *Dionisius Exiguus*, and into that of *Isidorus Mercator* hath; *Osius saith, If a Bishop moued with choler against a priest or deacon of his, would cast him forth of the church, it must be prouided, that being innocent he be not condemned or excommunicated; and therefore the excommunicated person, shall haue power to interpeale, the Bishops of the next Prouince, and procure his cause to be heard by them.* And the greeke edition, besides manie other differences, hath it thus: *The excommunicated person shall haue power, to haue recourse to the Bishop Metropolitan of the same Prouince: and if the Bishop Metropolitan be absent, to addresse himselfe to the Metropolitan of the next prouince, and to require that his cause may be diligentlie examined.* A thing which euidently sheweth, that the Greeke editiõ was not taken from the latine edition which was currẽt, be it in the time of Pope *Zosimus*, be it in the time of *Dionisius Exiguus*, but it is the antient originall greeke edition of the councell, of which some clauses were lost in the latine edition, from the time of Pope *Zozimus* and *Dionisius Exiguus.* Cõ. Cart. 6. c. 6. Cõ. Sar. c. 17.

The fifth counter-batterie is, that not only all the greeke editions as that of *Photius, Simon Logotheta, Zonara, Balsamõ, Alexius* and other greeke canonists containe the same canons of the councell of *Sardica*; but also all the other Easterne editions, aswell *Russian, as Syrian, Armenian, Egiptian*, and *Ethiopian*, as it appeares: for the *Syrian* editions by the *Syriack* collections of the canons which is at *Rome* in the Bibliotheque of the great Duke *Cosmo*, yet liuing; whither the great Duke *Ferdinand* his Father made to be brought all the *Syrian* bookes that he could recouer in the East; And in regard of the *Ethiopian* Edition, by the Code of the *Ethiopian* canons which is at *Rome*, in the howse of the *Ethiopians*, and for the rest by the copies which are to be found in all the prouinces of the East; by meanes whereof, the canons of the Councell of *Sardica*, must haue bene currant in the East, longe before *Justinians* tyme, the naturall *Egiptian* Churches which wee call *Cophtichs* and *Ethiopians*, hauing seperated themselues from the greeke and latine churches from the time of the councell of *Chalcedon*, and haue had since the time noe communion with them. And finallie the sixth counterbatterie is, that *Theodoret* who liued neere one hundred yeare before *Justinian* and that *Iohn* Patriarke of *Constantinople*, who liued in the same age with *Iustinian*, inserted into the collection of the Greeke Councells, the canons of the Councells, of *Sardica* with the other canons of the Greeke church, (for in the greeke Librarie of Queene *Catherine* of *Medicis*, which was brought from *Con-*

stantinople

stantinople to *Florẽce*, *by Demetrius*, *Gara*, *Lascaris*, & other greekes flying frõ the sack of *Constãtinople*, and which is now vnited with the librarie of the most Christian kinge, there is found an old Synagogue a manuscript of the canons, reduced into fiftie titles by *Theodoret* Bishop of *Cyre*, vnder which there is annexed a concordance of the imperiall lawes of *Iustinian* with the canons contained in these fiftie titles, made by *Iohn Scolasticus* Patriarke of *Constantinople*; in both which workes, the canons of the coũcell of *Sardica* are quoted and inserted equallie with the other canons of the Greeke church. Now that this Synagogue (which was the name that they gaue to the antient collections of councells, as it appeares by the report of *Socrates*, who cites the collections of Councells made by *Sabinus*, vnder the title of a Synagogue of the councells) is truly antient, and certainly *Theodorets*, is not to be doubted. For besides this, that the manuscript which is verie antient, beares this title; *Synagogue of the Canons reduced into fiftie titles by Theodoret Bishop of Cyre*; And besides that the stile of the author is wholie agreeable to the stile of *Theodoret*; there are manie thinges to shewe that this collection could not but bee made in *Theodorets* time, that it is so, first the author testifies in his exordium, that there were but ten Synods celebrated since the Apostles to his time: *There haue bene* (said hee) *ten great Synods of the Fathers since the Apostles*. And propounding a while after in the forme of a table the canons of the same ten councells, whereof his worke is compiled, he placeth that of *Nicea* first, and that of *Chalcedon* last in this order.

Socrat. l. 1. c. 5 & l. 2. c. 13. hist. Ec.

1. *Of the 318. holie Fathers assembled at Nicea vnder the Consulship of the Illustrious Paulinus and Iulianus, the yeare of the death of Alexander 606. the 19 of the month of Decius; that is to saie, the 13. before the Kadends of Iune; 20. Canons.*
2. *Of the blessed fathers assembled at Ancyra*, more antient then those *of Nicea* but placed after them because of the dignitie, *and authoritie of a generall Councell; 25. Canons.*
3. *Of the holie fathers assembled at the Synod of Neocesarea, in time also before that of Nicea, and later then that of Ancyra; but for honors-sake placed after that of Nicea; 14. Canons.*
4. *Of the fathers assembled at Sardica, after the Fathers of the councell of Nicea: 21. Canons.*
5. *Of the fathers assembled at Gangres: 20. Canons.*
6. *Of the fathers assembled at Antioch: 25. Canons.*
7. *Of the fathers assembled at Loadicea in Phrigia: 59. Canons.*
8. *Of the fathers assembled at Constantinople: 7. Canons.*
9. *Of the fathers assembled at Ephesus: 7. Canons.*
10. *Of the fathers assembled at Chalcedon: 27. Canons.*

From whence it appeares, that this Author must haue written a little while after the councell of *Chalcedon*, which is the time wherein *Theodoret* writt his dialogues against the *Euthycians*, and before the fifth generall councell, which was holden vnder *Iustinian* the first: and the sixth which was holden vnder *Constantine Pogonat*: and the councell surnamed *Trulliã* which made canons vnder the name of both the others: and by consequent that he was long before *Photius*, and all the other compilers of the greeke collections, whose copies are to be found, be it in the *East*, or in the west. Secondly he saith that he is not the first that hath compiled the canons in a volume, for as much as before him, there had bene some, that had made a collection distributed into sixtie titles: but that he is the first that hath distributed them into titles distinguisht by the dates of the matters; A thing that shewes, that he is more antient then the old *Nomocanon* reduced into fiftie titles, before the tyme of *Photius* whereof *Balsamon* speakes. Thirdlie he inserts none with the Canons of the Councells but only the Canons of S. BASILL: And hee saith more, that before him they had neuer bene inserted; which testifies, that he is more antient, then the councell intituled *Trullian*: and then all the collections of *Photius*, and other later greeke copies, wherein there are inserted the canons of manie other greeke fathers, and amongst others of S. CYRILL. Fowrthly, he makes noe mention in his worke, of the Canons of the councell of *Carthage*, an euident testimonie that he is more antient then *Iustinian*, who cites in his edict of faith, the Canons of the councell of *Carthage*; then the councell of *Constantinople*, surnamed *Trullian*: then the *Nomocanon* of *Photius*; and then all the other late greeke compilations, in the which the canons of the councell of *Carthage*, are inserted and incorporated. Moreouer he assignes but three Canons to the first Coũcell of *Constantinople*, which is the number that the old greeke and latine manuscripts cõtaine: and that *Dionisius exiguus*, (who saith he hath taken his translation vpon the greeke originall,) assignes to it, and giues but twentie seauen Canons to the Councell of *Chalcedon*, which is the number that the same *Dionisius*, and the other antiẽt greekes and latines attribute thereto, and that the historie of the Councell as wee haue aboue proued shewes, ought to be attributed thereto; for the twentie eight hauing bene propounded by the fathers of the councell, at the instance of *Anatolius*, the Popes legats opposed them selues to it, and Pope *Leo* refused to confirme it, and the Emperor and *Anatolius* himselfe desisted from pursuing it, in such sorte as it began not to take place amongst the Canons of *Chalcedon* till a long time after; from whence it is, that S. GREGORIE the *Great* saith: That the synod of *Chalcedon* had bene falsified in one place by those of *Constantinople*: And as for the two later Canons they are two canons made vpon particular occurrences, which haue bene transferred from the fowrth act of the councell, into the catalogue of the canons. By meanes whereof, it is necessarie that the author of this collection, should be more antient then S. GREGORIE the *Great*: and then the councell of *Constantinople*, surnamed *Trullian*, in whose times the twentie eigth Canon had alreadie bene inserted into the catalogue of the canons of the Councell of *Chalcedon*: and then the copies whereof *Photius*, *Zonara*, *Balsamon*, and other later Greekes haue made vse, within all which this addition is inserted. Besides he assignes but seauen Canons to the Councell of *Ephesus*, omitting the eigth which had bene made against *Iohn* Patriarke of *Antioch*, in fauour of the Bishops of *Cyprus* during the Schisme of the councell of *Ephesus*, and of *Iohn* Patriarke of *Antioch*, and which is inserted in all the greeke collections of *Photius*, *Zonara*, *Balsamon* and others. From whence it appeares, that the compiler of this Synagogue was one of the Bishops of the Patriarkship of *Antioch* who had during the schisme taken parte with *John* Patriarke of *Antioch* against the Councell of *Ephesus*: and who reunited themselues with the councell of *Ephesus*, when *Iohn* Patriarke of *Antioch* and the Bishops of his Patriarkship returned to it. By meanes whereof they receiued not this Canon with the other Canons of the Councell, for as much as it had bene made against their Patriarke; and during the schisme, and by contumacie, and vpon hearing of one partie only. And finally the Author which hath begun this collection, and hath illustrated it with conferring the imperiall lawes, annexing to the end of euery title, legall concor-

Dionys. Exiguus in Cod. Can. Theo. An. ad Calcem hist. Eccle. Theod. in edit. Rob. Steph. col. 1. 1. Gre. Mag. l. 5. ind 14. ep. 14.

dans

dances, answerable to the matter of the titles, had bene tyme-fellowe with *Iustinian* himself, and writt a little after his death, as appeares by the preface that he put before his concordances, which containes these wordes: *To the glorie of our great God and sauiour Iesus Christ, I haue now cõferred the sacred canons of the holie and blessed Apostles, and of the holie Fathers, who haue followed their tracks in euerie Synod, with a choyce of texts that I haue transcribed from the sacred new constitutions of Iustinian of holie memorie, publiht dispersedly after the Code, the which not onelie are agreable to the canons of the orthodox fathers, but also communicate to them the authoritie of the imperiall power, with an addition of legall right, and pleasing to God, which prouides in the imitation of God, what is profitable for euerie humã creature.* And by the end of the worke to which are annexed these words, written in greeke breuiatures; *The end of the Chapters of the new constitutions, concerning Ecclesiasticall decisions by Iohn Archbishop of Constantinople, which had bene Scolasticus.* For this *Iohn* Archbishop of *Constantinople*, surnamed heeretofore *Scholasticus* whom the aduersaries of the Popes authority acknowledge for one of the collectors of the greeke councells, was establisht by *Iustinian* himselfe in the *Sea* of *Constantinople* in the steede of *Eutychius*, and deceased twelue yeares after the death of *Iustinian*. And it derogates not from this, that *Balsamon* reiects all the *Nomocanons*; that is to saie, all the marriages of lawes and canõs which haue bene made before that of *Photius*: And amongst the rest, one *Nomocanon*, which distributes the lawes and canons into fiftie titles. For be it that he speake of that of *Iohn* Patriarke of *Constantinople*, surnamed *Scholasticus*: be it that he speake of an other later, he reiects it not, for not hauing bene antient enough, but for being too antient: for as much, as manie lawes of the Emperor *Iustinian* which are there inserted, haue ceased to be in vse hauing bene abrogated by the later Emperors: yet lesse is this repugnant to it, that the canons intituled from the Apostles are quoted in this synagogue, vnder the number of eigthie fiue canons: Whereas *Doonisius exiguus*, and after him *Cresconius* report but of fiftie. For bsiedes this that the greeke code of *Dionisius* (as hath bene aboue noted) was very lame and defectiue, it is certaine, that the Greekes both before *Theodoret*, and before *Dionisius Exiguus* retained eightie fiue, as appeares by these wordes of the councell of *Constantinople* surnamed *Trullian*: *Wee ordaine, that the eightie fiue canons which haue bene receaued and confirmed by the holie Fathers, who haue preceded vs, and haue bene giuen vs by them vnder the name of the canons of the holie and glorious Apostles, remaine from hence forward firme and vnmoueable.* And by the councell of *Constantinople* holden vnder *Nectarius* in the cause of *Agapius* and of *Bagadius* more then sixtie yeares before *Theodoret*, that the councell *Trullian* canoniseth in these wordes; *Wee seale also the canons of the holie fathers, which reassembled thẽselues anew in this religious & imperiall cittie vnder Nectarius Archbishop of the same cittie, & vnder Theophilus Archbishop of Alexandria.* Which coũcell holden vnder *Nectarius* in the cause of *Agapius* and *Bagadius*, cites the seauentie sixth Canon of the Apostles: for I will not renewe the difference that hath bene since Pope *Gelasius* betwene the greeke and latine church in regard of these Canons intituled from the Apostles. It sufficeth to defend the antiquitie of this Synagogue, that from before the time of *Theodoret*, the Greekes held eigthie fiue canons for Apostolicall canons: and this may be said, touching the sixth obiection, lett vs dispatch the two others.

Dionys. Exiguus in Co Cã. Crescon. in Coll. Can.

Conc. in Trull. c. 2.

The seauenth obiection, that the Popes aduersaries propound against the authoritie of the canons of the Councell of *Sardica*, is that Pope *Adrian* the first in the epitomy of the canons that he addresses to *Charlemaine*, saith, that the Canons of the councell of *Sardica* are not to be found amongst the Greekes, and that Pope *Nicholas* the first, in his Epistle to *Photius* Patriarke of *Constantinople* and to the *Constantinopolitans*, writes, *The Councell of Sardica which you saie you haue nott.* To this obiection then, wee answere two thinges, the one that if *Photius* who was author of the schisme which lasts to this daie betweene the greeke and Latine Church, should haue said by malice, and to couer his intrusion into the Patriarkship of *Constantinople*, which he had vsurped vpon *Ignatius*, true and lawfull Patriarke, that the Greekes had not, or receiued not the Councell of *Sardica*, it were noe great meruaile; no more then that the Bishops of *Egypt* writt to the Emperor *Leo*, to couer their heresie that they knew not the Synod of the hundred & fifteen fathers: that is to saie, the first generall Synod of *Constantinople*, in the which neuerthelesse, *Timothie* the first, their Patriarke, had assisted and presided. For *Photius* hauing intruded into the Patriarkship of *Constanstinople* against the Canons of the Coũcell of *Sardica*, which forbad Laymẽ to vsurpe ecclesiasticall charges, there is noe doubt, but he would willingly haue auoided that which condemned him. And the other, that it is a mistaking in Pope *Nicholas*, who deceaued himself vpon the Epitomy of the Canons of Pope *Adrian*, who was deceiued vpon *Dionisius* his collection For not only the Councell of *Constanstinople*, surnamed *Trullian*, that the Greekes intituled the sixt generall Councell, & which was more then an hundred and fiftie yeares before Pope *Adrian*, & more thẽ two hundred before Pope *Nicolas* & before *Photius*, & that *Photius* himself canoniseth & registers it in his nomocanon as an vniuersall œcumenicall Coũcell, writes, *Wee seale also the Canons that haue bene publisht by the fathers, assembled at Sardica & Carthage, & by those which reassembled thẽselues the second time in this Religious and imperiall Cittie, vnder* Nectarius *Archbishop of this imperiall Cittie, and Theophilus Archbishop of Alexandria.* But *Photius* himself in his *Nomocanon* insertes allmost vnder euery title, the canõs of the coũcell of *Sardica*, & those particularly of the Episcopall appeales to the sea Apostolike: & after *Photius*, *Simõ Logotheta*, *Zonara*, *Balsamõ*, *Alexius Blastares*, *Harmenopolus*, & other later greeke Canonists. The eigteenth & last obiection, that the aduersaries of the church make against the authoritie of the canõs of the coũcell of *Sardica*, is, that the practises of episcopall appeales, which are the subiect of the third, fourth, and fift Canon of the Coũcell of *Sardica*, hath bene long vnknowne to the Easterne Church. For proofe whereof they alleadge six instances; the first is, that *Socrates* speaking of *Cyrill* Bishop of *Hierusalem* who had appealed from the Councell of *Palestina* holden vnder *Acacius* Archbishop of *Cesarea* to a greater iudgment, that is to saie, to the iudgement of the Councell of *Seleucia*, saith that *Cyrill* practised the first, and onely one of this kind of proceeding, making vse against the custome of the ecclesiasticall Canon, of appeales, as in a lay iudgement. The second that the first Councell of *Constantinople*, that was called the second generall one, ordained that after the Synod of the Prouince, the Synod of the Patriarkship might examine in the second instance of the cause of Bishops, but that if after the Synod of the Patriarkship anie one should dare to importune the eares of the Emperor, or of secular Princes, or disquiet the generall synod, that he bee no more receaued to pursue his accusatiõ. The third that the Emperor *Iustiniã* saith, that frõ the sentẽces of the Patriarkes there is noe appeale, no more then from the sentences of the Prouosts of the Pretory. The fourth, that the Emperor *Iustinian* ordaines, that if a Clearke attempt anie Cause against his Bishop, he bee iudged by his Metropolitan; and in case, the one of the parties refuse to obey the iudgement, the Patriarke of the diocese shall end it. The fifth that the Emperors *Leo* and *Constantine* declared, that

Nicol. 1. ad Phot.

Concil. in Trull. c. 2.

Socrat. hist. Eccl. l. 2. c. 40.

Concil. Const. 1. c.

the ſentence of the Patriarke, was not ſubiect to appeale, as being the Prince of Eccleſiaſticall iudgements. And the ſixth that *Photius* in his *Nomocanon* ſaith, there is noe appeale from the ſentence of the Patriarkes.

To the firſt then of thoſe obiections; which is, that *Socrates* ſaith, that *Cyrill* Biſhop of *Ieruſalem*, was the only and firſt man, who againſt the Eccleſiaſticall canõ made vſe of an appeale; wee bring two Anſweres; the one that thoſe wordes, are not the wordes of *Socrates* but the wordes of an hereticall author from whom *Socrates* reports them; to wit, from *Sabinus* who to calumniate ſaint CYRILL, who although for feare of *Conſtantius* the *Arrian* Emperor, he did then communicate outwardly with the *Arrians* neuertheleſſe was in doctrine and beleefe a catholicke; reproaches it to him that he had appealed rom the Councell of *Ceſarea*, in *Paleſtina* wherein he had bene depoſed by the *Arrians*, and had put in his appeale to the Councell of *Seleucia* holden by the *Arrians*, but wherein there were manie couert catholicks, and which communicated not with the *Arrians*, but in the receipt of the Sacraments, and differd wholie from them in faith. The truth of his Anſwere appeares, both by this, that *Socrates* in the beginning of this hiſtorie ſaith, that he hath abridged it from the collection of *Sabinus*; *Let the Readers*, ſaith he, *curious to know things in particular; ſearch them in the collections of* Sabinus, *where they are at large ſett downe; wee running ouer them, haue but extracted heads*. And by the canon whereto this Author ſaith that *Cyrill* contradictes, which was a canon of the Councell of *Antioch* holden in the dedication; which Councell *Socrates* was ſo farr from thinking it lawfull, as contrariwiſe, not only in the ſame hiſtorie, he makes an Apoſtrophe againſt the memorie of *Eleuſius*, who had qualified the Biſhops of the Councell of *Antioch* with the title of Fathers, and aſkes him; *How, ô Eleuſius doſt thou call theſe Fathers, that were aſſembled at Antioch and denieſt that title to their Elders?* And a little after; *that if thoſe that were aſſembled at Antioch haue rooted out their Fathers, thoſe that followe them followe Paricides*; but alſo in the cauſe of ſaint CHRISOSTOME he ſaith, that the canon of the Councell of *Antioch* which was produced againſt him, had bene forged by the *Arrians*. And in deede, how could *Socrates* haue held the Biſhops appeales for a new thing, and cõtrarie to the canon of the Church, hee that alleadgeth for a reproach of nullitie againſt the Councell of *Antioch*, that the lawe of the Church imported that thoſe thinges that were done without the Biſhop of *Romes* conſent, were nullities? And who had ſaid, ſpeaking of *Paule* Biſhop of *Conſtantinople*, of *Aſclepas* Biſhop of *Gaza* in *Paleſtina*, of *Marcellus* primat of *Ancyra* in *Galatia* and other Biſhops depoſed by the Councell of *Antioch*, and other Councells of the Eaſt, and yet had had recourſe to the Pope, the Biſhop of *Rome*, becauſe of the prerogatiue of his Church, armed them with confident letters, and writt into the Eaſt, and reſtored them euery man to his place; and that a longe while before, the action of *Cyrill*, and of the Councell of *Seleucia*. The other anſwere is, that *Sabinus* himſelf did not pretend to ſaie by that, that *Cyrill* had done a new thing, and cõtrarie to the lawes of the Church; or as the words of *Sabinus* imported from a leſſe Tribunall to a greater; that is to ſaie, from the Councell of *Paleſtina*, to that of *Seleucia*, in appealing from one *Synod* to an other. For the Councell of *Antioch* it ſelf vpon which *Sabinus* grounds himſelf, ordaines that a Biſhop cõdẽned may haue recourſe to a greater *Synod*. But for this that he had in his appeale, followed the forme of ſecular appeales for as much as he had taken, to ſpeake according to the ſtile of this time, a releefe of appeale from the imperiall Chancerie, that is to ſaie, had taken letters from the

Socrat. hiſt. Eccl. l. 2. c. 39.

Socrat. hiſt. Eccl. l. 6. c. 18.

Socrat. hiſt. Eccl. l. 2. c. 8.

Socrat. ibidem c. 15.

Emperor, to oblige the Bishops of the Councell of *Seleucia* and particularly the *Acacians* who being *Arrians* and fauourd by the Officers of the Emperor, who assisted at the Councell who were *Arrians*, would not haue suffered that the cause of *Cyrill* who had bene condemned by *Acafius* in the Councell of *Palestina*, should againe haue bene put to triall to receaue his Appeale, and to renew the examination of his cause. This appeares both by the beginning of the historie of the Councell of *Seleucia*, where it is said that diuers letters of the Emperors were brought, whereof some ordained that they should first treat of matters of faith, and others that they should first handle the causes of accused Bishops: And by the very words of *Sabinus* against *Cyrill* which are; *As soone as he had bene deposed hauing sent a libell of appeale to those that had deposed him, he appealed to a greater iudgement; to which appeale, the Emperor Constantius added his suffrage, and this Cyrill did only, & the first against the Custome of the ecclesiasticall Canon, making vse of Appeales, as in lay iudgments.* By which words, *Sabinus* intended not to saie; that *Cyrill* was the first that appealed from a lesser Synod to a greater, but that hee was the first the vsed the forme of secular appeales in Ecclesiasticall iudgement; that is to saie, that had recourse to the Emperor to cause his appeale to be accepted: And therefore hee saith not that he was the first that vsed appeales; but that hee was the first that vsed them as in laie Iudgments. And this finallie appeares by the same Canon of the Councell of *Antioch*, the transgression whereof *Sabinus* obiects to S. CYRILL; which Canon forbids not that wee may appeale from a lesser Synod to a greater, contrariwise ordaines it in expresse words, but forbids that they should haue recourse to the Emperors authoritie, and setts downe the deffence in these words. *If any Priest deposed by his owne Bishop, or anie Bishop deposed by a Synod, presume to importune the eares of the Emperor; whereas he should haue recourse to a greater Synod, and referr the right that he supposeth he hath to a greater number of Bishops, let him not be receaued to iustification.* From whence it appeares, that this that *Sabinus* reprehended in Cyrill, was not that he had appealed from the Synod of *Palestina* to a greater Synod; to witt, to that of *Seleucia*, which was compounded of all the East, but for hauing recourse to the Emperor, & for hauing obtained letters from him, to cause his appeale to be accepted, which is that, that he calls to vse appeales, as in lay iudgments, for as much as in lay iudgments, the Emperor gaue letters to oblige the seconde Iudges to receaue the appeale, and the first to yeeld to it,

Socr. hist. Eccl. l. 2. c. 40.

Conc. Antioch. Can. 12.

TO the second instance, which is, that in the first generall Councell of *Constantinople* it was ordained that those that would accuse a Bishop, should accuse him to the Synod of the Prouince, and if the Synod of the Prouince did not content them, they should haue recourse to the Synod of the Patriarkship, and that after it should noe more be lawfull, neither to importune the eares of the Emperor, nor to disquiet a generall Councell: wee answere that he speakes of the accusers of Bishops, and not of Bishops accused, that is to saie, that he pretends not to ordaine, that it should not be lawfull for a Bishop accused, to appeale frō the Patriarkall Synod, to the Generall Councell, or to the Pope, who was the head thereof and represented it: but that it should not be lawfull for the accuser, after the Cause had bene adiuged in the first instance by the prouinciall Councell, and in the second by the Patriarchall Coūcel, to pursue it elsewhere, no not before a Generall Councell, as appeares by the Conclusion of the Canon, which is, *If anie one despising the thinges aforesaid, shall dare to importune the eares of the Emperor, or the iudgement of the secular*

Concil. Const. 1. Can. 6.

magistrates, or disunite the Generall Councell &c: let him be no more anie waie receaued in his accusation, Otherwise, how could saint CHRYSOSTOME, being deposed a while after this Councell, by a Councell holden at the instance of the Emperor and the Empresse in the Suburbs of *Constantinople*, haue appealed to a Generall Councell: And how a little after, seeing himself depriued of the Pope of a Generall Councell, because of the obstacle that the Emperor of the East (and the Empresse his wife, without whom a Generall Councell could not be celebrated) gaue to it, could he haue appealed to the Pope? And how could the Emporor *Valentinian*, haue said, that *Flauianus*, Bisho of *Constantinople*, had appealed to the Pope according to the custome of Councells? And how could the Councell of *Chalcedon*, holden at the gates of *Constantinople*, haue approued of the appeale of *Theodoret* Bishop of *Cyre* a cittie of the Patriarkship of *Antioch* to the Pope, and the iudgment of restitution be giuen by the Pope vpon his Appeale?

Sozom. hist. Eccl. l.8.c.17.

In ep. præamb. Conci. Chalced c.25.

Concil. Chalced, Act.1.

To the third Instance which is, that the Emperor *Iustin*, ordaines, that clerkes should be first iudged by their Bishop, and then by their metropolitans, and then by the Patriarkes of the Nation, and should obey the things decided by him as if from the beginning he had bene the iudge; for as much as against the sentence of such Bishops, the former Emperors had ordained, that there should be noe appeale: Wee answere, that he speakes of the causes of inferior clerkes who in the first instance ought to be iudged by their Bishops; in the second by the metropolitans, and in the third, by the Patriarke; and not of the causes of Bishops And whereas he saith, that against: the sentence of such Bishops, the former Emperors haue ordained, that there should be noe appeale; wee say with *Balsamon*, that the place is corrupted; and thas it must bee reads; *against such sentence of Bishops*; to witt, against the sentences of Bishop giuen in lay-matters; and it must bee interpreted of the appeale to the secular Tribunall; as appeares by the same lawe of the Emperors *Arcadius, Honorius* and *Theodosius*; to which that of *Iustin*, remitts the Readers; which ordaines that the sentences of Bishops, should be as those of the Prouostes of the Pretory: from whence it is not lawfull to appeale. *Wee ordaine* (said the Emperors, writing to *Theodorus* Prouost of the Pretorie) *that the Episcopall sentence shall remaine firme in the behalfe of those which haue desired to be iudged by the Bishops, add that like reuerence be giuen to their iudgements, as to yours, from whence it is not lawfull to appeale*. And by the report that *Photius* made of the same law in these wordes: *The ninth constitution of the fourth title of the first booke, of the code saith; That the sentences of Bishops, should bee as those of the prouostes of the Pretory, from whence it is not lawfull to appeale*; that is to saie, that it is noe more lawfull to appeale from the sentences of Bishops, to the imperiall Tribunall; then from those of the Prouost, of the Pretory: for the Emperors might well ordaine, that for things temporall, there should be noe appeale from the Bishops to them; but not that for things speritual there should be noe appeale frō Bishops, to the superior ecclesiasticall Tribunalls.

Cod. l.1. tit.4.l.4.

To the fourth instance, which is that the Emperor *Iustinian*, ordaines, that if anie clerke or layman, attempt an action against a Bishop for what cause soeuer, the cause should be iudged before the metropolitan, and that if any one contradict the things iudged, the cause should be referred to the Blessed Archbishop and Patriarke of the diocesse, and there according to the lawes and canons he must end it. And a little before, that if two Bishops of one selfe Sinod, haue a

Con-

conteſtatiõ one againſt the other, the Metropolitan with two of the Biſhops of the *Synod;* that is to ſaie of the Epiſcopall ſocieties of the Prouinces, shall iudge thereof; and that if one of the parties contradict it, the bleſſed Patriarke of the nation shall decide it, without that either of the parties can contradict it: Wee anſwere, that he ſpeakes of the cauſes of Biſhops, where there interuenes noe depoſition, the finall depoſition of Biſhops, hauing bene aliwaies ſubiect to appeales, be it to the Pope or to a Generall Councell; as appeares by the hiſtorie of *Liberatus*, time-fellowe with *Iuſtinian*, who ſaith that *John*, Patriarke of *Alexandria*, hauing bene depoſed at the inſtance of the Emperor *Zeno*, by the *Synod* of the Prouince, appealed to the Pope: And by ſaint ATHANASIVS, who reports theſe words out of the Epiſtle of Pope *Iulius*; *They muſt write to all of vs, that by all of vs that may be iudged which is iuſt: For thoſe that were diſquieted, were Biſhops.* And againe; *Are you ignorant that it is the cuſtome to write firſt to vs, and that from hence should proceede, the deciſion of things? And therefore yf there were anie ſuſpition conceaued againſt the biſhop there, it muſt haue bene written off to the Church here.* And beſides wee ſaie, thas whereas he ordaines, that the Patriarke should end cauſes, he intends he should end them in regard of ſecular indgements; that is to ſaie, that after the Patriarke, no ſecular iudge, should dare to examine it, nor should anie of the parties contradict before anie Secular Iudge; as when he ſaith in the former Paragraphe; *that if it be an Eccleſiaſticall cauſe which is attempted againſt anie clearke, the ſecular Iudges should not intermeddle in it, but, the Bleſſed Biſhop muſt end it:* For he intends not heereby to ſaie that there can be noe appeale from the Biſhop, to ſuperior eccleſiaſticall Iudges; but that there should be noe appeale from the Biſhop to the Prince and the ſecular Magiſtrat. And it is not to be ſaid, that the Pope ſaint GREGORIE the firſt, cites the conſtitution of *Iuſtinian*, whereof there hath bene aboue mention in the cauſe of the Biſhop *Steuen*, who ſeemed to be accuſed of a crime meriting depoſition; to witt of the crime of treaſon; for beſides that thoſe that make this allegation, forget to add to it the traine of ſaint GREGORIES text which is, *That if they ſaie contrariwiſe, that there is noe Metropolitan nor Patriarke, it muſt be anſwered that the cauſe ought to be iudged and decided by the Sea Apoſtolicke, which is the head of all the Churches.* That S. GREGORIE, alleadgeth this lawe, it is not to applie it to the meritt of *Steuens* cauſe, but to shewe that *Steuen* ought to be drawne in iudgement before the Councell of his Prouince, and not before the Councell of an other prouince. And indeede, how could S. GREGORIE haue pretended that in maior cauſes; that is to ſaie, wherin there were handled either the finall depoſition of Biſhops, or matters of Faith, the Patriarks ſentences not to be ſubiect to appeale; he that cries out; *Do not you know, that in the cauſe that John the prieſt had* (hee meanes *John* a prieſt of *Chalcedon*, who had bene condemned for a matter of faith at *Conſtantinople*,) *againſt our brother and Colleague, Iohn Biſhop of Conſtantinople, he hath had recourſe according to the canons to the Sea Apoſtolick, and that it hath bene defined by our iudgement?*

Liberat. in Breuiar. c. 17. Athan. apol. 2. Id. ibidem. Greg. Ma. l. 11. ind. 6 ep. 54. Gre. Mag. l. 4. ep. 82.

To the fifth Inſtance, which is that the Emperors LEO and *Conſtantine* ſaie that the Sentence of the Patriarke is not ſubiect to appeale, and is not to be retracted by an other Iudge, as being the Prince of Eccleſiaſticall iudgement: Wee ſaie, that thoſe two Emperors who haue written ſince the Schiſme of the Greeke Church, ſpeake of the Patriarke by excellencie; that is to ſaie of the Patriarke,

Leo & con. apud Leũ.

of *Constantinople*, whom they beleeue to holde the place of Pope in the East; for they esteemed the sentences of other Patriarkes to be subiect to appeales; but they beleeued that the sentences of Patriarkes vniuersall; that is to saie, according to them, of the Pope, and of the Patriarke of *Constantinoplee* whom they associated with the Pope in the Right of vniuersall Patriarke, for as much as *Constantinople*, was a second *Rome*, and the Patriarke of *Constantinople*, for this occasion, according to them, a second Pope, were not subiect to appeale. This appeares both by the tenth Article of the sixth title, were they saie, the iudgement of all Metropolitanshipps and Bishopricks, belonge to their proper Patriarke; but to him of *Constantinople*, it is lawfull to confirme, and reforme, and determine, the contestations bredd in other Seas. And by *Balsamon* who writes vpon the fifth canon of the Councell of *Antioch*, that this comdemnation is ment of *Synods* not subiect to appeale, as of the Pope, and of the Patriarke of *Constantinople*.

Phot. in Nomo can. To the sixth and last Instance, which is that *Photius* saith, that from the Patriarks there is noe appeale, wee answere it is not *Photius* that speakes, for *Photius* inserts not in his *Nomocanon*, but the only texts of the constitutions of the Emperors, without mingling anie thing of his owne; but that these are the words of the constitution of *Iustine*, vnckle to *Iustinian*, to which wee haue aboue answered, who saith alluding to the eighth lawe of the fourth title of the code, *for against such Episcopall sentences, as it hath bene ordained by our elders, there is noe appeale*; Of which words, the Greeke Bookebinders or Exemplifiers haue made, *for against the sentences of such Bishops*; that is to saie, of the Patriarks, *there is noe appeale*. Together that if *Photius* the author of the Schisme, that still continues betweene the latine and Greeke Churches had written these words to defend the inuasion made vpon the Sea of *Ignatius*, true and lawfull Patriarke then aliue. and to hinder the appeale that *Ignatius* had put in against *Photius*, and his pretended *Synod*, to the Pope; from taking effect, it would haue borne noe weight. But so farr is it from being soe, as not only *Photius*, but after him *Simon Logotheta*, *Zonara*, *Balsamon*, *Alexios*, *Blastares*, *Harmenopolus*, and other greeke canonists, insert into their collections, the canons of the Coucell of *Sardica*, and particularly the third, fourth, fifth, & by which the Episcopall appeales of all the prouinces, are yeelded to the Pope, but also that vnder the verie title of the retractation of the sentences of Bishops, vnder which he registers this constitution of *Iustine*, he quotes third, fourth, fifth canon of the Councell of *Sardica*, which ordaine that the Episcopall appeales should be remitted to the Pope. For to this that *Zonara*, to preserue the Easterne appeales to the Patriarke of *Constantinople* saith that the Councell of *Sardica*, in making the Rule of the Episcopall appeales, intended to yeeld noe more to the pope, but the westerne Appeales, Wee saie besides this, that this exceptiō defaulketh not *Africa*, which made a parte of the westerne prouinces, and was subiect to the Prouost of the Pretory of *Italie*; it is against the precise intention of the Councell of *Sardica*, which publisht this Rule expresselie, to abrogate the canon of the Councell of *Antioch*, and to iustifie the restitution that Pope *Iulius* had made of saint ATHANASIVS Patriarke of *Alexandria*, and of *Paule* Bishop of *Constantinople*, & of *Marcellus* primate of *Ancyra* in *Galatia*, and of *Asclepas* Bishop of *Gaza* in *Palestina*, who had bene deposed from their Seas, by the Councells of *Tyre*, of *Hierusalē* of *Antioch*, & other Easterne Coūcels: *Iuliū* (saith *Zosom*) *receiued Athanasius Bishop of Alexādria Paule Bishop of Constātinople Marcellus*

Zonar. in con. Sard. c. 5.

Bis-

Bishop of Ancyra in Galatia, Asclepas Bishop of Gaza in Palestina, and Lucius Bishopp of Andrinople into his communion; and because that to him for the dignitie of his Sea, the care of all things belonged, he restored to each of them his Church. And elsewhere speaking of the Fathers of the Councell of *Sardica* they answered that they would not seperate themselues from the communion of *Athanasius* and of *Paule*, and Principally for as much as *Iulius* Bishop of *Rome* had examined their cause, and had not condemned them. And therefore *Balsamon* seeing that this euasion could not subsist, hath inuented an other, which is that the councell of *Sardica* had indeede yeelded to the Pope, the appeales of all Bishops, but that *Constantinople* hauinge since bene erected to the title of the secōd *Rome*, the right of appeales hath bene deuided betwene the Pope, and the Patriarcke of *Constantinople*: *Those thinges* (said *Balsamon* commenting the third canon of the councell of *Sardica*) *which are heere defined of the Pope, ought also to bee extended to the Patriark of Constantinople, because by diuers Canons* (he meaneth the canons of the councell of *Chalcedon*, and of the conncell surnamed *Trullian*, by which he pretendes that he Bishop of *Constantinople* was made equall to the Pope excepting precedence) *he hath bene honored with priuiledges in all things equall to those of the Pope.* And againe, commenting the fift canon of the same councell of *Sardica*; *This priuilege belongeth not to the Pope alone, that it should be necessarie that euerie condemned Bishop haue recourse to the Sea of Rome, but it ought also to be vnderstood of the Sea of Constantinople.* And *Nilus* Archbishop of *Thessalonica*; *The twētie eight canō of the councell of Chalcedō, and the thirtie sixt of the sixth synod, honoring the Sea of Constantinople with the same priuiledges as the Sea of Rome, yeelde also manifestlie the appeales to the Sea of Constantinople.* And so much for the Councell of *Sardica*.

Sozom. hist. Eccl. l. 3. c. 7

Id. ibid. c. 10.

Balsam. in Concil. Sardic c. 3.

Id. Ibidem l. 5.

Nil. de Prim. Pap l. 2.

CAR-

CARDINALL PERRONS

REPLIE TO THE

KING OF GREAT BRITAINE.

THE FOVRTH BOOKE.

THE ESTATE OF THE CHVRCH

IN THE EAST.

CHAPT. I.

The continuance of the Kings answere.

Had anie one presumed to alter or disguise euer so little the faith approued by the vvhole world: it vvas easie euen for a Child to surprise and discouer in his noueltie him that should bring in a different doctrine, and the robber of the truth being surprised, all the pastors of the vvorld if it vvere needefull rowsed themselues vp, and being once stirred vp gaue themselues noe rest, till they had taken avvay the euill from amongst them, and had prouided for the securitie of Christs flocke. This vvas heeretofore the designation and felicitie of the Catholicke church, but vvhich indured not manie ages.

THE REPLIE.

APPELLES answered one daie to one of this Schollers that had painted a *Venus* loaded with pearles, carkanets and iewells; because thou couldst not paint her faire, thou hast painted her rich: so though this discription be not adorned with truth, which is the simple naked and naturall beautie of historie, it is eloquent and adorned with rich and magnificent wordes: But S. BASILL and S. HIEROM, paint out the estate of Religion in their time, in the east much otherwise: S. BASILL when he saith: *To what shall we compare the state of the present times certainlie to a Sea-fight, when Sea Captaines chafed with the warr, and inflamed to the combate, set one vpon an other with a violent hate, and nourisht with old iniuries.* And a while after. *The troubles stirred vp by the Princes of the earth, swallow vp the people more horribly, then all kinds of whirlewindes and tempests, and a darke and sad night possesses the Churches, the lights that God had placed to illuminate the soules of men being banisht from their Seas.* And S. HIEROME when he writes; *Because the East striking against it selfe by the antient furie of the people, teares in little morsells the vndeuided coate of our lord wouen on high, and that the foxes destroie the vine of Christ in such sort, as it is difficult amongst the drie pitts that haue noe water, to discerne where the sealed fountaine and the inclosed garden is; for this cause I haue thought, that I ought to consult whith the Chaire of Peter, and the faith praised by the mouth of the Apostle.* And a while after; *Now in the west the sunn of iustice is risen; and in the East that Lucifer which was fallen, hath sett vp his Throne aboue the starrs; you are the light of the world; you are the salt of the earth, you are the vessells of gold & of Syluer: and the vessells of earth or wood, doe here attend the rod of iron and the eternall fire.*

Basil. Magn.

Hieron. ad Damas. ep. 57. Id. ibidem.

And the historie of the following ages doth euen the same. For when *Eutyches* rose vp, and after he had bene iudged in the first instance by *Flauianus* Bishop of *Constantinople*, appealed or pretended to haue appealed to the Pope, and was againe iudged and deposed in the second instance by him; what came of it? The Emperor *Theodosius* gouerned by *Crysaphius* an abettor of *Eutyches*, caused a Councell to be held, vnder the title of Generall at *Ephesus*, where by force and by strong hand he caused, *Dioscorus* the Patrõ of *Eutyches* heresie to preside, the legates of the Pope for this cause, quitting the place, fled. In that Coũcell *Eutyches* was restored; *Flauianus* deposed and slaine, after he had neuerthelesse appealed from his condemnation to the Pope and the *Eutychian* heresie was subscribed by *Dioscorus* Patriarke of *Alexandria*, *Maximus* Patriarke of *Antioch*, *Iuuenall* Patriarke of *Hierusalem*, and almost by all the Bishops of the Councell, some by their good wills, and others by force. The Pope againe takes the cause of the faith in hand, pursues the holding of a new Councell which was that of *Chalcedon*, were that heresie is condemned and *Dioscorus* and *Eutyches* and all his abettors deposed and excommunicated, and in *Dioscorus* steed there was substituted in the patriarkshipp of *Alexandria*, *Proterius* a catolicke and partaker with the Councell of *Chalcedon*: to *Proterius* there succeeded *Timothie* an *Eutychian* and paracide of his Predecessor, who againe sett on foote the *Eutychian* heresie in the Sea of *Alexandria* and in *Egipt*, and disannulled there the decrees of the Councell of *Chalcedon*; a while after, into the Sea of *Antioch*, there entred PETER surnamed the *Tanner*, likewise an enemie to the Councell of *Chalcedon*, and professor of the heresie of *Eutyches*. Likewise there came to *Constantinople Acacius*, who communicated with *Peter* Bishop of *Antioch*: and there was installed in the Empire *Zeno* an *Eutychian* and disannuller of the Councell of *Chalcedon*; and all the Easterne Church miserablie rent by the factions of those that held, some for the Councell, and some against it, and others, neither for nor against it, whom they called neuters, so longe that after some changes of Patriarks, sometimes Catholicks, and some times *Eutychians*, all the naturall Churches of *Egypt*, and those of *Ethiopia*, that is to saie, all that acknowledged the *Egiptian* Patriarke of *Alexandria* haue remained and perseuered still to this daie in the profession of the *Eutychian* heresie. Such was then in the east (vnder the Emperors, abusing their authoritie) the designation and felicitie of the Church, and such was the facilitie euen for Children (except those that cast their eyes vpon the communion of the *Roman* Church) to knowe the robbers of the truth, and for pastors to driue awaie the euill from among them, For as for the west, the Patriarshipp of the *Roman* Church, hath alwaies had this particular blessing that within the limitts of the extent thereof, the Catholicke Church, notwithstanding the infidelitie of the Emperors, had bene without comparison more visible and more eminent, (as being the Ensigne Colonell, and that whereto the others ought to haue regard, and vnder which they should gather themselues) then in the other Patriarkships. From whence it is that what S. HIEROM writes in the forme of a historie of former times when he saith to Pope *Damasus*. *The wicked children hauing dispersed their patrimonie, amongst you onelie is preserued vncorrupted, the inheritance of the fathers*: S. LEO seemeth to saie it, in forme of a prophecie of those that are to followe, who pronounces, *That none of the Patriarchall-seas* (sauing that of *Rome*) *shall remaine firme and stable.*

Leo ep. 8. & in ep. præamb. Concil. Chalced. c. 4.

Val ent. epist. ad Theodos. in præamb. Cõc. Chalc c. 25.

Hieron. ad Damas. ep. 57.

Leo ad Marcian. Aug. ep. 52.

What the diuision of the Empire hath wrought to the diuision of the Church.

CHAP. II.

The continuance of the Kinges answere.

FOR after the Empire being ouerthrowne, and the forme of the common wealth changed, new gouernments haue risen vp, manie in number, different in manners, distinct in languages, lawes, and institutions. The diuision of the Empire hath drawne after it, the diuision of the Catholicke Church, and all those thinges that wee saie nowe to haue serued singularly to the preseruation of the vnion and externall Communion of the Catholicke Church, haue ceased by little and little.

THE REPLIE.

THE diuision of the Empire, hath not caused the diuision of the Church, especiallie in the West; for whatsoeuer multitude of gouernments haue had place there, vnder the title of Empire, Kindome, Principalitie, and Common wealth, and whatsoeuer difference of manners, languages, lawes, and institutions, that haue raigned there, the Church hath bene no more visible in the tyme when the Empire was one and ruled ouer all the East and west, then it hath bene vnder this diuersitie of Princes and gouernments Also the vnitie of the Church was not foretold by the Prophets, only for the time wherein there should be but one tẽporall monarcke in the world, if euer that title could haue belonged to anie Prince, but also for that tyme wherein there should bee seuerall kinges and Administrators of Estates, according to this Prophecie of the Psalmist: *The Kings and Kingdomes shall agree in one to serue our Lord.* Which caused S. AVGVSTINE to saie, vnder colour that in the whole world, Kingdomes are often deuided; yet for all that, Christian vnitie is not deuided, for as much as the Catholicke Church remaines on either part. And indeede, that the vnitie of the Church depends not from the vnitie of the Empire but from the relation to a visible center of the Ecclesiasticall communion, it appeared sufficiently euen in the time of the greatest vnitie and extent of the Empire, when the Christians which were vnder *Firmus* King of the *Barbarians* in *Africa*, vnder *Mania* Queene of the *Sarazins*; vnder *Cosroes* King of *Persia*, states all distinct, yea the most part of the time, enemies to the *Romane* Empire: And after in *Damascus* and other neighbouring Prouinces vnder the Kings, of the *Agarenians*, did all agree in the vnion and communion of the Catholicke Church. For as for the deuisions which are at this daie in the East, euery one knowes, that that of *Egypt* and *Ethiopia*, hath begun from the time of the vnitie of the Empire; And that of the *Armenians* likewise; as appeares by the decisiõs made against them in the Canõs of the Cõucell holden vnder *Iustinian Rhinotmete*: And that of the *Nestorians*, and *Iacobites* which haue yet to this day their sect in *Mesopotamia* & other partes of *Asia* likewise. And as for the Greeke Church, it is certaine, that although it began to be diuided since the separation of the Empire, neuerthelesse the cause of the diuision, was not the diuision of the

Psalm. 101. Aug. l. de vnit. Eccl. c. 12.

Empire vnder which it perseuered yet manie yeares in vnitie with the Latine, but the Schisme betweene the two competitors of the Patriarkship of *Constantinople Ignatius* and *Photius*, to which to make it the more lasting, heresie was added, and which the Emperors, (according as they haue bene good or euill) haue indeuoured themselues to fomēt or stopp, and there haue not wanted generall Councells, euen of the two seuerall Churches, to extinguish this diuision when they haue desired it. For histories are full of these examples, witnes that which was holden at *Constantinople* vnder the Emperor *Basilius* for the restitution of *Ignatius*, that which was holden vnder Pope *Innocent* the third which wee call the great Councell of *Latteran*, to reunite the Greeke church with the Latine; and that which was holden for the same effect at *Florence* vnder *Eugenius* the fourth at which the Emperor and the Patriarke of Greece assisted in person. As also the diuision of the Empire, and the rule of the Greeke Emperors & after, of the *Mahometan* Princes, did not hinder the Churches that acknowledged the Patriarke of the *Syrian* tongue, whom we call *Maronites*, from perseuering in the communion of the *Roman* Church. In such sort, as this varietie and diuision of sects in the East, can not be attributed to the defect of the vnitie of the Empire, since in the time that the Empyre was most vnited, these troubles and innouations had such place therein, as *Socrates* and *Sozomene* doe in the tyme of the Emperor *Canstantius*, set the mount *Tuscis* in *Illiria*, for a bound betweene the quiet peace of the Church, and the tempest and turbulencie of hereticks. But it ought to be attributed to the want of constancie of the Easterne people, or rather to the blessing of God vpon the *Roman* church, which would shew that this prophecie, *Thou art Peter, and vpon this Rock, I will build my Church, and the gates of hell shall not preuaile against it*, hath had some more speciall effect for the Sea of S. PETER, then for those of the other Patriarkes, according to that oracle of the great *Leo: Besides the stone that our Lord hatt sett for a foundation, noe other building shall be stedfast.*

Math. 16

Leo ep. 52.

Of the interpretation of these vvords: Thou art Peter, and vpon this Rock, I will build my Church.

CHAPT. III.

The continuance of the Kings answere.

SINCE that time, the Catholicke Church, in truth hath not ceast to be, for it shall allwaies bee, and the gates of hell shall not preuaile against her, who is founded on Christ the true stone, and in the faith of PEETER and of the other Apostles.

THE REPLIE.

THat some times the Fathers expound these words; *Vpon this Rock, I will build my Church*, of the Faith of S. PETER, and say that the Church was built vpon the confession of PETER: And that some times they expound it of the person of PETER and saie that the Church hath bene founded vpon the person of PETER, they are not contrarie expositions, the one excluding the other, but conioynt the one including the other, for they intend the Church (to speake the

Rock in French is, *Pierre*, in Greeke πετρος in Syriack *Cepha* which words in the self same languages are the name of *Peter*.

Schoole language) is built causallie vpon the confession of PETER; and formallie vpon the ministrie of the person of PETER; that is to saie, the confession of PETER was the cause werefore Christ chose him, to constitute him for the foundation of the ministrie of his Church: *By that* (saith saint HILLARIE) *the blessed Confession hath obtained his reward: and that the person of saint Peter, hath bene that vpon which our Lord hath properlie built his Church.* Soe as to saie that his Church is built vpon the confessiō of PETER, is not to denie that it is built vpō the person of PETER but it is to expresse the cause wherefore it is built vpon him; noe more then to saie with saint HIEROME, that PETER walked not vpon the waters, but Faith, is not to denie, that saint PETER walked trulie, properly, and formallie, vpon the water; but it is to expresse, that the cause that made him walke there, was not the actiuitie or naturall vertue of his person, but the faith that he had giuen to the words of Christ. And therefore, as these two propositions, the faith of PETER walked vpon the waters, and the person of PETER walked vpon the waters, are both true, but in a different sence, for the faith of PETER walked vpon the waters causallie, as the Schoolemē saie; that is to saie, it was the cause that the person of saint PETER walked there, and the person of saint PETER walked there trulie, properlie, and formallie; so these two propositions the Church was built vpon the confession of PETER, and the Church was built vpon the person of PETER, are both ioyntly true, but in different sence; for the confession of PETER is the causall foundation of the Church, that is to saie, it is the cause for which the Church is built vpon the person of PETER, rather then vpon that of anie other Apostle, for as much as the primacie of this confession not proceeding nor preuented from or by anie humane instruction, but proceeding immediatlie frō the pure reuelation of God, the other Apostles being silent & not knowing what to answere, was the cause, in fauour whereof Christ chose (preferring him before all others) saint PETER to constitute him the foundation of his Church. And the person of *Peter* is the formall foundation of the Church; that is to saie, him vpon whose ministrie, by preferring him before all others, Chirst hath built and edified his Church. But the differenc of these two expositions is that the one is immediate and the other mediate; the one direct and the other collaterall; the one literall, and the other morall the one originall, and perpetuall, and the other accessorie and temporall; the one consigned from the beginning, and the other introduced by occasion. For before the *Arrians* were risen vp; that is to saie before the age of *Constantine* and of the first Councell of *Nicea*, the interpretation that was current in the Church, was that, not of the confession of PETER, but of the person of PETER. As when *Tertullian* saith in his Booke of Prescriptions against heretikes; *Was there anie thing cōcealed from Peter who was called the stone of the building of the Church?* And ORIGEN *See what is said to the great foundatiō of the Church, and the solid stone vpon which Christ hath built his Church.* And elsewhere, *Peter vpon whō the Church of Christ hath bene built, against which the gates of hell shall not preuaile.* And in the comentarie vpon the *Epistle* to the *Romans* trāslated by saint HIEROME: *When the Soueraigne authoritie of feeding the Sheepe was giuen to Peter, and that vpon him as vpon a stone, the Church was built, the confessiō of anie other vertue was not exacted of him, but onlie that of Charitie.* And S. CYPRIAN, *Peter whom the Lord chose first, and vpon whom he built his Church.* And againe; *God is one, and Christ is one, and the Church is one, and the Chaire is one, built by the voyce of our Lord vpon Peter.* But after the coming of *Constantine*, when the *Arrians* had lifted themselues vp against the diuinitie of Christ, the

Hilar. in Matt. c. 16.
Hieron. ad Pammach. aduers. error. Ioann. Hierosol. ep. 61.
Tertull. de præscript. c. 32.
Origen. in Exod. c. 14 hom. 5.
Orig. apud Euseb. hist. Eccl. l. 6. c. 15.
Id. in epist. ad Roman. c. 6. l. 5.
Cyprian. ep. 71.
Idem. ep. 4.

Fathers

Fathers finding no passage in the scripture, more expresse to proue vnto them that IESVS CHRIST was the sonn of God, not by adoption, but by nature, then this Confession of sainct PETER, *Thou art Christ the Sõne of the liuing God*, in which they held, that the word *(liuing)* had bene expressely inserted, to shew that IESVS CHRIST, was the sonn of God by generation; for as much as to engender, as saie the Philosophers, is proper to liuing thinges, they tooke care as much as was possible for them, to exalt the dignitie of this confession. And because that in fauour thereof, and for it S. PETER had bene constituted, *foundation of the Church*, they licensed themselues to call it by *Metonimy*, that is to say, by translation of the name from the effect to the cause, the foundation of the Church, that they might haue the more occasion to declaime against those that destroyed it, in reproching thẽ that they ruined the foundatiõ of the Church that is to saie, the confession in fauour whereof, and for whose cause he that had made it, had bene constituted foundation of the Church, but neuerthelesse, to shew that they intended not, in doeing this to exclude the person of PETER from being the formall foundation of the Church, that which the same fathers had said in one place of the confession of PETER, as causall foundation of the Church, they said it in an other, yea often times in the same place, of the person of PETER, as formall foundation of the Church. This appeares by saint HILARIE, who disputing in his workes of the Trinitie against the *Arrians*, after he had said, *This faith is the foundation of the Church, by this faith the gates of hell are disabled against her; this faith hath the keyes of the heauenlie Kingdome*: Adds immediately after, to declare that this should be intended of the faith of sainct PETER causallie and meritoriouslie, but of his person formallie; that is to saie, that this confession hath only bene the meritorious cause, for which sainct PETER hath receiued these things, but that it is the person of PETER, that hath properly and formallie receiued them: *This is hee, that in the silence of all the other Apostles, acknowledging beyond the capacitie of human infirmitie, the Sonn of God, by the Reuelation of the Father hath merited by the Confession of his blessed faith, a supereminent place. And a little after. Hee hath confessed Christ to be the Sonn of God, and for that he is called blessed, This is the Reuelation of the Father, this is the foundation of the Church; this is the assurauce of eternitie, from hence he had the keyes of the Kingdome of heauen; from hence his earthly iudgments become heauenly.* And a little before; *After the confession of the Sacrament, the blessed Symon is submitted to the edification of the Church, receiuing the keyes of the heauenly Kingdome.* And in his comentaries vpon the verie place of the words of IESVS CHRIST, *The confession of Peter hath receaued a trulie worthie reward.* And a little after: *in the title of a new name, blessed foundation of the Church, and worthie Stone of her edification, that destroyed the lawes of hell, and the gates of the deepes, and all the prisons of Death: O blessed Porter of heauen, to whose arbitrement, the keyes of the eternall entrie are deliuered, whose iudgments on earth haue authoritie to preiudge in heauen.* And elsewhere. *Christ had so great a zeale to suffer for the Saluation of human kinde as Peter the first Confessor of the Sonn of God, the foundation of the Church, the Porter of the heauenly kingdome, the iudge of heauen vpon earth, disswading him, he called him by the name of Satan!* And soe sainct CHRYSOSTOME interprets it; that is to saie, sometimes of his faith, *Vpon this stone* (said hee) *that is to say, vpon the faith of this confession*: And sometimes of his person: *Hee promiseth* (saith he) *to make a fisherman more solid then anie kinde of stones.* And vpon the fiftith Psalme, heare what he saith to PETER, *That Pillar, that foundation, and therefore called Peter*

Mat. 16. | Hilar. de Trinit. l. 6 | Ibidem. | Ibidem. l. 10 | Hilar. in Matt. c. 16. | Id. ibidem. | Id in Psal. 131. | Chryso. in Matt. c. 16.

Cyrill.de Trinit.l.4 *as made a Rocke by faith*: And againe, *that Pillar of the Church, that basis of the faith, that head of the Apostolick flock*. And saint CYRILL doth euen the same, sometimes of his faith, *He hath* (said hee) *called the immutable faith of Peter his disciple, a Rocke*, and sometimes of his person, *he foretold him he should noe more be calld Symon but Peter; signifiing most aptlie by that word, that vpon him as vpon a Rocke and a stedfast stone, he should build his Church*. And this may be said of the first point of this Article, which is of building of the Church, vpon the faith, or vpon the person of PETER: Let vs passe forward to the secōd which is of that of the other Apostles. The Church saith his maiestie, is founded vpon the Confessiō of PETER & the other Apostles. Here it is needefull to distinguish the diuers vses that this word, *foundation of the Church*, receaues in the Scripture; for it is one thing to be the foundation of the faith of the Church, and an other thing to be the foundatiō of the Ministrie of the Church. And againe, the foundation of the faith of the Church, is of two sortes, for there is an obiectiue foundation of the faith of the Church, and a suggestiue foundation of the faith of the Church. I call that an obiectiue foundation of the faith of the Church, which is the first obiect that the Church is obliged to knowe and embrace for doctrine, of faith; and that is Christ, of
1.Corinth. c.3.vers.11 whom S. PAVLE saith, *None can laie anie other foundation besides that which is alreadie laid, that is Christ*. For the first thing that enters into the obiect of the Christian faith, as it is Christian, is Christ *God and Man crucified for our Sinns*; And all the other doctrins of Faith haue noe other place then as superedifications and accessories to that. I call that a suggestiue foundation of faith of the Church vpō which the Church grounds and assures the beleefe of those things which she holdes for doctrines of faith, and this againe is double, the one principall and originall, to wit, the holy
Ioan.14. vers.26. Ghost, of whom our Lord saith; *Hee shall suggest to you all thinges that I haue told you*, and the other instrumentall and organicall; to wit, the voice and pen of those, that he hath chosen to declare vnto vs the misteries of faith, with certaine and infallible authoritie. And in this sence, not only all the Apostles and Euangelists, but also all the prophets, are foundations of the faith of the Church according to this Apostolicall sentence;
Eph. 2. vers. 20. *Wee are edified vpon the foundation of the Prophets and of the Apostles*. And in this same sence sainct PAVL said in the second to the *Corinthians*,
2.Cor. c. 11.vers 5 & c.12. vers. 11. *That he had bene nothing inferior to the most excellently great of the Apostles*. And in the Epistle to the *Galatians*, *That he had not receiued his Ghospell from men, but from God*: *And that those that seemed to be something*; that is to saie, those that for the more particular familiaritie that they had with our Lord, it seemed they should bee more eminent in the doctrine of Faith, and should bee the Pillars of Faith, *had taught him nothing*. For to be something according to the stile of those of the east, is a word not of contempt, but of great and extraordinarie estimation.

I call him foundatiō of the ministrie of the Church, that hath the supereminēce and superintendencie of the gouernment and ministrie of the Church, which I haue distinguisht frō the foūdatiō of the Faith, not but that the primitiue and originall Ministrie of the Church, comprehends the Office of reuealing the Faith; and that the perpetuall and ordinarie ministrie of the Church, comprehends the office of preseruiug and pro-
1.Timoth. c.3. vers.15 pagating the Faith, from whence it is that sainct PAVL calleth the Church, *The pillar and foundation of faith*: But because the foundation of the Ministrie extends further; and manie, as sainct LVKE amongst others, haue bene foundations of the Faith of the Church, who neuer-

thelesse haue not bene foundations of the Ministrie of the Church. Now it is of this kinde of Foundation, to witt of the Foundation of the ministrie of the Church, that is treated off in these words of our Lord: *Thou art Peter, and vpon this Rock I will build my Church*; as it appeares by what followes of the keyes, and of the power to binde and loose. This qualitie then of foundation of the gouernment and ministrie of the Church to dispute; whether since it haue bene extended and communicated to the whole Bodie of the Apostles, it is an other point. For what S. PAVL saith: *If they be ministers of Christ, I am so more then they*, is to be vnderstood of the excesse in the labour of the Ministrie, and not in the authoritie. But at the least, when our Lord pronounced these wordes, *Thou art Peter and vpon this Rock I will build my Church*: It is certaine that in that instant and in those wordes, it was conferred to none but to sainct PETER; for the wordes are all pronounced in singular termes, and excluding pluralitie, *Blessed art thou Symon Sonn of Jona, and I saie vnto thee, that thou art Peter, and vpon this Rock I will build my Church: and I will giue thee the keyes of the kingdome of heauen*. Which sainct AMBROSE declares, who after he had said, *This man* to wit, PETER *when he had heard; but yee; what saie yee that I am? presently not forgetfull of his place he made the primacie*, adds to it, *It is then this Peter that answered before the rest, but for the rest, and therefore he is called Foundation*. Which sainct CYPRIAN likewise acknowledges in these wordes: *Vpon him beinge one, he built the Church*. And it is not to be said, that the Condition of Foundation of the Church hauing bene giuen to sainct PETER in fauour and for recompence of his Confession, all the other Apostles that had part in his Confession, ought also to haue their part therein. For the qualitie of foundation of the Church was not giuen to sainct PETER in fauour of his Confession simplie, for then it should be common to all the faithfull; but in fauour of the primacie of his Confession, wherein the other Apostles had noe actual part, but only by consent and non repugnancie, for as much as sainct PETER only answered, as illuminated immediately from God, the others being silent and not knowing what to saie, and learning it but my the meanes of sainct PETERS Answere: *Hee was* (saith sainct HILARIE) *made worthie of first knowing what there was of God, in Christ*. And sainct CYRILL of *Hierusalem*: *All the other Apostles being silent, for this doctrine was aboue their reach, Peter the Prince of the Apostles, and the Soueraigne herald of the Church, not of his owne inuention, neither perswaded by human reason, but illuminated in his soule by God the Father, said to him: thou art Christ the Sonn of the liuing God*. And sainct ATHANASIVS manie yeares before them: *For if the Father reuealed to Peter those thinges whereof our Lord demaunded him, &c. there is noe doubt but the same Lord who inquired, as if he had first reuealed to Peter those things that he had knowne from the Father, he askes him humanly, to shew in inquiring carnally that Peter that should tell them knew them diuinelie*.

2. Corinth c. 11. vers. 23.

Matth 16. vers. 18.

Ibid. vers. 19.

Ambros. de incarnat. Sacram. c. 4

Cypr. de vnit. Eccl.

Hilar. in Matt c. 16.

Cyrill. Catech. 11.

Athan. contr. Arian. Orat. 4.

FOR that in the sixth of S. IOHN, S. PETER answeres in common for all the Apostles: *Wee beleeue and knowe, thou art Christ the Sonn of the liuing God*, besides that the Latine editions haue not the word, *liuing*, Wee saie it was a later thing, for as much as when sainct PETER answered, *Wee beleeue and know that thou art Christ the Sonne of the liuing God*, hee had bene alreadie constituted head and Prince of the other Apostles, and in this qualitie he answered alone for all the rest, as sainct CYRILL testifies in these wordes; *By one that presided, or that was preeminent, all answered: and had alreadie receiued the promisses of our Lord, that vpon him he would build his Church*. As

Cyrill in Ioan. lib. 4 c. 28.

S. CYPRIAN declares in these wordes, *Peter speakes heere vpon whom the Church had bene built.* And therefore as the Apostles had part in the primacie of this confession only by adherence and non-repugnancie, so our Lord gaue them part in the authotitie he had giuen to *S. Peter by adherence and communication* with S. PETER; that is to saie, vnder condition of cōmunicating and adhearing and remayning in vnitie with saint PETER. And yet this part that he promised and gaue them in the rule and ministrie of the Church, was afterward, to witt, as in right in the eighteenth of saint MATHEW; *What yee bind on earth, shall be bound in heauen.* And as the installment into the possession in the twentith of saint IOHN *Receiue the holie Ghost, whose sinns yee forgiue, shall be forgiuen*, to the end to shew that to sainct PETER ōly the cōditiō of being a *Rock*, that is to sa, rule and foundation of the building of the Church had bene principallie and originally giuen; and that afterwards it was extended to the other Apostles, it was by aggregation and association, and by communicating and adhering with him, and as hauing relation and correspondence to him, as to the Center and middle forme of the veritie of the Church. For as God gaue first his spiritt to *Moyses*, and after tooke of the Spiritt that he had giuen to *Moyses*, and gaue thereof to the seauentie two Elders, not that God tooke awaie from *Moyses* anie portion of the spiritt that he had giuen him, not that the spirit of God was diuisible, but to the end to establish and shew a relation of vnitie, dependencie, and adherencie of the seauentie two Elders to *Moyses*. Soe in some sort (for I compare not the two histories wholie) our Lord gaue first the whole authoritie of the ministrie and the Chaire Apostolicke, to saint PETER alone; I intend as in right, and not in actuall possession, which he receaued not till after the Resurrection, and after gaue it to all the twelue Apostles in common, to the end to shew the relation of dependencie, vnitie, and adherence, that they ought to haue with saint PETER, whom vpon this occasion *Macharius* an antient *Egiptian* diuine, calls the successor of *Moyses*; *Afterward* (said hee) *to Moyses, succeeded Peter, to whom the new Church of Christ and the true priesthood hath bene committed*. Which hath caused the Fathers to saie, that there was but one Chaire, which was the Chaire of PETER; but that in this Chaire all the Apostles were placed, to witt, by the adherence, communion, and vnitie that they had with S. PETER. *In the Episcopall Chaire* (saith saint OPTATVS *Mileuitanus*) *there is sett the head of all the Apostles Peter, from whence he also hath bene called Cephas, to the end, that in this only Chaire, vnitie might be preserued in all, least the other Apostles should attribute to themselues, euery one his Chaire a parte, but that he might be a Schismaticke & Sinner, that against this onelie Chaire, should erect an other.* And therefore also the surname of PETER, by which this Condition of being the foundation of the rule of the Church is designed, hath bene giuen to him only to beare it in the title of a proper name, and not to anie other Apostle, to shew that to him by excellencie and eminencie ouer all the rest, appertained the thing whereof he alone bore the name. For since our Lord should by the word PETER designe the condition of being the ministeriall foūdation of the Church, for what cause should he affect it to *Peter* alone to beare it in the title of a proper and ordinarie name, and not giue it to anie other, if he were not to be a foundation of the Church in an other manner then the rest? Which S. BASILL hath in such sort acknowledged, as desiring to shew the difference which is betweene the substance and the hipostaticall proprieties of anie subiect, he alleadgeth for example of the substance, the substāce of humanitie, which is commō to PETER & PAVL.

Cyp. ep. 69

Mach. hom 26.

Opt Mileuit. contra Parmen. l. 2.

Although

although (said he) *the appellations be different, yet the substance of Peter and Paule, and of all men is one*; and alleadgeth amongst the examples of the hypostaticall indiuiduall and incommunicable conditions of PETER, that is to saie, which are particular to him onely, and are not common to him with saint PAVL, nor with anie other, the condition of being the foundation of the Church; *Because*, said he, *the names of men signifie not their substances, but the proprieties whereby each of them is designed in particular. From thence it is, that when wee heare the name of Peter, we vnderstand not his substance, &c. but conceiue the sence of the proprieties which are perticular to him. For as soone as wee heare this word, wee vnderstand Peter the Sonne of Ionas, he that was of Bethsaida, he that was Brother to Andrew; he that of a Fisherman was made an Apostle, he that by reason of the supereminencie of his Faith, receiued vpon him the edification of the Church.* Basil. contra Eunom l. 2. Id. ibid.

AND for this same cause to saint PETER onely there hath bene conferred singularlie separately and apart, the authoritie of the rule of the Church, and to all the rest onely in common and ioyntlie with him to the end to shew, that he was the originall, the source the center and the beginning of the vnitie of the Church, and that no other out of his Communion could exercise the rule and ministrie thereof, but that the rest had right to exercise it, it is onely as associated, and aggregated with him, and as grafted and inserted vpon him. For our Lord neuer said singularly to anie of the Eleuen; *Thou art Peter, and vpon this Rocke I will build my Church, and I will giue thee the keies of the Kingdome of heauen*; *nor, I haue praied for thee that thy faith shall not faile*: And finallie, *Thou being conuerted, confirme thy Bretheren*, nor, *louest thou me more then these? feede my sheepe*: But only hath said in generall to all the Bodie of the Apostles, sainct PETER being Colleague, present, and comprehended therein, that which he had said before to saint PETER alone, as to the head, *That which yee shall binde on earth, shall be bound in heauen, and they whose sinns yee forgiue, shall be forgiuen*. Which hath moued saint CYPRIAN to saie, that Christ hath instituted saint PETER the originall of vnitie: PETER (saith he) *vpon whom Christ hath built his Church, and instituted him the originall of vnitie*. And againe, *One chaire built vpon Peter by the voyce of our Lord*. And for this occasion as although in a tree, there be but the stocke, and the bodie of the tree only that succeedes, and is tied by direct continuance with the roote, neuerthelesse the other branches are tied to it by oblique and collaterall succession and continuance. Soe though there bee but only the Bishop of Rome that is saint PETERS successor in direct succession, neuerthelesse all the Bishops are esteemed in some sort to be sett in saint PETERS Chaire, and to be in a manner saint PETERS successors; to witt by oblique and indirect succession, because of the communication that they haue with the Chaire of S. PETER. But the Bishops are neuer said, neither in their whole bodie, nor separately to be successor to anie other particular Apostle; but are said either in generall to bee the Apostles successors, or in particular, successors to S. PETER, as to him that for being the head of the Apostleship, containes in vertue all the Apostolicke Bodie, so as neuer anie one Bishop hath called himself, successor to anie other Apostle, except those that haue succeded locallie to anie one of the other Apostles; as the Bishops of *Hierusalem* are in title successors to saint IAMES. Matt. 18. vers. 18. Ioan. 20. vers. 23. Cypr. de vnit. Eccl. Id. ep. 40.

BVT against this exposition, the aduersaries to the Primacie forme thriteen oppositions; the first, that our Lord adds presently after,

speaking to Peter, *Goe behind me Sathan* The seconde that he cries out; *If anie one amongst you desire to bee greatest, he shall be the least.* The third that S. PETER forbids from domineering ouer the flockes. The fourth that the Apostles sent PETER and IOHN into *Samaria.* The fifth that S. IAMES voted last in the Councell of *Hierusalem.* The sixth that S. PAVLE, names S. IAMES before S. PETER. The seauenth that the same S. PAVL saith, that the Ghospell of the Gentiles was committed to him, as that of the circumcision to PETER. The eighth that he saith S. PETER walked not right in the Ghospell. The ninth that he saith he resisted him to his face, because he was reproueable. The tenth that S. CYPRIAN writes, that the other Apostles were the same that Peter was. The eleauenth that EVSEBIVS reportes out of S. CLEMENT *Alexandrinus*, that PETER, IAMES, and IOHN contested not amongst themselues for the honor, but made IAMES Bishop of the Apostles. The twelfth that Sainct CHRISOSTOME writeth, that the other Apostles yeelded the Throne to IAMES. And the thirteenth, That the same S. CHRISOSTOME writes,
Matt.16. vers.23. that the Principalitie was committed to IAMES. To the first then of these obiections, which is, that our Lord said a while after to S. PETER, *Goe behind me Satan;* Wee answere. S. HIEROME hath solued it in these
Hieron. in Matt.c.16. words: *This blessing, beatitude, and edification of the Church vpon Peter, is promised to Peter in future times, and not giuen to him in time present. I will build* (said he) *my Church vpon thee.* To the seconde which is, that our Lord
Matt.c.20 vers.26. & Marc.c.10. vers.43. cryes elsewhere; *If anie one amongst you desire to be greatest, let him be the least,* Wee answere, he doth there forbidd the desire, and not the effect of the Primacie; the Ambition, and not the thing, the φιλοπρωτευέιν, and not the πρωτευέιν, witnes this traine that followes, *as the Sonn of man is come into the world, not to be serued, but to serue;* By which he pro pounds himself to his disciples for an example not of an Anarchy, but of Superioritie accompanied with humilitie. To the third Which is that S. PETER
1 Petr. c.5. vers 3. Matth.20. vers. 25. & Marc.10. vers. 24. Hieron. 16 in Ezech. c. 18. writes; *not domineering ouer the flocks,* Wee answere, that the Greeke word signifieth a violent *Dominion,* (such as that whereof our Lord said: *The kings of the nations domineere ouer them,* And such as S. HIEROME representeth it in these words: *The Princes of the Churches are wont to oppresse the Poeple with arrogance, of whom it is written, they haue constituted thee Prince, be not puft vp, but be amongst them, as one of them:* And not a presidencie and fatherlie direction, such as was that of *Samuell* ouer the people of *Israell*, who after he had exercised the Gouernment of *Israell*, and iudged the people many yeares, iustified himself in the end, saying: *I haue*
Samuel apud Iren.l. 4. aduers hæres.c 44 *nuersed with you from my youth to this daie; answere me in the presence of God, and of his annoynted, if I haue taken anie mans bullock or his Asse, or if I haue commaunded by force and oppressed any one of you.* And such as
Hebr. 13. vers. 17. Rom. 12. vers 9. Matth. 24 Ambr. de fide l.5.c.1. that whereof sainct PAVL said, *Obey your prelats and be subiect to them.* And elsewhere; *Let him that presides, preside in all diligence.* And our Lord himself, *which is the wise and faithfull seruant, that our Lord hath constituted ouer his familie? It is Peter* (saith sainct AMBROSE) *chosen by the iudgement of our Lord to feede his flocke, who hath merited to heare, feede my lambes, feede my sheepe.* To the fourth which is, that the historie of the Actes testifies, that the Apostles when it was in agitation to forme the Church of *Samaria*, sent thither PETER and IOHN: wee answere, it was a mission of request, as that when the *Israelites* sent *Phinees* their high priest, and the princes of the tribes, and not a mission of authority. To the fifth which is, that S. IAMES voted last in the Councell of *Hierusalem:* Wee answere, that in Councells, contrary to the order of secular companies, those that preside vote first. And namely

sainct

saint HIEROME saith, that saint PETER, from whose words S. IAMES tooke his Rule; *Was the Prince of this decree.* To the sixth, which is, that S. *Paule* writes, that *James Cephas, and Iohn, seeing the grace that God had conferred vpon him, gaue to him and to Barnabas the right hands of felloWshipp*: Wee answere, that the greeke edition of *Complutum* and manie seuerall Readings, Greeke and Latine haue it *Cephas, James* and *John*. Witnesse S. CHRISOSTOME, who in his comentarie vpon the Epistle to the *Galatians*; reades *Cephas, Iames*, and *John*; and *Theodoret*, who in his comentarie vpon the fifteenth chapter of the Epistle to the *Romans*, alleadging this passage, reports it in these words: *The Apostle teacheth this manifestly in the Epistle to the Galatians, for he saith; Peter Iames and John, Who seeme to be the pillars, gaue the right hands of felloWship to me and to Barnabas*: And saint AVGVSTINE who as well in the text as in the comentarie reades, *Cephas, James*, and *Iohn*, And saint HIEROME, who not only both in the text and the comentarie reades *Cephas, Iames* and *Iohn* but euen in his writings against *Heluidius*, citeth the text of saint PAVLE in these words: *Cephas Iames and Ishn.* And moreouer elswhere speaking of saint PAVLS Ordination to the Apostleship saith. *Paule Was ordained Apostle of the Gentils, by Peter, and James, and Iohn.* And therefore when it is found written in anie place; *Iames, Cephas*, and *Iohn*, as in the poeme of *Theodoret* vpon the Epistle to the *Ephesians*; and in that of the Epistle to the *HebreWes*; wee saie that this order is to haue reference to the prioritie of the knowledge that *James* receiued of the fruites of the grace of saint PAVLE: for as much as when *Paule* and *Barnabas* came the first tyme from *Antioch*, into *Hierusalem* they found but only saint IAMES, because saint PETER was in prison. And indeede not only throughout the scripture where saint PETER is named with the other Apostles, he is first named; or if he be last named, it is in increasing and rising by degrees: As when saint PAVLE saith; *The other Apostles and the bretheren of our Lord, and Cephas*. But also, when there is question of making the Generall catalogue of the Apostles, saint PETER is alwaies first placed, and *Judas* last, and all the rest without order, or at least without the title of second or third to shew that there was not only handled simplie primacie of order, but of dignitie; and he is not only set downe first, but he is sett first with the expression of the word first. *The first* (saith S. MATTHEW) *is Peter*; which *Beza* findes so to presse him, as he chargeth falshood vpon this place of the Ghospell. *I suspect* (saith *Beza*) *that this Word* (FIRST) *hath bene added by some one that would establish the primacie of Peter*; for that saint ANDREW was called before saint PETER, because saint ANDREW (as saint EPIPHANIVS saith) was the eldest. From whence it is, that *Bethsaida*, is called the cittie of *AndreW* and of *Peter*. This was in the first vocation described by saint IOHN, and before our Lord had said to saint PETER; *Thou shalt be called Peter*; in which word contained implicitly, the promise to make him VICAR of the true *Rock*, and to constitute him, ministeriall head of the Church; and not in the second vocation described by saint MATHEW, and made after the imposition of the name of *Peter*; in the which as S. EPIPHANIVS saith; *Peter preceded his brother.*

Hieron. ad Aug. ep. 89
Galat. 2.
Hieron. de script. Eccl. in Paulo
Act. 12.
1. Corint. 9
Matt. 10.
Beza in Matt. c. 10.
Epiph. hæres. 51.
Idem ibid
Matth. 16.
Epiph. vbi supra.

To the seauenth which is that saint PAVL writes, That the Ghospell of the circumcisiõ had bene committed to PETER, and the Ghospell of the vncircumcision to him: Wee answere, this clause is not a diuision of the authoritie of ministrie, but a more especiall testimony of the blessing of God vpon S. PETER to persuade the *JeWes*, and vpon saint PAVLE to perswade the *Gentills*: otherwise S. PAVLE, had bene

Galat. 2. vers. 7.

excluded

excluded from preaching the Ghospell to the *Iewes*; and neuerthelesse wheresoeuer he came, addressed himself first to the *Iewes*: and saint PETER from declaring the Ghospell to the *Gentiles*, yet neuerthelesse, it was by his ministrie, that God first opened the gate of the Church to the *Gentiles*; as appeares both by the historie of the conuersion of *Cornelius*, and by the protestation that he made to the Councell of *Hierusalem* in these wordes: *You know that God from the daies of old hath willed to call the Gentiles by my mouth.* To the eighth which is, that the same S. PAVLE saith: that saint PETER abstayning to eate with the *Gentiles* vpon the coming of the *Iewes*, walked not with right stepps in the Ghospell: Wee answere, that it was, as *Tertullian* saith; a vice not of doctrine, but of conuersation, and which consisted more in the occasion, then in the thing; since saint PAVLE himself, made himself, after ward a *Iewe* to the *Iewes*, and a *Gentile* to the *Gentiles*, that hee might gaine all; and circumcised *Timothie*, and purified himself in the temple. To the ninth which is, that he adds, that hee resisted S. PETER to his face, or in his presence, which is a phrase which we are accustomed to vse, to expresse a resistance to anie more eminent person because he was reprouable, or according to the Greeke and S. HIEROME, reproued: Wee answere, this resistance was not a reprehension of authoritie, but a reprehension of charitie, as those of *Iethro* to *Moyses*, or of S. BERNARD to Pope *Eugenius*, that is to saie, a reprehension that excluded not the superioritie of the reproued ouer the reprouer: Witnes these wordes of saint *Aug. you see what saint Cyprian saith, that the holie Apostle Peter, in whom there shined soe great a grace of the Primacie, being reproued by saint Paule, did not answere that hee had the Primacie, and would not be reproued by new men later then himself.* And againe, *The Apostle PETER hath left a more rare example of humilitie to posteritie, in teaching men not to disdaine reproofe from their inferiors, then Paule in teaching the meaner to resist the greater, sauing charitie for the defence of the truth.* And these of saint CHRISOSTOME, giuing the reason of the humilitie that S. PETER shewed in this action *And from hence it coms* (saith hee) *that Paule reproues, and Peter beares it; to the end, that while the Master reproued holdes his peace schollers may change their opinion.*

[Act.10.v.3. Act.15.v.7. — Galat.2.v.14. — Tertull. de prescript. c.23. — 1. Cor. 9. Act. 16. Act. 12. Gal.2. — Hieron. in epist. ad Galat.c.2. — Exod.18. — Bernard. de considerat l.4. — August. de baptism. cont. Donat.l.2. — Chrys. in ep.ad Galat.c.2.]

TO the tenth obiection which is, that S. CYPRIAN saith, *that the other Apostles were the same that Peter was, indued with like authoritie and power.* It is true but saint CYPRIAN speakes there of the internall and essentiall power of the Apostleship, and of the externall and accidentall power to the Apostleship, that is to saie, that they were equall as concerning power, but not concerning the order of the exercise of the power: for the vnderstanding whereof it must be knowne, that there are two things requisite to exercise the Apostleship lawfullie, the one to exercise it with authoritie: for those that exercise it without power, as the false Apostles were vsurpers, and sacrilegious persons, witnes this sentence of saint PAVL, *None attributes honor to himself, but he that is called like Aaron.* the other to exercise it in vnitie. For those that had exercised it out of vnitie had bene schismaticks, although they had true commission and authoritie to exercise it. *At Rome* (saith Optatus *Mileuitanus*:) *there hath bene placed a Chaire for Peter, that vnitie might bee preserued by all, least the other Apostles should attribut to euery one his owne.* And againe; he repeateth the knowledge that sainct PETER had of the diuinitie of the Sonn of God; the promise that hee had made him, to die with him; and how he had thrice denied him; And adds: *yet neuerthelesse, for the good of vnitie, he had not merited to be separated from the number of the Apostles.* And a little after: *They remained all innocent, and a Fisherman receiued*

[Cypr. de vnit. Eccl. — Hebr.5. — Opt. Mileuit. contr. Parm.l.2.]

the keyes, that the negotiation of vnitie might be formed, &c. without which thing, vnitie which is soe necessarie, could not bee. Now to preserue that vnitie, in which the internall and essetinall authoritie of the Apostleship ought to be exercised, it was necessarie first to haue a subiect, which should be as the center, the head, and roote, of this vnitie, and by relation and adherence whereto all the colledge of the Apostles, and all the Bodie of the Church might be manitained in vnitie. For the thinges which are plurall by themselues, and are not one with locall vnitie, cannot without loosing their vndiuided pluralitie, be reduced to a visible vnitie, vnlesse by relation to some thing, which by it self may be visiblie one. And secondlie, to maintaine this vnitie it is necessarie further, beside the internall authoritie, essentiall to the Apostleship, there should be an other externall authoritie, and accessory to the Apostleship, which might haue the superintendencie ouer the care of the preseruation of vnitie, to cause the Apostles te exercise their Apostleship in vnitie. And as the office of the cause is to rule his effect, he that should be the beginning and originall of this vnitie, should likewise haue the superintendencie ouer the rest, for what concernes the preseruation of vnitie; and by consequence, that to him should belonge, the supereminent iurisdiction ouer things necessarie to the maintenance of vnitie; that is to saie, ouer things necessarie to preuent schisme, and hinder the disorder and confusion of the exercise of the ministrie; as are the distinction, and distribution, either mediat or immediate of iurisdiction; the suspension & limitation of the exercise of the ministrie, and other such like. Not that the Apostles for their maintenance in vnitie, had neede that the effect of this Authoritie should be practised so euidently ouer them as ouer their sucessors, because of the assistance that they had euery one in particular of the Spirit of God; but to the end to propound to the Church a forme and a modell of the order that she should keepe after their decease: euen as although there were noe neede of a Councell in the time of the Apostles, to decide questions of Religion whereof euerie particular Apostle might be informed with all fullnes and certaintie; neuerthelesse the holie Ghost would that they should vse this forme in the matter of legall things, to leaue it for a patterne to the Church of the succeeding ages in like occurrences. It was then the internall authoritie, and essentiall to the Apostleship, which consisted in the power of reuealing matters of faith, with assurance of infallibilitie to make canonicall writings, to institute the first mission of pastors, remitt sinns, to giue the holy Ghost, and other the like, that saint CYPRIAN spake of when he said, that all the Apostles were indued with equall authoritie, and not of the externall authoritie and accidentall to the Apostleship, which was instituted to cause it to bee exercised in vnitie.

THIS appeares first because he touches before and after the originall of vnitie: *The Lord,* (saith he) *buildes the Church vpon him being one, and commaunds him to feede his sheepe. And although he conferr like power after his Resurrection vnto all his Apostles, and said to them. As my Father sent me, so send I you,* &c *yet to manifest vnitie, he constitutes the Chaire, one, and disposeth by his authoritie, that the originall thereof shall take beginning from one. That certainly that Peter was, the other Apostles were also, indued with a like share of authoritie and power; but the originall takes his beginning from one, that the Church & the Chaire may appeare to be one.* And a little after, according to the antient manuscripts, and the citations of *Iuon* and *Gratian, He that abandons the Chaire of Peter vpon which the Church is built, can he bee confident of being in the Church?* And elsewhere. *Peter vpon whom one God hath built the Church, and from whom*

Cypr. de vnit. Eccl.

Idem ibidem.

Id.ep.55.

he hath instituted the originall of vnitie. This appeares secondly because he calls the *Roman* Church, *the Chaire of Peter,* and the principall Church from whẽce Sacerdotall vnitie proceedes. This appeares thirdly because saint HIEROME after he had repeated the same sentence of S. CYPRIAN in these words: *Thou wilt tell me that the Church is built vpon Peter, though the like be done in an other place vpon others, and that the fortitude of the Church, doe leane equallie vpon all* Adds; *but amongst twelue, one is chosen, to the end, that a head being appointed, the occasion of Schisme might bee taken awaie.* To teach vs that in all other things, the Apostles, were equall to saint, PETER, except in those that had regard to the preuention of Schisme, and the preseruation of vnitie, for the consideration whereof he had bene constituted head of the Apostles. And finallie because *Optatus Mileuitanus* countryman to the one; to witt, saint CYPRIAN; and timefellowe to the other; to witt saint HIEROME, cries out. *Thou canst not denie, but that at Rome, the Episcopall Chaire hath bene placed by the Apostle Peter; &c. in which the vnitie was obserued by all; to the end, that all the Apostles should not attribute to themselues, to each one his Chaire, but that he should be a sinner and Schismaticke, who against the onelie Chaire, should erect an other.* And a little after: *from whence is it then, that you would vsurpe to yourselues, the keyes of the Kingdome, you that by your presumptions and audacious sacriledges, combat against the Chaire of Peter?*

Hieron ad- uers. Iouinian. l. 2.

To the eleuenth obiection, which is that *Eusebius,* ill translated by *Ruffinus* reportes from *Clemens Alexandrinus,* that *Peter, James,* and *Iohn,* establi hed *Iames,* brother to our Lord, Bishop of the Apostles: Wee answere, that it is from a faultie Grammar, a faultie diuinitie. For the greeke text saith, of *Hierusalem* and not of the Apostles. *Peter,* (saith he) *James, and John contested not for glorie* (or *opinion.* for greeke word signifies either) *but vnanimouslie constituted Iames brother of our Lord Bishop of Hierusalem;* that is to saie, *James,* and *John,* did noe more stand vpon it to dispute for honor with S. PETER as they had formely done, but vnited themselues with him, to consecrate *Iames,* Bishop of *Ierusalem*; whereto the words of CHRISOSTOME agree, about the iealousie that *James* and *John* formerly had of the Primacie of S. PETER; *Harken* (said hee) *how this same Iohn that latelie demaunded these thinges, afterward wholie yeelds the primacie to Peter.*

Opt. Mileuit contr. Parm l. 2.

TO the twelfth obiection, which is that S. CHRYSOSTOME vpõ the proposition made by S. PETER in the first of the *Acts,* to substitute an other Apostle in steede of *Iudas,* writes; *See the modestie of James, he had bene made* (the greeke saith, he hath bene made) *Bishop of Hierusalem, yet he saith not a word vpon this occasion. Consider also the singular modestie of the other disciples, how they yeelded the Throne to him, and debated noe more among themselues.* Wee answere, that this obiection is *Andabates* fence. For this concession of a Throne, hath reference not to S. IAMES, but to S. PETER, who whilst he spake, S. IAMES was soe modest, (as although he were so excellent, that he was after made Bishop of *Hierusalem*) he opened not his mouth, and the other Apostles as *James* and *Iohn,* Sõns of *Zebedeus,* which had formerly bene iealous of S. PETER, debated the Primacie with him noe longer, but yeelded him Presidencie. This appeares as well by the text of the history where there is noe tracke of respect giuẽ to S. IAMES but to S. PETER onlie, as by the time wherein S. IAMES was created Bishop of *Hierusalem.* For the first act that the Apostles did after the Ascension of our Lord, was the substitution of MATHIAS insteede of *Iudas,* in the historie whereof sainct CHRYSOSTOME saith these words. And *Clemens Alexandrinus* and *Eusebius* testifie, that the promotion of

Euseb. hist. Ecc. l. 2. c 1

saint *Iames* to the Bishopricke of *Hierusalem,* happened afterward. By meanes whereof the Apostles could not in that action; that is to saie, in the election of MATHIAS yeeld Presidēcie to saint IAMES because of the Bishoprick of *Hierusalem*. And the same is confirmed both by this that saint CHRISOSTOME had written vpon the twentith chapter of saint MATTHEW: *Marke (*said hee*) how this same Iohn that latelie made, such demaunds, after wholie yeeldes the Primacie to saint Peter*. And by this that he adds presently after the place obiected: *This mā* (saith hee, speaking of saint PETER) *first constitutes a doctor, and saith not, wee are enough to teach, far was he from vaine glory*. And a little after; *he takes the first authoritie of the affaire, as he that had all other put into his hands, for to him Christ had said:* And thou being once conuerted confirme thy bretheren. And by this that he protests in the beginning of his discourse: *Peter, (*saith hee*) both as full of zeale, & as hauing receaued from Christ the flocke into his keeping, and as the first of the Colledge, alwaies first beginns to speake.*

Chrysost. in Matt. hō 66.
Id. in Act. Apost. hom 3.
Id. ibid.

To the thirteenth obiection which is, that saint CHRISOSTOME writes vpon the fifteenth of the Acts, that the principalitie was committed to *Iames;* It is true, but he speakes there onlie of the *Principalitie* of the *Hierosolomitan* Church; if indeede the greeke word doe in that place intēd principalitie and not beginning, and that the sence be not, that IAMES had bene establisht from the beginning; that is to saie, that he was of the ancient Apostles, and not of the new, as saint PAVL; and neuerthelesse, that he tooke noe exceptiōs to S. PAVL, for speaking betweene S. PETER and him. For what soeuer that Greeke word signifies, it is certaine it can signifie nothing but the principalitie of the particular Church of *Hierusalem,* and not the principalitie of the vniuersall Church; which S. CHRISOSTOME himself testifies elswhere to haue bene grāted to saint PETER, in these words: *For if anie one aske me* (said hee) *how did Iames obtaine the Sea of Hierusalem? I will answere that Christ hath constituted Peter Master, not of that Sea but of all the world.* And againe, *Christ had foretold Peter great things, and had put the whole world into his hands, and had pronounced martirdome to him, and shewed him greater loue then to the rest.* And indeede S. CHRISOSTOME alleadgeth not this principalitie, to shew the modestie of saint *Iames* in this, that he was not offended that saint PETER had spoken before him, but to shew the modestie of saint IAMES in this, that he was not offended, that saint PAVL, spake betweene saint PETER; and him: A manifest proofe, that he treates not of the vniuersall principalitie, but of the principalitie of the particular Church of *Hierusalem,* of which he makes mention in this place because those that had moued the trouble for which the Coūcell was holden, were the Iewes and Pharisees of *Hierusalem* conuerted to Christianitie; who were iealous to see that the Gentiles were receaued into the Church, without obliging themselues to the obseruation of the lawe; And because saint IAMES had more especiall credit in their behalfe, because he was not only their Bishop, but Bishop of the Cittie, which but a while before was Metropolitan of the lawe, and consequently it seemed he should be touched with a more strict interest to the obseruation of the lawe, then anie other, and also that he had not gone about with sainct PETER and sainct PAVL to receiue the Gentiles into the Church, and by this meanes had not lost his creditt in the behalfe of the legalists: *It was (* saith sainct CHRYSOSTOME) *a profitable prouidence, that those thinges were done by those that were not to reside in Hierusalem, and that he that taught the Hierosolomitans was not refusable, and that his opinion might not be departed from.* For these causes then sainct IAMES had by accident a greater authoritie in the behalfe of the

Chrysost. in Ioan. 21. hom. 87.

authors

authors of this Scandall, then the other Apostles; to preserue the which he did (saith saint CHRISOSTOME) that which those ought to doe, that are constituted in great authoritie; that is to saie, he suffered saint PETER to speake more seuerelie, and himself spake more gentlie. But that compared simplie with saint PETER, hee was either equall or superior in iurisdiction, saint CHRISOSTOME is so farr, from
Chryso. in Ioan. hom. 87. hauing euer thought it, that contrariwise he cries out a lowde; *Peter was the Prince of the Apostles, and the mouth of the disciples, and the head of the Colledge, and for this occasion Paule went vp to visitt him, letting the rest alone.*
Id. ibid. And a little after; *Christ put into his hands, the Prouostship of his bretheren, and vpbraids him not with his deniall of him, nor reprocheth him with what was past; but saith to him, if thou louest me, be president of thy bretheren, and the same loue that thou hast in all things shewed to me, and whereof thou hast boasted shew it now; and that life that thou hast said, thou wouldst laie downe for me, laie it downe for my sheepe.* And in the homilie thirtith three vpon saint MATHEW; *The first and the Corypheos of the Apostles, was a man ignorant and without learning.* And in the homily fiftie fift, *Not onely the Apostles were Scandalized, but also the Corypheos,* (that is to saie, *Soueraigne*) *of them all, Peter.*
Chryso. de sacerd. l. 2. And in the second booke of the Priesthood; *Christ committed the care of his sheepe to Peter, and Peters Successors.* And in this doe all the rest of the Fathers agree aswell Greeke, as latine. *Thou seest* (saith saint GREGORIE
Greg. Nazianz. orat. 26. *Nazianzene) amongst the disciples of Christ, all sublime and worthie of election that one of them is called the Rock and that the foundations of the Church are committed to him; and the other is more beloued, and leanes vpon the bosom of Iesus, and the rest suffer the difference.* And saint AMBROSE, *The Lord* (said hee) *by*
Ambros. in Luc. l. 10. c. 24 *these words, louest thou me more then these, asked the question not to learne but to teach, being readie to be himself exalted into Heauen, which was he whom he would leaue to vs for the Vicar of his loue.* And a little after; *And because that of them all he onlie protests, he is preferrd before them all.* And elsewhere.

With a full floud of teares the Churches Rocke;
Did cleanse his Crime, at crowinge of the Cocke.

Hoc ipsa petra Ecclesiæ canente culpam diluit. Optat Mileuit. cōtra Parm. l. 2. Cyrill. Alexandr. in Ioan. l. 12. c. 64.
And S. EPIPHANIUS; *Christ hath appointed Peter to be the guide, and leader of his Disciples.* And *Optatus Mileuit. In the Roman Chaire there is sett Peter, the head of all the Apostles.* And againe; *Against the gates of hell, we reade that Peter our Prince, hath receaued the wholesome keyes.* And S. CYRILL of *Alexandria: Peter as the Prince and head of the rest, first cryed out, thou art Christ the sonne of the liuing God.* Euen vntill then, it was a thing so well knowne vnto antiquitie, that sainct PETER was the visible head of the Church, and of Christian religion, as the verie Pagans, and *Porphirius* amongst the rest, as sainct HIEROME reportes it, reproched it to Christians, *that S. Paul had*
Hiero. August. ep. 89. *bene so rashe, as to reproue Peter the Prince of the Apostles, and his master,* And they fained, (as saith sainct AUGUSTINE) that the Oracles of their false Gods, hauing bene inquired of, concerning Christian Religion, answered this blasphemie: *that Christ was innocent of the imposture of the Christiās*
August de Ciuit. Dei c. 53. *but that Peter who was a Magitian, for the loue he bore to his Master, had inuented Christian Religion.* And this may be said of the comparison betweene PETER and the other Apostles, for I will not now treate of the other frequent markes of the preheminēce and authoritie of S. PETER, which are in the Euangelicall and Apostolicke historie: As that our Lord
Matt. 17. commaunded him *to paie the tribute for himself, and for him*: that he vn-
Act. 1. dertooke the care of the replacing of an other Apostle in *Iudas* his
Act. 2. steede, all the Colledge of the Apostles suffring themselues to bend
Act. 5. and to be lead by his words: that he is nominated as for preheminence, and ranked a part, *Peter and the Eleuen*: that they bore the

sicke

ſicke into the Apoſtles waie, *that Peters ſhadowe might paſſe ouer them*: that that he alone, iudged *Ananias* and *Saphira* to death: that to him alone is reuealed the introduction of the nations into the Church, and other the like: for as much as it is not my purpoſe, to examine the other places of ſcripture; but onely thoſe that his maieſtie hath alleadged; and to examine thoſe, not by ſcripture, but by the Fathers, whoſe obiection me thinkes, I haue ſufficiẽtly ſatisfied. And as for *Origẽs* interpretatiõ which extends this text to all Chriſtians in generall, and ſaith, that whoſoeuer confeſſeth that Chriſt is the Sonn of God, is made a foundation of the Church, it is an interpretation morallized from this paſſage, to bring it into ſence, although ſtrained and wreſted, whoſe fruite may be applied to all the hearers, and not a ſerious and litterall interpretation as the ſame *Origen* that makes vſe of it teſtifies, when he expounds it expreſſly and literallie of the perſõ of *Peter*. There remaines the third point, which is, that the Church is built vpon Chriſt: now in this point we are all of accord with his Maieſtie: but yet wee graunt not that S. PETER leaues to be the viſible and miniſteriall Foundation of the Church; for the Philoſophers teach vs, that thinges ſubordinate combat not one an other, but imbrace & preſuppoſe one & other; & therefore to ſaie that Chriſt is the foundation of the Church, and to ſaie, that S. PETER is the foundation of the Church, are not repugnant propoſitions, but vnanimous and compatible. For wee doe not pretend, that they are foundations of the Church after one and the ſame ſort; but we hold, that Chriſt is the foundation of the Church by himſelf, and by his owne authoritie, and S. PETER only by commiſſion, no more then to ſaie with *Moyſes*, that God only was the guide of the people of *Iſraell* in their paſſage from *Egipt* to the land of *Chanaan*; and to ſaie with S. STEVEN, that *Moyſes* guided the people in the Wilderneſſe. *This was he* (ſaid he) *that was with the Church in the deſert*: Are not things incompatible, for god was the guide of the people of *Iſrael* by his proper vertue; and *Moyſes* by commiſſion and lieuetenancie from God. Likewiſe to ſaie that the Vice-Roy of *Ireland*, is the foundation of the gouernment and policie of *Ireland*, And to ſaie that the excellent Kinge of Great *Brittaine*, is the foundation of the ſtate and policie of the ſame *Ireland*, are not things incompatible, for the excellent King of Great *Brittaine*, is ſo by his proper authoritie; and the Vice-Roy is ſoe by commiſſion, lieuetenancie, and repreſentation. Although notwithſtanding that the literall intention of this paſſage, *Vpon this Rock I will build my Church*, is no way to deſigne by the word, *Rock* the perſon of Chriſt, but that only of *Peter*, as it appeares by ſix euident reaſons.

Act. 10. — Origen in Matt. c 16 Tract. 1. — Exod 15. Act. 7. — Matt. 16.

THE firſt, that our lord hauing foretold to S. PETER, that he would change his name, not by the attribution of a ſimple Epithete, as he did to the Sonns of *Zebedee*, whom he called the *Sonns of thunder*: but by the impoſition of a name ordinarie and permanent, in ſaying to him, *Thou ſhalt be called Cephas*, puts him noe where in poſſeſſion of this promiſe, nor explaines to him noe where, the cauſe of the impoſition of this name, but in this paſſage; *Thou art Peter, & vpõ this Rock I will build my Church*, Now this paſſage cãnot explaine the ſence of the word *Peter*, if in the secõd part of the paſſage, the word, *Rock*, be not taken in the ſame ſence, and for the ſame ſubiect for which it is taken in the firſt: and by conſequence this clauſe, *vpon this Rock I will build my Church*, cannot there be interpreted of the perſon of Chriſt, but on the only perſon of S. PETER.

Marc. 3. — Ioan. 1.

The ſecond that our Lord meanes in this place, to render an exchange for the words that S. PETER ſpake of him, as may appeare by this preface,

And I tell thee, which for this cause *Beza* hath translated into these words, *And I tell thee reciprocallie.* Now S. PETER in his propositiõ had done two things; the one to declare the appellatiue name of our Lord, which is Christ, & the other to explaine the sence and energy of the same name of CHRIST, in saying, *Thou art Christ the Sonne of the liuing God.* And therefore the lawe of the Antithesis & correspõdencie wills, that not only our lord should declare the name that he had promised to giue him, in saying to him; *Thou art Peter*; but also should explaine the sence & energy of this name in saying to him; *and vpon this Rock I will build my Church.* Which could not be vnlesse by the word *Rock* in this second clause there were literally vnderstood the person of S. PETER, and not that of CHRIST.

THE third, that it had bene a thing extremely from the purpose, to haue made mention of the name of *Peter* for the language that our Lord meant to speake to S. PETER, if by this clause, *and vpon this Rock*, he had not intended to speake of the person of *Peter*. For the word *Rock* hath no metaphoricall relation to the keyes, but to the building.

The fourth, that it had bene an inconstant grammaticall consequence, and euil knitt, to saie, *And I declare to thee, that thou art Peter, and vpon this Rocke which is my self, I will build my Church: and I will giue to thee the keyes of the Kingdome of heauen.* The fifth, that the connexion of the pronowne *(this)* with the repetition of the word (*Petra*) before exprest, sheweth that it is a relatiue pronowne, and whose relation is determined to the antecedent alreadie exprest; by meanes whereof this pronowne could not be diuerted from the naturall vse of the relatiue, that the repetition of the antecedent giues it to an vse of a demõstratiue pronowne, but by the application of an externall gesture of demonstration, either exprest in the text of the historie, or by the verie explication of the historian. As when our Lord after he had spoken of the *Iewish* Temple, said *Destroie, this temple, and within three daies I will build it vp againe*; The Euangelists to hinder the pronowne from being taken for a pronowne relatiue, as the repetition of the word *Temple* alreadie before expressed would haue informed the auditors, adds: *this he spake of the Temple of his Bodie*; a thing which is not in this passage.

AND the sixth and principall, that it is most certaine, that our Lord in these words: *thou art Peter, and vpon this Peter or Rocke* intended to allude to the name of S. PETER. Now all allusions which are made to names, are either allusions of confirmation, or allusions of correction. I call allusiõs of confirmation, those which are made to confirme or approue the imposition of the name which had bene first giuen; As when *Vopiscus* called the Emperor *Probus, trulie Probus*; that is to saie, *trulie an honest man*; and *Carus; truly Charus*; that is to saie, *trulie deare.* And saint ATHANASIVS, called *Osius, truly Osius*; that is to saie *trulie holy.* And the Councell of *Constantinople* holden vnder *Menas*, called *Agapet, truly Agapet*; that is to saie, *trulie beloued.* I call allusions of correction, those which are made to correct and reprehend the imposition of the name first giuen, to shewe that the effect of the name agrees not with him that beares it. And these allusiõs of correction againe are of two sortes; the one are made by simple negation or antithesis, as when Noemi said, *Call me no more* Noemi that is to saie, *Agreable*, but call mee, *mara*, that is to saie, *bitter.* And the other are made by translation; as when the name that hath bene first imposed vpon anie one, is transferred to an other: As when saint *Augustine*, speaking of *Absalon*, whose name signified, *the peace of the* Father saith; *That the true Absalon is Jesus Christ*; it is an allusion of translation, and consequentlie of correctiõ by which he transferrs the name of *Absalon* to *Jesus Christ*, and shewes

Epist. in Prob. imp. Id. in Car. imp. Athan. ad imperat. Constant. apolog. Conc. Cõst sub Men. Act. 1.

that

that it had not iustlie bene imposed vpon *Absalon*, From whence it ariseth that if our Lord in saying; *Vpon this Rock I will build my Church*, intended by the word *Rock*, the person of saint PETER: he ment to make an allusion of approbation, but if hee intended his owne, he ment to make an allusion of translation, and consequently of correction. Now besides, that it must be impertinent, that our Lord should make an allusion of correction vpon a name imposed by himselfe, it is manifest that in honorable names, allusions of approbation and confirmation are in steede of complements and gratifications, and allusions of correction are in steede of reprehensions and chasticemēts. Then to know whether our Lord did there meane to make an allusion of approbation, and by the word *Rock* intend the person of S. PETER, or to make an allusion of correction and translation, and by the word *Rock* intend his owne, there needes but to see, whether he meant by these words to cherish, gratifie, and recompence S. PETER, or to shake him vp and chastice him. For if by the word *Rock* he vnderstood the person of S. PETER, he ment to cherish, and recōpence him, but if thereby he vnderstood his owne, he meant to be rough with him, and to correct him. Now both the foregoeing confession of S. PETER; *Thou art Christ the Sonn of the liuing God*; and the preface of our Lords words; *Blessed art thou Symon the Sonne of Iona*, and this marke of recompence, and reciprocall vicissitude of title and elogie, translated by *Beza* himself into these wordes, *I saie reciprocallie to thee*, cannot without sacrilege suffer a doubt, but that he intēded not in that place to be harsh with him, and to chastice him, but to gratifie and recompence him, *The blessed confession*, (saith S. HILLARIE) *hath receaued the reward*, nor consequētlie but that our lord intēded to make an allusiō of cōfirmation *not of correction*, that is to saie, that he designed by the word *Rock* not his owne persō, but the persō of S. PETER. And against this ought not to be obiected that S. PAVL writes, *The Rock was Christ*. For metaphoricall names, are not takē alwaies in the sams sēce, nor for the same thinges, but varie their significatiōs according to the seuerall relations, whereunto they are imployed: which hath caused S. THOMAS to saie, that in metaphors there is not so much regard to be had from whence they are takē, as to what they are taken: and therefore although the word *Rock* sometimes signifies Christ in the scripture, it would neuerthelesse be a blinde impertinencie, to will that wheresoeuer the scriptures vseth it, it should be intēded of Christ. For sometimes the word *Rock* is imploied according to the relatiō that the *Rock* of a quarry hath to the morcels of stone that are drawne out of it. And in this sence, *Abraham* is called *Rock*: Looke (saith *Esaie vpon the Rock from whence you haue bene cutt; vpō Abraham your Father*; sometimes it is imployed according to the relation of the drynesse & barennes that rockes haue to the seede that is cast vpon them; and in this sence hard and indocile partes are intended by the word *Rock*: *Part of the seed* (said our Lord) *fell vpon the Rock*. Sometimes it is imployed according to the relatiō of the stedfastnes and soliditie that *Rocks* haue in the buildings which are founded vpon them; And in this fence our lord saith to S. PETER, *Vpō this Rock I will build my Church*, alluding to the custome of ātiquitie, who vsed when they were to build temples, to choose to build them vpō *Rocks* for their firmnes, rather then vpon other places. From whence it is, that the place wherevpon the Temple of *Delphus* was built, was called the *Delphian Rocks*: and that the men of a certaine Cittie of *Asia* to be preferred in the building of a Temple to the Emperor *Tiberius*, represented to him, that their cittie was situate vpon a Rocke: And therefore our lord intending to build his Church vpon S. PETER;

Bez. in Matt. 16.

Hilar. in Matt. c. 16

Esa. 51.

Luc. 8.

Matt. 16.

ſaid to him according to the *Hebrew*, and the *Syriacke; Thou art a Rock, and vpon this Rock I will build my Church.* Sometymes it is imployed, according to the relation that *Rocks* haue to the ſources and fountaines that ſpring from them; and in this ſence the Apoſtle ſaith, *They dranke of the ſpirituall Rock which followed them, and that Rock was Chriſt*. By meanes whereof, to inferr from this, that in theſe words, *the Rock was Chriſt*, when it is ſpoken of the *Rock* referr'd to the water that ſprang from it; Chriſt was intended by the word *Rock*; that heere, where it is ſpoken of the word *Rock* referrd to the metaphor of the miniſteriall building of the Church, it ſhould be neceſſarie to vnderſtand it of the perſon Chriſt, and not of of that of ſaint PETER, were an inconſequent conſequence. And it is not to be ſaid, that in the parable of the man that built his howſe vpon the rocke, by the word *Rock*; Chriſt is vnderſtood, for the litterall ſence of the word *Rock* in this place is noe other then to ſignifie a good and firme foundation; and that this is expounded of Chriſt, it is by allegorie. Now there is great difference betweene the litterall ſence of places mingled with metaphoricall termes, and the allegoricall ſence. For from the litterall ſence of places, mingled with metaphoricall termes arguments may be made, and conſequences may be drawne from one paſſage to an other; and from the allegoricall ſence, not. And then if ſaint PAVL had ſaid euen according to the relation, to the miniſteriall building of the Church, *the Rock was Chriſt*, hath not our Lord vſually communicated his names to his miniſters? And did not *Iacob* annoint the ſtone in *Bethell* in the figure of Chriſt, as prefiguring that Chriſt ought to be the ſtone whereof God prophecied by the mouth of *Eſay: Behold, I will ſet vp in Sion a Rock well founded:* And neuertheleſſe doth not the ſame *Iacob* ſaie, that *Joſeph* was the Paſtor and the *Rocke* of *Iſrael*, making vſe of the word *Euen* in both of them? That is to ſaie, doth he not communicate by word, the ſame word *Rock* of *Iſraell* to *Ioſeph*, that he had communicated by figure to Chriſt? And if they ſtagger about the difference which is betweene the word *(Euen)* & the word *(Tsur)* or *Petra*, which ſignifies *Rock*, although *Beza* doe not diſtinguiſh it, when he tranſlates; *Thou ſhalt be called Cephas*. which is interpreted, *lapis*. Doth not *Tertullian* write according to the vſe euen of the word, *Tsur*, or *Petra*, *He hath giuen to the deareſt of his diſciples to Peter, the name of one of his figures:* And doth not S. HIEROME write vpon the ſame place of S. MATTHEW, *As our Lord who is the light, hath giuen to his Apoſtles, that they ſhould be the light; ſo to Peter beleeuing in the Rock-Chriſt, he hath giuen to be the Rocke. And therefore according to the metaphor of Rock, it is ſaid to him with good right. I will build my Church vpon thee.* And elsewhere, *Not only Chriſt was the Rock, but hee hath giuen to Peter, that hee ſhould alſo be the Rock.* And ſaint BASILL: *Although Peter be alſo the Rock, neuertheleſſe hee is not the Rock as Chriſt, but hee is the Rock as Peter; forasmuch as Chriſt is eſſentiallie the vnmoueable Rock; and Peter is ſo by the Rock; for our Lord giues his dignities without diſpoyling himſelfe of them, &c. He is the Rock, he makes the Rock.* And ſaint EPIPHANIVS; *He hath made the firſt of his Apoſtles the firme Rock, wherevpon the Church is built.* And againe; *It is hee that hath heard from him, Peter, feede my lambes: and to whom the keeping of the Flock hath bene committed,* And PROSPER: *This moſt ſtrong Rock, hath receaued from the principall Rock communication both of vertue and name.* For whereas ſaint AVGVSTINE after hee had interpreted in manie places the *Rock* of the perſon of PETER, as in theſe words of the comentarie vpon the ſixtie ninth Pſalme. *Peter who is in this confeſſion, had bene called the Rock vpon which the Church ſhould be built.* And in theſe words of the *Pſalmes*

Tertul. aduerſ. Marcion. l. 4. c 13. Hieron. in Matt. c. 16. Baſil. hom. de pœnit.

Epiph. l. Anacorat.

Proſp. de vocat gent. l. 2. c. 28.

against *Donatus* his partie, *Reckon the Prelates from the sea of Peter, And in this order of the Fathers, see who haue succeeded one an other, this is the Rock, that the prowde gates of Hell cannot ouerthrow*. And in these words of the comentarie vpon sainct IOHN, *Peter this Rock answered in the name of all*; and in those words of the Epistle eightie six. *Peter the head of the Apostles, the Porter of heauen, the foundation of the Church*: remitts it finallie in his retractations to the readers choyse, whether of these two interpretations hee thinkes to be most probable, to witt, either to interpret it of the person of PETER, or to interpret it of the person of CHRIST, moued with this, that the Latine text hath: *Tu es Petrus*, and not, *Tu es Petra*. This is a grammaticall error partlie proceeding from the defect of knowledge in the *Hebrew* and the *Syriack* tongues, in which there is noe difference betweene *Petrus* and *Petra*: But the text hath it throughout. *Thou art Cephas and vpon this Cephas*, that is to saie in Latine, *Tu es Petra, & supra hanc Petram*, and in French, *Tu es rocher, & sur ce rocher, Thou art a rock, and vpon this rock*: & partlie for want of experience in the practise of the greeke tongue, in which the words πέτρως and πέτρα, signifie one selfe-same thing; from whence it is, that manie Greekes haue called the Sunne πέτρος, that is to saie, *stone*, by allusion to the doctrine of *Anaxagoras*, who held that the Sunn was a stone. By meanes whereof the Greeke interpreter of S. MATTHEW hath pretended to put noe difference in sence, but only in kinde, betweene these words πέτρος and πέτρα and meant to saie no other thing but what wee vnderstand in *French* by these words; *Tu es roc, & sur ce rocher, ie bastiray mon Eglise*. And therefore alsoe saint BASILL produces the first part of the clause in these words: *Thou art the Rock*, σὺ πέτρα εἶ hauing regard to the wordes of our Sauiour, in which the cōdition of the *Hebrew* and *Syriake* tongues permitt not to make the distinction of gender, as S. HIEROME notes in these words: *Not (saith hee) that* Petrus, *and* Petra *signifie differing things, but because that which in latine we call* Petra, *the hebrewes and Syrians, because of the affinitie of their tongues, call it Cephas*, And this *Beza*; though an enemie to the true sence of this passage, is constrained to confesse in these words: *The Lord speaking in Syriack, hath not vsed diuersitie of name, but in both places hath said Cephas*; as in our vulgar French the word, *Pierre*, is said as well of the proper, as of the appellatiue And for this same cause, he translates the place of the first Chapter of saint Iohn into these termes: *Thou shalt bee called Cephas, which is interpreted* Petra, *that is to saie, Rock, or Stone*. And not soe much as the doctors of the Iewes but doe acknowledge, that our Lord in calling *Peter*, *Cephas*, did intend to call him *Rock*, and to constitute him for the foundation of the Church: as appeares by these words of *Rabbi Helias* in his *Tisbi*, vpon the exposition of the word *Cephas*: *Iesus, the Nazarean (saith hee) called Simon sonn of Bariona, Cephas, which signifies fortitude: for the interpretation of the* Hebrew *word sela, is* Cepha, *which signifies in manie places, fortitude, meaning that he was the head and fortitude of his religion, and therefore he called him* Cephas. And to this there doe agree all the famous editions of scriptures, in what tongue soeuer, as well printed, as manuscripts. For not only the Hebrew editiō of the Ghospell of saint MATTHEW published by *Munster*, saith, *Thou art* Cepha, *and vpon this* Cepha; *Thou art a Rock, and vpon this Rock*. And the *Syriack* publisht by *Moses* of *Merdin* in *Mesopotamia*, and republisht by *Tremellius*: *Thou art Kipho, and vpon this Kipho, thou art a Rock, and vpon this Rock*. But also the *Arabicke* hath it, *Thou art Ascara, and vpon this Ascara: thou art the stone, and vpon this stone*. And the *Persian*. *Thou art zeng, and vpon this zeng: thou art the Rock, and vpon this Rock*. And the *Armenian*, thou art *Vimi, and vpon this Vimi: thou art the stone, and vpon this*

Aug. In Ioa. tract. 11.

Arsen. in Eurip.

Basil. vbi supra.

Hieron. in epist. ad Galat c. 2.

Beza in Matth. c. 16.

Tu vocaberis Cephas quod declaratur Petra Bez. ibid.

stone. And the *Ruthenian*, *Egiptian*, and *Ethiopian*, euen the same. Neuerthelesse, though the want of the *Hebrew* and *Syriack* tongues, suffered S. AVGVSTINE to fall into this mistake, to thinke that the primitiue word *Rocke*, was not there attributed to sainct PETER, but only the deriuatiue, and that *Petrus* signifieth not *Rock*, but *Rockey* or *Stonie*, he hath alwaies acknowledged, be it by vertue of the other places of the scripture, or be it by vertue of the perpetuall traditiō of the Church the same thing that wee conclude out of this passage, to witt, the Primacie of saint PETER. For interpretating a while after these wordes; *And I will giue thee the keyes of the Kingdome of heauen*: of the donation of the keyes made to the Church in the person of PETER, he saith the Church did then receaue in the person of PETER the keyes, because PETER figured the Church. And yeelding elsewhere a reason, why the person of PETER figured the Church; he declares that it is because of his Primacie. *Hee beares* (saith hee) *by a figuratiue generalitie, the person of the Church, because of the primacie he had amongst the rest of the disciples.* By which word, *Primacie*, he intends according to the stile of the scripture, the superintendencie and principalitie, as it appeares by these words of Wisedome. *I haue had Primacie in all nations*, And by these wordes of the same saint AVGVSTINE *Peter denominated from the Rock happie, bearing the figure of the Church, holding the principallitie of the Apostleshipp*. And againe. *Who knowes not, that this Principallitie of the Apostleship, ought to be preferred before whatsoeuer other Bishoprick.* And elsewhere; *in the Roman Church hath alwaies flourisht, the Principalitie of the Sea Apostolicke.*

Eccl. c.2.

Epist-162.

Of the indiuisibilitie of the Church.

CHAP. IV.

The continuance of the Kinges answere;

BVT it hath begun to diminish in luster, as being deuided into manie partes, as for externall Communion, wholie seperate one from an other.

THE REPLIE:

Two *Opuntine* Bretheren deuided the inheritance of their Father with such rigor, as they deuided euen to a cupp and to a Coate. It is in a sorte, thus with the heretickes, they doe indeede deuide the Chalice that our Father hath left vs by Testament, and whereof *Dauid* singeth. *The Lord is the portion of my inheritance and of my Chalice*; that is to saie, they doe indeede diuide the Sacraments of Christ; but the coate of Christ, which is his Church, they cannot diuide, for it is alone and indiuisible. *When the raigne of Israell,* saith S. CYPRIAN, *should be diuided, the Prophet Achias diuided his Rayment: But because the poeple of Christ cannot bee diuided, his coate wouen of a peece, and keeping it selse whole, was not diuided by those that possessed it. The coate of Christ indiuisibly vnited preseruing itself whole, shewed the indissoluble Concord of our poeple, of vs, who haue put on Christ. By the Sacrament & signe of his coate he hath declared the vnitie if his Church, Who then is he so impious, so faithlesse, and so disturbed with the fury of discord, that beleeues that the vnitie of God. the Coate of our Lord, the Church of Christ, can be deuided, or dare to deuide it?* Not but that the multitude of the

Psalm. 15

Cypr. de vnit. Eccl.

persons

persons whereof the Church is compounded, and which analogicallie is in steede of matter to it, may be deuided; but this diuision is but a materiall diuision of the Church, and not a formall diuision; no more then the diuision that the false mother would haue made of the Child, had bene a formall diuision; for as much as the being, and the forme of the whole had not remained in either of the partes, but a materiall diuision.

For the Church as well as naturall organicall bodies, may be materiallie diuided, but formallie it cannot be diuided; that is to saie, the members and parts may indeede be seperated from their whole, but after the seperation, they are noe more members and parts of the Church, but equiuocallie, and by abuse of language, euen as the members and partes of a Bodie indued with a life animall and sensitiue, when they come to be seperated from their whole, are noe more members and partes but equiuocally; forh as much as they participate noe more of the forme of the bodie, wich cannot be possessed but in vnitie, nor reside but in one only masse vnited and continued. By meanes whereof the Church after the diuision of the externall communion, resides only in one of the partes; to witt in that from which the others haue diuided themselues, and not in the others; for the Church is either one or none. *My Doue* (saith the Spouse) *is an onelie one*. And *Dauid*: *Hierusalem that is builded as a Cittie, whose participation is in vnitie*. And saint PAVL: *One bodie and one Spirit as you are called in one hope of your vocation*. & *Optatus Mileuitanus*; *There is one Church which can not be at once amongst you and amongst vs*. It resteth then, that it be in one place. And saint CHRISOSTOME; *The name of the Church, is not a name of diuision, but a name of vnion and agreement*. And saint AVGVSTINE; *He is one, the Church is vnitie; nothing answeres to one but vnitie*. And elsewhere; *Let euerie other inheritance be deuided amongst coheires; the inheritance of peace cannot be diuided*. And therefore when the Fathers saie, that hereticks, and Schismaticks deuide the Church; they intend, either that they deuide it as much as lyes in them, that is to saie, that they indeuor to diuide it, or that they deuide it materiallie and not formallie, that is to saie, that they make thereof manie Societies, but not manie Churches.

Cant. 6. Psalm 121. Ephes. 4. Optat Mileuit. cōtr. Parmen. l. 2. Chrys. in c. ad Corinth c. 1. hom. 1. Aug in ps. 101. Idem.

Of the effect that diuision brings to the Church.

CHAPT. V.

The continuance of the Kings answere.

AND also which is principallie to be lamented, it is happened by this dissipation, that there is lesse force in the seperate parts then there was in the whole to resist the enemie of mankinde, who as Christ teacheth vs, is awake and attentiue vpon euerie occasion, to mingle the good seede with darnell and tares.

THE REPLIE.

AFTER the deuision of the externall communion, all the soule, the forme and essence of the Church rests in one onlie of the societies, which remaine after the diuision, and not in the others which are no more trulie partes of the Church, but only equiuocallie, euen as when a member is separated from a liuing and sensible Bodie, all

the

the essence, the Soule, and forme of the creature, remaines in the Bodie, from whence that separation hath bene made, and not in the part that hath bene separated from it, which is noe more a part of the Bodie but equiuocallie and inproperlie. And therefore after the separation of hereticks, all the same strength, vigor, and vertue, which was in the Bodie of the Church before the separation, remaines in the part from whence the separation is made, as she that inherits the condition of all, and not in the others; in such sort, as she hath noe lesse force to resist the corruption that the enemie of mankinde would bring in, but contrariwise oftentimes more, for as much as the constancie of the Charitie of those which remaine in the Church, is made the more vnited and the more eminent by the separation of the rest according to this sentence of saint PAVLE; *There must be heresies that the Good may be manifested*. And therefore saint AVGVSTINE writes, *That the Church makes vse of hereticks for the approbation of her doctrine; and of schismaticks, for the demonstration of her stedfastnes*. And elsewhere; *That those that goe forth from the Bodie of the Church are as euill humors, by whose purgation the Bodie is eased*. By meanes whereof his Maiestie ought not to pretend that the alienations of the partes which are seperate from the Bodie of the Church, haue left in her from whom they are seperated, the lesse vigor to resist the enemie of mankinde, and to maintaine her self vncorrupted, then there was in the whole Bodie before; but contrariwise to presuppose that the same vertue which resided in the whole Bodie, is reunited in the part that succeedes it.

As when one of our eyes hath lost his former light
His splendors faire effect, shines in the other sight
And th'extinguisht beame, adds to the cleere eyes store
Who sees alone as much, as both could see before.

Also it cannot be found, that since the separation of the *Roman* Church and the Greeke faction quoted by his Maiestie, which is the greatest seperation that euer was made, the *Roman* Church receaued anie doctrine which was not holden by all the Bodie of the Catholike Church when this diuision happened; and noe more till then, since the separation of the *Egiptians* and *Ethiopian* Prouinces.

Of the pretended corruption of the Church.

CHAPT. VI,

The continuance of the Kings answere.

AND what wee now see with our eyes to be happened, yea and handle it with our handes; it is a ridiculous thing, and more then absurd to dispute, if heretofore it could be, or now can be done.

THE REPLIE,

THere was neuer anie age wherein those that seperated themselues from the Church, haue not beleeued that they saw cleerly and euidently that she was corrupted and full of palpable and Cymerian darknes, otherwise they had not seperated themselues from her. The figure of this preiudication, preceded in the rashnes of *Oza*, who beleeued that the Arke was about to fall, and vpon that beleefe, put out his hand to lifte it vp, for which he was punisht with death: And followed in the incredulitie of the Apostles, who while our Lord slept, thought that the Barke wherein they were with him, was about to perishe; in indignation whereof he chidd them for their little faith, and taught them, that he that keepes *Israell*, doth neither slumber nor sleepe: and the historie since hath cōtinued in all the pretended Reformers of the Church. For as *Pentheus*, in seeing his children, thought hee had seene Beares, Tigers, Serpents, and other wild beastes, and did not perceiue that the euill was not in them, but in his sight: Soe the heretickes in all ages, in seeing their mother; that is to saie, the Church, thought they had seene a troope of Dragons, Lyons, and wild-beasts; and vpon that occasion haue put themselues to flight, not discerning that the euill was not in the Church, but in their eyes. And that it is soe; did not the *Luciferians* saie, *That the Catholicke Church had bene conuerted into a brothell, and was become the whore of Antichrist?* And did not the *Donatists, call the Apostolicke chaire, the chaire of Pestilence?* And did they not crie out, *that the Catholicke Church was become the shield of Romulus?* And saith not saint AVGVSTINE of them, *I iustly persecute him that detracts from his neighbour, wherefore shall I not more iustlie persecute him that publickly blasphemes the Church &c. when he saith she is a whore?* And the *Pelagians* when there was alleadged to them, the number and the multitude of the Catholicks, did they not answere, *that to finde anie thing, a multitude of blinde men auailed nothing?* And neuerthelesse, who knowes not at this daie, that they were the blinde men, and not the Church; And then this pretended corruptiō of the Church being the theame of the question debated by vs, to cause that to passe, as a thing graunted, it is to put for a principle, that which his maiestie ought, if it please him to reserue to be iudged at the end, & not presuppose at the beginning of the disputation. For to saie that there is no thing but is altered and corrupted by age, this argument is good for those thinges that are preserued by ordinarie and naturall faculties, but not for those that are assisted by extraordinary and supernaturall helpe; and to whom these words of *Dauid* may be applied, *Thy youth shall be renewed as the youth of an Eagle.* Now the Church, is of this number, for our Lord saith of her without exception of time, *Thou art wholly faire, and there is noe spott in thee*, and shee sings and will sing to the end of the world. *I am black, but I am faire*; that is to saie, I am black in manners, but faire in doctrine. And therefore S. AVGVSTINE compares her to *Sara*, who when she was old, left not to be faire. And for this same cause, sainct HIEROME citing these wordes of *Salomon, that the eye that mockes his Father, or despiseth the age of his mother, the Crowes of the valley shall pull it out*, interprets them of hereticks who despise the age of the Church: *Assoone* (saith hee) *as the eye of the hereticks mocks the creator his father, or despiseth the age of the Church his mother, the cursed and vncleane birds shall peck it out.*

Hieron. aduers. Luciferian. Aug. contr. liter. Petil. l. 2. c. 51. Idem cont. Crescon. c. 13

Psalm. 102

Cantic. 1. Ibidem. Aug. contr. Faust. Manich. l. 22. c 28.

Prou. 30. Hieron. in Prou. c. 30.

Of the exclusion of hereticks from the Bodie of the Catholick Church.

CHAPT. VII,

The continuance of the Kings answere.

HE *Roman* Church then, the Greeke, the *Antiochian*, the Egyptian, the Abyssine, the Muscouite; and manie others, are members more excellent in truth, in doctrine, and sinceritie of faith, the one then the other: but yet members of the Catholicke Church whereof the Masse and contexture, as for externall forme, is alreadie long agoe dissolued and disassembled.

THE REPLIE:

AND what shall then become of that his maiestie lately said, that the specificall forme, and essentiall marke of the Church is truth of doctrine, and that there is noe communion betweene light and darknes, and betweene Christ and Belial. And that he that leaues Christ who is truth it self; leaues the Church which is the
1.Tim.3. & Hieron. in Zach.l.1.c.3 foundation of truth: if not onlie the *Greekes, Antiochians*, and *Muscouites*, who are hereticks in the point of the processiõ of the holie Ghost, which the most excellẽt King doth with vs hold for an article of Faith. & which in this qualitie is inserted into ATHANASIVS his Creede, and into the Creede of the Coũcell of *Cõstãtinople*, as it is read in the westerne Church, which his maiestie professeth to imbrace; but also the *Egiptians* and, *E-*
Cõc. Chalced Act.1. & in relat. ad Leo. *thiopians* (which followe the sect of *Eutyches* anathematised and cast out of the Church by the Councell of *Chalcedon*, neere twelue hundred yeares ag oead doeerre in the doctrine of the person of Christ, which is the fun-
1.Corint.3. damentall doctrine of the Church, and that whereof S. PAVLE saith, *None can laie anie other foundation besides Christ*,) are Churches and partes of the Catholicke Church? A *Lacedemonian* answered an inhabitant of the Isle of *Delphos*, who told him that the woemen were not deliuered of Child in their Isle, but trauelled out of it to be brought to bed, and that their dead, were not buried there, but that they were carried forth of it to their Sepulcher: And how then is it your countrie, said hee, if you be neither borne nor buried there? Soe, how is it, that the Sect of hereticks,
Cõc. Chalcẽd. vbi sup 2. Ioan. v 7 Ibid. v. 12 and namely those of the *Egiptians*, and *Ethiopians*, with whom the Coũcell of *Chalcedon* forbidds vs to communicate vpon paine of Anathema, and of whom saint *John* himself tells vs; *If anie one confesse not that Jesus Christ is come in the flesh, he is a seducer and Antichrist*. And againe, *If anie one bring not this Doctrine, receiue him not into your howses, and saie not to him, well be it with thee; for whosoeuer saith vnto him, well be it with thee, communicates in his wicked workes;* should obtaine the being and title of the Church, that is to saie, of the Spirituall countrie of the Faithfull, if to be borne in the grace of God, and to breathe, their first aire of spirituall, life; wee must, first goe forth of their Societie; and if to obtaine Saluation, and to rest in peace after death, wee must, first renounce their communion. God said to the Church, by the mouth of *Salomon*; *Thou art wholie faire, and there is noe spott in thee*; that is to saie, as for doctrine and conditions

of communion. And by the mouth of *Esaie*; *None incircumcised or vncleane, shall anie more passe through thee*: that is to saie, None that publickly professe a polluted or impure doctrine. *Hee* saith by the mouth of *Ezechiell*, describinge the future state of the christiã church: *I will establsih an alliãce of peace with my sheepe, and will cause the euill beastes of the* Earth *to cease*: Which the *Sibilla* seemes to haue expressed in these words, repeated by *Virgill*; and that sainct AVGVSTINE saith, might fitlie be applied to the Church.

Ezech. 34. Aug. contr. Faust. Manich. l. 13. c. 1.

Serpents shall cease swoll'n vp with th'impure blood,
Of poysenous herbes, in their deceiptfull bud.

And how then should the mock Councells of hereticks, which sainct HIEROME calls, *Venens of wilt beasts*; & whose doctrine he calls, *the wine of Sodome mingled witd the gall of Aspes*, be Churches & partes of the Church? or how should the Church to whom God hath spirituallie giuẽ the same prerogatiue, thar the historians attribute corporallie to the Isle of *Creete*, to witt, that it can suffer noe venomous beast in it; that is to saie, noe dogmatizing heretick, communicate her name and societie with the venemous sects of hereticks? Hee saith by the mouth of *Osea*, *I will espouse thee in faith*: And by that of Sainct PAVLE; *the edification of God is in faith*. And the most Excellent King himselfe protesteth, that the essentiall forme of the Church is faith. And how then can the sects not only of the *Egiptians*, and *Ethiopians*, but of all the hereticks which makes, as saith S. PAVLE, a Shipwracke of faith, be Churches, and in the Church? Hee saith by his owne mouth; *the gates of hell shall not haue victorie ouer the Church*. And S. EPIPHANIVS and S. HIEROME interpret those *Gates of Hell* to be heresies. And how then can it be, that the hereticall societies into whose communion wee cannot enter without yeelding our selues tributarie to the gates of hell, should be Churches, and partes of the Church? For though vices in manners belong also to the powers of hell, neuerthelesse because the vices are but in the persons of those that committ them, and not in the communion of the Church, for as much as the Church exacts not from anie of her members, the condition of being vicious to receaue them into her communiõ, they shall but conquer those particular persons that are spotted therewith, and not the Church, of the which God hath said by the Prophets: *Hierusalem shalbe called the cittie of truth, and the mountaine of the* Lord *of Hostes and the sanctified hill*. And by an other, *the howse of Israel shall noe more from hence forward be foyled*, whereas heresie infects the communions of the Societie where it remaines, none being to enter into anie hereticall societie without obliging themselues to the doctrine whereof she makes profession, and vnder whose condition she receaues men into her communion, and by consequent makes the gates of Hell victorious ouer the congregatiõ wherein shee remaines. He cõmaũds vs to hold those that heare not the Church, for Heathens and Publicãs, he forbidds vs then, from accounting the societies of hereticks, which heare not the Catholique Church, for Churches and partes of the Church, but for Societies of Infidells and Heathens. He saith to vs, *That whosoeuer gathers not with him, scatters*: the hereticks then that gather not with him, gather not but scatter, and so their assemblies are noe more Churches, but dispertions. He cries out to vs by the Organ of saint PAVLE, *That whosoeuer declares against what we haue receiued, shouldbe an anathema*. Hee wills then that heretickes should be held by the Church for anathema, and consequently excluded from the communion both internall and externall of the

Hier. in Ezech. l. 8 c. 27 & in Esai l. 7. c. c. 22. & l. 2. in Ose. c. 7.
Hieron in Esai l. 2. c. 5 & l. 16. c. 58.
Ibid.
Matth. 16.
Epiph l. Anacor.
Hieron. in Matt. c. 16.
Zach. 8.
Ezech. 43.

Church

Church. He teacheth vs by the same Oracle, that the Church is our mother, and not our mother as the first *Eue* was, who engendred her children dead to Saluation, but as the second *Eue*, who engendred her children liuing: From whence it is, that saint AMBROSE and saint HIEROME call the Church the true *Eue*, mother of the liuing. And how then is it that hereticall sects, who amongst the conditions vnder which they receiue men into their communion, oblige them to hold killing doctrines, should attribute to thēselues the title of a Church? Hee teacheth vs that the Fathers of the Earth, will not giue their children a Scorpion for an egge, or a Serpent for a Fishe. And how then is it, that the Church should giue hers poyson insteede of wholesome food? or that hereticall sects, whose wine, saith saint HIEROM, *is the furie of Dragons, and the incurable furie of Aspes*, should bee Churches? Hee teacheth vs that the Church is the Waie, the Gate, and Entrie into the Kingdome of Heauen; yea for this cause himself often calls it, the *Kingdome of Heauen*; it is then of the Essence of the Church, that Saluation might be therein obtained, and the waie howe to come to the Kingdome of Heauen; and consequently, that amongst the conditions, vnder whose obligation she receiues men into her communion there be none repugnant to Saluation. Now contrarywise it is of the Essence and of the definition of hereticall and Schismaticall Societies, that amongst the conditions vnder which they receiue men into their communion, there are conditions repugnant to Saluation: otherwise they could not be hereticall & Schismaticall: And so it is of the Essence and of the definition of the Church, not to be hereticall: and it is of the Essence and of the definition of hereticall Societies contrarywise, not to be Churches, nor partes of the Church, and they cannot be called Churches, nor members of the Church, but falselie and equiuocallie, as a dead member that is cutt off from the Bodie, is noe member but equiuocallie and by abuse of speeche; or as a dead man, or a man either formed in picture, or raised in a Sculpture, is noe man but equiuocally, & by abuse of speech. By meanes whereof, it is to erre against the Essence and definition of the Church, to hold them for Churches, or to reckon them in the totalitie of the catholick Church and to this all the Fathers agree. *Heresies* (saith *Clemens Alexandrinus*) *are equiuocallie called Churches*. And saint CYPRIAN: *Nouatianus doth as Apes doe, who would seeme to be men, though they be not soe: so will he seeme to haue a Church, though he haue none*. And againe; *When the Nouatians demaunded; beleeuest thou the remission of sinns by the holie Church? they lye in their Interrogatorie, for they haue noe Church*. And the *Elibertine* Councell; *If anie one passe from the Catholick Church vnto heresie and returne againe to the Church, &c.* And the Councell of *Sardica*: *Wee cast out of the limits of the Catholicke Church those, that affirme Christ to be God, and not verie* God. And saint HIEROME: *Heretickes make in their Church by false appellation, that which they made when they were yet heathen*. And againe: *Noe hereticall congregation can be called the Church of Christ*. And elsewhere: *In what Church hath he beleeued? in that of the Arrians; but they haue none*. And in the same worke: *If thou hearest in anie place of men denominated from anie other then from Christ, as Marcionites. Valentinians, Montagniers, or Campites, knowe, that there is not the Church of Christ*. And *Optatus Mileuitanus*: *Out of the onelie Church, which is the true Catholick Church, others amongst hereticks, are esteemed to be, and are not*. And againe. *There is one onely Church, which cannot be amongst you and amongst vs; it remaines then, that she must be in one place*. And S. AVGVSTINE: *you are with vs in the creede, and in the other Sacraments of our Lord, &c, but you are not with vs in the Catholique Church*. And againe; *There is one Catholique Church, vpon*

Amb l. 2 lucæ c. 3. Hier. in Ezech. l. 5. c. 16. & in Amos. l. 3 c. 9.

Hier l. 2. in Esai. c. 11

Clem. Alexandr. stromat. l. 1 Cypr. ad Iulian ep. 73. Conc. Elibert. c. 22.

Conc. Sard ep. ad omnes Episc.

Id. aduers. Luciferian

Id. ibid.

which other heresies impose other names, although themselues be all called by particular names which they dare not disauowe: From whence it appeares, in the iudgement of Iudges not preoccupate with fauour, to whom the name of Catholicke, whereof they are all ambitious, ought to be attributed. And elsewhere: *The Church of the saints, is the Catholique Church: the Church of the Saints, is not the church of Hereticks: She hath bene predesigned before she was seene, and hath bene exhibited that she might bee seene.* And in the Booke of Faith and of the creede: *Neither doe the Hereticks belonge to the Catholick church because she loues God; nor the Schismatickes because She loues her neighbour.* And in the Booke against the Fundamentall Epistle: *In this Church finallie, the name of Catholique detaines me, which this Church alone, amongst so manie and so great heresies, hath so preserued, as when a stranger askes where they assemble to the Catholick Church; there is noe hereticke dare shewe his Temple or his howse.* And in his Treatise vpon saint IOHN: *All hereticks and Schismaticks are gone out from vs; that is to saie, are gone out from the Church. Faustinus was not President to a Church, but to a faction. The holie Ghost hath not glorified Christ with a true glorie, but in the Catholick Church*: for elsewhere addeth hee; *be it amongst hereticks, be it amongst Pagans, his true glorie vpon earth cannot bee.* And vpon saint MATTHEW. *Jewes, and all other hereticks which doe indeede confesse that there is a holy Ghost, but denie that he is in the bodie of Christ, which is his onely Church, no other certainelie but onely the Catholicke, are without doubt, like the Pharises, who though they did confesse, that there was an holie Ghost, yet denied him to be in Christ.* And in the Booke of the method to cathecise the not instructed, *Wee must*, saith hee, *garnish and animate the infirmitie of man against temptations and scandalls, be it without, or be it within the Church; without, against Gentiles, or Iewes, or hereticks, and within against the Strawe in the Barne of our Lord.* And againe, *Let not the Enemie seduce thee, not only by those that are without the Church, whether Pagans, or Iewes, or Hereticks; but euen by those that thou seest in the Church euill liuers.* And in the fowrth Councell of *Carthage*, where he assisted in person: *Let not the Conuenticles of Hereticks be called Churches, but mock-Councells.* And the verie lawe of the Emperors: *Hereticks rashlie presume to call their Conuenticles, Churches.* Now if this haue place in other heresies; to witt, that the beeing and title of a Church, is denied to them, how much more in that of the *Eutychians*; that is to saie, of the *Egyptians*, and *Ethiopians*, which destroy not the walles, the roofe, and the couering onely, but the foundation of the Edifice of Faith, vpon the which all the other partes of the doctrine are built; to witt, Christ the corner stone, and maintaine that in Christ there is but one Nature; that is to saie, confound and steepe the Essence of the humanitie in that of the diuinitie? Doth not saint AVGVSTINE crie out. *Those that beleeue not that Christ is come in the fleshe, &c. and that he is risen againe in the same Bodie wherein he hath bene crucified and buried, although they should be in all the countries ouer the which the church is spread are not in the Church.* How can then the true Church haue cōmunion with this Sect? and how can this Sect, bee a member, and a true part of the Church? And how can it bee, that of the *Roman* Church which holdes the contrarie doctrine, and of this Sect, there should be framed one common Bodie of the catholicke Church? and to goe about to ioyne them together, in one selfe-same Societie of a catholicke Church, and more to add vnto them all other hereticall and schismaticall sects; How is it anie other thing, then to goe about to ioyne like *Mezentius* dead bodies with liuing bodies, and to make of the spouse of Christ, & of the doue of Christ which is the only catholicke Church, a monster, and a Prodigie compounded of all the impious horrible and contradictorie heresies, that

Id. id Psal. 149.

Id. de fid. &c. Symbol. 10. c. Contr. Ep. quam &c. Fund. c. 4. Ib. tract 100. de cap. 16. Id. de verb. Dom. in Euang. Matth. serm. 11. Id. de Catech. ru. c. Id. c. 27.

Conc. Carthag. 4. c. 71. Cod. l. 1. tit. 5. de heresi. l. 5. & Cod. Theod. l. 16. l. 2.

Aug. de vnit. Eccles. c. 4.

haue rent the Coate and mysticall Bodie of Christ, and to putt communion betweene Christ and *Beliall*, and betweene light and darknes? The Catholicke Church then, is not a Masse and common Societie which containes in it, the confusion of all Sects, and of all the multitude of those that are called Christians; but it is a particular Societie amongst all those Societies, which beares the name of Catholicke or totall Church; not because it containes in deed all the rest: *You will* (saith *Optatus Milenitanus* to the *Donatists*) *bee alone all the whole, who are not so much, as in the whole*. And saint AVGVSTINE: *Whosoever defends a part separate from the whole, cannot vsurpe the title of a Catholick: but because she containes them in right, and holds habituallie the place of the whole, in regard of them*. For the Church holds the place of the whole habituallie in regard of hereticall and schismaticall Sects, and by her eminencie; for as much as none of the other, considered euerie one a part, equalls her in number and in multitude. *Howbeit* (saith Saint AVGVSTINE,) *that there are manie heresies of Christians which would be all called Catholickes. There is neuerthelesse one Church, if you cast your Eies vpon the extent of the whole world, more aboundant in multitude*; and because vnto her alone, belonges the prerogatiue of being successiuely spread ouer the whole earth, in beginning from *Hierusalem*, whereas none of the others hath the priuiledge; but that the most part of them (like that kinde of Ape which the Greekes call *Callithrix*) cannot liue but in that climate, and vnder the same influence, wherein they were bredd: And beyond this, because all the rest hauing gone forth from her, and she hauing as saint AVGVSTINE saith, still remained in her stock and roote, holdes the places and right of the whole, in regard of all the rest; noe more nor lesse, then that part of the tree in which the life stood, and roote rests, holdes the place of the whole habituallie in regarde of those that haue bene separated from it: *They vnderstand not* (saith hee) *that amongst the Sects of the Christians there is one true and wholesome, and in sort Germinall and radicall Christian societie, from whence they haue separated themselues*. And finallie, because all the rest are obliged, if they will obtaine saluation, to reinsert and reincorporate themselues into the bodie of the Catholick Church; *Holde most stedfastlie* (saith FVLGENTIVS) *that noe heretick or schismatik, if he bee not reconciled to the Catholick Church, before the end of his life, can bee saued*. Otherwise, if all the hereticall and schismaticall Societies which professe the name of Christ, might iustlie enioy the title of the Church, and were actuallie parts of the Church, wherefore had the Fathers imployed these sentences against hereticks and schismaticks, *That out of the Church there is noe saluation: that out of the Church there may be had the faith and Sacraments and all thinges else, Saluation excepted: that who hath not the Church for his Mother, cannot haue God for his Father: that hee that communicates with the vniuersall Church, is a Catholicke, and he that communicates not therewith, is an hereticke and Antichrist*. And howe could the excellent King himselfe haue protested, That *he beleeues without colour or fraude, that the is one only Church, in deede and in name Catholicke and vniuersall, spread ouer the whole world, out of which there can be noe Saluation hoped for; and condemneth and detests those, that heretofore or since haue seperated themselues, either from the Faith of the Catholicke Church, and are become heretickes, as the Manichees; or from her communion, and are become Schismatickes, as the Donatists*, if the Catholicke Church did comprehend all the Hereticks and all Schismaticks, among which there was neuer anie more pernicious, then those that destroy

Optatus Mileuit. cont. Parm l.2.

Aug. de vtilit. credēt c.7.

Aug contr. Faust. l.13 c.12.

Fulgent. de fid. ad Petr. c.39

Conc. Carthag. 4. c.1. August. de gest. cū Emerit. Cypr. de vnit. Eccles.

the human nature of Christ, the only organ of our Saluation, as the *Egiptians* and *Ethiopians* doe? For whereas his maiestie auowes that the frame & contexture of the Church is alreadie longe agoe dissolued & dissãsẽbled betweene thẽ & vs, but adds, in regard of externall forme S.IOHN in saying to vs; *If anie one bring thee not this doctrine, saie not so much to him as, well bee it with thee; for whosoeuer shall say to him, well be it with thee, shall communicate in his wicked works*; forbidds vs all communion, as well internall as externall with thẽ. And elsewhere, we haue alreadie shewed, that when externall and Sacramentall communion is interdicted on both sides; that is to saie, where there is a reciprocall excommunication and an erection of Altar against Altar, there cannot be vnitie either internall or externall. *If wee be in vnitie* (said S. AVGVSTINE) *what makes two Altars in the Cittie*: And Sainct CYPRIAN *The Church which being Catholick is one, maintaines herself whole, and is ioyned together, with the cement of Prelates adhering to one an other*. 2. Ioan. Cypr. ad Pupp. Gellius l. 9 c. 2.

But against these decisions of the scripture and Fathers, there doe arise fowre obiections: The first that the word Church, doth grammaticallie signifie assemblie, and consequently that all assemblies are Churches, and so all Christian assemblies, are Christian Churches, Now this obiection is good in gramar, and to interpret prophane authors, but not in diuinitie, nor to interpret christian Authors, amongst whõ the word Church hath noe more this vast and large Grammaticall signification as it had before. For as when *Hormodius* and *Aristogiton*, had freed the common wealth of *Athens* from the slauerie of the thirtie tyrants, the *Athenian* Senate to consecrate their names and to make them reuerenced to Posteritie, ordained that from thence forward, they should neuer be imposed vpon, or communicated to anie other. Soe after our Lord had giuen to his Church, the priuiledge to conquer Hell, and to deliuer mankinde from the tyrannie and oppression of the deuill, that name is become consecrate and affected to her alone, and it hath bene forbidden to communicate it, anie more to anie other Societie, either Pagã, hereticall, or Schismaticall. *Let not the Conuenticles of hereticks* (saith the fowrth Councell of *Carthage*) *be called Churches, but Mock-Councells*. And the verie lawe of the Emperors, *That the Donations made to hereticall Conuenticles which they presume rashlie to call Churches, be applied to the reuerend Catholick Church*. Conc. Carthag 4 c. 71. Codic. l. 1. tit. 5. de hæret c 5.

THE second, that S. PAVLE writing to the *Galatians*, and to the *Corinthians*, calls their Societies, *Churches*; and neuerthelesse the *Galatians* erred in faith imbracing the circumcision with the Ghospell; and the *Corinthians* in not beleeuing the Resurrectiõ; but the snare here is manifest. For there is great difference betweene the doctrine of a Church, and the doctrine of anie particular person, which is deuided from the doctrine of the same Church. The doctrine of a church is that which is held by the bodie of that Church, & vnder the cõdition whereof either expresse or tacite, she receiues men into her cõmunion, & not the doctrine which euery particular mã straying frõ the commõ doctrine of the same church holdes against the opinions of the Bodie. Now it cannot be found that the Societie of the church of the *Corinthians* did euer hold that the dead did not rise againe, nor that she had exacted that beleefe from those that entred into her communion; but onelie that amongst the *Corinthians* there were some that did not beleeue the resurrection of the dead: *If Christ*, (saith S. PAVLE) *be preached to haue risen againe from the dead, how is it that there are some amongst you that saie, there is no resurrection of the dead?* And that S. PAVLE, made his remonstrance in common, it was to hinder them from being seduced by them which spake this language; *Suffer not your selues* (said hee) *to bee seduced; euill words corrupt good manners.* But not that he supposed they beleeued it; contrarywise hee exhorts them to remaine firme in that which they beleeued, *And therefore my Bretheren* (said hee) *be stedfast and vnmoueable.* And for the *Galatians*, soe farr off was it, that that error which saint PAVL cryed out against was the doctrine of the Church of the *Galatians*, as it was the doctrine of those which rebelled against the faith of the Church of the *Galatians*; which doctrine saint PAVL disputes as if all the *Galatians* had imbraced it, not that they did doe soe, but to hinder them from doeing soe; as he testifies to them in these wordes: *I haue this confidence of you in our* Lord, *that you will haue noe other beleefe, but that he that troubles you shall beare his iudgement whosoeuer hee be.* And againe, *If a man be found in anie crime, doe you which are spirituall, instruct him in the spiritt of mildness.* And that this is the true intent of saint PAVL, saint AVGVSTINE teacheth vs when hee writes to *Vincentius Rogatist*: *Thou might'st saie euen as well that manie of the Churches of Galatia were not when the* Apostle *cryed out. O foolish Galatians who hath bewitched you*: And a while after; *The Canonicall scriptures haue bene wont to make their reprehension in such sort, as it may seeme the word is addressed to all and neuertheless it concernes but some fewe.*

Ibid. c. 6.

Aug. ep. 48

Id. ibid.

THE third is that saint AVGVSTINE disputing against the *Donatistes*, writes, *That the Church begetts all Christians by Baptisme* from whence they would inferr, that all those then that are baptized, as well Catholiks as hereticks, are in the Church, but he bringes with it expressely this distinction, *either in her selfe, or without her selfe*; to shewe that the Church begetts none but Catholicks onely in her selfe, as *Sara* begate but *Isaack* onely in herselfe; and that the rest the Church begets without her selfe: For although *Ismael* were not begotten in the Bodie of *Sara* but in the bodie of *Agar*, yet he was in a sort begotten by *Sara*, for as much as he was begotten by her that belonged to *Sara* and was *Saras* nuptiall right; to witt, by the seede of *Abraham*. Soe then the hereticks be begotten by Baptisme out of the Church, neuerthelesse it is the Church that begetts them euen out of the Church, for as much, as the baptisme whereby they are begotten, and which those that baptise them haue carryed out of the Church, belonges to the Church, and is of the coniugall rightes of the church, and not heresie. By which meanes, when they returne to the church, there is noe neede that the church should baptise them againe; *The Church* (saith hee) *begetts all Christians by baptisme be it in her-selfe, that is to saie, in her bowells or without her selfe, that is to is to saie, of her husbands seede, be it in her selfe, or in the bond-woeman.* Whereby soe farr is hee from teaching, that heretickes are in the church, as contrarywise he plainelie affirmes heereby: that they are out of the church. For the thing wherein catholicks and the Donatists were at agreement was, that hereticks were out of the church, and the thing where about they disagreed was, that the Donatists held, that Baptisme could not be out of the church, and consequently, that hereticks could not haue it: And catholicks contrariwise maintained, that Baptisme might to be out of the church: and consequently, that hereticks though they were out of the church left not to haue it. *The Church* (saith saint AVGVSTINE) *compared to Paradise, teacheth vs, that Baptisme may be had without her, but the Saluation of the beatitude none can receaue or haue out of her, for the floods of the fountaine of Paradise rann aboundantlie forth of it* And in the Booke following: *What is* (saith hee) *this doctrine that an*

Aug. de baptism. cōtr Donatists l. 1. c 14.

Aug. vbi supra.

August. de baptism. contr. Donatists l. 4. c. 1.

heretick

heretick is pretended to haue noe baptisme, because he hath noe Church. And againe. *It is a wonder that there are some that saie, that baptisme and the Church cannot be separated and deuided, the one from the other*, And elsewhere, *But of the Church and against the Church they haue holden the sacraments of Christ, and as in a ciuill warr they haue fought, bearing our owne Banners against vs*. From whence we may discouer the impertinencie of those that conclude, that because hereticall Sects haue baptisme, therefore they are Churches.

THE fowrth obiection is, that sainct HIEROME speaking in the person of the Church, saith to *Hilarie* a *Luciferian* Deacon, *I am a harlott, but yet I am thy mother, I committ adultrie with Arius, and I did soe before with Praxeas, Ebion, Cerinthus*. But it shalbe heereafter manifested that this is a ridiculous equiuocation; by which they attribute that to S. HIEROME as spoken in his owne sence, which he spake according to the sence of his aduersary; that is to saie, according to the sence of the hereticke against whom he disputeth. For to this that some add, that a lying man, leaues to be trulie a man although he be not a true man; that is to saie, a veritable man, and then that a Church, leaues not to be truly a Church, although she be not a true Church, it is a Sophisme of the truth of the essence to the truth of the word, and of the word *verus*, to the word *Verax*, there being none so young a scholler, but knowes that to speake vniuocallie; whosoeuer is truly a man, is a true man, for as much as being, and truth, are conuertible, from whence it is that sainct AMBROSE vseth these wordes, *true Israelite, and trulie Israelite*, as termes equiualent. And that sainct AVGVSTINE saith; *Euerie soule is by that a soule, by which it is a true soule*. And therefore as the Fathers affirme, that there is none but the Catholicke Church, that is a true Church. *From thence*, saith sainct AVGVSTINE, *it appeares, that the true Church is concealed from noe bodie*. Soe they also saie, that there is none but the Catholicke Church, that is truly a Church. *If you did teach* (saith sainct AVGVSTINE to the *Manichees*) *that mariage were good, but virginitie better, as doth the Church, which is trulie the Church of Christ, the holie Ghost had not predesigned you*. And whereas it is replied, that a man for being lesse or more sound, leaues not to be a man: and soe that a Church for being lesse or more pure, leaues not to be a Church, it is an other manifest Sophisme, for health is not the essentiall forme of a man, nor sicknes the priuation of the essentiall forme of a man, but an accident which consequentlie may receaue more and lesse, whereas puritie of faith according to his maiesties owne confession, is the essentiall forme of the Church; and the impuritie of Faith, the priuation of the essentiall forme of the Church. By meanes whereof noe Societie can hold among the conditions of her Communion and doctrine impure in Faith, and contrarie to saluation, but shee looseth at the same time, the being and title of a Church. And therefore the diuersitie of the communions, whereinto the Church was deuided when *Luther* rose, must not be alleadged for a pretence to be ignorant where the true Church then was. For since the Church ought to be perpetually visible and eminent, and that then there were noe Christiã communions visible in the world but ours, & that of the *Grecians*, vnder which are cõprehended the *Muscouites*, & the *Antiochians*, & that of the *Egiptians*, & *Ethiopians*, which is but one, & that of the *Armenians*, & that of the *Nestorians*; & that it is of the essence, & of the necessitie of the Church, that she should be pure and impolluted in faith; and that all those others by the common confession of vs and of the Protestants, are heretickes, and corrupt; it is not needefull to goe to

Delphus to learne, that either the Church was perished, which (as wee haue aboue shewed) could not be, or that it was our communion which was the Church.

Of the qualitie wherein the Catholick Church attributes to her-selfe the name of the whole.

CHAP. VIII.

The continuance of the Kings answere.

AND therefore the most excellent King is much amazed when hee sees the Churches which haue bene members of the whole Bodie, drawe to themselues, all the right of vniuersalitie.

THE REPLIE:

IT hath alreadie bene aboue shewed, that by the Catholicke Church, the Fathers neuer intended the Masse and totall conclusion of the multitude of Christians: but a speciall societie, distinct from the beleefe, and from the communion of all hereticall and schismaticall sects, and which in regard of the Masse, and generall confusion of all the multitude of Christians, held actuallie but the place of a part, and held only the place of the whole actuallie, in regard of the particular Churches which were comprehended in deede in her communiō. For there was neuer anie age since the apostles built the church, but there haue bene some heretickes, which haue gone forth from the Bodie of the Church, neuerthelesse making profession of the name of Christ: *They haue* 1 Ioan. 2. Epist. Iud. vers. 11 *gone forth from vs* (saith S. IOHN) *but they were not of vs*. And S. IVDE, *Cursed bee they, for they perish in the contradiction of Chore, people which separated them selues, men, animalls hauing not spiritt.* And S. AVGVSTINE: *All hereticks and Schismaticks are gone forth from vs, that is to saie* (saith hee) *are gone forth of the Church.* But amongst this difference of societies, making profession of Christian Religion, there was alwaies one more eminent in multitude then the rest, which hath alwaies remained in her stocke and roote, and from whence all the rest are gone forth, to whom also the name of Catholicke hath bene preserued, not because she held actuallie the place of whole in regard of the rest; but onlie of all habituallie as the stocke, in regard of the boughes which haue bene pluckt off; for as much as in all the separations, she remained in the same estate wherein all the Bodie was before the separation, and consequentlie hath iustlie inherited the name of totall Church, and succeeded onelie in the right and application of the whole, as being she alone that represents it. *The Church.* (saith S. AVGVSTINE:) *Combating against all heresies, may be resisted, but she cannot be ouer-* Aug. de Symb. ad Catech. l. c. 5. *throwne: all heresies are gone forth from her, as vnprofitable branches cutt off from their vine, but she remaines in her roote, in her vine, in her charitie, the gates of hell shall not preuaile against her.* Which amazeth me, that is maiestie should be amazed, *that the Churches which haue heretofore bene members of the whole Bodie, should drawe to themselues all the Right of the vniuersalitie.* For the word Catholicke, was neuer common to all Christians, but onely to a part of

Christians; to witt, to that wherein there remained the actuall totalitie of that which rested in the iust possession of the title of the Church, and which in regard of the partes separated, retained noe more the effect, but only the right of the whole, as representing her, that before each separation, was the whole. And therefore, so farr was S. AVGVSTINE from extending the totalitie of the Catholicke Church, to the multitude of all the sectes of Christians, as contrariwise, after hauing reported the opinions of the eightie eight heresies, he adds, *What the Catholicke Church holdes against all these thinges, is a superfluous demaund, since it is sufficient for to knowe, that she holdes the contrary to these thinges.* And a while after, *There may also be, or be made other heresies, besides these which are reported in this worke of ours whereof who shall holde anie one, shall be noe Catholick Christiā.* And elsewhere; *The Catholick and the heretick, are deuided the one against the other.* And againe. *They cannot beginn to be Catholick, till they haue left to be heretické.* And therefore when the hereticall Sects separate themselues from the Catholicke Church, and deuide themselues from the part that consents not to heresie, they hinder not the title of Catholicke, nor the Right of vniuersalitie from being preserued in her alone, and from belonging to her alone, noe more then when in a common weale, the factious part, and which separated it-selfe from the state, and reuoltes against the true preseruers of the Estate, come to be deuided from that which remaines in the lawfull administration of the Estate, this diuision hinders not the part which restes vnited with the Estate from preseruing the right and title of the vniuersallitie of the cōmon-wealth, and those thinges which are done by it alone, from being accounted to be done by the whole Bodie of the common-wealth; Whose whole being is preserued in this part alone, the other by the desertion thereof, hauing lost all the part it had in the name and effect of the common-wealth.

Of the sence wherein the Roman Church is called Catholicke.

CHAP. IX.

The continuance of the Kinges answere,

TO attribute to themselues the title of Catholicke, as proper to themselues alone.

THE REPLIE,

WHEN wee vse this traine of Epithetes, the Catholicke, Apostolicke, *Roman* Church, we intend not by the word *Roman*, the particular Church of *Rome*, but all the Churches which adhere and are ioyned in communion with the *Roman* Church, euen as by the *Iewish* Church wee intended not the tribe of *Iuda* only, but the lines of *Leui* and *Beniamin*, and manie relikes of the lines which were ioyned therewith. For S. IOHN BAPTIST, was of the tribe of *Leuy*, and sainct PAVL of that of *Beniamin*, & *Anna* of the tribe of *Aser*, and neuerthelesse they were all of the people of the *Iewes*, and of the *Iewish* Church; but they were called *Iewes* and *Iewish* people because of the adherence and communion that they had with the principall Tribe, which was that of *Iuda*. Soe all the other Churches which communicate with the *Roman* in what soeuer part they are constituted, are comprehended vnder the common word of the *Roman* Church, when wee saie the Catholicke Apostolicke and *Roman* Church, because they hold the *Roman* Church for the center and originall of their communion. And in this sence saint AMBROSE saith that his brother inquired if the Bishop of one of the citties of *Sardica*, where he desired to be baptised, consented with the Catholicke Bishops, that is to saie, added hee, with the *Roman* Church. And in this sence, saint HIEROME saith, that the Church of *Alexandria*, glorifies her selfe, that she participates with the *Roman* Faith; And in this sence *Iohn* Patriarke of *Constãtinople* writes to Pope *Hormisdas*; *Wee promise not to recite amongst the sacred mistiries the names of those which are separate from the communion of the Cathoick Church, that is to saie, that consent not in all thinges with the Sea Apostolick*. And in this sence *Beda* vseth these words: *Our mother the Roman Church*. In this same sence they comprehend vnder the *Greeke* Church not only the natuaall *Greekes*, but the *Russians*, and *Muscouites*, although they be distinct in nation, and in language from the Greekes, yea, euen haue their Seruice in a tongue quite different, for asmuch as they adhere to the *Greeke* Church. Not that the particular *Roman* Church, may not also in a certaine regard, be called Catholicke. For the word Catholicke is taken in three sortes, to witt, either formallie, or causallie, or participatiuelie. Formally the only vniuersall Church, that is to saie, the Societie of all the true particular churches, vnited in one selfe-same communiõ, is called catholicke. Causallie, the *Roman* church is called Catholicke for as much as she infuseth vniuersalitie into all the whole bodie of the Catholicke church. That it is soe, to cõstitute vniuersalitie, there must be two thinges, one that may analogicallie be insteede of matter thereto, to witt, the multitude; for where there is no multitude there can be noe vniuersalitie: And the other to be in-steede of forme thereto, to witt, vnitie; for a multitude without vnitie, makes noe vniuersalitie: *Take awaie* (saith sainct AVGVSTINE) *the vnitie from the multitude, and it is a tumult, but bring in vnitie, and it is the people*. And therefore the *Roman* Church, which as center and beginning of the ecclesiasticall communion, infuseth vnitie, which is the forme of vniuersalitie into the Catholicke Church; and by consequent, causeth vniuersalitie in her, may be called catholicke causallie, though in her owne being, she be particular: noe more nor lesse then the Galley, to which all the other Gallies of a Fleete haue relation of dependancie and correspondencie, is called the Generall, although she bee but one particular Galley, because it is she, that by the relation that all others haue to her, giues vnitie to the totall and generall bodie of the Fleete. And finallie particular Churches are called Catholicke, participatiuely, because they agree and participate in doctrine and communion with the catholicke Church. And in this sence the Church of *Smyrna* addresseth her Epistle: *To the Catholick Church of Philomilion; and to all the Catholick Churches which are throughout the world.*

August. de verb. Domin. secundum Luc. serm. 26.

Of the causes wherefore the Roman Church, hath cutt of the rest from her communion.

CHAP. X.

The continuance of the Kings answere.

ND to exclude from their communion, all the rest which dissent from them in anie thinge, or refuse the yoake of slauerie.

THE REPLIE.

THE most excellent King, may be pleased to remember two things, one that antient authors haue written, that oftentimes for one only word contrarie to Faith, manie heresies haue bene cast out of the bodie of the Church: And the other, that the societies of the *Egiptians* and *Ethiopians* haue not bene excluded out of the Church, for refusinge that which his maiestie call the yoake of slauerie; that is to saie, the Superintendencie of the *Roman* Church, but for hauing imbraced the Sect of *Eutyches*, who with all his partakers, was cutt off from the Church by the Councell of *Chalcedon*; and that euen to this daie, they are all readie, and haue often offerred, to acknowledge the Pope, whom they confesse to bee the Successor of the Prince of the Apostles, if they might be receiued into the communion of the *Roman* Church, without obliging them to anathematize *Eutiches* and *Dioscorus*. And as for the diuision of the Greeke Church; the true cause thereof hath bene, the Schisme fallen out betweene *Ignatius*, lawfull Patriarke of *Constantinople*, whom the Pope preserued in his communion; and *Photius* intruded into the Patriarkship by the fauour of the Emperor; to which Schisme the Greekes added for an obstacle of reunió, as the crabb cast the stone into the oyster, to hinder it from shutting itselfe againe; the difference of the procession of the holy Ghost; and of Schismatickes became flatt heretickes. This was the true cause of the seperation of the Greekes, and not the yoake of slaueries of the *Roman* Church; of the which neither *Ignatius*, nor anie of his Catholicke Predecessors, had euer complayned.

Of the sence wherein the hereticks belonge not to the Catholick Church.

CHAP. XI.

The Continuance of the Kings Answere.

ND so on the suddaine to pronounce presumptuouslie, that they belonged not in anie thing to the Catholicke Church.

THE

THE REPLIE.

his deniall is intended in deede, and not in Right; for we doe not denie, but that the heretickes belong by right to the Church; that is to saie, that the Church hath to exercise her authority ouer them, and to iudge, censure, and excommunicate them: but wee saie that they belonge not in deede, to the Catholick church, that is to saie, that they are not actually comprehended and contained in the catholicke Church, and are not members and partes thereof: And it is not wee that saie this, but saint AVGVSTINE who writes it in these words: *And therefore neither the heretick, belongs to the Catholick Church, because she loues God; nor the Schismatick, because she loues her neighbour.*

Of the proceeding of the other sects.

CHAP. XII.

The continuance of the Kings answere.

ND it is not you alone, that attribute to yourselues this right, others also doe the same for at this daie, a word the king cannot speake without groaning, there are manie particular Churches, which beleeue themselues onelie to be the particular people that they call the Church, if you giue them strength like the Romans, they would alreadie haue done as that hath done, and would iudge the rest no lesse seuerelie.

THE REPLIE.

HAT those are, wee are not to Answere, let the dead bury their dead; only wee maie saie, their conclusion would be good, if their hypothesis were true, for if they were true churches, euery Societie which should be excluded out of their communion, should be excluded from the title of the Church, and from the right of being able to call thēselues a part of the Catholick Church, for as much as the Church as hath bene aboue said, is either one, or none.

Of the perswasion, that the other sects pretend to haue, of the truth of their Church by scriptures.

CHAP. XIII.

The Continuance of the Kings Answere.

HAT shall I saie more, that there are at this daie, many sects which are celebrated, the sectaries whereof are most stedfastlie persuaded, that they alone see some thing into holie writt, and, as saieth the Poet, that they alone are vnderstanding, and that the rest hunt after a shaddowe.

THE REPLIE.

HARPASTE, *Seneca's* domestical foole, hauing lost her sight, would not beleeue it was she that was become blinde, but perswaded herselfe, that it was growne darke: It is iust soe with all heretickes, they thinke it is the Church that is become darke and full of obscuritie, and not themselues which are become blinde. To finde anie thing answered the *Pelagians* to saint AVGVSTINE, when he alleadged the multitude of Authors for the Catholicke Church, *A multitude of blind persons serue to no vse.* And by that only his maiestie may iudge, how necessarie it is not to abandon nor prostitute the exposition of the scripture to the iudgement of euery particular person, since there is not that man that when he will make himselfe iudge of it, doth not beleeue himselfe only cleere sighted, and that the rest as *Homer* saith; *embrace nothing but darknes*. For the Scripture consisting, according to saint HIEROME, *not in the reading, but in the vnderstanding,* and men not being able to assure themselues of the vnderstanding of the Scripture by their particular Spirit, *for as much as,* saith saint PETER, *as the exposition of the Scripture is not made by priuate interpretation*: it is necessarie to determine the differences that are bredd by the interpretation of the Scripture to haue besides the Scripture a Iudge externall, and interposed betweene that and vs, who may secure vs of the true sence thereof, and that this iudge should haue other markes, and be notable by other externall meanes, then by that of the doctrine contested, since it is from that iudgement, that wee ought to learne the decision of the true sence of Scripture in pointes disputable; otherwise questions in Religion, could neuer be determined, no more then differences in ciuill controuersies, if wee should leaue the deciding of the sence of the wordes of the lawe, to the preoccupated vnderstanding of the Aduocates and parties, & that there were noe iudge ordained aboue them, and sett betweene the lawe and them, to interpret it.

Hier. cōtra Lucit.

2. Petr.

Of the sence wherein hereticks haue disputed the word Catholicke.

CHAP. XIV.

The continuance of the Kinges answere.

IT is verie true, that there hath bene noe age, wherein there hath not bene conuenticles to raise Sectes & parasynaxes, which haue bragged of the name of the Catholicke Church, and haue drawne ignorant persons to them by this allurement.

THE REPLIE.

THAT the ancient Sectes and Parasynaxes of heretickes haue effected the title of Catholicke, it was not to pretend in good earnest, that it belonged to them, nor to drawe ignorant persons to them by that allurement, but to dispute it with the catholicke Church, and to hinder least by the possession of this

name

name, she should preserue her menbers from being defrauded and seduced by hereticks. And euen so not to dispute it with her in that sence wherein she attributes it to herselfe to witt, as an Epethete of communion, but to dispute it in the qualitie of an Epithete of doctrine. For heretickes haue alwaies sufficiently knowne, that this taken in the true sence, could neither be giuen nor maintained to their Sects. And therefore they spake not of this word, but either in seeming to mocke and scorne at it, as when *Sympronion* saith to saint PACIAN, *that none vnder the Apostles were called Catholickes*. And when *Fulgentius* the *Donatist* said, *that the word Catholicke was an human fiction*. And that the *Donatists* according to the report of *Vincentius Lirinensis*, cryed out to the Catholicks: *Come, come, o you miserable madd people, commonlie called Catholicks*: or in disguising the sence of the word, and applying it to signifie the qualitie of doctrine, and not the communion of the Church, as the *Donatists* which called themselues Bishops of the Catholicke truth; and to whom S. AVGVSTINE said, *you are those that hold the Catholicke faith not from the communion of the whole world, but from the integritie of the diuine Sacraments*. For when they suffered it to bee admitted in a true sēce, they were as speedilie as shamefullie driuen from it. *I asked him* (saith S. AVGVSTINE, speaking of *Fortunatus* the *Donatist*) *if hee could giue letters cōmunicatory, which wee called formed whither I would, &c. But because the thinge was manifestly false, they shifted from it by confusion of language*. And elsewhere. *Wee must* (saith hee) *hold the Christian Religion, and the communion of that Church which is called Catholick, not onlie by themselues, but by their Enemies. For whether the hereticks themselues, and the foster children of schismes, will or nil not, when they speake not with those of their Sects, but with others, they call the Catholick Church, noe otherwise then Catholick. Neither could they be vnderstood if they did not discerne it by that name, by which the whole world calls it*. And againe. *This Church alone, amongst soe manie and soe great heresies, hath so maintayned this name, as when a stranger askes an hereticke, where they assemble to communicate in the Catholicke Church, none of them dares to shew his Temple or his howse*. And the reason the title of catholick was not an allurement wherewith heretickes drewe ignorant persons to them, but the firme bond by which the true Church drewe to her, and retained in her communion all the true faithfull, called to the hope of life eternall, and amongst other this Eagle of doctors S. AVGVSTINE, who saith, *That I omitt this sincere wisedome which you beleeue not to be in the catholicke church. There be manie other reasons which doe most iustlie retaine me in her lappe: the consent of people and nations retaines me, the authoritie begunn by miracles, nurst by hope, increased by charitie, confirmed by antiquitie, retaines me, the succession of Prelates, euen from the Sea of Peter, to whom our lord committed his sheepe to be fedd after his resurrection, vntill the present Bishop, detaines me: And finallie, the verie name of Catholicke, retaines me*. And a little after; *these so manie and so great most deare bondes of the Christian name, doe iustlie detaine faithfull men in the Catholick Church, although for the slownes of our vnderstanding, of the defect of meritts in our liues, truth doth not yet shew her, else with manifest euidence.*

Pacian. ad Sympron. ep. 1.

Vincent. Lirin. cont. heres. c. 26.

Aug. ep. 48

Aug. ep. 163

Aug de vera Relig. c. 7.

Aug. cont. ep. fund. c. 4

Id ibidem.

Ibidem.

Of

Of the cases wherein the Communion in vow with the Catholick Church, may be imputed as actuall.

CHAP. XV.

The continuance of the Kinges answere.

BVT this notable calamitie is particular to the last times, whereto wee are arriued, that the Catholick Church which must bee communicated with, either reallie and by effect, or at the least voluntarily and in vowe, is lesse illustrious at this daie then antiently she was, and lesse exposed to the view of men and more subiect to bee contested.

THE REPLIE.

ARISTOTLE, that great Philosopher, which steeped his pen, say the Greekes, in séce, in steede of inke; teacheth vs, that the cittie is before the cittizen; to witt, not in prioritie of time, for a cō-mon-weale can not be without a cittizen, but in prioritie of nature; that is to saie, that the being of the cittizen dependes from that of the cittie, and not the being of the cittie, from that of the cittizen: from whence it appeares, that the forme that giues being in the first place to the cittie, and then by participation to the cittizen, must reside in the cittie, in the most perfect manner that it can reside, and not in the most imperfect. And soe although it suffice to preserue to a cittizen the being of a cittizē that in default of being able to participate actuallie in the communion of the common- wealth; as when he is hindred by anie locall obstacle, either of beeing in a strange prison, or remayning in a strange countrie, he commnicate there habituallie, and in desire, which is an imperfect manner of communicating; it sufficeth not that the communion where by the common wealth is framed and preserued in being, should be a simple habituall communion and in vowe; but it is necessarie that it should be a true and actuall commnnion. For when a Cittizen is hindred by anie locall impossibilitie from communicating actuallie with his Common wealth, he leaues not to preserue the being of a cittizen, prouided that hee communicate therewith habituallie, that is to saie in vowe and in desire, and communicate not in a politicke communion with anie contrarie societie. But when the communion of the bodie of a common-wealth comes to be dispersed, and that there is noe more anie comerce or actuall communion in the estate, then the common wealth is extinct and hath noe more being; and the communion that is habituall and in desire of the cittizens dispersed, and noe more communicating one with an other, cannot preserue it. Now euen that ought to be said of the Church, whereof the Psalmist singes propheticallie; *Hierusalem which is built as a cittie, whose participatiō is in vnitie*: to witt, that although the cō-munion habituall and in vow, suffice for a particular person in case of im-possibilitie for the actuall, to make him imputatiuelie a member of the Church, that is to saie, to cause this imperfect communion to serue him

Arist. Politic. c. 2.

psal. 121

to saluation, in default of the other: Neuerthelesse the Church cannot be framed nor preserued, in the beeing of a Church, by a communion only habituall and in vowe, but by a reall and actuall communion: The which as soone as it comes wholie to cease and to perishe in the Church, the Church perisheth, and ceaseth to be. And therefore this distinction of actuall communion, and communion in vowe, serues well to shewe, that anie one may be imputatiuelie in the Church without participating actuallie in the visible communion of the Church; prouided, that this defect come from an impossibilitie of participating therein actualie: but not to shew, that the bodie of the Church can subsist, and preserue the being and true title of a Church, without visible and actuall communion. For contrariwise, that this imperfct manner of being in the Church, serues to his saluation that is hindred by anie locall obstacle from being able to be there actually, it is because the true and actuall communion which as in the Church, is imputed to him by the desire that he hath to participate thereof, which could not be imputed to him, if it were not reallie some where; and besides, this desire of participation must be stript from all other impediments, sauing that which proceedes from lo- and corporall impossibilities, in such sort, as all those which are not withheld by distance of place, or other like obstacle ineuitable to them, from participating in the actuall communion of the Church cannot be said to communicate there in vow, nor to be there imputatiuely. For nothing dispenceth with men for communicating with the Catholicke Church onely in vow and in will, and not reallie and by effect, if it be not the exclusion of time and place, and besides in the article of death; noe more then anie thing can excuse a man from being baptised onelie in vow and in will, and not reallie and by effect; but the condition of being excluded by the impossibilitie of time and of place, and also in the Article of death from the meanes how to be baptised. And because, when the obstacle proceedes from externall impediments onely; & that if there were locall or temporall commoditie, he that communicates with the Church in vowe, would communicate therewith actuallie, this desire of communion, may be imputed for true communion, and called a communion in vow. But when the obstacle proceedes from internall impediments from him that pretendes to communicate there in vow, as of repugnancie to the beleefe, and to the discipline, and the lawes, vnder the conditions whereof, the Catholick Church receiues into her communion those that she receaues thereinto, in such sort, as all corporall obstacles being taken awaie, and hee being in place where hee may assist at the Catholicke Church, & communicate with her, hee will not doe it; this conditionall desire of communicating with her, in case she would change the conditions of her communion, cannot be called communion in vowe, but discommunion; otherwise there would be no heretickes that would not communicate with the Catholick Church, for there is noe hereticke but would offer to communicate with her, prouided she would change the clauses and conditions of her communion, and would reforme her self to the conditions of his Sect. To communicate then in vowe with the Catholicke Church, is not to be hindred from communicating reallie therewith, by any obstacle proceeding from him that communicates therewith in vowe; nor by anie condition that he reproues in the Catholicke Church, nor by being vnited in communion with anie other Sect, whose cōmunion is repugnāt to the doctrine of the Catholicke Church. For whosoeuer cōmunicates with another sect, wherewith the catholike

Church

Church communicates not, can not be said to cõmunicate in vowe with the Catholicke Church. And therefore S. AVGVSTINE speaking of some good people, who sometimes are vniustlie excõmunicated & cast forth of the Church, affirmes that they cease not to enioy the friute of the communion of the Church; that is to saie, that they are reputed to communicate with the Church in vow, when there is on their parte noe obstacle from communicating actuallie therewith, and that they make noe congregation of Cõuenticles out of the Church: *Often times also* (saith hee) *diuine prouidence permitts that honest people should be cast out of the Christian congregation by some ouer turbulent sedition of carnall men, which iniurie to them done, when they beare it patientlie, for the peace of the Church, and attempt no innouation of Schismes, nor of heresies, they teache men with how true affection, and with how great sinceritie, and charitie, God must be serued.* Of such men then, the purpose is either to returne the tempest being ceased, or if they be not permitted, whether because the same tempest continues; or whether least by their returne, there may arise the like, or one more cruell; they yet preserue the will to serue euen those to whose motions and perturbations, they haue giuen waie, defending without anie congregation of Conuenticles to the death, and helping by their testimonie, the faith which they know to bee preached in the Catholicke Church: *Those the Father which sees them in secrett, will crowne in secret.* From whence it appeares, that those which cõmunicate with anie other Societie separate from the Church, and hold anie other doctrine, but that which is held in the Catholicke Church & who are hindred from communicating with the Catholicke Church by obstacles proceeding on this part, and by repugnancie to the conditions vnder the obligation whereof people are receiued into the Catholicke Church; cannot bee said to communicate in vow with the Catholick Church.

Of the equiuocation of termes diminutiue imployed for negatiues.

CHAP. XVI.

The continuance of the Kings answere.

BOTH lesse exposed to the viewe of men, and most subiect to Contestation.

THE REPLIE:

THE Poets faine, that the *Cyanian* or *Simplegade* Islandes, which are two Isles in the Mediteranean Sea, doe sometimes meete together, and ioyne themselues in such sorte, as they seeme to bee but one; therefore *Homer* calls them, wandring, and *Pindar*, animated, because they are described so moueable and vagabond. The same may be said, of the visible and inuisible Church of the *Protestants*; to witt, that sometimes they propoũd them as two Churches distinct, & separate & sometimes they drawe them together, and make them communicate together, and compound of them one selfe-Bodie and Societie. For when the oracles of the Prophetts & Apostles are produced to thé, touching the

Theocrit. Concurrẽtia Saxa. iuuenal. Cent.1.c.4 Vide Staplet.l.1.c.7

perpetuall puritie and integritie of the Church; and that they are demaunded where all these promises haue bene fulfilled since soe manie and soe manie ages; their onlie refuge is to frame two Churches; the one visible, and the other inuisible, and to saie, that the puritie of Religion hath alwaies bene preserued in the inuisible, which hath remained exempt from the contagion and from the abhominations of the visible, but that it hath bene extinguished and abolished for a longe time in the visible. And then as this ecclipse according to them is ceased, and that they come to cast their eyes vpon anie companie which begins to hold visible, that which they beleeue their inuisible Church inuisiblie to haue held, then they constitute noe more but one Church and one communion of the visible Church, and of the inuisible Church. Now what other *Protestants* doe vnder the terme of inuisible Church, his maiestie is brought to doe it vnder these wordes lesse exposed to mans viewe, and more subiect to contestation: by which noe other thing can be seriouslie vnderstood, but that when *Luther* came into the world, the true Church was wholie inuisible, and not only that she was wholie inuisible, but that she was wholie perished. For if when *Luther* came into the world, amongst manie Societies that contested for the title of the Church, there had bene one lesse illustrious and eminent then she had antiently bene, but yet visible, which ought to be discerned from the rest, by this essentiall marke, that in the pointes wherein she differed from them, she hath for her the worde of God. Where did that Church reside? Lett them giue it to vs, that wee may giue ourselues to it. But if she were inuisible, and that before the coming of *Luther* there were a flocke vnknowne in the eyes of men, but knowne to God, which held the same doctrine that *Luther* brought; besides that I will aske how the members of that Church could be saued, not making anie profession of their Faith; since our Lord saith, *Who shall denie me before men, I will denie him before God my Father*: And
Matt. 10. sainct PAVL; *Wee beleeue with our hartes to iustice, but wee con-*
Rom. 10. *fesse with our mouthes to Saluation*. This Church then when *Luther*, rose vp had no neede to receaue anie change in the pointes which are at this daie in controuersie, nor to take anie instruction from *Luther* or his disciples, but onelie to declare her self, and with her *Gyges* Ring, to make herselfe from inuisible, visible. And to cry out, this is my beleefe, this was the doctrine that I held before *Luther* spake. Now this is soe farr from benig soe, as *Luther*, protests, that none before him euer discouered the truth of the doctrine that he hath declared: And all those that came thither perswaded by the preaching of him and of his disciples, and without euer bragging of the precedent possession of the same doctrine; neither had this sufficed, for the same Church must haue said, *Luther* hath not yet passed forward enough hee is not yet arriued to the whole summe of my doctrine. For wee know how much *Caluin*, and *Zuinglius*, haue added to the doctrine of *Luther*. And so there not being, when *Luther*, came into the world, a Societie, neither visible, nor inuisible, which held *Luthers* doctrine, and much lesse *Caluins*, in the pointes controuerted betweene them and vs, it must necessarily followe, that the Church was then perished, for since the excellent King, will haue it that the only assured marke to discerne which, either of the Church which hee calls, *English*, or of ours, is the true Church, be it that which is the essentiall forme of the Church, and that he pretends to be doctrine; it is necessary that he suppose

that the difference, which are betweene the Church that hee calls, *English*, and ours, be questions which take awaie the essentiall forme of the Church, and destroy the being of a Church: And by consequence, that that of the one or other Societie, which errs in these pointes, shall bee depriued of the essentiall forme of a Church, and destitute from the being of a Church. And then if when *Luther* came into the world, there were noe Societie neither visible nor inuisible, which held that that the *English* Church holdes at this daie in the pointes disputed betweene her and vs, it followes there was then noe Church.

Of the authoritie of the worke intituled imperfect.

CHAP. XVII.

The Continuance of the Kings Answere.

AND therefore the excellent King thinkes, that he ought with soe much the more Care in so great a floud of different opinions, withdrawe himselfe into the mountaines of the holie Scripture. Aug. in psal. 124

THE REPLIE.

WHEN *Nauplius* King of the Island of *Eubœa* now called *Negrepont* would at the returne frō the Seige of *Troy*, cause the fleete of the *Greekes* to be shipwrackt, to reuenge the death of his Sonn *Palamides*, hee sett by night, torches in forme of a beacon vpon one of the mountaines of his Island, at the foote whereof, the Sea was full of bankes, cliffes, and rockes, so to drawe their shipps by the hope of a safe hauen, to runn, hazard and perish in those shores. Soe when antient heretickes, whom saint AVGVSTINE calls, *mountaines for Shipwracke*, would cause the Catholickes to make shipwracke in Faith, the more their doctrines haue bene pernicious and mortall, the more they haue adorned and illustrated them, with texts and lampes of the scripture: This appeares in the heresie of the *Arrians*, who painted and coloured their error with more then fortie passages of the Bible, and by this art attempted to call men backe from the externall and sensible markes of the Church, which could not bee pretended by false ensignes, by those who had them not, to reduce them to the only marke of the scripture, the interpretation whereof, by their subtletie they made subiect to as manie deceipts as there were wordes. But aboue all this is verified in the writer, from whom his Maiestie borrowes this language, who was one of the most passionate Champions of the *Arrians*, For though he cites these wordes without naming the Father, neuerthelesse, both the termes wherein they are couched, and the tracke of those who haue alleadged them before him; to witt, *Caluin* in some of the prefaces to his institution, & the author of the Booke of the Eucharist, in the preface to his worke, cannot suffer vs to doubt, but that they were taken from the author of the worke intituled *Imperfect*; falselie attributed to Sainct CHRYSOSTOME. Now that this Author was not onelie an open Arrian, but one of the most eager and violent Champions of the Arrians; it appeares by this, that he calls the

Author oper imperf in Matth. hom. 19.

Trinitie; triangular impietie and *the doctrine of the homousians* (that is to saie, of those that held the *Consubstantialitie* of the Father and the sonne) *Heresie*. Not but that I knew well, that he is sometimes alleadged euen by Catholickes, with the title of saint CHRISOSTOME, vnder whose name he had bene first printed at *Basle*. But because it is one thinge to alleadge him in places where hee disputes not against the Church, wherein he is excellent, and aboue all in the discourse of manners, and an other to alleadge him in the places, where hee combates with deliberate purpose against the doctrine of the Catholicke Church of his age, as he doth in that, from whence the words are taken which his maiestie produceth. For behold the expresse termes of the passage; *When you shall see the impious heresie, which is the armie of Antichrist sett in the holie places of the Church; then let them which are in Iudea, flie into the Mountaines; that is to saie, let them that are in the christian Societie, haue recourse to the scriptures*. And a little after; *The Lord then knowinge, that so great a confusion of things should arriue in the last daies; for this cause commaunds that the Christians, who are in the Christian Societie, being willing to receaue the stedfastnes of the true faith, should haue recourse to noe other thing but to the Scriptures; otherwise, if they cast their eyes elsewhere, they shall be scandalized and perish, not discerning which is the true Church*. Now that by this impious heresie, and by this Armie of Antichrist, he intends the Catholicke Church, and the communion of them, which beleeue the equalitie of the Father and the sonne, he plainelie shewes when he saith in the same Homilie; that *the great spirituall euills which haue come vpon the Church haue happened in the time of Constantine and Theodosius, and that the armie of Antichrist is the heresie and the abhomination of desolation, which hath since them possest the holie places of the Church*; that is to saie, the Basilickes that *Theodosius* cōmaunded to be deliuered vp to the Catholickes; And whē he saith in the former Homilie, that *the heresie of the Homousians* (that is to saie, of those that hold Christ to be consubstantiall which his Father) *Fights not only against the Church of Christ, but euen against the other heresies which hold not the like*. And in the nineteneth Homilie, when hee calls the worshippers the Trinitie; *Those that honor the triangular impietie*. Whereby it appeares, that this passage if so farre from giuing fauour to his Maiesties intention, as contrariwise it manifestes how dangerous a thing it is to seeke to reduce the markes of the Church, to the onelie doctrine drawne from the scripture by the interpretation of euerie particular person, since the *Arrians* in the point which of all others should be most expresse in the scriptures for the catholickes; to witt, in the point of the diuinitie of Christ; for if there be anie thing cleree in a Testament, it should be the qualitie of the testator; refused all the other markes of the Church, and all the other waies of disputation, and burnt with desire to fight by the onely texts of the Scripture, disarmed from the traditions of the Church.

Author. oper. imperf in Matth. hom. 49.

Eus[e]b. de vit. Const. l. 3. Author oper. imperf hom. 48.

Of the vnderstanding of these words of S. Augustine: to seeke the Church in the words of Christ.

CHAP. XVIII.

The continuance of the Kings answere.

AND to seeke (according to the Councell that S. AVGVSTINE heretofore gaue to the *Donatists*) the Church in the Words of Christ.

THE REPLIE:

WHEN S. AVGVSTINE said in the booke, of the vnitie of the Church, *there is a question betweene the Donatists and vs, where the Church is; what shall wee then doe: shall wee seeke her in our owne wordes, or in the wordes of her head, our* Lord *Iesus Christ: I thinke wee ought rather to seeke her in his word from him that is truth, and well knowes his owne Bodie:* And a while after: *I would not haue the Church demonstrated by humane instructions but by diuine oracles.* And againe: *Let vs then seeke her in the canonicall scriptures.* He did not intend, that to seeke the Church in the scriptures, betweene the Catholicks and the *Donatists*, was to seeke the doctrine of the Church in the scriptures; that is to saie, to examin by the scriptures the point of doctrine, which was contested betweene the Church and the *Donatists*; but to seeke the markes, and externall and visible characters of the Church in the scriptures; to the end, that the Church being discerned by those markes the truth of the doctrine contested, might be after knowne by the disposition of the Church. For the vnderstanding whereof it must be noted, that there were two questions betweene the Catholickes and the *Donatistes*; the one, of the Bodie of the Church, to know on what party either of the Catholickes, or of them, the true societie of the Church resided: The other, of the doctrine of the Church; to witt, the which they, or the Catholickes held the true doctrine, concerning the Baptisme of heretickes. The first question then, which is, of the Bodie of the Church, saint AVGVSTINE wills it should be iudged by the scripture alone, for as much as in the precise controuersie, wherein the question was, which of the two societies was the Church, the voice of the true Church cannot be discerned. But the second question, which is that of the doctrine contested betweene the Catholicks and the *Donatists*, he would haue it decided by the onlie deposition of the Church, as a faithfull guardian and depositarie of the Apostolicke tradition. To seeke then according to saint AVGVSTINE betweene the Catholickes and the *Donatists* the Church in the Scriptures, was not to search the doctrine of the Church in the contentious points of Faith in the Scripture, but to seeke the visible markes and notes by which the Church ought to be exteriorly discerned in the Scripture. For the *Donatists* to proue that their Church was the true Church, and not the Catholicke Church, alleadged human actes, and human proofes, to witt, that the Catholicke Church had receaued into her communion, without anie expiation,

Aug. de vnit. Eccles. c.2.

Ibidem c.3

Ibidem

and purgation of preceding pennance, those that had deliured the holie Bookes to be burnt, and had sacrificed to the false Gods in the time of persecution; and therfore that she was polluted with their contagion, and was perished. And then that the onely faction of *Donatus* which had remained pure from this contagion, was the true Church. And saint AVGVSTINE contrariwise saith, that against all these words, which were human proofes and words; for if he that ordained *Cecilianus*, had deliuered vp the holy Bookes in persecution time, it was a thing to be proued by human testimonies, that is to saie, by actes of notaries and clerkes euen prophane; the Catholickes had the wordes of Christ, wherein the workes of the Church were described, to witt, that she ought to be visible, eminent, vniuersall, perpetuall, and that to examin the Church according to these markes it was to seeke her in the words of Christ: and to examine her according to the production of the *Donatists*, it was to seeke her in humane wordes, *What are*, saith hee, *our words wherein wee must not seeke her*; &c. *All that wee obiect one against an other of the deliuerie of the holie Bookes, of the sacrificing to Idolls, and of the persecutions; those are our wordes*. And a while after; *I would not, that the Church should be demonstrated by human instructions; but by diuine oracles: for if the holie Scriptures haue designed the Church to be in Africa, alone, and in a smalle number of Roman inhabitants, making their conuenticles in Rockes and mountaines, and in the howse and territorie of a certaine Spanish Ladie; then whatsoeuer records can be produced, there are none but the Donatists that haue the Church. If the Scripture assigne it to a little number of Mauritanians, in the Cesarian prouince; you must goe to the Rogatists. If in a smalle troupe of Bizacenians and Tripolitans & prouincialls, the Maximinianists haue mett with her. If those of the East alone, wee must seeke her amongst the Arrians, Macedonians, Eunomians, and others, if there be others; for who can number the heresies, as proper and particular of euerie particular Prouince? But if by the diuine and most certaine testimonies of the Canonicall scriptures, she be designed in all nations, whatsoeuer they produce, and whensoeuer it be produced by those that saie, there is Christ, if wee be sheepe, let vs rather heare the voice of our Shepheard saying, beleeue them not. For euerie one of those is not to be found, but this which is ouer all, is to bee found in the selfe same places, where the others are. And therefore lett vs seeke her in the holie Canonicall scriptures.* The places thē of the scripture, where S. AVGVSTINE would haue the Donatists to seeke the Church, are these. *In thy seede, all the nations vpon the earth shalbe blessed, The children of the forsaken shalbe in much greater number, then those of her, that hath a husband. This Ghospell must be declared ouer the whole world, and then the end shall bee. I am with you to the consummation of ages*: And other such like. And the arguments that he bringes to manifest the Church by the Scriptures are these: *The cittie of God*, saith he, *hath this for a certaine marke, that she cannot be hidden: she is thē knowne to all nations; the sect of Donatus is vnknowne to manie nations, then that is not shee*. Item. *You haue the Church which ought to be spread ouer all, and to growe till the haruest. You haue the Cittie, whereof hee that built it hath said, the Cittie built vpon the mountaine cannot be hidd. It is she then that is most euident, not in anie one part of the world, but ouer all*. And other the like. But as for the point of doctrine; I saie againe, and I saie it boldlie, that saint AVGVSTINE neuer intended, either that the question of the Church betweene the Catholiques and the *Donatists*, should be tryed by the doctrine, nor that the article of the doctrine contested betweene thē should be decided by scripture, but that the point of the Church, should be examined by the externall and visible markes, that of the externall and visible markes, by the Scripture, and the difference of doctrine, by the reporte of the Church, that is to saie, by the tradition of the Apostles

Aug. de vnit Eccl. c. 2. Ibid. c. 3.

Ibid. c. 7. & 19. & ep. 165. Ibidem. Ibid. c. 15. & ep. 165. & ep. 48. Idem in Io tract. 102. & contra litter. Petil. l. 3. c. 50 Aug. contr. litt. Petil l. 2. c. 104. Idem de vnit. Eccl. c. 26.

is to denie, that in disputatiōs against other heresies, whē pointes are handled which are heere esteemed to be expressedlie treated of by the canonicall Scriptures, but that hee often called vpon their iudgment. For who doubtes but that where the Scripture is cleere & expresse, wee must haue recourse thereto? But wee said that he neuer thought, neither in generall that all things belonging to Religion, were treated off in scripture, nor in particular, that the contention betweene the Catholickes and the *Donatists*, concerning Baptisme, was of that quality. And wee maintaine, that for soe manie yeares, wherein hee combated with them about this article when there was question of Searching the cause to the bottome, hee neuer produced one proofe out of Canonicall scripture. Indeede, he hath often alleadged places of Scripture, to make some approaches to it, and to beate downe certaine defences, to solue by scripture the arguments that the Donatists brought out of Scripture, to maintaine that the custome of the Church in the point contested was according to Scripture, in as much as (*According*) signifies not against the Scripture, to establie generall theses and preparatiues, to proue the propositions that had some simpathy and affinitie with that which hee disputed. As for example, he doth indeede proue by scripture, that what is found and intire amongst heretickes, must not be repeated againe, when they returne to the Church; but that Baptisme is found and intire amongst them, he doth noe were proue by Scripture. He proues indeede by Scripture, that there may be ecclesiasticall thinges out of the Church, but that Baptisme is of that number, he nether doth nor can proue by Scripture. He proues indeede by scripture, that it is against the commaundement of God, if heretickes haue receaued the Baptisme of Christ in their owne partie, to rebaptise them; for wee also reade that our Lord answered Sainct PETER. *Hee that is wholie washt, neede washe but his feete*: But that heretickes receiue the Baptisme of Christ in their Sects, and not a polluted and prophane washing, which is all the knott of the question, he noe were proues by scripture. For as hee notes elsewhere, *Peter* of whom this is written, had not bene baptised by heretickes, he prooues indeede by scripture, that they who are out of the interior and Spirituall vnitie of the Church as *Judas* and wicked Catholickes, doe not for that leaue to conferr true Baptisme, but that they who are neither inwardlie nor outwardlie in the Church, who are out of the vnitie of the profession of Faith, and of the communion of the Sacraments of the ecclesiasticall bodie, can conferr it, he proues noe where by scripture. And in Summe, the thinges which belong to the Solutions of arguments to probable and coniecturall preparatiues, to shewes of possibilitie and non repugnancie, to soften and dispose the spiritt of the Readers, he doth indeede prooue by scripture, but the impression of the last forme, the assumption and hypothesis of the sillogisme, the proofe of this precise and speciall point, that Baptisme whereof Sainct IOHN cryes, *None may receaue anie thinge except it be giuen him from heauen*; That Sainct PETER saith *to be administred into remission of Sinnes*, That Sainct PAVL calls *the washing of regeneration, and the renewing of the holie Ghost*, and whereof hee writes, *One faith, and one Baptisme*. And againe; *All they that are baptized haue put on Christ*, That this Sacrament I saie, may be conferred out of the Church, which is the fullnes of Christ, which is the sealed Fountaine, which is the only dwelling of the holie Ghost, which is shee alone that hath

Aug. de Bapt. contr Donat. l. 2. 7.

Augu. de gust cum Emerit. & cont. Cresc l. 1. c. 30. Id. de Bapt. contra Donat. l. 4. c, 6. & alibi

Aug. contr. Cresc. l. 1. c 31. Idem de vnit. Eccl. c. 18.

Act. 2. Ad tit 3. Ephes 4. Galat. 3.

receiued the keyes, and the authoritie to remitt sinnes, that this can subsist amongst hereticks, who haue neither faith nor guift from heauen, nor the holie Ghost: you can neuer finde that in soe maine yeares as saint AVGVSTINE the principall opposite and ouerthrowe of this heresie hath contested her, he hath neuer manifested, nor could hee, nor he hath not pretended to proue by anie passage of Scripture, but by the only vnwritten traditions of the Apostles, and the generall practise and vniuersall attestation of the Church. *Wee must* (saith hee) *obserue in these thinges what the Church of God obserues; The question now betweene you and vs is, which of yours or ours, is the Church of God.* And againe; *Wherefore, although in truth there be noe example to be produced of this out of the canonicall Scripture, yet we leaue not to maintaine euen in this case, the truth of the Scriptures, when we obserue what hath bene approued by all that Church, that the authoritie of the canonicall Scripture recommendeth.* And in an other place; *This is neither openlie nor euidentlie read neither by you nor by me &c. But if anie one indued with wisdome and recommended by the testimonie of our Lord Iesus Christ, were to be found in the world and that hee had bene consulted by vs vpon this question, wee ought noe waie to doubt to doe what he should tell vs, for feare of being iudged repugnant, not so much to him, as to our Lord Jesus Christ by whose testimonie hee had bene recommended; Now he giues testimonie to his Church* And in the worke of Baptisme against the same *Donatists*: *The Apostles* (saith hee) *haue prescribed nothing in this matter, but this custome ought to be beleeued to haue taken the originall thereof, from their tradition, as there are manie thinges which the vniuersall Church obserues, and which are therefore, not without cause beleeued to haue bene commaunded by the Apostles, although they be not written.* From whence, the contrarie appeares to what his maiestie pretends to inferr from this passage; to witt, that the scripture only destitute of the vnwritten Apostolicke tradition, cannot decide all pointes of Faith nor refute all heresies. For the point in agitation betweene the Catholicks and the *Donatists* concerning the truth & realitie of the baptisme giuen by hereticks, was a point of faith, and wherein obstinate error would make an heresie. The proofe of this is, first that the doctrine of Baptisme importes so much to the faith, as where there is noe true baptisme, there is noe true Church: S. PAVL teaching vs, *that God clenseth his Church through the washing of water in the word.* Now there where the Church is destroyed, there is destroyed this article of the Faith of the Creede; *I beleeue the holie Catholick Church.* And secondlie, that the vnitie of Baptisme belonges so to faith, as S. PAVL saith; *there is one faith, and one Baptisme.* And that the creede of *Cōstātinople* setts amōgst the Articles of the Confession of the Faith: *We confesse one baptisme in the remission of sinns*: in such sort as if the Donatists erred in disanulling the baptisme of heretickes, and rebaptizing them, they destroyed the faith of the vnitie of baptisme, and anathematised the character of Christ, which had alreadie bene imprinted in the baptized by baptisme. And if the Catholicks erre in approuing the baptisme of heretickes, and in not rebaptisinge them when they came to them, they sinned against the Faith of the necessitie of Baptisme for the constitution of the Church, and consequently had noe Church. And neuerthelesse, neither could this point of Faith be proued, nor the contrarie heresie confuted by Scripture, only destitute of the helpe of tradition. And although *Optatus Mileuitus* in the beginning had attempted it; neuerthelesse, the successe hath made saint AVGVSTINE (who hath gone further in this question) see and confesse, that to compose it, there was a necessitie of hauing recourse to the vnwritten Apostolicke tradition. And what saint AVGVSTINE alleadgeth in generall against *Petilianus* must not be obiected against this, If anie one

Idem de vnit. Eccl. c. 19

Idem de Bapt. contr. Donat. l. 5. c. 23.

Ephes. 5.

Ephes. 4.

Cōc. Const 1.

Aug. contr. lit. Petil. l. 3 c. 6.

of Christ, or of the Church, or of ought belonging to the faith or to life, declare further then this that you haue receaued in the legall and Euangelicall scriptures, let him be anathema. For himselfe declares elsewhere, as it shall appeare hereafter that this word of S. PAVL *further*, signifies against, or to the preiudice of: *The Apostle* (saith hee) *hath not said*, more then, *but*, further, *for if he had said*, more then, *hee had condemned himselfe, He that desired to come to the Thessalonians to supplie what was wanting in their Faith. Now hee that supplies, adds that which was not in the thing, but takes not awaie what was therein before.*

Of the vnderstanding of the words of S. Chrysostome in the thirtie third homilie vpon the Acts.

CHAP. XIX.

The continuance of the Kinges answere,

EVEN soe S. CHRISOSTOME, as well elsewhere as of deliberate purpose in the thirtie third homilie vpon the Acts, handling this question, how the true Church may be discerned amongst manie Societies, which attribute this name to themselues, doth teach that there are two instruments to iudge and decide this question: First the word of God, and afterward the antiquitie of the doctrine, not inuented by anie late bodie, but alwaies knowne since the beginning of the Church, when she was but breeding.

THE REPLIE.

THERE are fowre obseruations to be made vpon this Article; the first, that sainct CRYSOSTOME giues not this Rule to discerne the true Church from all societies that differ from her in what point soeuer; but onlie to discerne her from those, that differ from her, in the point of Christs diuinitie; wherein it is noe wonder if the scripture be more cleere and expresse then in anie other. The second, that this marke to discerne the Church, he giues not to those, that are alreadie preoccupated with the opinion of anie of the Christian sects but to the Pagans which were not anticipated with passion, for anie of the parties that combated about the pointes of Christs diuinitie, and for this reason might seeme to iudge the more impartiallie. The third, that sainct CHRYSOSTOMES ayme is not to treate seriouslie there, of the markes of the Church with the Pagans, but to stopp their mouthes; and to shew, that whereas they said, that they would turne Christians, but that they knew not on which part to range themselues: these were but pretences, and not true language. The fowrth, that hee stopps not there, but acknowledging that this meanes, because of the subtletie and shiftes of hereticks, is not sufficient, requires and exactes an other, that is to saie, that hee reduceth in the last instance, all the summe of the question, to this point; that, that is the true Church which hath remained stedfast and immutable in her communion, and from whence all the others are gone forth, and that came forth from none. *A Pagan* (saith hee) *comes and saith, I would turne Christian, but I know not to whom I ought to adhere; for there are amongst you manie strifes, seditions, and tumultes, I know not which opinion I should choose, nor which I ought to preferr; euerie one saith, I followe* Chrysost. in Act. ho 33.

the truth; whom shall I (that am vtterlie ignorant in the Scriptures) beleeue, seeing both sides, (as well the Catholickes, as the Sects of the *Arrians*, as it shall appeare heereafter) *protest the same thinge? That certainly* answereth hee, *makes much for vs; for if wee saie wee must beleeue reasons, thou shalt not without cause be troubled; but if wee saie, wee must beleeue the Scriptures, and they be simple and true, it is easie for thee to iudge thereof; if anie one conforme himselfe to them, he is a Christian; if anie striue against them, he is farr from this rule. But what will become of it,* saith the Gentile, *if the other coming also, saie the scripture affirmes this thinge, and thou saist it affirmes an other thinge, and that you wrest the scripture into diuers parts each drawing the vnderstanding of the words thereof to his owne side? &c. Then,* saith S. CHRISOSTOME, *we will inquire of the Pagan, if what he saith, be pretences and excuses, and aske him, if he condemne the Gentiles? Hee must saie some thinge, for he will not desire to come to vs, till first he condemne them; wee will aske him then for what cause he condemnes them; for he will not condemne them without cause. It is manifest that he will saie, because their Gods are Creatures, and are not the vncreated God. This is well answere wee, for if this bee found in other heresies* (a clause which euidently shewes, that he spoke onely of those heresies which opposed, the deitie of Christ, which were those wherewith the East was afflicted) *and wee affirme the contrarie, what neede more words? Wee all confesse that Christ is God, but see who combats against it, and who combates not against it; wee call him God, and pronounce of him thinges worthie of God; that he hath power, that he is not seruile, that he is free, that he doth all thinges of himself; and they the contrary.* And then finallie, seeing that this attempt succeeded not sufficiently; *It is not possible,* saith hee, *but he that heares without preoccupation, should be perswaded; For as if there were a Rule according to which all thinges should be squared, there were noe neede of great consideration, but it would be easie to discerne him that should make wrye lines; Euen see is it nowe: But wherefore then, would he saie, doe they not see it? Preiudication and human causes doe manie thinges: that replies hee, they saie also of vs. And how can they saie it? for wee haue not seperated ourselues, nor haue made noe schisme, nor diuision in the Church; Wee haue noe heresiarchs, wee name not ourselues after the name of anie man. wee haue noe leaders, as to one Marcion, to an other Manicheus, to an other Arius, to an other, an other heresi-founder. But if wee take the appellatiō of anie particular, it is not from those that began anie heresie, but of those that preside ouer vs, and gouerne the Church: Wee haue noe doctors vpon earth, God forbid, wee haue one alone in heauen. This also will hee saie, the others likewise affirme it, but the name that they beare* (answereth hee to witt, of *Marcionites*, or of *Manichees* or of *Arrians*) *conuinceth them and stopps their mouthes.* By which words it appeares, that the last analysis and resolution of the question, is all determined in this point; that, that is the true Church, which hath remained vnmouable and stedfast in her communion, & from whom all the others haue gone forth, and is gone forth from none; which is also the marke that S. AVGVSTINE giues it when he saith. *The Catholicke Church combating against all heresies, may be opposed but she cannot be ouerthrowne, all heresies are come forth from her, as vnprofitable branches cutt off from their Vine, but she remaines in her vine, in her roote, in her Charitie.* And S. PACIAN Bishop of *Barcelona* before him, when he writes. *Now to knowe whether she hath bene principallie built vpon the foundation of the prophetts, and of the Apostles in Iesus Christ the corner stone: Consider whether she began before thee, whither she hath growne before thee: if she be not withdrawne from her first foundation: whether in separating herselfe from the rest of the Bodie, she haue not constituted to herselfe her Masters and her particular instructions: if she haue argued anie thing vnaccustomedlie: if she haue formed anie point of new right, if she haue declared to her Bodie the diuorce of peace, then lett her be esteemed to be departed from Christ, and to be constituted*

[Margin: Chrysost. ibidem.]

[Margin: August. de Symbol. ad Cathec. l. 1 c. 5.]

[Margin: Pacian. ad Sympron. ep. 3.]

tuted forth of the prophetts and Apostles. And therefore, although the point of the assentiall deitie of Christ, deserue to be more cleerelie exprest in Scripture, then anie other, as the qualitie of the Testator, ought to bee more cleerelie exprest in the Testament, then anie other; neuerthelesse, for as much as the heretickes by their malice and subtletie, shift off the places of Scripture alleadged to this purpose; the Fathers after they had tried all their strength to bring them backe to reason by Scripture, were constrained (seeing they could not make them yeeld vp their weapons by that waie) to chāge their battery, & haue recourse to the authoritie of the Church. *Behold* (saith saint ATHANASVS) *wee haue shewed the succession of our doctrine from father to sonn; you new Cayphas what Progenitors of your phrases and your termes, will you bringe vs?* And saint HILARIE: *Lett vs consider soe manie holie fathers; what will become of vs if wee anathematize them? for we bringe thinges to this point, that if they haue not bene Bishops, we are none, since we haue bene ordained by them.* And the same saint ATHANASIVS: *It is sufficient that these things are not of the Catholicke Church, and that the Fathers were not of that beleefe*. From whence it appeareth, that if the point of Christs diuinitie had neuer bene exprest in Scripture, they held the light of the perpetuall testimonie of the Church for a sufficient proofe of this article. For whereas saint CHRISOSTOME compares the Scripture to a Rule, according whereto all things should be squared; besides this that, according signifies there not against, he inteds that Scriptures rule all thinges either mediately, or immediately; that is to saie, either by it selfe, or by the meanes whereto it remitts vs, as hee testifies himselfe in these wordes; *From whence it appeares, that the Apostles deliuered not all thinges in vriting, but also manie thinges vnwritten: Now either of these are worthie of equall credit*.

Athan. in Decret. Synod. Nicen. contr. Arian.

Hilar. de Synod.

Athan. ep. ad epitect. contra hæret.

Chrysost. in 2 ad Thessal. c. 2.

Of the Rules to iudge admitted by sainct Chrysostome and S. Augustine.

CHAP. XX.

The continuance of the Kings answere.

THese two Rules to iudge, the King with the English Church embracing them with an earnest desire, pronounceth that hee acknowledgeth that doctrine finallie both to be true, and also necessarie to saluation; that running from the Springe of the holie Scripture by the consent of the ancient Church, as by a channell hath bene deriued downe to this time.

THE REPLIE.

NEither doe saint CHRISOSTOME and saint AVGVSTINE restraine the meanes to iudge of all the doctrine of the Church to these two onelie meanes, by exclusion of the third, to witt, of Apostolicke Tradition, since saint AVGVSTINE saith, *this is plainelie read neither by thee nor by me*. And againe, *The Apostles haue prescribed nothing in this, yet the custome opposit to Cyprian ought to bee beleeued to haue taken originall out of their tradition, as it is in manie thinges that the vniuersall Church, doth obserue: And for this cause indeede well beleeued to haue bene commaunded by the Apostles though they haue not bene written; And that saint*

Augu. de vnit. Eccl. c. 19.

Idem de baptism contr. Donat. l. 5. c. 23.

CHRYSOSTOME *saith that from thence it appeares, that the Apostles haue not giuen all thinges in writinge, but some also without writinge; whereof both sortes, are in like manner worthie of creditt.* And elsewhere; *It is not in vaine, that the Apostles haue giuen it by tradition, to offer sacrifice for the dead; they know how much aduantage and profitt encreaseth to them thereby.* Neither is the question in the disputation which is now handled betweene his maiestie and vs, of the examination of the right, but of the examination of the fact, that is to saie, wee are not to inquire by conferring the conclusions of Faith with their principles, which of the *English* doctrine or ours, is the truth, which is a question of right, whose triall, besides that it must be long, goes out of the listes, & frō the state of the questiō that we treate of. But to inquire by the continuāce & cōformitie with the auncięt Catholicke Church, whether our Church be the same Church as was in the time of S. AVGVSTINE and of the fowre first Councells, which is a question of fact; in which must be handled, not what ought to be beleeued, but what hath bene beleeued. For his maiestie being of agreement, that there was an obligation of communicatiō with the antient Catholicke Church, which flourisht in the time of the foure first Councells, and that whosoeuer was separate from the communion of that Church, was an hereticke or a Schismaticke: And the question is whether I might except from the praises of his maiestie the title of Catholicke, which is the first cause of this comparison consisting in the knowing not whether the Church of those ages, had beleeued well or euill, which is a question of right; but whether the Church of the last ages, from which his maiestie, or those that haue bene before him, haue separated themselues be the same Church by an vninterrupted succession both of persons and of doctrine, as that was in the time of S. AVGVSTINE, which is a question of fact, and capable of being proued by historie alone, soe as the subtletie of spiritts can finde noe shift for it now, to leape from the question of fact, to the question of right; And in steede of examining, whether the Catholicke Church of this time, had the same beleefe in the pointes controuerted betweene vs and our aduersaries, as the Church in the time of the foure first Councells had: to dispute whether the Church of those ages hath beleeued well, and with what reseruations and mollifications her beleefe must be receiued, it is to goe forth from the state of the question, and to change the order and meanes of the disputation.

Of the application of the Thesis of this obseruation to his Hipothesis.

CHAP. XXI.

The continuance of the Kinges answere

Then to make an end of this discourse, the king answeres to the first obseruation, that it can not be applied to the Hipothesis proposed, without manie defects. For so farr is this *English* Church from hauing departed from the faith of the ancient Catholicke Church, which she honours and reuerences, as she is not so much as departed from the Faith of the *Roman*, Church, in as much as she consents with the Catholicke Church.

THE REPLIE:

I Appeale from *Phillip* to *Phillip*; that is to saie, from the most excellent King, to himselfe: for what doth my first obseruation import; yea, according to the abridgement that this maiestie hath made of it, but *that the name of Catholicke doth not only denote faith, but also communion with the Catholick Church; and therefore, that the antient Writers, would not suffer those to be called Catholickes, who had separated themselues from the communion of the Church, although they retained the Faith thereof*: Now, how then is it, that the most excellent King alleadgeth to shewe, that this obseruation cannot be applied to his Hypothesis, without manie errors, that he is not departed, neither hee nor his Church, from the faith of the antient Church? For the obseruation wherein it is handled being, that to be Catholicke, it is not sufficient not to be separate from the Church of the Catholicke faith; but also not to be separated from the communion of the Catholicke Church: is it not fufficient to applie it to the Hipothesis, and to except the most excellent Kinge from the title of Catholicke, that his Maiestie hath separated himselfe, not from the Faith, if soe be he had not done soe but frō the onlie cōmunion of the Catholicke Church? And if the most excellent King saith, that she from whom he hath separated himself, is not the same Catholicke Church as she was in the time of the Fathers, and of whom the Fathers said, that out of her communiō the title of Catholicke, nor the reward of saluation could not be obtained must he not shew that there is an alteration happened in thinges which are of the essence of the Church, and without which the verie being of the Church cannot be preserued: and besides this, that he must finde out and cause to appeare, an other societie, wherein the succession of the doctrine and of the ministrie, both of the communion and of the prerogatiues of the antient Catholieke Church hath continued, and whereto he hath ranged himselfe; to the end that adhering thereto, he may saie, that he hath not separated himselfe from the communion of the antient Catholicke Church, but is returned into it?

Of the personall succession of the Bishops.

CHAP. XXII.

The Continuance of the Kings Answere.

IF wee seeke for the succession of persons, wee haue in being the name of Bishops, and the succession vninterrupted from the first.

THE REPLIE.

IT sufficeth not to constitute the personall successiō of Bishops that some are entred, in the steede of others; but they must bee entred with the same forme, and with the same conditions essentiall to a Bishopricke, that their predecessors entred withall. Noe more then it sufficeth to make the Priests of *Jerobo ā* Successors to the true Leuiticall Priests that he had driuen awaie that they came into theirplaces, not being come in with cōditions necessarie to succeede thē.

And therefore whether the mission of the Bishops which are at this daie in *England*, be a true ecclesiasticall mission, & made by ecclesiasticall authoritie, and with the iust ecclesiasticall formes, or rather a politick mission, I forbeare to dispute. Onlie I will saie, that there are two kindes of successions in the personall continuance of a Bishops Sea, the one, the succession of authoritie; and the other, the succession of the character. Whereof it is cleere, that the *English* according to the principles commõ to them and vs, haue not the one; and it is euidēt, that according to their owne particular principles, they cannot haue the other. For there doe meete together or concurr according to vs, two conditions in Episcopall mission; the one concerning the collation of authoritie, the other concerning the impression of the character, which comes from the part of the sacrament of order, which wee conceaue to imprint a Seale, which cannot be blotted out. Now the condition which concernes the character, which we will heere call sacramentall mission, may well be preserued out of the Church, for as much as the character cannot be blotted out, and consequently may be giuen, though vnlawfullie, yet reallie out of the Church, by them that haue carried it out of the Church. But that which cõcernes authoritie, which wee will call, notwithstanding the barbarisme of the word, authoritatiue missiõ, although it cānot be giuen in the Church without the other, yet it cannot be carried awaie nor giuen with the other out of the Church, and may be taken awaie by the Church from them, to whom she hath giuen it, when she shall iudge it necessarie to depose or degrade them. As the Councell of *Sardica* deposed *Narcissus*, *Menophantus*, and others, who notwithstanding, left not to preserue the character of the sacrament euen as the officers of a prince, when they ioyne themselues with a faction of rebells, may carry with them the Seale and the character of the Patent of their offices, and preserue it out of the state, and out of the common wealth; but they cannot carrie awaie the authoritie of their office with them. And therefore, when they that haue bene degraded by the Church, or ordained out of the Church returne to the Church, the lawfull authoritie to exercise their function must be restored to them, either by a particular rehabilitation, or by a publicke declaration that the Churches makes to receaue them into her communiõ with the exercise of their charges, which serues them for a generall rehabilitation: As when the *Arrians* returned to the Catholicke faith, the Church restored to their Bishops, the lawfull authoritie to administer the Bishop ricks whereof the ecclesiasticall lawes had depriued them, and rehabilitated them all at once, by the publicke declaration that she made to admitt them with the function of their charges. Ftom whence it appeares, that they that are ordained out of the Church, and by an other societie then by the true Church, although they be indeede Bishops as for the Character of the Sacrament, neuerthelesse, they are not Bishops, as for the function of authoritie; and as manie times as they shall pretend to vse their authoritie without being rehabilitated by the Church, soe often they commit sinn and sacriledge. *Let vs consider*, (saith S. HILARY, speaking of the Fathers of the Coũcell of *Nicea*) *what wee doe doe, wee that anathematize them, &c, For if they haue not bene Bishops we cā be none*. And S. ATHANASIVS; *It is impossible that the ordination of Secũdus as made by the Arriās, should haue anie force in the Catholicke Church*. And S. HIEROME; *There are at this daie noe Bishops in the world, sauing those that were ordained by the Synod*. And the lawe of the Emperors, speaking of the Bishops of the hereticks; *It is vnlawfull that they should make ministers, who are none themselues*. Whereby they doe not intend, that the Bishops

Hilar. de Synod. Athan. Apol. 2. Hier. contr Lucifer.

of

of hereticks who haue drawne their character from the Church, be not Bishops, as for the impression of the character, but that they are none as for the imposition of the authoritie. By meanes whereof, the *English* Bishops can pretend noe Episcopall succession from the Church of the antient Fathers, as for the succession of authoritie, for as much as if the Catholicke Church which was in *England* and in other places, when king *Henry* the eigth came to the crowne, were not the true Catholicke Church, the Bishops of the Catholicke communion, were not true and lawfull Bishops, as concerning authoritie, but only as concerning the character; and by consequence neither had themselues the succession of Episcopall authoritie, nor could transmitt it to those that haue taken it from them. *By what right* (saith sainct ATHANASIVS speaking of the *Arrians*) *can they be Bishops, if they haue bene ordained by those men, which themselues doe slander with heresie?* And contrariwise if the Church that was at the beginning of King *Henry* the eigth throughout *Europe*, and in manie other partes of the world, were the true Church, this selfe-same Church, hauing disannulled the episcopall authoritie in those from whom the *English* at this daie pretend to haue had their mission, and hauing deposed and anathematized them, they had no more lawfull episcopall authoritie & by consequéce could not cōferr it to others. And besides, if that Church were the true Church, the English Church at this daie which is gone out from her communion, can not be so, nor preserue in her the succession of Episcopall authoritie, which cannot be transferred out of the Church. And for the succession of the character the *English*, according to their doctrine, can in noe secte pretend to it; for they hold not (& if they would hold, they cannot doe it; for as much as they make profession to agree in the faith & in the sacraments with the Protestants of *France*) that order conferrs anie other thing then authoritie, nor that it imprints anie sacramentall character, which is that only, which in mission can be transferred & giuen out of the Church. And so if by their doctrine they could haue the succession of the character, they are fallen frō the right of making vse thereof. For they communicate with the Puritans of *France*, & hold their sheepe for true sheepe, and so their pastors for true pastors, and for their colleagues and fellowe bretheren. Now the ministers of *France*, are not ordained by anie Bishops, and so are noe Bishops, *For hee* (saith saint CYPRIAN) *cannot be a Bishop, who succeeding no bodie, hath bene ordained of himselfe*: And not being Bishops haue noe Church, since as saith the same sainct CYPRIAN, *The Church is in the Bishop, and the Bishop in the Church, and who is not with the Bishop is not in the Church*. By meanes whereof the *English* which communicate with them, and hold them for their colleagues and fellowe bretheren, inuolue themselues into the crime and contagion of all their ecclesiasticall defects: and consequenthe fall from all the rightes whereof those with whom they communicate, are depriued. I add to that, that to shew a Church to be successiuelie and representatiuely the antient Catholicke Church, it sufficeth not to shew that a part of that Church deriueth the personall successiō of her Bishops from the missiō of the antien Catholicke Church but all the Church that will pretéd the inheritāce & successiō of the tittle of catholike, must haue the successiō of her Bishops deriued frō the missiō of the antiēt catholick Church, *For the Bishops Sea is one*, as saith S. CYPRIAN, *whereof euerie one holdes his portiō vndiuidedly*: And elsewhere: *The Church is one, bound togeather by the cement of Bishops, adhering the one to the other*. Now the *English* doe not pretend alone, to cōstitute all the cōmunion of their Church, nor to be all the true and pure visible Catholicke Church, but doe comprehend into

Cypr. ad Magn. ep. 76

Id. ad Florent. Pupp. ep. 69.

Id. de vnit. Eccl.
Id. ad Pupp ep. 69

their communion the Proteſtantes of *France*, as partes of the Bodie of their Church. And therefore they cãnot ſaie, that the Catholicke Church to which they adhere, and wherewith they communicate, to bee by ſucceſſion and perſonall repreſentation, the ſame viſible Catholicke Church which was in the time of the fowre firſt Coũcells. Cõtrariwiſe from this that the other partes of the communion to which the *Engliſh* Church adheres, communicate not by ſucceſſion of perſons with the miſſion of the antient Catholicke Church, and conſequently are at the leaſt ſchiſmatikes; it iſſues that the *Engliſh* which communicate with them, cannot cõmunicate with the antient Catholicke Church for none, except in error of fact, can communicate with the Catholicke Church and with Schiſmatickes together. And finallie I ſaie, that ſince in all queſtions of Schiſmes wee muſt mount vp to the originall, following theſe wordes of ſaint AVGVSTINE to the *Donatiſts: The queſtion betweene you and vs is, where the Church of God ſhould be; wee muſt then begin at the originall, why haue you made a ſchiſme*: The accompt that the *Engliſh* Church will yeeld of the ſucceſſion of her Biſhops, ought to be brought to the originall of the Schiſme. Now therevpon I will aske his Maieſtie, where the firſt, after the riſing vp of *Luther* and *Caluin* began in *England* to ſeparate themſelues from the Catholicke Church, to imbrace other forme of Religion which they now hold, where was this Societie, wherein there was together to be found, both the ſucceſſion of Biſhops vninterrupted from the firſt, and the ſucceſsion of doctrine? For to goe out from the Church, then intituled Catholicke, they muſt range themſelues to an other Church, which muſt haue true doctrine, and true miniſtrie by adherence ad communion, to the which they might preſerue the title of Catholicke, and tranſmitt it to thoſe that ſhould come after them. Now where was then this Societie indued with the true doctrine, and the true ſucceſsion of Biſhops, when the *Engliſh* firſt ſeparated themſelues from the Church intituled Catholike? For I will not inquire who is the firſt, from whom ſhe ſaith that the *Engliſh* Biſhops can ſhew their vninterrupted ſucceſsion, if it be not S. AVGVSTIN Biſhop of *Canterburie*, whom S. GREGORIE ſent thither: Nor will I demaund for the preaching of what doctrine S. GREGORIE ſent him thither, if it were not for the preaching of the ſame doctrine that was there before the laſt ſeparation,

Of the ſucceſſion of doctrine.

CHAP. XXIII.

The continuance of the Kings anſwere.

IF the ſucceſſion of doctrine bee demaunded, lett vs make triall of it.

THE REPLIE:

THERE is great difference betweene ſimilitude of doctrine, and ſucceſsion of doctrine: Similitude of doctrine is a ſimple reporte of agreement betweene one doctrine & an other; but the ſucceſſion of doctrine properly takẽ, is a deriuation of do-

continued by a perpetuall vnintermitted chine of teachers, and persons taught. And therefore, the *Arrians* which are at this daie in *Polonia*, or in *Transilu ania*, may well pretẽd similitude of doctrine without the ancient *Arrians*, which were iu the time of the Councell of *Nicea*, but not Successiõ of doctrine; for as much as their doctrine hath not bene trãsmitted by a liuing perpetuall chaine of teachers and persons taught from the ancient *Arrians*, to them. For as the fire of the high places, was indeede one in similitude with that which came downe from heauen to serne for a beginninge to the fier of the mosaicell sacrifices, but not one in vnitie of Succession, there being but the only fier preserued for this effect in the Altar of *Hierusalem*, which was one in vnity of Succession with that: Soe a subsequent doctrine, may well be one in vnitie of Similitude with a precedent doctrine without anie flux of continuance to haue bene betweene them: but a Subsequent doctrine cannot be one in vnitie of Succession with a preceding doctrine, if it haue not bene deriued from it by a perpetuall channell of instruction, and by an vninterrupted traine of teachers and persons taught, which is that, that the Fathers as wee haue elswhere shewed; call consanguinitie or genealogie of doctrine; to witt a propagation of doctrine. deriued without interruption from Father to sonne, as by a tree of consanguinitie; euen as children are deriued by a perpetuall traine of generation, from their Fathers, from their Grandfathers, and from their great Grandfathers blood. And in this Sence, S. ATHNASIVS after he had combated the *Arrians* by the Scrptures, and acknowledged that their obstinancie made them indocill to his argumentes made vse of the Succession of doctrine: *Behold* (said hee) *wee haue proued the Succession of our doctrine deliuered from hand to hand, from Father to sonn, you new Iewes, and children of Caiphas, what Predecessors can you shew for your words*: And sainct PACIAN against the *Nouatians*: *I holding my self assured vpon the succession of the Church contenting myselfe with the peace of the antient congregation, haue neuer studied discord.* And so whether shee which is at this daie called the *English* Church, haue similitude of doctrine with the Fathers of the first fowre Councells, in the pointes which are in controuersie betweene her and vs, is that which is in question, and which we denie that she can proue; but that she hath succession of doctrine with the Church of the first fowre Councells, is a thing which cannot bee so much as Challenged. For there is noe man that dare saie, that the doctrine that the *English* Church holds at this daie in the points cõtested betweene her and vs, is come by a perpetuall and vninterrupted chaine of teachers and persons taught from the Church in the time of the first fowre Councells vnto her; seeing, that without goeing higher, in the beginning of the Raigne of King *Henry* the eigth she held directlie contrarie to what she holdes now. I omitt to saie that besides the succession of the ministrie and the succession of doctrine, there is an other third succession, which is that of communion, by which from age to age the most Antient in the Societie of the Church receiued into their communion, those that came in after them; and by this continuance and chaine of communion, the faithfull of subsequent ages communicated with them of preceding ages; a thing which can not be betweene the members of the antient Catholicke Church, and the members of her which at this daie calles her selfe the *English* Church, because their Predecessors haue excluded, disinherited and excommunicated them. For not onely in the more antient ages, the generall Bodie of the Catholicke Church, had excommunicated by retaile those which held some one point, other some an other of this Rapsodie of doctrines, which the *Puritans* call reformation, but particularly

Athan. in decret. Synod. Nicen. contra. Arian.
Pacian. contra Parm. ep. 3.

the *English* Church excommunicated in the time of Henry the eigth those, that held the doctrine, that she which is called the *English* Church now holdeth.

Of the holding of a Councell.

CHAP. XXIV.

The Continuance of the Kings Answere.

GIVE vs a free Councell, and which shall not depend of the will of one alone.

THE REPLIE.

IF by the word (alone) his maiestie intends the Pope, what Coũcell was euer more free in this regarde, then the second Councell of *Nicea*, which was celebrated in *Bythinia*, a Prouince of *Asia*, out of the West, and out of the Patriarkshipp of the *Roman* Church, and in an other Empire, and where there were none of all the *Latine* Church, but only two Priests, which represented the Popes person? Or what Councell was euer more free in the same regard, then the Councell off, *Constance*, wherein then when the differences of Faith were treated of because the Papacie was in question, not only the Pope did not assist there, but euen all the three pretended Popes, where deposed? For what was practised against *Iohn Husse* & *Hierome* of *Prage*, after they had againe fallen into the doctrine that they had abiured, was done, the Pope and his competitors in the Papacie, being absent, and while they proceeded in contumacie against him; euen when they publisht the decrees of rhe Superioritie of the Councell aboue the Pope. Or what Councell finallie was euer more free, then the Councell of F*lorence*; whereat there assisted the Emperor of the East, and the Patriarke of the Greeke Church, and a great number of Greeke Bishopps, who all had libertie to determine and giue their voyces; and euen those that gaue them against the commõ opinion of the Councell, persisted in their obstinancie, as *Marke* of *Ephesus* returned safely into their countrey? And neuerthelesse, in those three Councells, there were decided almost all those things, which are at this daie questioned in Christian Religion. For if to make a Councell free, it must be holden in the state of a Prince which fauours neither partie of the contestors, what Councell can be exempt from calumny? For doe not the *Arrians* put it amongst the reproaches of the Councell of *Nicea*, and of the first of *Const:* that they were holden vnder *Constantine* and *Theodosius*, who were abettors of their owne partie, and whose authoritie preuailed there? And did not the *Eutychians* reproach the Councell of *Chalcedon* for the authoritie of the Emperor *Marcian*, that had there fauored (say they) their aduersaries? From whence, euen to this day, they call those that hold the opinion of the Councell of *Chalcedon Melchites*, that is to saie, *Rogalists* or *Imperialists*? but if his maiestie intend by a free Councell, a Councell where the Pope neither assists personalie nor representatiuely; how can it be, that in a time wherein there is no Schisme in the Papacie, a Councell shall perfectly represent the vniuersall

Church, if the visible head of the Church, be neither there personallie, representatiuely, or confirmatiuely? And what will become of those antient *Maximes, That it is not lawfull to rule the Churches, or call the Councells, without the Bishop of Rome?* And againe; *that the ecclesiasticall lawe anulls all decrees made without him in Coũcells.* And then when the conditiõs requisit for the libertie of a Councell shall be resolued vpõ, what fruite cã be drawne from it if it be not agreed before it be assembled, that all that is decreed there, must be holdẽ for infallible? For if after such a Councell shall haue bene celebrated it rest still in the choyce of euery particular person to iudge, whether the Councell shall haue iudged conformablie to the word of God; who knowes not, that this is not to submitt their iudgment to a Councell, but to submitt a Councell to their iudgement, and so to haue things noe further aduanced after the celebration of a Councell, then before? Now how is it that those who hold that the vniuersall Church may erre, should hold that the authoritie of a generall Councell should be infallible, which hath noe authoritie of infallibillitie but in as much as it represents the vniuersall Societie of the visible Church, whereof it is the voice and organ, and of all the pastors, whereof it beares with it the tacit deputation? And how can those hold that the vniuersall Church, should be infallible & cannot erre, that hold, that indeede she hath erred, and that after soe manie ages there was noe visible part of the Church, which hath not bene plunged in a pitt of errors repugnant to saluation, and contrarie to faith? But whether his maiesties offers, ought to be examined in a formall Councell, or in a verball conference, wee are readie to assist at it, and to shew that the English Church in pointes contested betweene vs and her, hath neither Succession, nor Similitude of doctrine with the Church of the time of the first Councells.

Of the reduction of the Disputation, to the State of the Question.

CHAP. XXV

The continuance of the Kinges answere

THe English Church is readie to yeeld an accompt of her Faith, and to proue by effect, that the designe of the Authors of the Reformation, vndertaken in this Prouince, hath not bene to build anie new Church, as the ignorant and malicious haue slandered her, but to re-establish her that was fallen, in the best manner that might bee.

THE REPLIE.

IT is not the question in the proceeding that wee haue framed, to knowe whether the ayme of the Authors of the Reformatiõ of *England*, hath bene to make a new Church; or to restore that, which was fallen, and to sett it vp againe in a better forme; although the subsequent words of his maiestie where he saith, that the action of the *English* Church, hath bene a returne to the ancient Catholick Faith and a conuersion to Christ the onlie master of the Church: testifie that it hath bene a new refection and re-edification of the Church. For noe

it hath bene a new refection and re-edification of the Church. For noe Societie in whose faith there is an auersion from Christ, and from the ancient Catholicke beleefe, can possesse the beeing and the name of a Church. But in Summe, howsoeuer it be, it is not that, that is the question in the proceeding that we haue framed; but only to knowe whether the Catholicke Church, when the *English* portion separated it selfe from her, had so degenerated from the ancient Carholicke Church, which was in the tyme of the first fower Councells, in thinges importing the ruine of Saluation, and the destruction of the being of the Church, as she was noe more the same Church as she had bene in the time of those ages. And consequently, that it was noe more necessarie to obtaine the title of Catholicke, and the participation of Saluation to communicate with her but contrariwise was necessarie to be seperated from her and not to commnnicate with her. It is that, that is the question, it is that whereabout we must combat, and to shewe some condition, some doctrine, or custome, holden in the Catholicke Church at this daie, that may be pretended to be repugnant to saluation, and which destroyes the being of the true Church, that hath not bene in the Catholicke Church, in the time of the fower first Councells.

Of the inuention of order, in the iustification of the reformation before the proofe of the Deformation.

CHAP. XXVI.

The continuance of the Kings answere.

NOw they haue iudged amongst the best that which had bane giuen by the Apostles to the breeding Church, and which had bene in practise in the age neerest them.

THE REPLIE.

NEither is it the question of what they haue iudged, but of the change that is happened betweene the ancient Catholicke Church and the morderne, and of the importance of this change; that is to saie, whether there be happened anie change betweene the estate of the ancient Church, & the estate of the Church of the last ages, of such importance, as for that people might be permitted to separate themselues from her communion. Which cannot be, if some thinge haue not bene taken awaie from the forme of the antient Church, which was necessarie to saluation, or added thereto which was repugnant to saluation. For if the moderne Catholicke Church, were yet the same Church in matters of Faith and saluation, as it was in the time of the fowre first Councells, whatsoeuer reformation they haue pretended to make, hauing separated themselues from her, they cannot possesse the title of Catholicke whereof the question is; nor obtaine saluation. for as much as saith S. IRENEVS; *No reformation can be made that is of such importance, as*

Iren. adu. hæres. l. 4 c. 62.

the crime of schisme is pernicious. Besides *It must bee first determined, whether the Catholick Church were deformed in matters of faith and saluation, before the English Church can be thought to be reformed, in being seperated from her*. For the *English* Church could not seperate herselfe from the Catholick Church whereunto before she was ioyned in communion, if first it did not appeare to her by proofes necessatie and demōstratiue, that saluation could not be obtained in the Catholicke Church: that is to saie, she coulde not proceede to reforme her selfe, in separating herselfe from her whole, till it must first appeare to her: that the whole from whence she separated her selfe, were deformed and with a deformation incompatible with saluatiō. Now that could not appeare, that betweene the antient Catholicke Church of the time of the first fowre councells (which wee on both sides graunt to be the true Church, and whereof there remaines to vs monuments sufficient to instruct vs of the integritie of her doctrine, and of her Sacraments and ceremonies) and the Catholicke Church of this time, there had happened opposition in matters importing gaine or losse of Saluation. And therefore it is to that time, that we must cōfront the state of the Church of this time, and not leaue the ages of the fowre first Councells, of whose estate wee haue more light and monuments, then of the preceding ages, to goe vp to those of whose estate we haue recourse, not to finde therein more conformitie but to finde therein lesse instruction. For as for the Church in the time of the Apostles, besides that antiquitie affirmes, that the Apostles haue giuen manie thinges by tradition vnwritten to their disciples, his maiestie himselfe testifies that he is farr frō their opinion that beleeue the vniuersall historie of the primitiue Church to be all contained in the sacred, but onlie little Booke of the Actes of the Apostles.

Of the indefectibilitie of the Church.

CHAP. XXVII.

The continuance of the Kings answere.

THE King Confesseth, that his Church hath separated her selfe in manie points, from the faith and discipline, that the Roman Bishop doth at this daie hold and defēd with might and mayne. But the King and the English Church doe not interpret that to be, a defection from the antient Catholicke faith, but rather a returne to the antient Catholicke faith, which in the Roman Church had bene admirablie deformed in manie kindes, and a conuersion to Christ the only master of the Church.

THE REPLIE.

AND euen this confirmes our intention, to know that there is at this daie noe Catholicke Church; a thing directly against Gods promises, or that this that wee haue, is shee. For there could be noe other Catholicke Church, but her that was in the time of the first fowre Councells. Now shee, if shee haue bene interrupted (and she hath bene soe if ours which hath succeeded her, haue bene wanting in faith and in vnion with Christ, without which a Societie cannot be a Church) the *English* Church which succeedes her not, by an vninterrupted continuance, cannot be the same Church. For what Aristotle saith of Common-wealths, may also be said of the Church; to witt, that when a common-wealth hath interrupted the successiue continuance of her being, it is noe more one common-wealth in number, but an other common-wealth. Soe if the antient Catholicke Church hath interrupted the successiue continuance of her beeing, she is noe more one, and not being one, shee is noe more a Church, for the Church is one or none. And therefore the Fathers cry out, that if the Church be once perished, she can noe more, be borne againe. *If in* S. CYPRIANS *time* (saith saint AVGVSTINE) *the Church perished; from what Heauen ie Donatus fallen? from what Sea came hee forth? what earth hath sprunge him vp?* For to saie that the *English* Church accounts not her separation from the faith and from the discipline of the Pope, a defection from the antient Catholicke faith, but a returne to the antient Catholicke faith, and a conuersion to Christ, is not the question, viz. whether the *English* Church be conuerted to the antient Catholicke Faith. For as it hath bene aboue shewed, the name of catholicke, is not a name of simple beleefe, but of cōmunion. By meanes whereof, the *English* Church might haue all Faith: euen to the remouing of mountaines, yet if she communicated not with the Catholicke Church she could neither obtaine the title of Catholicke, nor the reward of life eternall; but should be schismaticall, and excluded from saluation. And therefore the state of the question in this which is presented, is not whether the *English* Church be return'd to the true faith, but whether the Church which possesseth at this daie the name of the Catholicke Church hath lost the being of the Catholicke Church; which she cannot haue done if in things important to saluation, and constructiue or destructiue to the being of a Church, she haue not varied from that of the time of the fowre first Councells, which wee on both sides confesse to haue bene the true Church, that is to saie, if she haue not taken awaie from the practise of the Church of those ages some thing necessarie to saluation, and without which saluation cannot be obtained; or if she haue not added to the practise of that Church something repugnant to saluation, and with which life eternall cannot be obtained. From whence it appeares, that the office of the *English* Church in this question, is to shew, not that she hath returned to the ancient Faith, which would alwaies exact the necessitie of a preceding dispute, to witt that the Church from whence she went out, hath diuerted her selfe from it; for the proofe of the auersion should precede the proofe of reuersion: but that the Church which wee at this daie intitle Catholicke hath soe diuerted her selfe from the faith of the Church of the time of the fowre first Councells, which both they and wee hold to haue bene the true Church, as she hath lost being and the iust title of a Church, and that saluation can noe more be obtained in her. And our office is contrariwise to maintaine, that the Church which is at this daie, differs not in anie thinge that can destroy saluation, and make her loose the beeing and the title of a true Church, from the ancient Catholicke Church, and that all the points that our Aduersaries obiect against vs, as such, and for which they take occasion to separate themselues from vs, vnder pretence that in our communion Saluation cannot be obtained, haue bene holden by the ancient Church.

Aug. de bapt. con. Donat. l. 3. c. 2.

Of

Of the sense wherein the Fathers haue intended that their doctrine had bene holden from the beginning.

CHAP. XXVIII.

The continuance of the Kinges answere

AND therefore, if anie one in consequence of this obseruation will inferr from thence, that the *English* Church, because she reiects some of the decrees of the *Roman* Church, is departed from the antient Catholicke Church, the King will not graunt him that till hee haue first proued by solid reasons, that all things that the *Romans* teach, haue bene approued from the beginning, and ordained by the antient Catholicke Church: And that noe man can doe this, now nor in the time to come, at the least that till nowe noe bodie hath done it is a thinge as certaine to the king, and to the Prelats of the *English* Church, as that the Sunn shines at noone daies.

THE REPLIE.

NEITHER is it the question, as I haue alreadie manie times said whether the *English* Church, haue departed from the doctrine of the antient Catholicke Church; but whether our Church be soe farr strayed from the doctrine of the antient Church, as she can noe more be reputed one selfe same Church with the antient Church and that we can noe more communicate with her, without losse of Saluation. For if she be still the same Church, and that amongst the conditions, vnder the obligation whereof, her communion is participated, there be noe doctrine nor custome which is opposite to Saluation; it is certaine, that out of her Societie, though one should haue Faith sufficient to remoue mountaines, yet they can neither possesse the Saluation, nor title of the Catholicke Church. Neither is it the question to knowe whether all thinges that the *Roman* Church holdes, and principallie those which she holdes to be necessary for Saluation, haue bene holden by antiquitie, and in this qualitie, which would be a longe and thornie disputation, because of the diuersitie of the acceptions of the word (*necessarie*) vnder the ambiguitie whereof, there would alwaies remaine a thousand cauills and shiftes. But whether all thinges that they obiect to vs as repugnant to saluation, and as occasions sufficient to cause separation from our communion, haue bene holden by the Catholicke Church from the time of the first fowre Councells. For in case they haue bene so, it is cleere that it is sacriledge in them, to separate themselues for their occasion from our communion. Not but that if this point were once cleered, it would be easier for vs then his maiestie conceaues, to proue that all thinges that the moderne Catholicke Church holdes as necessary to saluation, haue bene holden for such, and in the same ranke of necessitie by the antient Catholicke Church in the time of the first fowre Councells: but because the lawes of disputation, doe not permitt vs to ingage our selues to the triall of this point, before the cleering of the other, for feare of goeing out of the listes of the question, and of confounding the order of the conference. For whereas his Maiestie adds, that they haue bene approued & ordained frō the beginning, it hath bene manifested in the third obseruation of our Epistle, that to conuince, that a thing haue had place from first ages, it is sufficient, because of the fowre writinges of of that date that persecutions haue suffered to come downe to vs, to proue that it hath bene holden by the Church of the first fowre Councells, and that the Fathers that then liued testifie to haue receiued it, not as a thinge of a newe institution, but as a thing deriued to them by an vninterrupted succession from the age of the Apostles to the Church of their time, and that none of the preceding authors saie the contrary: His Maiesties owne selfe being agreed with vs in this, as hath often alreadie bene repeated, that the only little Booke of the Acts of the Apostles, is verie farr from contayning all the historie of the primitiue Church

Of the exceptions that the Kinge produceth to shewe that he hath not separated himselfe from the Church.

CHAP. XXIX.

The continuance of the Kings answere.

Finallie the King adds, that it is a great crime, to separate ones selfe from the Church but that he hath anie thing common with that crime, either hee or his Churchh ee vtterliie denes: for saith his maiestie wee fly not, but we are driuen away.

THE REPLIE.

AND why then doe Ministers soe earnestly exhort their hearers rather to indure all kindes of death, then to communicate in our Synaxes? And why then when they would dehort those of their partie from marrying with Catholickes, doe they alleadge those words of saint PAVL: *What communion is there of the faith-*
2. Cor. 6. *full, with an Infidell.* And ioyne also in their prayers, the Turkes, Papists and other Infidells? And why then doth his maiestie alleadge for a reason not to communicate with vs, these words of the reuelation: *Goe*
Apoc. 18. *forth of Babilon my people, for feare of communicating with her sinns*? For to offer to communicate with vs, when wee shall haue corrected those thinges that our Aduersaries pretend to haue bene deformed in our Church; who sees not; that that is not to offer to returne to vs, but to desire that wee should returne to them? And what sect hath there bene in the world that hath not offered to communicate with the Catholicke Church; prouided, that the Catholicke Church would renounce those pointes for which they were at difference; that is to saie, soe she would loose the condition of being the Catholicke Church.

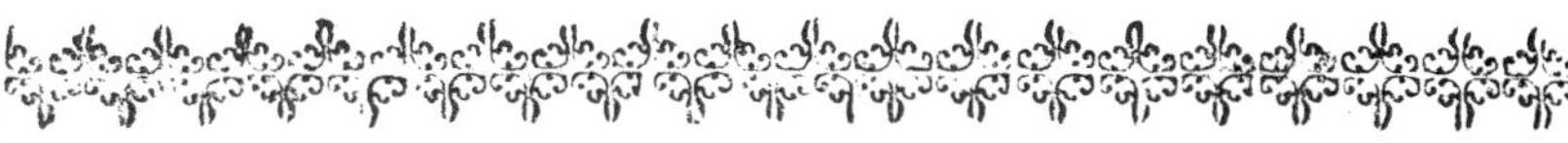

Of the demaunds made for Reformations since the fiue last ages;

Chapt. XXX.

The continuance of the Kings Answere.

AND your illustrious dignitie knowes, as he that is well informed thereof, how manie and how great personages in pietie and doctrine haue desired at least for this last fiue hundred yeares, the reformation of the Church, in the head and in the members. How manie greuous complaints of good kinges and princes, haue there bene heard deploring the estate of the Church in their ages? But what hath it auailed? For wee see not, that hitherto there hath bene anie one of those thinges corrected which were esteemed, before all others, to bee fitt for correction.

THE REPLIE.

THOSE demaundes of reformation in the head and in the members propounded before the last deuisiõs of the Church haue bene demaundes of reformation, not in the doctrine of Faith and of the sacraments, or vniuersall ceremonies of the Church, but in manners and in the practise of ecclesiasticall discipline, which euen these words of reformation both in the head and members, principallie vsed in the time of the Councells of *Constance* and of *Basile* testifie. Now as there is great difference betweene complayning of the personall practise of Iustice, and of the exercise of the Officers of a Kingdome, and desiring the reformation thereof, and betweene complayning of the lawes, ordinances, and constitutions of the state: soe there is great difference betweene complayning of the conuersation and manners of Ecclesiasticall persons, & betweene complayning of the doctrine and institutions of the Church. For when the corruption (to speake by hypothesis) is in the doctrine, or in the sacraments, or vniuersall ceremonies of the Church, none can remaine in the communion of the Church, without participating in that contagion; but when it is in the manners and in the practise of discipline, those onely that committ the faultes are culpable therein, and not the rest *who tolerate them as* sainct AVGVSTINE saith *for the good of vnitie, that which they detest for the good of equitie.* And to whom the more frequent and fowle such scandalls are, by soe much the more is the meritt of their perseuerance in the communion of the Church, and the martir-dome of their patience, as sainct AVGVSTINE calls it. For this only Sacrifice of choosing rather to support the remayning in communion with such persons, then to rent the coate of Christ, and to separate themselues from his Church to auoid their Societie, is the most pleasing Sacrifice that can be offered vp to God. Now the Church hath alwaies, not only since the last ages, but from all antiquitie, bene filled with such like complaints. For while she shall remaine in this world, she shall alwaies singe this verse of the Canticle; *I am black, but I am louelie,* That is to saie, black in manners, but louelie in doctrine; our Lord hauing deferred till his second Coming, the making her glorious and without spott. And not only so, but euerie one in his time,

Augu. ep. 162

Cantic. 1

hath alwaies beleeued himselfe to bee in the worst age of the Church for manners and for the practise of discipline, because they sawe the euills of their owne time, and did but heare the historie of other times; whereof the relation doth not soe liuely touch the eares, as the sight touches the eyes. But neuerthelesse, neither the euill hath alwaies gone on increasing, nor the good alwaies diminishing; but according to the diuersitie of the ages, the Church hath bene either more or lesse pure in manners. For, as for those, that in the beginning of these last diuisions either perswaded in some pointes by the innouators, or ioyned to the partie of the innouators themselues, haue attempted to seeke out some accommodation in matter of doctrine, and of the vniuersall Religion of the Church, to come to a reunion, perswading themselues, that as the Poet saith.

——————all men doe Sinn,
Without the walls of Troy, and eake within.

It will bee alwaies easie for vs to shew, that the desire of reconciliation rather then the knowledge of antiquitie and truth, hath caused them to speake this language.

Of the agreement or disagreement of the English reformers, with the Donatists.

CHAP. XXXI.

The continuance of the Kinges answere

ND therefore the *English* Church feareth not, that she can seeme in the iudgment of sincere arbitrators, to haue done anie thinge like to the *Donatists* in this separation. They out of a iollitie of harte, and without anie cause abandoned the Catholicke Church, approued by the consent of all nations, whereof they could neither blame the faith, nor the discipline.

THE REPLIE.

NEITHER was the Catholicke Church then actuallie approued by all nations, for these prophecies, *In thy seede shall all nations be blessed*; and, *This Ghospell must be preached ouer all the world*: shall not be fullie accōplisht as S. AVGVSTINE notes till the end of the world: But it might well be said by *Synecdoche*, & in regard of other Christian sectes, to be spread ouer all nations, because the extent thereof, was more eminent as it is nowe, then that of anie other Christian Societie; Neither was she approued by all men of all the Christian nations: For who knowes not how great the multitude of other heresies was, when the sect of the *Donatists* sprange vp; and how much greater then, when the passages of the Fathers, cited in the beginning of this obseruation, were pronounced against them? Of one side the *Arrians* possessed almost all the East: of the other side the number of the *Donatists* was such in *Africa*, as they held all at a time Councells of three hūdred Bishops: yea euē in the time of S. AVGVSTINE, there where whole natiōs that professed christianitie, which did not acknowledg the Catholick Church; as that of the *Gothes* & *Vandalls*. And in breefe eightie or an hundred other sects of Christiās; which were then in the world, diuided like *Sāpsons* Foxes by

(Genes. 28. Matt 24. August. ep. 165. de sermon. Dom. in Mont. i. 2.)

the heads, but tyed together by the tayles, did all agree to reproue the Catholicke Church. And whereas the excellent king addeth, that the *Donatists* could blame neither the faith nor discipline of the Catholicke Church; if by blaming, his maiestie intend to blame with reason, that is not particular to the *Donatistes*, for neuer anie Sect, either Schismaticall or hereticall could blame with reason the faith or discipline of the Church. But if by blaming he intend, accusing and slandring her, and beleeuing that they had iust occasion to doe soe, who euer blamed the faith and discipline of the Catholicke Church, more then the *donatists*? who called themselues the Bishops of thé Catholicke truth; and obiected to the Catholickes, that they erred in faith, in beleeuing that the holy Ghost, resided out of the Church; and in holding that Baptisme, which cannot be administred but by the operation of the holy Ghost, might be conferred out of the Church, and in the Societie of hereticks; who reprocht it to them, that they violated these oracles; *One faith, one Baptisme. It is lawfull to be baptised, if thou dost beleeue; be yee euery one of you baptised in the remission of Sinnes. Christ purgeth his Church, by the washing of water in the word. Who heares not the Church, lett him be as a publican and as a heathen. Baptisme is the washing of the regeneration of the Ghost. The Church is the close Garden, and the sealed Fountaine. Who gathers not with Christ scatters.* And other such like alleadged by them in so great number, as *Vincentius Lyrinensis* cryes out; *But perchance this new inuention* (that is to saie, the heresie of the Donatists) *will want defences; nay she was assisted with soe great strength of spirit; with so many flouds of Eloquence, with so great a number of protectors; with so much likelyhood, with so manie oracles of diuine lawe, but expounded in a new and naughtie manner, that it seemes to me, that such a conspiraice could neuer haue bene destroyed, if this same imbraced, this same defended, this same extolled profession of noueltie, had not in the end, left the cause of soe great a motion alone and abandoned.* And as for the discipline of the Church; did not they blame it, who taxed, the discipline of the Church, to haue receiued without expiation of preceding pennance, those that in the persecution time, had denied Christ, and communicated in the sacrifices of the Pagans, and consequently to haue bene polluted with the contagion of the Pagans; who accused her, for hauing receaued conuerted heretickes into her communion, without giuing them true Baptisme, which could not be giuen, according to them, but in the Church; and consequently, to haue polluted her communion with the contagion of vnbaptised, or vncircumcised spirituallie? and so to haue lost the being of the true Church which could not subsist without the true vse of the sacramēts? Who made profession in manners of a conuersation of life much better ruled, & more reformed, then that of the Catholickes; from whence it is that S. AVGVSTINE forbidds the catholicks, to reproche the *Donatists* with anie other thing, but that they were not Catholickes. Who called themselues, *the little flocke of the lord, the two tribes of the Kingdome of Iuda*; who said; *we hauing nothing, and possessing all things, wee account our soule to be our riches, and by our paines and our blood, we purchase the treasure of heauen*, And in breese, who supposed themselues to haue such reason for their separation, as they reputed the Catholickes not to be worthie of so much as the name of Christians, as hauing lost the true vse of Baptisme, whereby men are made Christiās & when they spake to them they said, *Caius Seius: Caia Seia* (*O man wilt thou be a Christian? O woeman wilt thou be a Christian*? And cryed to them. *Come o yee ignorant and wretched people, who are commonlie called Catholickes* And called the Chaire of *Rome* the *Chaire of pestilence*: and called the Catholicke Church, an *Harlott*, and an *Adulteresse*: and chose rather to suffer

Ephes. 4. Act. 8. Act. 2. Ephes. 5. Matth 18. Ad Tit. 3. Cantic. 4. Luc. 11. Vincent. Lirin. in commonit.

Idem cont. lit. Petilian l. 2. c. 99.

Idem. Vincent. Lyrin. cōtr hæres. c. 26

all kindes of persecutions and false Martirdomes, then to communicate with her. *If I persecute* (saith Saint AVGVSTINE) *iustlie him that detracts from his neighbour, why should I not persecute him, that detracts from the Church of Christ? and saith, this is not shee, but this is an harlott.* And againe, *If the punishment and not the cause made Martirdome, heauen should be full of your martirs*; And against whom contrariwise, the Catholickes in matter of doctrine, had not one passage of scripture for them, but only the Apostolicall vnwritten tradition, as S. AVGVSTINE himselfe confest in these wordes: *The Apostles* (saith hee) *in truth haue prescribed nothing of this, but this Custome ought to be beleeued to haue taken originall from their tradition; as there are manie things that the vniuersall Church obserueth, which are with good reason beleeued to haue bene giuen by the Apostles, although they be not in writing.* Was this to pretend to seperate themselues from the Church, out of iollitie of hart and without anie cause, and neither to blame the faith nor discipline of the Church.

Augu. concion. sup. gest. cum Emerit. Idem ibid.

August. de Bapt. contr Donat. l. 5. c. 23.

Of the authoritie of the rest of the Christian people, which denied to the Church the title of Catholick.

Chapt. XXXII.

The continuance of the Kings Answere.

THE *English* haue separated themselues by a cruell necessitie from that Church, that infinite Christian people (that I may speake as modestly as I possiblie can) doe not graunt to be the true vniuersall Church.

THE REPLIE.

THat the *English* Church hath bene iustly forced by a cruell necessitie, to depart from the Catholicke Church (wherein alone the stocke of vnitie doth reside, as our very aduersaries dare not saie, that the bodie of Catholicke vnitie was to be found in anie other Societie, when the *English* nation deuided themselues from her) saint AGVSTINE will not avow, who saith, *that there is no iust necessitie to deuide vnitie*: And lesse S. DIONISIVS of *Alexandria*, who was much antienter then saint AVGVSTINE, who writes; *Thou oughtest rather to suffer all kinds of death, then to deuide the Church of Christ.* For whereas his maiestie adds, that an infinite number of Christian people doe not grant her to bee the true & vniuersall Catholicke Church if these people can shew that there was an other, to whom this title belonged when *Luther* came into the world, wee will confesse her not to be soe, but if it be not in their power, not only to shewe, but to faine an other, then this must be shee. For the Catholicke Church is perpetuall, and their contradiction that are departed from her, can not raise anie doubt of her title, more then the contradiction of the antient *Arrians*, and other hereticks, could cause the antient Catholicke Church, to loose this title. For in that only that they haue departed from her, and can-

Aug. contr. ep. Parm. l. 2. c. 11 Dionys. Alexand. ep. ad Nouat. apud Eusebhist Eccl. 6 c. 45.

not shew that she hath deparrted from anie of all the other Societies which are in being, they teſtifie that she only is the true Catholicke Church, that is to ſaie, the true ſtocke and originall roote of the Church, from whom all others by their Schiſmes and diuiſions, are departed and gone forth.

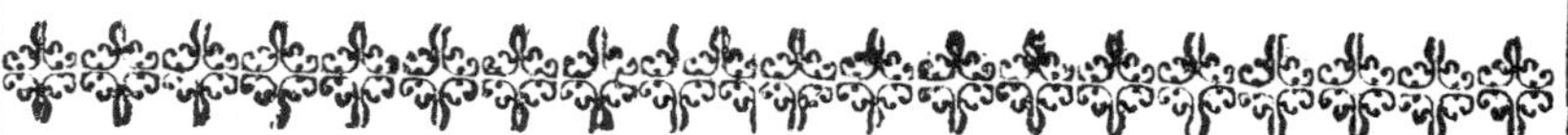

Of the teſtimonies of our writers.

CHAP. XXXIII.

The continuance of the King anſwere.

AND that manie of your writers themſelues, haue a longe while agoe, ingeniouſlie confeſſed, to haue much varied from the antient in the dogm'as, and in the forme of diſcipline and to haue patched and tacked together manie new thinges to the old, manie euill thinges to the good.

THE REPLIE.

THOSE writers haue bene ſuch as I haue aboue deſcribed, as *Eraſmus, Caſſander*, and others, who partly in preſumption, and partlie in ignorance of antiquitie, and partlie to gratifie thoſe Princes, in whoſe fauour they haue taken penn in hand, haue written thinges which would confound their faces if they were to maintaine them before anie that were verſed of purpoſe in the ſtudie of Antiquitie.

Of the begging of the principle contained in this hypotheſis.

CHAPT. XXXIV.

The continuance of the Kings anſwere.

WHICH is alreadie ſo knowne to all the world, as it is noe longer in the power of anie to denie it, or to be ignorant of it.

THE REPLIE.

THIS is to take for a principle of diſputation, that which is the ſubiect of the controuerſie: for not only all Catholickes, but alſo all the Chriſtian Societies in the world, more antient then the authors of this diuiſion, and who haue noe intereſt, neither for the one part nor for the other, and if they had anie, would haue it rather againſt the Church from which they are ſeparated, then for her, doe maintaine that all the principall pointes that the pretended reformers calumniate in the Roman Church, are of the true faith, and of the true diſcipline of the antient Catholicke Church.

Of the temporall causes of the separation of England.

CHAP. XXXV.

The Continuance of the Kings Answere.

ADD to this, that the Church of *England* had found the yoake of the *Roman* Bondage so hard vpõ her for some ages past, being incredible tormented frõ daie to day with new vexations, oppressions, and vnheard of exactions, as this only cause before iust iudges, may seeme to be able to free her from suspition of Schisme, and (as S. AVGVSTINE saith, speaking of the *Donatists)* wicked dismembring. For surely the *English* haue not separated themselues for iollitie of heart, from brotherly charitie as the *Donatists* did.

THE REPLIE:

IF it may please your maiestie to call againe to memorie the historie of the Schisme of *England*, you will finde, that all those thinges which were alleadged for pretence of the Churches diuision, haue noe waie bene the cause thereof: contrariwise that the *English* Church was more flourishing when this separation happened, and the King of *England* and his clergie more affectionate to maintaine the Faith and communion of the *Roman* Church, then euer they had bene before, as appeares by the Booke that he made in defence of the Church against *Luther*; the originall whereof he sent to *Rome* with these verses, such as they are, addressed to Pape *Leo* written with his owne hand;

Henry 8. King of England, sent this work to Leo the tenth as a witnesse both of his faith and friendship.

Harrie the English King, at once doth recommend,
This worke Leo to thee, which publick proofe shall lend,
To shew which way his faith, and friendship both doe bend:

But that it was the amorous passion of that King, who to satisfie the appetite which transported him, would cause a iust mariage to be broken, and marrie her that he loued, his first lawfull wife, and by whom he had issue being yet liuing; to which the Pope conceaued, that he could not with a safe conscience, giue consent: This was the true and onely cause of all this Iliad of euills.

Hinc illæ lachrymæ.

From hence gusht all these teares.

Of the comparison of the English Church, with the Iudaicall.

CHAP. XXXVI.

The continuance of the Kings answere.

NOT for feare of the euill which was eminent, but did not yet presse them like the tenn tribes of the people of the Iewes, but after hauing suffered manie ages after the supportinge of vnspeakable greeuances, they haue finallie shaken from their shoulders, that insupportable burthen which neither their strength was longer able to beare, nor would their conscience permitt them to doe it.

THE REPLIE:

HERE I might content myself with saying, that what was ordained and approoued by God, in the separation of the ten tribes of *Israell* from the Kingdome of *Iuda*, was the only diuision of State, and not that of Religion. *For God* (as saint AVGVSTINE saith) *commaunds neither Schisme nor heresie.* And by consequence, what pretence soeuer is added of present and not future euill, there can be noe consequence drawne from this example for the desertion of the Catholicke Church, *God* (saith saint AVGVSTINE) *bad that these tribes should be separated, not to diuide the Religion, but the Kingdome, and that by this meanes, vengeance might be taken vpon the Kingdome, of Iuda.* But for as much as the ordinarie refuge of those that separate themselues from vs, is to haue recourse to the Symptomes of the *Iewish* people, and to inferr from thence, the same conclusions of possibilitie of errour, and licence of separation for the Christian Church, and that to contradict this, wee haue not onely promised to shew that there neuer happened anie accident to the visible *Iewish* Church, wherefore they either ought or could separate themselues from her communion, but also that if anie such thing had happened, the cōsequence thereof could not bee applied to the Christian Church, which is grounded vpon other contracts, and vpon other prerogatiues It is best for vs here to quitt vs of our promise, and to search the question to the bottome, both concerning the *Thesis*, and the *Hypothesis*. In regard then of the *Thesis*, the aduersaries of Catholick religion set this foundation, that the Church in all times is subiect to the same Symptomes, and to the same accidents, & therevpon argue thus: The visible Church hath had three periods, the first vnder nature: the second vnder the lawe, and the third vnder Grace. Now vnder the two first she hath bene corrupted, and consequētly vnder the third she may be soe. Which is as if one should saie, there are three periods in the progresse of the generation of man. The first during the which man liues onlie the life of plantes, and is yet touched with noe other instinct the n simple appetite, which the Philosophers call naturall, common to herbes aud trees, which seemes to correspond to the condition of the first period of the Church, wherein she had yet noe lawe or rule, but the simple lawe of nature. The second during which he liues an animated and sensitiue life, which is proportioned to the state of the people of the *Iewes*; because as man in this second progresse, harh noe other knowing facultie but that of the sence, which is common to him with beastes; so all the obiects which were manifestlie propounded to the *Iewes*, and all the promises which were literallie made to them, were of sensible thinges And the last, wherein man takes possession of the life trulie human and reasonable, and is adorned and enobled with intellectuall knowledge, which hath analogy with the state of the Christiā Church, where the faithfull are consecrated to God by a perfect & lawfull forme of religion, and sticke noe longer in terrestriall and materiall obiectes; but exalting their thoughtes and their hopes, doe nourish & intertaine themselues with spirituall and incorruptible promises. Now vnder the first and second of those periods, the imperfect soule of man, which wee call an *Embricn*, is subiect to perish, corruptible and mortall; the soule of man therefore vnder the third period, is not incorruptible & immortall. For to produce for a reason of exception and dissimilitude, that the forme of a man during all the three periods of this progresse, is

not

not one selfe-same forme, the reason of the exception is void, for as much as the diuersitie of Gods promises, where it so falls out, hath noe lesse power to varie the Symptomes of the Church during the three periods of her being, then the diuersity of formes, to varie the conditions which accompanie the three periods of the generation of man. Now that the promises made to the Church vnder the last period, *which hath, bene establisht*, as S PAVL saith, *vpon better promises then the former*, be wholie different both in eminencie & perpetuitie from those that haue bene made to her vnder the two first, what Christian can call it in question? God first in regard of eminencie and multitude, did he not saie to Abraham; *in thy seede*; that is to saie, as S. PAVL expoundes it, in Christ, *shall all generations be blessed*: And againe, *thy seede shalbe as the starrs of heauen, and as the sands of the sea*? And *Aggeus* describing the future estate of the Church vnder the Enigma of the re-edification of the temple, doth hee not saie: *The glorie of this last howse, shall be much greater then that of the first*? And the Spouse in the canticles, speaking of the *Jewish* Church, doth she not singe: *our Sister is little, and she hath yet noe breasts*; that is to saie, is not yet in state to bringe forth, and nurse vp children? And doth not *Esaie* crie out: *Reioyce thou barren woman, that bearest not children, and thou that art no mother, cast forth cryes of ioy. For the children of the forsaken, shall be much more in number then hers that hath a husband*? And a while after: *Lengthen the cords of thy pauillions, and settle their posts, for thou shalt penetrate on the right hand, and on the left, and thy seede shall inheritt the nations*. And againe; *Cast thine eyes about thee, and behold all these are assembled for thee, they are come for thee: thy sonns shall come from farr, and thy daughters shall be borne vpon shoulders*. And doth not S. AVGVSTINE, disputing against the *Donatists*, crie out, *Feare you not, least the Jewes should aske you, where is that accomplished that your Paul hath expounded of your Church; reioyce thou barren woeman that thou bearest not, and cast out cryes of ioy that thou hast noe children; for the children of the forsaken are more in number, then hers that hath a husband*? *Preferring the multitude of the Christians before that of Iewes; if your little number be the Church of Christ*. And S. HIEROME against the *Luciferians*, *Where are these too Religious, or rather too prophane persons, that affirme there are more Synagogues then Churches*? And therefore doth not the same S. AVGVSTINE elegantlie compare the historie of the different times of the Church, to that of the birth of *Iacob*, for as much that as *Jacob* in his Birth, thrust forth first one arme, and then his head, and then all his Bodie, so the Church before she was borne, first thrust forth one arme that is to saie, a little part of her societie, which was the Synagogue, and then her head, which is Christ, and then all her Bodie, which is the Christian Church? But against that, the aduersaries of the multitude of the Church alleadge, that our Lord calls his Church *A little flocke*: & cōmaūds *to enter into the straight gate* it is true, but it makes nothing for them, for that our Lord calls his Church *a little Flocke*, it is in regarde of her birth, at the time whereof she was the least, the basest, and most contemptible of all societies, and not in regard of her progresse which himselfe compareth to that of a graine of mustard-seede; which being at the beginning the least of all seedes, becomes in the increase, the greatest of all plantes. *We are borne in that age* (saith S. AVGVSTINE) *and associated with the people of God in that time, wherein this plant, bredd from the graine of mustarde-seede, hath alreadie stretched forth her branches*. And that hee saith: *Enter in at the straight gate*: it is in respect of the conuersation of manners, and not of the profession of doctrine, as appeares by these wordes, *Manie called and few chosen*, And by these: *and the mariage chamber was full of inuited persons*; that is to saie, of those that were called. For though the number of the chosen be

Rom. 4. Genes. 22. Galat. 3. Genes. 22. Agg. 2. Cantic. 8. Esai. 54. vers. 1. Ibidem. v. 2 Esai. 49 v. 18. Aug. Vinc. ep. 48. Hieron. aduers. Luciferian Luc. 12. v. 32. Matth. 7. v. 14. Aug. in Psalm. 68. Matth. 22. v. 14. Ibidem. v. 10.

little, in regard of the wicked; neuerthelesse, considered in it self, it is verie great. *It is this Church* (saith saint AVGVSTINE) *of the little number whereof in comparison of the multitude of the wicked, it is said, that the waie that leades to life, is straight and close, and that those that walke it, are few in number.* And yet it is she againe, of whose multitude it is said: *Thy seede shalbe as the starrs of heauen, and as the sands of the sea.* For the same faithfull, holy and good, in comparison of the great multitude of the wicked, are a little number, and considered in themselues, are manie; for it is said, that of the children of the forsaken, are in greater number, then hers that hath a husband. And elsewhere: *Wherefore is it, o yee hereticks, that you glorie in your small number; if Christ died to the end to possesse the multitude for his inheritance?* But if the prerogatiues of the Christian Church be much other as for eminencie and multitude, then that of the Church of the *Iewes*, how much more in regard of lasting and perpetuitie, which are as often promised to the Christian Church, as denied to the Church of the *Iewes*; for who is ignorant that the *Iewish* Church had not receaued the same promises of lasting and perpetuitie, as haue bene made to the Christian Church? contrary-wise, if anie promises of lasting and perpetuitie, haue seemed to bee literallie addressed to the *Jewish* Church, they were made to her conditionallie, and not absolutely; and if anie haue bene made to her absolutely, they were made to her onely in shadowe and in figure; but the truth, like the truth of the promises of eternitie made to the Raigne of *Salomon*, belonged to him of whose Raigne *Salomons* was the figure. *Hieremie* saith and saint PAVL after him. *that the daies would come, wherein God would knitt vp a newe alliance with the familie of Juda, and with the familie of Israell; not according to the alliance that he contracted with their Fathers, when he tooke them by the hands and drewe them out of the land of Egipt:* Hee adds, *that if this contract once perisht from before the eyes of the* Lord *then all the seede of Israell should faile for euer; and there should be noe more people before him in anie age, but that the heauens on high should sooner bee measured, and the foundations of the earth belowe be sooner sounded:* Then finallie he concludes with these wordes; *the sanctuarie of the eternall, shall noe more be pluckt vp, and shall neuer more be destroyed and desolate in anie time to come.* EZECHIEL saith, *I will make a treatie of peace with them; J will haue an eternall confederacie with them, I will build them and multiplie them, and establish my sanctification in the middest of them for euer: my tabernacle shall bee amongst them, and I will be their God, and they shall bee my people, and the Nations shall knowe that I sanctifie Israel, when they shall see my sanctification in the middest of them for perpetuitie.* ESAY cryes out. *As in the daies of Noe I swore, that I would noe more powre downe the waters vpon the earth, soe I haue protested, that J will noe more bee angrie with thee, and that I will noe more looke vppon thee in my wrath. The mountaines shall be moued, and the hills shall shake, but my mercie shall not estrange it self from thee, and the peace of my alliance, shall neuer be transported from thee.* And in an other place; *When he that is driuen with the spirit of our Lord, shall become as an impetuous floud, and that the Sauiour shall arriue at Sion, to turne away the iniquities of Iacob; behold the alliance that shall be betweene them and me saith our Lord; my Spirit which is thy mouth and the words which I haue put in thy mouth, shall neuer depart from thy mouth nor from the mouth of they posterity; nor from the posteritie of thy posteritie, saith our* Lord, *from this time forth, for euer more.* And a little lower, *J will contract a perpetuall confederacie with them, and the people shall knowe their posteritie and their linage shall bee manifest in the middest of the Nations; and all that shall see it shall knowe, that this shall be the seede cherisht and fauourd by our* Lord. Now to what purpose were all these renouations of contracts and alliances,

Aug. ep. 48.

August. de vnit. Eccl. c. 8.

Hier. c. 31.

Ibidem, v. 36. & 37.

Ibidem v. 4.

Ezec. c. 37. v. 26. 27. & 28.

Esai. c. 54. v. 9.

Ibidem v. 10

Idem c. 59. v. 19. 20.

all these mentions of preheminencies and prerogatiues, if the Sincops and interruptions of the Church of the *Iewes* ought to make the lawe, and president for the Christian Church? To what purpose are all these clauses; *that the Gates of the Church should be continually open; that they shall be shutt neither daie nor night, that the multitude of nations may be brought in? That whereas she hath bene abandoned and odious, and that none frequented her, she shall be made the glorie of the wourld, and shall become the delight of generations? That she shall noe more be called the forsaken, and that her land shall noe more be called the desolate, but her name shall be the fauoritie of our Lord, and her land shall bee peopled and inhabited*? If the Christian Church should be exposed to the same ruines and desolations as the *Iewish*, which neuer receaued anie promises of perpetuitie; or if anie promises of perpetuitie may seeme to haue bene made to her onlie in shadowe and in figure, but their truth belonged to the Christian Church? To what purpose were all these promises of our Lord? Both by the mouth of *Esaie*: *As in the daies of Noe I swoare, I would noe more bring the waters of the flood againe vpon the earth; soe I haue sworne that I will noe more be angrie with thee.* And by that of *Zachary*. *I will noe more doe to this people, as I haue done in times past*. And by his owne: *The cittie built vpon a mountaine can not be hidden: the gates of hell shall neuer preuaile against her; This Ghospell of the Kingdome must first be preached ouer all the world, and then the end shall come. I am with you to the consummation of ages*, and other the like, if the Christian Church haue not quite other prerogatiues then the *Iewish* Church not onely in eminencie and multitude, but also in lasting and perpetuitie? Philosophers teach that passion is a waie tending and leading to corruption, and that what is incorruptible, is also reciprocallie impassible and inalterable, what wonder is it then, that the wayfarring preparation of the Religion of the *Iewes*, which was corruptible and subiect to perish, before it came to the terme of corruption, haue tryed manie passions, manie accidents, manie changes? that before it perisht, it haue vndergone manie weaknesses, Sincopes, and faintings: that this antient & decrepite howse which was one daie to be ruined (as the Apostle speaking of the old lawe teacheth vs *that that which weares and growes old, approacheth to ruine.*) haue somes times bene amazed and shaken? that this light, that was finallie to be extinguished & buried vnder a profoũd night and in perpetuall darknes, haue sometimes bene obscured and dimmed, and haue suffered defects and ecclipses? And contrariwise, that the state of the Christiã Church that the scriptures declare and prophecie to be incorruptible, and not subiect to perish, should be freed from all the passions, preserued from all these accidens, and dispenced withall and warranted from all these interruptions?

Esa. 45. Idem c. 60 · Esai 62 · Esai. 54. · Zachar. 11. · Matth 5. · Matth 16. · Matth. 24 · Matth. 28.

But we haue insisted too long vpon the thesis, let vs now come to the hypothesis, which is of the estate of the Church vnder the two first periods: and principallie, vnder that of the *Iewish* lawe. For in regard of the defects of the *Iewish* Church, the aduersaries to Christianitie, make nine notable obiections, which wee will confute in order one after an other. The first is taken from the historie of *Aaron*. *Aaron*, saie they, founded the Idoll, after which the people Idolatrized. It is true *Aaron*, not yet inuested with the high Priesthood, founded the golden calfe, after which the people, that is to saie, by *Synecdoche*, a part of the people, Idolatrized, for *Philo* the *Iew* doth particularly saie, that the maladie had not seised them all. But neither *Moyses*, who was the visible head of the *Israelites* Church, and in whose onely person resided till then the high Priestood; nor the whole bodie of the Leuiticall tribe, destined to the future guard of the

Exod. 32. Phil. Ibid.

Temple, and to the ordinarie ministrie of the lawe were touched with this crime. For as soone as *Moyses* cryed; *If anie one belonge to our Lord, lett him ioyne with me:* All the tribe of *Leui* gathered to him, to roote out the Idolaters. From whence it is, that *Moyses* giues these praises to *Leui*; *It is he that hath said of his Father, and of his mother, I haue not seene them: And who hath not acknowledged his Brothers, and hath noe more knowne his children; for they haue kept thy wordes;* And that God himselfe saith by the ministrie of *Malachy*; *The lawe of truth hath bene in the mouth of* Leui, *and in his lipps there was noe frowardnes; he hath walked with me in peace and equitie:* And that *Philo* the Iew, searching wherefore the Townes of refuge had bene taken of the tribe of the Leuites, saith, *that one reason was, because the Leuiticall tribe destined to guard the temple, had slaine the worshippers of the golden calfe*. And therefore saint PAVL citing the same historie, reduceth it to the number of some; *To the end*, saith he, *that you become not Idolaters, as some amongst them were;* to shew that this act was not vniuersall. For that the sinn was imputed in generall to all the people; it was not because they had all participated in it, but because they had not endeauored to reuenge and punish it in the act. And yet this action was not a iudiciarie action of the Church, or a rituall custome of the Synagogue, but a tumultuary seditiō of the people, which was extinguished the same daie, & consequently could not be reckoned for an interruptiō of the *Jewish* Church for as soone as the brute of the tumulte of the Idolators was raised, *Moyses* came downe from the mountaine to remedie it. Now what proportion is there betweene the tumulte of a daie, and such like clowdes of the *Iewish* Church (whose longest lasted, but the twentith part of an age, & by consequence, gaue noe occasion to saie of the *Jewish* Church that, that *Cornelius Tacitus* saith of the common-wealth of *Rome* vnder *Tiberius*, *Who is he that hath seene the common-wealth*) & the pretended ieterruptiō of the Catholicke Church, which according to the cōputation of her Aduersaries, hath bene ecclipsed in faith, & erred in saluation aboue fourhundred then yeares, & as they saie of *Epimenides*, that he fell into a sleepe yong, & awaked old; soe she fell a sleepe yong, to witt, īmediatly after the death of the apostles, & awaked old, that is to saie, vpō the end, & in the last waue of the world.

Exod.32 · Ibidem · Malach.2. · Phil.Iud. l. de Profug. · 1.Cor. 10.

The secōd obiection is takē from the historie of the symptomes, which hapened to the *Iewish* church, betweene the time of *Moyses*, & that of *David* where it is said, one while that *Micheas* made an Idoll, & that six hundred men of the tribe of *Dan*, hauing taken it, placed it in *Lais*, a cittie of the *Sydonians*, possessed by them; an other while, *that Gedeon made an Ephod in Ephra, and that all Israel went a whoring after it*: An other while, *that Israel transgrest, and abandoned the Lord*. An other while, that in the time of *Hely the word of God was precious:* that is to saie, rare: An other while, that in the time of *Saule, the arke had not bene required*, that is to saie, according to the innouators glosse, God had not bene consulted in his word. But for the historie of *Micheas* soe farr is it off, that from the act of *Micheas*, which was but a particular act, noe more then that of the six hundred *Israelites* of the tribe of *Dan*, there can bee anie inference drawne, that the visible seruice of God, was thē extinguished in all the people of *Israel*; as *Luther* affirmes, that this historie fell out, either at the latter end of *Josua*; or vnder the gouernment of *Othoniel*, an excellent seruant of God, wherein none can pretend, that the true seruice was extinguished in *Israel*. And the historian noting that this idoll remained in the cittie of *Lais*, as longe as the howse of our Lord remained in *Silo*, testifies that the howse of God, and the seate of the true seruice of God, was then in *Silo*. And whereas the people of *Israel* tooke occasion to goe a whoring after the *Ephod* of

Iudic.8.v.27 · Iosue 1. v. 11. · 1.Reg. 3.v. 1. · 1.Paral. 13. v.3.

Gedeon; and that the historie of Iudges saith; *All Israel went a whoriug after it*, it must be vnderstood of the *Israelites* of the cittie of *Ephra*, natiue place of Gedeon, and others neere to it; and that it is written in diuers places of the same history, *that Israel preuaricated and serued false Gods*; it is to be vnderstood by *Synecdoche*, of a part for the whole, following this sentence of S. AVGVSTINE. *The scripture hath this fashion of reproofe, that the word seemes to be addressed to all, yet concernes but some of them.* And indeede in the historie of *Josua*, not only the scripture saith; *The children of Israel violated the commaundement, and tooke of the Anathema*: But God himselfe pronounceth; *Israel hath sinned, and hath transgressed against my alliance they haue taken of the anathema, and haue stollen it and haue lyed and haue hidden it amongst their stuffe, and Israel cannot subsist before his enemies, but shall fly before them, for he is polluted with the anathema.* And notwithstanding there was but one onely man in al *Israell*, and he yet vnkowne, that had committed this crime, to witt, *Acham*. And whereas it is said in the first of *Samuel*, that in the time of *Eli, the word of God was precious*, that is to saie, rare; the author speakes not there in anie sort of the lawe, or of the written word, but of the oracles and visible predictions, that God had accustomed to giue by the prophets, as by these words, *And there was noe manifest vision*, may appeare. And whereas it is said in the first to the cronicles, *that in the time of Saule the Arke was not required*, that is to saie, according to the innouators glosse, that God was not consulted with, in this word. This is a wrong interpretation of the word, *requisiuimus*, which intends not there, *inquired of*, but *required*, and hath not reference to the word of God, but to the Arke and signifies noe other thing, but that in the time of *Saule*, they had not yet required the Arke from the cittie of *Kiriath Jearim*.

Aug. ep. 48 Iosue. 1. v. 11 Ibidem.

The third obiection is taken from the complaint of *Elias*. *Elias* (said the Aduersaries of the Church) *complained to God, that his Altars were beaten downe, and his prophetts slaine with the sword, and that he was left alone, and they likewise sought him, to put him to death*; *And God answered him, that he had reserued to himselfe seauen thousand.* Whereof *Elias* conceaued he had knowne none. And this when God could not be serued visible, but in *Iudea*, the Church as they conclude, was then inuisible. But how longe will they stũble at one selfe-same stone, and not learne to distinguish betweene the kingdome of *Israel*, were was the seate of schisme and heresie, & the kingdome of *Iuda*, where was the seate of the true Church? It is writtẽ that the herbe called *Eringus*, hath this hidden propertie, that if amongst a companie of Goates there be anie one that takes a leafe of it betweene his teeth, that Goate will immediatlie stopp, and with him all the Flocke; so as it is not possible to make anie one of thẽ goe forward, till first the leafe be pluckt out of his mouth. Soe after one of the aduersaries of the Church hath apprehended anie falshood or absurditie, all the rest as by a certaine charme, doe soe stopp and stumble at it, as it is not possible to make them goe forward, vnlesse you call back the first author, yea out of his graue to contradict himself and to recant publickly. *Melancton* being inquired off where the Church was twelue or thirteen hundred yeare agoe, since from that time by his accompt our communion was corrupted with Idolatrie and impietie, had recourse to the historie of *Elias*, to whom said hee for a while, the true Church was vnknowne and iuuisible. After this all those that haue handled the same questiõ, without inquiring whether this solution were true or false, without taking care to examin the place, haue soe tied themselues to it, as at this daie, it is their onely and common refuge in this extreamitie. It doth not importe vs answere they to knowe where the residence of the Church was in the ages

whereof

whereof you inquire. *Elias* who was a prophet, was alſo ignorant for a time, where she ſubſiſted; wee then may well be ignorant of it, who are neither Prophets, nor the children of Prophets; For he complained, that he was left alone: but of whom did *Elias* ſpeake when he ſaid, *They haue ſlaine thy Prophets with the ſword?* Was it not of *Achab* and of *Ieſabel*? and where was it that he ſaid *he was left alone?* was it not in the Kingdome of *Iſrael*? Now if ſaint AVGVSTINE ſpeaking of the Chriſtian Church it ſelfe, hath had reaſon to ſaie, *What an abſurditie is it not to conſider, that the Church, increaſing and multiplying ouer all the world, might ſuffer perſecution by the kinges of ſome Nations, when she did not ſuffer it by the reſt?* wherefore may not wee cry out, What an abſurditie is it to transferr what belōges to the Kingdome of *Iſrael*, where the true Church was perſecuted, to the Kingdome of *Iuda* where she was viſible, floriſhing, and eminent? For ſo farr of was the Church then from being tied and reſtrained to the Kingdome of *Iſrael*, as contrariwiſe, the true Seate, the only ſeate, the ſoueraigne ſeat of the ſeruice of God, and of the viſible exerciſe of Religion, wherein only ſacrifices might be lawfullie celebrated, the center of vnion and eccleſiaſticall communion, the heart, if I may ſaie ſo, and roote of the Church, was Situate out of the iuriſdiction of *Iſrael*. Nay more then ſo, all the ſacerdotall order, all the line of *Leui*, all the high-prieſts, prieſts and miniſters, to whom onely belonged the diſpenſation of the miſteries and ceremonies, all the magiſtrates and officers of the Church, all the Paſtors and ordinarie Doctors, without which she could not be viſible, nor retaine her iuſt markes and Sacraments, then made their reſidence out of the Kingdom of *Iſrael*. And to proue this, threeſcore yeares and more before *Elias* began to prophecie, the Kingdome of *Iſrael* had bene deuided into two Kingdomes, the one contayning the tribe of *Iuda*, which was without compariſon the greateſt and moſt principall, & that of *Beniamin*, to which was alſo ioyned the linage of *Leui* all intire, with infinite particulars of the other Tribes, who deſired to ſerue God purelie, holding the title of the Kingdome of *Iuda*, vnder the dominion of *Roboam*, the true and naturall heire; the other cōprehending the reſt of the tribes poſſeſſed by *Ieroboam*, a rebell & an vſurper, & poſſeſſed vnder the reſtrained name of the Kingdome of *Iſrael*. By meanes whereof, theſe two peoples haue alwaies had their eſtates and their kings aparte; yea, their religiōs alſo for the more part deuided. For to *Ieroboam* ſucceeded *Nadab*; to *Nadab Baaſa*; to *Baaſa, Ela*, to *Ela*, *Zambri*; to *Zambri*, *Amri*; to *Amri Achab*; All not only ſchiſmatickes, but Idolators and infidells. *Elias* then as ſubiect to *Achab* complained, that theſe Relickes of the Church, which remayned in *Iſrael*, theſe fewe of the faithfull which were left in the territorie of *Achab*, and which were wont euerie yeare to goe vp to profeſſe and to exerciſe their Religion in the Kingdome of *Iuda*, where the Temple and Prieſthood was, had bene rooted out by the tyrannie of Queene *Ieſabel*. And frō the departing frō thence there are men which cōclude without ſcruple of this feare, there was thē noe viſible Church, in the world. But heare the hiſtorie of the ſeperatiō of theſe two kingdomes: *He raigned* (ſaith the hiſtorie of the chronicles, ſpeaking of *Robo*ā) *ouer Iuda, & ouer Beniamin. The Prieſts alſo & the Leuites which were vnder the iuriſdictiō of* Iſrael, *came to him out of all the citties which had bene giuen to him for their habitation, leauing their poſſeſſiō and their inheritance, and paſſing and inhabiting in* Iuda *and in* Hieruſalē; *becauſe* Ieroboā *had driuen them out, hee & his Succeſſors, leaſt they should attend to the ſeruice of our Lord, hauing appointed prieſts of the high places to ſacrifice to the diuells and to the calues that he had cauſed to be ſett vp. Frō other places alſo of all the tribes of* Iſrael, *thoſe that ſett*

3.Reg. 19.

Aug. de ciuit. Dei, l.18.c.52.

Chronic. 11.

their hartes to seeke the God of Israel, went vp to Hierusalem to offer their sacrifices before the Lord God of their Fathers. Whereto *Josephus* adds these words, as pronounced by *Hieroboam* in forme of an oration to the people of *Israel*: *I thinke*, said hee, *none of you are ignorant, that there is noe place where God is not and that he reserues not to himselfe, anie appointed seate, but that euery where he heares those that pray to him, and casts his eyes vpon all that serue him. For this reason I haue not thought fitt, to suffer you to goe so farr to worship, and with so much paines, and also in an enemie cittie, as Hierusalem is. The temple that is there was built by a mortal man, neither more nor lesse then myselfe. Therefore I haue consecraced for you, two Calues of Golde, the one in Bethel, and the other in* Dan, *that goeing thither, according to the ease and oportunitie of the neighbourhood, you may there worship God more commodiouslie. Besides, you shall want noe priests and Leuites, whom I will establish from amongst you, that you may haue noe more neede of the tribe of* Leui, *nor of the familie of Aaron.* Behold then, that the Church was then so farr from being confined to the Kingdome of *Israel* as the Metropolitan Seate of the religion & seruice of God, which was *Hierusalem*, the place where sacrifices ought to be celebrated, which was the temple, the soueraigne tribunal of the adoration which was the Altar, the succession of *Dauid* from whom the *Messias* was to come, the high priest, and all the sacerdotall and Leuiticall Estate, which administred and represented the vniuersall Bodie of the Church, did remaine following the election and institution of God, in the partes of the Kingdome of *Iuda*, and out of that of the Kingdome of *Israel*. Which the holie Ghost had longe before declared by the mouth of the Psalmist in these termes not onlie historicall but also propheticall: *He hath,* (saith hee) *reiected the tabernacle of Joseph, and hath not chosen the tribe of Ephraim*; (that is to saie, the kingdome of *Israel*, which was called *Ephraim* for as much as *Jeroboam* as saith S. HIEROME who first raigned there was of the tribe of *Ephraim*;) *but hath chosen the tribe of Juda, and the mountaine of Sion, which he loued.* And after by that of *Ezechiel* in these, *Sonn of man* (saith the Lord) *take a peece of wood and write vpon it, Iuda and the children of Israel which are vnited to him and of his fellowshipp: and take an other and write vpon it; The word of Ioseph which is in the hand of Ephraim, and all the families of Israel, and of all those which are vnited to him.* And therefore the historie of *Tobie* saith, *that when all those of the tribe of* Nephthali *went to the golden calues that Ieroboam king of Israel had made, Tobie only fled the companie of all the rest, and went into Ierusalem to the temple of the lord, and there worshiped the* Lord *God of Israel offering all his first fruites and his tithes.* And therefore our Lord, when the *Samaritan* said to him, *our Fathers worshipped in this mountaine*; (that is to saie, in the mountaine of *Samaria* and of *Gerassim*) *and yee affirme that in Hierusalem is the place where wee ought to worshipp*, answered, that Saluation was on the *Jewes* side. And for this same cause, S. PAVL alleadging his extraction from *Abraham* according to the flesh, notes particularly that he was issued from the familie of *Beniamin*, as signifiing that he was extracted from the societie of those, in whose communion resided the true Bodie of the Church. *The tribe of Iuda* (saith S. AVGVSTINE) *and the line of Beniamin, had remained in the societie of the Temple, the Tribe of Leui which was that of the Priests, the tribe of Juda which was the royall line, and the line of Beniamin. Those only staied on Hierusalems partie, and in the communion of the Temple of God, when the separation had bene made by the reuolt of Salomons seruant. Doe not then imagine, that it is of little weight, that the Apostle adds, issued from the tribe of Beniamin, For it is as if he should haue said, communicating with Iuda, and not being depriued of, and separated from, the temple.* But behold yet more; which is, that the complaint

Ioseph. Antiquitat. Iudaic.l.8.

Psalm. 77. v.60.et.61

Hieron. in Hierem. c. 31.

Ezech.27.

Tob.1.

August in Psalm. 75.

of *Elias*, is soe farr from verifying this pretended interruption, and this generall ecclipse of the *Iewish* Church, as contrarywise it appeares, that at the same time at the same howre at the same moment, that *Elias* lamented the persecution of *Achab*, the true Religion florisht in *Iudea* with more glorie, puritie, and splendor, then euer she had done since the first *Salomon*, which was the figure of her true spouse, and the author of the materiall Temple, till the other that was declared to be greater then *Salomon*; that is to saie, vntill our Lord who built the spirituall Temple of the Catholicke Church. For in the same time, that *Achab* and *Iesabell*, persecuted *Elias*, *Iosaphat* sonn and Successor to *Asa*, raigned in *Iuda*. And to proue it soe the historie beares; that *Iosaphat* came to the crowne of *Iuda*, the fowrth yeare of the Raigne of *Achab* King of *Israel*. Now thete were six yeares and more of *Achabs* gouernement expired, when *Elias*, made his lamentation. For the great drought whereof, the hebrewes assigne the beginning to be in the third yeare of *Achab*, and which lasted three yeares and six moneths, according to the report of S. IAMES was then precisely finished; so as the complaint of *Elias*, not only falls out in the time of *Iosaphat*, but meetes exactly with the reuolution of the third yeare of his Empire, which was iust the same yeare, wherein he celebrated that famous circuit, and if I dare so stile it, that walking Parliament, and those great daies of Religion, where the most notable Princes of his estate and the principall priests and Leuites, were appointed to trauell, through all the citties of his Kingdome. Behold the time wherein *Elias* complaint happened. Now what *Iosaphat* was frō the beginning to the end of his life, how hee walked intirely in the way of *Asa* his Father, without turning from it in anie thing, but doeing what was pleasing to the Lord; how the Seruice of God was holily celebrated and administred vnder his authoritie, how the Almightie was with him, because he trode in the stepps of *Dauid* his Predecessor, and trusted not in Idolls, but in the God of his Father, walking in his precepts, and not according to the sinnes of *Israel*; how the priests and Leuites visited all the citties of his Kingdome, hauing the lawe of God in their handes, and instructing the people: and how there were iudges of the Sacerdotall order established in *Hierusalem* for ecclesiasticall causes; that when anie cōtrouersie should be presented concerning religiō, the cōmaundemētes the ceremonies, the iustifications, the people might be instructed not to sinne before the Lord; both histories aswell of the kinges, as of the chronicles, doe testifie. For the rest, with what temporall blessings God fauoured him, how much he abounded in glorie and in treasure, howe much he exceeded *Israel*, how dreadfull he was to the neighbouring nations, how the terror of the lord, said the scripture, was spread ouer all the Kingdomes of the earth, which were round about *Iuda*, so as they durst not make warr vpō *Iosaphat* how the *Philistins* paid him tribute, how he receiued pēsion & homage from the *Arabians*, how *Idumea* acknowledged him, what ordinary forces hee entertained for warr: to witt three hundred thousand chosen men vnder the charge of *Edna*, two hundred and fowre score thousand chosen souldiers vnder that of *Iohanna*, two hūdred & fourscore thousād mē of warr vnder the cōduct of *Amazia*, two hūdred & fourscore thousand Archers with *Eliada*, & an hundred & fourscore thousand light horsemē who followed *Iosabad* the historie & collectiō of the chronicles exactlie declares. Yet this fearefull number which amoūted vnto eleauē hūdred & threescore thousand mē of warr, did not cōprehend (saith the scripture) the garrisōs that he had in walled citties throughout his kingdome, neither were reckoned, an inestimable nūber of persōs vnable to beare armes, as of old mē woemē, & childrē, nor the tribe of *Leui* which

Iacob, 5.

Chron. 16

Ibidem

Ibidem.

exempt from the militarie ſtate, which neuertheleſſe was accuſtomed to people and poſſeſſe fortie eight citties. Now therevpon I demaund, if there be anie appearance to conclude, that the *Jewish* Church was then inuiſible, and if it be not flatlie to mocke the readers, to alleadge *Elias* to that purpoſe? For I will not ſaie, that in *Jſrael* it ſelf, if not the image, yet at leaſt the memorie of piety, was not ſo blotted out and extinguished, but that the examples thereof were ſtill freſh. And that this is ſo, the hi-
3.Reg.18. ſtorie recites, that when *Ieſabel* put the prophets to death, *Abdias* gouernor of *Achabs* howſe, ſaued one hundred in two ſeuerall caues, as the ſame *Abdias* had a while before reported to *Elias*: And that the verie
Ibidem daie before *Elias* flight, the generall ſtates of *Iſrael*, (called by *Achab*, at the inſtance of *Elias* vpon mount *Carmel*, to ſee the concluſion of *Baal's* prieſts) after they had kneeled downe, and cryed out, *the Lord is God, the Lord is God*, had fallen vpō the foure hūdred & fiftie falſe prophets, and had cutt them in peeces, *Achab* ſeeing it, and conſenting to it: As litle will I tell you, that *Elias* when he pronounced this lamentation, was not in the Kingdome of *Jſrael*, nor amidest the light and communication of men, but retired into a caue, in the mountaine of *Oreb* fourtie daies iourney from *Samaria*, the Metropolitan of *Iſrael*, where he ſpake not according to the exact knowledge of what was happened ſince his departure, but by a forme of indulgence to humane feare & frailtie, imagining, what the wrath of *Ieſabel*, new kindled by his occaſion, might haue effected againſt his Bretheren in his abſence: By meanes whereof, this multitude of faithfull *Iſraelites*, expreſt by the number of ſeauentie hundred a finite number for an infinite, was not vnknowne to thoſe, that inhabited in *Iſrael*. Onelie I will ſaie, that the generall extirpation of true godlynes in the territories ſubiect to king *Achab*, did not conclude therefore, that it was rooted out from all the tribes comprehended vnder the firſt diuiſion of *Jſrael*, ſince there were an infinitie of *Iſraelites* as hath aboue appeared, withdrawne in the forme of a voluntarie exile into *Hieruſalem* and into *Iuda*. For beſides thoſe that remoued thither in *Roboams* raigne, the ſcripture teſtifies, that *Aſa* father to *Ioſaphat*, neere twentie yeare before this perſecution, had gathered together the people of *Iuda* and of *Beniamin*, and all the ſtrangers of the tribes of *Ephraim*, of
Paralip. 15. *Manaſſes*, and of *Simeon*, becauſe manie of them, ſaith the ſame ſcripture, had come to him for refuge, ſeeing that the Lord their God was with him. Moreouer, the citties of the mountaine of *Ephraim*, conquered by the ſame *Aſa*, vpon the Kingdome of *Iſrael*; thoſe of *Bethel*, *Jeſana*, *Ephron* and others recouered by *Abia* his Father, after the battaile that he wan againſt *Ieroboam*, communicated in the true Religion with the people of *Iuda*, and the remnant of this medlie of *Jſraelites*, either ſubdued or sheltered, and dwellinge amongſt the *Iewes*, and communicating with them,
Luke 2. v. 36. laſted euen vntill the Birth of our Lord. In whoſe time ſainct LVKE ſtill notes, that the Propheteſſe *Anna*, who alſo was perpetually in the Temple, was of the line of *Aſer*. But whatſoeuer the Kingdome of *Jſrael* were, it ſufficeth that when *Elias* made this complaint, the Iewish Church flourisht with ſo much puritie and ſplendor in that of *Juda*, as it was neuer more pure, nor more viſible. Which *Elias* could not be ignorant of, ſince he was not only obliged with an expreſſe obligation he and all the reſt of Gods ſeruants which remained in *Jſrael*, to goe vp euerie yeare to certaine Feaſtes in *Hieruſalem*, to communicate in the Temple, and in the ſacrifices; but alſo had but then, newly paſſed by *Berſeba*, that bounded vpon the Kingdome of *Juda*, as he fledd from the tyrannie of *Jeſabel*.

The

The fourth obiection is taken from the historie of *Vria*, who by the commaundement of *Achaz* King of Iuda, sett vp a prophan Altar before the Temple. But besides this, that neither *Ezechias* Sonn & heire to the Kingdome of *Iuda*; nor *Esai* prince of the blood of *Iuda*, & Prophet, who by his extraordinarie Mission, and propheticall authoritie, a Succour promised in the old Testament, did supplie noe lesse truly the defect of the dutie of the ordinary Mission in the person of *Vria*, then the Poets fained fabulously that in the games of *Appollo*, the Grashopper had supplied the defect of *Eunomius* string; neither the Bodie of the sacerdotall and Leuiticall order, did participate in this sacriledge, but that all the Sacerdotall colledge, rather chose to suffer exile, then to consent to it. From whence it is, that when *Ezechias*, the first month of his raigne, caused the Delphicke oblations to be made in the behalfe of the people, he was constrained to make vse of the Leuites, to helpe to flea the beastes, because of the small number of Priests which were then about him, for as much saith S. HIEROME & the Hebrew glosse, *as they had bee dispersed in the time of King Achaz and were not yet returned*: And secondly so farr were the people of *Juda* from approuing it, as contrariwise they did for this cause soe abhor *Achaz*, as being dead, although his owne sonn succeeded him, they did not bury him in the sepulcher of his Fathers. Hieron. ad Vital. ep. 132.

THE fifth obiection is taken, from the foure hundred Prophetts that *Achab* caused to come and prophecie before *Josaphat*, who were all found false prophetts, and *Micheas* alone, a true Prophet. But neither did this 3. Reg. 22.
fall out in the kingdome of *Iuda*, where was the seate of the Church, but in the kingdome of *Israel*, neither were those Prophets, of the colledge of the Prophetts of *Baal*, and of the qualitie of those of whom before *Elias* had said: *Take all the Prophetts of Baal, and let not one man escape*. And of whom afterward *Elias* said to *Ioram* sonn of the same *Achab*; *What is there* 3. Reg. 18.
betweene me and thee? Goe to the Prophets of thy Father and of thy mother. And 4. Reg. 3.
therefore when *Iosaphat* would cause *Micheas* to come; hee asked him, *is* 3. Reg. 22
there not heere one Prophet of the Lord; to distinguish him from the Prophetts of *Baal*, by this word, *of the Lord*; which is the same difference, which *Iehu* afterwards vsed, when being desirous to put *Baal's* Priests to death, he said. *Take heede least there be anie of the seruantes of the* Lord *amongst you, but lett the seruant of Baal be only heere*. 4. Reg. 10.

The sixth obiection is taken from the historie of *Manasses* an Idolatrous Prince, and who caused all manner of abominations and false worshipp to be practised in Hierusalem and *Iuda*. But besides this, that hee came afterward to repentance, and then draue awaie all the Idolls and all the false Gods from *Hierusalem*, and commaunded the people of *Juda* to serue God, euen then when he exercised his greatest impieties, the church and the multitude of Gods true seruants, were not for all that inuisible. Contrariwise the scripture saith, *that he shedd so much innocent blood, as Hierusalem was filled therewith euen vp to the throate*. By meanes whereof, although 4. Reg. 21.
there had then bene no solemne assemblies in the Synagogues of *Juda*, and that all publicke exercise had bene suspended there, yet the slaughter of the faithfull yet warme & still breathing, and the voyce of their blood which smoaked and cryed for vengeance, as that of Abel before heauen and earth, permitted not that the true Religion should be vnknowne and inuisible there. For as manie executions and martirdomes as there were so manie sacrifices of praise and sweete smell were they, soe manie professions of Faith, soe manie sermons, so manie seales and sacraments of the true beleefe, which refresht and confirmed the memorie of the doctrine of saluation, euen in the spiritts of those, that persecuted it: for as much

much as all men knew, and themselues protested, the cause wherefore they were banisht, pursued and martyred. For the Church is not only illustrated by her Lillies, but also by her roses; that is to saie, she is not only euident by her quiet and peaceable exercises, which are the congregations to heare and adore the word of God, and to communicate in the sacramentes: but also by her militarie exercises dyed in blood, which are the martyrdomes and the executions suffered for the defence of the Faith which doe often no lesse increase her fame and renowne in the times wherein she is oppressed, then in the seasons wherein she enioyes more calme quiet, and fulfills without hindrance her ordinarie and accustomed
Aug.ep.48 workes. Soe as S. AVGVSTINE saith, *she is then eminent in her most stedfast champions.*

THE seauenth obiection is taken from the transmigration of *Babilon*, during with time, they pretend that the visible communion of the *Iewish* Church, was interrupted. But who knowes not, that the *Iewes* during this exile, had the true externall exercise of their religion, wherein they wrought their Saluation, & performed the visible obseruation of all their worships, seruices, and ceremonies, except of the Sacrifice alone, which could not be offered but in the Temple, and were euidently distinguished
Esth. 3. from other nations; witnes these wordes of *Aman* to *Assuerus*: *There is a people dispersed ouer all the Prouinces of thy Kingdome, and diuided into manie partes, that practises new lawes and ceremonies,* And these of the historian, *Manie other nations and sects ioyned themselues to their religion, and to their ceremonies.* For that this historie fell out in the time of the transmigration, it appeares by this, that it is said, that *Mardocheus* was one of those that had bene transported from *Hierusalem* in the time of *Nabuchodonosor*, and of *Iechonias*. And it is not cōtradictorie to this that *Assuerus* writes: *that Amā was a Macedonian, and would haue betraied the Empire to the Macedonians*: For the copie of the same epistle reported by *Iosephus* sixteene hundred yeares
Ioseph antiquit Iudaic.l.11.c 6. a gone, hath it *Allophilus*; that is to saie, a stranger: And that the Greeke & Latine Edition saith; a *Macedonian*, it proceedes from the *Syriacke* translation of the same Epistle, made after the death of *Alexander*: after which all strangers in *Asia*, were called *Macedonians*: as at this daie all those of the west, are called *Frankes* there: From whence it is, that the Syriacke edition saith: that *Assuerus* was cloathed in a *Macedonian* habit: that is to saie, in the habit of a stranger.

THE eigth obiection is taken from the writings of the Prophetts, who often deplored the dessolation of the seruice of God in their people. But either they spake of the portion of the Kingdome of *Israel* diuided from that of *Iuda*: and of the faction of the schismaticall *Israelites*, who were no more the Church, and to whom God protested by the mouth of
Ierem.3.v.8. *Ieremie, that he had giuen the libell of diuorce*: Or if they spake of that of the Kingdome of *Iuda*, S. AVGVSTINE teacheth vs, that they spake prophetically, and by an analogie of time, of the future Estate of the *Iewish* people, such as they should be after the death of our Lord: Or if they spake by *Synecdoche* and according to the stile of preachers, who censure the vices of particular persons in generall termes *to the end to reproue*, as S. AVGVSTINE saith of S. HILARY, *the more seuerelie that which they reproue more vniuersallie*: that is to saie, that they spake of certaine particular persons, who either abandoned the Religion of their Fathers, some to followe, that of the Pagans that sacrificed to Idolls, some to followe that of the Schismatickes, who sacrificed in the high places: or if they remained in the true religion and communion, liued wickedlie there as concerning manners. *They collect* (saith S. AVGVSTINE speaking of the *Donatists* he

might haue added the *Caluinists* to them) *either ignorantlie or fraudulentlie the places of Scripture, which are spoken either of the wicked, which are nimgled with the good, vntill the end, or of the destruction of the first people of the Iewes; and would wrest them against the Church of God; that she may seeme to haue failed, and to be perisht from the whole earth.*

The ninth and finall obiection, is taken from the comdemnation that the *Iewish* Church, made of the Sauiour of the world. But who sees not, that this was in the time wherein her contract was expired, and that of the Christian Church, did beginne? *The lawe and the prophetts*, saith our Sauiour, *vntill Iohn;* And sainct PAVLE, *Blindnes is partlie fallen vpon Israel, that the fullnes of the Gentiles might be introduced.* Now the lease that God had made of his vine to the *Iewish* Church, hauing bene but for a time; what wonder is it, that when this lease is come to expire, the prerogatiue that she had, by vertue of her contract, should cease; and that the master of the vineyard should lett forth his Vineyard to other hnsbandmen? and this sufficeth for the comparison of the Christian Church with the *Iewish*. For to ascend to the time before the lawe of *Moyses*, and to alleadge the little mention that is made there of the continuance of the Church, it is clere, that it had bene a thinge superfluous for the Scripture, to haue represented particularlie, the estate of the Church of those ages, the knowledge of the succession of the Church, not hauing bene necessarie, but after the last institution of the lawe, for the seruice whereof she is establisht as to the *Iewes* after the institution of the lawe of *Moyses*; and to the Christians after the institution of the Euangelicall lawe. Although both before and after the floud, there are manie monuments of it. For both before the floud this, that the sonns of God knew the daughters of men, shewes that there was an especiall people, which boare the title of the children of God: which title the interpretors would haue to be taken by the posteritie of *Seth*, to distinguish themselues from the posteritie of *Cain*, when *Seth* had begotten *Enos*; *and that they began*, saith the Scripture, *to all chemselues by the name of the Lord:* And the vniuersall corruption which fell out in the end, vpon all the other families, descended from *Seth*, except that of *Noe*, was a corruption of manners, and for which if wee beleeue saint HIEROME all those that perish with a temporall death in the floud, perisht not with an eternall death; And after the floud, that *Noe* liued almost to the sixtith yeare of *Abraham*, And *Sem* the Sonn of *Noe*, whom *Luther* calls the Pope of his Age, till after the death of *Iacob*: And that *Melckisedech* kinge of *Salem* was priest of the most high, and in his qualitie blest *Abraham*: & that *Rebecca* wife of *Isaach*, wẽt to enquire of God vpon the misterie of her childrẽ, shewes, that euẽ thẽ the true worship & visible seruice of God had place both before, & elsewhere, thẽ in the familie of *Abrahã*. But to cõclude, grant all the hypothesis to be such as the Protestãts pretend & that the Church had bene interrupted, both before the lawe & vnder the lawe: what would that make against the christiã church, to whõ Christ held this language: *As in the daies of Noe I swore, that I would neuer againe bringe the waters of the Floud vpon the Earth, soe I haue sworne, that I will noe more be angrie against thee: Thou shalt noe more be called the forsaken. I will noe more doe to this people as in former daies I will contract a new alliance with them, not according to the alliance I contracted with their Fathers, when I brought them out of the land of Egypt: The cittie of the Lord, shall noe more be pulled vp, nor destroyed: The glorie of this second howse shall bee much greater, then that of the first: The cittie built vpon the mount aine cannot be hidden: The gates of Hell shall not preuaile against my Church. I am with you to the consummation of ages. This Gho-*

Luc. 16. v. 16. Rom. 11. v. 25. Gen. 6. Gen. 4. Gen. 9. Gen. 11. Gen. 14. Gen. 25. Esai. 54. Esa. 26. Zach. 8. Agg. 2. v. 10. Mat th. 5. Matth. 16. Matth. 28. Matt. 24.

ſpell of the Kingdome muſt be preached through the whole world, and then the end ſhall come. Hee hath placed in his Church, the Apoſtles, Prophetts, Paſtors, and Doctors; &c: till wee all ſhall meete in the vnitie of faith. The Church is the firmament of truth: and other ſuch like.

Of the compariſon of the Charitie of the antient African Church and the moderne Roman Church.

CHAP. XXXVII.

The continuance of the Kinges anſwere

AND ſurely, the antient Church to recall the *Donatiſts*, that were refractory, to her communiō had accuſtomed by an admirable Charitie, to prouide, euen for the temporall commodities of the Bishops that should be conuerted, and of others alſo. And the *Roman* Church, to knitt againe the loue and good will, betweene her and the *English* Church, hath firſt employed the thunderboltes of Bulls, and afterward of force, ſometimes openly, and ſometimes vnder-hand.

THE REPLIE.

THE antient Catholicke Church of *Africa*, offered for the good of Charitie, and of the Eccleſiaſticall communion, to yeeld vp the Bishoprickes of *Africa*; not to thoſe *Donatiſt* Bishops, which ſtill remained on *Donatus* his partie, but to thoſe that would returne to the communion of the Catholicke Church. And the *Roman* Church hath excommunicated by her Bulls, not thoſe that will returne from the *English* diuiſion to the Catholick communion, but thoſe that after many admonitions, are obſtinate ſtill to remaine in the ſeparation, And therefore there is in this, no Antitheſis betweene the proceedings of the antient Catholicke Church, and thoſe of the moderne. For as concerning this word, *the thunderboltes of Bulls* by which ſome thinke to make the Popes cenſures the more odious, his maieſtie may remember if hee pleaſe, that it is an antient phraſe of ſpeeche that the Grecians vſe, who called the condemnations, euen of ſecular iudgementes, *thunderboltes* and to expreſſe, that one was condemned in iudgment, they would ſaie, he was T*hunder-ſtrucken.*

Of the innocencie of the Church in the matter of conſpiracies againſt his maieſtie,

CHAP. XXXVIII.

The continuance of the Kings anſwere.

RAYTORS manifeſtlie culpable of the paricide vndertaken in this prouince, she hath receiued into her lapp, and ſtill wholie protects them: thoſe that haue ſuffered iudgemēt for the ſame cauſe, she inrolles in the Catalogue of martyrs, and propugneth from daie to daie their innocencie, againſt all lawes, diuine and humane.

THE

THE REPLIE.

F anie of thoſe that were partakers of the abhominable cõſpiracie, proiected againſt his maieſtie be receiued at *Rome*, it is an error of fact, and not of Right, founded vpon a falſe information, that is to ſaie, vpon the beleefe, that they haue imprinted there, that they are not culpable of that attempt, as Princes are accuſtomed to receaue in the qualitie of innocent perſons, thoſe that haue recourſe to them out of other Prouinces, if the verball proceſſe of the crimẽ be not ſent to them, that they may informe themſelues of the truth or falſhood of the imputation. And this lawe is a lawe of refuge and freedome cõmon to the Eſtates of all Princes. But to beleeue that the Pope protects them in the qualitie of being culpable of this conſpiracie. I know to well how much I haue heard him deteſt it with his owne mouth. For as touching thoſe that haue bene excluded in *England*, that that is (for whoſe innocencie not with ſtanding diuers write) is alwaies grounded vpon the fact, and not vpon the right; that is to ſaie, pretending they were not complices nor conſenting thereto, and not maintayning the action to be other then damnable and deteſtable. Contrarywiſe that they are iuſtified by this waie, be it true be it falſe (for it is hard in ſuch a caſe to impoſe a lawe vpon the ſuſpition of abſent perſons) it is a manifeſt teſtimonie, that the action is abhorred, and comdemned. And when as his maieſtie adds, that the *Roman* Church, enrolls them in the catalogue of martyrs, if anie pariicular men defend their ſuppoſed innocencie hyperbolically, it is alwaies vpon this ſuppoſition whether true or falſe, that they were not complices in the fact. But as for the *Roman* Cburch, I neuer yet heard tell, that she hath canonized anie martir of the ſeauenteenth age.

Of the writings of the illuſtrious Cardinall Bellarmin.

CHAP. XXXIX.

The continuance of the King anſwere.

THe Cardinall *Bellarmine* himſelf, I will ſaie it againſt my will, but I ſaie truth, amongſt the protectors of the Paricides, holdes the rancke of the head of a faction who newlie againe to the end to allure the excellent King hath imployed this argument of wondrous efficacie, to perſwade that the Kingdome of *England* belonges to the Pope, and that the kinge of *England* is ſubiect to the Pope, euen in temporall thinges, and in his Feodary. I omitt the other complaintes of the kinge, and the *Engliſh* Church, as well old as newe, which now haue noe neede of commemoratiõ.

THE REPLIE.

THE proteſtation that I haue made, non to handle anie thing in this worke, but what is purely ſpirituall, obligeth me not to vndertake the defence of the Illuſtrious and moſt learned cardinall *Bellarmine*, but in caſes of this qualitie. It ſufficeth me for the reſt to ſaie, that himſelfe aduertiſes the Readers that what he propounds of the indirect authoritie of the Pope in temporalls, he propounds it not as a doctrine of faith, and whereof either ſide muſt be held vnder the paine of excommunication or anathema by meanes whereof this question should not hinder the reunion of those who desire to returne to the Church. For as for the annuall present that it is written, *England* was wont to make to the *Sea* Apostolicke, if his maiesties Predecessors would by anie marke of publicke acknowledgment testifie their particular deuotion towards saint PETERS Sea that could bring noe more dimunition to their temporall glory, then the submission of *Alexander* the great brought to him when he prostrated himselfe before the high Priest of the *Iewish* lawe; or that of the Emperor *Justinian* the second, when hee prostrated himselfe in *Asia* before Pope *Constantine*, making this acknowledgment not to men but to God, who saith by the mouth of *Esay* to his Church, whereof saint PETER in his Successors, is the head and visible figure: *Kings shall worship thee with their face on the ground.* Contrarywise it will be found, that the kings of *England*, haue bene more esteemed and feared since then, then euer they were before, Iointlie, that whensoeuer it shall please this great king to make so faire a present to the Church as to giue her his heart and person, I assure my selfe, the Pope will shewe (if these temporall acknowledgments bee displeasing to his Maiestie) that it is himselfe as S. PAVL saith, that he desires, and not the things that belong to him.

The end of the first Part.